AN INVITATION TO FAMILY LAW

PRINCIPLES, PROCESS AND PERSPECTIVES

Third Edition

By

Carl E. Schneider
Chauncey Stillman Professor of Law &
Professor of Internal Medicine
University of Michigan

Margaret F. Brinig
Sorin Professor of Law
Notre Dame Law School

AMERICAN CASEBOOK SERIES®

Mat # 40498668

610 Opperman Drive
P.O. Box 64526
St. Paul, MN 55164–0526
1–800–328–9352

ISBN–13: 978–0–314–16939–6
ISBN–10: 0–314–16939–3

TO JOAN

O ye gods! Render me worthy of this noble wife.

William Shakespeare
Julius Caesar, II, i, 318–319.

TO MARY, WENDY, KATIE, JILL AND BRIAN

Behold, children are a gift of the LORD,
The fruit of the womb is a reward.

Psalm 127:3.

*

Preface

A preface to a casebook may once have been unnecessary, since casebooks were relatively similar. This is no longer true, and it is particularly untrue of this casebook. We want therefore to explain briefly our purpose and our method.

We have two primary purposes. The first is to help you learn family law. Of course, that means introducing you to the legal doctrines that make up that subject. Fortunately, those doctrines are not gruesomely technical or complex, and they are thus learned pretty readily. We have tried to make learning them as comfortable and efficient as possible by describing them straightforwardly, sometimes through cases, but sometimes through text.

However, another part of learning family law is as hard as learning the doctrine is easy—considering, as Oliver Wendell Holmes put it, "the ends which the several rules seek to accomplish, the reasons why those ends are desired, what is given up to gain them, and whether they are worth the price." As Holmes suggests, those questions are worth asking about any field. But family law is law stretched to—perhaps beyond—its limits. Family law tries to regulate people in their least regulable behavior, in their most tumultuous moments, in their most private lives. Family law, then, deals with questions that have baffled human beings throughout history. This casebook tries to equip you to look analytically, critically, and insightfully at the heart of family law: the rules and assumptions the field employs in answering those questions.

Some of what you will read in our casebook will ask you to think about what family law ought to be. Thus we will regularly and extensively try to criticize family law and to explore ways to improve it. But we will also strive to understand family law as it is. We do this not because family law is right as it is, but because one function of any casebook is to help you understand the law.

Our second primary purpose is to help you learn law. That is, we try to use family law to help you think about some issues that are basic to the way the law generally relates to society. Thus the casebook concentrates on a number of "themes." One problem with the way law is conventionally taught is that students rarely have a chance to see the forest of law instead of the trees of each subject area. Some problems in writing and applying law recur from area to area, but professors seldom pause to deal with them as special problems which people have specially thought about. These recurring problems are our "themes." Most chapters specifically address a theme as well as a subject-matter area. Thus chapters consider subjects like the usefulness of contract as an organizing principle of law and life, the social and legal idea of privacy, the nature and desirability of rights thinking; the proper extent of judicial discretion, and so on.

We treat one particular kind of recurrent legal problem in a special way. We have tried to identify five functions that law in general serves and to explore those functions more directly and expressly than casebooks and courses usually do.

These themes and functions all raise standard questions every lawyer should have thought about. They are in fact questions that most law students have dealt with. The problem is that law students are generally asked to deal with them sporadically and indirectly. In other words, these questions form the implicit basis for much discussion of specific problems in the substantive area being taught, but students are often not told explicitly what the jurisprudential problem is and are generally not exposed to literature that expressly confronts it. Our goal is to bring these problems more expressly to your attention, to provide some cogent discussion of them, but to anchor these efforts in specific family-law issues.

Our casebook is different from most others in yet another way. The themes and functions we have just described together form an analytic framework that can be deployed to understand the whole range of family law problems. Our goal, then, is to provide you with a set of ideas that will serve you over the years as you confront the many novel issues in family law that you will encounter in the half-century during which you are likely to practice.

We have written the kind of casebook we have been describing partly because we believe family law offers a rewarding way of integrating much of the learning students are expected to accomplish in law school. In addition, however, we are responding to the fact that family law has undergone extraordinarily rapid change over the last three decades. The field thus is in particular need of reflection and evaluation after the burst of reform and revision.

Of course, to some extent, *all* casebooks are intended to help you learn how to think about legal problems generally and the substantive area with which the book deals. One way they might accomplish these two purposes is to analyze every legal problem which the book covers as extensively as possible, so that you might learn how to think about legal problems by studying the examples such discussions would constitute and so that you might learn about the substantive area by studying what a knowledgeable person had to say about it. But you will have noticed that casebook authors spurn this course.

There are reasons for this. First, casebook publishers do not allow authors the space such a tactic would require, nor are students anxious to concede professors the time it would demand. Second, casebook authors feel that that tactic would make it too easy for the student to read the material without engaging it. Casebook authors are overridingly eager to encourage students to reflect for themselves about what they are reading, to practice thinking like a keen and critical lawyer about legal issues, and to develop their own ideas about the material.

Many casebook authors try to solve these problems by asking lots of questions. Their questions are designed to seduce and provoke the reader into thinking carefully and freshly about the problems the book considers and, by doing so, to learn how to "think like a lawyer." This approach is surely legitimate, but it places onerous burdens on the student. Our experience—as onetime law students and now as professors—is that students often feel that they lack time to engage each question fully, that there are a daunting number of questions, and that the questions are baffingly opaque. Furthermore, students sometimes fear that the casebook author's learning is deliberately being concealed by the often delphic questions.

We have adopted a middle course. Like many of our colleagues, we have tried not to do your thinking for you. Following the conventional practice, we have used questions to stimulate you to do your own thinking. However, we have also striven not to leave you stunned by wave after wave of questions whose purport is irritatingly obscure and whose intent seems malevolent. Instead, we have regularly organized questions so that they unfold a series of alternative ways of thinking about a problem. That is, we will frequently begin with a general question and follow it with a set of subsidiary questions which intimate several (sometimes conflicting, sometimes complementary) possible answers to the general question. We hope this way of asking questions will exemplify for you the way a lawyer should begin analyzing a problem by asking a series of questions about it, will give you some guidance in thinking about the substantive issues family law raises, but will encourage you to engage deeply with those issues.

In any event, *we urge you to take the questions seriously. They are at the heart of the book.* Taking the questions seriously does not mean finding the right answer to them. We believe that few of these questions have a right answer. This is not a casebook that sets you problems with verifiably correct results. Rather, the questions raise issues that people have been grappling with since societies first came to be organized. If Plato and Aristotle, if Mill and Marx could not find irrefutable answers to them, there is no reason you and we should expect to. But for the same reasons these questions cannot be indubitably answered, they are worth considering. In short, in posing questions, we are not trying to hide the ball; we are attempting to find it ourselves and to help you find it.

Our belief that family law is more often characterized by conceptual than doctrinal difficulty has shaped several other features of this book. It has, for instance, led us to prefer to organize discussion around a single leading case or problem. That case or problem is usually supplemented by various kinds of materials of traditional and non-traditional, legal and non-legal sorts. This arrangement is intended to make it easier to reach underlying issues in class discussion, since the class need not be distracted by the admirable but frequently rehearsed exercise of assimilating the various fact situations and opinions of several cases. This arrangement also makes it possible to delve much deeper into opinions than the usual allotment of fifteen or twenty minutes per case allows.

This organization is possible partly because it is not a primary purpose of this casebook to train you to synthesize doctrine out of a line of cases. Vital though that skill is, it is taught (and commonly taught well) throughout the first year of law school and in much of the second and third years. Concentrating on a single leading case also makes it a little easier to present unedited documents. This is important because, since legal writing is often poorly taught and sometimes not taught at all in law schools, students should try to learn about constructing legal documents and legal arguments by seeing it done, and you do not really see it done unless you see the whole document.

Our concern for plumbing family law's perplexities has also meant that we have not been ashamed to use a number of standard cases. Thus, like thousands of family law students, you will read *Reynolds v. United States, McGuire v. McGuire, Marvin v. Marvin, Griswold v. Connecticut, Roe v. Wade, Painter v. Bannister,* and *Wisconsin v. Yoder.* They are, after all, standard because they are both important cases and good pedagogical instruments. They are, many of them, also cases that people have been thinking about for years, so that richer and wiser ideas have gathered around them than around most cases. For these reasons, they are as well cases that are part of a common vocabulary.

All this means that this is not one of those casebooks which turns every class into four cases and a cloud of dust. We urge you, then, not to delude yourselves into believing that you are not learning law unless you are reading a string of cases. We offer cases aplenty when they are the best teaching vehicles. We also use a number of statutes (particularly the UMDA and the ALI Principles). We do so not just because those statutes—model or actual—represent considered and systematic views of their subject, and not just because they are law of a particularly authoritative kind, but because few things are more critical to your legal education than learning how to read statutes. Unfortunately, both faculty and students resist engaging with statutes for the understandable but inadmissible reason that statutes are not as much fun to work with as cases. Nevertheless, if you are in law school to prepare yourself for the real work of a lawyer, learning to read statutes acutely, adeptly, and adroitly is crucial. This is your chance.

We believe casebooks are for teaching students about the law. Thus this book is neither an encyclopedia for family lawyers nor a research guide for legal scholars. This means two things. First, rather than surveying every nook and cranny, every highway and byway, every jot and tittle of family law, we have selected its most central and revealing issues and ideas and concentrated on them. Second, we have never understood why so many casebooks force students to search for wisps of text in a thicket of citations to cases and articles few students have time or appetite to read. We have found students are more disheartened than inspired by globs of citations. We are not even convinced that extra reading is the best way to spend study time. That time is generally better spent rereading the casebook and wrestling with its questions.

We have, therefore, eliminated (without specific indication) the less consequential citations in the pieces we have reprinted and have rationed the number of citations in the parts we wrote ourselves. We have also eliminated (again without specific indication) the less momentous footnotes in the material we have used. (In addition, once we have cited a source, we do not provide specific page numbers when we shortly thereafter quote the source again. Sufficient unto the day is the evil thereof.)

Of course, we do not want to discourage you from doing further reading; we just want that reading to be rewarding. To help you locate reading that repays the effort, we have selected articles and books not mentioned in the text and briefly described them in bibliographies that follow each chapter.

Like any casebook, this one asks you to think intently about a series of intricate, baffling, and sometimes rather abstract problems. But working on problems like those can be wearing and wearisome. Furthermore, family law involves particularly human kinds of problems. It regulates, and incorporates the stories of, real people. We have therefore tried as assiduously as we could to inject the relief of human interest into these materials. Some of the cases we think you will find deeply interesting at the most basic levels. But we have also tried to infiltrate into the materials stories about what actually happened in the cases you will read, poems, and even witticisms, all designed to enliven your studies and remind you of their human element even while deepening your understanding of family law.

We have also sought to make this book more stimulating and instructive by providing a wide variety of kinds of approaches and materials. As we have already said, throughout the book we combine doctrinal and thematic readings. Further, our techniques vary from place to place. The chapter on divorce, among other things, raises some of the ethical questions that arise in the course of practicing family law. The chapter on spouse abuse asks you to put yourself in the position of several different kinds of legal actors, law-makers as well as law-enforcers. The chapter on marital property rests primarily on a few leading cases and principles; our chapter on child custody presents a symphony of concrete cases. The chapter on the contractualization of family law relies crucially on a contrast between contracts in business life and contracts in family life. The chapter on child abuse uses legal cases to survey the whole range of a social problem. That chapter also asks you to grapple at length with the facts of a typical case and to put yourself in the shoes of each of the many lawyers the case engaged. The chapter on child support asks you to confront some very practical problems in the enforcement of law. The final chapter asks you to pull together all that you have learned in the course.

This leads us to a last word about family law. It treats one of the happiest parts of human existence—the rewards of life among the people who love us most and whom we love most. Yet law, much more than economics, the dismal science, deals with people in some of the most degraded parts of human existence—the failures, betrayals, and corruptions of family life. Family law cases present people so cudgeled by misfortune, so savaged by cruelty, so much wanderers in the wilderness of the world, that we too readily lose touch with what marriage and parenthood mean to most people most of the time. We urge you to step back regularly from these materials to try to place them in the larger context of life as you have observed it.

This leaves us to make only one further comment about this volume. We have tried to strike a blow for freedom from the inanities of the *Bluebook*. Thus, for the reasons given in Richard A. Posner, *Goodbye to the Bluebook,* 53 U Chi L Rev 1343 (1986), we follow the *University of Chicago Manual of Legal Citation* (Lawyers Co-operative, 1989), in all the materials we have prepared. Of course, citations left in cases follow their original format.

Bibliography

Many of this book's basic purposes are described in Carl E. Schneider, *The Next Step: Definition, Generalization, and Theory in American Family Law*, 18 Mich J L Ref 1039 (1985). Some of its pedagogical assumptions are lightly sketched in Carl E. Schneider, *The Frail Old Age of the Socratic Method*, 47 Law Quadrangle Notes 40 (Winter 1994).

Acknowledgments

The following authors and publishers gave us permission to reprint excerpts from copyrighted material; we gratefully acknowledge their assistance.

George A. Akerlof, Janet L. Yellen and Michael L. Katz, 'An Analysis of Out-of-Wedlock Childbearing in the United States', The Quarterly Journal of Economics, 111:2 (May, 1996), pp. 276-317. © 1996 by the President and Fellows of Harvard College and the Massachusetts Institute of Technology.

American Law Institute, Principles of the Law of Family Dissolution, Analysis and Recommendations, 2002.

Katharine T. Bartlett, Feminism and Family Law, 38 Fam L Q 475 (1999).

Jason Begay, Foster Program Pairs: American Indians' Goal is to Retain Culture and Values, Duluth News Tribune, August 2, 1999.

Thomas E. Carbonneau and Laura duPaix, A Consideraiton of Alternatives to Divorce Ligitaiton, 1986 U Ill L Rev 119. The copyright to the University of Illinois Law Review is held by The Board of Trustees of the University of Illinois Law Review.

David Chambers, Making Fathers Pay, 90-114 (University of Chicago Press 1979). © 1979 by David L. Chambers. All rights reserved.

Marsha Garrison, Law Making for Baby Making: An Interpretative Approach to the Determination of Legal Parentage, 113 Harv L Rev 835 (2000). Copyright © by the President and Fellows of Harvard College. All rights reserved.

Marsha Garrison, Autonomy or Community? An Evaluation of Two Models of Parental Obligation, © 1998 by the California Law Review. Reprinted from California Law Review.

Trina Grillo, The Mediation Alternative: Process Dangers for Women. Reprinted by permission of the Yale Law Journal Company from The Yale Law Journal Vol 100, page 1545.

AP Herbert, Holy Deadlock, Permission granted by A.P. Watt, Ltd. on behalf of Crystal Hale and Jocelyn Herbert.

Institute of Judicial Administration, Inc. and the American Bar Association Juvenile Justice Standards Project, Standards Relating to Abuse and Neglect.

Robert W. Mnookin, The Guardianship of Phillip B.: Jay Spears' Achievement, 40 Stan L Rev 841 (1988).

Robert H. Mnookin, Child Custody Adjudication: Judicial Functions in the Face of Indeterminacy, 39 Law & Cont Probs 226 (1975).

National Conference on Uniform State Laws, Uniform Marriage and Divorce Act and Uniform Premarital Agreement Act.

Robert A. Pratt, Crossing the Color Line: A Historical Assessment and Personal Narrative of Loving v. Virginia, 41 Howard LJ 229 (1988).

Milton C. Regan, Family Law and the Pursuit of Intimacy, Copyright © New York University Press, 1993.

Elizabeth S. Scott, Rational Decisionmaking for Marriage and Divorce, 76 Va L Rev 9 (1990).

Elizabeth S. Scott and Robert E. Scott, Parents as Fiduciaries, 81 Va L Rev 2401 (1995).

Amy Tan, "Rice Husband," from The Joy Luck Club by Amy Tan, copyright © 1989 by Amy Tan. Used by permission of G.P. Putnam's Sons, a division of Penguin Group (USA) Inc.

Lee Teitelbaum, Family History and Family Law, 1985 Wisconsin L Rev 1335. Copyright © 1985 by The Board of Regents of the University of Wisconsin System: Reprinted by permission of the Wisconsin Law Review.

Lee Teitelbaum and Lauara DuPaix, Alternative Dispute Resolution and Divorce: Natural Experimentation in Family Law, which originally appeared at 40 Rutgers L Rev 1093 (1998).

Michael S. Wald, Children's Rights: A Framework for Analysis, 12 UC Davis L Rev 255 (1979). This work, copyright 1979 by Michael S. Wald, was originally published in 12 U C Davis L Rev 225 (1979), copyright 1979 by The Regents of the University of California. Reprinted with Permission.

Lenore Weitzman, The Social and Economic Consequences of No-Fault Divorce. Originally published in 28 UCLA L Rev 1126. Copyright © 1983, The Regents of the University of California. All Rights Reserved.

Lenore B. Weitzman, The Marriage Contract (Free Press 1981); which first appeared in Legal Regulation of Marriage: Tradition and Change, 62 Cal L Rev 1281 (1974).

James Q. Whitman, The Two Western Cultures of Privacy: Dignity Versus Liberty. Reprinted by permission of The Yale Law Journal Company and William S. Hein Company from *The Yale Law Journal*, vol. 113, pages 1151-1221.

As all casebook authors must be, we are grateful to the students on whom we practiced. And as all authors must be, we are grateful to the colleagues who have given us the benefit of their time and wisdom. Dean May, Marsha Garrison, Marie Deveney, Suellyn Scarnecchia and Carol Weisbrod were all kind enough to read and comment on portions of the manuscript for the first edition. Lynn Wardle was brave enough to teach from it while it was in manuscript and to detail his reaction to it. And the late Lee Teitelbaum and Carol Weisbrod both deserve special admiration for their persistent encouragement of this casebook while they were working on one of their own. Since the first edition, we have received very helpful comments and advice (and terrific questions) from Hon. Michael McConnell, and Professors Jon Macey and Angela Onwuachi-Willig. Finally, we are grateful to our research assistants. They have now become too numerous to list in full, but on the latest edition, Elizabeth Ahrold, Francis Budde, Jordan Esbrook, Regina Ori and Brian Raimondo labored long and hard. Kati Jumper at the University of Iowa provided superb and careful assistance to this project.

*

Summary of Contents

PART IV. CONCLUSION

*

Table of Contents

PART III. PARENT AND CHILD

*

Table of Cases

The principal cases are in bold type. Cases cited or discussed in the text are roman type. References are to pages. Cases cited in principal cases and within other quoted materials are not included.

AN INVITATION TO FAMILY LAW

PRINCIPLES, PROCESS AND PERSPECTIVES

Third Edition

*

Part I

HUSBAND AND WIFE

Hail wedded Love, mysterious Law, true source Of human off-spring, sole propriety In Paradise of all things common else. By thee adulterous lust was driv'n from men Among the bestial herds to range, by thee Founded in Reason, Loyal, Just, and Pure, Relations dear, and all the Charities Of Father, Son, and Brother first were known.

John Milton
Paradise Lost

We begin our study of family law with an examination of the way the law treats what American society has historically regarded as the core of the family—the relationship between a husband and a wife. In Chapter 1, we will ask what marriage means and how the law regulates it. The law reveals its view of marriage most clearly in the way it treats divorce and hence we will devote particular attention to that subject. In Chapter 2, we will pause to equip ourselves with an overview of the kinds of analytical problems family law regularly presents. In Chapter 3, we will begin to grapple with one of the major issues of our subject—the principle of family autonomy. We will approach that issue particularly in terms of the greatest challenge to it: spouse abuse. Chapter 4 presents questions of the economics of marriage and divorce, and will lead us to look especially at how property and income are divided after divorce. Chapter 5 deals with one of the major modern challenges to traditional ideas about marriage as an institution, for in that chapter we will examine the use of contract as an ordering device for spousal relations. Part I will close with Chapter 6's examination of the apparent convergence between marriage and non-marital cohabitation.

Chapter I

AN HONORABLE ESTATE: INTRODUCTION TO THE LAW OF HUSBAND AND WIFE

Among the Phrygian hills there stands an oak
together with a linden . . . .
And Jupiter came there in mortal guise;
and with his father; though he'd set aside
his wings, came Mercury, Atlas' grandson . . . .
They asked for shelter at a thousand doors;
and at a thousand they were shunned and spurned.
But one house took them in: a modest place . . . .
And, in that hut, there lived an aged woman,
the pious Baucis, and with her, Philemon,
as old as she was; they were wed when young
within that hut; and there they had grown old . . . .
And when the two gods from the sky arrived,
they stooped on entering—the door was low.
The old man, setting out a bench on which
his Baucis had been quick to spread rough cloth,
invited them to sit, to rest their limbs . . . .

Meanwhile, the aged couple noticed this:
the wine bowl, which had served so many cups,
seemed to replenish its own self . . . .
Dismayed—
this sight was unbelievable—afraid,
both Baucis and the old Philemon prayed . . . .
Then they got set to kill their only goose . . . .
And then the gods told Baucis and Philemon
that they were not to kill the goose. They said:
"We're gods indeed; your sacrilegious neighbors
have earned the punishment they will receive,
but you'll be saved from that catastrophe . . . ."
Then Jove, the son of Saturn, said with calm:
"You, just old man, and you, his worthy wife,
tell me what you desire most." Philemon
spoke briefly to his Baucis, then declared
unto the gods their choice, the wish they shared:

"We want to be your priests, to guard your shrine;
and since, for such long years, we two have lived
in harmony, we pray that the same hour
in which one dies, may also be taken the other,
that I may never see her sepulcher
and she may never have to bury me."
Their wish was honored. And as long as life
was granted them, they served within the shrine.
But weary with their long, long years, one day
as they were standing near those sacred steps,
recounting times gone by in that dear place,
old Baucis saw that boughs were covering
Philemon, even as the old Philemon
saw his dear Baucis covered by green boughs.
One treetop covered both their faces now;
but they—as long as they still could—called out
in unison, "Farewell, dear mate, farewell . . ."
until at the same instant, bark had sealed
their lips.

Ovid
Metamorphoses

This first chapter has two purposes. The first is to introduce you to some of the basic questions family law confronts: Why does the law try to regulate the family? How should it do so? In what ways should it not try to do so? The chapter's second purpose is to begin to examine the relationship that has traditionally been at the core of the family—marriage. Ideally, we would start with a full-scale sociological and anthropological examination of marriage's functions. Time and space, however, prevent us. Instead, we refer you to Margaret F. Brinig, Carl E. Schneider and Lee E. Teitelbaum, *Family Law in Action* (Anderson, 1999). Here, then, we will examine two brief selections which should stimulate your own ideas about those functions. We will then review a statutory framework for marriage and ask what the law's relation to marriage is and should be. Next, we will assess marriage as a social and legal institution through the lawyerly device of studying three of its heterodox forms. In a closing section, we will further probe the institution of marriage by looking at the law of divorce.

SECTION 1. WHOM GOD HATH JOINED TOGETHER: THE LAW OF ENTRY INTO MARRIAGE

THIS IS THE QUESTION

MARRY

Children—(if it please God)—constant companion, (friend in old age)

Not MARRY

No children, (no second life) no one to care for one in old age.—What is the

MARRY

who will feel interested in one, object to be beloved and played with—better than a dog anyhow—Home, and someone to take care of house—Charms of music and female chit-chat. These things good for one's health. Forced to visit and receive relations but terrible loss of time.

My God, it is intolerable to think of spending one's whole life, like a neuter bee, working, working and nothing after all.—No, no won't do.—

Imagine living all one's day solitarily in smoky dirty London House.—Only picture to yourself a nice soft wife on a sofa with good fire, and books and music perhaps—compare this vision with the dingy reality of Gr[ea]t Marlboro St.

Marry—Marry—Marry

Not MARRY

use of working without sympathy from near and dear friends—who are near and dear friends to the old except relatives.

Freedom to go where one liked—Choice of Society and little of it. Conversation of clever men at clubs.—

Not forced to visit relatives, and to bend in every trifle—to have the expense and anxiety of children—perhaps quarrelling.

Loss of time—cannot read in the evenings—fatness and idleness—anxiety and responsibility—less money for books etc.—if many children forced to gain one's bread.—(But then it is very bad for one's health to work too much)

Perhaps my wife won't like London; then the sentence is banishment and degradation with indolent idle fool—

Q.E.D.

Charles Darwin, 1837 or 1838
Notes to himself.
(In January 1839, he married.)

A. MARRIAGE AS A SOCIAL AND LEGAL INSTITUTION

Such should conjugal love be, still the same, and as they are one flesh, so should they be of one mind, ... one consent, Geryon-like, coalescere in unum, have one heart in two bodies, will and nill the same.

Robert Burton
Anatomy of Melancholy

(1) What Does Marriage Mean to the Married?

Perhaps the most familiar, influential, succinct, and eloquent description of marriage as a social (and moral) institution is the Book of Common Prayer's marriage service. (For one modest measure of its influence, see W Va Code § 48–12b, (1998) which prescribes a strikingly similar ceremony.) In addition, it reminds us of religion's crucial part in building the Western view of marriage. As you read it, you should ask what kind of institution it seeks to create, and whether that institution is a desirable one.

THE BOOK OF COMMON PRAYER
SOLEMNIZATION OF MATRIMONY

¶ *[T]he Minister shall say,*

Dearly beloved, we are gathered together here in the sight of God, and in the face of this company, to join together this Man and this Woman in holy Matrimony: which is an honourable estate, instituted of God in the time of man's innocency, signifying unto us the mystical union that is betwixt Christ and his Church: which holy estate Christ adorned and beautified with his presence and first miracle that he wrought in Cana of Galilee, and is commended of Saint Paul to be honourable among all men: and therefore is not by any to be entered into unadvisedly or lightly, but reverently, discreetly, advisedly, soberly, and in the fear of God. Into this holy estate these two persons present come now to be joined. If any man can show just cause, why they may not lawfully be joined together, let him now speak, or else hereafter for ever hold his peace.

¶ *And also speaking unto the Persons who are to be married, he shall say,*

I require and charge you both, as ye will answer at the dreadful day of judgment when the secrets of all hearts shall be disclosed, that if either of you know any impediment, why ye may not be lawfully joined together in Matrimony, ye do now confess it. For be ye well assured, that if any persons are joined together otherwise than as God's Word doth allow, their marriage is not lawful.

¶ *The Minister, if he shall have reason to doubt of the lawfulness of the proposed Marriage, may demand sufficient surety for his indemnification: but if no impediment shall be alleged, or suspected, the Minister shall say to the Man,*

M. Wilt thou have this Woman to thy wedded wife, to live together after God's ordinance in the holy estate of Matrimony? Wilt thou love her, comfort her, honour, and keep her in sickness and in health; and, forsaking all others, keep thee only unto her, so long as ye both shall live?

¶ *The Man shall answer,*

I will.

¶ *Then shall the Minister say unto the Woman,*

N. Wilt thou have this Man to thy wedded husband, to live together after God's ordinance in the holy estate of Matrimony? Wilt thou obey him, and serve him, love, honour, and keep him in sickness and in health; and, forsaking all others, keep thee only unto him, so long as ye both shall live?

¶ *The Woman shall answer,*

I will.

¶ *Then shall the Minister say,*

Who giveth this Woman to be married to this Man?

¶ *Then shall they give their troth to each other in this manner. The Minister, receiving the Woman at her father's or friend's hands, shall cause the Man with his right hand to take the Woman by her right hand, and to say after him as followeth.*

I *M.* take thee *N.* to my wedded Wife, to have and to hold from this day forward, for better for worse, for richer for poorer, in sickness and in health, to love and to cherish, till death us do part, according to God's holy ordinance; and thereto I plight thee my troth.

¶ *Then shall they loose their hands; and the Woman with her right hand taking the Man by his right hand, shall likewise say after the Minister:*

I *N.* take thee *M.* to my wedded Husband, to have and to hold from this day forward, for better for worse, for richer for poorer, in sickness and in health, to love and to cherish, and to obey, till death us do part, according to God's holy ordinance; and thereto I plight thee my troth.

¶ *Then shall they again loose their hands; and the Man shall give unto the Woman a Ring. And the Minister taking the Ring shall deliver it unto the Man, to put it upon the fourth finger of the Woman's left hand. And the Man holding the Ring there, and taught by the Minister, shall say,*

With this Ring I thee wed, and with all my worldly goods I thee endow: In the Name of the Father, and of the Son, and of the Holy Ghost. *Amen.*

¶ *Then, the Man leaving the Ring upon the fourth finger of the Woman's left hand, the Minister shall say,*

Let us pray.

Our father, who art in heaven, Hallowed be thy Name. Thy Kingdom come. Thy will be done on earth, As it is in heaven. Give us this day our daily bread. And forgive us our trespasses, As we forgive those who trespass against us. And lead us not into temptation; But deliver us from evil. *Amen.*

O Eternal God, Creator and Preserver of all mankind, Giver of all spiritual grace, the Author of everlasting life; Send thy blessing upon these thy servants, this man and this woman, whom we bless in thy Name; that, as Isaac and Rebecca lived faithfully together, so these persons may surely perform and keep the vow and covenant betwixt them made, (whereof this Ring given and received is a token and pledge), and may ever remain in perfect love and peace together, and live according to thy laws; through Jesus Christ our Lord. *Amen.*

¶ *Then shall the Minister join their right hands together, and say,*

Those whom God hath joined together let no man put asunder.

¶ *Then shall the Minister speak unto the company.*

Forasmuch as *M.* and *N.* have consented together in holy wedlock, and have witnessed the same before God and this company, and thereto have given and pledged their troth, each to the other, and have declared the same by giving and receiving a Ring, and by joining hands; I pronounce that they are Man and Wife, In the Name of the Father, and of the Son, and of the Holy Ghost. *Amen.*

¶ *And the Minister shall add this Blessing.*

God the Father, God the Son, God the Holy Ghost, bless, preserve, and keep you; the Lord mercifully with his favour look upon you, and fill you with all spiritual benediction and grace; that ye may so live together in this life, that in the world to come ye may have life everlasting. *Amen.*

Notes and Questions on The Personal and Moral Basis of Marriage

(1) What kinds of "impediments" ought to prevent two people from being married?

(2) What kind of a relationship does this ceremony create? In legal terms? In moral terms? In social terms? What does the ceremony mean when it says the couple have made a "covenant"? See Margaret F. Brinig, *Status, Contract and Covenant*, 79 Cornell L Rev 1573 (1994).

(3) The exchange of promises contained in the marriage ceremony resembles a legal contract. But what are its terms? What happens if the contract is breached? If one party secretly intends not to perform one of the contractual terms?

(4) What kinds of responsibilities for each other does the service require the husband and wife to assume? Are these responsibilities a necessary part of a marriage? Are they responsibilities that it is reasonable to ask couples to assume? What kind of economic relationship does the service contemplate? Is it a just one?

(5) What differences do you see between the promises the man and the woman make? Is any of those differences defensible? What consequences for the marriage might those differences have? Are those differences integral to marriage? What consequences for the marriage would eliminating them have?

(6) The man and the woman promise to "forsake all others." Why? Is this a wise requirement? A realistic one? The Victorian novelist Anthony Trollope believed, as many people in many times have, that a "disposition to love" can be "governed." Doing so, a critic summarizing Trollope argues,

> does not exclude spontaneity and has nothing to do with repression because it is not like pulling the strings of a purse to shut in the disorder. It is an effort to interpret experience in one fashion rather than another and to find satisfaction in a different quarter.... That "there are things that should not be thought of" is therefore a constant refrain in Trollope's novels and in connection with all activities and being "unable to help what one thinks" is a sign not of a passionate nature but of moral ignorance and weakness.

Shirley Robin Letwin, *The Gentleman in Trollope: Individuality and Moral Conduct* 134 (Harvard U Press, 1982). Are those views plausible?

For reflections on them, see Mike W. Martin, *Love's Constancy*, 68 Philosophy 63 (1993); Susan Mendus, *Marital Faithfulness*, 59 Philosophy 243 (1984).

(7) The service contemplates that the marriage will last "until death us do part." Why? Is this a wise requirement? A realistic one? Can people reasonably be expected to love each other so endlessly?

(8) Are there promises which the wedding service does not include but ought to? Promises that it does include but shouldn't?

(9) The marriage ceremony you have just read is now several centuries old. Today, many couples write their own ceremonies. Suppose that you were to write one, what would it say?

(10) Marriage is a specially personal and intimate relationship. Does it make sense to begin it with a socially standardized set of promises?

(11) Why might a couple in love decide to marry, particularly since it is now relatively easy for a couple to live together without marriage?

(2) What Does Marriage Mean to Society?

Reading the wedding service has led us to ask what marriage might mean for the people who enter into it. But why is marriage a social institution, one which "society" and "the law" seek to shape, sustain, and strengthen? One brief and provocative statement of some of the possible reasons comes from the English philosopher and legal reformer Jeremy Bentham in his *Principles of the Civil Code (1843)*:

> Under whatever point of view the institution of marriage is considered, the utility of this noble contract is striking. It is the bond of society, the foundation of civilization.
>
> Marriage, considered as a contract, has drawn women from the hardest and most humiliating servitude; it has distributed the mass of the community into distinct families; it has created a domestic magistracy; it has trained up citizens; it has extended the views of men to the future, through their affection for the rising generation; it has multiplied the social sympathies. In order to estimate all its benefits, it is only necessary to imagine, for a moment, what would be the condition of Man without the institution.

Another brief and provocative statement of some of the reasons society may have an interest in marriage comes from one of the great classics of sociology—Emile Durkheim, *Suicide: A Study in Sociology* (The Free Press, 1951):

> After all, what is marriage? A regulation of sexual relations, including not merely the physical instincts which this intercourse involves but the feelings of every sort gradually engrafted by civilization on the foundation of physical desire. For among us love is a far more mental than organic fact. A man looks to a woman, not merely to the satisfaction of the sexual impulse. Though this natural proclivity has been the germ of all sexual evolution, it has become increasingly complicated with aesthetic and moral feelings, numerous and varied, and today it is only

the smallest element of the total complex process to which it has given birth. Under the influence of these intellectual elements it has itself been partially freed from its physical nature and assumed something like an intellectual one. Moral reasons as well as physical needs impel love.... But just because these various inclinations, thus changed, do not directly depend upon organic necessities, social regulation become necessary. They must be restrained by society since the organism has no means of restraining them. This is the function of marriage. It completely regulates the life of passion, and monogamic marriage more strictly than any other. For by forcing a man to attach himself forever to the same woman it assigns a strictly definite object to the need for love, and closes the horizon.

This determination is what forms the state of moral equilibrium from which the husband benefits. Being unable to seek other satisfactions than those permitted, without transgressing his duty, he restricts his desires to them. The salutary discipline to which he is subjected makes it his duty to find his happiness in his lot, and by doing so supplies him with the means. Besides, if his passion is forbidden to stray, its fixed object is forbidden to fail him; the obligation is reciprocal. Though his enjoyment is restricted, it is assured and this certainty forms his mental foundation. The lot of the unmarried man is different. As he has the right to form attachment wherever inclination leads him, he aspires to everything and is satisfied with nothing. This morbid desire for the infinite which everywhere accompanies anomie may as readily assail this as any other part of our consciousness.... When one is no longer checked, one becomes unable to check one's self. Beyond experienced pleasures one senses and desires others; if one happens almost to have exhausted the range of what is possible, one dreams of the impossible; one thirsts for the non-existent. How can the feelings not be exacerbated by such unending pursuit? For them to reach that state, one need not even have infinitely multiplied the experiences of love and lived the life of a Don Juan. The humdrum existence of the ordinary bachelor suffices. New hopes constantly awake, only to be deceived, leaving a trail of weariness and disillusionment behind them. How can desire, then, become fixed, being uncertain that it can retain what it attracts; for the anomie is twofold. Just as the person makes no definitive gift of himself, he has definitive title to nothing. The uncertainty of the future plus his own indeterminateness therefore condemns him to constant change.

Notes and Questions on the Social Basis of Marriage

(1) What does it mean to say that marriage "is the bond of society, the foundation of civilization"? Is it true? How? It is often said that the family is society's basic building block. But why isn't the individual the basic block? What functions does the family perform that could not be performed by other social institutions? For some wisdom on some of these questions, see Lee E. Teitelbaum, *Placing the Family in Context*, 22 UC Davis L Rev 801 (1989).

(2) What might Bentham mean in saying that marriage has "drawn women from the hardest and most humiliating servitude"? Was he right? Does it benefit women today? How or how not?

(3) What is "a domestic magistracy"? Is it a good thing?

(4) How, if at all, has marriage "multiplied the social sympathies"?

(5) What in fact "would be the condition of Man without the institution"?

(6) Why must sexual relations be regulated? Is it true that the "various inclinations" surrounding love "must be restrained by society"?

(7) What kind of view of human nature do you think Durkheim has?

(8) Why has the law made marriage a legal as well as a social institution? What social and legal functions does marriage serve? Consider the following review of what marriage has meant in the past, and means today:

MARGARET F. BRINIG AND JUNE CARBONE THE RELIANCE INTEREST IN MARRIAGE AND DIVORCE

62 Tulane Law Review 855 (1988)

I. FROM FAMILY TO INDIVIDUAL: THE TRANSFORMATION OF MARRIAGE AND DIVORCE

In considering the role of marriage and divorce, one must examine the fundamental changes in the nature of the institutions. During the centuries in which land continued to be the principal source of wealth, the family operated as the basic unit in society. Marriage functioned as a highly structured, indissolvable, hierarchical institution, responsible for not only the affairs of its members but also the management of the major source of wealth and productivity—land.

During this period, society treated the family as an irreducible unit, led by the husband. Upon marriage, the wife lost any independent legal existence. The family assets were held in the husband's name; only he had the capacity to sue, be sued, own property, and enter into contracts. He was responsible for the family finances, care of dependents, and education of the children. The bride, frequently a teen-age virgin marrying an established stranger twice her age, promised to love, honor, and obey. She was financially, psychologically, and practically dependent on her husband. The law reinforced male authority in the name of marital indivisibility; there would be no piercing of the marital veil to correct abuses in the conduct of marital responsibilities.

For both men and women, marriage was the major determinant of wealth and status. For men, marriage secured the legitimacy of their offspring, and with legitimacy and primogeniture, the right of succession and authority over the family's holdings. For women, marriage provided the only available form of support and the only socially sanctioned role outside the convent. Women had few opportunities for an independent economic existence, and in societies that prized virginity, little opportunity for remarriage once the union was consummated.

This combination of economic and social factors produced an enormous dependence on the stability of marriage both for the individuals involved and for society. The law responded by refusing to recognize "divorce" at all. The ecclesiastical courts recognized only divorce *a mensa et thoro,* effectively providing for a legal separation. The marital obligations apart from cohabitation remained unchanged. The husband continued to support the family and manage its affairs. He retained ownership and control of the family's assets and authority over the children. The wife's entitlement to support continued only "*vixerit dum sola et casta,*"—that is, only so long as she remained "*chast and single.*" However long the separation continued, the husband and wife remained part of the same family. The law protected those arrangements that depended on the continuation of the marriage: the indivisibility of family property, the legitimacy and inheritance rights of the children, the authority over family holdings, and the support of dependents.

Recognition of absolute divorce primarily affected the possibility of remarriage. Henry VIII notwithstanding, it was the spectacle of the faithful spouse remaining bound to the marriage while the other spouse flouted its obligations that guaranteed the obsolescence of divorce *a mensa et thoro*. With divorce *a vinculo matrimonii*, the innocent spouse who could establish that his or her mate had engaged in adultery, cruelty, or desertion (namely, unilateral activity incompatible with the continuation of the marriage) was entitled to release from his or her own marital obligations. Fault was central to this determination. If both parties were at fault, no divorce could be granted because neither party could justify release from the marriage.

The determination of fault secured the release of the innocent spouse's marital obligations while legally confirming the other's continuing obligations. Thus, if a husband succeeded in divorcing his wife, he was released from his duty to support her while retaining ownership of the family property and custody of the children. Correspondingly, if a wife successfully divorced her husband, she was released from her marital obligations of obedience, chastity, and service to her husband. He retained ownership of all property in his name, which ordinarily included all jointly acquired property, subject to a duty to support her from the proceeds. Thus, the "innocent husband" returned to the unencumbered position he had been in before marriage, freeing him—both legally and financially—to marry again. The "innocent wife" secured continuation of the support she expected from the marriage and needed to avoid becoming a ward of the state.

By the end of the nineteenth century, a wholesale change had occurred in the role of marriage and divorce. Commercial ventures had replaced land as the primary source of wealth. Men worked increasingly outside the home, with their wives assuming a greater role in running the household in their absence. Children, now less important as heirs to the indivisible family estate or as economic assets adding to the family income, were raised far more by their stay-at-home mothers. Single women enjoyed increased opportunities for employment outside the home, and married women acquired a measure of control over their separately acquired property.

The result of these economic changes was increasing recognition of men and women's individual identity within the family while marriage continued as a highly specialized, hierarchical (if no longer authoritarian) and not quite so indissolvable institution. Confirming the wife's increasingly independent identity, the Married Women's Property Acts granted married women the capacity to own property, to sue and be sued, and to enter into contracts. Upon divorce, women could recover their separately held property and pay for separately incurred debts. As the responsibility for child rearing shifted from father to mother during the marriage, custody presumptions shifted in favor of the mother at the time of divorce.

At the same time, however, the law confirmed male dominion over the family's commercial ventures. Upon marriage, women were expected to give up any outside employment to attend to family affairs. The husband's domicile controlled that of his wife; she could be divorced for desertion if she did not follow him. Commercial enterprises in which both spouses participated were subject to the husband's control. A wife was entitled neither to compensation for assistance given to her husband's business, nor to restitution for goods and services supplied. Upon divorce, since the husband retained ownership of all jointly held property, the wife remained entitled to and dependent upon his support.

Thus, marriage remained an institution governing the relationship between two parties performing highly specialized and—at least financially—unequal roles. But neither economic productivity nor individual well-being depended to the same degree on the indissolvability of the institution. Even a small measure of economic independence persuaded more women to end unhappy marriages. With increasing life expectancies and declining social stigma, the prospects for remarriage increased for both spouses. Rules against collusion proved ineffective in divorce suits. With less draconian consequences, the parties became more willing to collaborate in establishing fault, and the courts more willing to grant divorces. Nonetheless, the allocations made upon divorce were still tied to findings of fault and still designed to protect the major interests at stake: the indivisibility of commercial ventures, support for the dependent spouse, and custody for the wife as the parent most directly involved in the children's upbringing.

If the nineteenth century produced major changes in marriage and divorce, the twentieth century witnessed a wholesale revolution. By the last part of the twentieth century, the major source of wealth had long since ceased to be land or family held ventures. Large organizations, whether public or private, determined productivity. Entitlements to jobs, earning power, pensions, and government benefits have become the major sources of income. Families no longer govern the major sources of wealth nor necessarily determine their members' lifelong financial prospects.

As dependence on the family generally has decreased, the division of labor within the family has become less specialized. Employment outside the home has become increasingly common for women of all ages and marital status. During the same period, life expectancy has increased, the number of children per family has fallen, nuclear families have become more common, and labor saving devices have made household chores less onerous. Childrearing, housekeeping, and care of older or infirm relatives no longer take up the overwhelming part of an adult woman's lifespan. Women are accordingly freer to pursue other activities and, with their own income, are less dependent on the support of their husbands.

With the family no longer the exclusive determinant of status and wealth, the justification for marriage has changed from social obligation to mutual affection. Societal norms no longer regard it as a sufficient reason to marry that the spouse has parental approval, that he or she come from a "good family," that he be able to support her "in the style to which she has been accustomed," or that she be able to promote his well-being through her ability as a homemaker or entertainer. The basis of modern marriage is love. And when love disappears, when there is no longer mutual affection, society dictates no reason to stay married.

In modern society, divorce plays an altogether different role. Divorce is a matter of individual choice, following not from the abdication or breach of marital duties, but from the end of mutual affection. Where each spouse has the right to leave, the identification of "fault" is meaningless. Divorce is no longer the unilateral release of a spouse from his or her marital obligations justified by the breach of the other spouse. It is a determination—precipitated perhaps by the actions of one spouse, but nonetheless applicable to both—that marital differences have become irreconcilable. Modern divorce law eventually followed this social transformation, with all states now recognizing "no fault" divorce. Even where fault grounds are still available, most couples agree to the dissolution of their union without a pro forma assignment of blame.

With these changes in the nature of marriage and divorce, the allocations made at the time of the divorce serve different purposes. Without a societally imposed duty to continue the marriage, modern divorce courts emphasize the severance of marital bonds rather than the identification of which obligations are to continue. With less specialization in marital roles, the husband is no longer given ownership of the property while the "innocent" wife receives alimony. Most states allow each spouse to reclaim the property he or she brought into the marriage, and to retain gifts or bequests, while providing approximately equal division of property acquired during the marriage. With both spouses presumed independent upon divorce, and with no determination of culpability for the marital breakup, the courts intervene primarily to resolve the division of jointly held property. They are reluctant to impose any continuing relationship on the couple once the divorce has become final. Formerly indivisible family ventures are not included in the property settlement while the most important sources of modern wealth—entitlements to future income—remain the province of individuals.

The result is an uneasy coexistence of two systems that together describe only a minority of modern marriages. In traditional marriages where the wife continues to depend upon her husband's income, modern divorce law keeps open the possibility of permanent alimony justified by dependence. When both spouses are capable of self-support, the law provides for an approximately equal property division. But in an increasing majority of marriages, wives are neither dependent nor equal.

Whether because of sex discrimination, the division of marital responsibilities, or individual differences in ability, ambition, education, training, or social encouragement, husbands are likely to earn more than their working wives. For their part, women continue to assume a large share of the family's domestic responsibilities, a share compounded with the arrival of children. The longer the marriage, the more likely even working women are to be dependent on their husband's income to maintain their standard of living, the more likely they are to have sacrificed to some degree their own financial future to further the marriage, and the less likely their prospects for remarriage become. In addition, men are, perhaps for the first time, making similar sacrifices to support their wives' careers or to participate in raising the children. The existing system of marriage and divorce provides no scale for balancing these sacrifices, and while modern commentators have decried the resulting inequities, there has been no comprehensive analysis of the interests at stake.

(3) What Is the Law of Entry Into Marriage?

Now that we have begun to think about the social and legal functions of marriage, we need a brief introduction to the modern statutory framework of marriage law. One problem in teaching and learning about areas of law that, like family law, are primarily the responsibility of the states is, of course, that each state has its own statutes. To solve this problem, and to focus on larger trends in the law, we have generally used the Uniform Marriage and Divorce Act to exemplify the statutory structure of family law. We have used it for this purpose because it typifies many modern trends.

The UMDA is the offspring of the National Conference of Commissioners on Uniform State Laws, which was responsible for drafting the Act, and of the American Bar Association, which approved the Act. Both organizations grew out of the professionalization of the American bar in the late-nineteenth century. Both organizations were concerned with rationalizing, organizing, and unifying the laws of the states. The leading result of this concern was, of course, the Uniform Commercial Code. The UMDA is another such consequence. Its provisions defining marriage follow. (For an example of a statute enacting the UMDA's provisions, see Mont Code Ann § 40–1–103 (2005)).

THE UNIFORM MARRIAGE AND DIVORCE ACT

Marriage

SECTION 201. ***[Formalities.]***

Marriage is a personal relationship between a man and a woman arising out of a civil contract to which the consent of the parties is essential. A marriage licensed, solemnized, and registered as provided in this Act is valid in this state. A marriage may be contracted, maintained, invalidated, or dissolved only as provided by law.

SECTION 203. ***[License to Marry.]***

When a marriage application has been completed and signed by both parties to a prospective marriage and at least one party has appeared before the [marriage license] clerk and paid the marriage license fee of [$_______], the [marriage license] clerk shall issue a license to marry and a marriage certificate form upon being furnished:

(1) satisfactory proof that each party to the marriage will have attained the age of 18 years at the time the marriage license is effective, or will have attained the age of 16 years and has either the consent to the marriage of both parents or his guardian, or judicial approval; [or, if under the age of 16 years, has both the consent of both parents or his guardian and judicial approval;] and

(2) satisfactory proof that the marriage is not prohibited; [and]

[(3) a certificate of the results of any medical examination required by the laws of this state].

SECTION 204. ***[License, Effective Date.]***

A license to marry becomes effective throughout this state 3 days after the date of issuance, unless the [_______] court orders that the license is effective when issued, and expires 180 days after it becomes effective.

SECTION 205. ***[Judicial Approval.]***

(a) The [_______] court, after a reasonable effort has been made to notify the parents or guardian of each underaged party, may order the [marriage license] clerk to issue a marriage license and a marriage certificate form:

[(1)] to a party aged 16 or 17 years who has no parent capable of consenting to his marriage, or whose parent or guardian has not consented to his marriage; [or

(2) to a party under the age of 16 years who has the consent of both parents to his marriage, if capable of giving consent, or his guardian].

(b) A marriage license and a marriage certificate form may be issued under this section only if the court finds that the underaged party is capable of assuming the responsibilities of marriage and the marriage will serve his best interest. Pregnancy alone does not establish that the best interest of the party will be served.

(c) The [______] court shall authorize performance of a marriage by proxy upon the showing required by the provisions on solemnization.

SECTION 206. *[Solemnization and Registration.]*

(a) A marriage may be solemnized by a judge of a court of record, by a public official whose powers include solemnization of marriages, or in accordance with any mode of solemnization recognized by any religious denomination, Indian Nation or Tribe, or Native Group....

(b) If a party to a marriage is unable to be present at the solemnization, he may authorize in writing a third person to act as his proxy.

SECTION 207. *[Prohibited Marriages.]*

(a) The following marriages are prohibited:

(1) a marriage entered into prior to the dissolution of an earlier marriage of one of the parties;

(2) a marriage between an ancestor and a descendant, or between a brother and a sister, whether the relationship is by the half or the whole blood, or by adoption;

(3) a marriage between an uncle and a niece or between an aunt and a nephew, whether the relationship is by the half or the whole blood, except as to marriages permitted by the established customs of aboriginal cultures.

(b) Parties to a marriage prohibited under this section who cohabit after removal of the impediment are lawfully married as of the date of the removal of the impediment.

(c) Children born of a prohibited marriage are legitimate.

SECTION 208. *[Declaration of Invalidity.]*

(a) The [______] court shall enter its decree declaring the invalidity of a marriage entered into under the following circumstances:

(1) a party lacked capacity to consent to the marriage at the time the marriage was solemnized, either because of mental incapacity or infirmity or because of the influence of alcohol, drugs, or other incapacitating substances, or a party was induced to enter into a marriage by force or duress, or by fraud involving the essentials of marriage;

(2) a party lacks the physical capacity to consummate the marriage by sexual intercourse, and at the time the marriage was solemnized the other party did not know of the incapacity;

(3) a party [was under the age of 16 years and did not have the consent of his parents or guardian and judicial approval or] was aged

16 or 17 years and did not have the consent of his parents or guardian or judicial approval; or

(4) the marriage is prohibited.

(b) A declaration of invalidity under subsection (a)(1) through (3) may be sought by any of the following persons and must be commenced within the times specified, but in no event may a declaration of invalidity be sought after the death of either party to the marriage:

(1) for a reason set forth in subsection (a)(1), by either party or by the legal representative of the party who lacked capacity to consent, no later than 90 days after the petitioner obtained knowledge of the described condition;

(2) for the reason set forth in subsection (a)(2), by either party, no later than one year after the petitioner obtained knowledge of the described condition;

(3) for the reason set forth in subsection (a)(3), by the underaged party, his parent or guardian, prior to the time the underaged party reaches the age at which he could have married without satisfying the omitted requirement.

Alternative A

[(c) A declaration of invalidity for the reason set forth in subsection (a)(4) may be sought by either party, the legal spouse in case of a bigamous marriage, the [appropriate state official], or a child of either party, at any time prior to the death of one of the parties.]

Alternative B

[(c) A declaration of invalidity for the reason set forth in subsection (a)(4) may be sought by either party, the legal spouse in case of a bigamous marriage, the [appropriate state official], or a child of either party, at any time, not to exceed 5 years following the death of either party.]

(d) Children born of a marriage declared invalid are legitimate.

(e) Unless the court finds, after a consideration of all relevant circumstances, including the effect of a retroactive decree on third parties, that the interests of justice would be served by making the decree not retroactive, it shall declare the marriage invalid as of the date of the marriage. The provisions of this Act relating to property rights of the spouses, maintenance, support, and custody of children on dissolution of marriage are applicable to non-retroactive decrees of invalidity.

Notes and Questions on the Law of Entry Into Marriage

(1) If marriage is a "personal relationship," why may it be "contracted, maintained, invalidated, or dissolved only as provided by law"?

(2) If marriage is a "personal relationship," why is a marriage license required? Given the social importance often accorded to mar-

riage, why is a marriage license available on demand? Most states require a waiting period of a few days between the application and issuance of the license or, like the UMDA, after its issuance. Is that period long enough? Should states also require some form of counseling before issuing a license (as some religions do)?

(3) Section 201 says that marriage is a relationship "arising out of a civil contract." To what extent are the UMDA sections you have just read consistent with the law of contract?

(4) Professor Clark reports that no American statute and only one case authorizes ships' captains to perform marriages on the high seas. He also notes that, again contrary to popular understandings, the "conventional view is that a ceremonial marriage is valid notwithstanding that it is not consummated." Homer H. Clark, Jr., 1 *The Law of Domestic Relations in the United States* 93 (West, 1987).

(5) Would (ought) a person with Down's Syndrome and an IQ of 50 lack "capacity to consent to the marriage"? Does the following "Comment" help: "Courts ... will undoubtedly continue to apply existing stringent standards by holding that a declaration of invalidity is appropriate only if the petitioner offers clear and definite evidence that one of the spouses lacked 'sufficient mental capacity to understand intelligently the marriage contract ... and the obligations it imposed upon him' "? For a refusal to annul the marriage of a "mildly" retarded man, see *Edmunds v. Edwards*, 287 NW2d 420 (Neb 1980).

(6) If woman induces a man to marry her by fraudulently saying she is pregnant, may the marriage be declared invalid? For a negative answer see *Hill v. Hill*, 398 NE2d 1048 (Ill 1979). Can you formulate a general theory of what promises constitute fraud for purposes of annulling a marriage?

(7) Why does the UMDA place age limits on marriage? Are you convinced by the following: "Presumably the purposes of setting a minimum age for marriage are to prevent unwise marriages of immature persons, to reduce the divorce rate and promote marital stability, it being generally acknowledged that youthful marriages are more likely to end in divorce than other marriages, and to provide children with the care of mature and responsible parents"? Homer H. Clark, Jr., 1 *The Law of Domestic Relations in the United States* 162 (West 1987).

(8) Would a marriage contracted without a marriage license be valid under the UMDA? Holding yes under a similar statute is *Carabetta v. Carabetta*, 438 A2d 109 (Conn 1980).

(9) Professor Clark writes, "The divorce decree terminates for the future a valid existing marriage. Annulment, however, constitutes a declaration that no marriage ever occurred, due to an impediment existing at the time of the ceremony.... Today the distinction has become blurred and its logic is seen to be very largely an illusion. Many so-called void or voidable marriages have important legal consequences for the parties. We seem to be on the way back to the medieval position,

according to which annulment was merely a way of ending a marriage, and was called divorce." Homer H. Clark, Jr., 1 *The Law of Domestic Relations in the United States* 221 (West 1987). Does the UMDA contribute to such a development?

SECTION 2. LAWFULLY BE JOINED TOGETHER: EVALUATING MARRIAGE

I am, in truth, very thankful for not having married at all.... If I had had a husband dependent on me for his happiness, the responsibility would have made me wretched.... If my husband had not depended on me for his happiness, I should have been jealous. So also with children.... The veneration in which I hold domestic life has always shown me that that life was not for those whose self-respect had been early broken down, or had never grown.... My strong will, combined with anxiety of conscience, makes me fit only to live alone; and my taste and like are for living alone. The older I have grown, the more serious and irremediable have seemed to me the evils and disadvantages of married life, as it exists among us at this time: and I am provided with what it is the bane of single life in ordinary cases to want,—substantial, laborious and serious occupation.

Harriet Martineau
Harriet Martineau's Autobiography

We have been reading about a fairly traditional view of what marriage is and about the current legal requirements for entering marriage. But we need a richer sense of the purpose of marriage as a legal and social institution and of the community's relation to marriage as a legal and social institution. As you are by now well aware, one standard way to evaluate a legal idea is to try out logical extensions of the idea to see how far it can carry you. We will put traditional marriage to such a test by looking at three heterodox versions of that idea: polygamous, incestuous, and same-sex marriage.

A. EVALUATING MARRIAGE: POLYGAMY

If the purpose of dinner is to nourish the body, a man who eats two dinners at once may perhaps get more enjoyment but will not attain his purpose, for his stomach will not digest the two dinners.

If the purpose of marriage is the family, the person who wishes to have many wives or husbands may perhaps obtain much pleasure, but in that case will not have a family.

If the purpose of food is nourishment and the purpose of marriage is the family, the whole question resolves itself into not eating more than one can digest, and not having more wives or husbands than are needed for the family—that is, one wife or one husband.

Leo Tolstoy
War and Peace

(1) Reynolds v. United States

We will approach polygamous marriage primarily through the celebrated case of *Reynolds v. United States*, in which the Supreme Court held that the federal government was not constitutionally prohibited from banning Mormon polygamy in the territories. Assessing the judicial and social reaction to Mormon polygamy is made difficult for most of us by our unfamiliarity with Mormon religion and history. Therefore we have provided a short (very short) exposition of both. Because it is brief, and because much of the historical story is still controverted, you will need to read further for a fuller and better picture. Our account itself is primarily drawn from two books, both of which we recommend. They are Lawrence Foster, *Religion and Sexuality: Three American Communal Experiments of the Nineteenth Century* (Oxford U Press, 1981), and Klaus J. Hansen, *Mormonism and the American Experience* (U Chi Press, 1981). Professor Foster offers a fascinating and insightful look at nineteenth-century and Mormon thought about family life, Professor Hansen a general description of the rise and doctrine of Mormonism. A biography of George Reynolds, the protagonist of the following case, is *Prisoner for Conscience' Sake* by Bruce A. Van Orden (Deseret Book Co, 1991).

The story begins when, in the early nineteenth century, New Englanders began to settle in western New York State. They brought with them their New England religious ideas; they encountered the economic and social dislocations of antebellum business and family life. The region so caught fire with religious and social fervor that it was called the "Burned–Over District." It witnessed numerous religious revivals; the flourishing of communal experiments like Oneida, the Shakers, and the Fourierists; the beginnings of the women's rights movement; and a passionate abolitionism. It was also the home of Joseph Smith.

In the 1820s and '30s, Smith began the enterprise of founding Mormonism. From the beginning, that religion was importantly concerned with problems of family, sexual, and social disorder. From quite early on, Smith, who was much influenced by the Biblical Hebrews, contemplated introducing polygamy. It was tried on a limited scale during the Mormon stay at Nauvoo, Illinois. The church's commitment to polygamy was publicly announced in 1852, five years after the Mormons arrived in Salt Lake City.

The Mormons were not (nor are they) sexual liberationists, and their new form of marriage has been described as "puritan polygamy." Early Mormon writings roundly denounced fornication and adultery and described the patriarchal family as a bulwark against social disorder. Polygamy was a means of being fruitful and multiplying and a return to Old Testament practice. By some it was taken as a commandment. As the famous English traveler Richard Burton wrote, "All sensuality in the married state is strictly forbidden beyond the requirement for ensuring progeny,—the practice, in fact, of Adam and Abraham."

Marriage was central to Mormon theology. (It still is, but—we stress—this paragraph treats the theological background of the beliefs that were relevant to *Reynolds*.) One purpose of marriage was to provide souls with tabernacles, so that they might live on earth in a probationary state. Marriages also had consequences for one's life after death. After the Judgment there was a hell and three degrees of glory—in descending order the celestial, the telestial, and the terrestrial—each of which had its own divisions. When "sealed" (sanctioned) by the church, marriages extended into the celestial state through eternity. In heaven, husbands and wives of such marriages were to be surrounded by their immediate families and all their descendants (and by people who did not marry). Eventually, they could attain Godhood. Polygamy was important in part because multiple wives helped provide tabernacles for souls and greater kingdoms for patriarchs in heaven. It was also important in the theology of the time because, as Professor Hansen writes, "[T]he highest degree of glory in the celestial kingdom, the attainment of Godhood, was reserved for those who had entered into polygamous relationships."

Polygamy was also thought to accord with differences between men and women. As one polygamist husband wrote, " 'A woman needs but one man at a time. . . . She has no right to be any other man's wife while he lives for she has given herself to him. The husband belongs to no woman, and can lawfully receive other women, if they come to honorably [sic]. Then it is his right and duty to love them all that belong to him. Such a course is no more wrong than it is for a woman to love several children of her own at the same time." Quoted in Jessie L. Embry, *Mormon Polygamous Families: Life in the Principle* 127–28 (U Utah Press, 1987).

Given the special circumstances of the Mormon experiment with polygamy (the exigencies of settling a new land, the pressures of proselytizing for a new religion, the threat of criminal prosecutions), polygamy's success or failure in Utah would hardly be dispositive of its success or failure elsewhere. Nevertheless, you may find a bit of information about the workings of Mormon polygamy helpful in thinking about the institution of marriage generally. Unfortunately, of course, the evidence on the subject is unsatisfactory, and historians disagree about what to make of it. Professor Foster's account, which is among the best, mixes sympathy and skepticism. He notes evidence that polygamy was not entirely popular even among Mormons. Wives had to struggle with ambivalent feelings about their husband's relations with other wives; husbands had to strive to treat wives equally. As a daughter of one polygamous marriage and wife of another wrote,

> I am sure that women would never have accepted polygamy had it not been for their religion. No woman ever consented to its practice without great sacrifice on her part. There is something so sacred about the relationship of husband and wife that a third party in the family is sure to disturb the confidence and security that formerly existed.

Only fifteen to twenty percent of Mormon families were ever polygamous, and the proportion declined steadily from an early peak. (Professor Foster speculates that one reason was that in Utah there were not more women than men.) Professor Foster suggests that Mormons entered polygamous marriages primarily for religious reasons (although a desire for status and money played a part, particularly with last-and-youngest wives). He quotes one observer in 1880 who said that Mormon women considered polygamy " 'as a religious duty and schooled themselves to bear its discomforts as a sort of religious penance, and that it was a matter of pride to make everybody believe they lived happily and to persuade themselves and others that it was not a trial; and that a long life of such discipline makes the trial lighter.' "

On the other hand, Professor Foster finds little evidence that Mormon women felt degraded by polygamy. "Viewed as an honorable and desirable state, plural marriage could give women a sense of pride and importance." He notes that, like other Victorians, "Mormons stressed the positive and vital social role that women could play in the home and the family. . . ." Id. He sees polygamy as having a specially important role in a society where the men were frequently away for long periods on church missions, for it meant that polygamous wives could find companionship and help from their husband's other wives.

Professor Foster thinks polygamy may have been a means of "desexualizing and redirecting the husband-wife relationship so that relations between the sexes became first and foremost goal-directed," the goal being "the rapid and efficient establishment of religious and communal order." Polygamy did so "[b]y partially breaking down exclusive bonds between husband and wife and by undercutting intense emotional involvement in family affairs in favor of Church business. . . ."

Jessie L. Embry argues that "Mormon polygamous families were not much different than Mormon monogamous families and other non-Mormon families of the same era." Ms. Embry quotes Brigham Young as saying, " 'It is the calling of the wife and mother to know what to do with everything that is brought into the house, laboring to make her home desirable to her husband and children, making herself an Eve in the midst of a little paradise of her own.' " Ms. Embry finds such Victorian ideas about gender roles "far more important in determining life cycles for men and women and boys and girls than how many wives were married to the same husband." (She adds, however, that "this division of labor was sometimes enhanced even more because the priesthood holder—the man—was supposed to be the head of the home.") She reports a wide variety of practices in polygamous households. Some husbands scrupulously secured their first wife's assent to a second wife; other husbands simply announced their decision to marry again. Some plural wives lived together; many lived in separate homes (though usually in the same community). Some families divided their funds evenly among the wives; some used other formulas. Sometimes the first wife apportioned the funds; more often the husband did. Some co-wives established a mother-daughter relationship; some a sororal one (indeed as many as 30% may actually have been sisters); some could establish only a hostile relationship; some had hardly any relationship at all. Ms.

Embry agrees with Professor Foster that polygamy diluted the emotional importance of marriage and strengthened the emotional importance of children to women, and she suggests it may have weakened the father's relationship to his children.

Ms. Embry writes that "[l]iving in polygamy and overcoming natural jealousies and selfishness took considerable effort." Like Professor Foster, she points to the religious motive for entering polygamy and for understanding marital relations within it. Thus she quotes one polygamous wife: " 'When people had what I call the spirit of polygamy they were happy and they raised good and happy families. They had bitter times of course. No woman can help being jealous of another and if all the wives did not have the spirit of polygamy then there was suffering. It was a hard principle to live, but when it was lived at its best, it was truly a divine principle. Women learned to control themselves and develop resources within themselves that they would not have done otherwise.' "

Mormons had long met vehement opposition. The opposition came in part from the facts that Mormons claimed an aggressively exclusive view of religious truth, that they seemed to be instituting a separatist and nearly theocratic self-government within the United States, and that they seemed to have the economic power to turn their vision into reality. But Professor Foster suggests that "the primary conscious motivation for the nineteenth-century attacks on the Mormons was hostility toward polygamy and other behavior that diverged from American cultural norms.... For many Americans, the question appears to have been to what extent social practices perceived as deeply offensive to public morals could be justified by classifying those practices as part of a religion." Early rumors about polygamy provoked intense hostility from non-Mormons. This hostility continued after the Mormons moved to Utah and publicly embraced polygamy. In 1856, both Democratic and Republican platforms condemned polygamy; the Republican platform denounced it and slavery as "twin relics of barbarism."

In 1862, Congress passed the Morrill Act, which provided that "every person having a husband or wife living, who shall marry any other person, whether married or single, in a Territory of the United States ... shall ... be adjudged guilty of bigamy." In 1882, the Edmunds Act established fines and five-year prison sentences for polygamists and barred them from voting or serving on juries or in public office. The Edmunds Act failed to accomplish its purpose, and in 1887 Congress passed the Edmunds–Tucker Act, which, *inter alia*, dissolved the church and made forfeit most of its property. In May 1890, the Supreme Court upheld the government's attempts to enforce the Act. In September of that year, the President of the Mormon Church ended the practice of polygamy, and many ideas which had been part of the belief in polygamy were transmuted into an emphasis on the religious and social importance of the monogamous family. Two critics of the federal campaign against the church summarize its effects this way: "Over a thousand Mormons were convicted of practicing polygamy.... On a larger scale, the role of the Mormon church as a guiding force in all aspects of

Mormon life was destroyed. The church that Washington permitted to survive was shorn of its secular powers, and church experimentation with novel forms of social organization ... were abandoned. For better or worse, thenceforth the civil and religious powers in Utah were clearly separated, and Mormons became by and large indistinguishable from other Americans." Edwin Brown Firmage and Richard Collin Mangrum, *Zion in the Courts: A Legal History of the Church of Jesus Christ of Latter-day Saints, 1830–1900* 130 (U of Ill Press, 1988).

A legal centerpiece of Mormon resistance to federal force was *Reynolds v. United States*. George Reynolds was an English immigrant who was Brigham Young's secretary. He settled in the Utah Territory in 1865 and soon married Mary Ann Tuddenham. Nine years later, while still married to her, he married Amelia Jane Schofield. Charges of violating the Morrill Act by committing bigamy were brought against him, quite possibly as an arranged test case. Mormon doctrine held that the United States Constitution is divinely inspired, and Mormons believed, as Brigham Young said, that " 'there is not a single constitution of any single state, much less the constitution of the Federal Government, that hinders a man from having two wives....' " However, Reynolds was convicted, partly because of testimony against him by Amelia Jane Reynolds. His conviction was overturned by the Utah Supreme Court because the grand jury that had indicted him had been the wrong size. After a second trial, Reynolds was again convicted. Professors Firmage and Mangrum report, "In his brief to the Supreme Court, Reynolds's attorneys spent little time discussing First Amendment protection of polygamy. Instead, they challenged the size of the grand jury that had indicted him, the improper admission and exclusion of jurors, the admission of his polygamous wife's testimony from his first trial, and the bench's instructions to the jury to consider the larger consequences of polygamy." The Supreme Court rejected all Reynolds' arguments. Reynolds paid a $500 fine and served nineteen months of a two-year sentence. "After being released ..., Reynolds was received among the Mormons as a 'living martyr,' and in 1890 [ironically, the year the church disavowed polygamy] became one of the General Authorities of the church." And, in 1885, he married Mary Goold.

REYNOLDS v. UNITED STATES

Supreme Court of the United States, 1878
98 US 145

WAITE, J.... On the trial, the plaintiff in error, the accused, proved that at the time of his alleged second marriage he was, and for many years before had been, a member of the Church of Jesus Christ of Latter–Day Saints, commonly called the Mormon Church, and a believer in its doctrines; that it was an accepted doctrine of that church "that it was the duty of male members of said church, circumstances permitting, to practice polygamy; ... that this duty was enjoined by different books which the members of said church believed to be of divine origin, and among others the Holy Bible, and also that the members of the church believed that the practice of polygamy was directly enjoined upon the male members thereof by the Almighty God, in a revelation to Joseph Smith, the founder and prophet of said church; that the failing or refusing to practice polygamy by such male members of said church, when circumstances would admit, would be punished, and that the penalty for such failure and refusal would be damnation in the life to come." He also proved "that he had received permission from the recognized authorities in said church to enter into polygamous marriage; . . . that Daniel H. Wells, one having authority in said church to perform the marriage ceremony, married the said defendant on or about the time the crime is alleged to have been committed, to some woman by the name of Schofield, and that such marriage ceremony was performed under and pursuant to the doctrines of said church."

Upon this proof he asked the court to instruct the jury that if they found from the evidence that he "was married as charged—if he was married—in pursuance of and in conformity with what he believed at the time to be a religious duty, that the verdict must be 'not guilty.' "This request was refused, and the court did charge "that there must have been a criminal intent, but that if the defendant, under the influence of a religious belief that it was right,—under an inspiration, if you please, that it was right,—deliberately married a second time, having a first wife living, the want of consciousness of evil intent—the want of understanding on his part that he was committing a crime—did not excuse him; but the law inexorably in such case implies the criminal intent."

Upon this charge and refusal to charge the question is raised, whether religious belief can be accepted as a justification of an overt act made criminal by the law of the land. The inquiry is not as to the power of Congress to prescribe criminal laws for the Territories, but as to the guilt of one who knowingly violates a law which has been properly enacted, if he entertains a religious belief that the law is wrong.

Congress cannot pass a law for the government of the Territories which shall prohibit the free exercise of religion. The first amendment to the Constitution expressly forbids such legislation. Religious freedom is guaranteed everywhere throughout the United States, so far as congressional interference is concerned. The question to be determined is, whether the law now under consideration comes within this prohibition.

The word "religion" is not defined in the Constitution. We must go elsewhere, therefore, to ascertain its meaning, and nowhere more appropriately, we think, than to the history of the times in the midst of which the provision was adopted. The precise point of the inquiry is, what is the religious freedom which has been guaranteed.

Before the adoption of the Constitution, attempts were made in some of the colonies and States to legislate not only in respect to the establishment of religion, but in respect to its doctrines and precepts as well. The people were taxed, against their will, for the support of religion, and sometimes for the support of particular sects to whose tenets they could not and did not subscribe. Punishments were prescribed for a failure to attend upon public worship, and sometimes for entertaining heretical opinions. The controversy upon this general subject was animated in many of the States, but seemed at last to culminate in Virginia. In 1784, the House of Delegates of that State having under consideration "a bill establishing provision for teachers of the Christian religion," postponed it until the next session, and directed that the bill should be published and distributed, and that the people be requested "to signify their opinion respecting the adoption of such a bill at the next session of assembly."

This brought out a determined opposition. Amongst others, Mr. Madison prepared a "Memorial and Remonstrance," which was widely circulated and signed, and in which he demonstrated "that religion, or the duty we owe the Creator," was not within the cognizance of civil government. Semple's Virginia Baptists, Appendix. At the next session the proposed bill was not only defeated, but another, "for establishing religious freedom," drafted by Mr. Jefferson, was passed. 1 Jeff. Works, 45; 2 Howison, Hist. of Va. 298. In the preamble of this act (12 Hening's Stat. 84) religious freedom is defined; and after a recital "that to suffer the civil magistrate to intrude his powers into the field of opinion, and to restrain the profession or propagation of principle on supposition of their ill tendency, is a dangerous fallacy which at once destroys all religious liberty," it is declared "that it is time enough for the rightful purposes of civil government for its officers to interfere when principles break out into overt acts against peace and good order." In these two sentences is found the true distinction between what properly belongs to the church and what to the State.

In a little more than a year after the passage of this statute the convention met which prepared the Constitution of the United States. Of this convention Mr. Jefferson was not a member, he being then absent as minister to France. As soon as he saw the draft of the Constitution proposed for adoption, he, in a letter to a friend, expressed his disappointment at the absence of an express declaration insuring the freedom of religion (2 Jeff. Works, 355), but was willing to accept it as it was, trusting that the good sense and honest intentions of the people would bring about the necessary alterations. 1 Jeff. Works, 79. Five of the States, while adopting the Constitution, proposed amendments. Three—New Hampshire, New York, and Virginia—included in one form or another a declaration of religious freedom in the changes they desired to have made, as did also North Carolina, where the convention at first declined to ratify the Constitution until the proposed amendments were acted upon. Accordingly, at the first session of the first Congress the amendment now under consideration was proposed with others by Mr. Madison. It met the views of the advocates of religious freedom, and was adopted. Mr. Jefferson afterwards, in reply to an address to him by a committee of the Danbury Baptist Association (8 id. 113), took occasion to say: "Believing with you that religion is a matter which lies solely between man and his God; that he owes account to none other for his faith or his worship; that the legislative powers of the government reach actions only, and not opinions,—I contemplate with sovereign reverence that act of the whole American people which declared that their legislature should 'make no law respecting an establishment of religion or prohibiting the free exercise thereof,' thus building a wall of separation between church and State. Adhering to this expression of the supreme will of the nation in behalf of the rights of conscience, I shall see with sincere satisfaction the progress of those sentiments which tend to restore man to all his natural rights, convinced he has no natural right in opposition to his social duties." Coming as this does from an acknowledged leader of the advocates of the measure, it may be accepted almost as an authoritative declaration of the scope and effect of the amendment thus secured. Congress was deprived of all legislative power over mere opinion, but was left free to reach actions which were in violation of social duties or subversive of good order.

Polygamy has always been odious among the northern and western nations of Europe, and, until the establishment of the Mormon Church, was almost exclusively a feature of the life of Asiatic and of African people. At common law, the second marriage was always void (2 Kent, Com. 79), and from the earliest history of England polygamy has been treated as an offence against society. After the establishment of the ecclesiastical courts, and until the time of James I, it was punished through the instrumentality of those tribunals, not merely because ecclesiastical rights had been violated, but because upon the separation of the ecclesiastical courts from the civil the ecclesiastical were supposed to be the most appropriate for the trial of matrimonial causes and offences against the rights of marriage, just as they were for testamentary causes and the settlement of the estates of deceased persons.

By the statute of 1 James I (c.11), the offence, if committed in England or Wales, was made punishable in the civil courts, and the penalty was death. As this statute was limited in its operation to England and Wales, it was at a very early period re-enacted, generally with some modifications, in all the colonies. In connection with the case we are now considering, it is a significant fact that on the 8th of December, 1788, after the passage of the act establishing religious freedom, and after the convention of Virginia had recommended as an amendment to the Constitution of the United States the declaration in a bill of rights that "all men have an equal, natural, and unalienable right to the free exercise of religion, according to the dictates of conscience," the legislature of that State substantially enacted the statute of James I, death penalty included, because, as recited in the preamble, "it hath been doubted whether bigamy or poligamy be punishable by the laws of this Commonwealth." 12 Hening's Stat. 691. From that day to this we think it may safely be said there never has been a time in any State of the Union when polygamy has not been an offence against society, cognizable by the civil courts and punishable with more or less severity. In the face of all this evidence, it is impossible to believe that the constitutional guaranty of religious freedom was intended to prohibit legislation in respect to this most important feature of social life. Marriage, while from its very nature a sacred obligation, is nevertheless, in most civilized nations, a civil contract, and usually regulated by law. Upon it society may be said to be built, and out of its fruits spring social relations and social obligations and duties, with which government is necessarily required to deal. In fact, according as monogamous or polygamous marriages are allowed, do we find the principles on which the government of the people, to a greater or less extent, rests. Professor Lieber says, polygamy leads to the patriarchal principle, and which, when applied to large communities, fetters the people in stationary despotism, while that principle cannot long exist in connection with monogamy. Chancellor Kent observes that this remark is equally striking and profound. 2 Kent, Com. 81, note (*e*). An exceptional colony of polygamists under an exceptional leadership may sometimes exist for a time without appearing to disturb the social condition of the people who surround it; but there cannot be a doubt that, unless restricted by some form of constitution, it is within the legitimate scope of the power of every civil government to determine whether polygamy or monogamy shall be the law of social life under its dominion.

In our opinion, the statute immediately under consideration is within the legislative power of Congress. It is constitutional and valid as prescribing a rule of action for all those residing in the Territories, and in places over which the United States have exclusive control. This being so, the only question which remains is, whether those who make polygamy a part of their religion are excepted from the operation of the statute. If they are, then those who do not make polygamy a part of their religious belief may be found guilty and punished, while those who do, must be acquitted and go free. This would be introducing a new element into criminal law. Laws are made for the government of actions, and while they cannot interfere with mere religious belief and opinions, they may with practices. Suppose one believed that human sacrifices were a necessary part of religious worship, would it be seriously contended that the civil government under which he lived could not interfere to prevent a sacrifice? Or if a wife religiously believed it was her duty to burn herself upon the funeral pile of her dead husband, would it be beyond the power of the civil government to prevent her carrying her belief into practice?

So here, as a law of organization of society under the exclusive dominion of the United States, it is provided that plural marriages shall not be allowed. Can a man excuse his practices to the contrary because of his religious belief? To permit this would be to make the professed doctrines of religious belief superior to the law of the land, and in effect to permit every citizen to become a law unto himself. Government could exist only in name under such circumstances.

In *Regina v. Wagstaff* (10 Cox Crim. Cases, 531), the parents of a sick child, who omitted to call in medical attendance because of their religious belief that what they did for its cure would be effective, were held not to be guilty of manslaughter, while it was said the contrary would have been the result if the child had actually been starved to death by the parents, under the notion that it was their religious duty to abstain from giving it food. But when the offence consists of a positive act which is knowingly done, it would be dangerous to hold that the offender might escape punishment because he religiously believed the law which he had broken ought never to have been made. No case, we believe, can be found that has gone so far.

Notes and Questions on Subsequent Cases

Cleveland v. United States, 329 US 14 (1946), considers a prosecution of polygamists under the Mann Act, 36 Stat 825, 18 USC § 2421 (2000). That act, which was originally aimed at prostitution rings, criminalizes transporting in interstate commerce "any woman or girl for the purpose of prostitution or debauchery, or for any other immoral purpose." In an opinion by Justice Douglas, the Court sustained the conviction of fundamentalist Mormons who had taken plural wives across state lines:

> As ... stated in *Mormon Church v. United States*, 136 U.S. 1, 49, "The organization of a community for the spread and practice of polygamy is, in a measure, a return to barbarism. It is contrary to the spirit of Christianity and of the civilization which Christianity has produced in the Western world." ... The establishment or maintenance of polygamous households is a notorious example of promiscuity. The permanent advertisement of their existence is an example of the sharp repercussions which they have in the community. We could conclude that Congress excluded these practices from the Act only if it were clear that the Act is confined to commercialized sexual vice. Since we cannot say it is, we see no way by which the present transgressions can be excluded. These polygamous practices have long been branded as immoral in the law. Though they have different ramifications, they are in the same genus as the other immoral practices covered by the Act.

329 US at 19.

More recently, the Tenth Circuit decided *Potter v. Murray City*, 760 F2d 1065 (1985). Royston Potter had been a policeman in Murray City. He was also a polygamist. Utah's constitution proscribes polygamy. Potter was fired for failing to "support, obey and defend" that constitution. He sued under 42 USC § 1983 and lost. The court held that *Reynolds* was still good law. It observed that *Wisconsin v. Yoder*, 406 US 205 (1972) (which we will read later), had cited *Reynolds* for the proposition that " 'activities of individuals, even when religiously based, are often subject to regulation by the States in the exercise of their undoubted power to promote the health, safety, and general welfare....' " The court further reasoned that *Reynolds* had been cited with approval in cases after *Yoder*, that the state had a "compelling interest ... in upholding and enforcing its ban on plural marriage to protect the monogamous marriage relationship," and that there was no authority for extending the right to privacy to include polygamy.

(2) Thinking About Polygamy and the Institution of Marriage

To help you think about the issues surrounding polygamy and the implications of those issues for the institution of marriage, here are three comments on those subjects. The first is a feisty utilitarian criticism of polygamy by Jeremy Bentham. The second is a criticism by the philosopher David Hume. The third is John Donne's gentler view.

JEREMY BENTHAM
PRINCIPLES OF THE CIVIL CODE

1802

That such an arrangement [polygamy] may sometimes be desirable to the man, is possible; but it never can be so to the wives, whose interest would be sacrificed.

1. The effect of such a license would be to aggravate the inequality of conditions. The superiority of wealth has already too great an ascendancy, and this institution would make it still greater. A rich man, forming an alliance with a woman without fortune, would take advantage of her position to prevent his having a rival. Each of his wives would find herself in possession only of the moiety of a husband, whilst she might have constituted a source of happiness to another man, who, in consequence of this iniquitous arrangement, would be deprived of a companion.

2. What would become of the peace of families? The jealousies of the rival wives would spread among the children. They would form opposed parties, little armies, having each at their head an equally powerful protectrix, at least, with respect to her rights. What a scene of contentions! what fury! what animosity! From the relaxation of the fraternal bonds, there would result a similar relaxation of filial respect. Each child would behold in his father a protector of his enemy. All his actions of kindness or severity, being interpreted by opposite prejudices, would be attributed to unjust feelings of hatred or affection. The education of the children would be ruined in the midst of these hostile passions, under a system of favour or oppression, which would corrupt the one party by its rigours, and the other by its indulgences. In the East, polygamy and peace are found united, but it is slavery which prevents discourd: one abuse palliates another; every thing is tranquil under the same yoke.

There results from it an increase of authority to the husband: what eagerness to satisfy him! what pleasure in supplanting a rival by an action which is likely to please him! Would this be an evil or a good? Those who, from a low opinion of women, imagine that they cannot be too submissive, ought to consider polygamy admirable. Those who think that the ascendancy of this sex is favourable to suavity of manners—that it augments the pleasures of society—that the gentle and persuasive authority of women is salutary in a family—ought to consider this institution as very mischievous.

DAVID HUME
OF POLYGAMY AND DIVORCES

1740

As marriage is an engagement entered into by mutual consent, and has for its end the propagation of the species, it is evident, that it must be susceptible of all the variety of conditions, which consent establishes, provided they be not contrary to this end.

A man, in conjoining himself to a woman, is bound to her according to the terms of his engagement: In begetting children, he is bound, by all the ties of nature and humanity, to provide for their subsistence and education. When he has performed these two parts of duty, no one can reproach him with injustice or injury. And as the terms of his engagement, as well as the methods of subsisting his offspring, may be various, it is mere superstition to imagine, that marriage can be entirely uniform, and will admit only of one mode or form. Did not human laws restrain the natural liberty of men, every particular marriage would be as different as contracts or bargains of any other kind of species....

The advocates for polygamy may recommend it as the only effectual remedy for the disorders of love, and the only expedient for freeing men from that slavery to the females, which the natural violence of our passions has imposed upon us. By this means alone can we regain our right of sovereignty; and, sating our appetite, re-establish the authority of reason in our minds, and, of consequence, our own authority in our families. Man, like a weak sovereign, being unable to support himself against the wiles and intrigues of his subjects, must play one faction against another, and become absolute by the mutual jealousy of the females. *To divide and to govern* is an universal maxim; and by neglecting it, the Europeans undergo a more grievous and a more ignominious slavery than the Turks or Persians, who are subjected indeed to a sovereign, that lies at a distance from them, but in their domestic affairs rule with an uncontroulable sway.

On the other hand, it may be urged with better reason, that this sovereignty of the male is a real usurpation, and destroys that nearness of rank, not to say equality, with nature has established between the sexes. We are, by nature, their lovers, their friends, their patrons: Would we willingly exchange such endearing appellations, for the barbarous title of master and tyrant?

In what capacity shall we gain by this inhuman proceeding? As lovers, or as husbands? The *lover*, is totally annihilated; and courtship, the most agreeable scene in life, can no longer have place, where women have not the free disposal of themselves, but are bought and sold, like the meanest animal. The *husband* is as little a gainer, having found the admirable secret of extinguishing every part of love, except its jealousy. No rose without its thorn; but he must be a foolish wretch indeed, that throws away the rose and preserves only the thorn.

But the Asiatic manners are as destructive to friendship as to love. Jealousy excludes men from all intimacies and familiarities with each other. No one dares bring his friend to his house or table, lest he bring a lover to his numerous wives. Hence all over the east, each family is as much separate from another, as if they were so many distinct kingdoms. No wonder then, that Solomon, living like an eastern prince, with his seven hundred wives, and three hundred concubines, without one friend, could write so pathetically concerning the vanity of the world. Had he tried the secret of one wife or mistress, a few friends, and a great many companions, he might have found life somewhat more agreeable. Destroy love and friendship; what remains in the world worth accepting?

The bad education of children, especially children of condition, is another unavoidable consequence of these eastern institutions. Those who pass the early part of life among slaves, are only qualified to be, themselves, slaves and tyrants; and in every future intercourse, either with their inferiors or superiors, are apt to forget the natural equality of mankind. What attention, too, can it be supposed a parent, whose seraglio affords him fifty sons, will give to instilling principles of morality or science into a progeny, with whom he himself is scarcely acquainted, and whom he loves with so divided an affection? Barbarism, therefore, appears, from reason as well as experience, to be the inseparable attendant of polygamy.

JOHN DONNE
VARIETY (ELEGIE XVII)

The heavens rejoyce in motion, why should I
Abjure my so much lov'd variety,
And not with many youth and love divide?
Pleasure is none, if not diversifi'd:
The sun that sitting in the chaire of light
Sheds flame into what else soever doth seem bright,
Is not contented at one Signe to Inne,
But ends his year and with a new beginnes.
All things doe willingly in change delight,
The fruitfull mother of our appetite:
Rivers the clearer and more pleasing are,
Where their fair spreading streames run wide and farr;
And a dead lake that no strange bark doth greet,
Corrupts itself and what doth live in it.
Let no man tell me such a one is faire,
And worthy all alone my love to share.
Nature in her hath done the liberall part

Of a kinde Mistresse, and imploy'd her art
To make her loveable, and I aver
Him not humane that would turn back from her:
I love her well, and would, if need were, dye
To doe her service. But followes it that I
Must serve her onely, when I may have choice
Of other beauties, and in change rejoice?
The law is hard, and shall not have my voice.
The last I saw in all extreames is faire,
And holds me in the Sun-beames of her haire;
Her nymph-like features such agreements have
That I could venture with her to the grave:
Another's brown, I like her not the worse,
Her tongue is soft and takes me with discourse:
Others, for that they well descended are,
Do in my love obtain as large a share;
And though they be not fair, 'tis much with mee
To win their love onely for their degree.
And though I faile of my required ends,
The attempt is glorious and it selfe commends.
How happy were our Syres in ancient time,
Who held plurality of loves no crime!
With them it was accounted charity
To stirre up race of all indifferently;
Kindreds were not exempted from the bands:
Which with the Persian still in usage stands.
Women were then no sooner asked than won,
And what they did was honest and well done.
But since this title honour hath been us'd,
Our weake credulity hath been abus'd;
The golden laws of nature are repeald,
Which our first Fathers in such reverence held;
Our liberty's revers'd, our Charter's gone,
And we're made servants to opinion,
A monster in no certain shape attir'd,
And whose originall is much desir'd,
Formlesse at first, but growing on it fashions,
And doth prescribe manners and laws to nations.
Here love receiv'd immedieable harmes,
And was dispoiled of his daring armes.
A greater want than is his daring eyes,
He lost those awfull wings with which he flies;
His sinewy bow, and those immortall darts
Wherewith he'is wont to bruise resisting hearts.
Onely some few strong in themselves and free
Retain the seeds of antient liberty,
Following that part of Love although deprest,
And make a throne for him within their brest,
In spight of modern censures him avowing

Their Soveraigne, all service his allowing.
Amongst which troop although I am the least,
Yet equall in perfection with the best,
I glory in subjection of his hand,
Nor ever did decline his least command:
For in whatever forme the message came
My heart did open and receive the same.
But time will in his course a point discry
When I this loved service must deny,
For our allegiance temporary is,
With firmer age returnes our liberties.
What time in years and judgement we repos'd,
Shall not so easily be to change dispos'd,
Nor to the art of severall eyes obeying;
But beauty with true worth securely weighing,
Which being found assembled in some one,
Wee'l love her ever, and love her alone.

Notes and Questions on Polygamous Marriage

Reynolds raises a number of constitutional questions we will later investigate, particularly in Part II. Here, we want to survey some of *Reynolds'* normative problems unconstrained by the intricate doctrines and interpretational dilemmas that complicate constitutional law. In thinking about the following questions, then, you should consult general principles even if you are already familiar with the relevant constitutional doctrine.

At the beginning of a family law course, we confront several basic questions about government's regulation of the family. First, what purposes does the social institution of the family serve? Second, why might government support that social institution? Third, what is the proper extent of governmental regulation of the family? The following questions should help you probe those questions in the context of *Reynolds*.

(1) How would you construct an argument against state regulation of polygamy?

(a) Is state regulation of polygamy illegitimate when it conflicts with the polygamist's specifically religious views? If so, does your argument mean that people with religious motives for polygamy may do so but people with other reasons may not? Should one's religious views give one privileges the rest of society doesn't have? How do you evaluate the *Reynolds* Court's arguments that religious freedom does not extend to polygamy?

(i) Is the *Reynolds* Court's distinction between religious beliefs and religious practices tenable? Why does the Court make that distinction?

(ii) If the distinction between religious beliefs and religious practices is untenable, how (if at all) should courts go about deciding which religious practices are exempt from governmental regulation? Should courts, for instance, balance the religious claim against the asserted state interest? How? Can the strength of the religious claim or the state interest be measured? Can the strength of the claim and the interest be measured so as to make the two strengths comparable? If so, how? If not, how can the claim and the interest be "balanced"?

(b) Is state regulation of polygamy illegitimate because it violates basic ideas about human freedom? If so, what are those basic ideas? How do you know what they are? Why does regulation of polygamy violate them? Even if they are violated, can the state's interests in regulation justify the violation?

(c) Is state regulation of polygamy illegitimate because principles of pluralism hold that people need freedom to organize themselves into heterodox groups? What are our ideas about pluralism? What is pluralism? When should claims based on pluralism overcome justifications based on the state's interests?

What does the Mormon example say about these questions? Professor Foster writes that Mormon polygamy "was a fundamental protest against the careless individualism of romantic love, which seemed to threaten the very roots of family life and social solidarity." He sees the Mormons as "attacking and attempting to overcome the rampant, exploitative Jacksonian individualism which surrounded them. They were seeking a total solution, more akin to medieval ideals in which religious and social life were inextricably intertwined, and the good of the community took precedence over individual self-interest." If the Mormons were such a community, how is their claim to exemption from regulation strengthened or weakened?

(d) Is state regulation of polygamy illegitimate because the state lacks any legitimate reasons to regulate polygamy? This question leads us directly to our next question:

(2) You have just read an opinion which justifies state regulation of polygamy. However, that opinion was particularly directed toward responding to a religious challenge to such regulation and was written in a nineteenth-century context. How might one justify state regulation of polygamy against a secular challenge in the late twentieth century?

(a) Does the state have an interest in assuring everyone some statistical possibility of a marriage partner? Recall Bentham's argument that if polygyny were permitted, rich men would be likelier than poor men to have wives. Is prohibiting polygamy a proper and effective way of serving this interest? (In 1993, Herman, Minnesota, addressed such a problem by advertising a ratio of eligible males to females of 78/4. Hundreds of women came to the county fair to look over the town and its famous bachelors. *Minneapolis Star Tribune*, July 31, 1994, col 1B.)

(b) Does the state have an interest in preventing the exploitation of plural spouses? Are plural spouses likelier to be exploited than spouses in a monogamous marriage? Is it the state's business if they are? Is prohibiting polygamy a proper and effective way of serving this state interest? How does the Mormon experience with polygamy speak to these questions?

John McMurtry suggests that it is monogamy which promotes "conjugal insecurity, jealousy and alienation" by "[o]fficially underwriting a literally totalitarian expectation" of sexual exclusivity that is bound to be disappointed and that will be habitually violated, all of which will lead to anxiety and fear on both sides. *Monogamy: A Critique*, in Robert Baker and Frederick Elliston, eds, *Philosophy and Sex* 120, 125–26 (Prometheus Books, 1975). He contends that the "sexual containment and isolation" monogamy requires lead to the aggression sexual frustration causes and to "[a]pathy, frustration and dependence within the marriage bond." Is this persuasive?

McMurtry further argues that monogamous marriage is "simply a form of private property" in which the "essential principle" is "*the maintenance by one man or woman of the effective right to exclude indefinitely all others from erotic access to the conjugal partner*." Is McMurtry's evidence for the view that "the language of the marriage ceremony is the language of exclusive possession ('take,' 'to have and to hold,' 'forsaking all others and keeping you only unto him/her,' etc.), not to mention the proprietary locutions associated with the marital relationship (e.g., 'he's mine,' 'she belongs to him,' 'keep to your own husband,' 'wife stealer,' 'possessive husband,' etc.)" convincing? In your Property class, you asked what makes something property. What characteristics of property does marriage have? What characteristics does it lack? If it is not property, does it fit within some other legal category? For a discussion of some of these questions, see Richard Posner, *Sex and Reason* 112–18 (Harv U Press, 1993).

Is McMurtry correct that "the real secret of our form of monogamous marriage ... [is] that it serves the maintenance of our present social system" because it is "indispensable to the persistence of the capitalist order"? Is monogamy historically associated with capitalism? What might deter a non-monogamous society from capitalism? If monogamy *is* indispensable to capitalism, does this justify the state in prohibiting polygamy?

(c) Does the state have an interest in making it likelier that children will grow up in homes free of the jealousies and tensions that may be part of polygamous households? Recall Bentham's question about what "would become of the peace of families" under polygamy. Is prohibiting polygamy a proper and effective way of serving this state interest? Or is McMurtry right in arguing that monogamy "necessarily constricts, in perhaps the most unilateral possible way consistent with offspring survival, the number of adult sources of affection, interest, material support and instruction for the young"?

(d) A recent Canadian report suggests repealing the ban on polygamy in part to promote the cultural pluralism created by a rising tide of immigration from Africa and the Middle East, where polygamy is legally and religiously sanctioned. Polygamous marriages, though not recognized in Canada, might create some rights in women who had entered into them lawfully elsewhere. See Dean Beeby, Study Recommends Repealing Polygamy Ban in Canada, The Globe and Mail (Toronto, Can), Jan. 12, 2006, 2006 WLNR 705814.

Does a community have an interest in defining itself in socially and culturally important ways? Is ordaining a particular kind of marriage one of those ways? Does prohibiting polygamy properly and effectively serve this state interest?

(e) Does the state have an interest in nurturing social institutions that offer people guides to social behavior? The sociologist Peter L. Berger writes, "Today it is not so much that individuals become convinced of their capacity and right to choose new ways of life, but rather that tradition is weakened to the point where they *must* choose between alternatives whether they wish it or not.... [O]ne of the most archaic functions of society is to take away from individuals the burden of choice." *Toward a Critique of Modernity*, in *Facing up to Modernity* 77 (Basic Books, 1977). What does Professor Berger mean by "the burden of choice"? Is it ever desirable to ease that burden? Is monogamous marriage an institution that helps alleviate the burden of reinventing social life? Would the institution and function be importantly weakened if polygamous marriage became itself an institutionalized possibility? Is prohibiting polygamy a proper and effective way of serving this interest?

(f) Does the state have an interest in effectuating its citizens' strongly felt preference to live in a community in which polygamy is prohibited? Obviously we might refuse to effectuate some kinds of preferences however strongly felt they were, but are the citizenry's strongly felt preferences thus irrelevant? Is a distaste for polygamy the kind of preference we ought not effectuate? Is it relevant that the disapproval of polygamy has long and strong historical roots? Is prohibiting polygamy a proper and effective way of serving this interest?

(g) Does the state have an interest in preventing the practice of polygamy on the grounds that it degrades women as a class? Bentham, recall, argued that those "who, from a low opinion of women, imagine that they cannot be too submissive, ought to consider polygamy admirable." Is he right? How does polygamy, or at least polygyny, degrade women? Would polyandry degrade men? Even if polygamy degrades women, should women who wish to marry polygamously be free to do so? How does the Mormon experience with polygamy speak to these questions? Is prohibiting polygamy a proper and effective way of serving this interest?

Assume that Bentham is wrong about polygamy's consequences. But assume that Lawrence Foster is correct that Mormon polygamy was "an attempt to restore earlier patriarchal patterns in marriage that were under attack in the period." Would that have justified the state in prohibiting polygamy? Recall *Reynolds*: "Professor Lieber says, polygamy leads to the patriarchal principle, ... which, when applied to large communities, fetters the people in stationary despotism, while that principle cannot long exist in connection with monogamy."

At the time of *Reynolds*, American feminism was split between liberal and conservative factions. The relatively conservative American Woman Suffrage Association held that "[m]onogamy is the rock upon which the church of Woman's Equality is founded" and that equality for women depended partly on ending polygamy. The relatively liberal National Woman Suffrage Association also opposed polygamy, but thought it just one kind of deplorable marital relations practiced in the United States. The feminist reaction to Mormon polygamy was further complicated by the Utah Territory's status as one of the few places women could vote (although not hold office, and although the right had grown out of an attempt by non-Mormons to strike at polygamy). For a fine and fascinating study of Mormon polygamy, utopian communities, and women's groups, see Carol Weisbrod and Pamela Sheingorn, *Reynolds v. United States: Nineteenth Century Forms of Marriage and the Status of Women*, 10 Conn L Rev 828 (1978).

(h) Does the state have an interest in preserving the monogamous family as the "basic building block of society"? Even if the family is the basic building block, does the family have to be based on monogamy? Is prohibiting polygamy a proper and effective way to serve this interest?

(3) While evaluating state regulation of polygamy, you may have noticed that every justification hinged on assumptions about people and society for which there is little good evidence. How should that fact affect legal thinking about polygamy?

(a) Should the state be unable to regulate families without strong and systematic evidence that regulation is justifiable? If so, what constitutes such evidence? Must it be gathered by trained social scientists? What burden of proof must be met? A preponderance of the evidence? Clear and convincing? Beyond a reasonable doubt? Can social science ever reach high levels of confidence in its conclusions? What if, as regularly happens, social scientists disagree among themselves?

(b) Should the state be able to rely on a widespread social belief that polygamy is wrong? A virtually universal belief?

(c) Should the state be able to rely on a long-standing social tradition of regulating polygamy? Why or why not?

(4) Suppose a court held that the first or fourteenth amendment embodied a right to polygamous marriage. Would the holding invalidate all bigamy laws? Would it have to offer any protection for a spouse whose partner decided to contract another, simultaneous marriage?

B. EVALUATING MARRIAGE: INCEST

For the King ripped from her gown the golden brooches That were her ornament, and raised them, and plunged them down Straight into his own eyeballs, crying, "No more, No more shall you look on the misery about me, The horrors of my own doing! Too long you have known The faces of those whom I should never have seen, Too long been blind to those for whom I was searching! From this hour, go in darkness!" And as he spoke, He struck at his eyes—not once, but many times; And the blood spattered his beard, Bursting from his ruined sockets like red hail.

Sophocles
Oedipus Rex

We have just assessed the social and legal institution of marriage by examining one heterodox form—polygamy. We will now look at another such form—marriage between closely related partners. The anthropologist Claude Lévi-Strauss wrote, "The universal prohibition of incest specifies, as a general rule, that people considered as parents and children, or brother and sister, even if only by name, cannot have sexual relations and even less marry each other." *The Family*, in Henry L. Shapiro, ed, *Man, Culture, and Society* 276 (Oxford U Press, 1971). People often assume the incest prohibition serves genetic purposes. Lévi-Strauss reported that "while consanguineous marriages are likely to bring ill effects in a society which has consistently avoided them in the past, the danger would be much smaller if the prohibition had never existed, since this would have given ample opportunity for the harmful hereditary characters to become apparent and be automatically eliminated through selection...." In any event, genetic explanations are, for our purposes, the least interesting. For now, please, put to one side any genetic basis for prohibiting incestuous marriage.

We will consider the prohibition on incestuous marriage by reading one case and one comment. The comment is, again, from Bentham. The case is *Israel v. Allen*. Before you read it, let us mention one reason we selected it. Casebook authors usually seek opinions which illuminatingly discuss a legal problem. Law students thus have a skewed sample to use in weighing the usual standard of clarity and care in judicial opinions. The opinion in *Israel*, however, is representative in its quality of many judicial opinions generally and many family law opinions particularly, and we include it partly for that reason.

ISRAEL v. ALLEN

Supreme Court of Colorado, 1978
577 P2d 762

PRINGLE, CHIEF JUSTICE.... Plaintiffs, Martin Richard Israel and Tammy Lee Bannon Israel, are brother and sister related by adoption and are not related by either the half or the whole blood.

Raymond Israel (the natural father of Martin Richard Israel) and Sylvia Bannon (the natural mother of Tammy Lee Bannon Israel) were married on November 3, 1972. At the time of their marriage, Martin was 18 years of age and was living in the State of Washington; Tammy was 13 years of age and living with her mother in Denver, Colorado. Raymond Israel adopted Tammy on January 7, 1975.

Plaintiffs desire to be married in the State of Colorado. Defendant, Clerk and Recorder of Jefferson County, however, denied plaintiffs a license to marry based on section 14–2–110(1)(b), C.R.S.1973:

> "*Prohibited marriages.* (1) The following marriages are prohibited: ... (b) A marriage between an ancestor and a descendant or between a brother and sister, whether the relationship is by the half or the whole blood or by adoption; ..."

A complaint seeking declaratory relief was filed in the district court. The district court found that marriage is a fundamental right and that no compelling state interest is furthered by prohibiting marriage between a brother and sister only by adoption. Thus, the court held that that part of section 14–2–110(1)(b) which prohibited the marriage of a brother and sister by adoption was unconstitutional as a denial of equal protection and, therefore, severed from the statute the words "or by adoption."

I

... While the practice of adoption is an ancient one, the legal regulation of adoptive relationships in our society is strictly statutory in nature. The legislative intent in promulgating statutes concerning adoption was, in part, to make the law affecting adopted children in respect to equality of inheritance and parental duties *in pari materia* with that affecting natural children. It is clear, however, that adopted children are not engrafted upon their adoptive families for all purposes. *See, e.g.*, the criminal incest statute, which does not include sexual relationships between adopted brother and sister.

Nonetheless, defendant argues that this marriage prohibition provision furthers a legitimate state interest in family harmony. We do not agree. As the instant case illustrates, it is just as likely that prohibiting marriage between brother and sister related by adoption will result in family discord. While we are not, strictly speaking, dealing with an affinity based relationship in this case, we find the following analysis equally applicable to the situation presently before us:

> "According to the English law, relationship by affinity was an impediment to marriage to the same extent and in the same degree as consanguinity. While this principle, derived from the ecclesiastically administered canon law, still strongly persists in England, in the United States the statutory law governing the marriage relationship nowhere so sweepingly condemns the marriage of persons related only by affinity.... The objections that exist against consanguineous marriages are not present where the relationship is merely by affinity. The physical detriment to the offspring of persons related by blood is totally absent. The natural repugnance of people toward marriages of blood relatives, that has resulted in well-nigh universal moral condemnation of such marriages, is quite generally lacking in application to the union of those related only by affinity. It is difficult to construct any very logical case for the prohibition of marriage on grounds of affinity ..." 1 *Vernier, American Family Laws* 183.

We hold that it is just as illogical to prohibit marriage between adopted brother and sister....

JEREMY BENTHAM
PRINCIPLES OF THE CIVIL CODE

If we examine the interior of a family, composed of persons who differ among themselves in respect of age, sex, and relative duties, strong reasons will present themselves to our minds for prohibiting certain alliances between many individuals of this family.

I see one reason which directly pleads against allowing such marriages at all. A father, a grandfather, or an uncle holding the place of a father, might abuse his power in order to force a young girl to contract an alliance with him which might be hateful to her. The more necessary the authority of the parent is, the less temptation should be given to its abuse.

This inconvenience extends only to a small number of incestuous cases, and it is not the most weighty. It is in the corruption of manners, in the evils which would result from transitory connexions without marriage, that the true reasons for prohibiting certain alliances must be sought.

If there were not an insurmountable barrier against marriages between near relations, called to live together in the greatest intimacy, this close connexion, these continual opportunities, even friendship itself and its innocent caresses might kindle the most disastrous passions. Families, those retreats in which repose ought to be found in the bosom of order, and where the emotions of the soul, agitated in the scenes of the world, ought to sink to rest—families themselves would become the prey of all the inquietudes, the rivalries, and the fury of love. Suspicion would banish confidence; the gentlest feelings would be extinguished; and eternal enmities and revenges, of which the idea alone makes one tremble, would usurp their place. The opinion of the chastity of young women, so powerful an attraction to marriage, would not know upon what to repose, and the most dangerous snares in the education of youth would be found even in the asylum where they could be least avoided....

It is very seldom that the passion of love develops itself within the circle of individuals among whom it ought properly to be prohibited; a certain degree of surprise seems necessary for exciting this sentiment, a sudden effect of novelty; and it is this which the poets have cleverly expressed by the ingenious allegory of the bow and arrows, and the blindfolding of Cupid. Individuals, accustomed to be seen and to be known from the age which is incapable of conceiving or inspiring desire, will be seen with the same eyes to the end of life—this inclination will find no determinate period for its commencement. The affections have taken another course; they are, so to speak, a river which has dug its own bed, and which cannot change it.

Nature therefore agrees sufficiently well with the principle of utility; still it is not proper to trust to it alone. There are circumstances which may give birth to the inclination, and in which the alliance might become an object of desire, if it were not prohibited by the laws, and branded by public opinion....

The inconveniences of these alliances are not felt by those who contract them; the evil is altogether in the example. A permission granted to one, makes every body else feel the prohibition as tyrannical. Where the yoke is not the same for all, it appears more weighty to those who bear it.

Notes and Questions on Incestuous Marriage

(1) The result in *Israel* may well be right, but the opinion seems problematic. Consider, for example, its failure either to deal with the state's argument or to develop other possible objections to its own decision. What, then, do you think the state's argument about "family harmony" was? What is Bentham's argument about that issue? How might relationships within a family develop after an incestuous marriage?

(2) Suppose the Israels could show that none of the state's argument about family harmony applied in their particular family. Would the state's attorney have any remaining arguments?

(3) In evaluating the problems of families in which the parents are in their second marriage, Professor Cherlin mentions that of "resolving the sexual tensions that can emerge between step-relatives in the absence of a well-defined incest taboo." Andrew J. Cherlin, *Marriage, Divorce, Remarriage* 87 (Harv U Press, 1981). Should *Israel* have been decided differently in light of that observation?

(4) In discussing polygamy, we asked whether the state had a strong enough interest to justify its regulation of marriage generally and its prohibition of polygamy particularly. Can the state justify its prohibition of incestuous marriage? Consider the following categorization of possible state interests:

> A decision made on moral grounds turns on whether particular conduct is "right" or "wrong," whether it accords with the obligations owed other people or oneself. Incest might be prohibited on moral grounds because it is instinct with coercion or because it violates natural or divine law which prescribes standards of right and wrong. A decision made on psychological grounds turns on whether particular conduct promotes psychological health. Incest might be prohibited on psychological grounds because the prohibition eases resolution of the Oedipal conflict. A decision made on social grounds turns on whether particular conduct promotes the effective functioning of society as a whole. Incest might be prohibited on social grounds because "the prohibition of incest establishes a mutual dependency between families, compelling them, in order to perpetuate themselves, to give rise to new families." A decision made on economic grounds turns on whether particular conduct promotes economic efficiency. Incest might be prohibited on economic grounds because such a prohibition, by discouraging endogamy, encourages capital formation.

Carl E. Schneider, *Moral Discourse and the Transformation of American Family Law*, 83 Mich L Rev 1803, 1827–28 (1985).

(5) Suppose that the Israels' marriage would be unproblematic, but that the state's "family harmony" argument is correct and that allowing the Israels to marry would in some way affect the welfare of other families in the future. Is that a sufficient reason for preventing the Israels from marrying?

C. PUTTING TRADITIONAL MARRIAGE TO THE TEST: SAME–SEX MARRIAGE

> *[W]hen one of them finds his other half, whether he is a lover of youth or a lover of another sort, the pair are lost in an amazement of love and friendship and intimacy, and one will not be out of the other's sight, as I may say, even for a moment: These are they who pass their lives with one another; yet they could not explain what they desire of one another. For the intense yearning which each of them has towards the other does not appear to be the desire of intercourse, but of something else which the soul desires and cannot tell, and of which she has only a dark and doubtful presentiment.*
>
> **Plato**
> *Symposium*

(1) The Constitutional Claim

Until the 1970s, courts and legislatures assumed that "marriage" necessarily described a relationship between a man and a woman. Indeed, as of 1974, the sodomy statutes of 43 states and the District of

Columbia made even private adult homosexual conduct criminal. In 1974, a three-judge U.S. District Court declined to issue a declaratory judgment against one such statute, saying that homosexuality "is obviously no portion of marriage, home or family life" and that "[i]f a State determines that punishment therefore, even when committed in the home, is appropriate in the promotion of morality and decency, it is not for the courts to say that the State is not free to do so." *Doe v. Commonwealth's Attorney*, 403 F Supp 1199, 1202 (E D Va 1975), aff'd mem, 425 US 901 (1976). As you may know, the Supreme Court reached a similar result in *Bowers v. Hardwick*, 478 US 186 (1986), which was overruled by *Lawrence v. Texas*, 123 S Ct 2472 (2003), a case we will read in Chapter 7.

In the 1970s, however, social attitudes toward homosexuality began to change, many state legislatures decriminalized sodomy statutes, some courts developed (state and federal) constitutional doubts about sodomy statutes, and homosexuals began to seek marriage licenses. For many years, courts upheld the state's refusal to issue those licenses against claims that such refusals constituted discrimination on the basis of sex. In 1993, however, the Hawaii Supreme Court decided *Baehr v. Lewin*, 852 P2d 44, which concluded that Hawaii's refusal to permit homosexuals to marry violated the equal protection clause of the state's constitution. The legislature disagreed, and in 1998 Hawaii adopted the following constitutional amendment. "Section 23. The legislature shall have the power to reserve marriage to opposite-sex couples." The legislature also enacted a "reciprocal beneficiaries" law which "endows non-married couples, who register as 'reciprocal beneficiaries,' with many of the same rights and benefits married couples receive under Hawaii law. These rights and benefits, previously reserved for married couples only, include, but are not limited to, family health care benefits for state workers; hospital visitation rights; property and inheritance rights; the right to sue for the wrongful death of a reciprocal partner; and the right to protection from the domestic violence of a reciprocal partner.... [T]he Act also, in some instances, forces a private employer to supply health care benefits to reciprocal beneficiaries if the private employer supplies health care benefits to married couples." Note, *Hawaii's Reciprocal Beneficiaries Act: An Effective Step in Resolving the Controversy Surrounding Same Sex Marriage,* 37 Brandeis L J 81 (1998–99). Haw Rev Stat § 572C–4 (1998) provides that people become reciprocal beneficiaries if: "(1) Each of the parties be at least eighteen years old; (2) Neither of the parties be married nor a party to another reciprocal beneficiary relationship; [and] (3) The parties be legally prohibited from marrying one another under chapter 572. . . ."

In the meantime, however, litigation was brewing in Vermont which culminated in the opinion of *Baker v. Vermont*, 744 A2d 864 (Vt 1999), which found unconstitutional "the exclusion of same-sex couples from the secular benefits and protections offered married couples." The result of Baker was a civil union statute, found infra at p. 81. Civil union has also been adopted in Connecticut, Section 10 of Public Act 05–10 (2005); Maine, 2003 Me. Laws 672, codified in scattered sections of the Maine code; New Jersey, N.J. Stat. Ann. § 26:8a–1 et seq; and California, 2003 Cal. Stat. 421 (A.B. 205), codified as sections of the California Family Code. Denmark, Norway, Sweden, Iceland, and Finland allow same-sex couples to register partnerships, which has the same legal effect as opposite-sex marriages. Inching Down the Aisle: Differing Paths Towards the Legalization of Same–Sex Marriage in the U.S. & Europe, 116 Harv. L. Rev. 2004, 2004–05, 2008 (2003). France, Germany, and New Zealand have also created civil unions, and the United Kingdom recently introduced civil partnerships. Mark E. Wojcik, *The Wedding Bells Heard Around the World: Years From Now, Will We Wonder Why We Worried About Same–Sex Marriage?*, 24 N Ill U L Rev 589, 677 (2004).

Four countries permit same sex marriage: the Netherlands, Belgium, Spain, and Canada. Canada did so after courts there held that providing only civil unions did not satisfy the Canadian Charter of Rights and Freedoms. *Halpern v. Toronto*, 2003 Carswell On. 2159; *M. v. H.*, 1999 Carswell Ont 1348, 2 SCR 3, [1999] SCJ No 23. In the United States, a New Jersey trial court rejected claims that equal protection requires the recognition of same-sex marriage, but the case was appealed to the New Jersey Supreme Court and an opinion has not yet been issued. See *Lewis v. Harris*, 2003 WL 23191114 (NJ Super, L Div, Hudson Co 2003) (unpublished opinion), aff'd, *Lewis v. Harris*, 875 A2d 259 (App Div 2005). New York has also rejected claims for marriage rights in *Samuels v. New York State Department of Health*, 811 NYS2d 136, 2006 WL 346465 (N.Y.A.D. 3 Dept.), 2006 NY Slip Op. 01213, and *Hernandez v. Robles*, 26 A.D.3d 98, 805 NYS2d 354 ([2005]), as have Indiana (*Morrison v. Sadler*, 821 NE2d 15 (Ind App 2005)) and Arizona (*Standhardt v. Superior Court of Arizona*, 77 P3d 451 (Ariz App 2003)). Currently cases are pending in Iowa and in Washington, where a lower court found that Washington's failure to provide marriage rights to same sex couples violates the state constitution. *Varnum v. Brien*, filed in the Iowa District Court for Polk County; *Andersen v. King County*, No. 04–2–04964–4–SEA, 2004 WL 1738447 (Superior Court of Washington for King County).

Only one U.S. state permits same-sex couples to marry, without creating a separate status for them; in 2003, plaintiffs in Massachussetts prevailed in a challenge to that state's denial of marriage to same sex couples. We follow this case with the New York Appellate Division case of *Samuels v. New York* (2006), typical of those states ruling that restricting marriage to persons of different genders does not violate a state constitution.

GOODRIDGE ET AL. v. DEPARTMENT OF PUBLIC HEALTH

Supreme Judicial Court of Massachusetts, 2003
798 NE2d 941

MARSHALL, C.J.

Marriage is a vital social institution. The exclusive commitment of two individuals to each other nurtures love and mutual support; it brings stability to our society. For those who choose to marry, and for their children, marriage provides an abundance of legal, financial, and social benefits. In return it imposes weighty legal, financial, and social obligations. The question before us is whether, consistent with the Massachusetts Constitution, the Commonwealth may deny the protections, benefits, and obligations conferred by civil marriage to two individuals of the same sex who wish to marry. We conclude that it may not. The Massachusetts Constitution affirms the dignity and equality of all individuals. It forbids the creation of second-class citizens. In reaching our conclusion we have given full deference to the arguments made by the Commonwealth. But it has failed to identify any constitutionally adequate reason for denying civil marriage to same-sex couples....

Whether the Commonwealth may use its formidable regulatory authority to bar same-sex couples from civil marriage is a question not previously addressed by a Massachusetts appellate court. It is a question the United States Supreme Court left open as a matter of Federal law in Lawrence [v. Texas, 123 S. Ct. 2472 (2003)] at 2484, where it was not an issue. There, the Court affirmed that the core concept of common human dignity protected by the Fourteenth Amendment to the United States Constitution precludes government intrusion into the deeply personal realms of consensual adult expressions of intimacy and one's choice of an intimate partner. The Court also reaffirmed the central role that decisions whether to marry or have children bear in shaping one's identity. The Massachusetts Constitution is, if anything, more protective of individual liberty and equality than the Federal Constitution; it may demand broader protection for fundamental rights; and it is less tolerant of government intrusion into the protected spheres of private life.

Barred access to the protections, benefits, and obligations of civil marriage, a person who enters into an intimate, exclusive union with another of the same sex is arbitrarily deprived of membership in one of our community's most rewarding and cherished institutions. That exclusion is incompatible with the constitutional principles of respect for individual autonomy and equality under law.

The plaintiffs are fourteen individuals from five Massachusetts counties. As of April 11, 2001, the date they filed their complaint, the plaintiffs Gloria Bailey, sixty years old, and Linda Davies, fifty-five years old, had been in a committed relationship for thirty years; the plaintiffs Maureen Brodoff, forty-nine years old, and Ellen Wade, fifty-two years old, had been in a committed relationship for twenty years and lived with their twelve year old daughter; the plaintiffs Hillary Goodridge, forty-four years old, and Julie Goodridge, forty-three years old, had been in a committed relationship for thirteen years and lived with their five year old daughter.... ; and the plaintiffs David Wilson, fifty-seven years old, and Robert Compton, fifty-one years old, had been in a committed relationship for four years and had cared for David's mother in their home after a serious illness until she died.

The plaintiffs include business executives, lawyers, an investment banker, educators, therapists, and a computer engineer. Many are active in church, community, and school groups. They have employed such legal means as are available to them—for example, joint adoption, powers of attorney, and joint ownership of real property—to secure aspects of their relationships. Each plaintiff attests a desire to marry his or her partner in order to affirm publicly their commitment to each other and to secure the legal protections and benefits afforded to married couples and their children....

In March and April, 2001, each of the plaintiff couples attempted to obtain a marriage license from a city or town clerk's office.... In each case, the clerk either refused to accept the notice of intention to marry or denied a marriage license to the couple on the ground that Massachusetts does not recognize same-sex marriage. Because obtaining a marriage license is a necessary prerequisite to civil marriage in Massachusetts, denying marriage licenses to the plaintiffs was tantamount to denying them access to civil marriage itself, with its appurtenant social and legal protections, benefits, and obligations.

On April 11, 2001, the plaintiffs filed suit in the Superior Court against the department and the commissioner seeking a judgment that "the exclusion of the [p]laintiff couples and other qualified same-sex couples from access to marriage licenses, and the legal and social status of civil marriage, as well as the protections, benefits and obligations of marriage, violates Massachusetts law." The plaintiffs alleged violation of the laws of the Commonwealth....

The department, represented by the Attorney General, admitted to a policy and practice of denying marriage licenses to same-sex couples. It denied that its actions violated any law or that the plaintiffs were entitled to relief. The parties filed cross motions for summary judgment.

A Superior Court judge ruled for the department....

After the complaint was dismissed and summary judgment entered for the defendants, the plaintiffs appealed....

... G. L. c. 207, governing entrance to marriage, is a licensing law. The plaintiffs argue that because nothing in that licensing law specifically prohibits marriages between persons of the same sex, we may interpret the statute to permit "qualified same sex couples" to obtain marriage licenses, thereby avoiding the question whether the law is constitutional.

We interpret statutes to carry out the Legislature's intent, determined by the words of a statute interpreted according to "the ordinary and approved usage of the language." The everyday meaning of "marriage" is "[t]he legal union of a man and woman as husband and wife," Black's Law Dictionary 986 (7th ed. 1999), and the plaintiffs do not argue that the term "marriage" has ever had a different meaning under Massachusetts law. This definition of marriage, as both the department and the Superior Court judge point out, derives from the common law. Far from being ambiguous, the undefined word "marriage," as used in G. L. c. 207, confirms the General Court's intent to hew to the term's common-law and quotidian meaning concerning the genders of the marriage partners.

The intended scope of G. L. c. 207 is also evident in its consanguinity provisions. Sections 1 and 2 of G. L. c. 207 prohibit marriages between a man and certain female relatives and a woman and certain male relatives, but are silent as to the consanguinity of male-male or female-female marriage applicants. The only reasonable explanation is that the Legislature did not intend that same-sex couples be licensed to marry. We conclude, as did the judge, that G. L. c. 207 may not be construed to permit same-sex couples to marry.

III

A

The larger question is whether, as the department claims, government action that bars same-sex couples from civil marriage constitutes a legitimate exercise of the State's authority to regulate conduct, or whether, as the plaintiffs claim, this categorical marriage exclusion violates the Massachusetts Constitution....

The plaintiffs' claim that the marriage restriction violates the Massachusetts Constitution can be analyzed in two ways. Does it offend the Constitution's guarantees of equality before the law? Or do the liberty and due process provisions of the Massachusetts Constitution secure the plaintiffs' right to marry their chosen partner? In matters implicating marriage, family life, and the upbringing of children, the two constitutional concepts frequently overlap, as they do here. Much of what we say concerning one standard applies to the other.

We begin by considering the nature of civil marriage itself. Simply put, the government creates civil marriage. In Massachusetts, civil marriage is, and since pre-Colonial days has been, precisely what its name implies: a wholly secular institution. No religious ceremony has ever been required to validate a Massachusetts marriage.

In a real sense, there are three partners to every civil marriage: two willing spouses and an approving State. While only the parties can mutually assent to marriage, the terms of the marriage—who may marry and what obligations, benefits, and liabilities attach to civil marriage—are set by the Commonwealth. Conversely, while only the parties can agree to end the marriage (absent the death of one of them or a marriage void ab initio), the Commonwealth defines the exit terms.

Civil marriage is created and regulated through exercise of the police power. "Police power" (now more commonly termed the State's regulatory authority) is an old-fashioned term for the Commonwealth's law-making authority, as bounded by the liberty and equality guarantees of the Massachusetts Constitution and its express delegation of power from the people to their government. In broad terms, it is the Legislature's power to enact rules to regulate conduct, to the extent that such laws are "necessary to secure the health, safety, good order, comfort, or general welfare of the community"....

Marriage also bestows enormous private and social advantages on those who choose to marry. Civil marriage is at once a deeply personal commitment to another human being and a highly public celebration of the ideals of mutuality, companionship, intimacy, fidelity, and family...Because it fulfils yearnings for security, safe haven, and connection that express our common humanity, civil marriage is an esteemed institution, and the decision whether and whom to marry is among life's momentous acts of self-definition.

Tangible as well as intangible benefits flow from marriage. The marriage license grants valuable property rights to those who meet the entry requirements, and who agree to what might otherwise be a burdensome degree of government regulation of their activities. The Legislature has conferred on "each party [in a civil marriage] substantial rights concerning the assets of the other which unmarried cohabitants do not have."

The benefits accessible only by way of a marriage license are enormous, touching nearly every aspect of life and death. The department states that "hundreds of statutes" are related to marriage and to marital benefits. With no attempt to be comprehensive, we note that some of the statutory benefits conferred by the Legislature on those who enter into civil marriage include, as to property: joint Massachusetts income tax filing; tenancy by the entirety (a form of ownership that provides certain protections against creditors and allows for the automatic descent of property to the surviving spouse without probate); extension of the benefit of the homestead protection (securing up to $300,000 in equity from creditors) to one's spouse and children; automatic rights to inherit the property of a deceased spouse who does not leave a will; the rights of elective share and of dower; entitlement to wages owed to a deceased employee;...; the right to share the medical policy of one's spouse; thirty-nine week continuation of health coverage for the spouse of a person who is laid off or dies; preferential options under the Commonwealth's pension system; preferential benefits in the Commonwealth's medical program, MassHealth; the equitable division of marital property on divorce; temporary and permanent alimony rights; the right to separate support on separation of the parties that does not result in divorce; and the right to bring claims for wrongful death and loss of consortium, and for funeral and burial expenses and punitive damages resulting from tort actions

Exclusive marital benefits that are not directly tied to property rights include the presumptions of legitimacy and parentage of children born to a married couple and evidentiary rights, such as the prohibition against spouses testifying against one another about their private conversations, applicable in both civil and criminal cases. Other statutory benefits of a personal nature available only to married individuals include qualification for bereavement or medical leave to care for individuals related by blood or marriage; an automatic "family member" preference to make medical decisions for an incompetent or disabled spouse who does not have a contrary health care proxy;... priority rights to administer the estate of a deceased spouse who dies without a will, and requirement that surviving spouse must consent to the appointment of any other person as administrator; and the right to interment in the lot or tomb owned by one's deceased spouse...

It is undoubtedly for these concrete reasons, as well as for its intimately personal significance, that civil marriage has long been termed a "civil right." See, e.g., *Loving v. Virginia*, 388 U.S. 1, 12 (1967) ("Marriage is one of the 'basic civil rights of man,' fundamental to our very existence and survival"). The United States Supreme Court has described the right to marry as "of fundamental importance for all individuals" and as "part of the fundamental 'right of privacy' implicit in the Fourteenth Amendment's Due Process Clause." *Zablocki v. Redhail*, 434 U.S. 374, 384 (1978). See *Loving v. Virginia*, supra ("The freedom to marry has long been recognized as one of the vital personal rights essential to the orderly pursuit of happiness by free men").

Without the right to marry—or more properly, the right to choose to marry—one is excluded from the full range of human experience and denied full protection of the laws for one's from the full range of human experience and denied full protection of the laws for one's "avowed commitment to an intimate and lasting human relationship.". Because civil marriage is central to the lives of individuals and the welfare of the community, our laws assiduously protect the individual's right to marry against undue government incursion. Laws may not "interfere directly and substantially with the right to marry." *Zablocki v. Redhail*, supra at 387.

Unquestionably, the regulatory power of the Commonwealth over civil marriage is broad, as is the Commonwealth's discretion to award public benefits. Individuals who have the choice to marry each other and nevertheless choose not to may properly be denied the legal benefits of marriage. But that same logic cannot hold for a qualified individual who would marry if she or he only could.

B

For decades, indeed centuries, in much of this country (including Massachusetts) no lawful marriage was possible between white and black Americans. That long history availed not when the ...United States

Supreme Court ... held that a statutory bar to interracial marriage violated the Fourteenth Amendment, *Loving v. Virginia*, 388 U.S. 1 (1967). As ... *Loving* make[s] clear, the right to marry means little if it does not include the right to marry the person of one's choice, subject to appropriate government restrictions in the interests of public health, safety, and welfare. In this case, as in ... *Loving*, a statute deprives individuals of access to an institution of fundamental legal, personal, and social significance—the institution of marriage—because of a single trait: skin color in *Perez* and *Loving*, sexual orientation here. ...

The Massachusetts Constitution protects matters of personal liberty against government incursion as zealously, and often more so, than does the Federal Constitution, even where both Constitutions employ essentially the same language....

The individual liberty and equality safeguards of the Massachusetts Constitution protect both "freedom from" unwarranted government intrusion into protected spheres of life and "freedom to" partake in benefits created by the State for the common good. Whether and whom to marry, how to express sexual intimacy, and whether and how to establish a family—these are among the most basic of every individual's liberty and due process rights. See, e.g., *Lawrence, supra* at 2481; *Planned Parenthood of Southeastern Pa. v. Casey*, 505 U.S. 833, 851 (1992); *Zablocki v. Redhail*, 434 U.S. 374, 384 (1978); *Roe v. Wade*, 410 U.S. 113, 152–153 (1973); *Eisenstadt v. Baird*, 405 U.S. 438, 453 (1972); *Loving v. Virginia, supra*. And central to personal freedom and security is the assurance that the laws will apply equally to persons in similar situations. "Absolute equality before the law is a fundamental principle of our own Constitution. The liberty interest in choosing whether and whom to marry would be hollow if the Commonwealth could, without sufficient justification, foreclose an individual from freely choosing the person with whom to share an exclusive commitment in the unique institution of civil marriage....

The plaintiffs challenge the marriage statute on both equal protection and due process grounds. With respect to each such claim, we must first determine the appropriate standard of review. Where a statute implicates a fundamental right or uses a suspect classification, we employ "strict judicial scrutiny." For all other statutes, we employ the " 'rational basis' test." For due process claims, rational basis analysis requires that statutes "bear[] a real and substantial relation to the public health, safety, morals, or some other phase of the general welfare." For equal protection challenges, the rational basis test requires that "an impartial lawmaker could logically believe that the classification would serve a legitimate public purpose that transcends the harm to the members of the disadvantaged class."

The department argues that no fundamental right or "suspect" class is at issue here, and rational basis is the appropriate standard of review. For the reasons we explain below, we conclude that the marriage ban does not meet the rational basis test for either due process or equal protection. Because the statute does not survive rational basis review, we do not consider the plaintiffs' arguments that this case merits strict judicial scrutiny.

The department posits three legislative rationales for prohibiting same-sex couples from marrying: (1) providing a "favorable setting for procreation"; (2) ensuring the optimal setting for child rearing, which the department defines as "a two-parent family with one parent of each sex"; and (3) preserving scarce State and private financial resources. We consider each in turn.

The judge in the Superior Court endorsed the first rationale, holding that "the state's interest in regulating marriage is based on the traditional concept that marriage's primary purpose is procreation." This is incorrect. Our laws of civil marriage do not privilege procreative heterosexual intercourse between married people above every other form of adult intimacy and every other means of creating a family. General Laws c. 207 contains no requirement that the applicants for a marriage license attest to their ability or intention to conceive children by coitus. Fertility is not a condition of marriage, nor is it grounds for divorce. People who have never consummated their marriage, and never plan to, may be and stay married. While it is certainly true that many, perhaps most, married couples have children together (assisted or unassisted), it is the exclusive and permanent commitment of the marriage partners to one another, not the begetting of children, that is the sine qua non of civil marriage.

Moreover, the Commonwealth affirmatively facilitates bringing children into a family regardless of whether the intended parent is married or unmarried, whether the child is adopted or born into a family, whether assistive technology was used to conceive the child, and whether the parent or her partner is heterosexual, homosexual, or bisexual. If procreation were a necessary component of civil marriage, our statutes would draw a tighter circle around the permissible bounds of nonmarital child bearing and the creation of families by noncoital means. The attempt to isolate procreation as "the source of a fundamental right to marry" . . . overlooks the integrated way in which courts have examined the complex and overlapping realms of personal autonomy, marriage, family life, and child rearing. Our jurisprudence recognizes that, in these nuanced and fundamentally private areas of life, such a narrow focus is inappropriate.

The "marriage is procreation" argument singles out the one unbridgeable difference between same-sex and opposite-sex couples, and transforms that difference into the essence of legal marriage. Like "Amendment 2" to the Constitution of Colorado, which effectively denied homosexual persons equality under the law and full access to the political process, the marriage restriction impermissibly "identifies persons by a single trait and then denies them protection across the board." *Romer v. Evans,* 517 U.S. 620, 633 (1996). In so doing, the State's action confers an official stamp of approval on the destructive stereotype that same-sex relationships are inherently unstable and inferior to opposite-sex relationships and are not worthy of respect.

The department's first stated rationale, equating marriage with unassisted heterosexual procreation, shades imperceptibly into its second: that confining marriage to opposite-sex couples ensures that children are raised in the "optimal" setting. Protecting the welfare of children is a paramount State policy. Restricting marriage to opposite-sex couples, however, cannot plausibly further this policy. "The demographic changes of the past century make it difficult to speak of an average American family. The composition of families varies greatly from household to household." *Troxel v. Granville,* 530 U.S. 57, 63 (2000). Massachusetts has responded supportively to "the changing realities of the American family," and has moved vigorously to strengthen the modern family in its many variations. Moreover, we have repudiated the common-law power of the State to provide varying levels of protection to children based on the circumstances of birth. The "best interests of the child" standard does not turn on a parent's sexual orientation or marital status. See e.g., *Doe v. Doe,* 16 Mass. App. Ct. 499, 503 (1983) (parent's sexual orientation insufficient ground to deny custody of child in divorce action).

The department has offered no evidence that forbidding marriage to people of the same sex will increase the number of couples choosing to enter into opposite-sex marriages in order to have and raise children. There is thus no rational relationship between the marriage statute and the Commonwealth's proffered goal of protecting the "optimal" child rearing unit. Moreover, the department readily concedes that people in same-sex couples may be "excellent" parents. These couples (including four of the plaintiff couples) have children for the reasons others do—to love them, to care for them, to nurture them. But the task of child rearing for same-sex couples is made infinitely harder by their status as outliers to the marriage laws. While establishing the parentage of children as soon as possible is crucial to the safety and welfare of children, same-sex couples must undergo the sometimes lengthy and intrusive process of second-parent adoption to establish their joint parentage. While the enhanced income provided by marital benefits is an important source of security and stability for married couples and their children, those benefits are denied to families headed by same-sex couples... Given the wide range of public benefits reserved only for married couples, we do not credit the department's contention that the absence of access to civil marriage amounts to little more than an inconvenience to same-sex couples and their children. Excluding same-sex couples from civil marriage will not make children of opposite-sex marriages more secure, but it does prevent children of same-sex couples from enjoying the immeasurable advantages that flow from the assurance of "a stable family structure in which children will be reared, educated, and socialized."...

No one disputes that the plaintiff couples are families, that many are parents, and that the children they are raising, like all children, need and should have the fullest opportunity to grow up in a secure, protected family unit. Similarly, no one disputes that, under the rubric of marriage, the State provides a cornucopia of substantial benefits to married parents and their children. The preferential treatment of civil marriage reflects the Legislature's conclusion that marriage "is the foremost setting for the education and socialization of children" precisely because it "encourages parents to remain committed to each other and to their children as they grow."

In this case, we are confronted with an entire, sizeable class of parents raising children who have absolutely no access to civil marriage and its protections because they are forbidden from procuring a marriage license. It cannot be rational under our laws, and indeed it is not permitted, to penalize children by depriving them of State benefits because the State disapproves of their parents' sexual orientation.

The third rationale advanced by the department is that limiting marriage to opposite-sex couples furthers the Legislature's interest in conserving scarce State and private financial resources. The marriage restriction is rational, it argues, because the General Court logically could assume that same-sex couples are more financially independent than married couples and thus less needy of public marital benefits, such as tax advantages, or private marital benefits, such as employer-financed health plans that include spouses in their coverage.

An absolute statutory ban on same-sex marriage bears no rational relationship to the goal of economy. First, the department's conclusory generalization—that same-sex couples are less financially dependent on each other than opposite-sex couples—ignores that many same-sex couples, such as many of the plaintiffs in this case, have children and other dependents (here, aged parents) in their care. The department does not contend, nor could it, that these dependents are less needy or deserving than the dependents of married couples. Second, Massachusetts marriage laws do not condition receipt of public and private financial benefits to married individuals on a demonstration of financial dependence on each other; the benefits are available to married couples regardless of whether they mingle their finances or actually depend on each other for support.

The department suggests additional rationales for prohibiting same-sex couples from marrying, which are developed by some amici. It argues that broadening civil marriage to include same-sex couples will trivialize or destroy the institution of marriage as it has historically been fashioned. Certainly our decision today marks a significant change in the definition of marriage as it has been inherited from the common law, and understood by many societies for centuries. But it does not disturb the fundamental value of marriage in our society.

Here, the plaintiffs seek only to be married, not to undermine the institution of civil marriage. They do not want marriage abolished. They do not attack the binary nature of marriage, the consanguinity provisions, or any of the other gate-keeping provisions of the marriage licensing law. Recognizing the right of an individual to marry a person of the same sex will not diminish the validity or dignity of opposite-sex marriage, any more than recognizing the right of an individual to marry a person of a different race devalues the marriage of a person who marries someone of her own race. If anything, extending civil marriage to same-sex couples reinforces the importance of marriage to individuals and communities....

We also reject the argument suggested by the department, and elaborated by some amici, that expanding the institution of civil marriage in Massachusetts to include same-sex couples will lead to interstate conflict. We would not presume to dictate how another State should respond to today's decision. But neither should considerations of comity prevent us from according Massachusetts residents the full measure of protection available under the Massachusetts Constitution. The genius of our Federal system is that each State's Constitution has vitality specific to its own traditions, and that, subject to the minimum requirements of the Fourteenth Amendment, each State is free to address difficult issues of individual liberty in the manner its own Constitution demands.

Several amici suggest that prohibiting marriage by same-sex couples reflects community consensus that homosexual conduct is immoral. Yet Massachusetts has a strong affirmative policy of preventing discrimination on the basis of sexual orientation. See G. L. c. 151B (employment, housing, credit, services); G. L. c. 265, § 39 (hate crimes); G. L. c. 272, § 98 (public accommodation); G. L. c. 76, § 5 (public education)....

The marriage ban works a deep and scarring hardship on a very real segment of the community for no rational reason. The absence of any reasonable relationship between, on the one hand, an absolute disqualification of same-sex couples who wish to enter into civil marriage and, on the other, protection of public health, safety, or general welfare, suggests that the marriage restriction is rooted in persistent prejudices against persons who are (or who are believed to be) homosexual. The Constitution cannot control such prejudices but neither can it tolerate them. Private biases may be outside the reach of the law, but the law cannot, directly or indirectly, give them effect. Limiting the protections, benefits, and obligations of civil marriage to opposite-sex couples violates the basic premises of individual liberty and equality under law protected by the Massachusetts Constitution,

IV

... We construe civil marriage to mean the voluntary union of two persons as spouses, to the exclusion of all others. This reformulation redresses the plaintiffs' constitutional injury and furthers the aim of marriage to promote stable, exclusive relationships. It advances the two legitimate State interests the department has identified: providing a stable setting for child rearing and conserving State resources. It leaves intact the Legislature's broad discretion to regulate marriage.

In their complaint the plaintiffs request only a declaration that their exclusion and the exclusion of other qualified same-sex couples from access to civil marriage violates Massachusetts law. We declare that barring an individual from the protections, benefits, and obligations of civil marriage solely because that person would marry a person of the same sex violates the Massachusetts Constitution. We vacate the summary judgment for the department. We remand this case to the Superior Court for entry of judgment consistent with this opinion. Entry of judgment shall be stayed for 180 days to permit the Legislature to take such action as it may deem appropriate in light of this opinion.

SPINA, J. dissenting....

1. *Equal protection* ... , the marriage statutes do not discriminate on the basis of sexual orientation. As the court correctly recognizes, constitutional protections are extended to individuals, not couples. The marriage statutes do not disqualify individuals on the basis of sexual orientation from entering into marriage. All individuals, with certain exceptions not relevant here, are free to marry. Whether an individual chooses not to marry because of sexual orientation or any other reason should be of no concern to the court....

Unlike the *Loving* and *Sharp* cases, the Massachusetts Legislature has erected no barrier to marriage that intentionally discriminates against anyone. Within the institution of marriage, anyone is free to marry, with certain exceptions that are not challenged. In the absence of any discriminatory purpose, the State's marriage statutes do not violate principles of equal protection. See *Washington v. Davis,* 426 U.S. 229, 240 (1976) ("invidious quality of a law claimed to be ... discriminatory must ultimately be traced to a ... discriminatory purpose"). This court should not have invoked even the most deferential standard of review within equal protection analysis because no individual was denied access to the institution of marriage.

Due process. The marriage statutes do not impermissibly burden a right protected by our constitutional guarantee of due process implicit in art. 10 of our Declaration of Rights. There is no restriction on the right of any plaintiff to enter into marriage. Each is free to marry a willing person of the opposite sex. Cf. *Zablocki v. Redhail,* 434 U.S. 374 (1978) (fundamental right to marry impermissibly burdened by statute requiring court approval when subject to child support order).

Substantive due process protects individual rights against unwarranted government intrusion. The court states, as we have said on many occasions, that the Massachusetts Declaration of Rights may protect a right in ways that exceed the protection afforded by the Federal Constitution. However, today the court does not fashion a remedy that affords greater protection of a right. Instead, using the rubric of due process, it has redefined marriage....

SOSMAN, J., dissenting

In applying the rational basis test to any challenged statutory scheme, the issue is not whether the Legislature's rationale behind that scheme is persuasive to us, but only whether it satisfies a minimal threshold of rationality. Today, rather than apply that test, the court announces that, because it is persuaded that there are no differences between same-sex and opposite-sex couples, the Legislature has no rational basis for treating them differently with respect to the granting of marriage licenses. Reduced to its essence, the court's opinion concludes that, because same-sex couples are now raising children, and withholding the benefits of civil marriage from their union makes it harder for them to raise those children, the State must therefore provide the benefits of civil marriage to same-sex couples just as it does to opposite-sex couples. Of course, many people are raising children outside the confines of traditional marriage, and, by definition, those children are being deprived of the various benefits that would flow if they were being raised in a household with married parents. That does not mean that the Legislature must accord the full benefits of marital status on every household raising children. Rather, the Legislature need only have some rational basis for concluding that, at present, those alternate family structures have not yet been conclusively shown to be the equivalent of the marital family structure that has established itself as a successful one over a period of centuries. People are of course at liberty to raise their children in various family structures, as long as they are not literally harming their children by doing so. That does not mean that the State is required to provide identical forms of encouragement, endorsement, and support to all of the infinite variety of household structures that a free society permits.

Based on our own philosophy of child rearing, and on our observations of the children being raised by same-sex couples to whom we are personally close, we may be of the view that what matters to children is not the gender, or sexual orientation, or even the number of the adults who raise them, but rather whether those adults provide the children with a nurturing, stable, safe, consistent, and supportive environment in which to mature. Same-sex couples can provide their children with the requisite nurturing, stable, safe, consistent, and supportive environment in which to mature, just as opposite-sex couples do. It is therefore understandable that the court might view the traditional definition of marriage as an unnecessary anachronism, rooted in historical prejudices that modern society has in large measure rejected and biological limitations that modern science has overcome.

It is not, however, our assessment that matters. Conspicuously absent from the court's opinion today is any acknowledgment that the attempts at scientific study of the ramifications of raising children in same-sex couple households are themselves in their infancy and have so far produced inconclusive and conflicting results. Notwithstanding our belief that gender and sexual orientation of parents should not matter to the success of the child rearing venture, studies to date reveal that there are still some observable differences between children raised by opposite-sex couples and children raised by same-sex couples. Interpretation of the data gathered by those studies then becomes clouded by the personal and political beliefs of the investigators, both as to whether the differences identified are positive or negative, and as to the untested explanations of what might account for those differences.... Even in the absence of bias or political agenda behind the various studies of children raised by same-sex couples, the most neutral and strict application of scientific principles to this field would be constrained by the limited period of observation that has been available. Gay and lesbian couples living together openly, and official recognition of them as their children's sole parents, comprise a very recent phenomenon, and the recency of that phenomenon has not yet permitted any study of how those children fare as adults and at best minimal study of how they fare during their adolescent years. The Legislature can rationally view the state of the scientific evidence as unsettled on the critical question it now faces: Are families headed by same-sex parents equally successful in rearing children from infancy to adulthood as families headed by parents of opposite sexes? Our belief that children raised by same-sex couples should fare the same as children raised in traditional families is just that: a passionately held but utterly untested belief. The Legislature is not required to share that belief but may, as the creator of the institution of civil marriage, wish to see the proof before making a fundamental alteration to that institution.

Although ostensibly applying the rational basis test to the civil marriage statutes, it is abundantly apparent that the court is in fact applying some undefined stricter standard to assess the constitutionality of the marriage statutes' exclusion of same-sex couples....

Shorn of these emotion-laden invocations, the opinion ultimately opines that the Legislature is acting irrationally when it grants benefits to a proven successful family structure while denying the same benefits to a recent, perhaps promising, but essentially untested alternate family structure. Placed in a more neutral context, the court would never find any irrationality in such an approach. For example, if the issue were government subsidies and tax benefits promoting use of an established technology for energy efficient heating, the court would find no equal protection or due process violation in the Legislature's decision not to grant the same benefits to an inventor or manufacturer of some new, alternative technology who did not yet have sufficient data to prove that that new technology was just as good as the established technology. That the early results from preliminary testing of the new technology might look very promising, or that the theoretical underpinnings of the new technology might appear flawless, would not make it irrational for the Legislature to grant subsidies and tax breaks to the established technology and deny them to the still unproved newcomer in the field. While programs that affect families and children register higher on our emotional scale than programs affecting energy efficiency, our standards for what is or is not "rational" should not be bent by those emotional tugs. Where, as here, there is no ground for applying strict scrutiny, the emotionally compelling nature of the subject matter should not affect the manner in which we apply the rational basis test.

OPINIONS OF THE JUSTICES TO THE SENATE

Supreme Judicial Court of Massachusetts, 2004
802 N.E.2d 565

[On December 11, 2003, the Massachusetts legislature adopted, pending decision by the Massachusetts Supreme Judicial Court, Senate Bill 275, "An Act Relative to Civil Unions." Section 2 of that bill seeks to "provide eligible same-sex couples the opportunity to obtain the benefits, protections rights and responsibilities afforded to opposite sex couples by the marriage laws of the commonwealth, without entering into a marriage." The bill includes a new Chapter 207A of the Massachusetts statutes establishing civil unions, open to same-sex couples eligible on grounds of age, non-relationship, and other standard categories, but not to opposite-sex couples. Section 3 of 207A provides that "Persons eligible to form a civil union with each other under this chapter shall not be eligible to enter into a marriage with each other under chapter 207."

The second bill adopted at the same time, Senate Bill 2176, seeks an opinion by the Supreme Judicial Court on the question of whether the pending statute (S.B. 2175) complies with the equal protection and due process requirements of the state constitution.]

. . . We have now been asked to render an advisory opinion on Senate No. 2175, which creates a new legal status, "civil union," that is purportedly equal to "marriage," yet separate from it. The constitutional difficulty of the proposed civil union bill is evident in its stated purpose to "preserv[e] the traditional, historic nature and meaning of the institution of civil marriage." Senate No. 2175, § 1. Preserving the institution of civil marriage is of course a legislative priority of the highest order, and one to which the Justices accord the General Court the greatest deference. We recognize the efforts of the Senate to draft a bill in conformity with the *Goodridge* opinion. Yet the bill, as we read it, does nothing to "preserve" the civil marriage law, only its constitutional infirmity. . . .

The same defects of rationality evident in the marriage ban considered in *Goodridge* are evident in, if not exaggerated by, Senate No. 2175. Segregating same-sex unions from opposite-sex unions cannot possibly be held rationally to advance or "preserve" what we stated in *Goodridge* were the Commonwealth's legitimate interests in procreation, child rearing, and the conservation of resources. Because the proposed law by its express terms forbids same-sex couples entry into civil marriage, it continues to relegate same-sex couples to a different status. The holding in *Goodridge,* by which we are bound, is that group classifications based on unsupportable distinctions, such as that embodied in the proposed bill, are invalid under the Massachusetts Constitution. The history of our nation has demonstrated that separate is seldom, if ever, equal. . . .

The bill's absolute prohibition of the use of the word "marriage" by "spouses" who are the same sex is more than semantic. The dissimilitude between the terms "civil marriage" and "civil union" is not innocuous; it is a considered choice of language that reflects a demonstrable assigning of same-sex, largely homosexual, couples to second-class status. The denomination of this difference by the separate opinion of Justice Sosman (separate opinion) as merely a "squabble over the name to be used" so clearly misses the point that further discussion appears to be useless. If, as the separate opinion posits, the proponents of the bill believe that no message is conveyed by eschewing the word "marriage" and replacing it with "civil union" for same-sex "spouses," we doubt that the attempt to circumvent the court's decision in *Goodridge* would be so purposeful.

SAMUELS v. NEW YORK STATE DEPARTMENT OF HEALTH

Supreme Court, Appellate Division, 2006
811 NYS2d 136

LAHTINEN, J.

Plaintiffs contend that the N.Y. Constitution requires defendant State of New York to permit same-sex couples to marry.[1] Briefly stated, plaintiffs are same-sex couples, some of whom assert that they requested a marriage license from a town clerk and were informed that such licenses would not be issued to same-sex couples. It is also alleged in the complaint, and defendants admit, that defendant Department of Health determined that marriage licenses may not be issued to same-sex couples and the Department so advised city and town clerks throughout the state. In April 2004, plaintiffs commenced this action seeking a judgment declaring the Domestic Relations Law unconstitutional to the extent that it prohibits marriage licenses from being issued to same-sex couples. Plaintiffs assert that the statutory restriction violates the due process, equal protection and free speech provisions of the N.Y. Constitution. After defendants answered, the parties moved for summary judgment. In December 2004, Supreme Court denied plaintiffs' motion, granted defendants' cross motion and dismissed the complaint. Plaintiffs appeal.

The Legislature has placed many parameters on marriage in New York (*see e.g.,* Domestic Relations Law §§ 5, 6, 7). Historically, the role

1. We note at the outset that several appellate courts in other jurisdictions have addressed a similar issue under their constitutions and, in some instances, the U.S. Constitution. They have arrived at varying conclusions, often by divided votes (*see e.g. Lewis v. Harris,* 875 A.2d 259 [N.J. Super. 2005]; *Morrison v. Sadler,* 821 N.E.2d 15 [Ind. 2005]; *Goodridge v. Department of Public Health,* 798 N.E.2d 941 [Mass. 2003]; *Standhardt v. Superior Court of Arizona,* 77 P3d 451 [Ariz. 2003]; *Baker v. Vermont,* 744 A.2d 864 [Vt. 1999]; *Dean v. District of Columbia,* 653 A.2d 307 [D.C. 1995]; *Singer v. Hara,* 522 P.2d 1187 [1974], *review denied* 84 Wash 2d 1008 [1974]; *Baker v. Nelson,* 191 NW2d 185 [Minn. 1971], *appeal dismissed* 409 U.S. 810 [1972]). In this state, the First Department recently held that maintaining the definition of marriage as being between one man and one woman does not violate the N.Y. Constitution (*Hernandez v. Robles,* 26 AD3d 98, 805 N.Y.S.2d 354 [2005]) and, although it addressed the issue in a somewhat different context, the Second Department has indicated a similar conclusion (*Langan v. St. Vincent's Hosp. of N.Y.,* 25 AD3d 90 [2005]).

of defining the boundaries of marriage " 'has always been subject to the control of the Legislature' and, even though a particular judge or judges may disagree with the wisdom of some aspects of the restrictions, it is an area "left to the Legislature to resolve." Nevertheless, if the Legislature runs afoul of well ingrained precepts of the Constitution, court intervention-no matter how unpopular—is proper (*see e.g. Zablocki v. Redhail,* 434 U.S. 374 [1978]; *Loving v. Virginia,* 388 U.S. 1 [1967]). The hurdle for one attacking the constitutionality of laws duly enacted by the elected representatives of the people is high. "[L]egislative enactments are presumed valid and ... one who challenges a statute bears the burden of proving the legislation unconstitutional beyond a reasonable doubt." It is with this background in mind that we turn to plaintiffs' constitutional arguments. We consider first plaintiffs' contention that substantive due process is violated by this state's statutes limiting marriage to one woman and one man. New York's Due Process Clause provides that "[n]o person shall be deprived of life, liberty or property without due process of law" (N.Y. Const., art. I, § 6). Protection for certain fundamental rights is implicit within this crucial constitutional clause.[2] And, in an appropriate case, the protections provided by New York's Due Process Clause will be afforded a more expansive interpretation than the U.S. Constitution. A law that impinges upon a fundamental right is subject to strict scrutiny, whereas one that does not "burden a fundamental right ... is valid if it bears a rational relationship to [a governmental] interest."

Courts use great caution when urged to recognize a new fundamental right or significantly expand an established one. The compelling reason for such caution was explained by the United States Supreme Court as follows:

"[W]e have always been reluctant to expand the concept of substantive due process because guideposts for responsible decisionmaking in this unchartered area are scarce and open-ended. By extending constitutional protection to an asserted right or liberty interest, we, to a great extent, place the matter outside the arena of public debate and legislative action. We must therefore exercise the utmost care whenever we are asked to break new ground in this field, lest the liberty protected by the Due Process Clause be subtly transformed into the policy preferences of the Members of this Court" (*Washington v. Glucksberg,* 521 U.S. 702, 720 [1997]).

2. With regard to the U.S. Constitution, rights not specifically set forth in the Bill of Rights, but found to be fundamental to the "liberty" element of due process, include those "to marry, *Loving v. Virginia,* 388 U.S. 1 (1967); to have children, *Skinner v. Oklahoma ex rel. Williamson,* 316 U.S. 535 (1942); to direct the education and upbringing of one's children, *Meyer v. Nebraska,* 262 U.S. 390 (1923); *Pierce v. Society of Sisters,* 268 U.S. 510 (1925); to marital privacy, *Griswold v. Connecticut,* 381 U.S. 479 (1965); to use contraception, *ibid.; Eisenstadt v. Baird,* 405 U.S. 438 (1972); to bodily integrity, *Rochin v. California,* 342 U.S. 165 (1952), and to abortion [*Planned Parenthood of Southeastern Pa. v.] Casey,* [505 U.S. 833 (1992)]" (*Washington v. Glucksberg,* 521 U.S. 702, 720 (1997)).

One of the primary safeguards in maintaining a cautious and principled substantive due process analysis is the requirement that an asserted right or liberty generally be " 'deeply rooted in this Nation's history and tradition' " (*id.* at 721, quoting *Moore v. City of Cleveland,* 431 U.S. 494, 503 [1977]). The Court of Appeals has explained that "[d]ue process of law guarantees respect for personal immunities 'so rooted in the traditions and conscience of our people as to be ranked as fundamental.' " When, as here, the N.Y. Constitution is asserted, it is appropriate to consider whether the history and traditions unique to this state point clearly to the need for additional protection beyond that afforded by the U.S. Constitution.

Plaintiffs seek to bring the right to marry the person of their choosing regardless of gender within the protection of the well-recognized fundamental right to marry (*see Zablocki v. Redhail,* 434 U.S. 374 [1978], *supra; Loving v. Virginia,* 388 U.S. 1 [1967], *supra; Skinner v. Oklahoma ex rel. Williamson,* 316 U.S. 535, 541 [1942]). However, we find merit in defendants' assertion that this case is not simply about the right to marry the person of one's choice, but represents a significant expansion into new territory which is, in reality, a redefinition of marriage. The cornerstone cases acknowledging marriage as a fundamental right are laced with language referring to the ancient recognized nature of that institution, specifically tying part of its critical importance to its role in procreation and, thus, to the union of a woman and a man. In *Skinner v. Oklahoma ex rel. Williamson*, Justice Douglas, writing for the United States Supreme Court, stated that "[m]arriage and procreation are fundamental to the very existence and survival of the race"(*id.* at 541). Drawing upon *Skinner,* Chief Justice Warren penned in *Loving v. Virginia* that "[m]arriage is one of the 'basic civil rights of man,' fundamental to our very existence and survival" (*id.* at 12). Justice Marshall, citing to *Skinner* and *Loving,* as well as other decisions of the Court, wrote in *Zablocki v. Redhail (supra)*:

"Long ago ... the Court characterized marriage as the most important relation in life and as the foundation of the family and of society, without which there would be neither civilization nor progress ... [T]he Court recognized that the right to marry, establish a home and bring up children is a central part of the liberty protected by the Due Process Clause ... and ... marriage was described as fundamental to the very existence and survival of the race."

In a similar vein, the Court of Appeals has observed about marriage: "However much this relationship may be debased at times it nevertheless is the foundation upon which must rest the perpetuation of society and civilization." To remove from "marriage" a definitional component of that institution (i.e., one woman, one man) which long predates the constitutions of this country and state[3] would, to a certain extent,

3. In *Griswold v. Connecticut* the United States Supreme Court stated that "[w]e deal with a right of privacy older than the Bill of Rights-older than our political parties, older than our school system. Marriage is a coming together for better or for worse,

extract some of the "deep roots" that support its elevation to a fundamental right. While such a change of a basic element of the institution may eventually find favor with the Legislature, we are not persuaded that the Due Process Clause requires a judicial redefinition of marriage. Accordingly, the Domestic Relations Law will survive plaintiffs' substantive due process challenge if it has a rational basis. Before we address that issue, we must determine whether the Equal Protection Clause mandates a higher level of scrutiny.

The N.Y. Constitution's Equal Protection Clause provides, in pertinent part, that "[n]o person shall be denied the equal protection of the laws of this state or any subdivision thereof" (N.Y. Const, art I, § 11). The Court of Appeals has noted that "the State constitutional equal protection clause ... is no broader in coverage than the Federal provision." "The general rule [in equal protection analysis] is that legislation is presumed to be valid and will be sustained if the classification drawn by the statute is rationally related to a legitimate state interest." Rational basis review, however, gives way to strict scrutiny for classifications based on race, national origin or those affecting fundamental rights and to intermediate or heightened scrutiny for certain classifications such as gender and illegitimacy. Plaintiffs urge that they should be declared a new suspect class entitled to at least intermediate level scrutiny and, also, that New York's marriage statutes create a gender-based discriminatory scheme.

As to the level of scrutiny regarding assertions of sexual orientation discrimination, we recently held, in *Matter of Valentine v. American Airlines* (17 AD3d 38, 42 [2005]), as follows:

"Courts, including the United States Supreme Court, have applied the rational basis standard, rather than strict or heightened scrutiny, when reviewing sexual orientation discrimination allegations (*see Romer v. Evans,* 517 U.S. 620, 631–633 [1996] [noting that courts have uniformly refused to apply higher level of scrutiny to sexual orientation discrimination])."

The doctrine of adhering to precedent is an important one, and it is rooted in part in the "humbling assumption ... that no particular court as it is then constituted possesses a wisdom surpassing that of its predecessors." We recognize, however, that following precedent is not an absolutely rigid rule and "in cases interpreting the Constitution courts will ..., if convinced of prior error, correct the error." Nevertheless, after review of the arguments advanced in the current case, we are not persuaded to reconsider or depart from our recent holding in *Matter of Valentine v. American Airlines*.

hopefully enduring, and intimate to the degree of being sacred." Since *Griswold* spoke of marriage within the context of restrictions on contraceptives, it is apparent that the Court was referring to opposite-sex marriage ("This law ... operates directly on an intimate relation of husband and wife.") This is not to suggest that all aspects of marriage have or must remain mired in an inflexible mold. The legal rights of the parties to the relationship have changed.

Nor are we persuaded by plaintiffs' contention that the Domestic Relations Law discriminates on the basis of gender. In *Valentine,* we addressed an analogous assertion about the Workers' Compensation Law and held that, since that law "is facially neutral and applies equally to males and females, we do not accept claimant's argument that [the statute] discriminates on the basis of gender." The same reasoning applies to the facially neutral Domestic Relations Law. Hence, the marriage laws will survive plaintiffs' equal protection claims-as well as their due process claims—unless they are unsupported by a rational basis.

"When reviewing using a rational basis standard, 'a classification must be upheld . . . if there is any reasonably conceivable state of facts that could provide a rational basis for the classification . . . [I]ndeed, a court may even *hypothesize* the motivations of the State Legislature to discern any conceivable legitimate objective promoted by the provision under attack.' " "Since the challenged statute is presumed to be valid, the burden is on the one attacking the legislative arrangement to negative every conceivable basis which might support it . . . *whether or not the basis has a foundation in the record.*" Succinctly stated, "[t]he rational basis standard of review is a paradigm of judicial restraint."

The interests urged as meeting the low threshold of a rational basis include, among others: preserving the historic legal and cultural understanding of marriage; recognizing heterosexual marriage as a social institution in which procreation occurs; and conforming with the current legal landscape nationwide. Certainly, the logic of each of these grounds is neither flawless nor finely tailored; however, it need not be. "[W]here rationality is the test, a State 'does not violate the Equal Protection Clause merely because the classification made by its laws are imperfect.' "

We consider first the preservation of the historic legal and cultural understanding of marriage. In *Lawrence v. Texas* (539 U.S. 558 [2003])—a case cited by plaintiffs throughout their arguments—Justice O'Connor stated in her concurring opinion that a "legitimate state interest" would include "preserving the traditional institution of marriage." The majority in *Lawrence* was careful to explain that its decision did not involve "whether the government must give formal recognition to any relationship that homosexual persons seek to enter." It is, indeed, a long legal road from finding a constitutionally based shield providing protection from criminal prosecution for certain adult consensual conduct carried out in private to using the Constitution as the means to redefine marriage. While history and the collective wisdom of our ancestors should not be lightly set aside, there are nonetheless occasions when old paradigms must cease. A primary example of a justified break with the past is *Loving v. Virginia*, a case upon which plaintiffs place significant reliance. There are, however, critical legal and factual distinctions between *Loving* and the current case. For example, the law in *Loving* did not seek to redefine the historical understanding of marriage, but instead involved a race-based barrier to a traditional one woman, one man union. *Loving* was, in many respects, about racial discrimination. ["There is patently no legitimate overriding purpose independent of invidious racial discrimination which justifies this classification"]). Race-based barriers strike at the heart of the Civil War amendments and are always subject to the strictest scrutiny. *Loving* implicated not only marriage, but did so with a barrier that was clearly subject to the highest level of scrutiny. That barrier was a direct descendant of the abhorrent conduct which was a cause of civil war in this nation and served as an impetus for several amendments to the U.S. Constitution.

Here, after the recent efforts to redefine marriage received considerable publicity and some judicial support, the United States Congress passed, and President Clinton signed into law, the Federal Defense of Marriage Act (see 1 USC § 7; 28 USC § 1738C), and nearly all state legislatures that have addressed the issue have similarly maintained the traditional definition of marriage (over 40 states have reportedly enacted statutes similar to the Federal Defense of Marriage Act and many have amended their constitutions). In light of the recent statement of Justice O'Connor in *Lawrence v. Texas*, the expressed restraint of the majority in that case, and with due respect for history and elected representatives, we are not persuaded that plaintiffs have established beyond a reasonable doubt that it is irrational for the Legislature to preserve the historic legal and cultural understanding of marriage (*see Hernandez v. Robles, supra* at 359).

Next, we address the further proffered rational basis—closely related to the prior one—of recognizing heterosexual marriage as a social institution in which procreation occurs. We start by accepting for purposes of this case the following observations (many, but not all, of which are not seriously disputed): precluding same-sex couples from marrying does not encourage opposite-sex couples to have and raise children; many same-sex couples currently raise children and both partners are good parents; the adoption of a child is not dependent upon a parent's sexual orientation or marital status; with the assistance of modern technology, conception of a child is possible outside of sexual intercourse and regardless of the woman's sexual orientation; and many opposite-sex couples who marry do not have children. In light of these observations, if the test being employed was not rational basis, the overinclusive and underinclusive nature of this basis would create considerable problems for defendants; a fact that defendants conceded at oral argument.

However, as previously stated, the test here is rational basis, where "distinctions may be made with substantially less than mathematical exactitude, and rationality is not impaired because a distinction is either over-inclusive or under-inclusive." It is an undisputed biological fact that the vast majority of procreation still occurs as a result of sexual intercourse between a male and a female. In light of such fact, "[t]he State could reasonably decide that by encouraging opposite-sex couples to marry, thereby assuming legal and financial obligations, the children born from such relationships will have better opportunities to be nurtured and raised by two parents within long-term, committed relationships, which society has traditionally viewed as advantageous for children" (*Standhardt v. Superior Court of Arizona, supra* at 287–288). Stated another way:

"One of the State's key interests in supporting opposite-sex marriage is not necessarily to encourage and promote 'natural' procreation across the board and at the expense of other forms of becoming parents, such as by adoption and assisted reproduction; rather, it encourages opposite-sex couples who, by definition, are the only type of couples that can reproduce on their own by engaging in sex with little or no contemplation of the consequences that might result, i.e. a child, to procreate responsibly.... The institution of opposite-sex marriage both encourages such couples to enter into a stable relationship before having children and to remain in such a relationship if children arrive during the marriage unexpectedly." (*Morrison v. Sadler,* 821 N.E.2d 15, 25 [Ind. 2005]).

While the parties and amici have cited numerous studies by a host of authors and purported authorities, some of which affirm the premise of this rationale and some of which dispute it, the Legislature is the better forum for sorting through this type of conflicting data on an important social issue. We agree with the opinion of the First Department and the majority of jurisdictions, which have found a rational basis for the historic definition of marriage.[11] It is not necessary to discuss the other offered rational bases.

Lastly, we are unpersuaded by plaintiffs' argument that the relevant restrictions placed by New York on the issuing of marriage licenses violated plaintiffs' constitutional right to free speech. "It is possible to find some kernel of expression in almost every activity a person undertakes—for example, walking down the street or meeting one's friends at a shopping mall—but such a kernel is not sufficient to bring the activity within the protection of the First Amendment." Stated another way, "[w]e cannot accept the view that an apparently limitless variety of conduct can be labeled 'speech'." Such is the situation here. However, even if it is assumed that the Legislature's actions in fulfilling its long-established duty of defining the parameters of marriage implicated plaintiffs' rights under free speech protection, "when 'speech' and 'nonspeech' elements are combined ... a sufficiently important governmental interest in regulating the nonspeech element can justify incidental limitations on First Amendment freedoms." ... This state's laws defin-

11. We note that an appeal of a lower court decision finding no due process or equal protection violation in the one woman, one man element of marriage was dismissed for want of substantial federal question by the United States Supreme Court in *Baker v. Nelson* (291 Minn 310, 191 NW2d 185 [1971], *appeal dismissed* 409 U.S. 810 [1972]). With regard to *Cooper,* the ground asserted by plaintiffs for rejecting *Cooper* as authority is the citation in that case to *Bowers v. Hardwick* (478 U.S. 186 [1986]), which was subsequently overruled in *Lawrence v. Texas* (539 U.S. 558 [2003], *supra*). *Cooper,* however, was decided after *People v. Onofre* (51 N.Y.2d 476 [1980]), in which the Court of Appeals struck down this state's statutes criminalizing adult consensual sodomy in a ruling that foreshadowed the United States Supreme Court's *Lawrence* decision. The Second Department adhered to its *Cooper* decision in the recent case of *Langan v. St. Vincent's Hosp. of N.Y.* (*supra*).

ing marriage are general in nature and do not target any speech or expressive conduct. The Legislature acted consistent with its constitutional role, and the parameters that it placed on marriage are undergirded by sufficient governmental interests to uphold marriage as historically understood and defined. In our opinion, the Legislature is where changes to marriage of the nature urged by plaintiffs should be addressed.

Notes and Questions on the Case Law

(1) Even the assumption that marriage is a heterosexual institution is not without its perplexities. What is a woman? What is a man? Is a transsexual man who has had a sex-change operation a woman? For a detailed judicial answer, see the decision of the trial judge in *Corbett v. Corbett* (otherwise Ashley), (1970) All ER 33. For a case involving a sex-change operation that took place after the marriage, see *Anonymous v. Anonymous*, 325 NYS2d 499 (NY Misc 1971). For a more recent case which reviews the available precedents (and which holds that there cannot—absent a change in legislative policy—"be a valid marriage between a man and a person born as a man, but surgically altered to have the physical characteristics of a woman"), see *Littleton v. Prange*, 9 SW3d 223 (Tex App 1999). For "the story of a crossing from fifty-two-year-old man to fifty-five-year-old woman, Donald to Deirdre," see Deirdre N. McCloskey, *Crossing: A Memoir* (U Chi Press, 1999). You may have already have encountered Professor McCloskey, for she is a prominent scholar of economics and economic history. For a fascinating novel exploring the life of an ambiguously sexed person, consider Jeffrey Eugenides, *Middlesex* (Picador, 2003).

(2) In the older cases, *Reynolds* through *Loving*, why is religion mentioned so often? Is it appropriate for discussions of the bible to appear in cases? Gender identity and the process of creating or obtaining this is an issue at the heart of debates over marriage. Kansas had a recent case involving this issue: *In Re Estate of Gardiner*, 42 P3d 120 (2002). The Kansas Supreme Court held that a male to female post operative transsexual "is not a woman within the meaning of the statutes and cannot validly marry another man." Therefore she could not receive a spousal share of her husband's estate when he died intestate. The Kansas court cited a Texas decision, which asked, "is a person's gender immutably fixed by our Creator at birth?" Evidently, the Kansas Supreme Court believes that it is.

(3) You have often heard that the answer to a question often depends on how the question is framed. Is that true here? Consider the difference between two statements of the issue in the case: (1) May males marry only females and not males, even though women may marry males? (2) May persons of the same sex marry? As an advocate, you would know which formulation you would need to choose. As a judge, which formulation ought you choose? And, of course, why?

(a) Knowing that it matters how you frame a question does not help you decide which of the two possible ways of framing the question is preferable. Hawaii, which considered same-sex marriages in *Baehr v. Lewin*, 852 P2d 44 (1993), adopted a version of the Equal Rights Amendment. Does the intent of the framers of the ERA help you here? (See Haw Const Art I, sec 3: "Equality of rights under the law shall not be denied or abridged by the State on account of sex.")

(i). Who were the framers? The people who drafted the ERA? The citizens of Hawaii who voted for it?

(ii). Once you know who the framers were, how do you discover what their intent was?

(b) Is *Loving v. Virginia*, 388 US 1 (1967), distinguishable? *Samuels* answers this question in the affirmative. *Loving* held a statute prohibiting interracial marriage unconstitutional. The Court in *Loving* said, "The fact that Virginia prohibits only interracial marriage involving white persons demonstrates that the racial classifications must stand on their own justification, as measures designed to maintain White Supremacy." Since Massachusetts before *Goodridge* and New York before *Samuels* presumably prohibited same-sex marriages of any sort, does this quotation suggest a factual difference between *Loving* and the same-sex marriage cases that should be dispositive? Bearing this quotation in mind, might one further argue that the central meaning of the fourteenth amendment—the prevention of invidious treatment of blacks—was involved in *Loving*, but that the central meaning of the ERA—the prevention of invidious treatment of women—is not involved in *Goodridge* or *Samuels*?

(4) It is often said (indeed the courts in *Goodridge* and *Samuels* said in various ways) that the state has an interest in marriage because the state has an interest in the next generation and a duty to protect its helpless members, especially children. One prominent proponent of same-sex marriage comments on "a difference that I think is inherent between homosexual and heterosexual adults. The latter group is committed to the procreation of a new generation. The former simply isn't." Andrew Sullivan, *Virtually Normal: An Argument About Homosexuality* 196 (Alfred A. Knopf, 1995). Since same-sex marriage cannot without assistive technology serve the procreative function, does the state have any interest in creating such a legal institution? In other words, aren't homosexual relations purely a private matter in which the state has no interest?

(a) Professor Eskridge may be reflecting this difference when he says, "In today's society the importance of marriage is relational and not procreational." William N. Eskridge, Jr., *The Case for Same–Sex Marriage: From Sexual Liberty to Civilized Commitment* 11 (Free Press, 1996). If this is true, what is the state's interest in regulating marriage? One lesbian opponent of same-sex marriage says, "Nor do I want to give the state the power to regulate my primary relationship." Paula Ettelbrick, *Since When Is Marriage a Path to Liberation?* in Andrew Sullivan ed, *Same-Sex Marriage: Pro and Con* 120–21 (Vintage Books, 1997). What would give the state the authority to do so?

(b) While same-sex marriage cannot serve the procreative function, it can serve the child-rearing function. Does this provide a basis for the state's interest in it?

(5) What is *Goodridge*'s precedential effect?

(a) What kind of precedent is *Goodridge* for the rest of the country? *Goodridge*, of course, rests not on the United States Constitution, but rather on Massachusetts's. Furthermore, the Massachusetts court avers "The Massachusetts Constitution protects matter of personal liberty against government incursion as zealously, and often more so, than does the Federal Constitution even where both Constitutions employ essentially the same language."

(b) What kind of precedent is *Goodridge* for Massachusetts? One commonly advanced reason not to recognize same-sex marriage is a slippery slope argument—that doing so is apt to lead to recognizing other heterodox forms of marriage. Polygamy is an often cited instance. Would *Baker*'s reasoning in fact extend to polygamy? For an argument that comes close to saying yes, see David L. Chambers, *Polygamy and Same–Sex Marriage,* 26 Hofstra L Rev 53 (Fall 1997). Yet more directly, consider the following:

> "It [polygamy] seems like a pretty good idea for professional women, who can proceed with their careers and have someone at home they can trust to watch their children. It solves the day care problem," Luci Malin, vice chairman of Utah NOW, said in a telephone interview yesterday.... "If NOW is about anything, it's about choice," Miss Malin said in *Women's Quarterly*, a publication of the Independent Women's Forum.

(6) If a civil union is recognized by another state, will that pave the way necessarily for recognition of plural (e.g., polygamous) or close affinity (incestuous) marriages? What if the closely related couple were related only by adoption, so there were not issues involving their children's genetic problems? Cheshire Calhoun, *Who's Afraid of Polygamous Marriage? Lessons For Same Sex Marriage Advocacy From The History of Polygamy* 42 San Diego L Rev 1023 (2005) (arguing that that more careful attention to the historical practice of polygamy strengthens the case for same sex marriage and that attention to the similarities between the social issues at stake in the antipolygamy campaign and the same sex marriage campaign can productively complicate our sense of what the fundamental issues are in the same sex marriage debate); a reply to this article is Stanford Levinson, *Thinking About Polygamy*, 42 San Diego L Rev 1049 (2005).

(7) Does Vermont or Connecticut have jurisdiction over a couple coming specifically to form the civil union that would be binding even in those states? Would Vermont or Connecticut have had the same jurisdic-

tion (or lack of it) for a marriage (between a man and a woman)? How does the jurisdiction needed for marriage differ from that needed for dissolution of a relationship (if it does)?

This is not an idle question; for example, of the more than 6,400 couples that had obtained civil unions in Vermont as of November 2003, 85% were not residents of Vermont. See Nathan M. Brandenburg, *Preachers, Politicians, and Same–Sex Couples: Challenging Same–Sex Civil Unions and Implications on Interstate Recognition*, 91 Iowa L Rev 319, 326 (2005).

Thirty-eight states have adopted statutes with similar language or intent, known as "mini-DOMAs." The Creighton Law Review came out with another symposium on the subject of recognition of marriages: Symposium on the Implications of Lawrence and Goodridge for the Recognition of Same–Sex Marriages and the Validity of DOMA, 38 Creighton L Rev (2005). Here's another article on the subject: Barbara J. Cox, *Same-Sex Marriage and Choice-of-Law: If We Marry in Hawaii, Are We Still Married When We Return Home?*, 1994 Wis L Rev 1033.

Despite these provisions, states have been called upon to interpret the provisions of same-sex unions in issues such as dissolution, child custody, and wrongful death. In Iowa, plaintiffs challenged the authority of an Iowa court to dissolve a civil union created in Vermont; the Iowa Supreme Court held that the plaintiffs (a pastor and state legislators) did not have standing. See *Alons v. Iowa District Court*, 698 NW2d 858 (Iowa 2005). In Virginia, the courts addressed a custody battle between two former partners in a Vermont civil union over their young daughter. See Rachel E. Shoaf, *Two Mothers and Their Child: A Look At The Uncertain Status of Nonbiological Lesbian Mothers Under Current Law*, 12 Wm & Mary J Women & L 267 (2005). In New York a court held that a partner in a civil union must be treated as a spouse for purposes of the state's wrongful death statute. *Langan v. St. Vincent's Hosp. of New York*, 765 NYS2d 411 (2003).

> NOW endorses "an expanded definition of family, including same-sex parents," so "it is very difficult to look at that and not support other configurations of families, including polygamous families," said Robin Frodge, a Utah member of NOW who serves on the national board.

The Washington Times, Aug. 12, 1997, at A1. Can homosexual and polygamous marriage be distinguished in some relevant way?

(8) Commenting on the kinds of reasoning the *Goodridge* court relied on, and speaking of the United States Supreme Court instead of the Massachusetts Supreme Court, Judge Posner writes,

> There is nothing wrong with these arguments, except—a crucial except, however—the tacit assumption that the methods of legal casuistry are an adequate basis for compelling every state in the United States to adopt a radical social policy that is deeply offensive to the vast majority of its citizens and that exists in no other country of the world, and to do so at the behest of an educated, articulate, and increasingly politically effective minority that is seeking to bypass the normal political process for no better reason than impatience, albeit an understandable impa-

> tience.... A decision by the Supreme Court holding that the Constitution entitles people to marry others of the same sex would be far more radical than any of the decisions cited.... Its moorings in text, precedent, public policy, and public opinion would be too tenuous to rally even minimum public support. It would be an unprecedented example of judicial immodesty. That well-worn epithet "usurpative" would finally fit.

Richard A. Posner, *Should There Be Homosexual Marriage? And If So, Who Should Decide?,* 95 Mich L Rev 1578, 1584–85 (1997). Does this reasoning apply to the Massachusetts Supreme Court in the same way as to the US Supreme Court? Is this idea part of the *Samuels* reasoning?

(9) The ordinary principle of American law is that a marriage legally contracted in one state will be recognized by any other state unless to do so would violate the latter state's public policy in some serious way. For example, a state will sometimes refuse to recognize a marriage which was validly contracted elsewhere but which violates that state's laws against incestuous marriage. Anticipating a decision in Hawaii, Alaska, or Vermont authorizing same-sex marriage, Congress passed legislation in 1996 popularly known as the Defense of Marriage Act (or DOMA). The first of its sections, 1 USCA § 7, defines marriage for all federal statutes or agency rules and regulations as "a legal union between one man and one woman" and restricts "spouse" to a heterosexual husband or wife. In 28 USCA § 1738C, DOMA provides, "No State, territory, or possession of the United States, or Indian tribe, shall be required to give effect to any public act, record, or judicial proceeding of any other State, territory, possession, or tribe respecting a relationship between persons of the same sex that is treated as a marriage under the laws of such other State, territory, possession, or tribe, or a right or claim arising from such relationship." This legislation recognizes and attempts to give binding authority to the attempt by more than 30 states to insulate themselves from constitutional challenges to their non-recognition of same sex marriages. For example, an Iowa law adopted in 1998 provides that "only a marriage between a male and female is valid." Iowa Code Ann § 595.2(1) (Supp 2000). Foreign marriages are recognized according to Iowa Code Ann § 595.20 if the parties meet the requirements for validity pursuant to section § 595.2(1) and if the marriage would not otherwise be deemed void. Academics have fervently debated whether states invalidating marriages under such statutes violate the full-faith and credit clause or the privileges and immunities clause. For a sample, see the Symposium on Interjurisdictional Marriage Recognition, 32 Creighton L Rev (1998).

More practically, states have struggled with whether or not to recognize civil unions contracted in Vermont for dissolution purposes. Reaching contrary results are *Rosengarten v. Downes*, 802 A 2d 170 (Conn App Ct 2002), and *Informal Opinion No 2004–1* (NY Atty Gen) For a lucid discussion of many of these issues, see Andrew J. Koppelman, *Interstate Recognition of Same Sex Marriages and Civil Unions: A Handbook for Judges,* 153 U Pa L Rev 2143, 2146–47 (2005). A number of states have also enacted constitutional amendments defining marriage as consisting only of the union of one man and one woman. See, e.g. Tex Const art 1 § 32. The Nebraska amendment goes still further and precludes all forms of government protection or domestic partnership or civil unions. *Citizens for Equal Protection v. Bruning*, 290 F Supp 2d 1004 (D. Neb. 2003) (denying motion to dismiss suit challenging, Neb. Const. art. 29). *Citizens for Equal Protection, Inc. v. Bruning*, 368 F Supp 2d 980 (D. Neb. 2005) (finding Nebraska's constitutional amendment related to same-sex marriage unconstitutional as a denial of Equal Protection and as a bill of attainder).

(10) Why did the plaintiffs in *Goodridge* and *Samuels* want to get married?

(a) The court in *Goodridge* repeatedly described marriage as an undiluted advantage. It saw the issue in the case as whether Massachusetts might exclude same-sex couples from the benefits and protections that its laws provide to opposite-sex married couples and referred to a broad array of legal benefits and protections incident to the marital relation.

(i) Is this an accurate way to look at marriage? Professor Eskridge writes, "Marriage is a bundle of rights, benefits, and *obligations*. No discussion can be complete without understanding the disadvantages of getting married." William N. Eskridge, Jr., *The Case for Same–Sex Marriage: From Sexual Liberty to Civilized Commitment* 70 (Free Press, 1996). What are those disadvantages?

(ii) Is this a desirable way to look at marriage?

(b) "In a law-drenched country such as ours, permission for same-sex couples to marry under the law would signify the acceptance of lesbians and gay men as equal citizens more profoundly than any other nondiscrimination laws that might be adopted. Most proponents of same-sex marriage, within and outside the gay and lesbian communities, want marriage first and foremost for this recognition." David L. Chambers, *What If? The Legal Consequences of Marriage and the Legal Needs of Lesbian and Gay Male Couples,* 95 Mich L Rev 447, 450 (1996).

(c) Did the parties in *Goodridge* and *Samuels* want to marry because marriage improves serious relationships? For more on this possibility, see the discussion that follows on the "politics" of homosexuality.

(11) Opening marriage to homosexuals as well as heterosexuals might be the most dramatic change in the institution in American history. How would such a change affect the institution in general? In other words, would it change heterosexuals' perception of their marriages in any way?

(a) Would it, as one writer enthusiastically predicts, "dismantle the legal structure of gender in every marriage"? Nan D. Hunter,

Marriage, Law and Gender: A Feminist Inquiry, 1 Law & Sexuality 9 (1991).

(b) Would it, as Professor Eskridge predicts, "be civilizing for the institution of marriage to welcome couples like Ninia Baehr and Genora Dancel. . . ."?

(c) Would it have no effect because it would be hard to tell the difference between heterosexual and homosexual marriage? One opponent of same-sex marriage says, "As a lesbian, I am fundamentally different from nonlesbian women. That's the point. Marriage, as it exists today, is antithetical to my liberation as a lesbian and as a woman because it mainstreams my life and voice. I do not want to be known as 'Mrs. Attached–To–Somebody–Else.' " Paula Ettelbrick, *Since When Is Marriage a Path to Liberation?* in Andrew Sullivan ed, *Same-Sex Marriage: Pro and Con* 120–21 (Vintage Books, 1997). Same-sex couples are much less likely to adopt traditional sex roles than are opposite-sex couples: M. Cardell, S. Finn, and J. Marecek, "Sex–Role Identity, Sex–Role Behavior, and Satisfaction in Heterosexual, Lesbian, and Gay Male Couples", *Psychology of Women Quarterly*, 5 (Spring 1981), 488–94, at pp. 492–93. Indeed, "research shows that most lesbians and gay men actively reject traditional husband-wife or masculine-feminine roles as a model for enduring relationships": L.A. Peplau, "Lesbian and Gay Relationships", in J.C. Gonsiorek and J.D. Weinrich, eds., *Homosexuality: Research Implications for Public Policy* (1991), 177, at p. 183."

In his *Economics of Same Sex Marriage* (forthcoming Harv J L & Pub Pol'y 2006) Douglas W. Allen argues that laws made around the model of heterosexual marriage (particularly child centered) will most likely not meet the needs of same-sex couples. To the extent they are disadvantaged, they will likely litigate, changing marriage as we now know it. Do you find this argument permissive? Is it a reason for not allowing same-sex marriage?

The "Politics" of Homosexuality and the Merits of Marriage

Underlying many of the arguments about same-sex marriage are views about two subjects. First, what the law's attitudes toward homosexuality should be. Second, what the law's attitudes toward marriage should be. All of this chapter—indeed, much of this casebook—is devoted to answering the latter question. Here we will begin to examine some current attitudes toward marriage. One of the most helpful attempts to provide systematic answers to the former question is Andrew Sullivan, *Virtually Normal: An Argument About Homosexuality* (Alfred A. Knopf, 1995). Mr. Sullivan identifies four "politics of homosexuality."

(1) *Prohibitionists* hold that "homosexuality is an illness that requires a cure, and that homosexual acts ... are transgressions [against 'the natural design of male and female as the essential complementary

parts of the universe'] which require legal punishment and social deterrence." Mr. Sullivan believes

> [p]rohibitionism is a force to be reckoned with, resonating with the instincts and convictions of the majority of mankind.... And at its most serious, it is not a phobia; it is an argument. As arguments go, it has a rich literature, an extensive history, a complex philosophical core, and a view of humanity that tells a coherent and at times a beautiful story of the meaning of our natural selves. It should surprise no one that it commands the most widespread support of any of the four arguments outlined in this book.

For prohibitionists, same-sex marriage ought not be permitted because "to legitimize homosexuality is to strike at the core of the possibility of civilization—the heterosexual union and its social affirmation...."

(2) *Liberationists* believe that "homosexuality as a defining condition does not properly exist because it is a construct of human thought, not an inherent or natural state of being." For liberationists, "the full end of human fruition is to be free of all social constructs, to be liberated from the condition of homosexuality into a fully chosen form of identity, which is a repository of individual acts of freedom." The liberationist condemns the prohibitionist's prohibitions. Nevertheless, the liberationist is no friend of same-sex marriage: "Marriage of all institutions is to liberationists a form of imprisonment; it reeks of a discourse that has bought and sold property, that has denigrated and subjected women, that has constructed human relationships into a crude and suffocating form. Why on earth should it be supported for homosexuals?"

The liberationist objection to marriage, Mr. Sullivan says, is that it is "a form of imprisonment." Marriage is a prison because it makes distinctions. Some people are married, some people are not married, some people cannot marry. Marriage not only makes distinctions, it makes invidious distinctions: "Marriage defines certain relationships as more valid than all others." Paula Ettelbrick, *Since When Is Marriage a Path to Liberation?* in Andrew Sullivan ed, *Same-Sex Marriage: Pro and Con* 119 (Vintage Books, 1997).

The prison is at least of two kinds. First, it can be a Puritan prison. Thus Professor Eskridge quotes Gay Liberation Front leaders in 1969: " 'We expose the institution of marriage as one of the most insidious and basic sustainers of the system. The family is the microcosm of oppression'.... By insisting on monogamy, marriage suppresses the sexual liberty that is a chief aim of gay liberation, the radicals maintained."

Second, marriage to liberationists can be a patriarchal prison. "Steeped in a patriarchal system that looks to ownership, property, and dominance of men over women as its basis, the institution of marriage has long been the focus of radical-feminist revulsion." Paula Ettelbrick, *Since When Is Marriage a Path to Liberation?* in Andrew Sullivan ed, *Same-Sex Marriage: Pro and Con* 119 (Vintage Books, 1997). "Recent laws forcing under-age women to marry the adult men who impregnate them, state legislatures passing laws that require a husband's consent to a woman's decision to have an abortion, laws promoting contract marriage and other strict rules around divorce—these are some recent instances of the use of marriage to regulate the lives of women." Paula L. Ettelbrick, *Legal Marriage Is Not the Answer,* Harv Gay & Lesbian Rev 34, 34 (Fall, 1997). This may explain why "[i]t is white gay men who seem to be most vociferous in promoting the same-sex marriage philosophy. While pandering to the public's obsession with marriage and a return to the past, these activists ignore the history of women's experience with marriage and misappropriate the history of the struggle against miscegenation laws." Id at 34.

Liberationists, then, are likely to believe that "the struggle for same-sex marriage gives up on the goal of gaining public acceptance of sexual diversity and of sexuality itself." Paula L. Ettelbrick, *Legal Marriage Is Not the Answer,* Harvard Gay & Lesbian Rev 34, 35 (Fall, 1997), and that the better approach "would be to expand the definition of family, rather than confine ourselves to marriage." Id at 35. Liberationists write of "families we choose" and explain that "most chosen families are characterized by fluid boundaries, eclectic composition, and relatively little symbolic differentiation between erotic and nonerotic ties." Kath Weston, *Families We Choose: Lesbians, Gays, Kinship* 206 (Colum U Press, 1991).

(3) *Conservatives*, to Mr. Sullivan, are "a variety of liberal: someone who essentially shares the premises of the liberal state, its guarantee of liberty, of pluralism, of freedom of speech and action, but who still believes politics is an arena in which it is necessary to affirm certain cultural, social, and moral values over others.... These conservatives want to strike a balance—and sometimes an extremely precarious one—between allowing individuals considerable freedom of moral action and protecting the fabric of society that makes such liberties possible in the first place." Conservatives "are not prohibitionists, because they are affronted both by the moral certitude of prohibitionism and by the curtailment of liberties that prohibitionism might encourage." Conservatives "find it abhorrent that homosexuals ... might be subject to harassment, violence, ill treatment, discrimination, or illness, for no fault of their own." Nevertheless, they oppose same-sex marriage because they "wish to guide public life in a way that clearly demarcates homosexual behavior as shameful and to be avoided." One reason, Mr. Sullivan suggests, is that they see "a homosexual life" as "one in which emotional commitments are fleeting, promiscuous sex is common, disease is rampant, social ostracism is common, and standards of public decency, propriety, and self-restraint are flaunted. They mean a way of life that deliberately subverts gender norms in order to unsettle the virtues that make family life possible, ridicules heterosexual life, and commits itself to an ethic of hedonism, loneliness, and deceit."

(4) Liberals see these issues in terms of the human rights of the individual homosexual. The "liberal's response is to create laws which protect this minority class from ... infringements on its freedoms: abolition of anti-sodomy laws, enforcement of antidiscrimination statutes

in employment and housing, discouragement of antihomosexual public expression in the form of hate crimes laws, and the like." Liberals, however, "argue that their primary concern is not to preserve liberty, but to create a society which holds certain values dear, to transform the culture to make it more open and inclusive, and to use the laws to educate people in this fashion. Hence the 'symbolic' effect of antidiscrimination statutes: they are designed not simply to protect the rights of a minority, but to educate a backward majority in the errors of its ways."

Mr. Sullivan's own approach is to argue in favor of same-sex marriage by standing the "conservative" argument against it on its head. He suggests that in a world in which homosexuals cannot marry, there are "very few social incentives of the kind of conservatives like . . . : there's little social or familial support, no institution to encourage fidelity or monogamy, precious little religious or moral outreach to guide homosexuals into more virtuous living." He thus argues that society

> has good reasons to extend legal advantages to heterosexuals who choose the formal sanction of marriage over simply living together. . . . Marriage provides an anchor, if an arbitrary and often weak one, in the maelstrom of sex and relationships to which we are all prone. It provides a mechanism for emotional stability and economic security. We rig the law in its favor not because we disparage all forms of relationship other than the nuclear family, but because we recognize that not to promote marriage would be to ask too much of human virtue.

In short, "[g]ay marriage is not a radical step; it is a profoundly humanizing, traditionalizing step."

Professor Eskridge seems to make a similar argument, as the subtitle of his book—"*From Sexual Liberty to Civilized Commitment*"—implies. For example, he hypothesizes that "to achieve committed relationships gay men need the discipline of marriage more than lesbians . . . Gay men are like Ulysses, who directed that he be bound to the ship's mast as it passed the Sirens. . . . Likewise, gay men realize that they tend to lose their balance and succumb to private sirens if they are not socially and even legally constrained." He writes, "Whatever gravity gay life may have lacked in the disco seventies it acquired in the health crisis of the eighties. What it lost in youth and innocence it gained in dignity. Gay cruising and experimentation, . . . gave way somewhat in the 1980s to a more lesbian-like interest in commitment. Since 1981 and probably earlier, gays were civilizing themselves. Part of our self-civilization has been an insistence on the right to marry."

More specifically, Professor Eskridge argues that "the biggest cost of marriage provides the best reason why gays and lesbians should seek legal recognition of their right to marry: marriage is easy to enter but hard to exit. . . ." He explains: "When Ninia Baehr and Genora Dancel were dating, each shared her feelings of warmth and love for the other. Such verbal assurances are useful, but actions speak more loudly. . . . Getting married signals a significantly higher level of commitment, in part because the law imposes much greater obligations on the couple and makes it much more of a bother and expense to break up." Getting married not only signals commitment. The "duties and obligations of marriage directly contribute to interpersonal commitment.... [O]ne function that marriage plays is to hold a union together during times of strife and disagreement and to force a sober second thought before a partner departs."

Professor Eskridge frankly says,

> The foregoing argument assumes that interpersonal commitment is good.... The promise and the reasonable expectation of commitment are valuable for a variety of reasons, starting with the personal security that comes from knowing that one can depend on someone else for better or for worse.... [C]ommitment provides an intense focal point for one to transcend the self and deepen one's identity through intimate interaction with another being.... However complicated by biology, the mutual love between parent and child is as much a consequence as a cause of the mutual expectation that the relationship will be a lasting one. An analogous point can be made about partnership relations; they will be different, and deeper, if they are conducted within a mutual understanding of lasting commitment.

Professor Eskridge observes that Alan P. Bell and Martin A. Weinberg, *Homosexualities: A Study of Diversity Among Men and Women* (Simon & Schuster, 1978)

> found that couples committed to an exclusive long-term relationship reported high self-acceptance and greater happiness than five years previously. The authors contrasted that happiness with the greater tension in couples enjoying a sexually open, and therefore, less committed, relationship. Because this latter comparison has not been replicated by subsequent studies, it cannot be considered anything but a hypothesis. What subsequent studies do confirm is Bell and Weinberg's initial conclusion, namely, that committed gay and lesbian unions generate a great deal of satisfaction for the participants and that commitment itself tends to increase satisfaction with the relationship.

In short, attitudes toward homosexuality influence people's views about same-sex marriage. But they are also shaped by people's views about marriage itself. Opponents and proponents seem to agree about one thing—that the social and legal institution of marriage significantly influences the way people think about and lead their lives. They disagree violently, however, about whether marriage as it is and marriage as it might be influence people in desirable ways. For a recent and informative piece discussing the arguments pro and con same-sex marriage, see generally Katherine M. Franke, *The Politics of Same Sex Marriage Politics*, 15 Colum J Gender & L 236 (2006).

(2) The Simulacra of Marriage

The plaintiffs in *Baehr* and *Baker* may well have felt that their relationships were already essentially the same as those of any married couple. They may well have felt, in other words, that they had the "functional equivalent" of a family as the law defines "family." Courts have occasionally said that where a relationship is the functional equivalent of a family relationship, it should be treated as one.

A well-known example of the functional-equivalence approach is the following case:

BRASCHI v. STAHL ASSOCIATES

Court of Appeals of New York, 1989
74 NY2d 201

I.

Appellant, Miguel Braschi, was living with Leslie Blanchard in a rent-controlled apartment located at 405 East 54th Street from the summer of 1975 until Blanchard's death in September of 1986. In November of 1986, respondent, Stahl Associates Company, the owner of the apartment building, served a notice to cure on appellant contending that he was a mere licensee with no right to occupy the apartment since only Blanchard was the tenant of record. In December of 1986 respondent served appellant with a notice to terminate....

II. ...

The present dispute arises because the term "family" is not defined in the rent-control code and the legislative history is devoid of any specific reference to the noneviction provision....

Rent control was enacted to address a "serious public emergency" created by "an acute shortage in dwellings," which resulted in "speculative, unwarranted and abnormal increases in rent"....

[S]ection 2204.6 of the New York City Rent and Eviction Regulations which authorizes the issuance of a certificate for the eviction of persons occupying a rent-controlled apartment after the death of the named tenant, provides, in subdivision (d), noneviction protection to those occupants who are either the "surviving spouse of the deceased tenant or *some other member of the deceased tenant's family* who has been living with the tenant [of record]" (emphasis supplied)....

[W]e conclude that the term family, as used in 9 NYCRR 2204.6(d), should not be rigidly restricted to those people who have formalized their relationship by obtaining, for instance, a marriage certificate or an adoption order. The intended protection against sudden eviction should not rest on fictitious legal distinctions or genetic history, but instead should find its foundation in the reality of family life. In the context of eviction, a more realistic, and certainly equally valid, view of a family includes two adult lifetime partners whose relationship is long term and characterized by an emotional and financial commitment and interdependence. This view comports both with our society's traditional concept of "family" and with the expectations of individuals who live in such nuclear units.... In fact, Webster's Dictionary defines "family" *first* as "a group of people united by certain convictions or common affiliation" (Webster's Ninth New Collegiate Dictionary 448 [1984]). Hence, it is reasonable to conclude that, in using the term "family," the Legislature intended to extend protection to those who reside in households having all of the normal familial characteristics. Appellant Braschi should therefore be afforded the opportunity to prove that he and Blanchard had such a household....

The determination as to whether an individual is entitled to non-eviction protection should be based upon an objective examination of the relationship of the parties. In making this assessment, the lower courts of this State have looked to a number of factors, including the exclusivity and longevity of the relationship, the level of emotional and financial commitment, the manner in which the parties have conducted their everyday lives and held themselves out to society, and the reliance placed upon one another for daily family services. These factors are most helpful, although it should be emphasized that the presence or absence of one or more of them is not dispositive since it is the totality of the relationship as evidenced by the dedication, caring and self-sacrifice of the parties which should, in the final analysis, control....

Appellant and Blanchard lived together as permanent life partners for more than 10 years. They regarded one another, and were regarded by friends and family, as spouses. The two men's families were aware of the nature of the relationship, and they regularly visited each other's families and attended family functions together, as a couple. Even today, appellant continues to maintain a relationship with Blanchard's niece, who considers him an uncle.

In addition to their interwoven social lives, appellant clearly considered the apartment his home. He lists the apartment as his address on his driver's license and passport, and receives all his mail at the apartment address. Moreover, appellant's tenancy was known to the building's superintendent and doormen, who viewed the two men as a couple.

Financially, the two men shared all obligations including a household budget. The two were authorized signatories of three safe-deposit boxes, they maintained joint checking and savings accounts, and joint credit cards. In fact, rent was often paid with a check from their joint checking account. Additionally, Blanchard executed a power of attorney in appellant's favor so that appellant could make necessary decisions—financial, medical and personal—for him during his illness. Finally, appellant was the named beneficiary of Blanchard's life insurance policy, as well as the primary legatee and coexecutor of Blanchard's estate. Hence, a court examining these facts could reasonably conclude that these men were much more than mere roommates....

[The concurring opinion of Judge Bellacosa is omitted.]

SIMONS, JUDGE (dissenting)....

The [relevant] interests are properly balanced if the regulation's exception is applied by using objectively verifiable relationships based on blood, marriage and adoption, as the State has historically done in the estate succession laws, family court acts and similar legislation.... The distinction is warranted because members of families, so defined, assume certain legal obligations to each other and to third persons, such as creditors, which are not imposed on unrelated individuals and this legal interdependency is worthy of consideration in determining which individuals are entitled to succeed to the interest of the statutory tenant in rent-controlled premises. Moreover, such an interpretation promotes certainty and consistency in the law and obviates the need for drawn out hearings and litigation focusing on such intangibles as the strength and duration of the relationship and the extent of the emotional and financial interdependency....

Finally, there are serious practical problems in adopting the plurality's interpretation of the statute. Any determination of rights under it would require first a determination of whether protection should be accorded the relationship (i.e., unmarrieds, nonadopted occupants, etc.) and then a subjective determination in each case of whether the relationship was genuine, and entitled to the protection of the law, or expedient, and an attempt to take advantage of the law....

Notes and Questions: Functional Equivalents of Marriage

(1) One function of social institutions like marriage is to tell the people involved in them, the world in general, and the law in particular that those people have a particular relation to each other. When people marry, they, the world, and the law know they have assumed particular special obligations. "Functional equivalence" approaches serve this end less well. How important is this?

(2) If we are to know what a "functional equivalent" of a family is, we must first know what a "family" is. Can you devise a definition that would adequately guide courts?

(3) Deciding whether a group of people are the functional equivalent of a family presumably involves a detailed inquiry into the nature and intimacy of their relationship. How practical is this, and how serious are the consequences of such an intrusion into their privacy?

(4) *In re Adoption of Swanson*, 623 A2d 1095 (Del 1993), presents another approach to securing legal recognition of intimate relations the law does not generally acknowledge. "When Richard Sorrels sought to adopt James Swanson, his companion of 17 years, they were respectively, 66 and 51 years of age. The adoption had two purposes—to formalize the close emotional relationship that had existed between them for many years and to facilitate their estate planning." The court said, "Adult adoptions intended to foster a sexual relationship would be against public policy as violative of the incest statute." However, the court noted that most jurisdictions "recognize that adult adoptions for the purpose of creating inheritance rights are valid," and it could "divine no reason why this petition should be denied." For a case coming out the other

way, see, e.g., *Matter of Adoption of Robert Paul P.*, 471 NE2d 424 (NY 1984).

(5) You have already read in *Baker* about the Hawaii "reciprocal beneficiaries" statute. Municipalities have been experimenting with "domestic partnership" approaches for some time. In 1984, "the Berkeley City Council adopted the first operative municipal domestic partnership policy, which ultimately allowed city employees to obtain health benefits for their registered domestic partners." William N. Eskridge, Jr., *The Case for Same–Sex Marriage: From Sexual Liberty to Civilized Commitment* 59 (Free Press, 1996). A number of other jurisdictions followed. Professor Eskridge reports that in "most jurisdictions, only a handful of employees have registered.... More economically meaningful have been domestic partnership policies adopted by hundreds of nonstate employers ..., for those policies typically allow the domestic partner to be added to their employees' fringe benefit packages on the same terms as spouses." The latest—and most widely noticed—of the domestic-partnership efforts is the following statute, which the Vermont legislature enacted in response to the Vermont Supreme Court's decision in *Baker*:

AN ACT RELATING TO CIVIL UNIONS

2000 Vermont Laws P.A. 91 (H. 847)

Section 1202. REQUISITES OF A VALID CIVIL UNION

For a civil union to be established in Vermont, it shall be necessary that the parties to a civil union satisfy all of the following criteria:

(1) Not be a party to another civil union or a marriage.

(2) Be of the same sex and therefore excluded from the marriage laws of this state.

(3) Meet the criteria and obligations set forth in 18 V.S.A. chapter 106.

Section 1203. PERSON SHALL NOT ENTER A CIVIL UNION WITH A RELATIVE

(a) A woman shall not enter a civil union with her mother, grandmother, daughter, granddaughter, sister, brother's daughter, sister's daughter, father's sister or mother's sister.

(b) A man shall not enter a civil union with his father, grandfather, son, grandson, brother, brother's son, sister's son, father's brother or mother's brother.

(c) A civil union between persons prohibited from entering a civil union in subsection (a) or (b) of this section is void.

Section 1204. BENEFITS, PROTECTIONS AND RESPONSIBILITIES OF PARTIES TO A CIVIL UNION

(a) Parties to a civil union shall have all the same benefits, protections and responsibilities under law, whether they derive from statute, administrative or court rule, policy, common law or any other source of civil law, as are granted to spouses in a marriage.

(b) A party to a civil union shall be included in any definition or use of the terms "spouse," "family," "immediate family," "dependent," "next of kin," and other terms that denote the spousal relationship, as those terms are used throughout the law.

(c) Parties to a civil union shall be responsible for the support of one another to the same degree and in the same manner as prescribed under law for married persons.

(d) The law of domestic relations, including annulment, separation and divorce, child custody and support, and property division and maintenance shall apply to parties to a civil union.

(e) The following is a nonexclusive list of legal benefits, protections and responsibilities of spouses, which shall apply in like manner to parties to a civil union:

(1) laws relating to title, tenure, descent and distribution, intestate succession, waiver of will, survivorship, or other incidents of the acquisition, ownership, or transfer, inter vivos or at death, of real or personal property, including eligibility to hold real and personal property as tenants by the entirety (parties to a civil union meet the common law unity of person qualification for purposes of a tenancy by the entirety);

(2) causes of action related to or dependent upon spousal status, including an action for wrongful death, emotional distress, loss of consortium, dramshop, or other torts or actions under contracts reciting, related to, or dependent upon spousal status;

(3) probate law and procedure, including nonprobate transfer;

(4) adoption law and procedure;

(5) group insurance for state employees under 3 V.S.A. Section 631, and continuing care contracts under 8 V.S.A. Section 8005;

(6) spouse abuse programs under 3 V.S.A. Section 18;

(7) prohibitions against discrimination based upon marital status;

(8) victim's compensation rights under 13 V.S.A. Section 5351;

(9) workers' compensation benefits;

(10) laws relating to emergency and nonemergency medical care and treatment, hospital visitation and notification, including the Patient's Bill of Rights under 18 V.S.A. chapter 42 and the Nursing Home Residents' Bill of Rights under 33 V.S.A. chapter 73;

(11) terminal care documents under 18 V.S.A. chapter 111, and durable power of attorney for health care execution and revocation under 14 V.S.A. chapter 121;

(12) family leave benefits under 21 V.S.A. chapter 5, subchapter 4A;

(13) public assistance benefits under state law;

(14) laws relating to taxes imposed by the state or a municipality other than estate taxes;

(15) laws relating to immunity from compelled testimony and the marital communication privilege;

(16) the homestead rights of a surviving spouse under 27 V.S.A. Section 105 and homestead property tax allowance under 32 V.S.A. Section 6062;

(17) laws relating to loans to veterans under 8 V.S.A. Section 1849;

(18) the definition of family farmer under 10 V.S.A. Section 272;

(19) laws relating to the making, revoking and objecting to anatomical gifts by others under 18 V.S.A. Section 5240;

(20) state pay for military service under 20 V.S.A. Section 1544;

(21) application for absentee ballot under 17 V.S.A. Section 2532;

(22) family landowner rights to fish and hunt under 10 V.S.A. Section 4253;

(23) legal requirements for assignment of wages under 8 V.S.A. Section 2235; and

(24) affirmance of relationship under 15 V.S.A. Section 7.

(f) The rights of parties to a civil union, with respect to a child of whom either becomes the natural parent during the term of the civil union, shall be the same as those of a married couple, with respect to a child of whom either spouse becomes the natural parent during the marriage.

Section 1205. MODIFICATION OF CIVIL UNION TERMS

Parties to a civil union may modify the terms, conditions, or effects of their civil union in the same manner and to the same extent as married persons who execute an antenuptial agreement or other agreement recognized and enforceable under the law, setting forth particular understandings with respect to their union.

Section 1206. DISSOLUTION OF CIVIL UNIONS

The family court shall have jurisdiction over all proceedings relating to the dissolution of civil unions. The dissolution of civil unions shall follow the same procedures and be subject to the same substantive rights and obligations that are involved in the dissolution of marriage in accordance with chapter 11 of this title, including any residency requirements.

Notes and Questions on Vermont's Civil Union

(1) The court's opinion in *Baker* seemed to regard marriage as all benefits and no burdens. Has this statute provided only the benefits and not the burdens?

(2) The Vermont Supreme Court said that the state had to provide a benefit that matched marriage. Does the civil union ordinance succeed? Professor Eskridge writes,

> Gay and lesbian partners want a level of commitment that domestic partnership does not provide.... [L]esbian and gay couples desire a link to the larger historical community, something marriage (in all its troubled richness) provides and the just-concocted domestic partnership does not.... Witnesses to the marriage ... commit themselves to supporting the union.... [T]he very choreography of marriage imbues it with a significance that flat, boring domestic partnership cannot easily match. The pomp, gravity, and religiosity of marriage might appall the avant-garde, but they lend the institution an air of sanctification that is meaningful to its participants.

(3) Is the civil union statute preferable exactly because it does not create marriage? One commentator comments, "The lesbian and gay community has laid the groundwork for revolutionizing society's views of family. The domestic-partnership movement has been an important part of this progress insofar as it validates nonmarital relationships. Because it is not limited to sexual or romantic relationships, domestic partnership provides an important opportunity for many who are not related by blood or marriage to claim certain minimal protections." In pursuing that opportunity, though, it is crucial "that we avoid the pitfall of framing the push for legal recognition of domestic partners (those who share a primary residence and financial responsibilities for each other) as a stepping-stone to marriage. We must keep our eyes on the goals of providing true alternatives to marriage and of radically reordering society's view of family...." Paula Ettelbrick, *Since When Is Marriage a Path to Liberation?* in Andrew Sullivan ed, *Same-Sex Marriage: Pro and Con* 123–24 (Vintage Books, 1997).

SECTION 3. LET NO MAN PUT ASUNDER: THE LAW OF DIVORCE

Let me not to the marriage of true minds
Admit impediments. Love is not love
Which alters when it alteration finds,
Or bends with the remover to remove:
Oh, no! it is an ever-fixed mark,
That looks on tempests and is never shaken;
It is the star to every wandering bark,
Whose worth's unknown, although his height be taken.
Love's not Time's fool, though rosy lips and cheeks
Within his bending sickle's compass come;
Love alters not with his brief hours and weeks,

But bears it out even to the edge of doom.
If this be error and upon me proved,
I never writ, nor no man ever loved.

William Shakespeare

Why should a foolish marriage vow,
Which long ago was made,
Oblige us to each other now
When passion is decayed?
We loved, and we loved, as long as we could,
Till our love was loved out in us both;
But our marriage is dead when the pleasure is fled:
'Twas pleasure first made it an oath.

If I have pleasures for a friend,
And farther love in store,
What wrong has he whose joys did end,
And who could give no more?
'Tis a madness that he should be jealous of me,
Or that I should bar him of another:
For all we can gain is to give ourselves pain,
When neither can hinder the other.

John Dryden

A. INTRODUCTION

After meeting Vronksy at his own door, Karenin drove, as he had intended, to the Italian opera.... On his return home he carefully looked at the coat-stand and, noticing that no military greatcoat hung there, proceeded to his own room as usual.... The feeling of anger with his wife, who would not observe the rules of propriety and fulfill the one condition he had laid on her—not to receive her lover in his house—gave him no rest. She had not complied with his stipulation, and he must punish her and carry out his threat to divorce her and take the boy away.... The Countess Lydia Ivanovna had hinted that this would be the best way out of the situation, and of late the procedure of divorce had been so perfected that Karenin saw a possibility of overcoming the formal difficulties....

He did not sleep the whole night, and his fury, growing in a sort of vast, arithmetical progression, reached its peak in the morning. He dressed in haste, and, as though carrying his cup of wrath full to the brim and fearing to spill any—fearing to lose with his wrath the energy necessary for an interview with his wife—he went to her room directly he heard she was up.

Leo Tolstoy
Anna Karenina

Every state now permits spouses to obtain a divorce on no-fault grounds. But there is still much to learn from studying the law of divorce. Much of family law—the law of marital property, alimony, child custody, and child support—applies only when a couple divorces. To comprehend that law, we need to understand its context—divorce. We need to know the traditional law of divorce. In many states divorce is available on fault as well as no-fault grounds. And the triumph of no-fault divorce is relatively recent and entirely central. We need to assess it, its implications, and its future.

(1) Three Introductory Problems

> *The Pharisees also came unto him, tempting him, and saying unto him, Is it lawful for a man to put away his wife for every cause? And he answered and said unto them, "Have ye not read, that he which made them at the beginning made them male and female, And said, For this cause shall a man leave father and mother, and shall cleave to his wife: and they twain shall be one flesh? Wherefore they are no more twain, but one flesh. What therefore God hath joined together, let not man put asunder."* . . .
>
> *"All men cannot receive this saying, save they to whom it is given. . . . He that is able to receive it, let him receive it."*
>
> Matthew 19: 3–12

We begin by considering some problems which raise many basic issues of the law of divorce. The question you should be asking about them is *not* whether the parties are legally entitled to a divorce. Under the regime of no-fault divorce, they may have a divorce, although getting it may take much time and trouble. However, in analyzing our present system of divorce, we need to begin by asking whether the parties in these problems are *morally* entitled to a divorce. In other words, what factors should the party seeking a divorce in each case consider when deciding whether it is right or wrong to seek a divorce?

(1) Consider the case of Mr. and Mrs. Appleby, of Milan, Michigan. He is fifty-eight, she is fifty-six; they have been married for thirty-five years. He has been a salesman all his life, she a housewife. Their only child, Meg, is now thirty-two and living in New Mexico. Mrs. Appleby has always spent most of her time at home, in large part because her husband insisted on it and became angry when she did not. Mrs. Appleby consequently has few friends of her own, and what social life the couple has revolves around Mr. Appleby's friends. Mr. Appleby has been spending less and less time at home, and Mrs. Appleby has become more and more distressed. One evening, he tells her that he has fallen in love with his nineteen-year-old secretary and wants to marry her. Mrs. Appleby's religion forbids divorce, she still loves her husband and doesn't want to be separated from him, and she feels that her situation and status in the world depend on being married. She therefore detests the idea of divorce. Mr. Appleby has never earned much and the Applebys have never saved much. If they are divorced, all his modest income will be consumed

supporting his new wife and her twin sons. Mrs. Appleby has a high-school education and hasn't been on the job market for thirty-five years.

(2) Mr. and Mrs. Bartleby, of Rome, New York, have been married for five years. Both are in their early thirties. Both earn good salaries. Both are ambitious. Both are extensively educated. Both have worked hard at their careers. Both have excellent prospects. Their second son, who is six months old, was born with a birth defect, and he requires special attention which Mr. Bartleby finds stressful and which seriously interferes with his work. Mr. Bartleby wants to institutionalize the child; Mrs. Bartleby disagrees. Mr. Bartleby says that if Mrs. Bartleby won't agree to institutionalize the child, he wants a divorce. She passionately believes (as the child's physicians have warned her) that institutionalization would deeply and irreparably harm the child and would devastate her. Yet she does not want a divorce. If Mr. Bartleby divorces her, she will have to institutionalize the child.

(3) Mr. and Mrs. Cuttleby, of Paris, Kentucky, are in their early twenties. After living together for several years, they were married a year ago. Mrs. Cuttleby works as a secretary at a Coca–Cola bottling plant, Mr. Cuttleby as a folder-operator for a book-manufacturer. He has come to doubt that their marriage was such a good idea. He used to look forward to coming home to see his wife; he finds he no longer does, since it means he can't spend the time he used to with his friends. He used to enjoy going out on weekend evenings with his wife; now they don't go out, since she wants them to save money for a down payment on a house. When he thinks about living the rest of his life with his wife, he wonders whether he couldn't find someone better. He has told her that he wants a divorce. She is astonished and bitter, but she doesn't want their marriage to end.

(4) Now reconsider the same cases, but imagine that the gender roles are reversed. Does the reversal affect your thinking?

(2) Divorce as a Problem in Law–Making

> *Not even the intercourse of the sexes is exempt from the despotism of positive institution. Law pretends even to govern the indisciplinable wanderings of passion, to put fetters on the clearest deductions of reason, and by appeals to the will, to subdue the involuntary affections of our nature. Love is inevitably consequent upon the perception of loveliness. Love withers under constraint; its very essence is liberty; it is compatible neither with obedience, jealousy, nor fear, it is there most pure, perfect, and unlimited, where its votaries live in confidence, equality, and unreserve.*
>
> **Percy Bysshe Shelley**
> *Postscript to Queen Mab*

We begin our consideration of divorce as a problem in law-making by continuing our reading of Hume's intriguing essay:

DAVID HUME
OF POLYGAMY AND DIVORCES

1742

Having rejected polygamy, and matched one man with one woman, let us now consider what duration we shall assign to their union, and whether we shall admit of those voluntary divorces, which were customary among the Greeks and Romans. Those who would defend this practice may employ the following reasons.

How often does disgust and aversion arise after marriage, from the most trivial accidents, or from an incompatibility of humour; where time, instead of curing the wounds, proceeding from mutual injuries, festers them every day the more, by new quarrels and reproaches? Let us separate hearts, which were not made to associate together. Each of them may, perhaps, find another for which it is better fitted. At least, nothing can be more cruel than to preserve, by violence, an union, with, at first, was made by mutual love, and is now, in effect, dissolved by mutual hatred.

But the liberty of divorces is not only a cure to hatred and domestic quarrels: It is also an admirable preservative against them, and the only secret for keeping alive that love, which first united the married couple. The heart of man delights in liberty: The very image of constraint is grievous to it: When you would confine it by violence, to what would otherwise have been its choice, the inclination immediately changes, and desire is turned into aversion. If the public interest will not allow us to enjoy in polygamy that *variety*, which is so agreeable in love: at least, deprive us not of that liberty, which is so essentially requisite. In vain you tell me, that I had my choice of the person, with whom I would conjoin myself. I had my choice, it is true, of my prison; but this is but a small comfort, since it must still be a prison.

Such are the arguments which may be urged in favour of divorces: But there seem to be these three unanswerable objections against them. *First*, What must become of the children, upon the separation of the parents? Must they be committed to the care of a step-mother; and instead of the fond attention and concern of a parent, feel all the indifference or hatred of a stranger or an enemy? These inconveniences are sufficiently felt, where nature has made the divorce by the doom inevitable to all mortals: And shall we seek to multiply those inconveniences, by multiplying divorces, and putting it in the power of parents, upon every caprice, to render their posterity miserable?

Secondly, If it be true, on the one hand, that the heart of man naturally delights in liberty, and hates every thing to which it is confined; it is also true, on the other, that the heart of man naturally submits to necessity, and soon loses an inclination, when there appears an absolute impossibility of gratifying it. These principles of human nature, you'll say, are contradictory: But what is man but a heap of contradictions! Though it is remarkable, that, where principles are, after this manner, contrary in their operation, they do not always destroy each other; but the one or the other may predominate on any particular occasion, according as circumstances are more or less favourable to it. For instance, love is a restless and impatient passion, full of caprices and variations: arising in a moment from a feature, from an air, from nothing, and suddenly extinguishing after the same manner. Such a passion requires liberty above all things; and therefore Eloisa has reason, when, in order to preserve this passion, she refused to marry her beloved Abelard.

> *How oft, when prest to marriage, have I said, Curse on all laws but those which love has made; Love, free as air, at sight of human ties, Spreads his light wings, and in a moment flies.*

But *friendship* is a calm and sedate affection, conducted by reason and cemented by habit; springing from long acquaintance and mutual obligations; without jealousies or fears, and without those feverish fits of heat and cold, which cause such an agreeable torment in the amorous passion. So sober an affection, therefore, as friendship, rather thrives under constraint, and never rises to such a height, as when any strong interest or necessity binds two persons together, and gives them some common object of pursuit. We need not, therefore, be afraid of drawing the marriage-knot, which chiefly subsists by friendship, the closest possible. The amity between the persons, where it is solid and sincere, will rather gain by it: And where it is wavering and uncertain, this is the best expedient for fixing it. How many frivolous quarrels and disgusts are there, which people of common prudence endeavour to forget, when they lie under a necessity of passing their lives together; but which would soon be inflamed into the most deadly hatred, were they pursued to the utmost, under the prospect of an easy separation?

In the *third* place, we must consider, that nothing is more dangerous than to unite two persons so closely in all their interests and concerns, as man and wife, without rendering the union entire and total. The least possibility of a separate interest must be the source of endless quarrels and suspicions. The wife, not secure of her establishment, will still be driving some separate end or project; and the husband's selfishness, being accompanied with more power, may be still more dangerous.

We continue our consideration of divorce as a problem in law-making by continuing our reading of Durkheim's intriguing opinions:

> Now divorce implies a weakening of matrimonial regulation. Where it exists, and especially where law and custom permit its excessive practice, marriage is nothing but a weakened simulacrum of itself; it is an inferior form of marriage. It cannot produce its usual effects to the same degree. Its restraint upon desire is weakened; since it is more easily disturbed and superceded, it controls passion less and passion

tends to rebel. It consents less readily to its assigned limit. The moral calmness and tranquillity which were the husband's strength are less; they are replaced to some extent by an uneasiness which keeps a man from being satisfied with what he has. Besides, he is the less inclined to become attached to his present state as his enjoyment of it is not completely sure: the future is less certain. One cannot be strongly restrained by a chain which may be broken on one side or the other at any moment. One cannot help looking beyond one's own position when the ground underfoot does not feel secure. Hence, in the countries where marriage is strongly tempered by divorce, the immunity of the married man is inevitably less. As he resembles the unmarried under this regime, he inevitably loses some of his own advantages. Consequently, the total number of suicides rises.

Notes and Questions on Analyzing the Basis of No–Fault Divorce

The following questions introduce two problems. First, what ought the law of divorce be? How readily should divorce be available? What procedures ought the law offer couples who seek a divorce? What impediments? What attitudes toward divorce (if any) ought the law attempt to inculcate? Second, what can the law of divorce tell us about the role of family law generally? How far can the law of divorce affect the way people actually live their lives? How ought the law try to structure people's lives in families?

(1) You have already considered the Appleby, Bartleby, and Cuttleby cases in moral terms. Let us now think about them in legal terms. How can Mr. Appleby, Mr. Bartleby, and Mr. Cuttleby argue that the state should not prevent their getting a divorce?

(a) Can they argue that whether to divorce is so intimate a decision that the state should not influence it? Why does the intimacy of a decision make state influence inappropriate, if the decision has consequences for someone besides the person making the decision? Does the intimacy of the marital relationship make it *more* desirable for the state to supervise it, since it increases a spouse's vulnerability?

(b) Can they argue that the decision to divorce a spouse is so consequential for the person making it that the state should not deter anyone from getting a divorce? In other words, can they argue that denying them a divorce would subject them to so much unhappiness that the state ought not do so? Can the state respond by pointing to the unhappiness their spouses and children may suffer if there is a divorce?

(c) Can they argue that the state cannot force them to love their spouses, that loving one's spouse is the essence of marriage, and that divorce is only a formality that declares finished in law what had already finished in fact? Is it true that the state cannot influence one spouse's feelings for another by regulating the terms of marriage? (What would Hume say about this?) Is it pointless to preserve a marriage where one spouse has stopped loving the other?

(2) Mrs. Appleby, Mrs. Bartleby, and Mrs. Cuttleby all oppose the divorces their husbands seek. Ought they have some kind of legal claim that would prevent or deter their husbands from getting divorces?

(a) To what extent are they justified in opposing the divorces their husbands seek?

(i) May they say that their husbands agreed to be married for life and cannot now renege on that agreement? Did their husbands make such an agreement? Should that agreement have legal force? Was it intended to have legal force, or to be merely precatory?

(ii) May they say that they relied on their husbands' courses of conduct and that those courses led them to believe that their husbands would not end their marriages?

(iii) May they say their husbands' divorces damage them in ways for which there is no adequate remedy except specific performance? What injuries might divorce inflict on them?

(b) To what extent ought the law provide a remedy for the injuries the wives assert?

(c) A number of states have concluded that no-fault divorce does not unconstitutionally impair vested contractual rights. See, e.g., *In re Marriage of Walton*, 104 Cal Rptr 472 (Cal 1972); *In re Marriage of Franks*, 542 P2d 845 (Colo 1975); *Ryan v. Ryan*, 277 So 2d 266 (Fla 1973). And the fact that Mrs. Appleby's religion forbids divorce does not give her a constitutional objection to her husband's divorce proceeding. See, e.g., *Wikoski v. Wikoski*, 513 A2d 986 (Pa Super 1986); *Williams v. Williams*, 543 P2d 1401 (Okla 1975).

(3) Not only do Mrs. Bartleby and Mrs. Cuttleby have an interest in whether they are divorced; their children do as well. It is now conventionally believed that divorces tend to harm the children of the marriage in ways that may persist for some time. Children suffer not only emotionally, but also (often) economically. How, if at all, should divorce law take the children's interests into account?

(a) Should the ability of parents of (young?) children to obtain a divorce be restricted? See, e.g., Theodore Haas, *The Rationality and Enforceability of Contractual Restrictions on Divorce*, 66 NC L Rev 879 (1988); Elizabeth Scott, *Rational Decisionmaking about Marriage and Divorce*, 76 Va L Rev 9 (1990); but see Linda J. Lacey, *Mandatory Marriage "For the Sake of the Children:" A Feminist Reply to Elizabeth Scott*, 66 Tulane L Rev 1435 (1992). Martin Zelder argues that the presence of children causes some marriages to end "inefficiently," since children are marital assets that cannot be divided during couples' bargaining over whether to divorce. By inefficient divorce, he means that the total good both spouses find for staying in the marriage outweighs the total benefit they will receive from divorcing. *Inefficient Dissolutions as a Consequence of Public Goods: The Case of No–Fault Divorce*, 22 J Legal Stud 503 (1993).

How much of any deterrent should be monetary? See Cynthia Starnes, *Divorce and the Displaced Homemaker: A Discourse on Playing with Dolls, Partnership Buyouts and Dissociation under No–Fault*, 60 U Chi L Rev 67 (1993). Should the deterrent be a waiting period? See Scott, *Rational Decisionmaking*, 76 Va L Rev at 9.

(b) Should the ability of parents of (young?) children to obtain a divorce be restricted where a specific likelihood of harm to the children could be shown?

(c) When parents disagree over who should have custody of their children after divorce, courts use the child's "best interest" to decide which parent should have custody. Children are sometimes represented in the dispute by a guardian ad litem. Should children also be represented in divorce proceedings? Should the guardian be able to argue in favor of delaying or even preventing the parents' divorce?

(4) What interests does the state have in regulating divorce? In answering this question, it may help you to recall the interests we suggested the state might have in regulating entry into marriage.

(a) An interest in deterring married couples from leaving a relationship they would be happier staying in?

(b) An interest in deterring a spouse from leaving a relationship when doing so would injure the other spouse?

(c) An interest in deterring parents from obtaining a divorce that would injure their children?

(d) An interest in promoting the belief that marriage is a life-long commitment?

(5) Assuming, *arguendo*, that the state has such interests, what might inhibit it from serving them through restrictive divorce rules?

(a) Is the state not as good a judge as the parties of their own interests? Not as good a judge as the spouse seeking the divorce of what is in the couple's interest? Not as good a judge as the parents of their children's interests?

(b) Is the state simply unable to enforce its will?

(c) Will the state's intervention exacerbate the already strained relations between the spouses?

(d) Can the state's interests be served in ways other than restricting access to divorce?

(6) Assume, *arguendo*, that Mr. Appleby, Mr. Bartleby, and Mr. Cuttleby are not morally entitled to a divorce and that the state has legitimate and powerful reasons to oppose their divorces. May the state effectuate those interests in any way?

(3) Divorce as a Problem in the Practice of Law

Divorce is nothing but the declaration that a marriage is dead and that its existence is only pretense and deception.... Now, as precise unmistakable proof is required for physical death, the legislator can declare an ethical death only in the presence of the most indubitable symptoms, since to conserve the life of ethical relationships is not only his right but also his duty....

Karl Marx
Criticism of a Criticism

PORTRAITS FROM THE PRACTICE OF FAMILY LAW

You have been reading, and you will be reading, about the law regulating the family. But it is a truism of legal realism that law gains its meaning from the people who interpret it. And the principal professional interpreters of family law are divorce lawyers. (Not judges. While divorce litigation is by far the largest category of civil litigation, almost all cases are settled *before* a judge rules on their merits.) Furthermore, family law is conspicuously an arena in which practical problems of working with clients, their families, and other lawyers often loom larger than conceptual problems of legal doctrine. In what follows, then, we proffer a brief précis of changes in the practice of family law and then summarize two leading studies of how divorce lawyers approach their work.

Our précis of changes in the practice of family law is drawn from Linda Henry Elrod, *Epilogue: Of Families, Federalization, and a Quest for Policy*, 33 Family L Q 843 (1999). She reports, "Tsunamis have hit the practice of law since 1900 with much of the impact being felt in the area of family law. The sheer volume of lawyers is a major change. The number has quadrupled since 1972; the profession is no longer predominantly white male as women and minorities have entered the profession in record numbers." What is more, "[t]he practice of family law becomes more challenging annually." Divorce

> has actually become much more complex as both federal and state statutes add new definitions of "property." Pensions, stock options, and the good will of professional practices were not considered in most divorces prior to 1980.... As divorce became more prevalent, so did premarital contracting to avoid judicial discretion if divorce occurred. As domestic violence issues came to the forefront and intrafamily immunity faded, family law added more tort litigation....
>
> Lawyers who once only needed to know "the law" now also need to at least understand the language of other professions. There has been an increasing interdisciplinary approach to family law. Family lawyers need to understand a spreadsheet, a pension valuation, a medical diagnosis contained in the DSM–IV, as well as the proper administration and interpretation of psychological testing.

The increasing complexity of family law "has resulted in lawyers following the lead of the medical profession—specialization. Over 15,000 lawyers indicate they specialize in family law; in 1980 there were only 700. Many more lawyers practice some family law. At least 4,000 attorneys specialize in divorce mediation." Specialization may be more important of another reason: "Clients who expect more expertise ... are more willing to sue for malpractice or file an ethical grievance."

All these developments

> have increased the costs of legal services and marriage dissolution. The cost and lack of availability of legal services has led to larger numbers of litigants appearing pro se, which imposes additional burdens on the judicial system. In only 41 percent of cases are both parties represented by attorneys....
>
> The current court system in most states is not prepared to deal with the staggering caseloads and the myriad of complex family problems that come before it. Courts dealing with family law issues have the greatest burdens and the fewest resources. The civil domestic docket is the fastest growing docket in most states, increasing 70 percent between 1984 and 1995. Child custody disputes rose 43 percent in the same time period. Over 3 million children were reported as abused or neglected to child protective services in 1995, triple the number from the 1970s....
>
> Lawyers are either learning mediation skills or learning how to counsel clients who are in mediation or arbitration. Private and court-sponsored alternative dispute resolution have developed in response to the failure of the adversarial system to adequately address complex problems of families, staggering caseloads, shrinking public resources and consumer demand for access and flexibility. While these dispute resolution alternatives are reducing some of the burdens on the system (and the parties), there is a potential for a two-tiered system of justice. Those who have money can afford either to go to court, hire a private arbitrator (a retired judge), or a mediator of their choice. Those without money must use the already overburdened court-annexed systems. For example, one-half of mothers using public mediation in one area were unemployed or earned wages below poverty level.

These last comments lead us to the first of our studies of how divorce lawyers approach their work. It is Kenneth Kressel, *The Process of Divorce: How Professionals and Couples Negotiate Settlements* (Basic Books, 1985). Professor Kressel interviewed a group of seventeen "highly elite" divorce specialists in and around New York City. He found "three key areas in which systematic differences of opinion among the lawyers were evident: attitudes toward the client, the objectives of legal intervention, and the nature and value of collaboration with mental health professionals." Relying on these three categories, he proposed six ideal types of divorce lawyers.

1. *The Undertaker.* Undertakers see their work as "a thankless, messy business," and they see their clients as emotionally "deranged." Undertakers tend to be cynical about human nature and pessimistic about the chances of attaining a desirable result in divorce cases.

2. *The Mechanic.* Mechanics are pragmatic legal technicians. They tend to assume that clients essentially know what they want and that the lawyer's job is to help them find out whether and how the law might permit it.

3. *The Mediator.* Mediators value rational problem-solving and negotiated compromise. They hope to cooperate with the other side and, particularly, the other side's lawyer. "Generally, there is an appeal to the client's 'better nature' or a view that what the client wants should be tempered with a sense of 'what's fair.' There may also be a posture of emotional neutrality or noninvolvement...." Mediators look for a "fair" settlement both sides can "live with." Professor Kressel suggests that, unlike "the undertaker and the mechanic, but like the three stances that follow, the mediator tends to downplay (but not deny) the adversarial aspect of his role. Only when provoked by the other side does the mediator accept the responsibility to fight." Mediators may see other professionals as useful in helping to tame the client's pugnacity.

4. *The Social Worker.* The social worker is particularly concerned for their clients' adjustment after divorce and for their social welfare in general. When the client is a woman, the social worker is likely to be specially concerned for her "marketability." "The main thing is to fully explore her ability to contribute to her own support.... [I]s she employable? Is she going to remarry? How is she going to live?" Social workers also tend to worry about clients' entire family and not just the clients themselves. The social worker does not make reconciling couples a first priority but sees it as a genuine obligation where it is possible. In short, for the social worker "a good outcome is perceived to be one in which the client achieves social re-integration."

5. *The Therapist.* The therapist is particularly aware of clients' emotional distress and tends to think that clients' legal problems cannot be handled well unless the lawyer engages with and tries to understand clients' emotional difficulties. This stance involves accepting and adjusting to the fact that clients are in a state of emotional strain and turmoil. One therapist, for example, says, "I don't see that there's any difference in my work and the work of the psychiatrist or psychologist." Part of understanding clients' motives is helping them explore the possibilities for a reconciliation. For the therapist, "A good outcome is conceptualized more or less as it would be in a therapeutically-oriented crisis intervention situation: personal re-integration of the client after a trying, stressful period."

6. *The Moral Agent.* The moral agent explicitly rejects neutrality and asks what is "right" and what is "wrong." Professor Kressel writes, "Perhaps the most striking aspect of the moral agent stance is the degree to which opposition to the client's wishes is viewed as not only legitimate, but positively mandated by the lawyer's role."

In another study (reported in the same book) Professor Kressel surveyed members of the Family Law Section of the New Jersey State Bar Association. This survey confirmed in important ways the findings of the first study. Professor Kressel divided this second group of lawyers into two clusters—"a group of twenty-two attorneys whom we called *advocates,* and another group of twenty-four respondents whom we called *counselors.*" The advocates were essentially undertakers, mechanics, and mediators; the counselors essentially social workers, therapists, and moral agents. Advocates were particularly interested in securing a good financial settlement for their clients. They liked divorce work because of the challenges it set for exercising legal skills to win victories for clients. They saw clients' neurotic behavior as a particularly troublesome barrier to settlement. They were likelier than counselors to see value in an adversarial relationship with the other lawyer. And, again compared to counselors, they were less likely to think it was their job to give clients emotional support. Compared with the advocates, counselors were more interested in finding a way for the spouses to cooperate after their divorce and in promoting the children's welfare. They were likely to receive their satisfaction from "the opportunity which divorce work provided them to learn about human psychology." They were likelier to think settlements are impeded by lawyers' lack of psychological training. They were also more inclined to think divorce mediation by "mental health professionals" might be a good thing.

Despite these differences, advocates and counselors shared similarities. Overall, "[t]he most salient concern of the respondents was to protect children; furthering the welfare of children was both the goal of settlement endorsed more strongly and the greatest source of satisfaction in divorce work.... [T]he respondents disassociated themselves from the view that the lawyer should be a hired legal gun out to do the client's bidding. Equity, not winning through intimidation, was the preferred objective."

Like a number of observers, Professor Kressel believes divorce lawyers have a difficult job and feel considerable strain. He says the New Jersey lawyers reported that "[t]he most significant problem in divorce practice was seen to be the unrealistic and divergent goals of the parties, and the highly charged atmosphere between them." More generally, "the lawyer-client relationship is likely to be rife with undercurrents of mutual wariness. Many of the tensions are directly attributable to the client's difficult psychological and financial circumstances." In divorce law, perhaps as much as in any area of law, lawyers have an excellent chance of working for clients who are deeply upset with themselves and with their adversaries (all too often, this is the right word). Many of the most elemental plans they have made for their lives will be collapsing around them. Furthermore, they are likely to feel ambivalent about the very goals for which they are purportedly litigating. Worse, little about litigation is likely to make them feel much better about those things.

To add insult to injury, these miserable people are going to be asked to pay for this wretched process. Professor Kressel writes, "Between one-third and two-thirds of divorce clients appear to be seriously dissatisfied with the fees which they paid to their lawyer.... [T]here is good reason to suspect that attorneys are not too thrilled about the way in which clients uphold their end of the bargain either." Of course, most people who divorce are not wealthy, and they cannot easily afford legal fees. What is worse, their cost of living is about to rise abruptly, since two people separately cannot live as cheaply as two people together. The relative poverty of divorce clients not only means the clients have serious worries and that the lawyer may not be paid promptly or even fully. It also means that lawyers will often feel they cannot do a really good job for their clients. To put the point differently, this is an area of law where processing the clients through as quickly as possible may be the most rational economic approach even though its other costs are painfully obvious. This may help explain the fact that, while "the majority of divorce clients are satisfied with the assistance they have received, [a]t least one-third . . . are strongly dissatisfied." This may also help explain why there is evidence "that perhaps as many as half or more of all divorcing couples do most of the settlement negotiations themselves, with only minimal assistance from lawyers."

In all this misery, the various formal ethical codes do not give satisfying guidance to lawyers representing family members. What does zealous representation mean in these circumstances, where the litigants were once in love, probably have at least ambivalent feelings towards each other, will often need to work together for many years to come, and are surrounded by innocent bystanders? As that question suggests, there is a tension between protecting a client's economic and other interests and resolving the disputes between the spouses gently and justly. It is often feared that lawyers resolve this tension by too eager an attention to the first goal, to the injury of the second. There is, however, considerable evidence that lawyers encourage their clients to settle and discourage them from bargaining abusively. Professor Kressel observes, "In the prevailing stereotype it is the client who is likely to end up the unsuspecting victim of the lawyer's competitive zeal. Several recent investigations suggest that more often than not lawyers prefer to avoid conflict, but find themselves pressured into assuming a combative posture by their aggressive clients."

Professor Kressel sees it as "part of the unwritten code that lawyers should play the role of mediators, resolving as much through compromise and cooperative problem solving as possible." This code, Professor Kressel suggests, is not just a widely-held norm. It is also sustained by the structure of the situation in which divorce lawyers work: "[T]he lawyers' dependence on each other for the successful resolution of the case, their anticipation of future interaction once the case is completed, and their concern for their professional reputation, all represent significant collegial bonds which run counter to the adversary spirit." (Similarly, it is sometimes said that English barristers are led to conform to the local standards of behavior because there are only a few of them and reputations are easily and decisively influenced by perceived misbehavior. It is also sometimes hypothesized that lawyers in big cities behave more offensively than lawyers in small cities because they are less sure that they will have to deal with the opposing lawyer again soon and that their reputation can be readily injured.) Thus Professor Kressel suggests, "The lawyer's most valuable potential ally in managing the client is likely to be the opposing attorney.... [T]he two lawyers may be able to inject enough reason and reality into the proceedings to produce a constructive negotiating climate." (In like manner, Professor Weitzman reports that over 95 percent of the lawyers in her sample had tried to discourage a client from seeking custody where the lawyer thought that the client would lose, that the client was being vindictive, or that the client would not be the better parent. Lenore J. Weitzman, *The Divorce Revolution: The Unexpected Social and Economic Consequences for Women and Children in America* 237 (Free Press, 1985).)

All this sounds quite reassuring. But Professor Kressel points out that the ethic of mediation and the counsellors' as opposed to the advocates' view of the divorce lawyer's role are not necessarily good for the client. He cites one study which suggests "that 'cooperation' in the guise of a too ready willingness to compromise can prevent a truly superior settlement, whereas 'competitive' tactics, in the form of a stubborn adherence to relatively high aspirations combined with flexibility regarding means, can work to everybody's advantage." He also cites evidence that both cooperative and competitive lawyers can do good work for their clients. Ultimately, while he concludes that "[t]he weight of the evidence ... clearly favors counselors," he warns that "client satisfaction with the legal process made only a trivial contribution to postdivorce adjustment and one which was less important than factors such as health, economic stress, and postdivorce dating behavior."

Another view of the work of professionals comes from Austin Sarat and William L. F. Felstiner, *Divorce Lawyers and Their Clients: Power and Meaning in the Legal Process* (Oxford U Press, 1995). It examined one side of forty divorce cases in a medium-sized city and a town. It used interviews but also relied on observation of discussions between lawyers and their clients. The lawyers generally did not have particularly great income, experience, or status, their clients generally were not especially prosperous, they were not spoken of as the most successful practitioners, and they had not attended prestigious law schools.

Professors Sarat and Felstiner confirm the view of divorce lawyers as preferring settlement to litigation: They concluded that

> the lawyers' message is overwhelmingly pro-settlement. They consistently emphasize the advantages of informal as opposed to formal resolution. Adjudication is presented in an unfavorable light, as an alternative to be avoided. Thus the image of the lawyer as 'shark,' eagerly stirring up trouble, fanning the flames of contention, does not describe the lawyers we observed. This is not to say that lawyers are uniformly cooperative or that they advocate meekness and acquiescence or 'peace' at any price. Such is not the case. Negotiations in the cases we studied were usually adversarial and were described by lawyers as a process of 'hard bargaining.'

Clients often resisted their lawyers' pressure to settle and maneuvered to move their cases toward hearings or trials. This meant the lawyers exerted that pressure at some peril. "Lawyers worry that as they advise clients to negotiate, compromise, and settle they will be seen as selling out rather than providing zealous advocacy."

Professors Sarat and Felstiner come from a perspective that led them to expect that lawyers (indeed, professionals of all kinds) would constantly seek to build and exploit their professional power over their client. Nevertheless, their research led them to paint a somewhat more complicated picture than perhaps they had anticipated. They say, "While lawyers appear to play the dominant role, using their knowledge of the law to validate some interpretations and brand others irrelevant, clients are rarely simply acquiescent. They bring their own ideas of relevance and their own interpretations of events to the lawyer's office and maneuver, more or less overtly, to get those ideas and interpretations heard and accepted."

Sarat and Felstiner see the process of representation as one in which both lawyers and clients repeatedly seek to establish their own particular views of the case. Each side has its own characteristic attitude: "[C]lients typically focus on the character and personality dispositions of their spouse and emphasize their spouse's most objectionable traits and personal defects. They frame these accounts in the language of rights, a language that 'encompasses the belief that one should not be abused, mistreated, taken advantage of, harassed, insulted, or denied access to the means for securing life's necessities.' " Lawyers, on the other hand, want to talk about what can be done and what should be done. They tend to think their task is to reach a settlement that is the best for the client given what is legally and economically possible. The lawyers do not think the rights and wrongs of the marriage are relevant to that task. They thus avoid responding to their clients' stories about those rights and wrongs. This upsets the clients, who think their lawyers don't understand what happened to them and don't care. And clients are already "suspicious about the depth of commitment their lawyers bring to their cases and about their own ability to control the content and timing of their lawyers' actions. They worry about lawyers who seem too busy to attend fully to the idiosyncracies of their cases, and about divided loyalties, limited competence, erratic judgment, and personality conflict."

The lawyers did, however, have to elicit information from their clients about their marriage and their current situation. Because the lawyers were worried about their clients' equanimity and therefore about the accuracy of the stories their clients told, the lawyers tried to find ways to test those stories without seeming skeptical. "[T]hese lawyers often appear hyper-rational, detached, disloyal, and callous in response to the emotional intensity of their clients' situations. Clients, put off and alienated by such suspicions and distance, appear even more unstable and unpredictable to their lawyers."

The relations between lawyers and clients were further complicated by another crucial fact: the clients often did not really know what they wanted. This is hardly surprising. Clients were not only terribly upset, they were usually confronting a completely new situation which they had not planned for and did not much want. In addition, they often desired conflicting things. Thus "interpreting clients' interests is a known quagmire. Clients often do not appear to know what they want, or may not want what they 'ought' to want. They seem to change their minds in unpredictable ways, or they may not change their minds when it is, from their lawyer's point of view, strategically wise to do so." Because "[c]lient's objectives often appear uncertain; their goals appear unclear; their sense of an appropriate resolution seems to be not well settled ... [,] lawyers spend considerable time trying to elicit from their clients what is, from the client's perspective, very difficult to articulate."

The lawyers not only found their clients' objectives uncertain; they also found them unrealistic. Economically and even socially, their clients were playing a zero-sum game with limited resources. They had many urgent reasons for wanting to win that game. But they had little basis for judging what was realistically possible. "Clients ... seem to be psychologically unprepared for the disappointments that are almost inevitably part of the settlement process. Lawyers treat client goals as exaggerated and lean on the client to be 'realistic' and understand that two people cannot live as well separately as they can together."

Lawyers and clients, then, engaged in a continuing struggle to define the terms of their relationship. But neither lawyers nor clients wanted to seize command overtly. Rather, they shared a "mutual aversion to confrontation" and seemed to "recognize that, were they to behave as if they were hierarchically empowered, they would undermine the legitimacy of what is generally considered to be a cooperative enterprise." Thus the clients almost never told their lawyers, I am the client, you are the lawyer, I am paying the bill, so do as I say. And lawyers almost never told their clients, I am the lawyer, I am the expert, you are the novice, so do as I say. Rather, lawyers, "urge, cajole, flatter, use rhetorical tricks, provide unqualified or contingent advice, predict harm, discomfort, frustration, or catastrophe."

Not only was the struggle to define the relationship more implicit than explicit. It was a struggle which neither lawyers nor clients systematically won. "Parallel meanings are constructed and allowed to coexist. Neither lawyer nor client acknowledges, or tries to resolve, the difference. Neither is able to validate their interpretation and have it accepted as the working assumption in their interaction. Neither is able to assert dominance over the other." In the end, therefore, "both lawyers and clients are sometimes frustrated by feelings of powerlessness in dealing with the other.... Often no one may be in charge: interactions between lawyers and clients involve as much drift and uncertainty as direction and clarity of purpose. It may be difficult, at any one moment, to determine who, if anyone, is defining objectives, determining strategy, or devising tactics."

Notes and Questions: Divorce and the Practice of Law

Imagine now that you are the lawyer who has been approached by (successively) each of the spouses in the Appleby, Bartleby and Cuttleby cases. What should be your goals in serving each of these six clients? What conflicts do you see among those goals? How should those conflicts be resolved? What problems do you foresee in reaching those goals? What should your relationship to your client be? What should your relationship be to the other people with whom you will deal? What satisfactions do you hope to find in serving these clients? What dissatisfactions may you feel? The following notes and questions are intended to help you think about these questions.

Before you answer these questions, you need to know a little about how divorces are actually handled. Of course, a court grants divorces and approves the decree which specifies how the parties' property is to be divided, whether alimony must be paid, who will have custody of the children, and what child support must be provided. However, it is not usual for these issues to be litigated. Rather, the conventional estimate is that 90 percent of all divorce cases are settled by the parties, whose agreement is then ratified by the judge.

(1) What should your goal in serving your client be?

(a) To help your client win? (Recall that the Preamble to the Model Rules of Professional Conduct says, "As advocate, a lawyer zealously asserts the client's position under the rules of the adversary system. As negotiator, a lawyer seeks a result advantageous to the client but consistent with requirements of honest dealings with others.") What does winning mean? Getting or preventing a divorce and getting custody of the children and the largest possible financial settlement? Getting everything your client asks for? Securing an arrangement that will best serve the client's long-range interests?

(b) To help your client reach a fair accommodation of the spouses' disagreements? How do you decide what "fairness" is?

(c) To promote a calm and cooperative resolution of the disputes? At what cost?

(d) To help your client through the divorce as quickly and painlessly as possible?

(e) To help your client toward psychological well-being?

(f) To help your client establish an optimal post-divorce relationship with his or her spouse and children?

(g) To promote a settlement which will minimize the likelihood the parties will return to court after the divorce?

(h) To promote a solution to the family's problems that will be best for each of the family members? How should you decide what "best" means?

(i) To discourage your client and your client's spouse from divorcing where possible? To promote a reconciliation?

(j) To help your client do what is right?

(k) To provide your client with inexpensive legal services?

(l) To pursue the goals your client specifies?

(2) If you believe that your goal should be more than one of the above possibilities, what conflicts do you see among your chosen goals? How should you resolve them?

(a) Suppose your client is Mrs. Bartleby. Immediately after you are hired, Mr. Bartleby's lawyer proffers a settlement which would give Mrs. Bartleby custody of their children (as she wants), but which you believe would give her financially much less than similar divorcing wives in your jurisdiction ordinarily get. Mr. Bartleby's lawyer says that if Mrs. Bartleby rejects this offer, it will be withdrawn and Mr. Bartleby will not only insist on as advantageous a financial arrangement as possible, but also on custody of his son. In addition, Mr. Bartleby privately tells his wife that he is prepared to fight it out on those lines indefinitely. What do you advise your client? What goals are served by your advice? Disserved?

(b) Suppose again that your client is Mrs. Bartleby. She says she wants you to do all you legally can to impede the divorce. Insofar as you can't impede it, she wants you to make it as costly and crucifying for Mr. Bartleby as possible. What do you advise your client? What goals are served by your advice? Disserved?

(3) To what extent is it part of your job to help your client decide what he or she wants?

(a) Your client is Mrs. Bartleby. She tells you she does not want to contest her husband's claim for ownership of their house. Legally, she would have a good claim to at least a half interest in it. Should you do more than describe to your client her legal situation? Should you ask her why she won't claim all she is entitled to? Should you try to persuade her to claim the house, if you feel that she will suffer economic hardship without it? If you feel that in the long run she will want the house? If you feel her children will be economically disadvantaged without it? That they will be socially disadvantaged?

(b) Your client is Mr. Appleby. You feel he is not morally entitled to a divorce. Should you try to dissuade him from seeking one? If he persists, should you refuse to represent him?

(c) Rule 2.1 of the Model Rules of Professional Conduct states, "In representing a client, a lawyer shall exercise independent professional judgment and render candid advice. In rendering advice, a lawyer may refer not only to law but to other considerations such as moral, economic, social and political factors, that may be relevant to the client's situation." Does this help you answer Questions 2 and 3 and their subsidiary parts? What, if anything, makes a lawyer competent to speak in his or her "professional judgment" to questions of morals, economics, society, and politics? The annotation to Rule 2.1 says that, "[a]lthough a lawyer is not a moral advisor as such, moral and ethical considerations impinge upon most legal questions and may decisively influence how the law will be applied." Is divorce such a circumstance? The annotation also says that, "[i]n general, a lawyer is not expected to give advice until asked by the client.... A lawyer ordinarily has no duty to ... give advice that a client has indicated is unwanted, but a lawyer may initiate advice to a client when doing so appears to be in the client's interest." Does this help you decide when to give advice and what kind of advice to give?

(4) How far ought you try to see that your client behaves fairly and to protect the members of your client's family?

(a) Your client is Mr. Appleby. He tells you that he wants you to protect his financial situation as completely as possible. His goal, in other words, is to leave the marriage with as many assets and as few obligations as possible. What do you tell him? What if he rejects your advice?

(b) Your client is Mrs. Bartleby, and you discover she is an alcoholic. You are convinced her alcoholism is impairing her ability to care for her children. She nevertheless tells you to seek custody of them. What do you tell her? What if she rejects your advice?

(c) Your client is Mr. Bartleby. Mrs. Bartleby is not alcoholic, and both parents could raise their daughter well. Your client wants custody. However, Mrs. Bartleby has been the child's primary caretaker, and you believe she would be a much better parent than Mr. Bartleby. What do you tell him? What if he rejects your advice?

(5) People considering a divorce usually go through much emotional turmoil long before seeing a lawyer, and the process of divorce is usually further disturbing. The sources of these emotional difficulties probably run deep. How should these considerations affect your relationship with your clients?

(a) If you detect signs of emotional distress, should you encourage your client to seek professional counselling? Should you do so even if you don't see any such signs, on the theory that emotional distress is likely even if it is not evident to the untrained eye and that counselling can help your client through the emotional travails of divorce?

(b) If you detect signs of emotional distress, should you try to get your client to unburden himself or herself to you, so that you can understand your client's situation more fully, respond to your client's actual wishes more sensitively, and identify your client's best interests more accurately?

(c) If you detect signs of emotional distress, should you try to respond as politely as possible, but not encourage your client to unburden himself or herself to you, on the grounds that you are not professionally equipped to interpret your client's emotional problems or to provide help for them?

(6) What kinds of ethical, moral, and practical limits should inhibit your pursuit of your goals?

(a) Your client is Mr. Appleby, and he has told you that he has warned his wife that if she attempts to delay his divorce that he will physically assault her. What, if anything, do you say or do? Does it help to know that Rule 1.6(b) of the Model Rules says that a lawyer may reveal information relating to representation of a client "to the extent the lawyer reasonably believes necessary: (1) to prevent the client from committing a criminal act that the lawyer believes is likely to result in imminent death or substantial bodily harm . . ."?

(b) Your client is Mr. Bartleby. Negotiations with Mrs. Bartleby's lawyer have gone wretchedly. Mr. Bartleby has not sought custody of his children. He has said he would not be interested in custody, and he has never commented on his wife's proposals for visitation. He now instructs you that he wants custody and that he wants you to secure it for him. How do you respond?

(c) Your client is Mrs. Bartleby. She and her husband are engaged in a custody dispute. She tells you that her husband had told her several years ago that he had once been convicted of an act of homosexual prostitution and that he is horribly ashamed of this conviction. She wants you to threaten to use it in negotiating over custody. What do you say and do? Does it help to know that Model Rule of Professional Responsibility 4.3 says: "In dealing on behalf of a client with a person who is not represented by counsel, a lawyer shall not state or imply that the lawyer is disinterested. When the lawyer knows or reasonably should know that the unrepresented person misunderstands the lawyer's role in the matter, the lawyer shall make reasonable efforts to correct the misunderstanding"?

(d) Your client is Mr. Appleby. Mrs. Appleby's lawyer is inexperienced and inept. He appears not to know of developments in your jurisdiction's law which would entitle Mrs. Appleby to a half interest in her husband's pension. The lawyer presents for your client's signature a divorce settlement which is highly satisfactory to your client and which gives Mrs. Appleby no claim on Mr. Appleby's pension. Because there are effectively no other assets to divide, and because she is not entitled to alimony, she will be much worse off than her husband. How do you respond?

(e) Suppose that all the facts of the preceding question apply, except that Mrs. Appleby is not represented by counsel. You and the judge have both advised her to hire a lawyer, but she has adamantly refused. What do you say and do?

(f) Your client is Mrs. Cuttleby. Securing an optimal financial arrangement for her will require research and bargaining for which neither she nor her husband can pay. What do you say and do?

(7) In the preceding questions, we have described the facts of each case for you. In actuality, of course, you would have to find out the facts for yourself. How would you do so?

(a) Your primary source of information would presumably be your client. What questions would you ask your client when he or she first visited your office? Many of your questions would deal with points of controversy between your client and his or her spouse. How reliable are your client's answers likely to be? What further questions might you ask your client to make your client's answers more reliable?

(b) The other person who knows the most about your client's marriage is your client's spouse. Can you get information from the spouse? Rule 4.2 of the Model Rules states: "In representing a client, a lawyer shall not communicate about the subject of the representation with a party the lawyer knows to be represented by another lawyer in the matter, unless the lawyer has the consent of the other lawyer or is authorized by law to do so."

(c) Should you seek information from your client's children?

(d) Should you ask your client for permission to acquire information from his or her psychological therapist?

(8) What should your attitude be toward your client's dealings with third parties?

(a) Your client may still be living with and is likely at least to be regularly talking to his or her spouse. Further, Professor Kressel reports "that perhaps as many as half or more of all divorcing couples do most of the settlement negotiations themselves, with only minimal assistance from lawyers." How should you regard your client's dealings with his or her spouse?

(b) Your client may be seeing some kind of psychological therapist or religious counselor who may wish to give your client advice about the divorce. How should you regard your client's dealings with such people?

B. STUDIES IN LEGAL CHANGE: THE LEGISLATIVE IMPLEMENTATION OF NO–FAULT DIVORCE

Those who talk most about the blessings of marriage and the constancy of its vows are the very people who declare that if the chain were broken and the prisoners left free to choose, the whole social fabric would fly asunder. You cannot have the argument both ways. If the prisoner is happy, why lock him in? If he is not, why pretend that he is?

George Bernard Shaw
Man and Superman

This study in legal change examines a remarkable reform—the transformation in the 1960s and '70s of the law of divorce. The change interests us because of its extraordinary scope, because it offers a basis for evaluating the present law of divorce, and because it is an example of legal change effected through reforms enacted by state legislatures.

However, before we see how no-fault divorce swept the country, we need to learn what preceded it. This will not only set the stage for our story, but will tell you something about fault-based divorce. In England (until 1857), courts did not have the authority to grant divorces. Only Parliament could do so, and it did so infrequently. Alternatively, spouses could seek an annulment (also difficult to obtain) or a divorce *a mensa et thoro* (from bed and board), which was like a legal separation and did not permit the spouses to remarry. In colonial America, the South essentially followed the English pattern, while New England was modestly more liberal. After Independence, states, particularly northern states, gradually began to permit courts to authorize divorces. There was also a less formal "divorce" by desertion and emigration to the wilderness. The pressure of this "shadow institution" led to increasing numbers of legislative divorces in eastern states, particularly Massachusetts, Pennsylvania, Maryland and Virginia. When these special acts overwhelmed state legislatures, they gradually empowered courts to grant divorces. Legislative divorces are discussed in Lawrence Friedman and Robert Perceval, *Who Sues for Divorce? From Fault Through Fiction to Freedom*, 5 J Legal Stud 61 (1976). In the latter part of the nineteenth century, legislative divorce disappeared.

Although some states in the middle of the nineteenth century had relatively liberal divorce statutes, the rule was that divorce was available only where one of the parties had committed a marital "fault." (Indeed, New York adamantly refused to permit divorces on any ground except adultery until 1967.) Typical "fault" grounds included adultery, cruelty, impotence, and desertion. Of these, cruelty was the most important, for, as Professor Clark comments, it "proved to be capable of nearly limitless expansion, in the face of pronouncements by appellate courts which would lead one to think that the definition of cruelty had not changed much for one hundred and fifty years. In many states, especially in the West, a divorce for cruelty [could] be had for the asking, providing it [was] uncontested." Clark, *Law of Domestic Relations* 341 (1968). The significant exception to the fault-based system was the rule, increasingly common by the 1960's, that divorce could be had where the parties had lived apart for a set period (commonly three to five years).

One of the most telling and diverting descriptions of the strict fault regime (and of the "guilty" spouse's defenses) is A.P. Herbert's novel *Holy Deadlock* (Doubleday, 1934), a witty vivisection of England's divorce laws, which, like New York's, permitted divorce only for adultery. (England expanded its list of marital faults in 1937 when King George VI assented to an act of Parliament which Herbert had proposed and whose passage was influenced by Herbert's book. You may recall that in the preceding year George VI's deplorable predecessor, Edward VIII, abdicated because Parliament refused to let him marry a (twice) divorced woman.) As Herbert's novel opens, John Adam has been married to Mary Eve for nine years, during the last two of which they have been amicably separated. He has just received a telegram from her:

> John Adam 19 Adelphi Terrace London darling do hope you will behave like a gentleman because really want to marry Martin impossible do anything this end all nonsense but think you know why and hurry please darling because very much in love tell you more later much love and kisses writing Mary.

John cheerfully agrees to be a gentleman. He joins his solicitor, Mr. Boom, at a restaurant for lunch and meets classical divorce law:

A.P. HERBERT
HOLY DEADLOCK

(Doubleday, 1934)

"So you want to know how you are to behave like a gentleman?" he said.

"Um," said Mr. Adam, gulping down an oyster.

"You realize, do you, that you are asking me to take part in a criminal conspiracy?"

"Good God, no!"

"You are asking me to assist you to arrange a collusive petition for divorce, to pervert the processes of justice, to withhold material facts from the court, to aid and abet perjury. I am an officer of the court, and for all these offenses I may be struck off the rolls. We may both be committed for contempt of court or sent to prison for conspiracy. And you the son of a civil servant. Have some more wine."

John listened with alarm to this recital.

"I only want to give poor Mary her freedom," he said. "It seems simple enough."

"It is never simple to give anyone freedom. It is only simple to shut people up. As you know, it is the simplest thing in the world to get married or get into jail. It is quite another thing to get out."

"What am I to do?" said John.

"Hush," said Boom. "The waiter is listening. My friend," he said to the waiter, "kindly withdraw a little way. I am about to take part in a criminal conspiracy. And bring another bottle of Chablis."

"Let me see," he continued. "You were married in 1920. You separated in 1927. Seven years. A fair trial. You have no children. Why have you no children?"

"I don't know," said John. "We didn't want any at first, and then, when we did, they didn't come."

"Unfortunate. But not a crime. Nor is it really relevant to the law of divorce. However, since you have no children, the affair should, as you say, be simple. You have no obligation to anybody but yourselves: and if you wish to release each other, why not?"

"Why indeed?" said Mr. Adam indignantly.

"Because the law is not a hass, as somebody remarked, but a mule. I think myself ..." Mr. Boom paused and wiped his large lips with a napkin.

"But surely ..."

"One moment," said Mr. Boom, "here is the wine ..." He beamed benevolently on his impatient friend; he was in no hurry: he was enjoying himself.

"I think myself," he continued, "that in such a case as yours the wise provisions of the Partnership Act, 1890, should be applicable."

"What the deuce are they?"

"You and your wife should be able to go to the court, hand in hand, and say: 'My lord, long ago, when we were very young, we entered into the difficult partnership called marriage. We made a mistake, but an excusable mistake. We made a long and honest attempt (seven years) to keep the partnership going. It's not a case of recklessness or wickedness. We've tried hard, but we cannot live happily together. Our nerves, our health, our work, and our usefulness to the state are suffering damage. The partnership is a failure. It has failed to provide children for the country or a reasonably contented life for ourselves. We wish to be free, either to live alone or marry again. And so, my lord, we ask you, in your discretion, to say that the partnership ought to be honourably dissolved under Section 35.' "

"That sounds reasonable enough ..." began Mr. Adam.

"And therefore it is no part of the divorce laws of England. Cheese? Coffee? Brandy?"

"No," said Mr. Adam. "What would happen if I went to the court and said that?"

"The judge would say: 'Pardon me, Mr. Adam, but has either of you committed adultery? We are not here, Mr. Adam, to secure your happiness, but to preserve the institution of marriage and the purity of the home. And therefore one of you must commit adultery. Has either of you committed adultery?' And if you answered 'No,' the judge would say: 'In that case, Mr. Adam, the court cannot help you. One of you two must go away and commit adultery and then come back and tell us all about it. We may then be able to do what your wish. *One* of you, not both. For if both of you behave in this way, the marriage must stand, according to the ecclesiastical doctrine of recrimination ... ' "

"What the deuce . . . ?"

"Recrimination? Why, if one spouse petitions for divorce on the ground of the other's adultery, it is in theory enough to show that he or she has committed adultery, too. *Tu quoque*—the retort of the schoolboy, and the canon law. The law regards physical fidelity as the vital element in the marriage bond. Thus, without an act of adultery on one side or the other it is impossible to obtain a divorce. And a single act of infidelity is sufficient cause for the dissolution of a long and happy marriage, though that act may be begun and ended in five minutes—a sudden, unpremeditated act, the fruit of a passing craziness, jealousy, temper, or desire. So dearly does the law regard the purity of the marriage bed. It is, as we lawyers say, of the essence of the contract. One would think, then, that where *both* parties have violated the fundamental clause of the contract, there was twice the reason for dissolving the partnership. Not a bit of it. We say that in that case there is no good ground for a divorce at all—except in special cases by the discretion of the court. Normally, the guilty couple must remain united in law, though the only bond between them in fact is that each is living in sin with somebody else. They are, as somebody said, 'joined together in unholy matrimony.' Or, shorter still, 'married alive!' "

"Are you raving?" said Adam. "Or am I?"

"Neither."

"Sorry."

"Not at all. Whenever I explain certain sections of the law my clients conclude that I must be mad or drunk. That is why I like to explain the worst parts here: for I would rather be thought intoxicated than insane."

"I think, after all," said Mr. Adam, "that I will have a brandy."

"Of course. The doctrine of recrimination, I find, very often leads to drink. Henri, another brandy! However, all this is academic. For I assume that you have not both committed adultery—by the way, I mustn't use that word. Charles complains that it shocks his waiters and frightens his lay clients away. Do you mind if we call it intimacy?"

"Intimacy?" repeated the publisher.

"Intimacy. Don't you ever read the divorce reports? 'Petitioner alleged that acts of intimacy took place at a West End hotel.' . . . 'Acts of intimacy took place!' Glorious! The language of Shakespeare! 'Misconduct' is the favourite euphemism in the papers, but that annoys me. It might mean drunkenness or persistent unpunctuality. 'Intimacy' makes me laugh. Nobody but the English could use such a word for such a purpose. I sometimes think of rewriting the classics in the language of the newspaper law reports. Paris was 'intimate' with Helen of Troy. Thou shalt not commit intimacy. Ha!"

Mr. Boom laughed heartily at his fancies and drank gently of his wine.

John Adam said patiently, "Well, what am I to do?"

"I've told you. One of you must commit intimacy—not both. And you must not consult together which one it is to be: for that would be collusion. By the way, tear up that telegram of your wife's. That's enough to put the king's proctor on your track. Most indiscreet."

"She always telegraphs. The first thing that comes into her head."

"Well, she must stop it."

"I couldn't stop it when we were together; it's hardly likely I can stop it now."

"And I suppose she sends them over the telephone, to ensure publicity?"

"Yes."

Mr. Boom sighed. "You and your wife are the kind of people who ought never to be allowed out without a solicitor. You say she's in love with this fellow—what's his name?"

"Seal. Martin Seal."

"I seem to know the name. Why don't you divorce her? That seems the simplest thing."

"He's on the B.B.C. and is afraid of losing his job. They're very particular."

"I remember now. He used to run the 'Children's Hour.' Uncle Somebody-or-other."

"Yes. He's one of the announcers now."

"I see. It would never do for the British public to hear the weather report from the lips of a co-respondent. But how about your own office? Are publishers of schoolbooks less moral than the B.B.C.?"

"It will be unpleasant, of course, but not fatal. I shall explain everything to my chief."

"Tell him you're only behaving like a gentleman?"

"Yes."

"With whom?"

"That's what I don't know."

"Nobody you want to marry?"

"Yes. As a matter of fact, there is."

"Well, then . . ."

John Adam flushed, and spoke with spirit. "I'm not going to drag her into that filthy court! She wouldn't agree if I did," he added.

"No intimacy yet? Pardon the impertinence—purely professional."

"No. And there won't be."

John described to his adviser the parentage, history, and character of the gentle Joan Latimer, second mistress of St. Bride's College for Girls.

"H'm," said Mr. Boom. "Do you suppose that your wife has committed intimacy with her Mr. Seal?"

"This is a very odd conversation," thought Mr. Adam.

"I've no idea," he said. "I don't suppose so."

"Why not?"

"She'd probably telegraph if she did—bless her! She could never keep anything back."

"We might inquire!"

"Well, we won't!" said Mr. Adam, stubborn. "I've not the smallest feeling against her. I'm not going to have her badgered by detectives. And I'm not going to have her name on the placards of the evening papers.... Please understand that."

"This is going to be a difficult case," said Mr. Boom.

"Three parties with principles, and one with a job at the B.B.C."

John Adam looked at him, as one bewildered. "Do you really mean," he said, "that what you call 'intimacy' is the only way out of this mess? Supposing I go to Mary's flat and beat her—really knock her about? Wouldn't that do?"

"Not at all," said Mr. Boom cheerfully. "More brandy? Even persistent physical cruelty is not sufficient ground for a divorce. It would help your wife to get a judicial separation, but she would be no more free to marry Mr. Seal than she is now. If you violently knock your wife about every night, the ordinary person will conclude that you have not much affection for her; but the law requires you to prove it by sleeping with another woman. For that is the only act of a husband that the law regards as really important. It would be the same if you were certified a lunatic: or become a habitual and besotted drunkard: or were sentenced for embezzlement to fourteen years' penal servitude: or were found guilty of murder but reprieved, and so let off with imprisonment for life. Such trifles mean nothing to the divorce laws of this Christian country. Adultery, misconduct, intimacy, or nothing—that's the rule. Human love and Christian marriage are rightly contrasted with the brutal mating of animals, which has no spiritual element, no mystical union of soul and mind. But if, as the law insists, the one thing that matters is the physical act of love, we are not, after all, so very different from 'the brute beasts that have no understanding.' "

"It's disgusting," said Mr. Adam.

"On the contrary," said Mr. Boom, "the whole idea is purity. I must say, John, that I find your objections to our excellent divorce laws a little childish. After all, until the year 1857 you would have had to secure an act of Parliament to get a divorce. By the Matrimonial Causes Act, 1857 . . ."

"What am I to do?" said John.

But Mr. Boom's discourse rolled on like a flood, irresistible.

"The trouble is, you see, that our law is an attempt to combine two irreconcilable notions. It's possible, and honest, to hold, as the Catholics do, that marriage is a holy sacrament, and therefore cannot be terminated by men or the courts of men: and we may, and should, respect those who govern their own lives upon that principle. It is possible, again, to hold that marriage is a civil contract, a practical arrangement by which two reasonable beings agree to share certain rights and duties, an arrangement made by men and dissoluble by men. And that ought to be the point of view of any secular court of law, which is an institution designed for the practical assistance of men on the material and not the spiritual side of their lives. What is impossible is to combine the two—to say that marriage is both a sacrament and a civil contract, governed at one moment by the principles of common law and at another by the remnants of ecclesiastical tradition—enforceable by one set of rules but not avoidable except by another. For that's making the worst of two worlds. But that's what we're trying to do—in England—not, or not so much, in Scotland. If you claim your just rights under a contract of marriage you're supported by the doctrines of the civil law—you can get damages, for example, from the man who goes off with your wife, as if she were a side of beef (that doesn't fit very well into the sacramental theory). But if you want to surrender your rights under the contract of marriage—or partnership—you're impeded by obstacles which have a purely ecclesiastical origin. For example, it's impossible to imagine a civil action in which, both parties having violated clauses which were essential to the real purpose of contract, the court would nevertheless insist that the contract should still endure and be binding on them both. But that's what we do to married couples in England—though not in dear old licentious Scotland. Our old friend Recrimination."

"What happens in Scotland?"

"The presence of guilt on both sides doesn't preclude a divorce, but the comparative guilt of each does affect the monetary arrangements. The spouse, for example, whose conduct provoked the backsliding of the other will suffer in costs, the amount of maintenance, and other ways. Both parties, therefore, can tell the whole truth without fear that it will cost them their freedom: and one, at least, has a direct monetary incentive to tell the whole truth."

"It pays to tell the truth. And so in Scotland they have no king's proctor, because, where there is not so much temptation to lie, no special officer is needed to detect the liar. Likewise, there's no six months' suspense between decree nisi and decree absolute. They're down on collusion, of course, but the court trusts itself to find out everything at the first shot, as other courts do."

"Very interesting," said Mr. Adam, "but it doesn't help me much."

"No," said Mr. Boom, and went on smoothly. "To go back to the Church influence, the odd thing is that you have the same trouble whether you're married in church or married at a register office. Which were you?"

"Register office. Mary insisted."

"I remember. You didn't have to say that you took your wife 'till death us do part'?"

"No."

"But you'll be treated by the law in exactly the same way as if you had—as if you'd been joined by God and had sworn a number of vows before the holy altar. One might, perhaps, have two sets of laws—one for the people who faced the church service, and another for the registered unions. Logical—but perhaps impracticable."

Mr. Boom ruminated a while.

"What am I to do?" said the distressed husband.

"I was coming to that. The position is that someone has to commit intimacy for the general good; someone has to behave impurely in order to uphold the Christian ideal of purity; someone has to confess in public to a sinful breach of the marriage vows, in order that the happily married may point at him or her and feel themselves secure and virtuous. The delinquent, you say, is not to be your own wife; therefore it must be yourself. You cannot commit intimacy by yourself: there must be a woman. But it is not, you say, to be the woman you would like to marry. Therefore you must be intimate with some woman whom you do not wish to marry. You must be a good boy and have a slice of bread and butter before you come to the jam. Now, is there any other woman you would care to be intimate with?"

John Adam stood up. "If you're going to laugh at me . . ." he angrily began.

"Sit down," said the large lawyer calmly. "I'm not laughing—far from it. I'm trying to make you study the chart before you put to sea. You've no idea what rocks are ahead. Few people have. For the poor devils who do make the passage keep quiet about it. You're all the same. You prance into my office and ask me to get you a divorce as you'd ask me to get you a dog license; and sooner or later you all open your innocent eyes and say, 'I'd no idea that it was all so difficult.' I'm fond of you, John, and I'm determined that you shall go into this business with your eyes wide open."

"They are," said Mr. Adam wearily.

"No, they're not. To begin with, there's a film of bogus chivalry over them. Does it occur to you that in order to behave like a gentleman to your present wife you propose to behave like a cad to your future wife? She is, I understand, a pure and sensitive young woman. You will not 'have relations' with her (another charming phrase, that) until you are married: such is her character that you couldn't if you would . . ."

"No."

"Quite. Yet you propose to go to this virtuous girl and say, 'Darling, take me to your arms. By means of an adulterous union with a strange woman I have obtained the right to woo you. The king's courts have certified that I am impure and our holy married life can now begin.' "

"Don't," groaned Mr. Adam. "It's ghastly."

"It's true."

"It can't be helped."

"Why not? What does it matter to you if the Seal fellow loses his job? Why should you worry about your wife? Nobody thinks twice about the divorce of a leading lady. Probably it will prolong the run of her play. They're in a hurry, and you, I gather, are not. Tell them you decline to behave like a gentleman. Put detectives on them and, if you get your evidence, divorce her."

"No," said John, and the chin came out. "You must understand," he went on shyly and slowly, "that, in spite of everything, the Mary part of my life still means a lot to me. I'm fond of her, I respect her; I couldn't hurt her, I couldn't spy on her; and as for detectives . . ." Mr. Adam's pale face expressed disgust.

"Very well," said Boom, with sympathy. "I might say that you were sacrificing the future to the past: but I don't. I understand. The position is, then, that you are determined to behave like a gentleman and commit adultery with a strange woman."

"Yes. How do I get one?"

Mr. Boom laughed deeply. "My dear fellow, this is Chancery Lane, not Jermyn Street. You mustn't ask your lawyer to provide you with a lover."

"But I don't understand . . ."

"At this point," said Boom, "I must remind you of my remarks about criminal conspiracy. The court does not approve of gentlemen who behave like gentlemen: it would be improper for me to provide you with a lady, and I am not sure that I ought, at this point, to give you advice. I can, however, throw out a few hints about the present practice. As a rule, the gentleman takes the lady to a hotel—Brighton or some such place—enters her in the books as his wife—shares a room with her, and sends the bill to his wife. The wife's agents cause inquiries to be made, and eventually they find the chambermaid who brought the guilty couple their morning tea. A single night used to be sufficient, but the president has been tightening things up, and we generally advise a good long week-end today. What you want to suggest, you see, is that there is a real and continuing attachment, not merely a casual fling or a put-up job. That is why Brighton is good, for all the wild lovers are supposed to go there, though I never saw anyone at the Capitol but clergymen and family parties. For the same reason it's better for the lady to be of your own class, or as near as possible. For, remember, you are supposed to have left a very attractive wife for love of the lady, and you must not put too much of a strain on the credulity of the court, though in an undefended suit the woman hardly ever appears. At one time her name didn't appear, but Hawkhurst has put a stop to that."

"Tell me," said Mr. Adam, hesitating, "do I actually have to–to–to–you know?"

"To sleep with the lady? Technically, no. But you must share the same room and you must be in the same bed in the morning, when the tea comes up."

"Good God!" said John. "What a world!"

"True," said Boom and slowly raised his great bulk from the chair. "Well, I must go back to the office."

"Half a minute. You haven't told me where to find the lady."

"Ah!" said Boom. "That's your affair. Good-bye, and good luck." He took a step up Chancery Lane and stopped. "I have heard," he said darkly, "that there are agents—and even agencies. Most improper."

"I'd no idea," said John, "That it was all so difficult."

"I warned you," said Boom, and he ambled away.

Fault-based divorce law continues to be important in a number of jurisdictions. You therefore need to know something more about fault grounds.

Adultery. Although the conduct constituting adultery seems self evident, its proof remains troublesome. For example, despite the old saying that adultery requires proof of "inclination and opportunity," the Virginia Supreme Court found adultery in one case where the behavior took place at the man's home but not in circumstances that were nearly identical except that the rendezvous was at the woman's home. Compare *Coe v. Coe*, 303 SE2d 923 (Va 1983)(adultery) with *Dooley v. Dooley*, 278 SE2d 865 (Va 1981)(no adultery). The other issue plaguing courts is the effect of adultery during the parties' separation. When the intercourse, even if proven, was clearly not the source of the parties' marital difficulties, *Smith v. Smith*, 378 S2d 11 (Fla App 1979), courts commonly award the divorce on no-fault grounds despite the adultery and allow a "guilty" wife alimony.

Cruelty. The prevalent view is that acts of cruelty are cumulative: Although repeated abuse may be forgiven, one last unforgiven act of violence makes them all relevant in the divorce hearing. This legal rule thus fits modern notions about patterns of spousal abuse, which tends to operate in cycles of violence and forgiveness, as we describe in Chapter 3. Spouses have frequently litigated about the degree and kind of cruelty required to establish a fault divorce. Although cruelty need not be physical, *Ringgold v. Ringgold*, 104 SE 836 (Va 1920), at least since no-fault divorces have been available courts have required far more than mere bickering and unpleasantness. See, e.g., *Fountain v. Fountain*, 644 S2d 733 (La App 1994). Cruelty must amount to conduct that makes staying in the marital home unreasonable and dangerous to the life or health of the spouse (or a minor child, according to W Va Code § 48–2–4(9) (1999). Cruelty frequently works in conjunction with the desertion ground, since it justifies leaving the marital home (i.e., is a defense to a claim of desertion) and can give the departing spouse a cause of action for "constructive desertion" as well. *Richardson v. Richardson*, 304 A2d 1 (Md App 1973).

Desertion. Desertion is usually defined as departure from the marital home without lawful excuse or justification and with the intent to remain permanently absent. Recent cases have considered the wife's right to remain in one locale when her husband moves. *Kerr v. Kerr*, 371 SE2d 30 (Va App 1988). Under the common law rule, her domicile was her husband's, so that in refusing to accompany him, she was the deserter. The modern rule is that if she has some reason for remaining in her present location, refusing to move alone does not constitute desertion.

Nonsupport. If a statute authorizes divorce for failure to support, it will apply equally to both spouses. Divorces under this claim are usually for egregious conduct by a spouse who can work and does not, or who can provide the basic necessities of life and fails to do so. *Griffin v. Griffin*, 42 S2d 720 (Miss 1949)(constructive desertion). Divorce is an alternative remedy to that sought in *McGuire v. McGuire*, 59 NW2d 336 (Neb 1953), which we will consider in Chapter 4, or to criminal remedies for failure to support.

Drunkenness or Addiction. Many states, e.g., Illinois, allow divorces on fault grounds for substance abuse that negates the essence of married life. Usually the condition cannot have been known prior to the marriage and cannot be shared by the complaining spouse. *Husband D. v. Wife D.*, 383 A2d 302 (Del Fam 1977). States usually require the plaintiff to have unsuccessfully attempted to get the addicted spouse to pursue treatment. See NJ Stat Ann § 2A:34–2(e) (1987).

Separation. This is the "no-fault" ground that has been added to traditional fault grounds in many states. The two issues that seem to be litigated *most* involve the intent to separate and the physical conditions of the separation. The statutory period does not begin to run unless at least one spouse intends to make the separation permanent for the statutory period. It does not begin, for instance, every time one spouse goes to war or leaves to further an education. *Sinha v. Sinha*, 526 A2d 765 (Pa 1987). The other question is whether the spouses may be separated for purposes of the statute when they still reside "under the same roof." States disagree. Compare *Flynn v. Flynn*, 491 A2d 156 (Pa

Super 1985)(allowed), with NJ Stat Ann § 2A:34–2(d) (1987) ("different habitations").

Restrictive divorce laws were buttressed by criminal and civil remedies for offenses against a marriage. Adultery was once widely a criminal offense: "A married person who has sexual intercourse with a person not his spouse or an unmarried person who has sexual intercourse with a married person shall be guilty of adultery and shall be punished by imprisonment in the state prison for not more than three years or in jail for not more than two years or by a fine of not more than five hundred dollars." Mass Gen Laws ch. 272 § 14 (1990). This statute's constitutionality was upheld in *Massachusetts v. Stowell*, 449 NE2d 357 (Mass 1983). Perhaps a quarter of the states formally retain such a statute.

There was also a civil remedy against someone who had alienated a spouse's affections: "The essential elements of a cause of action for alienation of affections are: (1) wrongful conduct of the defendant; (2) loss of affection or consortium; and (3) a causal connection between such conduct and loss.... The tort of criminal conversation allows one to maintain an action for damages if it is shown that his or her spouse committed adultery with the defendant; the only defenses to this cause of action are consent by the plaintiff or the statute of limitations." *Hunt v. Hunt*, 309 NW2d 818, 820 (S D 1981). Today, many states have legislatively or judicially abolished the cause of action for alienation of affections. Modern actions for alienation of affections are sometimes brought where the defendant had no sexual relations with the plaintiff's spouse. For example, *Bear v. Reformed Mennonite Church*, 341 A2d 105 (Pa 1975), involved a husband's suit against church elders for interfering with his family by requiring his wife and children to "shun" him. (The court held, "While the First Amendment may present a complete and valid defense to the allegations of the complaint, in the instant case, appellant has pleaded sufficient facts and created sufficient 'doubt' that would entitle him to proceed with his action in order that he may attempt to prove the requisite elements that would entitle him to relief....") *O'Neil v. Schuckardt*, 733 P2d 693 (Idaho 1986), concerned a suit for disrupting familial relations against various clergy and religious involved in the Fatima Crusade.

Until the mid–1960s, then, America could be said to have "fault-based" divorce. That is, divorce was an adversary proceeding in which one spouse alleged that the other had violated a marriage obligation in some serious way, usually adultery, desertion, or cruelty. By the mid–1970s, America could be said to have "no-fault" divorce. No-fault divorce meant that a spouse had only to allege, in some form, that the marriage had broken down. This change alone was striking, but it was accompanied by substantial changes in the law governing alimony, the division of marital property, and child custody. This transformation is yet more remarkable when one recalls that these changes could not be made nationally, but rather were the work of 50 state legislatures. No bureaucracy, no powerful interest group, made divorce reform its business. Indeed, the transformation of American divorce law occurred practically unnoticed. How, then, did it happen? We will describe Professor Herbert Jacob's explanation. His book, *A Silent Revolution: Routine Policy Making and the Transformation of Divorce Law in the United States* (U Chi Press, 1988), is well worth reading.

Part of the explanation for any change of such magnitude, Professor Jacob notes, lies in changes in society, and twentieth-century America had indeed been prolific of changes in family life. Longer life-spans and smaller families meant couples lived together longer, and lived together longer by themselves. Women entered the work force, not just before and after they had children, but while their children were young. Further, women had increasingly better-paying jobs. These economic changes both increased tensions within marriages and made it easier—economically, socially, and psychologically—for women to leave them. The revival of feminism in the early 1960s heightened these effects. Expectations of marriage—that it be intensely rewarding, that it be a partnership of equals—changed at the same time divorce came to seem less wrong and even less dysfunctional. These changes in social attitudes and structure were reflected in changing views about divorce laws themselves: In 1966, only 13 percent of the population believed divorce laws were too strict; in 1974, after no-fault divorce had become widely available, that figure had risen to one-third of the population.

Changing social facts, and even changing opinions about law, do not of their own force change law. What transmuted new attitudes toward divorce into new law? Professor Jacob suggests that the transformation began in New York. New York had long been notorious for having the most restrictive divorce law in the country; adultery was the only basis for divorce. New York was also notorious for having the most flouted divorce law in the country: the same kind of fraudulent adultery that was long the stuff of English novels and life (recall the excerpt from A.P. Herbert) was regularly confected in New York. The delicate-minded (and well-to-do) went to Reno instead, for Nevada had a short residency requirement. The gap between the law in books and the law in action distressed many of those who knew about it and particularly worried the lawyers and judges who collaborated in or countenanced the hypocrisy and perjury which made the system work.

The catalyst of divorce reform in New York was a public-relations man and law student who was a Democratic member of the New York legislature. Quite by chance, he came upon the issue and, hoping to gain attention and promote his career, took it as his own. He learned that divorce reform attracted little attention. But he did find an ally in an admiralty lawyer who was chairman of a special committee on family law of the elite Bar Association of the City of New York, which was concerned about the fraud that was so much a part of New York divorce law. The legislator and the lawyer went to Professor Henry Foster, of New York University Law School, a specialist in family law. Professor Foster drafted both a bill and a legislative committee's report on the bill, a report which spoke of fraud and public confidence.

In the legislature, the bill attracted bi-partisan support and little opposition, even from the Catholic Church. The Church's power had long been feared by New York reformers, but its political strength had been eroded and its attentions were directed to battles over abortion reform and parochial school aid. Legislators who disliked the bill because it made divorce easier were accorded an amendment providing for compulsory conciliation proceedings. The press ignored the bill. Thus, even though the Bar Association of the City of New York was the only interest group actively backing the bill, it became law in 1966. The reform was justified as improving the honesty of divorce proceedings, not as introducing no-fault divorce. But when, a few years later, the waiting period for divorce after separation was reduced to one year, it was widely said that no-fault divorce had come to New York.

While New York had had perhaps the most restrictive divorce law in the country, California had, at least in practice, one of the most liberal. Nevertheless, California's was a fault-based statute. In the early 1960s, a group of elite matrimonial lawyers from the San Francisco Bay area who felt that the law invited dishonesty and exacerbated hostility between divorcing spouses began to seek reforms. They were joined by a similar group from Los Angeles. They testified before a legislative committee to advocate reforms including no-fault divorce. In 1966, Governor Edmund Brown appointed a Commission on the Family which included members of both groups. Arguing that no-fault divorce was already effectively available, the Commission (in the most conservative of terms and tones) advocated eliminating fault grounds altogether as well as altering a number of other aspects of California's divorce law. In 1967, these proposals were in their essentials introduced into the legislature by a conservative Republican. As in New York, the bill was presented as primarily a technical and limited reform of the law, and it attracted little notice and little opposition. The bill passed and was signed into law by Governor Ronald Reagan.

The next stage of the transformation of divorce law involved the National Conference of Commissioners on Uniform State Laws. The NCCUSL was founded in 1892 as a quasi-public group of law professors, elite lawyers, and legislators and was funded by appropriations from the states and grants from private sources. It was intended to promote uniformity among the laws of the various states by proposing (in conjunction with the ABA) drafts of laws in areas in which uniform laws might be desirable. (The Uniform Commercial Code, of course, has probably been the NCCUSL's greatest success.) The NCCUSL had been interested in divorce law since its inception, and by the mid–1960s a group of elite divorce lawyers and law professors had convinced the Conference that the widespread dishonesty in divorce proceedings, the overly adversarial nature of divorce proceedings, and the great diversity of divorce standards among the states justified another try at formulating a uniform standard. Once again, in short, the problem was formulated by lawyers in relatively technical lawyer's terms.

Elite law reform organizations like the NCCUSL and the ALI usually operate through a committee staffed by a "reporter" who is commonly a law professor expert in the relevant field. In this case, the co-reporters were Professor Robert Levy, who was a family-law specialist at the University of Minnesota Law School, and Professor (later Dean) Herma Hill Kay, who taught family law at Boalt Hall (Berkeley's law school) and who had been active in the reform of California divorce law. The reporters drafted, and the committee and the Conference adopted, the Uniform Marriage and Divorce Act. The UMDA not only offered states a model no-fault divorce statute, it proposed an entire body of family law, one prominently including reforms of the law of marital property, alimony, and custody. Yet despite the UMDA's sweep, debate over it was primarily technical and ignored the many broad social issues which the UMDA implicated. Approval by the ABA's House of Delegates, while inhibited by institutional and personal conflicts, came in 1973, reasonably easily and again without discussion of the social issues which the statute ultimately dealt with.

The crucial portions of the UMDA's divorce provisions are:

UNIFORM MARRIAGE AND DIVORCE ACT

SECTION 302. *[Dissolution of Marriage; Legal Separation]*

(a) The [ ] court shall enter a decree of dissolution of marriage if:

(1) the court finds that one of the parties, at the time the action was commenced, was domiciled in this State, or was stationed in this State while a member of the armed services, and that the domicil or military presence has been maintained for 90 days next preceding the making of the findings;

(2) the court finds that the conciliation provisions of Section 305 either do not apply or have been met;

(3) the court finds that the marriage is irretrievably broken; and

(4) to the extent it has jurisdiction to do so, the court has considered, approved, or made provision for child custody, the support of any child of the marriage entitled to support, the maintenance of either spouse, and the disposition of property.

(b) If a party requests a decree of legal separation rather than a decree of dissolution of marriage, the court shall grant the decree in that form unless the other party objects.

SECTION 305. *[Irretrievable Breakdown]*

(a) If both of the parties by petition or otherwise have stated under oath or affirmation that the marriage is irretrievably broken, or one of the parties has so stated and the other has not denied it, the court, after hearing, shall make a finding whether the marriage is irretrievably broken.

(b) If one of the parties has denied under oath or affirmation that the marriage is irretrievably broken, the court shall consider all relevant factors, including the circumstances that gave rise to filing the petition and the prospect of reconciliation, and shall:

(1) make a finding whether the marriage is irretrievably broken; or

(2) continue the matter for further hearing not fewer than 30 nor more than 60 days later, or as soon thereafter as the matter may be reached on the court's calendar, and may suggest to the parties that they seek counselling. The court, at the request of either party shall, or on its own motion may, order a conciliation conference. At the adjourned hearing the court shall make a finding whether the marriage is irretrievably broken.

(c) A finding of irretrievable breakdown is a determination that there is no reasonable prospect of reconciliation.

It is hard to say how much influence the UMDA had and how much simply reflected the temper of the times. The endorsement of no-fault divorce by such respectable and conservative institutions certainly promoted a process of reform that had gathered considerable momentum: By 1974, 45 states had what could be described as no-fault divorce, and by 1985 every state had no-fault divorce grounds. This description of the extent of the change is somewhat misleading, however, since the definition of "no-fault" is somewhat uncertain. Pure no-fault statutes provide for divorce if the marriage has irretrievably broken down, but statutes permitting divorce after separation for a defined period are also often considered no-fault statutes. By the latter standard, some states had had no-fault divorce well before the 1960s.

Furthermore, 31 states retain fault grounds in addition to no-fault grounds for divorce. Linda S. Elrod and Timothy B. Walker, *Family Law in the Fifty States*, 27 Family L Q 515, 660 Table 4 (1994). In addition, marital fault is considered in awarding alimony in Florida, the District of Columbia, and Missouri, which have only no-fault grounds for divorce. Fault may also be an absolute bar to alimony in Louisiana, Virginia (if the fault is adultery) and South Carolina. Although the number of divorces actually granted on traditional fault grounds is quite small, fault is frequently used as a bargaining tool in these states. Marygold Melli et al, *The Process of Negotiation: An Exploratory Investigation in the Context of No–Fault Divorce*, 40 Rutg L Rev 1133 (1988).

The UMDA also contributed to the reform of the other significant components of divorce law: the laws of marital property, alimony, and child support. As you know, except in a few community property states, property had traditionally been divided according to who could be said to own it at the time of the divorce, a decision heavily influenced by the name in which the property was held. In the 1970s, this rule was increasingly abandoned in favor of systems more inclined to treat property as marital rather than individual, that explicitly recognized in economic terms non-financial contributions to a family's well-being, that required ignoring marital fault in allocating property, and that gave judges greater discretion to divide property "equitably." Alimony had, in principle, traditionally been available to wives innocent of marital fault until they remarried. This rule was increasingly abandoned in favor of rehabilitative alimony—alimony designed to help a spouse (whether maritally at fault or not) regain the ability to support himself or herself but unavailable after that ability had been attained. Finally, custody of children had traditionally gone to the mother. In the 1970s and '80s, the maternal presumption weakened and a trend toward various alternatives, including forms of joint custody, developed.

What, then, motivated this striking transformation of divorce law? First, it is worth noting two things that Professor Jacob argues did not affect it. The Roman Catholic Church, whose opposition to divorce was well established and well known, had, except in a few states, little influence on the legislative debates. Second, feminists had a somewhat greater impact, but their position on these issues was not then well developed, and there were feminists on both sides. Further, the women's movement was diverted from these issues by its involvement in other issues, like the ERA. Indeed, no interest group, to say nothing of any mass movement, was deeply committed to the reform of divorce law. Bar associations were involved in every state's reform effort, but not intensively: divorce law is a relatively low status kind of practice, and not all divorce lawyers favored no-fault divorce. Even the press widely ignored the reform. Because of the low visibility of divorce reform, it was not an issue which legislators could use to advance their careers.

So let us repeat the question. How was the transformation worked? The changes in social structure and social attitudes described above made the transformation certainly less controversial and perhaps plainly desirable. It was a reform that cost nothing and that gained in respectability and even appeal as more and more states adopted it. It was close to cost-free politically too, since the absence of publicity about it helped ensure the absence of opposition to it. In short, all these factors made it possible for a small number of reformers, often individuals, often lawyers with professional interests in divorce law, to work with a small number of legislators to achieve their goals. They succeeded because they did nothing to alter the factors we have just described: they carefully defined their proposals as conservative, incremental, and technical changes in the law and denied they were trying to deal with any significant social problems; they strove not to stir up interest group opposition and often worked assiduously to propitiate the likeliest powerful opponent, the Catholic Church; and they asserted their special expertise against the claims of laymen.

In sum, Professor Jacob argues, the transformation of American divorce law exemplifies "routine policy-making." Professor Jacob notes that we ordinarily think of policy as being made in a conflictual process in which aggressive interest groups contend fiercely. But legislatures could not accomplish all they need to if all policy were made in that fashion. In fact, much policy is made quite routinely: reforms are drawn narrowly and described as conservative, experts are prominently relied on, costs are kept low, and public attention is avoided.

Divorce reform exemplified routine policy-making, and its advocates did not intend to work great change. But whatever their intentions, their results were not trivial: The requirements for divorce were changed, the common-law principles for dividing property on divorce were widely abandoned, alimony became less available and available for shorter terms, and reforms in custody law made the practice of giving custody to the mother less automatic.

The story we have been telling about the reform of divorce law is, of course, unending. Its latest chapter came in May 2000, when the American Law Institute approved its project on the Principles of the Law of Family Dissolution. Although the Principles have not yet found their way into current legislation—except that the child custody standards already replace sections of the West Virginia Code (§ 48–11–206 (2000))—they reflect some currently influential views of family law and thus have generated considerable academic discussion, journal commentary, and legislative interest. We will discuss each of its principal provisions in detail in the appropriate Chapter. Here, we want to complete our brief history of divorce reform by giving you a sense of what the ALI project attempts.

The ALI Principles are ambitious and range even more broadly than the UMDA. They proffer rules for spousal support, marital property, alimony, premarital and post-marital agreements, domestic partnerships, child custody, visitation, and child support. Like the UMDA, the Principles reflect the views of several sectors of elite professional opinion. Since you will encounter the two sets of model provisions throughout this book, we pause here first to sketch the Principles and second to invite you to reflect on the differences between the UMDA and the Principles and on why the latter reject so much of the former.

Central among the UMDA's themes were eliminating fault, simplifying divorce, and promoting gender equality. The ALI pursues each of these. For example, the ALI seeks to eliminate fault (except for financial misconduct) from financial awards at divorce (in § 4.16 for property distribution, in § 5.02 for spousal support). This would change the law in at least half the states, but it is consistent with the trend set in the UMDA. The principles likewise generally eliminate "fault" (except for domestic violence) from child-custody decisions.

Perhaps less prominently, the ALI may be read as trying to simplify divorce. For instance, it repeatedly tries to eliminate judicial discretion, a move that might simplify divorce by making judicial rulings more predictable and by thus reducing the couple's bargaining over the terms of their divorce. The Principles at least intend to give spouses more freedom to decide for themselves what the terms of any divorce will be.

Finally, the ALI is entirely committed to a vision of gender equality. For example, its default rule in dividing marital property is equality. In addition, it seeks to recompense spouses for the losses they suffer from their contributions to the marriage, a proposal it expects to see most used by wives who have sacrificed their careers to care for their families. Further, the Principles try to keep mothers from being economically worse off than fathers after divorce by reforming the method used to establish child-support payments. Current child-support guidelines generally use the percentage of income spent on children in intact families as the standard for setting awards. The Principles' child support formulas initially attempt to ensure all concerned the same standard of living they would enjoy if the parents had equal incomes. As the Reporter's Comments to § 3.05, at page 29, suggest, "When parents have equal incomes before the payment of child support, neither should be better or worse off economically than the other after the assignment of custodial and support duties. Application of this principle also guarantees that, in such circumstances, the child will not suffer disproportionately at divorce, as compared to either parent."

On the other hand, there are thematic and specific differences between the UMDA and the ALI Principles. Not the least of these is the ALI's insistence on reducing the power of judges. This is accomplished in two ways. First, the Principles regularly invite couples to substitute their agreements for the law's rules. To put the point differently, the Principles prefer contract to status. (See § 7.02). The substantive Principles, then, are intended only as an alternative for whatever the cohabiting, married, or divorcing couple may agree to themselves. These contracts are to be examined with the judicial scrutiny given important agreements in the commercial setting and are not to be overturned if the parties had time to think about them, the guidance of independent counsel, and some knowledge of each other's assets and income (§ 7.05). Domestic partners, spouses, and divorcing parents will not, to be sure, have complete freedom, particularly when child support and child custody are concerned or when the agreement will work a substantial injustice (§ 7.07). They may not by agreement change their state's grounds for divorce, alter the law on the role of fault in allocating marital property or awarding spousal support, or penalize the party filing for divorce or legal separation (§ 7.12). Nevertheless, all these parties are to have a greater freedom of contract than the UMDA ever contemplated.

The second way the Principles reduce the power of judges is by limiting judicial discretion. The UMDA, you will discover, was prone to give judges generous swaths of authority and to guide judges only by listing numerous factors to guide decisions. The Principles instead write elaborate rules from which judges are not to stray. Indeed, one commentator writes, "Judicial discretion is largely eliminated." J. Thomas Oldham, *ALI Principles of Family Dissolution: Some Comments*, 1997 U Ill L Rev 801, 814.

The Principles' treatment of child custody (which the Principles call "allocation of custodial and decisionmaking responsibility for children") and child support illustrates both these techniques. The Principles prefer that parents work out custodial agreements of their own that give substantial responsibility and custodial time to both parents. (§ 2.07). And instead of rules that allow courts broad discretion to make decisions "in the best interests of the child" or that presume children will do best if parents have joint custody of them, the court is instructed to replicate as closely as possible the way the couple cared for their children before the divorce, § 2.09(a). (The court must, however, also try to ensure that even parents who were largely absent from their children's company during the marriage spend time with them after it.)

Having attempted to give couples a freer rein to negotiate, the Principles also try to reduce their incentives to bargain strategically. In particular, the Principles try to deter parents from claiming custody simply as a bargaining chip to use in negotiating for a better financial award. The Principles suppose that, since a judicial order would replicate the parties' pre-separation custody patterns, it would do a parent no good to suddenly claim an interest in the child.

We have been describing Professor Jacob's analysis of a rather technical process of legislative reform. But underlying that process were some imposing social changes, changes which have deeply affected American family life and family law. The following excerpt describes them.

JUNE CARBONE AND MARGARET F. BRINIG, RETHINKING MARRIAGE: FEMINIST IDEOLOGY, ECONOMIC CHANGE, AND DIVORCE REFORM

65 Tulane Law Review 953 (1991)

By the later part of the twentieth century, the nineteenth-century solution to the problems of early industrialization stood in the way of continued economic evolution. While nineteenth-century industrialism required more educated workers than did an agrarian society, the greatest demand was for the unskilled and semiskilled. The ideal of complementarity had encouraged middle-class men to make the investment in education and training necessary to fill the relatively few but important managerial positions in early capitalism, while persuading married middle-class women to stay out of the labor market. On the other hand, in the "postindustrial" economy that characterized post-war America, management-intensive light industry and service sector employment replaced heavy manufacturing and agriculture, increasing the demand for educated, literate, English-speaking workers. With middle-class men already fully employed, middle-class women provided the most readily available supply of new labor. At the same time, the traditional demands on women as wives and mothers were decreasing. With the decline in infant mortality, women had fewer children, and care of the home had long since ceased to require fresh baked bread, hand sewn clothing, and daily trips to the market. The "problem that has no name" that Betty Friedan described in *The Feminine Mystique*, the book that galvanized the women's movement in the early sixties, was the failure of the roles of wife and mother to continue to provide a satisfying lifetime occupation. With the increasing demand for women's services in the labor force and the decreasing need for women to devote themselves to a lifetime of domestic tasks, a reassignment of responsibilities was in order. Just as nineteenth-century men went from the relatively undifferentiated role of farmer and husband to a highly specialized division of labor, so would twentieth-century women experience an increasingly specialized division of labor.

The first impact that the modern women's movement had on gender roles was to supply an ideology facilitating the large-scale entry of married middle-class women into the labor market. "Liberal" feminists did so by emphasizing sameness. Drawing on the ideal of equality generated by the civil rights movement, mid-century feminists denied the existence of any significant differences between men and women. Observable differences were attributed to nurture, not nature. The new ideal of equality replaced the older ideal of complementarity, tearing down the distinctions between commercial and domestic, between male and female spheres of influence. Separate was now viewed as inherently unequal. "Liberated" women, freed from an ideology that defined them exclusively in terms of their domestic roles, were encouraged to become lawyers, electricians, and accountants. At the same time, the traditional domestic role, and those who continued to pursue it, were devalued.

Divorce reform has both contributed to this transformation, and been shaped by it. As Herma Hill Kay recently reminded us, the movement to eliminate fault as a prerequisite for divorce preceded the modern women's movement. Fault, typically defined in terms of adultery, desertion, or extreme cruelty, became untenable as the exclusive grounds justifying divorce when society no longer dictated that an unhappy couple stay together in order to advance a larger set of societal interests. By the time California enacted the first no-fault act in 1969, fault-based divorce had been obsolete for half a century. Most divorces were uncontested and were granted on the basis of perfunctory testimony of marital fault. The principle that divorce could proceed from the agreement of the parties was so well established that the major argument advanced for divorce reform was not an ideological one, but rather the practical need to "free the administration of justice ... from the hypocrisy and perjury that had resulted from the use of marital fault as a controlling consideration in divorce proceedings."

The success of the no-fault movement nonetheless had a major impact on women's participation in the labor market because, in both symbolic and practical terms, it remade the marital agreement. Until the mid-twentieth century, the marital bargain exchanged the wife's services for her husband's support. Once the exchange occurred, the wife's position became significantly weaker than her husband's. Her prospects for remarriage declined with age. Whatever employment opportunities she had at the beginning of the marriage were limited by years as a homemaker. Her husband, in contrast, retained the career and other financial investments that had generated the family income and, with his sources of income intact, enjoyed favorable prospects for remarriage. Because husbands and wives' positions were not symmetrical, enforcement of the husbands' lifelong promise of support was necessary to encourage wives to make the career sacrifices that guaranteed their economic dependence. With expanding economic opportunities for women, marriage, child-bearing, and the traditional domestic role would become less attractive without reaffirmation of the husband's marital promises.

The no-fault movement, however, rather than affirming the traditional marital bargain, rendered it unenforceable. The elimination of fault as a *prerequisite* for divorce left open the question of the financial allocations to be made upon divorce. Fault, redefined in terms of breach of marital obligations, might be irrelevant to the dissolution of the marriage but still be very important in the financial settlement; just as breach of a commercial contract, while insufficient to justify specific performance of a particular obligation, might still be a basis for damages. However, because the no-fault movement had emphasized the difficulties of determining fault rather than its irrelevance as a prerequisite for divorce, and because the courts had trivialized the fault determination rather than acknowledge its obsolescence, determinations of marital misconduct in any form had acquired a bad name. Many states, in enacting no-fault legislation, followed California's lead, abolishing fault as grounds for divorce *and* precluding any consideration of marital misconduct in the financial allocations to be made.

The effect, probably unintended, of precluding consideration of fault was to change marriage from a lifetime commitment whose obligations were enforced, albeit selectively, through a form of specific performance, to a contract terminable at will. Either party could end the marriage; the other had no ability to prevent termination. Most of the states to address the matter have ruled that the reasons why the marriage ended are irrelevant. The husband's promise of life-long support became meaningless; the new standard emphasized the parties' self-sufficiency. Upon divorce, the property was divided, and dependent spouses were given transitional awards intended to encourage their financial independence. Protection of the standard of living enjoyed during the marriage, though discussed in the case law, disappeared from practice. The result, as Lenore Weitzman documents, was a divorce system that left men financially better off and women worse off than they had been when they were married.

This divorce system complemented the message of liberal feminism. The nineteenth-century ideal of complementarity defined the wife's role in terms of domesticity. Marriage law protected her from the resulting financial dependence by making divorce difficult and by promising financial security to wives who upheld their end of the bargain. With dramatically rising divorce rates, modern women had no certainty that their marriages would last nor even the promise of financial protection in the event they did not. Young women in the mid-eighties, whether consciously "feminist" or not, agreed that they could no longer rely on marriage for their economic security. Young couples quickly began to view both spouses' incomes as essential to their economic well-being. The courts reinforced these conclusions by demanding that divorcing women, whatever their earlier expectations, however young their children, and however long their marriage, had to develop their own sources of income. By the beginning of the eighties, the separation of the commercial from the domestic and the definition of a wife's role exclusively in terms of domesticity were gone. Feminist theory led—and divorce reform pushed—even the married mothers of young children into the labor market.

This redefinition of roles, however, did not end with middle-class women joining their husbands in the single-minded pursuit of law firm partnerships. There was still the small matter of who was to take care of the children. The initial response appeared to be no one. As record numbers of women entered the labor force, middle-class women deferred marriage and child-bearing. American fertility rates reached a record low in 1976. Childrearing might no longer be a lifelong occupation, but it still interfered with medical residencies, mortgage payments, and geographic mobility. The new ideology provided no model for combining parenthood and profession. As Joan Williams recently observed, "[w]estern wage labor is premised on an ideal worker with no child care responsibilities."

The new feminism, or at least what Robin West calls "cultural feminism," tried to provide an answer. In 1982, Carol Gilligan published *In A Different Voice*. The book, a critique of empirical studies purporting to demonstrate that boys' moral development occurred earlier than girls', interpreted the differences in terms of differences between boys and girls' experience of the world. Gilligan concluded:

> [T]he standard of moral judgment that informs their [women's] assessment of self is a standard of relationship, an ethic of nurturance, responsibility, and care.... [M]orality is seen by these women as arising from the experience of connection and conceived as a problem of inclusion rather than one of balancing claims.

For men on the other hand, "the moral imperative appears rather as an injunction to respect the rights of others and thus to protect from interference the rights to life and self-fulfillment." Gilligan's celebration of difference, her claim that women contribute to a higher morality that cannot be measured by a model created by and for men, has been enormously influential, affecting feminist work in all areas of study.

Unsurprisingly, Gilligan tied her discussion of "difference" to the fact that women rear children and men do not. The "feminine" traits she celebrated are those connected with motherhood: nurturing, responsibility, and care. The literature Gilligan inspired calls for the use of feminist insights to transform virtually all areas of life and thought. It also suggests a re-evaluation of the domestic roles that liberal feminism encouraged women to devalue, if not abandon. Taken to its logical conclusion, the feminism of difference can be said to imply that women are more nurturing because they rear children; that because women are more nurturing, they value family and children more than their spouses do; because of those values, they are more likely to place the welfare of the family above their individual advancement; and that their subsequent choices to stay home with sick children, to choose more flexible jobs, and to interrupt their careers ought to be respected and protected.

While these conclusions may be controversial, Robin West has described Gilligan's book and the type of thinking it represents as "feminism's official story." We believe Gilligan's work has been so phenomenally influential because, once married middle-class women permanently entered the labor force, making the earlier ideology of domesticity obsolete, no model existed to reconcile the demands of home and the demands of the market. Women were working more, and middle-class women believed that they should be thinking in terms of careers as well as jobs. Yet, the first generation of middle-class women for whom full labor force participation was a possibility were having children and, as Joan Williams has observed, making choices that placed them at odds with the liberal feminist ideal of equality on male terms. The new feminism frees women from the need to succeed exclusively on those terms. It offers the hope of transforming the workplace to accommodate women's values as well as men's, and it justifies the choice of work and family, career and children, and the accommodations needed to permit both.

The rediscovery of motherhood as a defining component of women's lives and of the economic consequences of mothers' primary responsibility for the care of their children has led to a re-examination of the financial implications of no-fault divorce. In particular, Lenore Weitzman's empirical work has focused attention on the differential impact divorce has on men and women, and the disastrous consequences for the mothers of young children. The primary result has been a reconsideration of the bases for spousal support. The older justifications, which tied alimony to the husband's duty of support or to the divorce court's finding of fault, were gone. The new emphasis on transitional support designed to encourage financial independence failed to make adequate provision for women's contributions to childrearing. The emerging model, which we have elsewhere described as restitution based, justifies spousal support as compensation for the career sacrifices mothers make in the interests of their children or their husband's career.

The new divorce rules together with the new feminist ideal encourage women to choose both to stay within the labor force and to value childrearing above career pursuits. The new feminist ideal ridicules the very idea of separate spheres without eliminating differences in the assignment of responsibilities. Men and women are to perform the same jobs (postal worker, parent), but they need not perform them in the same way. In a parallel fashion, the new divorce rules discourage the traditional exchange of support for domestic services, while reaffirming the mother's primary responsibility for the care of the children and sanctioning career sacrifices, but only if temporary and if made on behalf of the children or the other spouse's career.

Translating these developments into the language of legal obligation, the marital contract is dead, not because it is indeterminate, but because society wishes to discourage rather than protect economic reliance on marriage. Restitution, at least on a selective basis, is alive and well because, while married middle-class women are to join their husbands in supplying the labor needs of the postindustrial economy, they are also to remain primarily responsible for the care of their children. Unresolved is the issue whether an as yet unrealized transformation of the workplace together with a symbolic, but financially inadequate, commitment to compensation for middle-class women's career sacrifices can adequately provide for either the workforce or the domestic needs of the future.

Notes and Questions on the Process of Law Reform

(1) Are you persuaded by Professor Jacob's explanation for this reform? What are its strengths? Its weaknesses? Is it complete without an understanding of the kind of factors described in the article by Professors Carbone and Brinig?

(2) In our federal system each state makes its own law of divorce. Yet no-fault divorce swept the country quickly. Why? In our modern society, should family law largely be the responsibility of the states? Do states any longer differ significantly? Are they in any sense "communities"?

(a) Professor Mary Ann Glendon argues that, in family law, "the American federal system has not operated as a laboratory in which various legal approaches could be tested in different states. On the contrary, opportunity for evasion of one state's marriage or divorce law by migration to another state has made it difficult for any one state to resist for long pressures for conformity to patterns of diminished regulation, once other states begin to move in that direction." *Abortion and Divorce in Western Law: American Failures, European Challenges* 105 (Harv U Press, 1987). How persuasive is this explanation of no-fault's rapid success?

(b) As Professor Glendon also argues, European countries moved toward no-fault divorce (although not as completely as the United States) about the same time as the United States. This suggests that something in an international *Zeitgeist* helped motivate the reform. What? Why did fault-based divorce come to seem undesirable and no-fault divorce desirable? With what social ideas and attitudes is each system of divorce associated?

(3) Professor Glendon argues that the American law of divorce "seems to have come about more by accident than design." She reports that in Europe, divorce reform is accomplished nationally, and reforms are carefully formulated by the central government and widely discussed by the public. In America, she says, "the practicing matrimonial bar has had much more influence on divorce law reform than it has had or sought in Western Europe. Often this influence has been direct and decisive, as when state legislatures have relied on the presumed expertise of family law sections of local bar associations to draft new legislation." As you know, Professor Jacob agrees that divorce reform in the United States occurred without central organization or widespread public debate and that lawyers had a leading part in it. Was this a good way for the reform to occur?

(a) Was divorce reform in fact a technical or professional question as to which lawyers had special expertise?

(b) Why was there relatively little public debate over no-fault divorce? Would the law of divorce look different had there been more public discussion? Are there defects in no-fault divorce which might have been avoided with more public debate?

C. EVALUATING THE CONTEMPORARY LAW OF DIVORCE

It is so far from being natural for a man and woman to live in a state of marriage that we find all the motives which they have for remaining in that connection, and the restraints which civilized society imposes to prevent separation, are hardly sufficient to keep them together.

Samuel Johnson
Letter to Sir Joshua Reynolds

Is no-fault divorce desirable? No one advocates returning to the old regime, but the present one has now attracted its critics. We will see what several of them have to say.

(1) Evaluating the Reform on Its Own Terms

As licentious as the world reputes me, I have (in good truth) more strictly observed the lawes of wedlock then either I had promised or hoped. It is no longer time to wince when one hath put on the shackles. A man ought wisely to husband his liberty, but after he hath once submitted himself into bondage, he is to stick unto it by the lawes of common duty, or at least enforce himselfe to keepe them. Those which undertake that covenant do deale therein with hate and contempt, do both injustly and incommodiously. If one do not alwaise discharge his duty, yet ought he at least ever love, ever acknowledge it. It is treason for one to marry unless he wed.

Michel de Montaigne
On Some Verses of Virgil

One of the most direct criticisms of no-fault divorce on its own terms is Lynn Wardle's *No-Fault Divorce and the Divorce Conundrum*, 1991 BYU L Rev 79. Professor Wardle argues that "no-fault grounds for divorce have failed substantially to achieve the main purposes for which they were enacted" and that their adoption has "been accompanied by increased rates of divorce, and by significant inequities in the economic consequences of divorce...." Professor Wardle examines four goals of no-fault divorce and asks whether each has been reached.

Reducing the Acrimony of Divorce. Professor Wardle says that, "while there unquestionably is less hostile litigation regarding the grounds for divorce under no-fault laws than there was under fault grounds, it appears that this has been due primarily to a transfer of hostility into other facets of the divorce proceeding [rather] than to any substantial reduction in the proceeding overall." In other words, he suggests that while couples no longer can fight as much over who is responsible for the marriage's failure, they instead fight over alimony, property, and custody. Thus he cites one study which concluded that since the adoption of no-fault divorce 53 percent of the surveyed matrimonial lawyers believed the number of custody disputes had increased and 44 percent believed the bitterness of custody disputes had increased. (Most of the remaining lawyers believed the frequency and bitterness of such disputes had remained the same.)

Professor Wardle says no-fault conveys the "valuable message ... that it is not *necessary* to formally and publicly charge fault (blame) for marital failure." But he thinks it "unrealistic not to expect some (many) divorcing human beings to look for outlets to express the hurt they feel upon rejection, to seek some formal expression of acquittal, support or revenge." He sees "one of the powerful functions of the courts" as providing "a means for the peaceful expression of such powerful feelings of vindication and retribution." He concludes, "It should come as no surprise that the closing of one door to judicial vindication and retribution in divorce has only led to the breaking open of others."

Reducing Perjury. Professor Wardle finds that no-fault divorce has reduced perjury as to the grounds of divorce. But he argues that instead "a significant credibility gap has developed between the notion of real judicial inquiry into whether a marriage is '*irretrievably* broken' or whether differences are '*irreconcilable*' and what occurs in typical no-fault divorce cases in actual practice." And he sees "indications that the adoption of no-fault grounds for divorce has only caused the lying to shift (as did the hostility) from the part of the proceeding dealing with the grounds for divorce to the collateral aspects, especially child custody and visitation disputes." In particular, he argues that "the practice of one parent falsely accusing the other parent of child abuse, especially child sexual abuse, appears to have increased since the adoption of no-fault divorce grounds."

Conforming the Law in Action to the Law in Practice. Professor Wardle notes that a central avowed purpose of no-fault divorce was to conform the law in action to the law in practice. But, he writes, "[r]ather than merely conforming the statutory law to divorce practice whereby no-fault divorce could be obtained (but did not have to be) by mutual consent (never unilaterally), the no-fault divorce reforms generally have introduced nonconsensual, unilateral no-fault divorce, and in forty percent of the states, no other method of marriage termination is permitted."

Conforming the Law to Current Ideas about Marriage and Privacy. Professor Wardle agrees that "reformers were correct when they asserted that ... the requirement that 'fault' be publicly charged and proven in every case in which divorce is sought no longer reflects modern ideas about marriage or marital failure." However, he recruits the arguments we have been reviewing in this chapter as evidence that fault is still important to the thinking of many spouses about divorce and thus that it cannot easily be eliminated from the law of divorce.

Professor Wardle also argues that the kind of privacy which modern divorce law has come to promote is not the kind that the reformers originally argued for: "The type of privacy that was asserted was the privacy of couples who had worked out their own differences and were seeking divorce mutually (or without any contest) not to have to publicly charge and prove the details of marital misconduct." However, today divorce is available on the demand of just one party. Thus a "more radical notion of individualistic privacy has supplanted [the] mutual privacy principle."

In any event, "the adoption of no-fault grounds has led to more, not less, public intrusion into individual and family privacy in regard to marriage termination." This is because, since the adoption of those grounds, "there is not only more litigation regarding collateral matters (such as custody and finances) at the time of divorce, but there also is significantly more follow-up litigation" in which "divorced parties are returning to court demanding further judicial scrutiny of the remaining vestiges of a previously terminated marriage."

The Unanticipated Consequences of No–Fault Divorce. First, like a number of other scholars, Professor Wardle argues that no-fault divorce has disadvantaged women, particularly custodial mothers. Since we will be discussing this argument below, we will not rehearse Professor Wardle's arguments on this score. Second, Professor Wardle notes that the "conventional wisdom is that the adoption of no-fault grounds for divorce have not caused divorce rates to increase." However, he cites a study which demonstrated a "real and significant causal relationship between adoption of no-fault and divorce rates in most states."

The Three Dilemmas of the Divorce Conundrum. Professor Wardle also believes that no-fault divorce deals badly with the conflicts posed by the "three dimensions of the divorce conundrum." He writes, "The first dilemma of the divorce conundrum arises from the need to balance two different policy goals: to alleviate the dislocation and suffering caused by marital failure by making the divorce process easier, and to promote marital stability and prevent or repair marital disruption." He suggests that "[n]o-fault divorce laws substantially further the divorce facilitation policy and significantly impair the marriage stability policy," since they make divorce easy to obtain.

The second dimension of the divorce conundrum is that divorce requires the law to deal simultaneously with "two different notions of fairness: fairness for the divorcing parties and their children, and fairness for spouses in ongoing marriages and their children. . . ." The heart of the difficulty here is that equality of the spouses is the standard we use to settle disputes when the parties are divorcing but that love is the standard we want parties to use during the marriage. "The problem with the language of equality is that it encourages thinking about a fragile, living relationship in terms that do not fairly characterize it until it is dead." In other words, "An accounting mentality, so essential to fairness-as-equality, can canker marital relationships that are striving for fairness-as-love."

The third dimension of the divorce conundrum is that there is a "tension between the public and private (or privacy) interests in divorce." Divorce is not simply a matter between consenting adults. It often involves spouses who don't want to be divorced and children who have no say in the matter at all. Yet spouses and children alike may be seriously harmed by divorce. And divorce injures more than just the members of the divorcing family. Like the costs of any widespread social problem, the costs of divorce are borne by all society.

The Expressive Consequences of No–Fault Divorce. Professor Wardle has one final criticism of no-fault divorce laws. It is that they promote a view of marriage that is defective in three ways. First, by making divorce available on demand, those laws promote the view that marriage is not a permanent commitment. This is in fact not the view of marriage most people have, nor is it the view that will best promote strong marriages, since people who take that view will be unlikely to devote the effort needed to make marriages work.

Second, no-fault laws, by making divorce available on demand, foster the illusion that divorce can be inconsequential and painless. In fact, though, the social and psychological processes and sequelae of divorce are painful to the spouses and their children, however much the legal processes of divorce are minimized.

Third, no-fault laws, by making divorce so readily available, disserve the people who seek divorce because they may not want to end their marriages. Rather they may be groping for help improving their marriages.

What Next? Professor Wardle intended to criticize the existing law of divorce rather than to propose an alternative. Are the criticisms fair? Many of them are based on the argument that no-fault divorce has not accomplished its purposes. Has it nevertheless accomplished other desirable goals which it did not set out to accomplish? Assuming the criticisms are correct, what alternatives to the existing law might meet them? What defects do those alternatives themselves have? Are the alternatives on balance preferable to the present law?

(2) Evaluating the Reform in Terms of Its Effects

The science of constructing a commonwealth, or renovating it, or reforming it, is, like every other experimental science, not to be taught a priori. Nor is it a short experience that can instruct us in that practical science, because the real effects of moral causes are not always immediate; but that which in the first instance is prejudicial may be excellent in its remoter operation, and its excellence may arise even from the ill effects it produces in the beginning. The reverse also happens: and very plausible schemes, with very pleasing commencements, have often shameful and lamentable conclusions.

Edmund Burke
Reflections on the Revolution in France

A particularly influential survey of the new law's effects has been Lenore Weitzman's *The Divorce Revolution: The Unexpected Social and Economic Consequences for Women and Children in America* (Free Press, 1985). Professor Weitzman argues that the new laws generally disserved women by reducing the sense that marriage is for life, by depriving wives of the bargaining chip fault-based divorce often gave them, and by ending the advantages the innocent wife had under no-fault divorce. She also contends that the currently popular "rehabilitative" alimony lasted less long than traditional alimony and that it often failed of its rehabilitative purpose. Finally, she notes that the weakening of the presumption that mothers get custody gave fathers a new bargaining chip.

Professor Weitzman thus argues that the net effect of no-fault divorce has been to weaken the position of wives in divorce negotiations and litigation. That weakened position is particularly grave given Professor Weitzman's dramatic conclusion that, a year after divorce, men's standard of living rises 42%, while women's falls 73%. In short, she writes that the "major economic result of the divorce law revolution is the systematic impoverishment of divorced women and their children."

Professor Weitzman's work has been widely attacked. Some of the most effective attacks have been on her description of the degree (although, crucially, not the direction) of differences in men's and women's living standards after divorce. One study, for example, concluded that "Weitzman's highly publicized findings are almost certainly in error.... Corrected estimates suggest a decline in [women's] economic status of about one-third, rather than the widely cited 73 percent figure." Saul D. Hoffman and Greg J. Duncan, *What Are the Economic Consequences of Divorce?*, 25 Demography 641, 644 (1988).

Professor Weitzman's conclusion that no-fault divorce has worsened women's situation has also been criticized. Professor Herbert Jacob's data, for example, indicate that any difference that no-fault divorce has made is slight and is in women's favor. Professor Marsha Garrison suggests that while the economic situation of divorced women may have worsened in the years since the no-fault reform, there is little evidence linking that change to no-fault divorce itself. *The Economics of Divorce: Changing Rules, Changing Results*, in Stephen D. Sugarman and Herma Hill Kay, eds, *Divorce Reform at the Crossroads* 75 (Yale U Press, 1990). She observes that, as a logical matter, it is not clear that fault-based divorce uniformly benefitted women, since it disadvantaged women who had committed a marital "fault." She notes that no-fault divorce proliferated at a time when attitudes and laws toward the family and women were widely changing. She concludes that any change during that period in the economic status of divorced women had to do with changes in the law specifically regulating the granting of alimony and the division of the spouses' property, not with no-fault divorce.

(3) Considering Alternatives to No–Fault Divorce: The European Model

> *Marriage is the beginning and the pinnacle of all culture. It makes the savage gentle, and it gives the most cultivated the best occasion for demonstrating his gentleness. It has to be indissoluble: it brings so much happiness that individual instances of unhappiness do not come into account. And why speak of unhappiness at all? Impatience is what it really is, ever and again people are overcome by impatience, and then they like to think themselves unhappy. Let the moment pass, and you will count yourself happy that what has so long stood firm still stands.... Marriage may sometimes be an uncomfortable state, I can well believe that, and that is as it should be. Are we not also married to our conscience, and would we not often like to be rid of it because it is more uncomfortable than a husband or a wife could ever be.*
>
> Johann von Goethe
> *Elective Affinities*

In *Abortion and Divorce in Western Law: American Failures, European Challenges* (Harv U Press, 1987), Professor Mary Ann Glendon has criticized American no-fault divorce by contrasting it with parallel reforms in European divorce law. She concludes that "most American states have gone further than any country except Sweden in making marriage freely terminable, but that the United States has lagged behind several other nations to which we often compare ourselves in dealing with the economic aspects of marriage dissolution." She describes the modal European statute as embodying a compromise in which no-fault grounds are simply added to existing fault grounds. Those grounds are "hedged in" by waiting periods as long as several years in many countries. Several of these statutes "have provisions granting courts the power to deny a unilateral nonfault divorce altogether if legal dissolution of the marriage would involve exceptional unfairness or hardship for a nonconsenting spouse who has committed no marital offense." Generally, these clauses are not used to prevent a divorce.

Professor Glendon suggests that these statutes may be hard to justify theoretically but that they "officially maintained the idea of marriage as an enduring relationship involving reciprocal rights and obligations. In the absence of mutual consent, this relationship could be terminated only when one spouse seriously breached his or her marital duties, or when the marriage had ceased to function over a long period of time."

(4) Considering Alternatives to No–Fault Divorce: The "Pre-commitment" Model

> *People often say that marriage is an important thing, and should be much thought of in advance, and marrying people are cautioned that there are many who marry in haste and repent at leisure. I am not sure, however, that marriage may not be pondered over too much; nor do I feel certain that the leisurely repentance does not as often follow the leisurely marriage as it does the rapid ones. That some repent no one can doubt; but I am inclined to believe that most men and women take their lots as they find them, marrying as the birds do by force of nature, and going on with their mates with a general, though not perhaps an undisturbed satisfaction, feeling inwardly assured that Providence, if it has not done the very best for them, has done for them as well as they could do for themselves with all the thought in the world. I do not know that a woman can assure to herself, by her own prudence and taste, a good husband any more than she can add two cubits to her stature; but husbands have been made to be decently good,—and wives too, for the most part, in our country,—so that the thing does not require quite so much thinking as some people say.*
>
> Anthony Trollope
> *Can You Forgive Her?*

Earlier in this section, we read David Hume's remark that "the heart of many naturally submits to necessity, and soon loses an inclination, when there appears an absolute impossibility of gratifying it." Legislators who are dismayed by high divorce rates have hoped that Hume was right and have searched for ways of making divorce more difficult in a society in which no-fault divorce triumphed. Legislatively, the most successful solution has been "covenant marriage." Beginning in the late 1990s, first Louisiana and then Arizona and Arkansas enacted statutes giving engaged couples two choices of marriage regimes. La Civ Code Art 9, §§ 102 et seq (enacted 1997); Ariz Rev Stat §§ 25–901 et seq (enacted 1998); Ark Code §§ 9–11–801 et seq. (enacted 2001). The first regime is the regime now conventional in the United States. The second is covenant marriage. In *Covenant and Contract*, 12 Regent U L Rev 9, 10–11 (1999), Margaret Brinig and Steven Nock spell out the difference between covenant and conventional marriage and divorce legislation this way:

> The covenant option specifically acknowledges that marriage is a lifelong commitment and, as enacted in Louisiana, differs from conventional marriage in a number of additional ways:

- Covenant marriage requires premarital counseling. Counseling must include discussions of the seriousness of marriage, the life-long commitment being made by the couple to their marriage, the obligation to seek marital counseling if problems arise later in the marriage, and the exclusive grounds for divorce or legal separation in a covenant marriage. Couples must sign an affidavit acknowledging their commitment and prove that they have received counseling on these issues.
- Likewise, divorce from a covenant marriage requires the couple to have sought marriage counseling and to have made a good-faith effort to resolve their differences.
- Although a no-fault divorce is still possible for covenant marriages, the new law requires that the couple live separate and apart for two years (vs. six months under the current marriage regime) or be legally separated for eighteen months.
- Dissolving a covenant marriage in less than two years requires one person to prove fault on the part of the other. Acceptable "faults" are the traditional ones: felony conviction, abuse, abandonment, or adultery. Irreconcilable differences, general incompatibility, irretrievable breakdown of the marriage, or "we just don't get along any more" are not acceptable grounds for divorce, so if these are the problem, then [the spouses] have to wait the full two years.
- Newly marrying couples must choose either the covenant or the standard regime. It is not true that the law requires new marriages to be covenants or abolishes the standard regime (a point about which there has been some confusion).
- And finally, the law allows currently married couples to convert (or as proponents prefer, "upgrade") to covenants.

The rationale for devices like covenant marriage is most fully explored in Elizabeth S. Scott, *Rational Decisionmaking About Marriage and Divorce*, 76 Va L Rev 9 (1990). Professor Scott criticizes the American law of no-fault divorce on two grounds. First, she suggests that, where divorce is too readily obtainable, people may seek a divorce which, on a longer view, they would not want:

> Divorce law distorts contemporary norms by failing to recognize that although many people aspire to self-fulfillment in marriage, their short-term and long-term goals may conflict. Ready dissolution of the currently unsatisfactory relationship may not promote self-realization over time. Further, the law's rejection of some characteristics of traditional marriage such as commitment, responsibility, and mutual dependence may have been precipitous. These qualities may be important in modern marriage, not as ends in themselves, but because the contribute to an exchange that promotes long-term personal fulfillment.

Second, Professor Scott argues that the American law of divorce allows couples who ought to stay married for the sake of their children to divorce too easily. She finds "little support in the extensive body of empirical research on divorce" for the "somewhat reassuring assumption" that "if either parent is sufficiently dissatisfied with the marriage to contemplate divorce, then children may be more harmed by the continuation of the unhappy marriage than by divorce." She summarizes that research this way:

> There is substantial evidence that the process of going through their parents' divorce and the resulting changes in their lives are psychologically costly for most children. At a minimum, divorce involves significant stress and upheaval. The adjustment of most children is disrupted substantially for a year or two after divorce; for some the disruption continues to exert a harmful influence for many years. The child usually has less contact with one parent, and sometimes with both, particularly if the primary caretaker goes to work for the first time. In the early years of a divorce, both parents tend to function poorly at a time when the child may especially need care and stability. Divorce may result in important changes in children's lives; children must often leave the family home, neighborhood, friends, and school. In many divorced families, reduced income results in significant economic deprivation.
>
> Social scientists have attempted to measure the effect of divorce on children by examining different indicators of adjustment. By almost any measure divorce appears to be harmful to children. Compared to children in intact families, and controlling for other variables associated with divorce, children of divorce exhibited more delinquent and antisocial behavior, used more mental health services, and performed worse in school. Both boys and girls tend to differ somewhat from children in intact families in sex role behavior.
>
> For one group of children, the assumption that divorce promotes their welfare may be valid. These are children whose parents engage in intense conflict with each other during marriage that is greatly alleviated by the divorce. Exposure to high levels of interparental conflict is associated with poor adjustment among children. There is evidence that children in single-parent homes with a low level of conflict experience better adjustment than children in intact families with a high level of conflict. There is no evidence, however, that divorce promotes children's adjustment if the conflict continues or if the level of open conflict in the intact family is moderate—despite the fact that one or both parents may be dissatisfied with the marriage. If the child is not confronted regularly with the parents' anger and hostility toward each other, then the continuity and stability of an intact family may promote better adjustment. It is plausible that, unless conflict escalates, "staying married for the sake of the children" may indeed be better for the children in many families.

In response to these considerations, Professor Scott introduces the idea of "[p]recommitment strategies [which] represent a conscious attempt to reduce one's future options because subsequent preferences may be impulsive or contrary to one's long-term interests." She suggests that "for many persons, marriage (and remaining married) represent 'rational' decisions that take into account long-term interests, and divorce results from choices that reflect short-term preferences." However, "[w]ithdrawal, boredom, pursuit of other relationships, immersion in career, and conflict over finances, children, and other family may all weaken the resolve to sustain a lasting relationship and may ultimately lead to marital breakdown." Recognizing this possibility, then, couples may make precommitments "to reinforce the objective of a stable, lasting marriage." These precommitments operate "as safeguards against overvaluation of the alternatives [to marriage] or exaggeration of the costs of marital dissatisfaction."

Precommitment strategies work in three ways. First, they may directly make divorce less attractive, either by attaching a penalty to it or by making the process unattractive. Second, by making marriage harder to leave and thus convincing couples they should make the best of their marriage, precommitment strategies may improve the quality of marriages. Third, by making marriage harder to leave, they may encourage people to think more carefully about marrying in the first place.

Professor Scott notes that

> fault-based divorce law, although inadequate in many ways, served a little noticed precommitment function that has been inadvertently sacrificed in the effort to modernize legal norms. Leaving a marriage was not easy under traditional law. It is plausible that even as the religious and moral basis for lifelong marriage weakened, legal barriers may have continued subtly to reinforce personal attitudes that marriage was a lasting relationship, attitudes that may have promoted cooperative behavior....
>
> The traditional scheme failed, not because it erected barriers to divorce, but because of the nature and scope of the barriers.... The restrictions were excessive because they impeded all divorces.... The restrictions under traditional law were inadequate in scope in that many unhappy spouses could largely avoid their impact by collusion between spouses, or by migratory divorce [that is, by temporarily establishing residence in a jurisdiction with liberal divorce laws]. The limits imposed on divorce by the fault regime were also normatively unsatisfactory, premised as they were on moralistic prescriptions for lifelong marriage, to be set aside only for grave offense by one spouse against the other. Finally, the fault grounds themselves offered a simplistic picture of marital breakdown that was inconsistent with contemporary understanding.

Professor Scott observes that precommitment strategies could either be made available to all spouses who wished to use them or could be mandatorily imposed. Voluntary precommitment strategies would be legally implemented by enforcing contracts in which those strategies were used. Such contracts might state economic sanctions for divorce. These could include "provisions for a stipulated level of child or spousal support, a designated division of property, or a direct fine, to benefit the children or the spouse who wants to continue in the marriage." These contracts might also require "an extensive period of delay [at least two years] before final divorce." Because of the difficulties inherent in marital contracting (which we will discuss in Chapter 5), Professor Scott suggests that standard-form contracts be provided.

Professor Scott also sees attractions in a mandatory scheme of precommitment strategies:

> A mandatory precommitment scheme potentially avoids many of the costs of a pure contractarian regime. Legislatively announced precommitments presumably reflect a socially defined consensus about appropriate barriers to divorce under different circumstances.... Legislatures can avoid the romantic distortion of persons actually entering marriage; the rules would likely reflect greater realism about human limitations in following life plans. Finally, legislative precommitments express societal aspirations for marriage and family through mechanisms that may influence behavior and attitudes more effectively than a permissive policy. A precommitment rationale supports mandatory rules creating premarital and predivorce waiting periods, rigorous support obligations and enforcement, required mediation or counselling, and family property trusts.

Professor Scott argues that it would take only a small change in the law to enforce contracts containing precommitment strategies. She would make precommitment strategies mandatory only to divorces involving minor children. More specifically:

> First, and most importantly, parents of minor children could be subject to substantial mandatory delay periods to promote more thoughtful divorce decisions and to make divorce less attractive. Thus, a two-year separation could be the only ground for divorce for this group. Parents could be bound to more substantial support obligations than currently and to property distribution schemes that are beneficial to children. Counselling, mediation, and mental health evaluation of the children might be required before divorce is permitted.

Steven L. Nock, of the University of Virginia department of Sociology, has been studying covenant marriage in Louisiana under a grant from the National Science Foundation. In the years since covenant marriage became an option, only two to three percent of Louisiana couples has elected the covenant regime. Many of the court clerks who dispense marriage licenses either do not know about the option or are hostile to it. Graduated Students posing as engaged couples have visited half the parishes (counties) in Louisiana. In more than half of the parishes, the students were not told of the covenant-marriage option, and in ten parishes they found "standard" marriage already chosen for them on the application form. See Steven Nock et al., *Covenant Marriage Turns Five Years Old*, 10 Mich J Gender & L 169 (2003). More recently, the team has focused on the qualitative differences between covenant and standard marriage. Although covenant marriage couples are on average more religious, better educated, and wealthier on entering marriage than their "standard" marriage counterparts, husbands and wives (and particularly husbands) change more during the early years of covenant marriage than the other couples. Nock and his coauthors report the husbands are more involved with children, less likely to be involved in (self-or spouse-reported) domestic violence, and more likely to be sexually happy. Not surprisingly, these couples also report a much smaller rate of divorce than the "standard" couples. Steven L. Nock et al, Intimate Equity. The Early Years of Covenant and Standard Marriages, Bowling Green University Working paper, No. 2003–04, available at http://www.bgsu.edu/organizations/cfdr/research/pdf/2003/2003_04.pdf.

(5) Considering Alternatives to No–Fault Divorce: The Tort Model

The last five years have seen an increase in arguments for and even legislative activity toward reintroducing fault into the divorce system. (One site that collects these proposals is *http://www.divorcereform.org.*) Some of its advocates hope that doing so will help discourage divorce by making it harder to obtain and by inducing couples to think more carefully about whether their marriage has become intolerable. Others believe that people who marry really do commit themselves for life and ought not be relieved of their promise without extraordinary reason. Still others believe that a fair result in divorce actions cannot be achieved unless fault is taken into account. When husbands and wives divorce, the court sets many of the basic terms of their social and economic relations. Some proponents of fault argue that courts cannot do this justly unless they take at least the most serious wrongs the husband and wife have done each other into account. As we have seen, there were substantial reasons for making divorce available even in the presence of fault. Thus some proponents of fault propose to continue to allow divorce on demand but to permit divorcing spouses to bring tort actions for particularly egregious marital wrongs as part of the divorce litigation.

This proposal raises several basic issues. First, should spouses *ever* be able to sue each other in tort? Historically, spouses were immune from tort suits against each other. This immunity came to be defended with

> a number of public policy arguments: a) Such suits disturb the harmony of the marital relationship. b) They involve the courts in trivial disputes between the spouses. c) They encourage fraud and collusion between spouses where the conduct constituting the tort is covered by insurance.... d) The criminal law provides an adequate remedy. e) The divorce law provides an adequate remedy. f) Such suits reward the defendant for his own wrong, since if the parties are living together, they both share in the benefits of any judgment. g) A further consideration not often mentioned in judicial opinions but perhaps in the minds of some judges is that it appears broadly inconsistent with family solidarity, or unseemly, to have husbands and wives suing each other.

Homer H. Clark, Jr., 1 *The Law of Domestic Relations in the United States* 632 (West, 1987).

Today, however, "[i]nterspousal immunity has been totally routed and is no longer the law in any state." Robert G. Spector, *Marital Torts: The Current Legal Landscape,* 33 Family L Q 745, 746 (1999). It has, however, been routed only in the sense that every state permits *some* kind of interspousal tort suits. As Professor Spector observes, "One of the startling aspects of these cases is that they have not produced a revision in doctrine to define where the limits of tort law occur in a spousal context. Courts usually articulate the notion that every act that is tortious between strangers should not necessarily be tortious between spouses." Professor Spector reports that "most interspousal tort suits today involve situations where one spouse has battered the other. All authorities agree that cases where one spouse has been the victim of physical violence clearly state a claim in tort." But courts are much less receptive to suits for other kinds of torts. They particularly stress the disruptive effect such cases will have on "marital harmony" when there is still a chance the couple can work things out. In some states, even though an abused spouse can bring an action, it will only be in cases of "extreme and outrageous" misbehavior that leaves no shred of marital harmony left to preserve. (These considerations closely resemble concerns about the "heartbalm" actions we will discuss in Chapter 6.) This leads us, then, to the second question raised by the proposal to allow divorcing spouses to sue each other in tort—*which* torts should be actionable in that context?

The third question the proposal raises is this: assuming interspousal tort suits are permissible, should they be entertained as part of a divorce action? The American Law Institute, in its Principles of Marital Dissolution, P.F.D. Part I (1997), found "no reason to duplicate the battery law" by incorporating it into the law of divorce. The Reporter for the Principles has written a number of articles suggesting use of the tort system to air this kind of problem. See, e.g., Ira Mark Ellman, *The Misguided Movement to Revive Fault Divorce, and Why Reformers Should Look Instead to the American Law Institute*, 11 Intl JL & Policy & Fam 216 (1997). On the other hand, during the Institute's meetings in 1998, a number of feminist speakers objected to the removal of consideration of spousal violence from property and support considerations (as well as custody, where it still does play a role). See 24 Fam L Rptr 1383, 1384 (1998). The Institute in the end voted to make property and support determinations take place "without consideration of marital fault," even family violence, and severely restricted considerations of moral issues even in custody proceedings.

At this point, we need to evaluate the use of the tort system as a response to marital fault by looking at the case law: Here are three representative cases.

DOE v. DOE

Court of Appeals of Maryland, 2000
747 A2d 617

ELDRIDGE, Judge.

The issue presented in this case is whether Maryland law recognizes tort actions filed by a husband against his wife for fraud and intentional infliction of emotional distress when the actions are based upon the wife's alleged adultery and subsequent misrepresentation of the paternity of children born during the marriage.

I.

Jane Doe, the petitioner, and John Doe, the respondent, were married on September 2, 1989. During their marriage, three children were born: J.D. Doe, born February 21, 1992, and the twins A.E. and Z.S. Doe, born July 10, 1993. Unbeknownst to Mr. Doe, beginning in 1990 Ms. Doe had been sexually involved with her art professor, M.G. Mr. Doe did not learn about the affair until July 1996, when he discovered a letter written by Ms. Doe to M.G., which stated, in part:

> "It remains my belief that at some point in the course [of] our relationship I disappointed you deeply, and that this is ... responsible for bringing about the distance which has complicated our interactions during the past few years. The commencement of this change seems to roughly correlate with the birth of our children.... You will always be the father of my children.... The divulging of their identities will be at your discretion."

After reading the letter and confirming his suspicions in a telephone conversation with M.G., Mr. Doe confronted Ms. Doe who denied the allegations. The next day, July 12, 1996, Mr. Doe filed in the Circuit Court for Baltimore County a complaint for absolute divorce. The complaint alleged that Ms. Doe had committed adultery, and requested that Mr. Doe be awarded custody of the children, child support, use and possession of the family home, a monetary award, and counsel fees.

After filing the divorce action, Mr. Doe inquired as to whether he was, in fact, the father of the three children. Ms. Doe had always acted as though Mr. Doe fathered the children, including having his name placed on their birth certificates. Mr. Doe alleged that he never questioned the paternity of the children until he found Ms. Doe's letter. Both parties agreed that they and the children would submit to blood testing in order to determine paternity. The results of the tests disclosed that Mr. Doe was the biological father of J.D., but that he was not the biological father of the twins.

Upon receiving the blood test results, Mr. Doe filed an amended complaint for absolute divorce and "other causes of action" in December 1996. In addition to the original count seeking divorce, custody, child support, and relief related thereto, counts II and III of the amended complaint sought damages for fraud and intentional infliction of emotional distress resulting from Ms. Doe's alleged adultery and misrepresentation of the paternity of the children....

Upon Mr. Doe's appeal, the Court of Special Appeals affirmed the dismissal of counts IV through VIII but reversed the dismissal of counts II and III. The intermediate appellate court held that neither the doctrine of interspousal immunity nor public policy barred Mr. Doe's causes of action for fraud and intentional infliction of emotional distress.... [T]he Court of Special Appeals in the present case took the position that this Court in *Lusby v. Lusby*, 283 Md. 334, 390 A.2d 77 (1978), had abolished the defense of interspousal immunity with respect to all intentional tort actions....

II.

Preliminarily, we shall address the scope of this Court's opinion in *Lusby* and the Court of Special Appeals' interpretation of the *Lusby* opinion.

Prior to *Lusby*, the doctrine of interspousal immunity in tort cases was clearly recognized as part of the common law of this State. This Court stated many years ago: "Maryland w[ould] not entertain a suit by one spouse against the other for his or her tort, committed during the marital status."

In *Lusby*, Ms. Lusby brought a tort action for damages against her husband. She alleged that while she was driving, her husband and two accomplices in another vehicle forced her to the side of the road at gunpoint. Her husband then "forcefully and violently" raped her and thereafter assisted the accomplices in attempting to rape her. After reviewing the cases cited above, this Court held that there was nothing in the common law of this State preventing a wife from recovering damages from her husband for the type of outrageous, intentional conduct there involved. Judge Marvin Smith for the Court set forth the Court's holding as follows:

> We find nothing in our prior cases or elsewhere to indicate that under the common law of Maryland a wife was not permitted to recover from her husband in tort when she alleged and proved the type of outrageous, intentional conduct here alleged.

The exception to interspousal immunity applied in *Lusby*, therefore, was explicitly confined to "outrageous" intentional torts. The limited scope of the *Lusby* holding was underscored by this Court's view that nothing in our prior cases, applying interspousal immunity, precluded recovery for the outrageous conduct of the defendant. In *Boblitz v. Boblitz*, 296 Md. 242, 273, 462 A.2d 506, 521 (1983), where the Court did change the common law by abrogating interspousal immunity in negligence cases, we reiterated the limited nature of the *Lusby* holding with regard to intentional torts....

The Court of Special Appeals' interpretation of the *Lusby* opinion in *Bender* and in the present case was erroneous. The holding in *Linton* that *Lusby* did not abrogate interspousal immunity as to all intentional torts, is correct. As discussed above, in *Lusby* this Court held that, under the common law of this State, interspousal immunity had never been applied where the conduct alleged was "outrageous" and intentional.

The respondent alternatively argues that the conduct alleged in the case at bar is sufficiently "outrageous" to fit within this Court's limited holding in *Lusby*. For the reasons set forth below, however, we need not reach this issue.

III.

A claim of immunity is a defense. It need be reached only if the plaintiff has alleged a viable cause of action. We shall hold that the actions pled by Mr. Doe in counts II and III are not viable. In those counts, Mr. Doe seeks to recover damages, under different tort labels, for the same type of conduct which formerly gave rise to the common law cause of action known as criminal conversation. That cause of action was designed to provide a remedy for husbands in Mr. Doe's situation. The action, however, has been abolished in this State on constitutional and public policy grounds. See *Kline v. Ansell*, 287 Md. 585, 414 A.2d 929 (1980).

As this Court discussed in *Kline* with regard to the tort of criminal conversation, "the underlying basis of recovery was the injury to the husband's feelings and particularly to his sense of his own and his family's honor." The particular harms sought to be remedied were the " 'defilement of the marriage bed,' " and a man's right " 'to beget his own children.' " In fact, as Blackstone pointed out, the damages recoverable under the common law action, which were "usually very large and exemplary," were often dependent upon "the husband's obligation by settlement or otherwise to provide for those children, which he [could not] but suspect to be spurious." . . .

Under earlier Anglo–Saxon law, inheritance, as well as social standing, was largely dependent upon the "lawful issue of pure blood." . . . Dean Prosser summarized the rationale of the action when he said that "the real basis of recovery clearly is the defilement of the marriage bed, the blow to family honor, and the suspicion cast upon the legitimacy of the offspring." Prosser, Law of Torts § 124, p. 875 (4th ed.1971).

At the time when the tort of criminal conversation first evolved, the possibility of children as a consequence of adultery was even more likely than it is today, considering modern developments in birth control and the growth in scientific knowledge concerning conception. In addition, husbands were unable to determine actual paternity unless they could rule out their own. The tort action of criminal conversation was the remedy provided under the law for these problems. The husband was awarded monetary damages to compensate him for his emotional, as well as financial, injuries, especially when children were involved. Although the birth of children and the corresponding possible misrepresentation of their paternity were not necessary elements of the tort, they were clearly among the injuries for which damages could be recovered. The common law criminal conversation cause of action envisioned the exact conduct, and the same injuries, as those alleged in the case at bar. . . .

As previously discussed, the common law criminal conversation action was available only to men. As a result, in *Kline*, this Court was faced with the choice of expanding the cause of action to women so that the tort would not violate the ERA, or abolishing it in its entirety for violating the ERA. Based upon public policy grounds similar to those cited by the General Assembly in abolishing the actions for alienation of affections and breach of promise to marry, this Court chose to abolish the action for criminal conversation.

Mr. Doe's causes of action asserted in counts II and III differ from the tort of criminal conversation in that the defendant in this case is his wife rather than her paramour. The paramour was the named defendant under the common law criminal conversation action, not because the wife was deemed a non-tortfeasor, but because a married woman could not sue or be sued by anyone without having her husband joined in the action. Regardless of whether Mr. Doe is suing Ms. Doe or her paramour, his asserted causes of action are based on the same conduct that formerly gave rise to a criminal conversation action, and he seeks damages for the same injuries recognized in a criminal conversation action. Consequently, the identical public policy considerations, which led to the abolition of criminal conversation, are applicable here....

If we were to allow Mr. Doe's alleged causes of action in counts II and III, the tort of criminal conversation would be revived through "artful pleading." This Court decided twenty years ago that public policy would not allow tort damages based upon adultery. That decision should not be ignored simply because the plaintiff has employed different labels and named a different defendant.

HAKKILA v. HAKKILA

Court of Appeals of New Mexico, 1991
812 P2d 1320

HARTZ, Judge.

In response to the petition of E. Arnold Hakkila (husband) for dissolution of marriage, Peggy J. Hakkila (wife) counter-petitioned for damages arising from alleged intentional infliction of emotional distress. Husband appeals from the judgment entered against him on the tort claim and from the award of attorney's fees in the divorce proceeding. We reverse the damage award and remand for further proceedings with respect to the award of attorney's fees.

I. FACTS

Husband and wife were married on October 29, 1975. Each had been married before. They permanently separated in February 1985. Husband filed his petition for dissolution of marriage the following month. Husband, who holds a Ph.D. in chemistry, had been employed at Los Alamos National Laboratory throughout the marriage. Wife, a high school graduate with credit hours toward a baccalaureate degree in chemistry and a vocational degree as a chemical technician, had been employed at the laboratory as a secretary for seven years and as a chemical technician for about seven and one-half years. She voluntarily terminated her employment in December 1979.

The district court found that "[wife's] emotional and mental health, especially since the parties' separation, has been shown to have been characterized by acute depression and one psychotic episode." The district court's findings noted conflicting testimony concerning wife's past and current mental condition. The district court summarized one psychologist's testimony as diagnosing wife "as subject to a borderline personality disorder pre-dating the parties' marriage," and summarized another's as diagnosing her as "an intellectualizing personality in the early years of her marriage and as suffering from acute depression since approximately 1981." Apparently all the experts agreed that wife was temporarily emotionally disabled at the time of the hearing. . . .

With respect to each of the matters listed by the district court in Finding No. 22, the record shows:

a. There was evidence of several incidents of assault and battery. In late 1984 when wife was pushing her finger in husband's chest, he grabbed her wrist and twisted it severely. In 1981 during an argument in their home husband grabbed wife and threw her face down across the room, into a pot full of dirt. In 1978 when wife was putting groceries in the camper, husband slammed part of the camper shell down on her head and the trunk lid on her hands. In 1976 and "sometimes thereafter" during consensual sexual intercourse husband would use excessive force in attempting to stimulate wife with his hands.

b. The one incident in which husband insulted wife in the presence of others was at a friend's Christmas party. At about 11:00 p.m. wife approached husband, who was "weaving back and forth with his hands in his pockets," and suggested that they go home. Husband began screaming, "You f______ bitch, leave me alone." Wife excused herself and walked home alone.

c. Wife also testified that when she and husband were home alone he would go into rages and scream at her. There was no evidence of his screaming at her in the presence of others except for the incident described in "b."

d. The locking-out incident occurred after husband returned from a trip. Wife had been at a friend's home where she had eaten dinner and had some wine. During an argument that had ensued when he returned, she grabbed his shirt and popped all the buttons off. She went downstairs and stepped outside. He closed and locked the door. She went across the street to a home of neighbors, who let her in. He then threw his clothes into a camper and drove off for the night. When he returned the next morning, they made up and made love.

e. On several occasions husband told wife that "you prefer women to men." He did not use the word "lesbian." He testified that he meant only that wife preferred the company of other women to his company. She did not testify that his remarks had sexual connotations.

f. Throughout the marriage husband made remarks such as, "You're just plain sick, you're just stupid, you're just insane."

g. With respect to the finding that husband "refused to allow [wife] to pursue schooling and hobbies," husband's brief-in-chief contends that no evidence supports the finding. Wife's answer brief does not respond to the contention, so we will not consider that finding as support for the judgment.

h., i. With respect to the final two items in the finding, husband acknowledges that their sexual relationship atrophied and that wife testified that (1) it was his decision not to engage in sexual relations more frequently, and (2) he blamed her for their poor sexual relationship.

II. SHOULD WE RECOGNIZE THE TORT OF INTENTIONAL INFLICTION OF EMOTIONAL DISTRESS IN THE MARITAL CONTEXT?

A. Introduction

Husband argues that as a matter of public policy one spouse should have no cause of action against the other spouse for intentional infliction of emotional distress. Wife responds that husband's argument is foreclosed in this court by the New Mexico Supreme Court's recognition of the tort.

We reject, at least for the time being, husband's suggestion. Nevertheless, the policy grounds opposing recognition of the tort in this context counsel caution in permitting lawsuits of this nature.

B. Supreme Court Precedents Do Not Resolve the Matter . . .

Wife contends that we must recognize the tort when committed by one spouse against the other because New Mexico has abandoned immunity for interspousal torts. Yet the abolition of immunity does not mean that the existence of the marriage must be ignored in determining the scope of liability. After explaining the reasons for abolition of interspousal immunity, the commentary to Restatement Section 895F points out:

> The intimacy of the family relationship may . . . involve some relaxation in the application of the concept of reasonable care, particularly in the confines of the home. Thus, if one spouse in undressing leaves shoes out where the other stumbles over them in the dark, or if one spouse spills coffee on the other while they are both still sleepy, this may well be treated as not negligence.

Id., comment h. The comment refers to Section 895G comment k, which explains that despite abolition of parental immunity:

> The intimacies of family life also involve intended physical contacts that would be actionable between strangers but may be commonplace and expected within the family. Family romping, even roughhouse play and momentary flares of temper not producing serious hurt, may be normal in many households, to the point that the privilege arising from consent becomes analogous.

Thus, the family relationship can be an important consideration in analyzing intrafamilial torts, both negligent and intentional. Despite the abolition of interspousal immunity, we must still evaluate wife's claims in light of the marital context in which they arose. Cf. Restatement § 46(2) (liability for outrage when conduct is directed at third person may depend on family relationship of plaintiff and third person).

C. Limitations on Liability for Intentional Infliction of Emotional Distress

To appreciate the importance of the marital context to the tort of outrage, one must examine the policy considerations underlying restrictions on the scope of the tort. Perhaps the most striking aspect of the tort is that liability does not flow from every act that intends to cause, and does cause, emotional distress. One restriction on the tort is the limitation that the conduct be "extreme and outrageous." Why this limitation? Why should not anyone who "intentionally or recklessly causes severe emotional distress to another" be subject to liability?

Several explanations have been offered. As Professor Magruder stated, "[I]t would be unfortunate if the law closed all the safety valves through which irascible tempers might legally blow off steam." Magruder, Mental and Emotional Disturbance in the Law of Torts, 49 Harv. L.Rev. 1033, 1053 (1936). Courts must recognize that we are not yet as civilized as we might wish. Many, if not all, of us need some freedom to vent emotions in order to maintain our mental health. The law should not require a degree of civility beyond our capacity. Indeed, it has been suggested that because of pervasive incivility in our society, judicial resources would be taxed if a cause of action were permitted for every intentional infliction of emotional distress. Givelber, The Right to Minimum Social Decency and the Limits of Evenhandedness: Intentional Infliction of Emotional Distress by Outrageous Conduct, 82 Colum.L.Rev. 42, 57 (1982) ("Givelber").

Intentionally making another person unhappy or upset may also serve useful purposes besides simply preserving the mental health of the perpetrator. As Professor Givelber notes, such conduct may be "justified either in pursuit of one's legal rights (e.g., debt collection) or in service of a greater social good (e.g., cross-examination at trial) or for the [recipient's] 'own good' (e.g., basic training)."

An additional reason for restricting the scope of the tort is that there may be a protected liberty interest in conduct that would otherwise be tortious. As Dean Prosser wrote, "There is still, in this country, such a thing as liberty to express an unflattering opinion of another, however wounding it may be to his feelings * * * *" Prosser, Insult and Outrage, 44 Cal.L.Rev. 40, 44 (1956) ("Prosser"). Similarly, the interest in personal autonomy apparently has led courts to reject a cause of action when a person intentionally causes emotional distress by engaging in an extramarital relationship. . . .

Finally, the requirement that the conduct be extreme and outrageous provides reliable confirmation of two other elements of the tort—injury and causation—thereby reducing the possibility of unfounded, or even fraudulent, lawsuits. When conduct is extreme and outrageous, it is more likely that the victim has actually suffered severe emotional distress, and it is more likely that the severe emotional distress suffered by the victim was actually caused by the perpetrator's misconduct rather than by another source.

D. Application of the Tort to Interspousal Conduct

Considerations that justify limiting liability for intentional infliction of emotional distress to only outrageous conduct also suggest a very limited scope for the tort in the marital context.

Conduct intentionally or recklessly causing emotional distress to one's spouse is prevalent in our society. This is unfortunate but perhaps not surprising, given the length and intensity of the marital relationship. Yet even when the conduct of feuding spouses is not particularly unusual, high emotions can readily cause an offended spouse to view the other's misconduct as "extreme and outrageous." Thus, if the tort of outrage is construed loosely or broadly, claims of outrage may be tacked on in typical marital disputes, taxing judicial resources.

In addition, a spouse's most distressing conduct is likely to be privileged. Partners who are pledged to live together for a lifetime have a right to criticize each other's behavior. Even though one may question the utility of such comments, spouses are also free to express negative opinions of one another. "You look awful" or even "I don't love you" can be very wounding, but these statements cannot justify liability. See Restatement § 46 illustration 13 (you look "like a hippopotamus").

Not only should intramarital activity ordinarily not be the basis for tort liability, it should also be protected against disclosure in tort litigation. Although the spouse who raises a claim of outrage has no right to complain of the exposure of matters relevant to the claim, courts must be sensitive to the privacy interests of the defending spouse. Any litigation of a claim is certain to require exposure of the intimacies of married life. This feature of the tort distinguishes it from intramarital torts already recognized in New Mexico. For example, a suit by one spouse against another arising out of an automobile accident poses no such risk. Nor does one ordinarily think of exposure of an incident of battery as implicating legitimate privacy interests. In contrast, in this case the judge found that it was extreme and outrageous conduct for husband to refuse sexual relations with wife. Should we really use this tort as a basis for inquiry into a matter of such intimacy? In determining the scope of the tort of outrage in the marital context, it is necessary to consider the privacy interests of the accused spouse.

Moreover, largely because so much interspousal communication is privileged (not in the evidentiary sense, but in the sense that it cannot be the basis for liability), a reliable determination of causation is difficult if not impossible when outrage is alleged in this context. The connection between the outrageousness of the conduct of one spouse and the severe emotional distress of the other will likely be obscure. Although the victim spouse may well be suffering severe emotional distress, was it caused by the outrageousness of the conduct or by the implied (and privileged) message of antipathy? What could be more devastating to one's spouse than to say, "I don't love you any more"—a statement that could not form the basis for a cause of action? Rejection alone can create severe emotional distress. Suicides by jilted lovers are legion. Every adult knows individuals who have sunk into disabling depression when a spouse seeks divorce. As a result, litigation of an interspousal claim of outrage could easily degenerate into a battle of self-proclaimed experts performing psychological autopsies to "discover" whether the cause of the emotional distress was some particular despicable conduct or simply rejection by a loved one. Of course, no such problem arises in the context of previously recognized intramarital torts. If one spouse commits battery on another or causes an accident by driving negligently, the injuries to the other spouse can readily be tied to the tortious conduct.

In summary, concerns that necessitate limiting the tort of intentional infliction of emotional distress to "extreme and outrageous" conduct—(1) preventing burdensome litigation of the commonplace, (2) protecting privileged conduct and (3) avoiding groundless allegations of causation—argue strongly in favor of extreme care in recognizing intramarital claims of outrage.

A cautious approach to the tort of intramarital outrage also finds support in the public policy of New Mexico to avoid inquiry into what went wrong in a marriage. New Mexico was the first state to provide for no-fault divorce on the ground of incompatibility. New Mexico apportions community property without regard to fault, and grants alimony without consideration of punishment to either spouse.

In addition, although the tort has not been formally abolished, our courts have expressed dissatisfaction with the tort of alienation of affection, which has features similar to the tort of outrage in the marital context.

E. Conclusion

Consequently, in determining when the tort of outrage should be recognized in the marital setting, the threshold of outrageousness should be set high enough—or the circumstances in which the tort is recognized should be described precisely enough, e.g., child snatching—the social good from recognizing the tort will not be outweighed by unseemly and invasive litigation of meritless claims.

Some jurisdictions have apparently set the threshold of outrageousness so high in the marital context as to bar all suits.

Thus far, however, New Mexico has not witnessed an onslaught of claims of outrage by one spouse against the other. There is no need at this time to adopt husband's recommendation that all such claims be barred.

III. DID WIFE PROVE OUTRAGE?

We now move to the specifics of the case before us. The merits of wife's claim can be disposed of summarily. Husband's insults and outbursts fail to meet the legal standard of outrageousness. He was privileged to refrain from intercourse. There was no evidence that the other conduct caused severe emotional distress, as opposed to transient pain or discomfort.

Indeed, this case illustrates the risk of opening the door too wide to claims of this nature. Despite the claim's lack of merit, husband was subjected to a six-day trial, to say nothing of discovery and other preparation, surveying the rights and wrongs of a ten-year marriage. Motions for summary judgment should be viewed sympathetically in similar cases. If the potential harms from this kind of litigation are too frequently realized, it may be necessary to reconsider husband's suggestion that the tort of outrage be denied in the interspousal context....

DONNELLY, Judge (specially concurring).

I concur in the result of the foregoing opinion confirming that under New Mexico precedent an interspousal claim of outrage or intentional infliction of emotional distress is actionable, that the evidence presented by wife in support of her tort claim did not meet the threshold requirement for such claim, and that the award of attorney's fees should be remanded for redetermination. I write separately because I believe a different analysis is required to evaluate wife's claim of intentional infliction of emotional distress in a marital setting.

This case raises a troublesome issue of first impression. Husband argues on appeal that public policy considerations should preclude a spouse from initiating a cause of action for intentional infliction of emotional distress predicated upon conduct arising during the marriage of the parties and from raising the tort claim in the divorce proceeding.

Following husband's initiation of divorce proceedings, wife counterclaimed for divorce on the ground of cruel and inhuman treatment and joined in her counterclaim a claim seeking recovery of damages against husband for intentional infliction of emotional distress based upon conduct alleged to have occurred during the marriage of the parties. Following trial, the trial court granted the divorce, finding that the parties were incompatible, awarded wife alimony in the amount of $1,050.00 per month until further order of the court, and also awarded wife monetary damages resulting from husband's intentional infliction of emotional distress.

> The damage award to wife on her tort claim provided that she should recover $5,000.00 in medical expenses, and the residence of the parties [having a market value of $136,000] free and clear from any interest of [husband's one-half community property interest] and any [existing] mortgage encumbrances, for lost wages for the past, present, and future and for past, present, and future physical and mental pain and suffering.

Decisions of both our supreme court and this court have recognized the actionability of the tort of intentional infliction of emotional distress. No New Mexico appellate decision, however, has directly considered the issue of whether a spouse can join a tort claim for intentional infliction of emotional distress with an action for dissolution of marriage. Other states which have considered this issue have reached diverse results....

The facts in this case, however, illustrate the problems confronting the trial court when a tort claim for intentional infliction of emotional distress is joined and tried together with an action for dissolution of marriage. The problems are compounded where a jury trial is demanded in the trial of the tort claim and where the action for dissolution of marriage also involves a claim of alimony. Here, the trial court granted an award of alimony to the wife, based upon a finding that she was in need of $1,050.00 per month to meet her economic needs. The alimony award appears to duplicate in part the compensatory damage award granted to wife on her claim of intentional infliction of emotional distress. The damages arising from wife's tort claim were awarded by the court based upon her "loss of possibility of gainful employment past, present, and future, and for her medical and psychological expenses past, present, and future." In addition to the general damage award rendered to wife incident to her tort claim, the trial court also awarded her special future medical damages in the sum of $5,000.00, and, among other things, damages to wife for her loss of earnings during the marriage. The earnings of a spouse during marriage, however, are presumptively community property. Thus, this portion of the damage award to wife conflicts with the marital property award....

MASSEY v. MASSEY

Court of Appeals of Texas, 1991
807 SW2d 391

STEPHENS, Justice.

On August 8, 1989, following a trial and jury verdict, the trial court signed its final decree of divorce and judgment, dissolving the 22–year marriage of Henry P. Massey and Gayle Scott Massey and dividing their community estate. In six points of error, Henry Massey appeals from those portions of the judgment dividing the parties' community property and awarding Gayle Massey monetary damages and attorneys' fees....

The Tort Claim

We first consider appellant's point of error six, particularly his contention that, absent a finding of physical injury, a cause of action for infliction of emotional distress may not be asserted in a divorce suit or, alternatively, if such a cause of action does exist, that the trial court's failure to grant his motion for severance and a separate trial of Gayle Massey's tort suit was reversible error.

Appellant contends that, without proof of physical injury, Texas does not recognize a cause of action for the intentional or negligent infliction of emotional distress in a suit for divorce .....

Our conclusions, after reviewing the history of the tort of intentional and negligent infliction of emotional distress, significantly differ from those of the court in *Chiles*. After a careful study of *Chiles* and related supreme court authority, we find that the tort of infliction of emotional distress, without physical injury, is recognized as a separate cause of action in Texas and that the status of that cause of action in the area of family law is unclear....

[I]n Price v. Price, 732 S.W.2d 316 (Tex.1987), the court re-examined the doctrine of interspousal immunity, which mandates that one spouse cannot sue another for negligent conduct, and unequivocally abolished the doctrine "as to any cause of action." ...

After rejecting the historical basis for the doctrine of interspousal immunity, that is, the fiction that husband and wife were one person, the *Price* court concluded that there was no longer:

> any policy justification for retaining this feudal concept of the rights of parties to a marriage.... It is difficult to fathom how denying a forum for the redress of any wrong could be said to encourage domestic tranquility. It is equally difficult to see how suits based in tort would destroy domestic tranquility, while property and contract actions do not ...

To determine whether the supreme court specifically intended that the doctrine be abolished in the context of suits for divorce, we need only read on:

> The doctrine of interspousal immunity has previously been abrogated as to some causes of action in this jurisdiction. We now abolish that doctrine completely as to any cause of action. We do not limit our holding to suits involving vehicular accidents only, as has been done by some jurisdictions and as has been urged upon us in this case. To do so would be to negate meritorious claims such as was presented in *Stafford v. Stafford*, 726 S.W.2d 14 (Tex.1987). In that case a husband had transmitted a venereal disease to his wife.... While we ruled for her, the issue of interspousal immunity had not been preserved for our review. To leave in place a bar to suits like that of Mrs. Stafford or other suits involving non-vehicular torts would amount to a repudiation of the constitutional guarantee of equal protection of the laws.
>
> Our result today is compelled by the fundamental proposition of public policy that the courts should afford redress for a wrong, and the failure of the rationale supporting the doctrine [of interspousal immunity] to withstand scrutiny.

Price, 732 S.W.2d at 319–20....

We hold that the tort of intentional or negligent infliction of emotional distress is an established cause of action that does not require proof of physical injury. The equally clear mandate of the supreme court in *Price v. Price* further confirms that a cause of action for infliction of emotional distress may be brought by one spouse against the other. A selective requirement of physical injury in family law cases which does not exist in any other area of the law would be discriminatory, denying equal protection to persons because of their status as partners in a marriage relationship.

Severance

We next address appellant's alternative argument that, if a cause of action does exist for infliction of emotional distress without physical injury, it may not be joined with a suit for divorce. Appellant contends that the trial court erred in failing to grant a separate trial on Gayle Massey's tort claim and that he was prejudiced thereby.

A plaintiff in his or her claim may join as independent claims any or as many claims, either legal or equitable or both, as he or she may have against the opposing party. Courts favor avoiding a multiplicity of suits and encourage resolution in one suit of all matters existing between the parties. Procedural matters such as joinder of parties and consolidation of claims are within the discretion of the trial court and will not be disturbed except for an abuse of discretion.

Gayle Massey's divorce and tort suits involved the same facts and parties. The court unquestionably had jurisdiction to consider the divorce action. The amount in controversy gave the trial court jurisdiction over the tort claim. Therefore, under rule 51(a) and absent an express prohibition, the cases could properly be tried together. We do not find that the trial court abused its discretion in failing to grant severance.

Appellant claims, however, that the denial of his motion for severance amounted to reversible error because it caused him prejudice. He believes the trial of the combined issues led to a double recovery by the wife who was awarded both a monetary judgment on her tort claim and an unequal portion of the community estate. This argument ignores the unique and separate roles played by the judge and jury in this divorce case.

While the jury may place a value on certain property, such as its valuation in this case of the Columbus State Bank stock, the division of property in a divorce action is exclusively within the province of the trial judge, not the jury. The trial court is charged with the responsibility of and granted wide discretion in dividing the community estate in a manner that he deems just and right, having due regard for the rights of each party and any children of the marriage.

The trial judge may order an unequal division of marital property where a reasonable basis exists for doing so. We will correct the trial court's division of marital property only when an abuse of discretion has been shown. Furthermore, it is the duty of the appellate court to indulge every reasonable presumption in favor of the proper exercise of discretion by the trial court in dividing the community estate.

The court may consider many factors in making an unequal division of property. These include education, respective earning power, business and employment opportunities, physical health, probable future need for support, the award of custody, the size of the parties' separate estates, the length of the marriage and fault in its breakup. While evidence of fault may be presented, the court is not obligated to consider it in dividing the marital estate.

There is no basis in this record for appellant's assumption that the court divided the property on the basis of fault. After the jury had returned its verdict, the court held a separate hearing on the division of property and the amount of child support, after which it entered its judgment dividing the parties' estate. The judgment recites the factors considered by the trial court in its division of the property. Fault is not among them. The court, being cognizant of the jury's separate award of damages for emotional distress, divided the community estate without consideration of fault. The award to the wife does not represent a double recovery. Therefore, we conclude that appellant was not prejudiced by the combined trial of the divorce and tort suits.

Next we consider appellant's complaint, also raised in point of error six, that the jury's findings that Henry negligently and intentionally inflicted emotional distress upon Gayle are contrary to the evidence. We treat a point of error so phrased as a challenge to the factual sufficiency of the evidence which requires us to review the evidence in its entirety.

The elements of the tort of negligent or intentional infliction of emotional distress are that (1) the defendant acted intentionally or recklessly; (2) the conduct of the defendant was extreme and outrageous; (3) the actions of the defendant caused the plaintiff emotional distress; and (4) the emotional distress suffered by the plaintiff was severe.

At trial, Gayle testified that, over the term of their marriage, Henry was abusive, explosive, and rageful. He constantly engaged in verbal abuse such as criticism and blaming, and he belittled her in front of her children. He had temper tantrums and physical outbursts which sometimes involved the destruction of property. Although he stopped short of physically assaulting her, Gayle testified that Henry's physical outbursts caused her to experience intense anxiety and fear.

Gayle and several of her witnesses recounted Henry's tight control over money and his threats that Gayle would be penniless if she divorced him. He doled out small sums of cash—$20 at a time—to Gayle for groceries; he would not let her write checks on their supposedly joint account; and when once she wrote a check in an emergency, he exploded and told her to never again come into the bank (where he was president); he bought her clothes for her and became enraged when once, on her own, she bought two $75.00 dresses. Gayle was allowed no voice in decisions, financial or otherwise, which affected her.

Gayle claimed Henry was abusive to her and the couple's daughter because they could not drive the family's ski boat. He allegedly screamed at her about her incompetency and physically pushed his daughter. Henry acknowledged the incident but offered an explanation for his behavior.

Gayle also testified that she felt viciously attacked by Henry's threats to tell her children and her friends of her extramarital affair and to take custody of her youngest daughter from her. (At the time of trial, both parties admitted to having had extramarital relationships at the end of their marriage.)

Henry allegedly belittled Gayle's numerous charity activities and was rude to her friends. He often embarrassed her in front of others. At trial, Henry admitted that he called Gayle's friends, identified himself as Gayle's lawyer, and then questioned the friends about Gayle and the divorce.

Henry testified that, as the president's wife, Gayle "had the run of the bank, anytime she wanted" and that there were no restrictions on Gayle's use of the checking account. However, he also admitted that the bank's records failed to include even one check signed by her. He said Gayle spent too much money—$400–$500 on dresses and $150 on shoes—but he was sure she needed those things. He claimed he made numerous profitable investments for Gayle's benefit and with her knowledge.

Some of the incidents testified to by Gayle were not remembered by Henry, but he did not dispute that certain abusive incidents occurred. However, he remembered almost all of those incidents differently from Gayle and he had explanations for each event. He testified that Gayle's psychologist "lied" about him. He agreed that he often used threats to get his way both in business and in his marriage and that threats often worked.

Henry alleged that Gayle was alcoholic. He told Gayle's psychologist that he bought Gayle's garbage from the garbage collectors (at $5 a bag) to check for wine bottles because he was concerned for her. After divorce was filed, Henry called Gayle's gynecologist to report her excessive drinking only out of concern for her. He described his devastation at the discovery of her affair.

Both Gayle and Henry were subjected to highly effective cross-examination.

Gayle's psychologist diagnosed Henry as having an "explosive personality disorder" and lacking impulse control. She characterized Gayle as "emotionally battered." She also described Gayle as paralyzed, passive, and intimidated. According to the psychologist, Gayle was extremely fearful and had learned to deal with Henry through avoidance, "walking on egg shells" so as not to trigger Henry's rage. The psychologist characterized much of Henry's behavior as stemming from a malicious intent to harm Gayle. She predicted that Gayle would need extensive psychotherapy in the future.

In rigorous cross-examination, the psychologist admitted that her characterization of certain acts as malicious might be based on incorrect assumptions. For example, if the couple were financially insolvent, Henry's supposed threats that Gayle would end up penniless would not be malicious. Similarly, if Henry contacted Gayle's doctor with allegations that she was alcoholic because he was concerned for her health, this conduct would not be malicious. The psychologist also stated that she had no better ability than the jury did to determine which party was telling the truth.

The jury found that Henry had intentionally and negligently inflicted emotional distress on Gayle and awarded her past and future damages in the amount of $362,000. However, the jury also found that Henry had not assaulted Gayle by threat of imminent injury nor acted with malice. In response to special issue number 11, they awarded no exemplary damages. In light of the evidence at trial, we conclude that the jury's findings were not the result of passion or prejudice.

Next Henry contends that the jury's verdict is contrary to the evidence because his conduct does not rise to the level of "outrageous" conduct necessary to support an emotional distress claim. Outrageous conduct is that conduct which exceeds all reasonable bounds of decency. See Restatement of the Law, Torts, § 46 comment g (Supp.1948). Whether behavior is "outrageous" is an issue of fact for a jury to decide.

Special issue number five was preceded by the following limiting instruction to which no objection was made:

> The bounds of decency vary from legal relationship to legal relationship. The marital relationship is highly subjective and constituted by mutual understandings and interchanges which are constantly in flux, and any number of which could be viewed by some segments of society as outrageous. Conduct considered extreme and outrageous in some relationships may be considered forgivable in other relationships. In your deliberation on the questions, definitions and instructions that follow, you shall consider them only in the context of the marital relationship of the parties to this case.

The jury found from the evidence that Henry Massey had intentionally inflicted emotional distress upon Gayle Massey during their 22–year marriage. . . .

Questions about Interspousal Torts as a Substitute for Fault in Divorce

As you have seen, courts have taken a variety of approaches to marital fault and to tort suits as a way of responding to it. Which view makes the most sense to you?

(1) Is it important to allow interspousal tort suits—standing alone or as part of a divorce action?

> (a) Consider the *Hakkila* marriage, obviously not a happy one. That unhappiness may well have been Mr. Hakkila's fault. Is it just for all courts to ignore the emotional abuse Mrs. Hakkila endured for many years? Does she have any way to legally vent her frustrations with him? Does it matter if she does? Will decisions like *Hakkila* encourage bad-tempered spouses to behave in worse ways? Will they have the perverse effect of causing more violence by people like Mrs. Hakkila?

(b) Does recognizing interspousal tort actions express and inculcate the view that abusive behavior within marriage is no more permissible than abusive behavior outside it?

(c) Will interspousal tort suits make any difference? Professor Spector reports that "in practice there are relatively few cases that are actually brought and even fewer where there has actually been a recovery." He explains, "Matrimonial attorneys overwhelmingly indicate that their clients are simply not interested in bringing marital tort cases." For one thing, "practically all clients show a distaste for the prolonging of the process that a civil case would entail." And "even when the client is willing to bring a separate tort action there may not be source of funds to pay the damages. Most homeowner insurance policies no longer cover intentional torts." Robert G. Spector, *Marital Torts:). The Current Legal Landscape,* 33 Family L Q 745, 761–62 (Fall 1999).

(d) Is it a good idea to separate divorce actions and any tort actions because removing all considerations of fault from divorce allows the court to concentrate on allocating responsibility for children (both custody and support) and dividing marital assets and losses in a dispassionate way? As you will recall, these were important goals of the divorce reform movement of the nineteen sixties and seventies. Do they still seem important?

(2) Is there something to be said for handling all the disputes of the spouses at the time of divorce?

(a) Even under the ALI rules, as we will see in Chapter 9, physical violence against a child or spouse must be considered in allocating custodial responsibility. Once the evidence of abuse becomes important in the divorce proceedings, can the divorce be handled fairly unless *all* questions of marital fairness are considered? Even in the minority of cases where minor children are not involved, an abused spouse may well feel that her aggressor's conduct during the marriage should affect the percentage of marital assets due her or the amount of support she should receive. Does combining divorce and tort actions make it easier, overall, to do justice between the spouses?

(b) Is it inefficient to handle the divorce action and the tort action separately?

(i) Would it be more efficient for the parties? In many cases, for example, a different attorney might be involved. In addition, the amount received through a tort verdict will usually be reduced by the contingency percentage for attorney's fees, while the divorce lawyer in most states cannot collect fees on other than an hourly basis (only indirectly related to the size of the other spouse's income or estate).

(ii) Would it be more efficient for the state to avoid the expense of two separate trials?

(c) In most states, divorces are handled by judges, sometimes specially trained family judges, while tort litigation is handled by the regular civil justice system (and often by juries). Which is better situated to evaluate the kinds of claims we have been discussing?

D. ALTERNATIVES TO DIVORCE LITIGATION: ARBITRATION, MEDIATION, AND CONCILIATION

> **Divorce as it exists at present is not a readjustment but a revenge. It is the nasty exposure of a private wrong.... Of course, if our divorce law exists mainly for the gratification of the fiercer sexual resentments, well and good, but if that is so, let us abandon our pretence that marriage is an institution for the establishment and protection of homes.**
>
> H.G. Wells
> *An Englishman Looks at the World*

As one might expect of a casebook on family law, our discussion of divorce has dealt primarily with the legal resolution of the disputes associated with ending marriages. However, the obvious difficulties of resolving such complex and bitter disputes judicially has led many people to seek alternative methods of dispute resolution. In this section, we will read a description of the alternatives, a defense of such methods, and a cautionary response to them. We will conclude by briefly reviewing some research.

(1) A Brief Introduction To Divorce Mediation

Learned Hand famously remarked, "I must say that, as a litigant, I should dread a lawsuit beyond almost anything else short of sickness and death." Being a litigant in a divorce is particularly dreadful. For one thing, the bitterness so common in divorce exacerbates the bitterness so common in litigation. For another, litigation is expensive, and most divorcing couples are not wealthy, and, worse, are about to become even less so.

No-fault divorce was intended to ameliorate both these problems. It was hoped that removing fault from divorce litigation would take from the table a subject that aggravated the hostility between the parties and that prolonged litigation and thus increased its cost. No-fault divorce may perhaps have helped in these ways. But litigation remains painful and expensive. This has led to calls for substituting mediation for litigation.

What is mediation? It is defined by the American Arbitration Association, the ABA, and the Society for Professionals in Dispute Resolution as

> a process in which an impartial third party—a mediator—facilitates the resolution of a dispute by promoting voluntary agreement (or "self-determination") by the parties to the dispute. A mediator facilitates communications, promotes understanding, focuses the parties on their

> interests, and seeks creative problem solving to enable the parties to reach their own agreement.

Mediation is intended to be a relatively unintrusive form of third-party involvement in a dispute. While judges and arbitrators impose outcomes on the disputants, mediators are supposed to help the parties reach a mutually satisfactory agreement.

Mediation ought to be superior to litigation in several ways. First, it should be more pacific. Litigation deliberately pits the parties against each other; mediation asks them to cooperate. Litigation looks to the acrid past; mediation searches for a sweeter future. Second, it should be cheaper. Litigation requires the help of lawyers, who are costly; mediation need not require this luxury. (Thus one study showed that mediating couples spent about one-fifth as much on legal fees as those that pursued an adversary divorce. Howard Ehrlanger, Elizabeth Chambliss and Marygold Melli, *The Process of Negotiation: An Exploratory Investigation in the Context of No-Fault Divorce*, 40 Wis L Rev 1133, 1142 (1988).) Litigation prolongs itself; mediation seeks not to. Court dockets are crowded; mediators are less inaccessible. Third, mediation should give the parties more control over their lives than litigation. Litigation imposes social standards of right; mediation asks the couples to establish their own standards.

If mediation works this way, its benefits might be quite significant. Many divorcing couples must continue to deal with each other after their divorce. Most such couples have young children and will share responsibility for them for many years. Some couples will have persisting economic relations. If mediation leaves them with less antagonism, more resources, and rules more to their liking than litigation, it will have increased the sum of human happiness.

The bar reacted to mediation with some skepticism. In particular, it raised three ethical concerns. First, it suggested that non-attorney mediators would violate "unauthorized practice of law" rules by interpreting statutes and cases for the parties. Opinion of the Bar of the City of New York #80–23 (1980). Second, attorney-mediators would be unable to represent both (necessarily adversary) spouses and would therefore have conflicts of interest. Linda Silberman, *Professional Responsibility Problems of Divorce Mediation*, 16 Family L Q 107 (1982). Third, the bar thought attorneys might be bad mediators because their legal training would incline them to give legal advice rather than to counsel the afflicted. Oregon St Bar Comm'n on Legal Ethics Formal Op 488 (1983).

The bar's skepticism was returned full force by those who, with Shaw, believe that "[a]ll professions are conspiracies against the laity." Divorce usually does not raise particularly challenging legal issues, and mediators suggested that the bar was simply defending its turf against intruders. Some lawyers admitted as much. One lawyer put it pretty bluntly: "Mediation would be an outrage as far as I'm concerned. It would ruin our practice. Arbitration and mediation are a blot on the escutcheon. They'll put us all out of business. As far as I am concerned they ought to destroy all arbitrators and mediators tomorrow." Quoted in Kenneth Kressel and Allen M. Hochberg, *Divorce Attorneys: Assessment of a Topology and Attitudes Towards Legal Reform*, 10 J Divorce 1, 8–10 (1987).

Despite such concerns, the bar has in significant part reconciled itself to mediation. (Today, for example, it is possible to read favorable reports on mediation in family law from lawyers who are presidents of their state bar and experienced family law practitioners. Leonard L. Loeb, *New Forms of Resolving Disputes–ADR*, 33 Family L Q 581 (1999).) This is partly because, as you already learned in the Section entitled "Portraits From the Practice of Family Law," few lawyers adore the acrimony of family litigation. In addition, lawyers have learned that mediation need not be a threat to business, since lawyers themselves can be mediators.

Nevertheless, mediation is now more common than not in divorce cases, especially those involving children. About one-fourth of the states mandate mediation for custody and visitation issues. ALI Principles, § 2.08 & Comment b, at 99–10. For examples, see Cal Fam Code § 3170 (West 2006); Wis Stat Ann § 767.11 (2006). In half the states, courts have discretion to order mediation in child-custody and visitation disputes. In Iowa, for example, a court may order mediation so that the parties can determine whether joint custody is appropriate. Iowa Code Ann § 598.41(2)(d) (West 2005). In Virginia a spouse may move that a case be referred to mediation or the court may issue that order on its own motion. Va Code Ann § 20–124.2 (2006).

While mediation may be becoming the rule, there are still exceptions. These generally arise out of the beliefs (1) that mediation is inappropriate where one spouse wields too much power over the other and (2) that mediation depends on trust and is thus contraindicated if marital trust has been too greatly eroded. Some kinds of behavior are widely thought to have been so damaging to trust that mediation should not be attempted. For example: If one spouse has hidden assets throughout the marriage, mediation may well fail. Adultery likewise cripples trust. And when one spouse has abused the other or their children the spousal relationship is widely presumed to have be so dysfunctional that fair agreements cannot reliably be reached through mediation. Thus most jurisdictions do not require mediation for marriages in which there has been abuse. See, e.g., Cal Fam Code § 3181 (2006); Wis Stat § 767.11(8)(b) (West 2006). Some jurisdictions waive the requirement that spouses mediate their disputes in other circumstances, as when it may cause undue hardship or where it seems to place one of the parties or children in danger. E.g., Wis. Stat. § 767.11(5)(West 2006).

Mediation has not been left without its critics. Feminists have been among the most prominent doubters. (Feminists were also early supporters of mediation on the theory that it would handle disputes in the language of relationships rather than of individual rights.) Feminists' objections have essentially been threefold: First, some argue that women more than men value their relationships with their families and that this might lead them to make disadvantageous financial arrangements in order to preserve their relationship with their husbands or their children. Second, feminists fear that husbands will take advantage of their wives' relative lack of sophistication and power. Third, feminists believe women are more risk averse than men and that this may lead them to compromise their interests too readily.

A summary view of these attacks on mediation is to be found in Tina Grillo's criticism of mandatory mediation: *The Mediation Alternative: Process Dangers for Women*, 100 Yale LJ 1545, 1549–50 (1991). She concludes

> that mandatory mediation provides neither a more just nor a more humane alternative to the adversarial system of adjudication of custody, and, therefore, does not fulfill its promises. In particular, quite apart from whether an acceptable result is reached, mandatory mediation can be destructive to many women and some men because it requires them to speak in a setting they have not chosen and often imposes a rigid orthodoxy as to how they should speak, make decisions, and be. This orthodoxy is imposed through subtle and not-so-subtle messages about appropriate conduct and about what may be said in mediation. It is an orthodoxy that often excludes the possibility of the parties' speaking with their authentic voices.
>
> Moreover, people vary greatly in the extent to which their sense of self is "relational"—that is, defined in terms of connection to others. If two parties are forced to engage with one another, and one has a more relational sense of self than the other, that party may feel compelled to maintain her connection with the other, even to her own detriment. For this reason, the party with the more relational sense of self will be at a disadvantage in a mediated negotiation. Several prominent researchers have suggested that, as a general rule, women have a more relational sense of self than do men, although there is little agreement on what the origin of this difference might be. Thus, rather than being a feminist alternative to the adversary system, mediation has the potential actively to harm women.

(2) Research on Divorce Mediation

We have just described the arguments for and against mediation. What can empirical research tell us about those arguments? One of the most thoughtful and fair-minded summaries of that research is Kenneth Kressel, *The Process of Divorce: How Professionals and Couples Negotiate Settlements* (Basic Books, 1985). We will summarize it and supplement it with descriptions of more recent research when that seems profitable.

The first problem with evaluating mediation is that appropriate measures of success must be selected. One possible measure is customer satisfaction. Here Professor Kressel finds some reason for cheer. He says that a majority of the people who use divorce mediation seem to be generally satisfied with it and that this is probably a better result than the traditional legal system could claim. Professor Kressel noted that while people who had used mediation "were much more likely to say that the assistance they received improved communication, cooperation, understanding, and the ability to handle anger towards the ex-spouse," no more than half of them thought mediation had actually helped in this respect, about 40 percent thought mediation had made no difference in these ways, and the rest thought mediation had been harmful. And nine months after final orders were issued, any advantage mediation had on these measures was "slight." More generally, a "significant minority" (perhaps around a quarter or a third) "had distinctly negative things to report about the mediation experience."

Another possible measure of success is settlement rates. Professor Kressel believed that settlement rates probably range from 40 to 70 percent, which he characterized as "reasonably good" and as "roughly comparable to the settlement rates reported in studies of mediation in small claims court and across a range of civil disputes." A more recent book-length study, Eleanor M. Maccoby and Robert Mnookin, *Dividing the Child, Social and Legal Dilemmas of Custody* (1992), observes that in California custody cases mediation seems to have reduced litigation from ten percent of cases to less than two percent.

Another measure of success is how things seem to work out after the divorce. Professor Kressel reported that a somewhat higher proportion of the people who had reached a settlement through mediation reported their spouses to be in compliance after nine months than people who had not used mediation. This finding is corroborated by the later study of Robert E. Emery et al., *Child Custody Mediation and Litigation: Parents' Satisfaction and Functioning One Year After Settlement*, 72 J Consulting & Clinical Psychol 124, 128 (1994), which reported that fathers who mediated were likelier to meet their child-support obligations than fathers who did not. On the other hand, Professor Kressel saw little success in efforts to show that mediation actually improved the quality of the relationship between parents and children or the quality of children's lives after divorce. And he cited a number of studies which conclude that mediation does not reduce post-settlement litigation.

A final test of mediation's success is its ability to reduce the economic costs of divorce. Professor Kressel wrote, "Modest but distinctive savings in legal costs were ... associated with the use of mediation." More recent research by Richard D. Mathis and Lynelle C. Yingling, *Analysis of Pre and Post-test Gender Differences in Family Satisfaction of Divorce in Mediation Couples*, 17 J of Divorce & Remarriage 75, 84 (1992), found more than modest cost savings. They concluded that divorce fees and costs were 28% higher for those using lawyers or judges instead of mediators to handle either disputes about money or disputes about children and 49% higher when mediation was used to handle both kinds of disputes.

After we have decided what criteria to use in evaluating mediation, we need to decide how reliable the empirical research actually is.

Professor Kressel saw "numerous substantive and methodological grounds" for a "cautious interpretation of the evidence," particularly when it came to comparing mediation to the traditional approach. He concluded, "On balance, I do not think that the case [for mediation's "general workability"] has yet been made." Professor Kressel's doubt about the quality of the research that has been done began with the fact that there had been only a few studies, and all of those had looked at custody and visitation disputes, not at the other difficult issues which arise on divorce. Further, "[n]one of the existing studies controls for an array of nonspecific factors which might help explain the observed differences between the mediated and unmediated groups." The studies had a number of other methodological failings. For instance, typically "the less conflicted, more cooperatively oriented, and less disturbed couples end up in the mediation group, while the worst cases go into the 'control' or comparison groups." The studies also suffered from the uncertain effects of the facts that a large number of people refused to participate and that a significant number withdrew from the study once they had joined. Some of Professor Kressel's methodological concerns may have been ameliorated by the number and size of later studies. For example, the Maccoby and Mnookin study was undertaken at a time when all cases were mediated in California, so there could be no selection effect.

We said that feminists have become some of the most prominent critics of mediation. What can empirical research tell us about their criticisms? There is some evidence that men are more satisfied with mediation than women. Emery et al., supra at 128, found that men who mediated were more satisfied with their outcome one year after the divorce than fathers who litigated, while mothers who mediated were less satisfied than mothers who litigated. On the other hand, Richard D. Mathis and Lynelle C. Yingling, *Analysis of Pre and Post–Test Gender Differences in Family Satisfaction of Divorce in Mediation Couples*, 17 J of Divorce & Remarriage 75, 84 (1992), reported that although the husbands in their study had a higher increase in satisfaction due to mediation than their wives, their wives were happier than those who pursued the traditional settlement route.

What, though, of feminist concerns that women would win less favorable results in mediation than litigation? In general, empirical research has not substantiated those fears. For instance, Carol Bohmer and Marilyn L. Ray, *Effects of Different Dispute Resolution Methods on Women and Children After Divorce*, 28 Family L Q 223, 244 (Summer 1994), concluded that women and children were not worse off for mediating rather than litigating under the Georgia mediation system. There is even evidence that wives who mediate are even more satisfied with their ability to stand up for themselves than are their husbands or divorcing women who used the traditional adversary process.

Another way of investigating feminists' concerns is to examine the literature on psychological differences between men and women that might affect their ability to do well in mediation. Margaret F. Brinig,

Does Mediation Systematically Disadvantage Women?, 2 Wm & Mary J Women & L 1 (1995), argues that experimental and other empirical studies show that while women are indeed probably more risk averse than men (and therefore are more likely to settle rather than risk litigation), they are not altruistic in ways that would affect the results they reach. Professor Brinig also argues that that literature suggests that women are advantaged by having lower discount rates than men, which means they are more apt than men to look at long-range rather than short-range benefits in a settlement. More specifically, Robert C. Dingwall et al., *Gender and Interaction in Divorce Mediation*, 15 Mediation Q 277, 284 (1998), concluded that "women are neither generically advantaged nor disadvantaged by the process of mediation, although certain aspects of it may seem to have a more masculine character, particularly in the mediators' use of abstract-expert knowledge about children, which can make them seem more aligned with fathers than mothers." Fathers, the study finds, are more likely than mothers to refer to abstract as opposed to experiential knowledge about children and their needs. The study proposes that this "advantage" be balanced by "active solicitation of experiential knowledge from both parents."

(3) A Problem in Divorce Mediation

But enough generalities. Lawyers learn from cases, and it is time that we investigate the principles and problems of mediation through an example of it. We take our case from an article by a law professor who was also a divorce mediator. We reproduce, in chronological order, her reports of several mediation sessions observed.

TRINA GRILLO
THE MEDIATION ALTERNATIVE: PROCESS DANGERS FOR WOMEN

100 Yale Law Journal 1545 (1991)

Linda and Jerry had been married for five years when Kenny was born. They separated when he was fourteen months old. Even before the separation, Linda had had almost complete responsibility for Kenny since Jerry's job with the railroad took him out of town at least three nights per week on a schedule that was constantly changing. When Jerry was in town, he tended to spend time with his friends rather than with Linda and Kenny. After the separation, Jerry saw Kenny in a sporadic fashion until, when Kenny was two, Jerry moved 1000 miles away to another state. Jerry then kept in only infrequent contact with Kenny and paid little support for him until Jerry moved in with his girlfriend, whom he married when Kenny was three and one-half. Once Jerry remarried, he was anxious to have Kenny with him, and Linda began to send Kenny to Jerry for short visits.

[On one of these occasions,] Kenny had spent ten days with his father Jerry and was scheduled to return to his mother on a flight arriving on Thanksgiving afternoon. That morning, Jerry called Linda and told her that flying was expensive, and that he was returning to his ex-wife's area at Christmas anyway. He said he intended to keep Kenny with him until then; Kenny's stepmother would care for Kenny at their home. Linda, her Thanksgiving dinner in the oven and relatives scheduled to arrive, thought of going herself to pick up Kenny or going to court, but decided that the worst thing for Kenny would be a custody battle.

When Kenny returned at Christmas, his behavior was odd; for the first time in his life he was violent and aggressive toward other children. Upon questioning Kenny, Linda discovered that he had not been cared for by his stepmother during the day as promised, but had instead been sent to unlicensed daycare where the teacher had regularly used corporal punishment, to which Linda was passionately opposed and to which Kenny had never before been subjected.

[After the separation,] Linda had taken a low-paying job in a childcare center so that Kenny could be with her while she worked. Jerry continued to work the chaotic schedule required by the railroad. After determining that Linda and Jerry would share custody of Kenny, the mediator asked Jerry what schedule would work for him. Jerry said that he could not be tied down to a particular schedule because his job on the railroad required him to be available at short notice and out of town for long periods of time. When Linda protested that both she and Kenny needed a predictable schedule, and that she had spent her entire married life at the mercy of the whims of his employer, the mediator smiled sympathetically and said, "I guess you didn't get to divorce the railroad after all." ...

Linda was willing for Jerry to have frequent contact with Kenny. She did not feel, however, that it would be good for Kenny to live in two different homes, 1000 miles apart. The mediator told Linda that the most important thing for Kenny's future development was to have frequent and continuing contact with both parents. She said Jerry was entitled to have his son half the time; the only question was which half. Although the mediator recognized the difficulty of arranging for frequent long-distance travel for Kenny, she nonetheless recommended that Kenny spend alternate months with each parent. When Linda protested that, because of Jerry's work schedule, Kenny would have frequent and continuing contact with neither parent when he was staying with Jerry, the mediator made it clear that if Linda did not agree to sharing custody on the terms she suggested, she would recommend to the court that Jerry get sole custody....

In mediation, Linda asks that she be given primary custody of Kenny. She says that Jerry has been untruthful, unreliable, and has risked Kenny's emotional and physical well-being. She tries to argue that such a young child needs one home base, and that should be her home since she was effectively his sole parent for most of his first three years of life. The mediator does not allow her to make these points. Instead, she says that the past is not to be discussed; rather, they must plan together about the future. She says that whether Jerry participated in Kenny's life for his early years is irrelevant; he is here now. The Thanksgiving situation is past history, and she is sure that they both have complaints about the past. Blaming one another is counterproductive. The mediator tells Linda that she must recognize that the parent who has the child is responsible for choosing daycare. Linda must learn to give up control....

After a year spent in a custody arrangement under which Kenny lived alternate months with Linda and with Jerry, and following a second mediation, Linda gave up physical custody of Kenny to Jerry. She believed that the schedule was traumatic to Kenny, and felt that the mediator would recommend in Jerry's favor in a custody battle anyway based on the friendly parent principle.

Questions on Linda's View of Her Mediation

Professor Grillo says Linda was quite unhappy with her mediation. The following questions help you think about why and what her unhappiness might tell us about the risks of mediation. As you read the questions, you should think about whether Linda was unhappy because of problems intrinsic to mediation or because of problems with a particular mediator.

(1) Is Linda dissatisfied because of the mediator's refusal to discuss the couple's behavior in the past?

(a) Does she think Jerry's behavior is relevant because it demonstrates his lack of parental dedication?

(b) Does she think Jerry's behavior is relevant because it demonstrates she cannot trust him?

(c) Does she think her behavior is relevant because it has earned her custody of Kenny?

(2) Is Linda dissatisfied because in the scheme approved by the mediator she must continue to deal with Jerry and his employer's erratic schedules, as though her marriage were not over?

(a) Is she unhappy because she must suffer the hardships of both a divorced parent and the wife of a railroad employee?

(b) Is she unhappy because she thinks divorce should bring a "clean break"?

(3) Is Linda dissatisfied because Jerry's contributions as a provider are being counted the same way as her contributions as a primary caretaker?

(4) Is Linda dissatisfied because the mediator isn't paying enough attention to Jerry's decision to move?

(a) Is she unhappy because Jerry's decided to move without properly consulting her?

(b) Is she unhappy because Jerry's decision to move makes it hard for them to care properly for their child?

(5) Is Linda dissatisfied because she feels Jerry has abdicated day-to-day responsibility for Kenny even when he has custody of the boy?

(a) Is she unhappy because Jerry seems to have given his second wife so much of the responsibility for Linda's son?

(b) Is she unhappy Jerry has placed their son in unlicensed day care?

(6) Is Linda dissatisfied with Jerry's parental decisions, particularly those concerning corporal punishment?

(7) Would Linda have been happier had she and Jerry gone to lawyers and not a mediator? If she had gone to a different mediator?

Notes and Questions on Divorce Mediation

The following notes and questions are intended to help you answer more global questions: First, what should the role of the mediator be? Second, when and how is mediation preferable to litigation in divorce cases?

(1) What should the mediator's goal be?

(a) To help the spouses reach whatever agreement they mutually prefer?

(b) To help the spouses reach some particular agreement?

(i) An agreement the mediator thought wise?

(ii) An agreement the mediator thought a court would prefer?

(c) To equip spouses with the tools for working together productively after divorce?

(i) With the tools for resolving their future disputes on their own?

(ii) With the tools for treating each other in ways that reduce the conflict between them and thus the injury to their children such conflict can cause?

(2) What do you think this mediator's goals were?

(3) One way of thinking about mediators' goals is to ask whether mediators should be entirely neutral.

(a) It is often said that the best post-divorce arrangements are the ones the parties chose for themselves. It is even said that "[s]ocio-psychological advantages will result if divorcing parties are given a choice of remedies and some incentive to pursue them." Thomas E. Carbonneau, an advocate of divorce mediation, taken from *A Consideration of Alternatives to Divorce Litigation*, 1986 U Ill L Rev 1119. Will these advantages accrue to couples who were maneuvered or cajoled into an agreement by a mediator who was not neutral?

(b) It is, you will learn, a standard principle of family law that the government ought to "intervene" as little as possible in family life. Does that principle require mediators to be neutral? Professor Carbonneau suggests that a virtue of "non-adversarial proceedings [is that they] lessen state intrusion into the private life of each party." Is that advantage lost when mediators are not neutral?

(c) Is it possible for the mediator to be neutral?

(i) Is it always impossible for people to distance themselves from all their history and experience, from their race, their religion, their gender, their class, their calling? Is there any such thing as a truly "neutral" view of any human situation? Is it possible to escape the influence of one's ethnicity, gender, class, and so on?

(ii) Are some points of view almost built in to the mediator's world view? "To the extent that mediators believe that joint participation in family affairs is itself a valuable thing and that, even after divorce, the family remains an interacting communications network, they may prefer joint legal custody and the concomitant sense of preserving all of the parent-child relations that mark a stable family. Indeed, some mediators are quite explicit about their preference for this arrangement, believing that 'parents should be encouraged to share in joint legal custody.'" Lee E. Teitelbaum and Laura DuPaix, *Alternative Dispute Resolution and Divorce: Natural Experimentation in Family Law*, 40 Rutgers L Rev 1093 (1988).

(d) Is it desirable for the mediator to be neutral?

(i) Mediators will inevitably see people behaving badly. Should they seek to counteract bad behavior?

(ii) Mediators will inevitably see imbalances of power. Should they seek to counteract those imbalances? Is doing so breaking any rule of neutrality?

(iii) This mediator was working in California, and California has long had a presumption of joint custody, at least where parents can agree. Cal Fam Code § 3080 (West 1994). Is there a problem if the mediator's "non-neutrality" reflects state law?

(iv) Does a mediator obtain a perspective on families that judges may miss in formal litigation with its restrictive rules of evidence, its fixed standards of decision, and its zealous advocates? Would it be advantageous to take advantage of the insights the mediator might thus have gained? Is there any evidence that the mediator here had that kind of insight?

(e) Was this mediator neutral?

(4) The law sets up substantive standards by which to evaluate spouses' claims to property and to custody of their children and procedural standards to assure the litigants that their legitimate claims will be heard. Mediation has neither kind of standards. Does this deny spouses the "hearing" to which we ordinarily believe people are entitled when the government has some authority over their disputes?

(a) In this mediation, Kenny behaved in a disturbing way after he returned from visiting his father. Courts would probably consider that kind of reaction evidence of "detriment to the child" that a court would seriously consider in deciding custody disputes. The mediator prevented Laura from using this evidence. Was that proper?

(b) One of the most striking things about Professor Grillo's case is the mediator's determination to exclude discussion of things past. Is that determination appropriate?

(i) Is it necessary in order to move the couple away from their hostility and toward a better future for themselves and their child?

(ii) Is it inappropriate because the couple may need to discuss their past in order to diminish their bitterness in the future? Professor Wardle, as you remember, argued in *No-fault Divorce and the Divorce Conundrum*, 1991 BYU L Rev 79, that custody battles may be the contemporary replacement for divorce grounds as the turf over which parties "vent" their marital unhappiness. His comment was that "it appears that this has been due primarily to a transfer of hostility into other facets of the divorce proceeding" (and he cited evidence from matrimonial lawyers about the increase in the number of and bitterness in custody disputes.)

(iii) Is it inappropriate because the couple's past is psychologically, morally, and legally relevant to their plans for the future?

(c) Would these "due process" problems be solved by allowing spouses who were unhappy with mediation to appeal? Penelope Eileen Bryan, *Women's Freedom to Contract at Divorce: A Mask for Contextual Coercion*, 47 Buff L Rev 1153 (1999), suggests, "Judicial frustration with overcrowded dockets, judicial deference to family privacy, judicial distaste for divorce cases, and a pervasive preference for private settlement encourage judges to refuse to vacate unfair agreements." Is this regrettable? For one case where a stipulated divorce agreement was found unconscionable, see *Crawford v. Crawford*, 524 NW2d 833 (ND 1994). For one where it was not, see *Flynn v. Flynn*, 597 NE2d 709 (Ill Ct App 1992). Both these cases involved attorney negotiated rather than mediated agreements.

(5) As you will have grasped, one of the principal criticisms of mediation is that it may give the stronger spouse too much influence over the terms of their divorce. Should the mediator try to offset that influence in some way?

(a) Does this mediator try to do so?

(b) To the extent the mediator allows Linda to express herself, Linda seems to be a fairly good advocate. Some evidence suggests that the linguistic styles of the parties to mediation may be more important than their physical or financial power in determining whether they are effective. Randy Frances Kandel, *Power Plays: A Sociolinguistic Study of Inequality in Child Custody Mediation and a Hearsay Analog Solution*, 36 Ariz L Rev 879 (1994). Professor Kandel suggests that people's power in mediation depends partly on their ability to recall and quote dialogue and argues that resulting imbalances in power may be lessened through a hearsay exception and better mediator training.

(6) Do you see any role for Linda and Jerry's attorneys in this custody proceeding?

(a) Does mediation eliminate the need for divorce attorneys except to make sure the legal document drawn will survive legal challenges?

(b) What might lawyers bring to drafting the agreement that mediators might not?

(i) Would they be more likely to ask the couple to think about what would be fair?

(ii) Would they be more likely to take a longer view of the situation?

(iii) Would they have different insights drawn from their own experience about what agreements work and which provoke misery and litigation? What experience would they draw from? Law school? Litigation? Precedent?

(c) If lawyers are to be involved, should they be present at the mediation?

(i) Would the parties be more inhibited, or freer, if the lawyers were present?

(ii) Would the lawyers disrupt the work of a "therapeutic" mediator? Would the lawyers disrupt venting, even that allowed by a "facilitative" mediator?

(iii) Would Linda have been better off had her lawyer been present?

(d) Would lawyers cost more than they were worth?

(7) Many jurisdictions have rules constraining lawyers from professionally affiliating themselves with non-lawyers. Would it be a good idea for lawyers to become partners with lay mediators? Should mediators be attorneys? A representative statute setting the qualifications for media-

tors is Neb Rev Stat Ann § 43–2905 (2005). Standards of Practice for Lawyer Mediators in Family Disputes, Stnd III, cons. (A) & (C) (1984), requires that a mediator not "represent either party during or after the mediation" and that "the mediator must be impartial" and "facilitate the ability of the parties to make their own agreement, while raising questions of fairness, equity and feasibility of proposed options for settlement." The American Bar Associations Section on Dispute Resolution Model Standards are available online at http://www.abanet.org/ftp/pub/dispute/modstan.txt.

(8) A number of dispute resolution organizations have established ethical codes to govern the conduct of lawyers who mediate. These codes have been promulgated by the ABA, The Academy of Family Mediators (AFM), the Association of Family and Conciliation Courts (AFCC), The Society of Professionals in Dispute Resolution (SPIDR). These codes are available on the Internet Web sites of the various groups, such as http://www.mediators.org/afmstnds.html (AFM standards).

(9) Almost universally, what happens in mediation is supposed to be confidential. In particular, neither the mediator nor the parties may use the information they received during the mediation session in court. Will Linda be hurt by such a rule?

(a) Generally, the only exceptions to this rule are that the mediator may report whether an agreement has been reached and can (or must) disclose information pertaining to child abuse or sexual abuse. See, e.g., Colo Rev Stat Ann § 13–22–307(2) (2005).

(b) In California and Delaware, nothing said in the mediation conference can be used against a party in court, but the mediator can recommend who should have custody or what the visitation schedule should be. See Del Fam Ct Civ Rule Ann 16(b) (2005); Cal Fam Code Ann §§ 3177, 3183 (2006).

(10) One criticism of settlements (the common outcome of mediation) is that they don't allow new law to be forged. See, e.g., Marc Galanter and Mia Cahill, *"Most Cases Settle": Judicial Promotion and Regulation of Settlements*, 46 Stan L Rev 1339, 1350 tbl 1 (1994); and Owen Fiss, *Against Settlement*, 88 Yale LJ 1073 (1984). Is this an important criticism to make about divorce mediation?

(a) Is custody an area where we need new law? Or is it so fact-specific that appellate law is rarely crucial?

(b) Is the duty of attorneys to please the client or to advance legal knowledge? See Carrie Menkel–Meadow, *Whose Dispute Is It Anyway? A Philosophical and Democratic Defense of Settlement (In Some Cases)*, 83 Geo LJ 2663 (1995).

(11) Ann Estin, *Bonding After Divorce: Comments on Joint Custody: Bonding and Monitoring Theories*, 73 Ind L J 441, 451–52 (1998), suggests giving mediators some of the powers of arbitrators. She reports on a practice involving couples in Colorado who would ordinarily fit the pattern Professor Kressel feels is least likely to profit from mediation:

those who fought bitterly over custody even after their divorce. Usually such couples arm themselves with attorneys and litigate, litigate, litigate. The Colorado program hopes to force such couples to reach agreements themselves rather than calling in a judge. Attorneys convinced suitable clients to agree (in their settlement agreements) to submit custody disputes to experienced mediators who would schedule the sessions "almost immediately." These "arbitrator-mediators" had the authority to mediate any dispute the couples brought to them and to decide any unresolved issues left at the end of any session. Professor Estin reports that though the couples used the neutral extensively during the first few weeks, "My colleagues tell me that this system works because it is cost effective and more responsive to the parents' needs than are repeated hearings in front of a judge. Ideally, it also works as a behavior-modification device. As parents begin to anticipate how the mediator-arbitrator will decide particular issues, they begin to limit their complaints and requests to those that are likely to be deemed reasonable. Ultimately, then, they either learn to settle disputes themselves or to work more effectively together to eliminate them."

BIBLIOGRAPHY

The History and Sociology of the Family. Particularly enjoyable on the history of the family is Edward Shorter, *The Making of the Modern Family* (Basic Books, 1975). Soberer, but perhaps as controversial, is Lawrence Stone, *The Family, Sex and Marriage in England 1500–1800* (Harper & Row, 1977). A standard history of the American family and especially women's role in it is Carl N. Degler, *At Odds: Women and the Family in America from the Revolution to the Present* (Oxford U Press, 1980). For a pioneering study of the history of family law, see Michael Grossberg, *Governing the Hearth: Law and the Family in Nineteenth-Century America* (UNC Press, 1985). One accessible place to begin learning about the sociology of the family is Theodore Caplow, et al, *Middletown Families: Fifty Years of Change and Continuity* (U Minn Press, 1982). Other useful surveys of the sociology of the American family are Arlene Skolnick, *Embattled Paradise: The American Family in an Age of Uncertainty* (Basic Books, 1991), and Arlene S. Skolnick and Jerome H. Skolnick, *Family in Transition* (Little, Brown, 1980). A more strictly demographic study is Frances K. Goldscheider and Linda J. Waite, *New Families, No Families?: The Transformation of the American Home* (U Cal Press, 1991). Linda J. Waite explores the differences in result between marriage and cohabitation in *Does Marriage Matter?*, 32 Demography 483 (1995). A gloomy view of the modern family (one that uses the Scandinavian family to think about the future of the American family) is David Popenoe, *Disturbing the Nest: Family Change and Decline in Modern Societies* (Aldine de Gruyter, 1988). A study that relishes the trends Popenoe dislikes is Judith Stacey, *Brave New Families* (Basic Books, 1990).

Marriage. On what people know about the law of marriage when they wed, see Lynn A. Baker, *Promulgating the Marriage Contract*, 23 U

Mich J L Reform, 217 (1990); and Lynn A. Baker and Robert E. Emery, *When Every Relationship Is Above Average: Perceptions and Expectations of Divorce at the Time of Marriage*, 17 L & Human Behavior *439* (1993). Margaret F. Brinig, Carl E. Schneider, and Lee E. Teitelbaum, *Family Law in Action: A Reader* 69–79 (Anderson, 1999), includes excerpts dealing with courting. For a lovely collection of twentieth-century poetry on marriage, see Michael Blumenthal, *To Woo and to Wed: Poets on Love and Marriage* (Poseidon Press, 1992). For a lovely collection of literature on that subject, see Amy A. Kass and Leon R. Kass, eds, *Wing to Wing, Oar to Oar: Readings on Courting and Marrying* (U Notre Dame Press, 2000). For an historical account of marriage, see Nancy Cott, *Public Vows: A History of Marriage and The Nation* (Harvard U Press, 2002). Michael Grossberg, *Guarding the Altar, Physiological Restrictions and the Rise of State Intervention in Matrimony*, 25 Am J Legal Hist 197 (1982), contains a number of valuable historical insights into state laws regulating marriage and setting out grounds for annulment. Lynn D. Wardle, *Rethinking Marital Age Restrictions*, 22 J Family L 1 (1983), argues that if adolescents may make critical decisions involving contraception and abortion without parental consent, they should not be forbidden from marrying. Margaret F. Brinig, Carl E. Schneider, and Lee E. Teitelbaum, *Family Law in Action: A Reader* 219–292 (Anderson, 1999), surveys patterns of marriage and divorce and examines how divorces are obtained). Pages 79–92 discuss many of the less common marriage forms presented in Chapter 1. For an argument in favor of covenant marriage by one of its early promoters, see Katherine Spaht, *For the Sake of the Children: Recapturing the Meaning of Marriage*, 73 Notre Dame L Rev 1547 (1998). A report on the progress of covenant marriage and how the concept of covenant is viewed in various cultures is John Witte, Jr. and Eliza Ellison, eds., *Covenant Marriage in Comparative Perspective*, Eerdmans, 2005. A sociological study of covenant marriage in Louisiana is reported in Nock, Steven L., Laura Sanchez, Julia C. Wilson, and James D. Wright. "Intimate Equity: The Early Years of Covenant and Standard Marriages," *Department of Sociology, University of Virginia*. Charlottesville, VA, 2003, available online at http://www.bgsu.edu/organizations/cfdr/research/pdf/2003/2003_04.pdf. Elizabeth S. Scott and Robert E. Scott, *Marriage as Relational Contract*, 84 Va L Rev 1226 (1998), offers an informed and imaginative application of sophisticated thinking about commercial contracts to marriage arrangements. For a book-length discussion of the difference between contract and covenant in the context of family law, see Margaret F. Brinig, *From Contract to Covenant* (Harv U Press 2000).

Same-Sex Marriage. For a thoughtful examination of the subject, see William N. Eskridge, Jr., *A History of Same–Sex Marriage*, 79 Va L Rev 1419 (1993), and the commentaries by Milton C. Regan, Jr., and Nancy D. Polikoff that follow it. For discussions of the issues that will be involved when challenges are made to covenant marriage rules or civil unions, see Andrew Koppelman, *Same-Sex Marriage, Choice of Law, and Public Policy*, 76 Tex L Rev 921 (1998); Mark Strasser, *Baker and Some*

Recipes for Disaster: On DOMA, Covenant Marriages, and Full Faith And Credit Jurisprudence, 64 Brooklyn L Rev 307 (1998). For a look at the implications of the *Troxel* case, which we will consider in Chapter 7, see Nancy D. Polikoff, *The Impact of Troxel v. Granville on Lesbian and Gay Parents*, 32 Rutg LJ 825 (2001). For a novel about a gay man and his struggles to find relationship in an academic community and acceptance in his own family, with an interesting sub-plot about the Shaker utopian community, see Michael Dowling, *Perfect Agreement* (Berkeley Books 1997). A novel about family ties generally focusing on the role played by a gay young man is Jane Hamilton's *The Short History of a Prince* (Random House, 1998).

Polygamy. A fascinating study of contemporary (heterodox) Mormon polygamy is Irwin Altman and Joseph Ginat, *Polygamous Families in Contemporary Society* (Cambridge U Press, 1996).

The Law of Divorce. A particularly fine collection of essays is Stephen D. Sugarman and Herma Hill Kay, *Divorce Reform at the Crossroads* (Yale U Press, 1990). For a study by a leading English scholar, see John Eekelaar, *Regulating Divorce* (Oxford U Press, 1991). A journalist's study of divorce litigation is Emily Couric, *The Divorce Lawyers: The People and Stories Behind Ten Dramatic Cases* (St. Martin's Press, 1992). Jeffrey Evans Stake, *Mandatory Planning for Divorce*, 45 Vand L Rev 397 (1992), searches for ways to lead people to think more carefully about entering and leaving marriage. For empirical and theoretical discussions of whether no-fault divorce increased divorce rates, see Margaret F. Brinig and F.H. Buckley, *No-Fault Laws and At–Fault People*, 18 Intl J L & and Econ 325 (1998); and Leora Friedberg, *Did Unilateral Divorce Raise Divorce Rates? Evidence from Panel Data*, 88 Am Econ Rev 608 (1998), both of which find there was some long-term increase. In *Divorce Laws and the Structure of the American Family*, 35 J Legal Stud 143 (2006), economist Stéphane Mechoulan demonstrates the difference between no-faults effect on marriages contracted before and after the legislation.

The Sociology of Divorce. An eminent sociologist provides an uncommonly broad-ranging study in William J. Goode, *World Changes in Divorce Patterns* (Yale U Press, 1993). How people come to divorce is the subject of Diane Vaughan, *Uncoupling: Turning Points in Intimate Relationships* (Vintage, 1986). In Yoram Weiss and Robert J. Willis, *Match Quality, New Information, and Marital Dissolution*, 15 J Lab Econ S293 (1997), two "transactional" economists enlarge upon the pathbreaking work of Gary Becker to predict divorce from patterns in courtship. In Norval D. Glenn and Michael Supancic, *Social and Demographic Correlates of Divorce*, 46 J Marr & Fam 563 (1984), two important sociologists of the family discuss what causes divorce. Two influential statements of the harmful effects of divorce on children are Judith S. Wallerstein and Sandra Blakeslee, *Second Chances: Men, Women, and Children a Decade After Divorce* (Ticknor & Fields, 1989), and Judith S. Wallerstein and Joan Berlin Kelly, *Surviving the Breakup: How Children and Parents Cope with Divorce* (Basic Books, 1980). Frank

F. Furstenberg, Jr., and Andrew J. Cherlin, *Divided Families: What Happens to Children When Parents Part* (Harv U Press, 1991), is an admirable study of research on the lives of children after divorce. More recently, Elizabeth Marquardt reports on the effects of even "good" divorces in *Between Two Worlds: The Inner Lives of Children of Divorce* (Crown 2005). For a study of divorce from the mother's perspective, see Terry Arendell, *Mothers and Divorce: Legal, Economic, and Social Dilemmas* (Cal U Press, 1986). A more literary view of divorce is A. Alvarez, *Life After Marriage: Love in an Age of Divorce* (Simon & Schuster, 1981). And a more journalistic one is Jonathan Gathorne–Hardy, *Marriage, Love, Sex and Divorce: What Brings Us Together, What Drives Us Apart* (Summit Books, 1981). A vastly detailed investigation of its special topic is Annette Lawson, *Adultery: An Analysis of Love and Betrayal* (Basic Books, 1988). On the social and psychological dynamics of divorce, see Diane Vaughan, *Uncoupling: Turning Points in Intimate Relationships* (Vintage, 1986). For a more literary and diverting, if now dated, view of divorce in America, see Joseph Epstein, *Divorce in America: Marriage in an Age of Possibility* (E.P. Dutton, 1974).

Alternative Dispute Resolution. Two different kinds of feminist critique of mediation are Cheryl Regehr, *The Use of Empowerment in Child Custody Mediation: A Feminist Critique*, 11 Med Q 361 (1994); and Randy Frances Kandel, *Power Plays: A Sociolinguistic Study of Inequality in Custody Mediation and a Hearsay Analog Solution*, 36 Ariz L Rev 879 (1994). For empirical and theoretical discussions of risk aversion and altruistic behavior and how these might affect bargaining, see Margaret F. Brinig, *Does Mediation Disadvantage Women?*, 2 Wm & Mary J of Women and the Law 1 (1995).

Chapter II

A PAUSE TO REFLECT: THE THEMES AND FUNCTIONS OF FAMILY LAW

The remoter and more general aspects of the law are those which give it universal interest. It is through them that you not only become a great master in your calling, but connect your subject with the universe and catch an echo of the infinite, a glimpse of its unfathomable process, a hint of the universal law.

Oliver Wendell Holmes
The Path of the Law

No area of law is simply a collection of random, unrelated doctrines. Any area of law responds to a finite set of social demands, performs a limited set of functions, encounters recurring problems, and fixes on a small set of standard responses. Any field, however haltingly and ineptly, tries to rationalize and unify its rules. The lawyer who wants to understand an area of law must therefore identify and comprehend its recurrent patterns and purposes. This casebook makes that task one of its primary goals. This chapter begins that task by sketching twelve themes that recur in family law and by identifying five functions family law (and perhaps all law) performs. We will continue that task by devoting each chapter not just to a subject of family law, but also to a particular theme of family law.

SECTION 1. THE THEMES OF FAMILY LAW

Theory is the most important part of the dogma of the law, as the architect is the most important man who takes part in the building of a house.

Oliver Wendell Holmes
The Path of the Law

In family law, as in any other area of law, some issues show up again and again. In this casebook, we will particularly consider twelve of these themes. Of course, there are a number of equally significant themes we might have added to the list, and we will give some of these a good deal of thought. But we have given special attention to twelve themes by addressing each of them explicitly in the chapter which raises the problems surrounding the theme in the most illuminating way. Most chapters, then, will include readings designed to help you think about a theme in general and about its application to family law.

The purpose of this chapter, then, is to identify the twelve themes and to sketch their outlines. Yet if each of these themes will be extensively explored in the appropriate chapter, why read about them as a group now? We see several compelling benefits in doing so. First, it will often be helpful to think about each theme in the context of the problems raised in many of the chapters, not just one. This chapter allows you to think about such themes even before the chapter in which they are explicitly raised. Second, one characteristic of these themes is that they deal with problems that are important not just in family law but in other areas of law as well. We sketch the themes in advance to remind you how much you already know about them from your study of other areas of law and to encourage you to bring what you know about them to your study of family law. Third, the chapter on the law of husband and wife which you have just read raises in a narrow compass and in an accessible way many basic questions about the purpose and problems of family law. In other words, the past chapter is prologue to the rest of the book. Our preview of the themes of family law provides a vehicle for reviewing that crucial chapter, and particularly its emblematic case, *Reynolds v. United States*, in terms of the themes that will recur throughout the book. Or, in yet other words, this chapter attempts to solve a problem confronted by all casebooks, namely, that most areas of law make sense only when you understand the whole area, but you can understand the whole area only one piece at a time. This chapter attempts to give you a conceptual overview that will reveal some of the pieces in their places as early as possible.

A. THE DOCTRINE OF FAMILY AUTONOMY: A PERVASIVE THEME

We begin our survey by examining three themes that are so pervasive that they can hardly be isolated as themes. The first of these is the "theme" of family autonomy. The doctrine of family autonomy, as you will shortly learn, holds that the state should intervene in the family as little as possible, that as much as possible the state should leave the family to its own devices. In American family law, that doctrine has achieved considerable prominence.

We will discuss the doctrine of family autonomy at some length in the next chapter. But the theme will appear, although not as the only actor, in each chapter. It has had a starring role in Chapter I, since we have been centrally asking how far the state's power to regulate the formation and definition of families should extend. It will be the eponymous character in the chapter on state intervention in the marriage. It will be the ghost of Hamlet's father in the chapter on marital responsibilities, since that chapter will always be concerned with how far the state should enforce those responsibilities. It will return to center stage in the chapter on contracts in family law, for they can be seen as an attempt to confine the scope of state regulation of marriage in favor of private ordering. It will play a crucial and complex part in the chapter on the unmarried couple, since a basic question that chapter considers is not just whether the state should defer to private decisions about intimate relationships; the question is also how the state can best defer. It again becomes the protagonist when we move to the chapter on the constitutional view of families and the concept of rights, since the question what rights family members have is often the same question as what limitations there ought to be on the power of the government. It has a featured role in the chapter on child custody, for there we will repeatedly ask whether there is a way of limiting the state's authority to decide conflicts over children. It will have at least as important a part in the chapter on child protection, although there we are more likely to be asking whether the family autonomy doctrine restricts the state too much rather than too little. It has only a supporting part in the chapter on child-support enforcement, but the question how far the state should go in enforcing even an obligation that is widely thought unexceptionable is not a small question, particularly when the issue is whether a parental agreement about support should be regulated by legislation. And, it has a respectable part in the ensemble performance that makes up the chapter on "parent, child, community, and state," for that chapter deals with the conflicting claims to authority over children of parents, their communities, and the state.

Despite (or because of) its importance, the role of family autonomy has its limits. There are obviously times when the state must intervene, and there will be times when people will disagree over what the state should do. Throughout the casebook, then, we will ask you to try to articulate the limits of the doctrine.

We will also ask you to articulate the nature and basis of the doctrine. We will ask, for example, whether the doctrine of family autonomy is simply another version of the principle of individual autonomy. Or does family autonomy draw on concepts of what it means to live intimately with other people that may even conflict with individual autonomy? We will investigate this possibility in many forms, as when we consider the long tradition of treating members of the family as a legal entity and when we ask what kinds of economic and social individual autonomy are given up when the individual joins a family.

In sum, a casebook on family law without the doctrine of family autonomy would be like *Hamlet* without the Dane. On the other hand, *Hamlet* without Claudius wouldn't be much of a play either. We will therefore ask a few questions about family autonomy and the law of husband and wife and then turn to the second pervasive theme of family law (and blessedly take advantage of the change of scene to drop the curtain on the now-played-out dramatic metaphor).

Notes and Questions on Family Autonomy

(1) Does the problem of family autonomy present itself in *Reynolds*, *Israel*, and *Goodridge*? If so, in what form? If the state prohibits sexual relations between the would-be spouses in those kinds of cases, the state surely seems to be "intervening." But what if it simply refuses to recognize each heterodox kind of marriage? Or might the state be "intervening" in "the family" by granting legal recognition to those marriages? In other words, might it be argued that, by the very acts of according legal consequences to a relationship, of inquiring into whether the acts of the parties in entering and conducting the relationship are such as to evoke legal consequences, and of supervising the relationship's dissolution the state is affecting the parties' relationship? Is *every* governmental decision to regulate or not to regulate families intervention in the sense that both kinds of decisions have consequences for families? Is this a useful sense of "intervention"? Are there differences between intervention by regulation and by failure to regulate? If so, are they important differences?

(2) Why were the parties in each of these cases seeking to enter a state-approved marriage? Why wouldn't it have been enough for them to consider themselves married? Of course, one reason might be that the legal status of marriage would shelter them from prosecution under a statute which in some form forbade non-marital sexual relations. Assume again, however, that the state would allow each set of parties to live as spouses but would simply withhold legal recognition of their relationship as a marriage. This in fact describes the reality at least as to non-incestuous adult heterosexual relations in most of America today, yet people still marry in droves. Why? What legal incentives are there to marry? What social incentives? Are there legal and social disincentives to marry?

(3) Why does the state sponsor the institution of marriage? Why doesn't the state simply let people live together and conduct sexual relations however they choose without attaching legal consequences to these choices? Are the reasons you can suggest substantial enough to justify the undoubted costs of state sponsorship and regulation of marriage?

B. THE PRINCIPLE OF INDIVIDUAL AUTONOMY: A SECOND PERVASIVE THEME

One of the most potent ideas in American law is the belief in the centrality of individual autonomy. Autonomy is not just institutionalized as a value of American law; it is cherished as the heart of American life. Americans of all stripes believe that at least some aspects of "private life" are not the law's business, even though they disagree about just which aspects those are. It is thus no surprise that questions about the scope of individual autonomy pervade and perplex family law.

Such questions appear most conspicuously in the context of government regulations of the behavior of "consenting adults." Governmental regulation of sexual activity has long been challenged on exactly those grounds, and it is on those grounds that governmental restrictions on abortion are questioned.

But although autonomy questions are usually thought of in terms of a contest between the individual and the state, family law presents those questions in a harder form. Family law deals with times people's autonomy has been compromised not just by the power of the state, but also by their duties to and reliance on members of their family. In addition, it deals with times people's autonomy has been limited by the social conventions and pressures amidst which they live. When we consider questions of divorce, alimony, and marital property, we may find that applying the principle of autonomy can become quite complex, since more than one person's autonomy is at issue. This problem becomes even more acute in the areas of child custody, child support, and child abuse, for there one of the parties at interest is a person whose claim to autonomy may be restricted by immaturity.

In short, one problem you should be alert to as you read these materials is that it can be difficult to maximize individual autonomy in family law, since the autonomy of one person so regularly conflicts with the autonomy of others. A second problem for you to consider is the possibility that it is not always desirable to maximize autonomy. After all, autonomy is not the only individual or social good, and thus unlimited autonomy is unlikely to be individually desired or socially desirable—or, of course, even possible. It may be, then, that what is needed is an optimal, not a maximal level of autonomy.

Indeed, it might even be paradoxically argued that too much autonomy restricts individual freedom. Peter Berger, for instance, writes that "it is not so much that individuals become convinced of their capacity and right to choose new ways of life, but rather that tradition is weakened to the point where they *must* choose between alternatives whether they wish it or not.... [O]ne of the most archaic functions of society is to take away from individuals the burden of choice." *Toward a Critique of Modernity*, in *Facing Up to Modernity: Excursions in Society, Politics, and Religion* 77 (Basic Books, 1977). The point here is not that the burden of choice is in any particular instance intolerable; rather, it is that the combined burdens can become intolerable, or at least become so numerous as to distract one from other significant choices and thus diminish one's autonomy in other areas.

Notes and Questions on Individual Autonomy

(1) Is *Reynolds* an affront or an aid to individual autonomy? Should we see the case as an instance of the state's thwarting one man's desire and decision to have several wives? Or should we see it as the state's effort to protect women against the social imposition of a duty which women at the time might have been anxious to escape? In the social

circumstances of the time and place, can Reynolds' wives be said be have made an "autonomous" decision to marry plurally? Did his first wife have any choice in the matter? What makes a decision "autonomous"?

(2) Similarly, is *Israel* an affront or an aid to individual autonomy? Was Tammy Israel's autonomy infringed by the state, which prevented her from marrying the man of her choice, or by Martin Israel, whose relationship with her might (depending on facts we do not know) have been coercive?

(3) In *Reynolds* and *Israel* it might be said that all the parties were acting autonomously, but that most people in the situation of Reynolds' wives and of Tammy Israel would not, as a social matter, be comparably free. Should the parties in *Reynolds* and *Israel* be asked to forego their autonomy claims in the interests of protecting the autonomy of those other people?

(4) Were the plaintiffs in *Goodridge* trying to exercise autonomy or involve the state in their relationship? Aren't they trying to involve the community in their relationship? And isn't that what the opinion claims is happening?

(5) Think again about the Appleby hypothetical. Mr. Appleby wanted his freedom; Mrs. Appleby wanted to stay married. Their two exercises of autonomous choice were in conflict. Can the principle of autonomy help us decide how this conflict should be resolved?

(6) Throughout Chapter 1, we encountered situations in which claims of individual autonomy were pitted against various kinds of social interests. What were those social interests? When do you think they were strong enough to overcome the autonomy claims?

C. GENDER AND FAMILY LAW: A THIRD PERVASIVE THEME

Family law is centrally about the role women do and should play in family life and in society. Traditionally, family law supposed that women's lives were centrally organized around their families. It essentially supposed, in other words, a model of the middle-class family in which women raised the family's children and kept the family's house while their husbands earned the income needed to provide for their families. Such women might be well-educated and might participate in civic and charitable affairs, but they would generally not participate in the labor market. Their lives, their fortunes, and their status revolved around home and family. Husbands were legally required to support their wives. Divorce was made difficult partly to prevent wives from being abandoned by their husbands. Husbands were expected to pay alimony unless their divorce was justified by their wife's marital fault. On divorce, mothers received custody of the family's children, while fathers were responsible for paying to support those children.

In the 1960s and '70s, the social basis of family law began to collapse both empirically and normatively. In particular, women streamed into the labor market. The women's movement argued with growing success for the equality of men and women in all spheres. And women came increasingly to be expected to find meaning in their lives outside the family. As the social basis of family law eroded, the search began for new principles of organization. The old principles, based in important ways on different roles for men and women, were rejected. But what was to take their place?

The debate over that question has been significantly influenced by the increasing numbers of women in law and in academic life. As women began organizing politically and writing professionally, they took as their subject all aspects of society, including themselves, their families, and family law. Feminist thought (or women's studies) now figures prominently in most universities, and law schools and legal journals are no exceptions.

This development is complicated, however, for within the women's perspective are several, sometimes conflicting, strains. One group—often called liberal feminists—insists on the transcendence of such values as equality and independence. They therefore resist laws whose means or effect will be to keep women in traditional roles, and they stress reforms in the workplace that will make it easier for women to take their place in public life.

A second group of feminists, on the other hand, maintains that women differ from men in important ways. These "relational" or "difference" feminists suggest that women are likelier than men to value compassion, concern, altruism, and human relationships. Such feminists are likelier than their liberal-feminist counterparts to advocate legal changes that make it easier for women to seek accomplishment in ways that honor those kinds of preferences and activities.

Finally, there is a strain of radical feminists. In general, they take a stronger line than the liberal and relational feminists. For example, some members of this school object to marriage itself. And in particular, they argue for introducing women's values broadly into social—and legal—discourse.

In short, one of the recurring issues in feminist thought and jurisprudence is whether women are intrinsically like men. This difference in focus defines the dominant schools of feminist thought, including feminist thought about family law. See, e.g., Robin West, *The Jurisprudence of Gender*, 55 U Chi L Rev 1 (1988). (Of course, many feminists do not fall neatly into any of these camps.)

Because the role of women is central to family law, we treat it pervasively as well as investigating it in a number of more specific contexts. We will, for example, put the principle of family autonomy to its harshest test by inquiring into the extent to which it ought to influence our thinking about spouse abuse, a social problem that is generally understood to be essentially about the abuse of wives by husbands. We will then move on to deal with the consequences of women's relatively weak position in the labor market. Historically, one legal response to (and cause of?) that weakness was to impose on husbands a duty to support their wives. What ought to be the fate of such a rule in an age of gender equality? Another historical response to that weakness was to extend the duty of support beyond divorce through the doctrine of alimony. Is such a doctrine still necessary because of women's position in the labor market, or is alimony's general consequence to perpetuate the dependence of women on men? Next, our study of dividing marital property on divorce will lead us to ask how the different kinds of contributions to families that men and women have historically made have been and ought to be valued. When we then come to consider the contractualization of family law, we will centrally ask whether that development represents a way for women to free themselves from disadvantageous legal rules and social customs or whether it represents another way of perpetuating gender inequality indirectly. We will pursue that question further when we look at the enforceability of contracts between unmarried cohabitants. The question of women's legal freedom will also be addressed in one of its most direct and controversial forms—when we consider the constitutionalization of family law and, most prominently, *Roe v. Wade*. Questions about the situation of women will retain much of their importance when we move to our material on parents and children. For instance, we will examine the present and proper status of the practice of generally awarding custody of children on divorce to mothers. And for another instance, we will look at the longstanding problem of enforcing the child-support obligations non-custodial fathers owe custodial mothers.

Notes and Questions on Gender and Family Law

(1) We said that the question whether women and men are essentially similar or importantly different helps define the schools of feminism. This question has important implications for family law. In particular, it has consequences for the extent to which the law should try to equalize the situation of men and women. The question will surface throughout this book as we consider alimony (Chapter 5), abortion (Chapter 7), and custody (Chapter 9). Does the idea of equality, undoubtedly important in the labor market, translate easily into the family law context? Should it? If women have traditionally performed significant roles in the household, especially in child rearing, and these roles importantly influence their labor market wages, should the law require that wages be equalized? Should it deny special legal protections for caretakers? For women who bear children as opposed to men who merely sire them?

(2) Another, related, issue is also at the heart of a "school" of feminism, the "radical feminist" approach. For example, consider this statement: "Women are not children, but coerced women are effectively deprived of power over the expressive products of their coercion." Catherine Mackinnon, *Feminism Unmodified: Discourses on Life and Law* 182–83 (Harv U Press, 1987). Does the fact that men have historically been more powerful than women (and may still be), change the way

we ought to look at marriage? At questions like surrogacy? Mediation? In other words, must marriage be redefined, or abandoned altogether, to minimize opportunities for coercion? Is surrogate motherhood an occasion of women's repression or empowerment (through gaining wages for what has not been considered market work)? Will informal dispute resolution at divorce result in women being systematically disadvantaged by their husbands?

(3) Is law an appropriate instrument for dealing with what is really a social problem? For example, should divorcing men, but not married men, have to compensate for women's generally lower market wages or relative lack of retirement assets? Should displaced homemakers in the next few years be denied alimony in order to encourage the proper investment in job market skills by (and therefore more pervasive independence and financial equality for) today's young women? See Cynthia Starnes, *Divorce and the Displaced Homemaker: A Discourse on Playing with Dolls, Partnership Buyouts and Dissociation under No–Fault*, 60 U Chi L Rev 67 (1993).

(4) At this point, you should find it helpful to review the issues raised in Question (2)(g) of Chapter 1's questions on polygamous marriage.

D. HUMAN NATURE AND FAMILY LAW: A FOURTH PERVASIVE THEME

The maxim that the knowledge man needs most is knowledge of himself was an article of the religious creed of the Greeks at least two and half millennia ago, and the injunction inscribed upon the temple at Delphos has not lacked iteration through the subsequent centuries. But to no generation of men can it have come with more force than to our own.

Arthur O. Lovejoy
Reflections on Human Nature

Few questions will so greatly shape an area of law as the questions what human nature is and how society ought in consequence to be organized. The following passage from an article by Professor Schneider states that view and provides questions you should keep in mind in reading this section:

> [W]hat views of human nature inform family law? This is surely a question of the utmost interest and importance. A family law that fears that people are naturally depraved must differ from one that hopes they are naturally virtuous. Yet this fascinating and crucial question seems never to have been addressed. How have changing views of human nature shaped family law? Is post-Freudian family law different from pre-Freudian family law? Much of the constitutional doctrine of privacy and its attendant scholarship rests on facile assumptions about what is necessary for human dignity and happiness. What are those assumptions? Do we actually believe them? Is belief in them class-bound? Are

they correct? If so, are family laws consistent with them? How much freedom in personal affairs do people need? How much do they want? How much should they have?

Carl E. Schneider, *The Next Step: Definition, Generalization, and Theory in American Family Law* 18 U Mich J Law Ref 1039, 1057–58 (1985).

(1) The Pessimistic View

Civilization has to use its utmost efforts in order to set limits to man's aggressive instincts and to hold the manifestations of them in check by psychical reaction-formations. Hence, therefore, the use of methods intended to incite people into identifications and aim inhibited relationships of love, hence the restriction upon sexual life, and hence too the ideal's commandment to love one's neighbour as oneself—a commandment which is really justified by the fact that nothing else runs so strongly counter to the original nature of man.

Sigmund Freud
Civilization and its Discontents

The traditional view of marriage that we explored in Chapter 1 is, of course, part of a larger view of human nature. We will therefore continue our investigation of the traditional view of marriage by looking at its underlying view of human nature. As you read, you should ask to what extent that view of human nature is still current. To the extent (and it is surely an important extent) that that view is no longer current (or at least predominant), you should ask yourself what has replaced it. To the extent that you believe that that view is wrong, you should ask what ought to replace it.

The view of human nature on which the traditional view of marriage most strongly, although not exclusively or necessarily, relies we will call—regretfully and for want of a better term—the pessimistic view. Let us now define it somewhat more fully, if abstractly and ahistorically. The pessimistic view draws on many traditions. It may see mankind's nature as evil; it at least believes people are easily led to harm themselves and other people by their own self-interestedness. Thus Aristotle believed that

> [l]iving under the dictates of passion, they [most people] chase the pleasures fit for such natures and the means of gratifying them, and they shun the pains which are the opposite of those pleasures. But the honourable and the truly delightful—of that they have no conception....

The Ethics of Aristotle 310 (Penguin, 1953).

Thus St. Paul wrote that he was

> carnal, sold under sin.... For I know that in my members (that is, in my flesh,) dwelleth no good thing: for to will is present with me; but how to perform that which is good I find not. For the good that I would I do not: but the evil which I would not, that I do.

Romans 7:14, 18–19.

Thus Voltaire expostulated,

> Men in general are foolish, ungrateful, jealous, covetous of their neighbor's goods; abusing their superiority when they are strong, and tricksters when they are weak.... Power is commonly possessed, in States and in families, by those who have the strongest arms, the most resolute minds and the hardest hearts. From which the moralists of all ages have concluded that the human species is of little worth; and in this they have not departed widely from the truth.

Dieu et les hommes, quoted in Arthur O. Lovejoy, *Reflections on Human Nature* 6 (Johns Hopkins Press, 1961).

And thus, as James Q. Wilson concludes,

> every society has tried to curb our elemental, and thus our especially powerful, passions. The clear implication is that learning, culture, norms—all of the components of the social bond—are quite precarious, for they are contrivances, not instincts, created for collective but not individual advantage and maintained by creaky and uncertain institutions rather than by powerful and always-present emotions.

The Moral Sense 24 (Free Press, 1993).

The pessimistic view is not necessarily hostile to the pleasures of the senses, though it can sometimes be and is even more often thought to be. The pessimistic view does, however, appreciate the power of those pleasures and recognizes that they can divert people from better ends and drive them toward worse ones. It therefore contrives to channel those pleasures into the service of good, as when it summons sexual passion to exalt love in marriage. Insofar as mankind's destructive propensities cannot be channeled into good, this view of human nature hopes to curb those propensities by social conditioning which seeks to internalize self-restraint.

The pessimistic view of human nature has long influenced American social and legal thought. As one scholar writes,

> The liberalism of the Framers ... did not view the end of the state as the equal protection of the right of each to think and do as he wished. Early liberals ... were confident that they could identify the activities and beliefs reason permitted and sometimes required, and that they could then draw lines distinguishing "liberty," which encompassed such rational activities and beliefs, from "license," the expressions of man's baser desires and passions....
>
> The claim that true liberty requires the rule of reason over the passions was a chief characteristic of the "moderate Enlightenment" liberalism embodied in the constitution....
>
> [U]ltimately, for the liberal intellectuals at least, the pleasures of the mind, the delights of wisdom and moral virtue, were still seen as higher than those of the body, and it was such rational perfection that men should seek most of all.

Rogers Smith, *The Constitution and Autonomy*, 60 Tex L Rev 175, 177–78 (1982). The pessimistic view of human nature expressly underlay colonial family law and implicitly undergirded family law throughout the nineteenth century. Late eighteenth-century law (the law of the Constitution's era) regulated the family intensively and intrusively and embodied such restrictions as prohibitions of fornication, cohabitation, adultery, abortion, sodomy, and incest, to say nothing of the virtual prohibition of divorce. Late nineteenth-century law (the law of the fourteenth amendment's era) preserved those prohibitions and added new ones, including Comstock laws regulating contraceptives and laws intensifying the regulation of abortion. In sum, the pessimistic view has been effectively attacked as a basis for family law only recently.

Let us now say a word about how important elements of three major intellectual traditions have contributed to and deepened the pessimistic understanding of human nature. The first of these traditions is Christianity. Powerful currents in both Catholicism and Protestantism have held that people are naturally sinful, that sin particularly manifests itself in family and sexual life, and that this human tendency must be constrained through an elaborate system of inhibitions, proscriptions, and renunciations. Although those currents may have flowed most notably from St. Augustine and John Calvin, they flow freely even today. And while the Christian version of this understanding of human nature has been the one most influential in American history, its ascetic aspects find their equivalents in many of the world's major religions and in aspects of classical philosophy.

The second tradition supplying intellectual sustenance to the pessimistic view of human nature is psychology. Psychology is obviously a two-edged sword, because it is also a leading contributor to an opposite and now perhaps dominant view of human nature and of a corresponding view of social policy that calls for relaxing social constraints. Yet for just this reason we need to recall psychology's darker strain. Men, Freud tells us in a chilling passage,

> are not gentle creatures who want to be loved . . . ; they are, on the contrary, creatures among whose instinctual endowments is to be reckoned a powerful share of aggressiveness. As a result, their neighbour is for them not only a potential helper or sexual object, but also someone who tempts them to satisfy their aggressiveness on him . . . , to use him sexually without his consent . . . , to humiliate him . . . , to torture and to kill him. Homo homini lupus. [Man is a wolf to man.]

Sigmund Freud, *Civilization and its Discontents* 58–59 (1930).

The third of the traditions is sociology. As Professor Grey observes, "[E]very thinker of the great central tradition of the last century's social thought has seen repressed sexuality and the authoritarian family structure as close to the core of our civilization. Conservative theorists have defended repression as necessary; revolutionaries have urged that society would have to be overthrown to free us from its tyranny." Thomas Grey, *Eros, Civilization and the Burger Court*, 43 Law & Contemp Prob 83

(1980). A classic statement of this view is, of course, Max Weber's celebrated *The Protestant Ethic and the Spirit of Capitalism*, which attributes the rise of the capitalist ethos to a stern religious asceticism: "Combined with the harsh doctrines of the absolute transcendality of God and the corruption of everything pertaining to the flesh, this inner isolation of the individual [caused by turmoil induced by the doctrine of predestination] contains ... the reason for the entirely negative attitude of Puritanism to all the sensuous and emotional elements in culture and in religion, because they are of no use toward salvation...." Max Weber, *The Protestant Ethic and the Spirit of Capitalism* 105 (Routledge, 1958). As capitalism developed, some of the religious element of that asceticism faded, but it left a "rational asceticism" which condemned impulsive enjoyment of life as leading "away both from work in a calling and from religion."

In his inimitably vivid way, one eminent Victorian—James Fitzjames Stephen—summarized his understanding of the pessimistic view (in the process of attacking an even more eminent Victorian—John Stuart Mill):

> The great defect of Mr Mill's later writings seems to me to be that he has formed too favourable an estimate of human nature. This displays itself in the chapter now under consideration [*On Liberty*, Chapter II] by the tacit assumption which pervades every part of it that the removal of restraints usually tends to invigorate character. Surely the very opposite of this is the truth. Habitual exertion is the greatest of all invigorators of character, and restraint and coercion in one form or another is the great stimulus to exertion....
>
> This leads me to say a few words on Mr Mill's criticism on "the great Calvinistic theory." ...
>
> Calvin's general doctrine ... is something like this. The one great offence of man lies in the fact that, having before him good and evil, his weaker and worse appetites lead him to choose evil.... Man has a fearful disease, but his original constitution is excellent. Redemption consists not in killing but in curing his nature. Calvin describes original sin as "the inheritably descending perverseness and corruption of our nature poured abroad into all the parts of the soul," bringing forth "the works of the flesh," or, in other words, vice in all its forms.... I think that if Calvin were translated into modern language it would be hard to deny this. Speak or fail to speak of God as you think right, but the fact that men are deeply moved by ideas about power, wisdom, and goodness, on a superhuman scale which they rather apprehend than comprehend, is certain. Speak of original sin or not as you please, but the fact that all men are in some respects and at some times both weak and wicked, that they do the ill they would not do, and shun the good they would pursue, is no less certain. To describe this state of things as a "miserable bondage" is, to say the least, an intelligible way of speaking. Calvin's theory was that in order to escape from this bondage men must be true to the better part of their nature, keep in proper subjection its baser elements, and look up to God as the source of the only valuable kind of freedom—freedom to be good and wise. To describe this doctrine as a

> depressing influence leading to the crushing out of the human faculties, capacities, and susceptibilities, is to show an incapacity to separate from theological and scholastic husks the grain on which some of the bravest, hardiest, and most vigorous men that ever trod the face of this earth were nourished. No theory can possibly be right which requires us to believe that such a man as John Knox was a poor heartbroken creature with no will of his own.

Liberty, Equality, Fraternity 81–83 (U Chi Press, 1991, originally published 1874).

The pessimistic view of human nature is associated with what might—again, rather imprecisely—be called an ascetic approach to sexual and family life, an approach that underlies and helps explain the relatively restrictive social and legal codes of behavior that have traditionally governed that life in the United States. The ascetic approach has four analytically distinct but often intermixed aspects. The first aspect might be called the prudential. In the prudential view, sexual relations are best kept restrained because of the risks of unrestraint. Such risks have typically included unwanted pregnancy and venereal disease and the danger that extra-marital sexual activities might unsettle the stability of the family. This aspect of the ascetic approach has a long history and has, of course, had something of a renaissance because—in important part—of AIDS.

In its second aspect, the ascetic approach holds that sexual restraint is desirable because sexual activity distracts people from what are thought of as higher goals. We have already seen Professor Smith ascribing such a view to the Framers of the Constitution. Stuart Hampshire traces it much further back: "Having only partially freed himself from Plato, Aristotle retains the model of the soul as corresponding to the due gradations of the social order: reason as the master and governing class, desire as properly the co-operative subordinate auxiliary class and our animal nature as a dumb proletariat." *Innocence and Experience* 34 (Harv U Press, 1989). Some of this attitude's adherents—John Stuart Mill, for example—tend to see the sexual side of human life as mindless and irrational, while tending to believe that what makes human life different from and better than other forms of life is that people can be rational and can make decisions that allow them to control their lives. Other adherents believe that sexual relations are dangerous because it is easy to be habituated to them and thus to lead a self-centered and unproductive life. Walter Lippman expressed some of this second aspect of the ascetic view when he said,

> Men like St. Paul and St. Augustine knew in the most direct way what sexual desire can do to distract the religious life; how if it is not sternly regulated, and if it is allowed to run wild, it intoxicates the whole personality to the exclusion of spiritual interests.... [W]hen Paul spoke of the law of his members warring against the law of his mind, and bringing him into captivity to the law of sin, he had made a realistic observation which any candid person can verify out of his own experience.

Walter Lippmann, *A Preface to Morals* 90 (The Macmillan Company, 1929). A striking and perhaps unexpected expression of the second aspect of the ascetic approach comes from the notebooks of Albert Camus:

> Sexual life was given to man, perhaps, to turn him aside from his true path. It is his opium. In it everything goes to sleep. Outside it things take on life again. At the same time chastity puts an end to the species which is, perhaps, the truth.
>
> Sexuality leads to nothing. It is not immoral, but it is unproductive. One can give oneself to it for a time when one does not wish to produce. But chastity alone is connected with personal progress.
>
> There is a time when sexuality is a victory—when it is released from moral imperatives. But it quickly becomes a defeat afterwards—and the only victory is won over it in its turn: that is chastity.

In its third aspect, the ascetic approach speaks to the relationship between individuals. This aspect holds that what is important in life is to treat other people decently and that this means, at least, treating them as people, not as things to be used. Non-affectional sexual and familial relations are regarded as treating people as things to be used, as a means instead of an end, and thus to be avoided. This view has obvious Kantian characteristics, but it is also to be found today in, for example, feminist criticisms of some attitudes toward the relations between men and women.

The first three aspects of the ascetic approach tend to be conceived in terms of the relations of specific individuals. The fourth aspect draws on the first three and looks at the larger social effects of an unconstrained human nature. As we have already noted, there is a powerful tradition in Western thought that sees in humanity's sexual nature "a stupendous source of energy, far exceeding any comparable store elsewhere in the animal kingdom. As a compound of physical and psychic forces, eroticized sexuality has an extraordinary infiltrating power and makes the human being the most sexual of all animals." Richard S. Randall, *Freedom and Taboo: Pornography and the Politics of a Self Divided* 3 (U Cal Press, 1989). This force can drive people to behave in all the kinds of destructive ways we have been cataloguing in the last few pages. What is needed then, adherents of this view argue, is to take that energy and divert it toward more constructive purposes.

We have been examining the ascetic view of human nature because it has crucially undergirded much of family law. But just what kinds of consequences has that view had for the field? Sometimes family law has sought to prohibit directly behavior that has been thought harmful. Laws prohibiting the sexual abuse of children exemplify such an expression of the ascetic view. Family law has also sought to deter undesirable behavior indirectly. Attempts to dissuade people from divorce by requiring them to undergo a waiting period are examples of this approach. Family law can also be seen as a systematic attempt to influence behavior by reinforcing in people attitudes that encourage restraint in family and sexual settings. In this sense, family law (at least in its traditional form) can be seen as implementing a "socializing strategy."

Professor Schneider describes the way such a strategy tries to work in the following passage:

> The socializing strategy may be assessed in terms derived from the work of Stuart Hampshire [see *Morality and Conflict* (B. Blackwell, 1983), particularly Chapter 4, *Morality and Pessimism*]. He observes that, while some systems of morality derive and acquire their unity from divine revelation or rational inquiry, morality can also derive and acquire its unity from a pattern of moral injunctions recognized in the experience, ideals, and practices of a group. This pattern of moral injunctions helps define a way of life, and that way of life helps give meaning to the life of the group and the lives of its members. Systems of morality of this kind, as Hampshire argues, typically include:
>
>> a number of different moral prohibitions, apparent barriers to action, which a man acknowledges and which he thinks of as more or less insurmountable, except in abnormal, painful and improbable circumstances. One expects to meet these prohibitions, barriers to action, in certain quite distinct and clearly marked areas of action; these are the taking of human life, sexual relations, family duties and obligations, and the administration of justice according to the laws and customs of a given society. In the face of the doing of something that must not be done, and that is categorically excluded and forbidden morally, the fear that one may feel is fear of human nature. A relapse into a state of nature seems a real possibility or perhaps seems actually to have occurred....
>
> In Hampshire's understanding, then, society is defined (in one significant but not exclusive way) by a series of emphatic moral prohibitions about the family, sexual relations, and violence. These prohibitions, while not necessarily related to each other in a purely logical sense, are related in people's minds through similarities in subject matter and through their integration into a way of life. The statutes challenged in privacy cases conspicuously deal with precisely those subjects, and on this view, they may be attempts to influence behavior by affirming those strategic moral prohibitions.

Carl E. Schneider, *State-Interest Analysis in Fourteenth Amendment "Privacy" Law: An Essay on the Constitutionalization of Social Issues*, 51 Law & Contemp Prob 79, 99 (1988).

Questions on Human Nature and Family Law

(1) Is the pessimistic view of human nature convincing? Does it accord with your experience? Even if it is convincing, does the ascetic approach to sexual and family life follow convincingly from it?

(2) The pessimistic view of human nature was a crucial part of the foundation of traditional family law. But that view is no longer intellectually and socially pre-eminent, nor is it the basis for much of the family law that has been emerging in the last two decades. What views of

human nature now oppose the pessimistic view and how are those views reflected in modern family law?

(2) The Therapeutic View

> *In short, we repudiated all versions of the doctrine of original sin, of there being insane and irrational springs of wickedness in most men. We were not aware that civilisation was a thin and precarious crust ... only maintained by rules and conventions skillfully put across and guilefully preserved. We had no respect for traditional wisdom or the restraints of custom.... It did not occur to us to respect the extraordinary accomplishment of our predecessors in the ordering of life (as it now seems to me to have been) or the elaborate framework which they had devised to protect this order.*
>
> John Maynard Keynes
> *My Early Beliefs*

When we discussed the ascetic view of human nature, we said that that view had lost its prepotence, and we asked you to try to describe views which were contenders to replace it. We will now briefly examine one such contender. What follows is an excerpt from an article in which Professor Schneider argued that there is a tendency for late-twentieth-century Americans to think about human nature in medical—and particularly in psychologic—terms:

CARL E. SCHNEIDER MORAL DISCOURSE AND THE TRANSFORMATION OF AMERICAN FAMILY LAW

83 Michigan Law Review 1803 (1985)

a. The complexities of the shift. The shift to psychologism has, of course, been described before, usually in apocalyptic woe or messianic joy. Nevertheless, the shift confounds description because it is intellectually fragmented and complex. Its patriarch and paradigm, surely, is Freud. But no important thought achieves social power undegraded, and Freud's thought has reached its present power in a gaudy array of vulgarizations which have, in the public mind, overwhelmed the sophisticated variants.

The shift further confounds description because it is also sociologically complex. Nevertheless, its scope and significance cannot be doubted. Thus three leading students of the shift announce "the introduction of the 'era of psychology.' " A 1957 study on which those scholars rely "spoke of a psychological orientation, as distinguished from material or moral orientations, and suggested that this way of looking at life experiences and life problems might increase significantly in the future." By 1976, they conclude, "this shift had indeed occurred."

b. From morals to medicine: the role of human happiness. For our purposes, a central feature of the psychologic view is that it replaces moral discourse with medical discourse and moral thought with therapeutic thought. That shift may usefully be understood in terms of the role attributed to human happiness in social life. The old view held that men and women were obligated to lead a good life as that was defined by religious or social convention. Happiness was not the purpose of these conventions, but was expected to be a by-product of performing one's duties. If it did not come, however, one would be consoled by knowing one had led the right kind of life. The psychologic view, at least in its ideal type, denies that there are religious or social conventions that are independently valid. It holds that life's goal is the search for personal well-being, adjustment, and contentment—in short, for "health." Adherence to a religious or social convention may serve that end, but if it does not, other paths to well-being should be tried and used. In short, says Rieff mordantly,

> [E]vil and immorality are disappearing, as Spencer assumed they would, mainly because our culture is changing its definition of human perfection. No longer the Saint, but the instinctual Everyman, twisting his neck uncomfortably inside the starched collar of culture, is the communal ideal, to whom men offer tacit prayers for deliverance from their inherited renunciations.

On the old view, the right life was difficult: one's duties were numerous and onerous (though not necessarily unpleasant); distractions from duty were numerous and dangerous. Thus codes of family morality were aspirational and ascetic. As Professor Rieff observes:

> Heretofore, the saving arrangements of Western culture have appeared as symbol systems communicating demands by stoning the sensual with deprivations, and were thus operated in a dynamically ambivalent mode. Our culture developed, as its general technique of salvation, assents to moral demands that treated the sensual part of the self as an enemy. From mastery over this enemy-self there developed some triumphant moral feeling; a character ideal was born.

The psychologic view concedes that "stoning the sensual with deprivations" can work, but doubts it will. That view sees the drive of the instincts as crucial to understanding human motivation, believes that confining the drive of the instincts tends to be unhealthy, and, more specifically, sees sexual expression as central to human happiness.

c. *Antinomianism, pragmatism, and nonbinding commitments.* In his search for health, psychologic man must be skeptical and analytic in method and pragmatic in evaluation. In particular, psychological man must learn not to judge himself, his relationships, or other people according to moral rules; to do so is dysfunctional, since it asks the wrong question ("Is it right?") and blinds him to the answers to the right question ("Does it work?"). In other words, psychological man cannot come to rest in any relationship, or any community, or any creed; he must keep asking whether they are working for him. This is the doctrine of "nonbinding commitments." Personal and familial relations, on this view, become "arrangement[s] of convenience designed to advance the personal satisfactions and self-fulfillment of [their] members."

d. The search for self and the psychologic view of human nature. In the psychologic view, happiness comes from discovering and expressing one's unique true self. That self is discovered by peeling off society's false impositions and is expressed by peeling off its false constraints. Among the false impositions and constraints to be peeled off in the search for the "more personalized self-consciousness" are the roles and statuses into which society places people. Thus Veroff, Douvan, and Kulka announce as one of their "central themes" that "[s]ocial organization, social norms, the adaptation to and successful performance of social roles all seem to have lost some of their power to provide people with meaning, identity elements, satisfaction. In fact, role and status designations have become objects of suspicion.... "

The psychologic attitude seems to imply an optimistic account of human nature, if its proponents thought people base and vile, they could hardly advocate a Hobbesian world without the Leviathan or be so cheery about man's quest to find and express himself. Much psychologic writing explicitly argues that human nature is benign enough that, freed of socially imposed constraints, men will behave better than they do now. This benignity is buoyed by faith in human malleability: if people behave badly, it is because of environmental factors, which can be manipulated, or because of patterns of thought and behavior, which can (on some therapeutic views) be changed even if they cannot be understood.

Yet psychologic man's view of human nature is profoundly ambivalent. Against the optimism described in the preceding paragraph are pitted a vivid sense of the power and ubiquity of the passions, a dark sense of their cruelty, and a resigned sense that character is irrevocably and inevitably formed by early and universal experiences. Psychologic man's strain of pessimism about individual human nature is matched by a strain of pessimism about the capacity of systematic social activity to enhance human happiness. Professor Allen, in explaining why psychologism has been inimical to penal rehabilitation, notes the movement's frequent anti-intellectualism, its absence of public purpose, and the perverse fact that it "has not generally nourished the autonomy of individuals but has expressed a weariness with self-hood." Even "contemporary expressions of confidence in human malleability are often accompanied by a pervasive pessimism about the effectiveness and integrity of social institutions."

e. A case study. Perhaps greater concreteness can be given to psychologic man by reporting one version of his rise. Professor Susman suggests that in the nineteenth century, "character" was the word most revelatory of the modal American type, but that in the twentieth century, that word was "personality." The nineteenth century held "that the highest development of self ended in a version of self-control or self-mastery, which often meant fulfillment through sacrifice in the name of a higher law, ideals of duty, honor, integrity. One came to selfhood through obedience to law and ideals." The words "most frequently related to the notion of character" were "*citizenship, duty, democracy, work, building, golden deeds, outdoor life, conquest, honor, reputation, morals, manners, integrity,* and above all, *manhood.*" The twentieth century, on the other hand, "stressed self-fulfillment, self-expression, self-gratification.... Its 'essentially antinomian ... vision ...' with its view not of a higher law but of a higher self, was tempered by the suggestion that the self ought to be presented to society in such a way as to make oneself 'well-liked.' " The adjectives most frequently associated with personality "suggest a very different concept from that of character: *fascinating, stunning, attractive, magnetic, glowing, masterful, creative, dominant, forceful.*"

Questions on Human Nature and Family Law

(1) This description of the therapeutic view of human nature, while we hope it is fair, is not particularly flattering. How might it be shown in a more favorable light? What are its important variants?

(2) What other views of human nature seem to you to be contending for pre-eminence in modern American society?

(3) What consequences for family law ought the ascetic and therapeutic views of human nature have?

(a) How ought marriage be differently structured depending on one's view of human nature?

(b) How ought one's view of human nature affect the law of divorce? How did your view of human nature affect your reaction to the Appleby, Bartleby, and Cuttleby hypotheticals?

E. DEFINING THE FAMILY

When we speak of our families, we think we know what we mean. We are probably right. But even in our own culture, "family" has many meanings, and other cultures have many others. The meaning of "family" matters in family law because the law attaches consequences to membership in families. Yet the law too lacks a clear definition of "family." In the preceding chapter, for example, we have discussed problems in the definition of marriage and have asked why three heterodox forms of marriage should not fall within the legal meaning of "family." Such questions will return to prominence in the chapter on the unmarried couple, where we will ask whether and when people who have not gone through a formal process of becoming a family ought nevertheless be treated as if they were one. Later, our chapter on child custody will ask what it takes to create the relationship between parent and child. The answer to that question may be obvious enough in most cases, but who, for instance, are the "mother" and "father" of a child conceived by artificial insemination from a known donor who waived his rights in the child, born of a surrogate mother, and contractually promised to a third party who paid both the donor and the surrogate for their services?

These questions cannot be answered without asking a set of intractable prior questions. Is a family defined by blood relations only? If so, what about husbands and wives? Is a family defined by its functions? If otherwise unrelated people live together and if their relations serve the functions of a family, are they a family? What are the functions of a family? Does something in "human nature" tell us how to define family? In other words, is there something universal in the nature of the family that helps define it, or is "family" a social construct? What purposes does the social construct serve? To what extent can the social construct be deliberately manipulated? Need there be a single definition of "family"? Who decides what a family is? The putative family members themselves? The social group (e.g., a church) of which the individuals are members? Society as represented by the government? Finally, what is society's interest in defining "family"?

The problems in defining the family we have discussed so far largely have to do with defining membership in the family. Another set of problems in defining the family has to do with the relations and obligations family members have to each other. In other words, we will ask not just what people constitute a family, but also what it means to be a family. These problems we will discuss explicitly in a number of places. For instance, we will be interested in the obligations of support spouses have to each other during the marriage and the financial obligations they retain when they decide to divorce. And we will scrutinize the legal duties parents have toward their children and the kinds of authority they have over them.

Here again we will discover difficult underlying questions. What, for example, is the source of familial obligations? Can those obligations be logically inferred from some widely accepted system of ethics? Can they be inferred only from religion or from social tradition? Can they be inferred from the social functions families serve? How should we identify those functions? Need they be the same in each family?

Throughout this casebook we will look intensively at both aspects of the definition of "family" and at how the social and legal understandings of that definition may be changing. For example, we will ask whether the relationship between grandparent and grandchild falls within the ambit of the legally (indeed constitutionally) defined family. We will consider whether the parents' authority over and responsibility for the child entitle them to know whether the child is going to have an abortion and to withhold consent for one. We will inquire whether adult children are and should be legally obligated to support their parents, whether spouses are and should be legally obligated to support each other in sickness as well as in health, and whether parents are and should be obliged to support children of whom they have lost custody.

Questions on Defining the Family

(1) Why were the relationships in *Reynolds, Israel*, and *Goodridge* arguably, not "familial"? Thinking in social, not legal, terms, what might make those relationships familial? Is it the fact of a long-term commitment between the parties? If so, how do family relationships

differ from relations between friends, and how deep and long-term must a commitment be to make a relationship familial? Is what makes those relationships familial the fact of a long-term commitment between parties who also share a sexual relationship? If so, are marriages in which the parties never had or have ceased having sexual relations non-familial? Is what makes those relationships familial the fact that the parties in each of the cases apparently thought of the relations as familial? If so, is it true that we socially regard as a family any group of people who call themselves a family? Ought we to do so? Ultimately, what is the difference between "family" and "friends"?

(2) Is what makes the parties in *Baker* not a family the fact that they are incapable of "generating" children? In other words, is a distinguishing characteristic of "family" its role as the institution in which children are born and raised? Does this mean that heterosexual spouses who cannot or do not have children are not a family? Or are such spouses a family because, while the institution of the family is created to assure that children are satisfactorily raised, to avoid inappropriate inquiries any two people may marry if they generally can produce children?

Can prohibiting incestuous and polygamous marriages also be explained in terms of the family as a child-rearing institution? That is, are related parties forbidden to marry because of the fear of untoward genetic effects on their children and are people forbidden to marry more than one person because of the fear that polygamous families may offer undesirable conditions for rearing children? Here, too, the prohibitions would rest on generalizations, since not all incestuous and polygamous marriages need produce children and since not all children of such marriages would suffer the anticipated harms. Does this mean the prohibitions are unjustifiable?

F. PRIVACY

Many people believe that privacy is a basic human need, that it is a social institution found, albeit in differing forms, in tribal and industrialized societies alike. Many people believe that privacy is necessary if family life is to prosper and that the family is an important social institution partly because it provides the privacy that people need. See, e.g., George Orwell, *1984* (New American Library, 1949).

Privacy has for some time been a legal as well as a social idea and goal. As early as 1890, Samuel D. Warren and Louis D. Brandeis (the Brandeis who was to become one of the most distinguished Supreme Court Justices) wrote an article entitled *The Right to Privacy*. They observed,

> The intensity and complexity of life, attendant upon advancing civilization have rendered necessary some retreat from the world, and man, under the refining influence of culture, has become more sensitive to publicity, so that solitude and privacy have become more essential to the individual; but modern enterprise and invention have, through invasions

> upon his privacy, subjected him to mental pain and distress, far greater than could be inflicted by mere bodily injury.

4 Harv L Rev 193, 196 (1890). Warren and Brandeis argued that the "principle which protects personal writings and any other productions of the intellect or of the emotions, is the right to privacy, and the law has no new principle to formulate when it extends this protection to the personal appearance, sayings, acts, and to personal relations, domestic or otherwise." Warren and Brandeis urged recognition of a remedy in tort for invasions of privacy.

As Dean Prosser noted, modern tort law now provides a remedy against four kinds of invasion of privacy:

> 1. Intrusion upon the plaintiff's seclusion or solitude, or into his private affairs.
>
> 2. Public disclosure of embarrassing private facts about the plaintiff.
>
> 3. Publicity which places the plaintiff in a false light in the public eye.
>
> 4. Appropriation, for the defendant's advantage, of the plaintiff's name or likeness.

William L. Prosser, *Privacy*, 48 Cal L Rev 383, 389 (1960). This concern for privacy recurs in American law. It rests (even if not alone) at the base of much of the law of testimonial privilege, including the Fifth Amendment's protection against self-incrimination. It may be at the heart (although again not alone) of the constitutional limitations on searches and seizures. It appears in new forms in response to the government's increasing ability to collect and store information about us, as the Privacy Act of 1974, 5 U.S.C. § 552A (2000), suggests.

On the other hand, privacy has its critics. They argue that privacy is over-valued. They say that a person who insists on privacy from intimates sacrifices true intimacy. They think that private relationships can protect harmful as well as beneficial behavior. They suggest that social insistence on privacy can conceal from "deviants" the social breadth, and inferentially the social acceptability, of their "deviance." Other critics of privacy take a different tack and contend that the term "privacy" is not meaningful, that it represents no coherent or distinctive idea. They argue that all the values "privacy" speaks to can be best understood on their own terms, without further reference to the concept of privacy.

Questions about how to resolve the conflicts over the nature and desirability of privacy and about what role any resolution should play in family law will recur throughout these materials. Unsurprisingly, the theme of privacy will appear most directly in our examination of the doctrine of family autonomy. There, we will ask how valuable privacy really is to the family. That is, we will ask how far the interest in family privacy ought to prevent the state from serving important interests, particularly in preventing spouse and child abuse. However, the theme of privacy will appear, indeed has already appeared, elsewhere. For example, we have seen that one important impetus to no-fault divorce was the belief that fault-based divorce provoked too great an intrusion into family privacy. Similarly, our discussion of non-marital cohabitation will consider the claim that the couple's interest in privacy militates against enforcing some kinds of claims they might make to the law's help in structuring and concluding their relationship. Yet another privacy concern will animate our discussion of the contractualization of family law, for we will ask whether making marital life the subject of explicit and semi-public negotiation, expression, and enforcement undesirably diminishes marital privacy. Finally, when we evaluate the constitutionalization of family law we will ask how well the term "privacy" describes the doctrine that the state's authority over the family is constitutionally limited. We will there (once again) confront the multiple meanings of "privacy" and ask just what kinds of privacy the constitutional doctrine of privacy does and should protect.

Questions on Privacy

(1) To what extent can the result in *Reynolds* be explained in privacy terms? Can it be argued that the state foresees particular problems (of the kind we have discussed earlier) with relationships in polygamous families, that the state foresees that those relationships will be difficult to supervise in part because of the privacy in which family relations take place, and that the state therefore seeks to prevent those problems from arising by preventing the marriage from taking place? Is this a legitimate response to the problems presented by privacy? Might it be plausibly argued that intimacy between husbands and wives depends on privacy which is interfered with by the presence of an additional spouse within the family?

(2) To what extent can *Reynolds* be criticized in privacy terms? Can it be argued that the ways people choose to organize their private lives ought to be free from government scrutiny? Is the choice of a marriage partner such a choice, given the "public" elements of the marriage ceremony and of marriage and given the states's sponsorship of marriage?

G. CONTRACT AS AN ORDERING DEVICE

You already know the significance of contract as a legal idea from your Contracts course, a course whose very presence in the first-year curriculum bespeaks the subject's centrality in American law. The idea of contract has often stood in American law for the concept of private ordering, for the principle that people should be free to arrange with each other the structure of their affairs and should be able to summon the power of the government to enforce that order. It has also stood for the proposition that society works most efficiently when people can contract freely. On the other hand, freedom of contract has also been associated with the domination of the economically weak by the economically strong and with an overly commercial view of life.

We will repeatedly consider how well the normative and practical attractions of contract fit family law. The chapter you have just read partly asks whether people should be free to enter the contract of marriage as freely as they enter other contracts. A later chapter will ask at length whether spouses should be able to alter the economic and social terms of the marriage contract as freely as they alter the terms of other contracts. A still later chapter will ask whether we should enforce "marital" contracts between people who are not married. Even in the material on the relationship between parents and children an underlying question will be the extent to which parents should be able to decide questions about their child's economic, social, and physical well-being through contractual arrangements between themselves.

Notes and Questions on Contract

(1) Superficially, at least, marriage resembles nothing so much as a contract. In *Reynolds, Israel*, and *Goodridge*, the law prevented people who wanted to enter into that contract from doing so. It is often said (although less often than previously) that freedom to enter contracts is an important part of our freedom to organize our own lives. Yet reflection will remind you that the law of contract itself incorporates a variety of limitations on the ability to make contracts. Can the results in our three cases be understood in terms of ordinary contract law?

(a) One basis for preventing people from contracting is that they in some way lack the capacity to understand or consent to a contract. Is any such contractual incapacity present in any of these cases?

(b) Another basis for preventing people from contracting is that the contract seems likely to injure the parties in some way they are unlikely fully to appreciate. Is any such risk present here? If so, is it great enough to justify keeping the parties (indeed, all parties in the class of people likely to be injured) from entering the contract?

(c) Yet another basis for preventing people from contracting is that the contract seems likely to injure third parties to the contract. Is any such risk present here? If so, is it great enough to justify keeping the parties (indeed, all parties in the class of people likely to be injured) from entering the contract?

(d) Another basis for preventing people from contracting is that the contract is *contra bonos mores*, that is, against "good morals." Can that be said of the marriages in any of our three cases? How are we to know what "good morals" are? If a contract is in fact "against good morals" yet does not fall within the strictures described in Questions (1)(a)-(c), should it be prohibited?

(2) *Reynolds* can be seen not just as a case about entering the contract of marriage, but also as one about altering the terms of that

contract. In other words, it could be said that when a man and woman enter the contract of marriage, the state sets some of that contract's terms, just as many states impose a nonwaiveable warranty of habitability in residential leases. In *Reynolds*, the imposed term is that neither party shall take another spouse. Could such a nonwaiveable contractual provision be justified on the grounds that it protects the legitimate interests and indeed expectations of both parties? Should the parties be able when they enter the marriage to alter by mutual agreement the state-established terms? Should they be able to alter those terms after they are married? Can you think of other situations in which the state limits the ability of contractors to set the terms to their own contracts? What sort of reasons does the state advance in those situations? Do they apply to the family situation?

H. RIGHTS

You will hardly need convincing that the concept of rights is preeminently important in the law. Rights, of course, can be of many kinds, ranging from a freedom to behave as one wishes in the absence of legal authority to the contrary, through a statutory entitlement to behave in certain ways or to receive certain benefits, to a constitutional or even a natural law freedom to behave as one wishes despite judicial or statutory commands to the contrary. We will be concerned with all these kinds of rights, but we will be particularly concerned with constitutional rights as they affect in the family.

This casebook is structured to give you an opportunity first to think about how the common law and statutes have structured family law generally and the law of husband and wife particularly and to evaluate that structure in terms of its social and moral desirability. The casebook then turns its attention to the constitutionalization of family law and asks you to think about a number of significant issues in the jurisprudence of rights: What is a constitutional right? Where does it come from? How is it found? How is it defined? To what extent ought it yield to state interests? Our vehicle for asking those questions will, of course, be the constitutional right to privacy, whose roots lie in the early twentieth century and whose apotheosis in the late twentieth century has been *Roe v. Wade*. After we have completed this study of rights thinking, we will proceed to study the law of parent and child with a constant eye to the question of the role of rights and rights-thinking in that law. We will discover that virtually every area of it—the law of child custody, of child support, of child abuse and neglect, and the law governing the allocation of authority for making educational and medical decisions for children—is at least susceptible to a rights analysis.

Questions on Rights

(1) The statutes in *Reynolds, Israel*, and *Goodridge* all authorized the government to behave in a way the citizens involved felt injured them. Did the citizens have some kind of right to a different decision? If

not, why not? If so, what kind of right? A statutory right? A constitutional right? A moral or natural law right? How would you define the right? That is, what is it a right to? What kinds of behavior does the right encompass? What governmental interests might limit the right? Who should have the power to define the right?

I. THE TENSION BETWEEN DISCRETION AND RULES

Law today regulates in complex ways the complex behavior of millions of people. This can be done efficiently (indeed, can be done at all) only through broadly applicable rules. Yet such rules must be ambiguous in some respects, must fail in some cases, and must be unfair in some situations. This leads rule-makers to accord discretion to the administrators and judges who apply the rules. Yet discretion can be abused, and as discretion grows the advantages of rules diminish. As you will already have discovered in innumerable class discussions, balancing these considerations is necessary in every area of law. The discretion juries have in fact-finding, that judges have in interpreting the law, that grand juries and district attorneys have in deciding to prosecute, and that administrative agencies have in writing and enforcing regulations are only some of the more vivid examples of the ways rules and discretion interact.

In family law, the problem of discretion is as acute as anywhere in the law. Family law, after all, attempts to regulate people in the most complex, most emotional, most mysterious, most individual, most personal area of life. It is absurdly difficult to write rules for this area that are clear and that will apply justly and effectively to everyone they are intended to affect. The history of family law is the history of attempts to solve this problem. For example, one reason for no-fault divorce was the conviction that courts cannot analyze the facts of a marriage well enough to judge it accurately and fairly. The law of alimony and marital property attempted for decades to divide property according to either the common-law or the community-property system; both systems became intolerably complex, and partly for that reason many jurisdictions have substituted an "equitable division" system that essentially confides the division of property to a judge who is guided only by the most general kinds of standards. The law of child custody rested for centuries on powerful, if rebuttable, presumptions about custody, presumptions which have now in principle been rejected in favor of a mélange of compromises between rules and discretion. The law of child abuse and neglect was long criticized as giving administrators and judges too much discretion to remove children from their homes, and attempts were instituted to describe precisely what circumstances justify such intervention. Yet these rules have themselves been assailed and amended because they can prevent officials from removing some endangered children from the homes of their cruel parents.

Notes and Questions on Discretion and Rules

(1) *Reynolds* may be based on the generalization that polygamous marriages are likely to lead, for instance, to jealousies within marriages and to unstable homes for children. Even those who accept this generalization, however, might well agree that it is only a generalization and that some successful polygamous marriages may occur. Assume, arguendo, that this generalization is correct and that it is the only basis for the prohibition on polygamous marriage. Ought the state provide some means for would-be polygamous couples to show that they would be the exception? Through what sort of legal institution ought the state evaluate such a claim? What sort of standards ought that institution use in evaluating the claim? Could guidelines be written to govern the decision, or should it be confided to the discretion of a judge? What would the accuracy of the evaluation be? Finally, is the generalization in fact true?

(2) As you will recall, the state argued in *Israel* that its interest in "family harmony" justified prohibiting Martin and Tammy from marrying. And as you will recall, the court found that the Israels' family harmony would be undisturbed by the marriage and that therefore the marriage could not be permitted. Consider, however, this explanation of the state's position:

> [S]urely the state's argument was not addressed just to [the Israels' happiness]. Rather, the state presumably meant that "family harmony" in society generally was promoted by keeping the possibility of sexual relations between family members as far from their minds as possible. In brief, the legislature sought to reinforce the incest taboo. It sought to do so by making marriage between any people in the relation of siblings entirely unthinkable, not just unthinkable for actual siblings.

Carl E. Schneider, *State-Interest Analysis in Fourteenth Amendment "Privacy" Law: An Essay on the Constitutionalization of Social Issues,* 51 Law & Contemp Prob 79, 97–98 (1988). Assume, then, that the state was arguing that the consequence of allowing a court to exercise discretion in deciding whether "people in the relation of siblings" could marry would weaken the effectiveness of the rule designed to prevent "genuinely" or abusively incestuous relations, even if that discretion were exercised wisely in individual cases. Is the state's argument persuasive? Even if the state's argument is persuasive, should Martin and Tammy be prevented from marrying in the interests of helping to preserve the incest taboo?

J. DUE PROCESS

The great expansion of governmental power in the last half-century has been accompanied by a great elaboration of the doctrine of (procedural) due process. That elaboration can be seen, for instance, in the criminal side in the expanded scope of the rights of defendants in criminal cases and on the civil side in the expanded obligation of the government to provide hearings before it deprives citizens of government benefits. See, e.g., *Mathews v. Eldridge*, 424 US 319 (1976). More generally, see William Van Alstyne, *Cracks in "The New Property": Adjudicative Due Process in the Administrative State*, 62 Cornell L Rev 445 (1977), and Jerry L. Mashaw, *Due Process in the Administrative State* (Yale U Press, 1985). A constellation of intractable questions surrounds the concept of due process. What are its goals? How ought those goals be ranked so that conflicts between them can be resolved? Which means of effectuating the doctrine's goals work best? How great are the costs of the various due-process devices? Are there alternatives to those devices? What government interests justify what restrictions on due process rights?

We will discuss due process most intensively in our chapter on child abuse and neglect. That chapter describes the troubling conflict between compelling the government to treat those accused of wrong-doing fairly and ensuring that parents do not harm their children. However, we will also consider due process in, for instance, our investigation of the claim that foster parents may not be deprived of the custody of their foster children without some measure of process. Similar issues are also raised by the state and federal programs for making non-custodial parents pay the child support they owe. A related set of problems has to do with how the law should structure adjudications between family members. This set of problems presents itself most acutely in relation to divorce proceedings. For example, can divorce litigation be structured so that it does not exacerbate the animosities the parties feel for each other? So that the children's interests are represented?

Questions on Due Process

(1) Consider again the argument we discussed in the section on discretion that the right to marry polygamously ought not be denied without letting the would-be spouses show their marriage would succeed. What kind of a chance should that be? Should there be a hearing? Should the couple have counsel? Should the state provide counsel if the couple cannot? Would the state be constitutionally compelled to do so? Who would represent the state? Could the parties call witnesses? Who should the decision-maker be? A judge in the court of general jurisdiction? A judge from a "family court"? A psychologist expert about marriages? A jury? What would the basis for appeals be? What would the prospects of accurately predicting the couple's marital future be? What would the costs—economic and otherwise—of such a proceeding be?

K. THE ENFORCEMENT PROBLEM

Because the law seeks to regulate something as recalcitrant as human behavior, it encounters ubiquitously and intensely the problem of enforcement. This problem appears with special clarity, of course, in the criminal law. There the law attempts to secure enforcement by the most extreme means—by fines, by prison, and even by death. Yet despite this artillery of sanctions, innumerable crimes are committed. But the enforcement problem is not limited to the criminal law. Many administrative agencies, for instance, seek to secure compliance through civil penalties—again, primarily through fines, although also through the loss of privileges, subsidies, licenses, and contracts. These penalties too leave many enforcement problems unsolved. Government also attempts to solve enforcement problems not through penalties, but through incentives, as when its tax code allows accelerated depreciation for certain kinds of investments. Of course, this mechanism has its drawbacks. The government can rarely afford to pay for complete compliance, not all governmental goals can be promoted through incentives, and incentives seem normatively inappropriate to some governmental goals (paying someone not to commit a battery, for example, is unattractive). Another way governments promote their regulatory goals is by recruiting surrogates. The government seeks to deter accidents caused by negligence partly by allowing private citizens to bring tort actions. That this enforcement device, like all the rest, leaves much enforcing to be done is suggested by, for example, the fact that the cost and distastefulness of litigation often prevent injured parties from bringing suit. Finally, government works even more indirectly by trying to induce people so much to internalize governmental goals and values that they do not wish to act in socially harmful ways (as the government understands "socially harmful").

The enforcement problems that family law confronts are probably as acute as those in any area of law. As Professor Schneider once wrote, "[F]amily law's difficulty enforcing its rules is virtually ubiquitous: Consider the problems society has experienced enforcing alimony orders, spouse-and child-support obligations, strict divorce statutes, spouse-and child-abuse laws, visitation rights, sodomy and fornication statutes, and prohibitions of abortion, contraception, and parental kidnapping." Carl E. Schneider, *The Next Step: Definition, Generalization, and Theory in American Family Law*, 18 U Mich J L Reform 1039, 1056 (1985). The reasons for family law's enforcement problems are too numerous to recount fully here, but they include the impediments to finding out about and supervising behavior that occurs largely in private, the reluctance (sometimes born of fear) of victims to complain, the frequent difficulty of punishing the offender without injuring or putting at risk the victim, and the fact that offenders are usually dealing with the most intensely emotional relationships in their lives and are often acting under emotional pressures they hardly understand. In light of these restrictions on governmental power, we will repeatedly be asking not just what the law ought to do, but whether the law can do it.

Notes and Questions on the Enforcement Problem

(1) On one hand, one might suppose that the law's enforcement problems would not be severe when it comes to regulating entrance into marriage, since the requirement of a marriage license allows the law to tend the gate to marriage relatively easily. However, the law's intention

in preventing polygamous, incestuous, and homosexual marriage may well go beyond a simple desire to prevent the legal marriage and extend to a desire to prevent marriage-like behavior, that is, to prevent a group of people from living as though they were polygamously married, and so forth. If that is in fact the law's desire, its enforcement problems are acute. Consider the problem of polygamy. One scholar reports that "no group seems to be more anti-polygamous than Utah Mormons." Nevertheless, he also reports that "surveys indicate there are approximately 30,000 [polygamous] Fundamentalists, as they prefer to be called, in the western United States, particularly in Utah, Arizona, and Montana." He notes that "when it became evident that a Murray, Utah, policeman was polygamous, he was fired (on the grounds that he was violating the state's anti-polygamy statute) but was not prosecuted because the local district attorney's office was 'busy with cases involving property loss or personal harm.' " Richard S. Van Wagoner, *Mormon Polygamy: A History* III–V (Signature Books, 1986).

What enforcement problems would a state encounter which decided to seriously attempt to prevent "non-marital polygamy"? To prevent incestuous relations? To prevent homosexual relations? What methods might such a state use? What costs would those methods entail? Would the costs be worth bearing?

L. PLURALISM

In a society as diverse as ours, the law must constantly ask whether to take cultural differences into account in writing and enforcing statutes, whether to promote that diversity, how far to promote it, and how. The most conspicuous way American law addresses those questions is through the First Amendment, especially its religion clauses. But those questions are also addressed in many other ways. Some programs seek to maintain cultural diversity, including the whole mass of federal, state, and local anti-discrimination legislation; the exemption of conscientious objectors from military service; various bilingual education programs; the American Indian Religious Freedom Act, 42 U.S.C. § 1996 (1995) (which declared it "the policy of the United States to protect and preserve for American Indians their inherent right of freedom to believe, express, and exercise [their] traditional religions"); and even our federal system of government and our practice of delegating some of the power of state government to counties and cities, both of which are intended to allow states and local communities leeway to follow their own cultural preferences. Other kinds of programs seek to temper cultural diversity by providing some core cultural commonalities; compulsory education is perhaps the most obvious example of such a program.

Because it deals with the education of children (and thus with the transmission of culture) and because it deals with the way people lead those parts of their lives most likely to be affected by cultural (and particularly religious) differences, family law confronts the kinds of questions sketched in the preceding paragraph as much as any area of law. For example, a department of social services considering whether to remove a child from a home because of what it perceives as parental abuse or neglect must ask first whether the parental behavior it objects to might be unobjectionable in the parent's own cultural terms and then whether the child ought nevertheless to be removed. And a district attorney deciding to prosecute a spouse-abuse case might find that that case raised similar questions about the extent to which the law should defer to or try to alter its subjects' cultural values. In this casebook we will deal with the pluralism issue most directly when we discuss *Wisconsin v. Yoder*, a case in which Amish parents claimed exemption from a compulsory-education statute on the grounds that exposing their children to education beyond the eighth grade would weaken their community.

Notes and Questions on Pluralism

(1) Consider once again Question (1)(a) and Question (1)(c) in Chapter 1's questions on polygamous marriage.

(2) In the course of thinking about *Reynolds* and discussing pluralism, you have encountered the term "community," a term you will encounter a number of times in these materials. What weight ought the values of "community" have in deciding a case like *Reynolds?*

(a) What is a "community?"

(b) What are "the values of community?"

(c) What are the relevant communities in a case like *Reynolds*? The United States? The territory (or state) of Utah? The Mormon Church? Any town in which Mormons live? Any neighborhood in which Mormons live? Any Mormon family?

(d) How ought "the values of community" affect the outcome of a case like *Reynolds*?

(3) It is not uncommon to read references to the "gay community." Consider again your answers to Question (2). Does the gay community fit your definition of "community"? Does the gay community have a claim to be serving the "values of community"? How ought "the values of community" affect the outcome of a case like *Goodridge*?

M. A CONCLUDING NOTE: FAMILY LAW AND LEGAL CHANGE

This completes our review of the twelve themes of family law which we will pay special attention to in this casebook. There are, surely, many others we do not have space to consider extensively. One of those remaining themes deserves special mention, however. As a law student, you have repeatedly been asked to examine the ways a court or legislature can work a change in the law. This "sub-theme" asks how legal change does and should occur and how the responsibility for legal change should be allocated among the various legal institutions. In studying this issue we will ask a number of subsidiary questions: What makes legal change desirable or undesirable? What is and should be the relationship between social and legal change? What affects the ability to effectuate legal change? What different kinds of competence do the various legal institutions have? How does each institution initiate or resist legal change?

In order to study these questions, we will at several points pause in the study of a substantive area to see how a legal institution worked or failed to work a change in the law. We have already looked at the enactment of no-fault divorce by state legislatures. We will later examine the judicial reform of abortion law through constitutional interpretation and the use of public-interest law firms to seek to alter the administration of foster-care systems.

Questions on Legal Change

(1) It is plain that social attitudes toward homosexuality have changed considerably in the last two decades. It is also true that the legal treatment of gays and lesbians has changed. To what extent should the court in *Goodridge* or the Vermont legislature have been affected by these changes? Should, for instance, the court's view of the legislature's intentions and of the meaning of the state and federal constitutions have been affected by the changes in social and legal attitudes? If the court believed the legislature acted unwisely in denying same-sex couples the ability to marry, should it have granted them that ability?

SECTION 2. THE FUNCTIONS OF FAMILY LAW

The most important improvements of the last twenty-five years are improvements in theory. It is not to be feared as unpractical, for, to the competent, it simply means going to the bottom of the subject.

Oliver Wendell Holmes
The Path of the Law

You have now been introduced to one of the most basic institutions of family law—marriage. You have been asked, at least implicitly, to think about why the law might wish to regulate family relations at all; that is, you have been asked to think about the functions of family law. In this Section, we will examine explicitly what you have been considering implicitly. We will to try to identify the functions that family law might perform. In a sense, this consideration may be premature; it is hard to see what functions family law may serve until you know just what doctrines family embodies. On the other hand, the functions of family law are probably similar to the functions of law generally, so you should have in those latter functions a good starting place for analyzing the former ones. In any event, thinking about them now crucially prepares you to read family law more critically later.

There must always be some artificiality dividing any area of law into functions, since most legal regulations serve several functions simultaneously, since the distinctions between the functions is often blurred, and since lawmakers usually have not thought explicitly in terms of law's functions. Nevertheless, there are several reasons to identify and analyze family law's functions. First, it should help you consider something every lawyer ought to have pondered—what the functions of law in general are. Second, it should help you evaluate family law's purposes. Third, it should help you evaluate family law's doctrines, since you will be able to ask what function each doctrine serves and how well a doctrine serves its functions. Finally, it should help you think normatively about family law, since you will be poised to ask whether each of its functions is legitimate in general and as applied.

A. THE PROTECTIVE FUNCTION

One of law's most basic functions (perhaps its most basic function) is to protect citizens against disturbances of the peace, that is, to protect citizens against harms done to them by other citizens. At the core of this function is protecting people from physical harm. The primary, but not exclusive, vehicle of this function is, of course, the criminal law, which penalizes most physical assaults. This element of the protective function vitalizes an important aspect of family law: The law of spouse abuse attempts to protect each spouse against physical assault by the other. And the law of child abuse seeks to protect children against parental assaults by their parents that exceed the legitimate scope of parental discipline.

The law also employs means other than the criminal law to protect citizens against physical harm. For example, the law of torts provides civil remedies for physical harm. That law tries both to deter harm and to make victims whole for any harm they have suffered. Much regulatory law is similarly intended. Thus, for example, extensive systems of law try to assure employees a safe place to work and consumers safe food to eat. Family law too employs means other than the criminal law to protect family members from physical harm. For instance, tort suits may sometimes be brought between family members. And legally required medical examinations before marriage seek to protect spouses from contracting venereal diseases from each other.

The law generally protects citizens from each other in many ways other than the purely physical. Much of civil (and some criminal) law serves to that goal. Courts do not simply enforce contracts; they also set some standards (however loose) of procedural and substantive fairness which prevent parties to a contract from taking some kinds of advantage of each other. The law of property provides some kinds of barriers to unfairness in transfers of interests in property. The law also protects some kinds of non-pecuniary interests, as when it gives remedies for libel and for invasions of privacy. Much of family law is likewise devoted to protecting family members from each other in non-physical senses. Family law is particularly concerned with protecting family members economically. It imposes on spouses some obligation to support each other and requires parents to support their children. It restricts spouses' ability to disinherit each other. It requires courts to supervise the division of property between the spouses on divorce and allows courts to impose some kinds of support obligations after divorce. Family law also tries to protect family members, particularly children, from non-economic harm. Thus parents may be restrained from injuring their children even in some non-physical ways, and courts may award custody of children of a divorcing couple to the parent who can best care for the child.

Each function of family law has its characteristic problems. One of the protective function's problems is whether the law is acting "protectively" or, rather, "paternalistically." In other words, the people the law protects may not want to be protected, or may not want to be protected in the law's way. Perhaps more often, some people in a category may need the law's protection, while others in it find that protection unnecessary and unwelcome.

B. THE FACILITATIVE FUNCTION

The protective function may generally be said to be part of what is called "public law." Public law is contrasted to "private law." As one scholar writes, "The former is concerned with the relationship between the individual or groups and the state, whereas the latter is concerned with the relationship between individuals or groups and each other." A.W.B. Simpson, *Invitation to Law* 101 (Blackwell, 1988). Most family law is private law. A central function of private law is not so much to regulate the behavior of citizens as to create mechanisms that facilitate their organizing their lives and affairs in whatever ways they prefer. Particularly clear examples of the facilitative function can be found in the law's relationship to economic behavior. Consider Max Weber's observation that "[e]very rational business organization needs the possibility of acquiring contractual rights and of assuming obligations through temporary or permanent agents. Advanced trade, moreover, needs not only the possibility of transferring legal claims but also, and quite particularly, a method by which transfers can be made legally secure and which eliminates the need of constantly testing the title of the transferor." 2 *Law and Society* 681 (Barnes and Noble, 1978). Modern corporations, in other words, need the modern law of negotiable instruments and agency. Yet those tools can only be reliably created through law, and many legal systems have not adequately provided such tools. A legal system that does provide such tools has significantly expanded the range of activities a business can effectively undertake. More generally, of course, the law of contracts classically and centrally serves the facilitative function by giving people a means of negotiating and enforcing, often in great detail, the terms of their relationship.

Family law serves the facilitative function in a variety of ways. The primary, and perhaps most problematic, way is by making available to couples some aspects of the law of contracts. However, it has historically been thought family life is not well-suited to contractual organization.

Thus we will regularly ask how far couples ought to be able to organize of their lives contractually.

The facilitative function's characteristic problem is that it is often in tension with the protective function. The more the law frees people to arrange their own relationships with other people, the more it leaves them at the mercy of those other people. As you know, a classic problem of contract law is the extent to which contractors should be protected from the consequences of a bad bargain. This problem has preoccupied courts dealing with marital contracts, for in such contracts people are particularly vulnerable.

C. THE ARBITRAL FUNCTION

In a better world, the protective and facilitative functions might work well enough that people would never find themselves irreconcilably opposed. This is not that world, however, and thus one of law's functions is to provide a way to resolve some kinds of disputes. To a minor extent and in a somewhat tangential way, this is done through the criminal law, which gives some injured parties the satisfaction of a public statement of the wrong done them. To a larger extent, though, the arbitral function is served by the law of torts, which allows people who disagree about what recompense one of them owes the other to settle their disagreement through the courts and to use the apparatus of the state to enforce that settlement. Finally, the law of contract provides a similar service to people who once entered into an agreement and who subsequently dispute how it should be interpreted and enforced.

Family law serves the arbitral function in a variety of ways. When spousal disputes become violent, the police, courts, and social services agencies may try to tame the dispute and provide alternative means to resolve it. And there is some authority for using tort law to settle disputes between family members. However, it is the law of divorce which provides the clearest example of family law's arbitral function. The major task of today's divorce courts is not to decide whether a spouse may obtain a divorce, but rather to adjudicate claims to marital property, to alimony, and to custody of the children of the marriage. The law has also increasingly made its arbitral services available to unmarried cohabitants whose relationship is ending.

At first glance, the arbitral function seems unproblematic: people have disputes, the law should help resolve them. However, the arbitral function is intensely problematic. A court confronting a dispute must have some standard for resolving it, and the substance of such standards is, in family law, regularly controversial. A court which has settled a dispute must enforce its decision, and we have already seen that such enforcement is often difficult. And the law is not always a desirable agent of dispute resolution. Even in business life, there has in recent decades arisen considerable interest in resolving disputes through means other than litigation. In family life there is particular reason to fear that the adversary system and the rigidities and miseries of the law are unsuited for resolving the disputes families face.

A characteristic problem of the arbitral function in family law has been the question whether the law is really a good forum for resolving disputes between family members. As you have seen, this question has been prominently raised in debates over divorce. In those debates, it has been suggested that the law's usual means of dispute resolution exacerbate rather than soothe family disputes, obscure truth rather than reveal it, and corrupt law rather than promote it. When considering the law's arbitral function, then, it is often productive to ask whether the law is well equipped to resolve the particular kind of dispute at issue and whether there is some better means of doing so.

Another useful question about the arbitral function is what substantive consequences result from the law's willingness to resolve a dispute. The law's unwillingness to resolve a dispute often leaves the parties to live with the status quo, and such an unwillingness often has systematic consequences. For example, if the law refuses to allow a non-parent to challenge a parent's custody of a child, the practical consequence will generally be that non-parents are, for better or worse, unable to remove children from their parent's custody.

The protective, facilitative, and arbitral functions are probably at the core of what many Americans regard as law's purposes, and they can probably be defined broadly enough to subsume all the other possible purposes of family law. But it can be argued that law performs two further functions that are analytically distinct. There are at least three reasons family law in particular can be said to have come to serve these two additional functions. The first reason grows out of a problem that all law encounters but that, as you will see, family law encounters particularly acutely. This is the enforcement problem: For reasons that we discussed above and that we will explore at some length, much harmful behavior in families is impervious or highly resistant to direct prohibition. In response to the enforcement problem, family law has adopted the two more-oblique functions we are about to discuss. The second reason family law may have adopted those two functions has to do with our aspirations for family life: Law-makers have often felt that family law ought not just to try to prevent harm within families, but ought also to promote happiness within them. The third reason family law may have adopted these two further functions arises out of the sense that "the family" is an important social institution whose working and whose success have large consequences for all society and that therefore government ought in its law-making to promote the family. What then are the two other possible functions of family law?

D. THE CHANNELLING FUNCTION

The law performs the channelling function by creating or (more often) supporting social institutions and practices which are thought to promote desirable ends. Generally, the law does not require that people use these institutions, although it may offer incentives and disincentives for their use. Primarily, rather, it is the very presence of these institutions, the social currency which they have, and the governmental support they receive which combine to make it seem reasonable and even natural for people to use them. Thus people can be said to be channelled into them. Business law provides vivid examples of such institutions—the corporation and the partnership.

Consider the corporation. People have long joined together for the purpose of investing in and doing business. And governments have long believed that such activity is desirable. To encourage it, governments have given legal recognition to a particular way of organizing to do business—the corporation. They have also endowed that particular form of organization with a special advantage—the advantage of limited liability. After years of use, this form has come to be familiar, to seem natural, to be easily used.

To some extent, the corporation as an economic and social institution simply serves the three functions of law we have already discussed. For example, the corporation may be said to serve the protective function by allowing people to invest in enterprises without putting their whole fortunes at risk, by providing protections for minority shareholders, or by creating an institution whose public nature makes it easier to regulate. The corporation may be said to serve the facilitative function by providing people a convenient and efficient way of organizing themselves into enterprises. And the corporation may be said to serve the arbitral function by providing mechanisms for resolving disputes among participants in an enterprise and for winding up their affairs should they decide to dissolve the enterprise.

But the corporate form does more than promote the protective, facilitative, and arbitral functions of the law. It also serves what might be called "efficiency" functions. For instance, the corporation relieves each person who wants to establish an enterprise of the need to figure out *de novo* the best way of organizing that enterprise. Much of that work will already have been done over the years by many other people, and that experience is embodied in the corporate form and in the law, literature, and practices that surround it. Because the corporate form is neither monolithic nor the only form in which an enterprise may be organized, the entrepreneur will have some choices to make. But the energy the entrepreneur must expend on choosing is diminished by the existence of standard alternatives among which to choose.

In addition, the corporate form makes the world more predictable for all who deal with a corporation. The investor, employee, creditor, debtor, vendor, or customer who deals with a corporation knows the basic facts about how that entity is organized and what it can and cannot do. A creditor, for example, knows that, unlike a partnership, a corporation's liability is limited to its own assets. And so on. Because people have established expectations about corporation they need not expend efforts to try to understand the form of the enterprise with which they are dealing. This not only saves them time and trouble, but it tends to make them more willing to join in or work with the enterprise. In short, both the corporation and those with whom it deals can benefit from the existence of a well-known, time-tested, socially accepted, and governmentally supported institution.

Similarly, family law may on some views be said to try to discourage harmful behavior within families, to encourage happiness in intimate relationships, and to promote social stability by establishing, promoting, and channelling people into social institutions that seem to conduce to those goals and by channelling people away from social institutions that seem to disserve them. A particularly vivid example of such an effort is to be found in the institution of marriage as traditionally conceived—as life-long, monogamous, and the exclusive forum for raising children. To be sure, that institution was not created by law; it has roots deep in the social and religious history of the West. But family law constructed a framework of rules designed to shape and sustain monogamous marriage: It created a set of rules designed to set standards for entry into marriage. It created procedures designed to tell couples how to know they were married and to tell the world when the couple was married. It devised rules (particularly fault-based divorce law) intended to make marriage commitments permanent. It invented special categories of property to reflect the special relationship of marriage. It articulated a set of prohibitions against non-marital sexual activity. It set (usually indirectly) rules for behavior within marriage—for example, rules imposing obligations of support.

In family law as in other areas, the channelling function is in part simply a specialized way of performing the law's protective, facilitative, and arbitral functions. For instance, the institution of marriage can be thought of as serving the protective function. The social institution of marriage which the law recruits attempts to impose obligations on spouses to treat each other well—to love and honor each other. (Recall here Andrew Sullivan's "conservative" argument for same-sex marriage which we described in Chapter I.1.C.) The law has tried to buttress this socially imposed obligation by criminalizing and (in some jurisdictions) aggressively prosecuting spouse abuse, by making cruelty a ground for divorce, and by taking cruelty into account in settling the spouses' economic affairs. Marriage inhibits us from abandoning each other, from betraying each other, from destroying our children's home. Marriage may also be seen as protecting children by increasing the likelihood that they will be cared for throughout their minority by both parents. Marriage serves the facilitative function by offering people a relationship with social and legal advantages which are primarily available precisely because the law has given marriage a special status. Marriage serves the dispute-resolution function by providing rules and a forum in which to adjudicate the disputes which accompany the end of a marriage.

But the channeling function of family law goes beyond being a specialized means of performing family law's other functions. It also serves "efficiency" functions. First, the institutions the channeling function establishes or recruits save people from having to invent the forms of family life. Imagine two nineteen-year-olds living in a state of nature who find themselves in love. Without established social institutions, they might have to work out for themselves how to express that love, how to structure their relationship, and how to decide what expectations they might reasonably have of each other for the future. The same couple in, say, the United States of the nineteen-fifties would find answers to all those questions in the institution of marriage. The couple would, of course, see other answers presented by other institutions. And the couple would not be compelled to marry. But if their relationship met the requirements of marriage, marriage would seem natural to them because most adults they knew participated in it, because of the strong social (and legal) support for it, and because they internalized its values. As one sociologist remarks, "When people make decisions, they tend to look not to a mathematical formula to determine what is to their best advantage, but to what others do, to what they have traditionally done, or to what they think others think they ought to do." Alan Wolfe, *Whose Keeper?: Social Science and Moral Obligation* 43 (U Cal Press, 1989). The institution, in other words, would be part of a readily accessible social vocabulary.

The channeling function can promote "social efficiency" not just by relieving people of the burden of working out afresh how to organize their lives. Another of its advantages in this respect arises from the fact that even if one could satisfactorily invent modes of living for oneself, one probably would not or would not want to live most of them alone. Rather, one would need to live them with other people. This suggests that people need to be able to understand and predict what other people are thinking and doing so that they can readily and safely interact and cooperate with each other. Social institutions (in the broad sense in which we have been using that term) help meet that need. As Martin Krygier writes, "There are many social situations where our decisions are strategically interdependent [with the decisions of other people].... [I]n such situations, norms will be generated which provide 'some anchorage; some preeminently conspicuous indication as to what action is likely to be taken by (most of) the others....' " *Law as Tradition*, 5 Law & Philosophy 237, 258–59 (1986)(emphasis in original). Those norms and the institutions they create, then, improve the ability of people to predict and thus to rely on, cope with, and cooperate with other people. They allow people to anticipate how other people will behave in the future and to plan their lives in accordance with those expectations.

More concretely, for example, the prevalence of marriage allows people to make some plans for the future even before meeting their spouses and to reach better understandings with their future spouses about their married lives. People dealing with married couples similarly benefit. On the most mundane level, for example, they know that when they say, "Can you come for dinner on the sixteenth?" the invitation will be taken as including both husband and wife. Less banally, the knowledge that a person is married is expected to warn people who are attracted to that person not to pursue an intimate relationship.

One might summarize the workings of the channelling function by imagining the situation of two people who are looking for recreation, who live in a society without tennis, and who are given three balls, two rackets, and one net. The two will no doubt be able to find some way of amusing themselves with these toys. But tennis is a good game partly because it has been developed over many years (in fact, centuries), and it is not likely (although it is possible) that the two will readily invent as good a game. In addition, where tennis is a social institution, the two will find they have a much broader range of people with whom to enjoy their recreation, to improve their game, and to boast of their successes and lament their failures. And part of the pleasure of playing tennis lies in knowing something of its history and in following its current progress. Tennis is, in other words, a social pleasure which can be fully enjoyed only if it is a shared and well-established institution.

Like the other functions of family law, the channelling function has characteristic problems. Among them is its tension with the theme of individual autonomy. On one view, human beings ought to be freed as far as possible from all social pressures. And on another view, the government ought to be given as little influence over individual decisions as possible. On such views, the channelling function appears suspect. In addition, the channelling function operates less precisely than some of the other functions of family law generally appear to. It will not always be clear just what social institution the law is recruiting or creating or just what characteristics and consequences that institution is supposed to and can have.

Also, perhaps more than the three functions of family law we have so far discussed, the channelling function's attractiveness depends on the substantive ends to which it is put. At the core of each of the first three functions lies a relatively uncontroversial idea. There are people—particularly children—the law is generally expected to protect. There are relationships the law is generally expected to facilitate. There are disputes the law is generally expected to arbitrate. But it may be less clear just where the law ought to channel people.

E. THE EXPRESSIVE FUNCTION

The channelling function works by creating institutions which people are "channelled" into. The expressive function works by deploying the law's ability to impart ideas through words and symbols. The expressive function has two (related) aspects: First, the expressive abilities of law may be utilized because doing so gratifies those speaking through the law. Second, the expressive abilities of law may be utilized in the hopes of affecting the behavior of people who hear the law speak.

Let us amplify this a bit. Expressive laws may be expressive in the narrowest sense: they may express the "personality" of citizens in the same way that a piece of art expresses the "personality" of the artist.

For example, one justification for laws outlawing racial discrimination is that they provide a means by which the citizens of a society can say to themselves and the world at large, "We are the kind of society that values racial justice." Expressive laws may be used in a somewhat different way: law may be used symbolically or expressively by groups wishing to affirm their status as full-fledged, or predominant, members of the larger society. This was presumably part of the reason for making Martin Luther King's birthday a legal holiday.

But expressive laws may be also be passed for more instrumental reasons. Their function then is not just or even not so much to influence behavior by requiring or forbidding people to perform a particular act, but to influence behavior by encouraging people to think in a particular way. This can be done by passing laws that are in some way symbolic or that use a particular language or set of ideas (so that those ideas are brought more fully into public discourse). These laws will often try to affirm or contradict an idea or a way of acting, to place the law's authority behind or against an idea a way of acting. Laws prohibiting racial discrimination, for instance, are intended to do more than increase the price people pay for discriminating and thereby to deter them, as rational calculators, from discriminating. Such laws are also intended to put discrimination beyond the social pale and to cause people to internalize values hostile to discrimination.

Of course, many, probably most, laws perform multiple functions. Thus most laws will be specifically intended to regulate behavior quite directly. But many laws will also attempt to buttress direct regulation through an expressive element. And some of these laws may also allow their proponents to express ideas for the non-instrumental gratifications that they may bring.

Family law might on some views be said to discourage harmful behavior within families, to encourage happiness in intimate relationships, and to promote "the family" as a successful social institution by deploying the law's capacities for expression. In other words, family law may seek to encourage people to think about their familial relationships in ways that conduce to human happiness by its choice of rules, ideas, and language. For example, Professor Scott and Professor Glendon both argued in Chapter 1 that the adoption of no-fault divorce makes an important statement (albeit unintentionally) about the nature of the commitment married people ought to have to each other. Similarly, people supported the ERA partly for expressive reasons. The ERA was taken as making a statement about the full-fledged inclusion of women in society. It was hoped that it would help change attitudes toward women in all areas of life. And it was expected to change the language and content of the public debate about the roles women play.

The characteristic problems of the expressive function resemble those of the channelling function. It may, for example, be felt that government should not use its special power and authority in the realm of expression. (For an extended discourse on this problem, see Mark G.

Yudof, *When Government Speaks: Politics, Law, and Government Expression in America* (U Cal Press, 1983).) Further, it will often be unclear just what the law is "expressing." The expressive message may be obscure to the people who write the law, and the people who are reading the law will bring their own special understandings to it, understandings that will differ from person to person and time to time. In addition, the attractiveness of the expressive function, like that of the channelling function, crucially depends on the ends to which it is put.

We have spoken with some definiteness about the protective, facilitative, and arbitral functions of family law and with some caution about its channelling and expressive functions. One reason for this difference is that, while law-makers think fairly explicitly about the first three functions, they often do not think explicitly about the latter two. One could thus say that, if by "function" we mean "intended purpose," the latter functions ought sometimes not to qualify. On the other hand, it is hard for family law to escape performing these functions, whether they are "intended" or not. As long as family law supports some social institutions, it will be performing the channelling function. And since law must "talk" in some form, since law by definition promulgates rules, family law will always perform the expressive function, even if inadvertently and incoherently.

It is, of course, possible to conceptualize family law's functions in other ways. Indeed, we encourage you to do so. In any event, as you read these materials, you should ask yourself what functions each family-law doctrine seeks to serve, how well it succeeds, and whether the function is in the particular case legitimate. This inquiry will often help you see problems with family law's functioning. It may also help you see explanations for some aspects of family law that would not otherwise be readily apparent.

BIBLIOGRAPHY

Gender and Family Law. For general discussions about teaching and writing from a feminist perspective, see Katherine T. Bartlett, *Feminist Legal Methods*, 103 Harv L Rev 829 (1990); Carrie Menkel–Meadow, *Portia in a Different Voice: Speculation on a Woman's Lawyering Process*, 1 Berkeley Women's L J 39 (1985); Carrie Menkel–Meadow, *Mainstreaming Feminist Legal Theory*, 23 Pac L J 1493 (1985); Carrie Menkel–Meadow, *Feminist Legal Theory, Critical Legal Studies, and Legal Education or "The Fem–Crits Go to Law School,"* 38 J of Legal Educ 61 (1988); Martha Minow, *The Supreme Court, 1986 Term—Foreword: Justice Engendered,* 101 Harv L Rev 10 (1987); Joan Scott, *Deconstructing Equality Versus Difference: Post–Structuralist Theory for Feminism*, 14 Feminist Studies 33 (1988); Jeanne Shroeder, *Abduction from the Seraglio: Feminist Methodologies and the Logic of Imagination,* 70 Tex L Rev 109 (1991); Jana B. Singer, *The Privatization of Family Law*, 1992 Wis L Rev 1445 (1992); Carol Weisbrod, *Practical Polyphony: Theories of the State and Feminist Jurisprudence*, 24 Ga L Rev 985

(1990); and Robin West, *Jurisprudence and Gender*, 55 U Chi L Rev 1 (1988).

Divorce and Feminist Thought. For discussions of marriage, divorce and the divorce process from feminist perspectives, see June Carbone, *Economics, Feminism, and the Reinvention of Alimony: A Reply to Ira Ellman*, 43 Vand L Rev 1463 (1990); June Carbone and Margaret F. Brinig, *Rethinking Marriage: Feminist Ideology, Economic Change, and Divorce Reform*, 65 Tulane L Rev 953 (1991); Jana B. Singer, *Divorce Reform and Gender Justice*, 67 NC L Rev 1103 (1989); Jana B. Singer, *Alimony and Efficiency: The Gendered Costs and Benefits of the Economic Justification for Alimony*, 82 Geo LJ 2423 (1994); Wanda Weigers, *Economic Analysis of Law and "Private Ordering": A Feminist Critique*, 42 U Toronto L J 170 (1992).

Household and Labor Force Work. For discussions of the conflicts between home and family work, see Nancy Dowd, *Work and Family: The Gender Paradox and the Limitations of Discrimination Analysis in Restructuring the Workplace*, 24 Harv CR–CL L Rev 19 (1989); Lucinda M. Finley, *Transcending Equality Theory: A Way Out of the Maternity and the Workplace Debate*, 86 Colum L Rev 1118 (1986); Victor Fuchs, *Women's Quest for Economic Equality* (Harv U Press, 1988); Kathleen Gerson, *Hard Choices* (U Cal Press, 1985). For a discussion of many of the ways that economics informs the study of families, see the collection of essays included in Antony W. Dnes & Robert Rowthorn, *The Law and Economics of Marriage and Divorce* (Cambridge Press, 2002).

Gender and Equality. For accounts by "equality" feminists, see Marsha Garrison, *Marriage: The Status of Contract* (Book Review), 131 U Pa L Rev 1039, 1060 (1983); Herma Hill Kay, *Equality and Difference: A Perspective on No Fault Divorce and its Aftermath*, 56 Cinn L Rev 1 (1987); Herma Hill Kay, *An Appraisal of California's No–Fault Divorce Law*, 75 Cal L Rev 291 (1987); Herma Hill Kay, *Models of Equality*, 1985 U Ill L Rev 39; Sylvia A. Law, *Rethinking Sex and the Constitution*, 132 U Pa L Rev 955 (1984).

Gender and Difference. For feminist writings concentrating on the "difference" perspective, see Nancy Chodorow, *The Reproduction of Mothering* (U Cal Press, 1978); Carol Gilligan, *In a Different Voice: Psychiatric Theory and Women's Development* (Harv U Press, 1982); Joan Tronto, *Beyond Gender Difference: To a Theory of Care,* 12 Signs: Journal of Women in Culture and Society 644 (1977); Nel Noddings, *Caring: A Feminine Approach to Ethics and Moral Education* (U Cal Press, 1984); and Joan Williams, *Gender Wars: Selfless Women in the Republic of Choice,* 66 NYU L Rev 1559 (1991).

Radical Feminism. For the radical feminist approach, see Mary Joe Frug, *Sexual Equality and Sexual Difference in American Law*, in *For Mary Joe Frug: A Symposium on Feminist Critical Legal Studies and Postmodernism*, 26 New England L Rev 665–682 (1992); Catherine A. Mackinnon, *Toward a Feminist Theory of the State* (Harv U Press, 1989).

The Expressive Function. For a particularly thoughtful and sensible evaluation of the expressive function, see Carol Weisbrod, *On the Expressive Function of Family Law*, 22 U Cal–Davis L Rev 991 (1989). For an examination of that function in the context of the relations between parents and children, see Katharine T. Bartlett, *Re-Expressing Parenthood*, 98 Yale L J 293 (1988). For an investigation of the expressive function in law generally, see Cass R. Sunstein, *On the Expressive Function of Law*, 144 U Pa L Rev 2021 (1987).

Human Nature. For the argument that Puritans and Victorians were not hostile to sexual expression but were anxious that it be confined to what was seen as its appropriate place, see, e.g. Edmund Leites, *The Puritan Conscience and Modern Sexuality* (Yale U Press, 1986); Peter Gardella, *Innocent Ecstasy: How Christianity Gave America an Ethic of Sexual Pleasure* (Oxford U Press, 1985); Peter Gay, *Education of the Senses: in The Bourgeois Experience from Victoria to Freud* (Oxford U Press, 1984). On the origins of the therapeutic view, see generally Philip Rieff, *Freud: The Mind of the Moralist* (U Chi Press, 1959). For an intriguing criticism of modern psychology for being "more hostile to the inhibitory messages of traditional religious moralizing than is scientifically justified," see Donald T. Campbell, *On the Conflicts Between Biological and Social Evolution and Between Psychology and Moral Tradition*, 1975 Am Psychologist 1103. For a classic discussion contrasting the ascetic and therapeutic views (very much to the detriment of the latter), see Philip Rieff, *The Triumph of the Therapeutic: Uses of Faith After Freud* (U Chi Press, 1966). For a sociological investigation of the modern American attitude toward human nature and obligation, see Robert N. Bellah, et al., *Habits of the Heart: Individualism and Commitment in American Life* (Harper and Row, 1985). For a more sympathetic view of the same subject, see Francesca M. Cancian, *Love in America: Gender and Self–Development* (Cambridge U Press, 1987). For extended reflections on human nature and family law, see Carl E. Schneider, *Marriage, Morals, and the Law: No–Fault Divorce and Moral Discourse*, 1994 Utah L Rev 503.

The Channelling Function. For a fuller description, see Carl E. Schneider, *The Channelling Function in Family Law*, 20 Hofstra L Rev 495, 498 (1992). Margaret F. Brinig, Carl E. Schneider and Lee E. Teitelbaum, *Family Law in Action: A Reader* 406–422 (Anderson, 1999), includes excerpts elaborating on the channelling and expressive functions of family law.

Chapter III

THE POWER VESTED IN ME: STATE INTERVENTION IN THE MARRIAGE

To try to regulate the internal affairs of a family, the relations of love or friendship, or many other things of the same sort, by law or by the coercion of public opinion is like trying to pull an eyelash out of a man's eye with a pair of tongs. They may put out the eye, but they never will get hold of the eyelash.

James Fitzjames Stephen
Liberty, Equality, Fraternity

SECTION 1. CONSENTED TOGETHER: FAMILY AUTONOMY AND THE PRINCIPLE OF PRIVATE ORDERING

[A] law may bind two members of the community very closely to each other; but that law being abolished, they stand asunder.

Such, however, is not the case with those feelings which are natural to mankind. Whenever a law attempts to tutor these feelings in any particular manner, it seldom fails to weaken them; by attempting to add to their intensity it robs them of some of their elements, for they are never stronger than when left to themselves.

Alexis de Tocqueville
Democracy in America

A. FAMILY AUTONOMY: AN INTRODUCTORY CASE

How small, of all that human hearts endure That part which laws or kings can cause or cure! Still to ourselves in every place consigned, Our own felicity we make or find: With secret course, which no loud storms annoy, Glides the smooth current of domestic joy.

Samuel Johnson
Lines added to Goldsmith's *Traveler*

One of the most frequently articulated and deeply felt principles of American family law is the doctrine of "family autonomy," the principle that the government should as a rule not "intervene in the family." We will discover, of course, that this principle is less absolute and more ambiguous than judicial rhetoric suggests. Let us, therefore, begin now to ask what the principle might mean and how far it ought to extend. Let us do so by reading one of the classic citations for the principle:

KILGROW v. KILGROW

Supreme Court of Alabama, 1958
107 S2d 885

GOODWYN, JUSTICE....

On August 29, 1957, Jack M. Kilgrow, appellee, filed a petition in the circuit court of Montgomery County, in equity, against his wife, Christine B. Kilgrow, seeking a temporary injunction restraining her from interfering with petitioner's "right to carry the said Margaret Kilgrow [alleged in the bill to be the parties' 7–year-old daughter] to Loretta School next Tuesday to resume her education" and also seeking, upon final hearing of the cause, "a decree permanently enjoining the respondent from interfering or attempting to interfere and prevent the said Margaret Kilgrow from continuing her education at Loretta School." There is also a prayer for general relief.

The petition alleges that the parties are over 21 years of age, are bona fide residents of Montgomery, Alabama, and reside at 910 South Lawrence Street; that they were lawfully married in Montgomery County, Alabama, on May 19, 1948; that to this marriage was born one child, named Margaret Kilgrow, a girl now 7 years of age and who is residing with petitioner and respondent. The petition also contains the following allegations:

> "3. During the 1956–57 school year, the said minor child of petitioner and respondent, Margaret Kilgrow, entered the first grade at Loretta School in Montgomery, Alabama, and continued throughout the school year. That the said Margaret Kilgrow made an excellent scholastic record at Loretta. That all her friends and playmates go to school at Loretta and that the said Margaret Kilgrow had a happy school year at Loretta and took an active part in all the school activities. That last spring at the end of the 1956–57 school year, she was enrolled in the Loretta School to begin the fall term of the 1957–58 school year to begin on September 3, 1957. That last week your petitioner carried his minor daughter, Margaret Kilgrow, to Loretta School to ascertain what books and supplies would be required at the beginning of the new school term beginning next week.
>
> "4. That it would be to the best interest and welfare of the said Margaret Kilgrow that she return to Loretta School to resume her grade

school education. That the respondent, Christine B. Kilgrow, mother of the said Margaret Kilgrow, is threatening to prevent petitioner from carrying his said minor daughter to Loretta and is threatening to interfere with the right of the petitioner to place his said minor daughter in Loretta School beginning Tuesday, September 3, 1957; and has told petitioner that she will remain away from her job for the purpose of preventing the said Margaret Kilgrow from returning to Loretta School next week. That the threats and avowed purpose of the said respondent to prevent the said minor child from returning to Loretta School is inimical to the welfare and best interest of the said minor child."

On September 6, 1957, the petition was amended by adding thereto paragraph 5 as follows:

"5. That since the filing of the original petition in this cause and on, to-wit, this date, September 3, 1957, your petitioner has gotten his minor daughter, Margaret Kilgrow, ready to carry her to Loretta School; that petitioner was going to carry his daughter down town to his place of business and wait the opening of Loretta School so that he could carry the child to the school; that petitioner drove his said minor child to town in the automobile with respondent and was intending to turn the automobile over to respondent so that she might go to work; that petitioner and respondent occupied the front seat and the child the back seat; that petitioner drove the automobile in front of his place of work and got out of the front seat and started to open the back door to get the child, whereupon respondent jumped under the steering wheel and drove the automobile away carrying the child with her, as a consequence of which the said child will not be able to enter Loretta School this morning and will not be able to enter the said school unless the respondent is enjoined and restrained from interfering with the placing of said child in the said school."

On September 9th the respondent demurred to the petition, assigning the following grounds:

"1. There is no equity in said bill of compliant.

"2. For aught that appears from the bill of complaint this is a matter wholly within the family circle and in no way is a matter over which this Court has jurisdiction."

The demurrer was overruled.

The respondent then filed an answer to the petition embodying therein grounds of demurrer questioning the jurisdiction of the court and answering the petition by admitting all of its allegations except those contained in paragraphs 3 through 5, which she denies and of which she demands strict proof. Thereupon, on September 9th a hearing was had before the trial court and testimony taken on behalf of both petitioner and respondent. At the conclusion of the hearing a decree was rendered granting to petitioner the relief prayed for. To the extent here pertinent, the decree provides as follows:

"Ordered, adjudged and decreed by the court that the said demurrer of the respondent to the petition as amended be and the same is hereby overruled.

"And now coming to the merits of the matter the court is of opinion that it has jurisdiction of this matter. While it is true that the father of a minor child has in general the right to direct the education of his minor child, this right is subject to review and correction by the court if not exercised for the best welfare of the child. The decision of the father is prima facie correct, but subject to be rebutted by proper proof from the other parent.

"The court has gone into the evidence in this case at length and has heard about ten witnesses all told, and upon a consideration of the same the court is of opinion that it is for the best interest of the minor child involved in these proceedings that she remain in the school where the father has placed her and that the mother refrain from interfering with the schooling of said minor child. It is, therefore,

"Ordered, adjudged and decreed by the court

"1) that it is for the best welfare of the child, Margaret Kilgrow, that she continue her studies where her father has placed her, in Loretta School.

"2) That Mrs. Christine B. Kilgrow be and she is hereby enjoined and restrained from interfering with the schooling of the said child at Loretta School, and that said child continue her schooling there until and unless this order be changed in proper proceedings."

Although the decree setting the hearing recited that it would be upon the motion for a preliminary injunction, it seems that the proceeding was conducted as though it were a final hearing on the merits. This is made clear by the decree itself; and the parties also have treated it as a final decree on the merits. We shall do likewise.

From the pleadings and evidence it clearly appears that the dispute between the parents grows out of the fact that the father and mother are of different religious faiths. Loretta is a school operated by the church of the father's religious faith. He wants the child to attend that school while the mother wants her to attend a public school.

There was introduced in evidence an antenuptial agreement whereby the parties agreed that all the children of their marriage "shall be baptized and educated" in the "religion" of the father, whether he be "living or dead."

As we see it, the decisive question presented is whether a court of equity has inherent jurisdiction (there being no statute involved) to resolve a family dispute between parents as to the school their minor child should attend, when there is no question concerning the custody of the child incident to a separation (either voluntary or pursuant to a court order) or divorce of the parents, and to enforce its decision against one of the parents by injunction. In other words, should the jurisdiction of a court of equity extend to the settlement of a difference of opinion between parents as to what is best for their minor child when the parents and child are all living together as a family group?

This appears to be a case of first impression in Alabama and there seems to be little authority bearing on the question from other jurisdictions. In fact, no case has been cited to us, nor have we found any, which has dealt with the precise problem before us.

There can be no doubt that if this were a proceeding to determine the child's custody the equity court would have jurisdiction for that purpose. In *Campbell v. Sowell*, 159 So. 813, 814, it is stated as follows:

> "It is generally recognized that, when a proceeding is instituted to determine the custody of the child, such child becomes at once a ward of the court."

But that is not the situation before us. There is no issue as to the child's custody. Here, the injunctive process is employed at the instance of the father to restrain the mother, who continues to live with the father as a member of the family group and who also has natural custodial rights over her minor child.

It seems to us, if we should hold that equity has jurisdiction in this case such holding will open wide the gates for settlement in equity of all sorts and varieties of intimate family disputes concerning the upbringing of children. The absence of cases dealing with the question indicates a reluctance of the courts to assume jurisdiction in disputes arising out of the intimate family circle. It does not take much imagination to envision the extent to which explosive differences of opinion between parents as to the proper upbringing of their children could be brought into court for attempted solution.

In none of our cases has the court intervened to settle a controversy between unseparated parents as to some matter incident to the well-being of the child, where there was no question presented as to which parent should have custody. In all of our cases the real question has been which parent should properly be awarded custody. Never has the court put itself in the place of the parents and interposed its judgment as to the course which otherwise amicable parents should pursue in discharging their parental duty. Here, the sole difference between the parties is which school the child should attend. And, that difference seems not to have affected the conjugal attitude of the parents one to the other.

The inherent jurisdiction of courts of equity over infants is a matter of necessity, coming into exercise only where there has been a failure of that natural power and obligation which is the province of parenthood. It is a jurisdiction assumed by the courts only when it is forfeited by a natural custodian incident to a broken home or neglect, or as a result of a natural custodian's incapacity, unfitness or death. It is only for compelling reason that a parent is deprived of the custody of his or her child. The court only interferes as between parents to the extent of awarding custody to the one or the other, with the welfare of the child in mind. And it is in awarding custody that the court invokes the principle that the welfare of the child is the controlling consideration. We do not think a court of equity should undertake to settle a dispute between parents as to what is best for their minor child when there is no question concerning the child's custody.

It would be anomalous to hold that a court of equity may sit in constant supervision over a household and see that either parent's will and determination in the upbringing of a child is obeyed, even though the parents' dispute might involve what is best for the child. Every difference of opinion between parents concerning their child's upbringing necessarily involves the question of the child's best interest.

What was said in *Knighton v. Knighton*, 41 So.2d 172, 175, is equally pertinent here:

> "It intrigues the imagination to contemplate the lengths to which such a power once attempted may be carried, and the difficulty to be encountered in the enforcement of such a decree. Considerations of policy and expedience forbid a resort to injunctive relief in such a case."

It may well be suggested that a court of equity ought to interfere to prevent such a direful consequence as divorce or separation, rather than await the disruption of the marital relationship. Our answer to this is that intervention, rather than preventing or healing a disruption, would quite likely serve as the spark to a smoldering fire. A mandatory court decree supporting the position of one parent against the other would hardly be a composing situation for the unsuccessful parent to be confronted with daily. One spouse could scarcely be expected to entertain a tender, affectionate regard for the other spouse who brings him or her under restraint. The judicial mind and conscience is repelled by the thought of disruption of the sacred marital relationship, and usually voices the hope that the breach may somehow be healed by mutual understanding between the parents themselves.

The prenuptial agreement as to the child's religious education has no bearing on the question of the trial court's jurisdiction in this case. The bill does not even attempt to make that agreement a basis for relief.

It is argued that any apprehension about opening wide the jurisdiction of equity is not on sound footing because, in Alabama, a child is required by statute to attend school. Thus, it is argued, the instant case has for its purpose the fulfillment of this mandatory duty. But there is absolutely no question here concerning the neglect or failure of either parent to see that the child attends school. (In so commenting we make it clear that we are not now passing on the validity or constitutionality of any law requiring attendance at school; nor is there occasion to discuss what bearing, if any, evidence of either parent's failure or neglect to provide schooling for the child would have on this case.)

In view of what we have said it is unnecessary to decide whether the decree, in effect ordering that the child attend a school of a particular religious denomination which, according to the evidence, involves mandatory teaching of the religious doctrines of that denomination, would be giving preference by law to a particular religious sect contrary to the

First and Fourteenth Amendments of the Constitution of the United States and § 3 of Article 1, Alabama Constitution of 1901.

The decree appealed from is due to be reversed and one rendered here dismissing the petition. It is so ordered.

Notes and Questions on Kilgrow *and Family Autonomy*

As we said earlier, and for reasons that you now see, *Kilgrow* is often cited for the proposition that the state ought not intervene in the affairs of a family in which the husband and wife continue to live together, i.e., for the doctrine of family autonomy. The following questions are designed to help you identify and assess the rationales for that basic doctrine. You should examine these questions with particular care, since we will regularly return to them in order to evaluate the strength of the family-autonomy doctrine in other areas of family law. So, why might the state wish to adopt a doctrine of family autonomy?

(1) Is the problem that a court or agency lacks, and will find it hard to get, information about any particular family's situation? That is, is the problem that information about the family is likely to be peculiarly within the control of the parties, so that disputes will simply turn into a swearing contest? Does the problem run even deeper: is the difficulty that a wise decision about a family requires as full as possible an understanding of the social, emotional, and moral past and present of the family and each of its members, that such understanding is complex and detailed beyond description, that it is often not consciously possessed even by the family members themselves, and that for all these reasons it cannot be satisfactorily conveyed to outsiders even while it is available to the family members themselves? In other words, do we prefer to leave familial decisions to families because they know themselves better than anyone else could?

(2) Is the problem that judges lack expertise in these decisions? In other words, do family disputes have a dynamic of their own, a dynamic that may be comprehensible to a psychologist but not to a judge? Would this problem be resolved by adopting the practice of many jurisdictions and establishing courts that specialize in family problems? By following the usual judicial practice and allowing both parties to introduce expert testimony as to the psychological elements of the case?

(3) Is the problem that no adequate standards can be devised to govern a court's or an administrative agency's decision?

(a) Is the problem that the situations of families are so various, complex, and unpredictable that no useful standards could be drawn up?

(b) Is the problem that in a large, pluralistic society no satisfactory social agreement could be reached about behavior in families?

(c) Is the problem that there are some kinds of considerations—like religious belief or ethnic tradition—which may be important in resolving family disputes but which the state may not properly take into account?

(d) Is the problem that family disputes ought not be decided according to the kind of impersonal standards which the law must use, but should be resolved according to the standards of accommodation, affection, and love which brought the family together in the first place?

(e) Even if there is some truth to the above four points, don't courts make decisions about children's welfare repeatedly in, for example, child-custody cases and in cases where a parent is accused of abusing or neglecting a child? Don't courts make decisions about fairness within marriages repeatedly when they divide marital property "equitably"? And if courts can resolve family disputes of this difficulty, why should there be an *a priori* rule presumptively barring courts from deciding disputes about families?

(4) Is the problem that enforcement of a judicial decree in family disputes is often impossible?

(a) Is the problem that much of the behavior that is the subject of family disputes takes place in private and that government cannot easily find out or supervise what is going on?

(b) Is the problem that much of the behavior that is the subject of family disputes is motivated by psychological forces which are both strong and obscure and which thus are so difficult for people to control that even governmental sanctions may have little effect?

(c) Is the problem that much of the behavior that is the subject of family disputes has to do with matters that family members will often feel are not the concern of outsiders (and particularly are not the concern of government), so that families will resist attempts to enforce governmental rules and decisions?

(d) Is the problem that governmental attempts to enforce rules or decisions may provoke the regulated person to retaliate against the very people the government is attempting to protect?

(5) Is the problem that the judicial process will exacerbate, not resolve, the family conflict? In particular, is the adversary system of justice likely to encourage the parties to regard each other antagonistically? Why should this be so? Isn't the problem within the family presumably that the family is unable to agree on its own, and wouldn't a third party be able to propose some kind of solution which might give the parties a face-saving way out? Isn't it better for a court to provide a forum for resolving family disputes before those disputes lead to a divorce? Wouldn't a non-adversarial proceeding meet the objection that the judicial process might exacerbate family conflicts?

(6) Is the problem that a judicial inquiry into the facts of a family dispute would necessarily injure a family by invading its privacy? In other words, is it not important to the successful functioning of a family that it be able to conduct its intimate affairs free of scrutiny, and is it

not inevitable that any governmental attempt to resolve family disputes or to enforce governmental regulations must lead to inquiries which will reveal those intimate affairs at least to officials and possibly to the world? On the other hand, why can't courts protect families against the revelation of private information by such devices as closed hearings and sealed records? Aren't there many situations in which courts inquire into "private" matters, both in family law (child-custody disputes and disputes over marital property, to say nothing of investigations of *Marvin v. Marvin* claims) and in the law generally (libel suits, for instance)?

(7) Is the problem that it is in some way normatively preferable for individuals to organize their lives, particularly their intimate lives, free of government supervision? Is the problem that it is in some way normatively preferable for families to organize their lives, particularly their intimate lives, free of government supervision? Are these two questions identical? Are they just ways of summarizing the previous points? Can this rationale apply where people cannot agree about how to organize their intimate lives, where the decision of one party may in some sense have been coerced, or where their decision harms a third party?

(8) Is the problem that we wish to preserve a pluralist society and that allowing families freedom to organize themselves as they wish is one way of promoting that goal? What does "pluralist society" mean? How does the doctrine of family autonomy promote it?

(9) Many of these points seem simply to be another way of saying that a family will ordinarily make better decisions about itself than a governmental agency. But even if that is true as a general matter, ought it to prevent courts from intervening in families that seem to be making poor decisions? Ought it to prevent courts from intervening in families over issues as to which governmental expertise may be greater than the family's? Should the "doctrine of family autonomy" be simply a prudential guideline for governmental agencies, not a powerful "doctrine," much less a "right"?

(10) We said at the beginning of these questions that they were intended to help you probe the basis for the doctrine of family autonomy. Can a satisfactory basis be found for such a doctrine? If so, what would it be? If not, why not? How well does the best basis you can articulate for the doctrine of family autonomy support the result in *Kilgrow*? How well would it support the doctrine in contexts other than *Kilgrow*'s?

(11) Most of the more recent cases that otherwise resemble *Kilgrow* concern parental conflict over religious values or education after the parties' divorce. In these situations, even when the matters are the subject of written agreements, courts hesitate to interfere with decisions made by the custodial parent unless those decisions amount to infringement of the noncustodial parent's first amendment rights. For an examination of this attitude, see Carl E. Schneider, *Religion and Child Custody*, 25 U Mich J L Reform 879 (1992).

(12) Between the privacy issues presented by *Kilgrow* and those of criminal abuse discussed later in this chapter lie a whole range of potential interspousal privacy matters. One of these is the question of the marital-communications privilege, considered in other law school courses. The early cases established tort immunity because the courts feared suits might involve such relatively normal marital exchanges as the "unwanted kiss." *Wait v. Pierce*, 209 NW 475 (Wis 1926) (Eschweiler, J, dissenting). Courts were also concerned with the risk of collusion and ultimately barred suits between family members when the wrongs were done while the family was intact. A tort suit could not be brought after marriage and before divorce or before emancipation of a child. Beginning with automobile cases, see *Lewis v. Lewis*, 351 NE2d 526 (Mass 1976), passing through intentional torts so outrageous there was "no domestic tranquility to be preserved," *Lusby v. Lusby*, 390 A2d 77, 78 (Md 1978), most states have now abrogated interspousal, but not parent-child, immunity. See, for example, *Merenoff v. Merenoff*, 388 A2d 951 (NJ 1978); Va Code § 8.01–220.1 (2006).

SECTION 2. LOVE HER, COMFORT HER, HONOUR AND KEEP HER: FAMILY AUTONOMY AND THE PRINCIPLE OF PRIVACY

You know marriage is honourable, a blessed calling, appointed by God Himself in Paradise; it breeds true peace, tranquility, content, and happiness, qua nulla est aut fuit unquam sanctior conjunctio [than which there is not nor ever has been any holier union], as Daphnaeus in Plutarch could well prove, et quae generi humano immortalitatem parat [which makes the human race immortal], when they live without jarring, scolding, lovingly as they should do.

Robert Burton
The Anatomy of Melancholy

A. SPOUSE ABUSE

He had never sworn at her before, and now she burst out into a flood of tears. It was to her a terrible outrage.... [H]ere the word had been uttered with all its foulest violence, with virulence and vulgarity. It seemed to the victim to be a sign of a terrible crisis in her early married life,—as though the man who had so spoken to her could never again love her, never again be kind to her, never again be sweetly gentle and like a lover. And as he spoke it he looked at her as though he would like to tear her limbs asunder.

Anthony Trollope
The Prime Minister

(1) An Introductory Case

The principle of family autonomy is put to one of its harshest tests by the problem of spouse abuse. Ought the principle be waived or tempered where one spouse assaults another? If so, on what theory? Does a decision to waive the principle say anything about the principle's soundness? To help us begin thinking about such questions, we will read a nineteenth-century case which makes the argument against waiver with uncommon and even troubling directness.

STATE v. RHODES

Supreme Court of North Carolina, 1868
61 NC 453

The defendant was indicted for an assault and battery upon his wife, Elizabeth Rhodes. Upon the evidence submitted to them, the jury returned the following special verdict:

> "We find that the defendant struck Elizabeth Rhodes, his wife, three licks, with a switch about the size of one of his fingers (but not as large as a man's thumb) without any provocation except some words uttered by her and not recollected by the witness."

His Honor was of the opinion that the defendant had a right to whip his wife with a switch no larger than his thumb, and that upon the facts found in the special verdict, he was not guilty in law. Judgment in favor of the defendant was accordingly entered and the State appealed.

READE, JUSTICE:

The violence complained of would without question have constituted a battery if the subject of it had not been the defendant's wife. The question is how far that fact affects the case.

The courts have been loath to take cognizance of trivial complaints arising out of the domestic relations—such as master and apprentice, teacher and pupil, parent and child, husband and wife. Not because those relations are not subject to the law, but because the evil of publicity would be greater than the evil involved in the trifles complained of; and because they ought to be left to family government. On the civil side of this court, under our divorce laws, such cases have been unavoidable, and not infrequent. On the criminal side there are but two cases reported. In one the question was, whether the wife was a competent witness to prove a battery by the husband upon her, which inflicted no great or permanent injury. It was decided that she was not. In discussing the subject the court said, that the abstract question of the husband's right to whip his wife did not arise. *State v. Hussey*, Busb. 123. The other case was one of a slight battery by the husband upon the wife after gross provocation. He was held not to be punishable. In that case the court said, that unless some permanent injury be inflicted, or there be an excess of violence, or such a degree of cruelty as shows that it is inflicted to gratify his own bad passions, the law will not invade the domestic forum, or go behind the curtain. *State v. Black*, 1 Winst., 266.

Neither of those cases is like the one before us. The first case turned upon the competency of the wife as a witness, and in the second there was a slight battery upon a strong provocation.

In this case no provocation worth the name was proved. The fact found was that it was "without any provocation except some words which were not recollected by the witness." The words must have been of the slightest import to have made no impression on the memory. We must therefore consider the violence as unprovoked. The question is therefore plainly presented, whether the court will allow a conviction of the husband for moderate correction of the wife without provocation.

Our divorce laws do not compel a separation of husband and wife, unless the conduct of the husband be so cruel as to render the wife's condition intolerable, or her life burdensome. What sort of conduct on the part of the husband, would be allowed to have that effect, has been repeatedly considered. And it has not been found easy to lay down any iron rule upon the subject. In some cases it has been held that actual and repeated violence to the person, was not sufficient. In others that insults, indignities and neglect without any actual violence, were quite sufficient. So much does each case depend upon its peculiar surroundings.

We have sought the aid of the experience and wisdom of other times, and of other countries.

Blackstone says "that the husband, by the old law, might give the wife moderate correction, for as he was to answer for her misbehavior, he ought to have the power to control her; but that in the polite reign of Charles the Second, this power of correction began to be doubted." Wharton says, that by the ancient common law the husband possessed the power to chastise his wife; but that the tendency of criminal courts in the present day, is to regard the marital relation as no defense to a battery. Chancellor Walworth says of such correction, that it is not authorized by the law of any civilized country; not indeed meaning that England is not civilized, but referring to the anomalous relics of barbarism which cleave to her jurisprudence. The old law of moderate correction has been questioned even in England, and has been repudiated in Ireland and Scotland. The old rule is approved in Mississippi, but it has met with but little favor elsewhere in the United States. *Ibid.* 485. In looking into the discussions of the other States we find but little uniformity.

From what has been said it will be seen how much the subject is at sea. And, probably, it will ever be so: for it will always be influenced by the habits, manners and condition of every community. Yet it is necessary that we should lay down something as precise and practical as the nature of the subject will admit of, for the guidance of our courts.

Our conclusion is that family government is recognized by law as being as complete in itself as the State government is in itself, and yet subordinate to it; and that we will not interfere with or attempt to control it, in favor of either husband or wife, unless in cases where permanent or malicious injury is inflicted or threatened, or the condition of the party is intolerable. For, however great are the evils of ill temper, quarrels, and even personal conflicts inflicting only temporary pain, they are not comparable with the evils which would result from raising the curtain, and exposing to public curiosity and criticism, the nursery and the bed chamber. Every household has and must have, a government of its own, modeled to suit the temper, disposition and condition of its inmates. Mere ebullitions of passion, impulsive violence, and temporary pain, affection will soon forget and forgive; and each member will find excuse for the other in his own frailties. But when trifles are taken hold of by the public, and the parties are exposed and disgraced, and each endeavors to justify himself or herself by criminating the other, that which ought to be forgotten in a day, will be remembered for life.

It is urged in this case, that as there was no provocation the violence was of course excessive and malicious; that every one in whatever relation of life should be able to purchase immunity from pain, by obedience to authority and faithfulness in duty. And it is insisted, that in *State v. Pendergrass*, which was the case of a schoolmistress whipping a child, that doctrine is laid down. It is true that it is there said, that the master may be punishable even when he does not transcend the powers granted; *i.e.*, when he does not inflict permanent injury, if he grossly abuse his powers, and use them as a cover for his malice. But observe, the language is, if he *grossly* abuse his powers. So that every one would say at once, there was no cause for it, and it was purely malicious and cruel. If this be not the rule then every violence which would amount to an assault upon a stranger, would have to be investigated to see whether there was any provocation. And that would contravene what we have said, that we will punish no case of trifling importance. If in every such case we are to hunt for the provocation, how will the proof be supplied? Take the case before us. The witness said, there was no provocation except some slight words. But then who can tell what significance the trifling words may have had to the husband? Who can tell what had happened an hour before, and every hour for a week? To him they may have been sharper than a sword. And so in every case, it might be impossible for the court to appreciate what might be offered as an excuse, or no excuse might appear at all, when a complete justification exists. Or, suppose the provocation could in every case be known, and the court should undertake to weigh the provocation in every trifling family broil, what would be the standard? Suppose a case coming up to us from a hovel, where neither delicacy of sentiment nor refinement of manners is appreciated or known. The parties themselves would be amazed, if they were to be held responsible for rudeness or trifling violence. What do they care for insults and indignities? In such cases what end would be gained by investigation or punishment? Take a case from the middle class, where modesty and purity have their abode but nevertheless have not immunity from the frailties of nature, and are sometimes moved by the mysteries of passion. What could be more harassing to them, or injurious to society, than to draw a crowd around their seclusion. Or take a case from the higher ranks, where education and culture have so refined nature, that a look cuts like a knife, and a word strikes like a hammer; where the most delicate attention gives pleasure, and the slightest neglect pain; where an indignity is disgrace and exposure is ruin. Bring all these cases into court side by side, with the same offense charged and the same proof made; and what conceivable charge of the court to the jury would be alike appropriate to all the cases, except, that they all have domestic government, which they have formed for themselves, suited to their own peculiar conditions, and that those governments are supreme, and from them there is no appeal except in cases of great importance requiring the strong arm of the law, and that to those governments they must submit themselves.

It will be observed that the ground upon which we have put this decision, is not, that the husband has the *right* to whip his wife much or little; but that we will not interfere with family government in trifling cases. We will no more interfere where the husband whips the wife, than where the wife whips the husband; and yet we would hardly be supposed to hold, that a wife has a *right* to whip her husband. We will not inflict upon society the greater evil of raising the curtain upon domestic privacy, to punish the lesser evil of trifling violence. Two boys under fourteen years of age fight upon the play-ground, and yet the courts will take no notice of it, not for the reason that boys have the *right* to fight, but because the interests of society require that they should be left to the more appropriate discipline of the school room and of home. It is not true that boys have a right to fight; nor is it true that a husband has a right to whip his wife. And if he had, it is not easily seen how *the thumb* is the standard of size for the instrument which he may use, as some of the old authorities have said; and in deference to which was his Honor's charge. A light blow, or many light blows, with a stick larger than the thumb, might produce no injury; but a switch half the size might be so used as to produce death. The standard is the *effect produced*, and not the manner of producing it, or the instrument used.

Because our opinion is not in unison with the decisions of some of the sister States, or with the philosophy of some very respectable law writers, and could not be in unison with all, because of their contrariety—a decent respect for the opinions of others has induced us to be very full in stating the reasons for our conclusion. There is no error.

Notes and Questions on Rhodes

(1) Is *Rhodes* a weaker or stronger candidate than *Kilgrow* for governmental intervention?

(2) When we discussed *Kilgrow*, we considered eight justifications for the principle of family autonomy. At this point you should carefully re-examine those justifications and ask how well they fit a case like *Rhodes*.

(3) One response to attempts to apply the family autonomy principle to cases of spouse abuse is to argue that that principle ought not apply

where behavior within a family is criminal. This response notes that the principle of family autonomy is not thereby greatly damaged, since a bright line—the violation of a criminal law—is available to prevent a slippery-slope expansion of the exceptions to the principle. The response further notes that it is difficult to make distinctions between various forms of criminal activity and that it is therefore hard to see why spouse abuse should ever be exempted from criminal prosecution. In what ways is spouse abuse different from other kinds of crime? Are those differences great enough to justify treating spouse abuse differently from other kinds of crime?

(2) Spouse Abuse as a Social and Legal Problem: Two Expository Exercises

The questions you have just studied attempt to help you examine the doctrine of family autonomy in one of its most problematic applications. The following exercises introduce some broad outlines of the social problem of spouse abuse and the various legal responses to it. The exercises pay special attention to the question of the extent to which the criminal justice system should, as many now urge and as some jurisdictions are now attempting, aggressively arrest and prosecute spouse abusers. Professor Franklin E. Zimring has suggested that the current importance of this question is to some extent anomalous:

> The movement to expand the reach of the criminal law over family violence is somewhat at odds with efforts to cut back on the application of penal law in other spheres. Over the broad sweep of decades, just when society began to recognize the limits of the criminal sanction in areas such as narcotics, gambling, and prostitution, there was a growing emphasis on using criminal law for the regulation of family violence. More striking, while the increased salience of family violence has led some observers to seek alternatives to criminal law sanctions, it has simultaneously led others to press for increased reliance on criminal sanctions.

Legal Perspectives on Family Violence, 75 Cal L Rev 521, 534 (1987). As you study these exercises, then, you should ask yourself how far the criminal law provides an adequate vehicle for addressing the problem of family violence. You should recall what you learned in your Criminal Law class about the purposes and limits of the criminal law and in your Torts class about the purposes and limits of the law of torts.

(a) First Exercise

Suppose that you are the Mayor of Cooley, a large metropolitan city in the large industrial state of Hutchins. Like most Americans, you have for some time been aware that the problem of domestic violence has been receiving a good deal of national attention. A suit has recently been brought against your police department charging it with failing to respond adequately to incidents of spouse abuse. You have come to believe that your administration must reconsider its policy on family violence. You resolve to begin by reformulating your spouse abuse program. You ask your staff what to do. Your staff advises you to hire a consultant who is an expert in the field. This is the consultant's report:

PROFESSOR G. LECTEUR
DEALING WITH SPOUSE ABUSE: CONSIDERATIONS FOR COOLEY

The State of Research

The first difficulty in devising a program to combat spouse abuse is that we know too little about the extent of spouse abuse, its causes, and its cures. This is an area which has received scholarly attention only recently. Thus, little research has been done and the quality of much of that research has been poor. As one summary reports, "A ... serious problem with family violence research is that it tends to be exceedingly weak methodologically."[1] As another summary adds, "[T]he evidence accumulated from this literature has been described as 'clouded,' 'limited,' 'rudimentary,' 'primitive,' and not meeting 'traditional standards of scientific inquiry.' "[2] Research on the incidence of family violence has been particularly hampered by the difficulty of acquiring information about so delicate and painful a subject. Research on programs dealing with family violence has been hampered by many difficulties, including, for example, the barriers to establishing control groups. Thus, while there is general agreement that "the goal is to bring about a cessation of family violence through either deterrence or dissuasion, ... so far, very little research has been conducted to demonstrate how to accomplish this so that the benefits outweigh the costs."[3]

The Incidence of Spouse Abuse

Our first encounter with the difficulties posed by the quality of research in this area comes in describing the extent of spouse abuse. As Joseph G. Weis writes, "substantial discrepancies among estimates of the prevalence, incidence, and correlates of family violence compromise the usefulness of the research results.... [P]ronounced differences in prevalence estimates are evident in studies of spousal violence. Extrapolations from official records have produced estimates ranging from thousands to millions of battered wives per year, while more direct survey methods report that 28 percent of couples (approximately fifteen million) experience violence at some point during their marriage."[4] This latter study found that more than a third of couples experienced a relatively serious kind of assault, including hitting, beating up, and assaults with a weapon. This same study found that roughly half the

1. Lloyd Ohlin & Michael Tonry, *Family Violence in Perspective*, in Lloyd Ohlin & Michael Tonry, eds, *Family Violence* 1, 4 (U Chi Press, 1989).

2. *Family Violence Research Methodology and Design*, in *Family Violence* at 117.

3. *Family Violence in Perspective*, at 12.

4. *Family Violence Research Methodology and Design*, in *Family Violence* at 119.

incidents of violence involved violence by both spouses, that roughly a quarter involved violence by the husband, and that roughly a quarter involved violence by the wife. The authors' study, however, argues that "men's greater average size and physical strength and their tendency toward greater aggressivity can give the same acts quite different effects when done by a woman and a man in terms of pain, injury, and threat." The authors also found men more likely to engage in the more dangerous forms of violence and to repeat their assaults.[5]

As Weis implies, some of the differences among the estimates of the incidence of spouse abuse may be related to differences in the study design. Another source of differences is the wide variation in definitions of spouse abuse. These definitions have included slapping, kicking, pushing, grabbing, throwing an object, biting, punching, beating, threatening with a weapon, using a weapon, forced sexual acts, violence against the property of the victim, and psychological abuse (including pathological jealousy and mental degradation).

Some data are also available on the incidence of spouse abuse among divorcing couples (as opposed to spouses in general). Va Code Ann § 20–91(6) (2006) permits divorce for cruelty where a spouse has "caused reasonable apprehension of bodily hurt." Margaret F. Brinig and Douglas W. Allen, *These Boots Are Made for Walking: Why Most Divorce Filers Are Women*, 2 Amer L & Econ Rev 126 (2000), reports that in 1995, about 6% of the people filing for divorce obtained a divorce on those grounds. (Nearly all of them were women.) Professors Brinig and Allen believe this figure understates the actual rate of spouse abuse among divorcing couples. First, some abused spouses presumably could not prove their cases and thus did not obtain a divorce on cruelty grounds. Second, since the doctrine of recrimination has not been abolished in Virginia for divorces sought on cruelty grounds, some plaintiffs' cases may have been dismissed because they also committed "marital fault." Finally, in some cases, Virginia plaintiffs bring actions for divorce on fault grounds but use the no-fault separation ground after bargaining. A survey of the first 130 divorce cases brought in Fairfax County in 1995 revealed that about three times as many people filed for divorce on cruelty grounds as received divorces on those grounds.

An estimate of the incidence of spouse abuse among divorcing couples that is probably at the high end is Demie Kurz, *For Richer, For Poorer: Mothers Confront Divorce* (Routledge, 1995). She surveyed 129 Philadelphia-area mothers who obtained divorces in 1986 and found about 19% gave violence as their reason for leaving the marriage. More than "70% of women of all classes and races experienced violence at the hands of their husbands at least once. Fifty percent of women experienced violence at least two to three times," and 37% said the abuse was "frequent or serious."

5. Irene Hanson Frieze & Angela Browne, *Violence in Marriage*, in *Family Violence* at 181.

The Correlates of Spouse Abuse

The research on spousal violence has not produced any satisfactory explanation of why some spouses abuse their marital partners. There is some evidence, however, about characteristics that are disproportionately (not inevitably) associated with spouse abuse:

> [One study] found that, of the forty-two characteristics or "risk markers" studied in female victims, only one—having witnessed violence between parents or care givers in childhood—was consistently correlated with being the victim of a male partner's violence. Variables not found to be consistently related to spouse-abuse victimization for women included being a full-time housewife, alcohol use, income or education level, personality integration, hostility, self-esteem, or the use of violence toward her children. Conversely, for husbands who were violent toward their female partners, three risk markers—witnessing of parental violence while growing up, sexual aggression toward the wife, and use of violence toward the children—were consistently found. Alcohol use, income level, occupational status, education level, and assertiveness were also consistent risk markers, although less strong.... In examining couples' characteristics, frequency of verbal altercations and marital dissatisfaction were consistently associated with marriages in which there was wife abuse. Low family income or social class, marital status (divorced, separated, cohabiting, and reconstituted couples), and religious incompatibility were also consistent risk markers of relationships having husband-to-wife violence.[6]

Professors Margaret Brinig and Steven Crafton looked empirically at what increased spouse abuse in *Marriage and Opportunism*, 23 J Legal Stud 969 (1994). They found that states had significantly fewer abuse crisis calls when they had a higher rural population, and significantly more abuse when fault was irrelevant in divorce or alimony. Some states tended to have higher reporting of abuse: this was positively related to the presence of strong religious groups and a high per capita income. The number of crisis calls per 1000 population ranged from a high of nearly 76 in Wyoming to a low of less than .53 in South Carolina.

It is sometimes asked why battered women do not leave their husbands. One reason may be that they fear that doing so will spark more abusive, and more dangerously abusive, behavior. This is the argument powerfully made by Martha Mahoney in *Legal Images of Battered Women: Redefining the Issue of Separation*, 90 Mich L Rev 1 (1991). Other possible reasons are suggested by the following list:

> Some women cannot leave because of economic dependence on their husbands; others have nowhere to go because they lack resources of their own simply to pack up and drive to a motel, and they have no other source of shelter that would not require money. This situation is further complicated if the woman has children she would want to take with her. Other factors that might make it difficult to leave would be loss of her job and social status and fear of disapproval from family or

6. Id at 185.

friends. By leaving, a woman gives up her identity as a wife, risks social disapproval, loses economic support, and loses any love she feels from her husband.[7]

Restraining Spouse Abuse: What Do Police and Prosecutors Do?

Much of the debate about spouse abuse today revolves around how police and prosecutors should and do handle the problem. Both police and prosecutors have been much criticized for doing too little to punish and prevent spouse abuse. Critics of the police begin by contending that when the police receive calls about domestic disturbances, they tend to give them low priority. The critics continue by suggesting that police usually treat spousal batteries differently from other batteries and that they separate the spouses and warn the assaulting spouse to desist but avoid making arrests. These critics further charge that the police are often not specially hostile to spouse abuse, that they regard it, within some limits, as a problem for the spouses to resolve, and that they sometimes condone it. Critics believe that perhaps as few as a third, an eighth, or even a smaller fraction of battered women call the police.[8]

One particularly forceful statement of these criticisms is the affidavits filed in *Bruno v. Codd*, 396 NYS2d 974 (Sup Ct Special Term 1977), a class-action suit filed "by 12 'battered wives' against clerks of the Family Court in New York City and officials of the New York City Department of Probation...." *Bruno v. Codd*, 393 NE2d 976 (NY 1979). The suit claimed that "police officers called to the scene of a husband's assault on his wife uniformly refuse to take action, even if the physical evidence of the assault is unmistakable and undenied," that Probation Department personnel "fail to advise *pro se* battered wives seeking orders of protection of their right to an immediate petition for such orders," and that "Family Court petition clerks have, upon several occasions, denied petitioning wives timely access to the sitting Judge, and have abused their discretion in determining whether the wives' complaints are sufficient to warrant preparation of a petition." For instance, the trial court noted that one battered woman's call to the police station assertedly elicited the following advice:

> "There is nothing we can do. Our hands are tied. The police can't act without an order of protection. Even if you had an order of protection, if your husband harassed you and you called the police he would be arrested and released the next day. This would probably provoke your husband and put you in more danger."

Another woman, "whose arm had just been sprained by her husband's attack, requested his arrest, and says she was informed by a police officer that 'there is nothing wrong with a husband hitting his wife if he does not use a weapon.'" In yet another affidavit, a woman alleges that her husband broke into her apartment and threatened her with a knife.

7. Id at 206.

8. Id at 202–3. Willingness to call the police in domestic violence cases seems to correlate positively with low educational levels and high frequencies of violence.

She says that she went to Family Court for an order of protection, only to be told by a probation officer that

> "I couldn't see a judge because I had no case, and that my husband could enter and leave my apartment whenever he wanted.... My husband had every right to break into my apartment. She also said that since there were no witnesses, there was no reason for an Order of Protection."[9]

A careful survey of these criticisms is by Delbert S. Elliott.[10] Elliott repeatedly warns that the studies currently available are seriously weak as bases for public policy. He notes, for instance, that the studies often fail to make explicit their definitions, that they often speak of family violence as a whole without breaking it down into its many components, that samples are often small and unrepresentative, that control groups are often lacking, that follow-up periods are commonly too short (especially considering evidence that arrest may have only short-term consequences), that too few studies actually look at offenders, and that studies regularly lack a theoretical and conceptual basis. Elliott warns, "only a handful of good descriptive studies document the response of criminal justice agencies to family violence crimes. There are even fewer sound evaluations of the effectiveness of particular responses."[11]

All that being said, Elliott concludes that the criticisms detailed above about police and prosecutorial handling of domestic violence cases may be correct, but that those criticisms are at this point not borne out by the available evidence. He suggests that one reason for this is that the evidence for those criticisms is drawn from the entire class of "domestic disturbance" calls, while family violence cases make up only one-third of those calls. He also indicates that changes in police practices since the early 1970s may have made the criticisms less apt.

Elliott finds evidence that victims of domestic violence are as likely to report the crime as victims of crime generally. He writes that the few available studies "suggest that arrest rates (felony and misdemeanor combined) during the periods covered by these studies have been less than 50 percent and may have been as low as 12 percent of reported violent family crimes."[12] (Other major categories of responses included mediation or referral, separation, and no action.) However, Elliott warns of the considerable methodological limits of the evidence. He also suggests that even if better studies produced the same results, they could be

9. The New York Court of Appeals eventually held that a consent judgment negotiated with the police afforded the plaintiffs substantially all the relief they reasonably could expect. By its terms the police have agreed hereafter to respond swiftly to every request for protection and, as in an ordinary criminal case, to arrest the husband whenever there is reasonable cause to believe that a felony has been committed against the wife or that an order of protection or temporary order of protection has been violated. Moreover, officers are to remain at the scene of the alleged crime or violation in order to terminate or prevent the commission of further offenses and to provide the wife with other assistance.

10. *Criminal Justice Procedures in Family Violence Crimes*, in *Family Violence* at 427.

11. Id at 470.

12. Id at 438.

explained in terms of the fact that in general, and not just in domestic violence situations, the police tend to avoid arrests. The decision to arrest in both domestic violence and in other forms of violence appears to be influenced by many factors, including the victim's willingness to sign a complaint, the seriousness of the battery, the seriousness of the injury, the identity of the person calling the police, the behavior of the offender when the police arrive (and particularly whether the offender assaults the police), the involvement of alcohol in the violent incident, the sex and race of the parties, and the socioeconomic character of the neighborhood.

Critics of the present treatment of spouse abuse cases are concerned with the behavior of prosecutors as well as that of the police. The critics say prosecutors dismiss the majority of family violence cases they receive, and the critics suggest that this in turn discourages the police from responding vigorously to family violence. Elliott confirms that prosecutors fail to prosecute a substantial proportion of these cases, but he concludes that prosecutors use the same factors in deciding whether to prosecute domestic violence cases as they use in deciding whether to prosecute cases of all sorts. Elliott cites evidence that the most common reason prosecutors decide not to pursue a case is a problem with witnesses or evidence, and he observes that such problems are particularly common in family violence cases. (There is evidence that 70 to 80 percent of misdemeanor family violence cases end when the victim declines to pursue the complaint.) In addition, "whatever the type of crime, the proportion of cases prosecuted is lower when the offender knows the victim. When the victim and the offender were friends or acquaintances, cases ended in conviction only half as often as when these cases involved strangers; when family relations existed, conviction rates ranged from one-fourth to one-half of those involving strangers."[13] Assault cases seem less likely than other cases to be carried through to conviction: "the Vera Institute study of felony arrests in New York City shows that 'a defendant who enters the criminal process charged with a *felony* assault is less likely to be convicted than defendants entering the process on other felony charges.' "[14]

What motivates victims in spouse abuse cases to drop charges? The victim may, for instance, be worried about the social and economic effects of having a spouse in jail. But what is of special concern is that the offender, knowing that the victim has the power to bring the prosecution to an end, may put pressure on the victim to do so. Elliott cites evidence to show that problems with using victims as complaining witnesses are not unique to family violence cases but present themselves wherever offender and victim know each other.

13. Id at 460. For a study of how assistant district attorneys in Santa Barbara decided how to handle domestic violence cases, see David Rauma, *Going for the Gold: Prosecutorial Decision Making in Cases of Wife Assault*, 13 Soc Sci Research 321 (1984).

14. Id at 326 (emphasis added). Only 10% of the original cases in that study's sample were ever decided, and those were often decided by plea bargains.

Restraining Spouse Abuse: What Ought Police and Prosecutors Do?

Much of Elliott's commentary is devoted to the often-made criticism that the police and prosecutors treat domestic violence differently from other kinds of crime. That Elliott concludes that the evidence does not support this proposition does not, of course, mean that there are not problems with the way police and prosecutors deal with crime of all sorts, including domestic violence. What sorts of programs are being tried that might deal with some of these problems?

A range of (sometimes overlapping) responses is available to police called to the scene of a domestic disturbance. First, they may do nothing. Second, they may attempt to mediate the dispute informally. Third, they may put the parties in touch with available social services. Fourth, they may separate the parties, as by assisting the victim in going to a shelter for battered women. Fifth, they may arrest the offender.

It has been suggested that the last of these choices may particularly reduce recidivism rates. For example, the U.S. Attorney General's Task Force on Family Violence recommended in 1984 that "the chief executive of every law enforcement agency should establish arrest as the preferred response in cases of family violence." This belief has led to the passage of ordinances like the following:

> A police officer shall arrest a person when the officer has reasonable cause to believe that person has, within the previous twenty-four (24) hours, assaulted a spouse, former spouse or other person residing or having resided in the same household, if the victim has visible signs of injury from the assault or if the assailant used or threatened to use a dangerous weapon.... The obligation to arrest shall exist only if the assailant is present or can be readily apprehended.

Ann Arbor (Michigan) Ordinances § 1:65 (1). The evidence about the success of such rules is tentative, complex, and even in part contradictory. Elliott comments:

> The accumulating evidence from all available studies ... supports the claim that arrest is more effective than advisement, separation, or no action in reducing subsequent violence in misdemeanor family violence cases. However, some cautions are in order. Evidence for the generalization of those findings is still quite limited. [T]he differential effect may be minimal for more serious offenders; ... the effect may be temporary. None of these studies involved a very long follow-up period, and the longer term effects are still unknown. Whether these results reflect specific deterrence, a displacement effect,[15] or some other explanation is not yet clear. Nor is it known how a presumptive or mandatory arrest policy will affect the criminal justice system more generally.... Many victims do not want their spouses or relatives arrested, and, knowing that a call to the police will result in an arrest, they may not call.[16]

15. By mentioning a "displacement effect," Elliott is raising the possibility that, although arrest may deter an offender from assaulting his spouse again, it might also contribute to the ending of that marriage and to the entry of the offender into another violent relationship.

16. Elliott, *Criminal Justice Procedures in Family Violence Crimes*, in *Family Violence* at 457. A leading study is Lawrence

A variety of programs has been proposed and adopted for dealing with the danger of coercion of witnesses and the other difficulties prosecutors encounter. In some jurisdictions, for instance, special prosecutorial offices have been established to press spouse-assault charges. These offices often work out principles for dealing with the abused spouse, principles which commonly include providing assurances of prosecutorial and police information and support to the abused spouse and encouraging that spouse to persevere in pressing charges. In other jurisdictions, prosecutors have established a policy of continuing prosecutions even if the abused spouse declines to testify or asks that the charges be dropped.

It is not yet known how successful such programs are. There is some initial evidence that prosecution is somewhat more effective in preventing recidivism than taking no action or diverting offenders into various kinds of social service programs for less-violent offenders. The study that produced this evidence did not suggest "that the deterrent effect of legal action increased with the stage of processing in the legal system or the potential severity of legal sanction. The most effective action as judged by the failure rates for those with low levels of prior violence involved an arrest."[17]

The most often criticized portion of those programs is the policy of prosecuting against the victim's wishes. Some scholars have expressed fears that a program of automatic arrest and prosecution may deter victims from reporting crimes in the first place. And Elliott reports on a fascinating (but sadly small and thus limited) study of twenty-five women who had filed criminal charges against their husbands. Their most frequent reason for doing so was that the police had advised them to do so; their other reasons often had to do with using prosecution as part of negotiations with their spouses. When they withdrew their complaints, it was often because the complaint had served its purpose of being a bargaining tool. Elliott comments that "these results ... suggest some caution in implementing policies that may inadvertently disempower victims."[18]

Other Kinds of Legal Approaches to Spouse Abuse

Various approaches to spouse abuse have been proposed and, in various forms and in various jurisdictions, adopted. What follows briefly describes a number of them.

In response to the criticism that police do not receive adequate training and too often take family disputes too lightly, it is widely recommended that more time should be taken in training police to deal with domestic violence and that the seriousness of such violence should be emphasized. These recommendations often add that internal police policies and procedures should be rewritten and that prosecutors should

W. Sherman and Richard A. Bert, *The Specific Deterrent Effects of Arrest for Domestic Assault*, 49 Am Soc Rev 261 (1984).

17. Id at 467.

18. Id at 466.

adopt policies designed to show the police (among others) that their arrests will have further consequences in the criminal justice system.

A somewhat different approach to preventing domestic violence allows victims to obtain a court order restraining the offender from abusing the victim or requiring the offender to leave and then to stay away from the victim's home. Although one study found that 72% of the women who had obtained such an order thought the order effective, the study concluded that there was no evidence for that belief. The following provisions of the California Domestic Violence Prevention Act[19] illustrate this approach:

> § 6300. Issuance on affidavit showing reasonable proof of past act or acts of abuse
>
> An order may be issued under this part, with or without notice, to restrain any person for the purpose of preventing a recurrence of domestic violence and ensuring a period of separation of the persons involved, if an affidavit ... shows, to the satisfaction of the court, reasonable proof of a past act or acts of abuse.
>
> § 6321. Exclusion from dwelling
>
> (a) The court may issue an ex parte [orders excluding someone from entering a home].
>
> § 6322. Enjoining additional specified behaviors
>
> The court may issue an ex parte order enjoining a party from specified behavior that the court determines is necessary to effectuate orders under Section 6320 [enjoining various kinds of personal behavior including intimidating, harassing and stalking] or 6321.
>
> § 6250. Grounds for issuance
>
> A judicial officer may issue an ex parte emergency protective order where a law enforcement officer asserts reasonable grounds to believe either or both of the following:
>
> (a) That a person is in immediate and present danger of domestic violence....
>
> § 6256. Expiration of order
>
> An emergency protective order expires at the earlier of the following times:
>
> (a) The close of judicial business on the fifth court day following the day of its issuance.

19. Cal Family Code §§ 6200 et seq (2006). The Act defines "domestic violence" as abuse against a spouse, former spouse, cohabitant or former cohabitant, a person with whom the respondent is having or has had a dating or engagement relationship, a person with whom the respondent has had a child or presumed child, or any other person related by consanguinity or affinity within the second degree. Cal Fam Code § 6211.

(b) The seventh calendar day following the day of its issuance.

§ 6271. Service, filing, and delivery of order

A law enforcement officer who requests an emergency protective order shall do all of the following:

(a) Serve the order on the restrained person, if the restrained person can reasonably be located.

(b) Give a copy of the order to the protected person or, if the protected person is a minor child, to a parent or guardian of the endangered child who is not a restrained person, if the parent or guardian can reasonably be located, or to a person having temporary custody of the endangered child.

(c) File a copy of the order with the court as soon as practicable after issuance.

§ 6272. Means of enforcement; Protection of officer from liability

(a) A law enforcement officer shall use every reasonable means to enforce an emergency protective order.

(b) A law enforcement officer who acts in good faith to enforce an emergency protective order is not civilly or criminally liable.

§ 6340. Ex parte orders; Order excluding party from dwelling

(a) The court may issue any of the orders [commencing with Section 6320] after notice and a hearing. . . .

(b) The court may issue an order described in Section 6321 excluding a person from a dwelling if the court finds that physical or emotional harm would otherwise result to the other party, to a person under the care, custody, and control of the other party, or to a minor child of the parties or of the other party.

§ 6342. Payment of restitution for loss of earnings and out-of-pocket expenses

(a) After notice and a hearing, the court may issue any of the following orders:

(1) An order that restitution be paid to the petitioner for loss of earnings and out-of-pocket expenses . . . incurred as a direct result of the abuse inflicted by the respondent or any actual physical injuries sustained from the abuse. . . .

§ 6343. Participation in counseling

(a) After notice and a hearing, the court may issue an order requiring the restrained party to participate in a batterer's program approved by the probation department as provided in Section 1203.097 of the Penal Code.

(b) The courts shall, in consultation with local domestic violence shelters and programs, develop a resource list of referrals to appropriate community domestic violence programs and services to be provided to each applicant for an order under this section.

§ 6344. Payment of attorney's fees and costs

(a) After notice and a hearing, the court may issue an order for the payment of attorney's fees and costs of the prevailing party. ...

§ 6380. Electronic transmission of data to Department of Justice; Domestic Violence Retraining Order System

(a) Each county, with the approval of the Department of Justice, shall, by July 1, 1996, develop a procedure, using existing systems, for the electronic transmission of data, as described in subdivision (b), to the Department of Justice. The data shall be electronically transmitted through the California Law Enforcement Telecommunications System (CLETS) of the Department of Justice by law enforcement personnel, or with the approval of the Department of Justice, court personnel, or another appropriate agency capable of maintaining and preserving the integrity of both the CLETS and the Domestic Violence Restraining Order System, as described in subdivision (e).... All data with respect to criminal court protective orders issued, modified, extended, or terminated under subdivision (g) of Section 136.2 of the Penal Code, and all data filed with the court on the required Judicial Council forms with respect to protective orders, including their issuance, modification, extension, or termination, to which this division applies pursuant to Section 6221, shall be transmitted by the court or its designee within one business day to law enforcement personnel ...

The court shall order the petitioner or the attorney for the petitioner to deliver, or the county clerk to mail, a copy of an order ... to each local law enforcement agency designated by the petitioner ... having jurisdiction over the residence of the petitioner, the residence of a party with care, custody, and control of a child to be protected from domestic violence, and other locations where the court determines that acts of domestic violence against the petitioner and any other person protected by the order are likely to occur.

§ 6388. Criminal penalty for violation of order

A willful and knowing violation of a protective order ... is a crime punishable as provided by Section 273.6 of the Penal Code [i.e., is a misdemeanor].

Another approach to spouse abuse is providing services to the abused spouse. In some places, crisis telephone services help victims with an immediate problem and guide them to other forms of assistance. Chief among these other forms is the shelter for battered women. These shelters offer victims a place to go to get away from their abusers, people (including other victims) to talk about their problems with, information about the alternatives available to them, and services including legal advice and psychological counseling. These shelters have received favorable evaluations from their users.

A further approach is to provide counseling to the offenders. There are a number of kinds of voluntary programs, and some of these will accept referrals (at varying levels of coercion) from courts. One such program "was intended as a legitimate alternative to prosecution for individuals who could be and ordinarily would be prosecuted.... Diversion [to the program] could be allowed, *at the prosecutor's discretion*," for first offenders without a significant record who had not seriously injured their victim, who seemed likely to complete the program successfully, who wanted to be in the program, and whose victims did not have reasonable objections.[20] The program lasted at least a year, and the original charges would be dismissed only if the defendant had not injured anyone during that period.

Yet a further approach is to increase the penalties for spousal assaults. Thus section 273.5 of the California Penal Code (2006) provides: "(a) Any person who willfully inflicts upon a person who is his or her spouse, former spouse, cohabitant, former cohabitant, or the mother or father of his or her child, corporal injury resulting in a traumatic condition, is guilty of a felony, and upon conviction thereof shall be punished by imprisonment in the state prison for two, three, or four years, or in a county jail for not more than one year, or by a fine of up to six thousand dollars ($6,000) or by both that fine and imprisonment."

An assault is, of course, tortious. Until recently the law of most jurisdictions accepted a doctrine of spousal immunity from personal (as opposed to property) tort actions. Now, however, most states permit such actions. Although this change in the law has probably had its greatest consequences in automobile negligence cases, it opens the way in principle for suits seeking compensation for spousal assaults.

Another civil approach to spouse abuse is conciliation or mediation. One critic of this approach describes it:

> In most disputes which reach mediation, no formal legal action has been initiated, or the criminal charges which have been filed are suspended or dismissed when the case is referred to a mediation program....
>
> Advocates of the conciliation model view mediation as preferable to formal dispute resolution mechanisms for a wide range of humanitarian, client-focused reasons. Factors making mediation attractive include: "1. Avoidance of unnecessary hostility.... 2. A measure of client autonomy in constructing the solutions.... 3. Avoiding the traditional two-attorney fight." Professor Frank Sander ... favors mediation over more formal options for cases in which the parties have a long-term relationship because those parties may work out an agreement addressing the

20. David Rauma, *Going for the Gold: Prosecutorial Decision Making in Cases of Wife Assault*, 13 Soc Sci Research 321, 324–25 (1984)(emphasis in original).

> on-going problems underlying the superficial dispute. Law professor Paul Rice proposes mediation as an alternative to the criminal justice system which frequently fails to prosecute "culpable 'victims,' "sentences without regard to victims' needs, imposes disproportionately small penalties for serious crimes, operates inefficiently, requires victims to attend multiple hearings, grants frequent continuances, and fails to inform witnesses of the status of a case.[21]

This critic notes that a "Civil Rights Commission report on domestic violence stated that '[m]ediation and arbitration should *never* be used as an alternative to prosecution in cases involving physical violence.' "[22] She concludes, "If those who advocate law enforcement are correct in suggesting that domestic abuse may best be eliminated through institutional behavior which holds the abusers responsible for the violence, then mediation is the least appropriate of available legal remedies for wife abuse."[23]

Finally, sometimes victims respond to abuse by killing their abusers. When the homicide occurs at the moment the abuser is using deadly force, the victim is justified in killing in self defense. Frequently, however, the abused spouse kills when not immediately threatened with death. For example, the victim may retaliate while the abuser sleeps. In the ensuing murder trial, some defendants have attempted to introduce the so-called Battered Women's Syndrome defense. This strategy has been successful in some states, *State v. Baker*, 424 A2d 171 (N H 1980); *Smith v. State*, 277 SE2d 678 (Ga 1981), although most reject it. Even without testimony about that defense, there are jury findings of not guilty in a disproportionately large number of these cases. See Note, *The Battered Wife Syndrome and Self-Defense: A Legal and Empirical Dissent*, 72 Va L Rev 619 (1986).

A Novel Suggestion

An intriguing proposal for reforming American criminal law comes in John Braithwaite, *Crime, Shame, and Reintegration* (Cambridge U Press, 1989). Braithwaite argues "that the key to crime control is cultural commitments to shaming in ways that I call reintegrative. Societies with low crime rates are those that shame potently and judiciously; individuals who resort to crime are those insulated from shame over their wrongdoing." He warns emphatically that shaming can be used counterproductively, but believes that "shaming controls crime when it is at the same time powerful and bounded by efforts to reintegrate the offender back into the community."

Shaming is hardly a novel idea. A number of cultures—Japan, most famously—make it part of their repertoire for deterring deviance and ameliorating its effects. Lawrence Sherman, a prominent advocate of mandatory arrest in domestic violence cases, recently studied responses

21. Lisa G. Lerman, *Mediation of Wife Abuse Cases: The Adverse Impact of Informal Dispute Resolution on Women*, 7 Harv Women's L J 57, 67–69 (1984).

22. Id at 111.

23. Id at 113.

to juvenile offenders in New Zealand and reports that those offenders and their chosen supporters meet with victims and their supporters. A neutral third party, usually a police officer, asks both contingents to describe what happened. Offenders almost always admit responsibility, and victims almost always forgive them. Offenders are supposed to make restitution, which may come in the form of services instead of money. Professor Sherman believes that this approach lowers recidivism better than conventional approaches and that it can help restore both victim and offender to their original relationships with each other and their community, Lawrence W. Sherman, *Domestic Violence and Restorative Justice: Answering Key Questions*, 8 Va J Soc Pol'y & Law 263 (2000).

Such a process has an analog in the Navajo Peacemaker Court, which was instituted in 1982 because the civil state courts offended Navajo tradition. As Navajo Justice Homer Bluehouse, put it, "[O]ne [person] goes out of the courtroom with his tail in the air, and the other goes out with his tail between his legs." Navajo philosophy centers around the concepts of *hozhó*—everything in its proper place and functioning in a harmonious relationship with everything else[24]—and of *Ké*—"all those positive virtues which constitute intense, diffuse, and enduring solidarity."[25] Traditional Indian justice requires perpetrators and victims to "talk out" the problem along with their family and clans. In domestic violence situations, the Peacemaker Court seeks to restore to victims their former selves—their state of *hozhó*— and perpetrators, with the assistance of their family and clan, do the restoring. For example, perpetrators may replace or repair destroyed property, compensate victims for lost work time, give them rides to work or the store, or provide them with meals. Offenders' families may offer victims child care or supervise offenders' visits with victims or the couple's children.

Of course, evidence of this kind must always be greeted skeptically. The history of crime and punishment is the history of astoundingly optimistic reports of reform and rehabilitation. And shaming relies heavily on cultural understandings and social practices which may prevail in one society but be absent in another. New Zealand is a far smaller and more homogeneous society than the United States, and that is even truer of the Navajo. Shaming would surely not work with all American offenders. Some American evidence, for example, suggests that mandatory arrest can even be counter-productive where offenders do not have a job or some other tie to a group whose esteem the offender is anxious to retain.[26]

Perhaps, then, we should add to the law's armory of responses to spouse abuse adaptations of Braithwaite's proposal. Perhaps, for exam-

24. James W. Zion & Elsie B. Zion, *Hozhó Sokeé—Stay Together Nicely: Domestic Violence Under Navajo Common Law*, 25 Ariz St LJ 407, 415 (1993).

25. James W. Zion, *Traditional Indian Solutions for Domestic Violence*, 13 Austl JL & Soc'y 167, 170 & n16 (1997).

26. See, e.g., Murray Straus & Richard J. Gelles, *The Costs Of Family Violence*, 102 Public Health Rep (Nov./Dec. '87).

ple, we might publish the names of spouse abusers. Or, to quote Braithwaite, "a responsibility of the probation officer could be to convince representatives of a young person's school, employer, sporting clubs, and other groups that are important to the offender to attend the court and offer their opinions on what they would be able to contribute to monitoring the offender's behavior in future and to her rehabilitation." Spouse abusers may be particularly good candidates for the shaming strategy, since they are likelier than some other kinds of criminals to have enough connections with respectable society to be pained by shame, that there would be people to take an interest in their cases, and that they might be reintegrated into the community.

Shaming may be a particularly useful technique in family law because it responds to structural difficulties in controlling the family. Because family behavior largely occurs in private and because of the severe enforcement problems, family law particularly needs ways of encouraging people to internalize the standards the state wishes to enforce. This shaming strategy seems well suited to change the cultural attitudes that underlie spouse abuse.

When I have discussed this idea with groups I have been asked to address, I have repeatedly encountered hostility to it. Yet surely people who abuse their spouses have done something wrong. Surely they ought to be ashamed of themselves. Why then the objection to shaming them?

The question can be pushed a step or two further. One point of punishment is to administer pain. Shame is a kind of pain. Why is it wrong for that kind of pain to be one means of punishment? Indeed, isn't shame *supposed* to be a feature of criminal punishment? Isn't what makes criminal sanctions different from civil sanctions that they carry with them moral condemnation? And isn't shame an appropriate response to just moral condemnation?

Furthermore, isn't shame crucially connected to deterrence? Deterrence works partly by threatening pain, and as I just said, shame is one kind of pain. More profoundly, doesn't deterrence work by causing people to internalize, to assimilate as part of their conscience, a belief that they should not do something? And doesn't the conscience work by making you ashamed when you do something you shouldn't?

One explanation for resisting shame as a punishment is that it punishes the innocent family as well as the guilty abuser. But how so? The innocent family members haven't done anything wrong, therefore they shouldn't share in the abuser's shame. Is this answer fully satisfactory? That it may be irrational for the family to feel ashamed doesn't mean that they won't feel ashamed (or that other people won't make them feel ashamed), and perhaps we should take these irrational feelings and reactions into account. In addition, is it wholly irrational for the families to feel ashamed? We expect family members to share each other's feelings, joys, and sorrows. We expect family members to invest in each other, to take pride in each other's accomplishments. Unless family members have decided to cast the abuser out of the family, they may share his shame in the same way they would share his other feelings and accomplishments. But in the end, won't *any* punishment affect the family as well as the offender, and doesn't the shaming technique do so less than the alternatives?

Another explanation for the hostility to this proposal goes back to some basic attitudes. Braithwaite quotes D.H. Bayley, *Social Control and Political Change* 124 (Woodrow Wilson School, Princeton U, 1985) as saying, "Individualism habituates people to resist any group sanctioning." But shouldn't individualism yield to justice?

Suggestions for How to Proceed Next

As this report is intended to indicate, the problem of spouse abuse is a complex one. A successful attack on the problem will also have to be complex, not to say thorough. I would recommend the following steps. First, I would advise you to make a preliminary decision about what kinds of policies you yourself would prefer. Then I recommend securing comments from the relevant city agencies. Then I would propose that your office hold hearings designed to solicit public comments and ideas. This way you will have a much better sense of the social and political problems with which you are dealing locally.

Questions: First Exercise

(1) Recall that you are Mayor of Cooley and that you need to formulate policies for dealing with spouse abuse. What further information might you want before doing so? What initial policies would you propose? Keep in mind that political and budgetary realities will impose some severe limits on your choices.

(2) Having received the consultant's report, the Mayor of Cooley has sent copies of it on to the following people for their comments: the Chief of Police, the District Attorney, the City Solicitor, the Director of the Department of Social Services, and the Resident Director of the Cooley Shelter for Battered Women. Assume that you are in turn legal counsel to each of these agency heads. How would you advise each department to respond? What institutional and legal concerns will each department have? What programmatic objectives is each department likely to have? What further information might each department want before it made a proposal?

(3) Assume now that you are the aide in the Mayor's office who has been assigned responsibility for the next step in implementing the Mayor's policy preferences (as modified by the responses of the different departments). Your task is to hold a public hearing. Whom do you think will testify at that hearing? Who do you want to invite to testify? What do you think will be said? What kinds of alterations in the Mayor's proposal might the hearings lead to?

(b) Second Exercise

You are the District Attorney of Cooley. You have just finished reading and making comments on Professor Lecteur's report. (In those comments, you noted that you have already taken some steps toward improving the treatment of family violence cases. For instance, you have persuaded the police and social service departments to file lengthy narrative reports of domestic violence incidents, reports which are sent to your office and given special attention.) You have recently received a file from one of your assistant district attorneys. She requests your approval to prosecute the husband described in the following file:

Cooley Police Department

Incident Report—Domestic Violence

Name of Officer: Q. C. Fregit, badge #9814
Date: July 6, 1999
Precinct: 3

On the evening of July 5, 1999, my partner D. B. Asportatis and I were notified by radio at 9:52 of a domestic disturbance at 5 Christiancy Terrace. We proceeded there as soon as we had finished the paperwork on a traffic stop we had just made. While we were completing that paperwork, we ran a check on the occupants of the address at which the domestic disturbance had been reported and learned that neither resident had any criminal record.

We arrived at 5 Christiancy at 10:35. We knocked at the front door. A white male who identified himself as A. B. Shrode opened the door. We identified ourselves and asked if we could come in. Mr. Shrode admitted us into the living room. There we found a white female who identified herself as Betsy Shrode sitting on a sofa and crying. We informed the Shrodes that we had had a complaint of a disturbance at their house, and we asked them what had happened. Mrs. Shrode did not say anything, and Mr. Shrode said nothing had happened, just a little disagreement. At this point, my partner took Mr. Shrode out on the porch to ask him a few questions, and I sat down in a chair next to Mrs. Shrode. I asked her whether she was o.k., and she informed me she was. I told her we were here to help her and asked again what had happened. She said she and her husband had been having an argument and that her husband had pushed her and she had fallen down. I could see that there was a bruise that looked recent and was about four inches in diameter on her arm. I asked her if she had gotten the bruise when her husband had pushed her, and she said no. I asked her whether she wanted to press charges, and she said no. I asked her if she wanted us to arrest her husband. She said that would just make things worse. My partner and Mr. Shrode then returned from the porch. We told Mr. Shrode that he'd better cool it and that if we had to come back he'd be in real trouble. We then departed the house.

As we were proceeding down the front steps, we were stopped by a woman who identified herself as Celia N. Eye, the Shrode's next-door neighbor. She asked us to come into her house, and when we were inside she informed us that she was the one who had called the police. She stated that she had observed the altercation between the Shrodes through the Shrodes' lighted window. She said that Mr. Shrode had pushed Mrs. Shrode hard and that she had struck a table before falling to the floor. However, Mrs. Eye reported that she had not been able to hear what had been said or see what had happened much before the push. She stated she would be glad to testify to what she had seen.

Department of Social Services
City of Cooley
State of Hutchins

Client Contact Report

Name of Case Worker: Henry Hull, M.S.W.
Date of Contact: July 17, 1999
Date of Report: July 19, 1999

Proceeding according to Departmental Policy 88–43, requiring that all police reports of domestic violence be followed up by this office, I visited Ms. Betsy Shrode at her home on Monday while her husband was at work. Ms. Shrode is a twenty-five-year-old white woman who worked as a secretary until she married Mr. Shrode. He is a twenty-nine-year-old white male who has a college education but who is employed in the maintenance department of the Cooley National Bank. The Shrodes have been married for two years. They have a one-year-old son.

Although Ms. Shrode stated she did not wish to talk about the night of July 5, in response to further questions she stated that she loved her husband very much and that he was an attentive and affectionate husband. She stated that he really depended a lot on her and that what had started the argument that night was that he thought she had been spending too much time with a male friend who lived in the neighborhood. She stated that Mr. Shrode had never struck her before, that he promised he would never strike her again, that she believed her husband, and that she herself regretted some things she had done and said that evening. She then quoted Matthew 18: 21–22: "Then came Peter to him, and said, Lord, how oft shall my brother sin against me, and I forgive him? till seven times? Jesus saith unto him, I say not unto thee, Until seven times: but, Until seventy times seven." I asked her whether she could talk about her problem with friends, but she said that her husband was her real friend. When I suggested she should talk to the prosecutor at least to give herself a stronger position in case she should have a problem again, she told me that she would never talk to a "prosecutor, a policeman, a judge, or anybody."

Ms. Shrode's demeanor suggested to me that she may be suffering from some degree of depression. Before I left, I asked Ms. Shrode whether she had recovered from her husband's assault. She said she had not been hurt and that she was fine. I could see no clear evidence of a bruise, although there was a slight discoloration on her right arm that might have been what was left of a bruise. I did, however, observe that on her right wrist she was wearing an Ace bandage in the way a person might do who has sprained her wrist. As I was going, I handed her my card and literature describing Departmental services for abused spouses, including the Cooley Shelter for Battered Women. She told me she was not a battered wife and did not want my brochures.

MEMORANDUM

TO: The District Attorney
FROM: Laetitia Minton, Assistant District Attorney
DATE: July 27, 1989
RE: Prosecution of A. B. Shrode, File # JS–07M378

This memorandum is written in pursuance of my recent appointment as Assistant D.A. responsible for screening spouse abuse cases to decide whether they should be prosecuted.

Yesterday, I visited Ms. Shrode to ask her to cooperate in the prosecution of her husband. She angrily said she does not want her husband prosecuted, and she ordered me to leave her house. However, her refusal to cooperate will not prevent us from gaining a conviction in this case, since the testimony of the neighbor (assuming she is still willing to testify) and of the police will readily suffice to obtain a conviction. There will also be the physical evidence of her apparently sprained wrist. Thus there only remains the question whether we *should* prosecute Mr. Shrode. I believe we should.

First, we should prosecute him because he broke the law. Section 211.1 of the Hutchins Penal Code reads:

(1) Simple Assault. A person is guilty of assault if he:

(a) attempts to cause or purposely, knowingly or recklessly causes bodily injury to another; or

(b) negligently causes bodily injury to another with a deadly weapon; or

(c) attempts by physical menace to put another in fear of imminent serious bodily injury.

Simple assault is a misdemeanor unless committed in a fight or scuffle entered into by mutual consent, in which case it is a petty misdemeanor. A person who has been convicted of a misdemeanor or a petty misdemeanor may be sentenced to imprisonment for a definite term which shall be fixed by the Court and shall not exceed one year in the case of a misdemeanor or thirty days in the case of a petty misdemeanor.

Mr. Shrode committed the crime this statute defines. We should prosecute him for it just as we would prosecute anyone else. Indeed, I would argue that the fact that Mr. Shrode's victim is his wife gives us *more* reason to prosecute him than to prosecute the ordinary assault offender. By marrying Ms. Shrode, Mr. Shrode took on special obligations (we would often say fiduciary obligations) to her which his assault grievously violated. His wrong is greater than that of other offenders.

In any event, we should prosecute Mr. Shrode because he has committed a crime which deserves to be punished. I appeal here to the retributive motive for punishment. I ask you to imagine a thought experiment proposed by Michael S. Moore in *The Moral Worth of Retribution*, in *Responsibility, Character, and the Emotions: New Essays in Moral Psychology* 179, 185–86 (Cambridge, 1987): "Imagine that ... [serious] crimes are being done, but that there is no utilitarian or rehabilitative reason to punish. The murderer has truly found Christ, for example, so that he or she does not need to be reformed ... and the crime can go undetected so that general deterrence does not demand punishment ... My hypothesis is that most of us still feel some inclination, no matter how tentative, to punish."

Second, we should prosecute him to prevent him from assaulting Ms. Shrode again, that is, for reasons of specific deterrence. Mr. Shrode must be made to realize that he has done something society regards as wrong. He must be made to realize that he will pay if he ever commits such a crime again. The best way of making him realize that is to make him pay this time.

Furthermore, we should prosecute Mr. Shrode because we have good reason to believe he will assault Ms. Shrode again. We know that because Ms. Shrode's situation resembles that of other women whose husbands have later gone on to continue their abusive behavior. It is not uncommon for such husbands to be affectionate at the beginning of the marriage but for that affection later to grow into jealous and controlling behavior. It is not uncommon for such wives to find themselves increasingly isolated from friends and family and the support they can provide, nor is it uncommon for them to feel helpless in the face of the violence they encounter and to feel clinically depressed in the face of the prospect of more unsolvable problems to come. Finally, we know that there "is clearly some evidence for the assertion that family violence crimes are likely to be repeated." Delbert S. Elliott, *Criminal Justice Procedures in Family Violence Crimes*, in Lloyd Ohlin & Michael Tonry, eds, *Family Violence* 427, 447 (U Chi Press, 1989).

Third, we should prosecute Mr. Schrode in order to prevent people like him from assaulting their spouses, that is, for reasons of general deterrence. One important contributing factor to spouse abuse is the too-common belief that spouse abuse, at least in its less severe forms, is not particularly wrong. We need to enlist the expressive power of law to make the statement that *all* spouse abuse is not just wrong, it is criminal. There is no better way of making this statement than by prosecuting even the less serious forms of spouse abuse.

The fact that Ms. Shrode opposes the prosecution should not stand in our way. For one thing, it is hard for us to know whether her situation is as benign as she describes it. It is not atypical for victims of spousal assault to deny or discount what has happened or for them to blame themselves for contributing to the assault. And a major problem in prosecuting spouse-abuse cases is the risk the abuser will use force or threats of force to coerce the victim to drop the charges. For all we know, Ms. Shrode really would prefer that we prosecute.

I believe that my case can be forcefully put in terms of the functions of family law. The queen of those functions, the one that is a condition precedent to all the rest, is the protective function. The law has already failed to protect Ms. Shrode from violence. The law must now take the only course open to it to vindicate its protective function; that is, the law must punish Mr. Shrode. This will in turn serve the protective function by deterring Mr. Shrode and others in his situation from erring again.

Another of the law's functions is the facilitative function. I do not think that function has any applicability in this case. There are some things the law should not facilitate, even if all family members wish it to, and spouse abuse is one of them. Nor, on similar grounds, is this an occasion for serving the law's arbitral function. The law should not see this as a dispute between the Shrodes in which both have legitimate positions to advance; rather, this is a situation in which Mr. Shrode has gone beyond the permissible limits of marital behavior.

The channeling function attempts to create and direct people toward social institutions that discourage harmful behavior and encourage happiness in intimate relationships. Our concern here is the social construction of marriage. In other words, we want people to enter marriage understanding that it is an institution in which some kinds of behavior are unthinkable. By prosecuting even relatively minor marital violence, we demonstrate that spouse abuse is just that kind of unthinkable behavior. That we would not prosecute the same behavior between acquaintances against the victim's wishes simply emphasizes the point that marriage is different.

The expressive function involves the law's capacity to speak. This capacity is important for two reasons. First, it is important because law provides a means for the citizenry as a group to express itself, and communal expression can per se be an important value. Here, it provides a means for the citizenry to express its feelings about the brutality of husbands against wives and men against women. Second, the expressive function is important because law provides a means of shaping social attitudes through its expression, because, that is, expression serves instrumental ends. Here, it provides a means of directly stating that spousal violence is socially intolerable in any form and thereby deterring such violence.

It is, further, important to realize that often the expressive function can not be escaped. In other words, the law's silence is itself often eloquently expressive. We live in a culture in which many people, even some women, believe that women should in important ways be subordinate to men and that it is not wrong, and sometimes is even right, for husbands to strike their wives. If we fail to prosecute Mr. Shrode, the message we will send is that society does not condemn those views.

Some of my ideas about spouse abuse in relation to deterrence and to the expressive and channeling functions have been put in a powerful and striking form by the English jurist, historian, and philosopher, James Fitzjames Stephen:

> [I]f in all cases criminal law were regarded only as a direct appeal to the fears of persons likely to commit crimes, it would be deprived of a large part of its efficiency, for it operates not only on the fears of criminals, but upon the habitual sentiments of those who are not criminals. A great part of the general detestation of crime which happily prevails amongst the decent part of the community in all civilized countries arises from the fact that the commission of offences is associated in all such communities with the solemn and deliberate infliction of punishment wherever crime is proved.
>
> The relation between criminal law and morality is not in all cases the same.... [But i]n all common cases they do, and, in my opinion, wherever and so far as it is possible, they ought, to harmonize with, and support one another....
>
> [T]he sentence of the law is to the moral sentiment of the public in relation to any offence what a seal is to hot wax. It converts into a permanent final judgment what might otherwise be a transient sentiment.... [T]he infliction of punishment by law gives definite expression and a solemn ratification and justification to the hatred which is excited by the commission of the offence.... The criminal law thus proceeds upon the principle that it is morally right to hate criminals, and it confirms and justifies that sentiment by inflicting upon criminals punishments which express it.
>
> I think that whatever effect the administration of criminal justice has in preventing the commission of crimes is due as much to this circumstance as to any definite fear entertained by offenders of undergoing specific punishment. If this is doubted, let any one ask himself to what extent a man would be deterred from theft by the knowledge that by committing it he was exposed, say, to one chance in fifty of catching an illness which would inflict upon him the same amount of confinement, inconvenience, and money loss as six months' imprisonment and hard labour.... I am also of opinion that this close alliance between criminal law and moral sentiment is in all ways healthy and advantageous to the community. I think it highly desirable that criminals should be hated, that the punishments inflicted upon them should be so contrived as to give expression to that hatred, and to justify it so far as the public provision of means for expressing and gratifying a healthy natural sentiment can justify and encourage it....
>
> The doctrine that hatred and vengeance are wicked in themselves appears to me to contradict plain facts.... Love and hatred, gratitude for benefits, and the desire of vengeance for injuries, imply each other as much as convex and concave.... No doubt they are peculiarly liable to abuse...., but unqualified denunciations of them are as ill-judged as unqualified denunciations of sexual passion. The forms in which deliberate anger and righteous disapprobation are expressed, and the execution of criminal justice is the most emphatic of such forms, stand to the one

> set of passions in the same relation in which marriage stands to the other.

History of the Criminal Law of England 79–82 (Macmillan, 1883).

In sum, it is in society's interest and Ms. Shrode's own interest for us to prosecute Mr. Shrode. As the training materials of the International Association of Chiefs of Police say, "A policy of arrest, when the elements of the offense are present, promotes the well-being of the victim. Many battered wives who tolerate the situation undoubtedly do so because they feel they are alone in coping with the problem. The officer who starts legal action may give the wife the courage she needs to realistically face and correct her situation." Quoted in *Criminal Justice Procedures in Family Violence Crimes*, in Lloyd Ohlin and Michael Tonry, eds, *Family Violence* 427, 435 (U Chi Press, 1989). We are the officers who can start the legal action that may give us all the courage to realistically face and correct our social situation.

MEMORANDUM

TO: The District Attorney
FROM: Felicity Bold, Assistant District Attorney
DATE: July 31, 1989
RE: Prosecution of A. B. Shrode, File # JS–07M378

Laetitia has discussed with me her proposal that we prosecute A. B. Shrode, and she has shown me her memo to you on the subject. I would like to respond to it in this memo.

As I have said many times before, I entirely agree with Laetitia that our office, the police, and the Department of Social Services should cooperate in setting up programs that will ensure that battered wives can make a free choice whether to prosecute their husbands and that will support them when they decide to do so. However, I do not agree that we should prosecute A. B. Shrode.

First, I agree with Laetitia that we should prosecute Mr. Shrode just the way we would prosecute anyone else. But one task of a prosecutor is to exercise prosecutorial discretion, and one place we regularly exercise that discretion is in dealing with fights between friends. If exactly the same battery and injury had occurred in a fight between friends in a bar, and the police had broken up the fight with the same kind of warning Shrode got, would we prosecute if the victim didn't want us to? Even if the parties were not friends, would we prosecute? I suggest we would be unlikely to do so, given the characteristics of this defendant. He has no prior criminal record. There is no evidence that he has been involved in any kind of violence before. He did not respond violently when the police were called. He seems to deny that deliberate violence, at least, occurred, and the witness is hardly in a position to testify as to his intent or any of the surrounding circumstances of the assault. Worse, we have no way of knowing what helpful things Ms. Shrode might be willing to testify to on Mr. Shrode's behalf. And even if we prosecuted the parties in the barroom fight, the sentence would probably not involve any prison time for someone like Mr. Shrodes.

Further, I cannot agree that a crime ought to be punished purely for retributive reasons. Such reasons seem to me to be no reasons at all, but merely an expression of a dangerous emotional response.

Second, I am not persuaded by Laetitia's specific deterrence argument because it is not clear to me what the risk of a recurrence is. I am particularly troubled by Laetitia's suggestion that, because Ms. Shrode appears to resemble some chronically abused spouses, we should assume that she is or will soon be a chronically abused spouse. For one thing, this reasoning puts a great deal of weight on research which is still in its infancy. For another thing, even that research often produces contradictory results, and it clearly suggests that the characteristics, motives, and behavior of abused spouses are much more complex and multifarious than Laetitia's memo assumes. For example, Laetitia implies that Ms. Shrode's unwillingness to accept help is not atypical of battered women and thus that it is evidence that Ms. Shrode *is* a battered woman. But one summary of research in the field reports that "[m]ost battered women do seek help for the violence or, more generally, for marital problems." Irene Hanson Frieze & Angela Browne, *Violence in Marriage*, in Lloyd Ohlin and Michael Tonry, eds, *Family Violence* 163, 201 (U Chi Press, 1989). For yet another thing, the research Laetitia invokes does not suggest that all abused spouses exhibit the same characteristics or that all persons exhibiting those characteristics are abused spouses. That research only finds a statistically significant association between abused spouses as a class and those characteristics. In sum, Laetitia's argument would lead us to treat victims of spouse abuse as stereotypes and not as individuals.

Third, I have some doubts about the general deterrence argument and the associated arguments drawn from the expressive and channeling functions of family law. For one thing, it is not as clear as Laetitia suggests that there is still widespread public condonation of spouse abuse. For example, one survey found that "[e]ighty-six percent of men and 91 percent of women disagreed with the statement that 'there are some conditions under which it is okay for a husband to slap his wife.' There was slightly more tolerance of wives slapping husbands. However, people in this study did cite self-defense, retaliation, and sexual infidelity as acceptable reasons for violence toward one's spouse." *Id* at 165. In any event, if we prosecute Mr. Shrode, will people draw the conclusion Laetitia suggests, or will they believe we have used the considerable criminal power of the law in a way they will think is disproportionate to the offense? In addition, for the law to deter, the law must rely on victims reporting future abuses. Will they do so if they know that every report will lead to arrest and prosecution?

Fourth, the fact that Ms. Shrode opposes prosecution is crucial. I agree with Laetitia that there is always a risk in these kinds of cases that the abuser will bully the victim into silence. But I don't think we should use that as a blanket reason to prosecute in all cases. Rather, we should be alert to the possibility that that has happened and act on whatever indications we get. Here there are no such indications.

Similarly, the fact that *some* abused spouses discount what has happened or blame themselves should not cause us to discount or deny whatever the victim says. To do so would lead us into frequent error. Worse, it would lead us to treat those victims as people incapable of making decisions for themselves. We must assume, in the absence of better information, that Ms. Shrode knows better than we do the risks she runs, the value of her continuing relationship with her husband, how offensive her husband's behavior as a whole is, and how to prevent him from injuring her in the future. Obviously we should offer all the help she wants, but we should not interfere in a situation she may understand better than we do. In sum, I think prosecution in the face of the victim's objection would be paternalistic, and I am reluctant to be paternalistic without strong evidence that our estimate of the victim's interests is clearly better than her own estimate.

Let me say a word about Laetitia's argument that the functions of family law will be best served by prosecuting Mr. Shrode. I have no quarrel with her argument that the protective function is preeminently important. However, the enforcement problems that are endemic in family law make it unclear that the protective function in this case will be best served by prosecuting. And I see more of a role for the facilitative and arbitral functions than Laetitia. I believe we should place our resources at Ms. Shrode's disposal in order to facilitate her resolution of their disagreement.

Some of my doubts about Laetitia's proposal stem from my doubts about whether it is best to treat all kinds of spouse abuse as a problem to be handled by the criminal justice system. It seems to me spouse abuse is at base caused by a combination of social and psychological factors the criminal justice system can ultimately do little to affect. On a wider social level, we should attack the problem on a broad front that includes education to change people's attitudes and social welfare programs to change people's circumstances. On an individual basis, we should treat as essentially a medical problem the conduct of people so psychologically damaged that they will physically injure members of their own family. Like Laetitia, I find that James Fitzjames Stephen has aptly expressed my thoughts. He wrote that the criminal law is "by far the roughest engine which society can use for any purpose," but that its "excessive harshness ... very greatly narrows the range of its application" and that its use often makes it "necessary to go into an infinite number of delicate and subtle inquiries which would tear off all privacy from the lives of a large number of persons." *Liberty, Equality, Fraternity* 151 (Cambridge U Press, 1967).

Insofar as this case is a problem for the criminal law, we should look not at all to the retributive purposes of punishment. We should consider deterrence, but also rehabilitation. We should want Mr. Shrode to realize that his behavior was wrong and from that realization to return to being a useful and peaceful member of society and his family. I don't think Laetitia has made a convincing case that prosecuting this assault will accomplish that purpose.

There is one further, most regrettable, consideration. We are a busy office with a small staff and a puny budget. If we prosecute this case, we will be taking resources away from (i.e., handling inadequately or plea bargaining out) more serious cases of many kinds, including some domestic violence cases. I doubt this is a good trade.

As I hope I have made plain, I doubt we can improve this family's situation by intervening in it. I therefore recommend we take no further action (since we have already made it amply clear to Ms. Shrode that help is available if she wants it). However, if you do not agree (and I readily concede that Laetitia makes some important arguments), I suggest that, instead of directly instituting a prosecution, we tell Mr. Shrode that we will prosecute if he does not cooperate with the Department of Social Services in finding appropriate counseling. Then if Mr. Shrode is a chronic spouse abuser, he will get treatment; if he is not, he will be left alone.

Questions: Second Exercise

(1) Having read the file, what will you as district attorney do about the case? What further information might you need? What further arguments might be made on either side? Consider again the rationales we adduced earlier for family autonomy. Do they shed further light on whether to prosecute? Assuming you decide to prosecute and you win a conviction, what sentence will you ask for?

(2) Suppose now you are a lawyer practicing in Cooley and Cooley has been able to adopt *all* the alternative approaches to spouse abuse mentioned in Professor Lecteur's report. This morning you received a visit from a woman who wishes to retain you. She has been married for nineteen years to her husband. For the last several years, the marriage has not been a happy one. Her husband has been drinking and has had trouble keeping a job. Your client has come to see you because her husband has on repeated occasions struck her with his fist, severely bruising her and causing her considerable pain and anxiety. He has also threatened to kill her if she ever tells anyone he has attacked her. What do you advise your client?

(3) Spouse Abuse Revisited: The Battered Woman Defense

A particularly troubling legal problem related to spouse abuse arises because of the battered woman syndrome and the homicide by the victim of the abuse that sometimes follows it. If a battered woman kills when the threat of death or grievous bodily harm is not imminent, has she killed in self-defense? We include two contrasting opinions in a well-known case:

NORTH CAROLINA v. NORMAN

Court of Appeals of North Carolina, 1988
366 SE2d 586

At trial the judge instructed on first degree murder, second degree murder, and voluntary manslaughter. The primary issue presented on this appeal is whether the trial court erred in failing to instruct on self-defense. We answer in the affirmative and grant a new trial.

FACTS

At trial the State presented the testimony of a deputy sheriff of the Rutherford County Sheriff's Department who testified that on 12 June 1985, at approximately 7:30 p.m., he was dispatched to the Norman residence. There, in one of the bedrooms, he found decedent, John Thomas "J.T." Norman (herein decedent or Norman) dead, lying on his left side on a bed. The State presented an autopsy report, stipulated to by both parties, concluding that Norman had died from two gunshot wounds to the head. The deputy sheriff also testified that later that evening, after being advised of her rights, defendant told the officer that decedent, her husband, had been beating her all day, that she went to her mother's house nearby and got a .25 automatic pistol, that she returned to her house and loaded the gun, and that she shot her husband. The officer noted at the time that there were burns and bruises on defendant's body.

Defendant's evidence, presented through several different witnesses, disclosed a long history of verbal and physical abuse leveled by decedent against defendant. Defendant and Norman had been married twenty-five years at the time of Norman's death. Norman was an alcoholic. He had begun to drink and to beat defendant five years after they were married. The couple had five children, four of whom are still living. When defendant was pregnant with her youngest child, Norman beat her and kicked her down a flight of steps, causing the baby to be born prematurely the next day.

Norman, himself, had worked one day a few months prior to his death; but aside from that one day, witnesses could not remember his ever working. Over the years and up to the time of his death, Norman forced defendant to prostitute herself every day in order to support him. If she begged him not to make her go, he slapped her. Norman required defendant to make a minimum of one hundred dollars per day; if she failed to make this minimum, he would beat her.

Norman commonly called defendant "Dogs," "Bitches," and "Whores," and referred to her as a dog. Norman beat defendant "most every day," especially when he was drunk and when other people were around, to "show off." He would beat defendant with whatever was handy—his fist, a fly swatter, a baseball bat, his shoe, or a bottle; he put out cigarettes on defendant's skin; he threw food and drink in her face and refused to let her eat for days at a time; and he threw glasses, ashtrays, and beer bottles at her and once smashed a glass in her face. Defendant exhibited to the jury scars on her face from these incidents. Norman would often make defendant bark like a dog, and if she refused, he would beat her. He often forced defendant to sleep on the concrete floor of their home and on several occasions forced her to eat dog or cat food out of the dog or cat bowl.

Norman often stated both to defendant and to others that he would kill defendant. He also threatened to cut her heart out.

Witnesses for the defense also testified to the events in the thirty-six hours prior to Norman's death. On or about the morning of 10 June 1985, Norman forced defendant to go to a truck stop or rest stop on Interstate 85 in order to prostitute to make some money. Defendant's daughter and defendant's daughter's boyfriend accompanied defendant. Some time later that day, Norman went to the truck stop, apparently drunk, and began hitting defendant in the face with his fist and slamming the car door into her. He also threw hot coffee on defendant. On the way home, Norman's car was stopped by police, and he was arrested for driving under the influence.

When Norman was released from jail the next morning, on 11 June 1985, he was extremely angry and beat defendant. Defendant's mother said defendant acted nervous and scared. Defendant testified that during the entire day, when she was near him, her husband slapped her, and when she was away from him, he threw glasses, ashtrays, and beer bottles at her. Norman asked defendant to make him a sandwich; when defendant brought it to him, he threw it on the floor and told her to make him another. Defendant made him a second sandwich and brought it to him; Norman again threw it on the floor, telling her to put something on her hands because he did not want her to touch the bread. Defendant made a third sandwich using a paper towel to handle the bread. Norman took the third sandwich and smeared it in defendant's face.

On the evening of 11 June 1985, at about 8:00 or 8:30 p.m., a domestic quarrel was reported at the Norman residence. The officer responding to the call testified that defendant was bruised and crying and that she stated her husband had been beating her all day and she could not take it any longer. The officer advised defendant to take out a warrant on her husband, but defendant responded that if she did so, he would kill her. A short time later, the officer was again dispatched to the Norman residence. There he learned that defendant had taken an overdose of "nerve pills," and that Norman was interfering with emergency personnel who were trying to treat defendant. Norman was drunk and was making statements such as, " 'If you want to die, you deserve to die. I'll give you more pills,' " and " 'Let the bitch die.... She ain't nothing but a dog. She don't deserve to live.' " Norman also threatened to kill defendant, defendant's mother, and defendant's grandmother. The law enforcement officer reached for his flashlight or blackjack and chased Norman into the house. Defendant was taken to Rutherford Hospital.

The therapist on call at the hospital that night stated that defendant was angry and depressed and that she felt her situation was hopeless. On the advice of the therapist, defendant did not return home that night, but spent the night at her grandmother's house.

The next day, 12 June 1985, the day of Norman's death, Norman was angrier and more violent with defendant than usual. According to witnesses, Norman beat defendant all day long. Sometime during the day, Lemuel Splawn, Norman's best friend, called Norman and asked Norman to drive with him to Spartanburg, where Splawn worked, to pick up Splawn's paycheck. Norman arrived at Splawn's house some time later. Defendant was driving. During the ride to Spartanburg, Norman slapped defendant for following a truck too closely and poured a beer on her head. Norman kicked defendant in the side of the head while she was driving and told her he would " 'cut her breast off and shove it up her rear end.' "

Later that day, one of the Normans' daughters, Loretta, reported to defendant's mother that her father was beating her mother again. Defendant's mother called the sheriff's department, but no help arrived at that time. Witnesses stated that back at the Norman residence, Norman threatened to cut defendant's throat, threatened to kill her, and threatened to cut off her breast. Norman also smashed a doughnut on defendant's face and put out a cigarette on her chest.

In the late afternoon, Norman wanted to take a nap. He lay down on the larger of the two beds in the bedroom. Defendant started to lie down on the smaller bed, but Norman said, " 'No bitch ... Dogs don't sleep on beds, they sleep in [sic] the floor.' " Soon after, one of the Normans' daughters, Phyllis, came into the room and asked if defendant could look after her baby. Norman assented. When the baby began to cry, defendant took the child to her mother's house, fearful that the baby would disturb Norman. At her mother's house, defendant found a gun. She took it back to her home and shot Norman.

Defendant testified that things at home were so bad she could no longer stand it. She explained that she could not leave Norman because he would kill her. She stated that she had left him before on several occasions and that each time he found her, took her home, and beat her. She said that she was afraid to take out a warrant on her husband because he had said that if she ever had him locked up, he would kill her when he got out. She stated she did not have him committed because he told her he would see the authorities coming for him and before they got to him he would cut defendant's throat. Defendant also testified that when he threatened to kill her, she believed he would kill her if he had the chance.

The defense presented the testimony of two expert witnesses in the field of forensic psychology, Dr. William Tyson and Dr. Robert Rollins. Based on an examination of defendant and an investigation of the matter, Dr. Tyson concluded that defendant "fits and exceeds the profile, of an abused or battered spouse." Dr. Tyson explained that in defendant's case the situation had progressed beyond mere " 'Wife battering or family violence' "and had become "torture, degradation and reduction to an animal level of existence, where all behavior was marked purely by survival...." Dr. Tyson stated that defendant could not leave her husband because she had gotten to the point where she had no belief whatsoever in herself and believed in the total invulnerability of her husband. He stated, "Mrs. Norman didn't leave because she believed, fully believed that escape was totally impossible.... She fully believed that [Norman] was invulnerable to the law and to all social agencies that were available; that nobody could withstand his power. As a result, there was no such thing as escape." Dr. Tyson stated that the incidences of Norman forcing defendant to perform prostitution and to eat pet food from pet dishes were parts of the dehumanization process. Dr. Tyson analogized the process to practices in prisoner-of-war camps in the Second World War and the Korean War.

When asked if it appeared to defendant reasonably necessary to kill her husband, Dr. Tyson responded, "I think Judy Norman felt that she had no choice, both in the protection of herself and her family, but to engage, exhibit deadly force against Mr. Norman, and that in so doing, she was sacrificing herself, both for herself and for her family."

Dr. Rollins was defendant's attending physician at Dorothea Dix Hospital where she was sent for a psychiatric evaluation after her arrest. Based on an examination of defendant, laboratory studies, psychological tests, interviews, and background investigation, Dr. Rollins testified that defendant suffered from "abused spouse syndrome." Dr. Rollins defined the syndrome in the following way:

> The "abused spouse syndrome" refers to situations where one spouse has achieved almost complete control and submission of the other by both psychological and physical domination. It's, to start with, it's usually seen in the females who do not have a strong sense of their own adequacy who do not have a lot of personal or occupational resources; it's usually associated with physical abuse over a long period of time, and the particular characteristics that interest us are that the abused spouse comes to believe that the other person is in complete control; that they themselves are worthless and they cannot get away; that there's no rescue from the other person.

When asked, in his opinion, whether it appeared reasonably necessary that defendant take the life of J.T. Norman, Dr. Rollins responded, "In my opinion, that course of action did appear necessary to Mrs. Norman." However, Dr. Rollins stated that he found no evidence of any psychotic disorder and that defendant was capable of proceeding to trial.

LEGAL ANALYSIS

In North Carolina a defendant is entitled to an instruction on perfect self-defense as justification for homicide where, viewed in the light most favorable to the defendant, there is evidence tending to show that at the time of the killing:

(1) it appeared to defendant and he believed it to be necessary to kill the deceased in order to save himself from death or great bodily harm; and

(2) defendant's belief was reasonable in that the circumstances as they appeared to him at the time were sufficient to create such a belief in the mind of a person of ordinary firmness; and

(3) defendant was not the aggressor in bringing on the affray, i.e., he did not aggressively and willingly enter into the fight without legal excuse or provocation; and

(4) defendant did not use excessive force, i.e., did not use more force than was necessary or reasonably appeared to him to be necessary under the circumstances to protect himself from death or great bodily harm.

Under this standard, the reasonableness of defendant's belief in the necessity to kill decedent and non-aggression on defendant's part are two essential elements of the defense. The State argues that defendant was not entitled to an instruction on self-defense. The State contends that since decedent was asleep at the time of the shooting, defendant's belief in the necessity to kill decedent was, as a matter of law, unreasonable. The State further contends that even assuming arguendo that the evidence satisfied the requirement that defendant's belief be reasonable, defendant, being the aggressor, cannot satisfy the third requirement of perfect self-defense or the requirement of imperfect self-defense that the act be committed without murderous intent. . . .

The question then arising on the facts in this case is whether the victim's passiveness at the moment the unlawful act occurred precludes defendant from asserting perfect self-defense.

Applying the criteria of perfect self-defense to the facts of this case, we hold that the evidence was sufficient to submit an issue of perfect self-defense to the jury. An examination of the elements of perfect self-defense reveals that both subjective and objective standards are to be applied in making the crucial determinations. The first requirement that it appear to defendant and that defendant believe it necessary to kill the deceased in order to save herself from death or great bodily harm calls for a subjective evaluation. . . . The trial was replete with testimony of forced prostitution, beatings, and threats on defendant's life. The defendant testified that she believed the decedent would kill her, and the evidence showed that on the occasions when she had made an effort to get away from Norman, he had come after her and beat her. Indeed, within twenty-four hours prior to the shooting, defendant had attempted to escape by taking her own life and throughout the day on 12 June 1985 had been subjected to beatings and other physical abuse, verbal abuse, and threats on her life up to the time when decedent went to sleep. Both experts testified that in their opinion, defendant believed killing the victim was necessary to avoid being killed. This evidence would permit a finding by a jury that defendant believed it necessary to kill the victim to save herself from death or serious bodily harm.

Unlike the first requirement, the second element of self-defense—that defendant's belief be reasonable in that the circumstances as they appeared to defendant would be sufficient to create such a belief in the mind of a person of ordinary firmness—is measured by the objective standard of the person of ordinary firmness under the same circumstances. Again, the record is replete with sufficient evidence to permit but not compel a juror, representing the person of ordinary firmness, to infer that defendant's belief was reasonable under the circumstances in which she found herself. Both expert witnesses testified that defendant exhibited severe symptoms of battered spouse syndrome, a condition that develops from repeated cycles of violence by the victim against the defendant. Through this repeated, sometimes constant, abuse, the battered spouse acquires what the psychologists denote as a state of "learned helplessness," defendant's state of mind as described by Drs. Tyson and Rollins. In the instant case, decedent's excessive anger, his constant beating and battering of defendant on 12 June 1985, her fear that the beatings would resume, as well as previous efforts by defendant to extricate herself from this abuse are circumstances to be considered in judging the reasonableness of defendant's belief that she would be seriously injured or killed at the time the criminal act was committed. The evidence discloses that defendant felt helpless to extricate herself from this intolerable, dehumanizing, brutal existence. Just the night before the shooting, defendant had told the sheriff's deputy that she was afraid to swear out a warrant against her husband because he had threatened to kill her when he was released if she did. The inability of a defendant to withdraw from the hostile situation and the vulnerability of a defendant to the victim are factors considered by our Supreme Court in determining the reasonableness of a defendant's belief in the necessity to kill the victim.

To satisfy the third requirement, defendant must not have aggressively and willingly entered into the fight without legal excuse or provocation. By definition, aggression in the context of self-defense is tied to provocation. The existence of battered spouse syndrome, in our view, distinguishes this case from the usual situation involving a single confrontation or affray. The provocation necessary to determine whether defendant was the aggressor must be considered in light of the totality of the circumstances. Psychologists and sociologists report that battered spouse syndrome usually has three phases—the tension-building phase, the violent phase, and the quiet or loving phase. During the violent phase, the time when the traditional concept of self-defense would mandate that defendant protect herself, *i.e.*, at the moment the abusing spouse attacks, the battered spouse is least able to counter because she is immobilized by fear, if not actually physically restrained.

Mindful that the law should never casually permit an otherwise unlawful killing of another human being to be justified or excused, this

Court is of the opinion that with the battered spouse there can be, under certain circumstances, an unlawful killing of a passive victim that does not preclude the defense of perfect self-defense. Given the characteristics of battered spouse syndrome, we do not believe that a battered person must wait until a deadly attack occurs or that the victim must in all cases be actually attacking or threatening to attack at the very moment defendant commits the unlawful act for the battered person to act in self-defense. Such a standard, in our view, would ignore the realities of the condition. This position is in accord with other jurisdictions that have addressed the issue.

NORTH CAROLINA v. NORMAN

Supreme Court of North Carolina, 1989
378 SE2d 8

MITCHELL, Justice....

The right to kill in self-defense is based on the necessity, real or reasonably apparent, of killing an unlawful aggressor to save oneself from *imminent* death or great bodily harm at his hands. Our law has recognized that self-preservation under such circumstances springs from a primal impulse and is an inherent right of natural law.

In North Carolina, a defendant is entitled to have the jury consider acquittal by reason of *perfect* self-defense when the evidence, viewed in the light most favorable to the defendant, tends to show that at the time of the killing it appeared to the defendant and she believed it to be necessary to kill the decedent to save herself from imminent death or great bodily harm. That belief must be reasonable, however, in that the circumstances as they appeared to the defendant would create such a belief in the mind of a person of ordinary firmness. Further, the defendant must not have been the initial aggressor provoking the fatal confrontation. A killing in the proper exercise of the right of *perfect* self-defense is always completely justified in law and constitutes no legal wrong.

Our law also recognizes an *imperfect* right of self-defense in certain circumstances, including, for example, when the defendant is the initial aggressor, but without intent to kill or to seriously injure the decedent, and the decedent escalates the confrontation to a point where it reasonably appears to the defendant to be necessary to kill the decedent to save herself from imminent death or great bodily harm. Although the culpability of a defendant who kills in the exercise of *imperfect* self-defense is reduced, such a defendant is *not justified* in the killing so as to be entitled to acquittal, but is guilty at least of voluntary manslaughter.

The defendant in the present case was not entitled to a jury instruction on *either* perfect or imperfect self-defense. The trial court was not required to instruct on either form of self-defense unless evidence was introduced tending to show that at the time of the killing the defendant reasonably believed herself to be confronted by circumstances which necessitated her killing her husband to save herself from *imminent* death or great bodily harm. No such evidence was introduced in this case, and it would have been error for the trial court to instruct the jury on *either* perfect or imperfect self-defense.

The jury found the defendant guilty only of voluntary manslaughter in the present case. As we have indicated, an instruction on imperfect self-defense would have entitled the defendant to nothing more, since one who kills in the exercise of imperfect self-defense is guilty at least of voluntary manslaughter. Therefore, even if it is assumed arguendo that the defendant was entitled to an instruction on imperfect self-defense—a notion we have specifically rejected—the failure to give such an instruction was harmless in this case. Accordingly, although we recognize that the imminence requirement applies to both types of self-defense for almost identical reasons, we limit our consideration in the remainder of this opinion to the issue of whether the trial court erred in failing to instruct the jury to consider acquittal on the ground that the killing was justified and, thus, lawful as an act of *perfect* self-defense.

The killing of another human being is the most extreme recourse to our inherent right of self-preservation and can be justified in law only by the utmost real or apparent necessity brought about by the decedent. For that reason, our law of self-defense has required that a defendant claiming that a homicide was justified and, as a result, inherently lawful by reason of perfect self-defense must establish that she reasonably believed at the time of the killing she otherwise would have immediately suffered death or great bodily harm. Only if defendants are required to show that they killed due to a reasonable belief that death or great bodily harm was imminent can the justification for homicide remain clearly and firmly rooted in necessity. The imminence requirement ensures that deadly force will be used only where it is necessary as a last resort in the exercise of the inherent right of self-preservation. It also ensures that before a homicide is justified and, as a result, not a legal wrong, it will be reliably determined that the defendant reasonably believed that absent the use of deadly force, not only would an unlawful attack have occurred, but also that the attack would have caused death or great bodily harm. The law does not sanction the use of deadly force to repel simple assaults.

The term "imminent," as used to describe such perceived threats of death or great bodily harm as will justify a homicide by reason of perfect self-defense, has been defined as "immediate danger, such as must be instantly met, such as cannot be guarded against by calling for the assistance of others or the protection of the law." Our cases have sometimes used the phrase "about to suffer" interchangeably with "imminent" to describe the immediacy of threat that is required to justify killing in self-defense....

The uncontroverted evidence was that her husband had been asleep for some time when she walked to her mother's house, returned with the pistol, fixed the pistol after it jammed and then shot her husband three times in the back of the head. The defendant was not faced with an instantaneous choice between killing her husband or being killed or seriously injured. Instead, all of the evidence tended to show that the defendant had ample time and opportunity to resort to other means of preventing further abuse by her husband. There was no action underway by the decedent from which the jury could have found that the defendant had reasonable grounds to believe either that a felonious assault was imminent or that it might result in her death or great bodily injury....

Additionally, the lack of any belief by the defendant—reasonable or otherwise—that she faced a threat of imminent death or great bodily harm from the drunk and sleeping victim in the present case was illustrated by the defendant and her own expert witnesses when testifying about her subjective assessment of her situation at the time of the killing. The psychologist and psychiatrist replied affirmatively when asked their opinions of whether killing her husband "appeared reasonably necessary" to the defendant at the time of the homicide. That testimony spoke of no *imminent* threat nor of any fear by the defendant of death or great bodily harm, imminent or otherwise. Testimony in the form of a conclusion that a killing "appeared reasonably necessary" to a defendant does not tend to show all that must be shown to establish self-defense. More specifically, for a killing to be in self-defense, the perceived necessity must arise from a reasonable fear of imminent death or great bodily harm.

Dr. Tyson additionally testified that the defendant "believed herself to be doomed ... to a life of the worst kind of torture and abuse, degradation that she had experienced over the years in a progressive way; that it would only get worse, and that death was inevitable." Such evidence of the defendant's speculative beliefs concerning her remote and indefinite future, while indicating she had felt generally threatened, did not tend to show that she killed in the belief—reasonable or otherwise—that her husband presented a threat of *imminent* death or great bodily harm. Under our law of self-defense, a defendant's subjective belief of what might be "inevitable" at some indefinite point in the future does not equate to what she believes to be "imminent." ...

We are not persuaded by the reasoning of our Court of Appeals in this case that when there is evidence of battered wife syndrome, neither an actual attack nor threat of attack by the husband at the moment the wife uses deadly force is required to justify the wife's killing of him in perfect self-defense. The Court of Appeals concluded that to impose such requirements would ignore the "learned helplessness," meekness and other realities of battered wife syndrome and would effectively preclude such women from exercising their right of self-defense. Other jurisdictions which have addressed this question under similar facts are divided in their views, and we can discern no clear majority position on facts closely similar to those of this case. *Compare, e.g., Commonwealth v. Grove*, 363 Pa.Super. 328, 526 A.2d 369, *appeal denied* , 517 Pa. 630, 539 A.2d 810 (1987) (abused wife who killed her sleeping husband not entitled to self-defense instruction as no immediate threat was posed by the decedent), *with State v. Gallegos*, 104 N.M. 247, 719 P.2d 1268 (1986) (abused wife could claim self-defense where she walked into bedroom with gun and killed husband who was awake but lying on the bed).

The reasoning of our Court of Appeals in this case proposes to change the established law of self-defense by giving the term "imminent" a meaning substantially more indefinite and all-encompassing than its present meaning. This would result in a substantial relaxation of the requirement of real or apparent necessity to justify homicide. Such reasoning proposes justifying the taking of human life not upon the reasonable belief it is necessary to prevent death or great bodily harm—which the imminence requirement ensures—but upon purely subjective speculation that the decedent probably would present a threat to life at a future time and that the defendant would not be able to avoid the predicted threat. . . .

That result in principle could not be limited to a few cases decided on evidence as poignant as this. The relaxed requirements for perfect self-defense proposed by our Court of Appeals would tend to categorically legalize the opportune killing of abusive husbands by their wives solely on the basis of the wives' testimony concerning their subjective speculation as to the probability of future felonious assaults by their husbands. Homicidal self-help would then become a lawful solution, and perhaps the easiest and most effective solution, to this problem. *See generally* Rosen, *The Excuse of Self-Defense: Correcting A Historical Accident on Behalf of Battered Women Who Kill*, 36 Am.U.L.Rev. 11 (1986) (advocating changing the basis of self-defense acquittals to excuse rather than justification, so that excusing battered women's killing of their husbands under circumstances not fitting within the traditional requirements of self-defense would not be seen as justifying and therefore encouraging such self-help killing); Mitchell, *Does Wife Abuse Justify Homicide?*, 24 Wayne L.Rev. 1705 (1978) (advocating institutional rather than self-help solutions to wife abuse and citing case studies at the trial level where traditional defenses to homicide appeared stretched to accommodate poignant facts, resulting in justifications of some killings which appeared to be motivated by revenge rather than protection from death or great bodily harm). It has even been suggested that the relaxed requirements of self-defense found in what is often called the "battered woman's defense" could be extended in principle to *any type of case* in which a defendant testified that he or she subjectively believed that killing was necessary and proportionate to any perceived threat. Rosen, [*supra*]. . . .

For the foregoing reasons, we conclude that the defendant's conviction for voluntary manslaughter and the trial court's judgment sentencing her to a six-year term of imprisonment were without error. Therefore, we must reverse the decision of the Court of Appeals which awarded the defendant a new trial.

Questions on the Battered Spouse Defense

(1) Should Judy Norman have been prosecuted in the first place? In other words, should there have been an exercise of prosecutorial discretion? Should the prosecutor have refrained from prosecuting because the defendant was not morally a guilty person? In the preceding section, you read an exchange of memos between two assistant district attorneys about the purposes of punishment in spouse-abuse cases. How would those various purposes be served or disserved by a decision not to prosecute? Why do you suppose the prosecutor did decide to prosecute?

(2) Should the jury have convicted Judy Norman? As you will recall, the jury convicted her only of manslaughter. In North Carolina, first degree murder is an "unlawful killing committed with malice and with premeditation and deliberation." Second degree murder is "the unlawful killing of a human being with malice and without premeditation and deliberation." Voluntary manslaughter is "an intentional killing without premeditation, deliberation or malice but done in the heat of passion suddenly aroused by adequate provocation or in the exercise of imperfect self-defense where excessive force under the circumstances was used or where defendant is the aggressor." Which of these best matches the facts as the courts described them? Would it have been appropriate for the jury to find the defendant not guilty? How would the various purposes of punishment be served or disserved by each of these decisions? For a recent examination of this kind of problem, see Andrew D. Leipold, *Rethinking Jury Nullification*, 82 Va L Rev 253 (1996).

(3) The judge sentenced the defendant to six years in prison. Was this the best sentence? Would a suspended sentence have been more appropriate? How would the various purposes of punishment be served by these two sentences?

(4) "On July 7, 1989, three months after the North Carolina Supreme Court's decision reinstated Mrs. Norman's conviction, North Carolina Governor James G. Martin commuted her sentence and ordered her released from prison." Kerry A. Shad, Note, State v. Norman: *Self-Defense Unavailable to Battered Women Who Kill Passive Abusers*, 68 NC L Rev 1159, 1162 n24 (1990). Was this the right thing to do? The right time to do it? How does it serve or disserve the various purposes of punishment? See, e.g., Linda L. Ammons, *Discretionary Justice: a Legal and Policy Analysis of a Governor's Use of the Clemency Power in the Cases of Incarcerated Battered Women*, 3 J L & Policy 2 (1994).

(5) The North Carolina Supreme Court seemed to be invoking the cliché that hard cases make bad law. If that cliché applies here it is because of uncertainty about where the intermediate appellate court's precedent would lead. For example, does the defense only belong to women, or could there be a battered man's syndrome that works the same way? A battered-child syndrome? See Battered–Child Syndrome Could Apply to Case of Boy Charged with Murder, *Knoxville News–*

Sentinel, Feb 6, 2000. Would a mother suffering from "battered woman's syndrome" be able to employ the defense against a charge that she had abused her children by failing to prevent her partner from injuring them? Could she, that is, justify her failure to act on the grounds that she was too afraid to stop the abuser? Could she argue that her own capacity was so diminished she could not keep from abusing her children herself? See *State v. Mott*, 931 P2d 1046 (Ariz 1997) (not a defense).

(6) Now that you have thought about the use of the criminal law in dealing with spouse abuse, you may find it profitable to reconsider the doctrine of family autonomy in light of what you have learned. Return, then, to the eight justifications for the doctrine we derived from *Kilgrow*. How do you assess them and the doctrine now?

B. THE PRINCIPLE OF PRIVACY

[B]ecause every self is in some measure a cabinet of horrors, civilized relations between selves can only proceed to the extent that nasty little secrets of desire, greed, or envy are kept locked up.

Richard Sennett
The Fall of Public Man

We said in Chapter II that in each chapter we will examine in some depth one of the themes of family law. In this chapter we begin that enterprise by pausing to consider a recurring issue in family law—the meaning, status, function, and worth of "privacy." The *Rhodes* court said it sought to avoid the "evil of raising the curtain upon domestic privacy." Why did the court say this? Why might we today worry about invasions of privacy? We will approach these questions by reading part of a thoughtful comparative approach to privacy:

1. Whether or not you agree with the outcome, does Whitman's piece persuade you how the Supreme Court may at the same time be willing to strike down laws relating to criminal sodomy while letting stand laws limiting marriage to different-sex couples?
2. As we think more and more globally, should we expect the continental and United States views of privacy to converge? Or are they endemic, as Whitman suggests, to our national identities, different legal development, or even different constitutions?

JAMES Q. WHITMAN THE TWO WESTERN CULTURES OF PRIVACY: DIGNITY VERSUS LIBERTY

113 Yale Law Journal 1151 (2004)

I. A Transatlantic Clash

In every corner of the Western world, writers proclaim "privacy" as a supremely important human good, as a value somehow at the core of what makes life worth living. Without our privacy, we lose "our very integrity as persons,'' Charles Fried declared over thirty-five years ago. Many others have since agreed that privacy is somehow fundamental to our ''personhood.'' It is a commonplace, moreover, that our privacy is peculiarly menaced by the evolution of modern society, with its burgeoning technologies of surveillance and inquiry. Commentators paint this menace in very dark colors: Invasions of our privacy are said to portend a society of ''horror,'' to ''injure [us] in [our] very humanity,'' or even to threaten ''totalitarianism,'' and the establishment of law protecting privacy is accordingly declared to be a matter of fundamental rights. It is the rare privacy advocate who resists citing Orwell when describing these dangers.

At the same time, honest advocates of privacy protections are forced to admit that the concept of privacy is embarrassingly difficult to define. ''[N]obody,'' writes Judith Jarvis Thomson dryly, ''seems to have any very clear idea what [it] is.'' Not every author is as skeptical as Thomson, but many of them feel obliged to concede that privacy, fundamentally important though it may be, is an unusually slippery concept. In particular, the sense of what must be kept ''private,'' of what must be hidden before the eyes of others, seems to differ strangely from society to society. This is a point that is frequently made by citing the literature of ethnography, which tells us that there are some societies in which people cheerfully defecate in full view of others, and at least a few in which the same is true of having sex. But the same point can be made by citing a large historical literature, which shows how remarkably ideas of privacy have shifted and mutated over time. Anyone who wants a vivid example can visit the ruins of Ephesus, where the modern tourist can set himself down on one of numerous ancient toilet seats in a public hall where well-to-do Ephesians gathered to commune, two thousand years ago, as they collectively emptied their bowels.

If privacy is a universal human need that gives rise to a fundamental human right, why does it take such disconcertingly diverse forms? This is a hard problem for privacy advocates who want to talk about the values of ''personhood,'' harder than they typically acknowledge. It is a hard problem because of the way they usually try to make their case: Overwhelmingly, privacy advocates rely on what moral philosophers call ''intuitionist'' arguments. In their crude form, these sorts of arguments suppose that human beings have a direct, intuitive grasp of right and wrong—an intuitive grasp that can guide us in our ordinary ethical decisionmaking. Privacy advocates evidently suppose the same thing. Thus, the typical privacy article rests its case precisely on an appeal to its reader's intuitions and anxieties about the evils of privacy violations. Imagine invasions of your privacy, the argument runs. Do they not seem like violations of your very personhood? Since violations of privacy seem intuitively horrible to everybody, the argument continues, safeguarding privacy must be a legal imperative, just as safeguarding property or contract is a legal imperative. Indeed, privacy matters so much to us that laws protecting it must be a basic element of human rights.

This kind of argument can certainly make a powerful impression on first reading, since it is true that we can all imagine some violation of our privacy that seems very horrible. This is especially so when the writings in question are composed by scholars with a real literary gift, like Fried. Nevertheless, no matter how anxiety-inducing it may be to read these authors, their arguments only carry real weight if it is true that the intuitions they evoke are shared by all human beings. Yet all the evidence seems to suggest that human intuitions and anxieties about privacy differ. We do not need to refer to the practices of exotic ancient or modern cultures to demonstrate as much: It is true even as between the familiar societies of the modern West. In fact, we are in the midst of significant privacy conflicts between the United States and the countries of Western Europe—conflicts that reflect unmistakable differences in sensibilities about what ought to be kept "private."

To the Europeans, indeed, it often seems obvious that Americans do not understand the imperative demands of privacy at all. The Monica Lewinsky investigation, in particular, with its numerous and lewd disclosures, led many Europeans to that conclusion. But the Lewinsky business is not the only example: There are plenty of other aspects of American life that seem to Europeans to prove the same thing. Let me offer a variety of examples from France and Germany, two countries that have been my focus in recent research, and that are my focus in this Article as well. Some of the things that bother French and German observers involve what Americans will think of as trivialities of everyday behavior. For example, visitors from both countries are taken aback by the ill-bred way in which Americans talk about themselves. As a French article warns visitors to the United States, America is a place where strangers suddenly share information with you about their "private activities" in a way that is "difficult to imagine" for northern Europeans or Asians. Americans have a particularly embarrassing habit, continental Europeans believe, of talking about salaries. It is "normal in America," an Internet site informs German tourists, for your host at dinner to ask "not just how much you earn, but even what your net worth is"—topics ordinarily quite off-limits under the rules of European etiquette. Talking about salaries is not quite like defecating in public, but it can seem very off-putting to many Europeans nevertheless.

But it is not just a matter of the boorish American lack of privacy etiquette. It is also a matter of American law. Continental law is avidly protective of many kinds of "privacy" in many realms of life, whether the issue is consumer data, credit reporting, workplace privacy, discovery in civil litigation, the dissemination of nude images on the Internet, or shielding criminal offenders from public exposure. To people accustomed to the continental way of doing things, American law seems to tolerate relentless and brutal violations of privacy in all these areas of law. I have seen Europeans grow visibly angry, for example, when they learn about routine American practices like credit reporting. How, they ask, can merchants be permitted access to the entire credit history of customers who have never defaulted on their debts? Is it not obvious that this is a violation of privacy and personhood, which must be prohibited by law?

These are clashes in attitude that go well beyond the occasional social misunderstanding. In fact, they have provoked some tense and costly transatlantic legal and trade battles over the last decade and a half. Thus, the European Union and the United States slid into a major trade conflict over the protection of consumer data in the 1990s, only problematically resolved by a 2000 "safe harbor" agreement. Europeans still constantly complain that Americans do not accept the importance of protecting consumer privacy. Those tensions have only grown in the aftermath of September 11. Something similar has happened with regard to discovery in civil procedure: American law allows parties to rummage around in each other's records in a way that seems obnoxious and manifestly unacceptable to Europeans. The result, in recent decades, has been a seething little war over discovery. The circulation of the nude photos of celebrities on the Internet has produced another such conflict, with Europeans acting alone to penalize Internet service providers.

For sensitive Europeans, indeed, a tour through American law may be an experience something like a visit to the latrines of Ephesus. Correspondingly, it has become common for Europeans to maintain that they respect a "fundamental right to privacy" that is either weak or wholly absent in the "cultural context" of the United States. Here, Europeans point with pride to Article 8 of the European Convention on Human Rights, which protects "the right to respect for private and family life," and to the European Union's new Charter of Fundamental Rights, which demonstratively features articles on both "Respect for Private and Family Life" and "Protection of Personal Data." By the standards of those great documents, American privacy law seems, from the European point of view, simply to have "failed."

But it is not just that Europeans resent and distrust the American approach to privacy: The reverse is also true. Anyone who has lived in the United States knows that Americans can be just as obsessively attached to their "privacy" as Europeans, sometimes defending it by resort to firearms. As for American law, it too is obsessed with privacy. Indeed, some of the most violently controversial American social issues are conceived of as privacy matters. This has been true of abortion for thirty years. With the Supreme Court's decision in *Lawrence v. Texas*, it is now true of homosexuality as well. It is simply false to say that privacy doesn't matter to Americans.

In fact, let us make no mistake about it: When it comes to privacy, there are plenty of European practices that seem intuitively objectionable to Americans. Some of these have to do with seemingly minor aspects of the anthropology of everyday life, most especially involving nudity. If the Europeans are puzzled by the ill-bred way in which Americans casually talk about themselves, Americans are puzzled by the ill-bred way in which Europeans casually take off their clothes. Phenomena like public nudity in the parks of German cities are particularly baffling to

Americans, but so are phenomena like the presence of female attendants in men's washrooms. It is genital nudity that Americans find most bizarre: One's genitalia are "privates" in the full sense of the word in America, and one does not ordinarily expose them in public, and certainly not before the opposite sex. Even breasts are supposed to be kept covered in the United States—as the occasional female European tourist has discovered, when arrested (or even jailed!) for sunbathing topless on an American beach. ("Those Americans are Out of their Minds!" howls a headline from a Swiss tabloid reporting one such incident from Florida.) Even American advertising, which doesn't stop at much, doesn't show bare breasts.

Public nudity may seem little more than a curiosity (though we shall see that it raises revealing problems in the European law of privacy). But here again, it is not just a matter of norms of everyday behavior; it is a matter of law. There are numerous aspects of European law that can seem not only ridiculous, but somewhat shocking to Americans. For example, continental governments assert the authority to decide what names parents will be permitted to give their children—a practice affirmed by the European Court of Human Rights as recently as 1996. This is an application of state power that Americans will view with complete astonishment, as a manifest violation of proper norms of the protection of privacy and personhood. How can the state tell you what you are allowed to call your baby? Nor does it end there: In Germany, everybody must be formally registered with the police at all times. In both Germany and France, inspectors have the power to arrive at your door to investigate whether you have an unlicensed television. Evidence that Americans would regard as illegally seized is routinely considered in continental adjudication. In France and Germany, according to a recent study, telephones are tapped at ten to thirty times the rate they are tapped in the United States—and in the Netherlands and Italy, at 130 to 150 times the rate. All of this will make many an American snigger at the claim that Europeans have a superior grasp of privacy. What kind of "privacy" is there, Americans will ask, in countries where people prance around naked out of doors while allowing the state to keep tabs on their whereabouts, convict them on the basis of unfair police investigations, peer into their living rooms, tap their phones, and even dictate what names they can give to their babies?

Evidently, Americans and continental Europeans perceive privacy differently. Privacy advocates sometimes try to downplay these differences. The felt need for privacy, they insist, is in fact universal, and the only real difference is that American protections are the product of piecemeal legislation, less systematically developed than European protections as yet, but nevertheless evolving in a European direction. There is certainly some truth in this: There are indeed important resemblances between the systems on either side of the Atlantic. Any proper account of comparative privacy law will have to explain many similarities as well as many differences.

Nevertheless, when all is said and done, it is impossible to ignore the fact that Americans and Europeans are, as the Americans would put it, coming from different places. At least as far as the law goes, we do not seem to possess general "human" intuitions about the "horror" of privacy violations. We possess something more complicated than that: We possess American intuitions—or, as the case may be, Dutch, Italian, French, or German intuitions. We must make some effort to explain this fact before we start proclaiming universal norms of privacy protection. In particular, we will not do justice to our transatlantic conflicts if we begin by declaring that American privacy law has "failed" while European privacy law has "succeeded." That is hogwash. What we must acknowledge, instead, is that there are, on the two sides of the Atlantic, two different cultures of privacy, which are home to different intuitive sensibilities, and which have produced two significantly different laws of privacy.

II. Dignity Versus Liberty

So why do these sensibilities differ? Why is it that French people won't talk about their salaries, but will take off their bikini tops? Why is it that Americans comply with court discovery orders that open essentially all of their documents for inspection, but refuse to carry identity cards? Why is it that Europeans tolerate state meddling in their choice of baby names? Why is it that Americans submit to extensive credit reporting without rebelling?

These are not questions we can answer by assuming that all human beings share the same raw intuitions about privacy. We do not have the same intuitions, as anybody who has lived in more than one country ought to know. What we typically have is something else: We have intuitions that are shaped by the prevailing legal and social values of the societies in which we live. In particular, we have, if I may use a clumsy phrase, juridified intuitions—intuitions that reflect our knowledge of, and commitment to, the basic legal values of our culture.

Indeed, to get a handle on our transatlantic privacy conflicts, we must begin by recognizing that continental European and American sensibilities about privacy grow out of much larger and much older differences over basic legal values, rooted in much larger and much older differences in social and political traditions. The fundamental contrast, in my view, is not difficult to identify. In one form or another, it is a contrast that has been noticed by observers of the transatlantic scene for a century. It is the contrast between two conceptions of privacy most recently distinguished by Robert Post: between privacy as an aspect of dignity and privacy as an aspect of liberty.

Continental privacy protections are, at their core, a form of protection of a right to respect and personal dignity. The core continental privacy rights are rights to one's image, name, and reputation, and what Germans call the right to informational self-determination—the right to control the sorts of information disclosed about oneself. These are closely linked forms of the same basic right: They are all rights to control your public image—rights to guarantee that people see you the way you want to be seen. They are, as it were, rights to be shielded against unwanted public exposure—to be spared embarrassment or humiliation. The prime enemy of our privacy, according to this continental conception, is the media, which always threatens to broadcast unsavory information about us in ways that endanger our public dignity. But of course, this concern does not end with media exposure. Any other agent that gathers and disseminates information can also pose such dangers. In its focus on shielding us from public indignity, the continental conception is typical of the continental legal world much more broadly: On the Continent, the protection of personal dignity has been a consuming concern for many generations.

By contrast, America, in this as in so many things, is much more oriented toward values of liberty, and especially liberty against the state. At its conceptual core, the American right to privacy still takes much the form that it took in the eighteenth century: It is the right to freedom from intrusions by the state, especially in one's own home. The prime danger, from the American point of view, is that "the sanctity of [our] home[s]," in the words of a leading nineteenth-century Supreme Court opinion on privacy, will be breached by government actors. American anxieties thus focus comparatively little on the media. Instead, they tend to be anxieties about maintaining a kind of private sovereignty within our own walls.

Such is the contrast that lies at the base of our divergent sensibilities about what counts as a "privacy" violation. On the one hand, we have an Old World in which it seems fundamentally important not to lose public face; on the other, a New World in which it seems fundamentally important to preserve the home as a citadel of individual sovereignty. What Europeans miss in Americans is a sense of the demands of public face; indeed, Europeans have been denouncing American law on that ground since at least 1903. When Americans seem to continental Europeans to violate norms of privacy, it is because they seem to display an embarrassing lack of concern for public dignity—whether the issue is the public indignity inflicted upon Monica Lewinsky by the media, or the self-inflicted indignity of an American who boasts about his salary. Conversely, when continental Europeans seem to Americans to violate norms of privacy, it is because they seem to show a supine lack of resistance to invasions of the realm of private sovereignty whose main citadel is the home—whether the issue is wiretapping or baby names. The question of public nudity presents the contrast in piquant form. To the continental way of seeing things, what matters is the right to control your public image—and that right may include the right to present yourself proudly nude, if you so choose. To the American mind, by contrast, what matters is sovereignty within one's own home; and people who have shucked the protection of clothing are like people who have shucked the protection of the walls of their homes, only more so. They are people who have surrendered any "reasonable expectation of privacy." ...

III. The European Tradition of Dignity: Leveling Up....

Where do the peculiar continental anxieties about "privacy" come from? To understand the continental law of privacy, we must start by recognizing how deeply "dignity" and "honor" matter in continental law more broadly. Privacy is not the only area in which continental law aims to protect people from shame and humiliation, from loss of public dignity. The law of privacy, in these continental countries, is only one member of a much wider class of legal protections for interpersonal respect. The importance of the value of respect in continental law is most familiar to Americans from one body of law in particular: the continental law of hate speech, which protects minorities against disrespectful epithets. But the continental attachment to norms of respect goes well beyond hate speech. Minorities are not the only ones protected against disrespectful epithets on the Continent. Everybody is protected against disrespect, through the continental law of "insult," a very old body of law that protects the individual right to "personal honor." Nor does it end there. Continental law protects the right of workers to respectful treatment by their bosses and coworkers, through what is called the law of "mobbing" or "moral harassment." This is law that protects employees against being addressed disrespectfully, shunned, or even assigned humiliating tasks like xeroxing. Continental law also protects the right of women to respectful treatment through its version of the law of sexual harassment. It even tries to protect the right of prison inmates to respectful treatment, as I have noted in a recent book, to a degree almost unimaginable for Americans....

What we see in continental law today is the result of a centuries-long, slow-maturing revolt against that style of status privilege. Over time, it has come to seem unacceptable that only certain persons should enjoy legal protections for their "dignity." Indeed, the rise of norms of respect for everybody—even minorities, even prison inmates—represents a great social transformation on the Continent. Everybody is now supposed to be treated in ways that only highly placed and wealthy people were treated a couple of centuries ago. Germany and France have been the theater of a leveling up, of an extension of historically high-status norms throughout the population. As the French sociologist Philippe d'Iribarne has elegantly put it, the promise of modern continental society is the promise that, where there were once masters and slaves, now "you shall all be masters!" ...

VIII. Warren and Brandeis Revisited

Indeed, continental ideas of privacy are just not much at home in American legal culture. To be sure, there is certainly American law on the books that sounds something like what we find on the books of Germany or France. American law has its famous four forms of the privacy tort, as analyzed by William Prosser in 1960: intrusion upon seclusion, appropriation of the name or likeness of another, public disclosure of private facts "not of legitimate concern to the public," and disclosure of private facts in such a way as to portray victims in a "false light." There is considerable legislation too, like the Video Privacy Protection Act of 1987, passed in reaction to journalistic investigations of Robert Bork, and various other acts and bills, both state and federal. American legislatures do pass privacy protection statutes of various kinds—especially, as Jeffrey Rosen has observed, in the wake of "heartstring-tugging" scandals. While many of these statutes treat the government as the principal threat to privacy, not all of them do. Though less than a third of the states have general laws on the protection of privacy, there certainly are state protections. There are even state constitutional protections for privacy. There are decisions giving protection to one's image—notably cases involving the nude or sexually charged images of young women who did not intentionally pose in a provocative way, or who are the victims of sexual assaults, or who otherwise seem to be living "a life of rectitude." There are cases involving nongovernmental invasions of the "privacy of [the] home," and especially of the privacy of the bedroom: Where the walls of the home are breached Americans can be sensitive. There is a lot of American scholarship that vigorously defends the European point of view. And of course, there is the famous article of Warren and Brandeis. . . .

This is indeed how we should understand the fate of "that most influential law review article of all," Warren and Brandeis's The Right to Privacy. Warren and Brandeis undertook the seminal, and still most cited, effort to introduce a continental-style right of privacy into American law. In theory, their right is still part of the law almost everywhere in America. Nevertheless, it is generally conceded that, after a century of legal history, it amounts to little in American practice today. The story of the relative failure of Warren and Brandeis is precisely a study in how poorly continental ideas do in the American climate. . . .

Freedom of expression has been the most deadly enemy of continental-style privacy in America. To cite once again our German scholar of 1959, the conflict has always been one between the values of Jefferson and the values of Goethe. Of all American liberty values, freedom of the press is the most poisonous for continental-style privacy rights. Starting with the famous *Sidis* case of 1940, American law began, in an American way, to favor the interests of the press at the cost of almost any claim to privacy. Perhaps the most striking examples come from the Supreme Court, with its decisions in *Cox Broadcasting Corp. v. Cohn* and *Florida Star v. B.J.F.* These were cases in which the media published the names of rape victims—in the latter case despite the fact that dissemination of the victim's name was a crime under state law. In both cases the Supreme Court found that the First Amendment protected media outlets against suit. Freedom of expression just about always wins in America—both in privacy cases and in cases involving infliction of emotional distress, like *Hustler Magazine, Inc. v. Falwell*, which denied recovery to preacher Jerry Falwell after Hustler published a particularly gross parody. This is the kind of question on which continental law, with its focus on personal honor, comes out differently.

That does not mean, of course, that American law never protects the control of one's image. But even where it does, it tends to do it in an American way. This is perhaps clearest in the doctrine of the "right of publicity." The "right of publicity" is a characteristic American doctrinal invention, which we owe to Melville Nimmer's work of the 1950s. In a sense, it is a doctrine of the protection of one's image. Nimmer argued that persons had an ownership right in their image, and that they could sue others who had misappropriated it. But it should be obvious that the notion of one's image as a piece of property, as a commercial commodity, is different in spirit from the continental protection of image. And indeed, while continental lawyers endorse this American innovation, they are careful to distinguish it from their own distinctive traditions. (Indeed, Americans themselves are confused by the question of whether the right of publicity really belongs within the realm of privacy protections or not.) And unsurprisingly, the American doctrine produces different results from continental doctrine. As critics complain, the "right of publicity" has tended to lose all of its moorings in the Warren and Brandeis idea of privacy, becoming essentially a vehicle for protecting the enterprises of celebrities like Bette Midler and Vanna White. Moreover, nothing in the doctrine of the "right of publicity" prevents Americans from alienating the rights in their image, no matter how humiliating their subsequent use may be. If your image is your property, you can sell it. In Europe, by contrast, as we have seen, sales of your nude image remain voidable—a very important doctrine, in particular, for protecting the interests of persons who, in moments of youthful folly, have allowed themselves to be photographed in embarrassing positions....

IX. The American Tradition: Protecting the Sanctity of the Home

But does this mean that Americans don't understand the moral imperative of privacy in the creation of "personhood"? Such is the conclusion that commentators repeatedly draw, both in Europe and in the United States. Yet I hope it is clear that the problem is more complex than that. If Europeans protect "privacy," it is not because they understand universal moral truths that Americans fail to understand. It is because they live in societies that have been shaped by certain kinds of cultural expectations and certain kinds of egalitarian ideals. After many generations of experience, Europeans have come to value a certain kind of personhood: a kind of personhood founded in the commitment to a society in which every person, of every social station, has the right to put on a respectable public face; a society in which privacy rights are not just for royalty, but for everybody. This is a concept of personhood that has been formed by the peculiarities of continental culture and continental history, and it has produced a law of privacy that has been formed by the same culture and history. For persons who live in these continental cultures, there will always be some practices that seem, in an intuitively obvious way, to represent violations of privacy. Yet the same practices may not seem like violations at all to non-Europeans.

As for Americans: They have their own concepts of personhood, their own traditions, and their own values. And the consequence is that there will always be practices that intuitively seem to represent obvious violations to Americans. Most especially, state action will raise American hackles much more often than European ones....

That tradition has now continued with *Lawrence v. Texas*, the Supreme Court's striking 2002 Term opinion on homosexuality: "Liberty," the *Lawrence* opinion begins, "protects the person from unwarranted government intrusions into a dwelling or other private places." This is familiar, indeed well-worn, American language, but it is not the only language that the decision speaks. It also speaks the language of dignity: *Lawrence* insists movingly on the right of gays not to be "demeaned," on their right to enjoy respect. But once again, as has so long been the case, the *Lawrence* Court finds no doctrinal hook on which to hang its talk of "respect." There is language about respect in Lawrence, but there is little that can be said to count in any certain way as law. One wonders indeed whether "respect," as discussed by the Court in *Lawrence*, really has much future in American law. One hopes that it does. There is some authority that insists on privacy protections for sexual orientation as an "intimate aspect of ... personality." In other circumstances, too, dignity sometimes seems to play an authentically important role in the application of Fourth Amendment norms. History suggests, though, that such arguments will fade in American discourse with time. This makes the prospects for a constitutionalized right to gay marriage, for example, dim.

What matters in America, over the long run, is liberty against the state within the privacy of one's home. This does not mean that the American approach to "privacy" is narrowly limited to Fourth Amendment search and seizure problems, of course. Lawyers do ingenious things, and the conception of privacy as liberty within the sanctity of the home can be extended in important ways. This has been notably true, of course, in the famous series of "constitutional privacy" decisions that began with *Griswold v. Connecticut*. At the limit, for those who accept the reasoning in *Roe v. Wade*, the modern right to "privacy" is the right to keep the government from intervening in our "private" decision about whether or not to abort an unwanted fetus; just as for others it is the right to keep the government from taking away our firearms. When private actors breach the walls of our homes, they too may sometimes raise our legal hackles—like the much-cited New Hampshire landlord of *Hamberger v. Eastman*, who bugged his tenants' bedroom.

Nevertheless, the fundamental limit on American thinking always remains: American "privacy" law, however ingenious its elaborations, always tends to imagine the home as the primary defense, and the state as the primary enemy. This gives American privacy law a distinctive coloration. Where American law perceives a threat to privacy, it is typically precisely because the state has become involved in the transaction. The case of *Hanlon v. Berger*—also commonly known as "the CNN case"—makes a fine example As we saw before, the Supreme Court found no violation of privacy rights when, in the Florida Star case, a newspaper published the name of a rape victim. The result was different in *Hanlon*: There the Court found a violation of privacy where a TV news crew went on a "ride-along" during a police raid. Once the police come into it, American intuitions shift. Another important example is *Whalen v. Roe*, the leading American informational privacy case. Predictably, that was a case involving government collection of private information. In general, the really easy cases in the American tradition are the ones involving, or resembling, criminal investigations. You can count on Americans to see privacy violations once the state gets into the act—in particular, where the issue can be somehow analogized to penetration into the home, or sometimes the body. Otherwise, you can never be sure. But you can count on Americans to see violations once the state is involved, and that means that there will always be continental practices that seem acceptable to Europeans but objectionable to us....

Nevertheless, they are real differences, and they do mean that there are always some continental practices that seem just as obviously untroubling to German or French people as they seem obviously wrong to Americans. I offered numerous examples at the beginning of this Article. For the sake of brevity, let me focus on just one before concluding: the law of names. Continental governments reserve to themselves the right to refuse to register certain given names that parents have chosen for their infants. This is done differently in different countries. In Germany, the local registry office, the Standesamt, maintains a list of permissible names. After reforms in 1993, the state has more limited powers in France. Today, local French officials can issue a complaint if parents choose a name that those officials deem to be not in the best interests of the newborn child. A court will then be seized of the matter, and will decide if the name is an acceptable one. If it rejects the parents' choice, the court itself is to choose a name for the infant in question, if necessary.

These are practices that seem strange indeed to Americans—how can a judge name your baby?—but they are widely defended by Europeans. Most commonly, Europeans say that the state simply must intervene to protect children against the stupidities of their parents. Indeed, to judge from my own conversations, the popular mind is vividly conscious of the problem of parental stupidity....

Nevertheless, however complex it may be, its very existence is simply weird to Americans. Indeed, if you tried to introduce a law of names into a state like Texas, you might face an armed rebellion. But does that mean that it is wrong or evil, by some universal standard, to have such a law of names? Europeans can see benefits in it—just as Americans can see benefits in extensive credit reporting. But the issue, here as in credit reporting, is not whether there are or are not identifiable benefits. The issue is whether a given privacy violation seems to fly in the face of fundamentally important social values. For Americans, the answer is very likely to be that the continental law of names does exactly that—flies in the face of important values of liberty. They may note that African Americans in particular, a historically oppressed population, express their independence partly through inventing unusual names for their children. But in any case, here as elsewhere, Americans will see an unacceptable violation of privacy where the state introduces itself into any "private" decision. Indeed, if drawn to defend themselves philosophically, Americans may use exactly the same imposing language of "personhood" that Europeans use in defending their conceptions of privacy. Is not the name fundamental to the making of the person?

X. Conclusion

I will not try to answer that last question, because the correct concept of personhood is not what is at stake here. What is at stake are two different core sets of values: On the one hand, a European interest in personal dignity, threatened primarily by the mass media; on the other hand, an American interest in liberty, threatened primarily by the government. On both sides of the Atlantic, these values are founded on deeply felt sociopolitical ideals, whose histories reach back to the revolutionary era of the later eighteenth century....

The same is true of the law of privacy. We cannot simply start by asking ourselves whether privacy violations are intuitively horrible or nightmarish. The job is harder than that. We have to identify the fundamental values that are at stake in the "privacy" question as it is understood in a given society. The task is not to realize the true universal values of "privacy" in every society. The law puts more limits on us than that: The law will not work as law unless it seems to people to embody the basic commitments of their society. In practice, this means that the real choice, in the Atlantic world at least, is between social traditions strongly oriented toward liberty and social traditions strongly oriented toward dignity. This is a choice that goes well beyond the law of privacy: It is a choice that involves all the areas of law that touch, more or less nearly, on questions of dignity.

We can respond to this choice by refusing to make it: We can opt for a world in which societies just do things differently. For example, we can declare that American gays can realistically expect only to have their liberty rights protected. The prospects for the kind of dignitary protections embodied in a law of gay marriage, we could say, are remote. After all, protecting people's dignity is quite alien to the American tradition. Or we can do what most moral philosophers want to do: We can reject the notion that different societies should have differing standards. But if we take that tack, we must face the fact that we will not succeed in changing either world unless we embark on a very large-scale revaluation of legal values.

In truth, there is little reason to suppose that Americans will be persuaded to think of their world of values in a European way any time soon; American law simply does not endorse the general norm of personal dignity found in Europe. Nor is there any greater hope that Europeans will embrace the American ideal; the law of Europe does not recognize many of the antistatist concerns that Americans seem to take for granted. Of course we are all free to plead for a different kind of law—in Europe or in the United States. But pleading for privacy as such is not the way to do it. There is no such thing as privacy as such. The battle, if it is to be fought, will have to be fought over more fundamental values than that.

Notes and Questions on Privacy

The following reflections and questions are intended to help you think about the meaning and status of privacy in family law.

(1) Do We Really Value Privacy? In recent years, the idea of privacy has been accorded much public respect, in the law and culturally. The ability of bureaucracies to collect data about people in the information age is widely acknowledged, dreaded, and regulated. As the passage we quoted in Chapter II from Warren and Brandeis anticipated, tort law has tried to limit intrusions into privacy. The search and seizure clause recognizes the importance of one kind of privacy, as does the privilege against self-incrimination. Privacy has even achieved the dignity of a constitutional right. Finally, we have seen family law using a concern for privacy as an important part of the justification for the doctrine of family autonomy.

But do we really value privacy? If we do, why has the scope of privacy contracted so remarkably in so many ways over the last fifty or even one hundred years? To be sure, there are senses in which we have more privacy now than we would have a century or two ago. These senses have primarily to do with our society's greatly increased wealth, which has meant that people are more likely to live in detached houses with yards, so that they are less exposed to the scrutiny of neighbors. People other than members of the nuclear family are less likely to live in those houses, and often houses are big enough so that residents all have their own rooms and so that residents need not see each other even when they are not in their own rooms. See generally M.P. Baumgartner, *The Moral Order of a Suburb,* (Oxford U Press, 1988).

On the whole, though, has not the scope of our privacy diminished? A vivid instance may be encountered by turning on your television. Evening talk shows are filled with celebrities anxious to retail the deficits of their childhoods, the defects of their parents, the disappointments of their careers, and the details of their amours. Morning television offers talk shows which specialize in finding people at some crisis in their intimate lives or whose intimate relations are particularly unusual. The host allows, inveigles, or even compels the guests to reveal their feelings about their situations as floridly as possible, and guests who let their emotions rip are not the least favored. More concretely:

> I once saw a Phil Donahue show in which a mother (voluntarily) met, for the first time, the daughter she had given up for adoption at birth. I once heard a National Public Radio "All Things Considered" program in which a man who had committed incest with his young daughter was, with his family, interviewed at length about their experiences. I am told that, in the case of a man who had hired a surrogate mother and who, when the baby arrived with birth defects, claimed that the baby was not

> his, all the parties involved went on television to receive the results of the paternity test.

Carl E. Schneider, *Moral Discourse and the Transformation of American Family Law*, 83 Mich L Rev 1803, 1850 n181 (1985). A paradigm of this practice came in 1973, when an American family, the Louds, permitted PBS to film their daily lives for a twelve-part documentary. Among the scenes was "an icy Pat Loud informing her philandering husband Bill that she wants a divorce." *Time*, August 22, 1983, at 74. Nor has the trend abated, as shows like the frankly named *Big Brother* testify.

The media generally are notably willing to inquire into the emotional and intimate lives of celebrities, people who happen to find themselves in the news, and even ordinary citizens. As is often remarked, even political reporting is now fascinated by the personal lives of politicians. The standard example is the contrast between the press's care not to photograph FDR in ways that revealed the effects of his paralysis (much less to reveal what it knew about his private life) and its thirst to catch, say, President William Clinton *in flagrante delicto*. As Warren and Brandeis tendentiously put it in their seminal article,

> The press is overstepping in every direction the obvious bounds of propriety and of decency. Gossip is no longer the resource of the idle and of the vicious, but has become a trade, which is pursued with industry as well as effrontery. To satisfy a prurient taste the details of sexual relations are spread broadcast in the columns of the daily papers. To occupy the indolent, column upon column is filled with idle gossip, which can only be procured by intrusion upon the domestic circle.

Samuel D. Warren and Louis D. Brandeis, *The Right to Privacy*, 4 Harv L Rev 193, 196 (1890). These developments have been exacerbated over the years by the proliferation of the media, which need ever more material. Competition for audiences drives the media to look for ways of expanding an audience.

The scope of legitimate inquiry into other people's lives has expanded. Social science research has institutionalized one form of intrusion into privacy. We are expected to answer the questions of people taking surveys. Students in schools are often convenient subjects for study. Commercial surveys call you at home. Political surveys are taken with complete regularity. (For instances of intrusions into privacy in the name of research, see Herbert C. Kelman, *Privacy and Research with Human Beings*, 33 J Social Issues 169 (1977).) Personnel tests (psychological, honesty, drug) are more extensively used, more probing, and perhaps more effective in revealing information. Changes in privacy are also driven by changes in ideas about what ought to be taught in schools. The idea of educating "the whole child" justifies dealing with intimate aspects of the child's life, as do courses like "guidance" and sex education.

The scope of privacy has diminished even within the boundaries of private life. Some kinds of privacy were once protected by putting subjects outside the bounds of ordinary conversation. But there are now few topics about which one is not expected to speak freely, at least to friends, often to the world at large. There is a stronger feeling that people ought to be on relaxed and open terms with each other even without extensive acquaintance. And, there is now "an emerging norm of 'full disclosure' in intimate relationships." Zick Rubin, et al., *Self-Disclosure in Dating Couples: Sex Roles and the Ethic of Openness*, 42 J Marriage & the Family 305, 305 (1980).

The scope of privacy has also been affected by the fact that, in general, rules of etiquette are fewer and have less force. One function of such rules is to allow people to follow socially established forms so that they can conceal their own views and feelings. When somebody says, "How are you?" the conventional response—"Fine, thank you. How are you?"—spares you from revealing your true feelings and from eliciting an intimate description of your interlocutor's health and mood. Similarly, using last names is a distancing device, permitting you not to feel you are on terms that require intimacy with people you do not know well and might not wish to know better. Driven partly by the continuing strength of American egalitarianism, such distancing devices steadily weaken.

Many of these changes can be understood in light of the fact that, over the last half century, and possibly longer, there has been a major change in American culture, one related to the shifts in views about human nature we have already encountered in this casebook: We increasingly analyze our lives and our relationships in psychological terms. This has had a significant effect on the scope of privacy.

First, the trend emphasizes the importance of private life and of private relationships and thus focuses our attention on them. Second, psychological thought makes a virtue of frank and full confrontation with one's inner self and deepest motivations. It ennobles honesty and openness in relationships. Thus people are encouraged to be self-revelatory. This increases the social pressure against privacy. And this in turn has a further consequence. When someone reveals himself or herself to you, you are then obliged to respond in kind. If you do not, you have withheld something when you have been given something, and you may be taken to have rejected an expression of friendship and trust.

Third, psychological thought discourages making feelings and intimate behavior proper subjects for guilt or even embarrassment. This diminishes the range of subjects about which people feel reluctant to talk or ask. Finally, psychological thought regards self-revelation as therapeutic. This means you are likely to encourage yourself to talk about yourself, and it means other people are likely to encourage you to do so. This explains some of the revelations one sees on television.

In sum, privacy in America seems diminished. (Because historical change of this kind can be hard to perceive, it may help to compare the novels of Anthony Trollope or Edith Wharton with, say, those of Philip Roth or television shows like "OC" or "Desperate Housewives.") So is it true that we value privacy? In what ways do we regard privacy as having undesirable consequences? What view of human nature is implied by the modern view of privacy? For help with these issues, consider the following questions.

(2) Does "Privacy" Really Mean Anything? Does "privacy" in fact mean anything? Is the idea coherent? What activities do ideas about privacy protect? Would you include matters relating to sex, religion, politics (at least voting is secret), money, health, and grades? What, if anything, do these activities have in common? Does the constitutional right of "privacy" protect the same things as the tort right of "privacy"? What does Whitman's article say about these issues?

(3) Is Privacy an Outmoded Value? Isn't privacy culturally determined and hence arbitrary? For most of European history and much of American history, for example, houses were small and had relatively few rooms; servants, apprentices, and boarders lived with the family; and several people might sleep in a single bed. Today, such living arrangements would be regarded as giving people too little privacy. If the things we think of as private are simply culturally determined, cannot they be changed by a cultural decision to do so? And might it not be desirable to narrow the scope of privacy? Consider the following arguments.

To begin with, privacy may be simply unnecessary. Why should people want to keep private things of which there is no reason to be ashamed? Why should people be able to keep private things of which they are ashamed? Is it honest to live one life in public and another in private? Is it healthy?

This leads us to a more serious question: Isn't privacy actively harmful? We may suggest several (and in some ways conflicting) senses in which this could be true. First, privacy can make people feel isolated and unhappy. People are social animals. They do not like to feel separated from the rest of society or even radically different from other people. But if some important subjects are barred from conversation or public knowledge, people may not know there are other people who are like them. They may thus be deprived of the comfort that comes from knowing that they are not alone and from getting to know people who share their characteristics. An often-given example is the adolescent boy who grows up in a time and place where sexual preference is not an accepted topic of conversation but who finds he has homosexual feelings. Isn't that loneliness part of the story behind the award-winning film "Brokeback Mountain?"

Second, and relatedly, isn't "privacy" simply another mechanism of social control, a means of keeping people from knowing what others are doing and learning that they are not alone? Isn't it true that because sexual matters are commonly considered private people of unorthodox sexual persuasions are isolated and kept ignorant?

Third, we associate privacy and shameful subjects. This can mean that private subjects become subjects for embarrassment. This can have deplorable consequences. For instance, people might be deterred from seeking psychotherapy they need by the embarrassment that can be associated with it. Or they might be reluctant to suggest using condoms.

Fourth, and more broadly, Richard Wasserstrom writes, *Some Arguments and Assumptions, in Philosophical Law*, Richard Bronough ed. (Greenwood Press, 1989), "We have made ourselves vulnerable—or at least far more vulnerable than we need be—by accepting the notion that there are thoughts and actions concerning which we ought to feel ashamed or embarrassed. When we realize that everyone has fantasies, desires, and worries about all sorts of supposedly terrible, wicked, and shameful things, we ought to see that they really are not things to be ashamed of at all."

Fifth, Wasserstrom makes another standard argument against privacy: "[F]orthrightness, honesty, and candor are, for the most part, virtues, while hypocrisy and deceit are not. Yet this emphasis upon the maintenance of a private side to life tends to encourage hypocritical and deceitful ways of behavior. Individuals tend to see themselves as leading dual lives—public ones and private ones.... This way of living is hypocritical because it is, in essence, a life devoted to camouflaging the real, private self from public scrutiny. It is a dualistic, unintegrated life that renders the individuals who live it needlessly vulnerable, shame ridden, and lacking in a clear sense of self."

Sixth is another standard attack on privacy, one based on a contrast between private life and public life. Proponents of this criticism fear that private life may become so central to people that public life suffers. Public life is, of course, in part political life. It is important because it is the way people take responsibility for their society and their fellows. Private life is the life led thinking about oneself, one's family, and one's close friends. These critics do not condemn thinking about one's family and friends or even about oneself. But they worry that people will become concerned about these things to the exclusion of the welfare of the society at large or strangers.

We are probably more dependent now than ever before on people we don't know, since modernization makes us less able to provide entirely for ourselves. Yet what is there except this mutual interdependence to make us concerned for each other? One answer is that strangers are people very much like oneself. But if the strangers too are private, it is hard to know enough about them to perceive those similarities or to be interested in their affairs.

The final objection to privacy differs from the rest. It suggests that privacy can get in the way of social control. Social control works partly by making people feel constrained from doing what they ought not do. The less privacy there is, the more people will feel constrained because they will be more exposed to critical eyes.

(4) What Advantages Might Privacy Have? The first advantage of privacy is the other side of the last disadvantage. Privacy can be an important means of protecting oneself from social pressures. If you have privacy, people can't know what you are doing, they can't criticize it, and they can't try to prevent it. Even if they find out about it, they may feel

constrained by social understandings about privacy from acting on their knowledge.

This advantage of privacy seems important even if what is being done in private is not shameful. Even if people ought not be ashamed of what they think and do, they often are. Privacy protects such people. Even if people are not ashamed of what they think and do, other people may try to penalize them for those things. Privacy protects them. (To illuminate the conflict between this advantage of privacy and the previous disadvantage, you might consider the controversy over "outing.")

Privacy may be important to us even if our thoughts are not shameful, even if we don't think of them as shameful, and even if nobody is likely to think they are shameful. Privacy, for instance, allows us to experiment with ideas and actions to see whether we wish to adopt them as our own without committing ourselves to them in public. This might be thought of as the "trial balloon" justification of privacy.

In addition, by sparing us from revealing our thoughts, privacy lets us deal with people we might otherwise struggle to cope with. For example, many societies have elaborate rules governing the relationship between couples and their parents-in-law. These rules create privacy barriers between in-laws. This smoothes a relationship between people who did not choose to be intimates and whose roles provide rich opportunities for conflicts. Privacy rules, in other words, allow in-laws to deal superficially but still politely with people it would be hard to deal with at a deeper level.

There are vestiges of such rules in American society. There is some feeling that the way parents choose to raise their children is private, both in the sense that they should have a good deal of autonomy in deciding how to do so and in the sense that they should not have to reveal how they are doing so. Commensurately, people who observe how parents are raising their children are supposed not to notice, or at least not to draw attention to the fact that they have noticed by commenting on what they have seen. Thus when your mother-in-law comes to visit you, she is not supposed to analyze the way you are raising your children. To the extent that these rules work, a dangerous topic of conversation is peacefully removed from the repertoire.

More broadly, privacy allows us to have different kinds of relationships with different people. You might see the couple who live next door often and enjoy seeing them. But you may not find you are entirely compatible with them at a more intimate level. Ideas about privacy protect you from having to go to that more intimate level, thereby allowing you to carry on one kind of friendship with them and another kind with people with whom you feel comfortable being more intimate.

Indeed, if everything you revealed about yourself to one person became public, you would soon stop telling anybody anything. Yet it seems desirable that you be able to tell some people intimate things because you will sometimes need to reveal intimate information in order to get help. This is one way of explaining rules about the confidentiality of revelations made to lawyers and doctors. In addition, people like to reveal things to other people because it makes them feel better. Revealing this information establishes a greater closeness with another person. It can also be a way of sharing emotional burdens. Privacy may make it easier to be intimate in a controlled way.

Yet further, if perhaps less obviously, principles of privacy protect us from having to talk about—and to think about—upsetting things that we would (at least at that moment) rather ignore. If Sigmund Freud is to be believed, early in our lives we discover that all of our instinctual drives cannot be satisfied. Ultimately, many of them and the frustrations and angers that arise from their being thwarted are repressed. They are repressed because we learn they are socially dysfunctional and even dangerous. However, they are still active in our minds. The necessary job of controlling these repressed feelings is eased if we are not reminded of them and made to deal with them inopportunely. Not only is it good for our psychic equilibrium that we not be made to think about some things, it is also good for our relationships with other people, as Richard Sennett reminds us in the epigraph to this section.

Horrible Freudian urgings are not the only feelings we may not wish to have to experience unwillingly. Consider the explosion of the Challenger space shuttle in which Christa McAuliffe was riding. Her parents were there for the occasion, and the television cameras filmed them watching their daughter die, and die horribly. This presents a privacy problem in two ways. First, and most obviously, it was an invasion of the McAuliffes' privacy. As the camera watched their faces, their emotions became increasingly legible. We could not help finding out what they were thinking and feeling about an intimate subject. Similarly, in the September 11 tragedy, we were unwillingly confronted with images of people throwing themselves out of the World Trade Center and the recordings of the last cell phone conversations people had with their loved ones.

But why should the survivors feel that this is an invasion of their privacy? Why should they care that we knew how they felt? Wasn't what they felt entirely normal, understandable, and even admirable? Part of the trouble is that their deepest feelings have been shared with the world. Yet the world is not prepared to respond in a commensurately compassionate way. It cannot fully share their grief. Thus the McAuliffes must have the unpleasant sensation of knowing that people must be responding "inappropriately" to their strong feelings. These are the mechanisms well described by Joan Didier in *The Year of Magical Thinking* (Knopf, 2005).

But another part of the trouble here is that the emotional shock the McAuliffes had just experienced was so great that they lost command of their ability to control their feelings and censor the information that they released about those feelings. They thus lost an important kind of control over their circumstances. In other words, we see here (again) how "privacy" may be related to "autonomy."

This leads us to the second way in which the filming of the McAuliffes' agony or the WTC disaster raises privacy problems: that filming invades the privacy of the people who were watching television. When you watched the McAuliffes' agony or the buildings' collapse, you could not help but begin to empathize with the survivors' situation. But true empathy was impossible without summoning up deep feelings and without recalling similar kinds of losses in your own life. The film of the McAuliffes or the coverage of 911 thus evoked in viewers the strong and painful feelings privacy might protect a person from having to feel. And as James Fitzjames Stephen wrote, "Privacy may be violated not only by the intrusion of a stranger, but by compelling or persuading a person to direct too much attention to his own feelings and to attach too much importance to their analysis." *Liberty, Equality, Fraternity* 160 (U Chi Press, 1991). Of course, to some extent viewers had an alternative—to try to feel nothing. But our feelings are not always under enough control to make such a response possible. And such a response is in important ways unattractive. It seems callous. It seems to deny the importance of the survivors' sorrow.

Finally, privacy prevents some subjects from assuming too dominant a place in social life. People with a pessimistic view of human nature, for example, may think believe that some of the classic subjects of privacy—the sexual side of human life, for instance—bid fair to become too central in human activity. Ideas about privacy, then, help allocate social energy.

One way of analyzing the advantages of privacy is to ask yourself, "Why are grades kept private?" Generally speaking, grades are nothing to be ashamed of. As long as you have worked hard and done your best, why should there be anything shameful about your grade? We can only do the best we can with the abilities we have. Grades are not intended to be and are not a measure of the whole worth of a person or even of a person's worth as a lawyer. Far from it. Further, knowing other people's grades could often be comforting. This is the "at least I'm in good company" argument. In any event, grades still are likely to be revealed in the place where they will make the most difference—in the job market. Why, then, are grades so rarely announced publicly?

What do all these ideas tell us about the privacy justification for the doctrine of family autonomy and as a reason for caution in intervening in a family to deal with spouse abuse? Do the arguments in favor of privacy that we have canvassed give weight to the idea that family members may suffer when their family affairs become public knowledge, or even when they just have to reveal those affairs to people who are not family members? In other words, should it help us see why, even if those circumstances are not objectively embarrassing, people might still wish to keep them private? Or, on the other hand, should the arguments against privacy suggest important reasons we might want to breach familial privacy in spouse-abuse cases? Is this an area where privacy predominantly thwarts needed social control?

As you read on, you should think about how ideas about privacy affect our thinking about other areas of family law. How, for example, do those ideas speak to the contractualization of family law? How much do we want spouses to work out the terms of their relationship explicitly and then to have their behavior examined publicly in terms of those negotiated contractual terms? Or how far do we wish parents to have to reveal the private feelings and fears that contribute to their decision to end the life of a damaged newborn child?

BIBLIOGRAPHY

Privacy. For a fascinating study of privacy in tribal, classical Greek, Old Testament, and ancient Chinese societies, see Barrington Moore, *Privacy: Studies in Social and Cultural History* (M.E. Sharpe, 1984). For an excellent collection of articles on the philosophy and law of privacy, see Ferdinand D. Schoeman, *Philosophical Dimensions of Privacy: An Anthology* (Cambridge U Press, 1984).

Family, Citizen and State. One of the most thorough and esteemed modern studies of the limits of state intervention in private life is Joel Feinberg's four volume study *The Moral Limits of the Criminal Law* (Oxford U Press, 1984–1988). These volumes are *Harm to Others, Offense to Others, Harm to Self,* and *Harmless Wrongdoing*. Another philosophical treatment is Donald VanDeVeer, *Paternalistic Intervention: The Moral Bounds on Benevolence* (Princeton U Press, 1986). One of the leading figures in the law and economics school provides a vigorous statement of the non-intervention view in Richard A. Posner, *Sex and Reason* (Harv U Press, 1992). Milton C. Regan reflects on autonomy and community in marriage in *Alone Together* (Oxford U Press, 1998). And Linda Hirshman and Jane Larson explore the boundaries and politics of sexual relations in *Hard Bargains: The Politics of Sex* (Oxford U Press 1998). A poignant story about bitterness and secrets in a middle class family is Annette Ansay's *Vinegar Hill* (Viking Penguin Books, 1994).

Domestic Violence. Linda Gordon, *Heroes of Their Own Lifes: The Politics and History of Family Violence: Boston 1880–1960* (Viking, 1988) is an examination of the history of all kinds of domestic violence. Margaret F. Brinig, Carl E. Schneider, and Lee E. Teitelbaum, *Family Law in Action: A Reader* 163–187 (Anderson, 1999) includes an empirical study of intimate violence. Jane M. Cohen, *Regimes of Private Tyranny: What Do They Mean to Morality and for the Criminal Law?*, 57 U Pitt L Rev 757 (1996), reports on jury nullification in murder cases where women have killed abusive spouses. Demie Kurz, *For Richer, For Poorer* (Routledge, 1995) reports on the frightening incidence of violence in troubled marriages, particularly those of indigents. Dennis P. Saccuzzo, *How Should the Police Respond to Domestic Violence: A Therapeutic Jurisprudence Analysis of Mandatory Arrest*, 39 Santa Clara L Rev 765 (1999), discusses, in another context, the mechanism by which violent offenders can be deterred from further harming the people with whom they live. Two chilling novels dealing with how an intelligent woman can stay in abusive relationships are Alice Hoffman, *Here on Earth* (Putnam, 1997) (a woman in New England); and Jane Hamilton's *Book of Ruth* (1990) (in which the prime tormentor is the heroine's mother-in-law).

Commitment in Relationships. As the title implies, Steven L. Nock, *Commitment and Dependency in Marriage*, 57 J Marriage & Family 503 (1995), discusses how commitment to each other and to the relationship makes marriage stable. Psychologists Judith S. Wallerstein and Sandra Blakeslee, in *The Good Marriage* (Warner Books 1995), present lengthy portraits of what makes various types of marriages survive and flourish over the long term. Ron Hansen's *Atticus* (1996) presents a fictional portrait of a loving father searching for his son's past after he learns of his death.

Jeffrey Rosen, *The Unwanted Gaze: The Destruction of Privacy in America* (Random House, 2000), discusses privacy in terms of human dignity, information flows, and the regulatory state.

Chapter IV

I THEE ENDOW: THE ECONOMICS OF MARRIAGE AND DIVORCE

The family, in its ideal conception and often in practice, is one place where the principle of maximizing the sum of advantages is rejected. Members of a family commonly do not wish to gain unless they can do so in ways that further the interests of the rest.

John Rawls
A Theory of Justice

SECTION 1. ONE FLESH: SUPPORT AND THE MARTIAL ENTITY

Therefore shall a man leave his father and his mother, and shall cleave unto his wife: and they shall be one flesh.

Genesis 2:24.

Tho' marriage makes man and wife one flesh, it leaves 'em still two fools.

William Congreve
The Double Dealer

A. THE DUTY OF SUPPORT

"I see what you are feeling," replied Charlotte,—"you must be surprised, very much surprised,—so lately as Mr. Collins was wishing to marry you. But when you have had time to think it all over, I hope you will be satisfied with what I have done. I am not romantic you know. I never was. I ask only a comfortable home; and considering Mr. Collins's character, connections, and situations in life, I am convinced that my chance of happiness with him is as fair, as most people can boast on entering the marriage state."

Jane Austen
Pride and Prejudice

Traditionally, family law imposed on the husband the duty to support his wife. It did so even if she could support herself. Reciprocally, she had a duty to keep house and raise the children. But given the principle of family autonomy, what legal consequences did these duties have? The following case investigates that question.

McGUIRE v. McGUIRE

Supreme Court of Nebraska, 1953
59 NW2d 336

MESSMORE, JUSTICE:

The plaintiff, Lydia McGuire, brought this action in equity in the district court of Wayne County against Charles W. McGuire, her husband, as defendant, to recover suitable maintenance and support money, and for costs and attorney's fees. Trial was had to the court and a decree was rendered in favor of the plaintiff.

The district court decreed that the plaintiff was legally entitled to use the credit of the defendant and obligate him to pay for certain items in the nature of improvements and repairs, furniture, and appliances for the household in the amount of several thousand dollars; required the defendant to purchase a new automobile with an effective heater within 30 days; ordered him to pay travel expenses of the plaintiff for a visit to each of her daughters at least once a year; that the plaintiff be entitled in the future to pledge the credit of the defendant for what may constitute necessaries of life; awarded a personal allowance to the plaintiff in the sum of $50 a month; awarded $800 for services for the plaintiff's attorney; and as an alternative to part of the award so made, defendant was permitted, in agreement with plaintiff, to purchase a modern home elsewhere.

The defendant filed a motion for new trial which was overruled. From this order the defendant perfected appeal to this court.

For convenience we will refer to the parties as they are designated in the district court.

The record shows that the plaintiff and defendant were married in Wayne, Nebraska, on August 11, 1919. At the time of the marriage the defendant was a bachelor 46 or 47 years of age and had a reputation for more than ordinary frugality, of which the plaintiff was aware. She had visited in his home and had known him for about 3 years prior to the marriage. After the marriage the couple went to live on a farm of 160 acres located in Leslie precinct, Wayne County, owned by the defendant and upon which he had lived and farmed since 1905. The parties have lived on this place ever since. The plaintiff had been previously married. Her first husband died in October 1914, leaving surviving him the plaintiff and two daughters. He died intestate, leaving 80 acres of land in Dixon County. The plaintiff and each of the daughters inherited a one-third interest therein. At the time of the marriage of the plaintiff and defendant the plaintiff's daughters were 9 and 11 years of age. By working and receiving financial assistance from the parties to this action, the daughters received a high school education in Pender. One daughter attended Wayne State Teachers College for 2 years and the other daughter attended a business college in Sioux City, Iowa, for 1 year. Both of these daughters are married and have families of their own.

On April 12, 1939, the plaintiff transferred her interest in the 80–acre farm to her two daughters. The defendant signed the deed.

At the time of trial plaintiff was 66 years of age and the defendant nearly 80 years of age. No children were born of these parties. The defendant had no dependents except the plaintiff.

The plaintiff testified that she was a dutiful and obedient wife, worked and saved, and cohabited with the defendant until the last 2 or 3 years. She worked in the fields, did outside chores, cooked, and attended to her household duties such as cleaning the house and doing the washing. For a number of years she raised as high as 300 chickens, sold poultry and eggs, and used the money to buy clothing, things she wanted, and for groceries. She further testified that the defendant was the boss of the house and his word was law; that he would not tolerate any charge accounts and would not inform her as to his finances or business; and that he was a poor companion. The defendant did not complain of her work, but left the impression to her that she had not done enough. On several occasions the plaintiff asked the defendant for money. He would give her very small amounts, and for the last 3 or 4 years he had not given her any money nor provided her with clothing, except a coat about 4 years previous. The defendant had purchased the groceries the last 3 or 4 years, and permitted her to buy groceries, but he paid for them by check. There is apparently no complaint about the groceries the defendant furnished. The defendant had not taken her to a motion picture show during the past 12 years. They did not belong to any organizations or charitable institutions, nor did he give her money to make contributions to any charitable institutions. The defendant belongs to the Pleasant Valley Church which occupies about 2 acres of his farm land. At the time of trial there was no minister for this church so there were no services. For the past 4 years or more, the defendant had not given the plaintiff money to purchase furniture or other household necessities. Three years ago he did purchase an electric, wood–and–cob combination stove which was installed in the kitchen, also linoleum floor covering for the kitchen. The plaintiff further testified that the house is not equipped with a bathroom, bathing facilities, or inside toilet. The kitchen is not modern. She does not have a kitchen sink. Hard and soft water is obtained from a well and a cistern. She has a mechanical Servel refrigerator, and the house is equipped with electricity. There is a pipeless furnace which she testified had not been in good working order for 5 or 6 years, and she testified she was tired of scooping coal and ashes. She had requested a new furnace but the defendant believed the one they had to be satisfactory. She related that the furniture was old and she would like to replenish it, at least to be comparable with some of her neighbors; that her silverware and dishes were old and were primarily gifts, outside of what she purchased; that one of her daughters was good about furnishing her clothing, at least a dress a year, or sometimes two; that the defendant owns a 1929 Ford coupé equipped with a heater which is not efficient, and on the average of every 2 weeks he drives the plaintiff to Wayne to visit her mother; and that he also owns a 1927 Chevrolet pickup which is used for different purposes on the farm. The plaintiff was privileged to use all of the rent money she wanted to from the 80–acre farm, and when she goes to see her daughters, which is not frequent, she uses part of the rent money for that purpose, the defendant providing no funds for such use. The defendant ordinarily raised hogs on his farm, but the last 4 or 5 years has leased his farm land to tenants, and he generally keeps up the fences and the buildings. At the present time the plaintiff is not able to raise chickens and sell eggs. She has about 25 chickens. The plaintiff has had three abdominal operations for which the defendant has paid. She selected her own doctor, and there were no restrictions placed in that respect. When she has requested various things for the home or personal effects, defendant has informed her on many occasions that he did not have the money to pay for the same. She would like to have a new car. She visited one daughter in Spokane, Washington, in March 1951 for 3 or 4 weeks, and visited the other daughter living in Fort Worth, Texas, on three occasions for 2 to 4 weeks at a time. She had visited one of her daughters when she was living in Sioux City some weekends. The plaintiff further testified that she had very little funds, possibly $1,500 in the bank which was chicken money and money which her father furnished her, he having departed this life a few years ago; and that use of the telephone was restricted, indicating that defendant did not desire that she make long distance calls, otherwise she had free access to the telephone.

It appears that the defendant owns 398 acres of land with 2 acres deeded to a church, the land being of the value of $83,960; that he has bank deposits in the sum of $12,786.81 and government bonds in the amount of $104,500; and that his income, including interest on the bonds and rental for his real estate is $8,000 or $9,000 a year. There are apparently some Series E United States Savings Bonds listed and registered in the names of Charles W. McGuire or Lydia M. McGuire purchased in 1943, 1944, and 1945, in the amount of $2,500. Other bonds seem to be in the name of Charles W. McGuire, without a beneficiary or co-owner designated. The plaintiff has a bank account of $5,960.22. This account includes deposits of some $200 and $100 which the court required the defendant to pay his wife as temporary allowance during the pendency of these proceedings. One hundred dollars was withdrawn on the date of each deposit.

The facts are not in dispute.

The defendant assigns as error that the decree is not supported by sufficient evidence; that the decree is contrary to law; that the decree is an unwarranted usurpation and invasion of defendant's fundamental and constitutional rights; and that the court erred in allowing fees for the plaintiff's attorney.

While there is an allegation in the plaintiff's petition to the effect that the defendant was guilty of extreme cruelty towards the plaintiff, and also an allegation requesting a restraining order be entered against the defendant for fear he might molest plaintiff or take other action detrimental to her rights, the plaintiff made no attempt to prove these allegations and the fact that she continued to live with the defendant is quite incompatible with the same....

In the instant case the marital relation has continued for more than 33 years, and the wife has been supported in the same manner during this time without complaint on her part. The parties have not been separated or living apart from each other at any time. In the light of the cited cases it is clear, especially so in this jurisdiction, that to maintain an action such as the one at bar, the parties must be separated or living apart from each other.

The living standards of a family are a matter of concern to the household, and not for the courts to determine, even though the husband's attitude toward his wife, according to his wealth and circumstances, leaves little to be said in his behalf. As long as the home is maintained and the parties are living as husband and wife it may be said that the husband is legally supporting his wife and the purpose of the marriage relation is being carried out. Public policy requires such a holding. It appears that the plaintiff is not devoid of money in her own right. She has a fair-sized bank account and is entitled to use the rent from the 80 acres of land left by her first husband, if she so chooses....

There being no legal basis for the plaintiff's action as required by the law of this jurisdiction, an allowance of attorney's fees is erroneous and not authorized.

For the reasons given in this opinion, the judgment rendered by the district court is reversed and the cause remanded with directions to dismiss the cause.

Reversed and remanded with directions to dismiss....

YEAGER, J, dissenting:

From the beginning of the married life of the parties the defendant supplied only the barest necessities and there was no change thereafter. He did not even buy groceries until the last 3 or 4 years before the trial, and neither did he buy clothes for the plaintiff.

As long as she was able plaintiff made a garden, raised chickens, did outside chores, and worked in the fields. From the sale of chickens and eggs she provided groceries, household necessities, and her own clothing. These things she is no longer able to do, but notwithstanding this the defendant does no more than to buy groceries. He buys her no clothing and does not give her any money at all to spend for her needs or desires. Only one incident is mentioned in the record of defendant ever buying plaintiff any clothing. He bought her a coat over 3 years before the trial....

The house in which the parties live is supplied with electricity and there is a gas refrigerator, otherwise it is decidedly not modern.

On these facts the district court decreed that plaintiff was legally entitled to use the credit of defendant and to obligate him to pay for a large number of items, some of which were in the nature of improvements and repairs to the house and some of which were furniture and appliances to be placed in the home. The total cost of these improvements and additions, as is apparent from the decree, would amount to several thousand dollars. As an alternative to a part of this the defendant was permitted, in agreement with plaintiff, to purchase a modern house elsewhere. The defendant was ordered to purchase a new automobile with an effective heater within 30 days. He was ordered to pay travelling expenses of plaintiff for a visit to each of her daughters at least once each year. It was decreed that plaintiff was entitled in the future to pledge the credit of defendant for what may constitute necessaries of life. The plaintiff was awarded a personal allowance in the amount of $50 a month. An award of $800 was made for services for plaintiff's attorney.

As grounds for reversal necessary to be considered herein the defendant says that the decree is not supported by sufficient evidence; that the decree is contrary to law; that the decree is an unwarranted usurpation and invasion of the defendant's fundamental and constitutional rights; and that the court erred in allowing fees for plaintiff's attorney.

In support of these assignments the defendant urges that there is no legal or equitable basis or authority for the maintenance of this action or one such as this. Substantially he says that these parties are husband and wife; that they are living together as such; and that plaintiff is not seeking separation or separate maintenance, therefore no relief is available to the plaintiff through the court.

There is and can be no doubt that, independent of statutes relating to divorce, alimony, and separate maintenance, if this plaintiff were living apart from the defendant she could in equity and on the facts as outlined in the record be awarded appropriate relief.

The principle supporting the right of a wife to maintain an action in equity, independent of statute, for maintenance was first announced in this jurisdiction in *Earle v. Earle*, 27 Neb. 277, 43 N.W. 118, 119, 20 Am.St.Rep. 667. In the opinion it was said: "While the statute books of this and other states amply provide for the granting of divorces in meritorious cases, yet we do not apprehend that it is the purpose of the law to compel a wife, when the aggrieved party, to resort to this proceeding, and thus liberate her husband from all obligations to her, in order that the rights which the law gives her, by reason of her marital relations with her husband, may be enforced. Such a conclusion would not generally strike the conscience of a court of equity as being entirely equitable."

Further in the opinion and in determination of the question it was said: "But however that may be, we are of the opinion that courts of equity should have and do have the jurisdiction to grant relief in cases of this kind without reference to the statutes of the state, but by and through the jurisdiction growing out of the general equity powers of the court." . . .

If relief is to be denied to plaintiff under this principle it must be denied because of the fact that she is not living separate and apart from the defendant and is not seeking separation.

In light of what the decisions declare to be the basis of the right to maintain an action for support, is there any less reason for extending the right to a wife who is denied the right to maintenance in a home occupied with her husband than to one who has chosen to occupy a separate abode?

If the right is to be extended only to one who is separated from the husband equity and effective justice would be denied where a wealthy husband refused proper support and maintenance to a wife physically or mentally incapable of putting herself in a position where the rule could become available to her.

It is true that in all cases examined which uphold the right of a wife to maintain an action in equity for maintenance the parties were living apart, but no case has been cited or found which says that separation is a condition precedent to the right to maintain an action in equity for maintenance. Likewise none has been cited or found which says that it is not.

In primary essence the rule contemplates the enforcement of an obligation within and not without the full marriage relationship. The reasoning contained in the opinions sustaining this right declare that purpose.

In *Earle v. Earle, supra,* it was said: "The question is, whether or not the plaintiff shall be compelled to resort to a proceeding for a divorce, which she does not desire to do, and which probably she is unwilling to do, from conscientious convictions, or, in failing to do so, shall be deprived of that support which her husband is bound to give her."

This reasoning has received the approval of this court in the later cited cases.

If there may not be resort to equity in circumstances such as these then as pointed out in the following statement from *Earle v. Earle, supra,* a dim view must be taken of the powers of a court of equity: "As we have already said in substance, there is not much to commend an alleged principle of equity which would hold that the wife, with her family of one or more children to support, must be driven to going into court for a divorce when such a proceeding is abhorrent to her, or, in case of her refusal to do so, being compelled to submit to a deprivation of the rights which equity and humanity clearly give her; that, in order to obtain that to which she is clearly entitled, she must institute her action for a divorce, make her grievances public, which she would otherwise prefer to keep to herself, and finally liberate a husband from an obligation of which he is already tired, but from which he is not entitled to be relieved."

Can a principle of equity which requires a wife to leave her home before becoming able to enforce the obligation of her husband to support and maintain her receive in reason a higher commendation than the hypothesis contained in this quotation? I think not.

It is thought that the following from the same opinion should be regarded as controlling here: "It seems to us that a declaration of such a doctrine as the law of the land would place it within the power of every man, who, unrestrained by conscience, seeks to be freed from his obligation to his wife and family, by withholding the necessary comforts and support due them, to compel her to do that for him which the law would not do upon his own application."

I conclude therefore that the conclusion of the decree that the district court had the power to entertain the action was not contrary to law.

I think however that the court was without proper power to make any of the awards contained in the decree for the support and maintenance of the plaintiff except the one of $50 a month.

From the cases cited herein it is clear that a husband has the obligation to furnish to his wife the necessaries of life. These decisions make clear that for failure to furnish them the wife may seek allowances for her support and maintenance. However neither these decisions nor any others cited or found support the view contended for by plaintiff that the court may go beyond this and impose obligations other than that of payment of money for the proper support and maintenance of the wife.

There is no doubt that the plaintiff had the right to charge her husband with her necessaries of life and that recovery could be had therefor. No award of a court of equity was necessary to establish this right. Nothing was accomplished by the declaration of that right. The provision relating thereto therefore had no proper place in the decree.

I am of the opinion that the power of the court in such instances as this should not be extended beyond the allowance of sufficient money to provide adequate support and maintenance.

This court, I think, has laid down a sound rule for the guidance of the court with regard to awards in such cases as this in *Chapman v. Chapman, supra* [74 Neb. 388, 104 N.W. 880], as follows: "We think that the judgment of the district court should be reversed and the cause remanded with instructions to receive such additional competent evidence pertinent to the subject of alimony as may be offered by either party, and to award to the plaintiff such sums, to be paid to her periodically by the defendant, as shall appear to be within his ability to pay and be adequate for her suitable maintenance."

As pointed out the district court made an allowance of $50 a month. In the light of generally well-known present day economy the conclusion is inevitable that this award is insufficient for the maintenance of the plaintiff. The record before us however does not supply adequate information upon which this court could make a finding as to what would be sufficient.

The plaintiff has cross-appealed contending that the allowance is not sufficient. It is concluded that the cross-appeal has merit and accordingly this phase of the case should be remanded to the district court for the taking of evidence in order that finding may be made as to what would be adequate for plaintiff's suitable maintenance....

Notes on McGuire

It may help to review Mrs. McGuire's situation under traditional family law. First, she could spend her own money to supplement the support Mr. McGuire provided. Second, she could pledge Mr. McGuire's credit to purchase "necessaries." (In some jurisdictions she could pledge her own credit, thereby obligating her husband's under the doctrine of necessaries.) Necessaries are items appropriate to the standard of living the couple has established. The doctrine of necessaries, however, generally could do little to assure the wife support, since the wife had to persuade the merchant to accept her husband's credit, and the merchant could not recover from the husband if the item purchased was not "necessary" by the standards of the family or if it had already been supplied.

The doctrine of necessaries still has vitality in a number of jurisdictions, especially for emergency medical treatment and occasionally for necessary legal services. *Schilling v. Bedford County Memorial Hospital, Inc.*, 303 SE2d 905 (1983); *United States v. O'Neill*, 478 F Supp 852 (E D Pa 1979); *State v. Clark*, 563 P2d 1253 (Wash 1977). The doctrine arose because at common law the wife had no property from which to pay for necessaries, and thus the doctrine was only available to wives. Today, however, the doctrine may be used by husbands as well. See, e.g., Va Code § 55–37 (2006); *Richland Mem Hosp v. Burton*, 318 SE2d 12 (SC 1984); Note, *The Unnecessary Doctrine of Necessaries*, 82 Mich L Rev 1767 (1984).

Mrs. McGuire's third alternative was bringing an action for support against her husband if he wholly failed to support her. A total failure of support amounts to a constructive desertion and thus to an effective end of the relationship and of the reasons for judicial non-intervention. Fourth, Mrs. McGuire could move out of the house and seek separate maintenance, *i.e.*, support for a wife living apart from her husband. However, if she moved out unjustifiably, she would lose her claim to separate maintenance, since she would then have abandoned her husband. Fifth, she could sue for divorce and for alimony, using, in most jurisdictions, Mr. McGuire's failure to support as one of the grounds. Sixth, she could use the statute in force in most states making it a crime to fail to support a wife. (Section 230.5 of the Model Penal Code, for instance, provides: "A person commits a misdemeanor if he persistently fails to provide support which he can provide and which he knows he is legally obliged to provide to a spouse, child or other dependent.") Such statutes, however, generally are taken to define non–support in much more stringent terms than Mrs. McGuire would meet.

These traditional remedies are available today to various extents in various jurisdictions. But the modern law of support during the marriage itself must today be understood in terms of the following constitutional decision of the Supreme Court.

ORR v. ORR

Supreme Court of the United States, 1979
440 US 268

BRENNAN, JUSTICE . . .

In authorizing the imposition of alimony obligations on husbands, but not on wives, the Alabama statutory scheme "provides that different treatment be accorded . . . on the basis of . . . sex; it thus establishes a classification subject to scrutiny under the Equal Protection Clause," *Reed v. Reed*, 404 U.S. 71, 75 (1971). The fact that the classification expressly discriminates against men rather than women does not protect it from scrutiny. *Craig v. Boren*, 429 U.S. 190 (1976). "To withstand scrutiny" under the Equal Protection Clause, "classifications by gender must serve important governmental objectives and must be substantially related to achievement of those objectives." *Califano v. Webster*, 430 U.S. 313, 316–17 (1977). We shall, therefore, examine the three governmental objectives that might arguably be served by Alabama's statutory scheme.

Appellant views the Alabama alimony statutes as effectively announcing the State's preference for an allocation of family responsibilities under which the wife plays a dependent role, and as seeking for their objective the reinforcement of that model among the State's citizens. Cf. *Stern v. Stern*, 165 Conn. 190, 332 A.2d 78 (1973). We agree, as he urges, that prior cases settle that this purpose cannot sustain the statutes. *Stanton v. Stanton*, 421 U.S. 7, 10 (1975), held that the "old notio[n]" that "generally it is the man's primary responsibility to provide a home and its essentials," can no longer justify a statute that discriminates on the basis of gender. "No longer is the female destined solely for the home and the rearing of the family, and only the male for the marketplace and the world of ideas," *id.*, at 14–15. See also *Craig v. Boren, supra*, at 198. If the statute is to survive constitutional attack, therefore, it must be validated on some other basis.

The opinion of the Alabama Court of Civil Appeals suggests other purposes that the statute may serve. Its opinion states that the Alabama statutes were "designed" for "the wife of a broken marriage who needs financial assistance," 351 S.2d at 905. This may be read as asserting either of two legislative objectives. One is a legislative purpose to provide help for needy spouses, using sex as a proxy for need. The other is a goal of compensating women for past discrimination during marriage, which assertedly has left them unprepared to fend for themselves in the working world following divorce. We concede, of course, that assisting needy spouses is a legitimate and important governmental objective. We have also recognized "[r]eduction of the disparity in economic condition between men and women caused by the long history of discrimination against women ... as ... an important governmental objective," *Califano v. Webster, supra*, at 317. It only remains, therefore, to determine whether the classification at issue here is "substantially related to achievement of those objectives." *Ibid.*

Ordinarily, we would begin the analysis of the "needy spouse" objective by considering whether sex is a sufficiently "accurate proxy," *Craig v. Boren, supra*, at 204, for dependency to establish that the gender classification rests " 'upon some ground of difference having a fair and substantial relation to the object of the legislation,' " *Reed v. Reed, supra*, at 76. Similarly, we would initially approach the "compensation" rationale by asking whether women had in fact been significantly discriminated against in the sphere to which the statute applied a sex-based classification, leaving the sexes "*not* similarly situated with respect to opportunities" in that sphere, *Schlesinger v. Ballard*, 419 U.S. 498, 508 (1975). Compare *Califano v. Webster, supra*, at 318, and *Kahn v. Shevin*, 416 U.S. 351, 353 (1974), with *Weinberger v. Wiesenfeld*, 420 U.S. 636, 648 (1975).

But in this case, even if sex were a reliable proxy for need, and even if the institution of marriage did discriminate against women, these factors still would "not adequately justify the salient features of" Alabama's statutory scheme, *Craig v. Boren, supra*, at 202–203. Under the statute, individualized hearings at which the parties' relative financial circumstances are considered *already* occur. See *Russell v. Russell*, 247 Ala. 284, 286, 24 So.2d 124, 126 (1945); *Ortman v. Ortman*, 203 Ala. 167, 82 So. 417 (1919). There is no reason, therefore, to use sex as a proxy for need. Needy males could be helped along with needy females with little if any additional burden on the State. In such circumstances, not even an administrative-convenience rationale exists to justify operating by generalization or proxy. Similarly, since individualized hearings can determine which women were in fact discriminated against vis–à–vis their husbands, as well as which family units defied the stereotype and left the husband dependent on the wife, Alabama's alleged compensatory purpose may be effectuated without placing burdens solely on husbands. Progress toward fulfilling such a purpose would not be hampered, and it would cost the State nothing more, if it were to treat men and women equally by making alimony burdens independent of sex. "Thus, the gender–based distinction is gratuitous; without it, the statutory scheme would only provide benefits to those men who are in fact similarly situated to the women the statute aids," *Weinberger v. Wiesenfeld, supra*, at 653, and the effort to help those women would not in any way be compromised.

Moreover, use of a gender classification actually produces perverse results in this case. As compared to a gender–neutral law placing alimony obligations on the spouse able to pay, the present Alabama statutes give an advantage only to the financially secure wife whose husband is in need. Although such a wife might have to pay alimony under a gender-neutral statute, the present statutes exempt her from that obligation. Thus, "[t]he [wives] who benefit from the disparate treatment are those who were ... nondependent on their husbands," *Califano v. Goldfarb*, 430 U.S. 199, 221 (1977)(STEVENS, J., concurring in judgment). They are precisely those who are not "needy spouses" and who are "least likely to have been victims of ... discrimination," *ibid.*, by the institution of marriage. A gender-based classification which, as compared to a gender-neutral one, generates additional benefits only for those it has no reason to prefer cannot survive equal protection scrutiny.

Legislative classifications which distribute benefits and burdens on the basis of gender carry the inherent risk of reinforcing stereotypes about the "proper place" of women and their need for special protection. Cf. *United Jewish Organizations v. Carey*, 430 U.S. 144, 173–174 (1977) (opinion concurring in part). Thus, even statutes purportedly designed to compensate for and ameliorate the effects of past discrimination must be carefully tailored. Where, as here, the State's compensatory and ameliorative purposes are as well served by a gender–neutral classification as one that gender classifies and therefore carries with it the baggage of sexual stereotypes, the State cannot be permitted to classify on the basis of sex. And this is doubly so where the choice made by the State appears to redound—if only indirectly—to the benefit of those without need for special solicitude.

Questions on **Orr**

(1) Is there any reason to abandon the principle of family autonomy when a cohabiting spouse seeks judicial assistance in compelling the other spouse to provide support? How do our seven justifications for the principle of family autonomy fit the problem of support?

(2) How ought *Orr* affect *McGuire*? Does *Orr* establish a mutual duty of support? What would a mutual duty of support mean?

(3) Although spouses today may contract out of many of the incidents of marriage, are there limits to this private law power? For example, can they agree that during marriage neither will be responsible for the support of the other? *See, e.g., In re Marriage of Higgason*, 516 P2d 289 (Cal 1973).

B. THE CONCEPT OF THE MARITAL ENTITY

No sociological change equal in importance to this clearly marked improvement of an entire sex has ever taken place in one century. Under it all, the crux of the whole matter, goes on the one great change, that of the economic relation. This follows perfectly natural lines. Just as the development of machinery constantly lowers the importance of mere brute strength of body and raises that of mental power and skill, so the pressure of industrial conditions demands an ever—higher specialization, and tends to break up that relic of the patriarchal age,—the family as an economic unit.

Charlotte Perkins Gilman
Women and Economics

An underlying assumption of family law generally and of family autonomy particularly is that it is possible and even useful to regard the family as an entity. Dean Lee Teitelbaum criticizes that assumption and its use in cases like *McGuire* in the following excerpt.

LEE E. TEITELBAUM
FAMILY HISTORY AND FAMILY LAW

1985 Wisconsin Law Review 1135

... The complexity of discourse about public and private spheres is matched by the difficulties of legal and historical talk about intervention and the family. It has been suggested at various points in this article that the family cannot be viewed as a social entity which has an existence apart from public activity. Law does not act upon the family as water acts on a rock. It is in some sense constitutive of the family, in some sense continually involved in the family's function, and in some sense itself influenced by the behavior of families.

Caution in talking about the relationship of law and the family is peculiarly important when conversation turns to notions of family autonomy or privacy. As we have seen, the ideas of family autonomy and privacy are regularly invoked to justify legal doctrines. When courts refuse to resolve intra-spousal financial disputes, that decision is founded on the principle of family autonomy. When courts say that they will not resolve disputes about child-rearing or permit state laws to regulate educational decisions arbitrarily, those outcomes are likewise said to serve interests of family autonomy or privacy. However, the practical consequence of many, if not all, of these decisions is to confer or ratify the power of one family member over others. While Professor Glendon sees cases like *McGuire v. McGuire* as leaving spouses free to work out their own roles within the family, one wonders in what sense the family as an entity was made free. Certainly Mrs. McGuire was not "free to work out her own role" in the marriage if Mr. McGuire had all the money. She could not get the new cloth coat she wanted, or new linoleum for the kitchen, or a warm heater for their old car. Her only choice lay without the marriage, in seeking a judicial separation or divorce. When the majority in *McGuire* say that "the living standards of the family are a matter of concern to the household," they mean only that they propose to leave the parties where they are. The "household" does not make decisions about living standards, unless that is informally agreed. Otherwise, the husband will make those decisions.

By the same token, "family autonomy" in connection with parent-child relations, to the extent it exists at all, tends to mean the authority of parents over their children. We do not know whether the child in *Pierce v. Society of Sisters* wanted to go to parochial school but, if a gratuitous remark in a recent Supreme Court decision is taken seriously, that did not matter: striking down the Oregon public school law insofar as it failed to credit parochial education simply affirmed the parent's choice with regard to a child's schooling. Indeed, it generally appears that decisions involving either parent's or children's rights do not address an entity but allocate individual power within a social unit in one way or another. In *Parham v. J.R.*, the Supreme Court considered whether procedural protections need attach to the decisions of parents to commit their children to institutions for the mentally retarded. Characterizing the arguments in favor of such protection as "statist," the Court decided that no formal hearing procedure was required, or indeed desirable, because such procedures would invade "parental authority over minor children." By contrast, *Planned Parenthood of Central Missouri v. Danforth* held that a state could not give parents a veto over their mature minor's decision to seek an abortion. In doing so, the Court plainly recognized that its decision presumed a family already fractured by the abortion. Finally, the Court held in *Bellotti v. Baird* that a negative parental decision about abortion even for a daughter who could not be considered "mature" must be reviewed by a court to determine whether denial of that procedure would serve the child's long-run interest.

Although the outcomes of these cases run in all possible directions, each allocates power to one family member or reserves it to the state. None creates decisional rights in an entity. The same observation could be made of statutory provisions formally addressed to maintaining or strengthening the family unit. Although proceedings with respect to children in need of supervision (beyond the control of their parents) are commonly explained as devices to strengthen a disrupted family, there is reason to believe that no such effect is possible. To the extent that parental wishes are enforced, the child's preferences are overwhelmed. At the same time, the use of a court procedure to test the "reasonableness" of parental commands tells the child that it is not bare parental authority, but authority mediated by public judgment, to which he or she must submit. The one thing these proceedings cannot provide for family, parent, or child is a sense of autonomy or privacy.

In relation to autonomy or privacy, the family is a "false concrete" or anthropomorphism that we invoke to talk in terms that do not literally apply. In this respect, talk of family autonomy or privacy is like talk of "societal needs" or the attraction of bodies by gravity. Anthropomorphisms tend to be used when the body of accepted principles does not adequately explain some phenomenon. In scientific thought, these occasions arose when "the knowledge of the time was insufficient to provide the right generalization, [and] imagination took its place and supplied a kind of explanation which appealed to the urge for generality by satisfying it with naive parallelisms. Superficial analogies, particularly analogies with human experiences, were confused with generalizations and taken to be explanations."

Anthropomorphisms in law also arise out of the limits of conceptualization, although with law such limits may be necessary rather than temporal. Modern western legal theory supposes that the relevant unit is the individual and that the central problem of legal order is the adjustment of relations between society, representing the general will or good, and individual wills or goods. Lacking an adequate conceptual framework for dealing with relationships, law converts relationships into units and attributes to them characteristics that fit poorly. Neither "privacy" or "autonomy" helpfully describes the relationships within the family, but are used rather to characterize the attitude of public authority to those relationships. To the extent the family is "private" or "autonomous," legal agencies do not directly superintend certain forms of conduct within that relationship.

Reliance on metaphorical discussion, in law as in science, has real dangers. One is that it falsely confirms the power of the conceptual framework by suggesting its capacity to deal adequately with all phenomena, and another is that it tends to obscure the relationships that underlie the metaphorical unit.

We have encountered instances of these tendencies earlier in this article. The use of metaphor to preserve a conceptual framework may be illustrated by reconsidering an earlier argument. To show that the "private" picture of nineteenth and twentieth century domestic life is flawed, considerable evidence of an increase in "public" regulation of the conduct of family members was adduced. The term "public" was associated with "intervention" in the family throughout the argument. That is conventional usage, but it also reveals something about our understanding of law.

The conventional idea of intervention, relied on earlier, depends on a particular conceptualization of law. We mean by intervention public activity through proscriptive or prescriptive rules: "Thou shalt not steal" or "Thou shalt support thy wife." Commands of these kinds are sharply distinguished from facilitative rules and from silence or abstention, which are considered instances of non-regulation. A rule that says "Fathers must leave at least one-third of their wealth to their children at death" is considered different in kind from one that says "Any testamentary provision made in a certain form will be enforced." Similarly, a rule reciting that "Husbands shall adequately support their wives" is different, not only in its content but in its nature, from one that says, "The state will not resolve financial disputes between spouses." The first of these pairs of rules would be considered an instance of intervention because each manifestly limits individual choice; the second of these pairs would ordinarily be regarded as facilitating or conferring autonomy.

To the extent that law is identified with intervention and thought of as commands, it deals poorly with relationships. Commends are addressed to and enforced against individuals, and they are obeyed or disobeyed by individuals. When individual choice is the subject matter of law, a command theory may seem to work well enough, because law can limit its concern to single instances of conduct that have the same significance regardless of their author. Legal systems in a differentiated society, as we have seen, typically adopt such a narrow focus and concern themselves only with a specific set of behaviors rather than with complex interactions. If, however, the significance of choice and conduct is found in relationships among individuals, problems arise. A prescriptive rule regarding spousal or parental conduct does not address a relatively unambiguous single act but a course of dealings in which innumerable significant variations exist. Rather than say that the legal system we employ does not operate adequately here, it is simpler to regard the family as a unit and say, "This is an entity which has a claim against legal intrusion. Therefore law will not regulate conduct here." By treating the family as if it were a person, we can explain the difficulties of legal regulation of relationships without questioning the general theory of legal regulation.

The entity approach also hides decisions about family relationships that are worth examining. Although only proscriptive and prescriptive rules are taken as cases of intervention, it is surely true that all forms of societal behavior—including facilitative rules and silence—involve policy choices. Moreover, the choice of strategies is not simply between domination (intervention) and freedom (non-intervention), but between two kinds of authority. When government acts by commands, it thereby authorizes an exercise of public authority. Government by the rule of law is understood as insisting upon the equality of persons under this authority, which can only be assured through separation of rule-making and rule-applying functions.

> The rule of law implies that legal commands are uniform and general; that they cover all situations within the class they define and apply to all persons within that situation.... To the extent that [these conditions] are fulfilled, justice is impersonal and abstracted from the immediate source of authority.

Facilitative rules and silence, by contrast, leave people to their own strengths and thereby authorize personal authority. If bargains will always be enforced, the making of that bargain reflects only the power, skill, and knowledge of the parties. When the parties are in fact unequal in these characteristics, the weaker party is subjected to the domination of the stronger. That domination is personal rather than public; law only ratifies the naturally existing or socially created inequalities which have led to the victory of one over the other.

By regarding the family as an entity which is left free by governmental silence, the effects of a policy permitting personal domination are obscured. When, to take only one example, Mrs. McGuire is left to her own resources in dealing with her husband, she is subject to his personal authority in seeking a car or a coat. No rules require that he treat her as other husbands treat their wives, or as he treated a former wife, had he been married previously. It does not in principle matter that her neighbors have bought cars, coats, or an electric range for their wives. She, like contracting parties under facilitative rules, lives in a Hobbesean state of nature where those with practical power may do much as they want with those who lack that power. Because we focus on "the family" rather than on Mrs. McGuire, however, her condition becomes invisible.

It may well be said that, in ignoring natural inequalities such as Mrs. McGuire's lack of bargaining power or the dependence of children generally on their parents, family law simply follows generally prevailing liberal theory. American social thought has assumed that while law must provide formal equality among persons, it is not concerned with correcting naturally occurring inequalities among men. Enlightenment theory, which exercised a stronger grip on nineteenth century American views than on European thought, insisted that the state must take men as they are if progress, understood as the unfolding of the self-interest of individual actors, would be achieved. The will theory of contract is only one manifestation of this emphasis on formal rather than substantive equality.

However, the frankly individualistic nature of this doctrine makes its application to families difficult. Certainly no one believed that the relations among families should be marked by the egoistic competition so greatly prized outside the household. The routine insistence in nineteenth and twentieth century discourse on the altruistic role of wives and the harmony of the ideal home, in which the husband could leave behind the strife of the jungle, contradicts any such view. Regarding the family as an entity helped to obscure the fact that when law dealt with families, it nonetheless continued the general practice of ignoring individual differences in power even though social expectations about conduct within the family were frankly inconsistent with expectations about behavior in other settings. Here, the entity metaphor serves double duty, at once supporting a conceptualization that works poorly and masking the effects of that theory on those whom it governs.

Finally, talk of family autonomy ignores the influence of law itself in creating the imbalances of power within the family. The allocation of labor by which women worked in the non-money sector of the economy was not adventitious. The principles of family autonomy supposed a harmonious relationship with certain (although sometimes changing) assignments of responsibility. An ideal family embodying those characteristics became a referent for law when it acted proscriptively and prescriptively. The divorce record research of both Nancy Cott and Robert Griswold reveal just how strong those expectations were and the ways in which they influenced the outcomes of cases. The notion of the family entity allowed courts to ignore manifestations of inequality during the marriage and suppressed the view that "natural" inequalities resulted from social rules enforced by public authority. The consequence was a belief that, upon divorce or separation, whatever inequalities emerged were the result of consent or incapacity on the wife's part rather than a situation created and due remediation by law.

Questions on the Family Entity

(1) *Dean Teitelbaum's argument generally.* Dean Teitelbaum's argument is an important introduction to some baffling problems. First, he forcefully directs our attention to a quandary that pervades family law and indeed law generally—the great difficulty that law has in conceptualizing groups and the law's consequent tendency to think of groups as though they were individuals. As Professor Dan Cohen writes, we are a

> society of organizations.... But whereas lawyers do recognize organizations as legal actors, they often tend to refer to them as if they were indistinguishable, from a legal point of view, from another familiar kind of "legal person," namely the individual human being.... Concepts, institutions, doctrines, and attitudes that originated in an individualistic context, and whose applicability to organizations is at best questionable, are frequently used indiscriminately and unreflectively to deal with organizations as well.

Meir Dan Cohen, *Rights, Persons, and Organizations: A Legal Theory for Bureaucratic Society* 5 (U Cal Press, 1986). Second, Dean Teitelbaum confronts us with the fuzziness of the border between "public" and "private." Third, he reminds us to consider the actual consequences of abstract rules.

Dean Teitelbaum not only addresses several general problems, he says significant things about some of the family-law questions with which we have been grappling. One way into his treatment of these questions is to ask what his primary point is. Is he suggesting that there is no such thing as family autonomy (since the law cannot help but make policy about the family) and that it is meaningless to talk about government intervention in the family (since such intervention is inevitable)? Is he saying it is pointless to talk about the family as an entity (since a family is undeniably a group of individuals)? Or is he making a more modest suggestion—that we shouldn't talk about family autonomy, government intervention, or the family as entity without being aware of the social complexity each of these terms attempts to summarize? What policy conclusions would follow from each interpretation of Dean Teitelbaum's arguments?

(2) *Dean Teitelbaum on the family as entity.* Dean Teitelbaum suggests that the idea of family as entity is delusionary because every time we purport to treat the family as an entity we are in fact confirming the power of one of the parties. Part of his evidence consists of cases allocating rights between parents and children. Is this evidence apt? When we talk about family autonomy in the context of parents and children, don't we fully intend and expect that parents will make decisions for children? As the Court said in *Parham v. J.R.*, 442 US 584, 602 (1979), "Our jurisprudence historically has reflected Western civili-

zation's concept of the family as a unit with broad parental authority over minor children." In the context of parents and children, then, are we really thinking about the family as an entity, or are we thinking about the choice between a decision made by the government and one made by parents? See Barbara Bennett Woodhouse, *"Who Owns the Child?": Meyer and Pierce and the Child as Property*, 33 Wm & Mary L Rev 995 (1992).

Dean Teitelbaum's other source of evidence for his suggestion that family law decisions confirm the power of a family member and not the family is surely more troubling. This is the evidence from cases like *McGuire. McGuire* is a strong case for Dean Teitelbaum, so probing Dean Teitelbaum's argument as it applies to *McGuire* may help us understand that argument better. Part of Dean Teitelbaum's argument is that when Mrs. McGuire "is left to her own resources in dealing with her husband, she is subject to his personal authority in seeking a car or a coat." On the basis of what you know about the case, how true is this? Mrs. McGuire did have some property of her own, although by no means as much as he did. She had $6,000 in a bank account and access to the income from an 80–acre farm. Judging from the rate of return on her husband's land, that income was probably around $1600 per year. (Around this time, an assistant professor at the University of Nebraska made approximately $3,000 annually.) These are economic resources. What other kinds of resources might she have had? Cf. William Shakespeare, *Macbeth*; Aristophanes, *Lysistrata*. Don't husbands and wives, because their lives are intertwined so closely in so many ways, live in a complicated web of power relationships which often give each spouse some kinds of power? Isn't it likely that there was social pressure on Mr. McGuire not to be such a skinflint? Mr. and Mrs. McGuire were probably not equally powerful. Mrs. McGuire's presence in court suggests that she was a good deal less powerful than he. But was she so powerless that she was simply "under his personal authority"? For one inquiry along these lines, see Douglas W. Allen and Margaret F. Brinig, *Sex, Property Rights and Divorce* (5 Eur J L & Econ 211, 1998).

Dean Teitelbaum also argues that Mrs. McGuire "lives in a Hobbesean state of nature where those with practical power may do much as they want with those who lack that power." But a Hobbesean state of nature is a world without law. Was that Mrs. McGuire's world? Mrs. McGuire knew that if she left her husband for cause, the law would then enforce his support obligation even though he would have lost her services and companionship. The law made non-support a basis for divorce. The law also protected her "retirement" (and thus freed her to spend some of her own money) by giving her dower rights in his land. In fact, isn't all this the kind of thing Dean Teitelbaum refers to when he says that the law "is in some sense constitutive of the family"? See Anthony Kronman, *Contract Law and the State of Nature*, 1 J L Econ & Organization 5 (1985).

The questions developed in the two preceding paragraphs may suggest that Dean Teitelbaum overstates his case when he talks about the law's "non-interference" as simply confirming the power of one member of the family. But is Dean Teitelbaum nevertheless right that none of the cases he cites "creates decisional rights in an entity"? One way of getting at this question is to ask what it would mean to "create decisional rights in an entity." Corporations, law firms, and churches, for example, can all be thought of as entities, but in what sense does the law create decisional rights in them, as opposed to the individuals that, directly or indirectly, make them up? Isn't it true for any of them, as with the family, that if the law leaves them to their own devices, the strong will be more likely to get their way than the weak? In short, don't Dean Teitelbaum's arguments apply to all entities? If so, don't his arguments prove too much, since treating corporations, law firms, and churches as entities embodies "the common-sense belief, embedded in ordinary language and common practices, in the unity and the reality of organizations," Meir Dan Cohen, *Rights, Persons, and Organizations: A Legal Theory for Bureaucratic Society* 26 (U Cal Press 1986), and is useful to the point of necessity in dealing legally with organizations?

One way to save Dean Teitelbaum's argument from this slippery-slope criticism is to find a relevant distinction between families and other kinds of entities. Is such a distinction that the latter commonly have established formal governmental mechanisms while the former rarely have? This is surely an important distinction, for it is the absence of any established decision-making procedures that makes it so troublesome to talk, as *Rhodes* does, of "family government." Nevertheless, does the presence or absence of formal procedures speak to Dean Teitelbaum's basic argument—that the idea of the family as an entity is delusionary because judicial decisions purporting to treat the family as an entity simply confirm the power of one of the parties? Formal procedures themselves, that is, can only provide channels through which one of the parties (or groups of parties) exercises power. Furthermore, formal procedures, like informal family decisions, have no necessary connection with equality of power among the parties: it is a cliche that managers, not owners, control large corporations; associates often have little power in a law firm, and even partners are not all equal; and many churches are governed by clerics, not congregations. Even if procedures establish complete formal equality, the reality of small-group or bureaucratic politics will always mean that some people are more influential than others. (This is what the sociologist Robert Michels called the iron law of oligarchy.) Indeed, one might say that the more unequal the relations between the members of the entity, the more useful it is to describe the entity as acting, since sufficient inequality can give the entity a unified, identifiable voice and direction.

In short, in all organizations power will be unequally distributed, but it can still be meaningful to think of organizations as entities. It is meaningful partly because a decision made through the interaction of a group of people—bureaucrats, lawyers, members of a congregation, or family members—who have come together for a particular purpose and who deal regularly with each other will generally differ from a decision made by any person acting alone. Even family members making a decision are likely to be influenced by their history within the family; by the web of social, economic, and psychologic relations referred to earlier; by their sense of the purposes families generally and their family particularly serve; by their expectation of dealing with the same relatives again; by the system of social and legal expectations about how family members will act; and so on.

Dean Teitelbaum warns that the metaphor we use in talking of the family as an entity can falsely confirm the power of a conceptual scheme and can obscure the real relationships underlying the metaphor. These dangers are surely genuine, but are they not dangers deliberately and even usefully risked? Consider the reason for the "non-intervention" doctrine. It is centrally based on two ideas: first, that the state cannot readily enforce decisions about families; second, that the state ought not make decisions for families. In other words, far from suggesting that the law has a conceptual scheme capable of dealing with family disputes, these rationales expressly state that the law ought not have such a conceptual scheme and could not effectively use it even if it had one.

The second rationale expressly states that the state *ought* not be interested in the real relationships underlying the metaphor—it states that if people want to live in grossly unequal relationships, they should be free to. Mrs. McGuire knew when she married Mr. McGuire that he had "a reputation for more than ordinary frugality" and that, given his age, he was probably not likely to change. There can be questions, of course, about whether such decisions are really "free." Perhaps Mrs. McGuire lived in social circumstances that so shaped her preferences that marrying Mr. McGuire was not a free choice. But who is free enough of social conditioning to decide what Mrs. McGuire's true preferences would or ought to be?

The non-intervention doctrine here, in other words, is closely equivalent to the doctrine that the First Amendment prevents courts from resolving disputes over church property where the dispute rests on questions of religious doctrine. That doctrine implicitly recognizes that intra-church struggles may result in injustices but concludes that injustices are a price worth paying for preventing the government from becoming entangled in questions of religious belief and church government. As with the family, the concern is both that the state ought not and cannot effectively regulate the church. The doctrine of non-intervention in the family, that is, strives exactly to avoid "ratifying" any particular social arrangement even while realizing that in some sense (it hopes only a very weak one) it must "ratify" every social arrangement it does not expressly prohibit.

Perhaps, though, this strategy exacts too high a price. Dean Teitelbaum seems to be implying that the economic disadvantages women as a class have commonly suffered are so great and so wrong that the law should not countenance them and that the disparities in power of wives and husbands are so great and so wrong that the law should end them.

However, one can accept the former argument and perhaps the latter without jettisoning the non-intervention doctrine. That is, one can work to end those economic disadvantages by social means (as the women's movement has sought in many ways to do) and by other kinds of legal means (anti-discrimination statutes or government–financed child care, for example). Whether one wants to jettison the non-intervention doctrine, then, would depend on one's view of the seriousness of women's economic and social disadvantages, of the possibility of ameliorating those disadvantages through general social and economic reform, and of the desirability of allowing people to run their lives in ways that seem wrong to the rest of us.

(3) *Dean Teitelbaum on "non-intervention."* This brings us to Dean Teitelbaum's argument that "non-intervention" is a meaningless idea, that "all forms of societal behavior—including facilitative rules and silence—involve policy choices." There is surely much truth in what Dean Teitelbaum says. Indeed, he is adverting to a problem encountered in a number of areas of law. Recall *Shelley v. Kraemer*, 334 US 1 (1948), in which the Supreme Court held that a court cannot enforce a racially restrictive covenant without violating the equal protection clause. The problem in the case was that, if the covenant had been understood as an arrangement between private parties, there would have been no state action, and thus the equal protection clause would not have been applicable. The Court found state action in the judicial decision and decree. But if there is state action every time a private decision is protected by law, a very great number of private decisions will become state action. The bottom of this slippery slope is the argument that since the state *could* prevent any particular private decision, the state always has acted, if only by not acting. Cf. *Burton v. Wilmington Parking Authority*, 365 US 715 (1961).

Judges and commentators have not worked out satisfactory solutions to this genre of conundrums. However, cannot one concede that Dean Teitelbaum's particular conundrum has some force without conceding that "non-intervention" in the family is meaningless? Isn't there a large difference between a rule that, for example, says that husbands and wives may not use contraceptives and the absence of any rule as to their sexual relations? Isn't there a large difference in the degree of actual governmental involvement the two approaches require? Won't husbands and wives themselves perceive the rule as intrusive (and won't its enforcement almost have to be literally intrusive) while perceiving the absence of a rule as not intrusive? The law may indeed be constitutive of families, but it doesn't constitute all the terms of the relationship except in the narrow sense of failing to constitute them.

SECTION 2. ALL MY WORLDLY GOODS: MARITAL PROPERTY AND ALIMONY

Faithfulness and constancy mean something else besides doing what is easiest and pleasantest to ourselves. They mean renouncing whatever is opposed to the reliance others have in us, whatever would cause misery to those whom the course of our lives has made dependent on us.

George Eliot
The Mill on the Floss

A. THE LAW OF MARITAL PROPERTY AND ALIMONY

The human condition is compounded of so much joy and so much sorrow that it is impossible to reckon how much a husband owes a wife or a wife a husband. It is an infinite debt, it can be paid only in eternity.

Johann von Goethe
Elective Affinities

The primary economic consequence of divorce is put in plain terms by the economist Victor R. Fuchs in *How We Live: An Economic Perspective on Americans from Birth to Death* 73 (Harv U Press, 1983): "Prior to divorce, two parents and their children share one household, thus benefiting from economics of scale in the use of space, equipment, and supplies, and from the cooperative endeavors of the partnership. After the divorce there are typically two households to maintain, the economies of scale are lost, and cooperative efforts at best become more difficult." In short, two apart cannot live as cheaply as two together. The following material charts the law's difficulties in coping with this brute fact.

In thinking about the settling of a couple's financial affairs on divorce, some important facts should be kept in mind. Roughly 90% of all divorces are resolved not by litigation, but by settlement. Such settlements are subject to judicial review, but this generally means little. (In light of the huge burden of domestic relations cases on courts—it is often said that 50% of the civil dockets in the United States are devoted to them—this is hardly surprising.)

It is also important to keep in mind that the law of marital property and alimony is irrelevant to most divorcing couples because they have nothing to divide. Professor Garrison, for example, emphasizes the "scarcity of valuable, individually owned assets. Less than half of the surveyed husbands owned property worth as much as $2500 even in the relatively wealthy contested sample; only about a third of the group owned property worth $10,000." Marsha Garrison, *Good Intentions Gone Awry: The Impact of New York's Equitable Distribution Law on Divorce Outcomes,* 57 Brooklyn L Rev 621, 657–58 (1991). Even in a sample of people whose divorces were contested and who were relatively wealthy, the median net worth (assets minus debts) was $23,591. A substantial number of sample couples, indeed, had negative net worth....

(1) The Traditional Law of Marital Property

Before we study today's marital property law, we need some sense of traditional marital property law, since that is what today's law reflects and reforms. Traditional marital property law had two categories—separate and community property systems. Each jurisdiction worked a somewhat different variation on the system it adopted, and each jurisdiction developed an elaborate body of law to resolve the many difficulties created by the combined exigencies of economic and family life. What you are about to read therefore generalizes prodigiously and describes the ideal type of each system, not the actual working of either one.

In separate property jurisdictions—those following the common law as modified by the Married Women's Property Acts—each spouse was taken to own property independently of the other. Spouses could, of course, own property jointly—as joint tenants, tenants in common, or tenants by the entirety—or they could enter into joint business arrangements and thus acquire property concurrently. Spouses could give each other gifts. But the basic principle was that what a spouse acquired separately a spouse owned separately. (Of course, in the hurly-burly and heedlessness of married life, questions about what was acquired separately and concurrently could become hopelessly difficult even where, *per impossibile*, evidence of a transaction was preserved.) Each spouse managed his or her own property. On the death of one spouse, the other was generally entitled to choose between taking under that spouse's will or taking an elective share, that is, receiving a statutorily determined fixed proportion (usually a third) of the estate.

In community property jurisdictions (of which there were at one time eight), the spouses each had a half-interest in community property. Roughly speaking, community property was property that was not brought into the marriage and that was not given or bequeathed to one spouse during the marriage. The basic idea was that acquests—what spouses acquired during the marriage by their efforts—were acquired by the efforts of both and thus should belong to both. Spouses in a community property jurisdiction had the equivalent of a tenancy in common (each had an undivided half interest, there was no right of survivorship) except that neither had a right of partition. Management schemes varied, and at one time the husband controlled the community property (and each spouse controlled his or her own separate property), but the core principle became that both spouses controlled community property. On the death of one spouse, the survivor retained ownership of half the community property. For this reason, there were no further protections for a disinherited spouse.

One can summarize the difference between separate and community property jurisdictions by saying that, in separate property jurisdictions property "earned" by one of the spouses during marriage belonged to that spouse, while in community property jurisdictions such property belonged equally to both. However, even in separate property jurisdictions spouses could hold property concurrently, and even in community property states some means of acquiring property made that property separately owned. Further, both systems essentially were default mechanisms that could be modified by private contracts. Antenuptial agreements were particularly important in community property states.

For most people, the marital property scheme mattered only on divorce. In principle, both separate property and community property systems had a common advantage in divorce situations—predictability. In principle, both systems embodied worthy social goals: separate property systems let spouses arrange their own economic affairs as they wished; community property recognized the mutuality that has long been an ideal of marriage. Let us briefly see, then, how the two systems handled divorce.

In principle, the court in a separate property jurisdiction allocated the property to which an individual spouse had title to that spouse and divided jointly owned property between the spouses. In other words, the court's function in principle was to work out who owned what and to confirm that ownership lay in that person. In practice, of course, it was often baffling to tell who owned what, especially since equitable ideas about ownership often had to be employed. Equitable ideas came into play, for example, when the spouses' intent as to ownership was unclear or when it was necessary to prevent one spouse from treating the other inequitably. Such ideas could be used when, for example, one spouse had made a gift to another, one spouse could be thought of as holding property for the use of the other, when spouses had made some kind of agreement about ownership when the property was acquired, and so on. For a statutory attempt to sort out property holdings, see 750 Ill Comp Stat Ann 5/503 (2005). Furthermore, some jurisdictions had statutes allowing courts to divide even separately owned property as the court saw fit to achieve an equitable result, and in some jurisdictions marital fault could be considered in allocating property. Rules about the division of property were further muddled by the tendency of courts to blur the distinction between dividing property (in theory purely an inquiry into who owns what), awarding alimony (in theory an inquiry into what support obligations one spouse owes the other after divorce and thus into what property may be taken from one spouse and given to the other), and setting child support (in theory an inquiry into what support obligations both spouses owe their child and thus what property—often a house—may be taken from the non-custodial parent and given to the custodial parent).

In community property jurisdictions, the court's job was to ascertain who owned what separately and then to divide evenly the community property. The court's job was no easier in community property than in separate property jurisdictions, if only because the former jurisdictions spouses could still own separate property. Questions thus readily arose about whether something was separate or community property. Further, courts in some jurisdictions could allocate community property to achieve an equitable result or to consider marital fault. Finally, courts in community property jurisdictions could blur the distinction between property, alimony, and child support.

In the last few decades, both systems have been criticized. One virtue of the separate property system, as you will recall, is that it could give couples freedom to arrange their economic affairs as they wished. It has increasingly been thought, however, that that freedom has disadvantaged wives. The argument has been that, in a society where men are likelier to bring in an income than women, are likely to be better paid than women, and are likely to know more about financial affairs, ownership of property is likelier to be in the name of the husband than the wife. Furthermore, the view has become increasingly favored that the husband's higher earnings are possible only because of the wife's uncompensated but economically significant contributions to his career and their household. The criticism, in other words, pointed to the problem of the wife who had been married for some time, who had lost or never acquired skills of a kind rewarded on the labor market, who had not been employed outside the home but had been fully employed raising children and keeping house, and who would after the divorce be the custodian of the couple's children.

It has also been increasingly thought that community property systems likewise had the faults of their virtues. In the great number of divorces in which neither spouse had much property, the rigidity of the community property system made it hard to work out equitable resolutions of the spouses' past and future economic problems and thus hard to embody the principle of marital mutuality. For example, a divorcing couple often had to sell their home in order to divide its value. Further, while a major advantage of community property systems ought to be their predictability, their complexity had become so baroque that predictability was elusive.

As divorce became more common, the problems of both systems became more significant. With both systems under attack, the time was ripe for reform.

(2) Equitable Distribution

The solution to which many jurisdictions have moved is usually called "equitable distribution." The

> sharp dichotomy between common law and community property traditions no longer prevails in the United States. All the common-law states now allow the divorce court to distribute spousal property between the divorcing parties on a basis other than common-law principles of ownership, under a doctrine known generally as "equitable distribution." Five of the eight community property states also instruct their divorce courts to divide the community property between the spouses "equitably" (rather than "equally"). Equitable distribution is the dominant rule today, followed everywhere but in the three "equal division" community property states.

ALI, *Introduction*, *Principles of the Law of Family Dissolution: Analysis and Recommendations* (2002). Alternative A of section 307 of the UMDA typifies the further reaches of the equitable distribution principle, and it is reproduced below. (Also reproduced below is Alternative B of section 307. How do the two differ?)

UNIFORM MARRIAGE AND DIVORCE ACT

Alternative A [This alternative is identical to Mont Code Ann § 40–4–202 (2005).]

[SECTION 307. [*Disposition of Property.*]

(a) In a proceeding for dissolution of a marriage, legal separation, or disposition of property following a decree of dissolution of marriage or legal separation by a court which lacked personal jurisdiction over the absent spouse or lacked jurisdiction to dispose of the property, the court, without regard to marital misconduct, shall, and in a proceeding for legal separation may, finally equitably apportion between the parties the property and assets belonging to either or both however and whenever acquired, and whether the title thereto is in the name of the husband or wife or both. In making apportionment the court shall consider the duration of the marriage, any prior marriage of either party, any antenuptial agreement of the parties, the age, health, station, occupation, amount and sources of income, vocational skills, employability, estate, liabilities, and needs of each of the parties, custodial provisions, whether the apportionment is in lieu of or in addition to maintenance, and the opportunity of each for future acquisition of capital assets and income. The court shall also consider the contribution or dissipation of each party in the acquisition, preservation, depreciation, or appreciation in value of the respective estates, and as the contribution of a spouse as a homemaker or to the family unit.

(b) In the proceeding the court may protect and promote the best interests of the children by setting aside a portion of the jointly and separately held estates of the parties in a separate fund or trust for the support, maintenance, education, and general welfare of any minor, dependent, or incompetent children of the parties.]

Alternative B [This alternative is identical to Ariz Rev Stat § 25.318 (1993).]

[SECTION 307. [*Disposition of Property.*] In a proceeding for dissolution of the marriage, legal separation, or disposition of property following a decree of dissolution of the marriage or legal dissolution by a court which lacked personal jurisdiction over the absent spouse or lacked jurisdiction to dispose of the property, the court shall assign each spouse's separate property to that spouse. It also shall divide community property, without regard to marital misconduct, in just proportions after considering all relevant factors including:

(1) contribution of each spouse to acquisition of the marital property, including contribution of a spouse as homemaker;

(2) value of the property set apart to each spouse;

(3) duration of the marriage; and

(4) economic circumstances of each spouse when the division of property is to become effective, including the desirability of awarding the family home or the right to live therein for a reasonable period to the spouse having custody of any children.]

(1) As you will have observed, Notes on Section 307 Alternative A differs from both separate-property and community-property systems in that, for purposes of allocating property on divorce, it (in principle at least) abolishes separate property. The court may, on divorce, allocate the property of either spouse to the other. Few jurisdictions go as far as the UMDA: some jurisdictions allow the court to divide only property (other than gifts or inheritances) acquired during the marriage. This has been called a "deferred community" system. And some jurisdictions say property should be divided equally, not equitably. Nevertheless, the basic principle behind these reformed systems is often said to be that marriage should be recognized as an economic partnership to which both spouses contribute. See, e.g., Bea Smith, *The Partnership Theory of Marriage: A Borrowed Solution Fails*, 68 Tex L Rev 689 (1990). This is expressed in Alternative A in the requirement that the court consider "the contribution of a spouse as a homemaker or to the family unit."

(2) Like the movement to no-fault divorce, the reform of property-division statutes had to survive constitutional attack. The argument that property division impairs vested property rights was rejected in, for instance, *Kujawinski v. Kujawinski*, 376 NE2d 1382 (Ill 1978); and *Eggemeyer v. Eggemeyer*, 554 SW2d 137 (Tex 1977).

Notes on What Equitable Distribution Means

Justice Holmes rightly said in his dissent in *Lochner*, "general propositions do not decide concrete cases. The decision will depend on a judgment or intuition more subtle than any articulate major premise." Few principles are more general than the principle of "equitable distribution." Of course, the UMDA purports to guide courts by listing (in Section 307) the factors courts are supposed to use in interpreting that term. But guidelines of that sort are hardly very confining or even very informative. Perhaps, then, we can give you a somewhat more tangible sense what "equitable distribution" might mean by describing several cases decided under an equitable distribution statute—Va Code 20–107.3 (1995).

In *Thomas v. Thomas*, 1996 WL 679985 (Va Ct App), the spouses kept their money separate. Each was supposed to pay specified expenses. Mr. Thomas was supposed to pay the mortgage, real estate taxes, insurance, and utility bills, although on numerous occasions he failed to do so. Mrs. Thomas, who was employed throughout the thirty-year marriage, cared for the parties' children, maintained the home, and supported her husband's career by entertaining his colleagues. She eventually sued him for divorce on grounds of cruelty and constructive desertion and was awarded seventy percent of the equity in the marital home (the couple's most substantial asset). The court noted that she made all the nonmonetary and many of the monetary contributions to the marital residence and that she had saved the home from foreclosure and maintained it for the family. The court's opinion does not separately consider each factor.

In *Lightburn v. Lightburn*, 1998 WL 169499 (Va Ct App), the parties' marriage lasted for only a year, but litigation involving equitable distribution went twice through the appellate system and took more than five years. The wife was a psychiatric counsellor who left her job at a private psychiatric hospital to join her husband in another town. When the marriage failed, she pulled up stakes once again and became a private counsellor. During the marriage, the husband retitled a parcel of the property he'd owned prior to the marriage as a tenancy by the entireties (which made the spouses joint tenants). Ultimately the appellate court decided she deserved a one-third interest in the marital home (which was located on the "entireties" property). The court wrote:

> Finally, we hold that the evidence was sufficient to support the trial court's factual finding regarding wife's non-monetary contribution to the family. The evidence regarding the personal and professional concessions made by wife to join husband at the marital residence and the associated practical inconveniences was sufficient to support the trial court's finding that her relocation constituted a significant non-monetary contribution to the well-being of the family.

Finally, in *Masri v. Masri*, 1999 WL 58604 (Va Cir Ct), the husband, a psychiatrist, supported the family during the first twenty-five years of their thirty-seven year marriage. All this changed in 1988:

> In 1988, Dr. Masri, who made all of the financial, business, and investment decisions for the family, experienced a rapid decline in his financial affairs. He made and engaged in what proved to be unwise investment decisions, bad loans, and failed joint ventures. By the end of 1991, the parties were in dire financial straits, most of their assets had been liquidated to keep the family "afloat," and Ms. Masri was forced to return to outside employment as a psychiatric nurse. Their fortunes continued to decline, however, and in 1993 they filed for bankruptcy. They lost their marital home in Colonial Heights, a cottage in Nags Head, North Carolina, a home in Lake Tahoe, Nevada, and, according to Ms. Masri, "everything else." In 1994, Dr. Masri was investigated for Medicaid and insurance fraud. He eventually pled guilty to one count of mail fraud and spent five months in federal prison. He also lost his medical license. While he was in prison, Ms. Masri did the best she could to pay the family bills, and she visited Dr. Masri every week.
>
> In 1995, Dr. Masri's medical license was returned to him. Although he was not allowed to participate in insurance plans because of his felony conviction, he was allowed to see patients. With their combined incomes, he and Ms. Masri were able to pay their bills and, although not nearly as financially comfortable as they had been, appeared to be making things work. On May 26, 1996, however, Ms. Masri returned home from work and found that Dr. Masri had left and that most of his clothes were gone. It was not until her daughter called her that she

learned that Dr. Masri had left the country and gone to the Middle East, where he is from. Although he had been making plans to leave for several months, he had given Ms. Masri no notice of his plans, and had never said anything to her to make her aware of his impending departure. As a result, Ms. Masri was suddenly forced to deal single-handedly with all of the accounts from Dr. Masri's psychiatric practice and all of the parties' marital debts, including an Internal Revenue Service lien of nearly $400,000 that resulted from erroneous refunds previously paid to the parties and spent before the error was detected.

The court said it consulted the statutory factors and awarded Dr. Masri's I.R.A. to Mrs. Masri and required him to repay various marital debts. This left the Masris with roughly equivalent shares of their property:

> In light of the history of this marriage, it is clear that [the statutory] factors are in Ms. Masri's favor. Indeed, this court can think of no other case which has ever come before it in which the statutory factors so heavily predominated in favor of one of the parties. From supporting the family during Dr. Masri's medical residency to sponsoring his application for U.S. citizenship to standing by him and visiting him in jail to paying the family bills when he suddenly and unilaterally left the country, Ms. Masri has gone far beyond what anyone should expect of a spouse. In fact, if the purpose of equitable distribution were to punish a guilty spouse or to reward a good one, the court would probably be justified in awarding 100% of the marital property to Ms. Masri. Punishment, however, is not the purpose of equitable distribution. Instead, it is to compensate a spouse for his or her contribution to the acquisition and care of marital property during the marriage.

We have sketched these three cases to probe the meaning of the principle of equitable distribution. How much do you think the judges in these cases were actually guided by the general proposition? By the guidelines that are supposed to shape their decisions? One test of those questions is to ask whether equitable distribution statutes accomplished the purposes for which they were introduced. This is not the kind of question law professors like to ask because answering it would require them to do degrading things like empirical research. A noble exception to this deplorable rule, however, is Marsha Garrison, *Good Intentions Gone Awry: The Impact of New York's Equitable Distribution Law on Divorce Outcomes,* 57 Brooklyn L Rev 621 (1991).

Professor Garrison reports that equitable distribution was introduced in New York in large part to produce awards more favorable to women. She concludes, however, that, "[o]verall, there was little change in the percentage distribution of marital property after the passage of the equitable distribution law." Worse, "[i]n contrast to the relative stability in property distribution before and after the equitable distribution law, dramatic change in the frequency and duration of alimony awards occurred after the passage of the new law. Over the research period, the proportion of cases in which alimony was awarded in the three research counties declined by fully 43%." And an "even more dramatic change occurred in the duration of alimony awards. In 1978 approximately four out of five alimony awards were permanent. In 1984 about half that number were; the majority of awards were for a limited duration. The change was, again, statistically significant and consistent across case categories and across counties." Professor Garrison found it particularly "ironic that the equitable distribution law has diminished the alimony prospects of long-married, economically disadvantaged wives—the consensus case for long-term alimony—more than those of any other group." Finally, to add insult to injury, "[a]fter the passage of the equitable distribution law, the length of the average contested proceeding increased" thus apparently driving the cost of divorce up.

Why did the law fail to do what it was intended to do? Professor Garrison believes that

> [t]he story of New York's equitable distribution law is one of how good intentions, uninformed by an awareness of current outcomes and codified in vague and uncertain directives, will produce confused, inconsistent, and unexpected results. The law was predicated on the assumption that divorced wives would benefit from a property distribution law because husbands owned the valuable property and wives thus failed to get more than a small property share at divorce. For the typical divorcing couple, both of these assumptions were erroneous: the average husband's individual net worth was scarcely more than that of his wife, and the typical wife already received half of the couple's meager assets.

Equitable distribution in New York may have failed of its purpose for other reasons as well. Some judges may have resisted it (unconsciously or not). But even judges who tried to obey the legislature's instructions may have found them opaque. Thus "[o]utcomes were highly variable under the new law and not significantly correlated with factors, such as marital duration or income, that might expectedly produce disparate results." In contrast, at least one factor the legislature probably did not think about seems to have been quite significant, since "whether the parties were represented by counsel was another, highly significant predictor of an alimony award. In 1984, for example, 30% of wives were awarded alimony when both parties were represented by counsel, while not one alimony award was made when neither party was represented by counsel."

It is natural to suppose law is like the centurion and can do as it will: "I say to this man, Go, and he goeth; and to another, Come, and he cometh; and to my servant, Do this, and he doeth it." But a thousand years ago, King Canute tried to disillusion his courtiers about his efficacy by commanding the waves to stop beating. And more than sixty years ago, Harry Truman predicted of Dwight Eisenhower, "He'll sit here, and he'll say, 'Do this! Do that!' *And nothing will happen.* Poor Ike—it won't be a bit like the Army. He'll find it very frustrating."

It is natural to suppose law can do as it will because law has imposing powers. It can spend. It can fine. It can imprison. It can kill. So armed, surely it can command obedience. Sometimes it can. But surprisingly often, laws disappoint. They rarely fail completely. But, with dismaying frequency, laws betray the expectations of their promulgators and their advocates.

You spend much of your time in law school reading, thinking, and talking about what legal doctrine ought to say. Does it matter? Sometimes. But, as the material we have just reviewed may suggest, sometimes it does not. And we often don't know when it does and when it does not. But as you examine the statutes and cases that follow, in this chapter and throughout this book, it is worth asking yourself whether the rules they announce are likely to have their intended effect.

(3) The Law of Alimony

The English law from which American family law descended was organized around the principle that marriage was a sacrament which consecrated a life-time commitment. Divorce was therefore not permitted. A marriage could, it was true, be annulled if it was defective (if, for example, an impediment like consanguinity existed at the time of the marriage). But the closest thing to modern divorce, a divorce *a mensa et thoro* (from bed and board), was merely a judicially supervised separation in which the spouses remained married and thus could not remarry. Because marriage was a sacrament, the law of marriage was until as late as 1857 administered by the ecclesiastical, not the royal, courts. (Toward the end of the seventeenth century it became possible to get a divorce by an act of Parliament—obviously an expensive and arduous undertaking, and even such a divorce could be obtained only after an ecclesiastical court had granted a divorce *a mensa et thoro* on grounds of adultery.) Since a divorce *a mensa et thoro* did not dissolve the marriage, it did not dissolve the husband's duty to support his wife, and the ecclesiastical courts enforced that duty after husband and wife were separated, assuming the wife's fault had not caused the separation. This was important, since the husband continued to control the wife's property.

As American family law began to emerge, it came to differ from the English law in two important ways. It had no ecclesiastical courts, and it permitted divorce *a vinculo matrimonii* (from the bonds of matrimony). Nevertheless, the American statutes borrowed the principle of alimony from English law. This left alimony without a clear basis, since alimony had been an expression of the husband's duty to support his wife, a duty that made no sense when he was no longer her husband.

Of course, our legal system would be remarkably different if its rules all rested on clearly understood principles, and the obscurity of alimony did not prevent it from being awarded in the United States. There were several (often unarticulated) reasons for this. First was a sense that, even though divorce was legally available, marriage was morally a lifelong commitment. (In the nineteenth century some scrupulous divorced people declined to remarry.) Second was the feeling that a husband who had caused a divorce ought not by his fault escape from the financial obligations he had assumed on marriage. Third was the discovery that dividing marital property was hard where the couple's assets were few or were otherwise not readily divisible and that alimony provided a kind of property division in monthly installments. Fourth, women's employment opportunities were poor, and there were few government programs to help the indigent. The fifth reason for continuing to award alimony despite the absence of a sound doctrinal basis was that, since mothers were commonly given custody of the children, alimony could be a form of child support.

Like the rest of family law, the law of alimony has changed significantly in recent decades. You should understand the traditional rules of alimony to see what has changed and because the traditional rules still influence some jurisdictions and are still law in others. Traditionally, then, decisions about alimony were confided to the discretion of the trial court, which was encumbered only by a few guidelines. First, the wife was entitled to enough alimony to live according to the standard established in the marriage, although her assets and her ability to earn an income generally could be considered in reducing the award. Second, the award was also to be determined by the husband's ability to pay. Third, in some jurisdictions alimony was unavailable where the husband was the successful plaintiff; in other jurisdictions alimony could be reduced or denied where the wife was at fault; and in yet others the husband's fault justified increasing alimony. Alimony awards could be for lump sums, but usually were not. Decrees could be modified when circumstances changed, and alimony ceased when the wife remarried.

The direction of change in alimony law is indicated by the UMDA, which calls alimony "maintenance," and a case from the Florida Supreme Court.

UNIFORM MARRIAGE AND DIVORCE ACT

Section 308. [*Maintenance.*] [This section appears as Mont Code Ann § 40–4–203 (2005).]

(a) In a proceeding for dissolution of marriage, legal separation, or maintenance following a decree of dissolution of the marriage by a court which lacked personal jurisdiction over the absent spouse, the court may grant a maintenance order for either spouse, only if it finds that the spouse seeking maintenance:

(1) Lacks sufficient property to provide for his reasonable needs; and

(2) Is unable to support himself through appropriate employment or is the custodian of a child whose condition or circumstances make it appropriate that the custodian not be required to seek employment outside the home.

(b) The maintenance order shall be in amounts and for periods of time the court deems just, without regard to marital misconduct, and after considering all relevant factors including:

(1) The financial resources of the party seeking maintenance, including marital property apportioned to him, his ability to meet his needs independently, and the extent to which a provision for support of a child living with the party includes a sum for that party as custodian;

(2) The time necessary to acquire sufficient education or training to enable the party seeking maintenance to find appropriate employment;

(3) The standard of living established during the marriage;

(4) The duration of the marriage;

(5) The age and the physical and emotional condition of the spouse seeking maintenance; and

(6) The ability of the spouse from whom maintenance is sought to meet his needs while meeting those of the spouse seeking maintenance.

PFOHL v. PFOHL

District Court of Appeal of Florida, Third District, 1977
345 S2d 371

HUBBART, JUDGE.

This is an action for dissolution of marriage in which the husband was awarded lump sum and rehabilitative alimony as well as attorneys' fees. The wife appeals and the husband cross appeals, raising questions which go to the propriety and sufficiency of such awards.

On May 28, 1966, the parties were married. At the time of the marriage, the wife owned a one third interest in a trucking company given to her by her father, which interest she sold in 1972 for seven million dollars. The husband had no assets going into the marriage except for a one half interest in one hundred shares of Sears Roebuck stock. He had been employed for four and one half years as a toy salesman for Strombecker Toy Co. earning a salary of approximately $9,000–$10,000 a year plus expenses and bonus. He resigned this job after one and a half years of marriage to satisfy the wife's wishes. She did not like his travelling which was necessary to pursue his line of work, and refused to move to New York with him to accept a promotion. Prior to the marriage, he had finished three years of college and received an honorable discharge from the marines. The couple had two sons, now ages 8 and 2.

The parties lived a life of extreme luxury and comfort during a marriage which lasted nine years prior to the parties' final separation. The wife supported the family at first through contributions from her father, and from 1972–75 from her own separate estate.

Both the husband and wife had an unlimited joint checking account. Both had access to the wife's extensive properties: a one hundred acre farm in Elgin, Illinois, purchased for $500,000; a five bedroom house in

Chicago; and two homes in Bal Harbour, Florida, purchased for $140,000 and $60,000 respectively. Both had access to a six bedroom home and an eighty acre farm in Crystal Lake, Illinois, in which the wife gave the husband one half interest.

The husband had all the major credit cards with unlimited credit plus charge accounts at many luxury stores where he regularly shopped. He maintained extensive clothing in their Florida and Illinois homes. Several times each year he paid substantial entry fees so he could participate in celebrity golf tournaments such as the Bob Hope and Andy Williams Classics.

The parties were members of seven luxury country clubs in Chicago and Miami for which the wife paid substantial initial membership sums and all the subsequent dues and bills incurred. They travelled extensively throughout the country and the world, and because of the wife's substantial interest in race horses, routinely travelled to the Kentucky Derby and other races in New York, California and Illinois. They were attended by servants in their homes in Florida and Illinois. They entertained extensively at home and various clubs at which they were members. They had full access to the seventy-five foot family yacht on which they maintained a full crew, contributing $3,000 a month to the operation of the vessel. In addition, they had two late model Cadillacs, a Buick station wagon and a speedboat.

The husband estimated that his living expenses during the marriage were over $5,000 a month. The wife estimated that the family's total monthly living expenses were approximately $15,000 including income taxes. The wife could not have provided the foregoing fantasy-land existence for the husband on anything less than enormous resources. At the time of the final hearing, she had a net worth of $4,250,000 including cash and marketable securities of $3,325,000 plus an annual net income of $200,000.

During the marriage the husband dabbled, but never seriously participated in, various business ventures provided by his wife's family. He was a figurehead president of the Antioch Insurance Agency for four years. Following this venture, he was a treasurer and director in the Antioch Savings and Loan Association from which he was eventually removed for failure to attend meetings.

The parties ceased living together as husband and wife on May 6, 1975. At that time the wife forbade the husband to return to their home in Florida or to live in any other of her properties. She removed his clothes therefrom and the husband has remained unemployed living with friends at a drastically reduced living style ever since. He unsuccessfully sought employment on several occasions in Florida and Chicago. There is evidence that the husband presently suffers from a mental disorder requiring professional treatment, but that at 37 he is in excellent physical health.

At the time of the dissolution, the husband held the following assets, all provided to him by the wife during the marriage: an undivided one half interest in an eighty acre farm in Crystal Lake, Illinois, his interest valued at $160,000; a 1974 and 1975 Cadillac valued together at a total of $12,000; and a twenty-five foot power boat valued at $6,000. In addition, he leaves the marriage with his original one half interest in one hundred shares of Sears Roebuck stock valued at $6,000 and an 80 percent ownership interest in a Ft. Lauderdale lounge known as the "Filling Station." The husband owes the wife $60,000 for the purchase of this lounge which at the time of the final hearing was up for sale for $110,000. He, therefore, has approximately $200,000 in assets, almost all of which are non-liquid and non-income producing.

The wife filed a petition for dissolution of marriage, seeking the dissolution of the marriage, custody of the parties' two minor children and an adjudication of her rights as to the $60,000 loan which she had made to the husband. The husband answered denying that the marriage was irretrievably broken as well as the allegations concerning the loan. He requested alimony, attorneys fees and suit monies. The wife replied denying the husband's need for alimony, suit monies, and attorneys fees, which reply was amended to assert adultery as a defense to his claim for alimony, suit monies and attorneys fees.

The case came on for final hearing in which the trial court heard extensive testimony and reviewed certain physical evidence. Thereafter, the court entered a final judgment dissolving the marriage, awarding custody of the children to the wife with rights of visitation for the husband and requiring the husband to pay the wife $60,000 from his share of the proceeds obtained from the sale of the "Filling Station" lounge in Ft. Lauderdale. These parts of the final judgment are not contested by either party on this appeal.

The court further ordered the wife to pay the husband $30,000 lump sum alimony and $5,000 a month rehabilitative alimony for eighteen months. Both parties contest these awards.

At a subsequent hearing, the court took testimony and heard arguments as to reasonable attorneys fees. Thereafter the court awarded $30,000 in attorneys fees and $1,191.36 in suit monies for the husband. The wife contests this award.

I

The major question presented for review is whether it is an abuse of discretion in a dissolution of marriage action for a trial court to award the husband $30,000 in lump sum alimony and $5,000 a month rehabilitative alimony for 18 months when: (1) the wife has a net worth of $4,250,000; (2) the parties shared an extremely high standard of living at first supported by the wife based on contributions to her from her father and thereafter based entirely on her own wealth during a nine year marriage; (3) the husband is 37 years old, unemployed with limited employment skills, in good physical, but impaired mental health, and in possession of approximately $200,000 in assets most of which were received during the marriage from the wife.

Both parties contend that the trial judge abused his discretion. The wife argues that the husband is not entitled to any alimony; the husband argues that the amount of lump sum alimony is inadequate and that permanent, rather than rehabilitative alimony should have been awarded. We reject all these contentions and hold that the alimony awards herein were well within the discretion of the trial judge to make under the circumstances of this case.

A

Alimony has been traditionally considered an allowance which a husband is required to make in order to maintain his wife in the event of separation or divorce and is based on the common law obligation of a husband to support his wife. In determining the amount of such alimony, the courts have established two criteria: (1) the husband's ability to pay, and (2) the needs of the wife, taking into consideration the standard of living shared by the parties to the marriage.

Quite properly, these are criteria of the broadest nature, not susceptible to a precise formula automatically translatable into dollars and cents. We are dealing with a tragically human problem which touches peoples' lives during a period of immense personal crisis. One cannot dispense substantial justice in such explosive cases as if the answer lies in a computer or a rigid rule book. Mathematical exactness is neither possible nor desirable. The trial court of necessity has a wide discretion to apply the established criteria in fashioning a fair and equitable alimony award in the infinite variety of cases which come before it. Absent a showing that the trial court exercised this discretion arbitrarily or unfairly, alimony awards made pursuant to such criteria must be sustained on appeal.

The so-called "no fault" divorce law enacted by the Florida Legislature in 1971, represents a significant, but not totally radical departure from the historic conception of alimony. Section 61.08, Florida Statutes (1975) provides as follows:

> "(1) In a proceeding for dissolution of marriage, the court may grant alimony to either party, which alimony may be rehabilitative or permanent in nature. In any award of alimony, the court may order periodic payments or payments in lump sum or both. The court may consider the adultery of a spouse and the circumstances thereof in determining whether alimony shall be awarded to such spouse and the amount of alimony, if any, to be awarded to such spouse.
>
> (2) In determining a proper award of alimony, the court may consider any factor necessary to do equity and justice between the parties."

Under this statute, it is provided for the first time that a wife may be required to support her husband through alimony payments. This is in keeping with the current social trend toward establishing a more equitable relationship between the sexes. The First District Court of Appeal pointed out in *Beard v. Beard*, 262 So.2d 269 (Fla. 1st DCA 1972):

> "In this era of women's liberation movements and enlightened thinking, we have almost universally come to appreciate the fallacy of treating the feminine members of our society on anything but a basis of complete equality with the opposite sex. Any contrary view would be completely anachronistic. In this day and time, women are well educated and trained in the arts, sciences, and professions as are their male counterparts. The law properly protects them in their right to independently acquire, encumber, accumulate, and alienate property at will. They now occupy a position of equal partners in the family relationship resulting from marriage, and more often than not contribute a full measure to the economic well-being of the family unit." *Id.* at 271–72.

The First District Court of Appeal further elaborated on this theme in *Thigpen v. Thigpen*, 277 So.2d 583 (Fla. 1st DCA 1973) as follows:

> "The new concept of marriage relation implicit in the so-called 'no fault' divorce law enacted by the legislature in 1971 places both parties to the marriage on a basis of complete equality as partners sharing equal rights and obligations in the marriage relationship and sharing equal burdens in the event of dissolution." *Id.* at 585.

Although this historic change in alimony law is far-reaching and we have not yet chartered its full effects, we can at least begin by stating that a husband's entitlement to alimony must stand on the same criteria as that of a wife. To be entitled to alimony, the husband must show a financial ability by the wife to pay for such an award coupled with a demonstrated need of the husband for support, taking into consideration the standard of living shared by the parties to the marriage.

Although in most marriages, the husband remains the sole provider of the family, with the wife making the home and raising the children, if any, an increasing number of marriages do not fit this mold. In some marriages, both parties work and jointly support the family, although the degree of support by either party may vary. In others, the wife is the sole support of the family unit with the husband fulfilling some non-economic role. It is in these non-traditional type marriages where the question of alimony for the husband may arise.

In the instant case, we are faced with such a non-traditional type of marriage. Although neither party did any serious work to financially support the family unit, the wife, rather than the husband, was the sole provider in this marriage. The husband resigned his employment at the request of the wife to live a life of luxury with his wife and family. Such fabulous wealth on the part of a woman who supports a marriage in which the husband is of modest means is not unknown in our society, but it certainly presents a case of unusual dimensions which we think the trial judge handled most reasonably upon the marriage's dissolution under the traditional criteria for awarding alimony.

B

As to the first criterion for awarding alimony, it is undisputed that the wife easily has the financial ability to pay for the alimony award in this case. She has a financial worth in excess of $4,000,000 and regularly maintains a checking account considerably greater than the total $120,000 alimony award for the husband. The award is therefore immune from attack as being beyond the financial means of the wife.

As to the second criterion for awarding alimony, the lump sum and rehabilitative alimony awards herein were commensurate with the need of the husband for temporary, although not permanent support, taking into consideration the standard of living shared by the parties to the marriage. The husband's limited employment opportunities, his impaired mental condition, and the very high standard of living to which the wife accustomed the husband to live during the marriage, are all critical factors in sustaining the trial court's exercise of discretion in fashioning the alimony award in this case.

The husband was a toy salesman for six years earning a modest salary which job he gave up at the request of the wife to devote full time to his life and the wife and family after a year and a half of marriage. Save for his limited service mainly as a figurehead in the businesses of his wife's family, he has been out of the employment market for the last seven and a half years of the marriage. At the time of the final hearing, he was unemployed, living with friends at a drastically reduced life style, having unsuccessfully attempted on a number of occasions to obtain employment, since the wife barred him from the marital homes. This impairment in a spouse's otherwise modest employment capacities caused in part by the supporting spouse's insistence that such work be terminated in favor of the family is a significant factor in sustaining an alimony award.

Added to this, is the husband's impaired mental condition. According to the uncontradicted testimony of an industrial psychologist, Dr. Marquit, the husband is suffering from a mental disorder which will require at least a year of intensive psychotherapy at considerable expense. He further testified that at present the husband is ill-suited for the employment market. We are in no position to second guess the trial judge's acceptance of this testimony based on his personal evaluation of Dr. Marquit as well as that of the husband. Certainly it is not beyond the realm of reasonable inference for the trial judge to have concluded that the husband's nine years of leisure class idleness followed by an abrupt end to his male Cinderella existence when the wife literally threw him out of her home, at least partially brought on his current mental problems for which some period of rehabilitation is necessary. Such mental impairment, although temporary rather than permanent in nature, is a significant factor in sustaining an alimony award.

The husband's financial needs must also be measured in part by taking into consideration the extremely high standard of living to which the wife accustomed the husband through nine years of marriage. The wife accustomed the husband to a life-style which costs over $5,000 a month to maintain during a marriage which can hardly be described as a "marry in June and sue the following September" situation. *Firestone v. Firestone,* supra. In view of this fact, we cannot say that the limited eighteen month rehabilitative alimony plus lump sum alimony fashioned by the trial judge herein was an abuse of discretion. It was reasonably commensurate with the parties' high life style without at the same time creating an unreasonable charge on the wife for the rest of her life.

The wife argues that she accustomed the husband to such a high life style based on money she received from her father. It is true that the wife supported the marriage at first through contributions from the wife's father, but from 1972–1975 she supported the family unit entirely from her own separate estate. In our judgment, it is irrelevant how the wife lawfully acquired the money on which she supported the husband and the family. The fact is she supported the family unit, not the husband. And despite the wife's protests, a high standard of living remains a significant factor in setting an alimony award, which result is unchanged by the fact that the paying spouse acquired his or her wealth by gift or inheritance. See: *Firestone v. Firestone,* 263 So.2d 223 (Fla. 1972).

Rehabilitative alimony has been awarded to supplement means already available in an amount reasonably required during the post-marriage period to maintain a spouse until he or she, in the exercise of reasonable efforts and endeavors, is in a position of self support. It necessarily presupposes the potential for self support which is presently impaired. Lump sum alimony has been awarded as a payment of a definite sum or property in the nature of a final property settlement which serves a reasonable purpose such as rehabilitation or where the marriage's duration or the parties' financial position would make such an award advantageous to both parties. The alimony awards herein fit these traditional patterns and purposes for alimony.

The wife argues that the husband's $200,000 in assets acquired mainly by gift from the wife during the marriage, disqualifies the husband from receiving any alimony. We disagree. Although this is a significant factor in upholding the trial court's refusal to make the alimony permanent, we cannot say that this compels the result urged by the wife, particularly in view of the husband's demonstrated need for temporary, rehabilitative support. Except for the Sears stock, the husband's assets are non-income producing. And it has been held that a spouse is not required to deplete capital assets in order to maintain a prior standard of living. Moreover, alimony awards have been upheld where the spouse seeking alimony possessed assets comparable to that of the husband in this case.

The wife throughout these proceedings has attacked the husband's life style as parasitic and has warned that he should not be able to parlay such an existence into a $120,000 alimony award. The same criticism could be made of a good many wives who upon dissolution of a tragically flawed marriage have received alimony awards. We pass no judgment on the morality or social value of the marriage herein. Many Americans might very well regard the conduct of either party to this marriage with some cynicism. The work ethic is, after all, deeply ingrained in our mores. But we must take the marriage as we find it without passing judgment on the life style of either party. In a free society, there is room enough for many kinds of marriages, including this one. If and when such a marriage dissolves, it must be accorded equal treatment according to the standards for determining alimony set for all marriage dissolutions.

Moreover, the limited nature of the alimony awards herein should allay any fears that it will encourage any type of parasitic conduct. The husband has hardly been given a meal ticket for life; he has been given a temporary and limited assist to rehabilitate himself to a position of eventual self-support based on a demonstrated need. In this, we can find no abuse of discretion.

C

Turning now to the husband's cross appeal, we are not persuaded that the husband's demonstrated needs are so great that the trial court abused its discretion in refusing to make the alimony award permanent rather than rehabilitative and in refusing to award a greater lump sum alimony. As the wife accurately points out, the husband is a relatively young, well-educated man of 37, has excellent physical health although temporarily impaired mental health, has $200,000 in assets of his own, has some employment skills if only limited ones, and lives alone without custody of the parties' two children. We can see no reason why he could not properly rehabilitate himself within eighteen months with the alimony awarded herein. In the event that substantial rehabilitation does not occur by the end of eighteen months despite the husband's reasonable and diligent efforts, the husband can petition the court for modification of the alimony award.

Questions on Pfohl

Pfohl uses the traditional standard for setting the amount of alimony—the payor's ability to pay and the payee's need as established by the marital standard of living. The following questions ask you to consider whether that standard is a good one.

(1) Is the traditional standard actually used here?

(2) *Pfohl* is an unusual case in some important ways. Do these matter?

> (a) It is one of the few cases where the traditional standard is not wholly impractical. In most marriages, that is, it takes all the couple's resources to sustain their standard of living, and two households can not possibly live at that standard. How helpful is a standard that can rarely be directly applied? What better standard can you devise?
>
> (b) *Pfohl* is also one of a few cases where it is the husband and not the wife who is seeking alimony. How, if at all, should this matter?

(3) Why should the old standard of living be the test? Why should Mr. Pfohl luxuriate in the standard to which he became accustomed? Why not use the standard he had before he married Mrs. Pfohl? Why should anyone be supported by someone else at more than the level just above indigence? Why should anyone be supported by someone else at all?

(4) Assuming that Mr. Pfohl is entitled to live at a generous standard of living, why shouldn't he be required to dip into capital to do it? Didn't he decide during the marriage to do nothing to increase his capital or his skills? Does it matter if his inaction was at her request?

(5) Assuming Mr. Pfohl needed some rehabilitation before he could work, why shouldn't he be required to dip into capital to pay for it?

(6) The "standard of living" principle can be both a floor and a ceiling for alimony payments. If the payor's income increases so that the marital standard can be enjoyed by both, the payee can have the periodic payment raised. However, unlike child support, the amount payable is never greater than the marital standard, despite the payor's prosperity following the marriage. *Conway v. Conway*, 395 SE2d 464 (Va App 1990). Why?

Rethinking the Grounds for Alimony

As you recall, the doctrinal basis for alimony has been uncertain ever since alimony began to be awarded in cases of true divorce instead of just in judicial separations. The following questions are designed to help you think about whether the reasons alimony nevertheless persisted still apply and whether alimony, either in the traditional or the rehabilitative version, ought still to be awarded.

(1) The first of the implicit grounds for preserving alimony was the sense that marriage was a life-long commitment. That sense was strained even in the nineteenth century as legal changes made divorce more accessible. It has been strained perhaps to the breaking point by no-fault divorce and the proliferation of divorce. Furthermore, it has become more usual to think of marriage not as a life-time commitment, but rather as, in Justice Douglas's words, "hopefully enduring," as a relationship which two people enter for companionship and personal fulfillment but which should end when it stops serving that purpose for either of them. After that point, wouldn't any attempt to impose continuing duties interfere with the parties' ability to enter new relationships? In other words, isn't any attempt to sustain the institution of alimony under the first of the old implicit grounds badly out of date?

(2) The second of the old implicit grounds was that husbands should not by their fault escape their marital obligations. But isn't this rationale also out-dated, since it relies on ideas about marital fault which are being eliminated from the law?

For an examination of how the concept of fault might play out in a no-fault state, consider the following case:

IN RE MARRIAGE OF WENDELL

Court of Appeals of Iowa, 1998
581 N.W.2d 197

CADY, CHIEF JUDGE.

Jeffrey Wendell appeals from the economic provisions of the district court's dissolution decree. He claims the trial court failed to reach an equitable distribution of the marital assets and failed to provide appropriate terms for the termination of alimony. We affirm.

Jeffrey and Susan Wendell married on October 22, 1985. After slightly over eleven years of marriage, the parties divorced on January 22, 1997. At the time of dissolution, Jeffrey was thirty-nine years of age and Susan was thirty-three years old. The parties have one child, Jedediah, born May 3, 1986.

Jeffrey brought to the marriage various personal property and bank accounts valued at $17,281. The trial court awarded Susan net assets in the amount of approximately $178,402, while Jeffrey received net assets totaling approximately $178,403. The district court also ordered Jeffrey to pay Susan rehabilitative alimony of $700 per month for a period of five years. The decree provided the alimony payments would terminate either upon the death of either party or the remarriage of Susan.

On appeal Jeffrey claims the trial court erred by ruling his premarital assets had been converted to marital assets and were subject to division. He also asserts the district court erred by failing to provide for termination of alimony in the event of Susan's cohabitation or employment.

. . .

III. Alimony

Jeffrey maintains alimony should terminate in the event Susan becomes self-sufficient following employment or if she cohabits. The district court limited early termination of the five-year alimony to death or remarriage by Susan. The district court specifically rejected Jeffrey's claims that alimony should also terminate upon self sufficiency or cohabitation.

It is common in Iowa for alimony provisions in a decree for dissolution of marriage to include conditions providing for alimony to automatically terminate prior to the specific duration upon death or remarriage of the recipient spouse. This practice results, most likely, from two related principles. First, alimony is presumed to automatically terminate upon the death of the recipient spouse. Second, although subsequent remarriage does not automatically terminate an alimony obligation, it does shift the burden to the recipient to show "extraordinary circumstances" to justify its continuation. Consequently, in many instances, this heavy burden effectively eliminates alimony following remarriage. This result comports with the underlying rationale for the shift of the burden of proof. Generally, it is contrary to public policy to permit a person to be concurrently supported by a spouse and a former spouse. Marriage, traditionally, imposes a reciprocal obligation of support on each spouse, and remarriage following divorce correspondingly releases a former spouse from any continuing traditional obligation of support....

The convergence of these two principles helps explain the prevailing judicial practice of adjudicating the termination of alimony upon death or remarriage at the time of the original decree for dissolution of marriage instead of leaving the issue for future litigation framed by the presumption and shifting burden. Further litigation can be avoided by simply deciding the issue up-front. We must decide if cohabitation and self sufficiency should similarly be included.

In considering whether it is appropriate to include cohabitation as a condition causing termination of alimony, we acknowledge cohabitation may have many of the attributes of a marriage relationship. Thus, the same rationale which explains the termination of alimony upon remarriage may also apply to cohabitation. In the past, this has motivated us to include cohabitation in some cases as an event to terminate alimony. See *In re Marriage of Bell,* 576 N.W.2d 618 (Iowa App. 1998). This case gives us an opportunity to reconsider this practice.

We begin by recognizing that even remarriage may not always be an appropriate triggering event for the termination of alimony. In some cases, it is appropriate to continue alimony after the remarriage of the recipient spouse. Generally, whether remarriage terminates alimony depends, primarily, on the purpose behind the award of alimony. Rehabilitative and reimbursement alimony, for example, are often unaffected by remarriage. See *In re Marriage of Francis,* 442 N.W.2d 59, 67 (Iowa 1989) (reimbursement alimony not subject to modification or termination until full compensation except upon recipient's death); *In re Marriage of Seidenfeld,* 241 N.W.2d 881, 884 (Iowa 1976) (alimony payments to wife for the purpose of further education should continue even if wife remarries); see also *In re Marriage of Wilson,* 449 N.W.2d 890, 893 (Iowa App. 1989) (retirement benefits distributed in the form of alimony do not terminate on remarriage of recipient).

Although remarriage may not always trigger the termination of alimony, it nevertheless remains a viable issue for determination at the time of the original decree. This is because the purpose of the alimony is known at the time the decree is entered, and the triggering event, remarriage, is readily identifiable.

Unlike remarriage, cohabitation is not an easily identifiable triggering event. It may be compatible with remarriage when cohabitants live together and assume various responsibilities towards each other. Yet, cohabitation has too many variables to be a defined future event, like remarriage, in a dissolution decree. Thus, we believe it would be inappropriate to use cohabitation as an event to automatically terminate alimony in an original dissolution decree. The question is better reserved for resolution in an action to modify the decree for dissolution of marriage.

Jeffrey claims cohabitation could be viewed as an event within the contemplation of the trial court at the time of the original decree and outside the scope of a modification action. He fears he will be precluded from litigation of the issue in the future.

We observe our decision today will generally foreclose an adjudication of the cohabitation issue at the time of the original decree. Although we have tied cohabitation to remarriage in the past, we will no longer use cohabitation as an event to terminate alimony. For this reason, it would not be outside the scope of a modification proceeding.

Like cohabitation, we believe events such as employment and self-sufficiency should also be reserved for a modification action. The imposition and length of an award of traditional alimony is primarily predicated on need and ability. If circumstances later arise to eliminate need prior to the time frame anticipated when the original decree was entered, modification may be sought. See Iowa Code § 598.21(8)(a) (dissolution decree can be modified upon a showing of a substantial change in circumstances, including changes in employment or earning capacity); *In re Marriage of Romanelli,* 570 N.W.2d 761, 764 (Iowa 1997) (husband petitioned for modification of alimony based on wife's full-time employment)....

AFFIRMED.

SACKETT, Judge (specially concurring).

The majority's struggle to determine whether and when cohabitation should terminate alimony or "how much sex is enough," ending with a determination that its conclusion "strikes an appropriate balance between the interest of the parties ... consistent with our prevailing companion principles and the underlying policy of the law," is outstanding rhetoric but does little to provide definite guidelines or address the current application of age-old principles stemming from a time when the husband was the wage earner, a woman's worth was determined by home-type jobs, and when our supreme court said, "Alimony is an allowance for maintenance of the wife." *Russell v. Russell,* 4 Greene 26, 29 (Iowa 1853). In those times, a husband need only support his former wife, a being suited for domestic chores, until another man in the form of a husband, and sometimes a lover, came along.

While statutes providing alimony only to women have been found unconstitutional, *Orr v. Orr,* 440 U.S. 268, 278–79 (1979), the fact is alimony awards to men remain rare. Obviously, in some part, it is the result of continuing attitudes men should support their families, and it is justified by continuing wage differentials between men and women.

Aged principles, long out-dated by the entry of women in the work place, should be totally discarded in favor of principles gauged on fairness and not sexual or marital status or so-called balancing considerations that are driven by uncertainty and serve to advance additional litigation following a dissolution and threaten the financial stability of the divorced parties.

Society would be best served by resolving the economic issues in a dissolution by division of property and pension rights, giving finality to the parties and curtailing substantial future litigation. Alimony should be awarded primarily in those cases where the only source for equitable division is from the future income of the advantaged spouse. Modifications should be limited to situations where the disadvantaged spouse's income substantially decreases through no fault of their own. In accordance with existing trends, alimony should be limited to situations where one spouse has sacrificed his or her own career opportunities by assuming responsibility for home and family, while recognizing a former marital partner should not, in most cases, be a life-long meal ticket.

If such is the case, what makes sacrifices made in a marriage less compensable because the disadvantaged spouse elects to marry or just have sex? I suggest nothing should. Our supreme court has recently recognized there are limited instances where alimony should not terminate on remarriage, establishing what is referred to as "reimbursement alimony."

Until we are ready to discard the trappings of traditional concepts of spousal support and assess it under the facts of current society, we can only continue to engage in confusing rhetoric and continue to leave divorced persons with substantial uncertainty as to their economic futures.

Questions on Wendell

(1) Neither the majority nor the concurrent opinion in Wendell would allow Jeffrey to stipulate that Susan's alimony would terminate if she cohabited "in a marriage-like relationship." How would you sum up the difference in the reasoning of the two opinions? Which view holds more appeal?

(2) What is it that Jeffrey is trying to avoid? Does he receive sympathy from the Supreme Court of Iowa? How realistic might his fears be? Are women likely to refrain from remarrying in order to retain support from former spouses?

(3) The majority opinion stresses the difficulty of predicting whether Susan in fact might be supported by her cohabiting partner. Is it true that cohabiting relationships are more diverse than marriages? In other words, should the court be concerned that they cannot predict the future well in these circumstances? Can Jeffrey accomplish what he says he wants by using Iowa Code § 598.21C (2005), which allows modification where there is a substantial change of circumstances including "possible support of a party by another person"?

(4) If not, is the reason because he wishes to deter Susan from entering other relationships, especially non-marital ones, or because court action at a later time would be costly to him?

(5) Another possible solution to the problem appears in the following legislation, Va. Code Ann. § 20–109 (2006):

A. Upon petition of either party the court may increase, decrease, or terminate the amount or duration of any spousal support and maintenance that may thereafter accrue, whether previously or hereafter awarded, as the circumstances may make proper. Upon order of the court based upon clear and convincing evidence that the spouse receiving support has been habitually cohabiting with another person in a relationship analogous to a marriage for one year or more commencing on or after July 1, 1997, the court shall terminate spousal support and maintenance unless (i) otherwise provided by stipulation or contract or (ii) the spouse receiving support proves by a preponderance of the evidence that termination of such support would be unconscionable.

This legislation, like Iowa's § 598.41 (a)(h), terminates support only after the fact, and thus appears to meet the Iowa Supreme Court's prediction problem. But do you also notice a difference in the burden of proof placed upon obligor spouses?

(6) Are cohabiting couples as likely to feel real obligations to support each other as married couples? A second marriage would carry with it reciprocal legal duties of support, while cohabitation does not. (There are exceptions to this rule, in "common law" relationships in Canada, and in domestic partnerships in California, where, by statute, the nonmarital relationship requires mutual support. C–23, the Modernization of Benefits and Obligations Act, R.S. C2 (2d Supp) SC 2000, c 12, § 115; Cal Fam Code § 297.5(a)(2006)).

(7) Is the dissent correct that sexuality after divorce should not be the concern of the other spouse, at least as far as alimony is concerned?

Is the modern rationale for alimony simply a recognition of sacrifices made in a marriage? Are these any less real if made by a spouse who is self-sufficient than one who is not?

(3) The third implicit ground was that alimony was a way of dividing marital property when assets were unavailable or hard to divide. But isn't the solution to that problem to address it directly, and to use installment payments for dividing property? Isn't using alimony as a substitute for property division the kind of imprecision that can lead to intellectual and practical confusion?

One possible response is that alimony differs from property division since it is theoretically always modifiable if circumstances change and since the obligation does not survive the death of either spouse. Although future earnings are a kind of property (related to what economists call human capital), they depend more than most investments upon the individual efforts of the wealth-holder. Does this make future earnings too hard to calculate? Of course, courts calculate future earnings when determining tort damages. But there the tortfeasor's "fault" justifies imposing the risks of inaccurate calculations. But fault has largely been expelled from the law of divorce.

(4) The fourth implicit ground was that divorced wives were ill-situated to support themselves. But aren't there two problems with this argument today?

(a) Our ideas about who should be responsible for supporting those who cannot support themselves seem to have changed. We may now regard such support as the government's responsibility, and the government's ability to meet that responsibility, which was slight in the nineteenth century, is now ample. Insofar as the government isn't meeting its obligation, is the solution to impose those duties on individuals or to improve the government's performance? In much of Europe, for example, divorced custodial parents automatically receive governmental allowances.

(b) The situation of women in society has changed in ways that affect thinking about alimony. First, women's employment opportunities are much greater and are improving. Women increasingly obtain educations that prepare them for careers and increasingly work during marriage. Second, rules specially designed to protect women may now seem paternalistic. Alimony has been attacked as an institution that encourages women to rely economically on men. Thus even if women are not yet as able to support themselves as men, isn't it undesirable to perpetuate an institution based on destructive attitudes about women?

(5) The fifth implicit ground was that alimony is another form of child support. But doesn't this ground fail for the same reason that the third did, because it tries to do indirectly what could more straightforwardly and less misleadingly be done directly?

(6) Does alimony channel the parties' behavior within marriage? Margaret F. Brinig and Steven Crafton argue that using alimony as a kind of damages for breach of the marital contract encourages investment in the relationship. *Marriage and Opportunism*, 23 J Legal Stud 869 (1994). Does alimony also repay unusual, but desirable, marriage investments? *See* Margaret F. Brinig and June R. Carbone, *The Reliance Interest in Marriage and Divorce*, 62 Tulane L Rev 855 (1988). Ought alimony be awarded to recompense, and thus encourage, sacrifices made to benefit the marriage at the expense of one spouses? For such a proposal, see Ira Mark Ellman, *The Theory of Alimony*, 77 Cal L Rev 1 (1989). For a criticism of that proposal, see Carl E. Schneider, *Rethinking Alimony: Marital Decisions and Moral Discourse*, 1991 BYU L Rev 197.

(4) The ALI Synthesis

In Chapter I, we said that the ALI recently proposed new rules to govern most of the principal areas of family law. We will now look at its proposals for dealing with the spouses' financial affairs on divorce. We describe the ALI's proposals a synthesis for two reasons. First, the ALI

Principles can be said to draw from both the community-property and equitable-distribution systems. Indeed, those systems have been converging in case and statutory law for some years. That is, equitable distribution states have for some time been adapting and adopting community property concepts like its treatment of acquests, bequests, earned property, and unearned property.

We call the ALI Principles a synthesis for a second reason. As you know, the law distinguishes at divorce between dividing marital property and awarding alimony. The Principles may be said to abandon this distinction. Economists say that the value of an asset lies precisely in its ability to earn income. The value of marital property is that it produces income for support; alimony is a kind of property interest. The ALI Principles, then, try to decide what a couple's entire economic relationship should be on divorce. In particular, those Principles do not so much ask "who owns what" as "whose sacrifices for the benefit of the marriage should now be recompensed." For an argument that the ALI appropriately treats property division and alimony together, see Margaret F. Brinig, *Property Distribution Physics: The Talisman of Time and Middle Class Law,* 31 Family L Q 93 (1997).

AMERICAN LAW INSTITUTE PRINCIPLES OF FAMILY DISSOLUTION

Chapter 4: Division of Property at Dissolution

Proposed Final Draft (February 14, 1997)

§ 4.02 Objective of Principles Governing the Division of Property

The objective of this Chapter is to allocate property by principles

(1) that respect both spousal ownership rights in their property and the equitable claims that each spouse has on the property in consequence of their marital relationship;

(2) that facilitate the satisfaction of obligations the spouses have under Chapter 3 to support their children and under Chapter 5 to share equitably in the financial losses arising from the dissolution of their marriage; and

(3) that are consistent and predictable in application.

§ 4.03 Definition of Marital and Separate Property

(1) Property acquired during marriage is marital property, except as otherwise expressly provided in this Chapter.

(2) Inheritances, including bequests and devises, and gifts from third parties, are the separate property of the acquiring spouse even if acquired during marriage.

(3) Property received in exchange for separate property is separate property even if acquired during marriage.

(4) Property acquired during marriage but after the parties have commenced living apart pursuant to either a written separation agreement or a judicial decree, is the separate property of the acquiring spouse unless the agreement or decree specifies otherwise.

(5) For the purpose of this section "during marriage" means after the commencement of marriage and before the filing and service of a petition for dissolution (if that petition ultimately results in a decree dissolving the marriage), unless there are facts, set forth in written findings of the trial court, establishing that use of another date is necessary to avoid a substantial injustice.

(6) Property acquired before marriage but during the course of a relationship immediately preceding the marriage that qualifies under § 6.[03], or would have qualified under that section had the parties not married but continued to cohabit for the same duration as the marriage, is treated as marital property.

§ 4.04 Income from and Appreciation of Separate Property

(1) Both income during marriage from separate property, and the appreciation in value during marriage of separate property, are marital property to the extent the underlying asset is subsequently recharacterized as marital property, pursuant to § 4.12.

(2) Both income during marriage from separate property, and the appreciation in value during marriage of separate property, are marital property to the extent the income or appreciation is attributable to either spouse's labor during marriage, pursuant to § 4.05.

(3) Income from and appreciation of separate property are separate property if they are not marital property under Paragraph (1) or (2).

§ 4.05 Enhancement of Separate Property by Spousal Labor

(1) A portion of any increase in the value of separate property is marital property whenever either spouse has devoted substantial time during marriage to the property's management or preservation.

(2) The increase in value of separate property over the course of the marriage is measured by the difference between the market value of the property when acquired, or at the beginning of the marriage, if later, and the market value of the property when sold, or at the end of the marriage, if sooner.

(3) The portion of the increase in value that is marital property under Paragraph (1) is the difference between the actual amount by which the property has increased in value, and the amount by which capital of the same value would have increased over the same time period if invested in assets of relative safety requiring little management.

[§ 4.06 Property Acquired in Exchange for Marital and Separate Property is omitted since the provisions are substantially those under existing law in most states. There is a rebuttable presumption that when one spouse sells separate property and acquires something else with the proceeds, the new property is marital.]

§ 4.08 Deferred Or Contingent Earnings and Wage Substitutes

(1) Property earned by labor performed during marriage is marital property whether received before, during, or after the marriage. Property earned by labor not performed during marriage is the separate property of the laboring spouse even if received during marriage.

(a) Vested pension rights are marital property to the extent they are earned during the marriage.

(b) Contingent returns on labor performed during marriage, including unvested pension rights, choses in action, and compensation contingent on post-marital events, are marital property to the extent they are earned during the marriage

(2) Benefits received as compensation for a loss take their character from the asset they replace.

(a) Insurance proceeds and personal injury recoveries are marital property to the extent that entitlement to them arises from the loss of a marital asset, including income that the beneficiary-spouse would have earned during the marriage. The dissolution court may make a reasonable allocation of an undifferentiated award between its marital and separate property components.

(b) Disability pay and workers' compensation payments are marital property to the extent they replace income or benefits the recipient would have earned during the marriage but for the qualifying disability or injury.

(3) Where the value of the marital-property portion of a spouse's entitlement to future payments can be determined at dissolution, the court may include it in reckoning the worth of the marital property assigned to each spouse. Where the value of the future payments is not known at the time of dissolution, where their receipt is contingent on future events or not reasonably assured, or where for other reasons it is not equitable under the circumstances to include their value in the property assigned at the time of dissolution, the court may decline to do so, and either

(a) fix the spouses' respective shares in such future payments if and when received, or,

(b) if it is not possible to fix their share at the time of dissolution, reserve jurisdiction to make an appropriate order at the earliest practical date.

Topic 3. Allocation of Property on Dissolution of Marriage

§ 4.09 Division of Marital Property Generally

(1) Except as provided in Paragraph (2) of this section, marital property and marital debts are divided at dissolution so that the spouses receive net shares equal in value, although not necessarily identical in kind.

(2) The spouses are allocated net shares of the marital property and debts that are unequal in value if, and only if,

(a) Pursuant to § 5.10, § 5.11, or § 5.14, the court compensates a spouse for a loss recognized in Chapter 5, in whole or in part, with an enhanced share of the marital property; or

(b) Pursuant to § 4.10, the court allows one spouse an enhanced share of the marital property because the other spouse previously made an improper disposition of some portion of it; or

(c) Marital debts exceed marital assets, and it is just and equitable to assign the excess debt unequally, because of a significant disparity in the spouses' financial capacity, their participation in the decision to incur the debt, or their consumption of the goods or services that the debt was incurred to acquire.

§ 4.10 Financial Misconduct as Grounds for Unequal Division of Marital Property

(1) If one spouse, without the other spouse's consent, has made gifts of marital property to third parties that are substantial relative to the total value of the marital property at the time of the gift, the court should augment the other spouse's share of the remaining marital property by one-half of the value of such gifts. This paragraph applies only to gifts made after a date that is set by counting back, from the date on which the dissolution petition is served, a fixed period of time specified in a rule of statewide application.

(2) If marital property is lost, expended, or destroyed through the intentional misconduct of one spouse, the court should augment the other spouse's share of the remaining marital property by one-half the value of the lost or destroyed property. This paragraph applies only to misconduct after a date that is set by counting back, from the date on which the dissolution petition is served, a fixed period of time specified in a rule of statewide application.

(3) If marital property is lost or destroyed through the negligence of one spouse, the court should augment the other spouse's share of the remaining marital property by one-half the value of the lost or destroyed property. This paragraph applies only to negligence that took place after service of the dissolution petition.

(4) If one spouse is entitled to a remedy under Paragraph (1) or (2), or would have been entitled to a remedy had concealed or conveyed property not been recovered, and if the court also finds that the concealment or conveyance either

(a) had the purpose of denying the first spouse his or her equitable share of the marital property at dissolution, or

(b) was undertaken with knowledge that such denial was its likely effect, the court should require the second spouse to compensate the first spouse for all reasonable costs, including professional fees, that were incurred to establish the improper concealment or conveyance. Such compensation may take the form of an enhanced share of the available marital property.

(5) Paragraphs (1), (2), and (3) may be applied to gifts, misconduct, or neglect that occurred prior to the date specified in the statewide rule required under those sections, if facts set forth in written findings of the trial court establish that their application to the earlier incidents is necessary to avoid a substantial injustice.

(6) If there is insufficient marital property for an adjustment in its allocation to achieve the compensation found appropriate under this section, the court may achieve an equivalent result by

(a) making an award to one spouse of some portion of the other's separate property, as allowed under § 4.11, or, if the available separate property is also inadequate for this purpose,

(b) requiring one spouse to make equitable reimbursement to the other in such installment payments as the court judges equitable in light of the financial capacity and other obligations of the spouse making reimbursement.

§ 4.11 Separate Property

(1) In every dissolution of marriage, all separate property should be assigned to its owner, except that when there is insufficient marital property to permit the reimbursement that would otherwise be required under the court may reassign the spouses' separate party in order to achieve the equivalent result.

(2) Separate property that is recharacterized as marital property under § 4.12 is allocated between the uses under § 4.09 and not under this section.

AMERICAN LAW INSTITUTE PRINCIPLES OF FAMILY DISSOLUTION

2002

Chapter 5. Compensatory Payments

§ 5.02 Objective

(1) The objective of this Chapter is to allocate financial losses that arise at the dissolution of a marriage according to equitable principles that are consistent and predictable in application.

(2) Losses are allocated under this Chapter without regard to marital misconduct, but nothing in this Chapter is intended to foreclose a spouse from bringing an independent claim to redress injuries from conduct that occurred during the marriage.

(3) Equitable principles of loss recognition and allocation should take into account all of the following:

(a) The loss of earning capacity arising from a spouse's disproportionate share of caretaking responsibilities for children or other persons to whom the spouses have a moral obligation;

(b) Losses that arise from the changes in life opportunities and expectations caused by the adjustments individuals ordinarily make over the course of a long marital relationship;

(c) Disparities in the financial impact of a short marital relationship on the spouses' post-divorce lives, as compared to their situation prior to marriage;

(d) The primacy of the income earner's claim to benefit from the fruits of his or her own labor, as compared to claims of a former spouse.

§ 5.03 Kinds of Compensatory Awards

(1) Compensatory awards should allocate equitably between the spouses certain financial losses that either or both incur and which are realized at dissolution when the family is divided into separate economic units.

(2) The following compensable losses are recognized in Topic 2 of this Chapter:

(a) In a marriage of significant duration, the loss in living standard experienced at dissolution by the spouse who has less wealth or earning capacity (§ 5.04).

(b) An earning capacity loss incurred during marriage but continuing after dissolution and arising from one spouse's disproportionate share, during marriage, of the care of the marital children or of the children of either spouse (§ 5.05).

(c) An earning capacity loss incurred during marriage and continuing after dissolution, and arising from the care provided by one spouse to a sick, elderly, or disabled third party, in fulfillment of a moral obligation of the other spouse or of both spouses jointly (§ 5.11).

(3) The following compensable losses are recognized in Topic 3 of this Chapter:

(a) The loss either spouse incurs when the marriage is dissolved before that spouse realizes a fair return from his or her investment in the other spouse's earning capacity (§ 5.12); and

(b) An unfairly disproportionate disparity between the spouses in their respective abilities to recover their pre-marital living standard after the dissolution of a short marriage (§ 5.13).

(4) A spouse may qualify for more than one kind of compensatory award, but duplicate compensation should not be provided for any loss, and

(a) as provided in §§ 5.04, 5.05, and 5.11, the combined value of all Topic 2 awards cannot exceed the maximum award that could be made under § 5.05 alone in any dissolution involving spouses with similar incomes; and

(b) as provided in §§ 5.12 and 5.13, awards are not available under Topic 3 to an individual whose aggregate entitlement under Topic 2 is substantial.

§ 5.04 Compensation for Loss of Marital Living Standard

(1) A person married to someone of significantly greater wealth or earning capacity is entitled at dissolution to compensation for the reduced standard of living he or she would otherwise experience, if the marriage was of sufficient duration that equity requires the loss, or some portion of it, be treated as the spouses' joint responsibility.

(2) Entitlement to an award under this section should be determined by a rule of statewide application under which a presumption of entitlement arises in marriages of specified duration and spousal income disparity.

(3) The value of the award made under this section should be determined by a rule of statewide application that sets a presumptive award of periodic payments calculated by applying a specified percentage to the difference between the incomes the spouses are expected to have after dissolution. This percentage is referred to in this Chapter as the *durational factor,* and should increase with the duration of the marriage until it reaches a maximum value set by the rule.

(4) The presumptions established under this section should govern unless there are facts, set forth in written findings of the trial court (§ 1.02), establishing that the presumption's application to the case before the court would yield a substantial injustice. An award may be made under this section in cases where no presumption of entitlement arises, if facts not present at the dissolution of most marriages of similar duration and income levels establish that a substantial injustice will result if there is no compensation, and those facts are set forth in written findings of the trial court (§ 1.02).

(5) The duration of an award of periodic payments made under this section should be determined as provided in § 5.06. Subsequent modification of the award's amount or duration is allowed as provided under §§ 5.07, 5.08, and 5.09. An award of periodic payments that would otherwise arise under this section may be replaced, in whole or in part, by a single lump-sum payment, as provided in § 5.10.

(6) In determining the duration of a marriage for the purpose of this section, the court should include any period immediately preceding the formal marriage during which the parties lived together as domestic partners, as defined in § 6.03.

§ 5.05 Compensation for Primary Caretaker's Residual Loss in Earning Capacity

(1) A spouse should be entitled at dissolution to compensation for the earning capacity loss arising from his or her disproportionate share during marriage of the care of the marital children, or of the children of either spouse.

(2) Entitlement to an award under this section should be determined by a rule of statewide application under which a presumption of entitlement arises at the dissolution of a marriage in which

(a) there are or have been marital children, or children of either spouse;

(b) while under the age of majority the children have lived with the claimant (or with both spouses, when the claim is against the stepparent of the children), for a minimum period specified in the rule; and

(c) the claimant's earning capacity at dissolution is substantially less than that of the other spouse.

(3) A presumption of entitlement governs in the absence of a determination by the trial court that the claimant did not provide substantially more than half of the total care that both spouses together provided for the children.

(4) The value of an award under this section should be determined by a rule of statewide application under which a presumption arises that the award shall require a set of periodic payments in an amount calculated by applying a percentage, called the *child care durational factor,* to the difference between the incomes the spouses are expected to have after dissolution.

(a) The rule of statewide application should specify a value for the child care durational factor that increases with the duration of the *child care period,* which is the period during which the claimant provided significantly more than half of the total care that both spouses together provided for the children.

(b) The child care period equals the entire period during which minor children of the marriage, or of the spouse against whom the claim is made, lived in the same household as the claimant, unless a different period is established by the evidence. In the case of stepchildren of the spouse against whom the claim is made, the child care period equals the entire period during which the minor children lived in the same household as both spouses, unless a shorter period is established by the evidence.

(5) A claimant may be entitled to both an award under this section and an award under § 5.04, but in no case shall the combined value of the child care durational factor, and the durational factor employed to determine the presumed award under § 5.04, exceed the maximum value allowed for the § 5.04 durational factor alone.

(6) The presumed value of the award, as set under Paragraph (4), should govern unless there are facts, set forth in the written findings of the trial court, establishing that the presumption's application to the case before the court would yield a substantial injustice.

(7) The duration of an award of periodic payments made under this section should be determined as provided in § 5.06. Subsequent modifi-

cation of the award's amount or duration is allowed as provided under §§ 5.07, 5.08, and 5.09. An award of periodic payments that would otherwise arise under this section may be replaced, in whole or in part, by a single lump-sum payment, as provided in § 5.10.

§ 5.06 Duration of Award of Periodic Payments Under §§ 5.04 and 5.05

(1) An award of periodic payments made pursuant to § 5.04 or § 5.05 may have a term that is fixed or indefinite, according to a rule of statewide application under which a presumption arises

(a) that the term is indefinite when the age of the obligee, and the length of the marriage, are both greater than a minimum value specified in the rule; and, when this presumption does not apply,

(b) that the term is fixed at a duration equal, for awards under § 5.04, to the length of the marriage multiplied by a factor specified in the rule and, for awards under § 5.05, to the length of the child care period multiplied by a factor specified in the rule.

(2) The term set by the presumption should govern in the absence of written findings of the trial court (§ 1.02) that show either

(a) that the term specified in the court's order is less likely than the presumed term to require subsequent modification or extension; or

(b) that the presumption's application to the particular case will yield a substantial injustice.

(3) An award of periodic payments, whether fixed or indefinite in term, may be modified, terminated, or extended as provided in §§ 5.07, 5.08, and 5.09.

(4) In determining the duration of a marriage for the purpose of this section, the court should include any period immediately preceding the formal marriage during which the parties lived together as domestic partners, as defined in § 6.03.

§ 5.07 Automatic Termination of Awards Made Under § 5.04 and § 5.05

An obligation to make periodic payments imposed under § 5.04 or § 5.05 ends automatically at the remarriage of the obligee or at the death of either party, without regard to the award's term as fixed in the decree, unless

(1) the original decree provides otherwise, or

(2) the court makes written findings establishing that termination of the award would work a substantial injustice because of facts not present in most cases to which this section applies.

[§ 5.08 Judicial Modification of Awards Made Under § 5.04 and § 5.05 is omitted because it is substantially like existing state law. Modifications may be, *inter alia*, made when extraordinary changes in the parties' finances cause their living standards to become further apart or closer together than an existing order contemplated.]

§ 5.09 Effect of Obligee's Cohabitation

(1) An obligation to make periodic payments under § 5.04 or § 5.05 is terminated, without regard to its duration as fixed in the decree, when the obligor shows that the obligee established a domestic-partner relationship with a third person, unless either

(a) the original decree provides otherwise, or

(b) the court makes written findings (§ 1.02) establishing that termination of the award would work a substantial injustice.

(2) An obligor seeking termination of periodic payments under Paragraph (1) must show the obligee's establishment of a domestic-partner relationship with a third person by proof of any of the following:

(a) a court in another proceeding determined in a final order that the obligee established a domestic-partner relationship, as defined in § 6.03;

(b) the obligee maintained a common household with the third person and their common child, as defined in § 6.03, for the cohabitation parenting period set under § 6.03(2);

(c) the obligee maintained a common household with the third person for the cohabitation period set under § 6.03(3), unless the obligee rebuts the resulting presumption of a domestic partnership, as provided under § 6.03(3);

(d) for a significant period of time, the obligee and the third person shared a primary residence and a life together as a couple, as those terms are defined in § 6.03(6) and (7).

(3) An obligation to make periodic payments under § 5.04 or § 5.05 is suspended when the obligor shows that the obligee maintained a "common household," as defined in § 6.03, with another person (who may be the obligor), for a continuous period, specified in a rule of statewide application, of at least three months, unless either

(a) the original decree provides otherwise, or

(b) the obligee shows that he or she and the other person do not share "a life together as a couple," as defined in § 6.03(7).

(4) An obligation suspended under Paragraph (3) should be reinstated for any remaining portion of its original term, if the obligee shows that the relationship upon which the suspension was based has ended, unless the obligor shows, under Paragraph (2), that the relationship, before ending, endured long enough to become a domestic partnership.

§ 5.12 Compensation for Contributions to the Other Spouse's Education or Training

(1) A spouse is entitled at divorce to reimbursement for the financial contributions made to the other spouse's education or training when

(a) the claimant provided funds for the tuition or other direct costs of the other spouse's education or training, or provided the principal financial support of the family while the other spouse acquired the education or training; and

(b) the education or training was completed in less than a specified number of years, set in a rule of statewide application, before the filing of the petition for dissolution; and

(c) the education or training for which reimbursement is sought substantially enhanced the obligor's earning capacity.

(2) No award may be made under this section against a spouse:

(a) who is entitled to an award under § 5.04 or § 5.05; or

(b) who would have been entitled to an award under those sections but for the enhancement of his or her earning capacity from education or training described in Paragraphs (1)(a), (1)(b), and (1)(c).

(3) If both spouses qualify for reimbursement under this section their claims are netted against one another.

(4) The award allowed under this section is calculated by

(a) adding the obligor's share of the family living expenses during the period of education or training to the obligor's direct educational costs, to determine the obligor's total education or training costs;

(b) subtracting from the total costs the income of the obligor during that period, the amount of any debts then incurred which remain outstanding at the time of divorce and which are assigned to the obligor, and expenditures made during that period from the obligor's separate property; and

(c) adjusting the difference for changes in the real value of the dollar between the time when the education was obtained and the time of divorce.

(5) An award under this section is nonmodifiable and takes the form fixed under § 5.14.

Questions on the Division of Property under the UMDA and the ALI Principles

(1) Is there any real difference between the UMDA and the ALI Principles for property distribution? Are the factors (under UMDA § 307(a) and ALI Principles § 4.05) that address a spouse's entitlement to property originally belonging to the other the same? For example, is "contribution of each spouse to acquisition of the marital property, including contribution of a spouse as a homemaker" (the UMDA) the same as "devoting substantial time to the management or preservation" of property (the ALI Principles' formulation)?

(2) The UMDA takes into account such factors as the "economic circumstances of each spouse" and the "duration of the marriage," while

the ALI presumes that property will be divided equally. Which system is closer to the parties' intent? Which is fairer?

(3) The ALI is much more precise than the UMDA about what constitutes separate property. Why? To give befuddled spouses notice? To guide befuddled judges? To increase the fairness of the division of the spouses' wealth?

(4) Both the UMDA and the ALI move toward eliminating marital "fault" from decisions about marital wealth. Why? Do the reasons for eliminating fault from the grounds for divorce apply equally well to eliminating fault here? Can you divide property "equitably" without considering how the spouses mistreated each other?

(5) It appears that "financial misconduct" may be relevant to decisions under either statute. What constitutes such misconduct? Emptying a joint bank account and giving it to your paramour is surely misconduct. But what about spending it on a failing business venture? On an irresponsible relative who squanders it on loose living? What if one spouse commits a crime, insists he's innocent, and exhausts the marital estate on lawyers' fees in one appeal after another?

(6) What kinds of debts should be the responsibility of only one spouse? What if one spouse takes out a loan for graduate education and the ensuing enhanced earning capacity benefitted both spouses for a considerable time? What about loans procured from the family of only one spouse?

(7) The ALI rules apply to non-marital as well as marital dissolutions. Does that make sense?

Questions on Alimony, Maintenance, and Compensatory Payments

(1) Why did the UMDA change its term for spousal support from alimony to maintenance? What did the change signal? Does it adequately reflect the UMDA's stress on need? Why does the term change again when the ALI addresses the subject? Does the "compensatory payments" signal the ALI's stress on spousal sacrifice? Might it be intended to give the payments a greater dignity? Will it have that effect?

(2) Can spouses receiving compensatory payments feel they deserve them, that they have a property right to them? Does the rationale for the payments matter?

(3) At one time, alimony payments were "for life, or until remarriage." Under the UMDA § 308(b)(2), they are supposed to last for "[t]he time necessary to acquire sufficient education or training to enable the party seeking maintenance to find appropriate employment." Under ALI § 5.06, duration is so complicated we cannot summarize it here but must ask you to look at it again. What accounts for the different durations?

(4) Does requiring that compensable losses be related to childcare or a difference in earning capacity make sense? What if the spouses want to

move to a location where income is lower but life is easier? Is this rational? Is it "economically rational," even if the move disrupts one spouse's career?

(5) The ALI recompenses losses.

(a) Does the ALI scheme over-reward stay-at-home wives, encouraging them not to work while children are small? Would this be bad?

(b) Do marital losses have anything to do with cohabitation or remarriage? If not, why should the obligation to make them end if the spouse owed them begins a new relationship?

(6) Would Mr. Pfohl receive compensatory support under the ALI?

(a) Did the Pfohls' marriage last long enough to justify such an award?

(b) Does it matter to the ALI calculation that Mrs. Pfohl never really had an earning capacity?

(c) Were Mr. Pfohl's emotional problems (those that kept him from being gainfully employed following the parties' separation) closely enough related to the parties' marriage to justify his obtaining a compensatory payment (if you believe the marriage was relatively short)? Mr. Pfohl apparently will be unable to work for some time. If his income (as opposed to earning capacity) is less than Mrs. Pfohl's, does his inability to keep the marital standard of living roughly equivalent justify a compensable award?

(d) If Mr. Pfohl quit his sales job at Mrs. Pfohl's request, was this a rational loss under the ALI? Was this a loss due to the marriage?

(e) Did Mr. Pfohl care for his children in a way that affected his employment?

B. ANALYZING THE LAW OF MARITAL PROPERTY AND ALIMONY

Business of various kinds they might likewise pursue, if they were educated in a more orderly manner, which might save many from common and legal prostitution. Women would not then marry for a support, as men accept of places under government, and neglect the implied duties, nor would an attempt to earn their own subsistence—a most laudable one!—sink them almost to the level of those poor abandoned creatures who live by prostitution.

Mary Wollstonecraft
A Vindication of the Rights of Women

(1) An Introductory Case

Now that we have learned the basics of the law regulating marital property and alimony, we are ready for a case that treats a revealing problem in that law, a problem that may be of some interest to you—how should professional degrees be treated upon divorce when one spouse has supported the other through a professional school? As you read the opinion in this case, you should ask several questions: What views of marriage does the court seem to believe the law should be based on and promote? What rationales for and goals of dividing marital property is the court advocating? How much do these goals and rationales reflect judicial views of marriage? Your views?

MAHONEY v. MAHONEY

Supreme Court of New Jersey, 1982
453 A2d 527

PASHMAN, JUSTICE.

Once again the Court must interpret this state's law regarding the distribution of marital property upon divorce. The question here is whether the defendant has the right to share the value of a professional business (M.B.A.) degree earned by her former husband during their marriage. The Court must decide whether the plaintiff's degree is "property" for purposes of *N.J.S.A.* 2A:34–23, which requires equitable distribution of "the property, both real and personal, which was legally and beneficially acquired ... during the marriage." If the M.B.A. degree is not property, we must still decide whether the defendant can nonetheless recover the money she contributed to her husband's support while he pursued his professional education. For the reasons stated below, we hold that the plaintiff's professional degree is not property and therefore reject the defendant's claim that the degree is subject to equitable distribution. To this extent, we concur in the reasoning of the Appellate Division. Notwithstanding this concurrence, we reverse the judgment of the Appellate Division, which had the effect of denying the defendant any remedial relief for her contributions toward her husband's professional education and remand for further proceedings.

I

When the parties married in Indiana in 1971, plaintiff, Melvin Mahoney, had an engineering degree and defendant, June Lee Mahoney, had a bachelor of science degree. From that time until the parties separated in October 1978 they generally shared all household expenses. The sole exception was the period between September 1975 and January 1977, when the plaintiff attended the Wharton School of the University of Pennsylvania and received an M.B.A. degree.

During the 16–month period in which the plaintiff attended school, June Lee Mahoney contributed about $24,000 to the household. Her husband made no financial contribution while he was a student. Melvin's educational expenses of about $6,500 were paid for by a combination of veterans' benefits and a payment from the Air Force. After receiving his degree, the plaintiff went to work as a commercial lending officer for Chase Manhattan Bank.

Meanwhile, in 1976 the defendant began a part-time graduate program at Rutgers University, paid for by her employer, that led to a master's degree in microbiology one year after the parties had separated. June Lee worked full-time throughout the course of her graduate schooling.

In March 1979, Melvin Mahoney sued for divorce; his wife filed a counterclaim also seeking a divorce. In May 1980, the trial court granted dual judgments of divorce on the ground of 18 months continuous separation.

At the time of trial, plaintiff's annual income was $25,600 and defendant's income was $21,000. No claim for alimony was made. The parties owned no real property and divided the small amount of their personal property by agreement.

The only issue at trial was the defendant's claim for reimbursement of the amount of support she gave her husband while he obtained his M.B.A. degree. Defendant sought 50% of the $24,000 she had contributed to the household during that time, plus one-half of the $6,500 cost of her husband's tuition.

The trial court decided that defendant should be reimbursed, holding that "the education and degree obtained by plaintiff, under the circumstances of this case, constitute a property right...." However, the court did not attempt to determine the value of plaintiff's M.B.A. degree. Instead, finding that in this case "[t]o ignore the contributions of the sacrificing spouse would be ... an unjust enrichment of the educated spouse," the court ordered the award of a "reasonable sum as a credit [for] ... the maintenance of the household and the support of plaintiff during the educational period." Plaintiff was ordered to reimburse his wife in the amount of $5,000, to be paid at the rate of $100 per month. The court did not explain why it chose this amount.

Plaintiff appealed to the Appellate Division, which reversed the award. 442 A.2d 1062 (1982). It not only rejected defendant's claim for reimbursement but also held that neither a professional license nor an educational degree is "property" for the purposes of the equitable distribution statute, *N.J.S.A.* 2A:34–23. In so holding, the Appellate Division stated that it was bound by *Stern v. Stern*, 331 A.2d 257 (N.J.1975), where the Court held that "a person's earning capacity ... should not be recognized as a separate, particular item of property within the meaning of *N.J.S.A.* 2A:34–23" (footnote omitted). The Appellate Division noted that if enhanced earning capacity is not property, then "neither is the license or degree, which is merely the memorialization of the attainment of the skill, qualification and educational background which is the prerequisite of the enhanced earning capacity...." The court noted that degrees and licenses lack many of the attributes of most property rights, and that their value is not only speculative, but also may be fully accounted for by way of alimony and equitable division of the other assets.

In rejecting defendant's claim for reimbursement, the Appellate Division disapproved of the attempt to measure the contributions of the parties to one another or to their marriage. The court cited with approval *Wisner v. Wisner*, 631 P.2d 115, 123 (Ariz.App.1981), where an Arizona appeals court stated:

> [I]t is improper for a court to treat a marriage as an arm's length transaction by allowing a spouse to come into court after the fact and make legal arguments regarding unjust enrichment....
>
> ... [C]ourts should assume, in the absence of contrary proof, that the decision [to obtain a professional degree] was mutual and took into account what sacrifices the community [of husband and wife] needed to make in the furtherance of that decision. [emphasis in original]

The Appellate Division saw no need to distinguish contributions made toward a spouse's attainment of a license or degree from other contributions, calling such special treatment "a kind of elitism which inappropriately depreciates the value of all the other types of contributions made to each other by other spouses...." Finally, the court noted that in this case each spouse left the marriage "with comparable earning capacity and comparable educational achievements." The court did not order a remand....

II

This case first involves a question of statutory interpretation. The Court must decide whether the Legislature intended an M.B.A. degree to be "property" so that, if acquired by either spouse during a marriage, its value must be equitably distributed upon divorce. In determining whether the Legislature intended to treat an M.B.A. degree as property under *N.J.S.A.* 2A:34–23, the Court gains little guidance from traditional rules of statutory construction. There is no legislative history on the meaning of the word "property" in the equitable distribution statute, *N.J.S.A.* 2A:34–23, and the statute itself offers no guidance. Therefore, statutory construction in this case means little more than an inquiry into the extent to which professional degrees and licenses share the qualities of other things that the Legislature and courts have treated as property.

Regarding equitable distribution, this Court has frequently held that an "expansive interpretation [is] to be given to the word 'property,' " *Gauger v. Gauger*, 376 A.2d 523 (1977). New Jersey courts have subjected a broad range of assets and interests to equitable distribution including vested but unmatured private pensions; military retirement pay and disability benefits; unliquidated claim for benefits under workers' compensation; and personal injury claims. But see *Amato v. Amato*, 434 A.2d 639 (App.Div.1981)(reversing trial court's equitable distribution award requiring wife to give husband 25% of any proceeds she might recover for medical malpractice that occurred during the marriage).

This Court, however, has never subjected to equitable distribution an asset whose future monetary value is as uncertain and unquantifiable as a professional degree or license. The Appellate Division discussed at some length the characteristics that distinguish professional licenses and degrees from other assets and interests, including intangible ones, that courts equitably distribute as marital property. Quoting from *In re Marriage of Graham*, 574 P.2d 75, 77 (1978), in which the Colorado Supreme Court held that an M.B.A. degree is not subject to equitable distribution, the court stated:

> An educational degree, such as an M.B.A., is simply not encompassed even by the broad views of the concept of "property." It does not have an exchange value or any objective transferable value on an open market. It is personal to the holder. It terminates on death of the holder and is not inheritable. It cannot be assigned, sold, transferred, conveyed, or pledged. An advanced degree is a cumulative product of many years of previous education, combined with diligence and hard work. It may not be acquired by the mere expenditure of money. It is simply an intellectual achievement that may potentially assist in the future acquisition of property. In our view, it has none of the attributes of property in the usual sense of that term. [442 A.2d 1062]

A professional license or degree is a personal achievement of the holder. It cannot be sold and its value cannot readily be determined. A professional license or degree represents the opportunity to obtain an amount of money only upon the occurrence of highly uncertain future events. By contrast, the vested but unmatured pension at issue in *Kikkert* entitled the owner to a definite amount of money at a certain future date.

The value of a professional degree for purposes of property distribution is nothing more than the possibility of enhanced earnings that the particular academic credential will provide. In *Stern v. Stern*, 331 A.2d 257 (1975), we held that a lawyer's earning capacity,

> even where its development has been aided and enhanced by the other spouse ... should not be recognized as a separate, particular item of property within the meaning of *N.J.S.A.* 2A:34–23. Potential earning capacity ... should not be deemed property as such within the meaning of the statute. [footnote omitted]

Equitable distribution of a professional degree would similarly require distribution of "earning capacity"—income that the degree holder might never acquire. The amount of future earnings would be entirely speculative. Moreover, any assets resulting from income for professional services would be property acquired after the marriage; the statute restricts equitable distribution to property acquired during the marriage. *N.J.S.A.* 2A:34–23.

Valuing a professional degree in the hands of any particular individual at the start of his or her career would involve a gamut of calculations that reduces to little more than guesswork. As the Appellate Division noted, courts would be required to determine far more than what the degree holder could earn in the new career. The admittedly speculative dollar amount of

> earnings in the "enhanced" career [must] be reduced by the ... income the spouse should be assumed to have been able to earn if otherwise

> employed. In our view ... [this] is ordinarily nothing but speculation, particularly when it is fair to assume that a person with the ability and motivation to complete professional training or higher education would probably utilize those attributes in concomitantly productive alternative endeavors. [442 A.2d 1062]

Even if such estimates could be made, however, there would remain a world of unforeseen events that could affect the earning potential—not to mention the actual earnings—of any particular degree holder.

> A person qualified by education for a given profession may choose not to practice it, may fail at it, or may practice in a specialty, location or manner which generates less than the average income enjoyed by fellow professionals. The potential worth of the education may never be realized for these or many other reasons. An award based upon the prediction of the degree holder's success at the chosen field may bear no relationship to the reality he or she faces after the divorce. [*DeWitt v. DeWitt*, 296 N.W.2d 761, 768 (Wis.App.1980)(footnote omitted)]

Moreover, the likelihood that an equitable distribution will prove to be unfair is increased in those cases where the court miscalculates the value of the license or degree.

> The potential for inequity to the failed professional or one who changes careers is at once apparent; his or her spouse will have been awarded a share of something which never existed in any real sense.

The finality of property distribution precludes any remedy for such unfairness. "Unlike an award of alimony, which can be adjusted after divorce to reflect unanticipated changes in the parties' circumstances, a property division may not [be adjusted]."

Because of these problems, most courts that have faced the issue have declined to treat professional degrees and licenses as marital property subject to distribution upon divorce. Several courts, while not treating educational degrees as property, have awarded the supporting spouse an amount based on the cost to the supporting spouse of obtaining the degree. In effect, the supporting spouse was reimbursed for her financial contributions used by the supported spouse in obtaining a degree. Cf. *Inman v. Inman*, 578 S.W.2d 266, 269 (Ky.Ct.App. 1979)(dental license held to be property but measure of wife's interest was amount of investment in husband's education).

Even if it were marital property, valuing educational assets in terms of their cost would be an erroneous application of equitable distribution law. As the Appellate Division explained, the cost of a professional degree "has little to do with any real value of the degree and fails to consider at all the nonfinancial efforts made by the degree holder in completing his course of study." Once a degree candidate has earned his or her degree, the amount that a spouse—or anyone else—paid towards its attainment has no bearing whatever on its value. The cost of a spouse's financial contributions has no logical connection to the value of that degree.

As the Appellate Division correctly noted, "the cost approach [to equitable distribution] is plainly not conceptually predicated on a property theory at all but rather represents a general notion of how to do equity in this one special situation." Equitable distribution in these cases derives from the proposition that the supporting spouse should be reimbursed for contributions to the marital unit that, because of the divorce, did not bear its expected fruit for the supporting spouse.

The trial court recognized that the theoretical basis for the amount of its award was not equitable distribution, but rather reimbursement. It held that "the education and degree obtained by plaintiff, under the circumstances of this case, constitute a property right subject to equitable offset upon the dissolution of the marriage." The court allowed a "reasonable sum as a credit ... on behalf of the maintenance of the household and the support of the plaintiff during the educational period." Although the court found that the degree was distributable property, it actually reimbursed the defendant without attempting to give her part of the value of the degree.

This Court does not support reimbursement between former spouses in alimony proceedings as a general principle. Marriage is not a business arrangement in which the parties keep track of debits and credits, their accounts to be settled upon divorce. Rather, as we have said, "marriage is a shared enterprise, a joint undertaking ... in many ways it is akin to a partnership." *Rothman v. Rothman*, 320 A.2d 496 (1974). But every joint undertaking has its bounds of fairness. Where a partner to marriage takes the benefits of his spouse's support in obtaining a professional degree or license with the understanding that future benefits will accrue and inure to both of them, and the marriage is then terminated without the supported spouse giving anything in return, an unfairness has occurred that calls for a remedy.

In this case, the supporting spouse made financial contributions towards her husband's professional education with the expectation that both parties would enjoy material benefits flowing from the professional license or degree. It is therefore patently unfair that the supporting spouse be denied the mutually anticipated benefit while the supported spouse keeps not only the degree, but also all of the financial and material rewards flowing from it.

Furthermore, it is realistic to recognize that in this case, a supporting spouse has contributed more than mere earnings to her husband with the mutual expectation that both of them—she as well as he—will realize and enjoy material improvements in their marriage as a result of his increased earning capacity. Also, the wife has presumably made personal financial sacrifices, resulting in a reduced or lowered standard of living. Additionally, her husband, by pursuing preparations for a future career, has foregone gainful employment and financial contributions to the marriage that would have been forthcoming had he been employed. He thereby has further reduced the level of support his wife might otherwise have received, as well as the standard of living both of them would have otherwise enjoyed. In effect, through her contributions, the supporting spouse has consented to live at a lower material level while her husband has prepared for another career. She has postponed, as it were, present consumption and a higher standard of living, for the future prospect of greater support and material benefits. The supporting spouse's sacrifices would have been rewarded had the marriage endured and the mutual expectations of both of them been fulfilled. The unredressed sacrifices—loss of support and reduction of the standard of living—coupled with the unfairness attendant upon the defeat of the supporting spouse's shared expectation of future advantages, further justify a remedial reward. In this sense, an award that is referable to the spouse's monetary contributions to her partner's education significantly implicates basic considerations of marital support and standard of living—factors that are clearly relevant in the determination and award of conventional alimony.

To provide a fair and effective means of compensating a supporting spouse who has suffered a loss or reduction of support, or has incurred a lower standard of living, or has been deprived of a better standard of living in the future, the Court now introduces the concept of reimbursement alimony into divorce proceedings. The concept properly accords with the Court's belief that regardless of the appropriateness of permanent alimony or the presence or absence of marital property to be equitably distributed, there will be circumstances where a supporting spouse should be reimbursed for the financial contributions he or she made to the spouse's successful professional training. Such reimbursement alimony should cover all financial contributions towards the former spouse's education, including household expenses, educational costs, school travel expenses and any other contributions used by the supported spouse in obtaining his or her degree or license.

This result is consistent with the remedial provisions of the matrimonial statute. *N.J.S.A.* 2A:34–23. A basic purpose of alimony relates to the quality of economic life to which one spouse is entitled and that becomes the obligation of the other. Alimony has to do with support and standard of living. We have recently recognized the relevance of these concepts in accepting the notion of rehabilitative alimony, which is consonant with the basic underlying rationale that a party is entitled to continue at a customary standard of living inclusive of costs necessary for needed educational training. *Lepis v. Lepis*, 416 A.2d 45 n. 9.

The statute recognizes that alimony should be tailored to individual circumstances, particularly those relating to the financial status of the parties. Thus, in all actions for divorce (fault and no fault), when alimony is awarded, the court should consider actual need, ability to pay and duration of the marriage. In a "fault" divorce, however, the court "may consider also the proofs made in establishing such ground in determining ... alimony ... that is fit, reasonable and just." *N.J.S.A.* 2A:34–23. There is nothing in the statute to suggest that the standards for awarding alimony are mutually exclusive. Consequently, the financial contributions of the parties during the marriage can be relevant. Financial dishonesty or financial unfairness between the spouses, or overreaching also can be material. The Legislature has not precluded these considerations. Nothing in the statute precludes the court from considering marital conduct—such as one spouse contributing to the career of the other with the expectation of material benefit—in fashioning alimony awards. The flexible nature of relief in a matrimonial cause is also evidenced by the equitable distribution remedy that is provided in the same section of the matrimonial statute.

The Court does not hold that every spouse who contributes toward his or her partner's education or professional training is entitled to reimbursement alimony. Only monetary contributions made with the mutual and shared expectation that both parties to the marriage will derive increased income and material benefits should be a basis for such an award. For example, it is unlikely that a financially successful executive's spouse who, after many years of homemaking, returns to school would upon divorce be required to reimburse her husband for his contributions toward her degree. Reimbursement alimony should not subvert the basic goals of traditional alimony and equitable distribution.

In proper circumstances, however, courts should not hesitate to award reimbursement alimony. Marriage should not be a free ticket to professional education and training without subsequent obligations. This Court should not ignore the scenario of the young professional who after being supported through graduate school leaves his mate for supposedly greener pastures. One spouse ought not to receive a divorce complaint when the other receives a diploma. Those spouses supported through professional school should recognize that they may be called upon to reimburse the supporting spouses for the financial contributions they received in pursuit of their professional training. And they cannot deny the basic fairness of this result.

As we have stated, reimbursement alimony will not always be appropriate or necessary to compensate a spouse who has contributed financially to the partner's professional education or training. "Rehabilitative alimony" may be more appropriate in cases where a spouse who gave up or postponed her own education to support the household requires a lump sum or a short-term award to achieve economic self-sufficiency. The Court specifically approved of such limited alimony awards in *Lepis v. Lepis*, 416 A.2d 45 (1980), stating that we did "not share the view that only unusual cases will warrant the 'rehabilitative alimony' approach." However, rehabilitative alimony would not be appropriate where the supporting spouse is unable to return to the job market, or has already attained economic self-sufficiency.

Similarly, where the parties to a divorce have accumulated substantial assets during a lengthy marriage, courts should compensate for any unfairness to one party who sacrificed for the other's education, not by reimbursement alimony but by an equitable distribution of the assets to reflect the parties' different circumstances and earning capacities. In *Rothman, supra*, the Court explicitly rejected the notion that courts should presume an equal division of marital property. 320 A.2d 496. "Rejecting any simple formula, we rather believe that each case should be examined as an individual and particular entity." *Id.* If the degree-holding spouse has already put his professional education to use, the degree's value in enhanced earning potential will have been realized in the form of property, such as a partnership interest or other asset, that is subject to equitable distribution.

The degree holder's earning capacity can also be considered in an award of permanent alimony. Alimony awards under *N.J.S.A.* 2A:34–23 must take into account the supporting spouse's ability to pay; earning capacity is certainly relevant to this determination. Our courts have recognized that a primary purpose of alimony, besides preventing either spouse from requiring public assistance, is "to permit the wife, who contributed during marriage to the accumulation of the marital assets, to share therein." *Lynn v. Lynn*, 379 A.2d 1046 (Ch.Div.1977), rev'd on other grounds, 398 A.2d 141 (App.Div.1979). Even though the enhanced earning potential provided by a degree or license is not "property" for purposes of *N.J.S.A.* 2A:34–23, it clearly should be a factor considered by the trial judge in determining a proper amount of alimony. If the degree holder's actual earnings turn out to diverge greatly from the court's estimate, making the amount of alimony unfair to either party, the alimony award can be adjusted accordingly.

III

We stated in *Stern, supra*, that while earning potential should not be treated as a separate item of property, [p]otential earning capacity is doubtless a factor to be considered by a trial judge in determining what distribution will be "equitable" and it is even more obviously relevant upon the issue of alimony. [66 N.J. at 345, 331 A.2d 257] We believe that *Stern* presents the best approach for achieving fairness when one spouse has acquired a professional degree or license during the marriage. Courts may not make any permanent distribution of the value of professional degrees and licenses, whether based upon estimated worth or cost. However, where a spouse has received from his or her partner financial contributions used in obtaining a professional degree or license with the expectation of deriving material benefits for both marriage partners, that spouse may be called upon to reimburse the supporting spouse for the amount of contributions received.

In the present case, the defendant's financial support helped her husband to obtain his M.B.A. degree, which assistance was undertaken with the expectation of deriving material benefits for both spouses. Although the trial court awarded the defendant a sum as "equitable offset" for her contributions, the trial court's approach was not consistent with the guidelines we have announced in this opinion. Therefore, we are remanding the case so the trial court can determine whether reimbursement alimony should be awarded in this case and, if so, what amount is appropriate.

The judgment of the Appellate Division is reversed and the cause remanded for further proceedings not inconsistent with this opinion.

Questions on Mahoney

(1) Would Mrs. Mahoney be eligible for alimony under the UMDA? Under traditional standards for granting alimony?

(2) Is Mr. Mahoney's degree property?

(a) Is the degree property under the UMDA? If it is not property, does that mean its existence will be irrelevant in a division of the Mahoney property under the UMDA?

(b) Is the degree property under New Jersey law? Is the degree in fact different in significant respects from "vested but unmatured private pensions, ... military retirement pay and disability benefits, ... unliquidated claims for benefits under workers' compensation, ... and personal injury claims"? Is the degree the same as a lawyer's earning capacity?

(c) In the absence of a statute or judicial precedent, how would you go about deciding whether a professional degree is "property"? *Is* a professional degree "property"?

(3) Assuming that Mr. Mahoney's degree is property under the UMDA, how should it be valued?

(4) Assuming that Mr. Mahoney's degree is property under the UMDA, what share of it, if any, would Mrs. Mahoney receive under the UMDA?

(5) What would Mrs. Mahoney have been entitled to under the ALI principles?

(6) The *Mahoney* court creates the doctrine of reimbursement alimony. What rationales for that doctrine does the court suggest, explicitly or implicitly? How persuasively does the court defend each of them? How persuasively can you defend them? Why does the court countenance awarding Mrs. Mahoney reimbursement alimony even while saying that it "does not support reimbursement between former spouses in alimony proceedings as a general principle"? Can you identify other possible rationales for the doctrine of reimbursement alimony?

(7) You have recently been approached by a committee of the League of Women Voters which is examining the State of Hutchins' marital property law. The committee is particularly interested in the problem of professional degrees. The committee asks for your opinion about how you would have the law treat this problem. What do you tell them? What principles for dividing professional degrees (besides reimbursement alimony) will you tell them about? What are the rationales for those principles? How will you advise them professional degrees should be treated?

(8) Reconsider now the various rationales for the doctrine of reimbursement alimony or for the division of professional degrees. How should Mr. Mahoney's degree be valued under each of those rationales? How should it be divided under each of those rationales?

(2) Is a Professional Degree Property?

As you will remember from *Mahoney* and from Section 307 of the UMDA, divorce courts are commonly instructed to divide the "property" or "property and assets" of the parties. As *Mahoney* indicates, most states decline to treat the degree or professional license as property but find some rationale for awarding the working spouse some amount that reflects the tuition, the lost income, or the support paid during the graduate or professional school. A few states, like Colorado, *In re Marriage of Graham*, 574 P2d 75 (1978), make no award because the degree is not distributable property and the working spouse by definition does not "need" maintenance to live at the standard enjoyed during the marriage. But even *Graham* has now been modified by *In re Marriage of Olar*, 747 P2d 676 (Colo 1987), which held that "need" requires the court to consider the parties' economic circumstances and reasonable expectations during the marriage. New York uniquely treats degrees, and other career enhancements occurring during marriage, as divisible property. See *O'Brien v. O'Brien*, 66 NY2d 576 (medical license); *Golub v. Golub*, 527 NYS2d 946 (1988) (appreciation in career of actress and model).

But what does "property" mean? The UMDA does not define "property." The Uniform Marital Property Act defines "property" in a way that may solve all the problems, for the UMPA defines "property" as "an interest, present or future, legal or equitable, vested or contingent, in real or personal property." Section 1(15). Nor does "property" have any established definite meaning in Anglo–American law generally. How then might we think about whether a professional degree is property? Three techniques are worth considering.

The first such technique, one common in legal reasoning, is analogy. Let us see what can be learned about whether marital degrees are property by studying the example of real property. The development of property in land provides a useful analogy because at some point land in England changed from "not property" to "property." After the Norman Conquest, that is, land was held directly of the king, it reverted to him on the tenant's death, it could not be bought or sold (without the king's permission), it could not be inherited, it could not be willed, and it was held only as an element in a personal relationship between the king and the tenant. At this point, land could usefully be said not to be property for anyone except the king. Gradually, however, all this changed. Land can now be bought, sold, given away, inherited, and willed, all without the permission of any person or institution. It can be held entirely without regard to the owner's social relationships. It is property.

On this analogy, a professional degree does not look much like property: it cannot be bought, sold, given away, inherited, or willed. It has no market value. It is personal to the holder, a certificate of the knowledge and skills he or she has acquired.

The second technique for discovering whether a professional degree is property is to consult conventional understandings of the term "property." This technique influences thinking in, for example, the law of takings, which prevents the government from taking without compensation perhaps all forms of conventional property (any continuing trespass on a restaurant's land, for example, must be compensated), but which does not protect all kinds of value (the construction of a highway that diverted business away from the same restaurant probably would not be a taking, however great the economic damage to the restaurant).

On this analysis too a professional degree doesn't look much like property. It would probably not occur to most people to think of a degree as property (partly, perhaps, because of the considerations we developed in thinking about the analogy to land). Rather, people tend to think of the degree as merely symbolic of the effort and education the degree represents. People are also aware of the ability and preparation it took merely to be eligible for professional training. Further, there is a long-standing practice in which funding an education (through fellowships, scholarships, employment, and family contributions) is separate from owning the degree. Contrast this to the practice of some athletes (boxers, for instance) of selling shares in themselves in return for support for their early training.

Similarly, goodwill of a business, in this case a highly specialized medical practice based on personal goodwill, represents future earning capacity and is therefore not divisible in a dissolution proceeding. Yoon v. Yoon, 711 NE2d 1265 (Ind 1999).

A third technique for discovering whether a degree is property is to ask what purposes "property" generally serves or serves in a particular legal context, and then to ask whether the form of value under consideration serves that kind of purpose. This technique, like the others, must be used carefully, since not everything that serves a particular purpose necessarily falls into the same category as everything else that serves that purpose. This technique was used to telling effect by, for example, Charles Reich in his influential article *The New Property*, 73 Yale L J 733 (1964), in which he argued that property's function is to limit the power of the state to control individuals, that the state had created and continued to control many new forms of value which had to an important extent supplanted the old forms, and that the new forms of value had to be treated as property if the institution of property were to remain strong enough to serve its protective function.

This technique *can* be used to justify treating professional degrees as marital property. The argument, very briefly, would be that the purpose of the division of marital property is to assure that both parties are as well off economically after the divorce as possible and that the economic efforts of each are as fairly rewarded as possible. Defining professional degrees as property increases the amount of money to be divided and thus gives courts more flexibility in serving both goals.

However, the fact that the technique can be used to justify treating professional degrees as marital property does not mean it should be. The other techniques have important virtues. For instance, both those techniques help preserve some consistent meaning to the word "property," and the conventional understandings technique helps keep the legal and popular meanings of property close, which may make it easier for the legally untrained to arrange their affairs. Furthermore, the third technique's attraction—its flexibility—is also its fault. All depends on how you define the goal of property generally and marital property particularly. Property performs many social functions besides the one Reich, for instance, draws on. (Most obviously, it is the basis for capitalism, an economic system thought attractive for its productiveness and efficiency.) And marital property serve many functions. To an examination of those functions we now turn.

(3) Interests in the Division of Marital Wealth

Mahoney raises in a novel and provocative form the general question how marital property should be divided upon divorce. While much has been written about dividing marital property, surprisingly little has been said about what interests we might serve in doing so. We will explore that question through the professional degree cases to help you assess how the division of marital property is and should be managed.

Because we have selected only one professional degree case, you cannot see that the cases as a whole are in disarray, widely disagreeing about how divorce courts should treat professional degrees. Even within the opinion in *Mahoney*, the court's confusion is palpable. What ends might a court serve in dividing marital property, and how might each end be served in a professional degree case? There are a surprising number of such ends. Each has something to say for itself. Yet, while some of them are compatible with some of the others, many of them conflict. The difficulty of systematically reconciling them, or even ranking them, is attested to by the failure of the UMDA, for instance, to try to do so. Even when purposes have been selected, it can be hard to say what treatment of any particular kind of property will serve those purposes. The following discussion, then, uses the problem of professional degrees to examine the possible goals that might be served in dividing marital property. As you read each section, you should not only try to evaluate the goal being studied, but also ask whether it conflicts with the other goals.

Need

Goal: Marital property should be divided to assure that the needs of each spouse are, to the degree possible, fully met.

Need is perhaps the purpose most plainly and fully expressed in the UMDA, which tells a court dividing marital property to look to each party's earning power, assets, and entitlement to alimony. But why should need be relevant in distributing marital property? On a traditional view of the purpose of dividing property in either a separate property or a community property system, the court's only function is deciding who owns the property, not who needs it more. (Any question of need in the traditional system would, in principle, be a question of alimony, not property division.) In other words, the court's function is in principle the same as in any other dispute over property—to determine the owner. The fact that the widow needs Blackacre and the land developer doesn't gives her no greater legal claim to the property than she otherwise has. Why should the property issue be different when a divorcing couple is involved? Why, in other words, should one spouse effectively be required to support the other after the marriage?

The obvious response to these questions is that in ordinary property disputes, the parties have only a business relation with each other, while marriage is a special relation that creates special obligations. But what special relation does marriage create, and how long does that relation endure, if at all, after the marriage? Even during marriage, we have seen that there is some doubt about one spouse's duty to support the other. That doubt arose partly because of the law's reluctance to intervene in the family to enforce that duty. But the doubt is intensified by changes in our social circumstances and attitudes. The support duty may have made some sense in the traditional system of marriage, where the husband was obliged to support his wife and the wife was obliged to keep the house and raise the children. But such marriages are now less typical, and they are not the kind of marriage the law seeks to encourage, as *Orr* implies. Now that the support duty seems to run both ways, isn't the law saying that both spouses ought to be ready and willing to take care of themselves? And doesn't the support duty make less sense and seem less necessary when women are increasingly able and inclined to support themselves?

If the support obligation is puzzling during marriage, isn't it inexplicable after marriage? That is, while it might make sense to require that partners in a marriage be partners economically and jointly contribute to the household, does it make any sense to do so after the marriage is over? Isn't the basis for the requirement of support during marriage in large part that each spouse gets something from the marriage and therefore ought to contribute to it? And isn't the purpose of marriage for each of the individuals in it to find emotional support and companionship? And when the purpose of the marriage can no longer be served, is there any reason support obligations should continue? Isn't the post-marital support obligation a relic of the time when marriage was thought to be a life-long commitment? That time is surely no more. Half of all marriages are expected to end in divorce, many of them quite quickly. The law recognizes these changed social facts by making divorce available essentially on unilateral demand. And other social institutions—the second-marriage family, for example—have arisen which rely on the termination of obligations (except perhaps child support) from first marriages.

Furthermore, isn't the post-marital support obligation out of step with much of our general thinking about people's obligations to each other? Isn't it now generally thought that the state, not individuals, should be responsible for succoring? Are the needy post-marital support duties anything more than the government's attempt to require a specific individual to do what society as a whole ought to do?

Let us put the preceding arguments in a different way. Isn't it the trend of modern family law to treat people not as members of families, but as individuals who decide, for their own purposes and periods, to enter into relationships with other individuals and who should be free to leave those relationships when that is best for them? And if this is so, shouldn't the duties they have to family members (except children, who cannot make decisions for themselves and protect their own interests) end when the relationship ends?

One response to this argument is to say that a post-marital support obligation is legitimate because one spouse has caused the other to weaken his or her position so as to justify relying on the other spouse for support. But these arguments go not to the need purpose, but to one of the contract or quasi-contract purposes we will address later.

Some of the difficulty with the need criterion may be seen by asking what level of need ought to be used to set awards. On one hand, "need" seems to imply some abstract standard, but it is hard to see what that standard should be. There is probably only one abstract standard readily available, and that is the poverty standard. This standard may be appropriate, at least in the sense that it is designed to protect people from falling below a standard at which it is impossible to live. However, for most beneficiaries it will represent a severe falling off from the standard to which they were accustomed. This suggests the obvious alternative standard, the one commonly used in setting alimony and child-support payments—the standard set by the couple during the marriage. But why is this standard more appropriate than the other plausible standards—the standard the spouse claiming marital property or alimony established before marriage, or the standard the couple reasonably expected to attain during the marriage? Furthermore, is the standard of living during the marriage at all realistic for establishing need after the marriage, given that the income of one spouse will almost never support both spouses at the old level when they are living separately?

These questions raise a further significant question: How long should the obligation of support to the level of need last? Only long enough for the supported spouse to achieve by himself or herself the established standard of need? For life? Once you have accepted the principle that one spouse is obligated to provide for the other spouse's "need," why should there be a limit on the obligation? The answer to this question presumably depends on the rationale for support to the level of need. So we must once again ask, what is that rationale?

How ought professional degrees be treated if need is one of the purposes of the division of marital property? This is a relatively easy question. Insofar as we want to eradicate need, the deeper the pocket from which to meet the need the better, and treating professional degrees as property deepens pockets. Just that consideration has been influential in the trend toward treating professional degrees as property divisible on divorce.

Affecting Marital Behavior: Altruism

Goal: Marital property should be divided to foster desirable behavior within marriage, particularly mutual trust, concern, and generosity.

One of the traditional reasons for valuing marriage is that in it people are, more than perhaps in any relationship except that of parents and children, supposed to behave altruistically. Knowledge of how the law requires marital property to be divided might affect how people behave within marriages, and arguably the law of marital property should be organized in such a way as to encourage altruistic behavior.

The first question this proposition raises is whether people ever know enough about marital property law to be affected by it during their marriage. No doubt many people have a rough sense of how their state's system works, particularly if they are well–to–do or if they have already been through one divorce. But will people have an accurate and detailed enough sense to perceive the ways in which the law is encouraging altruism? So will those ways loom large enough in the couple's mind (given all the other factors that will affect the couple) to alter their behavior?

The second question about encouraging altruism is whether the goal is proper. The trend of the law is toward barring government from influencing people in intimate and family situations. Perhaps encouraging altruistic behavior is uncontroversial enough that the ordinary strictures against government influence over family life should not apply. But it is not clear that the goal is uncontroversial: it may conflict, for instance, with the widely appealing goal of encouraging the autonomy of the spouses. Furthermore, even if encouraging altruism is uncontroversial, people are likely to differ sharply over what altruism within a marriage means and how far it should be encouraged.

The third problem with encouraging altruism within marriage through marital property law is related to the point which concluded the preceding paragraph: it is not clear *how* one might use marital property law for that purpose. Consider our problem of professional degrees. Mr. Mahoney could be arguing that Mrs. Mahoney intended her support for him to be a gift, an act of altruism. Mrs. Mahoney could argue in return that the altruistic thing for Mr. Mahoney to have done was to assume responsibility for meeting her expectations that she would benefit economically after he received his degree. If the court dividing their marital property held that Mrs. Mahoney's contribution to his support was not a gift, it might seem to be denying that spouses can contribute to each other's welfare in altruistic ways. If the court held that Mr. Mahoney need not recompense Mrs. Mahoney, it might seem to be denying that he intended to act altruistically.

One solution to this dilemma is to say that courts should at least protect spouses from injuries caused by their acts of altruism. This solution, however, takes us to the question of the extent to which sacrifice should be recompensed, an issue we will discuss shortly.

Fourth, it is sometimes suggested that women, as a whole, may be more interested in sharing and giving than their male counterparts. Should reimbursement therefore be required from men as a gender "leveling" device? See Carol Rose, *Women and Property: Gaining and Losing Ground*, 78 Va L Rev 421 (1992).

Affecting Marital Behavior: Autonomy

Goal: Marital property should be divided to foster the autonomy of the individual spouses.

As you will recall, one of the primary criticisms of the old separate property system was that it tended to reduce the wife to dependence, dependence which weakened her position within the marriage, inhibited her from leaving it, and made it hard for her to establish herself after it. This criticism rests partly on an understanding of the role of law in creating and sustaining social attitudes. This understanding draws us toward organizing marital property law so that people's attitudes and economic situations lead them to be autonomous.

This goal presents the same kind of problems as the goal of promoting altruism. First, can marital property law seriously affect the autonomy of spouses within a marriage? Second, is it proper for the state to seek to affect attitudes within a marriage? Third, what principles of division will foster autonomy? On one hand, it might be argued that Mrs. Mahoney reduced her own autonomy by relying on her husband for her long-term economic well-being, that the law should not encourage people to rely on spouses in that way, and that therefore the law should not award the supporting spouse an interest in the other's degree, at least in the absence of an explicit contractual understanding. The argument might be extended by suggesting that spouses should be encouraged to develop their own resources and abilities so that they have economic independence both during and after the marriage. On the other hand, it might be replied that what will most increase Mrs. Mahoney's autonomy now is to award her an interest in Mr. Mahoney's degree. In other words, the reply would suggest that autonomy is most justly increased when legitimate expectations are legally enforceable. (The question of what legitimate expectations means we will discuss shortly).

Equality

Goal: Marital property should be divided to maximize the equality between the spouses after divorce.

Equality as the goal of property division—that is, dividing property equally between the spouses—has several attractions. Indeed, those attractions are sufficiently great that equality is, in modified form, a primary goal of the community property system of dividing marital property. Superficially, at least, it looks fair. It seems to effectuate our desire that the law not prefer husband to wife or wife to husband. It seems to serve our belief that husbands and wives both contribute to their households, that all kinds of contributions should be recognized, and that it is uncomfortable to try to distinguish the value of one contribution from the value of another.

The difficulty with equality as a goal, however, is that it may not accomplish those objectives that make it attractive. Or, to put the difficulty somewhat differently, the goal of equality conflicts with almost all the other possible goals of the division of marital property. An equal division is an attempt to do equity, but that equity in individual cases will almost always be more complicated than a fifty-fifty split. A fifty-fifty split, for example, may not redress all the sacrifices one spouse has made for another, may not fulfill the legitimate expectations of the spouses, may leave a spouse's needs unmet, and so forth.

Some of the difficulties with equality may be seen by investigating some of the individual cases that might arise. The first involves a marriage like the Pfohls', in which one party entered rich and the other entered relatively poor. Why should the poor spouse benefit all the rest of his or her life from having been married for a few years to a rich person? One answer to this question could be found in the traditional view that marriage is a life long joining of husband and wife. But unilateral no-fault divorce and a large swath of contemporary mores make this answer unavailable for discussing the law's division of marital property. A usual justification for equality is that both spouses will have contributed to the couple's acquisition of wealth, but in the Pfohls' case that was plainly not so. This hypothetical, in other words, may suggest to us the reason community property states divide equally only acquests.

A second hypothetical asks whether equality is a proper criterion in a marriage of people with greatly unequal earning power. Suppose, in other words, that Lee Marvin and Michelle Triola had actually married. Why, at the end of the marriage, should he have to part with half of the acquests of the marriage when his income made it possible for the couple to acquire far more than half? The usual argument in favor of an equal division of acquests is that the contributions of husband and wife are actually equal even if they contribute unequal dollar amounts, since there are many ways in which a spouse may contribute to the economic success of the marriage without earning an income, as by keeping house and taking care of children or by helping with professional entertaining. But even though it may be difficult to put dollar values on such contributions, won't their economic value sometimes be much less than the economic value of the other spouse's contribution?

It is important to note that where equality is not a goal of a system of alimony, women are likely to emerge from marriage—as they now do—in an economically weaker situation than men. Ought it be a goal of the law of alimony to rectify that kind of inequality?

Women often pursue careers that are less rewarding economically because they devote themselves more completely to caring for the couple's children. After the divorce, the man's relationship with his children is likely to be diminished, while the wife's is likely to be enhanced. Again, this is a burden, but it is also a benefit. If she primarily took care of them during the marriage, she has received the benefit of a close relationship. Much depends on how the relationship with the children is conceived. Is it a burden, or a benefit? How should either conclusion affect the award of alimony?

Predictability

Goal: Marital property should be divided to maximize the predictability of the law.

Predictability has perhaps always been thought desirable. One reason is that, as much law and economics scholarship suggests, predictability decreases litigation, and litigation wastes scarce personal and social resources. For an application of this view to property distribution, see Margaret F. Brinig and Michael V. Alexeev, *Trading at Divorce: Preferences, Legal Rules and Transaction Costs*, 8 Ohio St J on Disp Res 279, 283–84 & n 29 (1993).

Another reason for valuing predictability is that predictable law gives people more control over their lives. A spouse deciding whether to seek a divorce, or spouses negotiating over the economic and personal issues that accompany divorce, will want to know as a baseline for thought or negotiation how a court would distribute what is, after all, the entire wealth of both parties. Predictability is also valued because it is related to fairness—a rule that is not predictable cannot securely be similarly applied to similarly situated parties.

It is a drawback of current divorce law that its trend is toward eliminating predictability in all its aspects except the availability of the divorce itself. Both the common-law and the community-property systems at least attempted to be predictable; their lack of success had to do with the complexities introduced into both systems by the desire to take people's different circumstances into account. Much law now, however, seems to abandon attempts at predictability and instead to confide discretion in courts quite uninformed by useful guidelines. For example, the UMDA's marital property provisions tell potential litigants only that a judge will seek an "equitable" result based on a long list of criteria whose intended applications are uncertain and whose relative weights are unspecified. (Consider, for instance, the requirement that the judge consider the length of the marriage. Which way does this criterion cut?)

If predictability is the value to be served, any clear rule as to professional degrees would probably suffice. On the other hand, predictability might be most enhanced by not treating professional degrees as property, since that rule would reflect the understanding in ordinary language that a professional degree is not property and would fit the law's ordinary understanding of what property is. This would reduce the risk that differences between ordinary language and the law's ordinary language on one hand and the treatment of professional degrees on the other hand would promote inconsistencies in the treatment of professional degrees. This would not necessarily mean the degree would be irrelevant in working out the economic relations of the parties, since the income the degree helped produce could be considered in setting alimony. The advantage of alimony over property division as the vehicle for recognizing the degree is that, while property is supposed to be divided once for all, alimony decrees may be changed as circumstances change. A difficulty with alimony, however, is that, as we have seen, the modern trend is away from long-term alimony. Thus if predictability is the goal and it is still felt professional degrees should be divided, it will become important what valuation method is used, since some methods produce more predictable results than others.

Of all the marital-property systems you have studied, the ALI's Principles seem to value predictability most: "The ALI draft specifies the circumstances under which parties qualify for an award and outlines in great detail how the amount of the award should be calculated. Discretion is largely eliminated." J. Thomas Oldham, *ALI Principles of Family Dissolution: Some Comments*, 1997 U Ill L Rev 801, 817 (1997). How successful is the ALI at offering spouses predictability? The ALI almost seemed to strive to make its rules complex. What is more, those rules do not reflect what most Americans today would regard as intuitively obvious principles of property. How accurately, then, will judges apply them? How accurately will lawyers predict how judges will apply them? A pre-eminent disadvantage of predictability is a loss of flexibility to do justice in individual cases. Will judges create flexibility where none was intended? Even if lawyers and judges follow the ALI rules strictly, will couples ever know the rules before they contemplate divorce? Will most couples grasp the rules even during divorce proceedings? (Recall the description of how divorce lawyers and their clients which you read in Chapter 1.3.A.3.)

Finality

Goal: Marital property should be divided to maximize the finality of divorces.

Like predictability, finality is generally a value in the law, as the doctrines of collateral estoppel and res judicata and the principle of the statute of limitations suggest. Finality has been a particularly prominent value in the law of divorce. One motive for the reform of divorce law has been the desire to have the divorce process end as quickly and completely as possible. This motive appears, for example, in the spread of no-fault divorce itself and in the movement away from long-term alimony awards. The appeal of finality has several sources. First, marriages that are near divorce are presumably painful, and pain should be ended speedily and fully. Continuing financial relations between the parties can revive (monthly) the sense of injustice and injury the marriage (and the divorce) may have caused. Second, enforcing payments from one ex-spouse to the other (particularly, of course, enforcing alimony and child-support obligations) has historically proved difficult. Third, even apart from the enforcement difficulties, many people believe it is good to reduce the degree of government supervision of the lives of people after divorce, including the supervision of the financial obligations one former spouse owes the other. Fourth, finality frees the former spouses to organize their lives afresh.

What of finality and professional degrees? The problem is that professional degree cases are likely to arise early in the degree-holder's career, when he or she will be unable to make a large lump-sum payment. This increases the appeal of continuing payments, which conflicts with finality. A further problem is that under some valuation schemes it is difficult to know what the degree is worth until the holder has begun to use it. This also increases the appeal of continuing payments and thus also conflicts with the goal of finality. (Two resolutions of this kind of problem are to make the payments periodic, though vested, or to give the spouse a stated proportion of the degree's earnings as they are earned. This is the solution some states use for future pension payments. See, e.g., Va Code Ann § 20–107.3(G)(1)(1993)).

Recompensing Sacrifice

Goal: Marital property should be divided to make whole any sacrifice one spouse has made for the other.

The *Mahoney* court frequently invokes the sacrifice Mrs. Mahoney made and Mr. Mahoney's consequent obligation to recompense her for it. The ALI Principles are remarkable for singling out certain kinds of sacrifices for repayment. Like our other goals, recompensing sacrifice is alluring. If property division should give both spouses their rightful share of the property each brought to or acquired during the marriage, shouldn't spouses' sacrifices affect any allocation of property?

A crucial difficulty with sacrifice, however, is that we don't recompense all sacrifices. For example, the ALI recognizes sacrifices one spouse makes for the other's career, for "care of the marital children," and for care of dependent relatives. But spouses make many other kinds of sacrifices that they regard as important but that the ALI does not recompense. Put in general terms, the problem is this: Married life is an elaborate system of compromises, trades, accommodations, and gifts. Some of these are financial, others not. But economic or not, all of them go to make up the balance of exchanges which the parties during the marriage worked out. It seems troubling to select out a few of these compromises and require that they, but not the other compromises which made up the rest of the system, be recompensed on divorce.

One might propose that only evidently *economic* sacrifices should be recompensed, perhaps because economic compromises can generally be measured fairly readily while non-economic compromises resist measurement. Is this argument from judicial efficiency satisfactory? Would it unfairly abstract some elements of a couple's relationship for compensation but not others? Does it accord with the way people actually think about their relationships? If the rule (of compensating only economic sacrifices) came to be understood, how would it affect people's behavior?

Perhaps economic sacrifices are particularly likely to have been made with the expectation of recompense. However, this argument takes us to the goal of rewarding expectation, which we will deal with shortly. It also rests on an assumption about conduct within marriages which is possibly a good generalization, but which will often be false—that spouses expect (and should expect?) compensation for the things they do for each other. In any event, the trend of marital property law is toward recognizing the value of non-economic contributions to a household.

There is a further difficulty with the argument that economic (but only economic) sacrifice should be recompensed—we do not recompense all economic sacrifices. Consider the following hypothetical. Two years after their marriage, Jerry and Peggy decide Jerry should go to law school. Jerry wants to go to the best law school he can get into, and he is accepted by a very good one located a thousand miles from their home. Peggy, however, is reluctant to leave her family and the town where she was born. Peggy insists that Jerry go to a recently established unaccredited local law school. Jerry unwillingly acquiesces. He is unwilling because he believes he will earn more as a graduate of the out-of-state law school than as a graduate of the local law school. Using money he inherited and that he earned by clerking while in law school, Jerry pays for his education and supports himself, while Peggy works to support herself. On graduation day, Peggy tells Jerry that she has fallen in love with David and that she is going to get a divorce. Jerry calculates that going to the law school he went to instead of the one he wanted to go to cost him $150,000 in present dollars in lifetime earning potential (to say nothing of a diminished range of career choices). Assume Peggy has just inherited $150,000. Should she be required to recompense Jerry's sacrifice? Assume she is penniless. Should she be required to recompense Jerry's sacrifice? The standard legal answer to those questions is presumably no. Does this make sense?

In response to this hypothetical, it might be suggested not that we should recompense all economic sacrifices, but that we should recompense all out-of-pocket economic sacrifices. Why such a distinction should be made is not entirely clear—perhaps because we assume that a sacrifice made in dollars is immediately recognizable as a sacrifice and that its beneficiary therefore ought to realize that he or she may be expected to make his or her spouse whole on divorce. This may take us away from the sacrifice purpose toward a contract or expectation rationale, but let us not worry about that now. Rather, let us inquire into whether all out-of-pocket economic sacrifices are or ought to be recompensed. Consider the following hypothetical. Joe and Sheila meet while both are in college, and when they are seniors they marry. The next year, Joe goes to graduate school to get his Ph.D. in philosophy. Sheila supports Joe for the seven years it takes him to get his degree. On his graduation day, they mutually agree to a divorce. Joe now has a slight chance of getting a badly paying and insecure job teaching philosophy; he has a good chance of not getting such a job at all. He is worse off than if he had never gone to graduate school, because had he not done so he would have continued to work for his college employer, IBM, which is no longer interested in having him back, since his technical skills are now hopelessly out of date. Must Joe be required to recompense Sheila for her sacrifice? On *Mahoney*'s sacrifice principles, surely he should, since Sheila sacrificed much more than Mrs. Mahoney. Does this make sense?

One response to this hypothetical is that Sheila expected no benefit from paying for Joe's education and thus should get none. Once again, however, this takes us to the expectations argument, thus seeming to show that sacrifice by itself is not the issue. In addition, it makes assumptions about Sheila's motives which may not be true—she might well have had her own reasons for wanting to be an academic's wife or to live in the bliss of an academic community. Or she may just have wanted Joe to be happy.

Another response to this hypothetical would argue that Mr. Mahoney was enriched by Mrs. Mahoney's sacrifice (since he could presumably get a better job or faster advancement after receiving his degree) while Joe was not enriched by Sheila's sacrifice (since his degree was effectively worthless economically). But while Joe was not enriched in the sense that his income was increased, he was enriched in the sense that he got what he wanted and what he could not have gotten without Sheila's sacrifice—an advanced education in philosophy and a chance at the career he preferred, however perilous it might be. This point can, furthermore, be readily put in economic terms—had she not supported him, he would have had to earn or borrow the money to pay for his educational and living expenses. He is now economically worse off than he was, but that is because he made an uneconomic career choice, a choice which does not negate the fact of Sheila's sacrifice.

Is then the operative theory that a spouse must reimburse only out-of-pocket economic sacrifices that result in a transfer of economic goods to the other spouse? If so, why does *Mahoney* find it "unlikely that a financially successful executive's spouse who, after many years of homemaking returns to school would upon divorce be required to reimburse her husband for his contributions toward her degree"? Is the point that only real sacrifice, a financial contribution which is felt by the donor, counts? Why? And how are we to decide which sacrifices are felt?

Suppose the theory is that a spouse must reimburse out-of-pocket sacrifices that result in a transfer of economic goods or benefits to the other spouse where the donating spouse has to give up something significant to make the sacrifice. Would it not be true for any but the richest couples that any spouse who supports another ought to be recompensed on divorce? In other words, shouldn't all the financial contributions of either spouse to the other be added up, the smaller figure subtracted from the larger, and the balance awarded to the party who paid more?

It may help to see how this would work in *Mahoney*. We know that in 1978 Mr. Mahoney earned $25,600 a year and Mrs. Mahoney earned $21,000. We don't know their salaries for the years of their marriage, but we may plausibly assume that each earned 5% less each preceding year. Figuring on that basis, Mr. Mahoney's salary would have totaled $172,328 during the marriage. Since he didn't work for 16 months during 1975–77, however, we may subtract $30,805, leaving a total of $141,523 that he contributed to the household. Mrs. Mahoney's salary would have totaled $141,364. On a sacrifice theory, why would either owe the other anything? (Particularly puzzling is Mrs. Mahoney's claim for half the cost of her husband's tuition, since the tuition was "paid for by a combination of veterans' benefits and a payment from the Air Force.")

Carried yet a step further, the question becomes why a person who has supported a spouse should not be recompensed for that support. One usual answer to that question—that spouses contribute in different ways to a marriage, sometimes in economic terms, sometimes in non-economic terms that have economic consequences, and sometimes in non-economic ways that are nevertheless important—takes us back to the question we asked at the beginning of the section on sacrifice, namely, why any single sacrifice should be singled out for compensation, and starts us back on the trail we have followed to this point.

A common theme in our problems with recompensing sacrifice is that underlying many ideas about marriage is the belief that husbands and wives may and ought to make gifts to each other out of love, without expecting to be compensated for them, and even that husbands and wives should sacrifice for each other. Requiring that every sacrifice be reimbursed seems to ratify a materialistic and unloving view of marriage, or, to put it perhaps less invidiously, a very individualistic view of marriage. Yet if you do not sometimes require spouses to reimburse sacrifice on divorce, you may allow the good nature of a generous spouse to be abused, thus seeming to ratify a law-of-nature view of marriage.

Expectation

Goal: Marital property should be divided to avoid disappointing the financial expectations one spouse had of the other.

In discussing the sacrifice theory, we were repeatedly driven toward an expectation theory. Indeed, *Mahoney*'s answer to some of the problems with the recompensing sacrifice theory may be gathered from the following comment: "Only monetary contributions made with the mutual and shared expectation that both parties to the marriage will derive increased income and material benefits should be a basis for such an award." In other words, the court itself seems sometimes to move from sacrifice to expectation. It is not clear what the court means by expectation. For analytic convenience, we will discuss contractual understandings (that is, mutual express agreements in which the parties both accept that the support is exchanged for value from the degree) in the next section and discuss here expectations that do not meet the explicitness of contractual understandings.

One problem with expectations that are not contractual is that they are likely to be brutally difficult to discover. Were the parties drawing on a once conventional social understanding that wives forego developing their own market talents in reliance on their husband's implicit promise of support? Is that what Mrs. Mahoney did? If mutual support is one of the essential duties of marriage, did Mrs. Mahoney expect to be reimbursed? Given no-fault divorce, did the parties have any reasonable expectations of each other?

Part of the awkwardness here lies in the likelihood that neither spouse had actually developed expectations of enough definiteness to allow a court years later to fulfill them. Even if the parties developed sufficiently definite expectations there will often be insufficient evidence to establish their existence reliably. One response to lack of evidence is to try to infer what the parties' expectations were from the behavior of the parties as that behavior would normally be understood. Drawing such inferences, however, is problematic in the best of times, and during periods (like this) of rapid social change and in countries (like this) in which widely varying social attitudes coexist, it is impossible to draw such inferences reliably. Further, each spouse will ordinarily have different yet reasonable expectations. It is probably significant, therefore, that the *Mahoney* court, while basing its holding in part on the Mahoneys' expectations, nowhere adduces any evidence about what their expectations actually were.

Another puzzlement about fulfilling expectations is that there are many expectations that we do not fulfill. Suppose, for instance, that Kathy marries Al directly after he gets his M.B.A. and has begun to work for IBM. Her expectations would have been precisely the same as the court thought Mrs. Mahoney's were, but would we say that those expectations ought to be protected to the extent of giving her an interest in his degree? The modern trend, of course, is to say no, as the move toward rehabilitative alimony suggests. Nevertheless, Kathy's expectations are better founded than Mrs. Mahoney's, since Kathy knows at least that Al has actually received a degree and has a more realistic idea of his intentions and prospects.

Perhaps the difference between the two cases is that Mrs. Mahoney detrimentally relied and Kathy did not. However, this argument is a version of the recompensing sacrifice argument and suffers from many of its weaknesses. In addition, the assertion that Kathy did not detrimentally rely is dubious—one might even say that her detrimental reliance was greater than Mrs. Mahoney's, since deciding to marry seems a greater investment (emotionally, socially, and quite possible economically) than the $15,250 for which Mrs. Mahoney asked. Furthermore, to be compensable detrimental reliance must be reasonable reliance, and it's not clear that it is reasonable to expect that schooling will produce economic rewards commensurate with the investment required, or even to expect that marriages will last. For that matter, was it reasonable for Mrs. Mahoney to have relied on an increased standard of living, given present divorce rates?

A final objection to the expectation argument is that it leads to a perverse distinction. On the expectation theory, if Mrs. Mahoney had not expected to benefit economically from supporting Mr. Mahoney, she would have gotten no recompense on divorce; because she did expect economic benefit (or so the court assumes) she does get recompense. To put the problem crudely: selfish people are rewarded, selfless people aren't.

Contract

Goal: Marital property should be divided according to the contractual arrangements spouses have made.

We saw that one failing of the expectation standard was its lack of definiteness. The obvious solution is to say that only expectations that meet the criteria for legally binding contracts should be heeded in dividing marital property. We will not dwell on the limitations of this solution, since we will survey the problems with using contracts between spouses in considerable detail in Chapter 5 and will examine analogous problems when we discuss contracts between unmarried cohabitants in Chapter 6. Let us summarize those problems briefly: Husbands and wives often will not write contracts at all, when they do write contracts they will often fail to foresee major issues, when they do foresee major issues they often will not think about breach and remedies, and when they do think about breach and remedies, they will often do so unrealistically. Looming over these problems are doubts about whether encouraging husbands and wives to think in contractual and financial terms inspires desirable attitudes about marriage.

On the other hand, there are things to be said for a contractual solution to the problem of dividing professional degrees on divorce. First, the decision to support a spouse through graduate education is, as these things go, a significant one, and one which is in many ways an economic decision whether it is contractualized or not. Second, the couples who encounter the question may be sophisticated enough to use contracts should they become legally enforceable and commonly employed. Third, the contractual solution would need to affect only those couples who wished to be affected, at least if only actual and not implied contracts are recognized. Of course, contractualization would have the faults of its virtues. In particular, it would do little for the unsophisticated spouse who is taken advantage of.

Following Title

Goal: Marital property should be divided according to the title in which property is held.

As you will recognize, this goal restates the principle of the separate property system. As such, its disadvantages will already be familiar to you. On the other hand, this goal can also be seen as a variant of the contractual and expectation solutions, a variant not without its appeal. One disadvantage beyond those you already know is that forms of wealth marital property that are not property in the traditional sense may not be easily dealt with under this principle. This can be particularly disadvantageous where the couple are not rich and hold much of their wealth, as people increasingly do, in forms like degrees and pensions.

We said this goal can be seen as a variant of the contractual and expectation solutions. Because of the variety of forms in which property may be held in Anglo–American law, spouses may go a long way toward structuring their ownership of property however they like. This structuring may be relatively less susceptible to the vagaries of judicial contractual interpretation than most systems. It has the advantage of giving spouses the opportunity at the time they acquire property to determine its ownership without some kinds of difficulty.

Marital Fault

Goal: Marital property should be divided taking into account the marital fault of the parties.

Traditionally, "marital fault" has meant behavior by one spouse which would give the other grounds for divorce. The modern trend, as you have seen, is toward excluding marital fault from all phases of the divorce process. How well, though, does the trend fit some of the goals we have discussed here? The trend may conflict, for example, with the contract goal, since adultery might well be considered (might be considered by the parties themselves) a breach of the contract. Adultery might reduce the attractiveness of fulfilling expectations or of recompensing sacrifice. But we can put the point more broadly. Underlying many of the arguments for awarding money to the supporting spouse is the sense (expressed in "equitable distribution" statutes) that the equities between the parties should help determine the allocation of their property. But in many marriages the equities will include traditional questions of marital fault and other forms of marital conduct.

Of course, even if we are sure marital conduct should be considered in allocating the parties' wealth on divorce, we might not be sure *how*. Should a single act of adultery wipe out a spouse's entire investment? Even if the adultery was, for example, unrelated to the particular investment at issue? Should a spouse's alcoholism vitiate the obligation? Is the contract surrounding the advanced degree a separate contract from the marital one that has been materially breached? And how, if at all, can marital "faults" be assigned economic weights?

The *Mahoney* court itself hints that equitable concerns motivated it, and perhaps the confusion of the opinion can partly be explained by the *sub rosa* force of its perception of Mr. Mahoney's behavior. Near the end of the opinion (and quite without any indication that there was evidence in the record to support its implication), the court said, "This Court should not ignore the scenario of the young professional who after being supported through graduate school leaves his mate for supposedly greener pastures." The court seems to be referring to a situation in which one spouse has, at some level of deliberateness, taken advantage of the other for economic reasons and, having gotten what he wanted, divorced her. What the court seems to invoke is something akin to fraud.

(4) Valuing the Professional Degree

Another way of gaining insight into whether a degree is property and into the complexities of dividing marital property is to ask how to value a professional degree at divorce. There is some pressure to solve that problem by asking how much an average professional degree of the kind at issue adds to the income of its average holder over his lifetime. This pressure is felt most strongly when the degree is regarded as property. Property generally has a reasonably ascertainable value, since there is a market for most of those kinds of value we think of as property, and calculating the value of a particular degree in terms of the usual buying power of the kind of degree at issue seems a straightforward way of calculating the asset's worth. This pressure is also felt when the expectation goal is used, since what is expected is the benefit of a lifetime's enhanced income.

Sensible as this method of valuing the degree seems, its virtue is its drawback. Its virtue is its simplicity—a table could be established giving the value of all kinds of degrees. Its drawback is that the circumstances of degree holders are far from simple. The value of the degree to any particular person depends on that person's native ability, pre-professional and professional education, diligence, career choices, and so on, to say nothing of factors like luck. Valuing a degree by its average benefit rather than its benefit to the particular holder thus makes inaccurate valuations inevitable. Inaccurate valuations are not only unfair; they may also push the degree holder toward making the best economic (rather than, perhaps, the best personal or social) use of the degree.

One court has attempted to value the contribution one spouse makes to the other spouse's acquisition of a degree that tries to avoid some of the problems we have been discussing while still considering the worth of the degree. *In re Marriage of Francis*, 442 NW2d 59 (Iowa 1989), was a medical-degree case with facts that made the wife's case rather more sympathetic than Mrs. Mahoney's. The court there reasoned that an investment in a professional degree, like any other asset that earns money, comes from two sources: labor and capital. Labor contributions come entirely from the spouse in school. Contributions to capital, on the other hand, can come from either spouse. These contributions may be in cash or in kind—through earnings in the labor force or relieving the student spouse of the labor of caring for the house and the children. Although the returns on labor vary enormously (as we said in the preceding paragraph), economists regard the returns on capital as quite predictable and easy to measure. (Financial institutions make such calculations all the time when they establish interest rates for lending money.) The expert witness who testified in *Francis* said the conventional ratio of labor to capital in investments is 70/30. The *Mahoney* court apparently believed Mrs. Mahoney contributed about 80% of the capital it took to acquire the degree (she contributed $24,000 in earnings and Mr. Mahoney contributed $6,500 he had acquired from military service). Thus to calculate the value of the Mahoney degree 80% (Mrs. Mahoney's contribution to capital) would be multiplied by 30% (the proportion of the value of the degree the *Francis* expert said was attributable to capital). The result (.24) would then be multiplied by the value of the average business degree. Presumably an award under this system would be higher than the $5000 awarded in *Mahoney*. It would be higher because the *Francis* measure is an expectation, or gains-based, measure, rather than a sacrifice, or loss-based, one. Is it also a fair one?

The written report of Professor Richard A. Stephenson, the expert who testified in Francis, shows how such a calculation might be made once the initial suppositions about the relative contributions to labor and capital had been made.

Professor Stephenson's report of June 2, 1988, includes the following tables:

Exhibit C

PRESENT VALUE OF FUTURE INCOME FOR AN M.D. IN FAMILY PRACTICE				
Year	Age	Estimated Income	Present Value Factor	Present Value of Estimated Income
1988	29	30000	1	30000
1989	30	55000	0.941	51765
1990	31	8000	0.886	70865
1991	32	101000	0.834	84204
1992	33	108000	0.785	84744
1993	34	115000	0.739	84928
1994	35	122000	0.695	84798
1995	36	128000	0.654	83735
1996	37	134000	0.616	82504
1997	38	140000	0.579	81127
1998	39	145000	0.545	79082
1999	40	150000	0.513	76997
2000	41	155000	0.483	74883
2001	42	163060	0.455	74143
2002	43	171539	0.428	73410
2003	44	180459	0.403	72685
2004	45	189843	0.379	71967
2005	46	199715	0.357	71256
2006	47	210100	0.336	70551
2007	48	221025	0.316	69854
2008	49	232519	0.297	69164

PRESENT VALUE OF FUTURE INCOME FOR AN M.D. IN FAMILY PRACTICE				
Year	Age	Estimated Income	Present Value Factor	Present Value of Estimated Income
2009	50	244610	0.280	68480
2010	51	257329	0.263	67804
2011	52	264277	0.248	65538
2012	53	271413	0.233	63348
2013	54	278741	0.220	61232
2014	55	286267	0.207	59186
2015	56	293996	0.195	57208
2016	57	301934	0.183	55297
2017	58	310086	0.172	53449
2018	59	318458	0.162	51664
2019	60	327057	0.153	49937
2020	61	335887	0.144	48269
				----------- 2244076
AFTER–TAX PRESENT VALUE = 2244076 TIMES .72 = 1615735				

Exhibit D

Present Value of Estimated Income for Average Male, Age 30–34, with Five or More Years of College

STEP 1:

Take 1985 value from government documents

Estimated value = $33,000

STEP 2:

Multiply by 28 to reflect 31 years of additional earning power. The 28 years reflects a relative decline in earning power after the age of 55.

$33,000 times 28 = $924,000

STEP 3:

Multiply by (1–the average estimated tax rate of 22%) to obtain the after-tax present value.

$924,000 (1—.22) = $720,720

SUMMARY: The value of $720,720 is the estimated after-tax present value as of 1985 of the future earnings of the average sale with five or more years of college in the 30–34 age bracket. It is a present value under the reasonable assumption that the wage growth rate in the future will equal the discount rate except for the years after age 55.

The many difficulties with valuing the degree give rise to the idea adopted by the *Mahoney* court—that supporting spouses should get back not what they expected—half the value of the degree—but what they contributed. This solution has the disadvantage of conflicting with a number of the goals to be served in dividing marital property. It also raises yet more difficult questions about valuation, about, that is, how the spouse's contribution should be measured. For example, the *Mahoney* court seems to think Mrs. Mahoney should get back half of all the family's expenses for the time Mr. Mahoney was in school. This makes sense if the proper measure is the amount he would have had to borrow to support himself while he went to school were he single. Does it make sense if Mrs. Mahoney has a duty to support her husband? Suppose he had quit work and, instead of going to school, had, with his wife's acquiescence, done nothing except half the housework? If support is a duty, should the measure of Mrs. Mahoney's reimbursement be whatever she paid toward his exclusively educational expenses, on the theory that those went beyond her support duty? Or does the support duty have any meaning?

Does it help to look at the working spouse's contribution as an investment for which a return is expected? Since the investment is speculative, should the return include a risk premium? Presumably the couple's next best option would have been a commercial loan for the student's living expenses and tuition. The working spouse would get some share of this investment, plus interest. Note that the divorce court would not treat such a loan as equivalent to a student loan, where principal and interest payments are deferred and the rates are low because the government benefits from the education, as the former spouse (or commercial bank) does not.

Questions on Equitable Distribution

(1) Does the principle of equitable distribution genuinely fit today's marriages in light of the following observations?

(a) The partnership idea which the equitable-distribution theory would seem to be based on a life long commitment, yet divorce is now frequent, and the law has been changed to make it quite easy to obtain. Marriages that end in divorce (the only ones that matter for purposes of discussion of how the law should allocate property on divorce) generally last a short time. In 1977, for example, the median period between marriage and separation was 4.9 years.

(b) As the materials we will read on the contractualization of marriage suggest, the modern trend is toward giving spouses as much control over their circumstances as possible. Yet equitable distribution principles have the opposite effect—they give control over the spouses' circumstances to a court.

(c) The heart of the criticism of the separate property system was that it left housewives poorly protected. But an increasingly large number of women now work outside the home.

(d) The modern trend is toward simplifying divorce. Yet equitable distribution lengthens and complicates divorce by increasing the uncertainty of the law.

(2) How would your analysis of *Mahoney* change if the couple had two young children?

(3) Having thought about what kind of relationships between spouses the law should encourage and about how divorce should be handled, you are ready to test your ideas by applying them in a concrete situation. Exactly what amount, if any, should Mrs. Mahoney receive on divorce?

(4) The difference between dividing marital property and awarding alimony is the difference between deciding what each spouse owns and deciding what continuing obligations one spouse owes the other. Alimony in its traditional form has increasingly fallen out of favor and has increasingly been replaced by rehabilitative alimony. However, the trend is toward dividing marital property in ways that take prominently into account the relative needs of the two spouses. So isn't traditional alimony still with us in the form of property division? Isn't this argument confirmed by the fact that property divisions are sometimes awarded in periodic payments, while alimony is sometimes awarded in lump sums? In thinking about this last question, keep in mind that alimony awards, unlike divisions of marital property, usually may be altered as circumstances change, may terminate upon the remarriage of the supported spouse, and may not be dischargeable in bankruptcy.

(5) A Closing Note

The theory that a wife who . . . bears her fair share of the joint burdens is yet "supported" by her husband, has been the bane of all society. It has made women feel that it is their right to be dependents and nonproducers. Thus, for women, all work has until lately come to be regarded as degradation.

Antoinette Brown Blackwell
Industrial Reconstruction

Particularly since the advent of equitable property distribution in the mid 1970s, legislatures and courts have grappled with a number of issues that the degree cases do not entirely resolve. The following notes raise some of those issues.

(1) *The nature of marital property and the timing of property acquisition*. A group of cases involving the purchase of winning lottery tickets shortly before divorce nicely illustrates these questions. Marital funds were used to buy the tickets, but were the winnings gainfully acquired? Can a marriage "dead in fact" still produce sharing that justifies classifying property as marital? What if the winning ticket was purchased after the couple separated but before divorce? Compare *Smith v. Smith*, 557 NYS 2d 22 (1990)(when ticket was purchased before separation, winnings were marital property that should be divided equally); with *Alston v. Alston*, 629 A2d 70 (Md 1993) (winnings from ticket

purchased after separation were marital property, but the other spouse got no share). Generally, the property acquired during separation is marital property. *Brandenburg v. Brandenburg*, 416 A2d 327 (NJ 1980).

(2) *Personal injury awards*. To the extent that the award is for pain and suffering, it may be separate property. *Amato v. Amato*, 180 NJ Super 210, 434 A2d 639 (1981) (not divisible); *Van de Loo v. Van de Loo*, 346 NW2d 173 (Minn App 1984); but see *Bywater v. Bywater*, 128 Mich App 396, 340 NW2d 102 (1983)(divisible). However, if the award is to replace lost wages or compensate for medical costs expended during the marriage, courts consider the award marital property at least in part. Tex Family Code Ann § 3.001(3) (2005); *Thomas v. Thomas*, 408 SE2d 596 (Va App 1991); *Brown v. Brown*, 675 P2d 1207 (Wash 1984); *In re Marriage of Smith*, 405 NE2d 884 (Ill App 1980). Of course, if the injury is due to the other spouse's intentional act, there is no recovery. Punitive damages have been awarded as marital property. The real problem occurs where the personal injury award is unitary.

(3) *Closely held family corporations*. Where an important marital asset is a minority interest in a closely held family corporation, courts face difficulties in making awards. One solution is to order a fixed amount payable over time that will not interfere with the management of the enterprise nor force a public sale of the business. *Stainback v. Stainback*, 396 SE2d 686 (Va App 1990).

(4) *Property transmuted from separate property*. If one spouse owns property separately, but it is sold and the proceeds are invested in joint names or it is commingled with marital funds, it may be transmuted into marital property. See, e.g., *Goldstein v. Goldstein*, 310 So 2d 361 (Fla App 1975). Under the "source of funds" rule followed in many states, if it was acquired separately but purchase money comes from separate and marital funds, the property will be proportionately allocated as separate and marital. *Schweizer v. Schweizer*, 301 Md 626, 484 A2d 267 (1984). In community property states, the spouse may have an equitable lien on the separate property of the other. *Jensen v. Jensen*, 665 SW2d 107 (Tex 1984).

(5) *Tax consequences*. Property division or transfer that occurs pursuant to a separation or divorce, or follows a divorce within a one year period, is treated by the Internal Revenue Code as a gift for income tax purposes (i.e., it is not a taxable event). The recipient spouse will therefore acquire the owner spouse's basis, and will pay capital gains taxes upon sale of the property. IRC § 1041. Alimony, on the other hand, is taxable to the recipient and deductible by the payor. IRC §§ 71 and 215. If money is paid over time, and is tied to events connected with the recipient's life (i.e., death or remarriage) and the duty of support, it may be treated as alimony. Heavily "frontloading" payments will have substantial tax consequences. IRC § 71(f).

BIBLIOGRAPHY

Marital Property. For welcome empirical data on equitable distribution, see Marsha Garrison, *Good Intentions Gone Awry: The Impact of New York's Equitable Distribution Law on Divorce Outcomes*, 57 Brooklyn L Rev 621 (1991). For a proposal that, "[u]nless there is an agreement to the contrary, marital property should only begin to be accumulated after a child is born or after a couple has remained married for a substantial period," see J. Thomas Oldham, *Is the Concept of Marital Property Outdated?*, 22 J Family L 263 (1983–84). For a description of the interaction of the common law and community property systems in the United States, see Judith T. Younger, *Marital Regimes: A Story of Compromise and Demoralization, Together With Criticisms and Suggestions for Reform*, 67 Cornell L Rev 45 (1981). Margaret F. Brinig, *Property Distribution Physics: The Talisman of Time and Middle Class Law*, 31 Family L Q 93 (1997), suggests that alimony and property distribution are species of the same thing—division of various assets of the marriage—and proposes a theory to govern that division.

Alimony and Maintenance. An article that was influential in gaining recognition for housewives' economic contribution to the family is Carole Bruch, *Property Rights of De Facto Spouses Including Thoughts on the Value of Homemakers' Services,* 10 Family L Q 101 (1976). Jana B. Singer, *Alimony and Efficiency: The Gendered Costs and Benefits of the Economic Justification for Alimony,* 82 Geo L J 2432 (1994), traces and analyzes the law-and-economics justifications for alimony.

Law, Economics and Alimony. In his Nobel address, *The Economic Way of Looking at Behavior*, 101 J Pol Econ 385 (1993), Professor Gary Becker talks about the expansion of economics into the family, particularly in the idea of marriage as specialization, the value of household work, and the development of human capital. June Carbone and Margaret Brinig, *Rethinking Marriage: Feminist Ideology, Economic Change, and Divorce Reform*, 65 Tulane L Rev 953 (1991), article traces the various rationales for alimony and proposes a new one. Carol M. Rose, *Women and Property: Gaining and Losing Ground*, 78 Va L Rev 421 (1992), uses a game theoretic approach, and argues that although women have made tremendous advancements in the labor market, they are remain disadvantaged primarily because they have a greater taste for cooperation than men. Cynthia Starnes, *Divorce and the Displaced Homemaker: A Discourse on Playing with Dolls, Partnership Buyouts and Dissociation under No–Fault*, 60 U Chi L Rev 67 (1993), uses the analogy of dissolving business partnerships to argue that wives who have cared for children ought to be better compensated for their contributions to the marriage. A business school professor, Allen M. Parkman, hypothesizes that women are driven to work outside the home partly in order to protect themselves against the risk of divorce in *Why are Married Women Working So Hard?,* 18 Intl J L & Econ 41 (1998).

Empirical Research on Post–Divorce Finances. Margaret F. Brinig, Carl E. Schneider, and Lee E. Teitelbaum, *Family Law in Action: A Reader* 294–301 (Anderson, 1999), discusses a large Canadian study of the income available to divorcing men and women. The American data on that topic are analyzed in Richard R. Peterson, *A Re–Evaluation of the Economic Consequences of Divorce*, 61 Am Soc Rev 528 (1996).

Housework, Property and Alimony. Arlie Russell Hochschild, *The Time Bind* (Metropolitan Books, 1997), discusses how both home and workplace have changed since the Second World War and why women continue to do the bulk of housework. In Joan Williams, *UnBending Gender* (Oxford U Press, 2000), a law professor expounds on her theory that the American concept of the "ideal worker" means that women will continue to earn less than their male counterparts. One attempt to deal with what seems like an inequity in the distribution of tasks between spouses is Martha M. Ertman, *Commercializing Marriage: A Proposal for Valuing Women's Work Through Premarital Security Agreements*, 77 Tex L Rev 17 (1998). Professor Ertman proposes that before marriage (and before any significant investment in the relationship or children) spouses should explicitly contract to prevent one from taking advantage of the other. Katharine T. Silbaugh, *Turning Labor into Love: Housework and the Law*, 91 Nw U L Rev 1 (1996), discusses why housework continues to be uncompensated, even if explicit contracts are made between spouses. Margaret F. Brinig, Carl E. Schneider, and Lee E. Teitelbaum, *Family Law in Action: A Reader* 135–48 (Anderson, 1999), includes articles discussing how couples divide their time in the household and labor force and what forms their bargaining might take. Steven L. Nock, *Commitment and Dependency in Marriage*, 57 J Marriage & Family 503 (1995), discusses how much spouses, particularly women, sacrifice in marriages that are stable. He also contrasts cohabitation and marriage. Katharine T. Silbaugh, *Marriage Contracts and the Family Economy*, 93 Nw U L Rev 65 (1999), argues that if housework is "beyond price," and therefore outside the scope of contracting, so is men's labor force participation.

Chapter V

THE VOW AND THE COVENANT: THE CONTRACTUALIZATION OF FAMILY LAW

In contrast to the older law, the most essential feature of modern substantive law, especially private law, is the greatly increased significance of legal transactions, particularly contracts, as a source of claims guaranteed by legal coercion. So very characteristic is this feature of private law that one can a potiori designate the contemporary type of society, to the extent that private law obtains, as a "contractual" one.

Max Weber
Economy and Society

SECTION 1. AN INTRODUCTORY CASE

It befel that a wedded pair had a dispute with each other.... Many meetings of friends were held, many reproaches exchanged, and no remedy could be found, but the wife must needs in her pride have her rights set down clearly, point by point, and the obediences and services that the friends told her she must pay to her husband set down and written in articles on the one hand, and this and that from her husband to her on the other hand, and thus might they dwell together, if not in love, at least in peace....

One day they were going on a pilgrimage and it behoved them to pass by a narrow plank over a ditch. The husband went first, then turned and saw that his wife was fearful and dared not come after him; and the husband was adread lest if she should come, the fear itself should make her fall, and kindly he returned to her and took and held her by the hand; and leading her along the plank, held her and talked to her.... Then fell he into the water, that was deep, and he struggled hard in the water ..., and he cried to his wife that with the help of her staff that she bore, she should ... save him. But she answered thus: "Nay, nay" quoth she, "I will look first in my charter whether it be written therein that I must do so, and if it be therein I will do it, and otherwise not." She looked therein, and because that her charter made no mention thereof, she answered that she would do naught and left him and went her way.

The Goodman of Paris

We have said *Kilgrow* is often cited for the principle of family autonomy. Yet *Kilgrow* holds, in effect if not in terms, that at least some contracts between husbands and wives are unenforceable. The non-enforcement of marital contracts has long been one of the means by which law has sought to serve the family autonomy principle. This is for reasons in part suggested by the opinion in *Kilgrow*. Yet the association of the unenforceability principle with the family autonomy principle is, from another point of view, paradoxical. After all, the great attraction of contract as an organizing idea in law has long been that it lets people structure their relationships according to their own preferences, not according to state-imposed rules. Thus two diametrically opposed principles—the principle of freedom of contract and the principle that many marital contracts are unenforceable—seem to be recruited to serve the same ends: promoting family autonomy. How can this be so? How can this apparent conflict be reconciled?

As *Kilgrow* and the preceding paragraph suggest, family law was once hostile to contract. Family law still retains some of that hostility. But we may well be going through a period in which family law is being "contractualized." In what follows, you will be asked to think about the usefulness of contract as a way of talking about family law problems and as an organizing idea for family law. In particular you will be asked to think about the relationship between the principle of family autonomy and the principle of contract. You should keep several questions in mind: Is contract a means by which people set rules for themselves instead of relying on society to set rules for them? Or is it a way of legalizing (of bringing within the scope of the law's authority) family relations and giving courts power over families by giving courts authority to interpret contracts? Is contract an appropriate way of getting people to think about their intimate relations, or does it commercialize and embitter those relations? Can contract provide useful organizing principles for dealing with relations which are highly complex and, in theory, eternal? Can satisfactory remedies be provided within the scope of the family?

We begin with a contract proposed by Professor Lenore Weitzman, a contract which Professor Weitzman reports is not hypothetical; its "terms were formulated by real people in [a] real relationship." We have chosen this contract as a vehicle for discussion since it includes provisions that range from the commonplace to the extreme.

LENORE J. WEITZMAN
LEGAL REGULATION OF MARRIAGE: TRADITION AND CHANGE

62 California Law Review 1169, 1281 (1974)

Susan, an aspiring lawyer, and Peter, an aspiring social worker, have devised the following contract to maximize both career opportunities and their personal relationship.

a. Educational and living expenses

Susan and Peter decide that they will take turns going to school, so that the nonstudent partner can support the other until he or she receives a degree. Because Susan will earn more money as an attorney, they decide that they will maximize their joint income if Susan goes to school first. They therefore agree that Peter will be solely responsible for Susan's educational expenses and support for three full years. Susan will assume these same responsibilities for the following two years. If their partnership should dissolve at any time during these first five years, their contract stipulates that each shall have the following financial obligations to the other: (1) If dissolution occurs during the first three years, Peter will pay Susan's remaining tuition (which may be up to three full years' tuition in graduate school) and pay her $4,200 a year for living expenses. (2) Thereafter, Susan will pay Peter's remaining tuition (up to two full years of tuition in a school of social work) and pay him $4,200 a year in living expenses. All living expenses will be paid at the rate of $350 a month. This amount will be tied to the cost-of-living index to allow for automatic increases.

b. Domicile

Susan and Peter agree to maintain a joint domicile for the first five years of their relationship, location to be determined by the student partner to maximize educational opportunity.

After the first five years, Susan and Peter will make decisions regarding domicile jointly, with no presumption that the career of either is of greater importance in making the decision. However, if they cannot agree on where to live, the decision will be Susan's—for a period of three years. Peter will then have the right to choose the location for the following three years. They will continue to rotate the domicile decision on a three-year basis. As both parties realize that their career opportunities may not coincide with this prearranged schedule, they may decide to exchange the right of decision for any given period or make another equitable agreement which would then be incorporated into this contract. Further, both parties will always retain the option of establishing a temporary separate residence, at their own expense, if this is necessary for their careers.

c. Property

During the first five years all income and property, excluding gifts and inheritances, shall be considered community property. The income-earning partner shall have sole responsibility for its management and control.

After the first five years an inventory will be taken of all community property. Thereafter each party's earnings, as well as any gifts or bequests or the income from any property held, shall be her or his separate property. Neither party will have any rights in any present or future property of the other. A list will be kept of all household items in order to keep track of their ownership; in the event Susan and Peter decide to make a joint purchase, this will be noted on the list. Any joint purchase of items of value over $100 will be covered by a separate agreement concerning its ownership. Each party will manage and control her or his separate property, and will maintain a separate bank account.

d. Household expenses

(This part of the agreement shall go into effect five years hence.)

Household expenses will consist of rent, utilities, food, and housekeeping expenses. Susan and Peter will each contribute 50 percent of their gross income to household expenses. Their contributions will be made in monthly installments of equal amounts, and placed in a joint checking account. Responsibility for the joint account and for paying the above expenses will be rotated, with each having this responsibility for a three-month period. Each partner will be responsible for his or her own cleaning expenses, and for food and entertainment outside of the household. Each will maintain a separate car and a separate phone and will take care of these expenses separately. If money in the joint account is not exhausted by household expenses, it may be used for joint leisure activities.

Both parties recognize that Susan's income is likely to be higher than Peter's and that 50 percent of her income will allow her more money for separate expenses. The parties therefore agree to review this arrangement six months after it goes into effect. If it seems that the arrangement placed an unfair burden on Peter, they will change the second line above to read: Each party's contribution to household expenses shall be as follows: Susan shall contribute 55 percent of her gross income; Peter shall contribute 40 percent of his gross income.

e. Housekeeping responsibilities

Housework will be shared equally. All necessary tasks will be divided into two categories. On even-numbered months Susan will be responsible for category 1 and Peter for category 2; and vice versa on odd-numbered months. Each party will do her or his own cooking and clean up afterwards for breakfast and lunch, as well as keeping her or his own study clean. Dinner cooking and clean up will be considered part of the housework to be rotated as specified above. In the event that one party neglects to perform any task, the other party can perform it and charge the nonperforming partner $15 per hour for his or her labor, or agree to be repaid in kind.

f. Sexual relations

Sexual relations are subject to the consent of both parties. Responsibility for birth control will be shared equally.

g. Surname

Both parties will retain their own surnames.

h. Children

While the parties have decided to have two children at some time in the future, birth control will be practiced until a decision to have a child has been reached. Since the parties believe that a woman should have control over her own body, the decision of whether or not to terminate an accidental pregnancy before then shall be Susan's alone.

If Susan decides to have an abortion, the party who had responsibility for birth control the month that conception occurred will bear the cost of the abortion. This will include medical expenses not covered by insurance, and any other expenses or loss of pay incurred by Susan. However, if Susan decides to have the child and Peter does not agree, Susan will bear full financial and social responsibility for the child. In that event, Susan also agrees to compensate Peter should he be required to support the child. If the parties agree to have a child and Susan changes her mind after conception has occurred, she will pay for the abortion. If Peter changes his mind after conception has occurred and Susan agrees to an abortion, he will pay for it. If she does not agree, Peter will share the social and financial responsibility for the child, just as if he had not changed his mind.

When the parties decide to have a child, the following provisions will apply: Susan and Peter will assume equal financial responsibility for the child. This will include the medical expenses connected with the birth of the child as well as any other expenses incurred in preparation for the child. If it is necessary for Susan to take time off from work in connection with her pregnancy or with the birth of the child, Peter will pay her one-half of his salary to compensate for the loss. If either party has to take time off from work to care for the child, the other party will repay that party with one-half of his or her salary. All child-care, medical, and educational expenses will be shared equally.

Since Peter expects to become a psychiatric social worker specializing in preschool children, he will have the primary child-care responsibility. He will take a paternity leave after the birth in order to care for the child full-time, until day-care arrangements can be made. Susan will compensate him at the rate of one-half of her salary. Responsibility for caring for the child on evenings and weekends will be divided equally.

Any children will take the hyphenated surname of both parties.

i. Dissolution

If there are children, both parties agree to submit to at least one conciliation session prior to termination. In addition, if a decision to dissolve the partnership is made, both parties agree to submit to binding arbitration if they are unable to reach a mutual decision regarding the issues of child custody, child support, and property division. A list of mutually agreeable arbitrators is attached to this agreement. While both agree that custody should be determined according to the best interests of the child, a presumption exists in favor of Peter, since he will have had superior training in the rearing of children. Each party agrees to assume half of the financial burden of caring for the child.

If there are no children, this household agreement can be terminated by either party for any reason upon giving the other party 60 days' notice in writing. Upon separation, each party will take his or her separate property and any jointly owned property will be divided equally. Neither party will have any financial or other responsibility toward the other after separation and division of property.

Notes and Questions on the Peter and Susan Contract

(1) Suppose Peter and Susan came to you to ask you to draft a contract like the one you have just read. What would you advise them?

(a) First, who is your client? Can you represent both Peter and Susan? Rule 1.7(b) of the ABA's Model Rules of Professional Conduct says,

> A lawyer shall not represent a client if the representation of that client may be materially limited by the lawyer's responsibilities to another client or to a third person, or by the lawyer's own interests, unless:
>
> (1) the lawyer reasonably believes the representation will not be adversely affected; and
>
> (2) the client consents after consultation. When representation of multiple clients in a single matter is undertaken, the consultation shall include explanation of the implications of the common representation and the advantages and risks involved.

Can you represent the interest of each adequately? What is the possible effect of such representations on the exercise of your independent professional judgment on behalf of each? What would you have to say to provide the full disclosure the rule calls for?

(b) If only one member of the couple is a client, what ought you do to protect his or her interests? Suppose you are Peter's lawyer. What would you advise him about the contract he wishes to sign? Is each provision fair? Is each provision in his interest? Are there other provisions you ought to suggest to him? Suppose you are Susan's lawyer. What do you advise her in those respects?

(2) Recall the various justifications for the court's "family autonomy" holding in *Kilgrow*. Now recall that *Kilgrow* involved a contract. Keeping *Kilgrow* and Peter and Susan's contract in mind, do you think

that those rationales for family autonomy are persuasive where the question is one of enforcing a contract the family itself has written?

(a) Can the information problem be solved or diminished by narrowing contractually the range of substantive issues and thereby narrowing the range of information needed? By such contractual devices as specifying in the contract what information will and will not be relevant, thereby limiting the range of evidentiary material needed and alerting the parties to the importance of that material?

(b) Can the problem of judicial expertise be diminished by converting questions from "What is best for the parties?" to "What does the contract provide?"?

(c) Can the standards problem be resolved or diminished by substituting contractually determined standards for state-supplied ones?

(d) Can the enforcement problem be resolved or diminished by contractually establishing standards which both the parties found reasonable, by specifying contractually the remedies the parties regard as effective, and by reducing the parties' resistance to enforcement by involving them in establishing (contractually) their own marital standards and procedures?

(e) Can the exacerbation problem be resolved or diminished by the same forces that were discussed in (d)?

(f) Can the privacy problem be diminished or resolved by specifying contractually what is and is not a subject of judicial inquiry? Can the contract be taken as a waiver of the family's privacy claims?

(g) The last three considerations all speak to the desirability of allowing people to organize their own lives. Isn't that exactly what contract law is intended to permit?

(3) What does Peter and Susan's contract suggest to you about using contracts to organize family life? How, in other words, would you answer the questions we posed in introducing the contract?

SECTION 2. MARRIAGE AND THE LAW OF CONTRACT

Economic independence for women necessarily involves a change in the home and family relation. But, if that change is for the advantage of individual and race, we need not fear it. It does not involve a change in the married relation except in withdrawing the element of economic dependence, nor in the relation of mother to child save to improve it. But it does involve the exercise of human faculty in women, in social service and exchange rather than in domestic service solely. This will of course require the introduction of some other form of living than that which now obtains.

Charlotte Perkins Gilman
Women and Economics

A. A SURVEY OF CONTRACTS RELATING TO MARRIAGE

By legal friendship I mean such as is formed on stated conditions, whether it be absolutely commercial, demanding cash payments, or more liberal in respect of time but still requiring a certain covenanted quid pro quo.

Aristotle
Nicomachean Ethics

(1) Introduction

Now that we have considered the problem of contracts in the family setting in a drastic and dramatic form, we must look at how the law in fact treats such contracts. We will do so by exploring each of the three major kinds of marital contracts, by asking how far legislatures and courts allow each kind to be enforced, and then by looking at the various legislative and judicial attempts to assure the fairness of marital contracts.

(2) The Types of Marital Contracts

(a) Antenuptial Agreements

An antenuptial agreement, as the term suggests, is an agreement made before a marriage. Upper-class marriage used to be crucially an economic and social alliance between families, some kinds of antenuptial agreements have long been common, namely, those allocating the spouses' property on their *deaths*. Such antenuptial agreements have been particularly favored in second marriages, where the parties are likelier to have assets and children to protect, and they have also been common solutions to the awkwardness that may arise in a marriage between a relatively rich and a relatively poor person. (When the relatively poor Jacqueline Kennedy and the relatively rich Aristotle Onassis married, they reportedly entered into a 170–point contract.) Antenuptial contracts allocating property after the death of the parties are thought to preserve the marriage by removing from it a prolific source of dispute. They have thus long been enforceable.

A second kind of antenuptial agreement arranges the economic relations of the parties after *divorce*. Courts have feared these agreements might make divorce more attractive to one party and more perilous to the other. Thus, antenuptial agreements setting support obligations on divorce have long and widely been held invalid. This rule has recently been widely rejected, however, commonly for the reasons of the Florida Supreme Court in *Posner v. Posner*, 233 S2d 381, 384 (1970):

> With divorce such a commonplace fact of life, it is fair to assume that many prospective marriage partners whose property and familial situation is such as to generate a valid antenuptial agreement settling their property rights upon the death of either, might want to consider and discuss also—and agree upon, if possible—the disposition of their prop-

erty and the alimony rights of the wife in the event their marriage, despite their best efforts, should fail.

Nevertheless, courts have generally imposed conditions on such agreements designed to protect the spouses from over-reaching or mis-calculation. For instance, many courts remain skeptical of contracts that limit the alimony that may be awarded on divorce (as opposed to contracts directed toward the distribution of property on divorce). Thus in *In re Marriage of Gudenkauf*, 204 NW2d 586, 587–88 (Iowa 1973), the court reiterated "the principle that the interspousal support obligation is imposed by law and cannot be contracted away." The court continued:

> This case illustrates the wisdom of the rule. Respondent (Hattie) was 66 at the time of trial with a life expectancy of more than 12 years. If she did not receive alimony she would leave the marriage with about $10,000 in savings, $64 monthly social security and no reasonable prospect of employment. She would be at the mercy of the uncertainties and vicissitudes of life. Walter, a 63 year-old farmer at the time of trial, would leave the marriage with a net worth of about $150,000.

As this may imply, courts have hesitated to enforce contracts limiting alimony obligations partly because they fear some spouses will be left unsupported and the state will have to support them.

Another example of the reluctance of some jurisdictions to enforce agreements regulating the affairs of the couple on divorce is illustrated by the Restatement (Second) of Contracts § 190 (1981): "A promise that tends unreasonably to encourage divorce or separation is unenforceable on grounds of public policy." One illustration:

> A and B, who are about to be married, make an antenuptial agreement in which A promises that in case of divorce, he will settle one million dollars on B. A court may decide that, in view of the large sum promised, A's promise tends unreasonably to encourage divorce and is unenforceable on grounds of public policy.

A third kind of antenuptial agreement governs the behavior of the parties *during* the marriage. These have generally been unenforceable, partly on the grounds that the economic incidents of marriage have been established as a matter of public policy, partly because of the problem of enforcing contracts dealing with the non-economic aspects of marriage, see, e.g., *Favrot v. Barnes*, 332 So2d 873 (La App 1976)(sexual intercourse), and partly because of the principle of family autonomy. Thus it is often said that the obligation of spousal support may not be statutorily altered, and the old rule that an antenuptial agreement may not alter "the essential incidents of marriage" still has real force. *In re Marriage of Higgason*, 516 P2d 289 (Cal 1973)(medical care). Even here, however, the permissible scope of antenuptial contracts is increasing, particularly regarding the economic aspects of the relationship.

(b) Reconciliation Agreements

These are contracts between spouses who have had marital difficulties and who feel a contract would help preserve their marriage. See, e.g., *Capps v. Capps*, 219 SE2d 901 (Va 1975)(interest in home the parties purchased). The primary conventional problems with these contracts are that their permissible scope is no greater than that of antenuptial agreements (and thus that non-economic behavior within the marriage is generally outside that scope) and that many jurisdictions hesitate to allow adjustments of the economic incidents of marriage. In addition, a number of states have statutes prohibiting enforcement, except in unusual situations, of contracts for domestic services.

(c) Separation Agreements

When a married couple have decided to separate and have agreed to the economic terms of a divorce, the contract embodying those terms is called a separation agreement. These contracts may allocate the property of the parties between them, may set the terms under which alimony will or will not be paid, may specify who should have custody of the children, may establish that neither was at fault in causing the separation, and may establish the amount and duration of child-support payments. Separation agreements have in some forms long been countenanced, on the theory that the contract does not conduce to divorce, since the parties have already decided to end their marriage. Separation agreements, it is also argued, can reduce the bitterness of divorce by allowing couples to settle their differences by negotiation, not litigation.

Even though separation agreements may not conflict as such with public policy, it is also the general policy of the law to supervise the terms under which divorcing parties separate. Courts have asserted their authority to disregard separation agreements when entering divorce decrees. Courts have been particularly prone to ignore the agreement where it concerns the children of the marriage. Courts may also be willing to scrutinize more carefully agreements which affect the support of the economically weaker party. Nevertheless, the trend is in the other direction. "In a growing number of states ... courts are required to accept the parties' agreement, absent evidence of fraud, duress, overreaching, or a determination of unconscionability." Sally Burnett Sharp, *Fairness Standards and Separation Agreements: A Word of Caution on Contractual Freedom*, 132 U Pa L Rev 1399, 1444 (1984).

In any event, the practical facts of divorce make it likely that couples will enter into some kind of separation agreement and that the court will enforce it. Litigation is expensive financially and excruciating psychologically, and the parties thus have an incentive to come to an agreement that makes litigation unnecessary. Litigation also costs judges time, and unless a spouse complains, they will ordinarily want to approve the parties' agreement. Because the separation agreement for spousal support is a final action, unlike a modifiable court order for support, enforcement of an out-of-state decree becomes easier in some states. Va Code § 20–109 (2005). It should for these reasons not be surprising that it is often estimated that, despite the frequently tumultuous emotional circumstances of divorce, roughly ninety percent of all divorce cases are ultimately uncontested.

B. ASSURING THE FAIRNESS OF MARITAL CONTRACTS

> *The perfect friendship or love is the friendship or love of people who are good and alike in virtue; for those people are alike in wishing each other's good, in so far as they are good, and they are good in themselves. But it is people who wish the good of their friends for their friend's sake that are in the truest sense friends.*
>
> **Aristotle**
> *Nichomachean Ethics*

(1) A Survey of the Law of Marital Contracts

At this point, we will survey some recurring problems in marital contracts. We will primarily use the separation agreement as our entryway.

Consideration and Mutuality. The parties must exchange valuable consideration, which may be relief from debts as well as the receipt of assets. For example, in *Capps v. Capps*, 219 SE2d 901 (Va 1975), the couple agreed that the husband would make the down payment and mortgage payments on the home the two had been renting, although the wife would sign the deed of trust and be made a joint owner. If either sued for divorce, legal separation, or any other action affecting the marriage, title would be returned to the husband, and the wife would be relieved of her responsibility for the mortgage. Four years later, the husband sued for divorce and was able to enforce the contract.

Finality. In some states, an agreement that provides for spousal support is treated as a final judgment. *Goldman v. Goldman*, 415 NYS2d 7 (1979); *Mitchell v. Mitchell*, 573 S2d 913 (Fla App 1990); *Brower v. Brower*, 604 A2d 726 (Pa Super 1992). Neither party may seek modification once the agreement is presented with divorce pleadings, and it will receive full faith and credit as a final decree even if the obligee seeks enforcement in another state. Cal Civ Code § 3651 (2006); Va Code § 20–109 (2006). Child support, however, is always modifiable.

Taxation. Taxation incident to divorce is a complicated subject, which warrants careful attention by domestic relations practitioners. Congress frequently changes the tax laws affecting divorce. Generally speaking, however, alimony is deductible by the payor and taxable to the payee under IRC § 71 (2000). Child support is neither taxable nor deductible (i.e., it is treated like child support within the intact family). If the parties lump together alimony and child support, it will be treated as alimony if it is clear the payments are tied to events in the payee spouse's life, rather than children's. Property division does not usually result in a taxable event: if property is transferred between the spouses, it is treated for income tax purposes as a gift, and the property's basis does not change. Personal exemptions for minor children belong as a rule to the custodial spouse, although the parties may agree otherwise.

Extensions Beyond Divorce Court's Power. One advantage of a separation agreement is that the parties may agree to things the divorce court could not itself order. For example, the parties may stipulate that alimony will be paid despite the recipient spouse's remarriage or the payor's death. They may set up trusts or require that one keep life insurance in force for the other or for the children of the marriage. The most common such arrangement, however, is to provide for payment of college tuition in states where the court's jurisdiction over the children ends when they reach the age of majority. The parties then must decide what reasonable expenditures must be: does the noncustodial parent have to pay for an expensive private education if there is a thriftier state school the child could attend? See, e.g., *Ingrassia v. Ingrassia*, 509 NE2d 729 (Ill App 1987); *Rohn v. Thuma*, 408 NE2d 578 (Ind App 1980).

Termination at Cohabitation. Even though some state statutes do not provide for this situation, many couples agree that support under their written agreement terminates at cohabitation. Of course, there may be uncertainty as to when "cohabitation" has occurred.

Clauses Against Public Policy. In addition to prohibiting clauses that "promote or facilitate divorce or separation," courts will usually not enforce attempts to relieve the noncustodial parent of child support: *Kelley v. Kelley*, 412 SE2d 465 (Va App), reversed, 449 SE2d 55 (Va 1994). In exchange for the father's share of a marital home worth $43,000, the mother agreed not to ask for child support and to indemnify the husband should any court order him to pay it. Five years after the parties' divorce, the father sued for definite and specific visitation rights and the mother counterclaimed for child support. The father moved for indemnification for child support payments pursuant to the separation agreement. The court held that child support was an obligation that could not be removed from the court's jurisdiction by the parties' agreement. See also *Huckaby v. Huckaby*, 393 NE2d 1256 (Ill App Ct 1979) (stepparent agreed to assume responsibility). For a holding that the agreement would be valid as between the parties, see *Department of Health v. Morley*, 570 S2d 402 (Fla Dist Ct App 1990).

Enforcement. The parties may use standard contractual remedies, including specific performance, to enforce their agreement. E.g., *Chattin v. Chattin*, 427 SE2d 347 (Va 1993) (insurance policy plus support of $1200/month for 6 1/2 years). Contempt will not be available except for child and spousal support. Support requirements also generate the substantial remedies required by federal law.

Modification. Like parties to premarital agreements, parties to separation agreements should plan for modification of their agreement in case circumstances change, particularly if spousal support or custody is involved or if the state statute provides that any modification may only be in accordance with the parties' agreement. Common provisions vary spousal support with the consumer price index, some ratio of the parties' joint earnings, or the completion of education. The parties may also provide for renegotiation after a specified period of time or may require sessions with an arbitrator or mediator if negotiation fails.

As courts and legislatures have increased the scope of enforceable agreements within the family, they have wanted to reduce the dangers of such agreements. Of course all the standard devices designed to deter unfair contracts—like rules relating to duress, misrepresentation, and undue influence—apply to intra-family contracts quite as much as they apply to contracts generally. Let us briefly review what you learned in your Contracts course about those three devices.

The defense of duress applies only where the contract has been entered into under physical coercion or under an improper threat which actually evoked the victim's assent and was grave enough to justify that assent. The usefulness of the defense primarily depends on the definition of "threat." In the commercial context, that term is imprecise enough, since it can be hard to draw the line between aggressive business practices and threats. Can that term be extended in the family context to include coercive behavior by one of the parties made possible by their special intimate relationship? For example, would a "threat" not to go through with the marriage unless the contract was signed amount to coercion? The usual rule is that a "threat" to act in an otherwise legal way is not a threat; rather, it is an announcement of a willingness to choose a path to which one is legally entitled. On the other hand, given the importance the parties may attach to being married, would not making acquiescence in a contract a prerequisite to marriage sometimes put very considerable pressure on the possible contractor?

A contract is voidable by a party who has been deceived by the other party's misrepresentation. But not just any misrepresentation will do:

> First, there must be an assertion that is not in accord with the facts. Second, the assertion must be either fraudulent or material. Third, the assertion must be relied on by the recipient in manifesting his assent. Fourth, the reliance of the recipient must be justified.

E. Allan Farnsworth, *Contracts* § 4.10, at 236 (Little, Brown, 1982). The usefulness of the doctrine of misrepresentation is limited by the usual principle of contract law that an active misrepresentation of some sort is generally required and that mere silence as to a material fact is not misrepresentation. On the other hand, there are exceptions to this principle. One such exception, according to the Restatement (Second) of Contracts § 161(b)(1981), is where one party "knows that disclosure of the fact would correct a mistake of the other party as to a basic assumption on which the party is making the contract" and where the nondisclosure "amounts to a failure to act in good faith and in accordance with reasonable standards of fair dealing." A second common exception is where there is a "relation of trust and confidence," such as the relationship between family members. Does that exception include the relation between an engaged but unmarried couple?

The doctrine that deals most directly with our question is not misrepresentation but rather undue influence:

> The concept of undue influence developed in courts of equity to give relief to victims of unfair transactions that were induced by improper persuasion. In contrast to the common law notion of duress, the essence of which was simple fear induced by threat, the equitable concept of undue influence was aimed at the protection of those affected with a weakness, short of incapacity, against improper persuasion, short of misrepresentation or duress, by those in a special position to exercise such persuasion ..... Two elements are commonly required: first, a special relation between the parties; second, improper persuasion of the weaker by the stronger.

Farnsworth, *Contracts* § 4.1, at 268. Farnsworth observes that the "classical case" of the kind of "special relation between the parties that makes one of them peculiarly susceptible to persuasion by the other" involves "a relation of trust or confidence in which the weaker party is justified in assuming that the stronger will not act in a manner inconsistent with the weaker's welfare." The relation of husband and wife is paradigmatically such a relation, and the relation between an engaged couple is said in many jurisdictions to be another. Indeed, some jurisdictions go further and talk of fiduciary duties between engaged couples. ("The prerequisite of a confidential relationship is the reposing of trust and confidence by one person in another who is cognizant of this fact. The key factor in the existence of a fiduciary relationship lies in control by a person over the property of another. It is evident that while these two relationships may exist simultaneously, they do not necessarily do so." *Vai v. Bank of Am. Nat'l Trust & Sav. Ass'n*, 364 P2d 247 (Cal 1961). While this states the difference between the two concepts in principle, courts are not always scrupulous in observing the distinction.) But even in the presence of a "confidential relationship" there will be the question whether one party used unfair persuasion that "seriously impaired the free and competent exercise of judgment" of the other. Farnsworth, *Contracts* § 4.1 at 270.

Because the three doctrines we have just surveyed are standard parts of contract law, they apply to marital contracts. However, because they were primarily developed for dealing with commercial contracts, they often have an uncertain or limited application to marital contracts. Legislatures and courts have therefore adopted or adapted some other features of contract law in hopes of diminishing the chances that a marital contract will be unfair. Thus antenuptial agreements must generally be in writing; the Statute of Frauds provides that "any agreement made upon consideration of marriage" is enforceable only if it is "in writing, and signed by the party to be charged therewith." (Some states impose other formalities, such as the requirement that the parties sign in the presence of witnesses or acknowledge the agreement before a notary.) As one treatise notes, "In most recent cases where one party has attempted to enforce an oral antenuptial contract, the courts have been very strict and generally unreceptive to the claims." Lynn D. Wardle, Christopher L. Blakesley and Jacqueline Y. Parker, *Contemporary Family Law* § 5:04, at 16 (Callaghan & Co, 1988).

Legislatures and courts have also adapted to the special situation of marital contracts the commercial doctrine of unconscionability. This adaptation is intended to accord with the particular situation of marital contracts better than standard commercial unconscionability doctrine or the doctrines of duress, misrepresentation, and undue influence. Recall first the version in section 2–302 of the Uniform Commercial Code: "If the court as a matter of law finds the contract or any clause of the contract to have been unconscionable at the time it was made the court may refuse to enforce the contract, or it may enforce the remainder of the contract without the unconscionable clause, or it may so limit the application of any unconscionable clause as to avoid any unconscionable result." But what is unconscionability? Unconscionability is often said to have two aspects. The first, substantive unconscionability, treats the fairness of the outcome the contract requires. The second, procedural unconscionability, treats the fairness of the process by which the contract was reached. Both aspects of unconscionability doctrine have been recruited to limit the range of antenuptial agreements. Most typically, this has been done by combining, sometimes conjunctively and sometimes disjunctively, the two aspects of unconscionability doctrine. We will, however, look at the two aspects separately.

Jurisdictions have made substantive unconscionability an element of the law of marital agreements in varying ways, and even within jurisdictions the rules of substantive unconscionability may depend on such factors as the subject of the agreement (e.g., whether it deals with the spouse's property or with support obligations). Some jurisdictions simply require courts to ask whether the agreement was "unconscionable," thereby leaving the question of what constitutes unconscionability to judicial discretion and common-law development. E.g., Uniform Marital Property Act § 10(g)(2). Other jurisdictions require that "fair and reasonable provision" be made for the spouse opposing the contract. E.g., *Del Vecchio v. Del Vecchio*, 143 S2d 17 (Fla 1962). This formulation is, of course, hardly more illuminating than stating that agreements should not be "unconscionable." Thus some courts have suggested factors to be considered: "It is clear that the reasonableness of any monetary provision in an antenuptial contract cannot ultimately be judged in isolation. Rather, reference may be appropriately made to such factors as the parties' respective worth, the parties' respective ages, the parties' respective intelligence, literacy, and business acumen, and prior family ties or commitments." *Rosenberg v. Lipnick*, 389 NE2d 385, 389 (Mass 1979).

The substantive-unconscionability aspect of marital agreements also presents the problem whether unconscionability is to be determined as of the time the agreement was made or the time it is enforced. The former standard is the one ordinarily applied in contract law and has some appeal in marital law: "Parties to an antenuptial agreement are concerned with entering into a marriage, and removing as much uncertainty as possible from the potential division of property in the event of the death of one of the parties or of the dissolution of the planned marriage between the parties." *Newman v. Newman*, 653 P2d 728, 733 (Colo 1982). On the other hand, the latter standard makes sense because marital agreements may operate over many years and a complicated and unpredictable variety of circumstances.

Jurisdictions vary in handling this problem. Thus New York law requires both that an agreement be "fair and reasonable" when it was made and not unconscionable at the time of final judgment. NY Dom Rel Law § 236(B)(3)(2006). One court establishes a presumption in favor of enforcing prenuptial agreements but announces that "prenuptial agreements will be enforced in their explicit terms only to the extent that circumstances at the time the marriage ends are roughly what the parties foresaw at the time they entered into the prenuptial agreement." *Gant v. Gant*, 329 SE2d 106, 116 (W Va 1985). Jurisdictions may also be more willing to look at circumstances as of the time of enforcement when the issue is maintenance than when it is division of marital property. Thus the *Newman* court said, "Even though an antenuptial agreement is entered into in good faith, with full disclosure and without any element of fraud or overreaching, the maintenance provisions thereof may become voidable for unconscionability occasioned by circumstances existing at the time of the marriage dissolution."

The challenges of deciding what substantive unconscionability means in marital agreements have encouraged jurisdictions to rely only secondarily on substantive unconscionability and to rely primarily on various versions of procedural unconscionability. These safeguards are generally intended to ensure that the spouse who cedes something has made a fully informed and adequately deliberate cession. These safeguards come in so many forms that there cannot be said to be a typical one, but the safeguards established in *Del Vecchio v. Del Vecchio*, 143 S2d 17, 20 (Fla 1962) are both illustrative and common:

> A valid antenuptial agreement contemplates a fair and reasonable provision therein for the wife, or, absent such provision, a full and frank disclosure to the wife, before the signing of the agreement, of the husband's worth, or, absent such disclosure, a general and approximate knowledge by her of the prospective husband's property.... If the provision made by the agreement is not fair and reasonable then it should be made to appear that the wife, when she signed, had some understanding of her rights to be waived by the agreement. In any event she must have signed freely and voluntarily, preferably, but not necessarily a required prerequisite, upon competent and independent advice.

Section 10 of the Uniform Marital Property Act (Wis Stat § 766.58 (2006)) has a similar thrust:

(6) A marital property agreement executed before or during marriage is not enforceable if the spouse against whom enforcement is sought proves any of the following:

(a) The marital property agreement was unconscionable when made.

(b) That spouse did not execute the marital property agreement voluntarily.

(c) Before execution of the marital property agreement, that spouse:

1. Did not receive fair and reasonable disclosure, under the circumstances, of the other spouses property or financial obligations; and

2. Did not have notice of the other spouses property or financial obligations.

Some of the procedural situations the *Del Vecchio* court and the drafters of the UMPA were concerned about are suggested by a subsequent Florida case, *Belcher v. Belcher*, 307 S2d 918, 920 (Fla App 1975):

> The parties first met on Christmas day, 1969, and were married on January 20, 1970; prior to the wedding day, negotiations were held to discuss and determine the terms of the antenuptial agreement; in fact, on January 20, the wedding ceremony had to be delayed because the parties were still in the attorney's office negotiating terms, and the agreement was not signed until very late that afternoon; the wife was represented by counsel and she and her attorney both attended and participated in the negotiating sessions and at the execution of the agreement; the marriage lasted approximately sixteen months. . . .

There are many formulations designed to clarify the extent of disclosure required. One goes:

> Fair disclosure is not synonymous with detailed disclosure such as a financial statement of net worth and income. The mere fact that detailed disclosure was not made will not necessarily be sufficient to set aside an otherwise properly executed agreement. Fair disclosure contemplates that each spouse should be given information, of a general and approximate nature, concerning the net worth of the other.

In re Estate of Lopata, 641 P2d 952, 955 (Colo 1982). The issue is further complicated by the fact that in assessing the disclosure required, courts commonly consider the worldly experience of the party receiving the information and the information about the disclosing spouse's finances the receiving spouse already has. A number of courts (including, as you may recall, the *Del Vecchio* court) seek to insure that the receiving party has the financial sophistication to understand the received information, to know what unreceived information to ask for, to understand the contract, and to grasp what rights are being contractually waived by taking into account the availability to the receiving spouse of independent counsel. Courts also look to the circumstances under which the disclosures are made and the contract is signed. For example, the kind of situation presented in the *Belcher* case, where the agreement was signed just before the wedding, tends to make courts skeptical of the agreement. One court summarized its technique by saying that it considers

> the situation of the parties, their ages, their respective holdings and income, their respective family obligations or ties, the circumstances leading to the execution of the agreement, the actions of husband and wife after the marriage as they tended to show whether the agreement was voluntarily and understandingly made, the needs of him or her who made relinquishment, including whether or not that one, after the death of the other, can live substantially as comfortably as before the marriage.

Hartz v. Hartz, 234 A2d 865, 872 (Md App 1967). Courts often justify these disclosure requirements by consulting the doctrine we discussed earlier that the relationship between the contractors is a "confidential" one. Other confidential relationships include those between agent and principal, director and corporation, and trustee and beneficiary. In a confidential relationship, the active party must serve the best interests of the benefitted party and must reveal information within his or her knowledge which the benefitted party would be helped by knowing.

Separation agreements generally are subject to procedural and substantive safeguards similar to those imposed on antenuptial agreements. They are further often required to be incorporated in the divorce decree, which a court must issue and which thus provides an opportunity for the court to inspect the agreement. In some jurisdictions separation agreements must be in writing or meet other formal requirements. On the other hand, disclosure requirements may depend on whether the spouses are in a confidential relationship. Courts often say spouses negotiating a separation agreement are in a confidential relationship, although the basis for doing so for separation agreements seems less clear than for antenuptial agreements, since in the former the spouses have presumably already had serious disagreements, agreed to separate, and lost a good deal of present trust and the expectation of future trust. Courts have, however, applied the confidential-relationship principle to separation agreements by reasoning that the husband, as the dominant party, is relied on by the wife or by reasoning that even divorcing spouses *ought* still to treat each other in ways that honor their past relationship. In addition, the presumption that a confidential relationship exists is sometimes statutorily imposed. The confidential relationship can generally be terminated by a repudiatory act, like hiring a lawyer to represent one of the spouses in a divorce. Finally, in some jurisdictions the existence of a confidential relationship can be a matter of fact to be decided case by case.

As with antenuptial agreements, courts assess the bargaining position of the parties and will not uphold agreements where there was fraud or duress. See, e.g., *Hale v. Hale*, 539 A2d 247 (Md Ct Spec App 1988); *Adams v. Adams*, 1994 WL 27367 (Va Ct App.) Disclosure is as important in separation agreements as in premarital agreements. The better practice is to attach schedules of assets held separately or jointly to the agreement. Finally, as with any contract, the agreement will be construed against the party who prepared it, particularly if the other was not represented by an attorney. The unrepresented party should be strongly cautioned, preferably in writing, to have an attorney examine the agreement.

A Note on Negotiation

As we mentioned in Chapter 1, couples resolve the vast majority of family law disputes without litigating. Most of these conflicts, like most other legal disputes, end when the lawyers for the opposing parties reach agreement.

The most influential article on divorce negotiation (and one of the most cited works on dispute-resolution generally) is by Robert Mnookin and Lewis Kornhauser, a law professor and an economist. *Bargaining in the Shadow of the Law: The Case of Divorce,* 88 Yale L J 969 (1979), is worth reading but is briefly summarized here.

Mnookin and Kornhauser write that parties bargain from "endowment points." In the divorce context, they begin bargaining knowing that if they do not reach an agreement, they will go to court and have the court make their settlement for them. The divorce and custody regimes set by statute and court interpretation provide this background for the divorcing parties. If they are rational, they should not settle for less than that expected court outcome (less the costs of litigating). Further, Mnookin and Kornhauser classify the subjects of bargaining into two categories: custodial time and money. They state that "over some range of alternatives, each parent may be willing to exchange custodial rights and obligations for income or wealth, and parents may tie support duties to custodial prerogatives with a minimal level of resources." *Bargaining in the Shadow* also suggests that women might be more risk averse than men when it comes to litigating custody. That is, they might trade assets they could expect in court in order to avoid even a relatively small chance that they would lose custody in court. In particular, risk neutral men might exploit their risk averse wives by threatening custody actions. This concept is further explored in Richard Neely's *The Hidden Cost of Divorce: Barter in the Court,* New Republic, February 10, 1986, at 13.

Mnookin and Kornhauser's gloomiest prediction was that when divorce laws changed from fault to no-fault, women would be injured in terms of custody time and property distribution. Their warnings echoed loudly in the academic literature. In the last several years, a number of articles have looked empirically at no-fault divorce and its consequences. In one, Marsha Garrison made an empirical study of New York divorces: *Good Intentions Gone Awry: The Impact of New York's Equitable Distribution Law on Divorce Outcomes*, 57 Brooklyn L Rev 621 (1991). It reported that alimony, property and custody settlements were not very different from those preceding the no-fault era. Professor Mnookin published an important book in 1992 with Eleanor E. Maccoby called *Dividing the Child: Social and Legal Dilemmas of Custody* (Harv U Press 1992). Like Lenore Weitzman's earlier piece, *The Social and Economic Consequences of No-Fault Divorce*, 28 UCLA L Rev 1181

(1981), this book studied the actual settlements reached in California divorce cases. Mnookin and Maccoby looked at court records, which they supplemented with interviews. They asked whether the settlements were different in litigated than in settled cases. If Mnookin's earlier theoretical work was correct and if women were more risk averse than their husbands, the amount they received on settlement should have been lower than if they litigated. In fact, the results were virtually identical.

In 1993, three pieces compared results in fault and no-fault states. Yoram Weiss and Robert Willis, in *Transfers Among Divorced Couples,* 11 J Lab Econ 629 (1993), found little difference in divorce settlements across states. They looked at individual (panel) data. Similarly, Michael Alexeev and Margaret Brinig, in *Trading at Divorce: Preferences, Legal Rules and Transaction Costs,* 8 Ohio St J Disp Res 279 (1993), studied 1987 divorce settlements in Virginia and Wisconsin, states with quite different family law regimes. They found nearly identical results in the two suburban counties they examined. Each of these studies found that wives received somewhere between 45 and 55 percent of the total marital assets while receiving a custody share of between 71 and 75 percent.

This empirical work suggests that more thinking about no-fault divorce needs to be done. In particular, should the fact that men and women apparently have different preferences about custody and marital assets be reflected in divorce laws? If so, how? If no-fault divorce did not affect couple's bargaining, did it affect divorce rates? The quality of marriage?

Margaret F. Brinig and Steven M. Crafton, in *Marriage and Opportunism*, 23 J Legal Stud 869 (1994), propose that the real consequences of no-fault divorce are not felt at the time of divorce, but rather before and during marriage. The no-fault regime seems to decrease the number and quality of marriages. Brinig and Crafton postulate that no-fault divorce decreases investment in marriage and increases opportunism, particularly by men. They demonstrate these results empirically using statewide data revealing a lower birth rate, lower marriage rate, and higher rate of spouse abuse in no-fault states. Professors Brinig and F.H. Buckley, in *No-Fault Laws and At–Fault People*, 18 Intl Rev L & Econ 325 (1998), show that there are differences in divorce rates, if the appropriate definition of no-fault is used, and find that the existence of a joint custody regime seems to impede divorce.

(2) Two Cases

IN RE MARRIAGE OF SPIEGEL

Supreme Court of Iowa, 1996
553 NW2d 309

TERNUS, J.

Background

A.J. Spiegel met Sara Jane Williams in 1978; they began dating the next year. Both parties had been previously married and divorced and both had children from these prior marriages. At the time of trial A.J. was fifty years of age and Sara was forty-seven. Their respective children were adults.

Sara graduated from high school in 1965 and earned a bachelor of arts degree in merchandising and design in 1969. She then worked as a salaried interior decorator. In 1983 Sara started her own interior decorating business and while doing so completed a masters degree program in textile design. Her business has shown relatively little profit, generating no more than $4000 of net income in its best year.

In contrast A.J., through Herculean efforts beginning long before the parties' marriage, started and developed an extremely successful business. When the parties married, this business, the Mi–T–M Company (Mi–T–M), reported total assets in excess of $13 million, with A.J. having a net worth of more than $2.8 million.

The parties became engaged in 1983, but delayed setting a wedding date. Sara broke the engagement sometime in 1986 when she heard rumors A.J. was seeing other women. The parties soon reconciled and again became engaged within several months. Again no wedding date was set.

In February 1988, A.J. first brought up the idea of a prenuptial agreement. Although it was untrue, he told Sara his bankers, lawyers, and accountants felt he needed such an agreement to protect financing for a Mi–T–M construction project. Sara flatly rejected the suggestion, stating under no circumstances would she be married with a prenuptial agreement. A.J. dropped the matter for the time being.

In May 1988, the couple set a wedding date for July 30, 1988. A.J. did not bring up the subject of a prenuptial agreement again until approximately ten days before the scheduled wedding. Sara became upset and stated she had not changed her mind. A.J. again dropped the subject but, without telling Sara, he continued prior discussions with his advisors, and directed his legal counsel to draft a prenuptial agreement and mail it to Sara.

When Sara received the document only five days prior to the wedding, she was decimated. She immediately phoned A.J. and asked why he was doing this to her. A.J. falsely repeated that a prenuptial agreement was not his idea but that of his business advisors. He tried to comfort Sara, explaining the agreement was just a piece of paper, that it would never come between them, and it was just to get the bankers "off his back."

The prenuptial agreement sent to Sara covered the parties' financial relationship and rights both during the marriage and in the event the marriage terminated due to death or dissolution. It basically waived any rights to which Sara would be entitled under Iowa law. The separate property of each would remain separate and any property acquired after the marriage would remain the separate property of the person who acquired it, except for any property specifically purchased in joint tenancy. The agreement also provided each party's salary would be considered separate property and the parties would maintain separate bank accounts for purposes of segregating their finances. Finally, the agreement eliminated the right to support or alimony in the event of dissolution.

A.J. told Sara to consult an attorney, and offered to pay the fee. In accordance with A.J.'s prompting, Sara employed legal counsel immediately and met with her attorney the next day. Sara's counsel explained each provision of the agreement to her, pointing out his concerns. He told her, "This agreement basically says that you get nothing."

In the short time available before the wedding, Sara's attorney was able to negotiate three changes: (1) Sara's right to a spousal statutory share of A.J.'s estate in the event of his death would not be waived in the agreement; (2) title to the couple's new home would be in joint tenancy and Sara would be entitled to one-half of the furnishings of the home; and (3) Sara would have title to the automobile she drove. Although Sara's attorney also sought concessions in the provisions dealing with Sara's rights in the event of dissolution, A.J. would not agree to any changes in that area. Sara's counsel told her before she signed the agreement that he had asked for a provision allowing alimony if the parties' marriage was dissolved and A.J. had refused to allow such a provision.

During the days of negotiation, Sara informed her attorney of A.J.'s representations that his financial advisors wanted the prenuptial agreement and the agreement was just a piece of paper and would not come between them. Her attorney warned her the agreement contained a provision stating the prenuptial agreement constituted "the entire agreement of the parties and no representations, terms, provisions, conditions or exceptions exist except those expressly set forth herein." He told her that because A.J.'s representations were not included in the document, they would not be considered legally binding and the agreement could be enforced against her in a dissolution proceeding.

On the afternoon of July 29, less than twenty-four hours prior to the wedding, Sara, A.J., and their respective counsel attended a tense and emotional meeting. A.J. represented to Sara that he had never actually read the terms of the agreement. For that reason Sara had her attorney read the agreement aloud line-by-line in A.J.'s presence, hoping that when he heard it and realized its import he would not ask her to sign the agreement. When reading the document failed to change A.J.'s mind, she turned to him and asked if this was what he really wanted (referring to her signing the agreement). When he replied "yes," Sara signed. Although Sara's attorney thought A.J. was unfair, her attorney did not think Sara signed the agreement under duress, fraud or undue influence.

A.J. and Sara were married the following day, July 30, 1988. Their marriage was rocky almost from the beginning. More fruitful, however, was A.J.'s business. During the parties' six-year marriage, A.J.'s net worth increased from $2.8 million to $9.6 million. A.J. earned over

$800,000 in salary from Mi–T–M in 1993. That year the company had net sales of $9.4 million and net income of $494,546. Sara's net worth, valued at $39,250 at the time of the marriage, increased slightly due to her joint ownership of the marital home.

During the marriage, the parties abided by the prenuptial agreement. They maintained separate finances and did not commingle their assets or incomes. At one point, Sara attempted to obtain additional financial assistance from her first husband for their daughters' college expenses. During that proceeding, she relied on the prenuptial agreement to show the limited funds that were available to her from A.J.

Sara filed a petition for separate maintenance on April 14, 1994, after A.J. stopped paying Sara any money to meet the monthly household expenses. A.J. counterclaimed for dissolution of the marriage. Following trial, the district court refused to enforce the prenuptial agreement, finding it was gained through fraud, duress, and undue influence. The decree awarded Sara a lump sum property distribution of $2,000,000 with an initial payment of $250,000, the remainder payable in monthly installments over five years, with interest of ten percent per annum. A.J. was also ordered to pay Sara $7000 per month alimony until either party's death or Sara's remarriage. The alimony obligation would terminate if A.J. retired, provided he did not retire until he was sixty-five years of age. A supplemental decree awarded A.J. possession of the marital home. Sara was also awarded $15,000 for attorney fees. The case is before us on A.J.'s appeal. Our review is de novo. . . .

Property Distribution

A.J. argues the trial court erred by failing to enforce the prenuptial agreement. Enforcement of the agreement would have the effect of depriving Sara of any interest in A.J.'s property. Iowa Code section 598.21(1) expressly permits the court to consider the provisions of a prenuptial agreement when deciding equitable property division issues. Thus, our first task is to determine the validity of the prenuptial agreement signed by A.J. and Sara.

Enforceability of prenuptial agreements. Iowa cases have long held prenuptial agreements are favored in the law. The purpose of such agreements is to fix and determine the interest that the parties have respectively in the property of the other. The motivation for a prenuptial agreement may vary from case to case, but often such agreements protect the interests of children by former marriages, and by doing so, settle property questions that might otherwise cause dissension in the marriage. They allow parties to structure their financial affairs to suit their needs and values and to achieve certainty. This certainty may encourage marriage and may be conducive to marital tranquility by protecting the financial expectations of the parties. The right to enter into an agreement regulating financial affairs in a marriage is important to a large number of citizens.

We have said prenuptial agreements are entitled to the same consideration and construction as other contracts. Nevertheless, our cases have imposed requirements which appear to qualify this general statement.

In an early Iowa case, we held the court will examine a prenuptial agreement to determine whether its terms were unjust or unreasonable. If the contract is unjust or unreasonable, the burden is on the proponent of the agreement to show it was fairly procured. Where the agreement is fairly and honestly made, it is enforceable like any other contract. Stating the same rule in a different way, we have said when parties enter into a prenuptial agreement in the absence of fraud, mistake or undue influence, the contract is binding. The test to be gleaned from these cases is that agreements that are substantively unfair are still binding if they were executed in a procedurally fair manner.

We have been unable to find a clear statement in the Iowa cases of the test for substantive fairness. A review of our cases shows, however, that over time our appellate courts have become increasingly reluctant to declare an agreement unreasonable. For example, in the 1899 *Fisher* case, the court appeared to conclude the prenuptial contract was unfair because it deprived the wife of all her marital rights. *Fisher*, 110 Iowa at 500, 80 N.W. at 551 (court considered procedural fairness in execution of agreement, apparently concluding contract terms were unjust and unreasonable). Just fifteen years later, however, the court was reluctant to declare a contract unreasonable even though it deprived the wife of any interest in her husband's estate.

> From the whole record, which we have carefully read, we reach the conclusion that Mrs. Emanuel knew of the terms of the marriage contract, freely entered into it, uninfluenced by fraud or deceit, and that we have not the right to say that it should not be binding. Noting the wife had provided faithful and devoted care to her invalid husband, the court observed such care "merits compensation, stating a moral view, but does not warrant us, as a means of providing it, to declare invalid an instrument limiting [the wife's] rights which to us seems to have been fairly entered into."

We held an agreement that gave the wife a meager allowance upon the husband's death was not unfair. Noting the wife had lived in humble circumstances before the marriage, the court concluded that from a purely financial angle, [the wife] gained by the marriage. In a more recent case decided by our court of appeals, the court upheld a prenuptial agreement in which each party waived all rights in the other's property and waived all rights of election to take against the other's will. The husband died, making no provision for his wife in his will. The court concluded the contract was not unjust or unenforceable, even though the wife was left with nothing, noting the waiver of rights in the agreement was mutual.

Our courts' gradual minimization of the extent to which we will review the terms of an agreement for fairness and equity may reflect the difficulty and arbitrariness of the task.

We are reluctant to interfere with the power of persons contemplating marriage to agree upon, and to act in reliance upon, what they regard as an acceptable distribution scheme for their property. A court should not ignore the parties' expressed intent by proceeding to determine whether a prenuptial agreement was, in the court's view, reasonable at the time of its inception or the time of divorce. These are exactly the sorts of judicial determinations that such agreements are designed to avoid. Rare indeed is the agreement that is beyond possible challenge when reasonableness is placed at issue.

A.J. has not suggested in this appeal that we abandon our requirement of substantive fairness. Consequently, that issue is not before us. Nevertheless, the observations of the Wisconsin court in attempting to apply an intense review of the substantive fairness of prenuptial agreements and the Pennsylvania court in rejecting any review for substantive fairness highlight the difficulties inherent in evaluating substantive fairness. These inherent difficulties also confirm the wisdom of the uncomplicated approach taken in our later appellate cases that consider an agreement substantively fair if its obligations and waivers are mutual or the economically disadvantaged party receives a financial improvement in his or her pre-marriage circumstances.

Our procedural fairness test—fairly, freely and understandingly entered into—reflects the usual concern that any waiver of rights be knowing and voluntary. Consistent with principles of waiver, we have always required a full disclosure or independent knowledge of the nature and extent of the parties' assets to ensure the agreement was fairly procured.

In summary, the rules governing the validity of prenuptial agreements are as follows. The person challenging the agreement must prove its terms are unfair or the person's waiver of rights was not knowing and voluntary. Applying the standard of our recent cases, we hold the terms of an agreement are fair when the provisions of the contract are mutual or the division of property is consistent with the financial condition of the parties at the time of execution. Of course, the affirmative defenses of fraud, duress and undue influence are also available to void a prenuptial agreement, as with any other contract.

Our liberal test of substantive fairness combined with the requirement of a knowing and voluntary waiver strikes a proper balance between the two competing interests at stake. First we are sensitive to the traditional desire to protect the party waiving valuable property rights from doing so without a full knowledge and understanding of the import of his or her actions. On the other hand, we must respect the right of competent persons to contract as they wish. Under the test stated above, Iowa courts will not be called upon to judge the moral fairness of the agreement and in doing so, assume the role of guardian for one of the parties.

With these legal principles in mind, we turn to the contentions of the parties in this case.

A. Fairness of agreement and its procurement. Sara argues the terms of the prenuptial agreement are inequitable and unfair to her because she gave up nearly everything to which she would normally be entitled under the law. On our de novo review we conclude Sara has not carried her burden to show the agreement is unfair.

First, we decline Sara's implicit suggestion that in such cases we review the circumstances of the parties to decide if she was given "enough" to satisfy our sense of fairness. To adopt such a standard would require us to declare invalid any prenuptial agreement that constituted a bad fiscal bargain for one party. As we discussed earlier, we will not so grossly interfere with the parties' freedom to contract.

Turning to the prenuptial agreement at issue here, we note Sara did not forfeit all marital rights: she retained her statutory rights in the event of A.J.'s death and received a joint interest in the marital home. As a result of this latter provision, Sara's net worth increased during the marriage.

Moreover, the relinquishment of marital rights in the event of dissolution was mutual, as were all other provisions of the agreement. There is no rule of law requiring A.J. to share his wealth simply because he had more to share than did Sara.

Sara has also failed to show she did not sign the agreement knowingly and voluntarily. She had independent counsel who informed her in detail of the rights she was giving up and the consequences of signing the agreement. As we discuss more fully below in the divisions dealing with duress and undue influence, Sara signed the agreement voluntarily, albeit reluctantly.

Sara argues the agreement did not assure that A.J. had fully disclosed the nature and extent of his assets to her prior to her execution of the contract. A list of A.J.'s assets and debts was attached to the contract; the agreement stated, however, that the values of A.J.'s property, particularly Mi–T–M, may be greatly in excess of the valuations shown on the exhibit. Neither Sara nor her attorney expressed any desire to have a more formal appraisal done of A.J.'s holdings; nor does Sara complain on appeal that the valuations on the exhibit were wrong. In fact, she relies on the net worth shown on the exhibit attached to the prenuptial agreement to support her claim the value of A.J.'s assets appreciated tremendously during the marriage. We have never required that a party have precise valuations of the other's assets; a general knowledge of the true nature and extent of the other's properties is sufficient. We conclude A.J. made an adequate disclosure of his financial condition.

We certainly do not admire A.J.'s lack of forthrightness in blaming others for the motivation behind the agreement. Neither do we admire the timing utilized in presenting Sara with the dilemma of canceling a wedding or submitting to the agreement. Pressure put on Sara, and its timing, may be criticized as unkind, but cannot be deemed illegal.

C. Fraud. Fraud requires proof that Sara justifiably relied on A.J.'s representations. Whether a person's reliance is reasonable is determined subjectively: whether the complaining party, in view of his own information and intelligence, had a right to rely on the representations.

Sara claimed at trial that if she had known A.J. wanted the prenuptial agreement "for himself," she would not have signed the agreement. She also asserted she thought A.J. would never enforce the agreement. We find Sara's reliance on A.J.'s statements unjustified. First, her attorney advised her the agreement could be held binding notwithstanding anything A.J. said privately.

Second, A.J. never told her he would not enforce the prenuptial agreement. To the contrary he was not only insistent that she sign the agreement, he refused her requests to modify the provisions dealing with her rights upon dissolution. Moreover, minutes before Sara signed the agreement, A.J. finally acknowledged to her that he, not just the bankers and accountants, wanted the agreement.

As Sara acknowledged at trial, A.J.'s representations prior to her signing the agreement were in essence that the agreement would not interfere with their marriage or their happiness. Of course, that is presumably the intent and hope of all couples who enter into such an agreement. It can hardly be equated with a representation that if these hopes are not realized, the document will have no effect on the terms of a dissolution. In other words, saying the prenuptial agreement will not affect the parties' relationship is not the same as saying it will not affect the termination of that relationship. Thus, Sara has failed to prove she justifiably relied on A.J.'s representations in signing the prenuptial agreement.

D. Duress. We follow the Restatement's rule concerning the effect of duress on the enforceability of a contract: " 'If a party's manifestation of assent is induced by an improper threat by the other party that leaves the victim no reasonable alternative, the contract is voidable by the victim.' "An essential element of duress is the victim had no reasonable alternative to entering into the contract. Here, Sara had a reasonable alternative—she could have canceled the wedding. Although she may have suffered embarrassment in doing so, we do not think social embarrassment from the cancellation of wedding plans, even on the eve of the wedding, renders that choice unreasonable. Another essential element of duress is that the threat be wrongful or unlawful. A.J.'s threat here, albeit unspoken, was he would not marry Sara if she did not sign the prenuptial agreement. We find this threat neither wrongful nor unlawful. For these reasons, Sara has failed to show she acted under duress in signing the prenuptial agreement.

E. Undue influence. Undue influence is influence that deprives one person of his or her freedom of choice and substitutes the will of another in its place. We do not find clear and convincing evidence in the record before us to support a finding Sara executed the prenuptial agreement as the result of undue influence. The discussion of the court in *Stetzel*, holding undue influence did not exist as a matter of law, is instructive:

> The fact that the adjuster was boorish and intruded upon plaintiff's privacy is not significant unless it resulted in depriving [plaintiff] of her independence of action and substituted his will for hers at the time the release was signed. There is a total absence of evidence that it did. In fact the record proves conclusively to the contrary. Plaintiff places great importance on her testimony that she did not want to sign. This is by no means the same as saying undue influence was exercised upon her. Plaintiff was a well educated, highly intelligent young lady. Her scholastic record was outstanding. Before signing the release she sought independent advice from her landlady, in whom she apparently had considerable confidence, and from an Iowa City lawyer—not counsel now representing her—whose help she now denounces. Whether his advice was good or bad is not the question we here consider. The fact that she sought and received independent advice is a proper matter to consider on the question of undue influence. In addition to all this is the testimony heretofore set out in which plaintiff concedes she knew the purpose of the instrument, read it, understood it, and realized its consequences before signing. We hold all these circumstances refute undue influence as a matter of law. *Stetzel*, 174 N.W.2d at 443.

We reach the same conclusions here. There is no evidence A.J.'s will was substituted for Sara's own judgment in deciding to sign the prenuptial agreement. Sara is an intelligent, well-educated business woman. She had the advice of competent counsel. "[S]he knew the purpose of the instrument, read it, understood it, and realized its consequences before signing." Under these circumstances, Sara did not prove undue influence.

We conclude the prenuptial agreement is binding on Sara. Sara's regret at having signed the agreement will not prevent its enforcement against her. This holding makes it unnecessary for us to consider A.J.'s challenge to the trial court's property settlement. That settlement must be in accordance with the prenuptial agreement.

Alimony

The $7000 monthly alimony award is the subject of a separate assignment. The right to this award, as mentioned, was also waived in the agreement, but requires special analysis. Formerly, and again at the present time, provisions waiving alimony in prenuptial agreements were and are void. But A.J. contends the provision in this agreement was written during a window of time when such a provision was allowed.

Prior to 1980, alimony waivers were considered void as against public policy, but this common-law rule was modified when an amendment to Iowa Code section 598.21 allowed courts to consider them. In 1992, as a part of the uniform premarital agreement act, Iowa Code section 596.5(2) was adopted, reestablishing our prior rule prohibiting these provisions....

Alimony is a stipend to a spouse in lieu of the other spouse's legal obligation for support. Alimony is not an absolute right, and an award thereof depends upon the circumstances of a particular case. When making or denying an alimony award, the trial court considers the factors set forth in Iowa Code section 598.21(3). Although our review of the trial court's award is de novo, we accord the trial court considerable latitude in making this determination and will disturb the ruling only when there has been a failure to do equity.

The amount of the alimony award here was substantial. Sara argues the award was reasonable when compared to other cases where the payor spouse had a high income. In [other] cases, however, the marriage was of considerable duration, twenty years, twenty-two years, and thirty-four years, respectively. Here, in contrast, the marriage lasted a mere six years.

In addition to the length of the marriage, it is appropriate for us to consider the age and health of the parties, their educational level and earning capacity, the feasibility of the party seeking alimony becoming self-supporting at a comparable standard of living, any property distribution made in the decree, the tax consequences and the provisions of any prenuptial agreement. Notably, section 598.21(3) does not include in its list of factors the premarital relationship of the parties. Consequently, even though Sara emphasizes the emotional support she gave A.J. during their lengthy courtship, we give no consideration to this support even though it probably enhanced A.J.'s efforts to build the wealth he now enjoys.

We think the substantial alimony award made by the trial court is inappropriate when all relevant factors are considered. The marriage was relatively brief. Sara is well-educated, owns her own business and is in good health. The parties agreed in the prenuptial agreement that Sara would receive no support from A.J. if the marriage was dissolved. On the other hand, during the parties' marriage, Sara refrained, at A.J.'s urging, from developing her business. Without doubt the marked success of A.J.'s business career from 1988 to 1994 must be ascribed to his own talent and enterprise. But A.J. solicited Sara's commitment to support him emotionally, socially and domestically in his career and she obliged—to A.J.'s admitted advantage.

In view of all the foregoing we think Sara should be awarded alimony, but we modify the trial court's award by reducing the amount of alimony from $7000 to $3000 per month. Alimony shall be payable from the date of the decree but should terminate ten years thereafter, or when Sara dies, remarries, or cohabitates with a person of the opposite sex.

Summary

We hold the prenuptial agreement is enforceable. Therefore, any property division must be in accordance with that agreement. We remand to the district court to determine Sara's interest in any joint property. We modify the district court's award of alimony by reducing it from $7000 to $3000 and as modified, affirm the award of alimony. Costs are taxed one-half to each party.

Questions on Spiegel, *the Principles of Contract, and the Meaning of Marriage*

(1) The court ultimately refused to override this contract, but a contrary result is hardly unimaginable. Could A.J. have done anything more to diminish the contract's vulnerability?

(2) Is this contract unfair?

> (a) Would Sara's situation have been better if she had never met A.J.? If she had lived with A.J. but not married him?
>
> (b) Did Sara do anything that gave her a moral claim to the asset that A.J. had (apparently) worked with exceptional energy and skill to create?
>
> (c) Is it unfair for couples to have unequal resources during a marriage? To have unequal resources after a marriage?

(3) Would it have been unfair *not* to enforce this contract? (More precisely, was it unfair that the contract was not wholly enforced?) A.J. seems to have made it amply clear that he did not want to marry Sara without the protection the contract offered him. He presumably changed his position drastically—i.e., he married Sara—relying on the contract. Nor was Sara a person so inexperienced in the ways of the world that he should have been on notice that she could not look after herself. She was forty-seven-years old; she had been married and divorced; she had had a career, and she founded and owned her own business. The court thought A.J. had plausibly disclosed his assets. A.J. knew Sara was familiar with the contract's terms. And, not least, he knew Sara was represented by counsel (indeed, he seems to have paid for her to be represented).

(4) What standard did the court use in deciding whether the contract was unfair?

> (a) At one point, the court seems to suggest that if an agreement is substantively unfair but was procedurally unobjectionable a court cannot invalidate it. Is that the court's test? Should it be?
>
> (b) At another point, the court talks about what "substantively unfair" means. Is that the court's test? Should it be? Is the problem that the marital arrangement A.J. wanted did not fit social understandings of the moral requirements of marriage?
>
> (c) Is the court suggesting that a contract must be *both* substantively and procedurally fair? Should this be the test?
>
> (d) If this were a conventional commercial contract, what would the test for unfairness be? Was this the court's test? Should it be?

(e) Should the court use something other than the commercial-contract test on the theory that Sara and A.J. are in a "confidential relationship"?

(5) Is the result of this case explicable because of the statutory restrictions against waiving alimony? What if there were no such rule? Why is alimony different from other aspects of the couple's economic relations?

(6) Can you imagine circumstances which might make this contract unenforceable?

(a) Should the court decline to enforce the contract if the couple had had children during the marriage? If Sara had helped raise A.J.'s children from a former relationship?

(b) Should the court decline to enforce the contract if A.J. had founded his business during instead of before the marriage?

(c) Should the court decline to enforce the contract if A.J. had repeatedly abused Sara during the marriage?

(7) Should it matter that A.J. was not honest in describing his motives for entering the contract? Was it correct for the court to invoke the parole evidence rule?

(8) Should Sara have an action against the attorney who represented her? Was she disadvantaged in this case because she *did* win some concessions? Was she disadvantaged by her use of the agreement (and the understanding of its import that use implied) to try to extract more college support money from her previous husband?

(9) What if the Spiegels had called off their wedding but called it back on a few months later without revoking the agreement they had signed or without executing a new one? See, e.g., *Hurt v. Hurt*, 433 SE2d 493 (Va App 1993) superceded by Va Code Ann § 20–153 (2005).

IN RE THE MARRIAGE OF BONDS

Court of Appeal, First District, California, 2001
2001 WL 1191386

LAMBDEN, J.

The Supreme Court in *In re Marriage of Bonds* (2000) 24 Cal.4th 1, 99 Cal.Rptr.2d 252, 5 P.3d 815 (*Bonds*) (abrogated by Stats. 2001, ch. 286) held that the prenuptial agreement between Susann Margreth Bonds (Sun) and Barry Lamar Bonds (Barry) was valid and remanded for us to consider the remaining issues: whether the trial court denied Sun due process when it refused to hear evidence regarding estoppel; whether the trial court erred in ruling that Barry had not given to Sun a gift of a one-half interest in three real properties purchased during the marriage; whether the trial court erred in ruling that Barry had not transmuted his separate property interest in three real properties to community property; and whether the trial court should reconsider its ruling to terminate spousal support. We conclude that the court erred in finding no transmutation.

BACKGROUND

The facts of this case are set forth in detail in *Bonds, supra,* 24 Cal.4th 1, 99 Cal.Rptr.2d 252, 5 P.3d 815, and only those facts relevant to the issues remaining are specified here. On November 7, 1987, Sun moved to Phoenix to live with Barry. Seven days later Barry proposed to Sun. The parties set their wedding date for February 6, 1988.

Barry and Sun went to the office of Barry's attorneys to review the premarital agreement written by Barry's attorneys on February 5, 1988. The agreement, among other things, contained at paragraph 11 a provision regarding transmutation, which stated as follows: "Except as otherwise provided by this agreement, property or interests now owned or hereafter acquired by the parties, which by the terms of this agreement is classified as the separate property of one of them, may become the separate property of the other or the parties' community/joint property only by written instrument executed by the parties whose separate property is thereby reclassified." Paragraph 10 in the agreement concerned separate property. It specified that the earnings of the husband and wife during their marriage would be separate property of that spouse.

The parties signed the agreement and married a couple of days later in Las Vegas, Nevada. After the marriage, Sun did not work outside the home. The parties briefly separated in January 1989, but reconciled after Barry filed for divorce.

In July 1989, Barry used his earnings to purchase an unimproved lot, lot 81, in Murietta, California. Title was taken as "Barry L. Bonds and Susann Margaret [*sic*] Bonds, husband and wife as community property." Neither Barry nor Sun signed the deed, but they both signed a deed of trust securing a construction loan for the property. The deed of trust referred to the owners of the property as "Barry Lamar Bonds and Sun Bonds, husband and wife as community property."

During this same year, 1989, Barry also bought a residence in Pennsylvania (Pennsylvania property). Barry specified that ownership of this property would be in the names of both Sun and himself, as husband and wife.

In 1991, lot 81 was exchanged for another piece of property, lot 8, in the same development in Murietta. Barry and Sun both signed the exchange contract. This contract referred to "Barry Lamar Bonds and Susann Margaret [*sic*] Bonds, Husband and Wife." The owners of lot 8 signed a deed granting their lot to Barry Lamar Bonds and Susann Margreth Bonds, "Husband and Wife." When Barry and Sun deeded lot 81, they described it as owned by "Barry Lamar Bonds and Susann Margaret [*sic*] Bonds, Husband and Wife." Barry built a house on lot 8.

Barry purchased a third lot in the Murietta development as an investment property. He took title to the investment property in the name of his corporation, MVP Plus, Inc. (Murietta investment property).

In March 1993, Barry purchased a home in Atherton, California. In a deed not signed by Barry or Sun, the sellers conveyed title to "Barry Bonds and Sun Bonds, husband and wife, AS JOINT TENANTS." Barry and Sun signed a deed of trust on this property securing a loan, which stated that title to the Atherton Home was held by "Barry Bonds and Sun Bonds, Husband and Wife."

Barry filed a petition for legal separation on May 27, 1994. Sun responded by requesting custody of the parties' two children, child and spousal support, attorney's fees, and determination of property rights.

The case was first heard before Commissioner George Taylor who later recused himself sua sponte after the media reported that he had requested an autograph from Barry. The case was transferred to the Honorable Judith W. Kozloski. The legal separation action was later converted to one for divorce, and a status-only dissolution judgment was entered on December 8, 1994.

They parties stipulated to bifurcate the trial to determine the agreement's validity prior to the determination of other issues. The trial court ruled that the agreement was valid.

The second phase of the trial related to the interpretation and enforcement of the prenuptial agreement. The trial court ruled at the outset of this phase that Sun could not submit evidence in support of her claim that Barry was estopped from asserting that the prenuptial agreement was valid. The court ruled that the premarital agreement prohibited oral modifications to its terms.

The court, on May 29, 1996, entered judgment on all issues except duration of spousal support. The court found, among other things, that all the real property purchased during the marriage remained Barry's separate property. Sun filed a notice of intention to move for a new trial or to vacate the prematurely entered judgment and then filed the motion five days later. The one day hearing on the duration of spousal support occurred on September 9, 1996, and the court issued a minute order terminating spousal support on December 30, 1998.

Sun filed a timely notice of appeal from both the judgment order and from the minute order regarding the duration of spousal support. We reversed, concluding that the prenuptial agreement was not entered into voluntarily and was therefore not valid. The Supreme Court granted review and held that the agreement was valid. The Supreme Court remanded for us to consider the remaining issues on appeal.

DISCUSSION

I. Estoppel

Sun argues that the court denied her due process because it refused to permit her to present any evidence that Barry was estopped from enforcing the premarital agreement. Sun wanted to pre-sent evidence that Barry had told her that the premarital agreement was a "joke" and that he had made the necessary arrangements to have it canceled. Sun contends that the trial court erred in ruling that any modification of the agreement had to be in writing, since this requirement does not apply to the equitable remedy of estoppel. Although the elements of estoppel are generally a factual determination, the error here, Sun argues, is one of law because she was prevented from presenting her facts.

Had she been able to present evidence, Sun asserts she would have presented evidence that she relied on Barry's representations that he had rescinded the prenuptial agreement. She maintains that Barry and she separated and reconciled on numerous occasions and Barry's representations that the premarital contract no longer existed prevented her from, among other things, renegotiating the terms of the agreement as a condition to reconciliation. Additionally, she claims that she relied on Barry's representations when she failed to ensure that he execute documents establishing that she had an ownership interest in the real property purchased during their marriage. Further, she asserts, Barry's conduct breached the parties' fiduciary relationship as a matter of law.

Barry argues that the trial court's ruling is proper because Family Code section 1614 provides: "After marriage, a premarital agreement may be amended or revoked only by a written agreement signed by the parties. The amended agreement or the revocation is enforceable without consideration." Since Sun's evidence of revocation consisted of oral statements made by Barry, the court, according to Barry, properly ruled that these statements were not admissible.

Sun responds that estoppel is not the same as modifying or revoking an agreement. Estoppel leaves the contract intact, but prevents a deceitful party from contractual benefits from and after the date of misrepresentation. She cites *Hall v. Hall* (1990) 222 Cal.App.3d 578, 582–587, 271 Cal.Rptr. 773 (*Hall*), which held that traditional exceptions to the statute of frauds continued to apply even after California adopted the Uniform Premarital Agreement Act (former Civil Code, § 5300 et seq.) in 1985. The court explained that, even prior to the enactment of the Uniform Premarital Act, "marriage itself or mere payment of money was not sufficient performance to take an oral prenuptial agreement out of the writing requirement of the statute, because these acts could reasonably be expected in any marriage." However, in the case before it, the wife not only paid the husband money, which would have been insufficient to take the case out of the statute of frauds, but also stopped work and applied for early Social Security and irretrievably changed her position in reliance of her husband's promise to provide her a house for the rest of her life. The court concluded that partial performance still acted as an equitable exception to the requirement that a prenuptial agreement must be in writing (former Civil Code, § 5311).

Sun asserts that she would not have reconciled with Barry if she had known the prenuptial agreement still had effect. She concedes that marriage is insufficient to establish detrimental reliance when based on partial performance, as in *Hall,* but she claims that it may be sufficient when the basis for estoppel is false and deceitful representations. She points out that in *Peek, supra,* which was cited by the *Hall* court, the husband orally promised the wife that he would convey to her property if she married him but, instead, he secretly conveyed it to his son. The court cited the principle that marriage does not amount to part performance. However, since the husband had committed a fraud, and the wife had irretrievably changed her condition on the basis of this fraud, the *Peek* court held that the wife could seek relief in equity. The court explained its holding by quoting a Massachusetts court: " 'The cases most frequently referred to are those arising out of agreements for marriage settlements. In such cases the marriage, although not regarded as a part performance of the agreement for a marriage settlement, is such an irretrievable change of situation, that if procured by artifice, upon the faith that the settlement had been made, or the assurance that it would be executed, the other party is held to make good the agreement, and not permitted to defeat it by pleading the statute.' "

Peek, however, was decided well before the enactment of the Uniform Premarital Agreement Act, and the court in *Hall* merely cited *Peek* for its holding that marriage is insufficient to establish partial performance. Further, here, Sun is not arguing that she would not have married Barry, but is asserting that she would not have remained married to him or reconciled with him. She therefore did not change her position in reliance of his promise to cancel the prenuptial agreement.

Further, we agree with Barry that permitting Sun's claim to proceed would defeat the entire purpose of the Uniform Premarital Agreement Act, which is to increase certainty by foreclosing oral evidence of modifications to, or revocations of, premarital agreements. To permit "he said/she said" disputes to invalidate a written agreement would promote instability, since such agreements would always be vulnerable to attack by oral testimony.

Sun also argues that she relied on Barry's promise to cancel the premarital agreement and therefore did not require him to execute a formal writing evincing his intent to give Sun a one-half interest in the Murietta, Atherton, and Pennsylvania properties. Sun does not cite to any place in the record where this argument was presented to the trial court, and " '[A] party is precluded from urging on appeal any point not raised in the trial court.' " Even if we were to presume this argument was preserved, we reject it. This is just another attempt to sidestep the requirements of the statute: a valid premarital agreement can only be modified or revoked by a writing. Further, Sun cannot establish detrimental reliance. As we discuss below, the deeds were sufficient to satisfy the requirements of the premarital agreement; therefore, a formal executed writing was not necessary.

II. Transmutation

A. *Writing Requirements Pursuant to the Prenuptial Agreement*

The court found that Sun had the burden to prove a transmutation and had "produced no written document at the trial executed by [Barry] which evidenced that [Barry] desired to have his separate property, or any portion thereof, reclassified as community property, or any portion thereof, reclassified as community property or [Sun's] separate property. The grant deeds and other documents presented by [Sun] do not constitute such a writing." The court further explained: "[Sun] has never claimed that she was unaware that she executed the Premarital Agreement. It is uncontroverted that [Sun] knew that the Murietta Lot and Murietta home and Atherton property were acquired and improved with [Barry's] earnings ... If [Sun] wished for an asset of [Barry's] to be reclassified, she had the ability to request of [Barry] that he execute a written document reclassifying said asset ... there was no evidence presented that [Sun] made any such request of [Barry] or that any such document was executed. Based upon the parties' Premarital Agreement, [Sun] had no reason to believe that she had an interest in the properties based upon the form of title alone."

Sun argues that paragraph 11 in the premarital agreement does not require any evidence of desire to reclassify a property; nor does it, according to Sun, require a written instrument between the parties. Rather, it only requires an instrument that has the effect of reclassifying property under the agreement as separate. Sun argues that this requirement was satisfied when Barry purchased the properties and both Sun and Barry signed written instruments classifying these purchases as community or joint property.

It is undisputed that the Atherton property, lot 81 in the Murietta development, and the Pennsylvania property were purchased with Barry's separate income. Paragraph 10 of the premarital agreement provided, in pertinent part: "We agree that all the earnings and accumulations resulting from the other's personal services, skill, efforts and work, together with all property acquired with funds and income derived therefrom, shall be the separate property of that spouse. The earnings from husband and wife during marriage shall be: separate property of that spouse ... "

However, the agreement also provided for either spouse to transmute his or her separate property. Paragraph 11 provides: "Except as otherwise provided by this agreement, property or interests now owned or hereafter acquired by the parties, which by the terms of this agreement is classified as the separate property of one of them, may become the separate property of the other or the parties' community/joint property only by written instrument executed by the parties whose separate property is thereby reclassified." Thus, the question before us is whether the evidence, as a matter of law, satisfied the requirements of paragraph 11.

Barry contends that Sun did not make an argument of transmutation regarding the Pennsylvania property in the trial court, and has thus waived raising this issue on appeal. Rather, Barry maintains, she introduced evidence relating to this property for the sole purpose of establishing Barry's pattern of conduct concerning real estate.

Sun concedes that she devoted more of her argument at trial to the California properties because they had not been sold at the time of trial, but she asserts that she did raise the question of the Pennsylvania property in her argument regarding transmutation. In her opening statement Sun stated the following: "[W]e will demonstrate a pattern of holding three residential properties, first in Pennsylvania and then in Southern California and then in Northern California ... " "[H]e elected to transfer all of these properties in their joint and community names...."

In addition, Sun's trial counsel asked accountant Susan Screen whether she had been able to locate the $207,125 in net proceeds resulting from the sale of the Pennsylvania house in existing bank accounts. After she responded that she had not, counsel asked her about the form of title on this property. Barry objected based on the best evidence rule, and ultimately the parties stipulated that the property was titled in joint names, as the deed already in evidence established this. Barry then questioned the relevance of this questioning, and Sun's counsel responded: " ... We do maintain that this is joint property. And that, therefore, under those—under those circumstances one half of that property properly belongs to Mrs. Bonds...."

We conclude that the foregoing was sufficient to preserve on appeal the question of the Pennsylvania property as joint property either because of transmutation or gift. The grant deed on the Pennsylvania property conveyed the property to Barry and Sun jointly as husband and wife and was signed by the both of them.

With regard to the Murietta properties, the grant deed conveying lot 81 to Barry and Sun as community property was not signed by Barry and Sun, but the property was later exchanged for lot 8, and Barry and Sun signed that grant deed, which itself classified and conveyed lot 81 as their jointly owned property. This designation appeared again in the contract regarding the exchange, and in deed of trust on lot 81, both of which were signed by Barry and Sun.

Sun argues that lot 81 was purchased with Barry's separate earnings, but the grant deed and deed of trust had reclassified this property into community property. Therefore, when lot 81 was exchanged for lot 8 in the Murietta development, it was community property that was used to purchase lot 8. This was confirmed when they took title to lot 8 in both of their names as "Husband and Wife."

Similarly, Sun argues that the Atherton house was purchased with Barry's separate property, but Barry and Sun executed a deed of trust on the property conveying their interest in the property to the trustee bank. They covenanted that they were "lawfully seized of the estate hereby conveyed and [have] the right to grant and convey the Property ... " The deed granting the Atherton property to Barry and Sun as joint tenants was signed on the same day as the deed of trust executed by

Barry and Sun, and both were recorded. Therefore, Sun argues, these substantially contemporaneous instruments should be read together to determine the nature of the transaction between the parties.

Barry argues that under paragraph 11 of the agreement, a transmutation may be established only by a transfer document signed by the party whose separate property is transmuted. He argues that none of the documents consists of a document signed by Barry transferring an interest from Barry to Sun. A writing claimed to be a transmutation under the statute must stand alone and cannot be supplemented with extrinsic evidence. Additionally, Barry argues that the writing must give fair notice to the transmuting party of the change effected by the writing.

We, however, are not concerned with the statutory requirements for transmutation. As Barry has so vigorously argued, the premarital agreement is valid. This agreement provided for the treatment of their property during marriage, and the division of their property and debts upon dissolution of the marriage. Therefore the writings must satisfy paragraph 11 of the agreement and, if they satisfy the premarital agreement, they need not meet the mandates of the statutes on transmutation.

We agree with Sun that paragraph 11 only requires a written instrument signed by the parties that has the effect of reclassifying property. Once Barry and Sun signed written instruments classifying these purchases, which had been Barry's separate property, as community or joint property, Barry's separate property became "reclassified." Thus, the grant deeds met the requirements of the premarital agreement. Although under the agreement it is not necessary to establish any intent, Barry's decision to purchase the Murietta investment property and put title in his corporation, MVP Plus, established that he did not always place title in both Sun's and his names. This therefore indicated that he intended for both Sun and him to take title in the three other properties as joint tenants.

Accordingly, we hold that the grant deeds and deeds of trust satisfied the requirements for transmutation under the premarital agreement executed by the parties.

* * *

III. Termination of Spousal Support

In our earlier decision we held that we would not consider the question of terminating spousal support because by invalidating the premarital agreement, Sun's economic situation would be significantly improved, changing the facts that were before the trial court. We therefore remanded for the trial court to consider this issue in light of the new facts. The Supreme Court affirmed the trial court's ruling that the agreement was valid and instructed us to determine whether this remand remains necessary.

Given our ruling that Sun is entitled to a one-half interest in the Atherton property, lot 8 of the Murietta property, and the Pennsylvania property, the facts regarding Sun's financial situation have changed significantly. Although it seems extremely unlikely that the trial court will modify its ruling in light of Sun's improved situation, we remand for the court to determine this issue in light of the parties' new circumstances.

Notes and Questions on Bonds

1. This premarital agreement act case is not the only case involving Barry Bonds. You may have discussed *Popov v. Hayashi*, 2002 WL 31833731 (Cal. Super Ct), in your property class. It involves property rights in the ball hit by Bonds for his 500th career home run. He has also been involved in an unsuccessful slander action brought by a podiatrist, *Carver v. Bonds*, 135 Cal App 4th 328, 37 Cal Rptr 3d 480 (2005) and controversy over possible steroid use. See Lance Williams and Mark Fainaru–Wada, What Bonds told BALCO Grand Jury, Fan Francisco Chronicle A1 (December 3, 2004).

2. In contemporary society, it is unfashionable to argue that one divorcing spouse may have a clear advantage over another in a bargaining situation even when one spouse is unrepresented. Does this explain the result in *Bonds*? Does the evolution of marriage from partnership to contract explain it? See Developments in the Law: *Marriage As* Contract *And Marriage As Partnership: The Future Of Antenuptial Agreement Law*, 116 Harv L Rev 2075, 2077 (2003).

3. The *Bonds* opinion spawned a flurry of law review and news articles. A number of factors were at work. First, feminists, while unwilling to admit that women were necessarily disadvantaged by business-savvy husbands, nonetheless felt that the *Bonds* court might have gone too far. People saw that this case might have been decided the way it was just because of Bonds' tremendous baseball talent and popularity. For two comments, see Brian H. Bix, *The Public and the Private Ordering of Marriage*, 2004 U Chi Legal Forum 295, 307–08; Howard Fink and June Carbone, *Between Private Ordering and Public Fiat: A New Paradigm for Family Law Decision–Making*, 5 J L & Fam Stud 1, 7 (2003).

4. Whatever the reason, the California legislature quickly amended its version of the Uniform Premarital Agreement Act, adding section (c) in 2001, which would invalidate a term eliminating spousal support to a spouse who was unrepresented during the contract making or if elimination turned out to be unconscionable at the time of enforcement (as opposed to at the time of contract). The Act now reads:

Cal Fam Code § 1612 (2005)

(a) Parties to a premarital agreement may contract with respect to all of the following:

(1) The rights and obligations of each of the parties in any of the property of either or both of them whenever and wherever acquired or located.

(2) The right to buy, sell, use, transfer, exchange, abandon, lease, consume, expend, assign, create a security interest in,

mortgage, encumber, dispose of, or otherwise manage and control property.

(3) The disposition of property upon separation, marital dissolution, death, or the occurrence or nonoccurrence of any other event.

(4) The making of a will, trust, or other arrangement to carry out the provisions of the agreement.

(5) The ownership rights in and disposition of the death benefit from a life insurance policy.

(6) The choice of law governing the construction of the agreement.

(7) Any other matter, including their personal rights and obligations, not in violation of public policy or a statute imposing a criminal penalty.

(b) The right of a child to support may not be adversely affected by a premarital agreement.

(c) Any provision in a premarital agreement regarding spousal support, including, but not limited to, a waiver of it, is not enforceable if the party against whom enforcement of the spousal support provision is sought was not represented by independent counsel at the time the agreement containing the provision was signed, or if the provision regarding spousal support is unconscionable at the time of enforcement. An otherwise unenforceable provision in a premarital agreement regarding spousal support may not become enforceable solely because the party against whom enforcement is sought was represented by independent counsel.

Does this term solve the problem posed by *Bonds*? Does the expansion of unconscionability doctrine from, for example, UCC 2–302 ("unconscionable at the time it was made") demonstrate something about the nature of family bargaining or about continuing gender stereotypes? Note the difference between this provision and that of the Uniform Premarital Agreement Act in its original form, found on page X (currently 416) of your book.

5. Iowa's statute, Iowa Code § 596.5(g)(2)(2005) is slightly different, providing that "The right of a spouse or child to support shall not be adversely affected by a premarital agreement." Would this have resolved the problem in *Bonds*? Would it have done so in a way less apt to distort the law of contract?

C. STATUTORY RESOLUTIONS

> *Moral friendship, on the other hand, has no stated conditions. If a gift or any other favour is bestowed upon a person, it is bestowed upon him as a friend; but the giver expects to receive as much or more in return, regarding it not as a gift but as a loan. If he does not come out of the contract as well off as he was when he entered into it, he will complain. The reason of his complaint is that, although all people, or nearly all people, wish what is noble, they choose what is profitable, and it is noble to do good without expecting a return, but it is profitable to receive a benefaction.*
>
> **Aristotle**
> *Nicomachean Ethics*

To help you understand and evaluate the trend toward broadening the permissible scope of contracts relating to marriage, we proffer two attempts to write statutes governing familial contracts: the Uniform Premarital Agreement Act (which has been adopted in 25 states and the District of Columbia) and the ALI Principles' Chapter 7 on Agreements. Before you examine them, though, let us say a word about reading statutes. Cases are often easier than statutes for law students to read. This is partly because when you read a case, the controversy between the parties alerts you to much of what to look for doctrinally. When you read a statute, however, you encounter doctrine whose complexities do not readily present themselves. Nevertheless, it is vital, it is crucial, it is *really, really, really essential* for lawyers to be able to read statutes comfortably, insightfully, imaginatively, and shrewdly. This must often be done abstractly. That is, when a statute is passed in your jurisdiction dealing with subjects which concern your clients, you should read the statute not just to see how it affects the immediate problems of your present clients, but to see how it will affect the future behavior of future clients. When you read a statute, therefore, actively ask questions like these: How does the statute alter the pre-existing law? What subjects does it leave unaddressed? What ambiguities of interpretation lurk behind the statute's language? What must your clients do to comply with the statute? What would they be well advised to do that are not statutorily compelled? What are the statute's purposes? To what extent are they achieved?

UNIFORM PREMARITAL AGREEMENT ACT

§ 1. Definitions

As used in this Act:

(1) "Premarital agreement" means an agreement between prospective spouses made in contemplation of marriage and to be effective upon marriage.

(2) "Property" means an interest, present or future, legal or equitable, vested or contingent, in real or personal property, including income and earnings.

§ 2. Formalities

A premarital agreement must be in writing and signed by both parties. It is enforceable without consideration.

§ 3. Content

(a) Parties to a premarital agreement may contract with respect to:

(1) the rights and obligations of each of the parties in any of the property of either or both of them whenever and wherever acquired or located;

(2) the right to buy, sell, use, transfer, exchange, abandon, lease, consume, expend, assign, create a security interest in, mortgage, encumber, dispose of, or otherwise manage and control property;

(3) the disposition of property upon separation, marital dissolution, death, or the occurrence or nonoccurrence of any other event;

(4) the modification or elimination of spousal support;

(5) the making of a will, trust, or other arrangement to carry out the provisions of the agreement;

(6) the ownership rights in and disposition of the death benefit from a life insurance policy;

(7) the choice of law governing the construction of the agreement; and

(8) any other matter, including their personal rights and obligations, not in violation of public policy or a statute imposing a criminal penalty.

(b) The right of a child to support may not be adversely affected by a premarital agreement.

§ 4. Effect of Marriage

A premarital agreement becomes effective upon marriage.

§ 5. Amendment, Revocation

After marriage, a premarital agreement may be amended or revoked only by a written agreement signed by the parties. The amended agreement or the revocation is enforceable without consideration.

§ 6. Enforcement

(a) A premarital agreement is not enforceable if the party against whom enforcement is sought proves that:

(1) that party did not execute the agreement voluntarily; or

(2) the agreement was unconscionable when it was executed and, before execution of the agreement, that party:

(i) was not provided a fair and reasonable disclosure of the property or financial obligations of the other party;

(ii) did not voluntarily and expressly waive, in writing, any right to disclosure of the property or financial obligations of the other party beyond the disclosure provided; and

(iii) did not have, or reasonably could not have had, an adequate knowledge of the property or financial obligations of the other party.

(b) If a provision of a premarital agreement modifies or eliminates spousal support and that modification or elimination causes one party to the agreement to be eligible for support under a program of public assistance at the time of separation or marital dissolution, a court, notwithstanding the terms of the agreement, may require the other party to provide support to the extent necessary to avoid that eligibility.

(c) An issue of unconscionability of a premarital agreement shall be decided by the court as a matter of law.

§ 7. Enforcement: Void Marriage

If a marriage is determined to be void, an agreement that would otherwise have been a premarital agreement is enforceable only to the extent necessary to avoid an inequitable result.

§ 8. Limitation of Actions

Any statute of limitations applicable to an action asserting a claim for relief under a premarital agreement is tolled during the marriage of the parties to the agreement. However, equitable defenses limiting the time for enforcement, including laches and estoppel, are available to either party.

§ 9. Application and Construction

This [Act] shall be applied and construed to effectuate its general purpose to make uniform the law with respect to the subject of this [Act] among states enacting it.

AMERICAN LAW INSTITUTE PRINCIPLES OF THE LAW OF FAMILY DISSOLUTION

2002

§ 7.01 Scope and Definitions

(1) [Defining types of agreements and other terms]

(2) Except where otherwise specified,

(a) this Chapter also applies to agreements between current or prospective domestic partners that alter or confirm the remedies available under Chapter 6 when their relationship dissolves;

(b) references in the black letter set forth in this Chapter to "marital property," "spouses," "marriage," and "divorce" apply by analogy to domestic-partner property, domestic partners, their relationship, and their relationship's dissolution; and

(c) references in this Chapter to a marital or premarital agreement apply by analogy to an agreement between domestic partners or prospective domestic partners.

(3) When used in the black letter set forth in this Chapter, *agreements* includes premarital agreements, marital agreements, and agreements between current or prospective domestic partners, but does not include separation agreements.

(4) An enforceable agreement, or separation agreement, must comply with both this Chapter and general principles of contract law, which this Chapter does not address, except that consideration is not required to create an enforceable agreement.

§ 7.02 Objective

The objective of this Chapter is to allow spouses, those planning to marry, and those who are or plan to become domestic partners, to accommodate their particular needs and circumstances by contractually altering or confirming the legal rights and obligations that would otherwise arise under these Principles, or other state law governing marital dissolution, subject to constraints that recognize competing policy concerns and limitations in the capacity of parties to appreciate adequately, at the time of the agreement, the impact of its terms under different life circumstances.

§ 7.03 General Provisions

(1) A term in an agreement is enforceable when contained in an agreement that is valid under the general requirements of contract law and under §§ 7.05 and 7.07, unless the term is unenforceable under § 7.10, § 7.11, or § 7.12.

(2) Enforceable terms in a valid agreement prevail over any contrary provisions of law that would otherwise apply at dissolution. Unenforceable terms of an agreement do not bind the parties or the court, but a court exercising judgment under another applicable provision of law may give an unenforceable term such weight as is appropriate and equitable under that provision.

(3) An agreement need not address all issues that arise at dissolution to be valid as to those issues it does address.

Topic 2

Requirements for an Enforceable Agreement

§ 7.05 Procedural Requirements

(1) An agreement is not enforceable if it is not set forth in a writing signed by both parties.

(2) A party seeking to enforce an agreement must show that the other party's consent to it was informed and not obtained under duress.

(3) A rebuttable presumption arises that a premarital agreement satisfies the requirements of Paragraph (2) when the party seeking to enforce the agreement shows that

(a) it was executed at least 30 days before the parties' marriage;

(b) both parties were advised to obtain independent legal counsel, and had reasonable opportunity to do so, before the agreement's execution; and,

(c) in the case of agreements concluded without the assistance of independent legal counsel for each party, the agreement states, in language easily understandable by an adult of ordinary intelligence with no legal training,

(i) the nature of any rights or claims otherwise arising at dissolution that are altered by the contract, and the nature of that alteration, and

(ii) that the interests of the spouses with respect to the agreement may be adverse.

(4) A rebuttable presumption arises that a marital agreement, or an agreement between domestic partners, satisfies the requirements of Paragraph (2) when it complies with Paragraphs (3)(b) and (3)(c). A marital agreement, or agreement between domestic partners, is unenforceable if either party rescinds it in a writing delivered to the other party within 30 days of its execution, except that, if the other party has previously parted with anything of value pursuant to the agreement, the rescinding party must restore it promptly upon rescission, or the rescission is not effective.

(5) To enforce terms that limit claims the other party would otherwise have to compensatory payments, or to share in marital property, a party must show that prior to the agreement's execution the other party knew, at least approximately, the moving party's assets and income, or was provided by the moving party with a written statement containing that information. The general standard set forth in the prior sentence is always satisfied by a showing that prior to signing the agreement the party seeking to enforce it provided the other party with a written statement accurately listing (i) his or her significant assets, and their total approximate market value; (ii) his or her approximate annual income for each of the preceding three years; and (iii) any significant future acquisitions, or changes in income, to which the party has a current legal entitlement, or which the party reasonably expects to realize within three years of the agreement's execution.

§ 7.07. When Enforcement Would Work a Substantial Injustice

(1) The court should not enforce a term in an agreement if its enforcement would work a substantial injustice within the meaning of this section.

(2) The court should consider whether enforcement of an agreement would work a substantial injustice if, and only if, the party resisting its enforcement shows that, since the time of the agreement's execution,

(a) more than a fixed number of years have passed, that number being set in a uniform rule of statewide application; or

(b) a child was born to, or adopted by, the parties, who at the time of execution had no children in common; or

(c) the circumstances have changed, the change is significant in evaluating the impact of the agreement on the parties or their children, and it is likely that individuals would be unable, at the time of execution, to anticipate the new circumstances, or their impact upon the individual's evaluation of the agreement's terms.

(3) The party claiming that enforcement of an agreement would work a substantial injustice has the burden of proof on that question. In deciding whether the agreement's application to the parties' circumstances at divorce would work a substantial injustice, the court should consider

(a) the magnitude of the disparity between the outcome under the agreement and the outcome under Chapters 4 and 5 of these Principles;

(b) when practical and relevant, the circumstances of the party claiming that enforcement of the agreement would work a substantial injustice, if the agreement is enforced, as compared to that party's likely circumstances had the marriage never taken place;

(c) whether the purpose of the agreement was to benefit or protect the interests of third parties (such as children from a prior relationship), whether that purpose is still relevant, and whether the agreement's terms were reasonably designed to serve it; and

(d) if the agreement was made before the parties had children in common, the impact of its enforcement upon those children.

(4) An agreement to waive the application of § 4.18 of these Principles (providing for the gradual recharacterization of separate property as marital property) may not be challenged under this section.

§ 7.10 Child Support

The right of a child to support may not be adversely affected by an agreement.

§ 7.11 Allocation of Custodial Responsibility and Decisionmaking Responsibility for Children

Terms of an agreement allocating custodial responsibility and decisionmaking responsibility for a couple's children, or addressing other matters within the scope of Chapter 2, are governed by §§ 2.09, 2.10 and 2.11 of that Chapter, and not by this Chapter.

§ 7.12 Other Limitations on an Agreement's Terms

A term in an agreement is not enforceable if it

(1) limits or enlarges the grounds for divorce otherwise available under state law;

(2) would require or forbid a court to evaluate marital conduct in allocating marital property or awarding compensatory payments, except as the term incorporates principles of state law which so provide; or

(3) penalizes the party who initiates the legal action leading to a decree of divorce or legal separation.

Questions on Two Statutory Resolutions

As statutes go, the Uniform Premarital Agreement Act and the ALI Principles on Agreements are simple and straightforward. But this should not prevent you from seeing the many puzzles they struggle to resolve. First, then, go back to the questions we asked in the paragraph preceding the Act and try to answer them. Then consider the two sets of questions we ask below. Finally, read the problem that follows and analyze the legal relations of the parties under the common law principles described to you in this section, under the UPAA, and under the ALI Principles.

(1) Like the cases, these statutes tend toward the position that if the contract was procedurally regular, it should be upheld. The law and lawyers are deeply convinced that procedure matters crucially. Does it? Really? Consider three of the usual components of procedural regularity.

(a) *Advance notice*. It is possible to imagine that if one spouse springs an agreement on the other at the last moment that the surprised spouse will be poorly prepared to analyze it acutely. But is there any reason to think that just because you have plenty of time to think about something that you will actually do so, much less that you will do so shrewdly and wisely? How well, for example, did you investigate and evaluate the college you went to and the law school you are now attending, both of which you had many months if not years to assess?

(b) *Disclosure*. Americans are deeply committed to the principle of human autonomy, to the principle that people ought to be able to decide for themselves how to live their lives. Yet it is a truth universally acknowledged that people regularly reduce themselves to the most wretched conditions. The law cannot stop them without being paternalistic. Yet their misery is pitiable. What is the law to do?

More often than not, the law's answer is "Disclose!" Are people buying worthless stocks? The securities law say, "Disclose!" Are people borrowing money at usurious rates? The consumer protection laws say, "Disclose!" Are people buying into quack remedies? The law of informed consent says, "Disclose!" And so if people are entering disadvantageous marital agreements, we say, "Disclose!"

Does disclosure really matter? Of course it may. Surely sometimes it does. But how often? The authors of this casebook frankly testify that more often than not they have purchased securities without really reading the prospectus, much less the many more informative statements the SEC evokes from issuers of securities. The evidence is that consumers widely ignore interest rate disclosure. Because doctors, unlike lawyers, are empiricists, they have inquired with admirable diligence into the success of informed consent. The evidence is this: In depressing numbers, patients do not understand what they are told, do not remember what they are told, and do not take what they are told into account when they make decisions. For that matter, large numbers of them prefer to confide their medical decisions to someone else. (This evidence is amassed and analyzed in wearisome detail in Carl E. Schneider, *The Practice of Autonomy: Patients, Doctors, and Medical Decisions* (Oxford U Press, 1998).) Is there any reason to think disclosure will work better in marital agreements?

(c) *Independent counsel.* So is the answer to make sure everyone has a lawyer? Is this the essential meaning of *Bonds*? Did Mrs. Spiegel listen to hers? Do you want to pay a lawyer to tell you not to trust the one person you love most in the world?

(2) So if procedure seems an uncertain protection for the vulnerable, why not look at the fairness of the contract itself? How far in this direction are these statutes willing to go? How far should they go? How far can they go? Isn't the whole reason to move toward contracts that we want people to be free to arrange their own lives and that we can't agree what's good for them?

One response to this suggestion is that we may not want to say people have "arranged their own lives" where they apparently failed to foresee changed circumstances. But suppose that people say they have deeply considered reasons—indeed, religious reasons—for entering into a marital contract that pleases them but offends others. How seriously should we take difference then? Consider, for example, *Spires v. Spires,* 743 A2d 186 (DC App 1999). Apparently the Spires' marriage had not been doing well. They signed a contract in which the husband agreed "to continue in this marriage" in exchange for numerous promises from his wife. She agreed to "conduct herself in accordance with all scriptures in the Holy Bible applicable to marital relationships germane to wives, and in accordance with husband's specific requests." She also agreed that, while she was to "govern the affairs of the children at her discretion," she would "always inform the husband of any particular dealings with the children, . . . and any input by the husband concerning the children shall be considered a request" to be "carried out in strict accordance." She agreed that any violation of any of the twelve articles she agreed to "shall be considered . . . abandonment of the marriage" which would bring into effect a settlement agreement calling for him to become the owner of their house and all the money in any of their bank accounts and to have custody of their children. She would receive one of their cars, all her own debts, and half their joint debts.

The court had no trouble deciding the divorce court could ignore this agreement.

(3) Section 7.12 will not allow parties to contract for a more restrictive divorce regime. What happens to contracts designed to give "teeth" to covenant marriage without avoiding full faith and credit problems? What if a couple married in Louisiana, set up a sum that would go to one spouse if the other filed for no-fault "irreconcilable differences" divorce,

and that spouse moved to an ALI Chapter 7 state? Is this section necessary for the Chapter to have coherence, or does it merely reflect a hostility toward covenant marriage?

(4) Should it matter whether the principle of upholding agreements if there's procedural regularity be treated the same way whether the parties are cohabiting, engaged, or married? For example, are spouses acting under the emotions of impending marriage or divorce capable of making the same kind of rational decisions as those in commercial contracts? What provisions of Chapter 7 remedy these problems? Secondly, are spouses acting in a fiduciary capacity? What if they are hostile and contemplating divorce? To repeat, should they be treated the same way as those "with stars in their eyes"?

(5) Are these statutes blows for or against the equality of women? (as far as bargaining is concerned)? Does the fact that women generally have lower incomes than men change this? What if the woman contemplating marriage is pregnant with the man's child? Does she still have an equal bargaining position?

Notes and Questions on Two Cases and Two Statutes

As you may have noticed when you read *Spiegel*, Iowa has adopted the Uniform Premarital Agreement Act. The UPAA grants couples a generous freedom to contract. The ALI's grant in Chapter 7 of the Principles is similarly generous. For example, the Principles try "to accommodate [the couple's] particular needs and circumstances by contractually altering or confirming the legal rights and obligations that would otherwise arise." § 7.02. There are, however, some differences between the UPAA and the ALI Principles. Should they dictate different results in *Spiegel* and *Hale*?

(1) Does the Spiegel contract meet the formal requirements of the two statutes?

(a) The UPAA simply provides that agreements must be in writing and signed by both parties. This is hardly a difficult provision to meet. Is it enough?

(b) The ALI's provisions, which are in § 7.05, are far more detailed and involve rebuttable presumptions. Would the Spiegel agreement have met them?

(i) The ALI presumes the agreement is valid if it is executed 30 days prior to marriage. Sara Spiegel first saw the agreement only five days before the wedding. How important is that time difference?

(ii) The ALI favors "a written statement accurately listing (i) his or her significant assets, and their total approximate market value; [and] (ii) his or her approximate annual income for each of the preceding three years." Did A.J.'s disclosure meet this standard?

(iii) Does the fact that Mrs. Spiegel's attorney examined the agreement moot these procedural problems? Does the fact that the attorney suggested and negotiated changes moot them?

(2) The UPAA contains an "unconscionability" provision in § 6(a)(2) that takes effect only if there isn't "fair and reasonable disclosure" of the parties' assets and obligations (or a waiver of disclosure) and the moving party could not have had "adequate knowledge" of the other's economic situation. Spousal support can be waived unless doing so would drive the spouse onto the welfare rolls. (Note that, as *Spiegel* points out, Iowa Code's § 596.5(2) does not allow waiver of alimony or child support.) In contrast, the Principles' § 7.07 sets out a detailed "substantial injustice" standard. Although the Spiegel agreement was apparently not unconscionable under the UPAA, would it have been "substantially unjust" under § 7.07 of the ALI?

(a) The ALI describes three criteria to use (disjunctively) in deciding whether the court should "consider whether enforcement of an agreement would work a substantial injustice." One of these is whether "a fixed number of years have passed." We don't know, since Iowa hasn't enacted the ALI provisions, what the statutory length of marriage might be under § 7.07(2)(a). The Spiegels lived together from 1988 to 1994. Is a six-year marriage long enough?

(i) Are the parties likely to have substantially altered their financial plans during this time?

(ii) Are they likely to have commingled their financial dealings?

(iii) Is there any evidence the Spiegels actually did any of these things?

(b) The second criterion is whether a couple who did not have a child when they wrote the contract acquired one thereafter. The Spiegels both had children from prior marriages but had none in common. Why, given your understanding of the ALI property provisions from Chapter 4, might the presence of minor children be important?

(c) The third criterion is changed circumstances. Did the Spiegel's circumstances change in relevant ways? In particular, was A.J.'s financial success unexpected?

(3) Sara Spiegel would have had the burden of proving the agreement was unconscionable. Could she have met the factors of § 7.07(3)? In particular:

(a) Was the disparity between what she bargained for and what she would have received otherwise great enough? The agreement certainly appears to be one-sided. But would Sara have shared in the growth of A.J.'s business without the agreement, since he began it before the marriage?

(b) Was Sara sufficiently worse off than if she had not married? What could Sara have looked forward to if she hadn't married A.J.? Her interior decorating business had not generated more than $4000 profit a year.

(c) Was the agreement intended to benefit any third parties? Was it to benefit A.J.'s children? At the time, A.J. told Sara it was to protect his business financing. Does his misleading her (since he apparently was protecting his fortune) matter?

(4) Did the Bonds contract meet the formal requirements of the two statutes (we will assume for the sake of the exercise that the UPAA did apply to that contract)? For example, did Sun Bonds understand the extent of her husband's assets? The opinion says "she was generally aware of her husband's wealth and property—she knew that they lived well."

(5) Did the Bonds contract meet the substantive standards of the two statutes?

(6) How far do the ALI and (*mutatis mutandis)* the UPAA go in protecting someone like Sun Bonds?

A Problem

Margaret is fifty years old and a copy editor at the Hutchins University Press. She earns $2,000 per month. Margaret's husband, Franz, works for a debt-collection agency, is forty years old, and also earns $2,000 a month. Margaret and Franz were married fifteen years ago, when she was thirty-five. Franz is seeking to divorce Margaret, since he is aggrieved at her having committed adultery with Clifford. A divorce would suit Margaret, since she wants to marry Clifford. However, she is afraid he doesn't want to marry her.

Margaret and Franz were married in a Jewish ceremony in which they entered into a contract called a "Ketubah." The Ketubah evidences both the bridegroom's intention to cherish and provide for his wife as required by religious law and tradition and the bride's willingness to carry out her obligations to her husband in faithfulness and affection according to Jewish law and tradition. The terms of their Ketubah authorized a rabbinical tribunal to counsel them in light of Jewish tradition and to summon either party at the request of the other. According to Jewish law, a wife is not considered divorced and may not remarry until a Jewish divorce decree, known as a "Get," is granted. Before a Get can be granted, both husband and wife must appear before the rabbinical tribunal. In violation of the Ketubah, Franz refuses to appear. Margaret wishes to compel Franz to do so, since she feels she cannot marry Clifford until she receives her Get.

Both Margaret and Franz had been married before, and five months before their wedding they signed a secular antenuptial agreement. Margaret suggested terms at a meeting with Franz and his attorney. The attorney told Margaret she would be better off with a lawyer of her own. Margaret said she had always taken care of herself and was perfectly capable of doing so now. The agreement provided that upon divorce Margaret would receive the car she was then driving, any gifts given her by Franz, all her separately owned property at the time of the marriage, $2,000 in cash, and half the balance, if any, of a joint savings account into which all of her earnings during the marriage were to be deposited. The agreement allowed Margaret no maintenance unless she were disabled and unable to work at the time of the divorce, in which case she would be entitled to $500 per month.

At the time of the divorce, which, as you may recall, came fifteen years after the marriage, Margaret owned no property separately, and Franz had given her no gifts of lasting value. The money in the joint savings account had been entirely used for buying a house, which was put in Franz's name. During the marriage, Margaret did all the housework. Franz devoted all his spare time to making improvements on the house, which had been a wreck when they bought it, but which he had single-handedly turned into a showpiece worth $150,000. Franz has no other assets, but expects his pension (which will be worth $10,000 a year when he retires) to vest in five more years. Margaret has no pension.

Having worked out answers to this problem, try once again to answer the questions in the paragraph preceding the UPAA.

A number of courts have considered the question of the husband's refusal to go before the rabbinical tribunal as promised in the Ketubah. The most famous case, *Avitzur v. Avitzur*, 446 NE2d 136 (NY 1983), finds that the "plaintiff is not attempting to compel defendant to obtain a Get or to enforce a religious practice arising solely out of principles of religious law. She merely seeks to enforce an agreement made by defendant to appear before and accept the decision of a designated tribunal." The court analogized the requirement to an agreement to arbitrate a dispute and upheld the contract. See also *In re Marriage of Goldman*, 554 NE2d 1016 (Ill App 1990), and *Aziz v. Aziz*, 488 NYS2d 123 (NY Sup 1985)(contract made according to Islamic law).

Some contractual provisions are not so easily enforced. In *Favrot v. Barnes*, 332 So 2d 873 (La App 1976), the husband unsuccessfully sued on a premarital agreement made on his insistence which limited the parties' sexual relations to once a week. In *In re Marriage of Higgason*, 516 P2d 289 (Cal 1973), each party waived all right to spousal support after or during the marriage. The husband, who incurred substantial medical costs in a tragi-comic series of post-marital events, successfully sued his wealthy wife, even though she had had the marriage annulled as voidable.

SECTION 3. EVALUATING THE CONTRACTUALIZATION OF FAMILY LAW

Pactum vincit legem et amor judicium.

(An agreement prevails over law and love over the judgment.)

A. MARRIAGE—FROM STATUS TO CONTRACT?

When custom and fashion coincide with the natural principles of right and wrong, they heighten the delicacy of our sentiments, and increase our abhorrence for every thing which approaches to evil.

Adam Smith
The Theory of Moral Sentiments

(1) Maine's Dictum

Max Weber wrote that "in no legal order is freedom of contract unlimited in the sense that the law would place its guaranty of coercion at the disposal of all and every agreement regardless of its terms." 2 *Economy and Society* 668 (U Cal Press, 1978). In this section, we will examine the usefulness of contract as an organizing idea in legal and social thought. More particularly we will ask what limits ought to be placed on freedom of contract in family law, and we will try to reach some preliminary conclusions about the extent to which the law should permit, encourage, or even compel people to organize their family lives in contractual terms. We undertake these inquiries for several reasons. First, in our role as students of how law works and develops, we want to see family law as a whole and to generalize about it insightfully. To do these things well, we must understand one of family law's central ideas—contract. Second, in our role as citizens, we want to be able to discuss how family law should develop, and therefore we need to comprehend how family law is developing—toward contract. Third, in our role as lawyers handling family law cases, we want to appreciate the general strengths and weaknesses of contract in family law so we may wisely counsel our clients on the risks and benefits of family contracts, so we may help our clients write successful contracts, and so we may persuade courts to interpret and enforce contracts in the way our clients prefer. Fourth, our investigation of contracts will let us reconsider some of the ideas we faced in our Contracts class. We begin, then, with one of the best-known generalizations ever made about law—a passage from Henry Sumner Maine that places contract thinking in an historical context:

HENRY SUMNER MAINE
ANCIENT LAW

(1861)

The movement of the progressive societies has been uniform in one respect. Through all its course it has been distinguished by the gradual dissolution of family dependency, and the growth of individual obligation in its place. The Individual is steadily substituted for the Family, as the unit of which civil laws take account. The advance has been accomplished at varying rates of celerity, and there are societies not absolutely stationary in which the collapse of the ancient organisation can only be perceived by careful study of the phenomena they present. But, whatever its pace, the change has not been subject to reaction or recoil, and apparent retardation will be found to have been occasioned through the absorption of archaic ideas and customs from some entirely foreign source. Nor is it difficult to see what is the tie between man and man which replaces by degrees those forms of reciprocity in rights and duties which have their origin in the Family. It is Contract. Starting, as from one terminus of history, from a condition of society in which all the relations of Persons are summed up in the relations of Family, we seem to have steadily moved towards a phase of social order in which all these relations arise from the free agreement of Individuals. In Western Europe the progress achieved in this direction has been considerable. Thus the status of the Slave has disappeared—it has been superseded by the contractual relation of the servant to his master. The status of the Female under Tutelage, if the tutelage be understood of persons other than her husband, has also ceased to exist; from her coming of age to her marriage all the relations she may form are relations of contract. So too the status of the Son under Power has no true place in the law of modern European societies. If any civil obligation binds together the Parent and the child of full age, it is one to which only contract gives its legal validity. The apparent exceptions are exceptions of that stamp which illustrate the rule. The child before years of discretion, the orphan under guardianship, the adjudged lunatic, have all their capacities and incapacities regulated by the Law of Persons. But why? The reason is differently expressed in the conventional language of different systems, but in substance it is stated to the same effect by all. The great majority of Jurists are constant to the principle that the classes of persons just mentioned are subject to extrinsic control on the single ground that they do not possess the faculty of forming a judgment on their own interests; in other words, that they are wanting in the first essential of an engagement by Contract.

The word Status may be usefully employed to construct a formula expressing the law of progress thus indicated, which, whatever be its value, seems to me to be sufficiently ascertained. All the forms of Status taken notice of in the Law of Persons were derived from, and to some extent are still coloured by, the powers and privileges anciently residing in the Family. If then we employ Status, agreeably with the usage of the best writers, to signify these personal conditions only, and avoid applying the term to such conditions as are the immediate or remote result of agreement, we may say that the movement of the progressive societies has hitherto been a movement *from Status to Contract.*

(2) What Did Maine Mean?

Maine's formulation has been influential and has contributed to the not-uncommon assumption that modern law is moving broadly and inevitably toward contract. Maine's formulation also has a pronounced normative element; Maine clearly regards the change as progressive. So we will want to ask exactly what trend Maine perceives, whether the trend is actually occurring in law generally, what its applicability to family law is, and whether it is desirable.

To understand Maine, we must assess his two main terms. What does "status" mean? One scholar defines it as "*a special condition of a continuous and institutional nature, differing from the legal position of the normal person, which is conferred by law and not purely by the act of the parties, whenever a person occupies a position of which the creation, continuance or relinquishment and the incidents are a matter of sufficient social or public concern.*" R.H. Graveson, *Status in the Common Law* 2 (Athlone Press, 1953)(emphasis in original). More simply, Professor Rehbinder says, "Status, using the ordinary person as a point of reference, meant either a reduced legal capacity or some special legal privilege." Manfred Rehbinder, *Status, Contract, and the Welfare State*, 23 Stan L Rev 941, 943 (1971). "Status" law, then, treats individuals as members of a group rather than as individuals; all members of a group are treated identically even though they may prefer not to be and even though they differ in important ways. Status groups are often thought of—by Maine, for instance—as ascriptive, that is, as groups to which you belong involuntarily, usually by birth. However, "status" is also used to refer to groups one may join by attainment (like socio-economic groups) or which one may join by choice (marriage?).

What does "contract" mean? A contract is often defined as an agreement for whose breach the law gives a remedy. This definition may strike you as hardly adequate, but by now you have an excellent working knowledge of what contract effectively means. Here, we are particularly interested in the historical and social contexts of contract. These contexts are neatly summarized by Professor Rehbinder: "When medieval society was replaced by bourgeois liberal society, law no longer fixed the individual in his place in a divinely ordained order; instead it aimed to enable him to determine freely and responsibly his social relations as an equal member in a homogeneous society consisting of all citizens. The tool to achieve this result was contract." Rehbinder, 23 Stan L Rev at 944–45. At the heart of contract is the idea that it allows individuals freely to organize their relations through negotiated agreements and to have those agreements enforced at law. Contract represents the ideal of private choice and private ordering.

How do status and contract differ? "The first, and most important difference is the scope of choice. One may be free to choose a status, but one does not necessarily have the right or the power to affect the impact of that status on legal capacity. Moreover, in choosing a status one has control over fewer variables in the transaction. A young man may freely join the army, but as a soldier he does not have much say in the way the army orders his life. Contracting parties have the opportunity, on the other hand, to determine for themselves the parameters of their transaction." Howard O. Hunter, *An Essay on Contract and Status: Race, Marriage, and the Meretricious Spouse*, 64 Va L Rev 1039, 1044 (1978). Thus the distinction Maine is usually taken to be drawing is one between, on one hand, a system of social ordering that treats individuals as members of a group whose relations are determined by their group membership and, on the other hand, one that treats individuals as people who may determine their relations with others by agreement. Put most starkly, the distinction is between restriction and liberty.

(3) Was Maine Right?

While influential, Maine's dictum has been challenged. For example, the distinguished American legal scholar Roscoe Pound wrote dismissively: "But Maine's generalization as it is commonly understood shows only the course of evolution of Roman law. It has no basis in Anglo–American legal history, and the whole course of English and American law to-day is belying it unless, indeed, we are progressing backward." Roscoe Pound, *The End of Law as Developed in Juristic Thought*, 30 Harv L Rev 219 (1917). So was Maine right?

One line of attack on Maine is to say that, even within the family sphere (of which Maine was most directly speaking), he over-emphasizes the early centrality of status. This argument notes that some aspects of family organization—for example, marriage and adoption—have long had a contractual element. Then as now, spouses could arrange their married life in any way they could agree on. And through the law of marriage settlements, trust, and contract, one could alter legally some of the economic components of traditional marriage. The argument adds that a number of important social relationships in pre-modern societies—for example, the relationships of master and servant or apprentice, lord and vassal, and patron and client—also had substantial contractual elements. In fact, Max Weber, while conceding that the role of contract in the marketplace had by modern times vastly expanded, argued that the role of contract in family law was once very considerable but had greatly diminished: "[T]he farther we go back in legal history, the less significant becomes contract as a device of economic acquisition in fields other than the law of the family and inheritance." 2 *Economy and Society* 671 (U Cal Press, 1978).

Another line of attack on Maine contends that, whatever may have been contract's power in early law, it plays a *decreasingly* powerful role in modern law and even in some of the most commercial areas of modern law. This argument has two different forms. One is suggested by the first sentences of a well-known book by a prominent contracts scholar: "We are told that Contract, like God, is dead. And so it is." Grant Gilmore, *The Death of Contract* 3 (Ohio St U Press, 1974). Professor Gilmore essentially contends that once "contract" represented a formally coherent body of law which was organized (in important part through the doctrine of consideration) around the idea of the bargained-for exchange and which provided the exclusive legal vehicle for exchange relationships, but that now that coherence, the centrality of the bargained-for exchange, and contract's exclusivity have all so much faded that, "[s]peaking descriptively, we might say that what is happening is that 'contract' is being reabsorbed into the mainstream of 'tort.' "As Professor Gilmore writes: "With the growth of the ideas of quasi-contract and unjust enrichment, classical consideration theory was breached on the benefit side. With the growth of the promissory estoppel idea, it was breached on the detriment side. We are fast approaching the point where, to prevent unjust enrichment, any benefit received by a defendant must be paid for unless it was clearly meant as a gift; where any detriment reasonably incurred by a plaintiff in reliance on a defendant's assurances must be recompensed. When that point is reached there is really no longer any viable distinction between liability in contract and liability in tort."

Professor Gilmore's book is impressive, but is it right? In your experience, does it accurately explain what is happening in contract? Do the developments Professor Gilmore describes remove from contract those elements that make it distinctive (primarily the element of choice and agreement) or do they simply add to those elements? How does the "death" of contract affect the purported movement from "status" to "contract"? Does the "death" of contract make "contract" less attractive to family law? Or does it simply mean that family law is moving toward a new kind of contract? What kind?

The second form of the argument that contract plays a decreasingly powerful role in modern law holds that long-term relationships between entities (employers and unions, manufacturers and suppliers, and so on) have now become more important than one-shot deals between entities, and that those long-term relationships cannot be structured by contract law as we lawyers know it. This argument is implicit in much that Professor Macaulay says in the article you will shortly be reading and is made explicit by P.S. Atiyah: "[M]any bilateral long-term relationships are part of a spectrum of which the discrete contract is one end, and the complete merger or take-over which creates a single organization is at the other end.... Even when the two bodies retain a sufficiently distinct identity to enter into contractual relationships it will often be found that, in practice, contract law and contractual ideas do not in substance regulate the relationship." *The Rise and Fall of Freedom of Contract* 724 (Oxford U Press, 1979).

Yet another line of attack on Maine is to argue that what we have seen in the century and a quarter since Maine wrote is not an expansion of the scope within which people may freely contract but a limiting of it.

Consider, for example, Professor Charles Donahue's description of the recent history of the law of landlord and tenant, a history that is conventionally said to describe a movement from property law (i.e., status) to contract:

> It is sometimes said that there is nothing wrong with landlord-tenant law that a healthy dose of contract doctrine would not cure. The *Javins* case, for example, purports to be an application of the law of contract to the landlord-tenant relationship. But is this really true? Take the analogy of the sale of goods to which the courts have recently compared the landlord-tenant relationship. Although the notion of a warranty of habitability has some analogy to the warranties for goods, where do we find any counterpart to the implied covenant to repair which lies at the heart of so many recent cases and legislation? . . . The proper analogy to what is going on in American landlord-tenant law is not, in my view, to be found in the law of contract, but in its opposite, the law of status. Viewed as part of the law of status much that is inexplicable about the current changes falls into place. The remedy against the landlord is not a remedy in damages; it is more like a penalty for his wickedness in offering to let below code premises. An implied covenant which cannot be changed by express agreement has no counterpart in the law of contract, but it makes sense as a status rule about the landlord-tenant relationship. The continual reference in the cases to the housing code sounds peculiar as contract law in the absence of evidence that the parties contracted with reference to the code, but it makes some sense if what is going on is viewed as the creation of status rules about the way rental housing must be.

Looked at more broadly, the contractual freedom of the landlord is even narrower and the status-based entitlements of the tenant are even greater than Professor Donahue suggests. For instance, the landlord's choice of tenants is narrowed by state and federal anti-discrimination statutes and by rules which let tenants enter into sub-leases. Zoning statutes may reduce the activities for which the landlord may lease his property. Rent-control provisions may constrict the ability of landlord and tenant to bargain. And statutes and case law may limit a landlord's ability to avoid liability for his torts.

Consider also Charles Reich's *The New Property*, 73 Yale L J 733 (1964). Reich argued that much wealth is now held not in traditional forms but in the form of government largesse or entitlements, like government contracts, social security, Medicare benefits, and so on. Much of the of new property identified by Reich attaches to statuses—the condition of being aged, retired, ill, or unemployed—and not to individual achievement and agreement. (One might argue that labor-law rules limiting an employer's ability to dismiss an employee extend some of these forms of new property to the private sphere.) As the government becomes an important actor in the economy and in providing benefits to its citizens, might administrative law and the law of procedural due process importantly supplant contract law?

The developments like the ones Professor Donahue and Professor Reich describe have something in common: they reflect an expanded scope of government regulation and thus a diminished scope for contractual agreements between citizens. As Professor Atiyah writes: "I suggest that there is today a growing recognition that, even where parties enter into a transaction as a result of some voluntary conduct, the resulting rights and duties of the parties are, in large part, a product of the law, and not of the parties' real agreement." Some scholars suggest that this kind of government regulation eventually leads to treating people according to their "status": "[D]uties are imposed on the employer in the relation of employer and employee, not because he has so willed, not because he is at fault, but because the nature of the relation is deemed to call for it." Roscoe Pound, *The End of Law as Developed in Juristic Thought*, 30 Harv L Rev 219 (1917). Or as Professor Rehbinder makes the point, "The law of the welfare state considers man within his social context and again undertakes the regulation of his legal relationship, but it differentiates according to the subject's position in the social system."

A diminished scope for contracting and an expanded scope for status can be produced both directly and indirectly. Among the obvious examples of direct limits on contract include landlord/tenant law, consumer-protection law, and labor relations. One example of indirect limits occurs when zoning laws make it pointless to enter certain kinds of covenants. Another example is provided by those situations in which the government "prescribes the terms of a [contractual] relation only in the absence of a specific agreement to the contrary.... In ordinary transactions, people cannot or will not stop to make special agreements 'to the contrary.' Therefore, they find themselves governed by the statute with its prescribed insurance policy, its prescribed bill of lading, warehouse receipt, stock-transfer, negotiable instrument, articles of partnership, its prescribed type of sale." Nathan Isaacs, *The Standardizing of Contracts*, 27 Yale L J 34, 38 (1917).

As you might suppose, not everyone accepts this criticism of Maine. For instance, one might say the regulation of contractual relations does not truly deprive them of their "contractual" character, or at least does not transform them from contractual to status relations: "[M]any other kinds of contracts have long had incidents attached to them by law, and those incidents are not always subject to be varied at the will of the parties. A mortgagor cannot enter into an agreement with the mortgagee which has the effect of making the mortgage irredeemable, or even tends that way by 'clogging the equity of redemption.' It would be a strong thing to say that this peculiar doctrine of English courts of equity has created a status of mortgagors." Frederick Pollock, *Introduction and Notes to Sir Henry Maine's "Ancient Law,"* 36 (1914). Is Pollock right? While the single change he describes may not have created a status of mortgagors, has the whole set of limits on mortgagor and mortgagee done so?

How ought we regard the movement away from contract that we have just been considering? One perspective would have us look again at

Maine's implicit linking of contract with freedom. Max Weber provides a standard criticism of that linkage:

> The development of legally regulated relationships toward contractual association and of the law itself toward freedom of contract, especially toward a system of free disposition within stipulated forms of transaction, is usually regarded as signifying a decrease of constraint and an increase of individual freedom.... However, the extent to which this trend has brought about an actual increase of the individual's freedom to shape the conditions of his own life or the extent to which, on the contrary, life has become more stereotyped in spite, or, perhaps, just because of this trend, cannot be determined simply by studying the development of formal legal institutions. The great variety of permitted contractual schemata and the formal empowerment to set the content of contracts in accordance with one's desires and independently of all official form patterns, in and of itself by no means makes sure that these formal possibilities will in fact be available to all and everyone. Such availability is prevented above all by the differences in the distribution of property as guaranteed by law. The formal right of a worker to enter into any contract whatsoever with any employer whatsoever does not in practice represent for the employment seeker even the slightest freedom in the determination of his own conditions of work, and it does not guarantee him any influence on this process. It rather means, at least primarily, that the more powerful party in the market, i.e., normally the employer, has the possibility to set the terms, to offer the job "take it or leave it," and, given the normally more pressing economic need of the worker, to impose his terms upon him. The result of contractual freedom, then, is in the first place the opening of the opportunity to use, by the clever utilization of property ownership in the market, these resources without legal restraints as a means for the achievement of power over others.

2 *Economy and Society* 729–30 (U Cal Press, 1978). If this criticism is correct, the purported limitations on contract may *improve* the genuineness of bargaining rather than limit it. That is, those limitations may place parties to a contract where they would have been had they had equal bargaining strength. This is the point Professor Isaacs was making in 1917: "The movement toward status law clashes, of course, with the ideal of individual freedom in the negative sense of 'absence of restraint' or *laissez faire*. Yet, freedom in the positive sense of presence of opportunity is being served by social interference with contract. There is still much to be gained by the further standardizing of the relations in which society has an interest, in order to remove them from the control of the accident of power in individual bargaining.... Freedom of contract is not synonymous with liberty, nor is status slavery."

We have seen that Maine's dictum may wrongly describe the movement of law in the past century. Can that dictum be reformulated to assimilate what is valid in his analysis and his critics'? One way is to say that contract has become weaker but has yielded to many forces besides "status." Thus Professor Atiyah comments, "It would be more accurate to say that there has been a movement from contract to administration, a movement from private to public law, a movement from bilateral to multilateral relationships, a movement from single, individualized transactions to long-term relationships."

Another reformulation would say that law has moved from status to contract and back. "If contract was the central legal symbol of the ideal laissez-faire state, status is the legal banner of the ideal welfare state." Hunter, 64 Va L Rev at 1049. This argument has obvious attractions, but is it too simple? Has the meaning of status changed enough to make the argument misleading? Professor Rehbinder suggests a refined version of it. He begins by noting the relative complexity of modern society: "It is easy to see why, in an age of mass transactions and therefore of increased interaction, the importance of intention and will in the doctrine of legal transactions is steadily reduced in favor of protection of reliance. As each role is meant at the same time to govern the behavior of the social partner, the social partner in turn must be able to rely upon an outward appearance that suggests the role attributes and role behavior of his partner in order to be able to act appropriately." Professor Rehbinder proceeds to build on the idea of the social role: "Rules of conduct attach to a social position, and role becomes the point of intersection between individual and society. A role represents a normative generalization. The human being is seen not as a unique entity, but as one among many holders of the same position." Each role is defined by socially established norms, and holders of the role are treated according to those social expectations. Professor Rehbinder concludes, "The development from status to contract is more accurately 'a movement from "ascriptive" status, fixed by birth and family rights, to status acquired on the basis of individual achievement.' "In short, "[f]reedom of the individual today consists less in a freedom of role creation than in a freedom of role choice."

How does marriage fit into the continuum between status and contract? The standard view is that marriage has both contract and status elements. One part of marriage is clearly contractual—the decision to enter the marriage. But the extent to which parties to a marriage may set rules for themselves, and particularly the extent to which they alter the rules set by the state, has long been controverted. The classic statement is the Supreme Court's opinion in

MAYNARD v. HILL

Supreme Court of the United States, 1888
125 US 190

FIELD, JUSTICE

Marriage, as creating the most important relation in life, as having more to do with the morals and civilization of a people than any other institution, has always been subject to the control of the legislature. That body prescribes the age at which parties may contract to marry, the procedure or form essential to constitute marriage, the duties and obligations it creates, its effects upon the property rights of both, present and prospective, and the acts which may constitute grounds for its dissolution....

It is also to be observed that, while marriage is often termed by text writers and in decisions of courts as a civil contract—generally to indicate that it must be founded upon the agreement of the parties, and does not require any religious ceremony for its solemnization—it is something more than a mere contract. The consent of the parties is of course essential to its existence, but when the contract to marry is executed by the marriage, a relation between the parties is created which they cannot change. Other contracts may be modified, restricted, or enlarged, or entirely released upon the consent of the parties. Not so with marriage. The relation once formed, the law steps in and holds the parties to various obligations and liabilities. It is an institution, in the maintenance of which in its purity the public is deeply interested, for it is the foundation of the family and of society, without which there would be neither civilization nor progress. This view is well expressed by the supreme court of Maine in *Adams v. Palmer*, 51 Me. 480, 483. Said that court, speaking by Chief Justice APPLETON:

> "When the contracting parties have entered into the married state, they have not so much entered into a contract as into a new relation, the rights, duties, and obligations of which rest not upon their agreement, but upon the general law of the state, statutory or common, which defines and prescribes those rights, duties, and obligations. They are of law, not of contract. It was a contract that the relation should be established, but, being established, the power of the parties as to its extent or duration is at an end. Their rights under it are determined by the will of the sovereign, as evidenced by law. They can neither be modified nor changed by any agreement of parties. It is a relation for life, and the parties cannot terminate it at any shorter period by virtue of any contract they may make. The reciprocal rights arising from this relation, so long as it continues, are such as the law determines from time to time, and none other." And again: "It is not then a contract within the meaning of the clause of the constitution which prohibits the impairing the obligation of contracts. It is rather a social relation like that of parent and child, the obligations of which arise not from the consent of concurring minds, but are the creation of the law itself, a relation the most important, as affecting the happiness of individuals, the first step from barbarism to incipient civilization, the purest tie of social life, and the true basis of human progress."

And the chief justice cites in support of this view the case of *Maguire v. Maguire*, 7 Dana 181, 183, and *Ditson v. Ditson*, 4 R.I. 87, 101. In the first of these the supreme court of Kentucky said that marriage was more than a contract; that it was the most elementary and useful of all the social relations; was regulated and controlled by the sovereign power of the state, and could not, like mere contracts, be dissolved by the mutual consent of the contracting parties, but might be abrogated by the sovereign will whenever the public good, or justice to both parties, or either of the parties, would thereby be subserved; that being more than a contract, and depending especially upon the sovereign will, it was not embraced by the constitutional inhibition of legislative acts impairing the obligation of contracts. In the second case the supreme court of Rhode Island said that "*marriage*, in the sense in which it is dealt with by a decree of divorce, is not a contract, but one of the domestic *relations*. In strictness, though formed by contract, it signifies the *relation* of husband and wife, deriving both its rights and duties from a source higher than any contract of which the parties are capable, and, as to these, uncontrollable by any contract which they can make. When formed, this relation is no more a contract than 'fatherhood' or 'sonship' is a contract."

Another way of trying to answer the question whether marriage is a status or a contract draws on the work of Max Weber. Weber distinguished between two kinds of contract—status contracts and purposive contracts. Status contracts

> involve a change in what may be called the total legal situation . . . and the social status of the persons involved .... [T]hese contracts were originally either straightforward magical acts or at least acts having a magical significance. For a long time their symbolism retained traces of that character, and the majority of these contracts are 'fraternization contracts.' By means of such a contract a person was to become somebody's child, father, wife, brother, master, slave, kin, comrade-in-arms, protector, client, follower, vassal, subject, friend, or, quite generally, comrade. To 'fraternize' with another person did not, however, mean that a certain performance of the contract, contributing to the attainment of some specific object, was reciprocally guaranteed or expected. Nor did it mean merely that the making of a promise to another would, as we might put it, have ushered in a new orientation in the relationship between the parties. The contract rather meant that the person would 'become' something different in quality (or status) from the quality he possessed before.

2 *Economy and Society* at 672 (U Cal Press, 1978). The purposive contract, on the other hand, is the contract as we conventionally think of it today. Weber distinguishes it from the status contract by saying:

> The agreements of fraternization as well as other forms of status contract were oriented toward the total social status of the individual and his integration into an association comprehending his total personality. This form of contract with its all-inclusive rights and duties and the special attitudinal qualities based thereon thus appears in contrast to the money contract, which, as a specific, quantitatively delimited, qualityless, abstract, and usually economically conditioned agreement, represents the archetype of the purposive contract. As a non-ethical purposive contract the money contract was the appropriate means for the elimination of the magical and sacramental elements from legal transactions and for the secularization of the law.

Id at 674.

Our evaluation of the contractualization of family law has looked at a set of legal categories—status and contract—that have molded people's thinking about the legal nature of marriage. Our examination has implicitly revealed several issues. First, we have seen Maine intimating that the natural progress of society is away from status toward contract and associating contract with liberty. This seems to imply that if spouses are to be free the law should accord them freedom of contract. Second, we have encountered criticisms of Maine's ideas about the natural progress of society and about the association of contract with liberty. This may imply that the freest, or perhaps the best, marriage is one where the parties are protected by governmental regulation. Third, we might gather from Max Weber's distinction between status and purposive contracts that we cannot treat all contractual situations as identical and that therefore we cannot easily generalize from the general role of contracts in society to the particular role of contracts in the family.

These issues revolve centrally around the paradigm contract—the commercial contract. Therefore one way to pursue our inquiry into these issues and into the usefulness of contract in family law is to scrutinize commercial contracts and how family contracts resemble them.

B. THE USEFULNESS OF CONTRACT LAW THINKING: THE COMMERCIAL CONTRACT AND THE FAMILY CONTRACT

Men being naturally selfish, or endow'd only with a confin'd generosity, they are not easily induc'd to perform any action for the interest of strangers, except with a view to some reciprocal advantage, which they had no hope of obtaining but by such a performance.

David Hume
A Treatise of Human Nature

(1) Macaulay's Data

You already know a good deal about the legal doctrines governing the commercial contract. But to understand the commercial contract, we need to know not just what the law says it is, but also how businesses actually use it. We will therefore begin our comparison of the commercial and the family contract by reading part of a celebrated piece by Stewart Macaulay which searches for the reality of contract. Professor Macaulay interviewed "68 businessmen and lawyers representing 43 companies and six law firms." As he uses "contract," it involves "two distinct elements: (a) rational planning of the transaction with careful provision for as many future contingencies as can be foreseen, and (b) the existence or use of actual or potential legal sanctions to induce performance of the exchange or to compensate for non-performance."

We selected this article for several reasons. First, it is a classic expression of a school of thought that has much to say to family law—the "law and society" movement. That movement holds that law is a social institution which both influences and is influenced by other social institutions and that those interacting influences should be studied in a broadly interdisciplinary way by scholars and accounted for by law-makers. Second, Macaulay's article disciplines the easy assumptions lawyers, judges, and law professors often make about how people behave. It proffers a fascinating view of how businesses treat that voluminous body of doctrine we learned in Contracts. Third, Macaulay's article is an excellent point of departure for examining contract in family law. If contract works well anywhere, it is presumably in commerce. If we look at contract in that context, we should be led to some useful insights into what contract does well and what it does poorly, into when contract is an appropriate means of social organization and when it is not.

As you the read the article, then, you should be asking how Macaulay's ideas might speak to the contract between Susan and Peter specifically and to the contractualization of family law generally. More concretely, you should ask: Why does Macaulay think businesses enter into contracts? Do those reasons apply to family contracts as well? What disadvantages does Macaulay think businesses see in arranging their affairs contractually? Do they apply to family contracts?

STEWART MACAULAY NON-CONTRACTUAL RELATIONS IN BUSINESS: A PRELIMINARY STUDY

28 American Sociological Review 55 (1963)

TENTATIVE FINDINGS

It is difficult to generalize about the use and nonuse of contract by manufacturing industry. However, a number of observations can be made with reasonable accuracy at this time. The use and nonuse of contract in creating exchange relations and in dispute settling will be taken up in turn.

The creation of exchange relationships. In creating exchange relationships, businessmen may plan to a greater or lesser degree in relation to several types of issues. Before reporting the findings as to practices in creating such relationships, it is necessary to describe what one can plan about in a bargain and the degrees of planning which are possible.

People negotiating a contract can make plans concerning several types of issues: (1) They can plan what each is to do or refrain from doing; e.g., S might agree to deliver ten 1963 Studebaker four-door sedan automobiles to B on a certain date in exchange for a specified amount of money. (2) They can plan what effect certain contingencies are to have on their duties; e.g., what is to happen to S and B's obligations if S cannot deliver the cars because of a strike at the Studebaker factory? (3) They can plan what is to happen if either of them fails to perform; e.g., what is to happen if S delivers nine of the cars two weeks late? (4) They can plan their agreement so that it is a legally enforceable contract—that is, so that a legal sanction would be available to provide compensation for injury suffered by B as a result of S's failure to deliver the cars on time.

As to each of these issues, there may be a different degree of planning by the parties. (1) They may carefully and explicitly plan; e.g.,

S may agree to deliver ten 1963 Studebaker four-door sedans which have six cylinder engines, automatic transmissions and other specified items of optional equipment and which will perform to a specified standard for a certain time. (2) They may have a mutual but tacit understanding about an issue; e.g., although the subject was never mentioned in their negotiations, both S and B may assume that B may cancel his order for the cars before they are delivered if B's taxi-cab business is so curtailed that B can no longer use ten additional cabs. (3) They may have two inconsistent unexpressed assumptions about an issue; e.g., S may assume that if any of the cabs fails to perform to the specified standard for a certain time, all S must do is repair or replace it. B may assume S must also compensate B for the profits B would have made if the cab had been in operation. (4) They may never have thought of the issue; e.g., neither S nor B planned their agreement so that it would be a legally enforceable contract. Of course, the first and fourth degrees of planning listed are the extreme cases and the second and third are intermediate points. Clearly other intermediate points are possible; e.g., S and B neglect to specify whether the cabs should have automatic or conventional transmissions. Their planning is not as careful and explicit as that in the example previously given.

The following diagram represents the dimensions of creating an exchange relationship just discussed with "X's" representing the example of S and B's contract for ten taxi-cabs.

	Definition of Performance	Effect of Contingencies	Effect of Defective Performance	Legal Sanctions
Explicit and careful	X			
Tacit agreement		X		
Unilateral assumptions			X	
Unawareness of the issue				X

Most larger companies, and many smaller ones, attempt to plan carefully and completely. Important transactions not in the ordinary course of business are handled by a detailed contract. For example, recently the Empire State Building was sold for $65 million. More than 100 attorneys, representing 34 parties, produced a 400 page contract. . . .

More routine transactions commonly are handled by what can be called standardized planning. A firm will have a set of terms and conditions for purchases, sales, or both printed on the business documents used in these exchanges. Thus the things to be sold and the price may be planned particularly for each transaction, but standard provisions will further elaborate the performances and cover the other subjects of planning. Typically, these terms and conditions are lengthy and printed in small type on the back of the forms. For example, 24 paragraphs in eight point type are printed on the back of the purchase order form used by the Allis Chalmers Manufacturing Company. The provisions: (1) describe, in part, the performance required, e.g., "DO NOT WELD CASTINGS WITHOUT OUR CONSENT"; (2) plan for the effect of contingencies, e.g., "in the event the Seller suffers delay in performance due to an act of God, war, act of the Government, priorities or allocations, act of the Buyer, fire, flood, strike, sabotage, or other causes beyond Seller's control, the time of completion shall be extended a period of time equal to the period of such delay if the Seller gives the Buyer notice in writing of the cause of any such delay within a reasonable time after the beginning thereof"; (3) plan for the effect of defective performances, e.g., "The buyer, without waiving any other legal rights, reserves the right to cancel without charge or to postpone deliveries of any of the articles covered by this order which are not shipped in time reasonably to meet said agreed dates"; (4) plan for a legal sanction, e.g., the clause "without waiving any other legal rights," in the example just given.

In larger firms such "boiler plate" provisions are drafted by the house counsel or the firm's outside lawyer. In smaller firms such provisions may be drafted by the industry trade association, may be copied from a competitor, or may be found on forms purchased from a printer. In any event, salesmen and purchasing agents, the operating personnel, typically are unaware of what is said in the fine print on the back of the forms they use. Yet often the normal business patterns will give effect to this standardized planning. For example, purchasing agents may have to use a purchase order form so that all transactions receive a number under the firm's accounting system. Thus, the required accounting record will carry the necessary planning of the exchange relationship printed on its reverse side. If the seller does not object to this planning and accepts the order, the buyer's "fine print" will control. If the seller does object, differences can be settled by negotiation.

This type of standardized planning is very common. Requests for copies of the business documents used in buying and selling were sent to approximately 6,000 manufacturing firms which do business in Wisconsin. Approximately 1,200 replies were received and 850 companies used some type of standardized planning. With only a few exceptions, the firms that did not reply and the 350 that indicated they did not use standardized planning were very small manufacturers such as local bakeries, soft drink bottlers and sausage makers.

While businessmen can and often do carefully and completely plan, it is clear that not all exchanges are neatly rationalized. Although most businessmen think that a clear description of both the seller's and buyer's performances is obvious common sense, they do not always live up to this ideal. The house counsel and the purchasing agent of a medium size manufacturer of automobile parts reported that several times their engineers had committed the company to buy expensive machines without adequate specifications. The engineers had drawn careful specifications as to the type of machine and how it was to be made but had neglected to require that the machine produce specified results. An attorney and an auditor both stated that most contract disputes arise because of ambiguity in the specifications.

Businessmen often prefer to rely on "a man's word" in a brief letter, a handshake, or "common honesty and decency" even when the transaction involves exposure to serious risks. Seven lawyers from law firms with business practices were interviewed. Five thought that businessmen often entered contracts with only a minimal degree of advance planning. They complained that businessmen desire to "keep it simple and avoid red tape" even where large amounts of money and significant risks are involved. One stated that he was "sick of being told, 'We can trust old Max,' when the problem is not one of honesty but one of reaching an agreement that both sides understand." Another said that businessmen when bargaining often talk only in pleasant generalities, think they have a contract, but fail to reach agreement on any of the hard, unpleasant questions until forced to do so by a lawyer. Two outside lawyers had different views. One thought that large firms usually planned important exchanges, although he conceded that occasionally matters might be left in a fairly vague state. The other dissenter represents a large utility that commonly buys heavy equipment and buildings. The supplier's employees come on the utility's property to install the equipment or construct the buildings, and they may be injured while there. The utility has been sued by such employees so often that it carefully plans purchases with the assistance of a lawyer so that suppliers take this burden....

It is likely that businessmen pay more attention to describing the performances in an exchange than to planning for contingencies or defective performances or to obtaining legal enforceability of their contracts. Even when a purchase order and acknowledgment have conflicting provisions printed on the back, almost always the buyer and seller will be in agreement on what is to be sold and how much is to be paid for it. The lawyers who said businessmen often commit their firms to significant changes too casually, stated that the performances would be defined in the brief letter or telephone call; the lawyers objected that nothing else would be covered. Moreover, it is likely that businessmen are least concerned about planning their transactions so that they are legally enforceable contracts. For example, in Wisconsin requirements contracts—contracts to supply a firm's requirements of an item rather than a definite quantity—probably are not legally enforceable. Seven people interviewed reported that their firms regularly used requirements contracts in dealings in Wisconsin. None thought that the lack of legal sanction made any difference. Three of these people were house counsel who knew the Wisconsin law before being interviewed. Another example of a lack of desire for legal sanctions is found in the relationship between automobile manufacturers and their suppliers of parts. The manufacturers draft a carefully planned agreement, but one which is so designed that the supplier will have only minimal, if any, legal rights against the manufacturers. The standard contract used by manufacturers of paper to sell to magazine publishers has a pricing clause which is probably sufficiently vague to make the contract legally unenforceable. The house counsel of one of the largest paper producers said that everyone in the industry is aware of this because of a leading New York case concerning the contract, but that no one cares. Finally, it seems likely that planning for contingencies and defective performances are in-between cases—more likely to occur than planning for a legal sanction, but less likely than a description of performance.

Thus one can conclude that (1) many business exchanges reflect a high degree of planning about the four categories—description, contingencies, defective performances and legal sanction—but (2) many, if not most, exchanges reflect no planning, or only a minimal amount of it, especially concerning legal sanctions and the effect of defective performances. As a result, the opportunity for good faith disputes during the life of the exchange relationship often is present.

The adjustment of exchange relationships and the settling of disputes. While a significant amount of creating business exchanges is done on a fairly noncontractual basis, the creation of exchanges usually is far more contractual than the adjustment of such relationships and the settlement of disputes. Exchanges are adjusted when the obligations of one or both parties are modified by agreement during the life of the relationship. For example, the buyer may be allowed to cancel all or part of the goods he has ordered because he no longer needs them; the seller may be paid more than the contract price by the buyer because of unusual changed circumstances. Dispute settlement involves determining whether or not a party has performed as agreed and, if he has not, doing something about it. For example, a court may have to interpret the meaning of a contract, determine what the alleged defaulting party has done and determine what, if any, remedy the aggrieved party is entitled to. Or one party may assert that the other is in default, refuse to proceed with performing the contract and refuse to deal ever again with the alleged defaulter. If the alleged defaulter, who in fact may not be in default, takes no action, the dispute is then "settled."

Business exchanges in non-speculative areas are usually adjusted without dispute. Under the law of contracts, if B orders 1,000 widgets from S at $1.00 each, B must take all 1,000 widgets or be in breach of contract and liable to pay S his expenses up to the time of the breach plus his lost anticipated profit. Yet all ten of the purchasing agents asked about cancellation of orders once placed indicated that they expected to be able to cancel orders freely subject to only an obligation to pay for the seller's major expenses such as scrapped steel. All 17 sales personnel asked reported that they often had to accept cancellation. One said, "You can't ask a man to eat paper [the firm's product] when he has no use for it." A lawyer with many large industrial clients said,

> Often businessmen do not feel they have "a contract"—rather they have "an order." They speak of "cancelling the order" rather than "breaching our contract." When I began practice I referred to order cancellations as breaches of contract, but my clients objected since they do not think of cancellation as wrong. Most clients, in heavy industry at least, believe that there is a right to cancel as part of the buyer-seller relationship. There is a widespread attitude that one can back out of any deal within some very vague limits. Lawyers are often surprised by this attitude.

Disputes are frequently settled without reference to the contract or potential or actual legal sanctions. There is a hesitancy to speak of legal rights or to threaten to sue in these negotiations. Even where the parties have a detailed and carefully planned agreement which indicates what is to happen if, say, the seller fails to deliver on time, often they will never refer to the agreement but will negotiate a solution when the problem arises apparently as if there had never been any original contract. One purchasing agent expressed a common business attitude when he said,

> if something comes up, you get the other man on the telephone and deal with the problem. You don't read legalistic contract clauses at each other if you ever want to do business again. One doesn't run to lawyers if he wants to stay in business because one must behave decently.

Or as one businessman put it, "You can settle any dispute if you keep the lawyers and accountants out of it. They just do not understand the give-and-take needed in business." All of the house counsel interviewed indicated that they are called into the dispute settlement process only after the businessmen have failed to settle matters in their own way. Two indicated that after being called in house counsel at first will only advise the purchasing agent, sales manager or other official involved; not even the house counsel's letterhead is used on communications with the other side until all hope for a peaceful resolution is gone.

Law suits for breach of contract appear to be rare. Only five of the 12 purchasing agents had ever been involved in even a negotiation concerning a contract dispute where both sides were represented by lawyers; only two of ten sales managers had ever gone this far. None had been involved in a case that went through trial. . . .

At times relatively contractual methods are used to make adjustments in ongoing transactions and to settle disputes. Demands of one side which are deemed unreasonable by the other occasionally are blocked by reference to the terms of the agreement between the parties. The legal position of the parties can influence negotiations even though legal rights or litigation are never mentioned in their discussions; it makes a difference if one is demanding what both concede to be a right or begging for a favor. Now and then a firm may threaten to turn matters over to its attorneys, threaten to sue, commence a suit or even litigate and carry an appeal to the highest court which will hear the matter. Thus, legal sanctions, while not an everyday affair, are not unknown in business.

One can conclude that while detailed planning and legal sanctions play a significant role in some exchanges between businesses, in many business exchanges their role is small.

TENTATIVE EXPLANATIONS

Two questions need to be answered: (A) How can business successfully operate exchange relationships with relatively so little attention to detailed planning or to legal sanctions, and (B) Why does business ever use contract in light of its success without it?

Why are relatively non-contractual practices so common? In most situations contract is not needed. Often its functions are served by other devices. Most problems are avoided without resort to detailed planning or legal sanctions because usually there is little room for honest misunderstandings or good faith differences of opinion about the nature and quality of a seller's performance. Although the parties fail to cover all foreseeable contingencies, they will exercise care to see that both understand the primary obligation on each side. Either products are standardized with an accepted description or specifications are written calling for production to certain tolerances or results. Those who write and read specifications are experienced professionals who will know the customs of their industry and those of the industries with which they deal. Consequently, these customs can fill gaps in the express agreements of the parties. Finally, most products can be tested to see if they are what was ordered; typically in manufacturing industry we are not dealing with questions of taste or judgment where people can differ in good faith.

When defaults occur they are not likely to be disastrous because of techniques of risk avoidance or risk spreading. One can deal with firms of good reputation or he may be able to get some form of security to guarantee performance. One can insure against many breaches of contract where the risks justify the costs. Sellers set up reserves for bad debts on their books and can sell some of their accounts receivable. Buyers can place orders with two or more suppliers of the same item so that a default by one will not stop the buyer's assembly lines.

Moreover, contract and contract law are often thought unnecessary because there are many effective non-legal sanctions. Two norms are widely accepted. (1) Commitments are to be honored in almost all situations; one does not welsh on a deal. (2) One ought to produce a good product and stand behind it. Then, too, business units are organized to perform commitments, and internal sanctions will induce performance. For example, sales personnel must face angry customers when there has been a late or defective performance. The salesmen do not enjoy this and will put pressure on the production personnel responsible for the default. If the production personnel default too often, they will be fired. At all levels of the two business units personal relationships across the boundaries of the two organizations exert pressures for conformity to expectations. Salesmen often know purchasing agents well. The same two individuals occupying these roles may have dealt with each other from five to 25 years. Each has something to give the other. Salesmen have gossip about competitors, shortages and price increases to give purchasing agents who treat them well. Salesmen take purchasing agents to dinner, and they give purchasing agents Christmas gifts hoping to improve the chances of making a sale. The buyer's engineering staff may work with the seller's engineering staff to solve problems jointly. The seller's engineers may render great assistance, and the buyer's engineers may desire to return the favor by drafting specifications which only the seller can meet. The top executives of the two firms may know each other. They may sit together on government or trade committees. They may know each other socially and even belong to the same country club. The interrelationships may be more formal. Sellers may hold stock in corporations which are important customers; buyers may hold stock in important suppliers. Both buyer and seller may share common directors on their boards. They may share a common financial institution which has financed both units.

The final type of non-legal sanction is the most obvious. Both business units involved in the exchange desire to continue successfully in business and will avoid conduct which might interfere with attaining this goal. One is concerned with both the reaction of the other party in the particular exchange and with his own general business reputation. Obviously, the buyer gains sanctions insofar as the seller wants the particular exchange to be completed. Buyers can withhold part or all of their payments until sellers have performed to their satisfaction. If a seller has a great deal of money tied up in his performance which he must recover quickly, he will go a long way to please the buyer in order to be paid. Moreover, buyers who are dissatisfied may cancel and cause sellers to lose the cost of what they have done up to cancellation. Furthermore, sellers hope for repeat orders, and one gets few of these from unhappy customers. Some industrial buyers go so far as to formalize this sanction by issuing "report cards" rating the performance of each supplier. The supplier rating goes to the top management of the seller organization, and these men can apply internal sanctions to salesmen, production supervisors or product designers if there are too many "D's" or "F's" on the report card.

While it is generally assumed that the customer is always right, the seller may have some counterbalancing sanctions against the buyer. The seller may have obtained a large down payment from the buyer which he will want to protect. The seller may have an exclusive process which the buyer needs. The seller may be one of the few firms which has the skill to make the item to the tolerances set by the buyer's engineers and within the time available. There are costs and delays involved in turning from a supplier one has dealt with in the past to a new supplier. Then, too, market conditions can change so that a buyer is faced with shortages of critical items. The most extreme example is the post World War II gray market conditions when sellers were rationing goods rather than selling them. Buyers must build up some reserve of good will with suppliers if they face the risk of such shortage and desire good treatment when they occur. Finally, there is reciprocity in buying and selling. A buyer cannot push a supplier too far if that supplier also buys significant quantities of the product made by the buyer.

Not only do the particular business units in a given exchange want to deal with each other again, they also want to deal with other business units in the future. And the way one behaves in a particular transaction, or a series of transactions, will color his general business reputation. Blacklisting can be formal or informal. Buyers who fail to pay their bills on time risk a bad report in credit rating services such as Dun and Bradstreet. Sellers who do not satisfy their customers become the subject of discussion in the gossip exchanged by purchasing agents and salesmen, at meetings of purchasing agents' associations and trade associations, or even at country clubs or social gatherings where members of top management meet. The American male's habit of debating the merits of new cars carries over to industrial items. Obviously, a poor reputation does not help a firm make sales and may force it to offer great price discounts or added services to remain in business. Furthermore, the habits of unusually demanding buyers become known, and they tend to get no more than they can coerce out of suppliers who choose to deal with them. Thus often contract is not needed as there are alternatives.

Not only are contract and contract law not needed in many situations, their use may have, or may be thought to have, undesirable consequences. Detailed negotiated contracts can get in the way of creating good exchange relationships between business units. If one side insists on a detailed plan, there will be delay while letters are exchanged as the parties try to agree on what should happen if a remote and unlikely contingency occurs. In some cases they may not be able to agree at all on such matters and as a result a sale may be lost to the seller and the buyer may have to search elsewhere for an acceptable supplier. Many businessmen would react by thinking that had no one raised the series of remote and unlikely contingencies all this wasted effort could have been avoided.

Even where agreement can be reached at the negotiation stage, carefully planned arrangements may create undesirable exchange relationships between business units. Some businessmen object that in such a carefully worked out relationship one gets performance only to the letter of the contract. Such planning indicates a lack of trust and blunts the demands of friendship, turning a cooperative venture into an antagonistic horse trade. Yet the greater danger perceived by some businessmen is that one would have to perform his side of the bargain to its letter and thus lose what is called "flexibility." Businessmen may welcome a measure of vagueness in the obligations they assume so that they may negotiate matters in light of the actual circumstances.

Adjustment of exchange relationships and dispute settlement by litigation or the threat of it also has many costs. The gain anticipated from using this form of coercion often fails to outweigh these costs, which are both monetary and non-monetary. Threatening to turn matters over to an attorney may cost no more money than postage or a telephone call; yet few are so skilled in making such a threat that it will not cost some deterioration of the relationship between the firms. One businessman said that customers had better not rely on legal rights or threaten to bring a breach of contract law suit against him since he "would not be treated like a criminal" and would fight back with every means available. Clearly actual litigation is even more costly than making threats. Lawyers demand substantial fees from larger business units. A firm's executives often will have to be transported and maintained in another city during the proceedings if, as often is the case, the trial must be held away from the home office. Top management does not travel by Greyhound and stay at the Y.M.C.A. Moreover, there will be the cost of diverting top management, engineers, and others in the organization from their normal activities. The firm may lose many days work from several key people. The non-monetary costs may be large too. A breach of contract law suit may settle a particular dispute, but such an action often results in a "divorce" ending the "marriage" between the two businesses, since a contract action is likely to carry charges with at least overtones of bad faith. Many executives, moreover, dislike the prospect of being cross-examined in public. Some executives may dislike losing control of a situation by turning the decision-making power over to lawyers. Finally, the law of contract damages may not provide an adequate remedy even if the firm wins the suit; one may get vindication but not much money.

Why do relatively contractual practices ever exist? Although contract is not needed and actually may have negative consequences, businessmen do make some carefully planned contracts, negotiate settlements influenced by their legal rights and commence and defend some breach of contract law suits or arbitration proceedings. In view of the findings and explanation presented to this point, one may ask why. Exchanges are carefully planned when it is thought that planning and a potential legal sanction will have more advantages than disadvantages. Such a judgment may be reached when contract planning serves the internal needs of an organization involved in a business exchange. For example, a fairly detailed contract can serve as a communication device within a large corporation. While the corporation's sales manager and house counsel may work out all the provisions with the customer, its production manager will have to make the product. He must be told what to do and how to handle at least the most obvious contingencies. Moreover, the sales manager may want to remove certain issues from future negotiation by his subordinates. If he puts the matter in the written contract, he may be able to keep his salesmen from making concessions to the customer without first consulting the sales manager. Then the sales manager may be aided in his battles with his firm's financial or engineering departments if the contract calls for certain practices which the sales manager advocates but which the other departments resist. Now the corporation is obligated to a customer to do what the sales manager wants to do; how can the financial or engineering departments insist on anything else?

Also one tends to find a judgment that the gains of contract outweigh the costs where there is a likelihood that significant problems will arise. One factor leading to this conclusion is complexity of the agreed performance over a long period. Another factor is whether or not the degree of injury in case of default is thought to be potentially great. This factor cuts two ways. First, a buyer may want to commit a seller to a detailed and legally binding contract, where the consequences of a default by the seller would seriously injure the buyer. For example, the airlines are subject to law suits from the survivors of passengers and to great adverse publicity as a result of crashes. One would expect the airlines to bargain for carefully defined and legally enforceable obligations on the part of the airframe manufacturers when they purchase aircraft. Second, a seller may want to limit his liability for a buyer's damages by a provision in their contract. For example, a manufacturer of air conditioning may deal with motels in the South and Southwest. If this equipment fails in the hot summer months, a motel may lose a great deal of business. The manufacturer may wish to avoid any liability for this type of injury to his customers and may want a contract with a clear disclaimer clause.

Similarly, one uses or threatens to use legal sanctions to settle disputes when other devices will not work and when the gains are thought to outweigh the costs. For example, perhaps the most common type of business contracts case fought all the way through to the appellate courts today is an action for an alleged wrongful termination of a dealer's franchise by a manufacturer. Since the franchise has been terminated, factors such as personal relationships and the desire for future business will have little effect; the cancellation of the franchise indicates they have already failed to maintain the relationship. Nor will a complaining dealer worry about creating a hostile relationship between himself and the manufacturer. Often the dealer has suffered a great financial loss both as to his investment in building and equipment and as to his anticipated future profits. A canceled automobile dealer's lease on his showroom and shop will continue to run, and his tools for servicing, say, Plymouths cannot be used to service other makes of cars. Moreover, he will have no more new Plymouths to sell. Today there is some chance of winning a law suit for terminating a franchise in bad faith in many states and in the federal courts. Thus, often the dealer chooses to risk the cost of a lawyer's fee because of the chance that he may recover some compensation for his losses.

An "irrational" factor may exert some influence on the decision to use legal sanctions. The man who controls a firm may feel that he or his organization has been made to appear foolish or has been the victim of fraud or bad faith. The law suit may be seen as a vehicle "to get even" although the potential gains, as viewed by an objective observer, are outweighed by the potential costs.

The decision whether or not to use contract—whether the gain exceeds the costs—will be made by the person within the business unit with the power to make it, and it tends to make a difference who he is. People in a sales department oppose contract. Contractual negotiations are just one more hurdle in the way of a sale. Holding a customer to the letter of a contract is bad for "customer relations." Suing a customer who is not bankrupt and might order again is poor strategy. Purchasing agents and their buyers are less hostile to contracts but regard attention devoted to such matters as a waste of time. In contrast, the financial control department—the treasurer, controller or auditor—leans toward more contractual dealings. Contract is viewed by these people as an organizing tool to control operations in a large organization. It tends to define precisely and to minimize the risks to which the firm is exposed. Outside lawyers—those with many clients—may share this enthusiasm for a more contractual method of dealing. These lawyers are concerned with preventive law—avoiding any possible legal difficulty. They see many unstable and unsuccessful exchange transactions, and so they are aware of, and perhaps overly concerned with, all of the things which can go wrong. Moreover, their job of settling disputes with legal sanctions is much easier if their client has not been overly casual about transaction planning. The inside lawyer, or house counsel, is harder to classify. He is likely to have some sympathy with a more contractual method of dealing. He shares the outside lawyer's "craft urge" to see exchange transactions neat and tidy from a legal standpoint. Since he is more concerned with avoiding and settling disputes than selling goods, he is likely to be less willing to rely on a man's word as the sole sanction than is a salesman. Yet the house counsel is more a part of the organization and more aware of its goals and subject to its internal sanctions. If the potential risks are not too great, he may hesitate to suggest a more contractual procedure to the sales department. He must sell his services to the operating departments, and he must hoard what power he has, expending it on only what he sees as significant issues.

The power to decide that a more contractual method of creating relationships and settling disputes shall be used will be held by different people at different times in different organizations. In most firms the sales department and the purchasing department have a great deal of power to resist contractual procedures or to ignore them if they are formally adopted and to handle disputes their own way. Yet in larger organizations the treasurer and the controller have increasing power to demand both systems and compliance. Occasionally, the house counsel must arbitrate the conflicting positions of these departments; in giving "legal advice" he may make the business judgment necessary regarding the use of contract. At times he may ask for an opinion from an outside law firm to reinforce his own position with the outside firm's prestige.

Obviously, there are other significant variables which influence the degree that contract is used. One is the relative bargaining power or skill of the two business units. Even if the controller of a small supplier succeeds within the firm and creates a contractual system of dealing, there will be no contract if the firm's large customer prefers not to be bound to anything. Firms that supply General Motors deal as General Motors wants to do business, for the most part. Yet bargaining power is not size or share of the market alone. Even a General Motors may need a particular supplier, at least temporarily. Furthermore, bargaining power may shift as an exchange relationship is first created and then continues. Even a giant firm can find itself bound to a small supplier once production of an essential item begins for there may not be time to turn to another supplier. Also, all of the factors discussed in this paper can be viewed as components of bargaining power—for example, the personal relationship between the presidents of the buyer and the seller firms may give a sales manager great power over a purchasing agent who has been instructed to give the seller "every consideration." Another variable relevant to the use of contract is the influence of third parties. The federal government, or a lender of money, may insist that a contract be made in a particular transaction or may influence the decision to assert one's legal rights under a contract.

Contract, then, often plays an important role in business, but other factors are significant. To understand the functions of contract the whole system of conducting exchanges must be explored fully. More types of business communities must be studied, contract litigation must be analyzed to see why the nonlegal sanctions fail to prevent the use of legal sanctions and all of the variables suggested in this paper must be classified more systematically.

Note on Macaulay

In a later article, Professor Macaulay wrote that studies of the use of contract in Poland, Great Britain, Indonesia, Japan, Korea, and Ethiopia suggest that the conclusions of the article you have just read are widely applicable: "In all of these societies—which differ so greatly in social structure, culture, and political and economic ideology—the picture looks much the same. Industrial managers and merchants seldom litigate to solve disputes about contracts, preferring to use other techniques of dispute avoidance and settlement." Stewart Macaulay, *Elegant Models, Empirical Pictures, and the Complexities of Contract*, 11 L & Soc Rev 507, 507 (1977).

(2) The Normative Attractions of Contract

We begin our examination of the commercial contract at the most general level, the normative attractions of contract as a means of social ordering. The first we are already familiar with—that contractual freedom helps assure human freedom. Contractual freedom might do so because (a) it implies that government is not setting norms but rather is allowing individuals to do so and (b) it provides individuals with tools for making their environment predictable. So important has this route to human freedom seemed that courts have said things like, "[I]f there is one thing which more than another public policy requires it is that men of full age and competent understanding shall have the utmost liberty of contracting, and that their contracts when entered into freely and voluntarily shall be enforced by Courts of justice. Therefore, you have this paramount public policy to consider—that you are not lightly to interfere with this freedom of contract." *Printing & Numerical Registering Co. v. Sampson*, L R 19 Eq 462, 465 (1875).

This line of reasoning achieved constitutional status in the United States in the late nineteenth and early twentieth centuries. That constitutional status has since been lost, and freedom of contract in most social and economic contexts has also lost much of its legal and political strength. Nevertheless, that strength has hardly evaporated, and enthusiasm for contract has begun to be widely applied to intimate affairs. Thus one advocate of the contractualization of family law argues: "Contract offers a rich and developed tradition whose principal strength is precisely the accommodation of diverse relationships. It is designed to regulate human interactions where the state recognizes and defers to divergent values, needs, preferences, and resources. Indeed, the deference to individual choice is strengthened, the pluralistic choices themselves are legitimized, by the state's readiness to enforce private expectations or resolve private disputes at the behest of a party to a relationship." Marjorie Maguire Shultz, *Contractual Ordering of Marriage: A New Model for State Policy*, 70 Cal L Rev 204, 248 (1982).

The second normative argument for contract is that it is a particularly efficacious means of social organization, both to the contractors and to society generally. It is efficacious because it allows the people who know their own interests best—the contractors themselves—to arrange their own affairs and because it promotes mutually advantageous exchanges. As applied to family law, the argument is that this efficacious means of social organization should be offered to people who are organizing their family lives. Consider, for instance, the allocation of wealth and of children on divorce:

> There are obvious and substantial savings when a couple can resolve distributional consequences of divorce without resort to courtroom adjudication. The financial cost of litigation, both private and public, is minimized. The pain of a formal adversary proceeding is avoided.... Moreover, a negotiated agreement allows the parties to avoid the risks and uncertainties of litigation, which may involve all-or-nothing consequences. Given the substantial delays that often characterize contested judicial proceedings, agreement can often save time and allow each spouse to proceed with his or her life. Finally, a consensual solution is by definition more likely to be consistent with the preferences of each spouse, and acceptable over time, than would a result imposed by a court.

Robert H. Mnookin and Lewis Kornhauser, *Bargaining in the Shadow of the Law: The Case of Divorce*, 88 Yale L J 950, 956–57 (1979).

In addition to these two general normative advantages of contract, the contractualization of family law may serve various particular goals, such as equality in marriage, gender equality, the "individualization of relationships," or healthy psychological development. Proponents of contractualization believe it serves these ends partly because it supplants rules thought to have contrary effects. These advocates also contend that contract is a mode of social organization which accords with good principles of personal relations: "Where key social scientists stress the importance of individualism, self-development, and self-fulfillment in personal relations, the law should not base its policies upon a model of marriage as a relationship where self must be forgotten or merged with the other." Shultz, 70 Cal L Rev at 264. Professor Shultz argues that a contractualized model of marriage discourages spouses from forgetting self and encourages them to recognize their own individuality.

As this last argument suggests, some of contractualization's proponents see it as a desirable part of a larger move toward a different legal conception of the family. Thus Professor Shultz has proposed that our whole legal view of marriage has been changed by such developments as the constitutional recognition of privacy rights related to marriage, changed legal attitudes toward gender equality and non-traditional sexual conduct, the rise of no-fault divorce, and the weakening of the view of marriage as an entity. She urges that these changes and contractualization have several things in common because "they respond to pressures toward diversity, individualism, and equality by reducing public control of conduct in intimate relations, because they treat marital partners as individuals capable of separate interests, injuries, and remedies, and because they recognize that legal dispute resolution in marriage may sometimes be desirable."

(3) The Practical Attractions of Contract

We have been discussing the normative advantages of contract as a means of social and familial organization. We now want to ask more particularly why businesses enter into contracts and thus why spouses might want to do so. People enter business contracts to promote a mutually profitable exchange. Since marriage consists of exchanges between spouses, marriage should be an appropriate subject for contract. But before we can evaluate this conjecture, our simple statement of the virtues of business contracts needs filling out. As we do so, we will construct a *prima facie* case for marital contracting.

First, people enter business contracts as part of the planning which is essential to business activity. Contracts promote planning in two basic ways. First, the process of contracting helps a business ensure that it and the people it deals with understand each other. The business must consider carefully what it wants, and the negotiations ought to surface misunderstanding of which the parties were unaware. The second way contract promotes planning is by helping businesses control their environment and ensure that the people with whom they are dealing will act predictably. Through negotiations, a business can attempt to persuade the entities it deals with to act in ways the business finds desirable.

Because contracts are (formally and informally) enforceable, a business can hope to rely on the behavior of those entities.

Do these advantages of contract apply to marriage? Perhaps so. Each of the major kinds of marital contract has centrally to do with planning, with establishing the expectations of each party. The antenuptial agreement establishes what the parties may expect of each other during marriage; the reconciliation contract adjusts those expectations so the marriage may continue; and the separation agreement specifies what the parties may expect of each other after marriage.

However, we know from Professor Macaulay's article that the planning function is often treated rather lightly even in business settings. Let us consider the occasions planning is done carefully to see whether those occasions find parallels in the marital context. Macaulay says exchanges are carefully planned when a business thinks planning and a potential legal sanction will have more advantages than disadvantages. A business may think so when contract planning serves its internal needs. Does a marriage contract serve the spouses' "internal needs"? Shouldn't prospective spouses (and prospective ex-spouses) think carefully about their financial and even social and psychological expectations?

"Also," Macaulay reports, "one tends to find a judgment that the gains of contract outweigh the costs where there is a likelihood that significant problems will arise." He adds, "One factor leading to this conclusion is complexity of the agreed performance over a long period. Yet another factor is whether or not the degree of injury in case of default is thought to be potentially great." Surely both these factors are present in marriage. The marriage relationship is immensely complex, and it is intended to be life-long; the economic, social, and psychological consequences of divorce are injurious indeed.

A second reason businesses make contracts is to facilitate dispute resolution. The contract states what is expected of each party; it specifies the remedy for breach; it sometimes specifies means of resolving the dispute, like mediation or arbitration. Again, this purpose seems apt for marriage. When a marriage ends (or, one might say, when the life-long commitment portion of the marriage contract is breached) questions of support, property, and child custody often arise. Many spouses feel the law lacks clear and sound rules for settling these questions. Worse, the spouses are often too angry to handle disagreements well. A contract that foresees disputes, resolves them when the parties are relatively dispassionate, and that specifies ways to manage any unforeseen problems has obvious attractions.

A third reason businesses make contracts is to recruit the law's coercive force in reaching their planning and dispute-resolution goals. One student of contract writes, "From the point of view of the parties themselves, the law of contracts is a valuable and important institution because it enables them to harness the state's powers of coercion for their own private ends. The state may be thought of as a kind of machine (an enforcement machine). There is no other like it; within its own territory, the state possesses matchless powers of compulsion. If this machine were privately owned, contracting parties would pay for its use, and the taxes the state collects to support its monopoly of violence in part represent disguised payments of exactly this sort." Anthony T. Kronman, *Contract Law and the State of Nature*, 1 J L Econ & Organization 5, 5 (1985). Many of the advantages of contract law we have discussed (e.g., promoting a mutually satisfying exchange, clarifying understanding, facilitating dispute resolution) might be available even if the government did not enforce the contract. But in each case the government's coercive power adds an element of reliability. And here once again there are many reasons to believe that element will help contracting spouses.

So far we have canvassed the normative and the practical advantages of contract as a means of organizing economic relations. We have outlined the argument that those advantages apply to organizing familial relations. Indeed, that argument has long since persuaded the law to provide for some marital contracts, and it is now moving the law toward permitting a number of others. But we now need to look at the other side of these issues. Once again, we will do so by examining the family contract in light of the business contract and by applying the lessons of Macaulay's article. Specifically, we will assess the disadvantages of commercial contracts, the relevant differences between the commercial and family settings, and the normative objections to family contracts.

(4) The Disadvantages of Business Contracts

One of Macaulay's most striking points is that businesses sometimes (often?) find that contracts lack the advantages we have postulated, that contracts are sometimes unnecessary and even dysfunctional. What are those circumstances, and do they apply to family contracts?

(a) The Necessity of Business Contracts

Probably Macaulay's most remarkable conclusion is that contracts are used much less often than we who have taken Contracts might suppose. Part of his explanation is that contracting has costs and that it is therefore avoided where it is unnecessary. He finds it is sometimes (often?) unnecessary. Is contract unnecessary in the family situation for the same reasons?

Two circumstances in which Macaulay reports contracts are unnecessary have to do with the need for planning and the consequences of contractual failure. "[U]sually there is little room for honest misunderstandings or good faith differences of opinion about the nature and quality of a seller's performance. Although the parties fail to cover all foreseeable contingencies, they will exercise care to see that both understand the primary obligation on each side.... Those who write and read specifications are experienced professionals who will know the customs of their industry...." Marriage is probably far too complicated for this argument for non-use to obtain. Good faith differences about the nature and quality of spousal performance easily arise, and most engaged or divorcing couples can hardly be called experienced professionals about their problems.

Macaulay also finds contracts unnecessary where, "[w]hen defaults occur[,] they are not likely to be disastrous because of techniques of risk avoidance or risk spreading. One can deal with firms of good reputation.... One can insure against many breaches of contract.... Buyers can place orders with two or more suppliers...." These ways of avoiding contract cannot be literally transferred to the family. Given *Reynolds*, a person cannot, for example, marry several spouses as a means of risk spreading. On the other hand, could one "deal with firms of good reputation"? That is, could one choose a spouse really carefully? Is this not a traditional argument for long engagements? See Margaret F. Brinig and Michael V. Alexeev, *Fraud in Courtship: Annulment and Divorce*, 2 Eur J L & Econ 45 (1994)(exploring reputation and annulment as protection against fraud).

A second reason Macaulay says contracts are sometimes "unnecessary" in business is that business norms serve some of the planning, enforcement, and conflict-resolution functions of contract. One reason "[b]usiness exchanges in non-speculative areas are usually adjusted without dispute" is that in business "[t]wo norms are widely accepted. (1) Commitments are to be honored in almost all situations; one does not welsh on a deal. (2) One ought to produce a good product and stand behind it." In addition, a norm requires people to treat each other fairly. " 'One doesn't run to lawyers if he wants to stay in business because one must behave decently.' "Are there norms (religious? social? legal?) which serve the same purpose in the marital setting? Are they specific enough to be helpful? Powerful enough?

A third reason Macaulay suggests contracts may be "unnecessary" in business is that non-contractual devices serve some of the enforcement and conflict-resolution functions (but not, notice, the planning function) of contracts. "[B]usiness units are organized to perform commitments, and internal sanctions will induce performance." External forces, particularly the need to maintain a good reputation, pressure businesses to fulfill contracts and resolve disputes. Interconnections between companies ranging from personal acquaintanceships to financial interlockings have the same effect. Buyers and sellers can deploy informal sanctions against each other, from the threat of not doing business to withholding payment, cancelling orders, holding a down payment hostage, and barring access to a unique product or service. Finally, businesses want to succeed with the transaction at issue and to continue to deal with each other. As one of Macaulay's interviewees says, " 'You don't read legalistic contract clauses at each other if you ever want to do business again.' "

Are such non-contractual devices available in the family setting? People may not be "organized" to perform commitments, but are there psychological and moral internal sanctions that induce performance? Is marriage a situation in which "guilt may accompany the promisor's imposition of harmful results on others"? Charles J. Goetz and Robert E. Scott, *Enforcing Promises: An Examination of the Basis of Contract*, 89 Yale L J 1261, 1272 (1980). Gary Becker extends this notion to families in his Nobel address, reprinted as *The Economic Way of Looking at Behavior*, 101 J Pol Econ 185 (1993). Are there external pressures on spouses to behave as if they had entered into a set of equitable agreements with each other? Do relatives, friends, clergy, therapists, and even employers impose such pressures?

The "interconnections" point deserves special attention. The interconnections between spouses are likely to be more extensive and compelling than the interconnections between businesses. Is marriage then a case where even without a legally binding contract "the promisor exhibits some welfare interdependence with the promisee; that is, he is to some extent altruistic and cares about costs incurred by the promisee," Goetz and Scott, (and is therefore more likely to keep his promises even if there are no formal enforcement mechanisms)? As Goetz and Scott say, "Intrafamilial promises and promises between close friends are most likely to exemplify this phenomenon." A similar point is made in Professor Kronman's discussion of whether people would write contracts if there were no government to enforce them. He proposes that parties to such an exchange would "reduce the risk of opportunism by taking steps to increase the likelihood that each will see his own self-interest as being internally connected to the welfare of the other." He names the technique of "encouraging the parties to develop sympathy, affection, or love for one another" the "method of union." He says this method can be socially institutionalized and powerful:

> [I]f the members of a community deliberately establish routines, designed to reinforce in one another the altruistic habit of subordinating their own individual welfare to the welfare of others, if they make a conscious effort to instill similar habits in their children as they mature, and if they do all this, in part, to reduce the tensions that would otherwise accompany their efforts to establish exchange relationships among themselves, they are pursuing the strategy of union.... Marriage is [an] ... example of an arrangement aimed at cultivating a spirit of solidarity on the part of those involved which may, in certain circumstances, be an effective instrument for reducing transactional insecurity.... [T]he object of marriage, and its effect, is to establish between the parties an identity of interest that makes it increasingly difficult for either to view the other at arm's length.

One objection to this approach is that contract is designed to deal with some of the hardest problems in marriages. Is the "method of union" strong enough to solve them? What legal rules might strengthen the method?

What about the informal-sanctions and continuing-to-do-business arguments? Parties to a marriage presumably want the marriage to succeed and want to continue to deal with each other, and they generally have a variety of informal sanctions. We discussed some of them when we assessed the marriage as an entity. They "range from hostile, retributive behavior to a mere loss of others' esteem to foreclosure of future beneficial dealings." Goetz and Scott. But are those sanctions and the desire to continue to deal powerful enough to do the job of contract (in concert, of course, with the other devices we have been discussing)? Are they less significant because many of the problems marital contracts deal with arise when the spouses are at their most hostile and when the marriage is ending?

Does it matter that some forms of marital contracts are unnecessary? "In marriage, as Professor Macaulay found to be the case in commercial contract relationships, legal dispute resolution would take place only in special circumstances. The bulk of contract law's impact on marriage thus would be of the indirect type . . . : a background influence on conduct and private dispute settlement, a vague threat keeping the parties reliable, a legitimation of certain ideologies, and a lever allowing the powerless to influence the powerful." Shultz. Would these benefits actually obtain? Assuming Macaulay is correct that contracting has costs, are these benefits great enough?

(b) The Dysfunctions of Business Contracts

Macaulay writes, "Not only are contract and contract law not needed in many situations, their use may have, or may be thought to have, undesirable consequences." Is contract sometimes dysfunctional in the family situation in the way Macaulay says it can be in business? We begin with Macaulay's observation that the planning function of contract has costs. "If one side insists on a detailed plan, there will be delay while letters are exchanged as the parties try to agree on what should happen if a remote and unlikely contingency occurs." In addition, detailed negotiations may prevent some doable deals from being done. And Macaulay thinks "carefully planned arrangements may create undesirable exchange relationships between business units," partly because "[b]usinessmen may welcome a measure of vagueness in the obligations they assume so that they may negotiate matters in light of the actual circumstances."

The problem of delay may seem less crucial in marriage than business. But will couples expend energy debating "remote and unlikely contingencies"? Will they distinguish between such contingencies and likelier ones? Professor Schneider remembers a student saying in a class discussion of marital contracting that she and her husband found they agreed over things they expected to disagree about and disagreed about the things they expected to agree about. Is this experience common? May even remote contingencies become controversial if they involve issues about which the parties have strong moral or psychological preferences? Will such controversies promote difficulties between the parties where none might otherwise have existed? Might these controversies rise to the level of "preventing doable deals from being done"? Would this be good, on the theory that if parties have difficulties of this sort before their marriage, they would have worse ones afterward? Is a "measure of vagueness" desirable in a marital relationship if the duration of marriage is so long and the relationship is so complex that no one can foresee disputes that will arise or the best ways of handling them?

Macaulay continues, "Adjustment of exchange relationships and dispute settlement by litigation or the threat of it also has many costs." Prominent among them are costs associated with hiring lawyers: Lawyers and litigation are expensive, and "[s]ome executives may dislike losing control of a situation by turning the decision-making power over to lawyers." In marital situations, the costs of lawyers and litigation are particularly burdensome, given the financial resources of most divorcing couples. Yet as scope for marital contracting increases and as the requirements imposed on marital contracts are made more elaborate in the interests of preserving fairness, legal advice becomes increasingly desirable. Are those costs worthwhile? Do they justify themselves by their services to the planning function? By preventing one party from exploiting the other? Do they cause the parties to lose control of the situation or help them retain it? Does hiring lawyers increase or soothe animosities between the parties?

Another set of costs Macaulay has in mind has to do with the legal remedies for breach of contract: "A breach of contract law suit may settle a particular dispute, but such an action often results in a 'divorce' ending the 'marriage' between the two businesses, since a contract action is likely to carry charges with at least overtones of bad faith." And, "the law of contract damages may not provide an adequate remedy even if the firm wins the suit; one may get vindication but not much money." Professor Kronman reminds us of some of the basic limits of contract remedies: money damages may not compensate plaintiffs for "remote" or "speculative" losses, and it is often hard to measure damages accurately. Specific performance is designed to solve some of those problems, yet it can mean little where the performer performs grudgingly or has become unable to perform adequately. Lloyd Cohen discusses this problem in *Marriage, Divorce and Quasi Rents Or "I Gave Him the Best Years of My Life"*, 16 J Legal Stud 267, 300 (1987)("no court can succeed in forcing an unwilling spouse to perform marital duties in a spirit of love and devotion").

The analogy Macaulay uses to marriage and divorce suggests tellingly some of the consequences for a marriage of taking a contract to court. On the other hand, how many kinds of marital contracts does this objection apply to? And is it necessarily undesirable that enforcing a contractual right leads to divorce? As to the limitations of contract damages, does much depend on the kind of contract the parties have made? For example, are the problems described above present where the parties are divorcing anyway and where their contract is limited to financial matters? The contract between Peter and Susan tries to deal with enforcement where those two situations are not present. How does it do so? Is it successful? How will time and unforeseen events affect problems of contract enforcement?

(5) Differences Between Business and Family Contractual Settings

We have now completed our investigation of ways the disadvantages of contract in business may also limit contracts in families. We need next to ask whether the family setting systematically differs from the typical business setting in ways that diminish the usefulness of contract.

One difference between family and business contracts that particularly concerns critics of the contractualization of family law is that, while business contracts are typically intended to last for a finite period, marital contracts are typically intended to last indefinitely. Of course there are open-ended business contracts, but they are commonly regularly renegotiable or easily canceled. And the long-term business contracts that lack those features are more problematic than the paradigm single-transaction contract. The problem with long-term contracts, of course, is that the longer the term, the harder it is to foresee the changing circumstances in which the contract will be applied and the more troubling the loss of flexibility the contract imposes. How will those problems affect marital contracts? Might one say that "contracts and promises are essentially risk-allocation devices," that "the whole point of the transaction would be lost if the arrangement could not be made binding for the future," P.S. Atiyah, *The Rise and Fall of Freedom of Contract* 3 (Oxford U Press, 1979), and that a loss of flexibility is thus simply inherent in the idea of contract? As one scholar writes, "The device of contract cuts both ways. It provides a method of working out an individual arrangement of rights and obligations according to the particular needs of the parties and is thus a way of creating flexibility in legal relations. Once, however, the agreement becomes definite and fixed, the parties lose the flexibility in the relationship which would, in the absence of the contract, be available on a day-to-day basis by negotiation and compromise." Banks McDowell, *Contracts in the Family*, 65 Boston U L Rev 43, 49 (1965). On the other hand, is flexibility vital in the family situation?

Of course, lawyers can take some care in drafting contracts to ensure that they provide for modification in the future. In fact, as an empirical matter, good lawyers are apt to do this. One obvious way in which things change in divorced families with minor children is that children age, and that, over time, parents' income and health may change, as might the preferences of the children about who should have physical custody. The experienced attorney might draft a separation agreement that provides for modification of child support if such events happen, for example, specifying that the noncustodial parent will pay some amount that will be adjusted on a ratio of the two parents' incomes, or as the cost of living increases, or as the child hits milestone ages such as 12 or 16. In a study of Johnson County, Iowa, divorces, Professor Brinig found that the more experienced the attorney (based on the number of the cases in that year handled by the attorney), the more likely the couple was to have some sort of adjustment provision. Not surprisingly, the couples who made agreements with automatic adjustment provisions were less likely to litigate over child support after divorce. Margaret F. Brinig, Unhappy Contracts: The Case of Divorce Settlements, 1 Rev L & Econ 241, 256–57 (2005). Alternatively, the agreement may include a dispute resolution procedure when a parent wants an adjustment, such as mediation.

These questions about anticipating change and preserving flexibility in the family context suggest a second systematic difference between business and family contracts. Is the family situation too complex for business-contract techniques to work well? The paradigmatic business contract involves an essentially discrete transaction. Thus Professor Leff spoke of "the limitedness of contract. There seems to be something significant to contract in the bordered relationship, 'the deal,' as opposed to more long-term, non-limit-bound interpersonal relationships like husband-wife and father-son." Arthur Allen Leff, *Contract as Thing*, 19 Am U L Rev 131 (1970). Professor Macneil writes, "We do find in real life many quite discrete transactions: little personal involvement of the parties, communications largely or entirely linguistic and limited to the subject matter of transaction, the subjects of exchange consisting of an easily monetized commodity and money, little or no social or secondary exchange, and no significant past relations nor likely future relations." Ian Macneil, *Contracts: Adjustment of Long–Term Economic Relations Under Classical, Neoclassical, and Relational Contract Law*, 72 NW U L Rev 854, 856–57 (1978). Classical contract law enhances this element of discreteness by, for example, encouraging parties to agree to a single written document which entirely states the terms of their relationship, by trying to provide "a precise, predictable body of law to deal with all aspects of the transaction not encompassed by the promises," and by providing for only limited kinds of damages. In the paradigmatic contract situation, then, it is relatively easy to plan, to describe what performance is required, to tell if the contract has been performed, to calculate damages, and to collect them. Flexibility over time is achieved by entering into a series of discrete transactions and adjusting each one to developments as they occur, rather than by trying to plan an entire relationship in a single document.

Contracting becomes more complicated when the contract involves, as many marital contracts do, continuing relations between entities dealing with each other for an extended period over more than one kind of issue. Consider this statement of the limits of contract:

> The members of a small, self-sufficient group are all parts, one of another; all are bound together by a complex network of reciprocal renditions and expectations. In such a human situation any attempt at an explicit verbalized definition of each party's expected performance, and the price to be paid him for it, would certainly not produce order and might produce chaos. The ineptitude of contract as an organizing principle in this type of case becomes especially clear when we take into account the shifting contingencies affecting such a group: storms, droughts, sudden attacks by tribes, and the like.

Lon Fuller and Melvin Eisenberg, *Cases and Materials on Contracts* 98 (West, 1988).

On the other hand, students of contract law have argued that the paradigmatic transactional contract is being supplemented by a different kind of contractual relation: "Parties frequently enter into continuing, highly interactive contractual arrangements.... The resulting 'relational contracts' ... encompass most generic agency relationships, including distributorships, franchises, joint ventures, and employment contracts." Charles J. Goetz and Robert E. Scott, *Principles of Relational Contracts*, 67 Va L Rev 1089, 1090–91 (1981). Goetz and Scott say, "A contract is relational to the extent that the parties are incapable of reducing important terms of the arrangement to well-defined obligations. Such definitive obligations may be impractical because of inability to identify uncertain future conditions or because of inability to characterize complex adaptations adequately even when the contingencies themselves can be identified in advance." Professor Shultz argues that even in commercial law "the law of contracts had to adapt to the need for flexibility within legal relationships.... For example, the common law of contract originally required specification of such key terms as price, quantity, and time of performance. The U.C.C., by contrast, allows various terms to be 'open' or indefinite...." Professor Shultz provides several examples of the change she sees: the U.C.C. rejects the common law's disfavor of requirements and output contracts. The doctrines of changed circumstances and commercial impracticability are more accommodating than the law of impossibility, which they are replacing. The principles of unconscionability and good faith introduce further flexibility. Damages for non-economic injury, like emotional distress, add further flexibility and recognition of complexity.

Professor Shultz draws on the work of Professor Macneil, who has been a leading proponent of the "relational contract," to point out that "marriage is exceptionally well captured by his relational type. The overriding importance of continuing relationships; the whole-person nature of the exchange; the presence of quantifiable and nonquantifiable elements; the expected range of interaction, from altruism to self-interest to conflict; the need for planning as a continuing process that focuses on flexibility of structure and procedure rather than on any single transaction; the emphasis on remedies that repair and restructure relationships rather than replace a specific failed performance—each of these characteristics of Macneil's relational contract type is an important characteristic of marriage." Does this mean contract law has adequate answers to the problems of organizing long-term and complex familial relationships? How much is even the long-term business relationship really like the marital one? Is the importance to the contractor as great? Is the "whole person" as much involved? Are the quantifiable elements that make a business contract possible as present in marriage? Is the bottom line quantifiable in business in a way it is not in marriage? Is the expected range of interaction as great? Is the presence of strong emotional and psychological components in marital relationships contrasted with the relatively weak emotional and psychological components in business contracts a relevant difference?

In addition, has business law really accommodated the needs of the relational contract even in business situations? Shultz notes that Macneil "urges that a new body of principles and rules be developed to govern the entire continuum from the presently emphasized transactional type to his newly articulated relational type." And she says that process "is already underway." Does this imply that there are many problems yet to be solved with organizing long-term complex relations contractually? Does Macaulay's evidence suggest the law can deal with the relational contract well? The contracts Macaulay discusses are relatively simple, since they involve sales, not a continuing course of dealings. If contracts are problematic even in that setting, will they be far more so in the more complex setting of the family?

A third possible difference between business and family contracts lies in the negotiations that precede them. The theory of contract is that bargaining accurately reflects the parties' interests and therefore leads to an optimal allocation of resources. Business contracting has a number of features which promote this kind of bargaining. First, the parties enter negotiations realizing they are responsible for getting as good a bargain for themselves as they can. *Caveat emptor* may have been weakened in recent years, but it is not dead, and it still reflects the practical perception that a bargainer should be skeptical, alert, and self-interested. Second, self-interestedness is made easier in business by the usual absence of intimate and intense personal and emotional ties between the parties. Third, where two businesses are contracting the parties are almost by definition professionals in dealing with financial matters and the particular area of business. (Where one of the parties is a consumer, special regulations often govern the negotiations in order to protect the consumer.) Fourth, the parties to a business transaction are commonly involved in a workaday transaction that is involving only part (albeit often an important part) of their lives. Indeed, the negotiators often negotiate for their firms rather than themselves (even though their success may affect their careers).

Contrast these conditions with those likely to obtain in a family contract. First, the parties to a marital contract (even, to some extent, the parties to a separation agreement) are generally expected to be concerned for the interests of the other party and to trust the other party. Second, the parties to a marital contract find self-interested vigilance impeded by affection and deep-rooted emotional and psychological ties. Third, the parties are often inexpert about financial affairs or even the other aspects of married life. Fourth, the parties to a family contract will be hard put to summon the (relative) dispassion of their business counterparts. For one thing, they will be going through a particularly stressful social and emotional experience. This is clearest in the context of separation agreements: "Dissolution of marriage is, of course, an inherently stressful and usually traumatic event. It is therefore extraordinarily productive of the kinds of psychologically vulnerable states in which parties may easily exercise, or fall victim to, various forms of unfair bargaining tactics." Sally Burnett Sharp, *Fairness Standards and Separation Agreements: A Word of Caution on Contractual Freedom*, 132 U Pa L Rev 1399, 1428 (1984). And even though a marriage is happier than a divorce, it can still be disorienting and stressful. Also impeding the parties' dispassionate contemplation of marital contracts is the fact their contract can deal with all the dearest things in their lives: not just their entire fortunes, but also their relations with their spouse and their children. Business people often have a lot at stake in transactions, but rarely *this* much.

In sum, the situation of the negotiators of marital contracts raises the possibility that, on one hand, they will not bargain vigorously for their own interests and that, on the other hand, they will be vulnerable to a partner who *is* willing to bargain vigorously. In the business context, negotiators can ask whether a proposed contract is unfair either by looking at the value the market sets for the goods being negotiated for or, where there is no market, at least by looking at the probable economic consequences of the transaction. In the family context, however, there generally is no market to consult, and the economic consequences of the transaction may be particularly hard to calculate (given the problems of duration and complexity) and in any event only part of what the parties are bargaining about.

We have been surveying some of the problems that may arise during bargaining over marital contracts. Is one response to these concerns that the problem lies not in marital contracting but rather in the attitudes associated with marriage that impede successful bargaining? In other words, ought our attentions be devoted, for instance, to making spouses more independent and thus less vulnerable?

(6) Some Normative Objections to Family Contracts

The considerations we have just been discussing lead us neatly to a set of normative objections to applying contract law in the family setting. The first of these objections reminds us that a primary justification of "freedom of contract" is that it promotes human freedom. In American constitutional law, that argument was ultimately rejected in the economic context. Is it persuasive in the family context? This question takes us back to the questions we asked about Maine's dictum. One commentator, drawing on some of the ideas we there discussed, writes that contract law "serves massively and systematically as an *intensifier* of economic advantage and disadvantage. It does this because people and businesses who are in strong bargaining positions or who can afford expensive legal advice, can and epidemically do exact of necessitous and ignorant people contractual engagements which the general law would never impose." Charles L. Black, Jr., *Some Notes on Law Schools in the Present Day*, 79 Yale L J 505, 508 (1970). If such engagements are exacted in marital contracts, they are probably exacted most frequently from three groups (which would probably be overlapping): First, (as our discussion in the preceding section suggests) people who are behaving altruistically and who thus run risks dealing with people who are not. Second, the partner who knows least about financial affairs and who is economically worse off. Third, women. This is partly because women are under present social circumstances likely to be among those less well off financially and financially less sophisticated. Weitzman adds another reason: "[W]omen in our present society are less assertive and they are less likely to negotiate a favorable bargain with a prospective spouse (or heterosexual cohabitant)." Lenore J. Weitzman, *The Marriage Contract: Spouses, Lovers and the Law* 247 (Free Press, 1981). And women's bargaining position may also be affected by social assumptions that they have family duties while their male counterparts assume them only as they wish to. Karen Czapanskiy, *Volunteers and Draftees: The Struggle for Parental Equality*, 38 UCLA L Rev 1415 (1991).

But is Professor Black's description of contract as an intensifier of inequality correct? Professor Weitzman argues that despite the problems outlined in the preceding paragraph, a weaker party is likely to be better off with a contract than without: "[T]he woman is surely better off knowing [of her relatively weak position] at the beginning of the relationship instead of blindly trusting the goodwill of her intended partner.... [I]f the terms of an unfair agreement are made known to a woman in advance, she might decide not to enter the relationship." She adds that "even the woman who has entered into a less than optimal contract is likely to be better off knowing that she will not be protected than one who is surprised to find herself in the inferior position that results from traditional legal marriage." Is this argument persuasive, given that one of the traditional purposes of these contracts is to require the less wealthy partner to give up a right she may be entitled to under standard divorce law?

The relationship between contract and freedom has another wrinkle. Some critics contend that the contractualization of family law will increase government power over private lives because it accords government power in interpreting and enforcing contracts. Professor Hunter writes: "Under the status construct now prevalent, the state superimposes the structure on the partners, but (except for problems relating to dissolution, death, or desertion) the state allows, even requires the parties to work out their own problems within the context of the marriage. This 'hands-off' policy keeps the state from directly intruding upon the private, day-to-day affairs of a couple.... [R]esolution of disputes necessarily will involve more direct interference by the state. The state will not be removed from the picture; it simply will intrude at a different point, and this intrusion could be more objectionable than intrusion by way of an ordering of status at the outset." Howard O. Hunter, *An Essay on Contract and Status: Race, Marriage, and the Meretricious Spouse*, 64 Va L Rev 1039, 1075–76 (1978).

In evaluating the normative objections to family contracts, we have reviewed the argument that they are not the optimal means of promoting freedom in marriage. You have now encountered three basic positions on the relationship between contract and freedom in family relationships. (1) That freedom is most enhanced by allowing spouses to work out for themselves the terms of their relationship and by according them the assistance of the state in enforcing those terms. (2) That freedom is most enhanced by according the state the power to regulate crucial terms of marital relationships in the way the parties themselves would do if they were free of the constraints and disabilities that now impede fair bargaining. (3) That freedom is most enhanced by allowing the parties to work out for themselves the terms of their relationship but denying the state the authority to intrude in the relationship by enforcing any such agreement or (except to some necessary extent on divorce) by setting the terms of the relationship regulatorily. Which of these positions is the most realistic?

A second normative objection to applying contract law in the family setting is that business contracts are associated with attitudes toward people that ought to be inimical to family law. First, the contractual paradigm is impersonal, while marriage is highly personal. "Contract law is centrally concerned with voluntary exchange, and, although exchange is by no means limited to the market, our law of contracts tends to treat the impersonal market transaction as the paradigm of all exchange relationships.... The impersonality of the market is reflected in many of the most basic features of contract law: the traditional unwillingness of courts to upset bargains for inadequacy of consideration, ... the preference for money damages over specific performance, ... the noncompensability of emotional harms, ... and the refusal to recognize financial hardship as a form of duress...." Anthony T. Kronman, *Paternalism and the Law of Contracts*, 92 Yale L J 763, 797 (1983). Professor Kronman is here amplifying an argument made years ago by Max Weber:

> The reason for the impersonality of the market is its matter-of-factness, its orientation to the commodity and only to that. Where the market is allowed to follow its own autonomous tendencies, its participants do not look toward the persons of each other but only toward the commodity; there are no obligations of brotherliness or reverence, and none of those spontaneous human relations that are sustained by personal unions. They all would just obstruct the free development of the bare market relationship, and its specific interests serve, in their turn, to weaken the sentiments on which these obstructions rest. Market behavior is influenced by rational, purposeful pursuit of interests. The partner to a transaction is expected to behave according to rational legality and, quite particularly, to respect the formal inviolability of a promise once given.... Such absolute depersonalization is contrary to all the elementary forms of human relationship.

1 *Economy and Society* 636–37 (U Cal Press, 1978). Is this description of contract law correct? Even if it is, does importing contract law into family law have deleterious effects? Could contract law be altered to mend its "impersonality" in family contexts?

The second problem with the attitudes contractualizing marriage may promote is that it may encourage people to think in terms of rights instead of affection. The argument here might build on a point Professor Macaulay makes about the effects of contract even on commercial relationships. About the planning function of contract, he says, "Such planning indicates a lack of trust and blunts the demands of friendship, turning a cooperative venture into an antagonistic horse trade." About contract's dispute-resolution function, he quotes a businessman: "You can settle any dispute if you keep the lawyers and accountants out of it. They just do not understand the give-and-take needed in business." If contract has these harmful effects in business, will it *a fortiori* have them in families?

Some evidence that contract-like thinking is incompatible with successful marriage is found in the work of Professors Margaret Brinig and Steven Nock. In Steven L. Nock and Margaret F. Brinig, "Weak Men and Disorderly Women: Divorce and the Division of Labor," in *Marriage and Divorce: A Law and Economics Approach* (Dnes and Rowthorn, eds., Cambridge U Press, 2002), Brinig and Nock analyze data from the National Survey of Families and Households, looking for the ways that couples reported household and labor force work patterns affect their marital stability five years later. Brinig and Nock found that increased time by either spouse in so-called "women's work"—laundry, cooking, cleaning, shopping—increased the probability that the couple would be divorced five years later, while increased time by either spouse in so-called "men's work"—home and yard maintenance and car repair—decreased that same probability. Even beyond these differences, though, were the couples' attitudes about their own and their partners' contributions. Women in fact worked more combined hours than men in the sample. The couples who recognized that the arrangement was somewhat unfair to the woman were more stable that couples who thought everything was "about right," and both were more stable than couples in which both partners thought the arrangement was unfair to them. Interestingly, couples who didn't keep track of the household work they or their partners did were more stable than those who did.

For further evidence of how a marriage can become an "exchange relationship," and what this means, we include the following fictionalized account by Amy Tan, taken from her *The Joy Luck Club* (Ivy Books, 1989):

AMY TAN
"RICE HUSBAND"
THE JOY LUCK CLUB
PUTNAM EDITION, 1989

Pages 149–165

To this day, I believe my mother has the mysterious ability to see things before they happen. She has a Chinese saying for what she knows. *Chunwang chihan:* If the lips are gone, the teeth will be cold. Which means, I suppose, one thing is always the result of another.

But she does not predict when earthquakes will come, or how the stock market will do. She sees only bad things that affect our family.

And she knows what causes them. But now she laments that she never did anything to stop them.

One time when I was growing up in San Francisco, she looked at the way our new apartment sat too steeply on the hill. She said the new baby in her womb would fall out dead, and it did.

When a plumbing and bathroom fixtures store opened up across the street from our bank, my mother said the bank would soon have all its money drained away. And one month later, an officer of the bank was arrested for embezzlement.

And just after my father died last year, she said she knew this would happen. Because a philodendron plant my father had given her had withered and died, despite the fact that she watered it faithfully. She said the plant had damaged its roots and no water could get to it. The autopsy report she later received showed my father had had ninety-percent blockage of the arteries before he died of a heart attack at the age of seventy-four. My father was not Chinese like my mother, but English–Irish American, who enjoyed his five slices of bacon and three eggs sunny-side-up every morning.

I remembered this ability of my mother's, because now she is visiting my husband and me in the house we just bought in Woodside. And I wonder what she will see.

Harold and I were lucky to find this place, which is near the summit of Highway 9, then a left-right-left down three forks of unmarked dirt roads, unmarked because the residents always tear down the signs to keep out salesmen, developers, and city inspectors. We are only a forty-minute drive to my mother's apartment in San Francisco. This became a sixty-minute ordeal coming back from San Francisco, when my mother was with us in the car. After we got to the two-lane winding road to the summit, she touched her hand gently to Harold's shoulder and softly said, "Ai, tire squealing." And then a little later, "Too much tear and wear on car."

Harold had smiled and slowed down, but I could see his hands were clenched on the steering wheel of the Jaguar, as he glanced nervously in his rearview mirror at the line of impatient cars that was growing by the minute. And I was secretly glad to watch his discomfort. He was always the one who tailgated old ladies in their Buicks, honking his horn and revving the engine as if he would run them over unless they pulled over.

And at the same time, I hated myself for being mean-spirited, for thinking Harold deserved this torment. Yet I couldn't help myself. I was mad at Harold and he was exasperated with me. That morning, before we picked my mother up, he had said, "You should pay for the exterminators, because Mirugai is your cat and so they're *your* fleas. It's only fair."

None of our friends could ever believe we fight over something as stupid as fleas, but they would also never believe that our problems are much, much deeper than that, so deep I don't even know where bottom is.

And now that my mother is here—she is staying for a week, or until the electricians are done rewiring her building in San Francisco—we have to pretend nothing is the matter.

Meanwhile she asks over and over again why we had to pay so much for a renovated barn and a mildew-lined pool on four acres of land, two of which are covered with redwood trees and poison oak. Actually she doesn't really ask, she just says, "Aii, so much money, so much," as we show her different parts of the house and land. And her laments always compel Harold to explain to my mother in simple terms: "Well, you see, it's the details that cost so much. Like this wood floor. It's hand-bleached. And the walls here, this marbleized effect, it's hand-sponged. It's really worth it."

And my mother nods and agrees: "Bleach and sponge cost so much."

During our brief tour of the house, she's already found the flaws. She says the slant of the floor makes her feel as if she is "running down." She thinks the guest room where she will be staying—which is really a former hayloft shaped by a sloped roof—has "two lop sides." She sees spiders in high corners and even fleas jumping up in the air—pah! pah! pah!—like little spatters of hot oil. My mother knows, underneath all the fancy details that cost so much, this house is still a barn.

She can see all this. And it annoys me that all she sees are the bad parts. But then I look around and everything she's said is true. And this convinces me she can see what else is going on, between Harold and me. She knows what's going to happen to us. Because I remember something else she saw when I was eight years old.

My mother had looked in my rice bowl and told me I would marry a bad man.

"Aii, Lena," she had said after that dinner so many years ago, "your future husband have one pock mark for every rice you not finish."

She put my bowl down. "I once know a pock-mark man. Mean man, bad man."

And I thought of a mean neighbor boy who had tiny pits in his cheeks, and it was true, those marks were the size of rice grains. This boy was about twelve and his name was Arnold.

Arnold would shoot rubber bands at my legs whenever I walked past his building on my way home from school, and one time he ran over my doll with his bicycle, crushing her legs below the knees. I didn't want this cruel boy to be my future husband. So I picked up that cold bowl of rice and scraped the last few grains into my mouth, then smiled at my mother, confident my future husband would be not Arnold but *someone* whose face was as smooth as the porcelain in my now clean bowl.

But my mother sighed. "Yesterday, you not finish rice either." I thought of those unfinished mouthfuls of rice, and then the grains that lined my bowl the day before, and the day before that. By the minute, my eight-year-old heart grew more and more terror-stricken over the growing possibility that my future husband was fated to be this mean boy Arnold. And thanks to my poor eating habits, his hideous face would eventually resemble the craters of the moon.

This would have been a funny incident to remember from my childhood, but it is actually a memory I recall from time to time with a mixture of nausea and remorse. My loathing for Arnold had grown to such a point that I eventually found a way to make him die. I let one thing result from another. Of course, all of it could have been just loosely connected coincidences. And whether that's true or not, I know the *intention* was there. Because when I want something to happen—or not happen—I begin to look at all events and all things as relevant, an opportunity to take or avoid.

I found the opportunity. The same week my mother told me about the rice bowl and my future husband, I saw a shocking film at Sunday school. I remember the teacher had dimmed the lights so that all we could see were silhouettes of one another. Then the teacher looked at us, a roomful of squirmy, well-fed Chinese–American children, and she said, "This film will show you why you should give tithings to God, to do God's work."

She said, "I want you to think about a nickel's worth of candy money, or however much you eat each week—your Good and Plentys, your Necco wafers, your jujubes—and compare that to what you are about to see. And I also want you to think about what your true blessings in life really are."

And then she set the film projector clattering away. The film showed missionaries in Africa and India. These good souls worked with people whose legs were swollen to the size of tree trunks, whose numb limbs had become as twisted as jungle vines. But the most terrible of the afflictions were men and women with leprosy. Their faces were covered with every kind of misery I could imagine: pits and pustules, cracks and bumps, and fissures that I was sure erupted with the same vehemence as snails writhing in a bed of salt. If my mother had been in the room, she would have told me these poor people were victims of future husbands and wives who had failed to eat *platefuls* of food.

After seeing this film, I did a terrible thing. I saw what I had to do so I would not have to marry Arnold. I began to leave more rice in my bowl. And then I extended my prodigal ways beyond Chinese food. I did not finish my creamed corn, broccoli, Rice Krispies, or peanut butter sandwiches. And once, when I bit into a candy bar and saw how lumpy it was, how full of secret dark spots and creamy goo, I sacrificed that as well.

I considered that probably nothing would happen to Arnold, that he might not get leprosy, move to Africa and die. And this somehow balanced the dark possibility that he might.

He didn't die right away. In fact, it was some five years later, by which time I had become quite thin. I had stopped eating, not because of Arnold, whom I had long forgotten, but to be fashionably anorexic like all the other thirteen-year old girls who were dieting and finding other ways to suffer as teenagers. I was sitting at the breakfast table, waiting for my mother to finish packing a sack lunch which I always promptly threw away as soon as I rounded the comer. My father was eating with his fingers, dabbing the ends of his bacon into the egg yolks with one hand, while holding the newspaper with the other.

"Oh my, listen to this," he said, still dabbing. And that's when he announced that Arnold Reisman, a boy who lived in our old neighborhood in Oakland, had died of complications from measles. He had just been accepted to Cal State Hayward and was planning to become a podiatrist.

" 'Doctors were at first baffled by the disease, which they report is extremely rare and generally attacks children between the ages of ten and twenty, months to years after they have contracted the measles virus,' " read my father. " 'The boy had had a mild case of the measles when he was twelve, reported his mother. Problems this year were first noticed when the boy developed motor coordination problems and mental lethargy which increased until he fell into a coma. The boy, age seventeen, never regained consciousness.' "

"Didn't you know that boy?" asked my father, and I stood there mute.

"This is shame," said my mother, looking at me. "This is terrible shame."

And I thought she could see through me and that she knew I was the one who had caused Arnold to die. I was terrified.

That night, in my room, I gorged myself. I had stolen a half-gallon of strawberry ice cream from the freezer, and I forced spoonful after spoonful down my throat. And later, for several hours after that, I sat hunched on the fire escape landing outside my bedroom, retching back into the ice cream container. And I remember wondering why it was that eating something good could make me feel so terrible, while vomiting something terrible could make me feel so good.

The thought that I could have caused Arnold's death is not so ridiculous. Perhaps he *was* destined to be my husband. Because I think to myself, even today, how can the world in all its chaos come up with so many coincidences, so many similarities and exact opposites? Why did Arnold single me out for his rubber-band torture? How is it that he contracted measles the same year I began consciously to hate him? And why did I think of Arnold in the first place—when my mother looked in my rice bowl—and then come to hate him so much? Isn't hate merely the result of wounded love?

And even when I can finally dismiss all of this as ridiculous, I still feel that somehow, for the most part, we deserve what we get. I didn't get Arnold. I got Harold.

Harold and I work at the same architectural firm, Livotny & Associates. Only Harold Livotny is a partner and I am an associate. We met eight years ago, before he started Livotny & Associates. I was twenty-eight, a project assistant, and he was thirty-four. We both worked in the restaurant design and development division of Harned Kelley & Davis.

We started seeing each other for working lunches, to talk about the projects, and we would always split the tab right in half, even though I usually ordered only a salad because I have this tendency to gain weight easily. Later, when we started meeting secretly for dinner, we still divided the bill.

And we just continued that way, everything right down the middle. If anything, I encouraged it. Sometimes I insisted on paying for the whole thing: meal, drinks, and tip. And it really didn't bother me.

"Lena, you're really extraordinary," Harold said after six months of dinners, five months of post-prandial lovemaking, and one week of timid and silly love confessions. We were lying in bed, between new purple sheets I had just bought for him. His old set of white sheets was stained in revealing places, not very romantic.

And he nuzzled my neck and whispered, "I don't think I've ever met another woman, who's so together . . . " and I remember feeling a hiccup of fear upon hearing the words "another woman," because I could imagine dozens, hundreds of adoring women eager to buy Harold breakfast, lunch, and dinner to feel the pleasure of his breath on their skin.

Then he bit my neck and said in a rush, "Nor anyone who's as soft and squishy and lovable as you are."

And with that, I swooned inside, caught off balance by this latest revelation of love, wondering how such a remarkable person as Harold could think I was extraordinary.

Now that I'm angry at Harold, it's hard to remember what was so remarkable about him. And I know they're there, the good qualities, because I wasn't that stupid to fall in love with him, to marry him. All I can remember is how awfully lucky I felt, and consequently how worried I was that all this undeserved good fortune would someday slip away. When I fantasized about moving in with him, I also dredged up my deepest fears: that he would tell me I smelled bad, that I had terrible bathroom habits, that my taste in music and television was appalling. I worried that Harold would someday get a new prescription for his glasses and he'd put them on one morning, look me up and down, and say, "Why, gosh, you aren't the girl I thought you were, are you?"

And I think that feeling of fear never left me, that I would be caught someday, exposed as a sham of a woman. But recently, a friend of mine, Rose, who's in therapy now because her marriage has already fallen apart, told me those kinds of thoughts are commonplace in women like us.

"At first I thought it was because I was raised with all this Chinese humility," Rose said. "Or that maybe it was because when you're Chinese you're supposed to accept everything, flow with the Tao and not make waves. But my therapist said, Why do you blame your culture, your ethnicity? And I remembered reading an article about baby boomers, how we expect the best and when we get it we worry that maybe we should have expected more, because it's all diminishing returns after a certain age."

An after my talk with Rose, I felt better about myself and I thought, Of course, Harold and I are equals, in many respects. He's not exactly handsome in the classic sense, although clear-skinned and certainly attractive in that wiry intellectual way. And I may not be a raving beauty, but a lot of women in my aerobics class tell me I'm "exotic" in an unusual way, and they're jealous that my breasts don't sag, now that small breasts are in. Plus, one of my clients said I have incredible vitality and exuberance.

So I think I deserve someone like Harold, and I mean in the good sense and not like bad karma. We're equals. I'm also smart. I have common sense. And I'm intuitive, highly so. I was the one who told Harold he was good enough to start his own firm.

When we were still working at Harned Kelley & Davis, I said, "Harold, this firm knows just what a good deal it has with you. You're the goose who lays the golden egg. If you started your own business today, you'd walk away with more than half of the restaurant clients."

And he said laughing, "Half? Boy, that's love."

And I shouted back, laughing with him, "More than half! You're that good. You're the best there is in restaurant design and development. You know it and I know it, and so do a lot of restaurant developers."

That was the night he decided to "go for it," as he put it, which is a phrase I have personally detested ever since a bank I used to work for adopted the slogan for its employee productivity contest.

But still, I said to Harold, "Harold, I want to help you go for it, too. I mean, you're going to need money to start this business."

He wouldn't hear of taking any money from me, not as a favor, not as a loan, not as an investment, or even as the down payment on a partnership. He said he valued our relationship too much. He didn't want to contaminate it with money. He explained, "I wouldn't want a handout any more than you'd want one. As long as we keep the money thing separate, we'll always be sure of our love for each other."

I wanted to protest. I wanted to say, "Not! I'm not really this way about money, the way we've been doing it. I'm really into giving freely. I want . . . " But I didn't know where to begin. I wanted to ask him who, what woman, had hurt him this way, that made him so scared about accepting love in all its wonderful forms. But then I heard him saying what I'd been waiting to hear for a long, long time.

"Actually, you could help me out if you moved in with me. I mean, that way I could use the five hundred dollars' rent you paid to me ..."

"That's a wonderful idea," I said immediately, knowing how embarrassed he was to have to ask me that way. I was so deliriously happy that it didn't matter that the rent on my studio was really only four hundred thirty-five. Besides, Harold's place was much nicer, a two-bedroom flat with a two-hundred-forty-degree view of the bay. It was worth the extra money, no matter whom I shared the place with.

So within the year, Harold and I quit Harned Kelley & Davis and he started Livotny & Associates, and I went to work there as a project coordinator. And no, he didn't get half the restaurant clients of Harned Kelley & Davis. In fact, Harned Kelley & Davis threatened to sue if he walked away with even one client over the next year. So I gave him pep talks in the evening when he was discouraged. I told him how he should do more avant-garde thematic restaurant design, to differentiate himself from the other firms.

"Who needs another brass and oakwood bar and grill?" I said. "Who wants another pasta place in sleek Italian modern? How many places can you go to with police cars lurching out of the walls? This town is chockablock with restaurants that are just clones of the same old themes. You can find a niche. Do something different every time. Get the Hong Kong investors who are willing to sink some bucks into American ingenuity."

He gave me his adoring smile, the one that said, "I love it when you're so naive." And I adored his looking at me like that.

So I stammered out my love. "You ... you ... could do new theme eating places ... a ... a ... Home on the Range! All the home-cooked mom stuff, mom at the kitchen range with a gingham apron and mom waitresses leaning over telling you to finish your soup.

"And maybe ... maybe you could do a novel-menu restaurant ... foods from fiction ... sandwiches from Lawrence Sanders murder mysteries, just desserts from Nora Ephron's *Heartburn.* And something else with a magic theme, or jokes and gags, or ..."

Harold actually listened to me. He took those ideas and he applied them in an educated, methodical way. He made it happen. But still, I remember, it was my idea.

And today Livotny & Associates is a growing firm of twelve full-time people, which specializes in thematic restaurant design, what I still like to call "theme eating." Harold is the concept man, the chief architect, the designer, the person who makes the final sales presentation to a new client. I work under the interior designer, because, as Harold explains, it would not seem fair to the other employees if he promoted me just because we are now marriedthat was five years ago, two years after he started Livotny & Associates. And even though I am very good at what I do, I have never been formally trained in this area. When I was majoring in Asian–American studies, I took only one relevant course, in theater set design, for a college production of *Madame Butterfly*.

At Livotny & Associates, I procure the theme elements. For one restaurant called The Fisherman's Tale, one of my prized findings was a yellow varnished wood boat stenciled with the name "Overbored," and I was the one who thought the menus should dangle from miniature fishing poles, and the napkins be printed with rulers that have inches translating into feet. For a Lawrence of Arabia deli called Tray Sheik, I was the one who thought the place should have a bazaar effect, and I found the replicas of cobras lying on fake Hollywood boulders.

I love my work when I don't think about it too much. And when I do think about it, how much I get paid, how hard I work, how fair Harold is to everybody except me, I get upset.

So really, we're equals, except that Harold makes about seven times more than what I make. He knows this, too, because he signs my monthly check, and then I deposit it into my separate checking account.

Lately, however, this business about being equals started to bother me. It's been on my mind, only I didn't really know it. I just felt a little uneasy about *something*. And then about a week ago, it all became clear. I was putting the breakfast dishes away and Harold was warming up the car so we could go to work. And I saw the newspaper spread open on the kitchen counter, Harold's glasses on top, his favorite coffee mug with the chipped handle off to the side. And for some reason, seeing all these little domestic signs of familiarity, our daily ritual, made me swoon inside. But it was as if I were seeing Harold the first time we made love, this feeling of surrendering everything to him, with abandon, without caring what I got in return.

And when I got into the car, I still had the glow of that feeling and I touched his hand and said, "Harold, I love you." And he looked in the rearview mirror, backing up the car, and said, "I love you, too. Did you lock the door?" And just like that, I started to think, It's just not enough.

Harold jingles the car keys and says, "I'm going down the hill to buy stuff for dinner. Steaks okay? Want anything special?"

"We're out of rice," I say, discreetly nodding toward my mother, whose back is turned to me. She's looking out the kitchen window, at the trellis of bougainvillea. And then Harold is out the door and I hear the deep rumble of the car and then the sound of crunching gravel as he drives away.

My mother and I are alone in the house. I start to water the plants. She is standing on her tiptoes, peering at a list stuck on our refrigerator door.

The list says "Lena" and "Harold" and under each of our names are things we've bought and how much they cost:

Lena		*Harold*	
Chicken, veg., bread, Broccoli, shampoo, beer	$19.63	Garage stuff	$25.35
		Bathroom stuff	$5.41
Maria (clean + tip)	$65	Car stuff	$6.57
Groceries (see shop list)	$55.15	Light Fixtures	$87.26
Petunias, potting soil	$14.11	Road gravel	$19.99
Photo developing	$13.83	Gas	$22.00
		Car Smog Check	$35
		Movies & Dinner	$65
		Ice Cream	$4.50

The way things are going this week, Harold's already spent over a hundred dollars more, so I'll owe him around fifty from my checking account.

"What is this writing?" asks my mother in Chinese.

"Oh, nothing really. Just things we share," I say as casually as I can.

And she looks at me and frowns but doesn't say anything. She goes back to reading the list, this time more carefully, moving her finger down each item.

And I feel embarrassed, knowing what she's seeing. I'm relieved that she doesn't see the other half of it, the discussions. Through countless talks, Harold and I reached an understanding about not including personal things like "mascara," and "shaving lotion," "hair spray" or "Bic shavers," "tampons," or "athlete's foot powder."

When we got married at city hall, he insisted on paying the fee. I got my friend Robert to take photos. We held a party at our apartment and everybody brought champagne. And when we bought the house, we agreed that I should pay only a percentage of the mortgage based on what I earn and what he earns, and that I should own an equivalent percentage of community property; this is written in our prenuptial agreement. Since Harold pays more, he had the deciding vote on how the house should look. It is sleek, spare, and what he calls "fluid," nothing to disrupt the line, meaning none of my cluttered look. As for vacations, the one we choose together is fifty-fifty. The others Harold pays for, with the understanding that it's a birthday or Christmas present, or an anniversary gift.

And we've had philosophical arguments over things that have gray borders, like my birth control pills, or dinners at home when we entertain people who are really his clients or my old friends from college, or food magazines that I subscribe to but he also reads only because he's bored, not because he would have chosen them for himself.

And we still argue about Mirugai, *the* cat—not our cat, or my cat, but *the* cat that was his gift to me for my birthday last year.

"This, you do not share!" exclaims my mother in an astonished voice. And I am startled, thinking she had read my thoughts about Mirugai. But then I see she is pointing to "ice cream" on Harold's list. My mother must remember the incident on the fire escape landing, where she found me, shivering and exhausted, sitting next to that container of regurgitated ice cream. I could never stand the stuff after that. And then I am startled once again to realize that Harold has never noticed that I don't eat any of the ice cream he brings home every Friday evening.

"Why you do this?"

My mother has a wounded sound in her voice, as if I had put the list up to hurt her. I think how to explain this, recalling the words Harold and I have used with each other in the past: "So we can eliminate false dependencies . . . be equals . . . love without obligation . . . " But these are words she could never understand.

So instead I tell my mother this: "I don't really know. It's something we started before we got married. And for some reason we never stopped."

When Harold returns from the store, he starts the charcoal. I unload the groceries, marinate the steaks, cook the rice, and set the table. My mother sits on a stool at the granite counter, drinking from a mug of coffee I've poured for her. Every few minutes she wipes the bottom of the mug with a tissue she keeps stuffed in her sweater sleeve.

During dinner, Harold keeps the conversation going. He talks about the plans for the house: the skylights, expanding the deck, planting flower beds of tulips and crocuses, clearing the poison oak, adding another wing, building a Japanese-style tile bathroom. And then he clears the table and starts stacking the plates in the dishwasher.

"Who's ready for dessert?" he asks, reaching into the freezer.

"I'm full," I say.

"Lena cannot eat ice cream," says my mother. "So it seems. She's always on a diet.

No, she never eat it. She doesn't like."

And now Harold smiles and looks at me puzzled, expecting me to translate what my mother has said.

"It's true," I say evenly. "I've hated ice cream almost all my life."

Harold looks at me, as if I, too, were speaking Chinese and he could not understand.

"I guess I assumed you were just trying to lose weight. . . . Oh well."

"She become so thin now you cannot see her," says my mother. "She like a ghost, disappear."

"That's right! Christ, that's great," exclaims Harold, laughing, relieved in thinking my mother is graciously trying to rescue him.

After dinner, I put clean towels on the bed in the guest room. My mother is sitting on the bed. The room has Harold's minimalist look to it: the twin bed with plain white sheets and white blanket, polished wood floors, a bleached oakwood chair, and nothing on the slanted gray walls.

The only decoration is an odd-looking piece right next to the bed: an end table made out of a slab of unevenly cut marble and thin crisscrosses of black lacquer wood for the legs. My mother puts her handbag on the table and the cylindrical black vase on top starts to wobble. The freesias in the vase quiver.

"Careful, it's not too sturdy," I say. The table is a poorly designed piece that Harold made in his student days. I've always wondered why he's so proud of it. The lines are clumsy. It doesn't bear any of the traits of "fluidity" that are so important to Harold these days.

"What use for?" asks my mother, jiggling the table with her hand. "You put something else on top, everything fall down. *Chunwang chihan.*"

I leave my mother in her room and go back downstairs. Harold is opening the windows to let the night air in. He does this every evening.

"I'm cold," I say.

"What's that?"

"Could you close the windows, please."

He looks at me, sighs and smiles, pulls the windows shut, and then sits down cross-legged on the floor and flips open a magazine. I'm sitting on the sofa, seething, and I don't know why. It's not that Harold has done anything wrong. Harold is just Harold.

And before I even do it, I know I'm starting a fight that is bigger than I know how to handle. But I do it anyway. I go to the refrigerator and I cross out "ice cream" on Harold's side of the list.

"What's going on here?"

"I just don't think you should get credit for *your* ice cream anymore."

He shrugs his shoulders, amused. "Suits me."

"Why do you have to be so goddamn fair!" I shout.

Harold puts his magazine down, now wearing his open-mouthed exasperated look. "What is this? Why don't you say what's really the matter?"

"I don't know ... I don't know. Everything ... the way we account for everything. What we share. What we don't share. I'm so tired of it, adding things up, subtracting, making it come out even. I'm sick of it."

"You were the one who wanted the cat."

"What are you talking about?"

"All right. If you think I'm being unfair about the exterminators, we'll both pay for it."

"That's not the point!"

"Then tell me, *please,* what is the point?"

I start to cry, which I know Harold hates. It always makes him uncomfortable, angry. He thinks it's manipulative. But I can't help it, because I realize now that I don't know what the point of this argument is. Am I asking Harold to support me? Am I asking to pay less than half? Do I really think we should stop accounting for everything? Wouldn't we continue to tally things up in our head? Wouldn't Harold wind up paying more? And then wouldn't I feel worse, less than equal? Or maybe we shouldn't have gotten married in the first place. Maybe Harold is a bad man. Maybe I've made him this way.

None of it seems right. Nothing makes sense. I can admit to nothing and I am in complete despair.

"I just think we have to change things," I say when I think I can control my voice. Only the rest comes out like whining. "We need to think about what our marriage is really based on . . . not this balance sheet, who owes who what."

"Shit," Harold says. And then he sighs and leans back, as if he were thinking about this. Finally he says in what sounds like a hurt voice, "Well, I know our marriage is based on a lot more than a balance sheet. A lot more. And if you don't then I think you should think about what else you want, before you change things."

And now I don't know what to think. What am I saying? What's he saying? We sit in the room, not saying anything. The air feels muggy. I look out the window, and out in the distance is the valley beneath us, a sprinkling of thousands of lights shimmering in the summer fog. And then I hear the sound of glass shattering, upstairs, and a chair scrapes across a wood floor.

Harold starts to get up, but I say, "No, I'll go see."

The door is open, but the room is dark, so I call out, "Ma?"

I see it right away: the marble end table collapsed on top of its spindly black legs. Off to the side is the black vase, the smooth cylinder broken in half, the freesias strewn in a puddle of water.

And then I see my mother sitting by the open window, her dark silhouette against the night sky. She turns around in her chair, but I can't see her face.

"Fallen down," she says simply. She doesn't apologize.

"It doesn't matter," I say, and I start to pick up the broken glass shards. "I knew it would happen."

"Then why you don't stop it?" asks my mother.

And it's such a simple question.

Questions on The Joy Luck Club

1. Does assuming that things in marriage are done with some expectation of reward create the kind of dysfunctional relationship Amy Tan writes about? But should household services remain uncompensated (financially) when the equivalent market services are compensated?

2. Does a contractual approach to "winding up" a marriage exacerbate the problems posed by the preceding questions? How else would you approach them?

A final normative problem with family contracts in the family setting is that contracting may encourage people to think purposively and deliberately about their relations instead of living those relations freely and spontaneously. This point, of course, will be persuasive only to the extent that you find the underlying view of marriage as a place for spontaneity persuasive. Once again, Professor Shultz provides the contrary argument: "When individuals select goals, specify the type of behavior necessary to reach those goals, and identify the rewards for the undertaking, they achieve both motivation and a sense of potency." She adds that doing so "has the additional benefit of making those dimensions of a relationship clear to each individual." On the other hand, does talking about and planning for marriage contingencies necessarily improve the quality of the relationship, and in any event is contract the best way of encouraging such discussion? Consider too the abolition of the action for breach of promise of marriage. It was abolished because it was thought undesirable to compel people to stick to decisions about how to live their intimate lives and because the action seemed to treat marriage as a commercial rather than a personal relationship (and for several other reasons as well). Do those arguments apply equally to contractualizing marriage?

C. THE USEFULNESS OF CONTRACT LAW THINKING: SOME CLOSING CONSIDERATIONS

Lady Bracknell: As a matter of form, Mr. Worthing, I had better ask you if Miss Cardew has any little fortune?

Jack: Oh, about a hundred and thirty thousand pounds in the Funds. That is all. Good-bye, Lady Bracknell. . . .

*Lady Bracknell (***sitting down again***): A moment, Mr. Worthing. A hundred and thirty thousand pounds! . . . Miss Cardew seems to me a most attractive young lady, now that I look at her. Few girls of the present day have any really solid qualities, any of the qualities that last, and improve with time. We live, I regret to say, in an age of surfaces.*

Oscar Wilde
The Importance of Being Earnest

We have considered several criticisms of the contractualization of family law. But a full-fledged evaluation of contractualization needs to evaluate all the criticisms and all the benefits of contractualization as a group. In this section, though, we provide you with several ways to approach that evaluation.

The first approach asks how great the benefits of family contracting are likely to be for the whole set of possible contracting families. The categories of contracting families include: (1) families that will have no serious disputes even without a contract, (2) families that can solve their disputes relatively easily even without a contract, (3) families that can't solve their disputes satisfactorily even with a contract, (4) families for whom contract remedies can provide no satisfactory relief, (5) families for whom the attempt to negotiate or enforce a contract will exacerbate rather than diminish conflict, (6) families for whom conflict will be reduced by the availability of contract, and (7) families who will be able to reach a goal because of the availability of contract that they would not otherwise have been able to reach. What proportion of the total number of married couples is likely to be in each group? How much benefit or detriment from the availability of contract will each group experience? Are there categories not listed that ought to be? Will members of each group enter into contracts even if they are available? Can you work out from these calculations a cost/benefit analysis of the contractualization of family law?

A second approach to evaluating marital contracts begins with the assumption that a contract centrally provides the parties some certainty about their future. How far can (and do) marital contracts provide such certainty? To a small extent, because many important subjects fall outside the scope of contracting? To a small extent, because the scope of contracting is uncertain? To a small extent, because courts can alter or overturn contracts they regard as unfair procedurally or substantively? To a small extent, because the matters such contracts regulate are so complicated and so subject to change over the long periods the marriage may last that contract cannot provide certainty? To a small extent, because contract law has become more accommodating of attempts to limit the enforceability of contracts? To a reasonable extent, because no contract ever provides real certainty? To a reasonable extent, because marital contracts may be drafted narrowly enough to provide certainty at least in a few specific but troublesome areas?

A third approach to evaluating contract in family law asks whether there are good reasons to limit the range of family contracts. Two types of arguments present themselves. The first has to do with limiting the freedom to contract to protect people who are not parties to the contract but are affected by it. That argument has two forms. One suggests limiting these contracts for a classic but narrow reason—the protection of third parties who are ill-situated to protect their own interests. In the family context this will primarily be the children of the marriage. The state surely has the authority and even the duty to protect children. But, generally, if parents make decisions for their children without entering into contracts, the state will not challenge those decisions unless they constitute abuse or neglect as the law defines those wrongs. Why the difference? In this respect, think again about *Kilgrow*. The second, more controversial form of the "third party" argument holds that society itself has a "third party" interest in the contract. This argument largely restates the many propositions about the state's interest in marriage which you now know.

The second type of argument about restricting the range of marital contracting justifies restrictions not because contracts may harm third parties but because they may harm the spouses. This argument seeks to prevent harm to "the marriage," and it thus incorporates many of the arguments we earlier referred to as making normative objections to the contractualization of family law. This argument also seeks to prevent harm to the individual partners of the marriage, and it thus goes to some of the problems of vulnerability we discussed in contrasting business and family contracts. In either form, the argument raises the whole set of classic arguments about paternalism.

A fourth approach to evaluating the contractualization of family law asks whether family law might secure some of the advantages of business contracting without its attendant disadvantages. The mildest version of this approach asks whether contracts that are legally unenforceable might be worth encouraging. After all, even businesses sometimes enter into contracts which they know are unlikely to be enforced or even enforceable: "Notwithstanding practical difficulties of securing legal enforcement, ... a contractual provision also has value simply as a communication of understanding between the parties as to their mutual rights and duties." Charles J. Goetz and Robert E. Scott, *Principles of Relational Contracts*, 67 Va L Rev 1089, 1117 (1981). Professor Shultz makes an argument something like this with marital contracts specifically in mind: "The actionable nature of promises is not the main part of their function any more than law is encompassed by litigation or court decision. Rather, the primary function of contracts is the structuring of private exchange relationships projected over time." Under such a proposal, lawyers might make their services available to clients who wished help in sorting out their affairs and who sought the experience of someone experienced in counselling.

A broader version of the attempt to find justifiable forms of contract in family law suggests contracts should be enforceable in those areas closest to business contracts. This fits the historical (and, to a large extent, the contemporary) treatment of contracts, since the main present (and past) area of marital contracting is marital finances. These areas are easier to contract about because the problem of monitoring performance is greatly reduced (assuming that the subject of the contract is the division of property on death or divorce) and because enforceable remedies are easier to come by, since money damages generally suffice. This is not to say the proposal is without difficulties. One might ask, for example, whether these areas are really subject to more easily articulated standards and whether these areas can be separated from the rest of marital life.

Yet another version of the attempt to achieve the advantages of business contracts without their disadvantages would call for enforcing contracts intended less to work out the relations between the spouses and more to establish the terms of the relationship between the couple on one hand and the world on the other. On this view, antenuptial agreements might be defended on the grounds that they allow the parties to choose for themselves what sort of marital property regime they prefer while they are married, and divorce settlements might be defended as a way of keeping a court from imposing its will on the parties when they separate. See, e.g., Margaret F. Brinig and June Carbone, *The Reliance Interest in Marriage and Divorce*, 62 Tulane L Rev 855 (1988).

Still another way to secure the blessings without the banes of contract might be to impose a statutory limit of, say, five years on all marital contracts, so that a contract would have to be regularly renegotiated to endure throughout the marriage. This would greatly reduce the problems of the duration of the contract and the complexity of its subject matter and would diminish the risks run by the weaker bargainer. By the same token, though, this would reduce the usefulness of the contract as a way of controlling the uncertainties of marriage and would reduce the attractiveness of the contract to the stronger bargainer. (This proposal is analogous to the time limitations some states put on covenants that run with the land and would be imposed for much the same reasons.)

Another version of the attempt to secure contract's benefits in a safer form would devise form contracts to suit the range of standard marital situations. Thus contracts might be constructed for spouses who favored the traditional pattern, who favored one of several non-traditional patterns, who were concerned about the perils of marriage between a wealthy and a poor person, and so on. These form contracts would have several advantages. They would be safe harbors, since there would not be doubt about their enforceability. They would reduce the costs of contracting, since extensive legal advice would generally not be needed to draft and interpret them. They would reduce the risks of unequal bargaining power, since they would be written to assure fairness between the parties. If a choice among the standard contracts were made mandatory on marriage, many issues of alimony, marital property, and child custody might be simplified. All these advantages, of course, come at the cost of flexibility, but only if couples are limited to the standard forms. In short, this proposal would institutionalize and make more palatable Professor Rehbinder's idea that freedom today consists in the ability to choose among social roles.

We have put off until last the most significant current method of having the cake of contract and eating it too. That method is to try to avert the risks of marital contracting through judicial supervision of each contract. To evaluate the method, we need first to ask what level of judicial scrutiny is necessary. How serious are the risks that contracting couples run? As we have said before, the issues over which the parties have bargained are extraordinarily important, involving as they do the heart of people's emotional lives and their entire fortunes. But does this mean the courts should supervise contracting particularly strictly or that courts should be particularly reluctant to intervene?

Courts have two methods of ensuring the fairness of marital contracts. The first is to ask whether the contract is "substantively" fair. This question presents the problem of standards, which is ironic, since a major justification for the contractualization of family law is to relieve the state of having to devise standards for judging the fairness of marital arrangements. For perspective on the problem, we will again compare the business and family laws of fairness.

The classic assumption of contract law is that courts will not look into the adequacy of consideration. One of the essential attractions of contract is that the people who best know their own wants decide what they are. If that principle works in business, where the market helps establish a relatively objective value, shouldn't it work even better in the less orderly world of family life?

One response to that question is to recall that even in business law there is the doctrine of unconscionability. Section 2–302 (1) of the UCC provides: "If the court as a matter of law finds the contract or any clause of the contract to have been unconscionable at the time it was made the court may refuse to enforce the contract...." But what does this mean? One classic judicial statement of its meaning reads, "Unconscionability has generally been recognized to include an absence of meaningful choice on the part of one of the parties together with contract terms which are unreasonably favorable to the other party." *Williams v. Walker–Thomas Furniture Co.*, 350 F2d 445, 449 (DC Cir 1965). Does this help? What does an "absence of meaningful choice" mean in the marital context? How are we to solve the standards problem of deciding when terms are "unreasonably favorable" to one spouse? Can we ask whether one party has paid the other too high a "price"? Even in the commercial context, "courts have avoided square holdings that an excessive price without more is unconscionable." E. Allan Farnsworth, *Contracts* 312 (Little, Brown, 1982). And even if excessive price is the standard, how is excessiveness to be determined without a market? "The idea of reviewing a bargain for fairness of terms implies that an objective value can be placed upon a bargained-for performance." Melvin Aaron Eisenberg, *The Bargain Principle and Its Limits*, 95 Harv L Rev 741, 745 (1982). Can this be done in the marital context?

One answer to that question is that courts measure fairness in non-market situations all the time and thus should be able to do it in marital situations. As Professor Eisenberg notes, "off-market contracts between a beneficiary and his trustee or between a fiduciary and his corporation are customarily subject to review for objective fairness." And speaking specifically about marital contracts, Professor Sharp writes, "[A]t a practical or functional level, there does appear to be general agreement that unfair marital contracts can be identified: in a broad sense, unfair agreements are those in which one party has received disproportionately more or less than what a court would have been likely to have ordered absent agreement between the parties." But if an unconscionable contract is one whose terms differ from those a court would have required, why bother to have contracts? Professor Sharp answers: "The point is not to preclude parties from contracting in such a fashion but to require that significant disparities in benefits or burdens be explained to the satisfaction of the court before it could approve the agreement." But does this still limit freedom to what a court thinks is reasonable? One court's answer (in the context of alimony but not of marital property) seems to be yes: "In our view, unconscionability in the context of the [Uniform Marriage and Divorce] Act as applied to a maintenance agreement exists when enforcement of the terms of the agreement results in a spouse having insufficient property to provide for his reasonable needs and who is otherwise unable to support himself through appropriate employment." *Newman v. Newman*, 653 P2d 728, 735 (Colo 1982). (As you may recall, the court is restating the UMDA alimony standard.)

There is also the question whether unconscionability is to be determined as of the time of the contract or as of the time of enforcement. If the former time is chosen, unanticipated circumstances may lead to untoward results. If the latter is chosen, much of the benefit of entering into a contract (making the future more certain and allocating risks between the parties) is diminished.

Thwarted in deciding whether a contract's terms are "unreasonably favorable" to one spouse, courts have looked not just to the contract's "substantive" character, but to the "procedural" character. What problems has this inquiry encountered?

Investigations into the procedural fairness of marital contracts are (as you will remember) generally informed by the doctrine that spouses and prospective spouses are in a confidential relation and thus obliged to act fairly, most importantly to disclose their financial situation fully. Does this ensure the fairness of marital contracts? There are several reasons to doubt it. In some jurisdictions the existence of the confidential relationship is a question of fact, and in some jurisdictions the confidential relationship ends when the marriage begins to disintegrate (as evidenced, for instance, by one party's filing for divorce or even saying the spouses should separate). These rules pose particular problems for separation agreements.

The confidential relationship doctrine rests on ideas about what one spouse owes another. It also rests on the fear that the parties have unequal bargaining power. But can we tell when that is true? Professor Mnookin says, "I am skeptical about our ability to identify when parties have equal bargaining power." He observes that bargaining power is affected by many factors whose net effects may be imponderable, including the parties' legal entitlements, their preferences, their attitudes toward risk, their differential ability to withstand the emotional and economic costs of negotiations, and their skill as negotiators. Robert H. Mnookin, *Divorce Bargaining: The Limits on Private Ordering*, 18 U Mich J L Ref 1015, 1024–26 (1985).

Another limitation of the confidential relationship doctrine (particularly for separation agreements) is, Professor Sharp argues, that "judicial review requirements [for separation agreements] as currently applied by courts fail ... to provide a meaningful review for either substantive or procedural fairness. The review process is almost wholly perfunctory in most states.... [I]t is extremely rare for a court to undertake sua sponte any review that would result in modification of any proposed agreement." She quotes one appellate court describing how separation agreements are often reviewed: "[T]he trial court is presented with an agreement which, on its face at least, appears to be reasonable. Since the dissolution proceeding is 'uncontested,' the parties offer no proof of economic circumstances. Although the trial court could request such proof on its own motion, [the statute] does not require it to do so. Such a request is apparently rare, perhaps because the court views the case as agreed. The trial court then approves the agreement as conscionable without really knowing the underlying facts." Might antenuptial agreements too often escape judicial scrutiny for practical if not for doctrinal reasons? For example, suppose a couple signed an agreement greatly disadvantageous to one spouse and operated on its basis for many years. Might the disadvantaged spouse then find that the law provided no adequate way of undoing the agreement or that going to court to challenge it is too expensive economically or emotionally?

Probably the most important current attempts to ensure procedural, and thus substantive, fairness, is that the parties fully disclose their financial situations. Can this requirement reliably achieve its objectives? This is unfortunately little discussed. Courts and commentators seem to assume disclosure works: "[I]t seems likely that parties who were fully aware of their rights and who were not subjected to unfair persuasion tactics would agree to accept disproportionate benefits and burdens only in the rarest of circumstances." Sharp. Really?

Requiring disclosure is certainly a common way to seek contractual fairness. "One of the oldest and most prevalent methods of regulating consumer transactions has been to require the seller to disclose to his consumer buyer various types of information about their contractual transaction.... The common law of misrepresentation and public law concerning deceptive advertising ... at times have been interpreted to require the disclosure of contractual information." Many installment-sales acts require disclosure of information, and so do, e.g., the UCC, truth-in-lending laws, and truth-in-packaging laws, to say nothing of the securities laws. Nevertheless, there is substantial evidence that the technique works badly. "Critics argue [that] ... the disclosed information either is not learned by consumers, or if it is, it is not used by them in reaching purchase decisions." William C. Whitford, *The Functions of*

Disclosure Regulation in Consumer Transactions, 1973 Wis L Rev 400, 403–04. Professor Whitford concludes that truth-in-lending legislation has only modestly enhanced consumer's awareness of percentage rates and little affected their shopping and that its few benefits were concentrated among those who need them least—the rich—and were practically invisible among those who need them most—the poor.

Might disclosure might work better in the marital context? What might deter a prospective spouse from considering a disclosure carefully? By the time the disclosure is made, is the couple already committed to the marriage and to the basic terms of the agreement? Do most couples believe that divorce is unlikely and that disclosures (and for that matter the entire contract) are therefore irrelevant? Are there people who, as Professor Eisenberg says, "may be of average intelligence and yet [who] may lack the aptitude, experience, or judgmental ability to make a deliberative and well-informed judgment concerning the desirability of entering into a given complex transaction"? Would a requirement that each party be represented by counsel solve each of these problems?

D. THE FUNCTIONS OF FAMILY LAW AND CONTRACT

> *But tho' this self-interested commerce of men begins to take place, and to predominate in society, it does not entirely abolish the more generous and noble intercourse of friendship and good offices. I may still do services to such persons as I love, and am more particularly acquainted with, without any prospect of advantage; and they may make me a return in the same manner, without any view but that of recompensing my past services. In order, therefore, to distinguish those two different sorts of commerce, the interested and the disinterested, there is a certain form of words invented for the former, by which we bind ourselves to the performance of any action.*
>
> David Hume
> *A Treatise of Human Nature*

We will close our study of the contractualization of family law by encouraging you to speculate about how it might serve the five functions of family law.

(1) The Protective Function

There is likely to be a tension between the protective function and contract law. The gravamen of contract law is to give people freedom to work out their lives for themselves. The impulse of the protective function is to prevent people from finding themselves in distressful circumstances. The more contractual liberty you have, the more vulnerable you are likely to be. Since marital contracts can dispose of the entire present and even future wealth of the parties as well as the custody of their children, the misery the protective function intends to prevent can be severe.

There is a continuum of ways of dealing with the tension between the protective function and contract. At one end of the continuum lies the decision that (except at the extremes—say, spouse or child abuse) the liberty interest in contract wholly outweighs the security interest in protection. Such a conclusion rests on familiar rationales, including the standards and enforcement arguments. At the other end of the continuum is the proposition that protecting weak people and the family as a social institution is so urgent that no contracting should be allowed. This policy can be implemented by substituting for individual contracts governmentally imposed rules designed to do justice in the generality of cases. This is in effect what marital property systems have historically attempted to do, insofar as it has not been possible to contract out of them. The policy favoring the protective function over contract can also be implemented by having courts decide case by case how to resolve disputes between couples. In the middle of the continuum lie attempts to accommodate contract and the protective function. These attempts are likely to permit spouses to contract but to give courts power to supervise and over-ride their contracts. This is what both statutes and case law intend to do in developing standards of procedural and substantive unconscionability. A more indirect technique is to write standards that are as clear and fair as possible for courts deciding divorce cases where there are no contracts that bargaining spouses would have a benchmark of fairness and could be made aware that they have certain minimal entitlements which they need not yield.

(2) The Facilitative Function

Much of the justification for the contractualization of family law is, of course, that it serves family law's facilitative function. You have just finished reading a chapter investigating the extent to which contractualization does. Therefore, all we need do here is to remind ourselves of that discussion. Doing so should remind us of at least two major questions about contract and the facilitative function: Does contract actually serve a function in marital situations? Is serving this function worth the costs contract imposes on the other functions of family law?

(3) The Arbitral Function

The arbitral function is concerned with resolving intra-familial disputes. Does contractualizing family law promote that goal? The argument that it does reasons that the standards, information, and enforcement problems that normally plague the arbitral function can be solved by contracts, since the parties then provide both standards and information and since the parties are made more amenable to judicial resolution of their disputes by having consented and contributed to it. There are, however, two arguments that measures other than contractualization are preferable means of serving the arbitral function. One reasons that it is better normatively and easier practically to resolve family disputes on the basis of fixed rules. The other reasons that there are many kinds of family disputes which the law should not become engaged in at all, but which should be left to the family to work out as it decides through non-legal means. This latter argument, in other words, amounts to an argument that the proper scope of the arbitral function is limited.

(4) The Channelling Function

Insofar as the channelling function directs people toward certain specific kinds of property or familial relations, a pure contracting system serves the channelling function rather weakly. Courts have some leverage in interpreting contracts, but channelling primarily shapes behavior before disputes come to the legal system. However, a modified contracting system might adopt the proposal we discussed earlier of setting up form contracts which, while giving people a choice of channels, would nevertheless steer people toward a limited set of them. A contracting system that relied heavily on default rules might perform the same function: "Once the underlying rules policing the bargaining process have been specified, contract rules serve as standard or common risk allocations that can be varied by the individual agreement of particular parties. These rules serve the important purpose of saving most bargainers the cost of negotiating a tailor-made arrangement." Charles J. Goetz and Robert E. Scott, *Principles of Relational Contracts*, 67 Va L Rev 1089, 1090 (1981).

On the other hand, the contractualization of family law could be seen as a way of channelling people toward certain attitudes toward marriage and toward certain ways of conducting oneself within marriage. This is the argument we investigated when we noted that many proponents of contractualization see it as promoting various non-traditional views of marriage.

(5) The Expressive Function

The expressive function can be served by both a contract system and a non-contract system. The difference will lie in the messages expressed. Given all that we considered in evaluating the contractualization of family law, what would the message of the contract system be? Consider particularly the issues raised by our discussion of the "normative" suitability of contract thinking, by the argument that contractualization promotes certain views of marriage, and by the contention that contractualization promotes a neutral view of how marriage should be organized. What would the message of discouraging marital contracting be? What would the message of encouraging it be? Of requiring it? How clearly would those messages be perceived? Will there be any expressive effect of contractualization if spouses generally decline to contract? Will the law's policy regarding contract matter if most people don't know about that policy until divorce?

BIBLIOGRAPHY

Contract Law Generally. Two thoughtful views of the modern state of contract law include Grant Gilmore, *The Death of Contract* (Ohio St U Press, 1974); and Ian R. Macneil, *The New Social Contract: An Inquiry into Modern Contractual Relations* (Yale U Press, 1980). An excellent study of many of the broader issues we have been discussing is P.S. Atiyah, *The Rise and Fall of Freedom of Contract* (Oxford U Press,

1979). For a first-rate summary of Max Weber's view of the role of contract in modern law and society, see Anthony T. Kronman, *Max Weber* chapter 5 (Stanford U Press, 1983). As you will have gathered, Weber's own ideas are to be found in Max Weber, 2 *Economy and Society: An Outline of Interpretive Sociology* 666–752 (Guenther Roth and Claus Wittich, eds, 1978). But while Weber was capable of writing clearly and forcefully (you may at some point already have read and enjoyed *The Protestant Ethic And The Spirit Of Capitalism*), his work on the sociology of law was incomplete when he died, and it can be pretty rough going. Kronman, however, makes Weber's ideas as lucid as they can be made. For an updated and international view of the argument made in Macaulay's article, see Stewart Macaulay, *Elegant Models, Empirical Pictures and the Complexities of Contract*, 11 L & Soc Rev 507 (1977).

Contract and Status. Perhaps the best treatment of Maine's generalization and its relevance to family law is Howard O. Hunter, *An Essay on Contract and Status: Race, Marriage, and the Meretricious Spouse*, 64 Va L Rev 1039 (1978). For an argument preferring status to contract in family law, see Margaret F. Brinig, *From Contract to Covenant* (Harv U Press 2000).

Issues of Contract in Family Law Today. For a description of the law currently governing antenuptial agreements, see J. Thomas Oldham, *Premarital Contracts are now Enforceable, Unless . . .*, 21 Houston L Rev 757 (1984); Judith T. Younger, *Perspectives on Antenuptial Agreements*, 40 Rutgers L Rev 1059 (1988); and Ann L. Estin, *Law and Obligation*, 43 Wm & Mary L Rev 989 (1995). For a review of the law governing separation agreements and an argument that law inadequately protects the parties to such contracts, see Sally Burnett Sharp, *Fairness Standards and Separation Agreements: A Word of Caution on Contractual Freedom*, 132 U Pa L Rev 1399 (1984). For extended arguments in favor of the contractualization of family law, see Marjorie Maguire Schultz, *Contractual Ordering of Marriage: A New Model for State Policy*, 70 Cal L Rev 204 (1982); Michael J. Trebilcock and Rosemin Keshvani, *The Role of Private Ordering in Family Law: A Law and Economics Perspective*, 41 U Toronto L J 533 (1991); Lenore J. Weitzman, *The Marriage Contract: Spouses, Lovers, and the Law* (Free Press, 1981); Lenore J. Weitzman, *Legal Regulation of Marriage: Tradition and Change*, 62 Cal L Rev 1169 (1974). Although it is now out of date, Banks McDowell, *Contracts in the Family*, 65 BU L Rev 43 (1965), is still worth reading for some thoughtful comments on contract in the family context. Brian Bix, *Bargaining in the Shadow of Love: The Enforcement of Premarital Agreements and How We Think About Marriage*, 40 Wm & Mary L Rev 145 (1998), suggests that many premarital agreements should be enforceable. For an argument that antenuptial contracting may occasionally be destructive of marriage itself, see Judith T. Younger, *Perspectives on Antenuptial Agreements*, 40 Rutgers L Rev 1059 (1988). Jana B. Singer, *The Privatization of Family Law*, 1992 Wis L Rev 1445 (1992), argues that contract may prove transition mechanisms between an older view of the family and a more just and equal society.

Bargaining in Family Settings. Amy L. Wax, *Bargaining in the Shadow of the Market: Is There a Future for Egalitarian Marriage?*, 84 Va L Rev 509 (1998), argues that women are likely to be in their strongest bargaining position before marriage because they have not yet made sacrifices for the marriage that weaken that bargain position. In Shelly J. Lundberg and Robert Pollak, *Separate Spheres Bargaining and the Marriage Market*, 101 J Pol Econ 998 (1993), two labor economists develop a model for how couples behave when they disagree.

Law and Society and Family Contracting. As our discussion suggests, one of the most striking accomplishments of the law-and-society school has been its demonstration that the law often has much less effect on people's behavior than lawyers like to believe. For examples of and discussion about that literature, see Robert C. Ellickson, *Order Without Law: How Neighbors Settle Disputes* (Harv U Press, 1991); Lynn A. Baker and Robert E. Emery, *When Every Relationship Is Above Average: Perceptions and Expectations of Divorce at the Time of Marriage*, 17 L & Human Beh 439 (1993); Carl E. Schneider, *Rethinking Alimony: Marital Decisions and Moral Discourse*, 1991 BYU L Rev 197, 203–209; Robert H. Mnookin, Robert A. Burt, David L. Chambers, Michael S. Wald, Stephen D. Sugarman, Franklin E. Zimring, and Rayman L. Solomon, *In the Interest of Children: Advocacy, Law Reform, and Public Policy* (W.H. Freeman, 1985); Carl E. Schneider, *Lawyers and Children: Wisdom and Legitimacy in Family Policy*, 84 Mich L Rev 919 (1986); Carl E. Schneider, *Social Structure and Social Control: On The Moral Order of a Suburb*, 25 Law & Society Rev 875 (1990). For a brief history of the law and society movement and an extensive survey and assessment of its elements, see *Law and the Social Sciences* (Leon Lipson and Stanton Wheeler, eds, Russell Sage Foundation, 1986).

Law and Economics and Family Contracting. For a discussion of the role of family law in terms of general theories of civil obligation, see Margaret F. Brinig and June Carbone, *The Reliance Interest in Marriage and Divorce*, 62 Tulane L Rev 855 (1988); June Carbone and Margaret F. Brinig, *Rethinking Marriage: Feminist Ideology, Economic Changes and Divorce Reform*, 65 Tulane L Rev 953 (1991); and Elizabeth S. Scott, *Rational Decisionmaking about Marriage and Divorce*, 26 Va L Rev 9 (1990). For a thoughtful law-and-economics assessment of the role of contracting in families, *see* Michael J. Trebilcock and Rosemin Keshvani, *The Role of Private Ordering in Family Law: A Law and Economics Perspective*, 41 U Toronto LJ 533 (1991), in which two Canadian lawyers write about marriage and surrogacy contracts and argue that the state should have only a very limited role in restricting individuals' freedom of action. In Margaret F. Brinig, Carl E. Schneider, and Lee E. Teitelbaum, *Family Law in Action: A Reader* 34–45 (Anderson, 1999), Ann Estin critiques the application of economics to family law.

Chapter VI

I PLIGHT THEE MY TROTH: THE UNMARRIED COUPLE

But in Archer's little world no one laughed at a wife deceived, and a certain measure of contempt was attached to men who continued their philandering after marriage. In the rotation of crops there was a recognised season for wild oats; but they were not to be sown more than once.

Archer had always shared this view: in his heart he thought Lefferts despicable. But to love Ellen Olenska was not to become a man like Lefferts: for the first time Archer found himself face to face with the dread argument of the individual case. Ellen Olenska was like no other woman, he was like no other man: their situation, therefore, resembled no one else's, and they were answerable to no tribunal but that of their own judgment.

Edith Wharton
The Age of Innocence

SECTION 1. THE TRADITIONAL VIEW

"Well, then, Jane, call to aid your fancy—suppose [that,] . . . [h]eart-weary and soul-withered, you come home after years of voluntary banishment; you make a new acquaintance—how or where no matter: you find in this stranger much of the good and bright qualities which you have sought for twenty years, and never before encountered; and they are all fresh, healthy, without soil and without taint. Such society revives, regenerates: you feel better days come back—higher wishes, purer feelings; you desire to recommence your life, and to spend what remains to you of days in a way more worthy of an immortal being. To attain this end, are you justified in overleaping an obstacle of custom—a mere conventional impediment, which neither your conscience sanctifies nor your judgment approves?" . . .

"Sir," I answered, "a wanderer's repose or a sinner's reformation should never depend on a fellow creature. Men and women die; philosophers falter in wisdom, and Christians in goodness: if any one you know has suffered and erred, let him look higher than his equals for strength to amend, and solace to heal."

Charlotte Bronte
Jane Eyre

The traditional doctrine respecting the property relations of cohabiting unmarried couples is well summarized by the following description:

> At common law marital property could only exist between people who were married.... An illicit sexual relationship did not, however, incapacitate the participants from dealing with each other and to have those dealings, to some extent, legally enforced.... Until quite recently American courts tended to approach the problem in the following ways: (1) Non-marital sexual relationships did not give rise to spousal rights (dower, curtesy, elective or intestate share, Social Security, workmen's compensation, etc.), exceptions being made in a few jurisdictions for "common law" marriages (basically a form of marriage by prescription ...) and/or "putative spouses" (a spouse who in good faith believed himself to be married but was not for some technical reason, frequently the invalidity of a prior divorce). (2) An express or implied-in-fact contract between unmarried participants in a sexual relationship was illegal and unenforceable if all or part of the consideration for the contract was the participation in the relationship. (3) Conveyances from, to and between unmarried participants in a sexual relationship were valid and enforced in the same manner and to the same extent that conveyances from, to and between parties that did not have such a relationship. This meant that a jurisdiction which was willing to go behind the legal title and partition jointly held property on the basis of the consideration actually furnished might do so in the case of unmarried participants in a sexual relationship, at least so long as the consideration was not "illegal."

Charles Donahue, Jr., Thomas E. Kauper, and Peter W. Martin, *Property: An Introduction to the Concept and the Institution* 641 (West, 1983). Our first case reviews the basic aspects of the traditional doctrine respecting the ability of cohabitants to arrange their relations contractually and provides a workman-like statement of the reasons the Illinois Supreme Court declined to alter it:

HEWITT v. HEWITT

Supreme Court of Illinois, 1979
394 NE2d 1204

UNDERWOOD, J.

The issue in this case is whether plaintiff Victoria Hewitt, whose complaint alleges she lived with defendant Robert Hewitt from 1960 to 1975 in an unmarried, family-like relationship to which three children have been born, may recover from him "an equal share of the profits and properties accumulated by the parties" during that period.

Plaintiff initially filed a complaint for divorce, but at a hearing on defendant's motion to dismiss, admitted that no marriage ceremony had taken place and that the parties have never obtained a marriage license. In dismissing that complaint the trial court found that neither a ceremonial nor a common law marriage existed; that since defendant admitted the paternity of the minor children, plaintiff need not bring a separate action under the Paternity Act (Ill.Rev.Stat. 1975, ch. 1063/4, par. 51 *et seq.*) to have the question of child support determined; and directed plaintiff to make her complaint more definite as to the nature of the property of which she was seeking division.

Plaintiff thereafter filed an amended complaint alleging the following bases for her claim: (1) that because defendant promised he would "share his life, his future, his earnings and his property" with her and all of defendant's property resulted from the parties' joint endeavors, plaintiff is entitled in equity to a one-half share; (2) that the conduct of the parties evinced an implied contract entitling plaintiff to one-half the property accumulated during their "family relationship"; (3) that because defendant fraudulently assured plaintiff she was his wife in order to secure her services, although he knew they were not legally married, defendant's property should be impressed with a trust for plaintiff's benefit; (4) that because plaintiff has relied to her detriment on defendant's promises and devoted her entire life to him, defendant has been unjustly enriched.

The factual background alleged or testified to is that in June 1960, when she and defendant were students at Grinnell College in Iowa, plaintiff became pregnant; that defendant thereafter told her that they were husband and wife and would live as such, no formal ceremony being necessary, and that he would "share his life, his future, his earnings and his property" with her; that the parties immediately announced to their respective parents that they were married and thereafter held themselves out as husband and wife; that in reliance on defendant's promises she devoted her efforts to his professional education and his establishment in the practice of pedodontia, obtaining financial assistance from her parents for this purpose; that she assisted defendant in his career with her own special skills and although she was given payroll checks for these services she placed them in a common fund; that defendant, who was without funds at the time of the marriage, as a result of her efforts now earns over $80,000 a year and has accumulated large amounts of property, owned either jointly with her or separately; that she has given him every assistance a wife and mother could give, including social activities designed to enhance his social and professional reputation.

The amended complaint was also dismissed, the trial court finding that Illinois law and public policy require such claims to be based on a valid marriage. The appellate court reversed, stating that because the parties had outwardly lived a conventional married life, plaintiff's conduct had not "so affronted public policy that she should be denied any and all relief," and that plaintiff's complaint stated a cause of action on an express oral contract. We granted leave to appeal. Defendant apparently does not contest his obligation to support the children, and that question is not before us.

The appellate court, in reversing, gave considerable weight to the fact that the parties had held themselves out as husband and wife for over 15 years. The court noted that they lived "a most conventional, respectable and ordinary family life" that did not openly flout accepted standards, the "single flaw" being the lack of a valid marriage. Indeed the appellate court went so far as to say that the parties had "lived within the legitimate boundaries of a marriage and family relationship of a most conventional sort," an assertion which that court cannot have intended to be taken literally. Noting that the Illinois Marriage and Dissolution of Marriage Act (Ill.Rev.Stat.1977, ch. 40, par. 101 *et seq.*) does not prohibit nonmarital cohabitation and that the Criminal Code of 1961 (Ill.Rev.Stat.1977, ch. 38, par. 11–8(a)) makes fornication an offense only if the behavior is open and notorious, the appellate court concluded that plaintiff should not be denied relief on public policy grounds.

In finding that plaintiff's complaint stated a cause of action on an express oral contract, the appellate court adopted the reasoning of the California Supreme Court in the widely publicized case of *Marvin v. Marvin*, quoting extensively therefrom. In *Marvin*, Michelle Triola and defendant Lee Marvin lived together for 7 years pursuant to an alleged oral agreement that while "the parties lived together they would combine their efforts and earnings and would share equally any and all property accumulated as a result of their efforts whether individual or combined." In her complaint she alleged that, in reliance on this agreement, she gave up her career as a singer to devote herself full time to defendant as "companion, homemaker, housekeeper and cook." In resolving her claim for one-half the property accumulated in defendant's name during that period, the California court held that "The courts should enforce express contracts between nonmarital partners except to the extent that the contract is explicitly founded on the consideration of meretricious sexual services" and that "In the absence of an express contract, the courts should inquire into the conduct of the parties to determine whether that conduct demonstrates an implied contract, agreement of partnership or joint venture, or some other tacit understanding between the parties. The courts may also employ the doctrine of quantum meruit, or equitable remedies such as constructive or resulting trusts, when warranted by the facts of the case." The court reached its conclusions because:

> "In summary, we believe that the prevalence of nonmarital relationships in modern society and the social acceptance of them, marks this as a time when our courts should by no means apply the doctrine of the unlawfulness of the so-called meretricious relationship to the instant case. . . ."

"The mores of the society have indeed changed so radically in regard to cohabitation that we cannot impose a standard based on alleged moral considerations that have apparently been so widely abandoned by so many."

It is apparent that the *Marvin* court adopted a pure contract theory, under which, if the intent of the parties and the terms of their agreement are proved, the pseudo-conventional family relationship which impressed the appellate court here is irrelevant; recovery may be had unless the implicit sexual relationship is made the explicit consideration for the agreement. In contrast, the appellate court here, as we understand its opinion, would apply contract principles only in a setting where the relationship of the parties outwardly resembled that of a traditional family. It seems apparent that the plaintiff in *Marvin* would not have been entitled to recover in our appellate court because of the absence of that outwardly appearing conventional family relationship.

The issue of whether property rights accrue to unmarried cohabitants can not, however, be regarded realistically as merely a problem in the law of express contracts. Plaintiff argues that because her action is founded on an express contract, her recovery would in no way imply that unmarried cohabitants acquire property rights merely by cohabitation and subsequent separation. However, the *Marvin* court expressly recognized and the appellate court here seems to agree that if common law principles of express contract govern express agreements between unmarried cohabitants, common law principles of implied contract, equitable relief and constructive trust must govern the parties' relations in the absence of such an agreement. In all probability the latter case will be much the more common, since it is unlikely that most couples who live together will enter into express agreements regulating their property rights. (Bruch, *Property Rights of De Facto Spouses, Including Thoughts on the Value of Homemakers' Services*, 10 Fam.L.Q. 101, 102 (1976).) The increasing incidence of nonmarital cohabitation referred to in *Marvin* and the variety of legal remedies therein sanctioned seem certain to result in substantial amounts of litigation, in which, whatever the allegations regarding an oral contract, the proof will necessarily involve details of the parties' living arrangements.

Apart, however, from the appellate court's reliance upon *Marvin* to reach what appears to us to be a significantly different result, we believe there is a more fundamental problem. We are aware, of course, of the increasing judicial attention given the individual claims of unmarried cohabitants to jointly accumulated property, and the fact that the majority of courts considering the question have recognized an equitable or contractual basis for implementing the reasonable expectations of the parties unless sexual services were the explicit consideration. The issue of unmarried cohabitants' mutual property rights, however, as we earlier noted, cannot appropriately be characterized solely in terms of contract law, nor is it limited to considerations of equity or fairness as between the parties to such relationships. There are major public policy questions involved in determining whether, under what circumstances, and to what extent it is desirable to accord some type of legal status to claims arising from such relationships. Of substantially greater importance than the rights of the immediate parties is the impact of such recognition upon our society and the institution of marriage. Will the fact that legal rights closely resembling those arising from conventional marriages can be acquired by those who deliberately choose to enter into what have heretofore been commonly referred to as "illicit" or "meretricious" relationships encourage formation of such relationships and weaken marriage as the foundation of our family-based society? In the event of death shall the survivor have the status of a surviving spouse for purposes of inheritance, wrongful death actions, workmen's compensation, etc.? And still more importantly: what of the children born of such relationships? What are their support and inheritance rights and by what standards are custody questions resolved? What of the sociological and psychological effects upon them of that type of environment? Does not the recognition of legally enforceable property and custody rights emanating from nonmarital cohabitation in practical effect equate with the legalization of common law marriage at least in the circumstances of this case? And, in summary, have the increasing numbers of unmarried cohabitants and changing mores of our society reached the point at which the general welfare of the citizens of this State is best served by a return to something resembling the judicially created common law marriage our legislature outlawed in 1905?

Illinois' public policy regarding agreements such as the one alleged here was implemented long ago in *Wallace v. Rappleye* (1882), 103 Ill. 229, 249, where this court said: "An agreement in consideration of future illicit cohabitation between the plaintiffs is void." This is the traditional rule, in force until recent years in all jurisdictions. Section 589 of the Restatement of Contracts (1932) states, "A bargain in whole or in part for or in consideration of illicit sexual intercourse or of a promise thereof is illegal."

It is true, of course, that cohabitation by the parties may not prevent them from forming valid contracts about independent matters, for which it is said the sexual relations do not form part of the consideration. Those courts which allow recovery generally have relied on this principle to reduce the scope of the rule of illegality. Thus, California courts long prior to *Marvin* held that an express agreement to pool earnings is supported by independent consideration and is not invalidated by cohabitation of the parties, the agreements being regarded as simultaneous but separate. More recently, several courts have reasoned that the rendition of housekeeping and homemaking services such as plaintiff alleges here could be regarded as the consideration for a separate contract between the parties, severable from the illegal contract founded on sexual relations. In *Latham v. Latham* (1976), 547 P.2d 144, and *Carlson v. Olson* (Minn.1977), 256 N.W.2d 249, on allegations similar to those in this case, the Minnesota Supreme Court adopted *Marvin* and the Oregon court expressly held that agreements in consideration of cohabitation were not void, stating:

"We are not validating an agreement in which the only or primary consideration is sexual intercourse. The agreement here contemplated all the burdens and amenities of married life."

The real thrust of plaintiff's argument here is that we should abandon the rule of illegality because of certain changes in societal norms and attitudes. It is urged that social mores have changed radically in recent years, rendering this principle of law archaic. It is said that because there are so many unmarried cohabitants today the courts must confer a legal status on such relationships. This, of course, is the rationale underlying some of the decisions and commentaries. If this is to be the result, however, it would seem more candid to acknowledge the return of varying forms of common law marriage than to continue displaying the naivete we believe involved in the assertion that there are involved in these relationships contracts separate and independent from the sexual activity, and the assumption that those contracts would have been entered into or would continue without that activity.

Even if we were to assume some modification of the rule of illegality is appropriate, we return to the fundamental question earlier alluded to: If resolution of this issue rests ultimately on grounds of public policy, by what body should that policy be determined? *Marvin*, viewing the issue as governed solely by contract law, found judicial policy-making appropriate. Its decision was facilitated by California precedent and that State's no-fault divorce law. In our view, however, the situation alleged here was not the kind of arm's length bargain envisioned by traditional contract principles, but an intimate arrangement of a fundamentally different kind. The issue, realistically, is whether it is appropriate for this court to grant a legal status to a private arrangement substituting for the institution of marriage sanctioned by the State. The question whether change is needed in the law governing the rights of parties in this delicate area of marriage-like relationships involves evaluations of sociological data and alternatives we believe best suited to the superior investigative and fact-finding facilities of the legislative branch in the exercise of its traditional authority to declare public policy in the domestic relations field. That belief is reinforced by the fact that judicial recognition of mutual property rights between unmarried cohabitants would, in our opinion, clearly violate the policy of our recently enacted Illinois Marriage and Dissolution of Marriage Act. Although the Act does not specifically address the subject of nonmarital cohabitation, we think the legislative policy quite evident from the statutory scheme.

The Act provides:

"This Act shall be liberally construed and applied to promote its underlying purposes, which are to: (1) provide adequate procedures for the solemnization and registration of marriage; (2) strengthen and preserve the integrity of marriage and safeguard family relationships." (Ill.Rev.Stat.1977, ch. 40, par. 102.)

We cannot confidently say that judicial recognition of property rights between unmarried cohabitants will not make that alternative to marriage more attractive by allowing the parties to engage in such relationships with greater security. As one commentator has noted, it may make this alternative especially attractive to persons who seek a property arrangement that the law does not permit to marital partners. This court, for example, has held void agreements releasing husbands from their obligation to support their wives. In thus potentially enhancing the attractiveness of a private arrangement over marriage, we believe that the appellate court decision in this case contravenes the Act's policy of strengthening and preserving the integrity of marriage.

The Act also provides: "Common law marriages contracted in this State after June 30, 1905 are invalid." (Ill.Rev.Stat.1977, ch. 40, par. 214.) The doctrine of common law marriage was a judicially sanctioned alternative to formal marriage designed to apply to cases like the one before us. In *Port v. Port* (1873), 70 Ill. 484, this court reasoned that because the statute governing marriage did not "prohibit or declare void a marriage not solemnized in accordance with its provisions, a marriage without observing the statutory regulations, if made according to the common law, will still be a valid marriage." (70 Ill. 484, 486.) This court held that if the parties declared their present intent to take each other as husband and wife and thereafter did so a valid common law marriage existed. Such marriages were legislatively abolished in 1905, presumably because of the problems earlier noted, and the above-quoted language expressly reaffirms that policy.

While the appellate court denied that its decision here served to rehabilitate the doctrine of common law marriage, we are not persuaded. Plaintiff's allegations disclose a relationship that clearly would have constituted a valid common law marriage in this State prior to 1905. The parties expressly manifested their present intent to be husband and wife; immediately thereafter they assumed the marital status; and for many years they consistently held themselves out to their relatives and the public at large as husband and wife. Revealingly, the appellate court relied on the fact that the parties were, to the public, husband and wife in determining that the parties living arrangement did not flout Illinois public policy. It is of course true, as plaintiff argues, that unlike a common law spouse she would not have full marital rights in that she could not, for example, claim her statutory one-third share of defendant's property on his death. The distinction appears unimpressive, however, if she can claim one-half of his property on a theory of express or implied contract.

Further, in enacting the Illinois Marriage and Dissolution of Marriage Act, our legislature considered and rejected the "no-fault" divorce concept that has been adopted in many other jurisdictions, including California. (See Uniform Marriage and Divorce Act secs. 302, 305.) Illinois appears to be one of three States retaining fault grounds for dissolution of marriage. Certainly a significantly stronger promarriage policy is manifest in that action, which appears to us to reaffirm the traditional doctrine that marriage is a civil contract between three parties—the husband, the wife and the State. The policy of the Act gives the State a strong continuing interest in the institution of marriage and prevents the marriage relation from becoming in effect a private contract terminable at will. This seems to us another indication that public policy disfavors private contractual alternatives to marriage.

Lastly, in enacting the Illinois Marriage and Dissolution of Marriage Act, the legislature adopted for the first time the civil law concept of the putative spouse. The Act provides that an unmarried person may acquire the rights of a legal spouse only if he goes through a marriage ceremony and cohabits with another in the good-faith belief that he is validly married. When he learns that the marriage is not valid his status as a putative spouse terminates; common law marriages are expressly excluded. (Ill.Rev.Stat.1977, ch. 40, par. 305.) The legislature thus extended legal recognition to a class of nonmarital relationships, but only to the extent of a party's good-faith belief in the existence of a valid marriage. Moreover, during the legislature's deliberations on the Act *Marvin* was decided and received wide publicity. These circumstances in our opinion constitute a recent and unmistakable legislative judgment disfavoring the grant of mutual property rights to knowingly unmarried cohabitants. We have found no case in which recovery has been allowed in the face of a legislative declaration as recently and clearly enacted as ours. Even if we disagreed with the wisdom of that judgment, it is not for us to overturn or erode it.

Actually, however, the legislature judgment is in accord with the history of common law marriage in this country. "Despite its judicial acceptance in many states, the doctrine of common-law marriage is generally frowned on in this country, even in some of the states that have accepted it." Its origins, early history and problems are detailed in *In re Estate of Soeder* (Ohio App 1966), 220 N.E.2d 547, where that court noted that some 30 States did not authorize common law marriage. Judicial criticism has been widespread even in States recognizing the relationship. "It tends to weaken the public estimate of the sanctity of the marriage relation. It puts in doubt the certainty of the rights of inheritance. It opens the door to false pretenses of marriage and the imposition on estates of suppositious heirs."

In our judgment the fault in the appellate court holding in this case is that its practical effect is the reinstatement of common law marriage, as we earlier indicated, for there is no doubt that the alleged facts would, if proved, establish such a marriage under our pre–1905 law. The concern of both the *Marvin* court and the appellate court on this score is manifest from the circumstance that both courts found it necessary to emphasize marital values ("the structure of society itself largely depends upon the institution of marriage") (*Marvin v. Marvin* (1976), 557 P.2d 106, 122) and to deny any intent to "derogate from" (557 P.2d 106, 122) or "denigrate" (*Hewitt v. Hewitt* (1978), 380 N.E.2d 454) that institution. Commentators have expressed greater concern: "[T]he effect of these cases is to reinstitute common-law marriage in California after it has been abolished by the legislature." (Clark, *The New Marriage*, Williamette L.J. 441, 449 (1976).) "*[Hewitt]* is, if not a direct resurrection of common-law marriage contract principles, at least a large step in that direction." Reiland, *Hewitt v. Hewitt: Middle America, Marvin and Common–Law Marriage*, 60 Chi.B.Rec. 84, 88–90 (1978).

We do not intend to suggest that plaintiff's claims are totally devoid of merit. Rather, we believe that our statement in *Mogged v. Mogged* (1973), 302 N.E.2d 293, 295, made in deciding whether to abolish a judicially created defense to divorce, is appropriate here:

> "Whether or not the defense of recrimination should be abolished or modified in Illinois is a question involving complex public-policy considerations as to which compelling arguments may be made on both sides. For the reasons stated hereafter, we believe that these questions are appropriately within the province of the legislature, and that, if there is to be a change in the law of this State on this matter, it is for the legislature and not the courts to bring about that change."

We accordingly hold that plaintiff's claims are unenforceable for the reason that they contravene the public policy, implicit in the statutory scheme of the Illinois Marriage and Dissolution of Marriage Act, disfavoring the grant of mutually enforceable property rights to knowingly unmarried cohabitants. The judgment of the appellate court is reversed and the judgment of the circuit court of Champaign County is affirmed.

Informal Marriage

Had Illinois not statutorily abolished common-law marriage, *Hewitt* would have been easily decided, for the case presents the classic elements of such a marriage—an agreement in which the parties accept that they are married and a mutual and open assumption of a married relationship. (The latter is in practice often used as evidence of the former.) Would there still be a common-law marriage if, as plaintiff alleged, Mr. Hewitt knew the parties weren't married? As *Hewitt* indicates, the doctrine of common-law marriage can be used to prevent injustice. Yet all but 11 states and the District of Columbia have abolished it. Why?

Common-law marriage was abolished in part because it was thought to be generally unnecessary. Its opponents argued that it had served a useful purpose when great distances made it harder to find someone to officiate at a legal marriage or when illiteracy made it harder for people to understand what to do to be legally married. But, the opponents continued, these circumstances have changed. Perhaps more important was the problem of fraudulent claims of marriage to which the institution was thought to give rise. As you will recall from Chapter 1, a purpose of legally supervised marriage is to assure that the parties, the world, and the courts know when two people are married and thus what legal obligations they have assumed and what benefits they are entitled to. The criticism of common-law marriage is that in it such assurances are lacking. Since there can be economic advantages to being married—particularly where inheritances or social-security benefits are at stake—there is an incentive to claim to have been married. The fear of fraudulent claims helps explain the requirement that couples hold themselves out to the world as married. In addition, some cases demand that plaintiffs prove their case by clear and convincing evidence, and a number of jurisdictions apply the Dead Man's Statute to bar testimony by plaintiffs of what a deceased common-law spouse said.

Another device to protect spouses in informal marriages is putative marriage. Putative marriage occurs in some civil-law jurisdictions when a wedding has taken place but, unbeknownst to the couple (or at least to the would-be putative spouse), some impediment bars the marriage. It is more broadly defined by the UMDA:

§ 209. [Putative Spouse]

Any person who has cohabited with another to whom he is not legally married in the good faith belief that he was married to that person is a putative spouse until knowledge of the fact that he is not legally married terminates his status and prevents acquisition of further rights. A putative spouse acquires the rights conferred upon a legal spouse, including the right to maintenance following termination of his status, whether or not the marriage is prohibited (Section 207) or declared invalid (Section 208). If there is a legal spouse or other putative spouses, rights acquired by a putative spouse do not supersede the rights of the legal spouse or those acquired by other putative spouses, but the court shall apportion property, maintenance, and support rights among the claimants as appropriate in the circumstances and in the interests of justice.

Questions on the Traditional View

(1) It is supposed to be an advantage of common-law adjudication that close attention is paid to the facts of each case. However, as the policy-making, as opposed to the adjudicative, function of appellate courts has come increasingly to the fore, the situation of the individual litigants can sometimes be forgotten. This may have happened in *Hewitt.* The court could have protected Mrs. Hewitt even while reaching the same policy conclusion. Can you think of ways it might have done so?

(2) We said that the *Hewitt* opinion is workman-like. Why? What is the structure of the opinion? What kinds of legal arguments does it use?

(3) Iowa is one of the jurisdictions that continues to recognize, albeit grudgingly, the common law marriage doctrine. See Iowa Code § 595.11 (2005)(providing that such marriages are valid, but that the parties and people aiding them shall pay $50 apiece to the state treasurer); Conklin v. MacMillan Oil Company, 557 NW2d 102 (Iowa App 1996)(recognizing the concept, but finding support for the commissioner's finding that the petitioner had never intended to be married by common law nor publicly declared she was married). Assuming that, as we learned in Chapter 1, a marriage valid in the state where it is created is usually recognized in other states, why didn't Victoria Hewitt simply get the divorce she sought originally? (The trial court found that a

common law marriage did not exist, but should she have appealed?) Was her problem that *Robert* never intended to be married? Or that she believed him and thought she *was* married, and therefore never promised to be his wife?

(4) Some academics argue that common law marriage should be revived, mostly to protect dependent partners (many of whom are women). Legislation like that in place in California, under its domestic partnership law, Cal. Fam. Code §§ 297.5 (2005) (providing that the California benefits and obligations for registered domestic partners are the same as marriage) or in Canada, Modernization of Benefits and Obligations Act of 2000, RSC 4 (2d Supp.), SC 2000, c 12, could also provide relief. For other commonwealth nations' approach to the problem see Principles of the Law of Family Dissolution, Reporter's Note to § 6.03, at 934 (2002). For academic arguments in favor of a resurrection of common law marriage, see Hon. John B. Crawley, Is the Honeymoon Over for Common–Law Marriage: A Consideration of the Continued Viability of the Common–Law Marriage Doctrine, 29 Cumb L Rev 399 (1998); Cynthia Grant Bowman, A Feminist Proposal to Bring Back Common Law Marriage, 75 Or L Rev 709 (1996). For a contrary argument, see Ryan P. Newell, Comment, "To Be Sure He is My Husband Good Enough" or is He?: An Analysis of Common Law Marriage in Pennsylvania, 109 Penn St L Rev 337, 355–57 (2004) (arguing that it is no longer necessary).

SECTION 2. THE REVISED VIEW

I conceive that from the abolition of marriage the fit and natural arrangement of sexual connection would result. I by no means assert that the intercourse would be promiscuous; on the contrary, it appears, from the relation of parent to child that this union is generally of long duration and marked above all others with generosity and self-devotion.... That which will result from the abolition of marriage will be natural and right, because choice and change will be exempted from restraint.

Percy Bysshe Shelley
Postscript to Queen Mab

The centerpiece of the revised view of the relations between unmarried cohabitants is, as you probably know, *Marvin v. Marvin*. Neither *Marvin* nor *Hewitt* represents the majority position for treatment of unmarried cohabitants. Most states steer a middle course between the two views, as is illustrated by *Morone v. Morone*, 413 NE2d 1154 (NY 1980). This typical view enforces express contracts between unmarried cohabitants as so long as they are not primarily founded on intimate sexual relations. Another illuminating case is *Kozlowski v. Kozlowski*, 403 A2d 902 (NJ 1979), which suggests that the parties need to know they are not married to establish a contractual recovery. Nevertheless, *Marvin* has played so prominent a role in the progress of this area of law that we have paid it special attention. We provide opinions from three stages of the case so that you will have a better sense than casebooks usually can provide of how cases and legal ideas develop.

MARVIN v. MARVIN

California Supreme Court, 1976
557 P2d 106

TOBRINER, J.

During the past 15 years, there has been a substantial increase in the number of couples living together without marrying.[1] Such nonmarital relationships lead to legal controversy when one partner dies or the couple separates. Courts of Appeal, faced with the task of determining property rights in such cases, have arrived at conflicting positions: two cases (*In re Marriage of Cary* (1973) 109 Cal.Rptr. 862; *Estate of Atherley* (1975) 119 Cal.Rptr. 41) have held that the Family Law Act (Civ.Code, § 4000 et seq.) requires division of the property according to community property principles, and one decision (*Beckman v. Mayhew* (1975) 122 Cal.Rptr. 604) has rejected that holding. We take this opportunity to resolve that controversy and to declare the principles which should govern distribution of property acquired in a nonmarital relationship.

We conclude: (1) The provisions of the Family Law Act do not govern the distribution of property acquired during a nonmarital relationship; such a relationship remains subject solely to judicial decision. (2) The courts should enforce express contracts between nonmarital partners except to the extent that the contract is explicitly founded on the consideration of meretricious sexual services. (3) In the absence of an express contract, the courts should inquire into the conduct of the parties to determine whether that conduct demonstrates an implied contract, agreement of partnership or joint venture, or some other tacit understanding between the parties. The courts may also employ the doctrine of quantum meruit, or equitable remedies such as constructive or resulting trusts, when warranted by the facts of the case.

In the instant case plaintiff and defendant lived together for seven years without marrying; all property acquired during this period was taken in defendant's name. When plaintiff sued to enforce a contract under which she was entitled to half the property and to support payments, the trial court granted judgment on the pleadings for defendant, thus leaving him with all property accumulated by the couple during their relationship. Since the trial court denied plaintiff a trial on the merits of her claim, its decision conflicts with the principles stated above, and must be reversed.

1. The factual setting of this appeal.

1. "The 1970 census figures indicate that today perhaps eight times as many couples are living together without being married as cohabited ten years ago." (Comment, *In re Cary: A Judicial Recognition of Illicit Cohabitation* (1974) 25 Hastings L.J. 1226.)

Since the trial court rendered judgment for defendant on the pleadings, we must accept the allegations of plaintiff's complaint as true, determining whether such allegations state, or can be amended to state, a cause of action. We turn therefore to the specific allegations of the complaint.

Plaintiff avers that in October of 1964 she and defendant "entered into an oral agreement" that while "the parties lived together they would combine their efforts and earnings and would share equally any and all property accumulated as a result of their efforts whether individual or combined." Furthermore, they agreed to "hold themselves out to the general public as husband and wife" and that "plaintiff would further render her services as a companion, homemaker, housekeeper and cook to ... defendant."

Shortly thereafter plaintiff agreed to "give up her lucrative career as an entertainer (and) singer" in order to "devote her full time to defendant ... as a companion, homemaker, housekeeper and cook;" in return defendant agreed to "provide for all of plaintiff's financial support and needs for the rest of her life."

Plaintiff alleges that she lived with defendant from October of 1964 through May of 1970 and fulfilled her obligations under the agreement. During this period the parties as a result of their efforts and earnings acquired in defendant's name substantial real and personal property, including motion picture rights worth over $1 million. In May of 1970, however, defendant compelled plaintiff to leave his household. He continued to support plaintiff until November of 1971, but thereafter refused to provide further support.

On the basis of these allegations plaintiff asserts two causes of action. The first, for declaratory relief, asks the court to determine her contract and property rights; the second seeks to impose a constructive trust upon one half of the property acquired during the course of the relationship.

Defendant demurred unsuccessfully, and then answered the complaint. Following extensive discovery and pretrial proceedings, the case came to trial. Defendant renewed his attack on the complaint by a motion to dismiss. Since the parties had stipulated that defendant's marriage to Betty Marvin did not terminate until the filing of a final decree of divorce in January 1967, the trial court treated defendant's motion as one for judgment on the pleadings augmented by the stipulation.

After hearing argument the court granted defendant's motion and entered judgment for defendant. Plaintiff moved to set aside the judgment and asked leave to amend her complaint to allege that she and defendant reaffirmed their agreement after defendant's divorce was final. The trial court denied plaintiff's motion, and she appealed from the judgment.

2. Plaintiff's complaint states a cause of action for breach of an express contract.

In *Trutalli v. Meraviglia* (1932) 12 P.2d 430, we established the principle that nonmarital partners may lawfully contract concerning the ownership of property acquired during the relationship. We reaffirmed this principle in *Vallera v. Vallera* (1943) 134 P.2d 761, 763, stating that "If a man and woman (who are not married) live together as husband and wife under an agreement to pool their earnings and share equally in their joint accumulations, equity will protect the interests of each in such property."

In the case before us plaintiff, basing her cause of action in contract upon these precedents, maintains that the trial court erred in denying her a trial on the merits of her contention. Although that court did not specify the ground for its conclusion that plaintiff's contractual allegations stated no cause of action,[2] defendant offers some four theories to sustain the ruling; we proceed to examine them.

Defendant first and principally relies on the contention that the alleged contract is so closely related to the supposed "immoral" character of the relationship between plaintiff and himself that the enforcement of the contract would violate public policy. He points to cases asserting that a contract between nonmarital partners is unenforceable if it is "involved in" an illicit relationship. A review of the numerous California decisions concerning contracts between nonmarital partners, however, reveals that the courts have not employed such broad and uncertain standards to strike down contracts. The decisions instead disclose a narrower and more precise standard: a contract between nonmarital partners is unenforceable only to the extent that it explicitly rests upon the immoral and illicit consideration of meretricious sexual services....

Although the past decisions hover over the issue in the somewhat wispy form of the figures of a Chagall painting, we can abstract from those decisions a clear and simple rule. The fact that a man and woman live together without marriage, and engage in a sexual relationship, does not in itself invalidate agreements between them relating to their earnings, property, or expenses. Neither is such an agreement invalid merely because the parties may have contemplated the creation or continuation of a nonmarital relationship when they entered into it. Agreements between nonmarital partners fail only to the extent that they rest upon a consideration of meretricious sexual services. Thus the rule asserted by defendant, that a contract fails if it is "involved in" or

2. The colloquy between court and counsel at argument of the motion for judgement on the pleadings suggesting that the trial court held the 1964 agreement violated public policy because it derogated the community property rights of Betty Marvin, defendant's lawful wife. Plaintiff, however, offered to amend her complaint to allege that she and defendant reaffirmed their contract after defendant and Better were divorced. The trail court denied leave to amend, a ruling which suggests that the court's judgement must rest upon some other ground than the assertion that the contract would injure Betty's property rights.

made "in contemplation" of a nonmarital relationship, cannot be reconciled with the decisions....

In summary, we base our opinion on the principle that adults who voluntarily live together and engage in sexual relations are nonetheless as competent as any other persons to contract respecting their earnings and property rights. Of course, they cannot lawfully contract to pay for the performance of sexual services, for such a contract is, in essence, an agreement for prostitution and unlawful for that reason. But they may agree to pool their earnings and to hold all property acquired during the relationship in accord with the law governing community property; conversely they may agree that each partner's earnings and the property acquired from those earnings remains the separate property of the earning partner.[3] So long as the agreement does not rest upon illicit meretricious consideration, the parties may order their economic affairs as they choose, and no policy precludes the courts from enforcing such agreements.

In the present instance, plaintiff alleges that the parties agreed to pool their earnings, that they contracted to share equally in all property acquired, and that defendant agreed to support plaintiff. The terms of the contract as alleged do not rest upon any unlawful consideration. We therefore conclude that the complaint furnishes a suitable basis upon which the trial court can render declaratory relief. The trial court consequently erred in granting defendant's motion for judgment on the pleadings.

3. Plaintiff's complaint can be amended to state a cause of action founded upon theories of implied contract or equitable relief.

As we have noted, both causes of action in plaintiff's complaint allege an express contract; neither asserts any basis for relief independent from the contract. In *In re Marriage of Cary, supra*, 109 Cal.Rptr. 862, however, the Court of Appeal held that, in view of the policy of the Family Law Act, property accumulated by nonmarital partners in an actual family relationship should be divided equally. Upon examining the *Cary* opinion, the parties to the present case realized that plaintiff's alleged relationship with defendant might arguably support a cause of action independent of any express contract between the parties. The parties have therefore briefed and discussed the issue of the property rights of a nonmarital partner in the absence of an express contract. Although our conclusion that plaintiff's complaint states a cause of action based on an express contract alone compels us to reverse the judgment for defendant, resolution of the *Cary* issue will serve both to guide the parties upon retrial and to resolve a conflict presently manifest in published Court of Appeal decisions.

3. A great variety of other arrangements are possible. The parties might keep their earning and property separate, but agree to compensate one party for services which benefit the other. They may choose to pool only part of their earnings and property, to forma partnership or joint venture, or to hold property acquired as joint tenants or tenants in common, or agree to any other such arrangement.

Both plaintiff and defendant stand in broad agreement that the law should be fashioned to carry out the reasonable expectations of the parties. Plaintiff, however, presents the following contentions: that the decisions prior to *Cary* rest upon implicit and erroneous notions of punishing a party for his or her guilt in entering into a nonmarital relationship, that such decisions result in an inequitable distribution of property accumulated during the relationship, and that *Cary* correctly held that the enactment of the Family Law Act in 1970 overturned those prior decisions. Defendant in response maintains that the prior decisions merely applied common law principles of contract and property to persons who have deliberately elected to remain outside the bounds of the community property system.[4] *Cary*, defendant contends, erred in holding that the Family Law Act vitiated the force of the prior precedents....

This failure of the courts to recognize an action by a nonmarital partner based upon implied contract, or to grant an equitable remedy, contrasts with the judicial treatment of the putative spouse. Prior to the enactment of the Family Law Act, no statute granted rights to a putative spouse. The courts accordingly fashioned a variety of remedies by judicial decision. Some cases permitted the putative spouse to recover half the property on a theory that the conduct of the parties implied an agreement of partnership or joint venture. Others permitted the spouse to recover the reasonable value of rendered services, less the value of support received.[5] Finally, decisions affirmed the power of a court to employ equitable principles to achieve a fair division of property acquired during putative marriage.

Thus in summary, the cases prior to *Cary* exhibited a schizophrenic inconsistency. By enforcing an express contract between nonmarital partners unless it rested upon an unlawful consideration, the courts applied a common law principle as to contracts. Yet the courts disregarded the common law principle that holds that implied contracts can arise from the conduct of the parties.[6] Refusing to enforce such contracts, the

4. We note that a deliberate decision to avoid the strictures of the community property system is not the only reason that couples live together without marriage. Some couples may wish to avoid the permanent commitment that marriage implies, yet be willing to share equally any property acquired during the relationship; others may fear the loss of pension, welfare, or tax benefits resulting from marriage. Others may engage in the relationship as a possible prelude to marriage. In lower socio-economic groups the difficulty and expense of dissolving a former marriage often leads couples to choose a nonmarital relationship; many unmarried couples may also incorrectly believe that the doctrine of common law marriage prevails in California, and thus that they are in fact married. Consequently we conclude that the mere fact that a couple has not participated in a valid marriage ceremony cannot serve as a basis for a court's inference that the couple intend to keep their earnings and property separate and independent; the parties' intention can only be ascertained by a more searching inquiry into the nature of their relationship.

5. The putative spouse need not prove that he rendered services in expectation of monetary reward in order to recover the reasonable value of those services.

6. "Contracts may be express or implied. These terms, however, do not denote different kinds of contracts, but have reference to the evidence by which the agreement between the parties is shown. If the agreement is shown by the direct words of the parties, spoken or written, the contract

courts spoke of leaving the parties "in the position in which they had placed themselves" (*Oakley v. Oakley, supra*, 185 P.2d 848, 850), just as if they were guilty parties "in pari delicto." . . .

Thus as of 1973, the time of the filing of *In re Marriage of Cary*, the cases apparently held that a nonmarital partner who rendered services in the absence of express contract could assert no right to property acquired during the relationship. The facts of *Cary* demonstrated the unfairness of that rule.

Janet and Paul Cary had lived together, unmarried, for more than eight years. They held themselves out to friends and family as husband and wife, reared four children, purchased a home and other property, obtained credit, filed joint income tax returns, and otherwise conducted themselves as though they were married. Paul worked outside the home, and Janet generally cared for the house and children.

In 1971 Paul petitioned for "nullity of the marriage." Following a hearing on that petition, the trial court awarded Janet half the property acquired during the relationship, although all such property was traceable to Paul's earnings. The Court of Appeal affirmed the award.

Reviewing the prior decisions which had denied relief to the homemaking partner, the Court of Appeal reasoned that those decisions rested upon a policy of punishing persons guilty of cohabitation without marriage. The Family Law Act, the court observed, aimed to eliminate fault or guilt as a basis for dividing marital property. But once fault or guilt is excluded, the court reasoned, nothing distinguishes the property rights of a nonmarital "spouse" from those of a putative spouse. Since the latter is entitled to half the "quasi marital property" (Civ.Code, § 4452), the Court of Appeal concluded that, giving effect to the policy of the Family Law Act, a nonmarital cohabitator should also be entitled to half the property accumulated during an "actual family relationship."

Cary met with a mixed reception in other appellate districts. In *Estate of Atherley, supra*, 119 Cal.Rptr. 41, the Fourth District agreed with *Cary* that under the Family Law Act a nonmarital partner in an actual family relationship enjoys the same right to an equal division of property as a putative spouse. In *Beckman v. Mayhew, supra*, 122 Cal.Rptr. 604, however, the Third District rejected *Cary* on the ground that the Family Law Act was not intended to change California law dealing with nonmarital relationships.

If *Cary* is interpreted as holding that the Family Law Act requires an equal division of property accumulated in nonmarital "actual family relationships," then we agree with *Beckman v. Mayhew* that *Cary*

is said to be an express one. But if such agreement can only be shown by the acts and conduct of the parties, interpreted in the light of the subject-matter and of the surrounding circumstances, then the contract is an implied one." Thus, as Justice Schauer observed in *Desny v. Wilder* (1956) 299 P.2d 257, in a sense all contracts made in fact, as distinguished from quasi-contractual obligations, are express contracts, differing only in the manner in which the assent of the parties is expressed and proved.

distends the act. No language in the Family Law Act addresses the property rights of nonmarital partners, and nothing in the legislative history of the act suggests that the Legislature considered that subject. The delineation of the rights of nonmarital partners before 1970 had been fixed entirely by judicial decision; we see no reason to believe that the Legislature, by enacting the Family Law Act, intended to change that state of affairs.

But although we reject the reasoning of *Cary* and *Atherley*, we share the perception of the *Cary* and *Atherley* courts that the application of former precedent in the factual setting of those cases would work an unfair distribution of the property accumulated by the couple. Justice Friedman in *Beckman v. Mayhew, supra*, 122 Cal.Rptr. 604, also questioned the continued viability of our decisions in *Vallera* and *Keene*; commentators have argued the need to reconsider those precedents. We should not, therefore, reject the authority of *Cary* and *Atherley* without also examining the deficiencies in the former law which led to those decisions.

The principal reason why the pre-*Cary* decisions result in an unfair distribution of property inheres in the court's refusal to permit a nonmarital partner to assert rights based upon accepted principles of implied contract or equity. We have examined the reasons advanced to justify this denial of relief, and find that none have merit.

First, we note that the cases denying relief do not rest their refusal upon any theory of "punishing" a "guilty" partner. Indeed, to the extent that denial of relief "punishes" one partner, it necessarily rewards the other by permitting him to retain a disproportionate amount of the property. Concepts of "guilt" thus cannot justify an unequal division of property between two equally "guilty" persons.[7]

Other reasons advanced in the decisions fare no better. The principal argument seems to be that "(e)quitable considerations arising from the reasonable expectation of ... benefits attending the status of marriage ... are not present (in a nonmarital relationship)." (*Vallera v. Vallera, supra*, 134 P.2d 761, 763.) But, although parties to a nonmarital relationship obviously cannot have based any expectations upon the

7. Justice Finley of the Washington Supreme Court explains: "Under such circumstances (the dissolution of a nonmarital relationship), this court and the courts of other jurisdictions have, in effect, sometimes said, 'We will wash our hands of such disputes. The parties should and must be left to their own devices, just where they find themselves.' To me, such pronouncements seem overly fastidious and a bit fatuous. They are unrealistic and, among other things, ignore the fact that an unannounced (but nevertheless effective and binding) rule of law is inherent in any such terminal statements by a court of law. The unannounced but inherent rule is simply that the party who has title, or in some instances who is in possession, will enjoy the rights of ownership of the property concerned. The rule often operates to the great advantage of the cunning and the shrewd, who wind up with possession of the property, or title to it in their names, at the end of a so-called meretricious relationship. So, although the courts proclaim that they will have nothing to do with such matters, the proclamation in itself establishes, as to the parties involved, an effective and binding rule of law which tends to operate purely by accident or perhaps by reason of the cunning, anticipatory designs of just one of the parties." (*West v. Knowles* (1957) 311 P.2d 689, 692 (conc. opn.).)

belief that they were married, other expectations and equitable considerations remain. The parties may well expect that property will be divided in accord with the parties' own tacit understanding and that in the absence of such understanding the courts will fairly apportion property accumulated through mutual effort. We need not treat nonmarital partners as putatively married persons in order to apply principles of implied contract, or extend equitable remedies; we need to treat them only as we do any other unmarried persons.[8] . . .

In summary, we believe that the prevalence of nonmarital relationships in modern society and the social acceptance of them, marks this as a time when our courts should by no means apply the doctrine of the unlawfulness of the so-called meretricious relationship to the instant case. As we have explained, the nonenforceability of agreements expressly providing for meretricious conduct rested upon the fact that such conduct, as the word suggests, pertained to and encompassed prostitution. To equate the nonmarital relationship of today to such a subject matter is to do violence to an accepted and wholly different practice.

We are aware that many young couples live together without the solemnization of marriage, in order to make sure that they can successfully later undertake marriage. This trial period, preliminary to marriage, serves as some assurance that the marriage will not subsequently end in dissolution to the harm of both parties. We are aware, as we have stated, of the pervasiveness of nonmarital relationships in other situations.

The mores of the society have indeed changed so radically in regard to cohabitation that we cannot impose a standard based on alleged moral considerations that have apparently been so widely abandoned by so many. Lest we be misunderstood, however, we take this occasion to point out that the structure of society itself largely depends upon the institution of marriage, and nothing we have said in this opinion should be taken to derogate from that institution. The joining of the man and woman in marriage is at once the most socially productive and individually fulfilling relationship that one can enjoy in the course of a lifetime.

We conclude that the judicial barriers that may stand in the way of a policy based upon the fulfillment of the reasonable expectations of the parties to a nonmarital relationship should be removed. As we have explained, the courts now hold that express agreements will be enforced unless they rest on an unlawful meretricious consideration. We add that in the absence of an express agreement, the courts may look to a variety of other remedies in order to protect the parties' lawful expectations.[9]

8. In some instances a confidential relationship may arise between nonmarital partners, and economic transactions between them should be governed by the principles applicable to such relationships.

9. We do not seek to resurrect the doctrine of common law marriage, which was abolished in California by statute in 1895. Thus we do not hold that plaintiff and defendant were "married," nor do we extend to plaintiff the rights which the Family Law Act grants valid or putative spouses; we hold only that she has the same rights to enforce contracts and to assert her equitable interest in property acquired through

The courts may inquire into the conduct of the parties to determine whether that conduct demonstrates an implied contract or implied agreement of partnership or joint venture, or some other tacit understanding between the parties. The courts may, when appropriate, employ principles of constructive trust or resulting trust. Finally, a nonmarital partner may recover in quantum meruit for the reasonable value of household services rendered less the reasonable value of support received if he can show that he rendered services with the expectation of monetary reward.[10]

Since we have determined that plaintiff's complaint states a cause of action for breach of an express contract, and, as we have explained, can be amended to state a cause of action independent of allegations of express contract,[11] we must conclude that the trial court erred in granting defendant a judgment on the pleadings.

The judgment is reversed and the cause remanded for further proceedings consistent with the views expressed herein.

CLARK, JUSTICE (concurring and dissenting).

The majority opinion properly permits recovery on the basis of either express or implied in fact agreement between the parties. These being the issues presented, their resolution requires reversal of the judgment. Here, the opinion should stop.

This court should not attempt to determine all anticipated rights, duties and remedies within every meretricious relationship—particularly in vague terms. Rather, these complex issues should be determined as each arises in a concrete case.

The majority broadly indicates that a party to a meretricious relationship may recover on the basis of equitable principles and in quantum meruit. However, the majority fails to advise us of the circumstances permitting recovery, limitations on recovery, or whether their numerous remedies are cumulative or exclusive. Conceivably, under the majority opinion a party may recover half of the property acquired during the relationship on the basis of general equitable principles, recover a bonus based on specific equitable considerations, and recover a second bonus in quantum meruit.

The general sweep of the majority opinion raises but fails to answer several questions. First, because the Legislature specifically excluded some parties to a meretricious relationship from the equal division rule of Civil Code section 4452, is this court now free to create an equal division rule? Second, upon termination of the relationship, is it equita-

her effort as does any other unmarried person.

10. Our opinion does not preclude the evolution of additional equitable remedies to protect the expectations of the parties to a nonmarital relationship in cases in which existing remedies prove inadequate; the suitability of such remedies may be determined in later cases in light of the factual setting in which they arise.

11. We do not pass upon the question whether, in the absence of an express or implied contractual obligation, a party to a nonmarital relationship is entitled to support payments from the other party after the relationship terminates.

ble to impose the economic obligations of lawful spouses on meretricious parties when the latter may have rejected matrimony to avoid such obligations? Third, does not application of equitable principles—necessitating examination of the conduct of the parties—violate the spirit of the Family Law Act of 1969, designed to eliminate the bitterness and acrimony resulting from the former fault system in divorce? Fourth, will not application of equitable principles reimpose upon trial courts the unmanageable burden of arbitrating domestic disputes? Fifth, will not a quantum meruit system of compensation for services—discounted by benefits received—place meretricious spouses in a better position than lawful spouses? Sixth, if a quantum meruit system is to be allowed, does fairness not require inclusion of all services and all benefits regardless of how difficult the evaluation?

When the parties to a meretricious relationship show by express or implied in fact agreement they intend to create mutual obligations, the courts should enforce the agreement. However, in the absence of agreement, we should stop and consider the ramifications before creating economic obligations which may violate legislative intent, contravene the intention of the parties, and surely generate undue burdens on our trial courts.

By judicial overreach, the majority perform a *nunc pro tunc* marriage, dissolve it, and distribute its property on terms never contemplated by the parties, case law or the Legislature.

The Marvin Case on Remand

On remand, Michelle Triola tried to demonstrate that she did in fact have a contractual relationship with Lee Marvin. The trial lasted nearly twelve weeks and produced 8,000 pages of testimony. At the end of it, the judge issued the following opinion. We reproduce it in some detail because it gives you a good sense of the kind of complexities that arise in litigating a dispute between cohabitants.

MARVIN v. MARVIN

Opinion of the Trial Court on Remand
Superior Court of Los Angeles County (1979)

MARSHALL, J.

FACTS

In June, 1964, the parties met while they both were working on a picture called "Ship of Fools," he as a star and she as a stand-in. (She also was employed as a singer at the "Little Club" in Los Angeles.) A few days after their first meeting, they lunched together, then dined together. In a short time they saw each other on a daily basis after work. Sexual intimacy commenced about 2 weeks after their first date. During these early meetings, there was much conversation about their respective marital problems. The defendant said that, although he loved his wife and children, communication between him and his spouse had failed and he was unhappy. Plaintiff said that her marriage had been dissolved but her husband sought reconciliation.

Plaintiff testified that defendant told her that as soon as two people sign "a piece of paper," (meaning a marriage certificate) they waved that paper at each other whenever any problem arose instead of attempting to settle the problem. Defendant allegedly said that a license is a woman's insurance policy and he did not like that. Defendant further stated to plaintiff that when two people loved each other, there is no need for a license. Plaintiff declared that she told him that she did not necessarily agree with him.

Plaintiff testified that she hoped to secure a part in "Flower Drum Song" and was to journey to New York City for that purpose, but defendant did not want her to go as, he said, it was hard to conduct a romance at long distance. She did not go to New York. She rented an apartment for approximately one month. Defendant stayed with her from time to time.

In October, 1964, the plaintiff rented and moved into a house. The defendant moved in with her although he also maintained a room at a nearby hotel and occasionally stayed at the home where he had lived with his wife and children. Plaintiff told defendant that they were not "living together." His response was, "What does it mean when your blouse and my suit come back (from) to the cleaners together?" He inquired, "Does it mean that I live here?" She testified that she replied, "Well, I guess it does."

Defendant allegedly repeated again and again, his opinion that a piece of paper, a marriage certificate, is not needed by people in love. Plaintiff testified that at first she thought he was crazy and asked him to explain. She did not think it would work without the "paper." Defendant responded that his marriage was lacking in communication and that he was unhappy about it.

The defendant went to San Blas, Mexico in November or December of 1964 for sport fishing. He later invited plaintiff to join him, which she did. There, the defendant allegedly told her that he was unhappily married, that he might be terminating his marriage, and that he and plaintiff could be together. She testified that she doubted his words. He declared again that a woman does not need a piece of paper, a marriage certificate, for security. He repeated his belief that whenever there was a misunderstanding, each waved the paper at each other instead of working hard at clearing up the misunderstanding. He allegedly said that he would never marry again because he did not like that kind of arrangement. He declared that he was almost positive that his marriage was not going to mend and asked whether plaintiff and defendant could share their lives. She inquired as to his meaning. He replied that after the divorce he would be left with only "the shirt on his back (and alimony)" but would she like to live on the beach. She initially responded she was going to New York. Two days later she asked defendant if he really thought living together without marriage would work out. He said that it would and she agreed to live with him.

Then defendant allegedly uttered the words which plaintiff contends constitute a contractual offer. He said, "what I have is yours and what you have is mine." She then accepted the alleged offer but declared that she had her own career and she did not want to depend on anyone. Defendant said that he had no objection to her career, that they still could share and build their lives. She told him that she loved him, that she would care for him and their home, and that she would cook and be his companion. She offered to learn how to fish, a sport of which he was quite fond, although she got seasick. He said that she would get over her seasickness.

The defendant was intoxicated in San Blas a "few times" to the point of losing control. She said that in subsequent years, 1965 and 1966, he lost control whenever he drank. She testified that she asked him to stop drinking and that he did not do so.

Defendant vigorously denies telling plaintiff, "what I have is yours and what you have is mine;" he declared that he never said he would support her for life and that he never stated "I'll take care of you always." He further denies saying that a marriage license is a piece of paper which stood in the way of working out problems. He testified that he decided to get a divorce from his wife after he arrived at his beach house, many months after his return from San Blas. During the examination of defendant under Evidence Code, Section 776, counsel for plaintiff read from defendant's deposition wherein defendant declared that he wanted a relationship of no responsibility and that the plaintiff agreed thereto.

The defendant rented and later purchased a house on the Malibu beach. Plaintiff moved in, bringing a bed, stereo equipment and kitchen utensils. A refrigerator and washing machine were purchased. She brought food, cooked meals for defendant, cleaned house (after the first year, she had the periodic help of a cleaning woman). On occasion, the couple had visitors and they in turn went together to the homes of friends. In the circle of their friends and their acquaintances in the theatrical world, the plaintiff was reputed not to be defendant's wife.

In the six years of their relationship, they did considerable traveling, over 30 months away from the beach house, for the most part on various film locations. Plaintiff usually accompanied the defendant except for the seven months devoted to the filming of "Dirty Dozen" in England (she visited him for about a month) and an exploratory trip to Micronesia preliminary to filming "Hell in the Pacific."

Plaintiff testified that her acquaintance with the theater began in 1957 as a dancer. She danced with several troupes. She states that she was a featured dancer in a group organized by Barry Ashton, who produced shows in Las Vegas. She further alleges that she was also a singer from about 1957 and appeared in nightclubs in several states and abroad. Her compensation was usually "scale," ranging from $285 to

$400 a week. As to motion pictures, she served as a "stand-in" or in background groupings until her appearance in "Synanon" (shortly after working in "Ship of Fools" where she met defendant) in which she spoke some lines but was not a featured performer.

After the parties moved into the beach house, plaintiff continued to have singing engagements, encouraged by the defendant who would frequently attend, bringing friends and buying drinks for them to lengthen their stay and thereby increase plaintiff's audience.

A decorator was hired to work on the beach house and, after some structural changes, a substantial amount of furniture was purchased. Plaintiff worked with the decorator; both consulted defendant on occasion as to the purchases and alterations.

In 1966, defendant contacted a friend in Hawaii and secured a singing engagement for plaintiff. Before she left for Hawaii, Santana Records, Inc. was organized by defendant and defendant paid for the recordation of four songs by plaintiff under the Santana label. With the assistance of her manager, Mimi Marleaux, plaintiff visited disc jockeys in Hawaii and promoted the record.

In the same year, 1966, defendant went to London to make a picture entitled "Dirty Dozen." During his stay in England he wrote eight letters to plaintiff wherein he expressed affection for the plaintiff and looked forward to her coming to London. In one letter, Exhibit 13, he portrays an imaginary scene wherein he was "found guilty of robbing a 33–year-old cradle" and he answers the judge, "absolutely guilty, your honor.... Yes sir, I accept life with her, thank you your honor and the court. Will the jury please get out of that cradle!"

After the filming of "Dirty Dozen" and the parties' return to Malibu, Miss Marleaux allegedly was present in the Malibu house when defendant said, after plaintiff told Marleaux she was sorry she let her (Marleaux) down (by the slump in her career), "I don't know what you're worrying about. I'll always take care of you...."

While in Hawaii, plaintiff alleges that there was a ninth letter wherein defendant demanded that she give up her career, cut short her promotion of her record in Hawaii and come to London and if she did not, the relationship would be ended. At one point in the suit, plaintiff declared that she could not locate the letter. She now contends that it was destroyed by defendant. Miss Marleaux recollects a telephone call by defendant to the same effect but defendant introduced bills which indicate he made no such call.

In March of 1967, defendant testified that he told plaintiff that she would have to prepare for separation and that she should learn a trade. The plaintiff responded that if he left her, she would reveal his fears, his worries to the public and his career would be destroyed. She also threatened suicide.

In 1967, the plaintiff accompanied defendant to Baker, Oregon, where the latter made a film called "Paint Your Wagon." The parties rented a house in Baker and established a joint bank account. Plaintiff signed most of the checks drawn on that account.

The plaintiff returned to Los Angeles while "Paint Your Wagon" was still being filmed in Oregon in order to confer with one of the defendant's attorneys, Louis Goldman. She asked him whether it would be any trouble to change her name to "Marvin" as their different names were embarrassing to her as well as defendant in a place like Baker. Goldman said if the change was approved by defendant, it was agreeable with him. She then requested him to arrange with defendant for the placement of some property or a lump sum in her name. She declared to him that she did not know whether the relationship would last forever, that she had talked to defendant about conveying the house to her but that he had said absolutely no. She requested Goldman to persuade defendant to do something for her. Goldman later telephoned plaintiff to inform her that defendant had refused to agree to any of her requests.

Goldman testified that plaintiff told him that neither she nor defendant wanted to get married, that each wanted to be free to come and go as they pleased and to terminate the relationship if they wished. The subject of defendant's frequent intoxication was discussed.

On cross-examination, plaintiff testified that they were "always very proud of the fact that nothing held us. We weren't—we weren't legally married." After the breakup she declared to an interviewer: "We used to laugh and feel a great warmth about the fact that either of us could walk out at any time."

Following the completion of "Paint Your Wagon" (after additional work in Los Angeles), defendant made a picture entitled, "Hell in the Pacific" on the island of Palau in Micronesia. The parties again opened a joint account on location and drew funds there from for payment of food, clothing, etc. The plaintiff issued the greater number of checks.

She alleges that defendant introduced her as "Mrs. Marvin" although most of the American community on the island knew that they were not married, including the crew filming the picture and the cast. The defendant denies that he so introduced her.

The parties returned to Palau for a second sojourn. The parties enjoyed the fishing and the defendant supervised and assisted in the completion of a fishing boat which he hoped would vitalize the Palauan fishing industry. The parties talked to an architect about building a house, part of which they could occupy and part of which could be rented to visitors of Palau for the fishing.

Marriage was far from the thoughts of the parties. On the second visit to Palau, plaintiff testified that defendant asked her to marry him but she thought he was joking and laughed. A few weeks later plaintiff allegedly asked defendant to marry her and *he* laughed.

On Palau, the parties met Richard Doughty, a member of the Peace Corps fishery department. Doughty testified that he had sexual relations with plaintiff approximately twenty times on the island, and additional times later in Los Angeles and Tucson. Plaintiff vigorously denied this and claimed that Doughty was a homosexual, offering supporting witnesses. This in turn was vigorously denied by Doughty who also offered witnesses who would rebut such a charge. Doughty's testimony was corroborated by Carol Clark who testified that plaintiff admitted to her that she (plaintiff) had "an affair" with him.

Doughty's testimony is weakened by his denial of such relationship when defendant's counsel, A. David Kagon, first questioned him prior to the trial. He explained that he decided to tell the truth at the trial because he did not wish defendant to be railroaded and because he now was more willing to accept responsibility after he had recovered from a serious illness.

La Verna Hogan, wife of the production manager of "Hell in the Pacific," accompanied plaintiff on a trip from Palau to Hawaii. They stayed overnight in Guam where plaintiff told Mrs. Hogan that she was to meet two men in Hawaii. Mrs. Hogan asked plaintiff why she was going to meet them in view of her relationship with defendant and plaintiff responded, "We (plaintiff and defendant) have an understanding. He does his thing and I do mine." Plaintiff denies any such Hawaiian meeting.

In 1969, defendant filmed "Monte Walsh" on locations approximately two hours from Tucson. He rented a house in Tucson for the ten to twelve weeks of shooting. Doughty secured employment in "Monte Walsh" as a dialogue coach and lived with the parties. A joint bank account was again opened and funded by Edward Silver, defendant's business manager. Plaintiff signed most of the checks.

At the end of the shooting of the pictures, "Hell in the Pacific," "Paint Your Wagon," and "Monte Walsh," the Palau, Baker and Tucson joint bank accounts were closed and balances transferred to defendant's account.

Plaintiff had a separate account in Malibu in which defendant's business manager deposited $400 per month for her personal use.

The plaintiff testified that in May, 1970, defendant left the Malibu beach house upon her request. Later, she was told by defendant's agent, Mishkin, that defendant wished that they separate (Mishkin had referred to a "divorce" but testified that he was mistaken in his use of the term). The plaintiff later sought and found defendant in La Jolla. There he told her, plaintiff alleges, that he would not give up drinking, that it was part of his life and that his relationship with plaintiff was no longer enjoyable because of her frequent admonitions as to his drinking.

In May, 1970, plaintiff went to the office of defendant's attorney, Goldman. He informed her that defendant wanted her out of the house and out of his life and that defendant would pay her $833 per month (net after deduction of taxes from a gross of $1050) for five years. Plaintiff testified that she told Goldman she could not exist on such a stipend. Goldman responded that defendant could not afford to pay more because of alimony which he paid to his former wife. Plaintiff testified that she replied that defendant had promised to take care of her for life. Goldman, however, testified that she had simply thanked him for the arrangement and said that $833 would be enough for her needs.

She returned to the beach house but finally departed after an emotional confrontation with defendant and his attorneys, Goldman and Kagon. Checks for $833 each began to arrive. According to defendant, the payments were made on condition that she removed herself from his life and not discuss with anyone anything she learned about the defendant during their relationship. Defendant said that plaintiff thought this was fair. According to the plaintiff, the checks were stopped when defendant saw an item about him in one of the Hollywood columns. Defendant did send one more check but again stopped payment because, plaintiff declares, defendant was angered by her suit against Roberts. She told her attorney (then Howard L. Rosoff) to dismiss the action but, when no more checks came, she reversed her instructions. According to Goldman, plaintiff said she had nothing to do with the item in the column (re defendant's marriage to Pamela breaking up). He testified that she also said that she would not do it again and to give her another chance. Goldman replied that defendant "was at the end of the road."

The plaintiff filed an application dated March 26, 1970 to change her name to Michelle Triola Marvin. The verified application declared that she had been known professionally as "Marvin" and that she used the name in her acting and singing career.

Plaintiff stated in her deposition that she never used the name "Marvin" professionally. She now declares that she meant (in her application) that she used "Marvin" *during* her career but only socially.

The plaintiff also declared in her deposition that she had asked for a written agreement as to property shortly after moving into the beach house. Defendant allegedly said an agreement was being prepared but they did not need any papers. The plaintiff said they did. Plaintiff said nothing further about the nonappearance of an agreement during 1968, 1969 and 1970.

The defendant stated in his deposition that he wanted a relationship of no responsibility and that the plaintiff agreed with him.

On trips out of town, plaintiff was introduced on occasion as Michelle Marvin to avoid embarrassment in hotels, but defendant contends he never introduced her as *Mrs.* Marvin. Bills were rarely addressed to Mrs. Lee Marvin, but rather to Michelle Marvin. In the Malibu community and the actor-producer circles in which they moved, the couple's relationship was known not to be that of husband and wife.

The plaintiff testified that she never told the defendant that she would hold herself out as his wife, that the parties never used the terms "husband and wife," those words were not in their vocabulary and that they never used the word "homemaker."

Defendant testified that in the winter of 1969 plaintiff wanted him to finance a European trip at $10,000–$15,000 per month as the price for separation. Later, she offered to "get out of your (his) life for $50,000" and he would never hear from her again. Still later, she requested $100,000. Plaintiff denies that she made any such offer.

Rather than review the great number of allegations by plaintiff as to defendant's drinking to excess, it is enough to observe that defendant admits that he was frequently intoxicated. It is a reasonable inference therefrom that in such condition he needed care and that plaintiff provided it.

TESTIMONIAL INCONSISTENCIES

The weight of the testimony of the plaintiff is lessened by several inconsistencies.

Plaintiff claims to have had considerable help from Gene Kelly in the procurement of employment in "Flower Drum Song" in New York City. He, however, denied that he hired plaintiff. He further testified that he never talked to plaintiff about "Flower Drum Song" in 1963 or 1964 and that at that time the play was not being performed in New York City. In later testimony plaintiff altered her allegation of employment by Kelly to an offer of letters of introduction by him. She also modified her declaration that she was going to New York City to appear in "Flower Drum Song" to say that she did not know whether it was then being performed on Broadway.

Plaintiff's contention of many weeks of employment in Playboy clubs in Chicago, Phoenix, Miami, New York City, San Francisco and three other clubs and repeated in Chicago, Phoenix and San Francisco is countered by evidence from Playboy records of only one engagement, in Phoenix, and then for only two weeks. In fact, Noel Stein testified that the San Francisco club did not open until years after plaintiff's alleged engagement there. As for her allegation of employment by "Dino's Lodge" for 24 weeks in 1961 and 1962, its manager from 1958 on, Paul Wexler, declares that he recollects no employment of her by "Dino's Lodge" before 1965.

The testimony of plaintiff as to her right to compensation from Bobby Roberts, the producer of "Monte Walsh," contains three variations as to the type of compensation sought. At first she was to receive a Rolls Royce, then a 10% finders fee and lastly 50% of the producer's fee in return for informing Roberts as to the availability of the Monte Walsh script. Also, she testified that she met Roberts and Landers in their offices on or about March 15, 1968 whereas she was in Palau from Christmas of 1967 to April or May of 1968.

According to the records of Sears Roebuck, an account had been opened in the name of Lee Marvin (Exhibit 117; the application was signed by Betty Marvin, defendant's former wife). Plaintiff testified, however, that an account was opened by her with defendant present in the name of "Mr. and Mrs. Marvin" or Lee Marvin. Sears records do not list her on any application nor as an authorized signator (Exhibit 119).

Plaintiff testified that she "never had an apartment while I was with Lee." However, Exhibit 151 dated May 1, 1965 and signed by plaintiff is a lease of an apartment at 8633 West Knoll Drive, West Hollywood. Plaintiff contends she signed the lease on behalf of her manager, Mimi Marleaux, and that she, the plaintiff, had no belongings there nor did she make any rent payments. Yet, testimony by Marleaux reveals that plaintiff did have some clothes in the apartment and that she, Marleaux, had only stayed a month or two in the apartment. On cross-examination, plaintiff admitted that she may have paid the rent and on direct rebuttal she testified that she did pay the rent two or three times. Exhibit 186 indicates that a Continental Bank signature card signed on December 28, 1965 bore the West Knoll address as plaintiff's residence. At a later time, that address was crossed off and that of the Malibu Beach house was inserted.

Plaintiff testified that she asked defendant for a written agreement to protect her rights. The defendant responded that it was not necessary and she believed him. In her deposition, however, she stated that she continued to request such agreement.

LAW

IS THERE AN EXPRESS CONTRACT? . . .

A review of the extensive testimony clearly leads this court to the conclusion that no express contract was negotiated between the parties. Neither party entertained any expectations that the property was to be divided between them.

Further, before mutual consent can exist, an intent to contract must be present. Also, the meaning of the agreement must be ascertainable and both parties must have the same understanding of its meaning. The basic statement on which plaintiff relies is the one which she says (and defendant denies) was made by defendant at San Blas—"What I have is yours and what you have is mine."

Considering the circumstances from which it allegedly sprung, the lack of intent to make a contract is immediately apparent. In 1964–1965 defendant was married; he had considerable unresolved financial problems; he had repeatedly informed plaintiff that he did not believe in marriage because of the property rights which a wife thereby acquires. Plaintiff could not have understood that phrase to accord the same rights to one who was *not* defendant's wife. If those words had been spoken, they were not spoken under circumstances in which either party would be entitled to believe that an offer of a contract was intended.

In addition, the meaning of the phrase is difficult to ascertain. Does it mean a sharing of future as well as presently owned property? Does it mean a sharing of the *use* of property or is title to be extended to both parties? Does it mean that all property is shared even though the relationship may be terminated in a week or weekend? These are all unanswered questions. It is more reasonable to conclude that the declaration is simply hyperbole typical of persons who live and work in the entertainment field. It was defendant's way of expressing his affection for the plaintiff. As the defendant testified, in his business terms of affection are bandied about freely; one "loves" everyone and calls everybody "sweetheart."

Also, after hearing defendant's views on marriage and noting his antagonism against a person acquiring any rights by means of a certificate of marriage, it is not reasonable to believe that plaintiff understood that defendant intended to give her such rights even without a certificate. Without intent to contract and with no clearly ascertainable meaning of the contractual phrase, no express contract exists.

During a meeting with Marleaux in the fall of 1966 and in the presence of the defendant, the plaintiff told Marleaux that she (plaintiff) was sorry she had let Marleaux down by not pursuing her career. Defendant then allegedly stated, "I don't know what you're worrying about. I'll always take care of you."

Corbin has this to say about remarks of that sort: "The law does not attempt the realization of every expectation that has been induced by a promise; the expectation must be a reasonable one. Under no system of law that has ever existed are all promises enforceable. The expectation must be one that most people would have, and the promise must be one that most people would perform." Surely plaintiff had no expectation that defendant would extend such care to her after separation, remembering defendant's antagonism to such automatic rights in a wife if the relationship failed (and to which she testified).

In addition, the phrase "I'll always take care of you" leaves many questions unanswered: Does defendant mean that plaintiff has the right to care even if separation is caused by plaintiff? What level of care? What if plaintiff marries, does the care continue? An offer as indefinite as this cannot be the basis of an enforceable contract.

Further, the alleged promise lacks mutuality; the plaintiff made no enforceable promise in response. Even if, *arguendo*, she had promised to forego her career, defendant could not have legally enforced such promise. Actually, plaintiff's career, never very brisk-paced, was sputtering and not because of any act of defendant; it came to an end unmourned and unattended by plaintiff who made no attempt to breathe life into it.

Doubt is cast upon the Marleaux testimony as to the alleged promise. The statement was allegedly made in the presence of Marleaux. The plaintiff testified that she remembers the event very clearly and that it was very important in her life. Yet in plaintiff's deposition of October, 1978, she was asked whether anyone other than the defendant was present and she responded, "I can't recall if anyone was present."

The phrase, "Yes sir, I accept life with her, thank you, Your Honor, and the court" contained in Exhibit 13 (a letter written from London in

1966) adds no legal basis for a contract. It was a letter portraying an imaginary court scene from which one can infer the affection of defendant for plaintiff but from which one certainly cannot believe an offer of a contract was intended.

IS THERE AN IMPLIED CONTRACT?

The conduct of the parties after the San Blas conversation certainly does not reveal any implementation of any contract nor does such conduct give rise to an implied contract. No joint bank accounts were established and no real property was placed in joint tenancy or tenancy in common. Plaintiff used a separate bank account for her allowance of $400 per month, her earnings from the Hawaii engagement and her settlement of the Roberts suit. When defendant bought real property, he placed it in his own name. Their tax returns were separate.

In plaintiff's letter to defendant dated November 2, 1971, she describes her activities after their separation, thanks defendant for his "financial help" (monthly payments for five years) and says nothing about any contract or agreement. In Ex. 155, a page from a book by plaintiff's counsel, he declares that plaintiff only asked him how to enforce defendant's promise to make payments pursuant to the five-year arrangement. Nothing was said then to counsel about any agreement to divide property. Plaintiff's attorney sent a letter to defendant's attorney, demanding recommencement of the payments for the five-year period. Plaintiff was quoted in an interview recorded in the Brenda Shaw article as follows: "We were always very proud of the fact that nothing really held us. We both agreed, and we were really pleased with the fact that you work harder at a relationship when you know that there is nothing really holding you." This evidence bars the finding of any contract.

The very fact that plaintiff pursued a claim for compensation from Roberts makes it plain that she expected no part of any earnings of defendant from the picture. Otherwise, why would she commence a lawsuit to recover a finder's fee or half of a producer's fee when she would have rights to half of the million dollars paid to defendant for the picture?

The evidence does not support plaintiff's contention that she gave up her career in order to care for defendant and on his demand that she do so.

She claimed that defendant demanded that plaintiff give up her career and join him in London or else the relationship would end. Looking at the facts, she did go to London but remained only a few weeks. She declares that she returned because defendant was drinking heavily, and it was then too late to resume promotion of her record. Yet in her 1978 deposition she stated that she returned because her manager wanted her to come home to promote her record and in fact she did attempt to do so, but discovered that the radio stations were not interested. As for loss of momentum, in the promotion of her record by reason of her London trip, witnesses for defendant as well as one for plaintiff testified that no loss occurred. Contrary to any ultimatum, a witness for defendant declared that the latter expressed hope that she would have a successful career.

Plaintiff testified that the ultimatum was delivered to her by letter.

However, her witness, Marleaux, declared that it came by way of telephone. One must doubt that the defendant issued an ultimatum (allegedly in the missing letter) demanding that plaintiff come to London when he writes in Ex. 12, "only a month and a half to go, w(h)oopee," indicating that plans for her coming to London had already been made by the parties.

The plaintiff's testimony as to defendant's drinking habits would indicate that he was virtually awash with alcohol. Yet during this same period, defendant starred in several major films, all demanding of him physical stamina, a high degree of alertness and verbal as well as physical concentration. Her portrayal of large-scale and all pervasive inebriation raises doubt as to her accuracy of observation.

An implied as well as an express agreement must be founded upon mutual consent. Such consent may be inferred from the conduct of the parties. Proof of introductions of plaintiff as Mrs. Marvin, and the occasional registrations at hotels as Mrs. Marvin and evidence of a relationship wherein plaintiff furnished companionship, cooking and home care do not establish that defendant agreed to give plaintiff half of his property. Those services may be rendered out of love or affection and are indeed so rendered in a myriad of relationships between man and woman which are not contractual in nature. They may be consideration for a contract to receive property but the other elements of such contract remain to be established. Discussion of an equitable basis for an award because of homemaking services is to be found in a later portion of his opinion.

The change of name to Marvin appears to have had one motivation: to avoid embarrassment when traveling. It ended the awkwardness occurring when, for example, plaintiff's passport was examined in customs. Coming at a time so close to the date of separation and after some indication of difficulties between the parties, the change of name does raise a question whether plaintiff sought relief from embarrassment or whether she wished to acquire the right to use defendant's name after separation.

The evidence of a contract as to property may be imputed from a change in the manner of holding, such as joint tenancy bank accounts, but not such joint accounts as were set up on the various filming locations (Tucson, Baker, Palau). These accounts were transient, employed solely for the convenience of attending to current needs away from California. The disposition of funds remaining after the film was completed underlined the single purpose of the accounts: upon completion the funds were placed not in a joint account in Los Angeles but in defendant's separate account.

Plaintiff's use of charge accounts certainly does not establish that defendant by his alleged consent to such use intended that half of his property be given to plaintiff.

Registering at hotels as Mr. and Mrs. Marvin does not indicate that defendant intended to give plaintiff one-half of the property. Such evidence may assist in proving a relationship which on its surface resembles marriage in areas away from home, but relationships resembling marriage may exist without any property arrangements. Hence more must be proved by a preponderance of evidence, that is, that plaintiff used the charge accounts *because defendant had agreed to give her half of the property*.

Plaintiff proved that she acted as companion and homemaker, that she prepared a number of defendant's meals and that she cleaned house or supervised a cleaning woman. That she did so in consideration of a contract, express, implied, or tacit, with respect to disposing of property, remains unproven. The existence of such property agreement has not been established by the requisite preponderance of the evidence. The decisions of *In re Marriage of Cary* (1973)109 Cal.Rptr. 862, and *Estate of Atherley* (1975) 119 Cal.Rptr. 41, afford no comfort to the plaintiff as their facts distinguish them from the instant case. In *Cary*, the disputed property was placed in the joint names of both parties, joint income tax returns were filed, money was borrowed and business was conducted as husband and wife. In *Atherley*, both parties pooled earnings accumulated for 13 years and bought property as joint tenants. Both worked and contributed funds to the construction of improvements on land bought with such earnings. None of these facts were established in this case: there was no pooling of earnings, no property was purchased in joint names, and no joint income tax returns were executed. Joint accounts set up on filming locations were only used as convenient and transient methods of payment of bills with the balance returned to the separate account of the defendant when the film was completed.

As for pooling of earnings, the bulk of plaintiff's compensation for singing was used to pay her musician and arrangers. When she did achieve a net income in the Hawaiian engagement, she placed the money in her separate account. Defendant's income was deposited in his own bank account and used to buy property in his own name. This case therefore bears little resemblance either to *Cary* or *Atherley*.

Finding no contract, the testimony of Doughty is not evaluated as that relates to an alleged breach of contract.

It is clear that the parties came together because of mutual affection and not because of mutual consent to a contract. Nothing else, certainly no contract, kept them together and, when that affection diminished, they separated.

EQUITABLE REMEDIES....

The plaintiff has, by her dismissal of her fourth and fifth causes of action—both for quantum meruit—removed that remedy from the court's consideration.

If a resulting trust is to be established, it must be shown that property was intended by the parties to be held by one party in trust for the other and that consideration was provided by the one not holding title to purchase the property. As Witkin puts it, there must be "circumstances showing that the transferee (holder of title) was not intended to take the beneficial interest."

No evidence has been adduced to show such consideration having been provided by the plaintiff to buy property. It may be contended that as the defendant did not need to expend funds to secure homemaking services elsewhere, she thereby enhanced the financial base of the defendant and enabled him to increase his property purchases. Such alleged enhancement, however, would appear to be offset by the considerable flow of economic benefits in the other direction. Those benefits include payments for goods and services for plaintiff up to $72,900 for the period from 1967–1970 alone. Exhibit 196 indicates that living expenses for the parties were $221,400 for the period from 1965 to 1970. Among such benefits were a Mercedes Benz automobile for plaintiff, fur coats, travel to London, Hawaii, Japan, Micronesia, and the pleasures of life on the California beach in frequent contact with many film and stage notables. Further, defendant made a substantial financial effort to launch plaintiff's career as a recording singer. No equitable basis for an expansion of the resulting trust theory is afforded in view of this evidence.

A constructive trust, pleaded in the second cause of action, is "equity's version of implied-in-law recovery" (see Bruch, *supra*, p. 125). However, the defendant earned the money by means of his own effort, skill and reputation. The money was then invested in the properties now held by him. It cannot be said in good conscience that such properties do not belong to him.

As Witkin points out, such a trust is an equitable remedy imposed where a person obtains property by fraudulent misrepresentation or concealment or by some wrongful act. No such wrongdoing can be elicited from the facts of this case....

In *Atherley*, the parties, Harold and Annette, lived together for 22 years; after 14 years Harold divorced a prior wife *ex parte* in Juarez, Mexico and then married Annette in Reno, Nevada. Both were employed and pooled their earnings in various bank accounts. They had been advised by a Los Angeles attorney that the Mexican divorce was valid. Both contributed services to the construction of improvements on land purchased by them. Funds used to purchase both land and materials can be traced to their accumulated earnings. Two bank accounts were established with funds accumulated by Harold and Annette. Upon the sale of an improved parcel, a promissory note representing part of the sales price was held in joint tenancy. None of these facts is present in the instant case.

In this case we have all assets bought solely with the earnings of the defendant. The plaintiff had no net earnings except from the Hawaiian engagement and those funds went into her own account. Plaintiff secured $750 from the settlement of her suit against Roberts and those funds also did not go into defendant's account. There were, on the other hand, funds that were expended by defendant to further plaintiff's career. The defendant also persuaded a friend to employ plaintiff in Hawaii. He brought people to hear her sing and bought drinks to keep them in attendance. It was the plaintiff who stopped trying to sell her record and get singing engagements. The evidence does not establish that such cessation was caused by defendant.

It would be difficult to deem the singing career of plaintiff to be the "mutual effort" required by the Supreme Court. Certainly, where both wanted to be free to come and go without obligation, the basis of any division of property surely cannot be her "giving up" her career for him. It then can only be her work as cook, homemaker and companion that can be considered as plaintiff's contribution to the requisite "mutual effort." Yet, where $72,000 has been disbursed by defendant on behalf of plaintiff in less than six years, where she has enjoyed a fine home and travel throughout the world for about 30 months, where she acquired whatever clothes, furs and cars she wished and engaged in a social life amongst screen and stage luminaries, such services as she has rendered would appear to have been compensated. Surely one cannot glean from such services her participation in a "mutual effort" between the parties to earn funds to buy property as occurred in *Cary* and *Atherley, supra.*

The Supreme Court doubtless intended by the phrase "mutual effort" to mean the relationship of a man and woman who have joined together to make a home, who act together to earn and deposit such earnings in joint accounts, who pay taxes together, who make no effort to gain an advantage by reason of the association, (such as informing a producer of a script for a fee and taking defendant's name without his consent), who have children if possible and bring them up together. *Cary* and *Atherley* in fact demand more of the partners; they require participation in money-earning activities. Plaintiff's fund-raising put money in her own account.

To construe "mutual effort" to mean services as homemaker, cook and companion and nothing else, would be tantamount to the grant of the benefits of the Family Law Act to the nonmarital partner as well as to the married person. This the Supreme Court has refused to do. Therefore, one must seek and find in each case those additional factors which indicate the expenditure of "mutual effort," such as those present in *Cary* and *Atherley*. Such factors are not present in this case.

The court is aware that Footnote 25, *Marvin v. Marvin, supra*, p. 684, urges the trial court to employ whatever equitable remedy may be proper under the circumstances. The court is also aware of the recent resort of plaintiff to unemployment insurance benefits to support herself and of the fact that a return of plaintiff to a career as a singer is doubtful. Additionally, the court knows that the market value of defendant's property at time of separation exceeded $1,000,000.

In view of these circumstances, the court in equity awards plaintiff $104,000 for rehabilitation purposes so that she may have the economic means to re-educate herself and to learn new, employable skills or to refurbish those utilized, for example, during her most recent employment and so that she may return from her status as companion of a motion picture star to a separate, independent but perhaps more prosaic existence.

MARVIN v. MARVIN

California Court of Appeals, 1981
122 Cal App 3d 871, 176 Cal Rptr 555

COBEY, ASSOCIATE J.

Defendant, Lee Marvin, appeals from that portion of a judgment ordering him to pay to plaintiff, Michelle Marvin, the sum of $104,000, to be used by her primarily for her economic rehabilitation.

Defendant contends, among other things, that the challenged award is outside the issues of the case as framed by the pleadings of the parties (see Code Civ. Proc., § 588) and furthermore lacks any basis in equity or in law. We agree and will therefore modify the judgment by deleting therefrom the challenged award.

Facts

This statement of facts is taken wholly from the findings of the trial court, which tried the case without a jury. The parties met in June 1964 and started living together occasionally in October of that year. They lived together almost continuously (except for business absences of his) from the spring of 1965 to May or June of 1970, when their cohabitation was ended at his insistence. This cohabitation was the result of an initial agreement between them to live together as unmarried persons so long as they both enjoyed their mutual companionship and affection.

More specifically, the parties to this lawsuit never agreed during their cohabitation that they would combine their efforts and earnings or would share equally in any property accumulated as a result of their efforts, whether individual or combined. They also never agreed during this period that plaintiff would relinquish her professional career as an entertainer and singer in order to devote her efforts full time to defendant as his companion and homemaker generally. Defendant did not agree during this period of cohabitation that he would provide all of plaintiff's financial needs and support for the rest of her life.

Furthermore, the trial court specifically found that: (1) defendant has never had any obligation to pay plaintiff a reasonable sum as and for her maintenance; (2) plaintiff suffered no damage resulting from her relationship with defendant, including its termination and thus defendant did not become monetarily liable to plaintiff at all; (3) plaintiff actually benefited economically and socially from the cohabitation of the parties, including payment by defendant for goods and services for plaintiff's sole benefit in the approximate amount of $72,900.00, payment by defendant of the living expenses of the two of them of approximately $221,400.00, and other substantial specified gifts; (4) a confidential and fiduciary relationship never existed between the parties with respect to property; (5) defendant was never unjustly enriched as a result of the relationship of the parties or of the services performed by plaintiff for him or for them; (6) defendant never acquired any property or money from plaintiff by any wrongful act.

The trial court specifically found in support of its challenged rehabilitation award that the market value of defendant's property at the time the parties separated exceeded $1 million, that plaintiff at the time of the trial of this case had been recently receiving unemployment insurance benefits, that it was doubtful that plaintiff could return to the career that she had enjoyed before the relationship of the parties commenced, namely, that of singer, that plaintiff was in need of rehabilitation—i.e., to learn new employable skills, that she should be able to accomplish such rehabilitation in two years and that the sum of $104,000 was not only necessary primarily for such rehabilitation, but also for her living expenses (including her debts) during this period of rehabilitation, and that defendant had the ability to pay this sum forthwith.

Moreover, the trial court concluded as a matter of law that inasmuch as defendant had terminated the relationship of the parties and plaintiff had no visible means of support, "in equity", she had a right to assistance by defendant until she could become self-supporting. The trial court explained that it fixed the award at the highest salary that the plaintiff had ever earned, namely, $1,000 a week for two years, although plaintiff's salary had been at that level for only two weeks and she ordinarily had earned less than one-half that amount weekly.

Discussion

1. *The challenged rehabilitation award is not within the issues framed by the pleadings.*

This is a judgment roll appeal in the sense that we have no transcript of the evidence taken at the apparently lengthy trial below. The issues in a lawsuit are, aside from those added by a pretrial order, either those framed by the pleadings or as expanded at trial. Here, however, since we do not have before us the evidence taken at trial and there was no pretrial order expanding the issues, we can look only to the pleadings to determine the issues between the parties.

Plaintiff's amended complaint, upon which this action went to trial, asks, with respect to the support of plaintiff by defendant, only that defendant be ordered to pay to plaintiff a reasonable sum per month as and for her support and maintenance. Plaintiff did not ask in this basic pleading for any limited rehabilitative support of the type the trial court apparently on its own initiative subsequently awarded her. Consequently, the special findings of fact and conclusions of law in support of this award must be disregarded as not being within the issues framed by the pleadings. When this is done, the challenged portion of the judgment becomes devoid of any support whatsoever and therefore must be deleted.

2. *In any event there is no equitable or legal basis for the challenged rehabilitative award.*

The trial court apparently based its rehabilitative award upon two footnotes in the opinion of our Supreme Court in this case. These are footnotes 25 and 26. . . .

There is no doubt that footnote 26 opens the door to a support award in appropriate circumstances. Likewise, under footnote 25, equitable remedies should be devised "to protect the expectations of the parties to a nonmarital relationship." The difficulty in applying either of these footnotes in the manner in which the trial court has done in this case is that, as already pointed out, the challenged limited rehabilitative award of the trial court is not within the issues of the case as framed by the pleadings and there is nothing in the trial court's findings to suggest that such an award is warranted to protect the expectations of *both* parties.

Quite to the contrary, as already noted, the trial court expressly found that plaintiff benefited economically and socially from her relationship with defendant and suffered no damage therefrom, even with respect to its termination. Furthermore, the trial court also expressly found that defendant never had any obligation to pay plaintiff a reasonable sum as and for her maintenance and that defendant had not been unjustly enriched by reason of the relationship or its termination and that defendant had never acquired anything of value from plaintiff by any wrongful act.

Furthermore, the special findings in support of the challenged rehabilitative award merely established plaintiff's need therefor and defendant's ability to respond to that need. This is not enough. The award, being nonconsensual in nature, must be supported by some recognized underlying obligation in law or in equity. A court of equity admittedly has broad powers, but it may not create totally new substantive rights under the guise of doing equity.

The trial court in its special conclusions of law addressed to this point attempted to state an underlying obligation by saying that plaintiff had a right to assistance from defendant until she became self-supporting. But this special conclusion obviously conflicts with the earlier, more general, finding of the court that defendant has never had and did not then have any obligation to provide plaintiff with a reasonable sum for her support and maintenance and, in view of the already-mentioned findings of no damage (but benefit instead), no unjust enrichment and no wrongful act on the part of defendant with respect to either the relationship or its termination, it is clear that no basis whatsoever, either in equity or in law, exists for the challenged rehabilitative award. It therefore must be deleted from the judgment. . . .

A Few Notes on Marvin

You may be curious about what happened to the people involved in the *Marvin* case. Here is a brief report.

Lee Marvin. Lee Marvin continued to make movies, including *Delta Force.* He also took a wife, his second, with whom he lived at least for a while in Phoenix. In 1987, he died of a heart attack at the age of 63. *Time's* obituary noted that he had made *The Man Who Shot Liberty Valance, The Dirty Dozen,* and *Cat Ballou,* but said that he "won perhaps his greatest renown" for *Marvin v. Marvin. Time* said that in that case Michelle Triola had won $104,000. September 7, 1987, at 64.

Michelle Triola. On August 24, 1981, *Time* said Michelle Triola had been "fined and placed on probation for shop lifting some bras and a sweater from a Beverly Hills store." The brief article reported that she was then forty-six years old and that she described herself as a public relations agent. On January 30, 1986, at page 24, the *Los Angeles Times* reported she had legally changed her name to "Marvin" and was living "in the Los Angeles area with comedian Dick Van Dyke."

Marvin Mitchelson. Marvin Mitchelson was Michelle Triola's lawyer in *Marvin.* The *Los Angeles Times* stated, on January 30, 1986, page 24, that it cost Mitchelson $100,000 to try the case but that Mitchelson said he had "made millions" out of the case because of the publicity generated for his office. The article added, "Charging $250 an hour, Mitchelson prefers to work on a 25% contingency basis or negotiated share of the result, and he charges retainers of $15,000 to $75,000 for divorces and $10,000 to $15,000 for palimony."

Mitchelson's practice has not been without its difficulties, however. On July 3, 1988, at section 1, page 10, the *New York Times* reported: "Last week, the State Bar of California charged that in six separate instances Mr. Mitchelson either charged clients 'unconscionable' amounts of money, failed to return unearned fees or performed his work badly. Bar officials are now investigating at least 12 additional complaints against him, and more are pouring in daily." The article stated that bringing frivolous appeals had cost Mitchelson a total of $40,000 in two appellate courts, that a number of clients had brought legal proceedings against him, and that six women, five of them former clients, had charged Mitchelson with sexual misconduct. The article said, "Over time, Mr. Mitchelson became to the law what Liberace was to music: an endearing egomaniac who spent lavishly, lived garishly and seemed almost to relish the ridicule of his more strait-laced peers. He drove a Rolls–Royce, lived in a 27 room mansion in Beverly Hills and furnished his office bathroom with a Jacuzzi, wallpaper depicting nymphets and pillows with images of his late mother." Mitchelson has experienced proceedings of various sorts brought against him by creditors, including Sotheby's and the Internal Revenue Service. The article quoted Mitchelson as arguing that the complaints only showed that some of his clients had unrealistic expectations. "While he has made various 'fee adjustments,' he said, only two malpractice cases against him have ever been tried, and he won both of them."

When the *Los Angeles Times*, January 30, 1986, at 25, asked Mitchelson about *Marvin*, he replied, "Every judge recognizes the *Marvin* concept. Every law school knows it. It is a landmark decision. It is legend. It is recognized all over the world."

Questions on Marvin

(1) For what set (or sets) of ideas is *Marvin* a victory? Feminism? Individualism? Contract? Marriage? Libertarianism? Legalization? Legalization in what sense? In the sense that an activity which was once illegal is now legal? That the law now regulates an area that was once unregulated?

(2) Before we discuss *Marvin* further, you should define its holding as precisely as possible. What exactly is its scope? Does the California Supreme Court define that scope accurately?

(3) The court suggests that the standard it introduces is easier to apply than the old standard ("involved with" a meretricious relationship). Is that true? What ambiguities do you expect in future *Marvin* cases? Does the court intend that the new standard will actually be applied?

(4) As you will remember from your contracts class, there are four kinds of contracts: express written contracts, express oral contracts, implied-in-fact contracts, and implied-in-law contracts. The *Marvin* court announces its willingness to enforce all four kinds. How does this differ from the principles of contract law that apply to marriage? What problems do you foresee in enforcing each kind of contract? In thinking about this last question, we suggest you consider the kinds in the order we have listed them, since the difficulties are mostly cumulative.

(5) Recall now the principle of family autonomy. That principle has been taken to discourage courts from enforcing intra-familial contracts. See, e.g., *Kilgrow v. Kilgrow*. Ought it be applied to *Marvin* situations?

(6) What kind of an institution does *Marvin* create? After *Marvin* is there any difference between being married and cohabiting? Should there be any difference? If so, what should the difference be?

(7) In Chapter 1 we discussed some of the reasons people might want to be married. We said that a number of legal advantages flow from marriage. Which, if any, of them should be available to a couple living in a "*Marvin*" relationship? The ability to file joint income-tax returns? To recover for loss of consortium and for wrongful death? Which, if any, of the legal disadvantages that flow from marriage should be imposed on a

couple who are living in a "*Marvin*" relationship? Support duties? Rules of division of marital property? Should the parties be able to contract out of those disadvantages? Even where a married couple could not?

(8) *Marvin* rests partly on the court's perception that social behavior had changed. How well-substantiated was this perception?

(a) The *Marvin* court rests its decision on what it perceives as a major change in social behavior and beliefs—a dramatic increase in the frequency and legitimacy of unmarried cohabitation. The only evidence the court cites (in footnote 1) is a student note which quotes the census as finding an eightfold increase in cohabitation over ten years but which does not indicate what the actual rate of cohabitation is, what the nature of that cohabitation is, whether the trend the court detects is likely to continue, and so on. The court, then, may well have relied on its informal perceptions about social behavior. Is this a reliable basis for making changes in public policy? Might that basis be skewed by the judges' class situation? Might the court's sense that cohabitation was widespread, for instance, have been affected by the fact that cohabitation occurs more frequently among the well-to-do (and the poor) than among other segments of society? See Andrew Cherlin, *Marriage, Divorce, Remarriage* (Harv U Press, 1981).

(b) Does the court ask any searching questions about the social fact (increased cohabitation) that it perceives? For example, could any of the increase be due to the demographic bulge of young people, the group most likely to be cohabit? How much of the increase is real and how much of it is the result of the greater willingness of cohabitants to tell interviewers they are cohabiting? How much of the increase is an increase in cohabitation between people with a sexual relationship? (The Census Bureau simply treats as cohabitants each household of two unrelated people of opposite sexes, and thus "cohabitants" may include "a male college student who rents a room in the home of an elderly widow, or an elderly man with a female live-in housekeeper or nurse.") Is the increase permanent? (Social change is not unidirectional. The 1980s were quite different from the 1960s, and the '90s were different from the '80s.) Even if the increase is permanent, what kind of cohabitation are we talking about? Is it prolonged and serious cohabitation, as was arguably true in *Marvin*, or is it often short-term? All these questions go to whether the change in the law *Marvin* represents was needed.

(c) Since in 2000 the Census Bureau changed its definition to "unmarried partner," we can have a more realistic count of how many people cohabit. That Census reports nearly 50 million coupled households in the United States. Of these, 54.5 million were married couples, and nearly 5.5 million were unmarried (of whom nearly 4.9 million were opposite-sex couples). Entirely consistent with the census count is another paper, based upon the Current Population Series, traces the rise in cohabitation almost precisely since Marvin

v. Marvin. Number of Cohabiting Couples Based Upon Two Indirect Measures, 1977–97 (1999), available at http://www.census.gov/population/documentation/twps0036/tab01.txt.

Year	POSSLQ	Adj. POSSLQ	Diff. (thousands)	Diff. as Percent POSSLQ
1977	968	1,097	129	13.3
1978	1,155	1,295	140	12.1
1979	1,353	1,531	178	13.2
1980	1,560	1,776	216	13.8
1981	1,808	2,059	251	13.9
1982	1,863	2,124	261	14.0
1983	1,891	2,173	282	14.9
1984	1,980	2,268	288	14.5
1985	1,983	2,304	321	16.2
1986	2,220	2,533	313	14.1
1987	2,334	2,780	446	19.1
1988	2,588	2,999	411	15.9
1989	2,764	3,215	451	16.3
1990	2,856	3,324	468	16.4
1991	3,039	3,493	454	14.9
1992	3,308	3,836	528	16.0
1993	3,510	4,014	504	14.4
1994	3,662	4,272	610	16.7
1995	3,667	4,312	645	17.6
1996	3,958	4,602	644	16.3
1997	4,125	4,856	731	17.7

Assuming the Census data is accurate, since the effect of the "baby boom" ended before this counting began, what might account for the continued increase? A provocative paper by Stéphane Mechoulan, Divorce Laws and the Structure of the American Family, 35 J Legal Stud 143 (2006), suggests that couples might be marrying later and cohabiting first because they have learned the lessons of no-fault divorce. Because divorce is easier (and more frequent), couples sort themselves better before they marry, marry later, and actually are far less likely to divorce than those who married 20 years before. But if Mechoulan is correct, and many of these couples are not intending their nonmarital relationships to permanently substitute for marriage, do the considerations of *Marvin* and *Hewitt* (for marriage-like relationships) make sense?

(9) *Marvin* requires courts to draw inferences from the words and behavior of cohabitants. A court's abilities to do so will rest on how well it can discover the meaning the parties themselves attribute to what they say and do. In a time of rapid social change, will courts encounter difficulties because of the absence of widely shared social understandings?

(10) *Hewitt* and *Marvin* exemplify contrasting attitudes about how courts ought to treat legislative pronouncements that may be relevant to the decision about which kinds of contracts are enforceable. What are

their attitudes toward the question? What is the basis for them? Which attitude is preferable?

(11) As we said in introducing *Marvin*, it and *Hewitt* essentially represent the extremes of the judicial continuum. Here is a brief summary of the current state of the law:

> The great majority of jurisdictions recognize express contracts, and only a handful of them require that the contract be written rather than oral. Jurisdictions split on whether to recognize implied contracts. Those that do recognize implied contracts differ in their inclination to infer contractual undertakings from any given set of facts. Some courts reach much further than others. In doing so, they appear to vindicate an equitable rather than a contractual principle.

ALI, *Principles of the Law of Family Dissolution: Analysis and Recommendations* 18 (Tentative Draft No. 4, April 10, 2000).

Breach of Promise to Marry

Lee Marvin's attorney argued that the California statute eliminating actions for breach of promise to marry also barred Michelle's suit. Whether this argument is persuasive or not, we should consider briefly the action for breach of promise.

MARGARET F. BRINIG
RINGS AND PROMISES

6 Journal of Law, Economics, and Organization 203 (1990)

The breach of promise action entitled a woman whose fiance had broken off their engagement to sue him in assumpsit for damages including the actual expenses she had incurred in reliance on the marriage. She might also recover for her embarrassment, humiliation, and loss of other marriage opportunities. The early action for breach of promise to marry was within the jurisdiction of the English ecclesiastical courts, and in many cases the filing of the action resulted in specific performance of the marriage contract rather than an award of damages since the man was financially coerced into marriage to prevent the suit. One of the reasons given in favor of abolishing the action was that these forced marriages ought not to be encouraged.

Until fairly recently, a woman's marriage was necessary to secure her social position, so that the "old maid" would not only be scorned because she was not attractive enough to snag a husband, but also would be disadvantaged because in later life she would not be secure financially. Marriage was the "one career open to her," and once she had made her choice of husbands, the woman's "options were suddenly, irrevocably gone." Margaret F. Brinig and June Carbone, "The Reliance Interest in Marriage and Divorce," 62 Tul L. Rev. 855, 872–74 (1988).

But there was more to the doctrine than this. Many if not most women who brought such actions had not only lost a husband, but also their virginity. Particularly during the time between the two World

Wars, a woman was expected to remain chaste until the time of her engagement. Once she was betrothed, however, sexual intimacy with her fiancé reportedly occurred nearly half the time. All this was well and good, but if the marriage never came about, she was irretrievably barred from offering an unblemished self to a new suitor, and suffered a loss in "market value." While a man could pretend inexperience, a woman's virginity or lack of it was a verifiable physical fact. One author notes that "our courts seem to demand only that the plaintiff be *virgo intacta*. All is a question of the condition of the flesh. The mind may be poisoned with filth, and the character hardened by ugly habits; in short, the spiritual hymen may have suffered many a breach, but if the physical one is not intact, the defendant will have no better alternative than to marry her or pay damages." W.J. Brockelbank, "The Nature of the Promise to Marry—A Study in Comparative Law," 41 Ill L Rev 1, 8 (1946). Because of the importance of premarital chastity, damages in breach of promise actions where seduction (intercourse) had occurred were far more substantial than in cases where no sexual intimacy was alleged. The trials themselves frequently became public spectacles because of testimony regarding the woman's previous chastity (or lack of the same). By the beginning of the depression, the breach of promise suit came to be regarded as legally sanctioned blackmail, a threat to marriage and the family. . . .

While the action for breach of promise remains on the books of a number of jurisdictions, it has gradually fallen out of favor, so that now there are only a few reported breach of marriage promise decisions from those few jurisdictions where the action remains viable. Why?

The first reason, of course, is the belief that engagement is what the law in other contexts calls a *locus poenitentiae*, a last chance for the couple to be sure they want to live together for the rest of their lives. Furthermore, the action for breach of promise seems to some people to treat marriage too much as an economic relationship. Additionally, because it was historically available only to women, it smacked of inequality between men and women.

Another reason for the waning of breach of promise has been the fear of fraudulent suits and blackmail. Because engagements usually take place in private, it is often hard to know when a promise to marry has been made. To get over this problem, courts allowed contracts to be implied in fact. Yet doing so considerably increased the risk that an unscrupulous person would falsely allege a promise to extort a settlement or win a suit. Also, the action tended to drive people into marriage when sexual activity had already taken place. Walter Wadlington, *Shotgun Marriage by Operation of Law,* 1 Ga L Rev 183 (1968).

Yet a further difficulty of the action is that damages are notoriously difficult to assess, a problem that is exacerbated by the availability of punitive damages and by the susceptibility of juries. Critics of the action contend that these factors have often led to unjustifiable damage awards (and thus to increased risks of blackmail).

Questions on Breach of Promise

(1) We have seen that marriage is once again becoming contractualized, and *Marvin* indicates that non-marital relations are likewise becoming contractualized. As this process continues, will it be appropriate to restore the action for breach of promise to greater importance?

(2) Do you see how the criticisms of the action for breach of promise might also be applied to the actions the court creates in *Marvin*?

SECTION 3. THE REVISED VIEW: A STATUTORY PROPOSAL

But sexual conventions are not statutes, and it is important to define quite clearly just what they are. In the older world they were rules of conduct enforceable by the family and the community through habit, coercion, and authority. In this sense of the word, convention tends to lose force and effect in modern civilization. Yet a convention is essentially a theory of conduct and all human conduct implies some theory of conduct. Therefore, although it may be that no convention is any longer coercive, conventions remain, are adopted, revised, and debated. They embody the considered results of experience: perhaps the experience of a lonely pioneer or perhaps the collective experience of the dominant members of a community. In any event they are as necessary to a society which recognizes no authority as to one which does. For the inexperienced must be offered some kind of hypothesis when they are confronted with the necessity of making choices: they cannot be so utterly open-minded that they stand inert until something collides with them. In the modern world, therefore, the function of conventions is to declare the meaning of experience. A good convention is one which will most probably show the inexperienced the way to happy experience.

Walter Lippmann
A Preface to Morals

Marvin announced that new social attitudes demand new law. But the *Marvin* court had only a few law-making tools at hand. Imagine that you had the freedom of a legislature to devise whatever law for cohabitants you thought wise. That is the experiment the elite lawyers of the American Law Institute essayed. Consider now their conclusions:

AMERICAN LAW INSTITUTE PRINCIPLES OF FAMILY DISSOLUTION

Tentative Draft No. 4, 2000

§ 6.01 Scope

(1) This Chapter governs the financial claims of domestic partners against one another at the termination of their relationship. Domestic

partners are two persons of the same or opposite sex, not married to one another, who for a significant period of time share a primary residence and a life together as a couple, as determined by § 6.03.

(2) A contract between domestic partners that (i) waives or limits claims that would otherwise arise under this Chapter or (ii) provides remedies not provided by this Chapter, is enforceable according to its terms and displaces any inconsistent claims under this Chapter, so long as it satisfies the requirements of Chapter 7 for the enforcement of agreements.

(3) Nothing in this Chapter forecloses contract claims between persons who have no claims under this Chapter, but who have formed a contract that is enforceable under applicable law.

(4) Claims for custodial and decisionmaking responsibilities, and for child support, are governed by Chapters 2 and 3, and not by this Chapter.

(5) Claims arise under this Chapter from any period during which one or both of the domestic partners were married to someone else only to the extent that they do not compromise the marital claims of a domestic partner's spouse.

§ 6.02 Objectives of the Rules Governing Termination of the Relationship of Domestic Partners

(1) The primary objective of Chapter 6 is fair distribution of the economic gains and losses incident to termination of the relationship of domestic partners by:

(a) Allocating property according to principles that respect both individual ownership rights and equitable claims that each party has on the property in consequence of the relationship, and that are consistent and predictable in application; and

(b) Allocating financial losses that arise at the termination of the relationship according to equitable principles that are consistent and predictable in application.

(2) The secondary objective of Chapter 6 is protection of society from social welfare burdens that should be borne, in whole or in part, by individuals.

§ 6.03 Determination That Persons Are Domestic Partners

(1) In general, *domestic partners* are two persons of the same or opposite sex, not married to one another, who for a significant period of time share a primary residence and a life together as a couple.

(2) Persons are domestic partners when they have maintained a common household, as defined in Paragraph (4), with their common child, as defined in Paragraph (5), for a continuous period that equals or exceeds a duration, called the *cohabitation parenting period*, set in a uniform rule of statewide application.

(3) Persons not related by blood or adoption are presumed to be domestic partners when they have maintained a common household as defined in Paragraph (4), for a continuous period that equals or exceeds a duration, called the *cohabitation period*, set in a uniform rule of statewide application. The presumption is rebuttable by evidence that the parties did not share life together as a couple, as defined by Paragraph (7).

(4) Persons "maintain a common household" when they share a primary residence only with each other and family members; or when, if they share a household with other unrelated persons, they act jointly, rather than as individuals, with respect to management of the household.

(5) Persons have a "common child" when each is either the child's legal parent or parent by estoppel, as defined by § 2.03 or § 3.02A.

(6) When the requirements of paragraph (2) or (3) are not satisfied, a person asserting a claim under this Chapter bears the burden of proving that for a significant period of time the parties shared a primary residence and a life together as a couple, as defined in Paragraph (7). Whether a period of time is significant is determined in light of all the Paragraph (7) circumstances of the parties' relationship and, particularly, the extent to which those circumstances have wrought change in the life of one or both parties.

(7) Whether persons shared life together as a couple is determined by reference to all the circumstances, including:

(a) The oral or written statements or promises made to one another, or representations jointly made to third parties, regarding their relationship;

(b) The extent to which the parties intermingled their finances;

(c) The extent to which their relationship fostered the parties' economic interdependence, or the economic dependence of one party upon the other;

(d) The extent to which the parties engaged in conduct and assumed specialized or collaborative roles in furtherance of their life together.

(e) The extent to which the relationship wrought change in the life of either or both parties;

(f) The extent to which the parties acknowledged responsibilities to one another, as by naming one another the beneficiary of life insurance or of a testamentary instrument, or as eligible to receive benefits under an employee benefit plan;

(g) The extent to which the parties' relationship was treated by the parties as qualitatively distinct from the relationship either party had with any other person;

(h) The emotional or physical intimacy of the parties' relationship;

(i) The parties' community reputation as a couple;

(j) The parties' participation in some form of commitment ceremony or registration as a domestic partnership that, under applicable law, does not give rise to the rights and obligations established by this Chapter;

(k) The parties' participation in a void or voidable marriage that, under applicable law, does not give rise to the economic incidents of marriage;

(l) The parties' procreation of, adoption of, or joint assumption of parental functions toward a child; and

(m) The parties' maintenance of a common household.

§ 6.05 Allocation of Domestic–Partnership Property

Domestic-partnership property should be divided according to the principles set forth for the division of marital property in § 4.15 and § 4.16.

§ 6.06 Compensatory Payments

(1) Except as otherwise provided in this section,

(a) a domestic partner is entitled to compensatory payments on the same basis as a spouse under Chapter 5, and

(b) wherever a rule implementing a Chapter 5 principle makes the duration of the marriage a relevant factor, the application of that principle in this Chapter should instead employ the duration of the domestic-partnership period, as defined in § 6.04(2).

(2) No claim arises under § 5.06 against a domestic partner who is neither a legal parent or a parent by estoppel (as defined in § 2.03 or § 302A) of the child whose care provides the basis of the claim.

Notes and Questions on Domestic Partnership

(1) Do the ALI Principles restate the law or do they advocate making new law?

(a) Are its goals those of current law? Its methods?

(b) How would *Marvin* be decided under the ALI Principles?

(i) The ALI actually uses *Marvin* as one of its illustrations: "The Paragraph (3) presumption arises, and the parties are domestic partners unless Lee can overcome the presumption with evidence that the parties did not share life together as a couple." Can Lee do so?

(ii) If Lee cannot do so, what will be the consequences?

(c) How would *Hewitt* be decided under the ALI Principles?

(2) How is domestic partnership similar to and different from marriage? The Comment to § 6.02 says that domestic partners within the meaning of the act "will, in function, closely resemble marriages and

their termination will therefore pose the same social and legal issues as does the dissolution of a marriage." To avoid the consequences of being treated as though they were married, domestic partners must contract out of those rules, although even this power is limited. Wow! Even *Marvin* was at pains to deny that it was treating cohabitation like marriage.

(3) How is domestic partnership similar to and different from putative marriage?

(4) How is domestic partnership similar to and different from common-law marriage?

(5) How are the ALI's domestic partnership rules similar to and different from Vermont's domestic partnership rules?

(6) Are the ALI rules an attempt to do for the couple what they would have wanted to do for themselves or do they impose an external standard of fairness on the couple? An ALI Comment says that § 6.03 "does not require ... that the parties had an implied or express agreement, or even that the facts meet the standard requirements of a quantum meruit claim. It instead relies, as do the marriage laws, on a status classification...." Wow again. What do you make of this?

(a) Does this suggest that § 6.03's standards for determining when a domestic partnership begins is *really* important?

(b) How does this fit with what you know of other patterns in the law?

(i) Remember the Maine dictum: "that the movement of the progressive societies has hitherto been a movement from Status to Contract." Recall that the movement in family law has certainly been in that direction. Recall why.

(ii) Remember the principle of family autonomy. How do the ALI's principles fit with our presumption against government "interference"? When people marry they voluntarily subject themselves to legal rules about fairness on divorce. That may make us feel more comfortable about subjecting them to those rules. Parting partners, however, have not at all done so. Should this make us uncomfortable about subjecting them to those rules?

(iii) Remember the standards problem. How fair are the ALI's rules as applied to married couples? As applied to domestic partnerships? Is a flat rule better here than individualized decisions?

(7) Since being domestic partners means being treated like spouses when the relationship ends, couples will have lively reasons for wanting to know when they have crossed that threshold. How clear will that moment be to them? How likely is it that couples will inadvertently become domestic partners?

(a) Is the law clear enough to warn couples when they are about to become effectively married? Under § 6.03, if you lived with a roommate for the cohabitation period you would cross the line automatically. You would then have the burden of showing you did not "share life together as a couple." Even if you didn't live with someone for the cohabitation period, your partner might be able to prove that for "a significant period" you shared "life together as a couple." This makes Paragraph (7)'s definition of "life together as a couple" pretty significant. What is that definition? How much guidance does it give you?

(b) Were a legislature to adopt ALI Chapter 6, would couples know about the new law's rules? Would the rules eventually become common knowledge? How accurate would social knowledge about those rules be? Do these rules fit well enough with contemporary social practice that knowledge of them might in some sense be imputed to the couple?

(c) Even if people knew about the Chapter 6 Principles after they had been enacted into law, would they change their behavior because of them? The drafters may expect that by creating onerous default rules they will drive people to enter contracts. Will they do so?

(i) Throughout this casebook we have littered examples of the many ways people ignore the law and its gifts and organize their lives in their own ways and using their own methods. Recall, for example, Macaulay's discussion of businesses and contracts.

(ii) Few people sign antenuptial agreements. Far fewer sign *Marvin* agreements. We have explored the reasons for this at imposing length. Do those reasons apply to domestic-partnership agreements? When people first begin to live together, do they make plans? When they continue to live together, do they make plans, particularly formal plans? Marriage announces to couples that they are doing something with life-long consequences. Custom encourages couples to make plans. What comparable announcement do cohabitors hear; what comparable encouragement do they receive?

(8) The ALI expects legislatures to set a "cohabitation parenting period" and a "cohabitation period." How long should those periods be?

(9) Are the drafters of the ALI Principles closet traditionalists who want to make cohabitation such a risky enterprise that people will be deterred from undertaking it?

(10) As you may recall from our Chapter 4, married couples seeking divorce generally have very few assets. There is, if anything, reason to think cohabitants have even fewer assets. How often, then, would you expect to see domestic-partner litigation?

(11) The ALI Principles are not law. They are the vision of law of a few law professors and lawyers. If you were a legislator, would you turn vision into reality?

SECTION 4. EVALUATING *MARVIN* THROUGH THE THEMES AND FUNCTIONS OF FAMILY LAW

"One instant, Jane. Give one glance to my horrible life when you are gone. All happiness will be torn away with you. What then is left? For a wife I have but the maniac upstairs: as well might you refer me to some corpse in yonder churchyard. What shall I do, Jane? Where turn for a companion, and for some hope?"

"Do as I do: trust in God and yourself. Believe in heaven. Hope to meet again there." . . .

"[W]hile he spoke my very Conscience and Reason turned traitors against me, and charged me with crime in resisting him. They spoke almost as loud as Feeling: and that clamoured wildly." "Oh, comply!" it said. "Think of his misery; think of his danger—look at his state when left alone: remember his headlong nature; consider the recklessness following on despair—soothe him; save him; love him: tell him you love him and will be his. Who in the world cares for you? or who will be injured by what you do?"

Still indomitable was the reply—"I care for myself. The more solitary, the more friendless, the more unsustained I am, the more I will respect myself. I will keep the law given by God; sanctioned by man.... Laws and principles are not for the times when there is no temptation: they are for such moments as this, when body and soul rise in mutiny against their rigour; stringent are they; inviolate they shall be."

Charlotte Bronte
Jane Eyre

Marvin has come to stand for a marked change in the law's attitudes toward unmarried cohabitants. The questions that followed *Marvin* were intended to help you gauge what that case held. The textual material that follows is intended to help you (1) evaluate the wisdom of the changes which *Marvin* symbolizes and (2) anticipate the many questions *Marvin* leaves to be decided case by case. Taken to its extremes, *Marvin* requires us to consider virtually the whole range of ideas we have thought about so far in the course. To make our consideration of *Marvin* easier, then, we have recruited two of our basic ordering devices—the themes and the functions of family law. We will take each of the themes and functions in turn to see what it can tell us about the *Marvin* principle.

A. *MARVIN* AND THE THEMES OF FAMILY LAW

"Good God! This is worse than all the vows of all the churches on earth. I had rather be legally married to you ten times over."

George Bernard Shaw

(on hearing the terms Annie Besant had proposed for a contract to govern their relationship)

(1) Family Autonomy

In some senses, the cohabitants (and any children) will be a family. Does the doctrine of family autonomy suggest the state ought not intervene in that family, even if intervention only means adjusting the economic relations of the cohabitants after they have separated? To answer this complicated question, recall the eight rationales for family autonomy we developed in discussing *Kilgrow*.

The Information Problem. The first rationale for family autonomy was that a court may find it hard to obtain information about any particular family's situation. To what extent will that be true in *Marvin* cases? The problems presented will differ according to the kind of contract the plaintiff seeks to enforce. Assume, for instance, the plaintiff alleges the couple made an express oral contract. The exact contents of that agreement of course become crucial. Yet information about them may be elusive. First, the words of the contract are likely to have been heard only by the parties themselves; witnesses, to say nothing of disinterested witnesses, are unlikely. Second, years are likely to have passed between the time the words were spoken and the time the court must determine what they were. Third, the words will have been spoken in a context of speech and actions which determine the meaning of the contractual words, and that context must be recovered if the contract is to be understood. Fourth, a contract may be amended or indeed abrogated by the (possibly oral) agreement of the parties, and the court must ascertain whether this has happened. Because human memory is fallible, and because people's memories are swayed by their own interests, courts will hear a good deal of flatly contradictory information with no very satisfactory way of establishing the truth. *Offield v. Davis*, 40 SE 910 (Va 1902) explores many of these issues in a diverting fact situation.

These problems are illustrated by *Marvin*. Its trial lasted eleven weeks, suggesting that while the court acquired a good deal of information, it also acquired a good deal of conflicting information, information replete with the problems we just charted. Consider, for instance, the exchange in San Blas in which Lee was supposed to have made his contractual offer—"what I have is yours and what you have is mine." The parties were the only witnesses to this crucial exchange. It occurred in 1964; the trial court did not render its opinion until 1979. The contractual words were part of a conversation which apparently had begun two days earlier. That conversation itself took place in the context of an extended discussion of marriage (in which Lee allegedly expressed hostility to binding obligations), of the relationship between Lee and Michelle, and of changes in the behavior of the two. The contractual offer was immediately met with a counter offer. Later there was another purported contractual offer, when Lee said "I don't know what you're worrying about, I'll always take care of you. . . . " This second contractual offer occurred in the setting of a jumble of words and activities having to do with Michelle's career.

Lee and Michelle differed radically in their accounts of whether the contractual words had been spoken, of the conversations that preceded and followed the contractual words, and of the behavior that followed and succeeded them. Lee, for instance, "vigorously denies telling plaintiff, 'what I have is yours and what you have is mine' "; he declared he never said he would support her for life and never stated "I'll take care of you always." He alleged he had said "he wanted a relationship of no responsibility and that the plaintiff agreed thereto." Some of the words Lee and Michelle exchanged were written, but since the writings were generally letters not intended to formulate legally binding obligations, they were rarely precise enough to help. And at least one letter said to contain probative information could not be produced by the party who invoked it. Finally, Lee alleged, and Michelle denied, that they had entered into a contract apparently abrogating whatever contracts had gone before, a contract in which Michelle agreed to accept monthly checks of $833 in exchange for removing herself from his life and saying nothing about their relationship to anyone.

Now assume the plaintiff alleges an implied-in-fact contract. Here the court must infer from the parties' behavior that they intended to enter into a contract. What difficulties may the court encounter in gathering information about that behavior? Some of that information is likely to have to do with financial transactions, and such transactions can be easier than most family activities for a court to inquire into, since there are usually written records. Some of that information will have to do with public behavior, like Lee and Michelle holding themselves out in some circumstances as man and wife. Some of that information, however, will have to do with their behavior in private, like Michelle's caring for Lee during his problems with alcohol or her performance as companion, homemaker, housekeeper, and cook. Even as to the more public aspects of their behavior, reliable evidence may be hard to come by, as the controversy over the extent to which Michelle held herself as married to Lee indicates.

Finally, assume the plaintiff alleges an implied-in-law contract. Here the court's task will be made easier because it need not decide whether the parties intended to contract, but must only ask what justice requires. On the other hand, deciding what justice requires may require the kind and range of information the court would need for a contract implied in fact.

So far, we have been considering only the problem of gathering information. But there is a second problem—evaluating what the information gathered means. Let us again consider each kind of contract seriatim. Oral contracts will present familiar problems of interpretation. Williston writes, "It is a necessary requirement in the nature of things that an agreement in order to be binding must be sufficiently definite to enable a court to give it an exact meaning." People speaking in family and *Marvin* contexts may not understand that their words have legal consequences and thus may not even attempt to formulate the contractual terms in the detail and with the precision needed. Further, who is as precise orally as in writing?

The two contractual offers—"What I have is yours and what you have is mine" and "I'll always take care of you"—illustrate these problems. What do the two offers, even assuming they were accepted mean? Should the first offer be taken literally? That is, was Lee proposing that he and Michelle trade assets? Surely not, yet that is what his words say. Taken more idiomatically, these words might mean Lee and Michelle should merge their assets, thereby making each the owner of half the total. But Michelle claimed he was offering to share with her the property he was to acquire in the future. Yet it is hard to find a future promise in the present tense of the offer. To make sense of such vague expressions of intent, courts are driven to look at the preceding and subsequent behavior of the parties. Thus the problems presented by express oral contracts will blend into the problems presented by contracts implied in fact. To them we now turn.

The problem with inferring a contract from behavior is that behavior is often highly ambiguous. Michelle, for example, alleged that part of her consideration for Lee's promises was her work as a companion, homemaker, housekeeper, and cook. Can one infer a contract from the fact that she performed those tasks (with help Lee paid for)? What evidence is there, or would there generally be, from these facts that the parties intended a contract? That Michelle did not intend these services as a gift? That Lee understood, or even should have understood, that she intended these services as a gift?

Nor does it necessarily help to look at some of the other things Michelle did. For example, she stopped working at her own career. But is this evidence she was relying on Lee to supply, even after their relationship ended, what she might otherwise have earned? Or is it evidence that she was willing to gamble that her relationship with Lee would last long enough that she would not need a career? Or is it evidence that she believed she could always restart her career if necessary? Or is it evidence that she believed she could do better at her career with Lee's backing but then lost interest? And whatever it tells us about Michelle's intentions, we also need to ask what it tells us about Lee's motives. Even if Lee did not, as he alleged, encourage her in her career, was he tacitly promising her support simply because he acquiesced in her decision to abandon her career? Or did he attribute to her one of the motives we have just canvassed?

Even if Michelle expected compensation for the services, what compensation could reasonably be inferred from the conduct of the parties? Should the value of the services be measured by their market value, that is, by what it would have cost Lee to hire someone to perform them? By Michelle's opportunity costs, that is, by the value of what Michelle could have earned had she not been providing services to Lee? By the extent to which Lee was helped in earning money? Of course, the ordinary measure of contract damages is the expectation interest. That is, Michelle would get what she bargained for. But we are trying to find out how much she bargained for by looking at the behavior of the parties. What, if anything, does that behavior tell us? One answer is that the measure of what Michelle expected in return for the services she provided was what she in fact got—support (economic, social, and personal) in a lavish style while they were living together, but not more.

One part of the judicial technique for resolving uncertainties of fact and interpretation is to consult the normative standards of behavior embodied in the law. If we are to find a contract implied in law, we will need also to examine those standards. These questions bring us, however, to the next rationale for the doctrine of family autonomy.

The Standards Problem. This rationale for the doctrine of family autonomy holds that the state should try not to intervene in the family because, at least outside a few basic areas, the law lacks adequate standards to govern its intervention. One response to this argument in the *Marvin* context, of course, is that this is one of those few areas, since the law has established standards to govern the disposition of wealth and support duties on divorce. But how well do those standards fit the *Marvin* situation? On one hand, they seem to fit it well, since in both situations a couple that has lived together has decided to live apart and must wind up its economic affairs. On the other hand, they seem to fit it badly, since one fact that is by definition true of the *Marvin* situation is that the parties have decided *not* to be married. If we are trying to enforce a contract between the parties, then, we might conclude we should not apply standard marital-property and alimony law, since that law is presumably what the parties rejected when they decided not to marry. Yet what do we apply instead? The standards of ordinary contract law seem unhelpful, since they generally assume the parties are bargaining over economic interests for economic gain. The *Marvin* court may, however, intend that that body of law be consulted on the theory that the "quasi-marital" and the economic aspects of the relationship can be severed. Is this wise? Does any other body of law present itself? Can courts develop one? What would it look like?

There is another barrier to using the standards of marital-property and alimony law in deciding *Marvin* cases. That is the argument that it is not in the state's interest to obliterate the distinction between marriage and cohabitation. Is this a persuasive argument? What is the nature of that interest? How strong is it?

The Privacy Problem. Another rationale for family autonomy is that scrutinizing the family's affairs injures its privacy, privacy the family needs to conduct its intimate affairs. *Marvin* does seem to contemplate inquiries that might seem problematic for the couple's privacy. First, it requires courts to discover whether sexual relations are a severable part of the consideration for the contract. Second, it commands a "searching inquiry" into whether the parties have attempted to avoid a marital relationship. Third, there must be the factual investigation we charted earlier into whether there was an express contract, an implied contract, a partnership, a joint venture, or some other kind of understanding.

Some of the compromises of privacy these cases present may be illustrated by *Marvin*. For example, whether Lee's most agonizing problems were to be made public seems to have been explicitly considered by both parties. Thus in March 1967 Lee said he wanted to end his relationship with Michelle, and she is said to have "responded that if he left her, she would expose his fears, his worries to the public and his career would be destroyed." Later, Lee offered Michelle a monthly payment in exchange for a promise not to "discuss with anyone anything she learned about [Lee] during their relationship." For another example, the privacy of people not party to the litigation was also invaded. This was best illustrated by the case of the Peace Corps worker on Palau who testified he had slept with Michelle on a number of occasions, whose testimony was answered by Michelle's claim he was gay, and who then sought to produce evidence rebutting that claim.

The privacy problem presented by *Marvin* cases is also illustrated by the notable number of those cases involving well-known people, including Liberace, Peter Frampton, Billie Jean King, William Hurt, and Martina Navratilova. For example, a particularly lurid claim was brought by one Vicki Morgan against the estate of Alfred Bloomingdale, a wealthy man who had been an informal advisor of President Reagan and whose wife had been a close friend of Mrs. Reagan. Morgan claimed Bloomingdale had entered into both oral and written contracts arising out of her relationship with him. A sense of the depth of the inquiry into the private life of the parties may be had from this newspaper report:

> In a 231–page deposition, made public as part of court records Monday, Morgan had said Bloomingdale's eyes glazed and he would drool during sexual sessions when he bound women and beat them until they cried....
>
> Morgan said she complained to Bloomingdale repeatedly about the beatings and finally got him to talk to her psychiatrist. She said she also helped Bloomingdale by warning him when he got too rough with other women during the sessions.

Detroit Free Press, September 29, 1982. (Morgan was subsequently murdered by a man described as "her live-in companion." *New York Times*, July 8, 1983, page 6. Her estate eventually recovered $200,000 from Bloomingdale's estate on the basis of a written contract embodied in a letter from Bloomingdale. *New York Times*, December 22, 1984, page 46.) Cases of this sort also hint at the question of the extent to which *Marvin* cases raise another classic privacy problem—extortion.

The Enforcement Problem. Still another rationale for the doctrine of family autonomy is that it can be difficult to enforce legal decisions in the family context. In its classic form, the enforcement problem is not particularly severe in *Marvin* cases, since those cases involve money, and as long as assets can be located (which is of course not always easy), judgments can be enforced.

The classic form of the enforcement problem, of course, is primarily directed toward situations (spouse abuse, for instance) where the state attempts to change someone's behavior. *Marvin* cases, however, present a different kind of enforcement problem, since here one private citizen is attempting to change the behavior of another private citizen. The issue in *Marvin* cases is whether the *Marvin* cause of action provides a plausible means of doing so. The presence of this form of the enforcement problem in *Marvin* situations may be inferred from a newspaper article which reported that despite "an initial flurry of palimony suits, . . . the palimony concept has largely fallen into disuse. . . . " *Los Angeles Times*, January 30, 1986, page 1. The article stated that these suits can take as long as five years to get to trial, that the plaintiff's case is often difficult to prove, that *Marvin* cases are expensive to litigate, and that lawyers will generally not accept payment in the form of contingency fees. The article said that the lawyer who had represented the Bloomingdale estate had refused to accept other *Marvin* clients: " 'People are usually after things the court can't give them. . . . Like revenge, justification. They are angry because the person they picked turned out to be a turkey.' "And the article quoted a family law specialist as saying, " 'As long as people thought there was going to be a pot of gold at the end of the rainbow, they were willing to pursue it. But now lawyers are being more careful. They have learned it is such a crap-shoot they are just not filing them.' "

The Exacerbation Problem. A further rationale for the family autonomy doctrine is that legal intervention in a family will exacerbate, not ameliorate, a family's tensions. On one hand, perhaps this problem is not serious in the *Marvin* context, since *Marvin* cases only arise when a relationship is ending. On the other hand, the availability of *Marvin* remedies may encourage couples to shape their relationships in ways that would exacerbate tensions between them. For example, *Marvin* principles might encourage couples to think of their relationship in economic and self-seeking terms. Here as elsewhere, the severity of the exacerbation problem depends on the severity of the problems the family would face if the state failed to supply a means of resolving their disputes.

Individual Autonomy. Yet another rationale for the family autonomy doctrine is that it promotes individual autonomy. This argument is most often made about the *Marvin* principles in the following way: Marriage is an institution organized and governed by law which constrains the way people in intimate relationships behave. Some people would prefer to organize their intimate lives in ways other than those established by the state for marriage. Extending state control of intimate relationships beyond marriage to include *Marvin* relationships deprives such people of the ability to choose non-marital intimate relationships. A response to the argument is that *Marvin* does not impose any particular kind of rules for the conduct of intimate relationships on the parties, but simply allows people to set the terms of their relationships. The response to the response is that even if this were all *Marvin* does, a relationship entirely without legal consequences is still transformed into a relationship with legal consequences. And even if *Marvin* only allows parties to write contracts, it still introduces an element of state control into the relationship in the form of the judicial power to interpret the parties' contract. But *Marvin* does more than those two things. *Marvin* permits courts to adjust the economic relations of the parties to do "justice." It is precisely having the state's ideas of justice imposed on them that the couple may be trying to escape in avoiding marriage.

Pluralism. A final rationale for the family autonomy doctrine is that it promotes pluralism. While this rationale may not have great application to the *Marvin* situation, the autonomy argument we just reviewed might well be adapted to fit the pluralism rationale. There might, for instance, be groups which wished to organize their family life in ways inconsistent with the legal institution of marriage and with *Marvin* principles, and in the absence of those principles members of such groups might be able to organize their families on lines of their own choosing.

For example, both the law of conventional marriage and the law of *Marvin* relationships will probably continue this trend of promoting gender equality. Yet a number of individuals and groups in American society reject, often on religious and moral grounds, gender equality as conventionally understood. Should such people be allowed to organize their intimate lives along patriarchal principles?

(2) Individual Autonomy

See the discussion under "Individual Autonomy" in the preceding section.

(3) Gender and Family Law

An important impetus for the *Marvin* principles comes from concerns about the way the law affects women that parallel concerns we encountered in our discussion of marital property. That discussion noted that the traditional law of marital property was subject to the criticism that social practice, if not necessarily the law itself, typically gave husbands more power over a couple's financial affairs than it gave wives. This meant that under the common-law principles of property division, the wife's economic contributions to the family were likely to be undervalued. Similarly, it has been argued that in *Marvin* relationships assets will often be held in the man's name even though the woman may have contributed to their acquisition and that women in *Marvin* relationships may be induced to give up careers or otherwise rely on their cohabitants yet find themselves unable to recover losses caused by that reliance.

Marvin attempts to provide a full range of remedies for those situations. Is the range of remedies adequate? What might make the remedies unsatisfactory? As the social situation of women changes, will

Marvin become unnecessary? Can *Marvin* be criticized as a paternalistic effort to protect women, an effort more likely to lead to their continued subordination than to end it? Are you persuaded by the following argument?

> Another ground for opposing the extension of family law to cohabitants is that the rules that have been applied are not in keeping with the notions of equality of women and of marital partnership. Underlying premises of a financial award to a woman cohabitant are that she was the weaker partner and needs the protection of the court against exploitation; that, once having cohabited, she is unable to be self-supporting again or at best her capacity for self-support has been harmed; and that she has earned a share of the man's wealth for he could not have accumulated as much without her help.
>
> It is anomalous that at a time when most women are establishing social and economic independence, a few should try to capitalize on the myth of the weak woman....
>
> The women's movement in relation to family law speaks with two voices. One argues that treatment in the past has been bad and that today's easy divorce laws fail to recognize the extent of women's non-monetary contribution to the maintenance of the family unit; women are exploited, their position in society is inferior to men's, and there should be greater recompense for this, namely a share of family assets on divorce and maintenance to the full from the ex-husband to offset the wife's handicaps in the labor market and in recognition of her valuable home-making and child-rearing services....
>
> The other voice of the women's movement claims simply equal treatment and equal opportunity for women and it challenges the notion that in general women are weaker and that they have been exploited. It rejects the analogy with slavery, for women have had for a long time the choice of work or house-wifery or both—nor were they forced into marriage and denied basic education.... As long as it is the law and the general expectation that women are dependents, to be kept, then this will be an obstacle to full acceptance in the world of work. Equal opportunity and equal treatment at work must mean equal responsibilities and standing for the men and women partners to a union. Maintenance and property awards to former cohabiting partners are not simply payment for the freedom to leave one woman for another but would also reinforce the outmoded view, upheld by the law, of the man as the head of the household and the woman as being under obligation to provide domestic services and child care, a view which is too unsatisfactory in its application to married persons to permit of its extension to the unmarried.

Ruth Deech, *The Case Against Legal Recognition of Cohabitation*, in John M. Eekelaar and Sanford N. Katz, *Marriage and Cohabitation in Contemporary Societies: Areas of Legal, Social and Ethical Change* 300, 303–04 (Butterworths, 1980).

(4) Human Nature and Family Law

For pessimists about human nature, *Marvin* raises a classic problem:

> Control or regulation of sexual energy through repression, inhibition, channeling, and rechanneling is a task of all social systems. Although protecting the family as the primary institution of reproduction, nurturance, and early socialization of the young is usually considered its chief end, some degree of regulation is necessary simply to have reliable expectations about the behavior of others. Not least, social regulation reinforces the often precarious internal controls every person has had to place on his or her erotic energies and desires.

Richard S. Randall, *Freedom and Taboo: Pornography and the Politics of a Self Divided* 128 (U Cal Press, 1989). Confining sexual relations to marriage has historically been one way American culture has tried to provide children with stable homes and couples with stable relations. One way to look at *Marvin* is to ask whether those goals are proper. Another way is to ask whether *Marvin* disserves those goals. Is *Marvin* in fact a way of inhibiting erotic energies and desires by bringing people living outside of marriage under the law's scrutiny and correction?

(5) Defining the Family

Traditionally, the law has regarded a husband and wife as a family but has not regarded unmarried cohabitants as a family. One argument that has implicitly or explicitly undergirded the case for *Marvin* is that unmarried cohabitants are just as much families as married couples and therefore should be treated as families. The argument usually relies on a functional definition of "family." That is, it says that the relationship between husband and wife performs a set of social, psychological, economic, and moral functions, that the relationship between unmarried cohabitants performs the same set of functions, and therefore that the relationships are the same. Is it true that the two kinds of relationships are functionally identical? Suppose cohabitation is functionally identical to marriage in some cases but not others. How should the definitional problem be resolved? What other ways of defining "family" do you see? What advantages and disadvantages do they have?

Even if marriage and cohabitation are functionally identical, or even if cohabitants are every bit as much a family as husbands and wives, should the law treat cohabitants the same way it treats husbands and wives? Is this required by the principle that similar cases should be treated similarly? Or is it legitimate (and desirable) that the law should create different categories of "family" which the law may treat differently?

(6) Privacy

At this point, please recall the discussion of privacy and *Marvin* in our discussion of the family-autonomy doctrine.

(7) Contract as an Ordering Device

The best way for you to think about *Marvin* contracts is probably to review our discussion of marital contracts. That discussion is too extensive to recapitulate here, but it may help to look briefly at some of the differences between marital and *Marvin* contracts to see whether contract is more or less attractive in the latter than the former context.

One such difference has to do with the fact that marital contracts must be in writing but *Marvin* contracts need not be. This seems important for a variety of reasons. First, the requirement of a writing helps ensure a high level of intentionality. That is, a couple that enters a written contract must have intended to enter into a contract, must have thought at some degree of explicitness about its terms, and must have realized at some degree of awareness that the contract could have consequences. A couple entering a *Marvin* contract, however, is not compelled to reach this level of intentionality. This difference should not be overdrawn, since many of the factors that used to decide whether cohabitants have entered into a *Marvin* oral or implied contract may, under some marital-property systems, be consulted when dividing marital property.

Another contrast between marital and *Marvin* contracts arises out of differences in timing. Many marital contracts are made at a particular point in the course of a couple's relationship—just before marriage. This is a natural point for considering the issues that are relevant to contracts between couples, for then people are making and realize they are making a major change in their lives. Furthermore, this "natural point" occurs when couples have decided to make a serious commitment. In addition, at this point we may hope that the couple's altruistic feelings will be at their highest, yet they will know each other well enough to have acquired some realistic sense of each other and the relationship. No such natural point presents itself in *Marvin* cases.

Another difference between marital and *Marvin* contracts is that the usual rule is for courts to investigate the fairness of the former but not the latter. It is in one sense relatively easy for courts to investigate the fairness of marital contracts, since courts can use as a standard the principles of marital-property division. However, no such standard exists for *Marvin* contracts. To put the point differently, a standard exists for investigating the fairness of marital contracts because we assume partners to a marriage have made the deepest kind of commitment to each other. No such assumption informs our thinking about *Marvin* contracts. Indeed, the reasoning of *Marvin* itself suggests that cohabitants' contracts are enforceable not because of those things that make their contract like a marriage contract, but rather because of those things that make it like a commercial contract.

One way of summarizing these points is to say that the law of marital contracts is sensitive to the special dangers of over-reaching and of improvidence that exist when couples in an intimate relationship arrange their affairs and that the law of *Marvin* contracts is not similarly sensitive. But which way does this difference cut? Is the law of marital contracts over-sensitive? Is the law of *Marvin* contracts under-sensitive? Can the law of *Marvin* contracts be adjusted to be more sensitive? What consequences would that have?

Another difference between marital and *Marvin* contracts arises out of differences in the underlying relationships. Many of our problems with marital contracts, for example, grow out of fears about trying to write a contract to govern a life-long and greatly complex relationship. It is a statistical fact that marriages generally last longer than cohabitants' relationships. Does this mean writing contracts for the latter may be easier than writing contracts for the former? Or will the cohabitants who write contracts be the people in the sturdier relationships?

Another of the differences between the two kinds of contracts that may grow out of differences in the underlying relationships has to do with our reluctance to encourage husbands and wives to think of their relationship in terms that contract law may encourage—that is, in economic terms and in terms of each party's rights. Are we less concerned about cohabitants thinking in those terms?

If we turn our perspective around, we might ask whether husbands and wives have more need of the power to contract than cohabitants. This argument would suggest that contracts are especially useful in a long-term and complex relationship, since one function of contracts is to allow people to reduce uncertainty by allocating risks before entering a project. The argument would continue by suggesting that, as a class, cohabitants are less likely to be entering long-term and complex relationships and are therefore less in need of contract. And cohabitants, even more than married couples, can achieve most of the property relations they might desire without resorting to contract.

(8) Rights

Our next theme concerns rights-thinking in family law. We have discussed one application of this theme to the *Marvin* problem—the tension between, on one hand, the desire to let cohabitants create contractual rights which set the terms of their relationship and, on the other hand, the desire not to encourage people to think of their relationship in terms of conflicting rights. Another application of the theme is presented by the question whether the fourteenth amendment requires that rights to enter into contracts accorded to married people be also accorded to unmarried people whose relationship serves the same purposes for them that marriage does for the married.

(9) The Tension Between Discretion and Rules

On one view, the *Marvin* principle does not present the tension between discretion and rules in any acute form. And insofar as a couple is able to write a contract clear enough to obviate the need for interpretation and to anticipate all the developments which might someday present difficult questions about the parties' intent, courts will be offered relatively little room to exercise discretion. But, as we have suggested, that's not easy. And, of course, the *Marvin* principle allows courts to enforce not just written contracts, but also oral and implied-in-fact contracts. This permits, indeed compels, courts to exercise considerable discretion in deciding whether a contract was entered into and in interpreting its terms: First, information about the parties' words and acts will be elusive. Second, it will often be unclear how those words and acts should be interpreted. Third, the legal standards for in interpreting *Marvin* contracts are uncertain, are stated in terms that leave great room for judicial discretion, and that may not be susceptible of precise statement.

Of course, judicial discretion is not necessarily bad. The circumstances of cohabiting parties must vary considerably, their contracts must fail to anticipate all the contingencies that will arrive, and the demands of equity must be complex. We say there is a tension between discretion and rules because both serve important functions. How this tension should be resolved in the *Marvin* context depends on several factors. For instance, if we think the main purpose of the *Marvin* remedy is to allow couples freedom to set the terms of their relationship, we may feel the broad scope of judicial discretion presents serious problems. If, on the other hand, we think the main purpose of the *Marvin* remedy is to prevent one cohabitant from taking advantage of the other, we may think that scope allows courts to find and prevent unfairness in all its forms.

(10) Due Process

We doubt that *Marvin* raises a real due process problem. It might be argued that where a court finds *Marvin* rights that arose before a jurisdiction had announced its adoption of the *Marvin* principle, the court has worked a due process wrong against a person whose property was being transferred to a cohabitant. However, since *Marvin* purports to be decided on the basis of common law and statutory principles, this argument would probably fail. Nor would it be novel for a court to apply retrospectively novel common law principles.

(11) Enforcement

At this point, please recall the discussion of enforcement and *Marvin* in our discussion of the family autonomy doctrine.

(12) Pluralism

At this point, please recall the discussion of pluralism and *Marvin* in our discussion above of the family autonomy doctrine.

B. *MARVIN* AND THE FUNCTIONS OF FAMILY LAW

I believe that the marriage institution, like slavery and monarchy, and many other things which have been good or necessary in their day, is now effete, and in a general sense injurious, instead of being beneficial to the community, although of course it must continue to linger until better institutions can be formed. I mean by marriage, in this connection, any forced or obligatory tie between the sexes, any legal intervention or constraint to prevent people from adjusting their love relations precisely as they do their religious affairs in this country, in complete personal freedom; changing and improving them from time to time, and according to circumstances.

Victoria Woodhull
The Beecher–Tilton Scandal Case

(1) Marriage as a Social Institution

[P]erhaps on my advice you will change your mind and renounce the single state, a barren way of life hardly becoming to a man, and surrender yourself to holy wedlock.... I shall show by the clearest of proofs that this alternative would be far more honourable, profitable, and pleasant for you, and, one might add, necessary even in this day and age.

Erasmus
A Praise of Marriage

Why has marriage been a favored institution throughout American history? Why has cohabitation been a disfavored alternative to it? This is a question we have been asking in various forms since Chapter 1. Some of the historical answers to that question grow out of ideas about sexual morality that have changed notably in recent decades. Can any other answers be found?

One approach to this query may be found by looking at it in terms of the functions of family law, particularly the channelling function. How, then, do marriage and cohabitation look if we regard the former as an institution into which we might wish to channel people and if we ask whether the latter is similarly becoming such an institution?

So, why is marriage such a fine thing that we might want to channel—and here we should pause to say "channel" and not "coerce"—people into it? The traditional answer to that question has several parts. One of them is religious—marriage is "an honourable estate, instituted of God in the time of man's innocency." Another part reflects the socially common belief that a lifetime commitment to one other person can yield rewards as deep as anything in human experience. Here, however, we want to explore a more secular and pragmatic "social policy" justification for the institution. Put crudely, that justification holds that marriage is better for individuals and thus for society than cohabitation. One proponent of this argument is a prominent demographer. She asks: "If cohabitation provides the same benefits to individuals marriage does, then is it necessary to be concerned about this shift?" She answers: "Yes, because a valuable social institution arguably is being replaced by one that demands and offers less." She continues:

MARSHA GARRISON
REVIVING MARRIAGE

Brooklyn Law School Legal Studies working Paper
No. 43 (Oct 2005), SSRN ID=829825

Love and marriage, love and marriage
Go together like a horse and carriage.

Lasting commitment, care, love, and emotional and economic support ... occur in a wide range of relationships. When the law ... reflect[s] this fact, we will have ended marriage as we know it.

Sammy Cahn,
Love and Marriage (1955)

Marriage, once linked to love and commitment as routinely as horse to carriage, has become controversial. Some experts argue that the married state is fundamental and foundational. As they see it, "[t]he erosion of marriage during the past four decades ... lies at the heart of many of the social problems with which the government currently grapples," and "government policy [thus] should promote ... healthy marriage." Others see marriage as nothing more than a label, and an old-fashioned label at that. These experts argue that the state should not only eschew marriage promotion, but abandon marriage regulation altogether. Citing declining rates of marriage and marital birth–the very same factors that lead marriage advocates to urge promotion strategies–these commentators argue that the state should pursue "just social policies that facilitate maximum economic well-being and emotional flourishing for all, not only for those who marry." To accomplish this aim, they argue that tax obligations, government benefits, and even spousal rights and duties should be based on relational facts rather than marital status. They question whether state-sanctioned marriage should even "survive" the[se reforms] as a kinship form.

Both the pro-and anti-marriage perspectives have attracted the attention of policy makers. Those in the United States have thus far stressed marriage promotion. 1996 welfare-reform legislation that provided incentives to the states to increase two-parent families and reduce nonmarital childbearing was based on an underlying marriage-promotion policy. More recently, the Bush administration has launched an initiative designed to support "healthy" marriages more directly by providing funds for marriage-skills education and reducing financial penalties that might deter marriage. Many of the states have also launched their own marriage-promotion initiatives.

Across the Canadian border, the policy trend has been quite different. The Canadian Parliament has revised both tax and old-age pension rules so that the same standards apply to married and "common-law" partners. More recently, the Canadian Law Reform Commission has recommended comprehensive revision of Canadian law to avoid "problems of coherence" arising from marital status classifications. A number of other nations have adopted one or another feature of the Canadian approach, and New Zealand has gone so far as to extend all of the personal rights and obligations that flow from marriage to couples who have been "de facto partners" for three years.

Cross-nationally, the marriage debate often pits traditionalists and religious conservatives against liberal advocates of tolerance and social diversity. Because these opposing camps approach the subject of marriage with different preconceptions and values, the argument has more often resembled an exchange of slogans than a reasoned debate. On one side, the pro-marriage camp yearns for "a restigmatization of illegitimacy and promiscuity" and contends that virtually all social ills, including "[t]he drug crisis, the education crisis, the problems of teen pregnancy and juvenile crime" can be traced "to one source: broken families." On the other, the anti-marriage group deplores "destructive labeling" and "gross oversimplifications about what makes for a good ... family"; it characterizes efforts to revitalize marriage not only as "moralistic" and "atavistic," but as signs of "denial, resistance, displacement, and bad faith....

Between these two entrenched camps stand the social scientists, who have been quietly and carefully collecting data on marital and nonmarital behavior, expectations, and outcomes. By now there is a large body of evidence bearing on the desirability of marital-status classifications, the claimed benefits of marriage, and the feasibility of effective marriage promotion. But on both sides of the debate, advocates often selectively seize on evidence that supports their preconceived points-of-view. This tendency is particularly evident in recent family law scholarship on marriage and cohabitation, which often ignores the evidence altogether.

This is most unfortunate, not only because it tends to produce pompous manifestoes instead of fact-based arguments, but also because it obscures common ground. There is much that opponents and proponents of marriage should–and, I believe, would–agree on if they could get past the slogans. If they were to unite on these issues, some good might come of it. At the very least, debate grounded in evidence should enhance the possibility of meaningful dialogue; this kind of public conversation has the "large advantage of allowing a convergence on particular outcomes by people unable to reach an accord on general principles." It promotes the development of family policies capable of garnering broad public support and allegiance.

In this paper, I undertake a review of the social-science evidence on marriage and cohabitation and an appraisal of what it reveals about the desirability of various marital status classifications and marriage-promotion efforts. I do so not as an advocate of either traditional marriage or relational diversity, but as a family law expert committed to a coherent, evidence-based family policy. I am prepared to follow the evidence to its logical conclusion. I am impassioned only in believing that family policy is too important to leave to the ideologues. . . .

B. Does Marriage Confer Public Benefits?

1. The Debate Among Family Law Experts

Does marriage provide public benefits? In the legal scholarship, no consensus has developed. Some family law experts have urged that marriage offers psychological and ontological benefits derived from its capacity to induce a state of "belonging" that buffers the anomie of postmodern life. Others have urged that, because marriage "implies a reasonably well-understood set of commitments," it serves as an efficient method of "signaling" intentions both to one's spouse and the community. Yet others have argued that, because marriage is a formal union buttressed by law and social norms, it offers the most reliable means of "ensuring financial security for dependent family members."

Legal scholars do not all agree that marriage provides public benefits, however. Some argue that state-sanctioned marriage is outmoded and counterproductive. Martha Fineman, for example, argues that the "metanarrative of romantic sexual affiliation has deflected or absorbed concern for nonhorizontal intimate connections, particularly the one between parent and child"; she contends that the "the target of state policies should be the caretaker-dependent tie, not that between sexual affiliates." Other marriage critics argue that marriage, like race, is discriminatory in that "marital status functions to elevate some individuals, and subordinate others, based on their membership in groups that they did not choose to join." Yet others contend that, while "the state has a role in protecting and promoting ... relational interests," all intimate adult relationships—sexual and nonsexual—"create unique vulnerabilities" that require "protect[ion] wherever and with whomever they arise"; they argue that the law should move toward a "general-purpose civil union aimed explicitly at protecting and supporting intimate caregiving units of all types created." Some critics even go so far as to argue that "the law's recognition of marriage mandates or facilitates behaviors that cause social losses."

Much of the legal scholarship is highly conclusory. For example, the Canadian Law Reform Commission, arguing that the law should move "beyond conjugality" toward a "comprehensive" approach that incorporates "not just the situation of spouses and common-law partners, but also the needs of persons in non-conjugal relationships, including caregiver relationships," offers no evidence for this grand proposition beyond the number of disabled Canadians and a statistical breakdown of their living arrangements. Some legal scholars accuse their opponents of "cherry-picking" the evidence, only to engage in the same tactic themselves. Others ignore the evidence altogether.

Because of its failure to develop an evidentiary base, marriage scholarship from the legal academy also tends to be highly abstract: marriage proponents posit emotional and informational gains from marriage but fail to specify the nature, size, or quality of these advantages; marriage opponents posit social detriments from state recognition of marriage, but are equally vague on just how these harms are produced. With no facts to buttress their claims, each side of the debate speaks only to the converted. Neither group has the capacity to sway those in the other camp, or even to elicit meaningful dialogue.

Legal scholars' failure to offer evidence does not mean that it is unavailable. The decline of marriage and marital childbearing has spurred an intensive social-science research effort aimed at investigating the very same issues raised by marriage advocates and critics. This research effort has not resolved all questions about the benefits and costs of marriage; for example, it cannot yet explain the decline in marriage across the industrialized world. But it does offer data bearing on most of the questions raised by marriage's critics and advocates. It is time to incorporate these data into the debate over marriage classifications and policies.

2. *Does the Married State Benefit Those Who Marry?*

The research evidence unequivocally shows health and happiness benefits associated with marriage. Researcher after researcher has reported that the married live longer and are less likely to become disabled than the unmarried; husbands and wives get more sleep, eat more regular meals, and visit the doctor more regularly; they abuse addictive substances and engage in risky behaviors less frequently. On average, married individuals rate their sex life, happiness, and mental health more highly than the unmarried. They experience less domestic violence and greater physical security. Although an unfortunately large proportion of the marriage research comes from the United States, cross-national surveys show that marriage is associated with higher levels of subjective well-being across the industrialized and even non-industrialized world.

Married individuals also do better economically than their unmarried counterparts. Even after controlling for age, married men earn more than either single men or cohabitants, and they are less likely to lose their earnings through gambling. Married couples also have a higher savings rate and thus accrue greater wealth than the unmarried.

However, despite the consistent association between marriage and health, wealth, and happiness, the research also shows that these benefits are concentrated in certain types of marriages.

First, remarriage appears to confer much smaller benefits than first marriage. Indeed, sociologist Steven Nock found that, while first marriage was associated with significant gains in men's annual income, weeks worked, and occupational prestige, remarriage was actually correlated with *negative* economic consequences: men who remarried worked less, earned less, and had less prestigious occupations than they did before their remarriages.

Second, the various health and well-being benefits associated with marriage are not uniformly experienced even across first marriages. Violent marriages are obviously dangerous marriages, and even verbal marital conflict appears to be unhealthy, particularly for women. Researchers have thus consistently charted negative health effects associated with marital discord and stress. Accordingly, the health and well-being benefits associated with marriage make a case only for low-conflict marriage. That is why the Bush administration has opted to promote "healthy" marriage, but not marriage per se.

Third, some of the psychological and health benefits associated with the married state may well result from the retreat from marriage described in Part One. Divorce removes conflicted marriages from the marital pool. The decline of "shot-gun" marriages entered to avoid an illegitimate birth also appears to have reduced the pool of unstable, unhappy relationships, and the rise of cohabitation may have further reduced the number of conflicted marriages by eliminating them before marriage takes place. The psychic benefits associated with marriage thus might decline were vigorous marriage-promotion policies to succeed in attracting significant numbers of these high-conflict couples back to the marital fold.

Finally, some of the benefits associated with marriage derive from "selection" effects. We have already seen that economic theory predicts, and empirical research confirms, a higher marriage rate among employed, high-income men. To the extent that those who marry are wealthier—or happier, or healthier—before marriage, they should maintain these advantages after marriage. The jury is still out on the extent to which the marriage "premium" derives from preexisting characteristics or the married state. But, preexisting characteristics are important and explain away some significant part of the marital advantage.

Selection effects do not account for all of the benefits associated with marriage, however. Researchers who have controlled for obvious confounding factors like age and education continue to report marital advantages. Longitudinal studies have also demonstrated marital impacts. These studies show that those who were happy when married are less happy when divorced. And at least for men, marriage brings a "sharp reduction in social evenings at bars or taverns" and "an enormous increase" in involvement with relatives and church-related activities. Married men give more to relatives and less to friends and acquaintances. At least their first marriages are associated with measurable positive changes in annual income, weeks worked, and occupational prestige. Their loss of a spouse is associated with less healthy behaviors. Researchers thus almost universally agree that some, as yet undetermined, fraction of the marital premium is real, although they also agree that it is concentrated in stable, low-conflict relationships.

Why would marriage produce health, wealth, and happiness benefits? Obviously, marriage provides companionship and social support, factors that themselves are consistently associated with health and happiness. However, cohabitation also provides companionship and social support. The consistent advantages associated with marriage provide evidence for the claim that marriage is a more felicitous state than cohabitation, but they do not clearly show the mechanisms by which those benefits are produced. Some sociologists, like the legal scholars who favor marriage, posit benefits flowing from public commitment and the behavioral expectations induced by legal and social norms; some also theorize that marriage signifies "that the partners have successfully fulfilled their adult social roles." These theories of how the marital advantage develops are difficult to empirically prove, and demographer Kathleen Kiernan has alternatively suggested that the marital advantage may instead derive from "stronger and more committed partnerships being selected into marriage." Kiernan argues that the stability and other advantages associated with marriage will simply disappear if cohabiting couples increasingly eschew marriage. On this view, cohabitation would absorb the marital success stories and thereafter become a more successful relationship model itself.

The fact that remarriage is not associated with the same benefits as first marriage provides some support for Kieman's theory. Were the benefits of marriage primarily derived from public commitments and behavioral expectations, we would anticipate that remarriage–which entails the same commitments and expectations–would produce equivalent advantages. It is possible, of course, that a marital failure may inhibit commitment and sharing expectations; there is evidence to support this proposition, too. The bottom line is that we simply do not know how the marital advantage is produced. We thus cannot say whether Kiernan is right or wrong in asserting that the benefits associated with marriage are simply artifacts, and not the product of commitment, social norms, or other aspects of marriage itself.

Assuming that commitment and social norms do play a significant role in producing the marital advantage, is it also far from obvious that law is needed to preserve these benefits. No social scientist has compared formal and informal marriage; we thus cannot say whether the psychic and economic benefits associated with marriage would be lost or significantly diminished if marriage were to become a private status unregulated by the state. It is logical to suppose that entry into a public legal status that confers binding obligations and mandates formal exit procedures represents a different, more carefully considered, and more secure experience than entry into an informal relationship. But we lack the data to prove that this is so.

On balance, then, the social science evidence supports the claim that marriage provides individual benefits that, in aggregate, enhance the public good. But the evidence does not offer a strong case for the promotion of marriage *per se:* marriage can be harmful as well as helpful; remarriage does not appear to confer the same benefits as first marriage; and some obvious marriage promotion strategies—stringent divorce laws that reduce exit from marriage, marriage incentives that produce more "shotgun" marriages—could easily increase the number of weak marriages and thus work more harm than good. Perhaps most importantly, because we do not know exactly how the advantages associated with marriage are produced, we do not know whether, or to what extent, legal support for formal marriage is necessary to preserve them.

3. *Does Marriage Benefit Children?*

Although the adult benefits associated with marriage seem to support marital conflict-reduction more than they do marriage promotion, the social science evidence shows that marriage benefits children, too. Children born to married parents experience much greater stability than children born to unmarried parents; indeed, cross-national research shows that, in most countries, children born to cohabiting parents are two to four times more likely to see their parents separate than are children of parents married at the time of birth. Because of the greater stability that marriage provides, marital children are exposed to many fewer financial, physical, and educational risks. Unsurprisingly, lower risks produce higher levels of well-being. There is also evidence that the advantages conferred by marital childbearing and rearing transcend the specific benefits associated with residential and economic stability. For example, married fathers appear to be more involved and spend more time with their children than unmarried fathers; if parental separation occurs, they see their children more often and pay child support more regularly.

The advantages of marriage appear to extend into a child's adulthood, and even to his or her children. Researchers have documented a strong link between growing up in a single-parent household and adult income, health, and emotional stability. A number of studies have also found that both men and women who experience a single-parent household as children are more likely, as adults, to experience marital discord and to divorce or separate. And researchers who examined links between divorce in the grandparent generation and outcomes for grandchildren have reported that even grandparental divorce is significantly associated with less education, more marital discord, more divorce, and greater tension in early parent-child relationships.

Marriage is associated with advantages to children at all income and education levels. The experts have found that, "even among the poor, material hardships were substantially lower among married couple families with children than among other families with children, including those with at least two potential earners.... [E]ven among families with the same income-to-needs ratios, those in married couple families experienced significantly less hardship. The marriage impacts were quite large, generally higher than the effects of education....

The marital advantage appears to hold across national and cultural boundaries. Even in Scandinavia, which has the longest experience with cohabitation as a mainstream family form, demographers continue to find that marital childbearing is associated with much greater childhood stability, smaller risks to youthful and adult well-being, and lower rates of divorce and nonmarital childbearing. For example, in Sweden, where state policies "tend to view cohabitation as equal to marriage, and many of the regulations of marriage are applied to cohabiting relationships," cohabiting parents are more than four times as likely as married parents to separate before their first child turns five. And despite an extraordinarily high level of public assistance to single parents—assistance that produces a child poverty rate of less than 3%—single parenthood remains a serious risk factor for children. The most compelling study, which analyzed almost a million cases and took account of possibly confounding factors such as socioeconomic status and parental mental health, found that Swedish children in single-parent households showed significantly increased risks of "all adverse outcomes analyzed, including psychiatric disease, suicide or suicide attempt, injury, and addiction."

However, just as the adult benefits associated with marriage are concentrated in low-conflict, enduring relationships, so are the advantages of marriage to children. Although children living in high-conflict marriages may still reap economic advantages from doing so, researchers have found that the continuation of a high-conflict marriage is *negatively* associated with children's health and happiness, just as it is for adults; indeed, longitudinal surveys show that "parents' marital unhappiness and discord have a broad negative impact on virtually every dimension of offspring well-being." Moreover, although "[p]arental divorce also appears to have negative consequences for offspring, ... these are not as pervasive as the effects of parents' marital quality. It thus appears that parental household.... If divorce were limited only to high-conflict marriages, then divorce would generally be in children's best interest."

Again mirroring the research on adults, remarriage to a stepparent also fails to confer the same advantages as a continuing marriage between the child's parents. Children living in step-families tend to score lower than children living in intact families on tests of emotional and social well-being. Stepparents tend to be less warm, less involved, and less active in children's lives than are biological parents in intact, marital households.

Not only are the advantages of marital child rearing concentrated in low-conflict, enduring relationships, but—again mirroring the research on adult marriage partners—selection effects explain away a large portion of the marital advantage:

> Having a child while single is three times as common for the poor as for the affluent. Half of poor women who give birth while unmarried have no high school diploma at the time, and nearly a third have not worked at all in the last year.... And the situations of the men that father their children are not much better. More than four in ten poor men who have a child outside of marriage have already been to prison or jail by the time the baby is born; nearly half lack a high school diploma, and a quarter have no job.... [A]lmost half of them earned less than $10,000 in the year before the birth.

These patterns may be less pronounced in Western Europe, but in the United States some commentators have urged that reproductive behavior now diverges along class lines: educated young adults with good prospects continue to link childbearing with marriage, while the poor, ill-educated, and troubled do not. And even within Western Europe the available data suggests that "unmarried parenthood" may be more closely associated with impoverishment than empowerment.

Unmarried parents also tend to report many more relational stresses than their married counterparts. Parents who are unmarried when their child is born are more likely than married parents to have children by another partner. Their children are much more likely to be unplanned. They report higher levels of conflict and distrust, more problems with drugs and alcohol, more physical and mental health problems, and more domestic violence. Indeed, the evidence shows that many unwed parents fail to marry precisely because their relationships are highly problematic.

The socioeconomic and relational attributes of those who marry explain a large proportion of marital advantage. One recent study that compared married and cohabiting parents found that about two-thirds of the marital advantage in child poverty and half the advantage in parental mental health was due to observable differences between adults who choose to cohabit and those who choose to marry; the potential advantage or marriage within cohabiting stepparent households was even smaller, and because only observable characteristics could be taken into account, the study simulations almost certainly "overstate the potential benefits of marriage promotion."

But the systematic differences between married and unmarried parents ensures that marrying off the parents of nonmarital children would be inadequate to provide their children with the same advantages that marital children now enjoy. Indeed, it seems probable that such a strategy would simply increase the number of high-conflict marriages—marriages that are *not* advantageous to children—and, in many cases, substitute marital for nonmarital separation. The likelihood of this result is enhanced by the fact that the very same characteristics that predict nonmarriage also predict marital instability. Divorce is more than twice as common among couples living below the poverty line as it is in the general population, and elevated divorce rates are also significantly associated with youth, educational disadvantage, unemployment, violence, conflict, and infidelity.

A shift from cohabitation and separation to marriage and divorce might still confer some modest benefits on children. Married fathers in intact families appear to spend more time with their children; after separation, they see their children more frequently and pay child support more regularly than unmarried fathers. There is also evidence that, even after controlling for observable characteristics like education, academic test scores, and premarital pregnancy, marriage contributes significantly to living standards, "not only relative to single parents living alone but also compared to parents in cohabiting relationships and single parents living with other adult relatives." However, the extent to which these differences are due to marriage itself or other, as yet unmeasured personal characteristics, is unclear. It is also unclear whether they would be replicated in a population of poor marriage prospects.

The fact that marriage by itself is incapable of curing, or even dramatically curbing, the problems associated with nonmarital childbearing does not mean that marriage is irrelevant to children's well-being. Indeed, the fact that the less advantaged increasingly choose to bear children outside marriage "may be differentially harming children from less advantaged backgrounds and reinforcing inequalities in other domains." But to provide lasting benefits to children, state policy must succeed not just in encouraging parents to marry, but also to marry well and stay married. Because the chances of such a sequence are dramatically reduced when couples are immature and their relationships troubled by infidelity, violence, substance abuse, and the stresses associated with poverty, a marriage-promotion policy could not accomplish much for children unless it focused on the linked goals of encouraging healthy marriages with good prospects of long-term success and discouraging childbearing outside of such relationships. The issue, as sociologist Isabel Sawhill has put it, "is timing":

> The problem is not that people don't marry. Ninety percent of all American women are married by the age of 45.... What we need instead is to stop people from having babies before they get married.

A defer-childbearing-until-marriage approach would aim at encouraging both young men and women to wait until they have finished school, obtained employment and found a low-conflict relationship with decent prospects of long-term success before they commence child bearing.

Such a policy, if successful, would confer benefits on parents as well as their children. Women who give birth to one nonmarital child are disproportionately likely to give birth to another, typically with another father. They are much more likely to live in poverty and to live in poverty for longer periods of time. They are less likely to marry or to have stable relationships. Some of these adverse consequences are undoubtedly the result of selection effects, but the evidence suggests that a portion of the disadvantage associated with nonmarital childbearing results from nonmarital childbearing itself.

Even if a marital child-bearing effort succeeded merely in delaying nonmarital birth until after women had completed their educations we would have accomplished something substantial. Teenage birth is particularly risky for both parents and children. Historically, about half of teenage mothers have gone on welfare within five years of giving birth. And their children suffer a wide range of adverse consequences:

> The offspring of teenage mothers are more likely to be poor, abused, or neglected than those of women who delay childbearing, and they are less likely to receive proper nutrition, health care, and cognitive and social stimulation. They are also at greater risk of lower intellectual and academic achievement and social behavioral problems—one study found that children of teenage mothers are almost three times as likely to be

incarcerated during their adolescence or early 20s as are the children of older mothers. Children born to teen mothers are less likely to graduate from high school and more likely to be unemployed and to become teenage parents themselves than those born to women who delay childbearing.

Were a pro-marriage policy to succeed in encouraging young mothers to defer childbearing until they were better able to provide for their children themselves, that alone would be a significant achievement.

4. *Does Marital Formality Provide Public Benefits?*

Stable, low-conflict marriage is associated with significant benefits to adults and far more dramatic benefits to children. We do not know whether informal, marriage-like unions are capable of producing the same advantages. For both adults and their children, it is logical to suppose that a public commitment that entails binding legal obligations and necessitates formal exit procedures would be experienced differently than an informal relationship; indeed, unmarried mothers themselves suggest that the ceremonial aspects of marriage are important and meaningful to them. But long-term, low-conflict cohabitation is sufficiently rare that we lack the data to establish how it compares with formal marriage. We thus cannot say for sure that formal registration is an important source of measurable benefit to either adults or children.

Formal registration does provide significant evidentiary benefits, however, benefits that are often overlooked in the debate over marriage. Formal marriage not only signals intention to a partner, friends, and family, it also signals intention to the state and the public. Moreover, it accomplishes both of these aims efficiently, unequivocally, and prospectively. After a couple marries, there is no question about what sort of relationship they intend. No litigation will be necessary to determine their status. No decision maker will be required to sift through heaps of self-serving testimony about promises made and understandings reached. One partner cannot surprise the other with by bringing a fraudulent claim nor can one partner surprise the other by trying to evade a just claim.

Informal marriage lacks these various advantages. It must be proven and thus offers only a retrospective status. Gaining that status will almost invariably necessitate costly litigation.

These basic disadvantages are compounded by the evidentiary problems inherent in fact-based determination of marital status. Marital intent is subjective; when not publicly expressed, it is extraordinarily hard to prove. This basic difficulty is exacerbated by the range of meanings associated with cohabitation and the fact that cohabitants often do not agree about the nature of their relationship. Researchers have found that, in 20–40% of cohabiting relationships, partners express different views on whether they plan to marry each other. Moreover, in one survey, about a third of the time, only one partner felt that the couple spent a lot of time together; and in 40% of the cases, one partner but not the other reported a high degree of happiness with the relationship. Given the lack of uniformity in cohabitants' understandings and behaviors, the mere fact of living together provides little evidence of what the relationship means. One partner might fully believe that the relationship is committed; the other might fully believe the reverse. A break-up can only enhance such disagreement, setting the stage for disappointed expectations and resulting litigation. These difficulties are bad enough when both cohabitants are able to testify at a hearing; they are even worse when the issue of marital understanding is tested in a proceeding brought after one partner dies.

These various evidentiary problems have fueled the movement away from the common law marriage doctrine. At one time, nearly two-thirds of the states recognized common law marriage; by 2002, only twelve jurisdictions did so, and two of the twelve had adopted strict limitations on its establishment. This decline reflects the sad fact that post-hoc, litigation-based determination of marital commitment often "leads to fraud and uncertainty in the most important of human relationships." The evidentiary problems posed by the common law marriage doctrine were minimized when nonmarital cohabitation was rare; they are magnified in an era, like this one, in which cohabitation is extraordinarily common and extremely variable in its meaning.

Because of the uncertainty, cost, a rule-evasion evidentiary problems inherent in informal marriage, there are strong public policy reasons to encourage formal marriage even if informal unions are capable of providing the same emotional and economic benefits to adults and children. Informal marriage cannot clearly, efficiently, and prospectively alter a couple's status in accordance with their intentions; formal marriage can and does. Informal marriage creates undesirable opportunities for fraud and rule evasion; formal marriage does not.

Conclusion

Marriage and marital childbearing are in decline for reasons that are poorly understood. Cohabitation sometimes represents informal marriage, but far more frequently serves as a substitute for being single or a stage in the process of deciding whether to make a marital commitment. Cohabitation thus is not the equivalent of marriage, and most marital-status classifications appropriately divide the married from the unmarried. However, because marital decision making may be (dis)incentives created by these classifications, policymakers face difficult choices in deciding whether, and to what extent, they should revise statutory classifications to avoid marriage disincentives.

The research evidence shows that marriage is associated with economic and emotional benefits to both adult partners and their children, but it also shows that the emotional benefits associated with marriage are produced only in low-conflict, well-functioning relationships. Marriage also provides important public benefits through its notarial function; ceremonial marriage clearly denotes the intention to form a durable union and to assume marital roles and responsibilities, while cohabitation has a range of meanings and often has different meanings even for the cohabiting pair.

The evidence thus suggests that the state should avoid classificatory schemes that penalize formal marriage unless there is evidence showing that the costs of such avoidance exceed the expected gains. The evidence also supports some marriage-promotion initiatives, in particular low-cost public education aimed at preserving low-conflict marriages and deterring nonmarital childbearing. These initiatives do not have the capacity to revive the world in which marriage and marital child-bearing were almost universal. But they might have significant marginal effects, they appear to be cost-effective, and they seem extremely unlikely to do harm.

In the United States, marriage-promotion initiatives should also be coupled with policies aimed at reducing the social disadvantages strongly associated with nonmarital birth and relational failure: the research data shows that the same conditions which promote nonmarriage and marital failure also promote an enormous array of problems in family functioning and outcomes. Indeed, because of the strong and consistent association between disadvantage and relational failure, it is not obvious that the state can effectively promote marriage without such policies.

(2) Marriage, Cohabitation, and the Functions of Family Law

> *What happiness there is in the union of husband and wife, than which none greater nor more lasting exists in all of nature! For while we are linked with our other friends by benevolence of mind, with a wife we are joined by the greatest affection, physical union, the bond of the sacrament, and the common sharing of all fortunes.*
>
> Erasmus
> *A Praise of Marriage*

Suppose, *arguendo*, that what Professor Garrison reports is true. What, if anything, should the law's response be? One obvious response is to say the law should encourage marriage. If marriage makes people happier, produces social benefits, and reduces social dislocations, law should favor it. How? In part, it depends on why marriage works these wondrous benefits. As you may already have gathered, Professor Nock believes it does so because marriage is a social institution:

> While one can imagine a variety of close personal affiliations uniting two adults, the variety of marriage affiliations is much narrower because marriage is an *institution,* culturally patterned and integrated into other basic social institutions, such as education, the economy, and politics. Marriage has rules that originate outside any particular union of two spouses and that establish *soft boundaries* around the relationship that influence the partners in many ways.... Married couples have something that other couples lack: they are heirs to a vast system of understood principles that help organize and sustain their lives.

As we have seen (most recently, in the epigraph to this Section from Victoria Woodhull), not everyone agrees with this description of the way families work. (In particular, some feminists see marriage as an institution that oppresses women. Professor Nock agrees that dependency in marriages is inevitable but argues that equity should be sought in mutual dependence.) But again let us assume *arguendo* that it is correct. Even if it is, we would not want to use the law to promote marriage unless we felt the advantages of marriage as an institution outweighed its disadvantages and outweighed the costs of using the law to promote it. We have been counting and weighing those disadvantages and costs throughout this casebook, so let us yet again assume *arguendo* that it is worth using law to try promote marriage as an institution.

Now the question is how we should do so. The traditional answer is that we channel people into marriage partly by (1) granting them benefits when they marry and (2) denying them benefits when they use alternatives to marriage like cohabitation. This gives people concrete incentives to marry instead of cohabit. And the more people react to those incentives the more natural it seems to everybody else to marry instead of cohabit. In addition, this process is an exercise in law's expressive function. The law is stating, and is widely understood to be stating, a preference that people marry rather than cohabit. In short, the channelling and expressive functions reinforce each other.

Marvin and especially the ALI Principles seem to depart from this strategy. They do so in two ways. First, they offer cohabitants some of the protections traditionally available only to the married, thus changing the incentive structure couples confront. Indeed, the ALI Principles apply the same rules to married couples and "domestic partners." True, once you marry you can count on receiving the law's protections for the married, while the unmarried do not receive them until some time has passed and the relationship has evolved in somewhat ill-defined ways. Nevertheless, the trend is toward treating spouses and cohabitants similarly. This leads us to the second way *Marvin* and the ALI Principles depart from the strategy once thought to promote marriage as a social institution. They seem to abandon any ambition to recruit the law's expressive powers to promote marriage.

But is there an alternative? Cohabitation is distinctly more common than before. Cohabitors enter into property arrangements courts are asked to resolve. The *Hewitt* response to such requests works results that come to seem increasingly intolerable. Have we, then, reached a point at which the law cannot comfortably be recruited to support a social institution because the social institution itself is not strong enough to sustain itself without exorbitant legal measures? "The amount of law is relatively small which a modern legislature can successfully impose. The reason for this is that unless the enforcement of the law is taken in hand by the citizenry, the officials as such are quite helpless.... For what gives law reality is not that it is commanded by the sovereign but that it brings the organized force of the state to the aid of those citizens who believe in the law." Walter Lippmann, *A Preface to Morals* 276–77 (The Macmillan Company, 1929).

But this question is not the end of our story. Whatever may be the fate of marriage as a social and legal institution, are we witnessing the birth of a new social and legal institution—cohabitation? Some courts have simply said to cohabitants, "We will enforce your property agreements just as we enforce anyone else's property agreements." But other courts, and even more aggressively the ALI, have said something like this: "We know what fairness between cohabitants requires and will go some ways toward imposing fairness on you." This is not the language of contract. This is the language of status and of social institutions. Consider the progression of the Washington courts as recounted in *Connell v. Francisco*, 898 P2d 831 (1995):

> A meretricious relationship is a stable, marital-like relationship where both parties cohabit with knowledge that a lawful marriage between them does not exist. *In re Marriage of Lindsey*, 101 Wash.2d 299, 304, 678 P.2d 328 (1984).
>
> Relevant factors establishing a meretricious relationship include, but are not limited to: continuous cohabitation, duration of the relationship, purpose of the relationship, pooling of resources and services for joint projects, and the intent of the parties.
>
> In *Lindsey*, this court ruled a relationship need not be "long term" to be characterized as a meretricious relationship. While a "long term" relationship is not a threshold requirement, duration is a significant factor. A "short term" relationship may be characterized as meretricious, but a number of significant and substantial factors must be present. See *Lindsey* (a less than 2–year meretricious relationship preceded marriage)....
>
> Historically, property acquired during a meretricious relationship was presumed to belong to the person in whose name title to the property was placed. "[I]n the absence of any evidence to the contrary, it should be presumed as a matter of law that the parties intended to dispose of the property exactly as they did dispose of it." *Creasman v. Boyle*, 31 Wash.2d 345, 356, 196 P.2d 835 (1948)....
>
> To avoid inequitable results under "the *Creasman* presumption", Washington courts developed a number of exceptions. [Courts implied partnerships, used constructive trusts, traced the source of funds, and deployed contract theory.]
>
> In 1984, this court overruled *Creasman*. *Lindsey*. In its place, the court adopted a general rule requiring a just and equitable distribution of property following a meretricious relationship.

What would—what will?—the new social and legal institution of cohabitation look like? One way of trying to glimpse its future is to imagine how we might understand *Marvin* in terms of the functions of family law. To that exercise we now turn.

The Protective Function

On one view, the protective function is at the heart of *Marvin*'s rationale. On this view, *Marvin* is intended to prevent the abuse of the power that one member of an intimate couple can acquire by reason of that intimacy over the other and that one person can have over another by reason of superior ability and experience in dealing with finances. *Marvin* allows a court which encounters such abuses to remedy them. Or, to put the point differently, *Marvin* allows courts which encounter a person who has (often for many years and in important ways) relied on an intimate to protect that person from the consequences of unfairly disappointed reliance. Proponents of this view, then, find *Marvin* desirable because it protects people who are vulnerable and because it provides the same protective services to intimates as it provides to husbands and wives on one hand and to people in commercial settings on the other.

The Facilitative Function

On another view, the facilitative function is at the heart of the rationale for *Marvin*. On this view, the problem *Marvin* is intended to cope with is that people in intimate relationships have as much need as husbands and wives or indeed parties to commercial contracts to arrange their affairs in the ways that particularly and peculiarly suit them. Contract is the paradigmatic tool of the facilitative function, since it allows people to write the terms of their own relationships and endows them with the state's power to enforce those terms.

The Arbitral Function

The arbitral function is also important to the justification of the *Marvin* principle. The effect of the old rule was to close the law's tribunals to people whose disputes, although as real and serious as those of many other people, were part of a sexual relationship. *Marvin* opens those tribunals to solve those disputes. Further, *Marvin* promotes the arbitral function by providing, to some extent, legal standards to be used in resolving the disputes.

The Channelling Function

Marvin may exemplify the channelling function at work. *Marvin* may promote a new legal and social institution into which people may be channelled. As that institution develops, it may provide people with subsidiary institutions from which to choose. That is, particular versions of the cohabiting relationship—one for people who intend a long-term commitment, another for people who intend to have children, another for people who do not want to share their wealth, and so on—may arise. People will thereby be relieved of the need to invent the basics of their relationship for themselves, and the law will be helped in interpreting their behavior and in enforcing their contracts.

The Expressive Function

Both proponents and opponents of *Marvin* believe it has noteworthy expressive aspects. As the opinion suggests, proponents tend to think *Marvin* makes statement about the new social and legal acceptability of non-marital relationships. Opponents believe what the court's opinion denies, that that statement will widely be taken to condemn traditional marriage. The opponents argue that by creating an institution that parallels marriage and that may be endowed with advantages marriage does not have (for instance, a greater degree of freedom to enter into spousal contracts), *Marvin* weakens the institution of marriage. Which argument is correct? How do you know? Might the expressive message of *Marvin* change over time? How?

BIBLIOGRAPHY

Cohabitation Generally. John M. Eekelaar and Sanford N. Katz, *Marriage and Cohabitation in Contemporary Societies: Areas of Legal, Social and Ethical Change: An International and Interdisciplinary Study* (Butterworths, 1980), proffers an unusually broad ranging and often thought provoking essays on the topics announced in the book's various titles. Similarly, the ramifications of cohabitation are discussed from various perspectives in Alan Booth and Ann C. Crouter, *Just Living Together: Implications of Cohabitation on Families, Children, and Social Policy* (Lawrence Ehrlbaum, 2002). A comparative European study appears in Kathleen. Kiernan, *Cohabitation in Western Europe: Trends, Issues and Implications*, 96 Population Trends 25 (2001) 2. For a suggestion that existing family institutions may be incomplete, especially for women, see Beverly Horsburg, *Redefining the Family: Recognizing the Altruistic Caretaker and the Importance of Relational Needs*, 25 U Mich JL Ref 423 (1992). Joan R. Kahn and Kathryn A. London, *Premarital Sex and the Risk of Divorce*, 53 J Marriage & Family 845 (1991), finds that people who cohabit or have sexual relations before marriage are less likely to have stable marriages. A intriguing book reporting on an empirical study of low-income women in Philadelphia, concluding while they still want marriage as an ideal, they will elect single motherhood despite its clear costs is Kathryn Edin and Maria Kefalas, *Promises I Can Keep: Why Poor Women Put Motherhood Before Marriage* (U Cal Press, 2005).

Courtship and Dating. A wonderful novel that, among other things, reflects upon intercultural relationships is Ann Patchett's *Bel Canto* (Harper Perennial, 2002).

Part I: Conclusion—A Pause To Reflect

Now, as in Tullias tombe, one lampe burnt cleare, Unchang'd for fifteene hundred yeare, May these love-lamps we here enshrine, In warmth, light, lasting, equall the divine. Fire ever doth aspire, And makes all like it selfe, turnes all to fire, But ends in ashes, which these cannot doe, For none of these is fuell, but fire too. This is joyes bonfire, then, where loves strong Arts Make of so noble individuall parts One fire of foure inflaming eyes, and of two loving hearts.

John Donne
The Good Night

Since we have now completed Part I, this is a good time for you to review. Here are a few questions to guide you.

(1) In Chapter I we examined the social and legal functions of marriage. What are those functions? How well does marriage serve them? What changes in the law might improve the institution?

(2) We have repeatedly looked at the law of husband and wife in terms of the themes of family law. What has our investigation suggested about those themes? For example, how do you assess the doctrine of family autonomy? How convincing are its rationales? What ought its limits be? What governmental interests justify intervention in families?

(3) We have also repeatedly looked at the law of husband and wife in terms of the functions of family law. What has our investigation suggested about those functions? Are all the functions legitimate? What demands does each make on family law? To what extent is each function served by family law as it now is? As it should be? What limits do you see in the ability of family law to serve the five functions? What conflicts do you see among the various functions?

Part II

THE FAMILY AND THE CONSTITUTION

The great ideals of liberty and equality are preserved against the assaults of opportunism, the expediency of the passing hour, the erosion of small encroachments, the scorn and derision of those who have no patience with general principles, by enshrining them in constitutions. . . .

Benjamin N. Cardozo
The Nature of the Judicial Process

We have now examined the law regulating marriage. We will soon investigate the law regulating parents and children. But first, a change of pace. The materials on marriage had little to say about the Constitution. We scanted the Constitution so that we could concentrate on some basic questions of doctrine and policy that shape family law without having to master simultaneously the elaborate doctrines that shape the constitutional law of the family. Family law has increasingly been constitutionalized, so we must consider the constitutional law of the family at some length. Now is the time to do so.

Chapter VII

THE CONSTITUTIONAL VIEW OF FAMILIES AND THE CONCEPT OF RIGHTS

Whoever attentively considers the different departments of power must perceive, that, in a government in which they are separated from each other, the judiciary, from the nature of its functions, will always be the least dangerous to the political rights of the Constitution; because it will be least in a capacity to annoy or injure them.... The judiciary ... has no influence over either the sword or the purse; no direction either of the strength or of the wealth of the society; and can take no active resolution whatever.

Alexander Hamilton
The Federalist No. 78

Two major shifts occur when we move from family law in its traditional form to family law in its constitutional form. First is a shift from state law to federal law. Regulating the family is classically a central part of the police power and has historically been confided to the states. The discovery that the Constitution speaks to family law transfers some of the responsibility for that law to an agency of the federal government—its courts. Of course, the shift to federal authority has been going on for some time, and the constitutionalization of family law is only one reason. A prime cause has been the federal government's expansion of the welfare state: programs like AFDC and Social Security have important implications for families. Various kinds of federal rules also have direct and indirect effects on families; the federal statute directed toward enforcing child-support payments (which we will examine in Chapter 10) exemplifies the former kind of effect, federal statutes prohibiting discrimination against women exemplify the latter. The federalization of family law has also been promoted by a number of federally funded programs in such areas as family planning. Finally, the government has affected family law in its role as a major employer. In *Hisquierdo v. Hisquierdo*, 439 US 572 (1979), for example, the Supreme Court held that the federal law governing military pensions pre-empted state marital-property law (although Congress later revised the relevant statutes to pre-empt that preemption). So commonplace has the federal government's role in family-law become that not long ago a sense-of-Congress resolution advised the states to ensure that grandparents have a right to visit their grandchildren when the grandchildren's parents divorce. In sum, the federalization of family law has proceeded a significant distance. As you read the rest of this book, you should ask how far that development has progressed and how far it should progress.

The second major shift we observe when we study the constitutional law of the family is from legislatures to courts. Family law is highly statutory: the requirements for marriage, for obtaining a divorce, for dividing marital property, for setting alimony, and for much else are largely set statutorily. These statutes are not especially detailed or complex, and they deliberately leave room for judicial discretion. But the movement from statutory to constitutional law still represents a notable change in the locus of power—in non-constitutional areas legislatures can change judicial doctrine they dislike, but no legislature can reverse a court's interpretation of the Constitution.

Our continuing interest in legal change leads us to look at these questions of institutional authority. We will consider the extent to which power over family law should be local or federal, the desirability and legitimacy of judicial power over family law, and the attractions and liabilities of thinking about family law in terms of the rights language constitutionalization relies on. We begin this inquiry, then, by scrutinizing the doctrinal basis of the constitutionalization of family law. As you read, ask whether the Constitution speaks to family law, how you know that the Constitution does or does not do so, and what the Constitution says about family law.

SECTION 1. THE ORIGINS OF THE CONSTITUTIONAL DOCTRINE OF PRIVACY

He reddened under the retort, but kept his eyes on her. "May is ready to give me up."

"What! Three days after you've entreated her on your knees to hasten your marriage?"

"She's refused; that gives me the right—"

"Ah, you've taught me what an ugly word that is," she said.

Edith Wharton
The Age of Innocence

A. THE DOCTRINE OF SUBSTANTIVE DUE PROCESS

For myself it would be most irksome to be ruled by a bevy of Platonic Guardians, even if I knew how to choose them, which I assuredly do not. If

> *they were in charge, I should miss the stimulus of living in a society where I have, at least theoretically, some part in the direction of public affairs.*
>
> **Learned Hand**
> *The Bill of Rights*

The Constitution speaks to family law primarily through the Fourteenth Amendment. Its crucial sentence reads, "No State shall make or enforce any law which shall abridge the privileges or immunities of citizens of the United States nor shall any State deprive any person of life, liberty, or property, without due process of law; nor deny to any person within its jurisdiction the equal protection of the laws." On its face, this sentence may not seem to address with complete clarity the issues we have discussed in this course. How, then, has the Fourteenth Amendment been understood to do so?

The clause directed to deprivation of life, liberty, or property without due process of law looks at first reading doubly inapt to family law. First, the clause seems to refer most straightforwardly to criminal sentences—capital punishment, jail, and fines—and possibly to government actions amounting to a taking of property. Second, the clause seems to speak only to *procedure*. In other words, one might suppose that, as long as the government's procedures are correct, it may perform any substantive acts it wishes. In fact, in the first three decades after the amendment was adopted, the Court declined to find substantive limits on government action in the Due Process Clause. Nevertheless, in those decades litigants continued to press substantive claims on the Court, and the climate of legal opinion gradually warmed to them. Professor Gunther writes:

> The growth of industrialization and corporate power in the post-Civil War years stirred popular demands and legislative responses. And the new regulatory laws, opponents argued, contravened not only the economic laissez faire theories of Adam Smith ... but also the social views of 19th century writers such as Herbert Spencer.... Spencer's emphasis on the survival of the fittest in his 1850 volume, *Social Statics*, and the echoes of Social Darwinism in the writings of American defenders of economic inequalities and a governmental hands-off policy, found their way into legal treatises and briefs.

Gerald Gunther, *Constitutional Law* 554 (Foundation Press, 1985).

Finally, in 1897, the Supreme Court overturned a state law under the authority of the doctrine that the Fourteenth Amendment places substantive limits on the police power. *Allgeyer v. Louisiana*, 165 US 578 (1897). The Court said,

> The liberty mentioned in that amendment means not only the right of the citizen to be free from the mere physical restraint of his person, as by incarceration, but the term is deemed to embrace the right of the citizen to be free in the enjoyment of all his faculties; to

> be free to use them in all lawful ways; to live and work where he will; to earn his livelihood by any lawful calling; to pursue any livelihood or avocation, and for that purpose to enter into all contracts which may be proper, necessary and essential to his carrying out to a successful conclusion the purposes above mentioned.

Substantive due process, and particularly freedom of contract, were to flourish for forty years. That flourishing came, at least for its opponents, to be symbolized by *Lochner v. New York*, 198 US 45 (1905). New York had made it a crime for a bakery to require its employees to work more than sixty hours a week or ten hours a day because:

> [t]he constant inhaling of flour dust causes inflammation of the lungs and bronchial tubes. The eyes also suffer through this dust, which is responsible for the many cases of running eyes among the bakers. The long hours of toil to which all bakers are subjected produces rheumatism, cramps and swollen legs.... Nearly all bakers are pale-faced and of more delicate health than the workers of other crafts, which is chiefly due to their hard work and their irregular and unnatural mode of living, whereby the power of resistance against disease is greatly diminished. The average age of a baker is below that of other workmen; they seldom live over their fiftieth year, most of them dying between the ages of forty and fifty.

198 US at 70–71 (Harlan, J., dissenting). The Court, however, said,

> The mere assertion that the subject relates though but in a remote degree to the public health does not necessarily render the enactment valid. The act must have a more direct relation, as a means to an end, and the end itself must be appropriate and legitimate, before an act can be held to be valid which interferes with the general right of an individual to be free in his person and in his power to contract in relation to his own labor.

198 US at 57–58. The Court concluded, "The act is not, within any fair meaning of the term, a health law, but is an illegal interference with the rights of individuals, both employers and employees, to make contracts regarding labor upon such terms as they may think best, or which they may agree upon with the other parties to such contracts." 198 US at 61.

Justice Holmes' dissent is famous:

> This case is decided upon an economic theory which a large part of the country does not entertain. If it were a question whether I agreed with that theory, I should desire to study it further and long before making up my mind. But I do not conceive that to be my duty, because I strongly believe that my agreement or disagreement has nothing to do with the right of a majority to embody their opinions in law. It is settled by various decisions of this court that state constitutions and state laws may regulate life in many ways which we as legislators might think as injudicious or if you like as tyrannical as this, and which equally with this interfere with the

liberty to contract. Sunday laws and usury laws are ancient examples. A more modern one is the prohibition of lotteries. The liberty of the citizen to do as he likes so long as he does not interfere with the liberty of others to do the same, which has been a shibboleth for some well-known writers, is interfered with by school laws, by the Post Office, by every state or municipal institution which takes his money for purposes thought desirable, whether he likes it or not. The Fourteenth Amendment does not enact Mr. Herbert Spencer's Social Statics. The other day we sustained the Massachusetts vaccination law. *Jacobson v. Massachusetts*, 197 U.S. 11. United States and state statutes and decisions cutting the liberty to contract by way of combination are familiar to this court. Two years ago we upheld the prohibition of sales of stock on margins or for future delivery in the constitution of California. The decision sustaining an eight hour law for miners is still recent. Some of these laws embody convictions or prejudices which judges are likely to share. Some may not. But a constitution is not intended to embody a particular economic theory, whether of paternalism and the organic relation of the citizen to the State or of *laissez faire*.

It is made for people of fundamentally differing views, and the accident of our finding certain opinions natural and familiar or novel and even shocking ought not to conclude our judgment upon the question whether statutes embodying them conflict with the Constitution of the United States.

General propositions do not decide concrete cases. The decision will depend on a judgment or intuition more subtle than any articulate major premise. But I think that the proposition just stated, if it is accepted, will carry us far toward the end. Every opinion tends to become a law. I think that the word liberty in the Fourteenth Amendment is perverted when it is held to prevent the natural outcome of a dominant opinion, unless it can be said that a rational and fair man necessarily would admit that the statute proposal would infringe fundamental principles as they have been understood by the traditions of our people and our law. It does not need research to show that no such sweeping condemnation can be passed upon the statute before us. A reasonable man might think it a proper measure on the score of health. Men whom I certainly could not pronounce unreasonable would uphold it as a first installment of a general regulation of the hours of work. Whether in the latter aspect it would be open to the charge of inequality I think it unnecessary to discuss.

The Court's zeal for substantive due process continued into the 1930's, when it (and other of the Court's conservative-activist doctrines) encountered the reformist temper of the times and the New Deal's efforts to subdue the Depression. The Court's decisions invalidating important New Deal programs became unpopular enough for President Roosevelt to ask Congress to let him appoint new (and presumably more liberal) Justices. Although Roosevelt failed, the Court of the mid–1930's generally retreated. (The reasons for that retreat are various and debated.) After 1937, the Court rejected substantive due process arguments with responses like, "Our recent decisions make plain that we do not sit as a super-legislature to weigh the wisdom of legislation." *Day–Brite Lighting, Inc. v. Missouri*, 342 US 421, 423 (1952).

B. THE EARLY FAMILY LAW CASES

I am not afraid to say that the principle of self-interest rightly understood appears to me the best suited of all philosophical theories to the wants of the men of our time, and that I regard it as their chief remaining security against themselves.

Alexis de Tocqueville
Democracy in America

The history we have briefly canvassed formed much of the background of the modern constitutional law of the family. To complete the background, though, we must examine four more cases. Two of them are from the glory days of substantive due process:

MEYER v. STATE OF NEBRASKA

Supreme Court of the United States, 1923
262 US 390

McReynolds, J.

Plaintiff in error was tried and convicted in the District Court for Hamilton County, Nebraska, under an information which charged that on May 25, 1920, while an instructor in Zion Parochial School, he unlawfully taught the subject of reading in the German language to Raymond Parpart, a child of ten years, who had not attained and successfully passed the eighth grade. The information is based upon "An act relating to the teaching of foreign languages in the State of Nebraska," approved April 9, 1919, which follows [Laws 1919, c. 249.]:

> "Section 1. No person, individually or as a teacher, shall, in any private, denominational, parochial or public school, teach any subject to any person in any language other than the English language."
>
> "Sec. 2. Languages, other than the English language, may be taught as languages only after a pupil shall have attained and successfully passed the eighth grade. . . ."

The Supreme Court of the State affirmed the judgment of conviction. . . . The following excerpts from the opinion sufficiently indicated the reasons advanced to support the conclusion.

"The salutary purpose of the statute is clear. The legislature had seen the baneful effects of permitting foreigners, who had taken residence in this country, to rear and educate their children in the language of their native land. The result of that condition was found to be inimical to our own safety. To allow the children of foreigners, who had emigrated here, to be taught from early childhood the language of the country of their parents was to rear them with that language as their mother tongue. It was to educate them so that they must always think in that language, and as a consequence, naturally inculcate in them the ideas and sentiments foreign to the best interests of this country. The statute, therefore, was intended not only to require that the education of all children be conducted in the English language, but that, until they had grown into that language and until it had become a part of them, they should not in the schools be taught any other language. The obvious purpose of this statute was that the English language should be and become the mother tongue of all children reared in this state. The enactment of such a statute comes reasonably within the police power of the state...."

The problem for our determination is whether the statute as construed and applied unreasonably infringes the liberty guaranteed to the plaintiff in error by the Fourteenth Amendment. "No State shall ... deprive any person of life, liberty, or property, without due process of law."

While this Court has not attempted to define with exactness the liberty thus guaranteed, the term has received much consideration and some of the included things have been definitely stated. Without doubt, it denotes not merely freedom from bodily restraint but also the right of the individual to contract, to engage in any of the common occupations of life, to acquire useful knowledge, to marry, establish a home and bring up children, to worship God according to the dictates of his own conscience and generally to enjoy those privileges long recognized at common law as essential to the orderly pursuit of happiness by free men. The established doctrine is that this liberty may not be interfered with, under the guise of protecting the public interest, by legislative action which is arbitrary or without reasonable relation to some purpose within the competency of the State to effect. Determination by the legislature of what constitutes proper exercise of police power is not final or conclusive but is subject to supervision by the courts.

The American people have always regarded education and acquisition of knowledge as matters of supreme importance which should be diligently promoted. The Ordinance of 1787 declares, "Religion, morality, and knowledge being necessary to good government and the happiness of mankind, schools and the means of education shall forever be encouraged." Corresponding to the right of control it is the natural duty of the parent to give his children education suitable to their station in life; and nearly all the States, including Nebraska, enforce this obligation by compulsory laws.

Practically, education of the young is only possible in schools conducted by especially qualified persons who devote themselves thereto. The calling always has been regarded as useful and honorable, essential, indeed, to the public welfare. Mere knowledge of the German language cannot reasonably be regarded as harmful. Heretofore it has been commonly looked upon as helpful and desirable. Plaintiff in error taught this language in school as part of his occupation. His right thus to teach and the right of parents to engage him so to instruct their children, we think, are within the liberty of the Amendment.

The challenged statute forbids the teaching in school of any subject except in English; also the teaching of any other language until the pupil has attained and successfully passed the eighth grade, which is not usually accomplished before the age of twelve. The Supreme Court of the State has held that "the so-called ancient or dead languages" are not "within the spirit or the purpose of the act." Latin, Greek, Hebrew are not proscribed; but German, French, Spanish, Italian and every other alien speech are within the ban. Evidently the legislature has attempted materially to interfere with the calling of modern language teachers, with the opportunities of pupils to acquire knowledge, and with the power of parents to control the education of their own.

It is said the purpose of the legislation was to promote civic development by inhibiting training and education of the immature in foreign tongues and ideals before they could learn English and acquire American ideals; and "that the English language should be and become the mother tongue of all children reared in this State." It is also affirmed that the foreign born population is very large, that certain communities commonly use foreign words, follow foreign leaders, move in a foreign atmosphere, and that the children are thereby hindered from becoming citizens of the most useful type and the public safety is imperiled.

That the State may do much, go very far, indeed, in order to improve the quality of its citizens, physically, mentally and morally, is clear; but the individual has certain fundamental rights which must be respected. The protection of the Constitution extends to all, to those who speak other languages as well as to those born with English on the tongue. Perhaps it would be highly advantageous if all had ready understanding of our ordinary speech, but this cannot be coerced by methods which conflict with the Constitution—a desirable end cannot be promoted by prohibited means.

For the welfare of his Ideal Commonwealth, Plato suggested a law which should provide: "That the wives of our guardians are to be common, and their children are to be common, and no parent is to know his own child, nor any child his parent.... The proper officers will take the offspring of the good parents to the pen or fold, and there they will deposit them with certain nurses who dwell in a separate quarter; but the offspring of the inferior, or of the better when they chance to be deformed, will be put away in some mysterious, unknown place, as they should be." In order to submerge the individual and develop ideal citizens, Sparta assembled the males at seven into barracks and intrusted their subsequent education and training to official guardians. Although such measures have been deliberately approved by men of great genius, their ideas touching the relation between individual and State were wholly different from those upon which our institutions rest; and it hardly will be affirmed that any legislature could impose such restrictions upon the people of a State without doing violence to both letter and spirit of the Constitution.

The desire of the legislature to foster a homogeneous people with American ideals prepared readily to understand current discussions of civic matters is easy to appreciate. Unfortunate experiences during the late war and aversion toward every characteristic of truculent adversaries were certainly enough to quicken that aspiration. But the means adopted, we think, exceed the limitations upon the power of the State and conflict with rights assured to plaintiff in error. The interference is plain enough and no adequate reason therefor in time of peace and domestic tranquility has been shown.

The power of the State to compel attendance at some school and to make reasonable regulations for all schools, including a requirement that they shall give instructions in English, is not questioned. Nor has challenge been made of the State's power to prescribe a curriculum for institutions which it supports. Those matters are not within the present controversy.

PIERCE v. SOCIETY OF SISTERS

Supreme Court of the United States, 1925
268 US 510

McReynolds, J.

These appeals are from decrees, based upon undenied allegations, which granted preliminary orders restraining appellants from threatening or attempting to enforce the Compulsory Education Act adopted November 7, 1922, under the initiative provision of her Constitution by the voters of Oregon.

The challenged Act, effective September 1, 1926, requires every parent, guardian, or other person having control or charge or custody of a child between eight and sixteen years to send him "to a public school for the period of time a public school shall be held during the current year" in the district where the child resides; and failure so to do is declared a misdemeanor. There are exemptions—not specially important—for children who are not normal, or who have completed the eighth grade, or who reside at considerable distances from any public school, or whose parents or guardians hold special permits from the County Superintendent. The manifest purpose is to compel general attendance at public schools by normal children, between eight and sixteen, who have not completed the eighth grade. And without doubt enforcement of the statute would seriously impair, perhaps destroy, the profitable features of appellees' business and greatly diminish the value of their property.

Appellee, the Society of Sisters, is an Oregon corporation, organized in 1880, with power to care for orphans, educate and instruct the youth, establish and maintain academies or schools, and acquire necessary real and personal property.

Appellee, Hill Military Academy, is a private corporation organized in 1908 under the laws of Oregon, engaged in owning, operating and conducting for profit an elementary, college preparatory and military training school for boys between the ages of five and twenty-one years.

No question is raised concerning the power of the State reasonably to regulate all schools, to inspect, supervise and examine them, their teachers and pupils; to require that all children of proper age attend some school, that teachers shall be of good moral character and patriotic disposition, that certain studies plainly essential to good citizenship must be taught, and that nothing be taught which is manifestly inimical to the public welfare.

Under the doctrine of *Meyer v. Nebraska* 262 U.S. 390, we think it entirely plain that the Act of 1922 unreasonably interferes with the liberty of parents and guardians to direct the upbringing and education of children under their control. As often heretofore pointed out, rights guaranteed by the Constitution may not be abridged by legislation which has no reasonable relation to some purpose within the competency of the State. The fundamental theory of liberty upon which all governments in this Union repose excludes any general power of the State to standardize its children by forcing them to accept instruction from public teachers only. The child is not the mere creature of the State; those who nurture him and direct his destiny have the right, coupled with the high duty, to recognize and prepare him for additional obligations.

PRINCE v. MASSACHUSETTS

Supreme Court of the United States, 1944
321 US 158

RUTLEDGE, J.

[Sarah Prince was the guardian of Betty Simmons, her nine-year-old niece. Prince, a Jehovah's Witness, took Betty out one evening to sell the *Watchtower* on the streets of Brockton, Massachusetts. In doing so, she violated Massachusetts child labor laws.]

Previously in *Pierce v. Society of Sisters*, this Court ... sustained the parent's authority to provide religious with secular schooling, and the child's right to receive it, as against the state's requirement of attendance at public schools. And in *Meyer v. Nebraska*, children's rights to receive teaching in languages other than the nation's common tongue were guarded against the state's encroachment. It is cardinal with us that the custody, care and nurture of the child reside first in the parents, whose primary function and freedom include preparation for obligations the state can neither supply nor hinder. And it is in recognition of this that these decisions have respected the private realm of family life which the state cannot enter.

[T]he family itself is not beyond regulation in the public interest, as against a claim of religious liberty. *Reynolds v. United States,* 98 U.S. 145. And neither rights of religion nor rights of parenthood are beyond limitation. Acting to guard the general interest in youth's well being, the state as *parens patriae* may restrict the parent's control by requiring school attendance, regulating or prohibiting the child's labor and in many other ways. Its authority is not nullified merely because the parent grounds his claim to control the child's course of conduct on religion or conscience. Thus, he cannot claim freedom from compulsory vaccination for the child more than for himself on religious grounds. The right to practice religion freely does not include liberty to expose the community or the child to communicable disease or the latter to ill health or death. The catalogue need not be lengthened. It is sufficient to show what indeed appellant hardly disputes, that the state has a wide range of power for limiting parental freedom and authority in things affecting the child's welfare; and that this includes, to some extent, matters of conscience and religious conviction.

But it is said the state cannot do so here. This, first, because when state action impinges upon a claimed religious freedom, it must fall unless shown to be necessary for or conducive to the child's protection against some clear and present danger, and, it is added, there was no such showing here. The child's presence on the street, with her guardian, distributing or offering to distribute the magazines, it is urged, was in no way harmful to her, not in any event more so than the presence of many other children at the same time and place, engaged in shopping and other activities not prohibited. Accordingly, in view of the preferred position the freedoms of the First Article occupy, the statute in its present application must fall. It cannot be sustained by any presumption of validity. And, finally, it is said, the statute is, as to children, an absolute prohibition, not merely a reasonable regulation, of the denounced activity.

Concededly a statute or ordinance identical in terms with § 69, except that it is applicable to adults or all persons generally, would be invalid. But the mere fact a state could not wholly prohibit this form of adult activity, whether characterized locally as a "sale" or otherwise, does not mean it cannot do so for children. Such a conclusion granted would mean that a state could impose no greater limitation upon child labor than upon adult labor. Or, if an adult were free to enter dance halls, saloons, and disreputable places generally, in order to discharge his conceived religious duty to admonish or dissuade persons from frequenting such places, so would be a child with similar convictions and objectives, if not alone then in the parent's company, against the state's command.

The state's authority over children's activities is broader than over like actions of adults. This is peculiarly true of public activities and in matters of employment. A democratic society rests, for its continuance, upon the healthy, well-rounded growth of young people into full maturity as citizens, with all that implies. It may secure this against impeding restraints and dangers within a broad range of selection. Among evils most appropriate for such action are the crippling effects of child employment, more especially in public places, and the possible harms arising from other activities subject to all the diverse influences of the street. It is too late now to doubt that legislation appropriately designed to reach such evils is within the state's police power, whether against the parent's claim to control of the child or one that religious scruples dictate contrary action.

It is true children have rights, in common with older people, in the primary use of highways. But even in such use streets afford dangers for them not affecting adults. And in other uses, whether in work or in other things, this difference may be magnified. This is so not only when children are unaccompanied but certainly to some extent when they are with their parents. What may be wholly permissible for adults therefore may not be so for children, either with or without their parents' presence.

Street preaching, whether oral or by handing out literature, is not primary use of the highway, even for adults. While for them it cannot be wholly prohibited, it can be regulated within reasonable limits in accommodation to the primary and other incidental uses. But, for obvious reasons, notwithstanding appellant's contrary view, the validity of such a prohibition applied to children not accompanied by an older person hardly would seem open to question. The case reduces itself therefore to the question whether the presence of the child's guardian puts a limit to the state's power. That fact may lessen the likelihood that some evils the legislation seeks to avert will occur. But it cannot forestall all of them. The zealous though lawful exercise of the right to engage in propagandizing the community, whether in religious, political or other matters, may and at times does create situations difficult enough for adults to cope with and wholly inappropriate for children, especially of tender years, to face. Other harmful possibilities could be stated, of emotional excitement and psychological or physical injury. Parents may be free to become martyrs themselves. But it does not follow they are free, in identical circumstances, to make martyrs of their children before they have reached the age of full and legal discretion when they can make that choice for themselves. Massachusetts has determined that an absolute prohibition, though one limited to streets and public places and to the incidental uses proscribed, is necessary to accomplish its legitimate objectives. Its power to attain them is broad enough to reach these peripheral instances in which the parent's supervision may reduce but cannot eliminate entirely the ill effects of the prohibited conduct. We think that with reference to the public proclaiming of religion, upon the streets and in other similar public places, the power of the state to control the conduct of children reaches beyond the scope of its authority over adults, as is true in the case of other freedoms, and the rightful boundary of its power has not been crossed in this case.

Our ruling does not extend beyond the facts the case presents. We neither lay the foundation "for any [that is, every] state intervention in the indoctrination and participation of children in religion" which may be done "in the name of their health and welfare" nor give warrant for "every limitation on their religious training and activities." The religious training and indoctrination of children may be accomplished in many ways, some of which, as we have noted, have received constitutional protection through decisions of this Court. These and all others except the public proclaiming of religion on the streets, if this may be taken as either training or indoctrination of the proclaimer, remain unaffected by the decision.

MURPHY, J., dissenting:

The state, in my opinion, has completely failed to sustain its burden of proving the existence of any grave or immediate danger to any interest which it may lawfully protect. There is no proof that Betty Simmons' mode of worship constituted a serious menace to the public. It was carried on in an orderly, lawful manner at a public street corner.

It is claimed, however, that such activity was likely to affect adversely the health, morals and welfare of the child. Reference is made in the majority opinion to "the crippling effects of child employment, more especially in public places, and the possible harms arising from other activities subject to all the diverse influences of the street." To the extent that they flow from participation in ordinary commercial activities, these harms are irrelevant to this case. And the bare possibility that such harms might emanate from distribution of religious literature is not, standing alone, sufficient justification for restricting freedom of conscience and religion.

[Justice Jackson's concurring opinion is omitted.]

A fourth and final antecedent of the constitutional law of the family may be briefly summarized: An Oklahoma statute required the sterilization of habitual criminals, *i.e.*, those convicted of three felonies. In *Skinner v. Oklahoma,* 316 US 535 (1942), the Court held the statute violated the Equal Protection Clause, since the definition of felonies seemed to have little to do with inheritable traits or moral culpability. In a much quoted passage, the Court said, "We are dealing here with legislation which involves one of the basic civil rights of man. Marriage and procreation are fundamental to the very existence and survival of the race. Strict scrutiny of the classification which a State makes in a sterilization law is essential, lest unwittingly, or otherwise, invidious discriminations are made against groups or types of individuals in violation of the constitutional guaranty of just and equal laws."

Questions on the Early Constitutional Cases

You are now familiar with the foundations of the constitutional doctrine of privacy. Before you read the cases which created that doctrine, pause to think about what basis the constitutional text and the cases you have just read provide for the doctrine:

(1) On their own merits, are these cases rightly decided?

(a) Suppose, for example, that a state decided that its various efforts to reduce social inequality had failed and that a primary cause of social inequality was inequality of schooling. To eradicate some of the most severe differences in the quality of education that children receive, the state has made it illegal to send children to private schools. The legislature has concluded that those schools provide children of the wealthy not only economic, but also social advantages which unfairly benefit them vis-à-vis children of the rest of society. There is an exception for conscientious objection on religious grounds. This statute is part of a long-term project to reduce social and economic inequality. It has included, among many reforms, ending local funding of schools and instituting zoning reforms designed to reduce the social segregation of the wealthy. This statute presumably violates *Pierce*. Is *Pierce* rightly decided?

(b) On its own terms, what is the problem with the *Meyer* statute? Shouldn't Americans be able to speak English, and doesn't the statute serve that goal? Note that the *Meyer* statute applies only to schools (and not, for instance, to parents who wish to teach their children a foreign language) and that even schools may teach foreign languages after the eighth grade.

(2) Consider these cases as a group. What do they have in common?

(a) Do these cases do more than announce a principle of freedom of contract in which we no longer believe? The precedents cited are basically freedom of contract like *Lochner*, and each of them relies markedly on freedom-of-contract reasoning.

Meyer, for instance, discusses the state's interference with "the calling of modern language teachers" as well as "the power of parents to control the education of their own" and the "opportunities of pupils to acquire knowledge." The defendant in *Meyer* was a teacher, and it was his rights which were at issue. Indeed, Justice Holmes was able to characterize the case thus: "The only issue is whether the means adopted deprive teachers of the liberty secured to them by the Fourteenth Amendment." *Bartels v. Iowa,* 262 US 404, 412.

Similarly, in *Pierce* "[p]laintiffs asked protection against arbitrary, unreasonable and unlawful interference with their patrons and the consequent destruction of their business and property." The plaintiffs were a system of parochial schools and a military school.

(b) Isn't the strongest common element a First Amendment one? Each of the cases is about freedom to learn or to teach. There is even at least a hint of religious motivation in each case.

(c) Can these cases stand for some constitutional principle of parental freedom from government interference in the upbringing of children? In the only case where the parent was a litigant the parent lost (*Prince*). In the only opinion which expressly referred to "the private realm of family life which the state cannot enter" (*Prince*) the state won: "[T]he state has a wide range of power for limiting parental freedom and authority in things affecting the child's welfare; and that includes, to some extent, matters of conscience and religious conviction." In fact, it might once even have been supposed that *Prince* overruled *Meyer* and *Pierce*. For an argument that these cases reflect traditional notions of parental authority, see Barbara Bennett Woodhouse, *Who Owns the Child?*, 33 Wm & Mary L Rev 995 (1992).

SECTION 2. THE EMERGENCE OF CONSTITUTIONAL PRIVACY AND THE ISSUE OF CONTRACEPTION

To evade the bondage of system and habit, of family maxims, class opinions, and, in some degree, of national prejudices; to accept tradition only as a means of information, and existing facts only as a lesson to be used in doing otherwise and doing better; to seek the reason of things for oneself, and in oneself alone; to tend to results without being bound to means, and to strike through the form to the substance—such are the principal characteristics of what I shall call the philosophical method of the Americans.

Alexis de Tocqueville
Democracy in America

After *Prince*, the idea that the Constitution spoke to family law lay dormant for two decades. The idea was revived when the Court encountered in *Griswold v. Connecticut* a unique statute which prohibited the use of contraceptives (and not, as in other states with contraception statutes, only their distribution). When Justice Douglas sat down to write his opinion, he confronted several jurisprudential problems.

Justice Douglas had been appointed by President Roosevelt partly because Douglas shared FDR's outrage at the Supreme Court's savaging of the New Deal. The Court's weapons had been a narrow interpretation of the Commerce Clause and a broad interpretation of the Fourteenth Amendment. The latter interpretation recruited the doctrines of substantive due process and freedom to contract we described earlier and which has come to be symbolized by the decision in *Lochner*. New Dealers like Douglas assailed the Court's flouting of the basic precept of democracy—that the people rule. These critics argued that federal courts are non-majoritarian institutions—that is, that federal judges are appointed, not elected and that they may not be removed from office except for gross misconduct. Not only are courts non-majoritarian, the argument continued, but judges come from an elite stratum of society and represent their own class interests. The Court's preemption of legislative authority was thought possible because the vagueness of the Fourteenth Amendment left judges free to write law as they wished.

Griswold was crucial to the constitutionalization of family law. However, Justice Douglas's imaginative reasoning in it has not endured. We have therefore provided you with an opinion that better foretold the reasoning the Court has instead found persuasive. This is Justice Harlan's dissent in *Poe v. Ullman*, an earlier case which involved the same statute but which the Court had dealt with on justiciability grounds. That dissent better states Justice Harlan's views about substantive due process than his opinion in *Griswold*. As you read these opinions you should ask how each Justice responded to the considerations we outlined in the preceding paragraph.

GRISWOLD v. CONNECTICUT

Supreme Court of the United States, 1965
381 US 479

DOUGLAS, J.

Appellant Griswold is Executive Director of the Planned Parenthood League of Connecticut. Appellant Buxton is a licensed physician and a professor at the Yale Medical School who served as Medical Director for the League at its Center in New Haven—a center open and operating from November 1 to November 10, 1961, when appellants were arrested.

They gave information, instruction, and medical advice to *married persons* as to the means of preventing conception. They examined the wife and prescribed the best contraceptive device or material for her use. Fees were usually charged, although some couples were serviced free.

The statutes whose constitutionality is involved in this appeal are §§ 53–32 and 54–196 of the General Statutes of Connecticut (1958 rev.). The former provides:

> "Any person who uses any drug, medicinal article or instrument for the purpose of preventing conception shall be fined not less than fifty dollars or imprisoned not less than sixty days nor more than one year or be both fined and imprisoned."

Section 54–196 provides:

> "Any person who assists, abets, counsels, causes, hires or commands another to commit any offense may be prosecuted and punished as if he were the principal offender."

The appellants were found guilty as accessories and fined $100 each, against the claim that the accessory statute as so applied violated the Fourteenth Amendment. The Appellate Division of the Circuit Court affirmed. The Supreme Court of Errors affirmed that judgment. 151 Conn. 544, 200 A.2d 479. We noted probable jurisdiction. 379 U.S. 926.

We think that appellants have standing to raise the constitutional rights of the married people with whom they had a professional relationship. *Tileston v. Ullman*, 318 U.S. 44, is different, for there the plaintiff seeking to represent others asked for a declaratory judgment. In that situation we thought that the requirements of standing should be strict, lest the standards of "case or controversy" in Article III of the Constitution become blurred. Here those doubts are removed by reason of a criminal conviction for serving married couples in violation of an aiding-and-abetting statute. Certainly the accessory should have standing to assert that the offense which he is charged with assisting is not, or cannot constitutionally be, a crime.

This case is more akin to *Truax v. Raich*, 239 U.S. 33, where an employee was permitted to assert the rights of his employer; to *Pierce v. Society of Sisters,* 268 U.S. 510, where the owners of private schools were entitled to assert the rights of potential pupils and their parents; and to *Barrows v. Jackson*, 346 U.S. 249, where a white defendant, party to a racially restrictive covenant, who was being sued for damages by the covenantors because she had conveyed her property to Negroes, was allowed to raise the issue that enforcement of the covenant violated the rights of prospective Negro purchasers to equal protection, although no Negro was a party to the suit. And see *Meyer v. Nebraska*, 262 U.S. 390. The rights of husband and wife, pressed here, are likely to be diluted or adversely affected unless those rights are considered in a suit involving those who have this kind of confidential relation to them.

Coming to the merits, we are met with a wide range of questions that implicate the Due Process Clause of the Fourteenth Amendment. Overtones of some arguments suggest that *Lochner v. New York*, 198 U.S. 45, should be our guide. But we decline that invitation as we did in *West Coast Hotel Co. v. Parrish*, 300 U.S. 379. We do not sit as a super-legislature to determine the wisdom, need, and propriety of laws that touch economic problems, business affairs, or social conditions. This law, however, operates directly on an intimate relation of husband and wife and their physician's role in one aspect of that relation.

The association of people is not mentioned in the Constitution nor in the Bill of Rights. The right to educate a child in a school of the parents' choice—whether public or private or parochial—is also not mentioned. Nor is the right to study any particular subject or any foreign language. Yet the First Amendment has been construed to include certain of those rights.

By *Pierce v. Society of Sisters, supra*, the right to educate one's children as one chooses is made applicable to the States by the force of the First and Fourteenth Amendments. By *Meyer v. Nebraska, supra*, the same dignity is given the right to study the German language in a private school. In other words, the State may not, consistently with the spirit of the First Amendment, contract the spectrum of available knowledge. The right of freedom of speech and press includes not only the right to utter or to print, but the right to distribute, the right to receive, the right to read, and freedom of inquiry, freedom of thought, and freedom to teach, the freedom of the entire university community. Without those peripheral rights the specific rights would be less secure. And so we reaffirm the principle of the *Pierce* and the *Meyer* cases.

In *NAACP v. Alabama*, 357 U.S. 449, 462, we protected the "freedom to associate and privacy in one's associations," noting that freedom of association was a peripheral First Amendment right. Disclosure of membership lists of a constitutionally valid association, we held, was invalid "as entailing the likelihood of a substantial restraint upon the exercise by petitioner's members of their right to freedom of association." *Ibid.* In other words, the First Amendment has a penumbra where privacy is protected from governmental intrusion. In like context, we have protected forms of "association" that are not political in the customary sense but pertain to the social, legal, and economic benefit of the members. In *Schware v. Board of Bar Examiners*, 353 U.S. 232, we held it not permissible to bar a lawyer from practice, because he had once been a member of the Communist Party. The man's "association with that Party" was not shown to be "anything more than a political faith in a political party" and was not action of a kind proving bad moral character.

Those cases involved more than the "right of assembly"—a right that extends to all irrespective of their race or ideology. *DeJonge v. Oregon*, 299 U.S. 353. The right of "association," like the right of belief (*West Virginia State Board of Education v. Barnette*, 319 U.S. 624), is more than the right to attend a meeting; it includes the right to express one's attitudes or philosophies by membership in a group or by affiliation with it or by other lawful means. Association in that context is a form of expression of opinion; and while it is not expressly included in the First Amendment its existence is necessary in making the express guarantees fully meaningful.

The foregoing cases suggest that specific guarantees in the Bill of Rights have penumbras, formed by emanations from those guarantees that help give them life and substance. See *Poe v. Ullman*, 367 U.S. 497, 516–522 (dissenting opinion). Various guarantees create zones of privacy. The right of association contained in the penumbra of the First Amendment is one, as we have seen. The Third Amendment in its prohibition against the quartering of soldiers "in any house" in time of peace without the consent of the owner is another facet of that privacy. The Fourth Amendment explicitly affirms the "right of the people to be secure in their persons, houses, papers, and effects, against unreasonable searches and seizures." The Fifth Amendment in its Self–Incrimination Clause enables the citizen to create a zone of privacy which government may not force him to surrender to his detriment. The Ninth Amendment provides: "The enumeration in the Constitution, of certain rights, shall not be construed to deny or disparage others retained by the people."

The Fourth and Fifth Amendments were described in *Boyd v. United States*, 116 U.S. 616, 630, as protection against all governmental invasions "of the sanctity of a man's home and the privacies of life." We recently referred in *Mapp v. Ohio*, 367 U.S. 643, 656, to the Fourth Amendment as creating a "right to privacy, no less important than any other right carefully and particularly reserved to the people." See Beaney, The Constitutional Right to Privacy, 1962 Sup.Ct.Rev. 212; Griswold, The Right to be Let Alone, 55 Nw.U.L.Rev. 216 (1960).

We have had many controversies over these penumbral rights of "privacy and repose." See, *e.g., Breard v. City of Alexandria*, 341 U.S. 622, 626, 644; *Public Utilities Comm. v. Pollak*, 343 U.S. 451; *Monroe v. Pape*, 365 U.S. 167; *Lanza v. State of New York*, 370 U.S. 139; *Frank v. State of Maryland*, 359 U.S. 360; *Skinner v. State of Oklahoma*, 316 U.S. 535, 541. These cases bear witness that the right of privacy which presses for recognition here is a legitimate one.

The present case, then, concerns a relationship lying within the zone of privacy created by several fundamental constitutional guarantees. And it concerns a law which, in forbidding the *use* of contraceptives rather than regulating their manufacture or sale, seeks to achieve its goals by means having a maximum destructive impact upon that relationship. Such a law cannot stand in light of the familiar principle, so often applied by this Court, that a "governmental purpose to control or prevent activities constitutionally subject to state regulation may not be achieved by means which sweep unnecessarily broadly and thereby invade the area of protected freedoms." *NAACP v. Alabama*, 377 U.S. 288, 307. Would we allow the police to search the sacred precincts of marital bedrooms for telltale signs of the use of contraceptives? The very idea is repulsive to the notions of privacy surrounding the marriage relationship.

We deal with a right of privacy older than the Bill of Rights—older than our political parties, older than our school system. Marriage is a coming together for better or for worse, hopefully enduring, and intimate to the degree of being sacred. It is an association that promotes a way of life, not causes; a harmony in living, not political faiths; a bilateral loyalty, not commercial or social projects. Yet it is an association for as noble a purpose as any involved in our prior decisions.

[The concurring opinions of Justice Goldberg, Justice White, and Justice Harlan are omitted, as is Justice Black's dissent.]

MR. JUSTICE STEWART, whom MR. JUSTICE BLACK joins, dissenting.

Since 1879 Connecticut has had on its books a law which forbids the use of contraceptives by anyone. I think this is an uncommonly silly law. As a practical matter, the law is obviously unenforceable, except in the oblique context of the present case. As a philosophical matter, I believe the use of contraceptives in the relationship of marriage should be left to personal and private choice, based upon each individual's moral, ethical, and religious beliefs. As a matter of social policy, I think professional counsel about methods of birth control should be available to all, so that each individual's choice can be meaningfully made. But we are not asked in this case to say whether we think this law is unwise, or even asinine. We are asked to hold that it violates the United States Constitution. And that I cannot do.

In the course of its opinion the Court refers to no less than six Amendments to the Constitution: the First, the Third, the Fourth, the Fifth, the Ninth, and the Fourteenth. But the Court does not say which of these Amendments, if any, it thinks is infringed by this Connecticut law.

We *are* told that the Due Process Clause of the Fourteenth Amendment is not, as such, the "guide" in this case. With that much I agree. There is no claim that this law, duly enacted by the Connecticut Legislature, is unconstitutionally vague. There is no claim that the appellants were denied any of the elements of procedural due process at their trial, so as to make their convictions constitutionally invalid. And, as the Court says, the day has long passed since the Due Process Clause was regarded as a proper instrument for determining "the wisdom, need, and propriety" of state laws. Compare *Lochner v. New York*, 198 U.S. 45, with *Ferguson v. Skrupa*, 372 U.S. 726. My Brothers Harlan and White to the contrary, "(w)e have returned to the original constitutional proposition that courts do not substitute their social and economic beliefs for the judgment of legislative bodies, who are elected to pass laws." *Ferguson v. Skrupa, supra*, at 730.

As to the First, Third, Fourth, and Fifth Amendments, I can find nothing in any of them to invalidate this Connecticut law, even assuming that all those Amendments are fully applicable against the States. It has not even been argued that this is a law "respecting an establishment of religion, or prohibiting the free exercise thereof." And surely, unless the solemn process of constitutional adjudication is to descend to the level of a play on words, there is not involved here any abridgment of "the freedom of speech, or of the press; or the right of the people peaceably to assemble, and to petition the Government for a redress of grievances." No soldier has been quartered in any house. There has been no search, and no seizure. Nobody has been compelled to be a witness against himself.

The Court also quotes the Ninth Amendment, and my Brother Goldberg's concurring opinion relies heavily upon it. But to say that the Ninth Amendment has anything to do with this case is to turn somersaults with history. The Ninth Amendment, like its companion the Tenth, which this Court held "states but a truism that all is retained which has not been surrendered," *United States v. Darby*, 312 U.S. 100, 124, was framed by James Madison and adopted by the States simply to make clear that the adoption of the Bill of Rights did not alter the plan that the *Federal* Government was to be a government of express and limited powers, and that all rights and powers not delegated to it were retained by the people and the individual States. Until today no member of this Court has ever suggested that the Ninth Amendment meant anything else, and the idea that a federal court could ever use the Ninth Amendment to annul a law passed by the elected representatives of the people of the State of Connecticut would have caused James Madison no little wonder.

What provision of the Constitution, then, does make this state law invalid? The Court says it is the right of privacy "created by several fundamental constitutional guarantees." With all deference, I can find no such general right of privacy in the Bill of Rights, in any other part of the Constitution, or in any case ever before decided by this Court.

At the oral argument in this case we were told that the Connecticut law does not "conform to current community standards." But it is not the function of this Court to decide cases on the basis of community standards. We are here to decide cases "agreeably to the Constitution and laws of the United States." It is the essence of judicial duty to subordinate our own personal views, our own ideas of what legislation is wise and what is not. If, as I should surely hope, the law before us does not reflect the standards of the people of Connecticut, the people of Connecticut can freely exercise their true Ninth and Tenth Amendment rights to persuade their elected representatives to repeal it. That is the constitutional way to take this law off the books.

POE v. ULLMAN

Supreme Court of the United States, 1961
367 US 497

HARLAN, J., dissenting....

I consider that this Connecticut legislation, as construed to apply to these appellants, violates the Fourteenth Amendment. I believe that a statute making it a criminal offense for *married couples* to use contraceptives is an intolerable and unjustifiable invasion of privacy in the conduct of the most intimate concerns of an individual's personal life....

I. ...

Were due process merely a procedural safeguard it would fail to reach those situations where the deprivation of life, liberty or property was accomplished by legislation which by operating in the future could, given even the fairest possible procedure in application to individuals, nevertheless destroy the enjoyment of all three. Compare, *e.g., Korematsu v. United States*, 323 U.S. 214. Thus the guaranties of due process, though having their roots in Magna Carta's *"per legem terrae"* and considered as procedural safeguards "against executive usurpation and tyranny," have in this country "become bulwarks also against arbitrary legislation."

[I]t is not the particular enumeration of rights in the first eight Amendments which spells out the reach of Fourteenth Amendment due process, but rather, as was suggested in another context long before the adoption of that Amendment, those concepts which are considered to embrace those rights "which are ... *fundamental*; which belong ... to the citizens of all free governments," for "the purposes [of securing] which men enter into society," *Calder v. Bull*, 3 Dall. 386, 388. Again and again this Court has resisted the notion that the Fourteenth Amendment is no more than a shorthand reference to what is explicitly set out elsewhere in the Bill of Rights....

Due process has not been reduced to any formula; its content cannot be determined by reference to any code. The best that can be said is that through the course of this Court's decisions it has represented the balance which our Nation, built upon postulates of respect for the liberty of the individual, has struck between that liberty and the demands of organized society. If the supplying of content to this Constitutional concept has of necessity been a rational process, it certainly has not been one where judges have felt free to roam where unguided speculation might take them. The balance of which I speak is the balance struck by this country, having regard to what history teaches are the traditions from which it developed as well as the traditions from which it broke. That tradition is a living thing. A decision of this Court which radically departs from it could not long survive, while a decision which builds on what has survived is likely to be sound. No formula could serve as a substitute, in this area, for judgment and restraint....

[T]he full scope of the liberty guaranteed by the Due Process Clause cannot be found in or limited by the precise terms of the specific guarantees elsewhere provided in the Constitution. This "liberty" is not a series of isolated points pricked out in terms of the taking of property; the freedom of speech, press, and religion; the right to keep and bear arms; the freedom from unreasonable searches and seizures; and so on. It is a rational continuum which, broadly speaking, includes a freedom from all substantial arbitrary impositions and purposeless restraints, and which also recognizes, what a reasonable and sensitive judgment must, that certain interests require particularly careful scrutiny of the state needs asserted to justify their abridgment. Cf. *Skinner v. Oklahoma*.

As was said in *Meyer v. Nebraska*, "this court has not attempted to define with exactness the liberty thus guaranteed.... Without doubt, it denotes, not merely freedom from bodily restraint...." Thus, for instance, when in that case and in *Pierce v. Society of Sisters*, the Court struck down laws which sought not to require what children must learn in schools, but to prescribe, in the first case, what they must not learn, and in the second, where they must acquire their learning, I do not think it was wrong to put those decisions on "the right of the individual to ... establish a home and bring up children" or on the basis that "The fundamental theory of liberty upon which all governments in this Union repose excludes any general power of the State to standardize its children by forcing them to accept instruction from public teachers only." I consider this so, even though today those decisions would probably have gone by reference to the concepts of freedom of expression and conscience assured against state action by the Fourteenth Amendment, concepts that are derived from the explicit guarantees of the First Amendment against federal encroachment upon freedom of speech and belief. See *West Virginia State Board of Education v. Barnette*, 319 U.S. 624, and 656 (dissenting opinion); *Prince v. Massachusetts*. For it is the purposes of those guarantees and not their text, the reasons for their statement by the Framers and not the statement itself which have led to their present status in the compendious notion of "liberty" embraced in the Fourteenth Amendment.

Each new claim to Constitutional protection must be considered against a background of Constitutional purposes, as they have been rationally perceived and historically developed. Though we exercise limited and sharply restrained judgment, yet there is no "mechanical yardstick," no "mechanical answer." The decision of an apparently novel claim must depend on grounds which follow closely on well-accepted principles and criteria. The new decision must take "its place in relation to what went before and further [cut] a channel for what is to come." The matter was well put in *Rochin v. California*, 342 U.S. 165, 170–171:

> "The vague contours of the Due Process Clause do not leave judges at large. We may not draw on our merely personal and private notions and disregard the limits that bind judges in their judicial function. Even though the concept of due process of law is not final and fixed, these limits are derived from considerations that are fused in the whole nature of our judicial process.... These are considerations deeply rooted in reason and in the compelling traditions of the legal profession." ...

II.

Appellants contend that the Connecticut statute deprives them, as it unquestionably does, of a substantial measure of liberty in carrying on the most intimate of all personal relationships, and that it does so arbitrarily and without any rational, justifying purpose. The State, on the other hand, asserts that it is acting to protect the moral welfare of its citizenry, both directly, in that it considers the practice of contraception immoral in itself, and instrumentally, in that the availability of contraceptive materials tends to minimize "the disastrous consequence of dissolute action," that is fornication and adultery....

[T]he very inclusion of the category of morality among state concerns indicates that society is not limited in its objects only to the physical well-being of the community, but has traditionally concerned itself with the moral soundness of its people as well. Indeed to attempt a line between public behavior and that which is purely consensual or solitary would be to withdraw from community concern a range of subjects with which every society in civilized times has found it necessary to deal. The laws regarding marriage which provide both when the sexual powers may be used and the legal and societal context in which children are born and brought up, as well as laws forbidding adultery, fornication and homosexual practices which express the negative of the proposition, confining sexuality to lawful marriage, form a pattern so deeply pressed into the substance of our social life that any Constitutional doctrine in this area must build upon that basis.

It is in this area of sexual morality, which contains many proscriptions of consensual behavior having little or no direct impact on others, that the State of Connecticut has expressed its moral judgment that all use of contraceptives is improper. Appellants cite an impressive list of authorities who, from a great variety of points of view, commend the considered use of contraceptives by married couples. What they do not emphasize is that not too long ago the current of opinion was very probably quite the opposite, and that even today the issue is not free of controversy. Certainly, Connecticut's judgment is no more demonstrably correct or incorrect than are the varieties of judgment, expressed in law, on marriage and divorce, on adult consensual homosexuality, abortion, and sterilization, or euthanasia and suicide. If we had a case before us which required us to decide simply, and in abstraction, whether the moral judgment implicit in the application of the present statute to married couples was a sound one, the very controversial nature of these questions would, I think, require us to hesitate long before concluding that the Constitution precluded Connecticut from choosing as it has among these various views.

But, as might be expected, we are not presented simply with this moral judgment to be passed on as an abstract proposition. The secular state is not an examiner of consciences: it must operate in the realm of behavior, of overt actions, and where it does so operate, not only the underlying, moral purpose of its operations, but also the choice of means becomes relevant to any Constitutional judgment on what is done....

III.

Precisely what is involved here is this: the State is asserting the right to enforce its moral judgment by intruding upon the most intimate details of the marital relation with the full power of the criminal law. Potentially, this could allow the deployment of all the incidental machinery of the criminal law, arrests, searches and seizures; inevitably, it must mean at the very least the lodging of criminal charges, a public trial, and testimony as to the *corpus delicti*. Nor could any imaginable elaboration of presumptions, testimonial privileges, or other safeguards, alleviate the necessity for testimony as to the mode and manner of the married couples' sexual relations, or at least the opportunity for the accused to make denial of the charges. In sum, the statute allows the State to enquire into, prove and punish married people for the private use of their marital intimacy.

This, then, is the precise character of the enactment whose Constitutional measure we must take. The statute must pass a more rigorous Constitutional test than that going merely to the plausibility of its underlying rationale. This enactment involves what, by common understanding throughout the English-speaking world, must be granted to be a most fundamental aspect of "liberty," the privacy of the home in its most basic sense, and it is this which requires that the statute be subjected to "strict scrutiny."

That aspect of liberty which embraces the concept of the privacy of the home receives explicit Constitutional protection at two places only. These are the Third Amendment, relating to the quartering of soldiers, and the Fourth Amendment, prohibiting unreasonable searches and seizures....

Perhaps the most comprehensive statement of the principle of liberty underlying these aspects of the Constitution was given by Mr. Justice Brandeis, dissenting in *Olmstead v. United States*, 277 U.S. 438, at 478:

> "The protection guaranteed by the [Fourth and Fifth] Amendments is much broader in scope. The makers of our Constitution undertook to secure conditions favorable to the pursuit of happiness. They recognized the significance of man's spiritual nature, of his feelings and of his intellect. They knew that only a part of the pain, pleasure and satisfactions of life are to be found in material things. They sought to protect Americans in their beliefs, their thoughts, their emotions and their sensations. They conferred, as against the government, the right to be let alone—the most comprehensive of rights and the right most valued by civilized men. To protect that right, every unjustifiable intrusion by the government upon the privacy of the individual whatever the means employed, must be deemed a violation of the Fourth Amendment...."

I think the sweep of the Court's decisions, under both the Fourth and Fourteenth Amendments, amply shows that the Constitution protects the privacy of the home against all unreasonable intrusion of whatever character....

[Here we have not an intrusion into the home so much as on the life which characteristically has its place in the home. But to my mind such a distinction is so insubstantial as to be captious: if the physical curtilage of the home is protected, it is surely as a result of solicitude to protect the privacies of the life within.... The home derives its pre-eminence as the seat of family life. And the integrity of that life is something so fundamental that it has been found to draw to its protection the principles of more than one explicitly granted Constitutional right....

Of this whole "private realm of family life" it is difficult to imagine what is more private or more intimate than a husband and wife's marital relations....

The right of privacy most manifestly is not an absolute. Thus, I would not suggest that adultery, homosexuality, fornication and incest are immune from criminal enquiry, however privately practiced. So much has been explicitly recognized in acknowledging the State's rightful concern for its people's moral welfare. But not to discriminate between what is involved in this case and either the traditional offenses against good morals or crimes which, though they may be committed anywhere, happen to have been committed or concealed in the home, would entirely misconceive the argument that is being made.

Adultery, homosexuality and the like are sexual intimacies which the State forbids altogether, but the intimacy of husband and wife is necessarily an essential and accepted feature of the institution of marriage, an institution which the State not only must allow, but which always and in every age it has fostered and protected. It is one thing when the State exerts its power either to forbid extra-marital sexuality altogether, or to say who may marry, but it is quite another when, having acknowledged a marriage and the intimacies inherent in it, it undertakes to regulate by means of the criminal law the details of that intimacy....

Since, as it appears to me, the statute marks an abridgment of important fundamental liberties protected by the Fourteenth Amendment, it will not do to urge in justification of that abridgment simply that the statute is rationally related to the effectuation of a proper state purpose. A closer scrutiny and stronger justification than that are required.

Though the State has argued the Constitutional permissibility of the moral judgment underlying this statute, neither its brief, nor its argument, nor anything in any of the opinions of its highest court in these or other cases even remotely suggests a justification for the obnoxiously intrusive means it has chosen to effectuate that policy. To me the very circumstance that Connecticut has not chosen to press the enforcement of this statute against individual users, while it nevertheless persists in asserting its right to do so at any time—in effect a right to hold this statute as an imminent threat to the privacy of the households of the State—conduces to the inference either that it does not consider the policy of the statute a very important one, or that it does not regard the means it has chosen for its effectuation as appropriate or necessary.

But conclusive, in my view, is the utter novelty of this enactment. Although the Federal Government and many States have at one time or other had on their books statutes forbidding or regulating the distribution of contraceptives, none, so far as I can find, has made the use of contraceptives a crime....

Notes on Griswold

Dr. Charles Lee Buxton was the chairman of the Yale Medical School's department of obstetrics and gynecology and an infertility specialist. He was also a member of the Connecticut Planned Parenthood League. His experience in Connecticut led him to believe that "the problem is that women who have private doctors can get all the information they want and get prescriptions [for birth control].... The real problem in Connecticut is that poor women who do not have private doctors cannot get that kind of care." Quoted in Fred W. Friendly and

Martha J.H. Elliott, *The Constitution: That Delicate Balance* 190 (Random House, 1984), from which much of this account is drawn. In the late 1950s, Dr. Buxton encountered two women. One was likely to encounter serious and the other mortal medical problems if she became pregnant. Hoping that litigation might secure an exception to the Connecticut law which would allow doctors to prescribe contraceptives in this situation, Dr. Buxton joined the two women in a constitutional challenge to that law. In *Poe v. Ullman*, 367 US 497 (1961), the Court held the case nonjusticiable because the law had been so long unenforced.

Mrs. Estelle T. Griswold was the executive director of the Connecticut Planned Parenthood League. While *Poe* was being litigated, the League decided to open a clinic in New Haven, in part to present a justiciable issue to the courts. On November 1, 1961, a clinic of which Dr. Buxton was medical director opened. To the relief of League officials, a man who worked near the clinic complained to the county prosecutor, the state police, and the mayor of New Haven about it. On November 4, two detectives knocked on the clinic door.

> "[I]t was one of the easiest types of investigations you could get involved in," Detective Berg remembers. Mrs. Griswold and Dr. Buxton gave the detectives a guided tour of the clinic, pointing out the condoms and vaginal foam they were dispensing. "It wasn't one of those investigations where you had to dig out the information.... It was sort of 'Here it is; Here we are; Take us in; We want to test this.' "

Eventually, Mrs. Griswold and Dr. Buxton were arrested, charged, and released on $100 bail. In exchange for a promise of the records of a few consenting patients, the prosecutor agreed not to seize the clinic's records. One of the consenting patients was Joan B. Forsberg, then the wife of a minister, later the Associate Dean of the Yale Divinity School. Another was Rosemary Ann Stevens, then a graduate at the Yale School of Public Health, later a department chair at the University of Pennsylvania. These two and a third consenting patient testified against Mrs. Griswold and Dr. Buxton, both of whom were convicted and fined $100.

At the Justices' conference after the case had been argued in the Supreme Court, the vote was seven to two against the statute, but there was less clarity what the rationale. What followed was a draft Justice Douglas sent to Justice Brennan. According to Bernard Schwartz, "Justice Brennan wrote [back] that the 'association' of married couples had little to do with the advocacy protected by the First Amendment freedom of association." *The Unpublished Opinions of the Warren Court* 237 (Oxford U Press 1985). Instead, "Justice Brennan suggested that the expansion of the First Amendment to include freedom of association ... be used as an analogy to justify a similar approach in the area of privacy."

Questions on Griswold

(1) In *Griswold*, the Court begins to discover a constitutional right of privacy which limits the state's authority to regulate "family" behav-

ior. Where does the Court find the right comes from? The Court refers to "penumbras," but what exactly is the nature of those penumbras? What is the structure of Justice Douglas' argument?

(2) The Court is anxious to avoid the charge that it is inventing law, to show that its result is commanded by a reasonable interpretation of the Constitution. But isn't the Court's technique extraordinarily flexible? For example, wouldn't that technique lead even more persuasively to a constitutional freedom of contract than to a right of privacy? One would begin with the fact that, in contrast to its silence about privacy, the Constitution speaks directly and expressly to the special status of contracts: "No State shall ... pass any ... Law impairing the Obligation of Contracts...." Article I, Section 10. One would then recruit the penumbral technique: The First Amendment protects the ability to think and speak for oneself; a broader protection of personal autonomy is both a reason for that amendment and necessary to fully effectuate its guarantees. Personal autonomy is, as we said in discussing marital contracts, importantly secured through contract. And as Justice Douglas argues, the amendment likewise protects the freedom of association, a classic element of the freedom of contract. The Fourteenth Amendment assures the protection of the laws, presumably including laws surrounding freedom to make contracts, a common-law right of long standing. Finally, centuries of laissez-faire history confirm that freedom of contract is a right "older than the Bill of Rights." So doesn't Justice Douglas' technique prove too much?

(3) Justice Douglas's "penumbra" technique is not the only technique that might be employed to discover a constitutional right, as Justice Harlan's opinion makes clear. Which of the following techniques are legitimate means of constitutional interpretation? Can a right to privacy be justified under any of them? Under some combination?

(a) Consulting the express language of the text itself? Is there any such language to consult?

(b) Consulting the structure of the Constitution? Is any relevant structural inference possible?

(c) Consulting the Framers' intent? Which Framers? How do you find out what their intent was?

(d) Consulting the "values" implicit in the Constitution? How do you find out what they are? How do you keep the inquiry from concluding that the Constitution protects all things that are good, true, and beautiful? Or does it?

(e) Consulting the values implicit in the concept of ordered liberty? What does that phrase mean?

(f) Consulting judicial precedent? Are there elements of commonality in *Meyer, Pierce* and *Prince* that would create a constitutional right of privacy? Would those elements of commonality justify extending that right to the marital situation in *Griswold*?

(g) Consulting the values to be discovered in the history of our country? Does the fact that laws regulating contraception, abortion, fornication, and so forth used to be pervasive suggest that those values do not require that a right of privacy be found in the Constitution?

(h) Consulting current social norms? How do you determine what they are? Why ought current social norms have constitutional status?

(4) We have been asking whether a right of privacy can be inferred from the Constitution, and if so, how. One test of any inferred right is (a) whether it states a principle powerful enough to rank as a fundamental right, (b) whether the right can be defined, and (c) whether the right has reasonable limits. Consider again whatever rights of privacy you developed in answering Question (3). Do they meet this test?

(5) The constitutional right that originates in *Griswold* is called a right of privacy. We have spent some time thinking about what privacy is in a social sense and its place as a legal concept. In what sense is privacy an apt term for the right? Even if it is apt applied to *Griswold*, is it apt applied to *Meyer* and *Pierce*?

(6) It is a standard rule that courts should avoid reaching a constitutional question if a case can be resolved on some non-constitutional basis. Could the Court in *Griswold* have overturned the statute without devising a new constitutional right?

(7) Imagine you are a lawyer reading *Griswold* directly after the case was decided. You will want to ask yourself what the case means. What is the broadest reading it could fairly have been given at the time? The narrowest? Suppose you have a teenage client who lives in a state where (a) contraceptives may not be distributed to minors except by prescription, (b) abortions are prohibited by the criminal law, and (c) no medical procedures may be provided to minors without the consent of their parents. Your client wants to know whether she can constitutionally be prohibited from obtaining contraceptives, from obtaining an abortion, and from obtaining an abortion without her parents' consent. What do you tell her?

It was not immediately clear that *Griswold* was a significant case, although commentators had hopes for it. The Connecticut statute was the only one of its kind in the country, it was unenforceable and had been unenforced, it was an "uncommonly silly law." The opinion relied on a novel technique of constitutional interpretation and emphasized the intrusion on the most intimate part of a special legal and personal relationship: marriage. *Griswold* could, in short, have fallen into that limbo of cases that seem to announce a significant constitutional departure but which are subsequently ignored or narrowly construed. *Shelley v. Kraemer*, 334 US 1 (1948), and *Stanley v. Georgia*, 394 US 557 (1969), exemplify such cases. The ease of reading *Griswold* narrowly made our next case crucial.

EISENSTADT v. BAIRD

Supreme Court of the United States, 1972
405 US 438

BRENNAN, J.

Appellee William Baird was convicted at a bench trial in the Massachusetts Superior Court under Massachusetts General Laws Ann., c. 272, § 21, first, for exhibiting contraceptive articles in the course of delivering a lecture on contraception to a group of students at Boston University and, second, for giving a young woman a package of Emko vaginal foam at the close of his address....

Massachusetts General Laws Ann., c. 272, § 21, under which Baird was convicted, provides a maximum five-year term of imprisonment for "whoever ... gives away ... any drug, medicine, instrument or article whatever for the prevention of conception," except as authorized in § 21A. Under § 21A, "[a] registered physician may administer to or prescribe for any married person drugs or articles intended for the prevention of pregnancy or conception. [And a] registered pharmacist actually engaged in the business of pharmacy may furnish such drugs or articles to any married person presenting a prescription from a registered physician." ...

The legislative purposes that the statute is meant to serve are not altogether clear. In *Commonwealth v. Baird, supra*, the Supreme Judicial Court noted only the State's interest in protecting the health of its citizens: "[T]he prohibition in § 21," the court declared, "is directly related to" the State's goal of "preventing the distribution of articles designed to prevent conception which may have undesirable, if not dangerous, physical consequences," 355 Mass., at 753, 247 N.E.2d, at 578. In a subsequent decision, *Sturgis v. Attorney General*, 358 Mass. 37, 260 N.E.2d 687, 690 (1970), the court, however, found "a second and more compelling ground for upholding the statute"—namely, to protect morals through "regulating the private sexual lives of single persons." The Court of Appeals ... did not consider the promotion of health or the protection of morals through the deterrence of fornication to be the legislative aim. Instead, the court concluded that the statutory goal was to limit contraception in and of itself—a purpose that the court held conflicted "with fundamental human rights" under *Griswold v. Connecticut*, 381 U.S. 479 (1965), where this Court struck down Connecticut's prohibition against the use of contraceptives as an unconstitutional infringement of the right of marital privacy.

We agree that the goals of deterring premarital sex and regulating the distribution of potentially harmful articles cannot reasonably be regarded as legislative aims of §§ 21 and 21A. And we hold that the statute, viewed as a prohibition on contraception per se, violates the rights of single persons under the Equal Protection Clause of the Fourteenth Amendment....

If under *Griswold* the distribution of contraceptives to married persons cannot be prohibited, a ban on distribution to unmarried persons would be equally impermissible. It is true that in *Griswold* the right of privacy in question inhered in the marital relationship. Yet the marital couple is not an independent entity with a mind and heart of its own, but an association of two individuals each with a separate intellectual and emotional makeup. If the right of privacy means anything, it is the right of the *individual*, married or single, to be free from unwarranted governmental intrusion into matters so fundamentally affecting a person as the decision whether to bear or beget a child. See *Stanley v. Georgia*, 394 U.S. 557 (1969). See also *Skinner v. Oklahoma*, 316 U.S. 535 (1942); *Jacobson v. Massachusetts*, 197 U.S. 11, 29 (1905).

Questions on Eisenstadt

(1) Does *Eisenstadt* follow from *Griswold*?

(a) What happened to the "penumbra" technique?

(b) In what relevant ways are the facts of the two cases distinguishable? What analytic consequences ought those differences have?

(c) *Eisenstadt* is an equal-protection case. Equal-protection cases ask whether similarly situated classes are treated differently. What are the classes in *Eisenstadt*? Are they similarly situated?

(2) Part of the Court's technique in *Eisenstadt* is to show not that regulating contraception is outside the state's authority, but rather that Massachusetts' particular statute did not serve the purposes attributed to it. We had to edit that portion of the opinion out. But could such a demonstration be made? Consider the following summary of a criticism of the case made by Professor Robert Nagel in his student note, *Legislative Purpose, Rationality, and Equal Protection* 82 Yale L J 123 (1972): The Court in *Eisenstadt*, Professor Nagel noted, spoke primarily in terms of the "fit" of the statute with each of its purposes. The Court analyzed the law purpose by purpose and concluded that the fit as to each purpose was unsatisfactory. But this technique failed to account for the fact that each purpose was necessarily served only to the extent that the other purposes were not impaired. For example, the Court found the statute discriminatory and overbroad because, "[i]f there is a need to have a physician prescribe contraceptives, the need is as great for unmarried persons as for married persons." But another purpose of the statute was preventing premarital sexual relations, and that purpose and the special social and constitutional status of married couples explained the different treatment of the two groups. Similarly, the Court said that some contraceptives were widely available if used to prevent disease and that this availability belied the statute's restrictive purposes. But the statute sought to serve those restrictive purposes only so far as they were not inconsistent with another statutory purpose, public health. Professor Nagel suggested:

The legislature's overall purpose might have been defined as follows: to discourage premarital sex by making contraceptives harder to obtain to the extent that this would not increase the risks of venereal disease; to provide for the medical supervision of the distribution of contraceptives to the extent that this would not increase the availability of contraceptives to the unmarried; and to discourage the use of contraceptives to the extent that this would not interfere with the private behavior of married persons.

(3) Recall whatever constitutional right of privacy you developed in answering Question 3 of the *Griswold* questions, or, if you believed it impossible to develop such a right, the nearest possibility. How would you modify it, if at all, in light of *Eisenstadt*?

SECTION 3. THE ESTABLISHMENT OF CONSTITUTIONAL PRIVACY AND THE ISSUE OF ABORTION

At the end of three weeks, as I was preparing to leave the fragile patient to take up her difficult life once more, she finally voiced her fears, "Another baby will finish me, I suppose?"

"It's too early to talk about that," I temporized.

But when the doctor came to make his last call, I drew him aside. "Mrs. Sachs is terribly worried about having another baby."

"She well may be," replied the doctor, and then he stood before her and said, "Any more such capers, young woman, and there'll be no need to send for me."

"I know, doctor," she replied timidly, "but," and she hesitated as though it took all her courage to say it, "what can I do to prevent it?"

The doctor was a kindly man, and he had worked hard to save her, but such incidents had become so familiar to him that he had long since lost whatever delicacy he might once have had. He laughed good-naturedly. "You want to have your cake and eat it too, do you? Well, it can't be done."

Then picking up his hat and bag to depart he said, "Tell Jake to sleep on the roof."

Margaret Sanger
Margaret Sanger: An Autobiography

A. CONSTRUCTING THE PRIVACY DOCTRINE: THE FINAL STEP

Scarcely any political question arises in the United States that is not resolved, sooner or later, into a judicial question. Hence all parties are obliged to borrow in their daily controversies, the ideas, and even the language, peculiar to judicial proceedings. . . . The language of the law thus becomes, in some measure, a vulgar tongue; the spirit of the law, which is produced in the schools and courts of justice, gradually penetrates beyond their walls into the bosom of society, where it descends to the lowest classes, so that at last the whole people contract the habits and the tastes of the judicial magistrate.

Alexis de Tocqueville
Democracy in America

Eisenstadt was not decided until March 22, 1972, and it did not carry the privacy doctrine beyond the confines of the regulation of contraceptives. The doctrine, in other words, had quite a limited scope until January 22, 1973, when the Court decided *Roe v. Wade*. We will scrutinize *Roe* and its progeny, partly because they were crucial to the privacy doctrine and partly because its doctrinal and historical importance was obvious when it was decided and which the Court therefore considered carefully. In addition, of course, *Roe* and its sequelae line the boundaries of a critical part of family law.

ROE v. WADE

Supreme Court of the United States, 1973
410 US 113

BLACKMUN, J.

Roe alleged that she was unmarried and pregnant; that she wished to terminate her pregnancy by an abortion "performed by a competent, licensed physician, under safe, clinical conditions"; that she was unable to get a "legal" abortion in Texas because her life did not appear to be threatened by the continuation of her pregnancy; and that she could not afford to travel to another jurisdiction in order to secure a legal abortion under safe conditions. She claimed that the Texas statutes were unconstitutionally vague and that they abridged her right of personal privacy, protected by the First, Fourth, Fifth, Ninth, and Fourteenth Amendments. By an amendment to her complaint Roe purported to sue "on behalf of herself and all other women" similarly situated....

VIII

The Constitution does not explicitly mention any right of privacy. In a line of decisions, however, going back perhaps as far as *Union Pacific R. Co. v. Botsford*, 141 U.S. 250 (1891), the Court has recognized that a right of personal privacy, or a guarantee of certain areas or zones of privacy, does exist under the Constitution. In varying contexts, the Court or individual Justices have, indeed, found at least the roots of that right in the First Amendment, in the Fourth and Fifth Amendments, in the penumbras of the Bill of Rights, *Griswold v. Connecticut*, 381 U.S., at 484, 485; in the Ninth Amendment, id., at 486 (Goldberg, J., concurring); or in the concept of liberty guaranteed by the first section of the Fourteenth Amendment, see *Meyer v. Nebraska*, 262 U.S. 390, 399 (1923). These decisions make it clear that only personal rights that can be deemed "fundamental" or "implicit in the concept of ordered liberty," are included in this guarantee of personal privacy. They also make it clear that the right has some extension to activities relating to marriage, *Loving v. Virginia*, 388 U.S. 1, 12 (1967); procreation, *Skinner v. Oklahoma*, 316 U.S. 535, 541–542 (1942); contraception, *Eisenstadt v. Baird*, 405 U.S., at 453–454; id., at 460, 463–465 (White, J., concurring in result); family relationships, *Prince v. Massachusetts*, 321 U.S. 158, 166 (1944); and child rearing and education, *Pierce v. Society of Sisters*, 268 U.S. 510, 535 (1925), *Meyer v. Nebraska*, supra.

This right of privacy, whether it be founded in the Fourteenth Amendment's concept of personal liberty and restrictions upon state action, as we feel it is, or, as the District Court determined, in the Ninth Amendment's reservation of rights to the people, is broad enough to encompass a woman's decision whether or not to terminate her pregnancy. The detriment that the State would impose upon the pregnant woman by denying this choice altogether is apparent. Specific and direct harm medically diagnosable even in early pregnancy may be involved. Maternity, or additional offspring, may force upon the woman a distressful life and future. Psychological harm may be imminent. Mental and physical health may be taxed by child care. There is also the distress, for all concerned, associated with the unwanted child, and there is the problem of bringing a child into a family already unable, psychologically and otherwise, to care for it. In other cases, as in this one, the additional difficulties and continuing stigma of unwed motherhood may be involved. All these are factors the woman and her responsible physician necessarily will consider in consultation.

On the basis of elements such as these, appellant and some amici argue that the woman's right is absolute and that she is entitled to terminate her pregnancy at whatever time, in whatever way, and for whatever reason she alone chooses. With this we do not agree. Appellant's arguments that Texas either has no valid interest at all in regulating the abortion decision, or no interest strong enough to support any limitation upon the woman's sole determination, are unpersuasive. The Court's decisions recognizing a right of privacy also acknowledge that some state regulation in areas protected by that right is appropriate. As noted above, a State may properly assert important interests in safeguarding health, in maintaining medical standards, and in protecting potential life. At some point in pregnancy, these respective interests become sufficiently compelling to sustain regulation of the factors that govern the abortion decision. The privacy right involved, therefore, cannot be said to be absolute. In fact, it is not clear to us that the claim asserted by some amici that one has an unlimited right to do with one's body as one pleases bears a close relationship to the right of privacy previously articulated in the Court's decisions. The Court has refused to recognize an unlimited right of this kind in the past.

We, therefore, conclude that the right of personal privacy includes the abortion decision, but that this right is not unqualified and must be considered against important state interests in regulation.

We note that those federal and state courts that have recently considered abortion law challenges have reached the same conclusion. A majority, in addition to the District Court in the present case, have held state laws unconstitutional, at least in part, because of vagueness or because of overbreadth and abridgment of rights. Others have sustained state statutes.

Although the results are divided, most of these courts have agreed that the right of privacy, however based, is broad enough to cover the abortion decision; that the right, nonetheless, is not absolute and is subject to some limitations; and that at some point the state interests as to protection of health, medical standards, and prenatal life, become dominant. We agree with this approach.

Where certain "fundamental rights" are involved, the Court has held that regulation limiting these rights may be justified only by a "compelling state interest," and that legislative enactments must be narrowly drawn to express only the legitimate state interests at stake. *Griswold v. Connecticut*, 381 U.S., at 485; see *Eisenstadt v. Baird*, 405 U.S., at 460, 463–464 (White, J., concurring in result).

In the recent abortion cases, cited above, courts have recognized these principles. Those striking down state laws have generally scrutinized the State's interests in protecting health and potential life, and have concluded that neither interest justified broad limitations on the reasons for which a physician and his pregnant patient might decide that she should have an abortion in the early stages of pregnancy. Courts sustaining state laws have held that the State's determinations to protect health or prenatal life are dominant and constitutionally justifiable.

IX

The District Court held that the appellee failed to meet his burden of demonstrating that the Texas statute's infringement upon Roe's rights was necessary to support a compelling state interest, and that, although the appellee presented "several compelling justifications for state presence in the area of abortions," the statutes outstripped these justifications and swept "far beyond any areas of compelling state interest." Appellant and appellee both contest that holding. Appellant, as has been indicated, claims an absolute right that bars any state imposition of criminal penalties in the area. Appellee argues that the State's determination to recognize and protect prenatal life from and after conception constitutes a compelling state interest. As noted above, we do not agree fully with either formulation.

A. The appellee and certain amici argue that the fetus is a "person" within the language and meaning of the Fourteenth Amendment. In support of this, they outline at length and in detail the well-known facts of fetal development. If this suggestion of personhood is established, the appellant's case, of course, collapses, for the fetus' right to life would then be guaranteed specifically by the Amendment. The appellant conceded as much on reargument. On the other hand, the appellee conceded on reargument that no case could be cited that holds that a fetus is a person within the meaning of the Fourteenth Amendment.

The Constitution does not define "person" in so many words. Section 1 of the Fourteenth Amendment contains three references to "person." The first, in defining "citizens," speaks of "persons born or naturalized in the United States." The word also appears both in the Due Process Clause and in the Equal Protection Clause. "Person" is used in other places in the Constitution: in the listing of qualifications for Representatives and Senators, Art. I, § 2, cl. 2, and § 3, cl. 3; in the Apportionment Clause, Art. I, § 2, cl. 3; in the Migration and Importation provision, Art. I, § 9, cl. 1; in the Emolument Clause, Art. I, § 9, cl. 8; in the Electors provisions, Art. II, § 1, cl. 2, and the superseded cl. 3; in the provision outlining qualifications for the office of President, Art. II, § 1, cl. 5; in the Extradition provisions, Art. IV, § 2, cl. 2, and the superseded Fugitive Slave Clause 3; and in the Fifth, Twelfth, and Twenty-second Amendments, as well as in §§ 2 and 3 of the Fourteenth Amendment. But in nearly all these instances, the use of the word is such that it has application only postnatally. None indicates, with any assurance, that it has any possible pre-natal application.

All this, together with our observation, *supra,* that throughout the major portion of the 19th century prevailing legal abortion practices were far freer than they are today, persuades us that the word "person," as used in the Fourteenth Amendment, does not include the unborn. This is in accord with the results reached in those few cases where the issue has been squarely presented. Indeed, our decision in *United States v. Vuitch*, 402 U.S. 62 (1971), inferentially is to the same effect, for we there would not have indulged in statutory interpretation favorable to abortion in specified circumstances if the necessary consequence was the termination of life entitled to Fourteenth Amendment protection.

This conclusion, however, does not of itself fully answer the contentions raised by Texas, and we pass on to other considerations.

B. The pregnant woman cannot be isolated in her privacy. She carries an embryo and, later, a fetus, if one accepts the medical definitions of the developing young in the human uterus. See Dorland's *Illustrated Medical Dictionary* 478–479, 547 (24th ed. 1965). The situation therefore is inherently different from marital intimacy, or bedroom possession of obscene material, or marriage, or procreation, or education, with which *Eisenstadt* and *Griswold*, *Stanley*, *Loving*, *Skinner,* and *Pierce* and *Meyer* were respectively concerned. As we have intimated above, it is reasonable and appropriate for a State to decide that at some point in time another interest, that of health of the mother or that of potential human life, becomes significantly involved. The woman's privacy is no longer sole and any right of privacy she possesses must be measured accordingly.

Texas urges that, apart from the Fourteenth Amendment, life begins at conception and is present throughout pregnancy, and that, therefore, the State has a compelling interest in protecting that life from and after conception. We need not resolve the difficult question of when life begins. When those trained in the respective disciplines of medicine, philosophy, and theology are unable to arrive at any consensus, the judiciary, at this point in the development of man's knowledge, is not in a position to speculate as to the answer.

It should be sufficient to note briefly the wide divergence of thinking on this most sensitive and difficult question. There has always been strong support for the view that life does not begin until live birth. This was the belief of the Stoics. It appears to be the predominant, though not the unanimous, attitude of the Jewish faith. It may be taken to represent also the position of a large segment of the Protestant community, insofar as that can be ascertained; organized groups that have taken a formal position on the abortion issue have generally regarded abortion as a matter for the conscience of the individual and her family. As we have noted, the common law found greater significance in quickening. Physicians and their scientific colleagues have regarded that event with less interest and have tended to focus either upon conception, upon live birth, or upon the interim point at which the fetus becomes "viable," that is, potentially able to live outside the mother's womb, albeit with artificial aid. Viability is usually placed at about seven months (28 weeks) but may occur earlier, even at 24 weeks. The Aristotelian theory of "mediate animation," that held sway throughout the Middle Ages and the Renaissance in Europe, continued to be official Roman Catholic dogma until the 19th century, despite opposition to this "ensoulment" theory from those in the Church who would recognize the existence of life from the moment of conception. The latter is now, of course, the official belief of the Catholic Church. As one brief amicus discloses, this is a view strongly held by many non-Catholics as well, and by many physicians. Substantial problems for precise definition of this view are posed, however, by new embryological data that purport to indicate that conception is a "process" over time, rather than an event, and by new medical techniques such as menstrual extraction, the "morning-after" pill, implantation of embryos, artificial insemination, and even artificial wombs.

In areas other than criminal abortion, the law has been reluctant to endorse any theory that life, as we recognize it, begins before live birth or to accord legal rights to the unborn except in narrowly defined situations and except when the rights are contingent upon live birth. For example, the traditional rule of tort law denied recovery for prenatal injuries even though the child was born alive. That rule has been changed in almost every jurisdiction. In most States, recovery is said to be permitted only if the fetus was viable, or at least quick, when the injuries were sustained, though few courts have squarely so held. In a recent development, generally opposed by the commentators, some States permit the parents of a stillborn child to maintain an action for wrongful death because of prenatal injuries. Such an action, however, would appear to be one to vindicate the parents' interest and is thus consistent with the view that the fetus, at most, represents only the potentiality of life. Similarly, unborn children have been recognized as acquiring rights or interests by way of inheritance or other devolution of property, and have been represented by guardians ad litem. Perfection of the interests involved, again, has generally been contingent upon live birth. In short, the unborn have never been recognized in the law as persons in the whole sense.

X

In view of all this, we do not agree that, by adopting one theory of life, Texas may override the rights of the pregnant woman that are at stake. We repeat, however, that the State does have an important and legitimate interest in preserving and protecting the health of the pregnant woman, whether she be a resident of the State or a nonresident who seeks medical consultation and treatment there, and that it has still another important and legitimate interest in protecting the potentiality of human life. These interests are separate and distinct. Each grows in substantiality as the woman approaches term and, at a point during pregnancy, each becomes "compelling."

A Note on Doctrine

It is important that the structure of fourteenth-amendment analysis be clear to you. Because the Court's analytic technique has varied from case to case, that structure can be opaque. Here, then, is a brief summary of the analytic principles as the Court most often states them. Ordinarily, a statute is presumed constitutional, since a court assumes that the legislature, as a co-equal or perhaps even (since it speaks for the people) superior branch of government, is acting constitutionally. The constitutionality of a statute is thus ordinarily assessed by a lax test—is the statute "rationally related" to a "legitimate state interest"? Courts almost always find this test is satisfied. However, the Court has identified two kinds of circumstances where it will apply a stricter test, a procedure commonly referred to as "strict scrutiny." (1) In applying either the Due Process Clause or the Equal Protection Clause, a court applies the stricter test when a fundamental interest is at stake. Fundamental interests include the right to travel and the right to equal access to the ballot, as well, of course, as the right to privacy. (2) In applying the Equal Protection Clause, a court applies the stricter test when the legislature has used a suspect classification. A classification is suspect when, as one classic formulation goes, it affects "a discrete and insular minority." Race is the prototypical suspect classification. What is this stricter test? That the challenged statute must be "necessary" to promote a "compelling state interest." Courts almost always find that a statute subject to this stricter test fails it. The question whether a fundamental interest is at stake thus becomes crucial.

This two-tier structure of analysis has increasingly been loosened and expanded. The Court seems to be creating an intermediate form of scrutiny where women, illegitimates, aliens, and perhaps the mentally retarded are involved. The Court has also, without acknowledging what it was doing, sometimes made rational-basis scrutiny stricter than usual, thus creating something closer to a sliding-scale than a two-tier analytic structure. The Court has also occasionally held that a state interest is "compelling": *Roberts v. United States Jaycees*, 468 US 609 (1984), found it a compelling state interest to enforce a statute prohibiting sex-discrimination; *Bob Jones University v. United States*, 461 U.S. 574 (1983), found it a compelling interest to eradicate racial discrimination; and *Roe* you know about. For a detailed discussion of these tests, see Carl E. Schneider, *State-Interest Analysis in Fourteenth Amendment "Privacy" Law: An Essay on the Constitutionalization of Social Issues*, 51 L & Contemp Probs 79 (1988).

Questions on the Origins of the Privacy Right

The following questions are designed to help you work out what *Roe* says about the origins of the constitutional right to privacy.

(1) In an omitted portion of the decision, the Court dissects the history of abortion regulations. Why? Does the Court's historical excursion speak to whether there is a constitutional right of privacy, or is that excursion purely informational?

(a) Does it matter what the ancients thought? In particular, does it matter that the Hippocratic Oath can be explained away as the Pythagorean minority view, given the two millennia of subsequent history?

(b) What is the relevance of the fact abortion before quickening was not a crime in the first decades of the nineteenth century? Why might pre-quickening abortion not have been criminalized? How ought the fact that pre-quickening abortion began to be criminalized over a century ago affect our view of the constitutionality of abortion regulation?

(c) Why does the Court consider it insignificant that post-quickening abortion was long criminal and often harshly punished? (For a study of the common law's attitude toward abortion, see Shelley A.M. Gavigan, *The Criminal Sanction as it Relates to Human Reproduction: The Genesis of the Statutory Prohibition of Abortion*, 5 J Legal Hist 20 (1984).)

(d) Whatever the extent of legal restrictions on abortions, is it likely that the Framers of the Constitution (or, more particularly, the Framers of the Fourteenth Amendment) thought the state was constitutionally constrained from regulating abortion?

(2) What is the point of the information Justice Blackmun supplies (in an omitted portion of the opinion) about the views on abortion of such groups as the AMA, the APHA, and the ABA? Is evidence about the public's attitudes toward abortion regulation relevant to whether a constitutional right of privacy exists? Is evidence about the attitudes of

professional associations probative of public attitudes? Is it specially relevant to the question whether a constitutional right of privacy exists?

(3) How helpful are the precedents the Court cites in constructing a constitutional right of privacy? (Recall that they are: *Skinner, Loving, Prince, Meyer, Pierce, Griswold*, and *Eisenstadt*.)

(a) What do these cases have in common? Enough to evidence a right not expressed in the text of the Constitution?

(b) What do you make of the Court's apparent concession that there is a difference between the precedents and the right to an abortion: "The situation [in *Roe*] ... is inherently different from marital intimacy, or bedroom possession of obscene material, or marriage, or procreation, or education ..."?

(4) What does the Court itself identify as the rationale for deciding there is a constitutional right to obtain an abortion?

(5) The Court speaks of "the detriment that the State would impose upon the pregnant woman by denying this choice." Is it that detriment which gives rise to the right? How does a detriment give rise to a right? Don't all governmental restrictions on action impose detriments? Even if it is only severe detriments that give rise to rights, why don't all severe detriments give rise to rights?

(6) If an *entirely* safe and *entirely* effective contraceptive were available at no charge to anyone who asked, would there still be a right to obtain an abortion?

(7) The Court considered, explicitly and implicitly, other justifications for the right to an abortion. What were these other justifications, and why did the Court reject them?

Questions on the State's Interests

These questions are designed to help you assess how the Court decided whether a compelling state interest justified the Texas statute.

(1) The Court spends a good deal of time asking whether the Fourteenth Amendment defines human life to include fetal life. Why?

(a) Is the exercise pointless, since the Framers surely never had occasion to consider the issue?

(b) Is the exercise pointless, since even if the Fourteenth Amendment includes fetal life in its definition of human life, abortion legislation may not therefore be constitutionally necessary?

(2) The Court suggests that "the law has been reluctant ... to accord legal rights to the unborn except in narrowly defined situations and except when the rights are contingent upon live birth." Are the occasions on which the law accords rights to the unborn few? Insignificant? In the context of abortion regulation, does it matter that, when the law accords legal rights to the unborn, it generally makes them contingent on the child's birth?

(3) The Court concludes Part IX of its opinion by saying "the unborn have never been recognized in the law as persons in the whole sense."

(a) What does "in the whole sense" mean? Is "in the whole sense" the relevant standard for abortion regulation?

(b) The Court describes fetal life as "potential" life. Why is protecting potential life not a compelling state interest?

(4) The Court says it is "not in a position to speculate" whether a fetus is a live human being. Does the Court avoid deciding the question?

(5) The Court says Texas may not "by adopting one theory of life . . . override the rights of the pregnant woman that are at stake."

(a) The Court might be implying that Texas has arbitrarily chosen a theory of life. How true is that?

(b) Why may not Texas adopt one theory of life? Isn't defining life a classic legislative function? *Can* Texas avoid adopting one theory of life?

(6) Why does the state's interest in fetal life change as the fetus nears term? Does this view assume a particular theory of life?

Questions on the Court's Regulatory Scheme

The following questions are designed to help you think about the regulatory scheme the Court creates.

(1) Why does the fact that the danger from abortion becomes greater than the danger from childbirth after the first trimester mean the state cannot regulate abortions during the first trimester? Wasn't one major objection to the prohibition of abortion that the prohibition made it impossible for the state to regulate first trimester abortions to protect the woman's health?

(2) Why does the ability of the child to live outside the mother's body define the point when the state's interest becomes compelling? Does the word "meaningful" add anything? Does it suggest that what the fetus had was some ("non-meaningful"?) kind of life? Does it suggest the Court will countenance state termination of lives the state takes not to be meaningful?

(3) The Court creates a right of abortion in the third trimester for a woman whose health would be threatened by carrying the fetus to term. What is the basis for that right?

(4) In discussing family autonomy, we noted that one of its justifications is that the family makes better decisions than the state. Will the pregnant woman make better decisions than the state? There is presumably little doubt she will know her own situation better than the state. Are there any ways she is not a better decision-maker?

B. STUDIES IN LEGAL CHANGE: THE JUDICIAL REFORM OF ABORTION LAW

The first requirement of a sound body of law is, that it should correspond with the actual feelings and demands of the community, whether right or wrong.

Oliver Wendell Holmes

(1) The Setting of *Roe v. Wade*

During the early twentieth century, the laws extensively regulating abortion which had been adopted in the latter half of the nineteenth century were widely accepted, although there was evidence that they were also widely disobeyed and that they were sometimes interpreted in ways that made abortions available on therapeutic grounds (that is, to protect the life or health of the woman) more broadly than the text of the law might have suggested was possible.[1] By the late 1950's, however, an abortion reform movement was blossoming. One early sign was the creation in hospitals of boards responsible for approving therapeutic abortions. These boards were made necessary in part by increasing questions among doctors about what abortions were ethically and legally justifiable. These boards brought the question how readily available abortions should be more sharply before the medical profession and the public.

One early fruit of this attention was section 230.3 of the Model Penal Code, which was originally considered in 1959 and which was approved in 1962:

1. *Unjustified Abortion.* A person who purposely and unjustifiably terminates the pregnancy of another otherwise than by a live birth commits a felony of the third degree or, where the pregnancy has continued beyond the twenty-sixth week, a felony of the second degree.

2. *Justifiable Abortion.* A licensed physician is justified in terminating a pregnancy if he believes there is a substantial risk that continuance of the pregnancy would gravely impair the physical or mental health of the mother or that the child would be born with grave physical or mental defect, or that the pregnancy resulted from rape, incest, or other felonious intercourse. All illicit intercourse with a girl below the age of 16 shall be deemed felonious for purposes of this subsection. Justifiable abortions shall be performed only in a licensed hospital except in case of emergency when hospital facilities are unavailable.

3. *Physicians' Certifications; Presumption from NonCompliance.* No abortion shall be performed unless two physicians, one of whom may be the person performing the abortion, shall have certified in writing the circumstances which they believe to justify the abortion.... Failure to

1. Our discussion of the pre-*Roe* campaign to reform of abortion laws draws on Kristin Luker, *Abortion and the Politics of Motherhood* (U Cal Press, 1984).

comply with any of the requirements of this subsection gives rise to a presumption that the abortion was unjustified.

The Model Penal Code is important because, since it was drafted and approved by a weighty group of elite lawyers, it is indicative of the thinking of important elements of society on abortion.

A second major step in the reform of abortion laws came in California. An article in the Stanford Law Review reported that California hospitals varied widely in their treatment of therapeutic abortions. This article helped inspire two freshman state legislators to sponsor abortion-reform legislation. One of them, who represented Beverly Hills, said, "[W]e weren't talking about abortion on demand, we were talking about cases of rape or incest or where continuation [of the pregnancy] ... involved substantial risk to the mother's physical or mental health.... I think it probably got the law passed relatively quickly—[the fact] that the existing state of the law was barbaric or archaic, not moderate." The California bill was supported by various legal and medical professional elites, including, organizationally, the AMA, the ABA, the American Academy of Pediatrics, the California Medical Association, and the California Bar Association. Part of the professional support for abortion reform came from doctors who wanted legislative confirmation of the liberal interpretation they had been giving the California therapeutic-abortion law. These doctors wanted support because a basic disagreement among doctors over the medical and moral grounds for abortion had become increasingly apparent. (These doctors' feelings of urgency were sharpened when the California State Board of Medical Examiners brought charges against seven doctors who had performed abortions for women who had been exposed to rubella, a disease that can lead to the birth of deformed children.)

Another part of that support came from people who felt a restrictive abortion policy was disproportionately severe to poor women, led to the corruption of the police and the courts, and brought law into disrepute. Yet another part of the support came from liberal religious groups. And still another part came from civic groups, including, for instance, the American Association of University Women, the Young Republicans, and the California Junior Chamber of Commerce, whose convention supported the bill by an 80 percent vote. The supporters of the bill organized themselves into the California Committee on Therapeutic Abortion. As Professor Luker tells us, "It included lawyers who would later be judges, physicians who were and would become heads of departments in major universities, and representatives from many of the local colleges and universities, law schools, and medical schools."

Although the California bill was primarily promoted through elite politics, those politics were affected by the elevation of the abortion question to widespread public attention. A major factor in that development was the case of Mrs. Sherri Finkbine, an Arizona woman who was the host of a local television show for children. In 1962, while she was pregnant with her fifth child, Mrs. Finkbine realized that the sleeping pills her husband had brought back from a trip to Europe contained Thalidomide. That drug had caused some European babies to be born defective, often with severely deformed limbs and severe internal problems. Mrs. Finkbine's physician told her her child was likely to be born deformed, and he recommended a therapeutic abortion. The hospital's therapeutic-abortion committee approved the abortion. Before she received it, however, she told her story to the press, since she wanted to alert other pregnant women who might have taken Thalidomide of its dangers. The abortion which had been scheduled was canceled because of doubt that Arizona law, which allowed therapeutic abortions only to preserve the life of the mother, permitted an abortion in her case. She and her husband then asked a court to order that the abortion be performed. The suit was dismissed as moot when the state said that it would not take action against an abortion performed to prevent Mrs. Finkbine from committing suicide under the pressure of having to bear and rear a seriously defective child. By this time, Mrs. Finkbine's situation was attracting national attention. Eventually she decided to go to Sweden for an abortion, one which she received only with some difficulty and one which revealed that the child would have been born so severely damaged that it would not have survived.

In 1967, the California bill was passed by the legislature and signed by Governor Ronald Reagan. It permitted abortions necessary to prevent a pregnancy a hospital therapeutic-abortion board determined would "gravely impair" the woman's physical or mental health and abortions where the pregnancy was a result of rape, statutory rape, or incest. It did not permit abortions to prevent the birth of deformed children.

The new law was not generally expected to affect the abortion rate greatly. However, within four years the rate had increased 2,000 percent. Professor Luker concludes, "[B]y 1970 it was becoming apparent that what had been proposed as a 'middle-way' solution had in fact become 'abortion on demand.' ... [B]y late 1970, of all women who applied for an abortion, 99.2 percent were granted one. By 1971 abortion was as frequent as it would ever become in California, and one out of every three pregnancies was ended by a legal abortion."

Meanwhile, the 1960's saw a change in the attack on traditional abortion laws. The argument increasingly came to be made that abortion was a woman's right and that abortion laws thus ought to be not reformed, but repealed. This argument, Professor Luker suggests, grew out of the general reformist temper of the times but had its particular roots in the increasing entry of women into the labor force, especially those parts of the labor force that had once been only rarely entered by women. Professor Luker writes,

> As the traditional intermeshing of women's paid employment and family activities began to break down, women found themselves segregated in what were now seen as relatively unattractive jobs or denied opportunities for rewards or advancement *because they were mothers or potential mothers*.... The mobilization of significant numbers of women around the issue of abortion laws can therefore be seen as an attack on a

symbolic linchpin that held together a complicated set of assumptions about who women were, what their roles in life should be, what kinds of jobs they should take in the paid labor force, and how those jobs should be rewarded.

The most significant result of this change in the abortion-reform sentiment came in New York. In 1970, that state repealed its old abortion statute and passed a new one whose only restrictions were that abortions could not be performed after the twenty-fourth week of pregnancy and that they had to be performed by a licensed physician.

By 1971, eighteen states had reformed their abortion laws. But by this time, reformist activity increasingly looked to the courts. As you know, that activity succeeded (more quickly than anyone had anticipated) in 1973, with *Roe v. Wade*. How did that case come to be litigated?

(2) Roe v. Wade

Linda Coffee and Sarah Weddington were the two principal lawyers for Jane Roe. Both graduated from University of Texas Law School in the late '60s. Both were Texans. Ms. Coffee was a member of the Order of the Coif and had been invited to join the law review in her senior year. When she graduated, she clerked for Judge Irving Goldberg of the U.S. Court of Appeals for the Fifth Circuit. She then joined a small Dallas law firm where she began to do bankruptcy work. Ms. Weddington had worked while still in law school for Professor John Sutton, who was developing what is now the ABA Code of Professional Responsibility. When Ms. Weddington (like Ms. Coffee) found that jobs for women were not easy to find in Dallas law firms, she decided to continue to work for Sutton after graduation. By the time she became involved in *Roe*, she was a Ft. Worth assistant city attorney.

After graduation, both women joined local feminist groups, and both became interested in changing the Texas abortion statute. They began to search for a plaintiff. Doing so was impeded by, among other things, the need to find a plaintiff who would present a justiciable controversy. Most possible plaintiffs were women who were anxious to have an abortion and who did not want to remain pregnant while their case was litigated. Eventually, Ms. Coffee was approached by the "Does." They are described in the opinion

> as a childless married couple, the woman not being pregnant, who have no desire to have children at this time because of their having received medical advice that Mrs. Doe should avoid pregnancy, and for "other highly personal reasons." But they "fear . . . they may face the prospect of becoming parents."

Ms. Coffee did not regard the Does as ideal plaintiffs, partly because Texas law permitted abortions to save the mother's life and thus might permit Mrs. Doe to have an abortion. On the other hand, it was hard to find a better plaintiff.[2]

2. The Court concluded that the Does' claim was not justiciable: "Their alleged injury rests on possible future contraceptive failure, possible future pregnancy, possible

However, just as Ms. Coffee was about to file a complaint for the Does, she learned of Norma McCorvey. Ms. McCorvey was the daughter of a man who, after a career in the army, had become a Dallas electrician and who had divorced his wife and left Norma and her younger brother in her mother's care. By the age of sixteen, Norma had left school, worked as a waitress, married a twenty-year old who hoped to become a rock star, and moved to Los Angeles. When she became pregnant, her husband had assaulted her, and she had moved back to Dallas. When the child was born, it was adopted by Norma's mother, who soon moved with the child and a new husband to Arkansas.

When Ms. Coffee met Ms. McCorvey, Ms. McCorvey told her that in 1969 she had been traveling in the South selling tickets with a carnival. She reported that in August the carnival had been in Georgia, that one night on the way back to the motel she had been raped, and that she had become pregnant. She said she was in no position to rear or support another child and wanted an abortion.

Ms. Coffee and Ms. Weddington were skeptical of Ms. McCorvey's claim that she had been raped (correctly skeptical, as Ms. McCorvey later acknowledged). However, they decided that Ms. McCorvey would make a good plaintiff and that the issue of the rape need not arise. They nevertheless offered to help Ms. McCorvey, who was by then four months pregnant, obtain an abortion if she wanted one. Ms. McCorvey declined and agreed to be their plaintiff. They warned her the case might take years to resolve, and they tried to deal with her concerns about publicity by proposing that she bring suit pseudonymously.

The two lawyers then had to plan a litigation strategy. The Fourteenth Amendment privacy argument did not look as powerful then as it does in retrospect. *Griswold* was recent and controversial. They therefore recruited arguments based on the First, Fourth, Fifth, Eighth, Ninth, and Fourteenth Amendments. They did not argue that the government could not regulate abortion, since they did not believe a court would accept that argument; they did, of course, contend that the Texas statute went too far in doing so. In any event, Ms. Coffee filed the initiating papers on March 3, 1970.

(3) The Sequelae of Roe v. Wade

Lawrence M. Friedman writes, "*Roe v. Wade* belongs to a very select club of Supreme Court decisions—those that sent shock waves through the country affecting every aspect of political life." *The Conflict over Constitutional Legitimacy*, in Gilbert Y. Steiner, ed, *The Abortion Dispute and the American System* (Brookings Inst, 1983). He continues, "The reaction was volcanic—a slow rumble, followed by eruptions. No one predicted so strong a response." What were those eruptions?

future unpreparedness for parenthood, and possible future impairment of health.... [W]e are not prepared to say that the bare allegation of so indirect an injury is sufficient to present an actual case or controversy." 410 US at 128.

(a) The Federal Response

Roe's opponents in Congress have attempted in a variety of ways to counteract the case. Most dramatically, they have introduced constitutional amendments that would, for example, establish a right to life beginning at fertilization, that would accord fetuses status as "persons" under the Fifth and Fourteenth Amendments or that would return authority to regulate abortion to the states or to the states and Congress concurrently. However, an amendment needs the assent of two-thirds of both the House and the Senate and of three-quarters of the states, and none of the abortion amendments has emerged from Congress.

Roe's opponents have also attacked it statutorily. Bills have been proposed, for example, that would deprive federal courts of jurisdiction to handle abortion cases and that would declare that human life begins at conception, a declaration that might then be used to justify legislation under section 5 of the Fourteenth Amendment limiting abortion. These bills too have failed to become law, largely because of opposition in the judiciary committees of both houses.

Roe's opponents have, however, been more successful in some of their more limited forays. Most prominently, they have prevented the expenditure of federal funds for abortions in a variety of contexts, notably including Medicaid. This last restriction was found constitutional in *Harris v. McRae*, 448 US 297 (1980).

The final strategy of opponents of *Roe* is to seek the appointment of Justices unsympathetic to the case. Despite twelve years of Republican Presidents, however, this strategy has failed.

(b) The State Response

After *Roe*, many state legislatures began to probe the limits of permissible regulation of abortion. These probings can most easily be traced by sketching the Court's reaction to some of them.

Planned Parenthood of Central Missouri v. Danforth, 428 US 52 (1976). This case approved Missouri's statutory definition of viability as "that stage of fetal development when the life of the unborn child may be continued indefinitely outside the womb by natural or artificial life-support systems," and it also approved Missouri's requirement of a patient's informed, written consent to an abortion. However, the case disapproved four other provisions of the statute: (1) a prohibition on abortions by saline amniocentesis after the first twelve weeks, (2) a requirement that doctors performing an abortion exercise the same professional skill to preserve the life of the fetus which the doctor would have had "to exercise in order to preserve the life and health of any fetus intended to be born and not aborted," (3) a requirement that wives obtain their husbands' written consent to an abortion, and (4) a requirement that girls under the age of eighteen obtain the written consent of a parent, unless the operation was necessary to save the girl's life.

Maher v. Roe, 432 US 464 (1977). In *Maher*, the Court assessed a regulation of the Connecticut Welfare Department that provided that state Medicaid benefits could be used for abortions in the first trimester only when they were medically (including psychiatrically) necessary. Justice Powell's opinion for the majority rejected the argument that the regulation impinged on the fundamental right expounded in *Roe*. That case, he said, "did not declare an unqualified 'constitutional right to an abortion....' Rather, the right protects the woman from unduly burdensome interference with her freedom to decide whether to terminate her pregnancy." The statute in *Roe*, for example, imposed criminal sanctions, and the consent provisions in the *Danforth* statute set potentially absolute barriers in the path of a woman's decision to have an abortion. The Connecticut regulation, however, created no such obstacles. Any obstacles an indigent woman encountered after the regulation was issued she would have encountered in its absence. This reasoning signaled no retreat from *Roe*, since "[t]here is a basic difference between direct state interference with a protected activity and state encouragement of alternative activity consonant with legislative policy."

Harris v. McRae, 448 US 297 (1980). In *McRae*, the Court had before it one of Congress's Hyde Amendments. Relying principally on *Maher*, the Court upheld it. Justice Stewart wrote that a woman's right under *Roe* to decide to have an abortion does not carry with it "a constitutional entitlement to the financial resources to avail herself of the full range of protected choices.... [A]lthough government may not place obstacles in the path of a woman's exercise of her freedom of choice, it need not remove those not of its own creation. Indigency falls in the latter category."

Bellotti v. Baird, 443 US 622 (1979). This case dealt with a Massachusetts statute that required that an unmarried mother younger than eighteen obtain parental permission to have an abortion and that allowed her to seek permission from a judge if she couldn't get it from her parents. The Court voted eight to one to hold the statute constitutionally unsound; the majority divided four to four in its reasons. Justice Powell's opinion has proved the more consequential. It stated that if a state "decides to require a pregnant minor to obtain one or both parents' consent to an abortion, it also must provide an alternative procedure whereby authorization for the abortion can be obtained." The Massachusetts statute met this requirement, but it had two constitutional faults. As the Court later described them: "(a) it permitted overruling of a mature minor's decision to abort her pregnancy; and (b) it requires parental consultation or notification in every instance, without affording the pregnant minor an opportunity to receive an independent judicial determination that she is mature enough to consent or that an abortion would be in her best interests." *H.L. v. Matheson*, 450 US 398, 408–09 (1981), quoting *Bellotti*, 443 US at 651.

H.L. v. Matheson, 450 US 398 (1981). This case presented the rather narrow question of "the facial constitutionality of a statute requiring a physician to give notice to parents, 'if possible,' prior to performing an abortion on their minor daughter, (a) when the girl is living with and dependent upon her parents, (b) when she is not emancipated by marriage or otherwise, and (c) when she has made no claim or showing as to her maturity or as to her relations with her parents." The Court upheld the statute because it gave "neither parents nor judges a veto power over the minor's abortion decision." The Court concluded by saying,

> That the requirement of notice to parents may inhibit some minors from seeking abortions is not a valid basis to void the statute as applied to appellant and the class properly before us. The Constitution does not compel a state to fine-tune its statutes so as to encourage or facilitate abortions. To the contrary, state action "encouraging childbirth except in the most urgent circumstances" is "rationally related to the legitimate governmental objective of protecting potential life."

Justice Powell and Justice Stewart joined the opinion "on the understanding that it leaves open the question whether [the statute] unconstitutionally burdens the right of a mature minor or a minor whose best interests would not be served by parental notification."

Akron v. Akron Center for Reproductive Health, 462 US 416 (1983). This case dealt with an Akron ordinance that imposed a variety of regulations on abortions. (1) One such regulation required that abortions done after the first trimester be performed in hospitals (as opposed, for instance, to outpatient facilities). The Court held *Akron* had thereby "imposed a heavy, and unnecessary, burden on women's access to a relatively inexpensive, otherwise accessible, and safe abortion procedure." (2) The Court invalidated a parental consent requirement which did not, at least with adequate clarity, " 'establish a procedure by which a minor can avoid a parental veto of her abortion decision by demonstrating that her decision is in fact informed. . . .' "

(3) The Akron ordinance contained an informed-consent provision which, as the Court described it, required that "the woman must be 'orally informed by her attending physician' of the status of her pregnancy, the development of her fetus, the date of possible viability, the physical and emotional complications that may result from an abortion, and the availability of agencies to provide her with assistance and information with respect to birth control, adoption, and childbirth." The Court "found it fair to say that much of the information required is designed not to inform the woman's consent but rather to persuade her to withhold it altogether." The Court added that an "equally decisive objection" to the ordinance was "its intrusion upon the discretion of the pregnant woman's physician." The Court thus held the provision invalid. (4) That provision also contained a requirement that the attending physician must inform a patient "of the particular risks associated with her own pregnancy and the abortion technique to be employed . . . [and] other information which in his own medical judgment is relevant to her decision as to whether to have an abortion or carry her pregnancy to term." The Court could not find evidence in the record "that the woman's consent to the abortion will not be informed if a physician

delegates the counselling task to another qualified individual," and the Court found this requirement unconstitutional.

(5) The Court overturned a provision requiring that an abortion not be performed until twenty-four hours after the woman had signed a consent form. The Court said "*Akron* has failed to demonstrate that any legitimate state interest is furthered by an arbitrary and inflexible waiting period." (6) Finally, the Court found impermissibly vague a provision of the ordinance that required that physicians performing abortions "insure that the remains of the unborn child are disposed of in a humane and sanitary manner."

Planned Parenthood Association of Kansas City, Missouri, Inc. v. Ashcroft, 462 US 476 (1983). This was a companion case to *Akron*. In it, the Court considered, *inter alia*, provisions of Missouri statutes requiring a pathology report on fetal tissue removed during an abortion and the presence of a second physician at an abortion whose task was to seek to "preserve the life and health of the viable unborn child; provided that it does not pose an increased risk to the life or health of the woman." There was no majority opinion, but the Court held both provisions constitutional.

Thornburgh v. American College of Obstetricians & Gynecologists, 476 US 747 (1986). This case dealt with a Pennsylvania statute. One provision of that statute required that doctors performing abortions provide a detailed report explaining why the doctor decided the fetus was not viable. In finding this provision unconstitutional, the Court said, "The scope of the information required and its availability to the public belie any assertions by the Commonwealth that it is advancing any legitimate interest." Another provision of the statute required that the doctor exercise the degree of care which would be exercised were a live birth intended and that the abortion technique be the technique which would pose the least risk to the chances of a live birth, unless that technique would be riskier to the woman. The Court held this provision unconstitutional because it seemed to expect a trade-off between the woman's health and the fetus's chances of survival.

Webster v. Reproductive Health Services, 492 US 490 (1989). This case upheld several controversial provisions of the Missouri statute, including its preamble, which stated that life begins at conception. It also upheld provisions requiring testing for viability once the fetus reached 20 weeks' gestational age.

(4) Roe Revised? Roe Reaffirmed?

For many years, there seemed a possibility that the Supreme Court might in some way recant its opinion in *Roe*. The likeliest opportunity to do so came in 1992, when the Court decided the following case. A sense of the persisting complexity of views about the Court, substantive due process, and abortion comes from the announcement of the Justices' positions:

O'CONNOR, KENNEDY, AND SOUTER, JJ., announced the judgment of the Court and delivered the opinion of the Court with respect to Parts I, II, III, V–A, V–C, and VI, in which BLACKMUN and STEVENS, JJ., joined, an opinion with respect to Part V–E, in which STEVENS, J., joined, and an opinion with respect to Parts IV, V–B, and V–D. STEVENS, J., filed an opinion concurring in part and dissenting in part. BLACKMUN, J., filed an opinion concurring in part, concurring in the judgment in part, and dissenting in part. REHNQUIST, C.J., filed an opinion concurring in the judgment in part and dissenting in part, in which WHITE, SCALIA, and THOMAS, JJ., joined. SCALIA, J., filed an opinion concurring in the judgment in part and dissenting in part, in which REHNQUIST, C.J., and WHITE and THOMAS, JJ., joined.

PLANNED PARENTHOOD OF S.E. PENNSYLVANIA v. CASEY

Supreme Court of the United States, 1992
505 US 833

O'CONNOR, J.

I

Liberty finds no refuge in a jurisprudence of doubt. Yet 19 years after our holding that the Constitution protects a woman's right to terminate her pregnancy in its early stages, *Roe v. Wade,* that definition of liberty is still questioned. Joining the respondents as amicus curiae, the United States, as it has done in five other cases in the last decade, again asks us to overrule *Roe*.

At issue in these cases are five provisions of the Pennsylvania Abortion Control Act of 1982 as amended in 1988 and 1989. 18 Pa. Cons. Stat. §§ 3203–3220 (1990). The Act requires that a woman seeking an abortion give her informed consent prior to the abortion procedure, and specifies that she be provided with certain information at least 24 hours before the abortion is performed. For a minor to obtain an abortion, the Act requires the informed consent of one of her parents, but provides for a judicial bypass option if the minor does not wish to or cannot obtain a parent's consent. Another provision of the Act requires that, unless certain exceptions apply, a married woman seeking an abortion must sign a statement indicating that she has notified her husband of her intended abortion. The Act exempts compliance with these three requirements in the event of a "medical emergency," which is defined in § 3203 of the Act. In addition to the above provisions regulating the performance of abortions, the Act imposes certain reporting requirements on facilities that provide abortion services....

After considering the fundamental constitutional questions resolved by *Roe*, principles of institutional integrity, and the rule of stare decisis, we are led to conclude this: the essential holding of *Roe v. Wade* should be retained and once again reaffirmed....

II

Constitutional protection of the woman's decision to terminate her pregnancy derives from the Due Process Clause of the Fourteenth Amendment. It declares that no State shall "deprive any person of life, liberty, or property, without due process of law." The controlling word in the case before us is "liberty." Although a literal reading of the Clause might suggest that it governs only the procedures by which a State may deprive persons of liberty, for at least 105 years, at least since *Mugler v. Kansas*, 123 U.S. 623, 660–661 (1887), the Clause has been understood to contain a substantive component as well, one "barring certain government actions regardless of the fairness of the procedures used to implement them." As Justice Brandeis (joined by Justice Holmes) observed, "despite arguments to the contrary which had seemed to me persuasive, it is settled that the due process clause of the Fourteenth Amendment applies to matters of substantive law as well as to matters of procedure. Thus all fundamental rights comprised within the term liberty are protected by the Federal Constitution from invasion by the States." . . .

Men and women of good conscience can disagree, and we suppose some always shall disagree, about the profound moral and spiritual implications of terminating a pregnancy, even in its earliest stage. Some of us as individuals find abortion offensive to our most basic principles of morality, but that cannot control our decision. Our obligation is to define the liberty of all, not to mandate our own moral code. The underlying constitutional issue is whether the State can resolve these philosophic questions in such a definitive way that a woman lacks all choice in the matter, except perhaps in those rare circumstances in which the pregnancy is itself a danger to her own life or health, or is the result of rape or incest. . . .

Our law affords constitutional protection to personal decisions relating to marriage, procreation, contraception, family relationships, child rearing, and education. Our cases recognize "the right of the individual, married or single, to be free from unwarranted governmental intrusion into matters so fundamentally affecting a person as the decision whether to bear or beget a child." *Eisenstadt v. Baird*. Our precedents "have respected the private realm of family life which the state cannot enter." *Prince v. Massachusetts*. These matters, involving the most intimate and personal choices a person may make in a lifetime, choices central to personal dignity and autonomy, are central to the liberty protected by the Fourteenth Amendment. At the heart of liberty is the right to define one's own concept of existence, of meaning, of the universe, and of the mystery of human life. Beliefs about these matters could not define the attributes of personhood were they formed under compulsion of the State.

These considerations begin our analysis of the woman's interest in terminating her pregnancy but cannot end it, for this reason: though the abortion decision may originate within the zone of conscience and belief, it is more than a philosophic exercise. Abortion is a unique act. It is an act fraught with consequences for others: for the woman who must live with the implications of her decision; for the persons who perform and assist in the procedure; for the spouse, family, and society which must confront the knowledge that these procedures exist, procedures some deem nothing short of an act of violence against innocent human life; and, depending on one's beliefs, for the life or potential life that is aborted. Though abortion is conduct, it does not follow that the State is entitled to proscribe it in all instances. That is because the liberty of the woman is at stake in a sense unique to the human condition and so unique to the law. The mother who carries a child to full term is subject to anxieties, to physical constraints, to pain that only she must bear. That these sacrifices have from the beginning of the human race been endured by woman with a pride that ennobles her in the eyes of others and gives to the infant a bond of love cannot alone be grounds for the State to insist she make the sacrifice. Her suffering is too intimate and personal for the State to insist, without more, upon its own vision of the woman's role, however dominant that vision has been in the course of our history and our culture. The destiny of the woman must be shaped to a large extent on her own conception of her spiritual imperatives and her place in society. . . .

III

A . . .

[W]hen this Court reexamines a prior holding, its judgment is customarily informed by a series of prudential and pragmatic considerations designed to test the consistency of overruling a prior decision with the ideal of the rule of law, and to gauge the respective costs of reaffirming and overruling a prior case. Thus, for example, we may ask whether the rule has proved to be intolerable simply in defying practical workability; whether the rule is subject to a kind of reliance that would lend a special hardship to the consequences of overruling and add inequity to the cost of repudiation; whether related principles of law have so far developed as to have left the old rule no more than a remnant of abandoned doctrine; or whether facts have so changed or come to be seen so differently, as to have robbed the old rule of significant application or justification.

So in this case we may inquire whether *Roe's* central rule has been found unworkable; whether the rule's limitation on state power could be removed without serious inequity to those who have relied upon it or significant damage to the stability of the society governed by the rule in question; whether the law's growth in the intervening years has left *Roe's* central rule a doctrinal anachronism discounted by society; and whether *Roe's* premises of fact have so far changed in the ensuing two decades as to render its central holding somehow irrelevant or unjustifiable in dealing with the issue it addressed.

1

Although *Roe* has engendered opposition, it has in no sense proven "unworkable," representing as it does a simple limitation beyond which a state law is unenforceable. While *Roe* has, of course, required judicial assessment of state laws affecting the exercise of the choice guaranteed against government infringement, and although the need for such review will remain as a consequence of today's decision, the required determinations fall within judicial competence.

2

The inquiry into reliance counts the cost of a rule's repudiation as it would fall on those who have relied reasonably on the rule's continued application....

[F]or two decades of economic and social developments, people have organized intimate relationships and made choices that define their views of themselves and their places in society, in reliance on the availability of abortion in the event that contraception should fail. The ability of women to participate equally in the economic and social life of the Nation has been facilitated by their ability to control their reproductive lives. The Constitution serves human values, and while the effect of reliance on *Roe* cannot be exactly measured, neither can the certain cost of overruling *Roe* for people who have ordered their thinking and living around that case be dismissed.

3

No evolution of legal principle has left *Roe's* doctrinal footings weaker than they were in 1973. No development of constitutional law since the case was decided has implicitly or explicitly left *Roe* behind as a mere survivor of obsolete constitutional thinking....

Roe ... may be seen not only as an exemplar of *Griswold* liberty but as a rule (whether or not mistaken) of personal autonomy and bodily integrity, with doctrinal affinity to cases recognizing limits on governmental power to mandate medical treatment or to bar its rejection. If so, our cases since *Roe* accord with *Roe*'s view that a State's interest in the protection of life falls short of justifying any plenary override of individual liberty claims....

Nor will courts building upon *Roe* be likely to hand down erroneous decisions as a consequence. Even on the assumption that the central holding of *Roe* was in error, that error would go only to the strength of the state interest in fetal protection, not to the recognition afforded by the Constitution to the woman's liberty....

The soundness of this prong of the *Roe* analysis is apparent from a consideration of the alternative. If indeed the woman's interest in deciding whether to bear and beget a child had not been recognized as in *Roe*, the State might as readily restrict a woman's right to choose to carry a pregnancy to term as to terminate it, to further asserted state interests in population control, or eugenics, for example. Yet *Roe* has been sensibly relied upon to counter any such suggestions. In any event, because *Roe*'s scope is confined by the fact of its concern with postconception potential life, a concern otherwise likely to be implicated only by some forms of contraception protected independently under *Griswold* and later cases, any error in *Roe* is unlikely to have serious ramifications in future cases.

4

We have seen how time has overtaken some of *Roe*'s factual assumptions: advances in maternal health care allow for abortions safe to the mother later in pregnancy than was true in 1973, and advances in neonatal care have advanced viability to a point somewhat earlier. But ... [t]he soundness or unsoundness of that constitutional judgment in no sense turns on whether viability occurs at approximately 28 weeks, as was usual at the time of *Roe*, at 23 to 24 weeks, as it sometimes does today, or at some moment even slightly earlier in pregnancy, as it may if fetal respiratory capacity can somehow be enhanced in the future....

C

The Court's duty in the present case is clear. In 1973, it confronted the already-divisive issue of governmental power to limit personal choice to undergo abortion, for which it provided a new resolution based on the due process guaranteed by the Fourteenth Amendment. Whether or not a new social consensus is developing on that issue, its divisiveness is no less today than in 1973, and pressure to overrule the decision, like pressure to retain it, has grown only more intense. A decision to overrule *Roe*'s essential holding under the existing circumstances would address error, if error there was, at the cost of both profound and unnecessary damage to the Court's legitimacy, and to the Nation's commitment to the rule of law. It is therefore imperative to adhere to the essence of *Roe*'s original decision, and we do so today.

IV ...

The woman's liberty is not so unlimited, however, that from the outset the State cannot show its concern for the life of the unborn, and at a later point in fetal development the State's interest in life has sufficient force so that the right of the woman to terminate the pregnancy can be restricted....

We conclude the line should be drawn at viability, so that before that time the woman has a right to choose to terminate her pregnancy. We adhere to this principle for two reasons. First, as we have said, is the doctrine of stare decisis....

The second reason is that the concept of viability, as we noted in *Roe*, is the time at which there is a realistic possibility of maintaining and nourishing a life outside the womb, so that the independent existence of the second life can in reason and all fairness be the object of state protection that now overrides the rights of the woman. Consistent with other constitutional norms, legislatures may draw lines which appear arbitrary without the necessity of offering a justification. But courts may not. We must justify the lines we draw. And there is no line other than viability which is more workable.... The viability line also has, as a practical matter, an element of fairness. In some broad sense it might be said that a woman who fails to act before viability has consented to the State's intervention on behalf of the developing child....

On the other side of the equation is the interest of the State in the protection of potential life.... The matter is not before us in the first instance, and coming as it does after nearly 20 years of litigation in *Roe*'s wake we are satisfied that the immediate question is not the soundness of *Roe*'s resolution of the issue, but the precedential force that must be accorded to its holding....

Yet it must be remembered that *Roe v. Wade* speaks with clarity in establishing not only the woman's liberty but also the State's "important and legitimate interest in potential life." That portion of the decision in *Roe* has been given too little acknowledgment and implementation by the Court in its subsequent cases. Those cases decided that any regulation touching upon the abortion decision must survive strict scrutiny, to be sustained only if drawn in narrow terms to further a compelling state interest. Not all of the cases decided under that formulation can be reconciled with the holding in *Roe* itself that the State has legitimate interests in the health of the woman and in protecting the potential life within her....

Roe established a trimester framework to govern abortion regulations. Under this elaborate but rigid construct, almost no regulation at all is permitted during the first trimester of pregnancy; regulations designed to protect the woman's health, but not to further the State's interest in potential life, are permitted during the second trimester; and during the third trimester, when the fetus is viable, prohibitions are permitted provided the life or health of the mother is not at stake. Most of our cases since *Roe* have involved the application of rules derived from the trimester framework....

We reject the trimester framework, which we do not consider to be part of the essential holding of *Roe*.... The trimester framework suffers from these basic flaws: in its formulation it misconceives the nature of the pregnant woman's interest; and in practice it undervalues the State's interest in potential life, as recognized in *Roe*....

The very notion that the State has a substantial interest in potential life leads to the conclusion that not all regulations must be deemed unwarranted. Not all burdens on the right to decide whether to terminate a pregnancy will be undue. In our view, the undue burden standard is the appropriate means of reconciling the State's interest with the woman's constitutionally protected liberty....

A finding of an undue burden is a shorthand for the conclusion that a state regulation has the purpose or effect of placing a substantial obstacle in the path of a woman seeking an abortion of a nonviable fetus. A statute with this purpose is invalid because the means chosen by the State to further the interest in potential life must be calculated to inform the woman's free choice, not hinder it. And a statute which, while furthering the interest in potential life or some other valid state interest, has the effect of placing a substantial obstacle in the path of a woman's choice cannot be considered a permissible means of serving its legitimate ends....

V

The Court of Appeals applied what it believed to be the undue burden standard and upheld each of the provisions except for the husband notification requirement. We agree generally with this conclusion, but refine the undue burden analysis in accordance with the principles articulated above. We now consider the separate statutory sections at issue....

C

Section 3209 of Pennsylvania's abortion law provides, except in cases of medical emergency, that no physician shall perform an abortion on a married woman without receiving a signed statement from the woman that she has notified her spouse that she is about to undergo an abortion. The woman has the option of providing an alternative signed statement certifying that her husband is not the man who impregnated her; that her husband could not be located; that the pregnancy is the result of spousal sexual assault which she has reported; or that the woman believes that notifying her husband will cause him or someone else to inflict bodily injury upon her. A physician who performs an abortion on a married woman without receiving the appropriate signed statement will have his or her license revoked, and is liable to the husband for damages....

In well-functioning marriages, spouses discuss important intimate decisions such as whether to bear a child. But there are millions of women in this country who are the victims of regular physical and psychological abuse at the hands of their husbands. Should these women become pregnant, they may have very good reasons for not wishing to inform their husbands of their decision to obtain an abortion....

The unfortunate yet persisting conditions we document above will mean that in a large fraction of the cases in which § 3209 is relevant, it will operate as a substantial obstacle to a woman's choice to undergo an abortion. It is an undue burden, and therefore invalid....

REHNQUIST, C.J., and WHITE, SCALIA, and THOMAS, JJ., concurring in the judgment in part and dissenting in part.

The joint opinion, following its newly-minted variation on stare decisis, retains the outer shell of *Roe v. Wade*, but beats a wholesale retreat from the substance of that case. We believe that *Roe* was wrongly decided, and that it can and should be overruled consistently with our traditional approach to stare decisis in constitutional cases....

SCALIA, WHITE, THOMAS, JJ., and REHNQUIST, C.J., concurring in the judgment in part and dissenting in part.

My views on this matter are unchanged from those I set forth in my separate opinions in *Webster v. Reproductive Health Services,* and *Ohio v. Akron Center for Reproductive Health*. The States may, if they wish, permit abortion-on-demand, but the Constitution does not require them to do so. The permissibility of abortion, and the limitations upon it, are to be resolved like most important questions in our democracy: by citizens trying to persuade one another and then voting. As the Court acknowledges, "where reasonable people disagree the government can adopt one position or the other." The Court is correct in adding the qualification that this "assumes a state of affairs in which the choice does not intrude upon a protected liberty," but the crucial part of that qualification is the penultimate word. A State's choice between two positions on which reasonable people can disagree is constitutional even when (as is often the case) it intrudes upon a "liberty" in the absolute sense. Laws against bigamy, for example—which entire societies of reasonable people disagree with—intrude upon men and women's liberty to marry and live with one another. But bigamy happens not to be a liberty specially "protected" by the Constitution.

That is, quite simply, the issue in this case: not whether the power of a woman to abort her unborn child is a "liberty" in the absolute sense; or even whether it is a liberty of great importance to many women. Of course it is both. The issue is whether it is a liberty protected by the Constitution of the United States. I am sure it is not. I reach that conclusion not because of anything so exalted as my views concerning the "concept of existence, of meaning, of the universe, and of the mystery of human life." Rather, I reach it for the same reason I reach the conclusion that bigamy is not constitutionally protected—because of two simple facts: (1) the Constitution says absolutely nothing about it, and (2) the longstanding traditions of American society have permitted it to be legally proscribed....

The ultimately standardless nature of the "undue burden" inquiry is a reflection of the underlying fact that the concept has no principled or coherent legal basis.... The "undue burden" standard is not at all the generally applicable principle the joint opinion pretends it to be; rather, it is a unique concept created specially for this case, to preserve some judicial foothold in this ill-gotten territory. In claiming otherwise, the three Justices show their willingness to place all constitutional rights at risk in an effort to preserve what they deem the "central holding in *Roe*." ...

In truth, I am as distressed as the Court is and expressed my distress several years ago, about the "political pressure" directed to the Court: the marches, the mail, the protests aimed at inducing us to change our opinions. How upsetting it is, that so many of our citizens (good people, not lawless ones, on both sides of this abortion issue, and on various sides of other issues as well) think that we Justices should properly take into account their views, as though we were engaged not in ascertaining an objective law but in determining some kind of social consensus. The Court would profit, I think, from giving less attention to the fact of this distressing phenomenon, and more attention to the cause of it. That cause permeates today's opinion: a new mode of constitutional adjudication that relies not upon text and traditional practice to determine the law, but upon what the Court calls "reasoned judgment," which turns out to be nothing but philosophical predilection and moral intuition. All manner of "liberties," the Court tells us, inhere in the Constitution and are enforceable by this Court—not just those mentioned in the text or established in the traditions of our society. Why even the Ninth Amendment which says only that "the enumeration in the Constitution of certain rights shall not be construed to deny or disparage others retained by the people"—is, despite our contrary understanding for almost 200 years, a literally boundless source of additional, unnamed, unhinted-at "rights," definable and enforceable by us, through "reasoned judgment."

What makes all this relevant to the bothersome application of "political pressure" against the Court are the twin facts that the American people love democracy and the American people are not fools. As long as this Court thought (and the people thought) that we Justices were doing essentially lawyers' work up here—reading text and discerning our society's traditional understanding of that text—the public pretty much left us alone. Texts and traditions are facts to study, not convictions to demonstrate about. But if in reality our process of constitutional adjudication consists primarily of making value judgments; if we can ignore a long and clear tradition clarifying an ambiguous text, as we did, for example, five days ago in declaring unconstitutional invocations and benedictions at public-high-school graduation ceremonies, if, as I say, our pronouncement of constitutional law rests primarily on value judgments, then a free and intelligent people's attitude towards us can be expected to be (ought to be) quite different. The people know that their value judgments are quite as good as those taught in any law school—maybe better. . . .

Notes and Questions: Casey *and the Privacy Doctrine*

(1) What is an "undue burden"? How workable, in other words, is the Court's new test? Does it, as the dissent suggests, invite yet more litigation? Does it give legislatures accurate guidance about how they might attempt to regulate the provision of abortions? Will the "undue burden" test actually result in different results from the ones the Court was already reaching under its earlier test?

(2) Does *Casey's* pragmatic reasoning—that to go back to a pre-*Roe* world would upset much of the progress women have made in the job market and elsewhere, or that to require women to consult with their husbands before abortion might lead to more spousal abuse—satisfy the competing demands of family and individual privacy typified by *McGuire* and *Griswold*?

(3) How persuaded are you by the equality argument: that the right to abortion is necessary in order to make women the constitutional

equivalents of men? Could *Roe* properly—or even better—have been based on the Equal Protection rather than the Due Process Clause of the Fourteenth Amendment? Given the controversial nature of substantive due process, why wasn't it decided on that basis? If it had been decided on that basis, should the Court's analysis of the state's interests been any different? What other areas of law and life might be subject to the same kind of analysis?

(4) Protests against abortion and violence directed against clinic employees continue to be problems. In *National Organization for Women v. Scheidler*, 510 US 1215 (1994), women's groups and health care clinics alleged that a coalition of anti-abortion groups were members of a nationwide conspiracy to shut down abortion clinics through a pattern of racketeering activity including extortion. They were allowed to proceed under the RICO (Racketeer Influenced and Corrupt Organizations) sections of the federal criminal code even though the alleged conspirators had no economic motive.

(5) What kind of precedent is *Casey* outside the law of abortion? Courts (see, e.g., *Compassion in Dying v. Washington*, 79 F3d 790 (9th Cir 1996)) and commentators have been particularly taken with one passage from *Casey*: "These matters, involving the most intimate and personal choices a person may make in a lifetime, choices central to personal dignity and autonomy, are central to the liberty protected by the Fourteenth Amendment. At the heart of liberty is the right to define one's own concept of existence, of meaning, of the universe, and of the mystery of human life." What does this passage mean? How much constitutional weight can it bear?

(5) Coda

The struggle between the Supreme Court, Congress, and many states continues. As one tendentious but informative observer reports:

> [E]ach year since 1995, Congress has enacted legislation to restrict late-term abortion, and each year President Clinton has either vetoed or threatened to veto it. During the sequence of votes and vetoes, each side has gone out of its way to make itself look bad. Pro-life members of Congress have proposed absolute bans that make no provision for protecting the life of the mother, which undermines their claim to revere life. Senator Diane Feinstein of California, in what was surely one of the all-time lows for American liberalism, brought to the Senate floor a bill intended to affirm a woman's right to terminate a healthy, viable late-term fetus.

Gregg Easterbrook, *Abortion and Brain Waves*, New Republic 21, 25 (January 31, 2000). The Supreme Court's encounter with this issue provoked what has become the customary profusion of opinions: Justice Breyer wrote an opinion for the Court. Justice Stevens filed a concurring opinion in which Justice Ginsburg joined. Justice O'Connor filed a concurring opinion. Justice Ginsburg filed a concurring opinion in which Justice Stevens joined. Chief Justice Rehnquist filed a dissenting opinion. Justice Scalia filed a dissenting opinion. Justice Kennedy filed a dissenting opinion in which Chief Justice Rehnquist joined. Justice Thomas filed a dissenting opinion in which Chief Justice Rehnquist and Justice Scalia joined.

STENBERG v. CARHART

Supreme Court of the United States, 2000
530 US 914

Breyer, J. . . .

[A Nebraska] statute reads as follows:

> "No partial birth abortion shall be performed in this state, unless such procedure is necessary to save the life of the mother whose life is endangered by a physical disorder, physical illness, or physical injury, including a life-endangering physical condition caused by or arising from the pregnancy itself." Neb.Rev.Stat. Ann. § 28–328(1) (Supp.1999).

The statute defines "partial birth abortion" as:

> "an abortion procedure in which the person performing the abortion partially delivers vaginally a living unborn child before killing the unborn child and completing the delivery." § 28–326(9).

It further defines "partially delivers vaginally a living unborn child before killing the unborn child" to mean

> "deliberately and intentionally delivering into the vagina a living unborn child, or a substantial portion thereof, for the purpose of performing a procedure that the person performing such procedure knows will kill the unborn child and does kill the unborn child." . . .

I. . . .

B

Because Nebraska law seeks to ban one method of aborting a pregnancy, we must describe and then discuss several different abortion procedures. . . .

The evidence before the trial court, as supported or supplemented in the literature, indicates the following:

1. About 90% of all abortions performed in the United States take place during the first trimester of pregnancy, before 12 weeks of gestational age. During the first trimester, the predominant abortion method is "vacuum aspiration," which involves insertion of a vacuum tube (cannula) into the uterus to evacuate the contents. . . . Vacuum aspiration is considered particularly safe. . . . As the fetus grows in size, however, the vacuum aspiration method becomes increasingly difficult to use.

2. Approximately 10% of all abortions are performed during the second trimester of pregnancy (12 to 24 weeks). In the early 1970's, inducing labor through the injection of saline into the uterus was the

predominant method of second trimester abortion. Today, however, the medical profession has switched from medical induction of labor to surgical procedures for most second trimester abortions. The most commonly used procedure is called "dilation and evacuation" (D & E). That procedure (together with a modified form of vacuum aspiration used in the early second trimester) accounts for about 95% of all abortions performed from 12 to 20 weeks of gestational age.

3. D & E "refers generically to transcervical procedures performed at 13 weeks gestation or later." The AMA Report, adopted by the District Court, describes the process as follows.

Between 13 and 15 weeks of gestation:

> "D & E is similar to vacuum aspiration except that the cervix must be dilated more widely because surgical instruments are used to remove larger pieces of tissue. Osmotic dilators are usually used. Intravenous fluids and an analgesic or sedative may be administered. A local anesthetic such as a paracervical block may be administered, dilating agents, if used, are removed and instruments are inserted through the cervix into the uterus to remove all fetal and placental tissue. Because fetal tissue is friable and easily broken, the fetus may not be removed intact. The walls of the uterus are scraped with a curette to ensure that no tissue remains."

After 15 weeks:

> "Because the fetus is larger at this stage of gestation (particularly the head), and because bones are more rigid, dismemberment or other destructive procedures are more likely to be required than at earlier gestational ages to remove fetal and placental tissue."

After 20 weeks:

> "Some physicians use intrafetal potassium chloride or digoxin to induce fetal demise prior to a late D & E (after 20 weeks), to facilitate evacuation."

There are variations in D & E operative strategy. However, the common points are that D & E involves (1) dilation of the cervix; (2) removal of at least some fetal tissue using nonvacuum instruments; and (3) (after the 15th week) the potential need for instrumental disarticulation or dismemberment of the fetus or the collapse of fetal parts to facilitate evacuation from the uterus.

4. When instrumental disarticulation incident to D & E is necessary, it typically occurs as the doctor pulls a portion of the fetus through the cervix into the birth canal. Dr. Carhart testified at trial as follows:

> "Dr. Carhart: ... 'The dismemberment occurs between the traction of ... my instrument and the counter-traction of the internal os of the cervix....
>
> "Counsel: 'So the dismemberment occurs after you pulled a part of the fetus through the cervix, is that correct?

"Dr. Carhart: 'Exactly. Because you're using—The cervix has two strictures or two rings, the internal os and the external os ... that's what's actually doing the dismembering....

5. The D & E procedure carries certain risks.... Nonetheless studies show that the risks of mortality and complication that accompany the D & E procedure between the 12th and 20th weeks of gestation are significantly lower than those accompanying induced labor procedures (the next safest midsecond trimester procedures).

6. At trial, Dr. Carhart and Dr. Stubblefield described a variation of the D & E procedure, which they referred to as an "intact D & E." Like other versions of the D & E technique, it begins with induced dilation of the cervix. The procedure then involves removing the fetus from the uterus through the cervix "intact," i.e., in one pass, rather than in several passes. The intact D & E proceeds in one of two ways, depending on the presentation of the fetus. If the fetus presents head first (a vertex presentation), the doctor collapses the skull; and the doctor then extracts the entire fetus through the cervix. If the fetus presents feet first (a breech presentation), the doctor pulls the fetal body through the cervix, collapses the skull, and extracts the fetus through the cervix .. The breech extraction version of the intact D & E is also known commonly as "dilation and extraction," or D & X. In the late second trimester, vertex, breech, and traverse/compound (sideways) presentations occur in roughly similar proportions....

8. The American College of Obstetricians and Gynecologists describes the D & X procedure in a manner corresponding to a breech-conversion intact D & E, including the following steps:

"1. deliberate dilatation of the cervix, usually over a sequence of days;

"2. instrumental conversion of the fetus to a footling breech;

"3. breech extraction of the body excepting the head; and

"4. partial evacuation of the intracranial contents of a living fetus to effect vaginal delivery of a dead but otherwise intact fetus."

Despite the technical differences we have just described, intact D & E and D & X are sufficiently similar for us to use the terms interchangeably.

9. Dr. Carhart testified he attempts to use the intact D & E procedure during weeks 16 to 20 because (1) it reduces the dangers from sharp bone fragments passing through the cervix, (2) minimizes the number of instrument passes needed for extraction and lessens the likelihood of uterine perforations caused by those instruments, (3) reduces the likelihood of leaving infection-causing fetal and placental tissue in the uterus, and (4) could help to prevent potentially fatal absorption of fetal tissue into the maternal circulation.... The District Court concluded ... that "the evidence is both clear and convincing that Carhart's D & X procedure is superior to, and safer than, the ... other

abortion procedures used during the relevant gestational period in the 10 to 20 cases a year that present to Dr. Carhart."

10. The materials presented at trial referred to the potential benefits of the D & X procedure in circumstances involving nonviable fetuses, such as fetuses with abnormal fluid accumulation in the brain (hydrocephaly).... (D & X "may be especially useful in the presence of fetal anomalies, such as hydrocephalus," because its reduction of the cranium allows "a smaller diameter to pass through the cervix, thus reducing risk of cervical injury"). Others have emphasized its potential for women with prior uterine scars, or for women for whom induction of labor would be particularly dangerous.

11. There are no reliable data on the number of D & X abortions performed annually. Estimates have ranged between 640 and 5,000 per year.

II

The question before us is whether Nebraska's statute, making criminal the performance of a "partial birth abortion," violates the Federal Constitution, as interpreted in *Planned Parenthood of Southeastern Pa. v. Casey* and *Roe v. Wade*. We conclude that it does for at least two independent reasons. First, the law lacks any exception " 'for the preservation of the ... health of the mother.' " Casey (joint opinion of O'CONNOR, KENNEDY, and SOUTER, JJ.). Second, it "imposes an undue burden on a woman's ability" to choose a D & E abortion, thereby unduly burdening the right to choose abortion itself. Id. We shall discuss each of these reasons in turn.

A

The *Casey* joint opinion reiterated what the Court held in *Roe*; that " 'subsequent to viability, the State in promoting its interest in the potentiality of human life may, if it chooses, regulate, and even proscribe, abortion except where it is necessary, in appropriate medical judgment, for the preservation of the life or health of the mother.' "

The fact that Nebraska's law applies both pre-and postviability aggravates the constitutional problem presented. The State's interest in regulating abortion previability is considerably weaker than postviability. Since the law requires a health exception in order to validate even a postviability abortion regulation, it at a minimum requires the same in respect to previability regulation.

The quoted standard also depends on the state regulations "promoting [the State's] interest in the potentiality of human life." The Nebraska law, of course, does not directly further an interest "in the potentiality of human life" by saving the fetus in question from destruction, as it regulates only a method of performing abortion. Nebraska describes its interests differently. It says the law " 'show[s] concern for the life of the unborn,' " "prevent[s] cruelty to partially born children," and "preserve[s] the integrity of the medical profession." But we cannot see how the interest-related differences could make any difference to the question at hand, namely, the application of the "health" requirement....

1

Nebraska responds that the law does not require a health exception unless there is a need for such an exception. And here there is no such need, it says. It argues that "safe alternatives remain available" and "a ban on partial-birth abortion/D & X would create no risk to the health of women." The problem for Nebraska is that the parties strongly contested this factual question in the trial court below; and the findings and evidence support Dr. Carhart. The State fails to demonstrate that banning D & X without a health exception may not create significant health risks for women, because the record shows that significant medical authority supports the proposition that in some circumstances, D & X would be the safest procedure....

On the basis of medical testimony the District Court concluded that "Carhart's D & X procedure is ... safer tha[n] the D & E and other abortion procedures used during the relevant gestational period in the 10 to 20 cases a year that present to Dr. Carhart." It found that the D & X procedure permits the fetus to pass through the cervix with a minimum of instrumentation. It thereby

> "reduces operating time, blood loss and risk of infection; reduces complications from bony fragments; reduces instrument-inflicted damage to the uterus and cervix; prevents the most common causes of maternal mortality (DIC and amniotic fluid embolus); and eliminates the possibility of 'horrible complications' arising from retained fetal parts."

The District Court also noted that a select panel of the American College of Obstetricians and Gynecologists concluded that D & X " 'may be the best or most appropriate procedure in a particular circumstance to save the life or preserve the health of a woman.' " ...

2

Nebraska, along with supporting amici, replies that these findings are irrelevant, wrong, or applicable only in a tiny number of instances. It says (1) that the D & X procedure is "little-used," (2) by only "a handful of doctors." It argues (3) that D & E and labor induction are at all times "safe alternative procedures." Id., at 36. It refers to the testimony of petitioners' medical expert, who testified (4) that the ban would not increase a woman's risk of several rare abortion complications....

3

We find these ... arguments insufficient to demonstrate that Nebraska's law needs no health exception. For one thing, certain of the arguments are beside the point. The D & X procedure's relative rarity ... is not highly relevant. The D & X is an infrequently used abortion procedure; but the health exception question is whether protecting women's health requires an exception for those infrequent occasions....

For another thing, the record responds to Nebraska's (and amici's) medically based arguments....

4

The upshot is a District Court finding that D & X significantly obviates health risks in certain circumstances, a highly plausible record-based explanation of why that might be so, a division of opinion among some medical experts over whether D & X is generally safer, and an absence of controlled medical studies that would help answer these medical questions. Given these medically related evidentiary circumstances, we believe the law requires a health exception....

In sum, Nebraska has not convinced us that a health exception is "never necessary to preserve the health of women." Rather, a statute that altogether forbids D & X creates a significant health risk. The statute consequently must contain a health exception. This is not to say, as Justice THOMAS and Justice KENNEDY claim, that a State is prohibited from proscribing an abortion procedure whenever a particular physician deems the procedure preferable. By no means must a State grant physicians "unfettered discretion" in their selection of abortion methods. But where substantial medical authority supports the proposition that banning a particular abortion procedure could endanger women's health, *Casey* requires the statute to include a health exception when the procedure is " 'necessary, in appropriate medical judgment, for the preservation of the life or health of the mother.' " ...

B

The Eighth Circuit found the Nebraska statute unconstitutional because, in *Casey*'s words, it has the "effect of placing a substantial obstacle in the path of a woman seeking an abortion of a nonviable fetus." It thereby places an "undue burden" upon a woman's right to terminate her pregnancy before viability. Nebraska does not deny that the statute imposes an "undue burden" if it applies to the more commonly used D & E procedure as well as to D & X. And we agree with the Eighth Circuit that it does so apply.

Our earlier discussion of the D & E procedure shows that it falls within the statutory prohibition. The statute forbids "deliberately and intentionally delivering into the vagina a living unborn child, or a substantial portion thereof, for the purpose of performing a procedure that the person performing such procedure knows will kill the unborn child." We do not understand how one could distinguish, using this language, between D & E (where a foot or arm is drawn through the cervix) and D & X (where the body up to the head is drawn through the cervix). Evidence before the trial court makes clear that D & E will often involve a physician pulling a "substantial portion" of a still living fetus, say, an arm or leg, into the vagina prior to the death of the fetus. Indeed

D & E involves dismemberment that commonly occurs only when the fetus meets resistance that restricts the motion of the fetus.... And these events often do not occur until after a portion of a living fetus has been pulled into the vagina.

Even if the statute's basic aim is to ban D & X, its language makes clear that it also covers a much broader category of procedures. The language does not track the medical differences between D & E and D & X—though it would have been a simple matter, for example, to provide an exception for the performance of D & E and other abortion procedures. E.g., Kan. Stat. Ann. § 65–6721(b)(1) (Supp.1999). Nor does the statute anywhere suggest that its application turns on whether a portion of the fetus' body is drawn into the vagina as part of a process to extract an intact fetus after collapsing the head as opposed to a process that would dismember the fetus. Thus, the dissenters' argument that the law was generally intended to bar D & X can be both correct and irrelevant. The relevant question is not whether the legislature wanted to ban D & X; it is whether the law was intended to apply only to D & X. The plain language covers both procedures.... Both procedures can involve the introduction of a "substantial portion" of a still living fetus, through the cervix, into the vagina—the very feature of an abortion that leads Justice THOMAS to characterize such a procedure as involving "partial birth." ...

In sum, using this law some present prosecutors and future Attorneys General may choose to pursue physicians who use D & E procedures, the most commonly used method for performing previability second trimester abortions. All those who perform abortion procedures using that method must fear prosecution, conviction, and imprisonment. The result is an undue burden upon a woman's right to make an abortion decision. We must consequently find the statute unconstitutional.

STEVENS, J., concurring.

Although much ink is spilled today describing the gruesome nature of late-term abortion procedures, that rhetoric does not provide me a reason to believe that the procedure Nebraska here claims it seeks to ban is more brutal, more gruesome, or less respectful of "potential life" than the equally gruesome procedure Nebraska claims it still allows.... [The holding of *Roe v. Wade*]—that the word "liberty" in the Fourteenth Amendment includes a woman's right to make this difficult and extremely personal decision—makes it impossible for me to understand how a State has any legitimate interest in requiring a doctor to follow any procedure other than the one that he or she reasonably believes will best protect the woman in her exercise of this constitutional liberty....

SCALIA, J., dissenting.

I am optimistic enough to believe that, one day, *Stenberg v. Carhart* will be assigned its rightful place in the history of this Court's jurisprudence beside *Korematsu* and *Dred Scott*. The method of killing a human child—one cannot even accurately say an entirely unborn human child—

proscribed by this statute is so horrible that the most clinical description of it evokes a shudder of revulsion. And the Court must know (as most state legislatures banning this procedure have concluded) that demanding a "health exception"—which requires the abortionist to assure himself that, in his expert medical judgment, this method is, in the case at hand, marginally safer than others (how can one prove the contrary beyond a reasonable doubt?)—is to give live-birth abortion free rein. The notion that the Constitution of the United States ... prohibits the States from simply banning this visibly brutal means of eliminating our half-born posterity is quite simply absurd....

In my dissent in *Casey*, I wrote that the "undue burden" test made law by the joint opinion created a standard that was "as doubtful in application as it is unprincipled in origin," "hopelessly unworkable in practice," "ultimately standardless." Today's decision is the proof. As long as we are debating this issue of necessity for a health-of-the-mother exception on the basis of Casey, it is really quite impossible for us dissenters to contend that the majority is wrong on the law—any more than it could be said that one is wrong in law to support or oppose the death penalty, or to support or oppose mandatory minimum sentences. The most that we can honestly say is that we disagree with the majority on their policy-judgment-couched-as-law. And those who believe that a 5–to–4 vote on a policy matter by unelected lawyers should not overcome the judgment of 30 state legislatures have a problem, not with the application of *Casey*, but with its existence. *Casey* must be overruled.

While I am in an I-told-you-so mood, I must recall my bemusement, in *Casey*, at the joint opinion's expressed belief that *Roe v. Wade* had "call[ed] the contending sides of a national controversy to end their national division by accepting a common mandate rooted in the Constitution," and that the decision in Casey would ratify that happy truce. It seemed to me, quite to the contrary, that "*Roe* fanned into life an issue that has inflamed our national politics in general, and has obscured with its smoke the selection of Justices to this Court in particular, ever since"; and that, "by keeping us in the abortion-umpiring business, it is the perpetuation of that disruption, rather than of any *Pax Roeana*, that the Court's new majority decrees." Today's decision, that the Constitution of the United States prevents the prohibition of a horrible mode of abortion, will be greeted by a firestorm of criticism—as well it should. I cannot understand why those who acknowledge that, in the opening words of Justice O'CONNOR's concurrence, "[t]he issue of abortion is one of the most contentious and controversial in contemporary American society," persist in the belief that this Court, armed with neither constitutional text nor accepted tradition, can resolve that contention and controversy rather than be consumed by it. If only for the sake of its own preservation, the Court should return this matter to the people—where the Constitution, by its silence on the subject, left it—and let them decide, State by State, whether this practice should be allowed. *Casey* must be overruled.

KENNEDY, J., dissenting.

For close to two decades after *Roe v. Wade,* the Court gave but slight weight to the interests of the separate States when their legislatures sought to address persisting concerns raised by the existence of a woman's right to elect an abortion in defined circumstances. When the Court reaffirmed the essential holding of *Roe*, a central premise was that the States retain a critical and legitimate role in legislating on the subject of abortion, as limited by the woman's right the Court restated and again guaranteed. *Casey*. The political processes of the State are not to be foreclosed from enacting laws to promote the life of the unborn and to ensure respect for all human life and its potential. [Here Justice Kennedy cited the joint opinion in *Casey* which he had joined.] . . .

The Court's decision today, in my submission, repudiates this understanding by invalidating a statute advancing critical state interests, even though the law denies no woman the right to choose an abortion and places no undue burden upon the right. . . .

I

The Court's failure to accord any weight to Nebraska's interest in prohibiting partial-birth abortion is erroneous and undermines its discussion and holding. The Court's approach in this regard is revealed by its description of the abortion methods at issue, which the Court is correct to describe as "clinically cold or callous." The majority views the procedures from the perspective of the abortionist, rather than from the perspective of a society shocked when confronted with a new method of ending human life. Words invoked by the majority, such as "transcervical procedures," "[o]smotic dilators," "instrumental disarticulation," and "paracervical block," may be accurate and are to some extent necessary; but for citizens who seek to know why laws on this subject have been enacted across the Nation, the words are insufficient. Repeated references to sources understandable only to a trained physician may obscure matters for persons not trained in medical terminology. Thus it seems necessary at the outset to set forth what may happen during an abortion.

The person challenging Nebraska's law is Dr. Leroy Carhart, a physician who received his medical degree from Hahnemann Hospital and University in 1973. Dr. Carhart performs the procedures in a clinic in Nebraska and will also travel to Ohio to perform abortions there. Dr. Carhart has no specialty certifications in a field related to childbirth or abortion and lacks admitting privileges at any hospital. He performs abortions throughout pregnancy, including when he is unsure whether the fetus is viable. In contrast to the physicians who provided expert testimony in this case (who are board certified instructors at leading medical education institutions and members of the American Board of Obstetricians and Gynecologists), Dr. Carhart performs the partial-birth abortion procedure (D & X) that Nebraska seeks to ban. He also performs the other method of abortion at issue in the case, the D & E.

As described by Dr. Carhart, the D & E procedure requires the abortionist to use instruments to grasp a portion (such as a foot or hand) of a developed and living fetus and drag the grasped portion out of the uterus into the vagina. Dr. Carhart uses the traction created by the opening between the uterus and vagina to dismember the fetus, tearing the grasped portion away from the remainder of the body. The traction between the uterus and vagina is essential to the procedure because attempting to abort a fetus without using that traction is described by Dr. Carhart as "pulling the cat's tail" or "drag[ging] a string across the floor, you'll just keep dragging it. It's not until something grabs the other end that you are going to develop traction." The fetus, in many cases, dies just as a human adult or child would: It bleeds to death as it is torn from limb from limb. The fetus can be alive at the beginning of the dismemberment process and can survive for a time while its limbs are being torn off. Dr. Carhart agreed that "[w]hen you pull out a piece of the fetus, let's say, an arm or a leg and remove that, at the time just prior to removal of the portion of the fetus, ... the fetus [is] alive." Dr. Carhart has observed fetal heartbeat via ultrasound with "extensive parts of the fetus removed," and testified that mere dismemberment of a limb does not always cause death because he knows of a physician who removed the arm of a fetus only to have the fetus go on to be born "as a living child with one arm." At the conclusion of a D & E abortion no intact fetus remains. In Dr. Carhart's words, the abortionist is left with "a tray full of pieces."

The other procedure implicated today is called "partial-birth abortion" or the D & X. The D & X can be used, as a general matter, after 19 weeks gestation because the fetus has become so developed that it may survive intact partial delivery from the uterus into the vagina. In the D & X, the abortionist initiates the woman's natural delivery process by causing the cervix of the woman to be dilated, sometimes over a sequence of days. The fetus' arms and legs are delivered outside the uterus while the fetus is alive; witnesses to the procedure report seeing the body of the fetus moving outside the woman's body. At this point, the abortion procedure has the appearance of a live birth. As stated by one group of physicians, "[a]s the physician manually performs breech extraction of the body of a live fetus, excepting the head, she continues in the apparent role of an obstetrician delivering a child." Brief for Association of American Physicians and Surgeons et al. as Amici Curiae 27. With only the head of the fetus remaining in utero, the abortionist tears open the skull. According to Dr. Martin Haskell, a leading proponent of the procedure, the appropriate instrument to be used at this stage of the abortion is a pair of scissors. Witnesses report observing the portion of the fetus outside the woman react to the skull penetration. The abortionist then inserts a suction tube and vacuums out the developing brain and other matter found within the skull. The process of making the size of the fetus' head smaller is given the clinically neutral term "reduction procedure." Brain death does not occur until after the skull invasion, and, according to Dr. Carhart, the heart of the fetus may continue to beat for minutes after the contents of the skull are vacuumed out. The abortionist next completes the delivery of a dead fetus, intact except for the damage to the head and the missing contents of the skull.

Of the two described procedures, Nebraska seeks only to ban the D & X. In light of the description of the D & X procedure, it should go without saying that Nebraska's ban on partial-birth abortion furthers purposes States are entitled to pursue. Dr. Carhart nevertheless maintains the State has no legitimate interest in forbidding the D & X. As he interprets the controlling cases in this Court, the only two interests the State may advance through regulation of abortion are in the health of the woman who is considering the procedure and in the life of the fetus she carries. The Court, as I read its opinion, accedes to his views, misunderstanding *Casey* and the authorities it confirmed....

Casey is premised on the States having an important constitutional role in defining their interests in the abortion debate. It is only with this principle in mind that Nebraska's interests can be given proper weight. The State's brief describes its interests as including concern for the life of the unborn and "for the partially-born," in preserving the integrity of the medical profession, and in "erecting a barrier to infanticide." A review of Casey demonstrates the legitimacy of these policies. The Court should say so.

States may take sides in the abortion debate and come down on the side of life, even life in the unborn:

> "Even in the earliest stages of pregnancy, the State may enact rules and regulations designed to encourage [a woman] to know that there are philosophic and social arguments of great weight that can be brought to bear in favor of continuing the pregnancy to full term and that there are procedures and institutions to allow adoption of unwanted children as well as a certain degree of state assistance if the mother chooses to raise the child herself." *Casey*, 505 U.S., at 872 (joint opinion of O'CONNOR, KENNEDY, and SOUTER, JJ.).

States also have an interest in forbidding medical procedures which, in the State's reasonable determination, might cause the medical profession or society as a whole to become insensitive, even disdainful, to life, including life in the human fetus. Abortion, *Casey* held, has consequences beyond the woman and her fetus. The States' interests in regulating are of concomitant extension. *Casey* recognized that abortion is, "fraught with consequences for ... the persons who perform and assist in the procedure [and for] society which must confront the knowledge that these procedures exist, procedures some deem nothing short of an act of violence against innocent human life." *Id.*, at 852, 112 S.Ct. 2791....

Casey demonstrates that the interests asserted by the State are legitimate and recognized by law. It is argued, however, that a ban on the D & X does not further these interests. This is because, the reasoning continues, the D & E method, which Nebraska claims to be beyond its intent to regulate, can still be used to abort a fetus and is no less dehumanizing than the D & X method. While not adopting the argument in express terms, the Court indicates tacit approval of it by refusing to reject it in a forthright manner. Rendering express what is only implicit in the majority opinion, Justice STEVENS and Justice GINSBURG are forthright in declaring that the two procedures are indistinguishable and that Nebraska has acted both irrationally and without a proper purpose in enacting the law. The issue is not whether members of the judiciary can see a difference between the two procedures. It is whether Nebraska can. The Court's refusal to recognize Nebraska's right to declare a moral difference between the procedure is a dispiriting disclosure of the illogic and illegitimacy of the Court's approach to the entire case.

Nebraska was entitled to find the existence of a consequential moral difference between the procedures. We are referred to substantial medical authority that D & X perverts the natural birth process to a greater degree than D & E, commandeering the live birth process until the skull is pierced. American Medical Association (AMA) publications describe the D & X abortion method as "ethically wrong." AMA Board of Trustees Factsheet on HR 1122 (June 1997), in App. to Brief for Association of American Physicians and Surgeons et al. as Amici Curiae 1 (AMA Factsheet). The D & X differs from the D & E because in the D & X the fetus is "killed outside of the womb" where the fetus has "an autonomy which separates it from the right of the woman to choose treatments for her own body." *Ibid.*; see also App. 639–640; Brief for Association of American Physicians and Surgeons et al. as Amici Curiae 27 ("Intact D & X is aberrant and troubling because the technique confuses the disparate role of a physician in childbirth and abortion in such a way as to blur the medical, legal, and ethical line between infanticide and abortion"). Witnesses to the procedure relate that the fingers and feet of the fetus are moving prior to the piercing of the skull; when the scissors are inserted in the back of the head, the fetus' body, wholly outside the woman's body and alive, reacts as though startled and goes limp. D & X's stronger resemblance to infanticide means Nebraska could conclude the procedure presents a greater risk of disrespect for life and a consequent greater risk to the profession and society, which depend for their sustenance upon reciprocal recognition of dignity and respect. The Court is without authority to second-guess this conclusion.

Those who oppose abortion would agree, indeed would insist, that both procedures are subject to the most severe moral condemnation, condemnation reserved for the most repulsive human conduct. This is not inconsistent, however, with the further proposition that as an ethical and moral matter D & X is distinct from D & E and is a more serious concern for medical ethics and the morality of the larger society the medical profession must serve. Nebraska must obey the legal regime which has declared the right of the woman to have an abortion before viability. Yet it retains its power to adopt regulations which do not impose an undue burden on the woman's right. By its regulation,

Nebraska instructs all participants in the abortion process, including the mother, of its moral judgment that all life, including the life of the unborn, is to be respected. The participants, Nebraska has determined, cannot be indifferent to the procedure used and must refrain from using the natural delivery process to kill the fetus. The differentiation between the procedures is itself a moral statement, serving to promote respect for human life; and if the woman and her physician in contemplating the moral consequences of the prohibited procedure conclude that grave moral consequences pertain to the permitted abortion process as well, the choice to elect or not to elect abortion is more informed; and the policy of promoting respect for life is advanced....

II

Demonstrating a further and basic misunderstanding of *Casey*, the Court holds the ban on the D & X procedure fails because it does not include an exception permitting an abortionist to perform a D & X whenever he believes it will best preserve the health of the woman. Casting aside the views of distinguished physicians and the statements of leading medical organizations, the Court awards each physician a veto power over the State's judgment that the procedures should not be performed. Dr. Carhart has made the medical judgment to use the D & X procedure in every case, regardless of indications, after 15 weeks gestation. Requiring Nebraska to defer to Dr. Carhart's judgment is no different than forbidding Nebraska from enacting a ban at all; for it is now Dr. Leroy Carhart who sets abortion policy for the State of Nebraska, not the legislature or the people. *Casey* does not give precedence to the views of a single physician or a group of physicians regarding the relative safety of a particular procedure....

Nebraska ... was entitled to conclude that its ban, while advancing important interests regarding the sanctity of life, deprived no woman of a safe abortion and therefore did not impose a substantial obstacle on the rights of any woman. The American College of Obstetricians and Gynecologists (ACOG) "could identify no circumstances under which [D & X] would be the only option to save the life or preserve the health of the woman." The American Medical Association agrees, stating the "AMA's expert panel, which included an ACOG representative, could not find 'any' identified circumstance where it was 'the only appropriate alternative.' "AMA Factsheet 1. The Court's conclusion that the D & X is the safest method requires it to replace the words "may be" with the word "is" in the following sentence from ACOG's position statement: "An intact D & X, however, may be the best or most appropriate procedure in a particular circumstance."

No studies support the contention that the D & X abortion method is safer than other abortion methods....

The Court cannot conclude the D & X is part of standard medical practice. It is telling that no expert called by Dr. Carhart, and no expert testifying in favor of the procedure, had in fact performed a partial-birth abortion in his or her medical practice.... Litigation in other jurisdictions establishes that physicians do not adopt the D & X procedure as part of standard medical practice. E.g., *Richmond Medical Center for Women v. Gilmore*, 144 F.3d 326, 328 (C.A.4 1998); *Hope Clinic v. Ryan*, 195 F.3d 857, 871 (C.A.7 1999). It is quite wrong for the Court to conclude, as it seems to have done here, that Dr. Carhart conforms his practice to the proper standard of care because he has incorporated the procedure into his practice. Neither Dr. Boehm nor Dr. Carhart's lead expert, Dr. Stubblefield (the chairman of the Department of Obstetrics and Gynecology at Boston University School of Medicine and director of obstetrics and gynecology for the Boston Medical Center) has done so....

Unsubstantiated and generalized health differences which are, at best, marginal, do not amount to a substantial obstacle to the abortion right. *Id.*, at 874, 876, 112 S.Ct. 2791 (joint opinion of O'CONNOR, KENNEDY, and SOUTER, JJ.). It is also important to recognize that the D & X is effective only when the fetus is close to viable or, in fact, viable; thus the State is regulating the process at the point where its interest in life is nearing its peak....

In deferring to the physician's judgment, the Court turns back to cases decided in the wake of *Roe*, cases which gave a physician's treatment decisions controlling weight. Before it was repudiated by *Casey*, the approach of deferring to physicians had reached its apex in *Akron*, where the Court held an informed consent requirement was unconstitutional. The law challenged in *Akron* ... was invalidated based on the physician's right to practice medicine in the way he or she saw fit; for, according to the *Akron* Court, "[i]t remains primarily the responsibility of the physician to ensure that appropriate information is conveyed to his patient, depending on her particular circumstances." Dispositive for the Court was that the law was an "intrusion upon the discretion of the pregnant woman's physician." The physician was placed in an "undesired and uncomfortable straitjacket." The Court's decision today echoes the *Akron* Court's deference to a physician's right to practice medicine in the way he sees fit....

Rather than exalting the right of a physician to practice medicine with unfettered discretion, *Casey* recognized: "Whatever constitutional status the doctor-patient relation may have as a general matter, in the present context it is derivative of the woman's position." ...

Instructive is *Jacobson v. Massachusetts*, 197 U.S. 11 (1905), where the defendant was convicted because he refused to undergo a smallpox vaccination. The defendant claimed the mandatory vaccination violated his liberty to "care for his own body and health in such way as to him seems best." He offered to prove that members of the medical profession took the position that the vaccination was of no value and, in fact, was harmful. The Court rejected the claim, establishing beyond doubt the right of the legislature to resolve matters upon which physicians disagreed....

JUSTICE O'CONNOR assures the people of Nebraska they are free to redraft the law to include an exception permitting the D & X to be performed when "the procedure, in appropriate medical judgment, is necessary to preserve the health of the mother." 5. The assurance is meaningless. She has joined an opinion which accepts that Dr. Carhart exercises "appropriate medical judgment" in using the D & X for every patient in every procedure, regardless of indications, after 15 weeks' gestation. *Ante* (requiring any health exception to "tolerate responsible differences of medical opinion" which "are present here."). A ban which depends on the "appropriate medical judgment" of Dr. Carhart is no ban at all....

In light of divided medical opinion on the propriety of the partial-birth abortion technique (both in terms of physical safety and ethical practice) and the vital interests asserted by Nebraska in its law, one is left to ask what the first Justice Harlan asked: "Upon what sound principles as to the relations existing between the different departments of government can the court review this action of the legislature?" *Jacobson*. The answer is none.

III

The Court's next holding is that Nebraska's ban forbids both the D & X procedure and the more common D & E procedure. In so ruling the Court misapplies settled doctrines of statutory construction and contradicts *Casey*'s premise that the States have a vital constitutional position in the abortion debate.... Like the ruling requiring a physician veto, requiring a State to meet unattainable standards of statutory draftsmanship in order to have its voice heard on this grave and difficult subject is no different from foreclosing state participation altogether....

IV

Ignoring substantial medical and ethical opinion, the Court substitutes its own judgment for the judgment of Nebraska and some 30 other States and sweeps the law away. The Court's holding stems from misunderstanding the record, misinterpretation of Casey, outright refusal to respect the law of a State, and statutory construction in conflict with settled rules. The decision nullifies a law expressing the will of the people of Nebraska that medical procedures must be governed by moral principles having their foundation in the intrinsic value of human life, including life of the unborn. Through their law the people of Nebraska were forthright in confronting an issue of immense moral consequence. The State chose to forbid a procedure many decent and civilized people find so abhorrent as to be among the most serious of crimes against human life, while the State still protected the woman's autonomous right of choice as reaffirmed in *Casey*. The Court closes its eyes to these profound concerns.

From the decision, the reasoning, and the judgment, I dissent.

Notes and Questions on Carhart

(1) How narrowly may the exception to protect the woman's "health" be written? Must it include an exception for emotional or psychological health? If so, is there any way to prevent the exception from swallowing up the rule? (The experience in many states that passed legislation before *Roe* that permitted abortions where necessary to protect the woman's health was that that restriction was not very confining.)

(2) What is the current status of *Casey*? Does *Carhart* work any change in that status?

(3) The saga of *Roe v. Wade* has made judicial review one of the principal constitutional issues of our time. That issue continues to be contested with exceptional passion. For example, the editors of the journal *First Things* published a symposium which they said "addresses many similarly troubling judicial actions that add up to an entrenched pattern of government by judges that is nothing less than the usurpation of politics. The question here explored, is whether we have reached or are reaching the point where conscientious citizens can no longer give moral assent to the existing regime." They continued:

> The proposition examined in the following essays is this: The government of the United States of America no longer governs by the consent of the governed. With respect to the American people, the judiciary has in effect declared that the most important questions about how we ought to order our life together are outside the purview of "things of their knowledge." ... The Supreme Court itself—notably in the *Casey* decision of 1992—has raised the alarm about the legitimacy of law in the present regime. Its proposed solution is that citizens should defer to the decisions of the court.

The Editors of *First Things*, *Introduction,* in Mitchell S. Muncy, ed, *The End of Democracy?: The Celebrated* First Things *Debate with Arguments Pro and Con and, "The Anatomy of a Controversy"* by Richard John Neuhaus 3, 5–6 (Spence Publishing, 1997).

(4) The United States today seems to continue to be experiencing sharp divisions over the question of abortion. Is there any way those apparently implacable disagreements might be compromised? Is this an issue as to which compromise is desirable? Important? What will happen if no compromise can be reached? Is the Court the right institution to try to find some compromise? Does the majority opinion in *Carhart* contribute to any such compromise?

A Problem

David Johnson brought suit against his employer, the University of Iowa ("University"), alleging that the University's Parental Leave Policy violated the Equal Protection Clause of the Fourteenth Amendment of the United States Constitution, the Equal Protection Clause of the Iowa Constitution, Title VII of the Civil Rights Act of 1964, and the Iowa Civil

Rights Act. The district court granted summary judgment to the defendants on all claims. *Johnson v. University of Iowa*, 408 F Supp 2d 728 (SD Iowa 2004). This opinion was affirmed by the Eighth Circuit Court of Appeals. 431 F3d 325 (8th Cir 2005).

In 2002, Johnson and his wife were expecting a baby girl. At that time, Johnson worked full-time in the Office of the Registrar at the University, and his wife worked part-time in the University's College of Nursing. While attending a class that explained the details of the University's Parental Leave Policy, Johnson was told that he, unlike his wife, could not use accrued sick leave to be paid for absences after the birth of their daughter.

The applicable portion of the Parental Leave Policy, as contained in Chapter 22 of the Operations Manual which governs the employment of Embree and Johnson, states:

22.8 PARENTAL LEAVE POLICY

a. Purpose. To permit parents who have care giving responsibilities to have time off to spend with a child newly added to the family and, to the extent permitted by state law, to be paid during such leave. To adapt an employee's work schedule and/or duties to help reduce conflict with parental obligations.

b. Entitlement to Leave.

(1) Twelve–Month Faculty, Professional, Scientific, and Non–Organized Merit System Staff.

(a) Biological mothers are entitled to leave for any period of pregnancy-related temporary disability, to be charged against accrued sick leave. Based on current medical practice, a leave of six weeks or less would not require the employee to provide disability documentation.

If an employee's accumulated sick leave is insufficient to cover the period of disability, the employee will, at the employee's request, be granted a leave of absence to be charged to vacation time, compensatory time, or a leave of absence without pay. Any request for absence beyond the period of disability is considered as a leave of absence without pay or as vacation.

(b) A newly adoptive parent, including a domestic partner, is entitled to one week (5 days) of paid adoption leave to be charged against accrued sick leave. Departments are encouraged to arrange for additional leave as necessary. Departments should work with prospective adoptive parents seeking to adopt through an adoption agency with specific requirements for parental leave, to the extent the adoption leave is not sufficient to undertake an adoption. Time not charged to accrued sick leave may be charged to accrued vacation or taken as leave without pay.

Johnson claimed that the University's paid leave policy discriminated against biological fathers of children (which he claimed was a suspect class) in violation of the equal protection clause of the Fourteenth Amendment and its counterpart in the Iowa Constitution, and violating Title VII or the Iowa Civil Rights Act. The court of appeals found, however, that because "biological fathers are not a suspect class and because the right to paid leave is not fundamental, the appropriate standard of review is the rational basis test." As you recall, a classification reviewed under this standard will be upheld "if it has some reasonable basis." Biological mothers, held the court, were receiving disability leave under the policy rather than parental leave (whether or not they were in fact disabled). The rational basis found by the Eighth Circuit was that adoptive parents face demands on their time and finances that may be significantly greater than those faced by biological parents. "For example, the benefits of the University's health insurance plan offset the medical costs arising when an employee or an employee's spouse gives birth. Adoptive parents receive no such insurance benefit to offset the costs of adoption. Adoptive parents may also be required to take time off from work to deal with adoption-related administrative concerns prior to the arrival of the child." Similarly, because there was no fundamental right to paid leave from an employer, the benefits given to adoptive parents only needed to survive a rational basis test to be upheld under Title VII. Since the University had articulated legitimate reasons for the classifications, they survived the challenge.

(1) The Johnson case illustrates distinctions laws involving parenting have made between women and men, same-sex versus opposite sex partnering, and adoption and birth parenting. What is the justification given for each of these distinctions? How does it play out during the child's development (pregnancy, childbirth, infancy, childhood)?

(2) Johnson's problem apparently involves both financial decisions made by the university (recognizing the smallest group who must be given benefits under the federal statute) and attitudes about women's autonomy coming from the abortion decisions. Can these really be reconciled? Should they be?

(3) The last question implies that gender politics (women's equality) plays a large role in at least this portion of family law. Should it? Does giving a woman prime decision-making power over pregnancy and childbirth (required by the abortion decisions we have already considered) disadvantage women in other territory, such as household bargaining or the labor force? Consider the following, which, with the *Johnson* case, may give some insight into continuing socially constructed gender differences:

ALPHA R. KATZEV, REBECCA L. WARNER, AND ALAN C. ACOCK
GIRLS OR BOYS? RELATIONSHIP OF CHILD GENDER TO MARITAL INSTABILITY

56 J Marriage & Family 89, 97 (1994)

While many effects discussed in this paper are small, they provide additional evidence that the gender of the children in the family has significant effects on the mother's perception of marital stability. It does matter whether a family has boys only, girls only, or a mix of both boys and girls. Having at least one boy reduced the mother's perception of the likelihood of separation or divorce. Previous research has found a greater proportion of couples with only daughters among those who had already divorced. We found evidence for similar effects of child gender on marital instability before marital dissolution took place.

We have argued that because boys continue to be more valued in our society, mothers with sons may feel more satisfied in their marriages and hence be less disposed to consider separation from their spouses. A second explanation may lie in the fact that boys of all ages experience more severe and longer lasting adjustment problems with family disruptions than girls do. The realization that divorce creates particular problems for the socialization of sons may factor into the mother's estimate of the likelihood that her marriage will end. In the present study, we were unable to test the relative importance of these two explanations for the direct effects of child gender on marital instability.

By far the strongest predictor of the likelihood of a separation was the mother's perception that the relationship was inequitable. Mothers who felt overbenefited in the relationship and those who felt disadvantaged were both more prone to consider divorce likely than were those who felt the division of marital responsibilities was fair to both partners....

The mechanism for the relationship between child gender and marital instability appears to lie in paternal involvement in family life, in that the time that fathers invested either in their children or in doing household chores was related to wives' perception of fairness about the division of household responsibility. But the effect of child gender was limited to fathers' interactions with children and hence may be focused on the institutionalized role fathers are viewed as playing in socializing sons....

Having at least one boy in the family increased the time fathers spent with the children as we predicted, but child gender did not directly affect the amount of gendered housework done by fathers....

SECTION 4. RECONSIDERING THE CONSTITUTIONALIZATION OF FAMILY LAW

The wisdom of the next social order, as I imagine it, would not reside in right doctrine, administered by the right men, who must be found, but rather in doctrines amounting to permission for each man to live an experimental life.... All governments will be just, so long as they secure that consoling plenitude of option in which modern satisfaction really consists.

Philip Rieff
The Triumph of the Therapeutic

A. RETREAT? REGRET? RETRENCHMENT?

About seventy-five years ago, I learned that I was not God. And so, when the people ... want to do something I can't find anything in the Constitution expressly forbidding them to do, I say, whether I like it nor not, "Goddamit, let 'em do it!"

Oliver Wendell Holmes, Jr.

(1) Privacy and Sodomy

In this Chapter, we have investigated the role the Constitution may play in family law. This has particularly meant that we have traced the career of the constitutional doctrine of privacy and of the principle of substantive due process. That doctrine and that principle perhaps reached their apex with *Lawrence v. Texas*, 539 US 558 (2003), which follows. As you have seen, the reaction to *Roe v. Wade* was explosive. The same-sex relationship cases may prove just as politically divisive.

LAWRENCE v. TEXAS

Supreme Court of the United States, 2003
539 US 558

JUSTICE KENNEDY delivered the opinion of the Court.

Liberty protects the person from unwarranted government intrusions into a dwelling or other private places. In our tradition the State is not omnipresent in the home. And there are other spheres of our lives and existence, outside the home, where the State should not be a dominant presence. Freedom extends beyond spatial bounds. Liberty presumes an autonomy of self that includes freedom of thought, belief, expression, and certain intimate conduct. The instant case involves liberty of the person both in its spatial and more transcendent dimensions.

I

The question before the Court is the validity of a Texas statute making it a crime for two persons of the same sex to engage in certain intimate sexual conduct.

In Houston, Texas, officers of the Harris County Police Department were dispatched to a private residence in response to a reported weapons disturbance. They entered an apartment where one of the petitioners, John Geddes Lawrence, resided. The right of the police to enter does not seem to have been questioned. The officers observed Lawrence and another man, Tyron Garner, engaging in a sexual act. The two petitioners were arrested, held in custody over night, and charged and convicted before a Justice of the Peace.

The complaints described their crime as "deviate sexual intercourse, namely anal sex, with a member of the same sex (man)." App. to Pet. for Cert. 127a, 139a. The applicable state law is Tex. Penal Code Ann. § 21.06(a) (2003). It provides: "A person commits an offense if he engages in deviate sexual intercourse with another individual of the same sex." The statute defines "[d]eviate sexual intercourse" as follows:

> "(A) any contact between any part of the genitals of one person and the mouth or anus of another person; or
>
> "(B) the penetration of the genitals or the anus of another person with an object."

§ 21.01(1).

The petitioners exercised their right to a trial *de novo* in Harris County Criminal Court. They challenged the statute as a violation of the Equal Protection Clause of the Fourteenth Amendment and of a like provision of the Texas Constitution. Tex. Const., Art. 1, § 3a. Those contentions were rejected. The petitioners, having entered a plea of *nolo contendere,* were each fined $200 and assessed court costs of $141.25.

The Court of Appeals for the Texas Fourteenth District considered the petitioners' federal constitutional arguments under both the Equal Protection and Due Process Clauses of the Fourteenth Amendment. After hearing the case en banc the court, in a divided opinion, rejected the constitutional arguments and affirmed the convictions. The majority opinion indicates that the Court of Appeals considered our decision in *Bowers v. Hardwick,* 478 U.S. 186 (1986), to be controlling on the federal due process aspect of the case. *Bowers* then being authoritative, this was proper.

We granted certiorari to consider three questions:

> "1. Whether Petitioners' criminal convictions under the Texas 'Homosexual Conduct' law-which criminalizes sexual intimacy by same-sex couples, but not identical behavior by different-sex couples—violate the Fourteenth Amendment guarantee of equal protection of laws?

> "2. Whether Petitioners' criminal convictions for adult consensual sexual intimacy in the home violate their vital interests in liberty and privacy protected by the Due Process Clause of the Fourteenth Amendment?
>
> "3. Whether *Bowers v. Hardwick*, 478 U.S. 186 (1986) should be overruled?"

The petitioners were adults at the time of the alleged offense. Their conduct was in private and consensual.

II.

We conclude the case should be resolved by determining whether the petitioners were free as adults to engage in the private conduct in the exercise of their liberty under the Due Process Clause of the Fourteenth Amendment to the Constitution. For this inquiry we deem it necessary to reconsider the Court's holding in *Bowers*.

There are broad statements of the substantive reach of liberty under the Due Process Clause in earlier cases, including *Pierce v. Society of Sisters*, 268 U.S. 510 (1925), and *Meyer v. Nebraska*, 262 U.S. 390 (1923); but the most pertinent beginning point is our decision in *Griswold v. Connecticut*, 381 U.S. 479 (1965) . . .

In *Griswold* the Court invalidated a state law prohibiting the use of drugs or devices of contraception and counseling or aiding and abetting the use of contraceptives. The Court described the protected interest as a right to privacy and placed emphasis on the marriage relation and the protected space of the marital bedroom.

After *Griswold* it was established that the right to make certain decisions regarding sexual conduct extends beyond the marital relationship. In *Eisenstadt v. Baird*, 405 U.S. 438 (1972), the Court invalidated a law prohibiting the distribution of contraceptives to unmarried persons. The case was decided under the Equal Protection Clause, but with respect to unmarried persons, the Court went on to state the fundamental proposition that the law impaired the exercise of their personal rights. It quoted from the statement of the Court of Appeals finding the law to be in conflict with fundamental human rights, and it followed with this statement of its own:

> "It is true that in *Griswold* the right of privacy in question inhered in the marital relationship . . . If the right of privacy means anything, it is the right of the *individual*, married or single, to be free from unwarranted governmental intrusion into matters so fundamentally affecting a person as the decision whether to bear or beget a child."

The opinions in *Griswold* and *Eisenstadt* were part of the background for the decision in *Roe v. Wade*, 410 U.S. 113 (1973). As is well known, the case involved a challenge to the Texas law prohibiting abortions, but the laws of other States were affected as well. Although the Court held the woman's rights were not absolute, her right to elect an abortion did have real and substantial protection as an exercise of her liberty under the Due Process Clause. The Court cited cases that protect spatial freedom and cases that go well beyond it. *Roe* recognized the right of a woman to make certain fundamental decisions affecting her destiny and confirmed once more that the protection of liberty under the Due Process Clause has a substantive dimension of fundamental significance in defining the rights of the person.

In *Carey v. Population Services Int'l,* 431 U.S. 678 (1977), the Court confronted a New York law forbidding sale or distribution of contraceptive devices to persons under 16 years of age. Although there was no single opinion for the Court, the law was invalidated. Both *Eisenstadt* and *Carey*, as well as the holding and rationale in *Roe,* confirmed that the reasoning of *Griswold* could not be confined to the protection of rights of married adults. This was the state of the law with respect to some of the most relevant cases when the Court considered *Bowers v. Hardwick.*

The facts in *Bowers* had some similarities to the instant case. A police officer, whose right to enter seems not to have been in question, observed Hardwick, in his own bedroom, engaging in intimate sexual conduct with another adult male. The conduct was in violation of a Georgia statute making it a criminal offense to engage in sodomy. One difference between the two cases is that the Georgia statute prohibited the conduct whether or not the participants were of the same sex, while the Texas statute, as we have seen, applies only to participants of the same sex. Hardwick was not prosecuted, but he brought an action in federal court to declare the state statute invalid. He alleged he was a practicing homosexual and that the criminal prohibition violated rights guaranteed to him by the Constitution. The Court, in an opinion by Justice White, sustained the Georgia law. Chief Justice Burger and Justice Powell joined the opinion of the Court and filed separate, concurring opinions. Four Justices dissented.

The Court began its substantive discussion in *Bowers* as follows: "The issue presented is whether the Federal Constitution confers a fundamental right upon homosexuals to engage in sodomy and hence invalidates the laws of the many States that still make such conduct illegal and have done so for a very long time." That statement, we now conclude, discloses the Court's own failure to appreciate the extent of the liberty at stake. To say that the issue in *Bowers* was simply the right to engage in certain sexual conduct demeans the claim the individual put forward, just as it would demean a married couple were it to be said marriage is simply about the right to have sexual intercourse. The laws involved in *Bowers* and here are, to be sure, statutes that purport to do no more than prohibit a particular sexual act. Their penalties and purposes, though, have more far-reaching consequences, touching upon the most private human conduct, sexual behavior, and in the most private of places, the home. The statutes do seek to control a personal relationship that, whether or not entitled to formal recognition in the law, is within the liberty of persons to choose without being punished as criminals.

This, as a general rule, should counsel against attempts by the State, or a court, to define the meaning of the relationship or to set its boundaries absent injury to a person or abuse of an institution the law protects. It suffices for us to acknowledge that adults may choose to enter upon this relationship in the confines of their homes and their own private lives and still retain their dignity as free persons. When sexuality finds overt expression in intimate conduct with another person, the conduct can be but one element in a personal bond that is more enduring. The liberty protected by the Constitution allows homosexual persons the right to make this choice.

Having misapprehended the claim of liberty there presented to it, and thus stating the claim to be whether there is a fundamental right to engage in consensual sodomy, the *Bowers* Court said: "Proscriptions against that conduct have ancient roots." In academic writings, and in many of the scholarly *amicus* briefs filed to assist the Court in this case, there are fundamental criticisms of the historical premises relied upon by the majority and concurring opinions in *Bowers*. Brief for Cato Institute as *Amicus Curiae* 16–17; Brief for American Civil Liberties Union et al. as *Amici Curiae* 15–21; Brief for Professors of History et al. as *Amici Curiae* 3–10. We need not enter this debate in the attempt to reach a definitive historical judgment, but the following considerations counsel against adopting the definitive conclusions upon which *Bowers* placed such reliance.

At the outset it should be noted that there is no longstanding history in this country of laws directed at homosexual conduct as a distinct matter . . .

Laws prohibiting sodomy do not seem to have been enforced against consenting adults acting in private . . .

The policy of punishing consenting adults for private acts was not much discussed in the early legal literature. We can infer that one reason for this was the very private nature of the conduct. Despite the absence of prosecutions, there may have been periods in which there was public criticism of homosexuals as such and an insistence that the criminal laws be enforced to discourage their practices. But far from possessing "ancient roots," American laws targeting same-sex couples did not develop until the last third of the 20th century. The reported decisions concerning the prosecution of consensual, homosexual sodomy between adults for the years 1880–1995 are not always clear in the details, but a significant number involved conduct in a public place . . .

In summary, the historical grounds relied upon in *Bowers* are more complex than the majority opinion and the concurring opinion by Chief Justice Burger indicate. Their historical premises are not without doubt and, at the very least, are overstated.

It must be acknowledged, of course, that the Court in *Bowers* was making the broader point that for centuries there have been powerful voices to condemn homosexual conduct as immoral. The condemnation has been shaped by religious beliefs, conceptions of right and acceptable behavior, and respect for the traditional family. For many persons these are not trivial concerns but profound and deep convictions accepted as ethical and moral principles to which they aspire and which thus determine the course of their lives. These considerations do not answer the question before us, however. The issue is whether the majority may use the power of the State to enforce these views on the whole society through operation of the criminal law. "Our obligation is to define the liberty of all, not to mandate our own moral code."

Chief Justice Burger joined the opinion for the Court in *Bowers* and further explained his views as follows: "Decisions of individuals relating to homosexual conduct have been subject to state intervention throughout the history of Western civilization. Condemnation of those practices is firmly rooted in Judeo–Christian moral and ethical standards." As with Justice White's assumptions about history, scholarship casts some doubt on the sweeping nature of the statement by Chief Justice Burger as it pertains to private homosexual conduct between consenting adults. See, *e.g., Eskridge, Hardwick and Historiography*, 1999 U. Ill. L.Rev. 631, 656. In all events we think that our laws and traditions in the past half century are of most relevance here. These references show an emerging awareness that liberty gives substantial protection to adult persons in deciding how to conduct their private lives in matters pertaining to sex. "[H]istory and tradition are the starting point but not in all cases the ending point of the substantive due process inquiry." ...

In our own constitutional system the deficiencies in *Bowers* became even more apparent in the years following its announcement. The 25 States with laws prohibiting the relevant conduct referenced in the *Bowers* decision are reduced now to 13, of which 4 enforce their laws only against homosexual conduct. In those States where sodomy is still proscribed, whether for same-sex or heterosexual conduct, there is a pattern of non-enforcement with respect to consenting adults acting in private. The State of Texas admitted in 1994 that as of that date it had not prosecuted anyone under those circumstances.

Two principal cases decided after *Bowers* cast its holding into even more doubt. In *Planned Parenthood of Southeastern Pa. v. Casey,* 505 U.S. 833 (1992), the Court reaffirmed the substantive force of the liberty protected by the Due Process Clause. The *Casey* decision again confirmed that our laws and tradition afford constitutional protection to personal decisions relating to marriage, procreation, contraception, family relationships, child rearing, and education. In explaining the respect the Constitution demands for the autonomy of the person in making these choices, we stated as follows:

> "These matters, involving the most intimate and personal choices a person may make in a lifetime, choices central to personal dignity

and autonomy, are central to the liberty protected by the Fourteenth Amendment. At the heart of liberty is the right to define one's own concept of existence, of meaning, of the universe, and of the mystery of human life. Beliefs about these matters could not define the attributes of personhood were they formed under compulsion of the State."

Persons in a homosexual relationship may seek autonomy for these purposes, just as heterosexual persons do. The decision in *Bowers* would deny them this right.

The second post-*Bowers* case of principal relevance is *Romer v. Evans,* 517 U.S. 620 (1996). There the Court struck down class-based legislation directed at homosexuals as a violation of the Equal Protection Clause. *Romer* invalidated an amendment to Colorado's constitution which named as a solitary class persons who were homosexuals, lesbians, or bisexual either by "orientation, conduct, practices or relationships," and deprived them of protection under state antidiscrimination laws. We concluded that the provision was "born of animosity toward the class of persons affected" and further that it had no rational relation to a legitimate governmental purpose.

As an alternative argument in this case, counsel for the petitioners and some *amici* contend that *Romer* provides the basis for declaring the Texas statute invalid under the Equal Protection Clause. That is a tenable argument, but we conclude the instant case requires us to address whether *Bowers* itself has continuing validity. Were we to hold the statute invalid under the Equal Protection Clause some might question whether a prohibition would be valid if drawn differently, say, to prohibit the conduct both between same-sex and different-sex participants.

Equality of treatment and the due process right to demand respect for conduct protected by the substantive guarantee of liberty are linked in important respects, and a decision on the latter point advances both interests. If protected conduct is made criminal and the law which does so remains unexamined for its substantive validity, its stigma might remain even if it were not enforceable as drawn for equal protection reasons. When homosexual conduct is made criminal by the law of the State, that declaration in and of itself is an invitation to subject homosexual persons to discrimination both in the public and in the private spheres. The central holding of *Bowers* has been brought in question by this case, and it should be addressed. Its continuance as precedent demeans the lives of homosexual persons.

The stigma this criminal statute imposes, moreover, is not trivial. The offense, to be sure, is but a class C misdemeanor, a minor offense in the Texas legal system. Still, it remains a criminal offense with all that imports for the dignity of the persons charged. The petitioners will bear on their record the history of their criminal convictions. Just this Term we rejected various challenges to state laws requiring the registration of sex offenders. We are advised that if Texas convicted an adult for private, consensual homosexual conduct under the statute here in question the convicted person would come within the registration laws of a least four States were he or she to be subject to their jurisdiction. This underscores the consequential nature of the punishment and the state-sponsored condemnation attendant to the criminal prohibition. Furthermore, the Texas criminal conviction carries with it the other collateral consequences always following a conviction, such as notations on job application forms, to mention but one example.

The foundations of *Bowers* have sustained serious erosion from our recent decisions in *Casey* and *Romer*. When our precedent has been thus weakened, criticism from other sources is of greater significance. In the United States criticism of *Bowers* has been substantial and continuing, disapproving of its reasoning in all respects, not just as to its historical assumptions. See, *e.g.,* C. Fried, *Order and Law: Arguing the Reagan Revolution—A Firsthand Account* 81–84 (1991); R. Posner, *Sex and Reason* 341–350 (1992). The courts of five different States have declined to follow it in interpreting provisions in their own state constitutions parallel to the Due Process Clause of the Fourteenth Amendment.

To the extent *Bowers* relied on values we share with a wider civilization, it should be noted that the reasoning and holding in *Bowers* have been rejected elsewhere. The European Court of Human Rights has followed not *Bowers* but its own decision in *Dudgeon v. United Kingdom.* See *P.G. & J.H. v. United Kingdom,* App. No. 00044787/98, 56 (Eur.Ct.H. R., Sept. 25, 2001); *Modinos v. Cyprus,* 259 Eur. Ct. H.R. (1993); *Norris v. Ireland,* 142 Eur. Ct. H.R. (1988). Other nations, too, have taken action consistent with an affirmation of the protected right of homosexual adults to engage in intimate, consensual conduct. See Brief for Mary Robinson et al., as *Amici Curiae* 11–12. The right the petitioners seek in this case has been accepted as an integral part of human freedom in many other countries. There has been no showing that in this country the governmental interest in circumscribing personal choice is somehow more legitimate or urgent.

The doctrine of *stare decisis* is essential to the respect accorded to the judgments of the Court and to the stability of the law. It is not, however, an inexorable command. In *Casey* we noted that when a Court is asked to overrule a precedent recognizing a constitutional liberty interest, individual or societal reliance on the existence of that liberty cautions with particular strength against reversing course. The holding in *Bowers,* however, has not induced detrimental reliance comparable to some instances where recognized individual rights are involved. Indeed, there has been no individual or societal reliance on *Bowers* of the sort that could counsel against overturning its holding once there are compelling reasons to do so. *Bowers* itself causes uncertainty, for the precedents before and after its issuance contradict its central holding.

The rationale of *Bowers* does not withstand careful analysis. In his dissenting opinion in *Bowers* JUSTICE STEVENS came to these conclusions:

> "Our prior cases make two propositions abundantly clear. First, the fact that the governing majority in a State has traditionally viewed a particular practice as immoral is not a sufficient reason for upholding a law prohibiting the practice; neither history nor tradition could save a law prohibiting miscegenation from constitutional attack. Second, individual decisions by married persons, concerning the intimacies of their physical relationship, even when not intended to produce offspring, are a form of 'liberty' protected by the Due Process Clause of the Fourteenth Amendment. Moreover, this protection extends to intimate choices by unmarried as well as married persons." 478 U.S., at 216, 106 S.Ct. 2841 (footnotes and citations omitted).

JUSTICE STEVENS' analysis, in our view, should have been controlling in *Bowers* and should control here.

Bowers was not correct when it was decided, and it is not correct today. It ought not to remain binding precedent. *Bowers v. Hardwick* should be and now is overruled.

The present case does not involve minors. It does not involve persons who might be injured or coerced or who are situated in relationships where consent might not easily be refused. It does not involve public conduct or prostitution. It does not involve whether the government must give formal recognition to any relationship that homosexual persons seek to enter. The case does involve two adults who, with full and mutual consent from each other, engaged in sexual practices common to a homosexual lifestyle. The petitioners are entitled to respect for their private lives. The State cannot demean their existence or control their destiny by making their private sexual conduct a crime. Their right to liberty under the Due Process Clause gives them the full right to engage in their conduct without intervention of the government. "It is a promise of the Constitution that there is a realm of personal liberty which the government may not enter." The Texas statute furthers no legitimate state interest which can justify its intrusion into the personal and private life of the individual.

Had those who drew and ratified the Due Process Clauses of the Fifth Amendment or the Fourteenth Amendment known the components of liberty in its manifold possibilities, they might have been more specific. They did not presume to have this insight. They knew times can blind us to certain truths and later generations can see that laws once thought necessary and proper in fact serve only to oppress. As the Constitution endures, persons in every generation can invoke its principles in their own search for greater freedom.

The judgment of the Court of Appeals for the Texas Fourteenth District is reversed, and the case is remanded for further proceedings not inconsistent with this opinion.

It is so ordered.

JUSTICE O'CONNOR, concurring in the judgment.

The Court today overrules *Bowers v. Hardwick,* 478 U.S. 186, 106 S.Ct. 2841, 92 L.Ed.2d 140 (1986). I joined *Bowers,* and do not join the Court in overruling it. Nevertheless, I agree with the Court that Texas' statute banning same-sex sodomy is unconstitutional. See Tex. Penal Code Ann. § 21.06 (2003). Rather than relying on the substantive component of the Fourteenth Amendment's Due Process Clause, as the Court does, I base my conclusion on the Fourteenth Amendment's Equal Protection Clause ...

The statute at issue here makes sodomy a crime only if a person "engages in deviate sexual intercourse with another individual of the same sex." Tex. Penal Code Ann. § 21.06(a) (2003). Sodomy between opposite-sex partners, however, is not a crime in Texas. That is, Texas treats the same conduct differently based solely on the participants. Those harmed by this law are people who have a same-sex sexual orientation and thus are more likely to engage in behavior prohibited by § 21.06.

The Texas statute makes homosexuals unequal in the eyes of the law by making particular conduct—and only that conduct—subject to criminal sanction. It appears that prosecutions under Texas' sodomy law are rare. This case shows, however, that prosecutions under § 21.06 *do* occur. And while the penalty imposed on petitioners in this case was relatively minor, the consequences of conviction are not. As the Court notes, petitioners' convictions, if upheld, would disqualify them from or restrict their ability to engage in a variety of professions, including medicine, athletic training, and interior design. Indeed, were petitioners to move to one of four States, their convictions would require them to register as sex offenders to local law enforcement.

And the effect of Texas' sodomy law is not just limited to the threat of prosecution or consequence of conviction. Texas' sodomy law brands all homosexuals as criminals, thereby making it more difficult for homosexuals to be treated in the same manner as everyone else. Indeed, Texas itself has previously acknowledged the collateral effects of the law, stipulating in a prior challenge to this action that the law "legally sanctions discrimination against [homosexuals] in a variety of ways unrelated to the criminal law," including in the areas of "employment, family issues, and housing." ...

A law branding one class of persons as criminal solely based on the State's moral disapproval of that class and the conduct associated with that class runs contrary to the values of the Constitution and the Equal Protection Clause, under any standard of review. I therefore concur in the Court's judgment that Texas' sodomy law banning "deviate sexual intercourse" between consenting adults of the same sex, but not between consenting adults of different sexes, is unconstitutional.

JUSTICE SCALIA, with whom THE CHIEF JUSTICE and JUSTICE THOMAS join, dissenting.

"Liberty finds no refuge in a jurisprudence of doubt." That was the Court's sententious response, barely more than a decade ago, to those seeking to overrule *Roe v. Wade,* 410 U.S. 113 (1973). The Court's response today, to those who have engaged in a 17-year crusade to overrule *Bowers v. Hardwick,* 478 U.S. 186 (1986), is very different. The need for stability and certainty presents no barrier . . .

Questions: Lawrence *and the Privacy Right*

1. Is there express support in the Constitution for same-sex sexual conduct?

2. Justice Kennedy refers to many of the case we have already read: *Griswold, Eisenstadt, Roe* and *Carey*. Does the decision in *Lawrence* follow more easily from these cases than *Bowers* did?

3. Is the answer to the *Lawrence* decision the difference in the attitudes in the United States toward same-sex relationships since *Bowers*? (note the discussion on the number of statutes in Part II) Should popularity among legislatures determine a statute's constitutionality? Whether or not conduct reaches the status of a "fundamental right?'

4. Will the decriminalization of sodomy lead to a difference in the attitudes of both straight and gay and lesbian couples about sexual identity and the acceptability of all kinds of relationships? Ryan Goodman suggests such a difference in his empirical study of the decriminalization of sodomy in South Africa. *Beyond the Enforcement Principle: Sodomy Laws, Social Norms and Social Panaoptics*, 89 Cal L Rev 643 (2001). In fact, South Africa's Constitutional Court opened the door for same-sex marriage by finding the restrictions to heterosexual couples unconstitutional in *Minister of Home Affairs v. Fourie*, Case 60/04, (Dec. 1, 2005). Will legalization of same-sex marriage ultimately lead to recognition of polygamy and other consensual adult relationships? Canada, which adopted same-sex marriage in An Act Respecting Certain Aspects of Legal Marriage for Civil Purposes, Bill C–38, 38th Parliament, 1st Session (2005), is debating the issue in early 2006. Dean Beeby, Study Recommends Repealing Polygamy Ban in Canada, www.canada.com (January 22, 2006) (discussing study of Martha Bailey of Queens' University law faculty).

5. Justice O'Connor, while seemingly willing to accept the prohibition against sodomy, rejects under equal protection any different treatment of homosexual and heterosexual conduct. Would this have been a sounder basis for the decision? Would it have been less likely to spur challenges to statutes restricting marriage to heterosexual couples?

6. Could one difference between the Courts in the time of *Bowers* and *Lawrence* be the growing acceptability of oral sex among young people? See Norval Glenn and Elizabeth Marquardt, *Hooking Up, Hanging Out and Hoping for Mr. Right: College Women on Mating and Dating Today*, an Institute for American Values Report to the Independent Women's Forum 4–6 (2001).

7. Does *Lawrence* mean, as the dissent suggests, that a constitutional decision invalidating all the "marriage between a man and a

woman" legislation (and the state constitutions that do the same) is inevitable? Consider the language both saying what the opinion is *not* doing ("whether the government must give formal recognition to any relationship that homosexual persons seek to enter") and saying that the criminal statutes are more than just about sex "just as it would demean a married couple were it to be said marriage is simply about the right to have sexual intercourse."

(2) Privacy and Health Care

In recent years, much of the Court's attention to the privacy principle has shifted from family law to health law. A crucial case in that shift was *Cruzan v. Director, Missouri Dep't of Health,* 497 US 261 (1990). Nancy Cruzan, a woman in her early thirties, had fallen into a persistent vegetative state—"a condition in which a person exhibits motor reflexes but evinces no indications of significant cognitive function"—after being injured in an automobile accident. Because she could not feed herself, surgeons "implanted a gastrostomy feeding and hydration tube." When her parents became convinced Cruzan would never regain consciousness, they asked the state hospital in which she lay to stop giving her food and liquid. When the hospital refused, the parents went to court.

The Missouri Supreme Court held that Cruzan's parents could not terminate her medical treatment " 'in the absence of the formalities required under Missouri's Living Will statutes or the clear and convincing, inherently reliable evidence absent here.' "The United States Supreme Court granted certiorari to decide whether a state can constitutionally set such a standard for terminating treatment of an incompetent patient. The Court's opinion (by Chief Justice Rehnquist) began by saying that competent people have a "constitutionally protected liberty interest in refusing unwanted medical treatment." It declined to decide whether that interest might be overcome by any state interests, but assumed (very much) *arguendo* that it would not be. The Court then asked whether incompetents must have the same right as competents. The Court decided they need not:

> The difficulty with petitioners' claim is that in a sense it begs the question: an incompetent person is not able to make an informed and voluntary choice to exercise a hypothetical right to refuse treatment or any other right. Such a "right" must be exercised for her, if at all, by some sort of surrogate. Here, Missouri has in effect recognized that under certain circumstances a surrogate may act for the patient in electing to have hydration and nutrition withdrawn in such a way as to cause death, but it has established a procedural safeguard to assure that the action of the surrogate conforms as best it may to the wishes expressed by the patient while competent.

The Court concluded that that procedural requirement was constitutionally tolerable. Missouri had an undoubted "interest in the protection and preservation of human life." The Court believed that Missouri's procedural requirement protected the personal choice between life and death and that in any event the state had an "unqualified interest in the preservation of human life to be weighed against the constitutionally protected interests of the individual." The Court also thought that Missouri "may permissibly place an increased risk of an erroneous decision on those seeking to terminate an incompetent individual's life-sustaining treatment," since an erroneous decision not to terminate treatment would only perpetuate the status quo, while an erroneous decision to terminate treatment would result in the patient's death and would not be correctable.

Finally, the Court considered the claim "that Missouri must accept the 'substituted judgment' of close family members even in the absence of substantial proof that their views [reflect] the views of the patient." The Court denied that *Michael H. v. Gerald D.* and *Parham v. J.R.* (see Chapter VIII) required such a result. Those two cases, the Court said, *allowed* a state to defer to family decisions; they did not *require* a state to do so. Further:

> Close family members may have a strong feeling—a feeling not at all ignoble or unworthy, but not entirely disinterested, either—that they do not wish to witness the continuation of the life of a loved one which they regard as hopeless, meaningless, and even degrading. But there is not automatic assurance that the view of close family members will necessarily be the same as the patient's would have been had she been confronted with the prospect of her situation while competent.

Justice Brennan's dissent (in which Justice Marshall joined) argued that a competent person not only has a liberty interest in being free of unwanted medical treatment, but that that interest was "fundamental," so that any infringement of it must be " 'supported by sufficiently important state interests and [be] . . . closely tailored to effectuate only those interests.' " Cruzan's incompetence did not "deprive her of her fundamental rights." Thus "the question is not whether an incompetent has constitutional rights, but how such rights may be exercised."

What was Cruzan's right? It was "a right to evaluate the potential benefit of treatment and its possible consequences according to one's own values and to make a personal decision whether to subject oneself to the intrusion." For Cruzan, "the sole benefit of medical treatment is being kept metabolically alive," while, for many people, the conditions under which she lived would be intolerable.

The state, on the other hand, "has no legitimate general interest in someone's life, completely abstracted from the interest of the person living that life, that could outweigh the person's choice to avoid medical treatment." In other words, if Cruzan had decided her life was not worth living, the state could not gainsay her decision, and thus would be left with no interests to protect. The state's only legitimate concern could be to assure Cruzan "as accurate as possible a determination of how she would exercise her rights under these circumstances." But the Missouri standard did not assure that accurate determination, since it biased the result in favor of treatment by requiring a high level of proof that a patient would actually want treatment discontinued.

Where the patient's wish in fact can not be discovered, Justice Brennan believed that a state "generally must either repose the choice with the person whom the patient himself would most likely have chosen as proxy or leave the decision to the patient's family."

Like Justice Brennan's dissent, Justice Stevens' dissent argued that the case implicated a fundamental right. However, Justice Stevens concluded from this that Missouri's statute "must, at a minimum, bear a reasonable relationship to a legitimate state end." And while Justice Brennan argued that Cruzan had a right to make a decision for herself, Justice Stevens seemed to argue that Cruzan had a right to a decision in her best interests. He wrote, "[T]he constitutional answer is clear: the best interests [of] the individual, especially when buttressed by the interests of all related third parties, must prevail over any general state policy that simply ignores those interests." Justice Stevens found "no reasonable ground for believing that Nancy Beth Cruzan has any *personal* interest in the perpetuation of what the State has decided is her life."

In any event, "the difficulties involved in ascertaining what her interests are do not in any way justify the State's decision to oppose her interests with its own." Justice Stevens seemed to imply that one way to ascertain her interests was to consult a "next friend." He later added that the "meaning and completion" of Cruzan's life "should be controlled by persons who have her best interests at heart."

Cruzan was an equivocal case which implied that patients had some kind of constitutional rights to make decisions but did not directly hold that they did. This left room for partisans of physician-assisted suicide to argue that the statutes prohibiting it were unconstitutional. That is precisely what the Ninth Circuit gleefully held in *Compassion in Dying v. Washington,* 79 F3d 790 (1996). However, a unanimous Supreme Court (unanimous in result but not, of course, in explanation) reversed the Ninth Circuit in *Washington v. Glucksberg*, 521 US 702 (1997).

Chief Justice Rehnquist's opinion for the Court began by "examining our Nation's history, legal traditions, and practices." It had no trouble concluding that none of those recognized any kind of right to assistance in committing suicide. On the contrary. The Court acknowledged that in *Cruzan* it had "assumed, and strongly suggested, that the Due Process Clause protects the traditional right to refuse unwanted lifesaving medical treatment." However, the Court insisted, it had

> "always been reluctant to expand the concept of substantive due process because guideposts for responsible decisionmaking in this unchartered area are scarce and open-ended." By extending constitutional protection to an asserted right or liberty interest, we, to a great extent, place the matter outside the arena of public debate and legislative action. We must therefore "exercise the utmost care whenever we are asked to break new ground in this field," lest the

liberty protected by the Due Process Clause be subtly transformed into the policy preferences of the members of this Court....

The Court went to pains to reject the argument that Justice O'Connor's rhapsodic language in *Casey* about defining one's own concept of existence created a broad-ranging right of personal autonomy:

> By choosing this language, the Court's opinion in *Casey* described, in a general way and in light of our prior cases, those personal activities and decisions that this Court has identified as so deeply rooted in our history and traditions, or so fundamental to our concept of constitutionally ordered liberty, that they are protected by the Fourteenth Amendment.... That many of the rights and liberties protected by the Due Process Clause sound in personal autonomy does not warrant the sweeping conclusion that any and all important, intimate, and personal decisions are so protected, and *Casey* did not suggest otherwise.

The Court thus concluded that "our decisions lead us to conclude that the asserted 'right' to assistance in committing suicide is not a fundamental liberty interest" and that prohibitions of it need only be "rationally related to legitimate government interests." The Court concluded without effort that states have ample interests in (among other things) preventing improvident suicides to justify prohibitions on assisted suicide.

Several lessons may usefully be drawn from this account of the Court's current approach to substantive due process. First, the Court has to a degree that is still difficult to assess abandoned much of the apparatus it originally used to analyze substantive due process cases. It seems reluctant even to talk about fundamental rights or a right to privacy. Instead, it invokes "liberty interests." It managed in *Cruzan* to provide a lengthy opinion that scrupulously avoided citing *Roe v. Wade*. It is unhappy with the much-criticized two-tier strict-scrutiny/no-scrutiny system it once seemed to favor. It seems to be more willing than before to take the state's interests seriously.

Second, when the Court asks whether an individual can assert a constitutional liberty interest, the Court is increasingly inclined to use the technique Justice Scalia defended in his plurality opinion in *Michael H.* and to define the asserted right quite narrowly. Thus the Court took the right claimed in *Glucksberg* not to be a right to self-determination, or a right to die with dignity, or a right to determine the time and manner of one's death. Rather, the Court asked what constitutional basis there might be for a right to commit suicide and, unsurprisingly, found none.

Third, the Court regularly announces its reluctance to find new privacy rights. It regularly recites the risks of substantive due process. The kind of passage we quoted a moment ago from *Glucksberg* has become increasingly familiar.

B. *LE DERNIER CRI* BUT NOT THE LAST WORD

All the ills of democracy can be cured by more democracy.

Alfred E. Smith

We conclude this Chapter by examining the Court's most recent foray into the constitutional law of the family as opposed to the adult couple. In these cases, there was hardly a question about whether some kind of right was at stake. On the contrary, the asserted right was based happily in the heartland of historical privacy rights. Nevertheless, the Court again found itself struggling to define just what the right might be, what it might mean, and who might possess it.

TROXEL v. GRANVILLE

Supreme Court of the United States, 2000
530 US 57

JUSTICE O'CONNOR announced the judgment of the Court and delivered an opinion, in which THE CHIEF JUSTICE, JUSTICE GINSBURG, and JUSTICE BREYER join. . . .

I

Tommie Granville and Brad Troxel shared a relationship that ended in June 1991. The two never married, but they had two daughters, Isabelle and Natalie. Jenifer and Gary Troxel are Brad's parents, and thus the paternal grandparents of Isabelle and Natalie. After Tommie and Brad separated in 1991, Brad lived with his parents and regularly brought his daughters to his parents' home for weekend visitation. Brad committed suicide in May 1993. Although the Troxels at first continued to see Isabelle and Natalie on a regular basis after their son's death, Tommie Granville informed the Troxels in October 1993 that she wished to limit their visitation with her daughters to one short visit per month. *In re Smith*, 137 Wash. 2d 1, 6, 969 P. 2d 21, 23–24 (1998); *In re Troxel*, 87 Wash. App. 131, 133, 940 P. 2d 698, 698–699 (1997).

In December 1993, the Troxels commenced the present action by filing, in the Washington Superior Court for Skagit County, a petition to obtain visitation rights with Isabelle and Natalie. The Troxels filed their petition under two Washington statutes, Wash. Rev. Code §§ 26.09.240 and 26.10.160(3) (1994). Only the latter statute is at issue in this case. Section 26.10.160(3) provides: "Any person may petition the court for visitation rights at any time including, but not limited to, custody proceedings. The court may order visitation rights for any person when visitation may serve the best interest of the child whether or not there has been any change of circumstances." At trial, the Troxels requested two weekends of overnight visitation per month and two weeks of visitation each summer. Granville did not oppose visitation altogether, but instead asked the court to order one day of visitation per month with no overnight stay. In 1995, the Superior Court issued an oral ruling and entered a visitation decree ordering visitation one weekend per month, one week during the summer, and four hours on both of the petitioning grandparents' birthdays.

Granville appealed, during which time she married Kelly Wynn. Before addressing the merits of Granville's appeal, the Washington Court of Appeals remanded the case to the Superior Court for entry of written findings of fact and conclusions of law. On remand, the Superior Court found that visitation was in Isabelle and Natalie's best interests:

> "The Petitioners [the Troxels] are part of a large, central, loving family, all located in this area, and the Petitioners can provide opportunities for the children in the areas of cousins and music.
>
> " ... The court took into consideration all factors regarding the best interest of the children and considered all the testimony before it. The children would be benefitted from spending quality time with the Petitioners, provided that that time is balanced with time with the childrens' [*sic*] nuclear family. The court finds that the childrens' [*sic*] best interests are served by spending time with their mother and stepfather's other six children."

Approximately nine months after the Superior Court entered its order on remand, Granville's husband formally adopted Isabelle and Natalie.

The Washington Court of Appeals reversed the lower court's visitation order and dismissed the Troxels' petition for visitation, holding that nonparents lack standing to seek visitation under § 26.10.160(3) unless a custody action is pending. In the Court of Appeals' view, that limitation on nonparental visitation actions was "consistent with the constitutional restrictions on state interference with parents' fundamental liberty interest in the care, custody, and management of their children." Having resolved the case on the statutory ground, however, the Court of Appeals did not expressly pass on Granville's constitutional challenge to the visitation statute.

The Washington Supreme Court granted the Troxels' petition for review and, after consolidating their case with two other visitation cases, affirmed. The court disagreed with the Court of Appeals' decision on the statutory issue and found that the plain language of § 26.10.160(3) gave the Troxels standing to seek visitation, irrespective of whether a custody action was pending. The Washington Supreme Court nevertheless agreed with the Court of Appeals' ultimate conclusion that the Troxels could not obtain visitation of Isabelle and Natalie pursuant to § 26.10.160(3). The court rested its decision on the Federal Constitution, holding that § 26.10.160(3) unconstitutionally infringes on the fundamental right of parents to rear their children. In the court's view, there were at least two problems with the nonparental visitation statute. First, according to the Washington Supreme Court, the Constitution permits a State to interfere with the right of parents to rear their children only to prevent harm or potential harm to a child. Section 26.10.160(3) fails that standard because it requires no threshold showing of harm. Second, by allowing "any person" to petition for forced visitation of a child at "any time" with the only requirement being that the visitation serve the "best interest of the child," the Washington visitation statute sweeps too broadly. "It is not within the province of the state to make significant decisions concerning the custody of children merely because it could make a 'better' decision." The Washington Supreme Court held that "[p]arents have a right to limit visitation of their children with third persons," and that between parents and judges, "the parents should be the ones to choose whether to expose their children to certain people or ideas." Four justices dissented from the Washington Supreme Court's holding on the constitutionality of the statute.

We granted certiorari and now affirm the judgment.

II

The demographic changes of the past century make it difficult to speak of an average American family. The composition of families varies greatly from household to household. While many children may have two married parents and grandparents who visit regularly, many other children are raised in single-parent households. In 1996, children living with only one parent accounted for 28 percent of all children under age 18 in the United States. U. S. Dept. of Commerce, Bureau of Census, Current Population Reports, 1997 Population Profile of the United States 27 (1998). Understandably, in these single-parent households, persons outside the nuclear family are called upon with increasing frequency to assist in the everyday tasks of child rearing. In many cases, grandparents play an important role. For example, in 1998, approximately 4 million children—or 5.6 percent of all children under age 18—lived in the household of their grandparents. U.S. Dept. of Commerce, Bureau of Census, Current Population Reports, Marital Status and Living Arrangements: March 1998 (Update), p. *i* (1998).

The nationwide enactment of nonparental visitation statutes is assuredly due, in some part, to the States' recognition of these changing realities of the American family. Because grandparents and other relatives undertake duties of a parental nature in many households, States have sought to ensure the welfare of the children therein by protecting the relationships those children form with such third parties. The States' nonparental visitation statutes are further supported by a recognition, which varies from State to State, that children should have the opportunity to benefit from relationships with statutorily specified persons—for example, their grandparents. The extension of statutory rights in this area to persons other than a child's parents, however, comes with an obvious cost. For example, the State's recognition of an independent third-party interest in a child can place a substantial burden on the traditional parent-child relationship. Contrary to Justice Stevens' accusation, our description of state nonparental visitation statutes in these terms, of course, is not meant to suggest that "children are so much chattel." Rather, our terminology is intended to highlight the fact that these statutes can present questions of constitutional import. In this case, we are presented with just such a question. Specifically, we are asked to decide whether § 26.10.160(3), as applied to Tommie Granville and her family, violates the Federal Constitution.

The Fourteenth Amendment provides that no State shall "deprive any person of life, liberty, or property, without due process of law." We have long recognized that the Amendment's Due Process Clause, like its Fifth Amendment counterpart, "guarantees more than fair process." *Washington v. Glucksberg*, 521 U.S. 702, 719 (1997) [in which the Court upheld the Washington statute forbidding physician suicide]. The Clause also includes a substantive component that "provides heightened protection against government interference with certain fundamental rights and liberty interests."

The liberty interest at issue in this case—the interest of parents in the care, custody, and control of their children—is perhaps the oldest of the fundamental liberty interests recognized by this Court. More than 75 years ago, in *Meyer v. Nebraska*, 262 U.S. 390, 399, 401 (1923), we held that the "liberty" protected by the Due Process Clause includes the right of parents to "establish a home and bring up children" and "to control the education of their own." Two years later, in *Pierce v. Society of Sisters*, 268 U.S. 510, 534–535 (1925), we again held that the "liberty of parents and guardians" includes the right "to direct the upbringing and education of children under their control." We explained in *Pierce* that "[t]he child is not the mere creature of the State; those who nurture him and direct his destiny have the right, coupled with the high duty, to recognize and prepare him for additional obligations." We returned to the subject in *Prince v. Massachusetts*, 321 U.S. 158 (1944), and again confirmed that there is a constitutional dimension to the right of parents to direct the upbringing of their children. "It is cardinal with us that the custody, care and nurture of the child reside first in the parents, whose primary function and freedom include preparation for obligations the state can neither supply nor hinder."

In subsequent cases also, we have recognized the fundamental right of parents to make decisions concerning the care, custody, and control of their children. See, e.g., *Stanley v. Illinois*, 405 U.S. 645, 651 (1972) ("It is plain that the interest of a parent in the companionship, care, custody, and management of his or her children 'come[s] to this Court with a momentum for respect lacking when appeal is made to liberties which derive merely from shifting economic arrangements' "(citation omitted)); *Wisconsin v. Yoder*, 406 U.S. 205, 232 (1972) ("The history and culture of Western civilization reflect a strong tradition of parental concern for the nurture and upbringing of their children. This primary role of the parents in the upbringing of their children is now established beyond debate as an enduring American tradition"); *Quilloin v. Walcott*, 434 U.S. 246, 255 (1978) ("We have recognized on numerous occasions that the relationship between parent and child is constitutionally protected"); *Parham v. J. R.*, 442 U.S. 584, 602 (1979) ("Our jurisprudence historically has reflected Western civilization concepts of the family as a unit with broad parental authority over minor children. Our cases have consistently followed that course"); *Santosky v. Kramer*, 455 U.S. 745, 753 (1982) (discussing "[t]he fundamental liberty interest of natural parents in the care, custody, and management of their child"); *Glucksberg*, supra, at 720 ("In a long line of cases, we have held that, in addition to the specific freedoms protected by the Bill of Rights, the 'liberty' specially protected by the Due Process Clause includes the righ[t] . . . to direct the education and upbringing of one's children" (citing *Meyer* and *Pierce*)). In light of this extensive precedent, it cannot now be doubted that the Due Process Clause of the Fourteenth Amendment protects the fundamental right of parents to make decisions concerning the care, custody, and control of their children.

Section 26.10.160(3), as applied to Granville and her family in this case, unconstitutionally infringes on that fundamental parental right. The Washington nonparental visitation statute is breathtakingly broad. According to the statute's text, "*[a]ny person* may petition the court for visitation rights *at any time*," and the court may grant such visitation rights whenever "visitation may serve *the best interest of the child*." § 26.10.160(3) (emphases added). That language effectively permits any third party seeking visitation to subject any decision by a parent concerning visitation of the parent's children to state-court review. Once the visitation petition has been filed in court and the matter is placed before a judge, a parent's decision that visitation would not be in the child's best interest is accorded no deference. Section 26.10.160(3) contains no requirement that a court accord the parent's decision any presumption of validity or any weight whatsoever. Instead, the Washington statute places the best-interest determination solely in the hands of the judge. Should the judge disagree with the parent's estimation of the child's best interests, the judge's view necessarily prevails. Thus, in practical effect, in the State of Washington a court can disregard and overturn *any* decision by a fit custodial parent concerning visitation whenever a third party affected by the decision files a visitation petition, based solely on the judge's determination of the child's best interests. The Washington Supreme Court had the opportunity to give § 26.10.160(3) a narrower reading, but it declined to do so.

Turning to the facts of this case, the record reveals that the Superior Court's order was based on precisely the type of mere disagreement we have just described and nothing more. The Superior Court's order was not founded on any special factors that might justify the State's interference with Granville's fundamental right to make decisions concerning the rearing of her two daughters. To be sure, this case involves a visitation petition filed by grandparents soon after the death of their son—the father of Isabelle and Natalie—but the combination of several factors here compels our conclusion that § 26.10.160(3), as applied, exceeded the bounds of the Due Process Clause.

First, the Troxels did not allege, and no court has found, that Granville was an unfit parent. That aspect of the case is important, for there is a presumption that fit parents act in the best interests of their children. As this Court explained in *Parham*:

> "[O]ur constitutional system long ago rejected any notion that a child is the mere creature of the State and, on the contrary, asserted that parents generally have the right, coupled with the high duty, to recognize and prepare [their children] for additional obligations.... The law's concept of the family rests on a presumption that parents possess what a child lacks in maturity, experience, and capacity for judgment required for making life's difficult decisions. More important, historically it has recognized that natural bonds of affection lead parents to act in the best interests of their children." 442 U. S., at 602 (alteration in original) (internal quotation marks and citations omitted).

Accordingly, so long as a parent adequately cares for his or her children (i.e., is fit), there will normally be no reason for the State to inject itself into the private realm of the family to further question the ability of that parent to make the best decisions concerning the rearing of that parent's children.

The problem here is not that the Washington Superior Court intervened, but that when it did so, it gave no special weight at all to Granville's determination of her daughters' best interests. More importantly, it appears that the Superior Court applied exactly the opposite presumption. In reciting its oral ruling after the conclusion of closing arguments, the Superior Court judge explained:

> "The burden is to show that it is in the best interest of the children to have some visitation and some quality time with their grandparents. I think in most situations a commonsensical approach [is that] it is normally in the best interest of the children to spend quality time with the grandparent, unless the grandparent, [*sic*] there are some issues or problems involved wherein the grandparents, their lifestyles are going to impact adversely upon the children. That certainly isn't the case here from what I can tell."

The judge's comments suggest that he presumed the grandparents' request should be granted unless the children would be "impact[ed] adversely." In effect, the judge placed on Granville, the fit custodial parent, the burden of *disproving* that visitation would be in the best interest of her daughters. The judge reiterated moments later: "I think [visitation with the Troxels] would be in the best interest of the children and I haven't been shown it is not in [the] best interest of the children."

The decisional framework employed by the Superior Court directly contravened the traditional presumption that a fit parent will act in the best interest of his or her child. In that respect, the court's presumption failed to provide any protection for Granville's fundamental constitutional right to make decisions concerning the rearing of her own daughters.... In an ideal world, parents might always seek to cultivate the bonds between grandparents and their grandchildren. Needless to say, however, our world is far from perfect, and in it the decision whether such an intergenerational relationship would be beneficial in any specific case is for the parent to make in the first instance. And, if a fit parent's decision of the kind at issue here becomes subject to judicial review, the court must accord at least some special weight to the parent's own determination.

Finally, we note that there is no allegation that Granville ever sought to cut off visitation entirely. Rather, the present dispute originated when Granville informed the Troxels that she would prefer to restrict their visitation with Isabelle and Natalie to one short visit per month and special holidays. In the Superior Court proceedings Granville did not oppose visitation but instead asked that the duration of any visitation order be shorter than that requested by the Troxels. While the Troxels requested two weekends per month and two full weeks in the summer, Granville asked the Superior Court to order only one day of visitation per month (with no overnight stay) and participation in the Granville family's holiday celebrations. See 87 Wash. App., at 133, 940 P. 2d, at 699; Verbatim Report 9 ("Right off the bat we'd like to say that our position is that grandparent visitation is in the best interest of the children. It is a matter of how much and how it is going to be structured") (opening statement by Granville's attorney). The Superior Court gave no weight to Granville's having assented to visitation even before the filing of any visitation petition or subsequent court intervention. The court instead rejected Granville's proposal and settled on a middle ground, ordering one weekend of visitation per month, one week in the summer, and time on both of the petitioning grandparents' birthdays. Significantly, many other States expressly provide by statute that courts may not award visitation unless a parent has denied (or unreasonably denied) visitation to the concerned third party....

Considered together with the Superior Court's reasons for awarding visitation to the Troxels, the combination of these factors demonstrates that the visitation order in this case was an unconstitutional infringement on Granville's fundamental right to make decisions concerning the care, custody, and control of her two daughters. The Washington Superior Court failed to accord the determination of Granville, a fit custodial parent, any material weight. In fact, the Superior Court made only two formal findings in support of its visitation order. First, the Troxels "are part of a large, central, loving family, all located in this area, and the [Troxels] can provide opportunities for the children in the areas of cousins and music." Second, "[t]he children would be benefitted from spending quality time with the [Troxels], provided that that time is balanced with time with the childrens' [*sic*] nuclear family." These slender findings, in combination with the court's announced presumption in favor of grandparent visitation and its failure to accord significant weight to Granville's already having offered meaningful visitation to the Troxels, show that this case involves nothing more than a simple disagreement between the Washington Superior Court and Granville concerning her children's best interests. The Superior Court's announced reason for ordering one week of visitation in the summer demonstrates our conclusion well: "I look back on some personal experiences.... We always spen[t] as kids a week with one set of grandparents and another set of grandparents, [and] it happened to work out in our family that [it] turned out to be an enjoyable experience. Maybe that can, in this family, if that is how it works out." As we have explained, the Due Process Clause does not permit a State to infringe on the fundamental right of parents to make childrearing decisions simply because a state judge believes a "better" decision could be made. Neither the Washington nonparental visitation statute generally—which places no limits on either the persons who may petition for visitation or the circumstances in which such a petition may be granted—nor the Superior Court in this specific case required anything more. Accordingly, we hold that § 26.10.160(3), as applied in this case, is unconstitutional.

Because we rest our decision on the sweeping breadth of § 26.10.160(3) and the application of that broad, unlimited power in this case, we do not consider the primary constitutional question passed on by the Washington Supreme Court—whether the Due Process Clause requires all nonparental visitation statutes to include a showing of harm or potential harm to the child as a condition precedent to granting visitation. We do not, and need not, define today the precise scope of the parental due process right in the visitation context. In this respect, we agree with Justice Kennedy that the constitutionality of any standard for awarding visitation turns on the specific manner in which that standard is applied and that the constitutional protections in this area are best "elaborated with care." Because much state-court adjudication in this context occurs on a case-by-case basis, we would be hesitant to hold that specific nonparental visitation statutes violate the Due Process Clause as a *per se* matter.*

Justice Stevens criticizes our reliance on what he characterizes as merely "a guess" about the Washington courts' interpretation of § 26.10.160(3). Justice Kennedy likewise states that "[m]ore specific guidance should await a case in which a State's highest court has considered all of the facts in the course of elaborating the protection afforded to parents by the laws of the State and by the Constitution itself." We respectfully disagree. There is no need to hypothesize about how the Washington courts *might* apply § 26.10.160(3) because the Washington Superior Court did apply the statute in this very case. Like the Washington Supreme Court, then, we are presented with an actual visitation order and the reasons why the Superior Court believed entry of the order was appropriate in this case. Faced with the Superior Court's application of § 26.10.160(3) to Granville and her family, the Washington Supreme Court chose not to give the statute a narrower construction. Rather, that court gave § 26.10.160(3) a literal and expansive interpretation. As we have explained, that broad construction plainly encompassed the Superior Court's application of the statute.

There is thus no reason to remand the case for further proceedings in the Washington Supreme Court. As Justice Kennedy recognizes, the burden of litigating a domestic relations proceeding can itself be "so

* All 50 States have statutes that provide for grandparent visitation in some form.

disruptive of the parent-child relationship that the constitutional right of a custodial parent to make certain basic determinations for the child's welfare becomes implicated." In this case, the litigation costs incurred by Granville on her trip through the Washington court system and to this Court are without a doubt already substantial. As we have explained, it is apparent that the entry of the visitation order in this case violated the Constitution. We should say so now, without forcing the parties into additional litigation that would further burden Granville's parental right. We therefore hold that the application of § 26.10.160(3) to Granville and her family violated her due process right to make decisions concerning the care, custody, and control of her daughters. . . .

JUSTICE SOUTER, concurring in the judgment.

I concur in the judgment affirming the decision of the Supreme Court of Washington, whose facial invalidation of its own state statute is consistent with this Court's prior cases addressing the substantive interests at stake. I would say no more. The issues that might well be presented by reviewing a decision addressing the specific application of the state statute by the trial court are not before us and do not call for turning any fresh furrows in the "treacherous field" of substantive due process.

The Supreme Court of Washington invalidated its state statute based on the text of the statute alone, not its application to any particular case. Its ruling rested on two independently sufficient grounds: the failure of the statute to require harm to the child to justify a disputed visitation order and the statute's authorization of "any person" at "any time" to petition and to receive visitation rights subject only to a free-ranging best-interests-of-the-child standard. I see no error in the second reason, that because the state statute authorizes any person at any time to request (and a judge to award) visitation rights, subject only to the State's particular best-interests standard, the state statute sweeps too broadly and is unconstitutional on its face. Consequently, there is no need to decide whether harm is required or to consider the precise scope of the parent's right or its necessary protections.

We have long recognized that a parent's interests in the nurture, upbringing, companionship, care, and custody of children are generally protected by the Due Process Clause of the Fourteenth Amendment. . . .

Our cases, it is true, have not set out exact metes and bounds to the protected interest of a parent in the relationship with his child, but *Meyer's* repeatedly recognized right of upbringing would be a sham if it failed to encompass the right to be free of judicially compelled visitation by "any party" at "any time" a judge believed he "could make a 'better' decision" than the objecting parent had done. The strength of a parent's interest in controlling a child's associates is as obvious as the influence of personal associations on the development of the child's social and moral character. Whether for good or for ill, adults not only influence but may indoctrinate children, and a choice about a child's social companions is not essentially different from the designation of the adults who will influence the child in school. Even a State's considered judgment about the preferable political and religious character of schoolteachers is not entitled to prevail over a parent's choice of private school. *Pierce*. It would be anomalous, then, to subject a parent to any individual judge's choice of a child's associates from out of the general population merely because the judge might think himself more enlightened than the child's parent....

JUSTICE THOMAS, concurring in the judgment.

I write separately to note that neither party has argued that our substantive due process cases were wrongly decided and that the original understanding of the Due Process Clause precludes judicial enforcement of unenumerated rights under that constitutional provision. As a result, I express no view on the merits of this matter, and I understand the plurality as well to leave the resolution of that issue for another day.

Consequently, I agree with the plurality that this Court's recognition of a fundamental right of parents to direct the upbringing of their children resolves this case. Our decision in *Pierce v. Society of Sisters*, 268 U. S. 510 (1925), holds that parents have a fundamental constitutional right to rear their children, including the right to determine who shall educate and socialize them. The opinions of the plurality, Justice Kennedy, and Justice Souter recognize such a right, but curiously none of them articulates the appropriate standard of review. I would apply strict scrutiny to infringements of fundamental rights. Here, the State of Washington lacks even a legitimate governmental interest—to say nothing of a compelling one—in second-guessing a fit parent's decision regarding visitation with third parties. On this basis, I would affirm the judgment below.

JUSTICE STEVENS, dissenting.

The Court today wisely declines to endorse either the holding or the reasoning of the Supreme Court of Washington. In my opinion, the Court would have been even wiser to deny certiorari. Given the problematic character of the trial court's decision and the uniqueness of the Washington statute, there was no pressing need to review a State Supreme Court decision that merely requires the state legislature to draft a better statute.

Having decided to address the merits, however, the Court should begin by recognizing that the State Supreme Court rendered a federal constitutional judgment holding a state law invalid on its face. In light of that judgment, I believe that we should confront the federal questions presented directly. For the Washington statute is not made facially invalid either because it may be invoked by too many hypothetical plaintiffs, or because it leaves open the possibility that someone may be permitted to sustain a relationship with a child without having to prove that serious harm to the child would otherwise result.

I . . .

The task of reviewing a trial court's application of a state statute to the particular facts of a case is one that should be performed in the first instance by the state appellate courts. In this case, because of their views of the Federal Constitution, the Washington state appeals courts have yet to decide whether the trial court's findings were adequate under the statute. Any as-applied critique of the trial court's judgment that this Court might offer could only be based upon a guess about the state courts' application of that State's statute, and an independent assessment of the facts in this case—both judgments that we are ill-suited and ill-advised to make.[3] . . .

We are thus presented with the unconstrued terms of a state statute and a State Supreme Court opinion that, in my view, significantly misstates the effect of the Federal Constitution upon any construction of that statute. Given that posture, I believe the Court should identify and correct the two flaws in the reasoning of the state court's majority opinion, and remand for further review of the trial court's disposition of this specific case.

II

In my view, the State Supreme Court erred in its federal constitutional analysis because neither the provision granting "any person" the right to petition the court for visitation, nor the absence of a provision

3. Unlike JUSTICE O'CONNOR, I find no suggestion in the trial court's decision in this case that the court was applying any presumptions at all in its analysis, much less one in favor of the grandparents. The first excerpt JUSTICE O'CONNOR quotes from the trial court's ruling says nothing one way or another about who bears the burden under the statute of demonstrating "best interests." There is certainly no indication of a presumption against the parents' judgment, only a " 'commonsensical' "estimation that, usually but not always, visiting with grandparents can be good for children. The second quotation, " 'I think [visitation] would be in the best interest of the children and I haven't been shown that it is not in [the] best interest of the children,' "sounds as though the judge has simply concluded, based on the evidence before him, that visitation in this case would be in the best interests of both girls. Verbatim Report of Proceedings in *In re Troxel*, No. 93–3–00650–7 (Wash.Super.Ct., Dec. 14, 1994), p. 214. These statements do not provide us with a definitive assessment of the law the court applied regarding a "presumption" either way. Indeed, a different impression is conveyed by the judge's very next comment: "That has to be balanced, of course, with Mr. and Mrs. Wynn [a.k.a. Tommie Granville], who are trying to put together a family that includes eight children, . . . trying to get all those children together at the same time and put together some sort of functional unit wherein the children can be raised as brothers and sisters and spend lots of quality time together." The judge then went on to reject the Troxels' efforts to attain the same level of visitation that their son, the girls' biological father, would have had, had he been alive. "[T]he fact that Mr. Troxel is deceased and he was the natural parent and as much as the grandparents would maybe like to step into the shoes of Brad, under our law that is not what we can do. The grandparents cannot step into the shoes of a deceased parent, per say *[sic]*, as far as whole gamut of visitation rights are concerned." Rather, as the judge put it, "I understand your desire to do that as loving grandparents. Unfortunately that would impact too dramatically on the children and their ability to be integrated into the nuclear unit with the mother."

However one understands the trial court's decision—and my point is merely to demonstrate that it is surely open to interpretation—its validity under the state statute as written is a judgment for the state appellate courts to make in the first instance.

requiring a "threshold ... finding of harm to the child," provides a sufficient basis for holding that the statute is invalid in all its applications. I believe that a facial challenge should fail whenever a statute has "a 'plainly legitimate sweep,' " *Washington v. Glucksberg*, 521 U.S. 702, 739–740 and n. 7 (1997) (Stevens, J., concurring in judgment). Under the Washington statute, there are plainly any number of cases—indeed, one suspects, the most common to arise—in which the "person" among "any" seeking visitation is a once-custodial caregiver, an intimate relation, or even a genetic parent. Even the Court would seem to agree that in many circumstances, it would be constitutionally permissible for a court to award some visitation of a child to a parent or previous caregiver in cases of parental separation or divorce, cases of disputed custody, cases involving temporary foster care or guardianship, and so forth. As the statute plainly sweeps in a great deal of the permissible, the State Supreme Court majority incorrectly concluded that a statute authorizing "any person" to file a petition seeking visitation privileges would invariably run afoul of the Fourteenth Amendment.

The second key aspect of the Washington Supreme Court's holding—that the Federal Constitution requires a showing of actual or potential "harm" to the child before a court may order visitation continued over a parent's objections—finds no support in this Court's case law. While, as the Court recognizes, the Federal Constitution certainly protects the parent-child relationship from arbitrary impairment by the State, we have never held that the parent's liberty interest in this relationship is so inflexible as to establish a rigid constitutional shield, protecting every arbitrary parental decision from any challenge absent a threshold finding of harm. The presumption that parental decisions generally serve the best interests of their children is sound, and clearly in the normal case the parent's interest is paramount. But even a fit parent is capable of treating a child like a mere possession.

Cases like this do not present a bipolar struggle between the parents and the State over who has final authority to determine what is in a child's best interests. There is at a minimum a third individual, whose interests are implicated in every case to which the statute applies—the child....

A parent's rights with respect to her child have thus never been regarded as absolute, but rather are limited by the existence of an actual, developed relationship with a child, and are tied to the presence or absence of some embodiment of family. These limitations have arisen, not simply out of the definition of parenthood itself, but because of this Court's assumption that a parent's interests in a child must be balanced against the State's long-recognized interests as parens patriae, and, critically, the child's own complementary interest in preserving relationships that serve her welfare and protection, *Santosky*, 455 U.S., at 760.

While this Court has not yet had occasion to elucidate the nature of a child's liberty interests in preserving established familial or family-like bonds, it seems to me extremely likely that, to the extent parents and families have fundamental liberty interests in preserving such intimate relationships, so, too, do children have these interests, and so, too, must their interests be balanced in the equation. At a minimum, our prior cases recognizing that children are, generally speaking, constitutionally protected actors require that this Court reject any suggestion that when it comes to parental rights, children are so much chattel. The constitutional protection against arbitrary state interference with parental rights should not be extended to prevent the States from protecting children against the arbitrary exercise of parental authority that is not in fact motivated by an interest in the welfare of the child.

This is not, of course, to suggest that a child's liberty interest in maintaining contact with a particular individual is to be treated invariably as on a par with that child's parents' contrary interests. Because our substantive due process case law includes a strong presumption that a parent will act in the best interest of her child, it would be necessary, were the state appellate courts actually to confront a challenge to the statute as applied, to consider whether the trial court's assessment of the "best interest of the child" incorporated that presumption. Neither would I decide whether the trial court applied Washington's statute in a constitutional way in this case, although, as I have explained, I think the outcome of this determination is far from clear. For the purpose of a facial challenge like this, I think it safe to assume that trial judges usually give great deference to parents' wishes, and I am not persuaded otherwise here.

But presumptions notwithstanding, we should recognize that there may be circumstances in which a child has a stronger interest at stake than mere protection from serious harm caused by the termination of visitation by a "person" other than a parent. The almost infinite variety of family relationships that pervade our ever-changing society strongly counsel against the creation by this Court of a constitutional rule that treats a biological parent's liberty interest in the care and supervision of her child as an isolated right that may be exercised arbitrarily. It is indisputably the business of the States, rather than a federal court employing a national standard, to assess in the first instance the relative importance of the conflicting interests that give rise to disputes such as this. Far from guaranteeing that parents' interests will be trammeled in the sweep of cases arising under the statute, the Washington law merely gives an individual—with whom a child may have an established relationship—the procedural right to ask the State to act as arbiter, through the entirely well-known best-interests standard, between the parent's protected interests and the child's. It seems clear to me that the Due Process Clause of the Fourteenth Amendment leaves room for States to consider the impact on a child of possibly arbitrary parental decisions that neither serve nor are motivated by the best interests of the child....

JUSTICE SCALIA, dissenting.

In my view, a right of parents to direct the upbringing of their children is among the "unalienable Rights" with which the Declaration of Independence proclaims "all Men ... are endowed by their Creator." And in my view that right is also among the "othe[r] [rights] retained by the people" which the Ninth Amendment says the Constitution's enumeration of rights "shall not be construed to deny or disparage." The Declaration of Independence, however, is not a legal prescription conferring powers upon the courts; and the Constitution's refusal to "deny or disparage" other rights is far removed from affirming any one of them, and even farther removed from authorizing judges to identify what they might be, and to enforce the judges' list against laws duly enacted by the people. Consequently, while I would think it entirely compatible with the commitment to representative democracy set forth in the founding documents to argue, in legislative chambers or in electoral campaigns, that the state has *no power* to interfere with parents' authority over the rearing of their children, I do not believe that the power which the Constitution confers upon me *as a judge* entitles me to deny legal effect to laws that (in my view) infringe upon what is (in my view) that unenumerated right.

Only three holdings of this Court rest in whole or in part upon a substantive constitutional right of parents to direct the upbringing of their children—two of them from an era rich in substantive due process holdings that have since been repudiated. See *Meyer v. Nebraska*, 262 U.S. 390, 399, 401 (1923); *Pierce v. Society of Sisters,* 268 U.S. 510, 534–535 (1925); *Wisconsin v. Yoder*, 406 U.S. 205, 232–233 (1972). The sheer diversity of today's opinions persuades me that the theory of unenumerated parental rights underlying these three cases has small claim to stare decisis protection. A legal principle that can be thought to produce such diverse outcomes in the relatively simple case before us here is not a legal principle that has induced substantial reliance. While I would not now overrule those earlier cases (that has not been urged), neither would I extend the theory upon which they rested to this new context.

Judicial vindication of "parental rights" under a Constitution that does not even mention them requires (as Justice Kennedy's opinion rightly points out) not only a judicially crafted definition of parents, but also—unless, as no one believes, the parental rights are to be absolute—judicially approved assessments of "harm to the child" and judicially defined gradations of other persons (grandparents, extended family, adoptive family in an adoption later found to be invalid, long-term guardians, etc.) who may have some claim against the wishes of the parents. If we embrace this unenumerated right, I think it obvious—whether we affirm or reverse the judgment here, or remand as Justice Stevens or Justice Kennedy would do—that we will be ushering in a new regime of judicially prescribed, and federally prescribed, family law. I have no reason to believe that federal judges will be better at this than state legislatures; and state legislatures have the great advantages of doing harm in a more circumscribed area, of being able to correct their mistakes in a flash, and of being removable by the people....

JUSTICE KENNEDY, dissenting. . . .

The first flaw the State Supreme Court found in the statute is that it allows an award of visitation to a non-parent without a finding that harm to the child would result if visitation were withheld; and the second is that the statute allows any person to seek visitation at any time. In my view the first theory is too broad to be correct, as it appears to contemplate that the best interests of the child standard may not be applied in any visitation case. I acknowledge the distinct possibility that visitation cases may arise where, considering the absence of other protection for the parent under state laws and procedures, the best interests of the child standard would give insufficient protection to the parent's constitutional right to raise the child without undue intervention by the state; but it is quite a different matter to say, as I understand the Supreme Court of Washington to have said, that a harm to the child standard is required in every instance.

Given the error I see in the State Supreme Court's central conclusion that the best interests of the child standard is never appropriate in third-party visitation cases, that court should have the first opportunity to reconsider this case. I would remand the case to the state court for further proceedings. If it then found the statute has been applied in an unconstitutional manner because the best interests of the child standard gives insufficient protection to a parent under the circumstances of this case, or if it again declared the statute a nullity because the statute seems to allow any person at all to seek visitation at any time, the decision would present other issues which may or may not warrant further review in this Court. These include not only the protection the Constitution gives parents against state-ordered visitation but also the extent to which federal rules for facial challenges to statutes control in state courts. These matters, however, should await some further case. The judgment now under review should be vacated and remanded on the sole ground that the harm ruling that was so central to the Supreme Court of Washington's decision was error, given its broad formulation. . . .

To say that third parties have had no historical right to petition for visitation does not necessarily imply, as the Supreme Court of Washington concluded, that a parent has a constitutional right to prevent visitation in all cases not involving harm. True, this Court has acknowledged that States have the authority to intervene to prevent harm to children, see, e.g., *Prince*, supra, at 168–169; *Yoder*, supra, at 233–234, but that is not the same as saying that a heightened harm to the child standard must be satisfied in every case in which a third party seeks a visitation order. It is also true that the law's traditional presumption has been "that natural bonds of affection lead parents to act in the best interests of their children," *Parham v. J. R.*, 442 U.S. 584, 602 (1979); and "[s]imply because the decision of a parent is not agreeable to a child or because it involves risks does not automatically transfer the power to make that decision from the parents to some agency or officer of the state," *id.*, at 603. The State Supreme Court's conclusion that the

Constitution forbids the application of the best interests of the child standard in any visitation proceeding, however, appears to rest upon assumptions the Constitution does not require.

My principal concern is that the holding seems to proceed from the assumption that the parent or parents who resist visitation have always been the child's primary caregivers and that the third parties who seek visitation have no legitimate and established relationship with the child. That idea, in turn, appears influenced by the concept that the conventional nuclear family ought to establish the visitation standard for every domestic relations case. As we all know, this is simply not the structure or prevailing condition in many households. See, e.g., *Moore v. East Cleveland*, 431 U.S. 494 (1977). For many boys and girls a traditional family with two or even one permanent and caring parent is simply not the reality of their childhood. This may be so whether their childhood has been marked by tragedy or filled with considerable happiness and fulfillment.

Cases are sure to arise—perhaps a substantial number of cases—in which a third party, by acting in a caregiving role over a significant period of time, has developed a relationship with a child which is not necessarily subject to absolute parental veto. See *Michael H. v. Gerald D.*, 491 U.S. 110 (1989) (putative natural father not entitled to rebut state law presumption that child born in a marriage is a child of the marriage); *Quilloin v. Walcott*, 434 U.S. 246 (1978) (best interests standard sufficient in adoption proceeding to protect interests of natural father who had not legitimated the child); see also *Lehr v. Robertson*, 463 U.S. 248, 261 (1983) ("[T]he importance of the familial relationship, to the individuals involved and to the society, stems from the emotional attachments that derive from the intimacy of daily association, and from the role it plays in "promot[ing] a way of life" through the instruction of children ... as well as from the fact of blood relationship." (quoting *Smith v. Organization of Foster Families For Equality & Reform*, 431 U.S. 816, 844 (1977) (in turn quoting *Yoder*, 406 U.S., at 231–233))). Some pre-existing relationships, then, serve to identify persons who have a strong attachment to the child with the concomitant motivation to act in a responsible way to ensure the child's welfare. As the State Supreme Court was correct to acknowledge, those relationships can be so enduring that "in certain circumstances where a child has enjoyed a substantial relationship with a third person, arbitrarily depriving the child of the relationship could cause severe psychological harm to the child," and harm to the adult may also ensue. In the design and elaboration of their visitation laws, States may be entitled to consider that certain relationships are such that to avoid the risk of harm, a best interests standard can be employed by their domestic relations courts in some circumstances....

It must be recognized, of course, that a domestic relations proceeding in and of itself can constitute state intervention that is so disruptive of the parent-child relationship that the constitutional right of a custodial parent to make certain basic determinations for the child's welfare becomes implicated. The best interests of the child standard has at times been criticized as indeterminate, leading to unpredictable results. See, e.g., American Law Institute, Principles of the Law of Family Dissolution 2, and n. 2 (Tentative Draft No. 3, Mar. 20, 1998). If a single parent who is struggling to raise a child is faced with visitation demands from a third party, the attorney's fees alone might destroy her hopes and plans for the child's future. Our system must confront more often the reality that litigation can itself be so disruptive that constitutional protection may be required; and I do not discount the possibility that in some instances the best interests of the child standard may provide insufficient protection to the parent-child relationship. We owe it to the Nation's domestic relations legal structure, however, to proceed with caution.

It should suffice in this case to reverse the holding of the State Supreme Court that the application of the best interests of the child standard is always unconstitutional in third-party visitation cases. Whether, under the circumstances of this case, the order requiring visitation over the objection of this fit parent violated the Constitution ought to be reserved for further proceedings. Because of its sweeping ruling requiring the harm to the child standard, the Supreme Court of Washington did not have the occasion to address the specific visitation order the Troxels obtained. More specific guidance should await a case in which a State's highest court has considered all of the facts in the course of elaborating the protection afforded to parents by the laws of the State and by the Constitution itself. Furthermore, in my view, we need not address whether, under the correct constitutional standards, the Washington statute can be invalidated on its face. This question, too, ought to be addressed by the state court in the first instance....

Notes and Questions on Troxel

(1) There are six opinions in this case, and there is no opinion for the Court. This has become a common pattern. Do the Justices have any obligation to mute their own individual preferences in order to provide guidance to lower courts, legislators, attorneys, and the public? Does it say anything about the legitimacy of the constitutional right the Court is interpreting that the Justices see it so very differently?

(2) What has happened to the usual structure of Fourteenth Amendment analysis? Do parents have "fundamental" constitutional rights? The plurality says there was "an unconstitutional infringement on Granville's fundamental right to make decisions concerning the care, custody, and control of her two daughters." But then where is the "compelling" state interest? Justice Thomas says the state "lacks even a legitimate governmental interest." Is this true? If not, what interests does the government seem to advance or the plurality to acknowledge?

(3) So, the Washington statute as applied in this particular case was unconstitutional. What is the least Washington would have to do to

make the statute entirely constitutional? To satisfy the plurality? To satisfy some majority of the Court?

(a) The plurality notes that the statute "effectively permits any third party seeking visitation to subject any decision by a parent concerning visitation of the parent's children to state-court review." Would the statute be constitutional if it limited standing to grandparents?

(b) The plurality says that as "long as a parent adequately cares for his or her children (i.e., is fit), there will normally be no reason for the State to inject itself into the private realm of the family to further question the ability of that parent to make the best decisions concerning the rearing of that parent's children." Does this mean a statute may not constitutionally permit grandparents to seek visitation unless the custodial parent is unfit? (We will see in Chapter 10 that unfitness is usually defined narrowly.)

(c) The plurality says "the court must accord at least some special weight to the parent's own determination." What formulation would meet that demand? Would that formulation also change the decisions of trial judges?

(d) Can there be anything like a reliable answer to our question about what it would take for a statute to win the Court's approval? The plurality says, "Because much state-court adjudication in this context occurs on a case-by-case basis, we would be hesitant to hold that specific nonparental visitation statutes violate the Due Process Clause as a *per se* matter."

(4) Why do you suppose Ms. Granville refused to allow her daughters to visit their grandparents for extended periods? The Supreme Court leaves this information tantalizingly concealed, but other courts have not been so discrete.

(a) In *Ridenour v. Ridenour*, 901 P2d 770 (NM Ct App 1995), the mother accused the grandmother of sexually abusing the child, and the grandparents accused the mother of abandoning the children, not supervising them properly, taking drugs, and more.

(b) In *Newman v. Phillips*, 1996 WL 480856 (Tenn Ct App 1996), the court reported that "early in Chelsea's life, the relationship between Ms. Phillips and her parents was fairly close and cordial. However, relations became strained, apparently after an unfortunate incident in April, 1994, when Mr. Newman attempted to discipline Chelsea, then about 2 ½ years old, by whipping her with a belt. After that incident, the parties engaged in a number of discordant and heated exchanges which ultimately resulted in Ms. Phillips' decision to discontinue contact with her parents."

(c) In *Hawk v. Hawk*, 855 SW2d 573 (Tenn 1993), the father worked in his father's (the grandfather's) bowling alley. The grandfather seems to have disapproved of the wife from the start, wanted the wife and husband to divorce, publicly cursed the wife, and frequently berated the husband for not "standing up" to his wife "as a man." The parents disagreed with the grandparents about disciplining the children, what the children should do, and when they should go to bed. The parents also worried about the children's uncle, a drug offender who saw the children when they visited the grandparents. Eventually the grandfather fired the father, tried to keep him from receiving unemployment benefits, and wanted to buy the parents' part of the family cemetery plot.

(5) In deciding *Troxel*, should the Court be influenced by the fact that *every* state has some sort of third-party visitation statute? If so, should the Court consider the politics of visitation statutes? Is there anything like a failure of the political process here? In ordinary constitutional terms, the answer to that question is surely "no." Parents are adults who are represented in vast numbers in legislatures. On the other hand, the political reality is that these statutes exist in large part because elderly Americans are politically well-organized and powerful. Parents have not begun to organize to protect their interests as parents in a similar way. Can that matter constitutionally?

(6) Is this a case where the best is the enemy of the good? In other words, even if grandparental visitation ought ideally to be judicially imposed in some cases, is a statute authorizing courts to order it desirable? Will the number of cases in which visitation ought to be ordered be small enough and the risk of ill-considered judicial orders be great enough that such a statute would produce more harm than good? The law must intervene to resolve questions of child custody, but need it intervene to protect the interests of grandparents? Do any of these considerations matter constitutionally?

(7) Recent law review articles suggest that not all state courts are striking down their visitation statutes, as Iowa has done twice, in *Santi v. Santi*, 633 NW2d 312 (2001) and *In re Marriage of Howard*, 661 NW2d 183 (Iowa 2003). *Howard* suggests because *Troxel* establishes a fundamental right to parent, to survive "the highest level" of federal constitutional scrutiny, a grandparent visitation statute must include more than disrupting circumstances such as divorce to overcome the "presumption in favor of a fit parent's decisions regarding their [sic] children." The court found that while divorce, "by necessity, permits the state to resolve immediate and direct disputes that arise between parents over custody and visitation," it is "not the sina qua non of a *compelling* state interest when non-parents seek to challenge parental decision-making." The compelling interest arises only "when substantial harm or potential harm" is visited upon children. The best interests test is therefore insufficient, even when the statute also specifies a preexisting "established substantial relationship" between grandparent and child. As the court puts it, there is a threshold requirement of unfitness. A selection of the (more than 50) law reviews include Michelle Ognibene, *A Constitutional Analysis of Grandparents' Custody Rights*, 72 U Chi L Rev 1473 (2005); Natalie Reed, *Third-Party Visitation Statutes: Why Are Some Families More Equal Than Others?*, 78 S Cal L Rev 1529 (2005);

Paula A. Lorfeld, *Have State Judiciaries Become Legislatures When Grandma Comes to Court? State Court Decisions in the Post-*Troxel *Era*, 5 Marq Elder's Advisor 241 (2004); Solangel Maldonado, *When Father (or Mother) Doesn't Know Best: Quasi–Parents and Parental Deference After* Troxel v. Granville, 88 Iowa L Rev 865 (2003); Kristine L. Roberts, *State Supreme Courts' Applications of Troxel v. Granville and the Reluctance to Declare Grandparent Visitation Statutes Unconstitutional*, 41 Fam Ct Rev 14 (2003).

(8) Some states have distinguished their statutes from the Washington legislation invalidated in *Troxel,* and upheld them if they were more specific about the persons who may seek visitation, the circumstances in which they may sue, and the burden of proof that the third parties must carry. See, e.g., *Stacy v. Ross*, 798 S2d 1275 (Miss 2001); *State ex rel. Brandon L. v. Moats*, 551 SE2d 674 (W Va 2001). As we will discuss shortly, there are also states taking up Justice Stevens' point stressing the child's interest in maintaining relationships. See *Rideout v. Riendeau*, 761 A2d 291 (Me 2000); see generally Shelley A. Riggs, *Response to* Troxel v. Granville: *Implications of Attachment Theory for Judicial Decisions Regarding Custody and Third Party Visitation*, 41 Fam Ct Rev 39 (2003).

(9) De facto parents are the subject of ALI Principles § 2.03 (1)(c), discussed in Chapter 9 [currently at 789]. Assuming grandparents have the right to petition to visit under a state statute that survives a post-Troxel challenge, what about de facto grandparents? In *Peters v. Costello*, 891 A2d 705 (Pa 2005), the Supreme Court of Pennsylvania considered whether a couple who had acted (in loco) for the child's mother from age 11 months to adulthood, largely under a legal custody order, but who had never adopted the mother, had standing to pursue visitation. The child, with her mother, had lived with the couple for four years until the mother lost custody to the father, whom she had never married. The court noted

> to deny appellees the right even to seek visitation under the Act, simply because they lack a biological or formal adoptive connection to Francesca and Felicity, would artificially minimize appellees' actual and substantial relationship to Francesca and Felicity and their actual contributions to their well-being where appellees have, for more than two decades, assumed the responsibilities attendant upon parenting Francesca and serving as *de facto* grandparents to Felicity. Appellees are not officious intermeddlers or mere "prior caretakers," as appellant would have it. As a result of their willingness to step in and actually perform the roles of parents and grandparents, they have distinguished themselves from all other persons lacking a biological or adoptive relationship with this child. In this regard, appellant's argument that the fact that Felicity has a living, biological maternal grandparent justifies denying appellees' standing to seek visitation misses the point. Francesca had and has a living, biological parent, too; but it was appellees who took on the responsibilities for raising Francesca, and thereby acquiring the

> attendant rights of parenthood. The universe of potential petitioners under the Act, while larger than the biological pool, nevertheless is rationally restricted only to those who have played an actual rearing role in the child's life. Accordingly, we hold that, for purposes of the Act, appellees are the equivalent of the child's maternal grandparents, and as such, appellees had standing to file a petition seeking visitation with their grandchild.

Does this holding open the floodgates of litigation to all sorts of people seeing continued connection with a child? We will consider such questions in connection with *Philip B.*, discussed in Chapter 8, and the adoption case of Baby Cornilious in Chapter 10.

Notes and Questions on Troxel, *Family Autonomy, and the Constitution*

This Part of the casebook has been devoted to understanding the role the Constitution plays in contemporary family law. That role is almost entirely the creation of judges, or more accurately, Justices. What—if anything—are they trying to accomplish? What, after several decades of adjudication, is the constitutional principle the Court infers from the due process clause? How useful is the Constitution in regulating the government's regulation of families?

Troxel raises these questions in a number of pointed ways. At this juncture, we may find it most profitable to observe that *Troxel* takes us back to the principle of family autonomy. The tradition of family law is the tradition of *family* autonomy, the principle that the government ought to "intervene" in the family as little as possible. The Court in *Troxel* overturns the statute, and this might indicate that the Court believed the Constitution protected families against encroachment by the state. However, there is a good deal of language in the plurality opinion which suggests it would be quite willing to countenance a less sweeping but similar statute. E.g.: "[I]f a fit parent's decision of the kind at issue here becomes subject to judicial review, the court must accord at least some special weight to the parent's own determination." Justice Stevens seems to intimate an even greater willingness to allow the state to supervise families: "The almost infinite variety of family relationships that pervade our ever-changing society strongly counsel against the creation by this Court of a constitutional rule that treats a biological parent's liberty interest in the care and supervision of her child as an isolated right that may be exercised arbitrarily."

Yet *Troxel* may seem an excellent case for announcing a constitutionalized version of the family autonomy principle. The following notes and questions, then, ask how *Troxel* might look analyzed in those terms. In other words, did James Fitzjames Stephen proffer the best justification for the Supreme Court's intervention in family law? "To try to regulate the internal affairs of a family, the relations of love or friendship, or many other things of the same sort, by law or by the coercion of public opinion is like trying to pull an eyelash out of a man's eye with a pair of tongs. They may put out the eye, but they never will get hold of the eyelash." Let us review our justifications for family autonomy to see how they fit in *Troxel*.

(1) *Is the problem that a court or agency lacks, and will find it hard to get, information about any particular family's situation? Troxel* is an illuminating case partly because it gives us wisps of the trial judge's perceptions of the case and hence some sense of the competence, knowledge, and acuity of the judges who really make decisions in family cases. We learn that

> the Superior Court made only two formal findings in support of its visitation order. First, the Troxels "are part of a large, central, loving family, all located in this area, and the [Troxels] can provide opportunities for the children in the areas of cousins and music." Second, "[t]he children would be benefitted from spending quality time with the [Troxels], provided that that time is balanced with time with the childrens' [*sic*] nuclear family."

The trial court had clearly collected more information than this. But how much more? How much would it need to make a really good judgment about the benefits of awarding the grandparents visitation rights?

(2) *Is the problem that judges lack expertise in these kinds of decisions?* Is there any indication in *Troxel* that the judge has any educated insight into the ways families work and children develop? If he did, how large a role did that insight play compared with the reveries about his childhood?

> The Superior Court's announced reason for ordering one week of visitation in the summer demonstrates our conclusion well: "I look back on some personal experiences.... We always spen[t] as kids a week with one set of grandparents and another set of grandparents, [and] it happened to work out in our family that [it] turned out to be an enjoyable experience. Maybe that can, in this family, if that is how it works out."

Expert witnesses did testify in *Troxel*. How much guidance are they likely to have brought the court?

(3) *Is the problem that no adequate standards can be devised to govern a court's or an administrative agency's decision?* Isn't this at the crux of the problem of *Troxel*? How are we to know what is in the children's best interests? The people closest to them seem to disagree. The "best-interests" standard is notoriously vague (or, as lawyers like to say, indeterminate). It seems exceptionally likely that it is often in the interests of children to maintain contact with their grandparents but also in the interests of children not to have the grandparents use the law to force their way into the children's household. In other words, the children in these cases usually have conflicting interests. This is the kind of tragic conflict abstract standards rarely resolve satisfactorily.

(4) *Is the problem that enforcement of a judicial decree in family disputes would be impossible?* The enforcement problems here are potentially quite unpleasant. Presumably no visitation order is necessary

unless the relations between the parent and the grandparents have become hostile. It's quite possible that the grandparents have so infuriated the mother that she will aggressively resist their attempts to enforce their visitation rights. Courts find visitation orders hard to enforce even when one of the parents is the visitor. How far will the trial court in *Troxel* be willing to go to enforce its order?

There is another twist to the enforcement problem. The dispute over visitation began in October 1993. The grandparents sued in December 1993. The trial did not take place until a year later. Some time in 1995, the trial court issued an oral ruling. The appellate court remanded for written findings of fact and conclusions of law. The trial court complied, and the appellate court reversed. The state supreme court finally issued a ruling on Christmas Eve, 1998. The US Supreme Court handed down its opinion on June 5, 2000. Of course, few if any of these cases will reach the Supreme Court, but litigation can certainly drag on for years. In visitation disputes, those years can effectively moot out the case.

(5) *Is the problem that the judicial process will exacerbate, not resolve, the family conflict?* In one sense, this seems quite likely. If the grandparents have no cause of action, the custodial parent can simply prevent them from visiting the children. The parent and the children need never see the grandparents. Their relations will be peaceful because they won't exist. The cause of action gives the grandparents a way of forcing a fight with the custodial parent. Once the grandparents have brought suit, the agony of litigation seems unlikely to endear the parent and the grandparents to each other. And if the parent is forced to cooperate in allowing the grandparents to visit the children it is easy to imagine many ways they might enrage each other.

(6) *Is the problem that a judicial inquiry into the facts of a family dispute would necessarily injure a family by invading its privacy? Griswold* speaks directly in the language of privacy in its ordinary—not its constitutional—meaning. Isn't that kind of privacy crucially at risk in *Troxel* cases? From the custodial parent's point of view, the grandparents are outsiders who are trying to break into a private household. *Troxel* suits, then, seem fated to violate familial privacy in two ways. First, the process of litigation is likely to force the parent and perhaps even the children to explain how they are living and why they do not want their household disturbed. In addition, the suit is likely to be the occasion of intrusions into the privacy of the plaintiff-grandparents. They may have consented, but that may not make the inquiry into their psychological and moral fitness to spend time with their grandchildren much more appealing. Second, grandparents who win visitation rights will have a picture window, kept uncurtained at the government's command, into the lives of the parents and children.

(7) *Is the problem that it is in some way normatively preferable for individuals to organize their lives, particularly their intimate lives, free of government supervision?* This is surely what the parents in *Troxel* cases will strongly feel. The grandparents, on the other hand, will point out

that they cannot organize their intimate lives in the way they want to *without* government intervention. Do we have some reason to think them entitled to that help?

(8) *Is the problem that we wish to preserve a pluralist society, and that allowing families freedom to organize themselves as they wish is one way of promoting that goal?* Doesn't it seem likely that no small proportion of the reasons parents may have for wanting to deny visitation to grandparents may concern conflicts over values the state is constitutionally impeded from evaluating? Grandparents and parents fight over the things that are important to people, like how the child is to be educated, what divinity the child should be taught to worship, what political principles should be taboo in the household, and what ethnic traditions should be most esteemed. (Is this why the Washington Supreme Court wrote in overturning the statute at issue in *Troxel*: "Some parents and judges will not care if their child is physically disciplined by a third person; some parents and judges will not care if a third person teaches the child a religion inconsistent with the parents' religion; and some judges and parents will not care if the child is exposed to or taught racist or sexist beliefs. But many parents and judges will care, and, between the two, the parents should be the ones to choose whether to expose their children to certain people or ideas." *In re Smith*, 969 P2d 21, 31 (1998).)

The Court returned to the nuclear (though divorced) family in *Elk Grove v. Newdow*.

ELK GROVE UNIFIED SCHOOL DISTRICT v. NEWDOW

Supreme Court of the United States, 2004
542 US 1

JUSTICE STEVENS delivered the opinion of the Court.

Each day elementary school teachers in the Elk Grove Unified School District (School District) lead their classes in a group recitation of the Pledge of Allegiance. Respondent, Michael A. Newdow, is an atheist whose daughter participates in that daily exercise. Because the Pledge contains the words "under God," he views the School District's policy as a religious indoctrination of his child that violates the First Amendment. A divided panel of the Court of Appeals for the Ninth Circuit agreed with Newdow. In light of the obvious importance of that decision, we granted certiorari to review the First Amendment issue and, preliminarily, the question whether Newdow has standing to invoke the jurisdiction of the federal courts. We conclude that Newdow lacks standing and therefore reverse the Court of Appeals' decision.

I

"The very purpose of a national flag is to serve as a symbol of our country," *Texas v. Johnson,* 491 U.S. 397, 405 (1989), and of its proud traditions "of freedom, of equal opportunity, of religious tolerance, and of good will for other peoples who share our aspirations," *id.,* at 437 (STEVENS, J., dissenting). As its history illustrates, the Pledge of Allegiance evolved as a common public acknowledgement of the ideals that our flag symbolizes. Its recitation is a patriotic exercise designed to foster national unity and pride in those principles.

The Pledge of Allegiance was initially conceived more than a century ago. As part of the nationwide interest in commemorating the 400th anniversary of Christopher Columbus' discovery of America, a widely circulated national magazine for youth proposed in 1892 that pupils recite the following affirmation: "I pledge allegiance to my Flag and the Republic for which it stands: one Nation indivisible, with Liberty and Justice for all." In the 1920's, the National Flag Conferences replaced the phrase "my Flag" with "the flag of the United States of America."

In 1942, in the midst of World War II, Congress adopted, and the President signed, a Joint Resolution codifying a detailed set of "rules and customs pertaining to the display and use of the flag of the United States of America. Chapter 435, 56 Stat. 377. Section 7 of this codification provided in full:

> "That the pledge of allegiance to the flag, 'I pledge allegiance to the flag of the United States of America and to the Republic for which it stands, one Nation indivisible, with liberty and justice for all', be rendered by standing with the right hand over the heart; extending the right hand, palm upward, toward the flag at the words 'to the flag' and holding this position until the end, when the hand drops to the side. However, civilians will always show full respect to the flag when the pledge is given by merely standing at attention, men removing the headdress. Persons in uniform shall render the military salute." *Id.,* at 380.

This resolution, which marked the first appearance of the Pledge of Allegiance in positive law, confirmed the importance of the flag as a symbol of our Nation's indivisibility and commitment to the concept of liberty.

Congress revisited the Pledge of Allegiance 12 years later when it amended the text to add the words "under God." Act of June 14, 1954, ch. 297, 68 Stat. 249. The House Report that accompanied the legislation observed that, "[f]rom the time of our earliest history our peoples and our institutions have reflected the traditional concept that our Nation was founded on a fundamental belief in God." H.R.Rep. No. 1693, 83d Cong., 2d Sess., p. 2 (1954). The resulting text is the Pledge as we know it today: "I pledge allegiance to the Flag of the United States of America, and to the Republic for which it stands, one Nation under God, indivisible, with liberty and justice for all." 4 U.S.C. § 4.

II

Under California law, "every public elementary school" must begin each day with "appropriate patriotic exercises." Cal. Educ.Code Ann.

§ 52720 (West 1989). The statute provides that "[t]he giving of the Pledge of Allegiance to the Flag of the United States of America shall satisfy" this requirement. The Elk Grove Unified School District has implemented the state law by requiring that "[e]ach elementary school class recite the pledge of allegiance to the flag once each day." Consistent with our case law, the School District permits students who object on religious grounds to abstain from the recitation. See *West Virginia Bd. of Ed. v. Barnette,* 319 U.S. 624 (1943).

In March 2000, Newdow filed suit in the United States District Court for the Eastern District of California against the United States Congress, the President of the United States, the State of California, and the Elk Grove Unified School District and its superintendent. At the time of filing, Newdow's daughter was enrolled in kindergarten in the Elk Grove Unified School District and participated in the daily recitation of the Pledge. Styled as a mandamus action, the complaint explains that Newdow is an atheist who was ordained more than 20 years ago in a ministry that "espouses the religious philosophy that the true and eternal bonds of righteousness and virtue stem from reason rather than mythology." The complaint seeks a declaration that the 1954 Act's addition of the words "under God" violated the Establishment and Free Exercise Clauses of the United States Constitution, as well as an injunction against the School District's policy requiring daily recitation of the Pledge. It alleges that Newdow has standing to sue on his own behalf and on behalf of his daughter as "next friend."

The case was referred to a Magistrate Judge, whose brief findings and recommendation concluded, "the Pledge does not violate the Establishment Clause." The District Court adopted that recommendation and dismissed the complaint on July 21, 2000. The Court of Appeals reversed and issued three separate decisions discussing the merits and Newdow's standing.

In its first opinion the appeals court unanimously held that Newdow has standing "as a parent to challenge a practice that interferes with his right to direct the religious education of his daughter." *Newdow v. U.S. Congress*, 292 F.3d 597, 602 (C.A. 9 2002) (*Newdow* I). That holding sustained Newdow's standing to challenge not only the policy of the School District, where his daughter still is enrolled, but also the 1954 Act of Congress that had amended the Pledge, because his " 'injury in fact' "was " 'fairly traceable' "to its enactment. On the merits, over the dissent of one judge, the court held that both the 1954 Act and the School District's policy violate the Establishment Clause of the First Amendment.

After the Court of Appeals' initial opinion was announced, Sandra Banning, the mother of Newdow's daughter, filed a motion for leave to intervene, or alternatively to dismiss the complaint. She declared that although she and Newdow shared "physical custody" of their daughter, a state-court order granted her "exclusive legal custody" of the child, "including the sole right to represent [the daughter's] legal interests and make all decision[s] about her education" and welfare. Banning further stated that her daughter is a Christian who believes in God and has no objection either to reciting or hearing others recite the Pledge of Allegiance, or to its reference to God. Banning expressed the belief that her daughter would be harmed if the litigation were permitted to proceed, because others might incorrectly perceive the child as sharing her father's atheist views. Banning accordingly concluded, as her daughter's sole legal custodian, that it was not in the child's interest to be a party to Newdow's lawsuit. On September 25, 2002, the California Superior Court entered an order enjoining Newdow from including his daughter as an unnamed party or suing as her "next friend." That order did not purport to answer the question of Newdow's Article III standing. See *Newdow v. U.S. Congress*, 313 F.3d 500, 502 (C.A.9 2002) (*Newdow* II).

In a second published opinion, the Court of Appeals reconsidered Newdow's standing in light of Banning's motion. The court noted that Newdow no longer claimed to represent his daughter, but unanimously concluded that "the grant of sole legal custody to Banning" did not deprive Newdow, "as a noncustodial parent, of Article III standing to object to unconstitutional government action affecting his child." The court held that under California law Newdow retains the right to expose his child to his particular religious views even if those views contradict the mother's, and that Banning's objections as sole legal custodian do not defeat Newdow's right to seek redress for an alleged injury to his own parental interests.

On February 28, 2003, the Court of Appeals issued an order amending its first opinion and denying rehearing en banc. *Newdow v. U.S. Congress*, 328 F.3d 466, 468 (C.A. 9 2003) (*Newdow III*). The amended opinion omitted the initial opinion's discussion of Newdow's standing to challenge the 1954 Act and declined to determine whether Newdow was entitled to declaratory relief regarding the constitutionality of that Act. Nine judges dissented from the denial of en banc review. We granted the School District's petition for a writ of certiorari to consider two questions: (1) whether Newdow has standing as a noncustodial parent to challenge the School District's policy, and (2) if so, whether the policy offends the First Amendment.

III

In every federal case, the party bringing the suit must establish standing to prosecute the action. "In essence the question of standing is whether the litigant is entitled to have the court decide the merits of the dispute or of particular issues." The standing requirement is born partly of " 'an idea, which is more than an intuition but less than a rigorous and explicit theory, about the constitutional and prudential limits to the powers of an unelected, unrepresentative judiciary in our kind of government.' "

The command to guard jealously and exercise rarely our power to make constitutional pronouncements requires strictest adherence when matters of great national significance are at stake. Even in cases concededly within our jurisdiction under Article III, we abide by "a series of rules under which [we have] avoided passing upon a large part of all the constitutional questions pressed upon [us] for decision." Always we must balance "the heavy obligation to exercise jurisdiction," against the "deeply rooted" commitment "not to pass on questions of constitutionality" unless adjudication of the constitutional issue is necessary.

Consistent with these principles, our standing jurisprudence contains two strands: Article III standing, which enforces the Constitution's case or controversy requirement, and prudential standing, which embodies "judicially self-imposed limits on the exercise of federal jurisdiction.," The Article III limitations are familiar: The plaintiff must show that the conduct of which he complains has caused him to suffer an "injury in fact" that a favorable judgment will redress. Although we have not exhaustively defined the prudential dimensions of the standing doctrine, we have explained that prudential standing encompasses "the general prohibition on a litigant's raising another person's legal rights, the rule barring adjudication of generalized grievances more appropriately addressed in the representative branches, and the requirement that a plaintiff's complaint fall within the zone of interests protected by the law invoked." "Without such limitations—closely related to Art. III concerns but essentially matters of judicial self-governance—the courts would be called upon to decide abstract questions of wide public significance even though other governmental institutions may be more competent to address the questions and even though judicial intervention may be unnecessary to protect individual rights."

One of the principal areas in which this Court has customarily declined to intervene is the realm of domestic relations. Long ago we observed that "[t]he whole subject of the domestic relations of husband and wife, parent and child, belongs to the laws of the States and not to the laws of the United States." So strong is our deference to state law in this area that we have recognized a "domestic relations exception" that "divests the federal courts of power to issue divorce, alimony, and child custody decrees." *Ankenbrandt v. Richards,* 504 U.S. 689, 703 (1992). We have also acknowledged that it might be appropriate for the federal courts to decline to hear a case involving "elements of the domestic relationship," even when divorce, alimony, or child custody is not strictly at issue:

> "This would be so when a case presents 'difficult questions of state law bearing on policy problems of substantial public import whose importance transcends the result in the case then at bar.' Such might well be the case if a federal suit were filed prior to effectuation of a divorce, alimony, or child custody decree, and the suit depended on a determination of the status of the parties."

Thus, while rare instances arise in which it is necessary to answer a substantial federal question that transcends or exists apart from the family law issue, see, *e.g., Palmore v. Sidoti,* 466 U.S. 429, 432–434,

(1984), in general it is appropriate for the federal courts to leave delicate issues of domestic relations to the state courts.[4]

As explained briefly above, the extent of the standing problem raised by the domestic relations issues in this case was not apparent until August 5, 2002, when Banning filed her motion for leave to intervene or dismiss the complaint following the Court of Appeals' initial decision. At that time, the child's custody was governed by a February 6, 2002, order of the California Superior Court. That order provided that Banning had " '*sole* legal custody as to the rights and responsibilities to make decisions relating to the health, education and welfare of' "her daughter. *Newdow II,* 313 F.3d, at 502. The order stated that the two parents should " 'consult with one another on substantial decisions relating to' " the child's " 'psychological and educational needs,' " but it authorized Banning to " 'exercise legal control' " if the parents could not reach " 'mutual agreement.' "

That family court order was the controlling document at the time of the Court of Appeals' standing decision. After the Court of Appeals ruled, however, the Superior Court held another conference regarding the child's custody. At a hearing on September 11, 2003, the Superior Court announced that the parents have "joint legal custody," but that Banning "makes the final decisions if the two ... disagree."[5]

Newdow contends that despite Banning's final authority, he retains "an unrestricted right to inculcate in his daughter—free from governmental interference—the atheistic beliefs he finds persuasive." The difficulty with that argument is that Newdow's rights, as in many cases touching upon family relations, cannot be viewed in isolation. This case concerns not merely Newdow's interest in inculcating his child with his

4. Our holding does not rest, as THE CHIEF JUSTICE suggests, see *post,* at 2313–2314, on either the domestic relations exception or the abstention doctrine. Rather, our prudential standing analysis is informed by the variety of contexts in which federal courts decline to intervene because, as [*Ankenbrandt*] contemplated, the suit "depend[s] on a determination of the status of the parties." We deemed it appropriate to review the dispute in *Palmore* because it "raise[d] important federal concerns arising from the Constitution's commitment to eradicating discrimination based on race." In this case, by contrast, the disputed family law rights are entwined inextricably with the threshold standing inquiry. THE CHIEF JUSTICE in this respect misses our point: The *merits* question undoubtedly transcends the domestic relations issue, but the *standing* question surely does not.

5. The court confirmed that position in a written order issued January 9, 2004:

"The parties will have joint legal custody defined as follows: Ms. Banning will continue to make the final decisions as to the minor's health, education, and welfare if the two parties cannot mutually agree. The parties are required to consult with each other on substantial decisions relating to the health, education and welfare of the minor child, including ... psychological and educational needs of the minor. If mutual agreement is not reached in these areas, then Ms. Banning may exercise legal control of the minor that is not specifically prohibited or is inconsistent with the physical custody."

Despite the use of the term "joint legal custody"—which is defined by California statute, see Cal. Fam.Code Ann. § 3003 (West 1994)—we see no meaningful distinction for present purposes between the custody order issued February 6, 2002, and the one issued January 9, 2004. Under either order, Newdow has the right to consult on issues relating to the child's education, but Banning possesses what we understand amounts to a tiebreaking vote.

views on religion, but also the rights of the child's mother as a parent generally and under the Superior Court orders specifically. And most important, it implicates the interests of a young child who finds herself at the center of a highly public debate over her custody, the propriety of a widespread national ritual, and the meaning of our Constitution.

The interests of the affected persons in this case are in many respects antagonistic. Of course, legal disharmony in family relations is not uncommon, and in many instances that disharmony poses no bar to federal-court adjudication of proper federal questions. What makes this case different is that Newdow's standing derives entirely from his relationship with his daughter, but he lacks the right to litigate as her next friend. In marked contrast to our case law on *jus tertii,* the interests of this parent and this child are not parallel and, indeed, are potentially in conflict.[6]

Newdow's parental status is defined by California's domestic relations law. Our custom on questions of state law ordinarily is to defer to the interpretation of the Court of Appeals for the Circuit in which the State is located. In this case, the Court of Appeals, which possesses greater familiarity with California law, concluded that state law vests in Newdow a cognizable right to influence his daughter's religious upbringing. The court based its ruling on two intermediate state appellate cases holding that "while the custodial parent undoubtedly has the right to make ultimate decisions concerning the child's religious upbringing, a court will not enjoin the noncustodial parent from discussing religion with the child or involving the child in his or her religious activities in the absence of a showing that the child will be thereby harmed." *In re Marriage of Murga,* 163 Cal.Rptr. 79, 82 (1980). See also *In re Marriage of Mentry,* 190 Cal.Rptr. 843, 849–850 (1983) (relying on *Murga* to invalidate portion of restraining order barring noncustodial father from engaging children in religious activity or discussion without custodial parent's consent). Animated by a conception of "family privacy" that includes "not simply a policy of minimum state intervention but also a presumption of parental autonomy," the state cases create a zone of private authority within which each parent, whether custodial or noncustodial, remains free to impart to the child his or her religious perspective.

Nothing that either Banning or the School Board has done, however, impairs Newdow's right to instruct his daughter in his religious views. Instead, Newdow requests relief that is more ambitious than that sought

6. "There are good and sufficient reasons for th[e] prudential limitation on standing when rights of third parties are implicated—the avoidance of the adjudication of rights which those not before the Court may not wish to assert, and the assurance that the most effective advocate of the rights at issue is present to champion them." *Duke Power Co. v. Carolina Environmental Study Group, Inc.*, 438 U.S. 59, 80 (1978). Banning tells us that her daughter has no objection to the Pledge, and we are mindful in cases such as this that "children themselves have constitutionally protectible interests." *Wisconsin v. Yoder,* 406 U.S. 205, 243 (1972) (Douglas, J., dissenting). In a fundamental respect, "[i]t is the future of the student, not the future of the parents," that is at stake.

in *Mentry* and *Murga.* He wishes to forestall his daughter's exposure to religious ideas that her mother, who wields a form of veto power, endorses, and to use his parental status to challenge the influences to which his daughter may be exposed in school when he and Banning disagree. The California cases simply do not stand for the proposition that Newdow has a right to dictate to others what they may and may not say to his child respecting religion. *Mentry* and *Murga* are concerned with protecting " 'the fragile, complex interpersonal bonds between child and parent,' " and with permitting divorced parents to expose their children to the " 'diversity of religious experiences [that] is itself a sound stimulant for a child,' " The cases speak not at all to the problem of a parent seeking to reach outside the private parent-child sphere to restrain the acts of a third party. A next friend surely could exercise such a right, but the Superior Court's order has deprived Newdow of that status.

In our view, it is improper for the federal courts to entertain a claim by a plaintiff whose standing to sue is founded on family law rights that are in dispute when prosecution of the lawsuit may have an adverse effect on the person who is the source of the plaintiff's claimed standing. When hard questions of domestic relations are sure to affect the outcome, the prudent course is for the federal court to stay its hand rather than reach out to resolve a weighty question of federal constitutional law. There is a vast difference between Newdow's right to communicate with his child—which both California law and the First Amendment recognize—and his claimed right to shield his daughter from influences to which she is exposed in school despite the terms of the custody order. We conclude that, having been deprived under California law of the right to sue as next friend, Newdow lacks prudential standing to bring this suit in federal court.

The judgment of the Court of Appeals is reversed.

Chief Justice Rehnquist, with whom Justice O'Connor joins, and with whom Justice Thomas joins as to Part I, concurring in the judgment.

The Court today erects a novel prudential standing principle in order to avoid reaching the merits of the constitutional claim. I dissent from that ruling. On the merits, I conclude that the Elk Grove Unified School District (School District) policy that requires teachers to lead willing students in reciting the Pledge of Allegiance, which includes the words "under God," does not violate the Establishment Clause of the First Amendment....

Notes and Questions on Elk Grove

1. Iowa's Supreme Court has struck down its grandparent visitation statute twice, in *Santi v. Santi*, 633 NW2d 312 (Iowa 2001) and *In re Marriage of Howard*, 661 NW2d 183 (Iowa 2003). *Howard* suggests that because *Troxel* establishes a fundamental right to parent, to survive

"the highest level" of federal constitutional scrutiny, a grandparent visitation statute must include more than disrupting circumstances such as divorce to overcome the "presumption in favor of a fit parent's decisions regarding their [sic] children." The court found that while divorce, "by necessity, permits the state to resolve immediate and direct disputes that arise between parents over custody and visitation," it is "not the sina qua non of a *compelling* state interest when non-parents seek to challenge parental decision-making." The compelling interest arises only "when substantial harm or potential harm" is visited upon children. The best interests test is therefore insufficient, even when the statute also specifies a preexisting "established substantial relationship" between grandparent and child. The statute must also "require a threshold finding of parental unfitness." Would a custodial parent ever be unfit? Because unfitness of a custodial parent is highly unlikely (although, hypothetically, a custodial parent could be fit in all other respects save the matter of grandparent visitation), does *Howard* mean that grandparents have effectively lost visitation rights in Iowa? Does *Troxel*, as modified by *Elk Grove*, require this of grandparent visitation statutes?

2. When the Court handed down *Elk Grove,* the opinion was greeted with keen disappointment by constitutional law professors since it dealt with standing and prudential issues rather than the establishment clause question raised by *Newdow*. When evaluated in combination with *Troxel*, does it nonetheless hold real significance for family law? In other words, does *Elk Grove* signal some limitations to the parental autonomy doctrine firmly established in *Troxel*? Note that the *Elk Grove* opinion was written by Justice Stevens, who wrote a dissenting opinion in *Troxel*, suggesting in Part II that "There is at minimum a third individual, whose interests are implicated in every case to which the statute applies..." Does a holding like the Iowa court's in *Howard* interfere with what *Elk Grove* recognizes are the daughter's rights? Or would the interests be less likely to be "potentially in conflict" if it were a custodial parent, like Sandra Banning in *Elk Grove*, who objected to the visitation?

3. You may have noticed that the flag salute legislation was passed shortly before *Lochner* the symbol of substantive due process and was modified at almost the same time as *Meyer* and *Prince* when concern about foreign nationals ran high. Do contemporary concerns about terrorism and military involvement in the Middle East color the *Elk Grove* opinions?

4. Does the California custody order, practically speaking, grant Michael Newdow any parenting (that is, not just "zoo daddy") rights? The clarification the Court gives is that Newdow is to be consulted and have input, and that Sandra Banning is to act as tiebreaker when the two cannot agree. Given the Court's holding, does Newdow have any real power to influence his daughter's upbringing? Does the Court's holding in *Elk Grove* change the rights of noncustodial parents in California despite its decision to decline jurisdiction over substantive family law?

Does *Elk Grove* alter the rights of noncustodial parents outside California? Will *Elk Grove* give incentives for individual fathers to seek custody rather than "visitation?" Will *Elk Grove* impact the joint physical custody movement, discussed in Chapter 9?

5. Should the Court revisit the "domestic relations exception" discussed both in *Ankenbrandt v. Richards* and *Elk Grove*? Does the Court do a particularly good job in family law cases? Are state supreme courts (like Iowa's in *Howard*) any more expert?

6. Is the statement the Court makes at the end of the paragraph beginning "Newdow contends ...", page 718, a departure from the autonomy rights given to parents in *Meyer*, *Pierce*, *Prince* and *Troxel*? Whose rights are now most important? Is *Elk Grove* really about Michael, Sarah or their (unnamed) daughter? For a case considering the problem from the child's perspective, see *Rideout v. Riendeau*, 761 A2d 291, 302 & n 16 (Me 2000); see generally Shelley A. Riggs, *Response to* Troxel v. Granville: *Implications of Attachment Theory for Judicial Decisions Regarding Custody and Third Party Visitation*, 41 Fam Ct Rev 39 (2003).

7. Why might it be important for a court to intervene in *Elk Grove* but not in *Troxel* or *Howard*? The Supreme Court has jurisdiction because of the First Amendment rights involved, but that doesn't resolve the autonomy question. Is the difference that the two parents are not in agreement? That they are already in litigation? That the daughter, "a Christian," although in elementary school may be old enough to have her own views? That the case may prove (may have already proven) highly embarrassing for the daughter? In other words, is this right to say or not say "under God" a First Amendment right being given to Newdow and Banning's daughter? We will visit these issues in a somewhat different context in Justice Douglas' dissenting opinion in *Wisconsin v. Yoder* in Chapter 12. (Note that Douglas' opinion in *Yoder* is quoted in footnote 4).

Notes and Questions on **Troxel** *and* **Elk Grove,** *the Family as Entity, and the Constitution*

Whose rights are at stake in *Troxel*? The mother challenged the statute, and thus it was the mother who claimed a constitutional right. And, as the Justices generally acknowledged, she could muster impressive precedential credentials. But why couldn't the grandparents claim their own constitutional rights? Consider *Moore v. City of East Cleveland*, 431 US 494 (1977). East Cleveland's zoning ordinance defined "family" in a way that did not include Mrs. Moore's household, in which she lived with her son and two grandsons who were cousins and not brothers. The Court held this definition unconstitutionally narrow. Does *Moore* support the grandparents' claim in *Troxel*? Don't the reasons the Court has regularly advanced for attributing rights to individuals justify attributing rights to grandparents?

For that matter, aren't children the most deeply interested parties in the dispute, and shouldn't they also have their claim to constitutional dignity? We ordinarily let parents make decisions for children, of course. Don't we do so because we think parents will make good decisions for them? If so, is that presumption true in situations where it seems so likely that parents will have become absorbed in their own battles with grandparents or each other? Isn't this, then, a situation where children's own constitutional claims should be recognized directly?

Questions of this kind can be put not just about *Troxel* and *Elk Grove,* but about most constitutional cases involving families. Why did the Justices not treat these questions more seriously? One possibility is that American constitutional doctrine is not well-equipped to handle them. That doctrine revolves around what we may call the "Mill paradigm" in which one individual confronts the state. As Professor Schneider writes,

> In such conflicts, we are predisposed to favor the person, out of respect for his moral autonomy and human dignity. We have, to use a legal expression, a presumption in favor of a decision by the person. This presumption is tolerable partly because society can afford to bear the risk of an incorrect substantive decision better than a person can....
>
> In family law, however, the Mill paradigm often breaks down, because in family law conflicts are often not between a person and the state but between one person and another person. In these conflicts, we cannot be guided by our presumption in favor of the person: both contenders have their claim to moral autonomy and human dignity; neither is a priori better situated than the other to bear the risk of improperly allocated authority. Our legal thinking about rights has conspicuously, if understandably, failed to develop a satisfactory alternative to the Mill paradigm with which to approach such conflicts. That failure is reflected in the painful awkwardness of the Supreme Court's treatment of, inter alia, statutes requiring a parent's consent to a minor child's abortion, statutes requiring a husband's consent to his wife's abortion, statutes prohibiting abortion, and claims that foster parents can acquire constitutional rights in other people's children....

Rights Discourse and Neonatal Euthanasia, 76 Cal L Rev 151, 157–58 (1988).

So how has the Court handled the absence of a satisfactory paradigm for handling family law problems through constitutional rights? Principally, it has tried to squeeze family cases into the Mill paradigm, however awkward the fit. In the beginning were *Meyer* and *Pierce*. There, the Court simply assumed that the parents and the children had the same interests. *Meyer* and *Pierce* begat *Griswold* and *Eisenstadt*. The Court based its opinion in the former on the sanctity of the marital entity and based the latter on the claims of individuals. *Griswold* and *Eisenstadt* begat *Roe* and *Casey*. The great problem of *Roe*, a problem the Court's opinion slides away from, is the argument that the interests of the mother and the fetus conflict. In *Casey* that conflict is dealt with even less directly.

In *Troxel*, it is difficult for the Court to avoid confronting the fact that the Mill paradigm is inapt. The statute in *Troxel* was designed to deal with situations in which there is a flat conflict between the custodial parent and the grandparents. The statute seeks to resolve that conflict in terms of yet a third set of interests, those of the children, who may have independent interests of their own or who may share the interests of either the parent or the grandparents (or, perhaps more plausibly, all three). What, then, is the Court's technique? Does the Court employ the same technique in *Elk Grove*?

BIBLIOGRAPHY

Laurence H. Tribe, *Abortion: The Clash of Absolutes* (Norton, 1990), is an examination of the issue by one of the most influential constitutional scholars. One of Professor Tribe's colleagues provides a provocative comparative study of the abortion controversy in Mary Ann Glendon, *Abortion and Divorce in Western Law: American Failures, European Challenges* (Harv U Press, 1987). The abortion controversy is put into yet a different perspective in Guido Calabresi, *Ideals, Beliefs, Attitudes, and the Law: Private Law Perspectives on a Public Law Problem* (Syracuse U Press, 1985). And that controversy is still once more re-interpreted in Rosalind Pollack Petchesky, *Abortion and Woman's Choice: The State, Sexuality, and Reproductive Freedom* (Northeastern U Press, 1985). A collection of essays (including an imaginative attempt to rewrite *Roe*), is Carl E. Schneider and Maris A. Vinovskis, eds, *The Law and Politics of Abortion* (Lexington Books, 1980). A look into the implications for family law of the cases you have read is Janet L. Dolgin, *The Family in Transition From* Griswold *to* Eisenstadt *and Beyond*, 82 Geo L Rev 1519 (1994). Joan Williams, *Gender Wars: Selfless Women in the Republic of Choice*, 66 NYU L Rev 1559 (1991), provides a look at the issues of abortion and labor participation by married women with children as examples of how their choices have been mischaracterized as selfish.

Kristin Luker, *Abortion and the Politics of Motherhood* (U Cal Press, 1984), is an excellent and illuminating study of activists on both sides of the issue.

A survey of the debate on the moral status of abortion is L. W. Sumner, *Abortion and Moral Theory* (Princeton U Press, 1981).

For examinations of the larger dispute over American culture generally and the role of the family particularly, see James Davison Hunter, *Culture Wars: The Struggle to Define America* (Basic Books, 1991); Brigitte Berger and Peter L. Berger, *The War Over the Family: Capturing the Middle Ground* (Anchor Books, 1984).

The literature on rights is, of course, gigantic. A few selections from the philosophical literature include Richard Tuck, *Natural Rights Theories: Their Origin and Development* (Cambridge U Press, 1979); Ian

Shapiro, *The Evolution of Rights in Liberal Theory* (Cambridge U Press, 1986); L.W. Sumner, *The Moral Foundation of Rights* (Oxford U Press, 1987). Mary Ann Glendon, *Rights Talk: The Impoverishment of Political Discourse* (Free Press, 1991) criticizes modern American rights discourse. Lawrence M. Friedman, *The Republic of Choice: Law, Authority, and Culture* (Harv U Press, 1990) finds more to like in it.

The Abortion Choice. For fictional insights into the difficult choices faced by a talented African–American woman who must deal with a pregnancy that's unplanned, see Terry McMillan, *Disappearing Acts* (Pocket Books, 1989).

Troxel Opinion. For a very thoughtful perspective on the meaning of Troxel in the context of the cases you have been reading in this chapter, see David D. Meyer, Lochner *Redeemed: Family Privacy after* Troxel *and* Carhart, 48 UCLA L Rev 1125 (2001).

Part III

PARENT AND CHILD

I lay awake for a long while, until the slow-moving moon passed my window on its way up the heavens. I was thinking about Antonia and her children; about Anna's solicitude for her, Ambrosch's grave affection, Leo's jealous, animal little love.... Antonia had always been one to leave images in the mind that did not fade, that grew stronger with time.... She lent herself to immemorial attitudes which we recognize by instinct as universal and true. I had not been mistaken. She was a battered woman now, not a lovely girl; but she still had that something which fires the imagination, could still stop one's breath for a moment by a look or feature that somehow revealed the meaning in common things. She had only to stand in the orchard, to put her hand on a little crab tree and look up at the apples, to make you feel the goodness of planting and tending and harvesting at last. All the strong things of her heart came out in her body, that had been so tireless in serving generous emotions.

It was no wonder that her sons stood tall and straight. She was a rich mine of life, like the founders of early races.

Willa Cather
My Antonia

Chapter VIII

AN INTRODUCTION TO THE LAW OF PARENT AND CHILD

Children sweeten labours, but they make misfortunes more bitter.

Francis Bacon
Of Parents and Children

SECTION 1. THE RELATIONSHIP BETWEEN PARENTS AND CHILDREN

If there is any truly natural law, . . . after the care every animal has for its own preservation and the avoidance of what is harmful, the affection that the begetter has for his begotten ranks second. And because Nature seems to have recommended it to us with a view to extending and advancing the successive parts of this machine of hers, it is no wonder if, turning backward, the affection of children for their fathers is not so great.

Michel de Montaigne
Of the Affection of Fathers for Their Children

A. AN INTRODUCTORY CASE

And the king was much moved, and went up to the chamber over the gate, and wept: and as he went, thus he said, O my son Absalom, my son, my son Absalom! would God I had died for thee, O Absalom, my son, my son!

II Samuel 18:33

We move now to consider the legal regulation of parents and children. Our introduction to it is a gripping case which vividly presents virtually the whole range of issues that we will study.

IN RE PHILLIP B.

California Court of Appeals, 1979
92 Cal App 3d 796, 156 Cal Rptr 48

A petition was filed by the juvenile probation department in the juvenile court, alleging that Phillip B., a minor, came within the provision of Welfare and Institutions Code section 300, subdivision (b), because he was not provided with the "necessities of life."

The petition requested that Phillip be declared a dependent child of the court for the special purpose of ensuring that he receive cardiac surgery for a congenital heart defect. Phillip's parents had refused to consent to the surgery. The juvenile court dismissed the petition. The appeal is from the order.

Phillip is a 12–year-old boy suffering from Down's Syndrome. At the birth, his parents decided he should live in a residential care facility. Phillip suffers from a congenital heart defect—a ventricular septal defect that results in elevated pulmonary blood pressure. Due to the defect, Phillip's heart must work three times harder than normal to supply blood to his body. When he overexerts, unoxygenated blood travels the wrong way through the septal hole reaching his circulation, rather than the lungs.

If the congenital heart defect is not corrected, damage to the lungs will increase to the point where his lungs will be unable to carry and oxygenate any blood. As a result, death follows. During the deterioration of the lungs, Phillip will suffer from a progressive loss of energy and vitality until he is forced to lead a bed-to-chair existence.

Phillip's heart condition has been known since 1973. At that time Dr. Gathman, a pediatric cardiologist, examined Phillip and recommended cardiac catheterization to further define the anatomy and dynamics of Phillip's condition. Phillip's parents refused.

In 1977, Dr. Gathman again recommended catheterization and this time Phillip's parents consented. The catheterization revealed the extensive nature of Phillip's septal defect, thus it was Dr. Gathman's recommendation that surgery be performed.

Dr. Gathman referred Phillip to a second pediatric cardiologist, Dr. William French of the Stanford Medical Center. Dr. French estimates the surgical mortality rate to be 5 to 10 percent, and notes that Down's Syndrome children face a higher than average risk of postoperative complications. Dr. French found that Phillip's pulmonary vessels have already undergone some change from high pulmonary artery pressure. Without the operation, Phillip will begin to function less physically until he will be severely incapacitated. Dr. French agrees with Dr. Gathman that Phillip will enjoy a significant expansion of his life span if his defect is surgically corrected. Without the surgery, Phillip may live at the outside 20 more years. Dr. French's opinion on the advisability of surgery was not asked.

I

It is fundamental that parental autonomy is constitutionally protected. The United States Supreme Court has articulated the concept of personal liberty found in the Fourteenth Amendment as a right of privacy which extends to certain aspects of a family relationship. (*Roe v. Wade* [right of privacy extends to child rearing and education]; *Wisconsin v. Yoder* (1972) 406 U.S. 205 232 [parental right to determine child's religious upbringing]; *Eisenstadt v. Baird* [right to marital privacy]; *Skinner v. Oklahoma* [right to marriage and procreation]; *Pierce v. Society of Sisters* [liberty of parents to direct education of their children]; *Meyer v. Nebraska* [liberty of parents to raise child].) "It is cardinal with us that the custody, care and nurture of the child reside first in the parents, whose primary function and freedom include preparation for obligations the state can neither supply nor hinder." (*Prince v. Massachusetts.*)

Inherent in the preference for parental autonomy is a commitment to diverse lifestyles, including the right of parents to raise their children as they think best. Legal judgments regarding the value of child rearing patterns should be kept to a minimum so long as the child is afforded the best available opportunity to fulfill his potential in society.... Parental autonomy, however, is not absolute. The state is the guardian of society's basic values. Under the doctrine of *parens patriae*, the state has a right, indeed, a duty, to protect children.... State officials may interfere in family matters to safeguard the child's health, educational development and emotional well-being.

One of the most basic values protected by the state is the sanctity of human life. (U.S. Const. 14th Amend., § 1.) Where parents fail to provide their children with adequate medical care, the state is justified to intervene. However, since the state should usually defer to the wishes of the parents, it has a serious burden of justification before abridging parental autonomy by substituting its judgment for that of the parents.

Several relevant factors must be taken into consideration before a state insists upon medical treatment rejected by the parents. The state should examine the seriousness of the harm the child is suffering or the substantial likelihood that he will suffer serious harm; the evaluation for the treatment by the medical profession; the risks involved in medically treating the child; and the expressed preferences of the child. Of course, the underlying consideration is the child's welfare and whether his best interests will be served by the medical treatment.

Section 300, subdivision (b), permits a court to adjudge a child under the age of 18 years a dependent of the court if the child is not provided with the "necessities of life." ... The trial judge dismissed the petition on the ground that there was "no clear and convincing evidence to sustain this petition."

The rule is clear that the power of the appellate court begins and ends with a determination as to whether there is any substantial evidence, contradicted or uncontradicted, which will support the conclusion reached by the trier of fact.... The "clear and convincing evidence" standard of proof applies only to the trial court, and is not the standard for the appellate review.

Turning to the facts of this case, one expert witness testified that Phillip's case was more risky than the average for two reasons. One, he has pulmonary vascular changes and statistically this would make the operation more risky in that he would be subject to more complications than if he did not have these changes. Two, children with Down's Syndrome have more problems in the postoperative period. This witness put the mortality rate at 5 to 10 percent, and the morbidity would be somewhat higher. When asked if he knew of a case in which this type of operation had been performed on a Down's Syndrome child, the witness replied that he did, but could not remember a case involving a child who had the degree of pulmonary vascular change that Phillip had. Another expert witness testified that one of the risks of surgery to correct a ventricular septal defect was damage to the nerve that controls the heartbeat as the nerve is in the same area as the defect. When this occurs a pacemaker would be required.

The trial judge, in announcing his decision, cited the inconclusiveness of the evidence to support the petition.

On reading the record we can see the trial court's attempt to balance the possible benefits to be gained from the operation against the risks involved. The court had before it a child suffering not only from a ventricular septal defect but also from Down's Syndrome, with its higher than average morbidity, and the presence of pulmonary vascular changes. In light of these facts, we cannot say as a matter of law that there was no substantial evidence to support the decision of the trial court.

II

In denying the petition the trial court ruled that there was no clear and convincing evidence to sustain the petition. The state contends the proper standard of proof is by a preponderance of the evidence and not by the clear and convincing test. The state asserts that only when a permanent severance of the parent-child relationship is ordered by the court must the clear and convincing standard of proof be applied. Since the petition did not seek permanent severance but only authorization for corrective heart surgery, the state contends the lower standard of proof should have been applied.

In the case of *In re Robert P.* (1976), 61 Cal.App.3d 310, 318, the court pointed out that a dependency hearing pursuant to section 600, need not result in a permanent severance of the parent-child relationship. Section 366 (formerly § 729) requires subsequent hearings at periods not exceeding one year until such time as the court's jurisdiction over such minor is terminated. *In re Robert P.* held that even though the severance need not be permanent the standard of proof was "clear and convincing" and not a "preponderance of the evidence." The statement in *In re Christopher B.,* (1978) 82 Cal.App.3d 608, cited by appellant, that clear and convincing proof is required only when the final result is to sever the parent-child relationship and award custody to a nonparent is dicta. The *Christopher* court did not remove the child from the parents' custody but simply retained jurisdiction to supervise proper maintenance of the child's environment. The "clear and convincing standard" was proper in this case.

III

Section 353 requires that at the beginning of the hearing on a petition, "[t]he judge shall ascertain whether the minor and his parent or guardian or adult relative, as the case may be, has been informed of the right of the minor to be represented by counsel, and if not, the judge shall advise the minor and such person, if present, of the right to have counsel present and where applicable, of the right to appointed counsel." ... Amicus Curiae contends the judge erred in failing to notify Phillip of his right to counsel, thus Phillip was not properly represented.

A minor has a statutory right to counsel. (§ 318.5.) If a minor is already represented by counsel, it is not crucial that a judge inform a minor of his right to counsel. "[I]f either the minor or his parents ... appear without counsel, the judge shall advise the *unrepresented* party of his rights under this section." (§ 318.5, subd. (d); italics added.)

In the present case, the facts show that a deputy district attorney was representing Phillip at the hearing. He was introduced to the judge as Phillip's attorney. The deputy district attorney proceeded to make an opening statement and continued to represent Phillip throughout the entire hearing.

The judge was under no statutory duty to inform Phillip of his right to counsel when it was evident to the court that Phillip was, in fact, represented by counsel.

The order dismissing the petition is affirmed.

Notes and Questions on Phillip B.

(1) When Phillip was born, parents of Downs Syndrome children were widely advised that their situation was hopeless and that they should be institutionalized or allowed to die. As one author reports,

> Previously, many cardiologists and cardiac surgeons were reluctant to recommend or perform cardiac surgery in children with Down syndrome. These physicians felt that children with Down syndrome were so severely intellectually handicapped that surgical intervention would not benefit them. Other arguments against cardiac surgery included the children's reduced life expectancy, their unemployability, and financial considerations. However, recent technological advances in cardiovascular surgery and society's altered viewpoint concerning persons with handicaps brought about a marked improvement in the management of congenital heart disease in children with Down syndrome.

Siegfried M. Pueschel, *Health Concerns in Persons with Down Syndrome*, in *New Perspectives on Down Syndrome* 113, 115, Siegfried M. Pueschel, et al., eds (P.H. Brookes Pub, 1987). There is evidence that in deciding to institutionalize Phillip, his parents took advice from a social worker and their pediatrician. Recall, too, that at the trial the parents placed into evidence a letter from a doctor who said that Phillip would not learn to read, write, or take care of himself and that he would lead "a life I consider devoid of those qualities which give it human dignity." What would you have done in the parent's situation?

(2) Nothing you have read about Phillip B. so far gives a clear idea of what it is like to be the parent or sibling of a seriously handicapped child. You may already have some idea, though, from your own experience or imagination. In any case, there is a genre of books about life with retarded and disabled children written by their parents that make the difficulties of that life unforgettable. A good introduction to this literature (written by the mother of a blind, retarded, hydrocephalic child with cerebral palsy), one that consults as well other kinds of writing on the subject, is Helen Featherstone, *A Difference in the Family: Life with a Disabled Child* (Basic Books, 1980). In three frank, riveting, and disturbing books about his autistic son, Josh Greenfeld reproduces selections from his diary: *A Child Called Noah* (Harcourt, Brace, Jovanovich, 1970), *A Place for Noah* (Harcourt, Brace, Jovanovich, 1978), *A Client Called Noah* (Harcourt, Brace, Jovanovich, 1986). Of special interest to law students, and of considerable independent merit, is John P. Frank, *My Son's Story* (Knopf, 1952). Frank was law clerk to Justice Hugo Black, a lawyer with Arnold and Porter, and a law professor. His book is a restrained and moving description of his and his wife's experience with their mentally retarded son. There are numerous of books on mentally retarded children. One comprehensive example is Daryl Paul Evans, *The Lives of Mentally Retarded People* (Westview Press, 1983).

(a) When Phillip was born, his parents already had one son, and they had another one after Phillip was born. How far should the parents have taken their other children into account in deciding whether to bring Phillip home and to consent to his heart surgery?

(b) To what extent should the parents have taken their own situation as a couple into account?

(c) There is evidence that throughout Phillip's early years his parents sought the advice of doctors, priests, teachers, and social workers. They took much of this advice. No court ever held that they, in the law's phrase, "abused or neglected" Phillip. Since the parents might be said to have acted correctly "procedurally," and since they won on the neglect claim in *In re Phillip B.*, should the "substantive" correctness of their decisions be open to judicial review?

(3) Parents have rights; the state has interests. What do children have?

Guardianship of Phillip B.

"What is truth? said jesting Pilate; and would not stay for an answer." Lawyers read short, flat descriptions of small slices of real people's lives. Short and flat but tendentious. We now turn to another view of another slice of the life of Phillip Becker. It is not so short and not at all flat. It is tendentious. It was written by one of the lawyers in the case (Robert Mnookin) on the occasion of the death of one of the other lawyers in the case (Jay Spears).

ROBERT H. MNOOKIN THE GUARDIANSHIP OF PHILLIP B.: JAY SPEARS' ACHIEVEMENT

40 Stanford Law Review 841 (1988)

On October 16, 1987, Phillip Becker–Heath, a Down syndrome young man, turned twenty-one years old. For six years he has lived with his adoptive parents, Pat and Herb Heath, in a comfortable home in San Jose, California. The Heaths are devoted to Phillip, who is now, more than ever, the center of their lives; their older sons are married, and their daughter is living on her own.

Phillip's life has settled into a comfortable routine. In the morning he gets himself up around 7:00, puts on his glasses and hearing aid, dresses himself, and helps "Mama Pat" with breakfast. The Heaths take him to the bus stop where he catches the county transit bus. The bus drops Phillip a few blocks from the Joseph McKinnon School in San Jose, and he walks the rest of the way on his own.

As part of his school program, Phillip works at the Santa Clara Valley Medical Center where he busses tables in the cafeteria. Earlier this year he worked in the Hewlett–Packard cafeteria as part of a special county program for the disabled. He is learning to read, albeit not without a struggle. A tutor works with Phillip at home to supplement the program at McKinnon. Pat expects his reading skills to improve rapidly because Phillip recently began to use a reading program that he runs himself on the Apple computer he received from the Heaths for Christmas.

Phillip loves sports. Because the congenital heart defect that had threatened to cut his life short was corrected by surgery in 1983, Phillip now actively participates in the Special Olympics. He enjoys bowling, basketball, softball, and soccer. Joe Montana's picture hangs in his bedroom, and Phillip and the Heaths look forward to watching the Forty–Niners' games on television. Phillip roots for "number sixteen."

Phillip is a warm, affectionate, and optimistic young man who, according to Pat, is "a little bit cocky, and at times a smart aleck." He is helpful around the house. His chores include taking out the trash and raking the leaves in the yard. The Heaths are committed to seeing that Phillip develops the skills, discipline, and confidence necessary to hold down a job and lead a productive and largely independent life, notwithstanding his handicap. Pat and Herb feel certain that he will do so. "Two aspects of his character," according to Pat, "serve him very well. He wants to be a 'good boy' and he loves to work." . . .

Because Jay [Spears] found the deepest meaning in his life as a lawyer in this case, I offer this necessarily personal (and hardly disinterested) account of the case that joined a spirited and determined developmentally disabled young man with a gifted, modest, and humane young lawyer whose life was so tragically cut short.

I.

The story of Phillip's early years is not a happy one. He was born in 1966. His parents, college-educated, upper-middle class people, were "deeply distraught" to learn that their newborn infant was afflicted with Down syndrome. At the time, they had one other child. (Subsequently, they had another.) After consulting with a state social worker and their pediatrician, they decided not to take Phillip home with them from the hospital. Instead, shortly after Phillip's birth, the Beckers placed him in a private board and care nursing facility in San Jose. "Although the facility was clean, it offered no structured educational or developmental programs. . . ."

The Beckers "initially visited Phillip frequently, but soon their visits became less frequent and they became more detached from him." When Phillip was three, his parents learned that he had a congenital heart defect that could probably be corrected by surgery when he became six. His parents never pursued the matter.

In 1972, when Phillip was five, he was transferred to We Care, a licensed, privately owned residential facility in San Jose for developmentally disabled children. Upon arrival at We Care, Phillip's health was poor and his physical and cognitive development seriously delayed. Phillip was unusually small and thin for his age, and his color was poor. He was not toilet trained and wore diapers. He still slept in a baby crib. He could barely walk, and could not climb stairs except by crawling. Because of a lack of early stimulation and therapy, he spoke very few words, and those with difficulty. Soon after Phillip arrived at We Care, a volunteer program under the direction of Jeanne Haight was organized to provide the children with a greater range of activities. As a volunteer, Pat Heath began working with Phillip on a daily basis. Her husband and their children soon joined in as well; and before long the entire Heath family took a special interest in Phillip. Together they helped prepare Phillip for a preschool program, engaged in educational games and other activities with him, and took him on outings.

During the next several years, while Phillip's parents increasingly detached themselves from him both physically and emotionally, the Heaths established a caring and increasingly close relationship with him. Phillip first visited the Heaths' home on Christmas day in 1972. Thereafter, the Heaths regularly brought him home on weekends. He had a room in their house. He called the Heaths "Mama Pat" and "Daddy Bert" and referred to their house as "my home." During the same period, the Beckers never brought Phillip to their home for an overnight visit; they visited him only a few times a year at We Care. They expressed the opinion that Phillip was so severely retarded that he "would always require institutionalization," and therefore must learn to adjust to communal living. They also claimed that allowing Phillip to form deep emotional bonds with his family as a child would only present adjustment difficulties for Phillip later, at least if he eventually survived his loved ones.

Conflict over the appropriate care of Phillip arose almost by accident. In 1977, Phillip underwent a heart catheterization to determine whether needed dental work was medically safe, given his congenital heart defect. The pediatric cardiologist, who had earlier diagnosed Phillip's ventricular septal defect, recommended that Phillip undergo heart surgery. The physician stated that the surgery was necessary to prevent what would otherwise be a progressively debilitating condition resulting in a "bed to chair existence" for Phillip and an early death by about age thirty. The heart surgery carried a 3 to 5 percent risk of death.

In the summer of 1977, Phillip's parents refused to consent to surgery. Although at the time of their refusal they had not consulted with any other physician, they later stated that they thought the cardiologist " 'painted' an inaccurate picture ... [and] that the surgery would be merely life-prolonging rather than life-saving, presenting the possibility that they would be unable to care for Phillip during his later years." Their decision appeared to be based on Phillip's retardation, for Mr. Becker was later to testify that he would consent to surgery if either of his other two sons had the same heart problem.

In early 1978, the District Attorney of Santa Clara County initiated a juvenile dependency proceeding on the grounds that, by refusing to consent to the heart operation, Phillip's parents had been medically neglectful. After a hearing that involved only two partial court days, the juvenile court dismissed the petition on the basis that the evidence was inconclusive. While the court rendered no written opinion, it expressed the view in its oral statements that the state had not shown surgery to be necessary to prevent immediate death, that the Beckers were thoughtful parents, and that the court could not claim to be morally or intellectually better able to weigh the competing concerns than were the Beckers. His decision was sustained on appeal. The Heaths were never called to testify in the juvenile court proceedings.

Phillip's story and the decision of the juvenile court attracted media attention in the fall of 1978. This publicity prompted the Beckers to file lawsuits for defamation and invasion of privacy, not only against the media, but also against the staff at We Care, the Heaths, Phillip's cardiologist, and various governmental agencies. In September 1978, Mr. Becker also withdrew consent for Phillip to visit the Heaths' home and asked that "they be denied personal visits with Phillip at We Care." The Beckers also attempted to remove him from We Care. These efforts were unsuccessful because government funds, not parental funds, largely provided support for Phillip. Transfer, therefore, required the approval of a regional center that monitors public assistance. Such consent was denied because, notwithstanding an extended search, no equally appropriate alternative facility was found.

Because they were volunteers at the facility, the Heaths were able to continue to visit Phillip daily, notwithstanding the Beckers' actions. The termination of overnight visits to the Heaths' home nevertheless severely traumatized Phillip. He apparently blamed himself and assumed he was being punished. Phillip promised Pat Heath, "Me be good," and would cry whenever he was told he could not come home to visit. Once he ran away to the Heaths' home. He began hitting himself, wetting his bed, and playing with matches. The quality of both his behavior and his speech declined.

II.

By November 1980, when the Heaths met Jay Spears, they were extraordinarily distressed. The juvenile court's action had been sustained on appeal, and the Heaths were fearful that the Beckers would succeed in making it impossible for them to maintain their relationship with Phillip. The Heaths were profoundly worried about Phillip's well-being and feared that the Beckers might harm Phillip further by moving him out of We Care. They needed the help of a lawyer.

That the Heaths were put in contact with Jay Spears was quite serendipitous. Because of a segment on the television show *Sixty Minutes* focusing on Phillip's plight, the Heaths met Kathleen and Laurie Fisher. Kathleen, an associate with a large San Francisco firm, wanted to represent the Heaths, with the help of her sister Laurie, who had just taken the California bar exam. Unfortunately, Kathleen discovered that she could not represent the Heaths because her firm already represented a media defendant that had been sued by the Beckers. Kathleen immediately thought of Jay Spears. She and Jay were old friends, and she expected that Jay would be very moved to learn about the circumstances of Phillip and the Heaths.

When Jay met with the Heaths he was an associate at Howard, Rice, Nemerovski, Canady, Robertson & Falk, a law firm in San Francisco. About four and a half years earlier he had graduated from Stanford Law School with an extraordinary record. Near the top of his class, he was elected to Order of the Coif, had served as Barbara Babcock's research assistant, and was President of the *Stanford Law Review*. Before joining Howard, Rice, he had spent two years as a law clerk, first for Judge David Bazelon on the D.C. Circuit, and then for Justice Potter Stewart on the United States Supreme Court. His was a golden resume.

Jay loved the Howard, Rice firm and its informality, collegiality, and, most of all, its people. But after two years in commercial litigation, he was not sure that he wanted to be a practicing lawyer. Jay had decided to be a litigator almost by default. Through my relationship with Howard, Rice, Jay and I had become friends. At the time he met the

Heaths, he was having serious doubts about whether he was cut out to be a trial lawyer. He had not been a competitive person who enjoyed the one-upmanship that so often characterizes litigation. Although he always pulled his weight in his early years at the firm, Jay did not take great pleasure in the pretrial discovery and motions practice that characterizes most commercial litigation. Nor did he relish conflict.

Jay eagerly embraced the opportunity to help the Heaths, and their plight filled him with energy. I recall when he contacted me in December 1980. Did I know about this case? What legal theory might be best used to achieve the Heaths' goals? I enthusiastically accepted his invitation to help, but pointedly told him that he would necessarily be doing the lion's share of the work because of my ongoing academic obligations. In early December we met in San Francisco and spent several hours talking together about the case. I suggested, and we then decided, that the best approach would be for the Heaths to initiate a guardianship proceeding, and for us to treat the matter as a "custody fight" under California's ancient guardianship statute. We would show that the Heaths were Phillip's "psychological parents" and that it would be detrimental to Phillip for the Beckers to retain custody.

The California guardianship statute is old and not particularly well drafted. It authorizes a court to appoint a guardian if such an appointment "appears necessary or convenient." The problem with the statute is that it provides no concrete standards for when it is "necessary or convenient" for a guardian to be appointed. While it had become clear under California law that there must be a showing of "detriment" before a guardian is appointed to replace a biological parent, there is relatively little guidance in either the statute or the case law to indicate the extent to which parental prerogatives should be favored, even though a court might believe the child would be better off with a guardian.

Courts are normally asked to appoint a child's personal guardian only if no parent is available to exercise custodial control. Conflicts over custody can take place in guardianship proceedings in a variety of circumstances, however. After the death of a custodial parent, a stepparent may petition to be appointed a child's guardian, and this petition may be contested by a divorced parent who has not been living with the child. Similarly, foster parents have at times used a guardianship petition to secure a legally predictable form of custody over the objections of the biological parents.

Phillip's case was complicated by the fact that there had already been a neglect proceeding, and a juvenile court had refused to find that the parents' refusal of consent to surgery constituted neglect. While there certainly was no collateral estoppel (the Heaths had not been parties to, nor had they even testified in, the neglect proceeding), the outcome of the neglect proceeding made it more difficult to establish detriment, even though, in our view, few parental actions could be more detrimental than the refusal to perform an operation essential to extending a child's life. Our task was also made more difficult by the fact that

Phillip had never resided with the Heaths. In nearly all of the reported guardianship cases in which a nonparent was appointed guardian over parental objection, the child had lived with the nonparent.

Once we had decided that we would file a guardianship petition, Jay focused on the task of building a factual case that demonstrated two things: (1) that from Phillip's perspective, the Heaths were his parents, *and* that he had no substantial psychological relationship with the Beckers, and (2) that Phillip's educational, social, psychological, and physical development had been and would be detrimentally affected unless the Heaths were given custody.

On December 22, 1980, Jay sent a memorandum to all the attorneys at Howard, Rice indicating that he had been asked to represent the Heaths in guardianship proceedings on a pro bono basis, and that I had offered to help. Obviously, the firm would receive no fees. Jay also asked that the firm advance the costs and proposed that the firm's name be used on the pleadings. Jay warned that the boy's father, an attorney, had sued everyone who had shown interest in Phillip and that by entering the case we "or the firm might be added to the list of defendants, which now stands at 45." A few days later Jay sent a second memorandum indicating that he had lined up pro bono representation by a young litigation partner in another major San Francisco firm who had agreed to represent the Heaths' lawyers on a pro bono basis if we were sued.

On February 23, 1981, we filed a petition asking the court to appoint Patsy and Herbert Heath as Phillip's guardians. We also filed a motion asking that a guardian ad litem and independent counsel be appointed to represent Phillip. The court appointed Sterling L. Ross, Jr., a University of Michigan law graduate with considerable experience representing disabled children and adults and their families. Without compensation, "Terry" Ross dedicated himself to representing Phillip in the proceedings that were to follow.

Because we believed a reasonable settlement might better serve the interests of all concerned, about a month after the petition was filed, Jay wrote to the attorney on the other side indicating that we would "very much prefer to avoid litigation if [the Heaths'] concerns could be satisfied by other means." We indicated that there were two concerns:

> First, they want Phillip to receive appropriate medical treatment for his heart condition. More specifically, they want him to have heart surgery *if* that course is medically advisable. Second, they seek continued contact with Phillip. So long as Phillip remains at We Care, they would be satisfied with an arrangement like the one that existed until 1978.

Jay added that he realized "that attitudes have hardened and suspicions run deep on both sides. But it would surely be in our clients' interests to put aside emotions and try to avoid litigation if we possibly can." Settlement proved impossible because the Beckers would not permit Phillip to have overnight visits at the Heath home, and they also asked that the Heaths pay the Beckers' attorneys' fees and costs.

As petitioners, the Heaths of course had the burden of establishing the appropriateness of their appointment as guardians. Between February and July 1, when the trial began, Jay spent hundreds of hours assembling the factual case. He succeeded, after a bitterly contested motion, in securing access to Phillip's records. He interviewed potential witnesses and experts and, with Pat Heath's help, organized a mass of materials in very short order.

This case was in no sense like the commercial litigation that was the "bread and butter" of Jay's firm practice. The hearing on the merits was scheduled to begin on July 1, less than five months after the petition was filed. Because Jay had available to him the testimony and depositions of Phillip's parents from the neglect proceeding, he shrewdly decided not to depose the Beckers before the trial. He correctly figured that he would be better prepared than the lawyers on the other side who might wish to avoid the expense of deposing the Heaths.

As July 1 approached, the case literally absorbed Jay's whole life. The Beckers and their attorneys showed a great deal of animosity. Shortly before the trial was to begin, Kathy Fisher saw Jay and recalled that he "looked awful." Kathy expressed some guilt that she had unloaded on him what had become a very demanding case. Jay reassured her that it had become the most meaningful professional experience of his life.

Guardianship of Phillip B. was Jay Spears' first trial. Like many associates (and even some young partners), this was the first time Jay ever examined and cross-examined witnesses before a judge. But Jay did have a wonderful mentor at his side—Marty Glick.

Marty Glick, a partner at Howard, Rice and a former California Rural Legal Assistance lawyer, had substantial trial experience. Marty sat beside Jay, discussed with him various tactical options, and examined some of the witnesses, including Warren Becker and the cardiologist. But Jay examined the expert witnesses and the Heaths, and cross-examined Mrs. Becker. Jay also made the opening and the principal closing arguments. During the 10–day trial, the tension in the courtroom was palpable. The case aroused extraordinary emotions, and both sides viewed the stakes as profound. The Heaths believed that they were fighting for Phillip's chance to have a life worth living. The Beckers believed they were defending their integrity as parents.

On August 7, 1981, Judge William Fernandez summoned the parties and their lawyers to the courtroom, which was filled with reporters and well-wishers. When the judge began reading his opinion, Jay and Marty had no idea what the result would be because during the trial, the judge had done nothing to tip his hand. Judge Fernandez wrote:

> California does not provide a method by which a mentally retarded child may state a preference. Other states have used a substituted judgment procedure to allow the court to state such a preference for the incompetent. This doctrine requires the court to ascertain as nearly as possible the incompetent person's "actual interests and preferences." . . . .

In our case the use of the substituted judgment method to arrive at Phillip's preference may best be stated in the form of a platonic dialogue with the court posing the choices to Phillip and Phillip's preference being ascertained from the more logical choice. The dialogue begins:

> The Court: "Phillip ... [your] first choice will lead you to a room in an institution where you will live. You will be fed, housed, and clothed but you will not receive any life prolonging medical care.... You will not be given an opportunity to add to your basic skills or to your motor skills and ... will be treated as if you are ... incapable of learning and not fit to enter into society. You will not be allowed to become attached to any person, in fact efforts will be made to prevent any such attachments. Your biological parents will visit you occasionally, but their love and caring for you will at best be ambivalent...."
>
> Your second choice Phillip will lead you to a private home where you will be bathed in the love and affection of your psychological parents.... You will be given private tutoring and one on one training.... Your psychological parents believe that you are educable and will do all in their power to help you receive the education you may need to care for yourself and to secure work when you are an adult. You will have a chance for life prolonging surgery as well as receiving all the medical care that you need. Even if life prolonging surgery cannot be performed, your psychological parents will always be there to comfort you and care for you in the dark times of your final illness. Best of all, your psychological parents will do all in their power to involve your biological parents in your habilitation and to unite both families together in ensuring for you a life that is worth living.

In my view, the dialogue would end with Phillip choosing to live with the Heaths.

Sad to say the foregoing legal analysis has no precedent in California law.

The judge went on to find that if detriment is defined as harm, then Phillip had suffered harm by the parenting of the Beckers: "severe emotional harm," "physical harm," "medical harm," and "the lasting harm by their stigmatization ... as permanently mentally ill and disordered." He concluded by reading:

> [T]his is not a hearing to determine surgery for Phillip. That must wait another time and a sound parenting decision. This is a hearing for the purpose of giving Phillip Becker another parenting choice. It is a hearing responsive to Phillip's need for habilitation, and responsive to his desire for a chance to secure a life worth living. *I will give him that chance.*

When Judge Fernandez finished, the court personnel, the reporters in the courtroom, the Heaths, and their attorneys were in tears, not only because of the joyous result, but also because of this extraordinary demonstration of humanity by a courageous judge.

That day the judge signed the guardianship papers, appointing the Heaths guardians. He also authorized a heart catheterization to be done to determine if surgery was still possible. A court order also authorized the Heaths to take Phillip home for reasonable visitation, and later for custody.

III.

The task now was to defend Judge Fernandez' decision on appeal. His opinion was profoundly moving, but came close to saying that he was going to give Phillip a chance, irrespective of California law. Jay, Marty, and I had a long meeting; and I strongly urged that, for purposes of appeal, we would be far better off if we prepared and presented to Judge Fernandez for his adoption very detailed and narrowly drawn findings of facts and conclusions of law. In this way, on appeal we would be relying not simply on the trial record and the judge's opinion, but also on the judge's specific findings. These findings would provide the foundation for our arguments on appeal. Jay, with some assistance from Marty, prepared 110 pages of findings, all of which were adopted by Judge Fernandez.

It took nearly a year for the record to be certified and for a briefing schedule to be established for the Beckers' appeal. I recently reread the appellate brief that we prepared in the guardianship proceeding. It is a 123–page brief, and Jay wrote nearly all of it. I wrote the 11–page legal argument that "the appointment of a guardian over parental objection is 'necessary or convenient' where the parents do not provide daily care, the parents have no substantial relationship with the child, and the child has a substantial and reciprocal relationship with the would-be guardian." The primary task of this section was to show that the result below could be upheld on a very narrow reading of guardianship law, consistent with prior California cases, that permitted the appointment of a guardian over parental objection only when: (1) the child had not been living with the objecting parent for a period of years before the hearing, (2) there is no substantial emotional bond between the child and the objecting parent, and (3) the person or persons seeking to be appointed guardians have substantial or reciprocal emotional bonds to the child based on continuous contact over a period of years.

But the real power in the brief was a remarkable 72–page factual statement that Jay wrote, with some help from Marty. It is eloquent, careful, and deeply moving. After reading Jay's factual statement, each point of which contains references to the findings and the record, no appellate court could have reasonably concluded that the trial court's appointment of the Heaths as Phillip's guardians was unsupported by substantial evidence.

The oral argument was held on October 26, 1982. Jay's argument, which is described in Jerry Falk's tribute, was magnificent. In January of 1983, the court of appeals issued its opinion. The California Supreme Court subsequently declined to review the case.

IV.

When the guardianship petition was filed in 1981, we and the Heaths feared that even if they won the case, it would be too late for Phillip to have corrective heart surgery. Unfortunately, the progressive nature of his disease made it less likely that surgery would be successful as time passed. About five weeks before the trial, Jay reported to the firm, after deposing two pediatric cardiologists, "we don't know for sure if Phillip is still operable." One doctor advised against surgery. The other testified there was a one-third chance of benefit, a one-third chance of detriment, and a one-third chance of no change.

> Bob Mnookin and I intend to continue the case through trial (now set for July 1). The medical issue is not as strong as we'd like, but even without *any* medical issue, we believe we have a decent chance of winning based on the parents' long neglect and the Heaths' proven devotion to Phillip.

Immediately after announcing his opinion, Judge Fernandez issued an order authorizing a heart catheterization to determine Phillip's present condition. The Beckers sought an extraordinary writ both to stay the transfer of custody to the Heaths and to prevent the catheterization. The court of appeals, in a careful opinion written by Joseph Grodin, upheld Judge Fernandez' orders in both regards. However, the California Supreme Court (in what can only be characterized as an act of remarkable judicial arrogance and recklessness), without a hearing or argument, issued a one-paragraph order that stayed the catheterization, notwithstanding our showing that time was of the essence to determine whether surgery was advisable. This order meant that there would be a 2-year delay until Phillip's heart condition could be carefully assessed.

The catheterization was finally performed in the summer of 1983, after Judge Fernandez' opinion was sustained on appeal. It showed that Phillip had miraculously developed a new blockage that had not damaged his heart and yet had protected his lungs from further damage. The doctors reported that surgery was clearly indicated. Over two years after Judge Fernandez' original decision, on August 19, 1983, Jay filed papers asking for an order authorizing heart surgery. The judge granted the order the next day, and in September Phillip underwent open heart surgery at the University of California hospital in San Francisco.

The night before surgery, Pat Heath kissed Phillip goodnight in the hospital and, feeling fearful, called Jay from a phone booth in the hospital lobby. She asked, "Are we doing the right thing? What if he doesn't make it? I'm afraid for him." Jay compassionately and calmly reassured Pat. "He told me that Phillip would make it. He gave me the faith I needed."

Phillip came through the surgery beautifully, and Jay visited him while he was still in the intensive care unit. It was now Pat's turn to reassure Jay who was a little squeamish and had what he characterized as a weak stomach. Jay went in, saw Phillip, and smiled broadly. After a few minutes, he handed Pat a bag of chocolate cookies and left.

After Judge Fernandez' decision had been sustained on appeal, but before Phillip's heart surgery, the Beckers and the Heaths entered into a settlement agreement. The Heaths agreed that they would "provide and assume full responsibility for the cost of Phillip's care, and shall relieve the Beckers of and indemnify them against any liability for said costs." They further agreed to permit either the Beckers or Phillip's brothers (after his brothers reached adulthood) to visit Phillip at least two days a year and to provide Phillip with Catholic last rites if he were near death. The Beckers agreed to dismiss with prejudice the state court actions against the Heaths and further agreed that "unless there is a substantial and material change in the facts and circumstances currently known to the Beckers, the Beckers agree to take no legal action to remove custody of Phillip from the Heaths or to contest, limit or terminate the Heaths' status as Phillip's guardians and/or conservators." Each party agreed to assume its costs on appeal.

The Heaths very much wanted to adopt Phillip; and in early 1984, they filed a petition requesting adoption. The Beckers would neither refuse nor grant consent, so that things remained at a standstill until Phillip turned eighteen, an event that created new legal options. At eighteen, the guardianship would, of course, end. Because of Phillip's disabilities, a conservatorship would be necessary. The Heaths promptly petitioned to become Phillip's limited conservators. We also petitioned for a decree of adoption.

Since Phillip was now an adult, it was necessary to proceed under the adult adoption statute, which provides that a court may issue a decree of adoption based on an agreement of adoption executed by the adopting parties. Because it was not clear that Phillip had the capacity to enter into such an agreement himself, we petitioned the court for an order authorizing the conservators to enter into a contract of adult adoption on behalf of their conservatee.

The court ordered an investigation; and the report plainly stated that although Phillip did not understand "the legalities" of the proceedings, he understood "perfectly the question 'Do you want Mr. and Mrs. Heath to continue to take care of you?' His answer, given repeatedly, was that he does." He clearly indicated that he wanted to live with the Heaths and join in family activities. In February 1985, after full notice to the Beckers, who indicated that they did not object, the Heaths adopted Phillip.

With Phillip's adoption, Jay Spears' remarkable legal triumph was now complete. The material from the various proceedings filled a dozen bankers' boxes sent to storage by Howard, Rice. There are eleven volumes of pleadings and half a dozen volumes of legal memoranda. Jay had put well over 2000 hours of effort into this matter; and the Howard, Rice law firm had contributed a total of 3025 hours which would have cost $419,082 at the then-current billing rates.

The article you have just read understates one thing—the extraordinary quality of the brief Mr. Spears and Professor Mnookin wrote in *Heath v. Becker*. It is as effective as any brief either of us has ever read. The appellate opinion in *Guardianship of Phillip B.*, 139 Cal App 3d 407, 188 Cal Rptr 781 (1983), is enormously influenced by that powerful document.

Unfortunately, the Beckers' brief was not comparably good. It is thus hard to learn how the Beckers saw the saga of their son. A few words from Mr. Becker have occasionally appeared in the press. In the October 10, 1983, New York *Times*, Section A, page 12, Mr. Becker is quoted as calling *Heath v. Becker* "an 'outrageous' intervention by the state 'in the rights of parents to make decisions concerning their children.' " Later in the article, we read, "Asked why he had resisted the operation so long, Mr. Becker said: 'It wasn't in his interest. It was risky. What's the point? It might extend his life for a few years, but for what purpose? He's almost 17 and he's still carrying a teddy bear. Who's going to take care of him when the Heaths are gone?' " A *Newsweek* article from September 3, 1979, page 49, reports that when Mr. Becker was asked if Phillip would be better off dead than alive, he replied, " 'Yes, I think it would be best for everyone.' "

The Beckers spoke for themselves about the case in a "My Turn" column for *Newsweek*, May 30, 1983. There, they said that after Phillip was born, they had visited him regularly, seen to it "that he was generally health, happy and well adjusted to his circumstances in life," visited him, taken him to church, and seen to his medical welfare. They said that "it was only after long, agonizing discussions with medical specialists and spiritual advisors that we refused to consent to risky, painful and questionable open-heart surgery." They pointed out that this decision was affirmed by a trial judge, appealed unsuccessfully to two state courts, and not reviewed by the Supreme Court. But despite this, Phillip was judicially taken from them and given "to a couple our age whom we had never met." They believed the case stands as a warning that a parent who has not abandoned, abused, or neglected a child can nevertheless lose him because someone else can convince a judge that he is more involved with the child than the parent and will make better decisions for him. The Beckers wrote, "Every day we are forced to live with the cruel realization that our son is alive, but we have lost him forever." (The New York *Times* reported on July 12, 1983, Section A, page 14, that the Beckers wrote the My Turn piece in settlement of a libel suit against *Newsweek.)*

The latest word we have about Phillip comes from Robert H. Mnookin and D. Kelly Weisberg, *Child Family, and State: Problems and Materials on Children and the Law* 791 (Aspen, 2000):

> In 1999 Phillip Becker–Heath turned 33 years old. He is doing well, has a girlfriend and continues to reside with the Heaths. He attends a

group program to learn independent living skills, although he has little interest in living on his own. He continues to work and to participate in the Special Olympics in bowling and golf. He was chosen to represent the state of California in the national Special Olympics in golf. He attends computer art design classes at night with other impaired adults. The Heath's daughter has been named co-conservator of Phillip, to care for him in the event of the Heath's deaths.

The Beckers never initiated further contact with Phillip after his heart surgery in 1983. Mr. Becker passed away from cancer in 1995. "They don't know what they missed," says Pat Heath. "He's absolutely been the joy of my life."

B. THE RATIONALE FOR PARENTS' RIGHTS

Honour thy father and thy mother: that thy days may be long upon the land which the Lord thy God giveth thee.

Exodus 20:12

You know from reading *Meyer, Pierce,* and *Prince* in Chapter 7 that parents have a constitutional claim to authority over their children. And you have seen in *In re Phillip B.* just how weighty that authority can be. But if we are to understand the legal consequences of that constitutional authority, we need to understand its rationale. We will begin to probe that rationale by reading two classic views of the parent's role. The first is by John Locke, whose writing on education and child-rearing were perhaps as influential in America as his writing on government (and whose *Second Treatise of Government* was a response to a view that saw government as having a parental relationship to the governed). The second is, once again, from Jeremy Bentham's *Principles of the Civil Code*.

JOHN LOCKE
THE SECOND TREATISE OF GOVERNMENT

(1690)

CHAPTER 6: OF PATERNAL POWER

53. Had but this one thing been well considered, without looking any deeper into the matter, it might, perhaps, have kept men from running into those gross mistakes they have made about this power of parents; which, however it might without any great harshness bear the name of absolute dominion and regal authority when, under the title of paternal power, it seemed appropriated to the father, would yet have sounded but oddly, and in the very name shewn the absurdity, if this supposed absolute power over children had been called parental, and thereby have discovered that it belonged to the mother too. For it will but very ill serve the turn of those men who contend so much for the absolute power and authority of the fatherhood, as they call it, that the mother should have any share in it. And it would have but ill supported

the monarchy they contend for, when by the very name it appeared that the fundamental authority from whence they would derive their government of a single person only, was not placed in one, but two persons jointly. But to let this of names pass....

58. The power, then, that parents have over their children arises from that duty which is incumbent on them, to take care of their offspring during the imperfect state of childhood. To inform the mind, and govern the actions of their yet ignorant nonage, till reason shall take its place and ease them of that trouble, is what the children want, and the parents are bound to. For God, having given man an understanding to direct his actions, has allowed him a freedom of will and liberty of acting as properly belonging thereunto, within he bounds of that law he is under. But whilst he is in an estate wherein he has not understanding of his own to direct his will, he is not to have any will of his own to follow. He that understands for him must will for him too; he must prescribe to his will, and regulate his actions; but when he comes to the estate that made his father a freeman, the son is a freeman too....

63. The freedom, then, of man, and liberty of acting according to his own will, is grounded on his having reason, which is able to instruct him in that law he is to govern himself by, and make him know how far he is left to the freedom of his own will. To turn him loose to an unrestrained liberty before he has reason to guide him is not to allow him the privilege of his nature to be free, but to thrust him out amongst brutes, and abandon him to a state as wretched, and as much beneath that of a man, as theirs. This is that which puts the authority into the parents' hands to govern the minority of their children. God hath made it their business to employ this care on their offspring, and hath placed in them suitable inclinations of tenderness and concern to temper this power, to apply it, as his wisdom designed it, to the children's good, as long as they should need to be under it.

64. But what reason can hence advance this care of the parents due to their offspring into an absolute arbitrary dominion of the father? whose power reaches no farther than by such a discipline as he finds most effectual to give such strength and health to their bodies, such vigour and rectitude to their minds, as may best fit his children to be most useful to themselves and others; and, if it be necessary to this condition, to make them work, when they are able, for their own subsistence. But in this power the mother, too, has her share with the father....

66. But though there be a time when a child comes to be as free from subjection to the will and command of his father, as the father himself is free from subjection to the will of anybody else, and they are each under no other restraint but that which is common to them both, whether it be the law of nature or municipal law of their country, yet this freedom exempts not a son from that honour which he ought, by the law of God and nature, to pay his parents. God having made the parents instruments in his great design of continuing the race of mankind, and

the occasions of life to their children, as he hath laid on them an obligation to nourish, preserve, and bring up their offspring, so he has laid on the children a perpetual obligation of honouring their parents, which containing in it an inward esteem and reverence to be shewn by all outward expressions, ties up the child from anything that may ever injure or affront, disturb, or endanger the happiness or life of those from whom he received his; and engages him in all actions of defence, relief, assistance, and comfort of those by whose means he entered into being, and has been made capable of any enjoyments of life. From this obligation no state, no freedom, can absolve children. But this is very far from giving parents a power of command over their children, or an authority to make laws and dispose as they please of their lives or liberties. "Tis one thing to owe honour, respect, gratitude, and assistance; another to require an absolute obedience and submission. The honour due to parents, a monarch in his throne owes his mother, and yet this lessens not his authority, nor subjects him to her government."

67. The subjection of a minor places in the father a temporary government, which terminates with the minority of the child; and the honour due from a child places in the parents a perpetual right to respect, reverence, support, and compliance too, more or less, as the father's care, cost, and kindness in his education has been more or less. This ends not with minority, but holds in all parts and conditions of a man's life. The want of distinguishing these two powers, *viz.*, that which the father hath in the right of tuition during minority, and the right of honour all his life, may perhaps have caused a great part of the mistakes about this matter. For, to speak properly of them, the first of these is rather the privilege of children, and duty of parents, than any prerogative of paternal power. The nourishment and education of their children is a charge so incumbent on parents for their children's good that nothing can absolve them from taking care of it. And though the power of commanding and chastising them go along with it, yet God hath woven into the principles of human nature such a tenderness for their offspring that there is little fear that parents should use their power with too much rigour; the excess is seldom on the severe side, the strong bias of nature drawing the other way. And therefore God Almighty, when he would express his gentle dealing with the Israelites, he tells them that though he chastened them, he chastened them as a man chastens his son (Deut. viii. 5)—*i.e.*, with tenderness and affection—and kept them under no severer discipline than what was absolutely best for them, and had been less kindness to have slackened. This is that power to which children are commanded obedience, that the pains and care of their parents may not be increased or ill rewarded. . . .

74. To conclude, then: though the father's power of commanding extends no farther than the minority of his children, and to a degree only fit for the discipline and government of that age; and though that honour and respect, and all that which the Latins called piety, which they indispensably owe to their parents all their lifetime and in all estates, with all that support and defence is due to them, gives the father

no power of governing—*i.e.*, making laws and exacting penalties on his children—though by all this he has no dominion over the property or actions of his son, yet it is obvious to conceive how easy it was, in the first ages of the world, and in places still where the thinness of people gives families leave to separate into unpossessed quarters, and they have room to remove or plant themselves in yet vacant habitations, for the father of the family to become the prince of it. He had been a ruler from the beginning of the infancy of his children: and since without some government it would be hard for them to live together, it was likeliest it should, by the express or tacit consent of the children, when they were grown up, be in the father, where it seemed without any change barely to continue; when indeed nothing more was required to it than the permitting the father to exercise alone in his family that executive power of the law of nature which every free man naturally hath, and by that permission resigning up to him a monarchical power whilst they remained in it. But that this was not by any paternal right, but only the consent of his children, is evident from hence—that nobody doubts but if a strange, whom chance or business had brought to his family, had there killed any of his children, which it was impossible he should do by virtue of any paternal authority over one who was not his child, but by virtue of that executive power of the law of nature which, as a man, he had a right to; and he alone could punish him in his family, where the respect of his children had laid by the exercise of such a power to give way to the dignity and authority they were willing should remain in him above the rest of his family.

Notes on Locke and the Social Contract Between Parent and Child

For many obvious reasons, we do not expect and do not want parents and children to organize their relations by bargaining over terms of a contract. Nevertheless, the material you have just read raises the possibility that the relationship between parents and children may be understood in terms of an implicit contract. John Locke, after all, is famous for proposing that society rests on a "social contract" to which people do not expressly consent but to which their implicit consent furnishes a basis for government.

At one time, as the reading from Locke implies, the terms of such a contract might have been fairly clear. Essentially, the parents implicitly contracted to support their children, to protect them during their years of incapacity, and to prepare them for adulthood. In return, the children implicitly contracted to contribute to the economic well-being of the household, to revere their parents all their lives and obey them during their minority, and to support their parents in their old age.

This contract was possible and even logical because of the social and economic circumstances of the time. In an agrarian economy, even quite young children were economic assets, since they could work around the farm or household. And in the days before Social Security, when no one had heard of 401(k)s, 403(b)s, IRAs, SRAs, or TIAA–CREF, children provided for their parents when they could no longer work. Even quite recently, elderly people frequently lived with their children's families. (Of course, there were fewer octogenarians or nonagenarians and more children in most families to share the expense of housing and caring for an aged parent. Daniels, *Family Responsibility Initiatives and Justice Between Age Groups*, 73 Law, Med, & Health Care 153, 157 (1985).) Thus parents once had an economic and social incentive for "optimal" investment in their offspring.

However, these economic and social circumstances have changed in ways that may raise questions about this implicit contract. As cottage industry and then factory production developed, feeding, clothing, and educating children became more consumption activities than financial investments. And when child-labor laws and compulsory-education statutes were enacted in the nineteenth century, even the small income most children could provide evaporated. Children have also become less central to the economic comfort of the elderly. As the country has become more prosperous, as pension systems have developed, as various social-security schemes have been established, and as wealth has increasingly come to be held in the form of financial assets, the elderly have increasingly become economically and socially less reliant on their children. In addition, it has become clear that many elderly people do not particularly wish to live with their children, but would rather live by themselves in Florida. Karen C. Holder and Timothy M. Smeeding, *The Poor, the Rich, and the Insecure Elderly Caught in Between*, 68(2) Milbank Q 191 (1990). When the elderly become too feeble to live alone, we increasingly expect, and their medical needs sometimes lead, them to enter nursing homes.

What, then, has happened to the incentive structure of the modern American family and the implicit contract between parents and children? Today, the parents' incentive for investing (psychologically and socially, as well as economically) in their children may look pretty subjective. Parents may "spend" time or money on their children because they love their children and wish all the best for them. They may invest in their children because they feel some sort of duty to do so. They may take pride in their children's achievements, either because these enhance the family reputation or their own immortality.

Is all this an adequate basis for the implicit contract between parent and child? Will it support our legal assumption that parents will act in the best interests of their children?

JEREMY BENTHAM
PRINCIPLES OF THE CIVIL CODE

(1789)

CHAPTER III: Guardian and Ward

The feebleness of infancy demands a continual protection. Everything must be done for an imperfect being, which, as yet, does nothing for itself. The complete development of its physical powers takes many years; that of its intellectual faculties is still slower. At a certain age it has already strength and passions, without experience enough to regulate them. Too sensitive to present impulses, too negligent of the future, such a being must be kept under an authority more immediate than that of the laws; it must be governed by punishments and rewards, which act, not at distant intervals, but continually, and which can adapt themselves to all the details of conduct during the process of education.

In order that a condition of life, or a profession, may be chosen for a child, he must of necessity be submitted to a particular authority. This choice is founded upon personal circumstances; upon the expectations, the talents, the inclinations of the pupil; upon his facility for adopting one business rather than another; in one word, upon probabilities of success. It is a question too complicated to be left to the decision of a public magistrate; it must be determined specially for every case; and such a determination would demand a knowledge of details, which the magistrate could not possess.

This power of protection and of government, over individuals thought incapable to protect and to govern themselves, constitutes *wardship*,—a kind of domestic magistracy, founded upon the manifest need of those who are submitted to it, and which ought to include all the powers necessary to the fulfillment of its object, and nothing more.

The powers necessary to education are those of determining the ward's method of life, and of fixing his domicile, with those means of reprimand and of correction, without which this authority would not be efficacious. The severity of these means may be the more easily limited, inasmuch as their application is more immediate, more certain, and more varied, and because domestic government possesses an inexhaustible fund of rewards; for at an age when nothing is acquired and everything is bestowed, there is no concession which may not take the form of remuneration. . . .

Wardship being a charge purely burdensome, it is made to fall upon those persons who have the greatest inclination to sustain it, and the greatest facility for doing so. This is eminently the case with the father and mother. Natural affection disposes them to this duty more strongly than the law; yet the law which imposes it upon them is not useless. It is because instances occur in which children are abandoned by their parents, that this abandonment has been made an offence. . . .

Some attention should be paid to those circumstances which ought to release particular individuals from the duty of wardship, such as advanced age, a numerous family, infirmities, or reasons of prudence and delicacy—such, for example, as a complication of interests.

Particular precautions against the abuse of this power are to be found among the penal laws. An abuse of authority as respects the person of the child belongs to the class of personal injuries; illicit gains at the expense of the ward's fortune fall into the class of fraudulent acquisitions. The only thing to be considered is the particular *circum-*

stance of the offence, namely, *the violation of confidence*. But though this renders the offence more odious, it is not always a reason for augmenting the punishment; on the contrary, as we shall see elsewhere, it is often a reason for diminishing it; the position of the delinquent being such that the discovery of the offence is easier, the reparation easier, and the alarm not so great. In the case of seduction, the character of guardian is an aggravation of the crime....

The most simple means of protection is to allow anybody to act as the friend of the ward in legal processes against his guardian, whether for mismanagement of the property, for negligence, or for violence. The law thus puts those who are too feeble to protect themselves under the protection of every man generous enough to undertake the charge.

Wardship, being a state of dependence, is an evil which ought to cease as soon as there is no danger that its cessation will produce a greater evil. But what should be the age of emancipation? As to that matter, we must be guided by general presumptions. The English law, which has fixed upon the age of twenty-one years, seems much more reasonable than the Roman law, which has appointed the age of twenty-five for that purpose, and which has been followed throughout almost the whole of Europe. At twenty-one the faculties of man are developed; he has a perception of his strength, he yields to counsel what he refuses to authority; and can no longer bear to be kept in leading-strings. So strong is this feeling, that the prolongation of the domestic power often produces a state of irritation and ill-nature equally uncomfortable for all concerned. But there are individuals who seem incapable of arriving at maturity, or who are much slower than others in reaching it. Cases of that nature may be easily provided for by prolonging the guardianship whenever occasion for it occurs.

Questions on the Rationales for Parental Rights

We now need to begin to think systematically about the relationship of parent and child and parents and the state. We will start by asking why we might attribute rights to parents. So that you may look afresh at parental rights, imagine yourself a member of a commission considering a constitutional amendment according rights to parents. Why might you want to do so? Not want to? You may find it helpful to reconsider the justifications for family autonomy we explored in Part I. Some of those justifications are often propounded to justify parental rights. The following questions remind you of them and then ask questions designed to help you think productively about them.

(1) The first justification for family autonomy was that a court or agency is likely to lack, and to find it hard to get, information about any particular family's situation. Is one justification for parental rights that parents will know their child and their child's situation better than anyone else can, since they will have cared for and lived with the child in the most complete way from his birth, and that no governmental agency will be well-situated to acquire equally good information?

(2) The second justification for family autonomy was that a court or agency is likely to lack expertise in making decisions about families. Is one justification for parental rights that decisions about children implicate questions about the dynamics of child development and of family interactions about which judges and bureaucrats are not expert? Are parents any more expert than judges and administrators? Are parents as well situated as judges and administrators to acquire information?

(3) The third justification for family autonomy was the difficulty of devising standards to govern judicial or administrative decisions.

(a) Is one justification for parental rights that children live in such various, complex, and unpredictable situations that no adequately comprehensive, detailed, and principled standards could be devised to guide courts or agencies in making decisions about children?

(b) Is one justification for parental rights that in a large pluralistic society no satisfactory social agreement can be reached about what kind of adults we want children to become, about what child-rearing techniques will rear what kind of adults, or about what child-rearing techniques are appropriate?

(c) Is one justification for parental rights that there are considerations—like religious belief or ethnic tradition—which may be desirable in rearing children but which the state may not properly consult?

(d) Is one justification for parental rights that decisions about children ought not be made according to the kind of impersonal standards the law must use but should be resolved according to the standards of accommodation, affection, and love parents naturally feel for their children? To what extent are those two standards incompatible?

(4) The fourth justification for family autonomy was the enforcement problem.

(a) Is one justification for parental rights that much of the interaction between parents and children occurs in private and government therefore cannot easily find out and supervise what is going on?

(b) Is one justification for parental rights that parental behavior reflects psychological motives that are both strong and often unrecognized and that thus are so difficult for people to control that even governmental sanctions may have little effect?

(c) Is one justification for parental rights that parents often feel their upbringing of their children is not the concern of outsiders (and particularly not the concern of government), so that parents will resist attempts to enforce government rules and decisions?

(d) Is one justification for parental rights that governmental attempts to enforce rules or decisions against parents may provoke parents to retaliate against the very people the government is trying to protect—the children?

(5) The fifth justification for family autonomy was the danger that governmental intervention will exacerbate family conflict. Is one justification for parental rights that governmental intervention, by bringing into the family outsiders from social workers to prosecutors, may disrupt the crucial stability of the relationship between parent and child? Is one justification for parental rights that children need their parents to be stable authority figures and that government intervention in the family injures parents as authority figures?

(6) The sixth justification for family autonomy was that government intervention in the family injures the family by diminishing its privacy. Is one justification for parental rights that judicial or administrative inquiry into the relationship of parent and child injures both parent and child by diminishing the privacy of both? Should parents be able to raise their children in privacy?

(7) The seventh justification for family autonomy was that it is normatively preferable for people to organize their own lives, particularly their own intimate lives. Is one justification for parental rights that it is normatively preferable for parents to organize their relationship with their children?

(8) The eighth justification for family autonomy was that allowing families freedom promotes pluralism. Is one justification for parental rights that allowing parents freedom to raise their children as they will permits them to perpetuate whatever communities, orthodox or heterodox, the parents prefer, thereby preserving the range of communities necessary to make society pluralist?

(9) The first six possible justifications for parental rights reason that giving parents power to make decisions for children is good for children. This may well be generally true, but does it justify attributing *rights* to parents? Sometimes the state would make *better* decisions for children than parents. The structure of rights analysis that you studied in Part II makes it quite difficult for the state to override rights. And as we conventionally understand rights, they create an area of liberty in which people may make whatever decision they wish, even if society regards that decision as incorrect. Since there will be times when the government must intervene in families to protect children, and since it will be difficult to specify those times in advance, do we want to give parents as effective a shield against government intervention as rights?

(10) We have been investigating the sources of parental rights, but we have not asked just what rights parents may have. Recall your position as a member of the commission to consider a constitutional amendment. How would you define the parental rights (if any) you believe the Constitution should contain?

(11) What interests does the state have that might sometimes override parental rights? As a member of the commission, how might

you try to identify the interests the state may legitimately assert for this purpose and the means to be used in assessing those interests?

Parents' Rights and Parents' Duties

Consider now an attempt to use a familiar legal category—the fiduciary relationship—to derive a convincing justification for the legal rights of parents and a cogent way of explaining the limits of those rights. This article is valuable for another reason—it introduces you to several of the major trends in contemporary thinking about the legal relationship between parents and children.

ELIZABETH S. SCOTT AND ROBERT E. SCOTT PARENTS AS FIDUCIARIES

81 Virginia Law Review 2401 (1995)

Traditionally, the law has deferred to the rights of biological parents in regulating the parent-child relationship. More recently, as the emphasis of legal regulation has shifted to protecting children's interests, critics have targeted the traditional focus on parents' rights as impeding the goal of promoting children's welfare. Some contemporary scholars argue instead for a "child-centered perspective," in contrast to the current regime under which biological parents continue to have important legal interests in their relationship with their children. The underlying assumption of this claim is that the rights of parents and the interests of children often are conflicting, and that greater recognition of one interest means diminished importance to the other.

One way of thinking about a legal regime that seeks to harmonize this conflict is to imagine that the parent's legal relationship to the child is shaped by fiduciary responsibilities toward the child rather than by inherent rights derived from status. Fiduciaries in law are agents who occupy a position of special confidence, superiority, or influence, and thus are subject to strict and non-negotiable duties of loyalty and reasonable diligence in acting on behalf of their principals. Characterizing parents as fiduciaries suggests that the parent-child relationship shares important features with other legal relationships that have been similarly defined, such as trustees and trust beneficiaries, corporate directors and shareholders, executors and legatees, and guardians and wards. Basic structural similarities are apparent. There are information asymmetries in this family relationship that are analogous to those of other fiduciary relationships. Moreover, satisfactory performance by parents, like that of other fiduciaries, requires considerable discretion, and children, like other principals, are not in a position to direct or control that performance. Here, as in other contexts, the challenge for legal regulation is to encourage the parent to act so as to serve the interests of the child rather than her own conflicting interests, and yet to do so in a context in which monitoring parental behavior is difficult....

I. Reconceptualizing the Parent–Child Relationship

A. *The Critique of Parents' Rights*

Legal deference to the claims of biological parents recently has come under attack in the courts, in the academic literature, and in the popular media. Cases such as the highly publicized dispute between the DeBoers and Daniel Schmidt over the custody of "Baby Jessica" [about which you will read in Chapter 9] contribute to a view that the law, frozen in ancient doctrine, accords unwarranted legal protection to biological parents in ways that are both directly harmful and symbolically corrosive to the interests of their children. For example, recognition of the rights of non-custodial biological parents can undermine a relationship between the child and a more suitable social parent. Further, the latitude given to parents in rearing their children is seen as excessive, allowing some parents to inflict unmonitored and unsanctioned harm on their children. More indirectly, to the extent that the law emphasizes parental rights, it encourages parents' inclination to put their own interests before those of their children, both in the intact family and on divorce or dissolution....

Outside of the adoption context, non-custodial biological parents often win custody contests with stepparents and other third parties who have functioned in a parental role. To the consternation of critics, traditional law gives little legal protection to the relationship between the faithful stepparent and the child if the biological parent is fit. Similarly poignant are cases in which a grandparent or other relative has assumed the care of a child who is neglected or informally abandoned by his parent. Months or even years later, the wayward parent who mends her ways may assert her parental rights and often successfully reclaim custody.

Critics of parental rights also decry the legal response to seriously deficient parental conduct. State agents are constrained from directly monitoring the quality of parental care by policies that support parental authority and family privacy. Many critics view these policies as leaving children vulnerable and without adequate protection from their parents' neglectful or abusive behavior. Even when children are in state custody, the spectre of parental rights casts a shadow. Foster care placement tends to extend indefinitely for a large percentage of these children, who are neither returned to their parents' custody nor available for adoption because parental rights are not terminated. Children get older (and less adoptable) while parents are given expansive opportunities to remedy the conditions that resulted in the removal. Meanwhile, children's relationships with foster parents receive little legal protection (and children are moved from one foster family to another) on the ground that a strong attachment might undermine family ties with the biological parents.

Considerable reform efforts, including comprehensive federal legislation, have focused on the problem of foster care "drift," but with few positive results. Policies promoting family reunification have had mixed success, because a large portion of parents are unable to resume care, or fail to do so adequately. Moreover, systemic efforts directed at facilitating termination of parental rights and adoption in appropriate cases have been largely unsuccessful. Terminating parental rights continues to be a costly and cumbersome process, owing to procedural and substantive requirements directed toward protecting parental interests. For the population of children in foster care, a large gap separates the cases in which parents can resume care of their child from the cases in which parenting is so clearly deficient that state agents pursue termination of parental rights. The interests of the children in this middle category, the critics argue, are poorly served by policies that protect parents' rights....

The critics of parental rights often focus on cases of horrendous parental conduct, or on contexts in which parents use a legal entitlement to claim (or reclaim) a relationship with their child which in some sense they have not earned. A more subtle critique focuses on the intangible but perhaps more pervasive effects of contemporary "rights talk" on family relationships. A rights framework is grounded in autonomy and protection of individual interests. Thus, it reinforces the parents' tendency to elevate self-interest over the interests of their child. As Carl Schneider suggests, thinking in terms of rights "encourages us to think about what constrains us from doing what we want, not what obligates us to do what we ought." Arguably, the legal emphasis on parental rights (and the cultural rhetoric that it generates) influences parents' behavior in a number of ways. It might affect the allocation of financial resources and parental efforts between family and personal pursuits, as well as the inclination to consider the child's welfare in making family decisions. An incentive to act selfishly can, of course, lead to abuse and neglect in extreme cases. A more subtle but destructive impact on the stability of family relationships results if parents are less motivated to preserve the family in the face of marital stress, or, if the family dissolves, to maintain a relationship with the child and provide financial support. The regime of no-fault divorce may exemplify the effects of a rights-based conception of the parent-child relationship. By making divorce easy, the law signals that, in making the decision to divorce, parents are not required to weigh the interests of their children.

B. *A Relational Approach*....

Simply shifting the focus of legal regulation toward greater protection of the needs of children is unhelpful, in our view. This is so not because such a perspective misunderstands the social goals that drive the regulation of parent-child relationships, but rather because a child-centered approach, standing alone, will not lead reliably to legal rules that effect those objectives. Presumably, the social goal at stake in the regulation of the parent-child relationship is to ensure children the care necessary for their development into healthy, productive adults. This goal is more likely to be achieved if the law focuses principally on the relationship between parent and child, rather than on the child's needs per se. Parents are not fungible child rearers. The link between parent and child has substantial and intrinsic value to the child; the substitution of another parent and/or termination of the relationship is accomplished only at considerable cost to the child. Moreover, as a general matter, the state is not well suited to substitute for parents in the job of rearing children. If the calculus used to determine the optimal state role focuses on the child's interest discounted by the (now less weighty) parental interest, the presumption that these interests are inherently in tension persists and the central importance of the relationship is likely to be obscured. Moreover, assuming that we are correct that parents presumptively are the "first best" child-rearers, an interest-balancing approach offers no grounding for a regulatory regime that promotes optimal parental performance.

Other critics of rights-based family law argue that the law should emphasize parental responsibility, rather than rights. Katharine Bartlett, for example, emphasizing the law's expressive function, argues that the law should express a "better view of parenthood," one that is grounded in the morality of benevolence and responsibility. In her view, responsibility is inherent in relationship, and describes a connection based on identification. Although parental responsibility is a component of a rights-based conception of family relationships, it serves primarily as a justification for rights. As such, the importance of responsibility and other relationship values is obscured and diminished.

In our view, Bartlett correctly identifies parental responsibility as a core component of a regulatory scheme that will better promote the interests of children. Although in many regards our analysis is compatible with communitarian principles, we propose to explore the issues of parental responsibility through a lens that is quite different from the more philosophically-based critiques developed by Bartlett and others. Our relational approach is more explicitly positive and instrumental in character. We seek to discover the means through which a scheme of legal regulation can best motivate parents to invest the effort necessary to fulfill the obligations of child-rearing....

II. Regulating Conflicts of Interest Between Parent and Child....

A. *The Structure and Control of Fiduciary Relationships*

Fiduciary relationships are a subset of agency relationships, a broad category of legal relationships in which one party undertakes to perform a service for another. A key goal in the regulation of agency relationships is to encourage the agent to serve her principal's interests as well as her own. Several characteristics of agency relationships contribute to the risk of self-interested actions. In contrast to performance under a simple contingent contract, the agent's performance is complex and cannot be reduced readily to specific obligations. Satisfactory performance demands considerable decisionmaking discretion, and monitoring the quality of the agent's performance may be difficult.

These factors are exaggerated in a fiduciary relationship because the principal will typically be even less able to control or monitor the fiduciary's performance than is the case in an ordinary agency relationship.... [T]ypically, beneficiaries—whether shareholders, trust beneficiaries or legatees—are presumed to lack the requisite information or expertise to understand and evaluate the fiduciary's performance, and acquiring such information is very costly. As a result, not only is it difficult to monitor the agent's diligence and effort in performing her assigned responsibilities, but the context carries a heightened risk of self-dealing as well. In general, the law characterizes as fiduciary those agency relationships in which the principal is particularly vulnerable and unable fully to protect and assert his own interests, thus providing the agent a peculiar opportunity and incentive either to shirk or cheat.

Fiduciary law seeks to change these incentives through mechanisms designed to encourage actors to pursue collective rather than personal goals. Legal duties of fiduciaries fall roughly into two categories: a duty of care—the agent must perform her responsibilities with reasonable diligence—and a duty of loyalty—the fiduciary must not place her personal interests above those of her principal. The objective, in either case, is first to encourage the fiduciary to take the beneficiary's interests properly into account in making decisions, and second to facilitate detection of her failure to do so....

Questions on Parents as Fiduciaries

(1) What would it mean to call parents "fiduciaries"? How might the law already do so? How might law have to be changed in order to do so? Essentially, the law only intervenes in an intact family when parents have drastically fallen short of pretty unexacting standards. When the law deals with divorced parents, it effectively asks little more than that they pay what they owe. Even parents who have abused or neglected their children are basically asked only to come up to the law's minimal standards of parental decency. The law would have unmarried fathers denied parental standing only when they have in some useful sense abandoned their children. In child-custody disputes, parents are not held to any particular standard, but are judged on a relative basis. Does all this strike you as pretty distant from the lofty standard of the fiduciary?

(2) As the Scotts describe it, the law of fiduciary obligation is a protean doctrine which assumes different forms depending on the relationship involved. None of the relationships to which it ordinarily applies much resembles that of parent and child. Indeed, the Scotts scrupulously chart a number of ways in which fiduciary and parent-child relationships differ significantly. For example, they note that fiduciaries can generally be replaced without intolerably disturbing things, while parents are not so readily discarded. The Scotts also suggest that it can be harder to gauge whether parents have acted in their child's interest than whether corporate directors have made a decision within the range of acceptable business practices. In short, is commercial law generally designed for an

area of life so different from family life as to make borrowing from it problematic for family law? What lessons about this question can you infer from our discussion of the law of commercial and family contracts?

(3) Is the fiduciary principle problematic as a general statement of what parents should do for their children? In its original, pure form, the fiduciary principle appears to require fiduciaries to put their loyalty to the client's interest above all else. As the famous (and inevitable) passage from Cardozo puts it,

> Joint adventurers, like copartners, owe to one another, while the enterprise continues, the duty of the finest loyalty. Many forms of conduct permissible in a workaday world for those acting at arm's length, are forbidden to those bound by fiduciary ties. A trustee is held to something stricter than the morals of the market place. Not honesty alone, but the punctilio of an honor the most sensitive, is then the standard of behavior. As to this there has developed a tradition that is unbending and inveterate. Uncompromising rigidity has been the attitude of courts of equity when petitioned to undermine the rule of undivided loyalty by the 'disintegrating erosion' of particular exceptions.

Meinhard v. Salmon, 164 NE 545, 546 (NY 1928). But should the interests of children always trump the interests of parents? In other words, is the fiduciary standard actually higher than the standard we might expect from parents? In commercial law, the fiduciary's relationship with the benefitted party is commonly of limited scope, but the relationship between parent and child involves broad areas of both of their lives. It may be practical to impose a high standard of selflessness within a limited strip of a person's life, but is it as practical to do so more globally? In other words, may parents have duties to each other, to their other children, and even to themselves that may conflict with "fiduciary" obligations to an individual child?

(4) Consider the questions we asked under the heading "Probing the Rationales for Parental Rights." Are not the first six of these rationales based on the belief that giving parents power is good for children? If this is so, are there important differences between a "parents' rights" approach, a "child-centered perspective," and a "fiduciary" approach?

SECTION 2. CHILDREN'S RIGHTS

> *The principal change that has occurred in my own outlook on child rearing has been the realization that what is making the parent's job most difficult is today's child-centered viewpoint. I don't merely refer to the few parents who kowtow to their tyrannical children or the larger number who have been intimidated by all the advice they've received from us pediatricians, psychologists, psychiatrists and pedagogues, and are hesitant to give their children the firm leadership they need, for fear they might do the wrong thing. I mean the tendency of many conscientious parents to keep their eyes exclusively focused on their child, thinking about what he needs from them and from the community, instead of thinking about what the world, the*

neighborhood, the family will be needing from the child and then making sure that he will grow up to meet such obligations. Even to hear this latter point of view expressed is a little startling to many Americans.

Benjamin Spock
Baby and Child Care (1973)

We have been discussing the rights of parents and the interests of children. But of course children have rights too. But what rights? The following article explores that question with some care.

LEE E. TEITLEBAUM
CHILDREN'S RIGHTS AND THE PROBLEM OF EQUAL RESPECT

27 Hofstra Law Review 799 (1999)

II. Traditional Rights Theories and Children

For liberal theorists, and often in law, rights are a reflection of a basic human right to equal respect in making decisions about one's life; a theory which, it has been argued, the Constitution is meant to express. This approach begins from the assumption that human beings have a special capacity to reason and engage in deliberative decision-making. They can evaluate arguments and form plans according to their rational acceptance or rejection of various possibilities. It is this capacity in each of us that is entitled to respect.

It is further assumed that each of us is entitled not only to respect but to the same respect due others. The principle of equal respect is variously articulated according to the context of the moral theory in which it is situated but it is also associated with the notion of autonomy. Both are found in Locke's propositions that "all men by nature are equal" and of the "equal right, that every man hath, to his natural freedom, without being subjected to the will or authority of any other man." ... Even theories of rights that do not separate claims of rights from the creation of social good (that is, utilitarian approaches) strongly emphasize the importance of liberty and the capacity for self-expression. To take the most familiar instance, Mill, whose views generally follow consequentialist principles, takes as the central purpose of his celebrated essay, *On Liberty*, the assertion of

> one very simple principle.... That principle is, that the sole end for which mankind are warranted, individually or collectively, in interfering with the liberty of action of any of their number, is self-protection. That the only purpose for which power can be rightfully exercised over any member of a civilized community, against his will, is to prevent harm to others. His own good, either physical or moral, is not a sufficient warrant. He cannot rightfully be compelled to do or forbear because it will be better for him to do so....

While so strong a commitment to individual choice is notoriously difficult to explain within a utilitarian framework, Mill's own position is that human nature is such that, because of the need for self-expression that follows upon the capacity for thought and reflection, men and women simply cannot be made happier by external restrictions on their development and spontaneity.

Several characteristics of these approaches to rights bear emphasis. Rights based on capacity, or moral agency, or ability to engage in neutral dialogue, seem ultimately to be understood as categorical. The entitlement to respect is founded on the ability to think rationally, form plans, and make choices. If an individual possesses this capacity or agency, he or she is entitled to respect for choices about life, and not just to respect in some degree, but to equal respect that is to the same degree of respect accorded to all other rights holders. Absence of this capacity is likewise categorical, in most views. If a rights holder is entitled to the same respect as all others, then one either has the same rights as others or has none of those rights. You may have other rights, if the society decides to give them to you. Animals are protected from cruelty, infants from starvation; but neither animals nor infants have rights to self-determination.

A second characteristic of the traditional understanding of rights is its political function. "Rights" have sometimes been described as a militant concept. Standard rights theories based on a respect for the choices of others create a "space" around the individual. To have a right to do something means at least that no one may intrude on your choice except in very limited circumstances. In fact, if I am a rights holder or a citizen, no one else has any general claim regarding my conduct, except when that conduct invades the space of the other, through coercion or injury....

It is not surprising that these formulations of rights theory find little place for talk about children. The right to equal respect or to liberty as a recognition of the special character of mankind's capacity for reason is only thought appropriate for those who possess the capacity for rational choice: a criterion commonly held to exclude children. Mill's position is again the most familiar. Immediately after his articulation of the famous liberty principle, Mill continues:

> It is perhaps hardly necessary to say that this doctrine is meant to apply only to human beings in the maturity of their faculties. We are not speaking of children.... Those who are still in a state to require being taken care of by others, must be protected against their own actions as well as against external injury.... Liberty, as a principle, has no application to any state of things anterior to the time when mankind has become capable of being improved by free and equal discussion.

Locke, likewise, observed that children were an exception to his general proposition that "all men by nature are equal." The human mind, at birth, is a "white [p]aper, void of all [c]haracters, without any

[i]deas." That paper will be inscribed by experience over time but, because children lack reason in at least their early years, parents, he said, "have a sort of rule and jurisdiction over them," although temporary and (perhaps) proportionate to the child's level of reason.... Amy Gutmann observes more simply that "it would be absurd to apply [the] principle of equal freedom to children."

III. Children's Rights in Legal Doctrine

It will occur to those familiar with Supreme Court doctrine and other bodies of law dealing with the rights of children that, whatever may be true for moral theorists, courts and legislatures have been quite ready to accept children as rights holders. Legislatures have created two kinds of rights especially applicable to children. All children are entitled to a variety of what might be called "welfare rights," such as to nutrition, food, shelter, education and the like. State laws also provide for statutory rights, where older children may, even before the age of majority, marry, secure a driver's license, and seek gainful employment. Courts have recognized constitutionally based rights for children in virtually every domain where such rights have been recognized for adults.

Recognition or creation of these various rights for children seems on its face inconsistent with a general claim that children cannot appropriately be regarded as rights holders. The inconsistency may lie in either of two directions. It may be that legal doctrines maintain the theoretical notion of rights described above but treat children as possessing the same rights as adults. Alternatively, legal doctrines may modify the notion of rights themselves in their application to young persons. A review of these bodies of law dealing with minors suggests that the former hypothesis cannot be supported.

A. Welfare Rights

The most pervasively recognized rights of children are positive rights, rights to receive social goods, which find expression in the laws of every state and in international declarations of human rights. Grants of positive rights are recognized grudgingly and with some suspicion in connection with adults, but are readily accepted in relation to young people. We are quite accustomed to talk of the rights of children to education, nutrition, shelter, and other social and personal goods. For example, the United Nations Declaration of the Rights of the Child ("United Nations Declaration") contains the following principle:

> The child is entitled to receive education, which shall be free and compulsory, at least in the elementary stages. He shall be given an education which will promote his general culture, and enable him, on a basis of equal opportunity, to develop his abilities, his individual judgment, and his sense of moral and social responsibility, and to become a useful member of society.

The right reflected in the United Nations Declaration, like those to shelter and nutrition, supposes an obligation on the part of others—parents or the state—to supply basic social goods. It is a positive right in the sense used by Salmond or Hohfeld: that is, an interest with respect to which there exists a duty imposed upon some other person, and has often enough been recognized, although not always enthusiastically, in Supreme Court decisions.

Recognition of these positive rights can be justified on various theoretical grounds. For social contractarians, they derive from a hypothetical social contract, as those things that every rational person would consider essential to have as a child. Even without the contractarian framework, a liberal may consider some such entitlements to be essential to achieving the capacity for rational choice on which membership in a liberal society is founded. Utilitarians can justify a broader range of such rights, as long as it appears that production of educated healthy children will maximize human happiness.

Adults have relatively few positive rights. Medicaid would illustrate the exceptional situation. But even where positive rights are available to adults, there is a very important difference between the posture of positive rights for adults and those rights for children. The adult holder of positive rights retains his autonomy with respect to those rights—he or she may take advantage of Medicaid, or may choose not to do so. By contrast, the United Nations Declaration does not end with creation of a governmental duty to provide education. It also presumes a duty on the child to accept the benefits of that right. Education is to be "compulsory" quite as much as it is to be free.

Claims of this sort, which I have called "integrative rights" elsewhere, are evidently based on principles concerning the needs rather than the preferences or choices of children, at the point at which the decision is made. A young person's choice to forebear from education, even with thanks, will not be accorded respect but rather will result in an incorrigibility petition to deprive her of physical liberty. A neglected child does not have the negative right to decline becoming a ward of the court and remain in an inadequate home, however dearly she may wish to do so. There is, in short, no question of equal respect for actual choices in this sense of rights.

Nor do these integrative rights express the individualism conveyed by liberty interests. Rights in the latter sense create a social and political distance between the holder and all others, including the state. Integrative rights point in precisely the opposite direction. As the United Nations Declaration itself makes plain, the thrust of the right to education is to become a useful member of the society. American juvenile court law has said exactly the same thing about the coercive intervention of that tribunal: the assumption of jurisdiction over delinquent and neglected children was explained as an effort by the court to place children on the road to "good, sound, adult citizenship" when their parents could not or would not do so.

B. Other Statutory Rights for Children

State positive laws also typically recognize certain rights for older minors that are not based on welfare interests. These laws permit older children to engage in activities that are generally permitted for adults and generally prohibited for minors. It is sometimes argued that these statutory legal entitlements demonstrate that legal rules do not follow the categorical approach to competency supposed by traditional rights theory. There is, it is said, no single age of majority but rather multiple ages: twenty-one for purchase of alcohol; eighteen for voting and purchasing tobacco; sixteen for most kinds of employment, for marriage, and eligibility for the death sentence; sixteen or even fourteen or fifteen for permission to drive; and "maturity" for deciding whether to terminate a pregnancy. These variations in ages of legal capacity are taken to suggest that "rights" are not all-or-nothing propositions as traditional theory supposes, but rather that legal practice and perhaps legal theory expects that different rights require different competencies.

While the argument below will suggest the desirability of considering competence to be more continuous than categorical, these legislative distinctions do not demonstrate that such a theory has already been accepted in practice. For one thing, these age limits do not generally reflect legislative conclusions about the relationship of levels of competence to age.

This is most dramatically true of the age at which people can buy alcoholic beverages. Many states lowered their drinking ages from twenty-one to eighteen after the adoption of the Twenty-sixth Amendment lowering the voting age. Currently, the drinking age in all states is twenty-one as the result of federal legislation requiring that they do so in order to qualify for highway construction funds. The initial reduction in the drinking age, if it had anything to do with the competence of eighteen-year-olds, arose from their supposed competence to vote rather than to use alcohol responsibly. The later increase in the drinking age followed not from a state legislative finding that eighteen-year-olds were after all incompetent to drink responsibly, but from a Congressional decision to that effect implemented by conditioning eligibility for highway funding on state acquiescence in that judgment. Nor is it clear that either conclusion would be supported by data about capacity to use alcohol responsibly in general or even about the specific risk that eighteen-year-olds present a greater risk in driving vehicles. Studies do show that lowering the drinking age increased fatalities somewhat among younger drivers. However, they also show that traffic fatalities among persons under twenty-one were lower than those for young adults between twenty-one and twenty-five. There was, however, no movement by those who wished re-election to raise the drinking age to twenty-five.

Even the adoption of the Twenty-sixth Amendment, lowering the age for voting in federal elections from twenty-one to eighteen, is hard to explain entirely as a judgment about adolescent competence to exercise the franchise. Although much of the debate took that turn, it has the flavor of a second-order justification for an essentially political decision that drafting eighteen-year-olds to fight in an unpopular war about which they had no right to vote was unacceptable or at least unappealing.

It is, moreover, important that most of these age-variant laws do not create rights in the usual adult sense. While a sixteen-year-old may marry in most states, he or she can only do so with parental permission. By the same token, a minor seeking a drivers permit typically must have the consent of a parent or guardian. And while a minor may be entitled to decide, or have a court decide, whether termination of a pregnancy is in her best interests, her parents are entitled to receive notice and must consent to that procedure unless a court decides that requiring parental notification or consent would be harmful to the child. To vest such authority with parents obviously contradicts the claim that legislatures have determined that minors are themselves competent to make decisions about these activities. Rather than create spheres of autonomy for minors, these laws transfer responsibility for decisions about competence with respect to these activities from public to private authority—here, the authority of parents....

With respect to these decisions and the reasons for them, older minors are subject not to rules of general applicability, but to the personal domination of their parents. However important and socially acceptable that domination may be in this setting, a regime in which authority may be exercised on the basis of the private values and beliefs of the person exercising authority cannot be reconciled with liberal rights theory. To take only the most familiar example, the vice of vague rules is that they allow officials an almost unlimited power to grant or deny freedoms, and "the very idea that one man may be compelled to hold his life, or the means of living ... at the mere will of another, seems to be intolerable in any country where freedom prevails, as being the essence of slavery itself." Subjection to the "mere will" of another captures, however, the kind of authority held by parents of minors above some age over decisions to marry or drive, and for many other purposes as well.

C. *Supreme Court Doctrine and Children's Rights*

The strongest declarations of minors' rights, and the classes of rights that seem most indistinguishable from rights in traditional political and moral theory, are found in decisions of the United States Supreme Court. The Court has by this point recognized rights claims for children in many areas where autonomy-based rights have been recognized for adults. The core meaning of liberty—freedom from physical confinement—was held applicable to children in *In re Gault* and reaffirmed in *Breed v. Jones. Gault* extended the privilege against self-incrimination to minors, not solely from concern for untrustworthy confessions but because children are entitled to decide whether and how they will participate in proceedings affecting their liberty.

First Amendment rights to political expression have also been recognized for very young children. *Tinker v. Des Moines Independent Community School District*, for example, held that the suspension of students (in that case ages eight, eleven, thirteen, fifteen and sixteen), for wearing armbands to protest the Vietnam War infringed on their right "to freedom of expression of their views." The right of children to receive information as well as to express themselves was recognized in *Erznoznik v. City of Jacksonville*, where the Court held:

> Speech that is neither obscene as to youths nor subject to some other legitimate proscription cannot be suppressed solely to protect the young from ideas or images that a legislative body thinks unsuitable for them. In most circumstances, the values protected by the First Amendment are no less applicable when government seeks to control the flow of information to minors.

Children, of course, have been held to possess some interest in privacy, reflected in rights of access to contraception and abortion. The Court has struck down categorical legislative rules requiring the consent of a parent of an unmarried minor as a condition to obtaining an abortion and prohibiting the distribution of contraceptives to minors.

When claimed by adults, these rights are typically understood as reflecting values of autonomy and choice. They are "negative rights"—rights not to be controlled by others in our choice about the good life. Edwin Baker, for example, argues that this view provides the most coherent theory of the First Amendment. "The liberty model holds that the free speech clause protects not a marketplace but rather an arena of individual liberty from certain types of governmental restrictions. Speech is protected not as a means to a collective good but because of the value of speech conduct to the individual."

Reproductive rights are, perhaps even more clearly, founded on recognition of the value of choice. "Although '[t]he Constitution does not explicitly mention any right of privacy,' the Court has recognized that one aspect of the 'liberty' protected by the Due Process Clause of the Fourteenth Amendment is 'a right of personal privacy, or a guarantee of certain areas or zones of privacy.' " The "right of personal privacy includes 'the interest in independence in making certain kinds of important decisions.' " The decision over whether or not to have a child is "at the very heart of this cluster of constitutionally protected choices." Further, "[i]f the right of privacy means anything, it is the right of the individual, married or single, to be free of unwarranted governmental intrusion into matters so fundamentally affecting a person as the decision whether to bear or beget a child."

The privilege against self-incrimination, in the adult context, also can be understood in terms of a zone of autonomy. The privilege is not solely or even primarily concerned with the accuracy of statements by those facing criminal prosecution, but rather with assuring that suspects may freely decide whether to cooperate in a proceeding affecting their liberty.

The above cases do seem to suggest that children are generally entitled to rights in the strong sense enjoyed by adults: to claims of self-determination and self-realization against all others, including the state. But how can the Supreme Court have held that children have autonomy-based rights in the midst of a legal setting that supposes that children are obliged to accept parental and governmental control regarding health, education, housing, and the like? Part of the answer to this dilemma is that, although rights to speech, procreation and the like are justified for adults in terms of their capacity for rational choice, the extension of these rights to minors has never been explained on grounds assuming the same capacity for choice.

In fact, discussion of the competence of children rarely appears in decisions extending procedural protection in delinquency cases, or even in decisions regarding privacy and First Amendment interests claimed by or on behalf of children. The Court has, on the one hand, recognized that minors enjoy some degree of liberty interest in virtually all areas where such interests are recognized for adults. On the other hand, these liberty interests have not usually been explained on grounds of adult-like capacity for choice.

Rather, the Court's analysis has begun textually with the observation that the Constitution talks of "persons." It has followed that minors have some claims arising from the due process clause, but not that the extent of state power to regulate is the same for minors and adults, as would be true on an assumption of equal capacity. On the contrary, the Court has long recognized greater governmental authority to regulate the activities of minors than would be allowable for adults. States may restrict religiously motivated activities of children when some danger exists, although adults probably could not be so controlled. They may require attendance at school by minors, and may limit minors' access to "objectionable" but not "obscene" material that could not constitutionally be kept from adults.

The greater authority of the state to regulate the decisions and conduct of minors reflects precisely the belief that adjudication of their claims to rights does not entail assumptions about equal capacity. Justice Stewart, concurring in *Ginsberg v. New York,* justifies protecting children from non-obscene publications in the following way:

> I think a State may permissibly determine that, at least in some precisely delineated areas, a child—like someone in a captive audience—is not possessed of that full capacity for individual choice which is the presupposition of First Amendment guarantees. It is only upon such a premise, I should suppose, that a State may deprive children of other rights—the right to marry, for example, or the right to vote—deprivations that would be constitutionally intolerable for adults.

Justice Brennan's plurality opinion in *Carey v. Population Services International* sounded the same theme. The privacy interest implicated (access to contraceptives) was at base an "interest in . . . making certain kinds of important decisions," and "the law has generally regarded minors as having a lesser capability for making important decisions."

This assumption is reflected as well in the standard of review employed by Justice Brennan in connection with privacy rights of minors. The issue is whether state restrictions "serve 'any significant state interest ... that is not present in the case of an adult,' "a test he characterizes as: "[l]ess rigorous than the "compelling state interest" test applied to restrictions on the privacy rights of adults. Such lesser scrutiny is appropriate ... because of the States' greater latitude to regulate the conduct of children."

Constitutional doctrine—even when it upholds children's rights that are founded on the principle of equal respect when recognized for adults—does not assume that children are as capable of mature choice or that they possess the same "negative rights," rights to be left alone, as do adults.

Supreme Court decisions do not make a great deal of this modification in the theory of rights for children. Since all rights are subject to regulation in some circumstances, it seems to follow easily that the rights of children can be regulated according to the abilities of their holders. In principle, however, there is more to it than that. We have already seen that rights in the adult setting are universal in scope. Your right to speech and my right to speech are identical; your privilege against self-incrimination and mine are formally identical. For some persons to have broader rights than others would be an unacceptable denial of the principle of equal respect. A regulation limiting speech where there is an immediate risk of violence must apply to all instances of such risk, which means that all speakers are subject to an identical range of limitation. The thrust of the Supreme Court cases discussed above, however, is precisely to say that the rights of children are more limited in their extension than those of adults. Whatever their status as rights, children's rights are understood differently than are the rights of adults.

Questions on the Claims of Children

Recall the question we asked earlier: Parents have rights; the state has interests. What do children have? Do children have particular kinds of legally protected interests? The following questions explore some of the forms such interests might take. As you read them, you should keep in mind several overarching questions: Is the particular "legally protected interest" a right? If so, what kind? A moral right? A "natural law" right? A statutory entitlement? A constitutional right? By whom is the legally protected interest to be effectuated? The state? The parents? A court-appointed guardian? How is the legally protected interest to be reconciled with parental rights?

(1) Do children have a legally protectable interest in life? How is that interest to be reconciled with the possibility that some lives are not worth living?

(2) Do children have a legally protectable interest in the conditions necessary to make their lives as fulfilling as possible? How are limits to be set to such an interest? How are such rights to be paid for? Which legal institution is best situated to declare and enforce such rights?

(3) Do children have a legally protectable interest in correct decisions about important questions in their lives? How are we to decide what "correct" means?

(4) Do children have a legally protectable interest in the same decision they would have made themselves about important questions in their lives? How should we determine what children would have decided for themselves if they cannot articulate their preferences? Suppose that they can articulate their preferences but seem too young to use wise judgment? Are we to make the decision they would make for themselves retrospectively as adults? How can we tell what that would be?

(5) Do children have a legally protectable interest in having a "personal," as opposed to a governmental, decision made for them? Need this be a decision by a relative? By someone intimate with the child?

(6) Do children have a legally protectable interest in having a decision made that is based on their religious views? How are those views to be determined?

Questions on the Rights of Children

You are an attorney who has specialized in representing children in custody cases. Tax reformers in the state of Hutchins have successfully pressed for a constitutional revision to rewrite the Hutchins Constitution. You have been placed on a committee to revise the law of individual rights. You are the chair of a committee to consider whether Hutchins should have a Children's Rights Clause. The committee has asked you to try your hand at drafting such a clause. What will it say?

(1) You have just read a series of interests children probably have. You were asked to think about whether those interests are legally protectible. You should now review those interests and decide whether any of them can profitably be made a right.

(2) Perhaps the easiest kind of right to create is a right to make a decision. This is, as Dean Teitelbaum writes, the kind of right most commonly accorded to adult and the kind of right best founded on familiar ideas in Western legal and moral philosophy. In addition, the right is administratively convenient in the sense that once it has been recognized the state need only defer to the right-holder's choice. Have you selected any such rights for children?

(a) Are children appropriate candidates for such a right? As Dean Teitelbaum points out, such rights are accorded to adults partly out of respect for their abilities to make wise decisions for themselves. Do children have comparable abilities? Do they think differently from adults? If so, how? For a more concrete discussion of this issue, see the questions that follow *Wisconsin v. Yoder* in Chapter 12.

(b) Even if some children make decisions as well as adults, very young children clearly do not. Does this matter? Are people entitled to choose for themselves even if they choose in ways that seem foolish?

(c) Even if we should accord rights to make decisions to children so young they seem likely to make foolish decisions, should we accord rights to children too young to understand their choices or to articulate their preferences? If so, who is to make decision for them?

(i) The state? Isn't the state exactly the entity rights are generally intended to restrict?

(ii) The child's parents? Isn't that pretty much where the power to make decisions for children is already confided? Aren't they the people the child is most likely to come into conflict with?

(iii) Someone appointed to be the child's "advocate"? How is such a person to know what is best for the child?

(3) We have already accorded rights to parents. Many of these rights are accorded them because we expect them to make decisions for children. What will be the status of these rights if your Clause is adopted?

(4) What language will you use to embody the rights you have selected?

(a) Should you borrow the UN Declaration of the Rights of the Child, which is quoted in Dean Teitelbaum's essay?

(b) Should you borrow the language of the Equal Rights Amendment? ("Equality of rights under the law shall not be denied or abridged by the United States or by any State on account of sex.")

(c) Should you borrow the following language, which one of the authors of this casebook has heard mooted as a possible version of a Child's Rights Amendment to the US Constitution?

The rights of persons under the age of 18 years shall include all the due process and protective rights possessed by those over the age of 18 years. Such rights may be limited only upon demonstration of a compelling state interest, and any such limitation shall be accomplished by the least intrusive means. Nothing herein shall be construed to diminish any rights of persons under the age of 18 years, nor to preclude the enhancement of the rights of such persons.

(d) Can you devise language of your own which accurately states your intentions in a way that courts will understand centuries into the future? What specific kinds of cases will your language apply to?

(5) Is it necessary to include a Children's Rights Clause in the Hutchins Constitution?

(a) Is it unnecessary because, as Dean Teitelbaum remarks, courts have already found a variety of ways of according children rights, even if those rights are not as extensive as adults'?

(b) Is it unnecessary because children will have fourteenth amendment rights anyway the theory that childhood is a suspect classification? Children can't vote, which makes them classic candidates for suspect-classification protection. Children are so much a historically stigmatized minority that they are the group to which other minorities compare themselves to show they are being mistreated. That is, if a group can show it is being treated like children, it will have demonstrated that it is being mistreated. Finally, children are in a number of important ways a discrete and insular minority.

(6) Are you so confident about your ideas of children's welfare that you believe those ideas should be made part of the virtually permanent fundamental law of your state?

We are now ready to consider the questions about the rights of parents and the rights of children in a case that presents them in an intriguing context.

IN RE SCOTT K.

Supreme Court of California, 1979
595 P2d 105

NEWMAN, JUSTICE.

A 17-year-old defendant appeals from an order declaring him a juvenile court ward and placing him on probation. The order was based on the court's finding that defendant unlawfully possessed marijuana for purpose of sale in violation of section 11359 of the Health and Safety Code. The question is whether a warrantless, parent-approved, police search of defendant's personal property was permissible.

Defendant's mother found marijuana in his desk drawer. She gave it to an off-duty police officer who lived in the neighborhood and told him that conversations with other parents led her to believe that her son might be selling marijuana. A week later that officer's report was given to Narcotics Officer Schian for follow-up. He telephoned the father to advise that he was about to arrest defendant. The conversation was as follows: "In substance, I advised the father that I was in charge of the follow-up investigation of the marijuana that his wife had turned over to the police officer; that an arrest would result from this situation, arrest of the son; that I intended to come out and arrest his son if his son was home, and then I received the information that he was working on his motorcycle in the garage.

"And I asked him, 'Is it all right with you then that I go to the garage and arrest your boy there and do you wish to join us out there then, or what shall we do to make it easy on maybe the rest of the family?'

"And he indicated, 'Why don't you just come on inside after you have arrested him?' "

Without warrant, Schian and other officers went to the garage. Schian arrested defendant and took him to the house, where the father gave permission to search defendant's bedroom. The search disclosed a locked toolbox. The father told Schian that he had no key and that it was defendant's box. When asked about the key, defendant replied he had lost it. Schian said, "Your father already told me I could break the toolbox open if I couldn't find a key, but it's not in my interest to destroy the lock. Let me see the keys you have in your pocket." Defendant gave Schian his keys, one of which opened the box. Inside were nine baggies of marijuana.

The trial court ruled the arrest illegal ... because no exigent circumstances existed and there was sufficient time for the officer to secure an arrest warrant. The court nonetheless denied a motion to suppress as evidence the marijuana found in the toolbox. It concluded that search of the box was independent from the arrest and was pursuant to a valid consent. The court reasoned that, because the father owned the house and had a duty to control his son's activities, he could permit the search at any time, whether or not his son was present or under arrest....

The People contend that a father has authority to inspect the belongings of a minor child to promote the child's health and welfare; also, that in consenting to the search this father was "merely using the police as an instrumentality to assist him in complying with his parental duty...."

SEARCH AND SEIZURE

Article I, section 13 of the California Constitution provides: "The right of the people to be secure in their persons, houses, papers, and effects against unreasonable seizures and searches may not be violated; and a warrant may not issue except on probable cause, supported by oath or affirmation, particularly describing the place to be searched and the persons and things to be seized." ...

By no means are the rights of juveniles coextensive with those of adults. Minors' rights are often legitimately curtailed when the restriction serves a state's interest in promoting the health and growth of children. (See *Prince v. Massachusetts*). In juvenile court proceedings, rights may not be asserted if they might disrupt unique features of the proceedings; for example, jury trial is not required. Search and seizure laws, however, hardly seem disruptive or otherwise inconsistent with the state's interest in child welfare. It is established that minors have a liberty interest that entitles them to due process whenever a state initiates action to deprive them of liberty. (*In re Gault*, 387 U.S. 1; *Goss v. Lopez* (1975), 419 U.S. 565, 574; *In re Winship* (1970), 397 U.S. 358,

367; *In re Roger S.*, 19 Cal.3d 921; *In re Arthur N.* (1976), 16 Cal.3d 226.) Enforcement of search and seizure protections helps ensure that the factfinding process conforms with standards of due process....

The minor here contends that, because the toolbox was his own property, warrantless police search violated both his right to privacy and his right to be free from unreasonable search and seizure. He was age 17, old enough to assert his rights. When the police asked him for the key he did not consent to the search; instead the father gave consent.

Though the record discloses some discord in the parent-child relation, no evidence suggests that the discord concerned control of the box. The facts rather support the son's claim that the box was his own.[1] His constitutional rights were at stake; and we need only consult the words of article I, section 13 of the California Constitution to see that its protection applies....

PARENTAL CONTROL AND MINORS' RIGHTS

The People argue that, because a parent is responsible for minor children and may himself inspect their property, police search of that property when pursuant to parental consent is reasonable and accordingly constitutional. Implicit is the notion that the father here could effectively waive his son's right to be secure in the son's effects. We reject that view.

In *Planned Parenthood of Central Missouri v. Danforth*, the United States Supreme Court rejected the argument that parental authority should prevail over a minor's decision to terminate pregnancy. "Any independent interest the parent may have in the termination of the minor daughter's pregnancy is no more weighty than the right of privacy of the competent minor mature enough to become pregnant."

This court has insisted that a minor's due process right be protected even when the right imposes a burden on parents or limits parental control. (*In re Ricky H.* (1970), 2 Cal.3d 513; *In re Roger S.*) In *Ricky H.* the trial court's decision accepting a minor's waiver of the right to counsel was reversed because the waiver was influenced by the fact that the nonindigent parents were obliged by statute to pay counsel fees. *Roger S.* held that, regarding admission to a mental hospital, a minor of 14 years or more possesses due process rights that may not be waived by the parent or guardian. It would be incongruous to conclude that parents, for good reason or no reason, may summarily waive their child's right to search and seizure protections.

THIRD PARTY CONSENT TO SEARCH

Our final question is whether the toolbox search was reasonable because the father's consent qualified under the third-party-consent exception to warrant requirements. A warrantless search is reasonable

1. The father told the police that the box belonged to his son. It was locked and the son had the key. The father later testified that the son obtained the box from a father-in-law and, though he (the father) had borrowed tools, he had never opened the box himself but always obtained the tools directly from the son.

when consent is granted by one who has a protectible interest in the property. Valid consent may come from the sole owner of property or from "a third party who possessed common authority over or other sufficient relationship to the premises or effects sought to be inspected." (*United States v. Matlock* (1974), 415 U.S. 164, 171.)[2]

California case law prior to *Matlock* is consistent with that "common authority" principle. Third-party-consent searches were held invalid in *People v. Cruz* (1964), 40 Cal.Rptr. 841, 395 P.2d 889 (apartment guests could not consent to search of property of others jointly residing there); *People v. Murillo* (1966), 50 Cal.Rptr. 290 (roommate's consent to search residence was not a valid consent to search attache case); *People v. Egan* (1967), 58 Cal.Rptr. 627 (stepfather's consent invalid for search of adult stepson's personal effects though they were located in bedroom of stepfather's home); *People v. Daniels* (1971) 93 Cal.Rptr. 628 (mother could not consent to search of adult son's suitcase in her home).

The trial court here held that the father's authority was based on the combined circumstance of his ownership of the home and his duty to control his son. Yet neither fact shows the requisite link between the father's interest and the property inspected. Common authority over personal property may not be implied from the father's proprietary interest in the premises. (*United States v. Matlock*). Neither may it be premised on the nature of the parent-child relation.

Juveniles are entitled "to acquire and hold property, real and personal" (*Estate of Yano* (1922) 206 P. 995, 997); and "a minor child's property is his own ... not that of his parents." (*Emery v. Emery* (1955), 289 P.2d 218, 225; see also Civ.Code, § 202.) Parents may have a protectible interest in property belonging to children, but that fact may not be assumed. When a warrantless search is challenged the People must show that it was reasonable. Here the People did not establish that the consenting parent had a sufficient interest under search and seizure law. The father claimed no interest in the box or its contents. He acknowledged that the son was owner, and the son did not consent to the search. Because those facts were known to the police there was no justification either for their relying on the father's consent to conduct the search or for their failure to seek the warrant required by law.

The trial court's order is reversed.

CLARK, JUSTICE, dissenting.

Scott's right under the California Constitution to be free from unreasonable searches and seizures was not violated when his father and mother enlisted police assistance in discharging their parental responsibilities and consented to the search of Scott's toolbox. But his parents'

2. As explained by the court, "(c)ommon authority is ... not to be implied from the mere property interest a third party has in the property ... but rests rather on mutual use of the property by persons generally having joint access or control for most purposes, so that it is reasonable to recognize that any of the co-inhabitants has the right to permit the inspection in his own right and that the others have assumed the risk that one of their number might permit the common area to be searched."

right to care for, discipline and control their minor children a liberty interest protected by the due process clause of the Fourteenth Amendment to the United States Constitution is violated by the decision reached by this court's majority today.

Admittedly, minors as well as adults possess constitutional rights. (*Planned Parenthood of Cent. Mo. v. Danforth.*) However, as the majority concede, the rights of minors are by no means coextensive with those of adults. In particular, the right to be free from unreasonable searches and seizures does not extend as far when a minor is involved. (*In re Christopher W.* (1973), 105 Cal.Rptr. 775.)

"(E)ven where there is an invasion of protected freedoms 'the power of the state to control the conduct of children reaches beyond the scope of its authority over adults.' " (*Ginsberg v. New York* (1968) 390 U.S. 629, 638; *Prince v. Massachusetts.*) Moreover, parents have powers greater than those of the state to curtail a child's exercise of the constitutional rights he may otherwise enjoy, for a parent's own constitutionally protected liberty includes the right to "bring up children" (*Meyer v. Nebraska*), and to "direct the upbringing and education of children" (*Pierce v. Society of Sisters*). As against the state, this parental duty and right is subject to limitation only "if it appears that parental decisions will jeopardize the health or safety of the child, or have a potential for significant social burdens." (*Wisconsin v. Yoder* (1972), 406 U.S. 205, 234.)

By bringing Scott's possession and possible sale of marijuana to the attention of the authorities, and by cooperating with them in the investigation of these offenses, Scott's parents certainly did not jeopardize his health or safety, nor did their actions "have a potential for significant social burdens." Quite the contrary. However, the majority's decision very likely will have such deleterious effects by diminishing the authority of parents to discipline and control their children.

The issue presented by this case was correctly analyzed in the majority opinion prepared for the Court of Appeal by Justice Kingsley. "There is a strong public policy protecting the interest of a parent in the care, discipline and control of a minor child. A parent who, as in this case, has reasonable grounds to believe that a minor child is engaged in serious criminal activity, must be allowed to investigate that belief, in order to determine the proper discipline and corrective action to be taken. If that investigation involves the search, with or without the minor's consent, of locked items, the search is justified as conduct in aid of the parental power of care and discipline. It follows that, if the father in this case had himself opened the toolbox, or if the father, exerting his parental authority, had secured the key from the minor and then opened the box, the search would have been lawful. That conclusion is supported by the cases involving searches of locked containers by school authorities. If the Loco parentis status of a school official permits a search of a locked container in order to protect against and prevent violations of the criminal laws, a fortiori, a parent has an equal right.

"The minor argues, however, that if the father, instead of securing the key himself and using it himself, involves a police officer in the process, the search thereby becomes tainted. We reject that theory. The material fact is not who actually secured the key and used it, but under whose authority the key was obtained and used. The record before us makes it clear that the authority here was that of the father. The police made it clear that they would not search the box unless the father consented; they acted only on that consent. What the father could do himself, he could do by an agent, whether that agent be a locksmith or a policeman."

The reasoning of the Court of Appeal is supported by *Vandenberg v. Superior Court* (1970), 8 Cal.App.3d 1048; a decision the majority of this court fail to mention. The petitioner in *Vandenberg*, like Scott, was a minor "living with his father, in the father's home, and subject to the ordinary rules regulating the relationship of parent and minor child." A deputy sheriff went to the Vandenberg residence, advised the father he was conducting a narcotics investigation, and received the father's permission to enter the home. After demonstrating to the father that his son had puncture wounds on his arms possibly indicative of narcotics usage, the deputy asked for the father's permission to search the house for narcotics. The father consented, despite his son's objection. In searching the bedroom jointly occupied by the father and son, the deputy found a paper containing a substance resembling heroin hidden among some towels.

The Court of Appeal held: "(A) father may grant permission to enter and search a bedroom jointly occupied by the father and his son and such consent is valid although the son may protest the search." Explaining its decision, the court stated: "In his capacity as the head of the household, a father has the responsibility and authority for the discipline, training and control of his children. In the exercise of his parental authority a father has full access to the room set aside for his son for purposes of fulfilling his right and duty to control his son's social behavior and to obtain obedience. Permitting an officer to search a bedroom in order to determine if his son is using or trafficking in narcotics appears to us to be a reasonable and necessary extension of a father's authority and control over his children's moral training, health and personal hygiene."

Questions on In re Scott K.

(1) Is this a good result? If we are to hold parents responsible for raising their children, should we also give parents this kind of authority over their children?

(2) What if Scott hung a sign on his door saying "No one over 20 admitted," and his mother usually left the laundry in the hall?

(3) Should the child's age make any difference? What if the child was eight and had a habit of taking things when she got angry at other

family members (or her teachers, or her friends). She only "stole" from the family, and hid all the scissors, hair bands, pens, paperback books, safety pins and other needed items under her mattress. Would her parents be justified in making a periodic "sweep" of her room, or would they be usurping her privacy? What if she kept the purloined items in a locked box (the one her grandmother had given her)?

(4) Does the fourth amendment right recognized here (but not in all states, see, e.g., *State v. Douglas*, 498 A2d 364, 371 (NJ App Div 1985)), coupled with the mature pregnant minor's right to obtain an abortion and the right of minors to seek certain medical treatments or birth control devices without parental consent establish an entirely different division of family rights and responsibilities than that envisioned by Locke, Bentham and the earlier cases?

SECTION 3. THE POWERS OF PARENTS AND THE CLAIMS OF CHILDREN: THE INSTANCE OF MEDICAL DECISIONS

It has been universally remarked that in our time the several members of a family stand upon an entirely new footing towards each other; that the distance which formerly separated a father from his sons has been lessened; and that paternal authority, if not destroyed, is at least impaired.

Alexis de Tocqueville
Democracy in America

A. A CONSTITUTIONAL VIEW OF PATIENTS, CHILDREN, AND DECISIONS

I think that in proportion as manners and laws become more democratic, the relation of father and son becomes more intimate and more affectionate; rules and authority are less talked of, confidence and tenderness are often increased, and it would seem that the natural bond is drawn closer in proportion as the social bond is loosened.

Alexis de Tocqueville
Democracy in America

We have now completed our introductory survey of the powers of parents and the claims of children. We now need to examine those powers and claims more acutely by studying them in a particular context—decisions about children's medical care.

PARHAM v. J. R.

Supreme Court of the United States, 1979
442 US 584

BURGER, CHIEF JUSTICE:

The question presented in this appeal is what process is constitutionally due a minor child whose parents or guardian seek state administered institutional mental health care for the child and specifically whether an adversary proceeding is required prior to or after the commitment.

I

. . . (c) Appellee J. R. was declared a neglected child by the county and removed from his natural parents when he was three months old. He was placed in seven different foster homes in succession prior to his admission to Central State Hospital at the age of 7.

Immediately preceding his hospitalization, J. R. received outpatient treatment at a county mental health center for several months. He then began attending school where he was so disruptive and incorrigible that he could not conform to normal behavior patterns. Because of his abnormal behavior, J. R.'s seventh set of foster parents requested his removal from their home. The Department of Family and Children Services then sought his admission at Central State. The agency provided the hospital with a complete sociomedical history at the time of his admission. In addition, three separate interviews were conducted with J. R. by the admission team of the hospital.

It was determined that he was borderline retarded, and suffered an "unsocialized, aggressive reaction of childhood." It was recommended unanimously that he would "benefit from the structured environment" of the hospital and would "enjoy living and playing with boys of the same age."

J. R.'s progress was re-examined periodically. In addition, unsuccessful efforts were made by the Department of Family and Children Services during his stay at the hospital to place J. R. in various foster homes. On October 24, 1975, J. R. (with J. L.) filed this suit requesting an order of the court placing him in a less drastic environment suitable to his needs.

(d) Georgia Code § 88–503.1 (1975) provides for the voluntary admission to a state regional hospital of children such as J. L. and J. R. Under that provision, admission begins with an application for hospitalization signed by a "parent or guardian." Upon application, the superintendent of each hospital is given the power to admit temporarily any child for "observation and diagnosis." If, after observation, the superintendent finds "evidence of mental illness" and that the child is "suitable for treatment" in the hospital, then the child may be admitted "for such period and under such conditions as may be authorized by law." . . .

III

In an earlier day, the problems inherent in coping with children afflicted with mental or emotional abnormalities were dealt with largely within the family. Sometimes parents were aided by teachers or a family doctor. While some parents no doubt were able to deal with their disturbed children without specialized assistance, others, especially those of limited means and education, were not. Increasingly, they turned for assistance to local, public sources or private charities. Until recently, most of the states did little more than provide custodial institutions for the confinement of persons who were considered dangerous.

As medical knowledge about the mentally ill and public concern for their condition expanded, the states, aided substantially by federal grants, have sought to ameliorate the human tragedies of seriously disturbed children. Ironically, as most states have expanded their efforts to assist the mentally ill, their actions have been subjected to increasing litigation and heightened constitutional scrutiny. Courts have been required to resolve the thorny constitutional attacks on state programs and procedures with limited precedential guidance. In this case, appellees have challenged Georgia's procedural and substantive balance of the individual, family, and social interests at stake in the voluntary commitment of a child to one of its regional mental hospitals.

The parties agree that our prior holdings have set out a general approach for testing challenged state procedures under a due process claim. Assuming the existence of a protectable property or liberty interest, the Court has required a balancing of a number of factors:

> "First, the private interest that will be affected by the official action; second, the risk of an erroneous deprivation of such interest through the procedures used, and the probable value, if any, of additional or substitute procedural safeguards; and finally, the Government's interest, including the function involved and the fiscal and administrative burdens that the additional or substitute procedural requirement would entail." *Mathews v. Eldridge*, 424 U.S. 319, 335 (1976).

In applying these criteria, we must consider first the child's interest in not being committed. Normally, however, since this interest is inextricably linked with the parents' interest in and obligation for the welfare and health of the child, the private interest at stake is a combination of the child's and parents' concerns. Next, we must examine the State's interest in the procedures it has adopted for commitment and treatment of children. Finally, we must consider how well Georgia's procedures protect against arbitrariness in the decision to commit a child to a state mental hospital.

(a) It is not disputed that a child, in common with adults, has a substantial liberty interest in not being confined unnecessarily for medical treatment and that the state's involvement in the commitment decision constitutes state action under the Fourteenth Amendment. We also recognize that commitment sometimes produces adverse social consequences for the child because of the reaction of some to the discovery that the child has received psychiatric care.

This reaction, however, need not be equated with the community response resulting from being labeled by the state as delinquent, criminal, or mentally ill and possibly dangerous. The state through its voluntary commitment procedures does not "label" the child; it provides a diagnosis and treatment that medical specialists conclude the child requires. In terms of public reaction, the child who exhibits abnormal behavior may be seriously injured by an erroneous decision not to commit. Appellees overlook a significant source of the public reaction to the mentally ill, for what is truly "stigmatizing" is the symptomatology of a mental or emotional illness. The pattern of untreated, abnormal behavior—even if nondangerous—arouses at least as much negative reaction as treatment that becomes public knowledge. A person needing, but not receiving, appropriate medical care may well face even greater social ostracism resulting from the observable symptoms of an untreated disorder.

However, we need not decide what effect these factors might have in a different case. For purposes of this decision, we assume that a child has a protectable interest not only in being free of unnecessary bodily restraints but also in not being labeled erroneously by some persons because of an improper decision by the state hospital superintendent.

(b) We next deal with the interests of the parents who have decided, on the basis of their observations and independent professional recommendations, that their child needs institutional care. Appellees argue that the constitutional rights of the child are of such magnitude and the likelihood of parental abuse is so great that the parents' traditional interests in and responsibility for the upbringing of their child must be subordinated at least to the extent of providing a formal adversary hearing prior to a voluntary commitment.

Our jurisprudence historically has reflected Western civilization concepts of the family as a unit with broad parental authority over minor children. Our cases have consistently followed that course; our constitutional system long ago rejected any notion that a child is "the mere creature of the State" and, on the contrary, asserted that parents generally "have the right, coupled with the high duty, to recognize and prepare [their children] for additional obligations." *Pierce v. Society of Sisters*. See also *Wisconsin v. Yoder*, 406 U.S. 205, 213 (1972); *Prince v. Massachusetts*; *Meyer v. Nebraska*. Surely, this includes a "high duty" to recognize symptoms of illness and to seek and follow medical advice. The law's concept of the family rests on a presumption that parents possess what a child lacks in maturity, experience, and capacity for judgment required for making life's difficult decisions. More important, historically it has recognized that natural bonds of affection lead parents to act in the best interests of their children. 1 W. Blackstone, Commentaries *447; 2 J. Kent, Commentaries on American Law *190.

As with so many other legal presumptions, experience and reality may rebut what the law accepts as a starting point; the incidence of child neglect and abuse cases attests to this. That some parents "may at times be acting against the interests of their children" creates a basis for caution, but is hardly a reason to discard wholesale those pages of human experience that teach that parents generally do act in the child's best interests. The statist notion that governmental power should supersede parental authority in all cases because some parents abuse and neglect children is repugnant to American tradition.

Nonetheless, we have recognized that a state is not without constitutional control over parental discretion in dealing with children when their physical or mental health is jeopardized. Moreover, the Court recently declared unconstitutional a state statute that granted parents an absolute veto over a minor child's decision to have an abortion. *Planned Parenthood of Central Missouri v. Danforth*, 428 U.S. 52 (1976). Appellees urge that these precedents limiting the traditional rights of parents, if viewed in the context of the liberty interest of the child and the likelihood of parental abuse, require us to hold that the parents' decision to have a child admitted to a mental hospital must be subjected to an exacting constitutional scrutiny, including a formal, adversary, pre–admission hearing.

Appellees' argument, however, sweeps too broadly. Simply because the decision of a parent is not agreeable to a child or because it involves risks does not automatically transfer the power to make that decision from the parents to some agency or officer of the state. The same characterizations can be made for a tonsillectomy, appendectomy, or other medical procedure. Most children, even in adolescence, simply are not able to make sound judgments concerning many decisions, including their need for medical care or treatment. Parents can and must make those judgments. Here, there is no finding by the District Court of even a single instance of bad faith by any parent of any member of appellees' class. We cannot assume that the result in *Meyer v. Nebraska* and *Pierce v. Society of Sisters*, would have been different if the children there had announced a preference to learn only English or a preference to go to a public, rather than a church, school. The fact that a child may balk at hospitalization or complain about a parental refusal to provide cosmetic surgery does not diminish the parents' authority to decide what is best for the child. Neither state officials nor federal courts are equipped to review such parental decisions.

Appellees place particular reliance on *Planned Parenthood*, arguing that its holding indicates how little deference to parents is appropriate when the child is exercising a constitutional right. The basic situation in that case, however, was very different; *Planned Parenthood* involved an absolute parental veto over the child's ability to obtain an abortion. Parents in Georgia in no sense have an absolute right to commit their children to state mental hospitals; the statute requires the superintendent of each regional hospital to exercise independent judgment as to the child's need for confinement.

In defining the respective rights and prerogatives of the child and parent in the voluntary commitment setting, we conclude that our precedents permit the parents to retain a substantial, if not the dominant, role in the decision, absent a finding of neglect or abuse, and that the traditional presumption that the parents act in the best interests of their child should apply. We also conclude, however, that the child's rights and the nature of the commitment decision are such that parents cannot always have absolute and unreviewable discretion to decide whether to have a child institutionalized. They, of course, retain plenary authority to seek such care for their children, subject to a physician's independent examination and medical judgment.

(c) The State obviously has a significant interest in confining the use of its costly mental health facilities to cases of genuine need. The Georgia program seeks first to determine whether the patient seeking admission has an illness that calls for inpatient treatment. To accomplish this purpose, the State has charged the superintendents of each regional hospital with the responsibility for determining, before authorizing an admission, whether a prospective patient is mentally ill and whether the patient will likely benefit from hospital care. In addition, the State has imposed a continuing duty on hospital superintendents to release any patient who has recovered to the point where hospitalization is no longer needed.

The State in performing its voluntarily assumed mission also has a significant interest in not imposing unnecessary procedural obstacles that may discourage the mentally ill or their families from seeking needed psychiatric assistance. The *parens patriae* interest in helping parents care for the mental health of their children cannot be fulfilled if the parents are unwilling to take advantage of the opportunities because the admission process is too onerous, too embarrassing, or too contentious. It is surely not idle to speculate as to how many parents who believe they are acting in good faith would forgo state–provided hospital care if such care is contingent on participation in an adversary proceeding designed to probe their motives and other private family matters in seeking the voluntary admission.

The State also has a genuine interest in allocating priority to the diagnosis and treatment of patients as soon as they are admitted to a hospital rather than to time–consuming procedural minuets before the admission. One factor that must be considered is the utilization of the time of psychiatrists, psychologists, and other behavioral specialists in preparing for and participating in hearings rather than performing the task for which their special training has fitted them. Behavioral experts in courtrooms and hearings are of little help to patients.

The *amici* brief of the American Psychiatric Association et al. points out at page 20 that the average staff psychiatrist in a hospital presently is able to devote only 47% of his time to direct patient care. One consequence of increasing the procedures the state must provide prior to a child's voluntary admission will be that mental health professionals will be diverted even more from the treatment of patients in order to travel to and participate in—and wait for—what could be hundreds—or even thousands—of hearings each year. Obviously the cost of these procedures would come from the public moneys the legislature intended for mental health care.

(d) We now turn to consideration of what process protects adequately the child's constitutional rights by reducing risks of error without unduly trenching on traditional parental authority and without undercutting "efforts to further the legitimate interests of both the state and the patient that are served by" voluntary commitments. We conclude that the risk of error inherent in the parental decision to have a child institutionalized for mental health care is sufficiently great that some kind of inquiry should be made by a "neutral factfinder" to determine whether the statutory requirements for admission are satisfied. That inquiry must carefully probe the child's background using all available sources, including, but not limited to, parents, schools, and other social agencies. Of course, the review must also include an interview with the child. It is necessary that the decisionmaker have the authority to refuse to admit any child who does not satisfy the medical standards for admission. Finally, it is necessary that the child's continuing need for commitment be reviewed periodically by a similarly independent procedure.

We are satisfied that such procedures will protect the child from an erroneous admission decision in a way that neither unduly burdens the states nor inhibits parental decisions to seek state help.

Due process has never been thought to require that the neutral and detached trier of fact be law trained or a judicial or administrative officer. Surely, this is the case as to medical decisions, for "neither judges nor administrative hearing officers are better qualified than psychiatrists to render psychiatric judgments." Thus, a staff physician will suffice, so long as he or she is free to evaluate independently the child's mental and emotional condition and need for treatment.

It is not necessary that the deciding physician conduct a formal or quasi-formal hearing. A state is free to require such a hearing, but due process is not violated by use of informal traditional medical investigative techniques. Since well-established medical procedures already exist, we do not undertake to outline with specificity precisely what this investigation must involve. The mode and procedure of medical diagnostic procedures is not the business of judges. What is best for a child is an individual medical decision that must be left to the judgment of physicians in each case. We do no more than emphasize that the decision should represent an independent judgment of what the child requires and that all sources of information that are traditionally relied on by physicians and behavioral specialists should be consulted.

What process is constitutionally due cannot be divorced from the nature of the ultimate decision that is being made. Not every determination by state officers can be made most effectively by use of "the procedural tools of judicial or administrative decisionmaking."

Here, the questions are essentially medical in character: whether the child is mentally or emotionally ill and whether he can benefit from the treatment that is provided by the state. While facts are plainly necessary for a proper resolution of those questions, they are only a first step in the process. In an opinion for a unanimous Court, we recently stated in *Addington v. Texas* that the determination of "whether [a person] is mentally ill turns on the meaning of the facts which must be interpreted by expert psychiatrists and psychologists."

Although we acknowledge the fallibility of medical and psychiatric diagnosis, we do not accept the notion that the shortcomings of specialists can always be avoided by shifting the decision from a trained specialist using the traditional tools of medical science to an untrained judge or administrative hearing officer after a judicial–type hearing. Even after a hearing, the nonspecialist decisionmaker must make a medical-psychiatric decision. Common human experience and scholarly opinions suggest that the supposed protections of an adversary proceeding to determine the appropriateness of medical decisions for the commitment and treatment of mental and emotional illness may well be more illusory than real.

Another problem with requiring a formalized, factfinding hearing lies in the danger it poses for significant intrusion into the parent–child relationship. Pitting the parents and child as adversaries often will be at odds with the presumption that parents act in the best interests of their child. It is one thing to require a neutral physician to make a careful review of the parents' decision in order to make sure it is proper from a medical standpoint; it is a wholly different matter to employ an adversary contest to ascertain whether the parents' motivation is consistent with the child's interests.

Moreover, it is appropriate to inquire into how such a hearing would contribute to the successful long-range treatment of the patient. Surely, there is a risk that it would exacerbate whatever tensions already exist between the child and the parents. Since the parents can and usually do play a significant role in the treatment while the child is hospitalized and even more so after release, there is a serious risk that an adversary confrontation will adversely affect the ability of the parents to assist the child while in the hospital. Moreover, it will make his subsequent return home more difficult. These unfortunate results are especially critical with an emotionally disturbed child; they seem likely to occur in the context of an adversary hearing in which the parents testify. A confrontation over such intimate family relationships would distress the normal adult parents and the impact on a disturbed child almost certainly would be significantly greater.

It has been suggested that a hearing conducted by someone other than the admitting physician is necessary in order to detect instances where parents are "guilty of railroading their children into asylums" or are using "voluntary commitment procedures in order to sanction behavior of which they disapprov[e]." Curiously, it seems to be taken for granted that parents who seek to "dump" their children on the state will inevitably be able to conceal their motives and thus deceive the admitting psychiatrists and the other mental health professionals who make and review the admission decision. It is elementary that one early diagnostic inquiry into the cause of an emotional disturbance of a child is an examination into the environment of the child. It is unlikely, if not inconceivable, that a decision to abandon an emotionally normal, healthy child and thrust him into an institution will be a discrete act leaving no trail of circumstances. Evidence of such conflicts will emerge either in the interviews or from secondary sources. It is unrealistic to believe that trained psychiatrists, skilled in eliciting responses, sorting medically relevant facts, and sensing motivational nuances will often be deceived about the family situation surrounding a child's emotional disturbance. Surely a lay, or even law–trained, factfinder would be no more skilled in this process than the professional.

By expressing some confidence in the medical decisionmaking process, we are by no means suggesting it is error free. On occasion, parents may initially mislead an admitting physician or a physician may erroneously diagnose the child as needing institutional care either because of negligence or an overabundance of caution. That there may be risks of error in the process affords no rational predicate for holding unconstitutional an entire statutory and administrative scheme that is generally followed in more than 30 states. "[P]rocedural due process rules are shaped by the risk of error inherent in the truthfinding process as applied to the generality of cases, not the rare exceptions." *Mathews v. Eldridge*, 424 U.S., at 344. In general, we are satisfied that an independent medical decision-making process, which includes the thorough psychiatric investigation described earlier, followed by additional periodic review of a child's condition, will protect children who should not be admitted; we do not believe the risks of error in that process would be significantly reduced by a more formal, judicial-type hearing. . . .

We are satisfied that the voluminous record as a whole supports the conclusion that the admissions staffs of the hospitals have acted in a neutral and detached fashion in making medical judgments in the best interests of the children. The State, through its mental health programs, provides the authority for trained professionals to assist parents in examining, diagnosing, and treating emotionally disturbed children. Through its hiring practices, it provides well–staffed and well–equipped hospitals and—as the District Court found—conscientious public employees to implement the State's beneficent purposes.

Although our review of the record in this case satisfies us that Georgia's general administrative and statutory scheme for the voluntary commitment of children is not *per se* unconstitutional, we cannot decide on this record, whether every child in appellees' class received an adequate, independent diagnosis of his emotional condition and need for confinement under the standards announced earlier in this opinion. On remand, the District Court is free to and should consider any individual claims that initial admissions did not meet the standards we have described in this opinion....

IV

(a) Our discussion in Part III was directed at the situation where a child's natural parents request his admission to a state mental hospital. Some members of appellees' class, including J. R., were wards of the State of Georgia at the time of their admission. Obviously their situation differs from those members of the class who have natural parents. While the determination of what process is due varies somewhat when the state, rather than a natural parent, makes the request for commitment, we conclude that the differences in the two situations do not justify requiring different procedures at the time of the child's initial admission to the hospital....

B. THREE HYPOTHETICALS

[P]arents love their children as part of themselves, whereas children love their parents as authors of their being. And parents know their children better than the children know their parentage.

Aristotle
Nicomachean Ethics

The materials you have been reading employ the problem of children's medical-care decisions to introduce our primary general issues: the relationship between parents and children; the relationship between parents, children, and the state; and the role of rights thinking in both relationships. You have now read enough about this subject to benefit by reflecting on it. To help you, we have prepared questions organized around three hypotheticals. As you read them, you should ask yourself the following questions: As a moral matter, may the parents in them refuse permission for the medical treatment proposed for their children's problems? As a legal matter, do the parents have a right to refuse permission? As a legal matter, may the state secure a court order requiring it?

(1) The Knightlys have just learned their one-day-old child has Downs Syndrome. They are told that the child's degree of mental retardation cannot be predicted at birth but that it will run from "very low mentality to borderline subnormal." The IQ of Downs Syndrome adults, they are told, generally runs from 25 to 60, though it will occasionally reach the 60 to 80 range. Downs Syndrome children are almost always trainable, but they are not always educable. Downs syndrome children may be specially susceptible to infection (one study reports that 30% of the deaths of the institutionalized people with Downs syndrome resulted from infection); 40% of them have congenital heart defects; many Downs children have problems hearing and seeing;

they are disproportionately likely to suffer from congenital hypothyroidism; they have dental problems with disproportionate frequency; they suffer from muscular and skeletal deficiencies; they tend to have diminished motor coordination capacities. In addition, people with Downs syndrome are thought to age more rapidly than normal and to be highly susceptible to Alzheimer's disease at an age as early as 30 or 40. They have, however, a reputation for being happy children. The Knightlys are told their child has an intestinal blockage which can be corrected with an operation of nominal risk. Without the operation, the child will die.

(2) The Allworthys have just learned their newborn infant suffers from spina bifida. That is, the child has an opening that has exposed the spinal neural tube and that is leaking cerebrospinal fluid. The Allworthys are told that, given the location of the opening, the child is likely to experience sensory loss and muscle weakness or even paralysis in the lower body. The child is also likely to suffer bladder and bowel incontinence. This condition needs to be treated within 24 hours of birth by surgery that closes the spinal opening and that inserts shunts to drain fluid. Preventing infection will be a major and continuing concern. This operation is likely to be the first of many, and even after these operations, the child will suffer from the severe physical handicaps listed above. Some untreated spina bifida cases live for as much as a year or more.

The Allworthys' decision is further complicated because, like a number of spina bifida cases, the child suffers from hydrocephalus, an enlargement of the head caused by cerebrospinal fluid in the brain. This condition can cause, and may already have caused, irreversible brain damage. The extent of this brain damage cannot now be immediately ascertained; it could be severe.

(3) The Goodlys have just been told that their newborn child has Trisomy 18. Their physician has read them the following prognosis.

> Diagnosis of the condition at birth is relatively easy because of the multiple physical abnormalities associated with the syndrome: incompletely developed, low-set ears; narrow, elongated skull; hypertonia; clenched hand, with overlapping fingers and malformed thumb; rock-bottom feet; low birth weight; short sternum; congenital heart disease; and severe gastrointestinal and renal deformities. Trisomic 18 neonates also display severe mental deficiency, difficulty in breathing, apnea, cyanosis, a poor sucking reflex, and a high-pitched cry. Life expectancy for such infants is short: 50% die in the first two months, only 10% survive the first year (with severe mental and physical retardation), and only 1% have a chance of surviving 10 years even with aggressive treatment and institutionalization.

Robert Weir, *Selective Nontreatment of Handicapped Newborns* 45 (Oxford U Press, 1984).

Questions on Deciding for Oneself and Deciding for Others

(1) Part of the problem raised by these hypotheticals has to do with whether and when anyone, disabled or not, should be allowed to refuse medical treatment necessary to preserve life. Let us therefore begin our investigation of the hypotheticals by considering the situation of a normal adult patient. You should initially consider the following questions in light of what good social policy would require, then in light of what the law might reasonably say about the problem, if anything.

(a) Ought a non-retarded adult patient with an intestinal blockage like the one in the Knightly hypothetical be permitted to refuse treatment? The standard principle of tort law was stated by Cardozo in 1914: "[E]very human being of adult years and sound mind has a right to determine what shall be done with his own body; and a surgeon who performs an operation without his patient's consent, commits an assault, for which he is liable in damages." *Schloendorff v. Society of the New York Hospital*, 105 NE 92, 93–94 (1914). Does this tort-law assumption establish the patients' authority to refuse whatever treatment they wish?

(i) Would the non-retarded adult patient's reasons matter? Would it, for instance, be legitimate for the patient to refuse to accept treatment without stating a reason? Should the patient be able to refuse if the treatment were in some sense "extraordinary"? That is, should the patient be permitted to refuse treatment where the treatment offered little chance of success or was experimental? Ought the patient be permitted to refuse treatment because the treatment would not cure the patient of an underlying disease whose burdens the patient no longer wished to bear? Because the patient wished to die for other reasons?

(ii) Would it be proper to allow the patient to refuse treatment because there is a distinction between killing and allowing nature to take its course, even where that course leads to death?

(iii) Would a refusal to accept life-saving treatment sometimes be grounds for a hearing patients' competence to make judgments for himself or herself? Could such a refusal be part of the evidence that the patient was not competent?

(b) The trouble with many of the preceding questions is that the issue might not arise because patients can simply decline to present themselves for treatment. Suppose, therefore, that the patient is a paraplegic living in a nursing home and does not wish to be treated because life as a paraplegic seems unendurable. Ought the patient be able to refuse treatment for this reason? For the reasons we canvassed in the preceding questions?

(c) The questions you have looked at so far involve a refusal to accept life-saving treatment. Harder problems may be raised by patients who wish to die but who will not die if left medically untreated. Here distinctions between extraordinary and ordinary treatment and between active and passive euthanasia become less relevant or even irrelevant. In considering the problems such patients present, consider the following questions. Suppose the paraplegic has no intestinal blockage, but finds life as a paraplegic unendurable and wishes not to be fed in order to die. Does this patient have the right to compel the nursing home to withhold food and water? To compel the nursing home to administer a lethal injection? (For an example of such a situation, see *Bouvia v. Superior Court*, 225 Cal Rptr 297 (Cal App 2 Dist 1986). It and similar cases are discussed at length in Marsha Garrison and Carl E. Schneider, *Law and Bioethics* (West, forthcoming).)

(d) We have framed these questions in terms of whether good social policy would *permit* the patient to refuse treatment or to seek death. However, the issue in these cases goes beyond what good social policy would allow and extends to the questions of what kind of entitlement patients have to refuse treatment. Do the patients in any of the above situations have a *right* to refuse treatment?

(i) If so, what do you mean by "right"? A moral entitlement? A statutory entitlement? A constitutional entitlement? A natural law entitlement?

(ii) If so, what is the basis for the "right"? In *Cruzan v. Director, Missouri Department of Health*, 497 US 261 (1990), the Court considered a Missouri statute that required anyone asking that food and water be withheld from a patient in a persistent vegetative state to show by clear and convincing evidence that that withdrawal was what the patient would have wanted. The Court said, "The principle that a competent person has a constitutionally protected liberty interest in refusing unwanted medical treatment may be inferred from our prior decisions."

What decisions did the Court have had in mind? What is the moral basis for Nancy Beth Cruzan's claim? Is she accorded the right out of respect for her personal autonomy, for her status as an independent moral agent? What does this mean? Is it, as our justifications for family autonomy might suggest, that the patient is likely to make a wiser decision than the state? Should the presumption that the patient will make a wiser decision than the state be irrebuttable? The *Cruzan* Court took the state's interests with unusual seriousness. What might they have been?

(e) If you believe the patients in the above situations have some kind of right to non-treatment, does it follow that a severely defective new-born infant has such a right? Is the basis for the adult's right and the child's right the same? If the patient is accorded a right either out of respect for his or her status as an independent moral agent or on the presumption that he or she will make a better decision than the state, does it make sense to accord the same right to an infant, who is not an independent moral agent and is too young to make or express a decision? Is a right to make a decision a right one acquires only as one grows old enough to make that decision wisely?

(2) One problem in child-medical-care decisions is exactly that the patients cannot make decisions for themselves. Who, then, should have the power to make medical decisions for them? The obvious answer is that those decisions should be made by parents. But this answer leaves important questions unanswered. For example, what criteria should parents use in making medical decisions for their children? Should parents attempt to act as proxies for their children, to make the same decisions the children would have made for themselves had they been competent to do so? Should parents attempt to make the decision they think is wisest for the child? Are parents exercising rights on behalf of their child, or are they exercising their own rights? What limits on parental decisions ought there be under any of the models of decision-making? To help answer these questions, let us begin with an adult patient who cannot act for herself but whose family and friends wish to act for her. We begin with that case since it in some ways presents easier questions than the case of a young child.

(a) Suppose the paraplegic in Question 1(b) with the intestinal blockage is in a coma and is unlikely to emerge for at least a very long time. Suppose further that the paraplegic is forty years old and that her father asks that the operation to remove the blockage not be performed. Should the father have to state a reason? If so, what kind?

(i) Suppose the father cites as his reason a document signed by the paraplegic before she fell into the coma asking that no operation ever be performed to save her life. Ought this document be enough to prevent the operation quite apart from the father's expression of his wishes? Should it matter what degree of formality the document met? When the document was signed? Can the document actually represent the patient's wishes at the time the document was signed? At the time its directions are to be carried out?

(ii) Suppose the father cites an oral request made before the paraplegic fell into the coma and made in the presence of a nurse and a doctor that the operation not be performed?

(iii) Suppose the father cites a strongly worded opinion expressed by the paraplegic before she was paralyzed that paraplegics who were made deeply unhappy by their condition ought not undergo operations to save their lives. Suppose further that the daughter has expressed an equally strongly worded opinion that she has been made deeply unhappy by her condition.

(iv) Suppose the father says the operation would be against the religious convictions of his daughter.

(v) Suppose the father says that because he knows his daughter well, he knows she would not want the operation.

(vi) If you thought the father's ability to decide for his daughter to refuse treatment ended sometime in this series of suppositions, is it because parents should be able to make decisions that will end the lives of their children only when they have some particularly strong reason to believe their decision genuinely reflects the child's preferences?

(vii) What does *Parham* say about why we let parents make crucial decisions for children? What do Locke and Bentham say?

(b) One way to investigate the strength and nature of the parent's authority is to ask whether it is possessed simply because parents are usually the nearest available relative. One way to ask that question is to examine the following suppositions: The paraplegic in the coma is a fifty-five-year old mother. It is her thirty-year-old son who is asking that the operation not occur. Suppose the son cites the same series of reasons the father cited in question (2)(a).

(c) We might pursue the questions raised in (2)(b) by investigating the decision-making authority and capacity of non-relatives.

(i) Suppose the paraplegic in the coma is a fifty-five-year old monk who has been in the same contemplative order for thirty years. It is his abbot, whom he has known for all those thirty years, who opposes the operation. Suppose the abbot cites the same series of reasons the father cited in question (2)(a).

(ii) Suppose there are no relatives and the proposed decision-maker is a close friend of thirty years. Suppose the friend cites the same series of reasons the father cited in question (2)(a).

(iii) Suppose the proposed decision-maker is an employer of thirty years and no family members or friends will make a decision. The friend cites the same series of reasons the father cited in question (2)(a).

(iv) Suppose the paraplegic who is in a coma has been living for the previous five years in an insane asylum and has for that period been declared legally incompetent to manage her own affairs. This time it is an attorney who has recently been appointed by a court to be her guardian who opposes the operation. The attorney cites the same series of reasons the father cited in (a).

(d) One feature each of these hypotheticals has in common is that the paraplegic was at some point capable of making decisions. Suppose the paraplegics in the preceding questions were never competent. Does your response to these questions change?

(e) If you believe a person should have been allowed to die in these cases, does it follow that the Knightlys, the Allworthys, and the Goodlys should be allowed to prevent life-saving treatment for their newborn children? What differences and similarities do you see between the situations in these questions and in the hypotheticals? What difference does it make that the decision is to be made by a parent?

(f) Why are we willing, if we are, to have the decision not to treat made by the parent, the child, the friend, the close associate, the employer, or the attorney?

(i) Is it because we believe those people have a particularly close knowledge of the patient and therefore a particularly reliable insight into what the patient "wants"?

(ii) Is it because we believe those people have a particularly great concern for the patient and are therefore in the best position to put themselves in the patient's place?

(iii) Is it because we believe that those people would be the people the patient would want to have making the decision?

(iv) Is it because we believe that the patient has a right to decide whether to die, that the patient should not lose the right simply because the patient cannot make decisions, that someone other than the government must exercise the right, and that those people are simply the most logical exercisers of it?

(v) Is it because we believe those people will somehow make the best decision for the patient? Is this because we believe an individual will make a better decision for the patient than an institution or a government and that the individuals in question are simply the most plausible decision-makers? Is that true? What makes one decision better than another for the patient?

(vi) Is it because we believe that those people themselves have an interest in the decision whether to treat the patient and that, within reasonable bounds, that interest should be recognized by giving those people the power to make a decision for the patient?

(3) How do the hypotheticals look from the perspective of ordinary criminal law? Causing the death of another human being is criminally punishable homicide. Where one person has a duty to care for another, as a parent has a duty to care for a child, a failure to fulfill that duty that causes death is also homicide. Further, child abuse-and-neglect statutes commonly make a failure to provide necessary medical treatment punishable. By their terms, do homicide and abuse-and-neglect statutes make the Knightlys, the Allworthys, or the Goodlys criminally liable for a failure to provide treatment?

(a) Is it proper that people in the Knightlys', the Allworthys', or the Goodlys' situation should risk criminal prosecution? On one hand, their position is already cruelly perplexing and painful. Since most parents will do their best to make the proper decision, it seems harsh to have them do so under the threat of prosecution. On the other hand, how would you write a homicide or child-abuse statute that did not criminalize a decision to deny a child medical treatment necessary to save the child's life?

(i) What reasons would you offer for not prohibiting such decisions criminally?

(ii) Considering the issue from the viewpoint of the law's expressive function, what message would a failure to criminalize such decisions (or at least some such decisions) impart?

(iii) How could a statute be written to distinguish permissible and impermissible non-treatment? Most people might agree that a failure to provide a reasonably safe operation to correct a defect like a blocked intestine in a normal child ought to be criminal. Many people would agree that a decision not to treat such a problem when the child was afflicted with severe birth defects ought not be criminal. But how do you draw the line between the ends of the continuum, and how do you put that line into words?

(b) Does it help you to know that parents in the Allworthys' and Knightlys' situation are virtually never prosecuted? Is this irrelevant, since it is not good to have statutes which leave so much discretion to prosecutors? Does it demonstrate that prosecutorial discretion and nullifying judges and juries adequately safeguard parents who try to make conscientious decisions while still not creating the problems we considered in the preceding paragraph?

(4) Suppose the Knightly, Allworthy, and Goodly children were born in a state hospital. After *Parham*, do they have some kind of due process right? Ordinarily, courts decide what process is due by considering "the private interests at stake, the government's interest, and the risk that the procedures used will lead to erroneous decisions." *Lassiter v. Department of Social Services*, 452 US 18, 27 (1981). How ought these criteria be applied here? Is the children's right a right to a dispassionate and disinterested decision-maker? Would the children's doctors be such decision-makers? A committee of doctors? The parents? Ought the children have independent representation? Some kind of formal procedure?

(5) To what extent should responsibility for this decision be placed on the children's physicians? Is the decision a medical one? Should the physicians have standing to seek a court order compelling the operation? Should they ever be legally obliged to seek such an order?

Questions on Parental Rights and Children's Care

Consider again the reasons for attributing rights to parents. Do they suggest that the Knightlys, the Allworthys, and the Goodlys have a right to decide whether the operation should take place?

(1) The first reason is that parents make better decisions for their children than the state because parents know their children and their children's situation better than the state. This may make sense applied to most parental decisions, but does it make sense applied to this one?

(a) Do the parents in these hypotheticals know their children, given that they are only a day old?

(i) Are the parents well-situated to know their children's future, given that to do so they must imagine what the life of a disabled child and adult would be like over many years?

(ii) Should the argument be more modest—that parents know better than anyone else the circumstances in which their children would be living for the next few years? Ought the parents' view of those circumstances determine whether their children will live or die? Part of the circumstances the parents presumably know is the economic situation of their families, the possible effect of a disabled child on the other children in the family, and the consequences for the parents of raising a disabled child. Is it legitimate for parents to consider such things? Is it fair that some otherwise identical disabled children will die and some will live because of differences in their parents' attitudes about these factors? Would we allow parents to consider them if the question were whether to treat a fourteen-year-old child in the situation of the Knightlys' or the Allworthys' child?

(2) The second justification for parental rights is that a court or agency is likely to lack expertise in making decisions about families. Here, however, can the state, not the parents, be called the better-equipped decision-maker? A central problem in making decisions about severely defective newborns is that many doctors are themselves not well-informed about the prospects for such children and that all the information anyone has is general predictive information. If this is true, isn't the state better situated to collect information and to evaluate it carefully than the average parent? Doesn't the state have the further advantage that it, unlike the average parent, has time to ponder the issue in advance and is under relatively little psychological pressure?

(3) The third justification for parental rights has to do with the difficulty of devising standards to govern decisions. How compelling an argument is this in the context of neonatal euthanasia?

(a) Part of the standards problem is the difficulty of writing rules that govern all the situations which might arise. However, do the rules have to anticipate all contingencies? Is it enough if general principles are laid down reflecting basic social judgments and the decision is confided to expert decision-makers? For instance, many hospitals have non-treatment decisions reviewed by a panel that commonly includes doctors, ethicists, and even lawyers. Could such a practice be legally mandated, and could the committee's written decisions be rationally reviewed by a court where necessary?

(b) Another part of the standards problem is that no satisfactory social agreement could be reached. What does that mean?

(i) Need we look for any level of social consensus beyond that ordinarily required in the law—that is, whatever solution regularly constituted governmental entities produce? Even if social consensus is difficult to achieve, does that mean a social issue should be removed from political consideration? Isn't the definition of life a social issue courts and legislatures have long decided?

(ii) Can't the standards problem be looked at from another angle? Recall our earlier discussions of the channelling function. One purpose of the channelling function is to relieve people of some of the burden of individual decision. Parents making decisions about defective newborns are faced with a cruel problem made worse by the absence of social guidelines and the consequent exacerbation of the loneliness and uncertainty of the decision. Might many parents welcome clearer social standards, even if those standards infringed on some understandings of parental rights?

(c) The third standards problem is that there are some considerations—like religious belief or ethnic tradition—that may be considered in making decisions about children but that the state may not properly take into account. Will any of these desirable considerations loom large in these parents' situation? Aren't those considerations, as a practical matter, likely to cut in favor of operating, not against?

Suppose, on the other hand, that religious considerations counsel against treatment. How far should such considerations foreclose the state from intervening? Consider the following case: A wholly normal infant needs an operation to open a blocked intestine. The operation can be performed with minimal risk. The parents are Jehovah's Witnesses and believe blood transfusions are sinful. The operation cannot safely be performed without a blood transfusion. May—should—the state obtain a court order requiring the operation? (Courts are commonly willing to grant such orders.)

(d) The fourth justification standards problem is that decisions about children should be informed by love, not impersonal rules. Can, however, the parents in our hypotheticals be confidently said to love their children, given that they have not yet come to know them? Is it even possible that their bitter disappointment and despair at the birth of these children who are so different from what they expected and hoped for as well as their bitter fears for their future will have caused them to dislike or even hate their children? Recall that what we are doing here is asking about whether parents in the Knightlys' situation have rights of decision. The question, therefore, is not whether the Knightlys specifically love their child, but whether parents in the Knightlys' situation so generally love their children that they should have rights to decide whether those children will live or die.

(4) The fourth justification for parental rights is the enforcement problem. What enforcement problems will be encountered in the neonatal euthanasia context? How severe will those problems be? Ought they deter the state from acting?

(a) One enforcement problem is that parents raise their children in private, and thus the government cannot easily find out what is going on or supervise it. Is that true here, where the decision whether to treat the child is made in consultation with other people (for example, doctors) and where many other people (for example, nurses) will know if the child is allowed to die?

(i) Many decisions parents make cannot readily be supervised. This includes numerous kinds of medical decisions, like those in which parents must be responsible for the child's medical treatment at home. But the Knightlys' case presents a one-time decision which can be entirely implemented by people outside the family. Furthermore, if the Knightlys continue to believe that their child should not live, the state can remove the child from their control. And there is in principle the possibility of criminal sanctions should the parents fail to preserve their child's health.

(ii) On the other hand, would a state-ordered operation affect the parents' feelings about their children and their willingness to care for them?

(b) A second enforcement problem is that parents are driven to deep and obscure psychological motives which may be difficult for them to understand and control. Ought this be dispositive where the child's life is at stake? Will most parents gradually come to terms with whatever initial psychological resistance they may have to caring for their disabled child? Are parents in a good position when they make the decision to know whether they will come to terms with any such resistance?

(c) The third enforcement problem is that parents may resist government supervention because of a conviction that the family's business is no one else's business. On the other hand, one troubling aspect of the enforcement problem is that it sometimes seems to suggest that a citizen's unwillingness to do what is right makes it wrong for the state to insist on what is right. Is that what happening here? Is the citizen's willingness to do what is right influenced by what the law is?

(5) The fifth justification for parental rights is that governmental intervention exacerbates family conflict. Is that a risk here? Part of the concern is that children need a stable authority figure and that state supervention of parental decisions injures parents in that role. Can this

be significant where the child is too young to know what is happening and where supervention is a one-time event? Is state supervision ever, except in extreme cases, a serious threat to the parent as an authority figure?

(6) The sixth justification for parental rights is that governmental intervention injures the family by diminishing its privacy. But is this a decision that should be made in private? Will privacy make the situation of the parents less painful? Or will it make the parent's situation more painful by placing a greater burden of responsibility on them and by isolating them from the compassion of the community? Will parents make a better decision if they think their decision will not be well known or judged?

(7) The seventh justification for parental rights is that it is normatively preferable for people to organize their own lives.

(a) In one form of this argument, the parental right would be analogous to the right to maintain intimate relations with spouses. Is that analogy convincing? Isn't an important difference that spouses are adults who can protect themselves, while children are not?

(b) Ought the law exalt as a right a power that includes the authority to make life or death decisions for helpless and burdensome people? The standard rule for child-custody cases is that the best interest of the child is essentially the law's sole criterion. Is that standard better than this rationale for parental rights?

(c) Would this rationale allow parents to take into account the effect of their child's existence on themselves? Would it be legitimate for them to consider their own strong desire that the child not live? To consider the financial consequences of having a Downs Syndrome, *spina bifida*, or trisomy 18 child? To consider the consequences for their marriage?

(8) The eighth justification for parental rights is that attributing rights to parents helps preserve a pluralist society. Should this rationale apply where the parents are not asserting a pluralism interest, or where, as seems likely to be true in neonatal euthanasia cases, parents are unlikely to assert a pluralism interest? Hasn't the state traditionally been responsible for defining life and death and for deciding when people may be caused or allowed to die? How far ought we go in protecting pluralism? What interests may the state have in limiting pluralism?

BIBLIOGRAPHY

Parents, Children, and Philosophy. For a philosophical study of the parent-child relationship, see Jeffrey Blustein, *Parents and Children: The Ethics of the Family* (Oxford U Press, 1982).

Medical Decisionmaking in Families. Margaret F. Brinig, Carl E. Scheider, and Lee E. Teitelbaum, *Family Law in Action: A Reader* 148–60 (Anderson, 1999), excerpts a number of articles showing how families actually make medical decisions. This topic is further pursued in Carl E. Schneider, *The Practice of Autonomy: Patients, Doctors, and Medical Decisions* (Oxford U Press, 1998).

Children with Disabilities. Two interesting and well-written novels dealing with the problems posed by disabled children living in families in which they are not the only children are Brett Lott, *Jewel* (Wash Square Press, 1991); and Wally Lamb, *I Know This Much is True* (Harper Perennial Books, 1998). The portrayals of the struggles of the mothers involved are also worth considering. Similarly, Ron McLarty's *The Memory of Running* (Viking Adult 2004) describes the problems of dealing with a disturbed young woman from the perspective of her now-adult brother.

Children and Decisions. For skeptical thoughts on the capacity of children to make their own decisions well, see Elizabeth S. Scott, *Judgment and Reasoning in Adolescent Decisionmaking*, 37 Villanova L Rev 1607 (1992), and Bruce C. Hafen, *Children's Liberation and the New Egalitarianism: Some Reservations About Abandoning Youth to Their "Rights,"* 1976 BYU L Rev 605, which notes the ways in which children, even adolescents, are have difficulty making mature choices.

Chapter IX

CHILD CUSTODY: INDETERMINACY, RULES, AND DISCRETION

Then came there two women, that were harlots, unto the king, and stood before him. And the one woman said, O my lord, I and this woman dwell in one house; and I was delivered of a child with her in the house. And it came to pass the third day after that I was delivered, that this woman was delivered also: and we were together; there was no stranger with us in the house, save we two in the house. And this woman's child died in the night; because she overlaid it. And she arose at midnight, and took my son from beside me, while thine handmaid slept, and laid it in her bosom, and laid her dead child in my bosom. And when I rose in the morning to give my child suck, behold, it was dead: but when I had considered it in the morning, behold, it was not my son, which I did bear. And the other woman said, Nay; but the living is my son, and the dead is thy son. And this said, No; but the dead is thy son, and the living is my son. Thus they spake before the king. Then said the king, The one saith, This is my son that liveth, and thy son is the dead: and the other saith, Nay; but thy son is the dead, and my son is the living. And the king said, Bring me a sword. And they brought a sword before the king. And the king said, Divide the living child in two, and give half to the one, and half to the other. Then spake the woman whose the living child was unto the king, for her bowels yearned upon her son, and she said, O my lord, give her the living child, and in no wise slay it. But the other said, Let it be neither mine nor thine, but divide it. Then the king answered and said, Give her the living child, and in no wise slay it: she is the mother thereof. And all Israel heard of the judgment which the king had judged; and they feared the king: for they saw that the wisdom of God was in him, to do judgment.

I Kings 3:16–28

SECTION 1. AN INTRODUCTORY CASE

[T]he little girl [was] disposed of in a manner worthy of the judgement seat of Solomon. She was divided in two and the portions tossed impartially to the disputants. They would take her, in rotation, for six months at a time; she would spend half the year with each. This was odd justice in the eyes of

those who still blinked in the fierce light projected from the tribunal–a light in which neither parent figured in the least as a happy example to youth and innocence. What was to have been expected on the evidence was the nomination, in loco parentis, of some proper third person, some respectable or at least some presentable friend. Apparently, however, the circle of the Faranges had been scanned in vain for any such ornament; so that the only solution finally meeting all the difficulties was, save that of sending Maisie to a Home, the partition of the tutelary office in the manner I have mentioned. There were more reasons for her parents to agree to it than there had ever been for them to agree to anything; and they now prepared with her help to enjoy the distinction that waits upon vulgarity sufficiently attested.

Henry James
What Maisie Knew

The common-law rule was that, in a dispute between father and mother, the father was entitled to the custody of his children. At the beginning of the nineteenth century, courts began to say custody should be awarded according to the best interests of the child. That has remained the standard, but it has been interpreted variously. Most significantly, a presumption (the tender-years presumption) arose that it was best for young children to be in the custody of their mother. That presumption is now under constitutional, common law, and legislative attack, and some states have instituted a presumption in favor of joint custody or of the "primary caretaker." The following materials introduce you to these and other problems in thinking about custody disputes. We begin with the celebrated case of

PAINTER v. BANNISTER

Supreme Court of Iowa, 1966
140 NW2d 152

STUART, JUSTICE.

We are here setting the course for Mark Wendell Painter's future. Our decision on the custody of this 7 year old boy will have a marked influence on his whole life. The fact that we are called upon many times a year to determine custody matters does not make the exercising of this awesome responsibility any less difficult. Legal training and experience are of little practical help in solving the complex problems of human relations. However, these problems do arise and under our system of government, the burden of rendering a final decision rests upon us. It is frustrating to know we can only resolve, not solve, these unfortunate situations.

The custody dispute before us in this habeas corpus action is between the father, Harold Painter, and the maternal grandparents, Dwight and Margaret Bannister. Mark's mother and younger sister were killed in an automobile accident on December 6, 1962 near Pullman, Washington. The father, after other arrangements for Mark's care had proved unsatisfactory, asked the Bannisters to take care of Mark. They went to California and brought Mark to their farm home near Ames in July, 1963. Mr. Painter remarried in November, 1964 and about that time indicated he wanted to take Mark back. The Bannisters refused to let him leave and this action was filed in June, 1965. Since July 1965 he has continued to remain in the Bannister home under an order of this court staying execution of the judgment of the trial court awarding custody to the father until the matter could be determined on appeal. For reasons hereinafter stated, we conclude Mark's better interests will be served if he remains with the Bannisters.

Mark's parents came from highly contrasting backgrounds. His mother was born, raised and educated in rural Iowa. Her parents are college graduates. Her father is agricultural information editor for the Iowa State University Extension Service. The Bannister home is in the Gilbert Community and is well kept, roomy and comfortable. The Bannisters are highly respected members of the community. Mr. Bannister has served on the school board and regularly teaches a Sunday school class at the Gilbert Congregational Church. Mark's mother graduated from Grinnell College. She then went to work for a newspaper in Anchorage, Alaska, where she met Harold Painter.

Mark's father was born in California. When he was 2½ years old, his parents were divorced and he was placed in a foster home. Although he has kept in contact with his natural parents, he considers his foster parents, the McNellys, as his family. He flunked out of a high school and a trade school because of a lack of interest in academic subjects, rather than any lack of ability. He joined the navy at 17. He did not like it. After receiving an honorable discharge, he took examinations and obtained his high school diploma. He lived with the McNellys and went to college for 2½ years under the G.I. bill. He quit college to take a job on a small newspaper in Ephrata, Washington in November 1955. In May 1956, he went to work for the newspaper in Anchorage which employed Jeanne Bannister.

Harold and Jeanne were married in April, 1957. Although there is a conflict in the evidence on the point, we are convinced the marriage, overall, was a happy one with many ups and downs as could be expected in the uniting of two such opposites.

We are not confronted with a situation where one of the contesting parties is not a fit or proper person. There is no criticism of either the Bannisters or their home. There is no suggestion in the record that Mr. Painter is morally unfit. It is obvious the Bannisters did not approve of their daughter's marriage to Harold Painter and do not want their grandchild raised under his guidance. The philosophies of life are entirely different. As stated by the psychiatrist who examined Mr. Painter at the request of Bannisters' attorneys: "It is evident that there exists a large difference in ways of life and value systems between the Bannisters and Mr. Painter, but in this case, there is no evidence that psychiatric instability is involved. Rather, these divergent life patterns seem to represent alternative normal adaptations."

It is not our prerogative to determine custody upon our choice of one of two ways of life within normal and proper limits and we will not do so. However, the philosophies are important as they relate to Mark and his particular needs.

The Bannister home provides Mark with a stable, dependable, conventional, middle class, midwest background and an opportunity for a college education and profession, if he desires it. It provides a solid foundation and secure atmosphere. In the Painter home, Mark would have more freedom of conduct and thought with an opportunity to develop his individual talents. It would be more exciting and challenging in many respects, but romantic, impractical and unstable.

Little additional recitation of evidence is necessary to support our evaluation of the Bannister home. It might be pointed out, however, that Jeanne's three sisters also received college educations and seem to be happily married to college graduates.

Our conclusion as to the type of home Mr. Painter would offer is based upon his Bohemian approach to finances and life in general. We feel there is much evidence which supports this conclusion. His main ambition is to be a free lance writer and photographer. He has had some articles and picture stories published, but the income from these efforts has been negligible. At the time of the accident, Jeanne was willingly working to support the family so Harold could devote more time to his writing and photography. In the 10 years since he left college, he has changed jobs seven times. He was asked to leave two of them; two he quit because he didn't like the work; two because he wanted to devote more time to writing and the rest for better pay. He was contemplating a move to Berkeley at the time of trial. His attitude toward his career is typified by his own comments concerning a job offer:

> "About the Portland news job, I hope you understand when I say it took guts not to take it; I had to get behind myself and push. It was very, very tempting to accept a good salary and settle down to a steady, easy routine. As I approached Portland, with the intention of taking the job, I began to ask what, in the long run, would be the good of this job: 1) it was not really what I wanted; 2) Portland is just another big farm town, with none of the stimulation it takes to get my mind sparking. Anyway, I decided Mark and myself would be better off if I went ahead with what I've started and the hell with the rest, sink, swim or starve."

There is general agreement that Mr. Painter needs help with his finances. Both Jeanne and Marilyn, his present wife, handled most of them. Purchases and sales of books, boats, photographic equipment and houses indicate poor financial judgment and an easy come easy go attitude. He dissipated his wife's estate of about $4300, most of which was a gift from her parents and which she had hoped would be used for the children's education.

The psychiatrist classifies him as "a romantic and somewhat of a dreamer". An apt example are the plans he related for himself and Mark in February 1963: "My thought now is to settle Mark and myself in Sausilito, [sic] near San Francisco; this is a retreat for wealthy artists, writers, and such aspiring artists and writers as can fork up the rent money. My plan is to do expensive portraits ($150 and up), sell prints ($15 and up) to the tourists who flock in from all over the world...."

The house in which Mr. Painter and his present wife live, compared with the well kept Bannister home, exemplifies the contrasting ways of life. In his words "it is a very old and beat up and lovely home...." They live in the rear part. The interior is inexpensively but tastefully decorated. The large yard on a hill in the business district of Walnut Creek, California, is of uncut weeds and wild oats. The house "is not painted on the outside because I do not want it painted. I am very fond of the wood on the outside of the house."

The present Mrs. Painter has her master's degree in cinema design and apparently likes and has had considerable contact with children. She is anxious to have Mark in her home. Everything indicates she would provide a leveling influence on Mr. Painter and could ably care for Mark.

Mr. Painter is either an agnostic or atheist and has no concern for formal religious training. He has read a lot of Zen Buddhism and "has been very much influenced by it." Mrs. Painter is Roman Catholic. They plan to send Mark to a Congregational Church near the Catholic Church, on an irregular schedule.

He is a political liberal and got into difficulty in a job at the University of Washington for his support of the activities of the American Civil Liberties Union in the university news bulletin.

There were "two funerals" for his wife. One in the basement of his home in which he alone was present. He conducted the service and wrote her a long letter. The second at a church in Pullman was for the gratification of her friends. He attended in a sport shirt and sweater.

These matters are not related as a criticism of Mr. Painter's conduct, way of life or sense of values. An individual is free to choose his own values, within bounds, which are not exceeded here. They do serve however to support our conclusion as to the kind of life Mark would be exposed to in the Painter household. We believe it would be unstable, unconventional, arty, Bohemian, and probably intellectually stimulating.

Were the question simply which household would be the most suitable in which to raise a child, we would have unhesitatingly chosen the Bannister home. We believe security and stability in the home are more important than intellectual stimulation in the proper development of a child. There are, however, several factors which have made us pause.

First, there is the presumption of parental preference, which though weakened in the past several years, exists by statute. Code of Iowa, Section 668.1. We have a great deal of sympathy for a father, who in the difficult period of adjustment following his wife's death, turns to the maternal grandparents for their help and then finds them unwilling to return the child. There is no merit in the Bannister claim that Mr. Painter permanently relinquished custody. It was intended to be a temporary arrangement. A father should be encouraged to look for help with the children, from those who love them without the risk of thereby losing the custody of the children permanently. This fact must receive consideration in cases of this kind. However, as always, the primary consideration is the best interest of the child and if the return of custody to the father is likely to have a seriously disrupting and disturbing effect upon the child's development, this fact must prevail.

Second, Jeanne's will named her husband guardian of the children and if he failed to qualify or ceased to act, named her mother. The parent's wishes are entitled to consideration.

Third, the Bannisters are 60 years old. By the time Mark graduates from high school they will be over 70 years old. Care of young children is a strain on grandparents and Mrs. Bannister's letters indicate as much.

We have considered all of these factors and have concluded that Mark's best interest demands that his custody remain with the Bannisters. Mark was five when he came to their home. The evidence clearly shows he was not well adjusted at that time. He did not distinguish fact from fiction and was inclined to tell "tall tales" emphasizing the big "I". He was very aggressive toward smaller children, cruel to animals, not liked by his classmates and did not seem to know what was acceptable conduct. As stated by one witness: "Mark knew where his freedom was and he didn't know where his boundaries were." In two years he made a great deal of improvement. He now appears to be well disciplined, happy, relatively secure and popular with his classmates, although still subject to more than normal anxiety.

We place a great deal of reliance on the testimony of Dr. Glenn R. Hawks, a child psychologist. The trial court, in effect, disregarded Dr. Hawks' opinions stating: "The court has given full consideration to the good doctor's testimony, but cannot accept it at full face value because of exaggerated statement and the witness' attitude on the stand." We, of course, do not have the advantage of viewing the witness' conduct on the stand, but we have carefully reviewed his testimony and find nothing in the written record to justify such a summary dismissal of the opinions of this eminent child psychologist.

Dr. Hawks is head of the Department of Child Development at Iowa State University. However, there is nothing in the record which suggests that his relationship with the Bannisters is such that his professional opinion would be influenced thereby. Child development is his specialty and he has written many articles and a textbook on the subject. He is recognized nationally, having served on the staff of the 1960 White House Conference on Children and Youth and as consultant on a Ford Foundation program concerning youth in India. He is now education consultant on the project "Head Start". He has taught and lectured at many universities and belongs to many professional associations. He works with the Iowa Children's Home Society in placement problems. Further detailing of his qualifications is unnecessary.

Between June 15th and the time of trial, he spent approximately 25 hours acquiring information about Mark and the Bannisters, including appropriate testing of and "depth interviews" with Mark. Dr. Hawks' testimony covers 70 pages of the record and it is difficult to pinpoint any bit of testimony which precisely summarizes his opinion. He places great emphasis on the "father figure" and discounts the importance of the "biological father". "The father figure is a figure that the child sees as an authority figure, as a helper, he is a nutrient figure, and one who typifies maleness and stands as maleness as far as the child is concerned."

His investigation revealed: " ... the strength of the father figure before Mark came to the Bannisters is very unclear. Mark is confused about the father figure prior to his contact with Mr. Bannister." Now, "Mark used Mr. Bannister as his father figure. This is very evident. It shows up in the depth interview, and it shows up in the description of Mark's life given by Mark. He has a very warm feeling for Mr. Bannister."

Dr. Hawks concluded that it was not for Mark's best interest to be removed from the Bannister home. He is criticized for reaching this conclusion without investigating the Painter home or finding out more about Mr. Painter's character. He answered:

> "I was most concerned about the welfare of the child, not the welfare of Mr. Painter, not about the welfare of the Bannisters. In as much as Mark has already made an adjustment and sees the Bannisters as his parental figures in his psychological makeup, to me this is the most critical factor. Disruption at this point, I think, would be detrimental to the child even tho Mr. Painter might well be a paragon of virtue. I think this would be a kind of thing which would not be in the best interest of the child. I think knowing something about where the child is at the present time is vital. I think something about where he might go, in my way of thinking is essentially untenable to me, and relatively unimportant. It isn't even helpful. The thing I was most concerned about was Mark's view of his own reality in which he presently lives. If this is destroyed I think it will have rather bad effects on Mark. I think then if one were to make a determination whether it would be to the parents' household, or the McNelly household, or X-household, then I think the further study would be appropriate."

Dr. Hawks stated: "I am appalled at the tremendous task Mr. Painter would have if Mark were to return to him because he has got to build the relationship from scratch. There is essentially nothing on which to build at the present time. Mark is aware Mr. Painter is his father, but he is not very clear about what this means. In his own mind the father figure is Mr. Bannister. I think it would take a very strong person with everything in his favor in order to build a relationship as Mr. Painter would have to build at this point with Mark."

It was Dr. Hawks' opinion "the chances are very high (Mark) will go wrong if he is returned to his father." This is based on adoption studies which "establish that the majority of adoptions in children who are changed, from ages six to eight, will go bad, if they have had a prior history of instability, some history of prior movement. When I refer to instability I am referring to where there has been no attempt to establish a strong relationship." Although this is not an adoption, the analogy seems appropriate, for Mark who had a history of instability would be removed from the only home in which he has a clearly established "father figure" and placed with his natural father about whom his feelings are unclear.

We know more of Mr. Painter's way of life than Dr. Hawks. We have concluded that it does not offer as great a stability or security as the Bannister home. Throughout his testimony he emphasized Mark's need at this critical time is stability. He has it in the Bannister home.

Other items of Dr. Hawks' testimony which have a bearing on our decision follow. He did not consider the Bannisters' age anyway disqualifying. He was of the opinion that Mark could adjust to a change more easily later on, if one became necessary, when he would have better control over his environment.

He believes the presence of other children in the home would have a detrimental effect upon Mark's adjustment whether this occurred in the Bannister home or the Painter home.

The trial court does not say which of Dr. Hawks' statements he felt were exaggerated. We were most surprised at the inconsequential position to which he relegated the "biological father." He concedes "child psychologists are less concerned about natural parents than probably other professional groups are." We are not inclined to so lightly value the role of the natural father, but find much reason for his evaluation of this particular case.

Mark has established a father-son relationship with Mr. Bannister, which he apparently had never had with his natural father. He is happy, well adjusted and progressing nicely in his development. We do not believe it is for Mark's best interest to take him out of this stable atmosphere in the face of warnings of dire consequences from an eminent child psychologist and send him to an uncertain future in his father's home. Regardless of our appreciation of the father's love for his child and his desire to have him with him, we do not believe we have the moral right to gamble with this child's future. He should be encouraged in every way possible to know his father. We are sure there are many ways in which Mr. Painter can enrich Mark's life.

For the reasons stated, we reverse the trial court and remand the case for judgment in accordance herewith.

Questions on Painter v. Bannister

(1) In his testimony, Dr. Hawks said, "Mark expressed a desire to stay with the Bannisters. He asked me to ask him about that. He was concerned he hadn't been asked." The trial judge reported that the Bannisters "state that Mark has declared his preference to stay with them." The judge, in his interview of Mark did not ask the boy this question for "obvious reasons." How should Mark's preference have been taken into account? Dr. Hawks testified that Mark was too young to formulate a reliable view of who should win custody. Was he right? Assume *arguendo* that he was. Could the court have put itself in Mark's place and made the decision that Mark would have made had he been old enough? What result would that have led to?

(2) What factors did the court in *Painter* consider in thinking about which custody award would be in Mark's best interests? How did the court weigh those factors? Was its weighing correct? What additional factors might the court have considered? How would you decide what weight should be given each factor?

(3) Are there factors in deciding what is in the child's best interests that are not suggested by *Painter* but that should be used in child-custody decisions? Do the following factors strike you as candidates?

> (a) The Bannisters could give Mark a home with two parents. Suppose that Mr. Painter was unmarried. Ought there be a presumption that the Bannisters, as a couple, should have custody? Other things being equal, are two parents better than one?
>
> (b) Suppose that (as seems likely) the Bannisters were better off economically than Mr. Painter and thus better able to give Mark the things money can buy in a capitalist society. Money may not buy happiness, but it does improve access to better health care, better education, a wider range of occupational choices, and so on. Should a court therefore be able to consider the relative wealth of contending custodians?
>
> (c) Suppose Mr. Painter had had several affairs with other women while he was married to Mrs. Painter. Should a court be permitted to treat such marital behavior as relevant in custody cases?

(4) We made *Painter v. Bannister* our principal case with a little trepidation. On first reading it can be too easy to dismiss the court's opinion as an expression of parochial prejudice. Even if you believe this is an appropriate reaction to the case, you need to read the court's opinion as sympathetically as possible. First, you may discover you were wrong. Second, you need to be able to read even wrong-headed opinions sympathetically, if only in order to respond to them effectively. What explanations for the court's result in *Painter* might be advanced beyond parochialism?

(5) Dr. Hawks made it amply clear that not only would it be better for Mark to stay with the Bannisters, but that it would surely harm Mark to return to his father. Mr. Painter produced no expert testimony. Given this unequivocal and uncontradicted expert testimony, how could a court award custody to Mr. Painter?

(a) Can a court confronted with uncontradicted expert testimony dismiss it as the trial court did, by saying that the psychologist's "attitude on the stand" made his testimony suspect? Should the appellate court have deferred to the trial court's observations? Or insist that the trial court explain why it disbelieved the testimony? Should the trial court's evaluation of the demeanor of expert witnesses be given less weight than its evaluation of the demeanor of other witnesses?

(b) Can a court confronted with uncontradicted expert psychological testimony rely on the cross-examination of the expert witness in rejecting that testimony? In *Painter*, there appears not to have been particularly effective cross-examination. Is a trial court or an appellate court in a good situation to evaluate the witness's testimony in such a case? In *Painter*, the trial court rejected the expert's testimony partly on the grounds that he had made "exaggerated statements." If the exaggerated statements had to do with questions of expert opinion and not with questions of fact, how did the trial-court judge acquire the expertise to decide that the psychologist was exaggerating? Should the appellate court accept the trial court's conclusions about the witness's exaggerated statements where the trial court did not (and perhaps thus inferentially could not) specify what they were?

(c) Can a court confronted with uncontradicted expert psychological testimony reject that testimony on the theory that the witness is an interested witness? That is, can the court simply say that the witness was being paid to testify on behalf of one of the parties and that all the witness's testimony is therefore suspect?

(d) Can a court confronted with uncontradicted expert psychological testimony reject that testimony on the theory that the study of human psychology has not advanced enough to make its conclusions adequate for use in making child-custody decisions?

(e) Can a court confronted with uncontradicted expert psychological testimony reject that testimony because it is based on or systematically promotes values the court believes are not the values on which child-custody decisions should be based? How might such an argument have been made in *Painter*?

(6) Consider the following remarks in terms of both expert and non-expert witnesses:

> There is room still to wonder whether the opportunity to evaluate the demeanor of witnesses at trial actually enhances the fact-finding process. The outward signs of lying are extraordinarily subtle and complex.

> The trial judge may easily be distracted by the effort to unravel the signals of demeanor in ways that even a subsequent study of the paper record cannot undo. Nonetheless, it is our firm tradition, and the belief of most today, that great regard is "due" the trial judge's opportunity to evaluate demeanor. It is difficult to show clear error in a decision to believe a single witness, or in a decision to disbelieve a single witness unless the witness is the seldom encountered perfect witness who is uninterested, unimpeached, and uncontradicted by any circumstance. It is nearly impossible to show clear error in a choice between two or more witnesses whose testimony is at all plausible.

Edward H. Cooper, *Civil Rule 52(a): Rationing and Rationalizing the Resources of Appellate Review*, 63 Notre Dame L Rev 645, 650–51 (1988).

(7) The essential principle of *Painter* may be that a child can be separated from a parent for so long and can form such strong ties with an alternative custodian that returning the child to the parent and separating the child from the alternative custodian may be so injurious as to justify leaving the child with the custodian. Is this principle itself incorrect? Is it correct but incorrectly applied in *Painter*? How would your view of this case be changed if the length of time Mr. Painter and Mark had been separated were different? If Mark's age at the beginning of the separation were different? If the reasons for the separation were different?

(a) Imagine a Mr. Painter who was twenty years old when Mark was born, who was unemployed, who had not graduated from high school, who was using drugs and alcohol, whose marriage was dissolving. Suppose that Mark had been born with a congenital defect that caused one leg to grow faster than the other and that this Mr. Painter had no way to get Mark to the hospital for treatment. Suppose further that Mr. and Mrs. Painter consented to a court order making the Bannisters Mark's legal guardian. Should this Mr. Painter be able to recover custody of Mark when his social and economic circumstances improved after three years? After five years? After ten years? Suppose this Mark had been ten years old at the time of the separation? (This hypothetical is drawn from *Matter of Guardianship of J.R.G.*, 708 P2d 263 (Mont 1985), which held that a guardianship created under these circumstances that had endured six years could be terminated where the guardian could not show "that the best interest of the child would be served by a continuation of the guardianship.")

(b) Suppose Mr. Painter had simply abandoned Mark and had returned to claim him after three years? After five years? After ten years? Suppose Mark had been one day old at the time of the separation? Ten years old?

(c) Suppose Mr. Painter had committed homicide and been jailed for three years? For five years? For life? For life with no possibility of parole? Suppose Mark had been one day old at the time of the separation? Ten years old?

(d) Suppose Mr. Painter had fallen seriously ill and been hospitalized for three years? Suppose Mr. Painter had fallen seriously ill mentally and been hospitalized for three years? Suppose the hospitalization had lasted for five years? Ten years? Suppose Mark had been one day old at the time of the separation? Ten years old?

(e) According to Joseph Goldstein, Anna Freud, and Albert J. Solnit, *Beyond the Best Interests of the Child* 107 (Free Press, 1973), after the Second World War, there were, thanks in large part to the Dutch resistance movement, perhaps 4,500 Jewish children in Holland whose parents had left them in the care of non-Jews. The parents of roughly 2,500 of these children survived the war. The Dutch government ruled that these children should be returned to their parents or should be placed in the custody of relatives. Only where no relatives were available (which was true for 360 children) were the non-Jewish foster parents allowed to retain custody. Was the Dutch government correct? (For a somewhat different account, see J.S. Fishman, *Jewish War Orphans in the Netherlands—The Guardianship Issue 1945–1950*, 27 The Wiener Library Bull 31 [1973–74].)

(f) A couple named Twigg and a couple named Mays had children at the same time in the same hospital. The Twigg's daughter Arlena had heart disease and after nine years died of it. It was then discovered that the hospital had (presumably inadvertently) given the Twiggs the Mays' child, and vice-versa. Should the Twiggs be able to recover their daughter Kimberly Mays from the custody of Robert Mays? *Twigg v. Mays*, 642 S2d 1373 (Fla Ct App 1994).

(8) Mr. Painter had been Mark's primary caretaker only for a short period. The Bannisters had been his primary caretakers for the three years preceding the Iowa Supreme Court's opinion. Ought there be a presumption that the Bannisters, as his primary caretakers, should have custody? If so, why? Because that would probably be in Mark's best interests? Because the Bannisters would probably have formed an intense relationship with Mark which it would be painful to break?

(9) Suppose that while the Bannisters could provide Mark with a female caretaker, Mr. Painter could not. Suppose it was Mrs. Painter, rather than Mr. Painter, who had placed Mark in the Bannisters' care after Mr. Painter had died. Should the fact that it then would have been Mark's mother rather than his father who was seeking custody have altered the result? On what principle?

(10) Suppose the Bannisters and Mr. Painter lived in the same town. Should the court award custody jointly to both the Bannisters and Mr. Painter? Award custody to one of the contenders but to award visiting rights to the other?

(11) Ought there have been, as in fact there was, a presumption that Mr. Painter, as Mark's natural parent, should have custody? How strong ought such a presumption be? Ought the presumption be irrebuttable? Rebuttable by strong arguments? Ought the presumption be

simply one of a variety of factors all of which should be taken into account? What was the strength of the presumption in *Painter*?

(a) Ought a natural parent always win custody unless he or she is an unfit parent? What kind of evidence ought it take to show unfitness? What quantum of evidence? (That is, should unfitness have to be shown by a preponderance of the evidence? By clear and convincing evidence? Beyond a reasonable doubt?) Could such a showing have been made in *Painter*?

(b) Ought a natural parent always win custody unless granting him or her custody would harm the child? How much harm ought it take to rebut the presumption? Could such a showing have been made in *Painter*?

(c) Ought a natural parent always win custody unless he or she has abandoned the child? What kind of evidence ought it take to show abandonment? What quantum of evidence? Could such a showing have been made in *Painter*?

(d) Ought a natural parent always win custody unless granting him or her custody would not be in the child's best interests? What kind of evidence ought it take to make that showing? What quantum of evidence? Could such a showing have been made in *Painter*?

(12) Can our rationales for parental rights tell us anything about whether Mr. Painter has a special claim to custody of Mark?

(a) Our first rationale is that parents know their children better than anyone else can. Is that true here? Mr. Painter was not (at least for any significant period) Mark's primary caretaker. At the time of the Iowa Supreme Court's decision Mr. Painter had not had extended contact with his son for slightly more than three years. The Bannisters, on the other hand, had been Mark's primary caretakers for the immediately preceding three years. By the time of the court decision, then, did they not know Mark better than Mr. Painter?

(b) Our second rationale for parental rights is that the lack of judicial expertise about child development helps justify judicial deference to parental choices. But is there any reason in this case to defer to Mr. Painter instead of to the Bannisters?

(c) Our third justification for parental rights has to do with the absence of standards for making decisions about children. The court must decide who is to have custody. Is the parental-rights argument here that automatically awarding custody to the natural parent relieves the court of devising standards for that choice? How strong an argument is this? Does it justify awarding custody to a natural parent even though doing so may injure the child?

(d) Our fourth justification for parental rights invokes the enforcement problem. How serious an enforcement problem is there here? The enforcement problem in family law grows partly from the difficulty of detecting violations of legislative rules or judicial orders.

That problem is absent here. Mr. Painter cannot disobey a judicial order without being noticed. The Bannisters have custody; Mr. Painter could take it from them only by kidnapping Mark. To avoid being caught, Mr. Painter would have to abandon his present house and job and attempt to find a new home and employment using a pseudonym. Would the difficulties of this probably deter Mr. Painter from flouting a judicial decision? Another part of family law's enforcement problem grows out of the danger that the person being enforced against may retaliate against the person the law is trying to protect. Is Mr. Painter likely to retaliate against Mark?

(e) Our fifth justification for parental rights is the danger that governmental intervention will disrupt the relationship between parent and child. But here, isn't the crucial stability in Mark's life now the stability of his relationship with his grandparents and not with his father?

(f) Our sixth justification for parental rights is that inquiry into the relationship of parent and child may injure both by diminishing their privacy. But once there is a custody dispute, is there any way you can avoid injuring privacy? Or would automatically awarding natural parents custody obviates the need for an inquiry? How strong an argument is this? Does it justify awarding custody to a natural parent even though doing so may injure the child?

(g) Our seventh justification for parental rights is that it is normatively preferable for parents to be able to organize their relationship with their children. The argument here is that parents have the same kind of interest in freely conducting their relationship with their children that spouses have in conducting their relationship with each other. However, a crucial difference between the parent-child and spousal relationships is that spouses can leave a marriage while children cannot usually to leave their parents. Given this difference, should parents be able to invoke this rationale for the parental right where the very question the court is deciding is whether it is in the child's interest for the parent to have custody?

(h) Our eighth justification for parental rights is that allowing parents freedom to raise their children promotes pluralism by allowing parents to perpetuate whatever communities they prefer. Does automatically awarding natural parents custody prevent courts from systematically making decisions that disfavor heterodox communities? How strong an argument is this? Does it justify awarding custody to a natural parent even though doing so may injure the child? Does it fit *Painter*?

(i) Do the justifications for parental rights fit the Bannisters as well as they fit Mr. Painter? Do parental rights arise out of the fact of biological parenthood or out of a parental relationship? Are the Bannisters' claims to quasi-parental rights given greater substance by the biological relationship between the Bannisters and Mark?

(13) In some jurisdictions, the appellate court reviewing a child-custody case may consider the case de novo. Other jurisdictions use an intermediate standard: "[T]his court's scope of review in a custody dispute is of the broadest type, and while we will not usurp the fact-finding function of the trial court, we are not bound by deductions or inferences made by the hearing judge from the facts as found." *Morris v. Morris*, 412 A2d 139, 145 (Pa Super 1979). Although the court in *Painter* did not discuss it, an "intermediate" standard of review was applicable in that case: "In Iowa, habeas corpus actions involving custody of minors are regarded as equitable in nature, reviewable *de novo*, but the trial court's findings are entitled to substantial weight." Case Comment, 79 Harv L Rev 1710, 1710 n 1 (1966). Other jurisdictions "will disturb the trial court's resolution of custody issues only if convinced that the record shows an abuse of discretion, or if controlling findings of fact are clearly erroneous." *Carle v. Carle*, 503 P2d 1050, 1052 (Alaska 1972). Did the appellate court accord the trial court in *Painter* adequate weight? Did that trial court abuse its discretion?

(14) After considering all these questions, do you think "the best interests of the child" was the proper standard to use in *Painter*? Why is it ordinarily used in child-custody disputes? Why, in other words, are the child's interests paramount, especially in view of the constitutional doctrine of parental rights and the fact that the interests and happiness of the adult contenders for custody are so much at stake?

(a) Is it because the best interests of the child are what each contender for custody wants to serve?

(b) Is it because the contending adults can generally protect their own interests, while children cannot protect theirs and thus need to have them protected by the court?

(c) Is it because there is a powerful social interest in having children brought up as successfully as possible?

(d) Is it because the child may be unrepresented in the proceedings and thus needs to be protected through the best interest standard?

(e) Is it because the interests of the contending adults are often indistinguishable or evenly balanced, and the interest of the child is the most logical next criterion to consult?

(f) Is it because the interests of the contending adults are likely to be taken into account implicitly when the best-interests standard is used, since it is likely to be in the interest of the child to be with the parent who is most strongly motivated to have him or her?

(g) Is it because the law ought to reflect the moral principle that parents should put their children's interests ahead of their own?

(15) After thinking about all these questions, are you persuaded by the often-made criticism of the best-interests standard that its indeter-

minacy makes it useless or even dangerous? Is the standard more indeterminate than many other legal standards? Is indeterminacy bad?

PAINTER v. BANNISTER: SOME FURTHER INFORMATION

The Trial Court's Opinion

In summary, the Court finds that the plaintiff, the father of Mark Painter, is a proper and fit person to have the care and custody of his own minor son, and that it is for the best interests of the son, Mark Painter, to be reared and educated in his own father's home; that the father is the person to properly maintain his son and to properly educate him. In making this finding the Court does not cast any reflections upon defendants, Mr. and Mrs. Bannister. The Court knows they are good people, they have and did provide a good home for their grandson, but that the greater equities are with the plaintiff, he being the natural father of Mark, and there being no evidence that he is an unfit father, there being no evidence that he abandoned the child, and the Court being convinced that the grandson's stay with the Bannisters was originally on a temporary basis and that it is for the best interests of the child, Mark Painter, that he be placed permanently in the care and custody of his father.

Mr. Painter's Brief on Appeal

The following are excerpts from Mr. Painter's brief to the Iowa Supreme Court.

The plaintiff, Harold W. Painter, is 34 years of age.... Plaintiff was born in California and from the time he was two and one-half years old was raised by his foster parents, Mr. and Mrs. Leo B. McNelly....

His childhood was stable and very satisfactory.... The McNellys on occasion had other foster children stay with them for short periods of time so that he grew up with other children around him.... The McNellys wanted to adopt the plaintiff but the father was not agreeable. He [presumably Harold Painter] flunked out of one high school because he didn't like it and the subjects that were taught. However, he did do well in the subjects he liked.

While in high school, plaintiff had a number of outside interests. He was involved in sports a great deal and on the wrestling and track team. He was president of the history class and debating societies. He was active in scouting and was in the Cub Scouts at 9, Boy Scouts until 12 where he achieved the rank of Star Scout.... During the time he lived with the McNellys, he saw his natural mother once a month and his father frequently came over once a week to visit him.

Plaintiff has attended two and one-half years of college.... His academic standing in college was very good having received mostly "A's." ... He majored mostly in literature and journalism and was editor of a school magazine and writer on the school newspaper.... He went to San Francisco City College for two years, and then went on to San Francisco State College, a four-year college. . . .

After leaving college, Plaintiff–Appellee took a job in a newspaper at Ephrata, Washington, where his mother lived and worked as a wire editor. He voluntarily left Ephrata [after] about a year because of the low pay and went to work for the Anchorage Times in May of 1956. . . . When he left the job [in Anchorage], he was city editor in charge of the newsroom.

In a letter to her husband, Jeanne once wrote, "I appreciate you even more than I did before. You are a wonderful husband. Every day I think of something more I like about you ... you should be told how wonderful you are, though." Jeanne went on to extol the Plaintiff in said letter saying how he was taking the lead on saving and spending money and how she could feel comfortably dependent upon him. She stated that she enjoyed being an equal partner and concluded her letter by saying "I just plain love you."

Jeanne prepared a Last Will and Testament. . . . In said Will, she nominates her husband as Executor and appoints him as the guardian of the person of their minor children. If Plaintiff should fail to qualify or cease to act, she appoints her mother, Margaret Bonnifield Bannister. . . .

[After his wife and daughter died], Plaintiff was in a state of shock and his state of shock continued at varying degrees for a long period of time. . . . When Plaintiff left Pullman, Washington he took Mark and moved to Glen Ellyn, California, and he and Mark stayed with his foster parents, the McNellys, and then acquired a house where he and Mark lived. . . . Mark stayed with the McNellys for a while because of the hours that Plaintiff worked but Plaintiff was dissatisfied with their care and did not want Mark to be cared for by a baby-sitter. The good friends of Plaintiff, the Lienhards, had offered to look after Mark and Plaintiff considered this for a temporary period of time until he could become resettled, but eventually thought it would be best to have the Bannisters take care of him in Iowa until he became resettled. . . .

Plaintiff allowed Mark to return to the Bannisters because "they had raised a woman who was quite remarkable, I think, in many respects. . . ." Plaintiff thought it was very important that Mark have a mother and that he not spend time with a baby-sitter. Plaintiff was still upset and wasn't sure what he was going to do. . . .

It was the understanding between the parties that Mark's return to Ames was to be a temporary one and that Plaintiff definitely wanted Mark back. . . . In Defendants' Exhibit 38, a letter to Mrs. McNelly written by Mrs. Bannister, she stated "[w]e didn't dare want to miss any opportunity we had even if it were only going to be temporary ... in Hal's first letter when he approached us on the possibility of taking Mark he definitely stated that he wanted us to get Mark started in his first year of school" and added, "but, of course, I want him back for he is a dear little boy."

Dr. Hawks' Testimony

Here are some brief excerpts from Dr. Hawks' testimony.

1. "I have seen Mark Painter and Dwight and Margaret Bannister professionally for the purpose of evaluating them. I spent approximately twenty-five hours studying these people, acquiring information on them. I have explored Mark's school record, facts and information that I could determine from the school. I have done testing . . . and I have conducted depth interviews with Mark over a period beginning with June 15 up until last night." Dr. Hawks reported that Mark's score on his IQ test was 120, and he speculated that Mark's IQ might actually be nearer 130.

   Dr. Hawks said that he also talked with Mark's teachers and the school-bus driver, "who was singled out by the teachers as being a very important person in Mark's life." Dr. Hawks further reported that he "was interested in knowing something about the Bannisters as citizens of Gilbert. Research, as well as my own experience, has substantiated the idea that the kind of people, the way people are regarded in their community, is indicative of the kind of support they can expect from their community in emergencies. It is also indicative of the kind of people they are. As an example of this, we know if we want to develop a sense of responsibility in the child, the best way to develop a sense of responsibility is not by necessarily giving chores, but by being responsible people yourself, so that you set a model by which a child builds his life. So that I did have discussions with people in Gilbert, as well as people with whom Mr. Bannister works, and found the Bannisters are very highly thought of. They are seen as mature contributing people in the segments of society in which they operate."

2. "The child aperception test, tells me some things about Mark. That he is an anxious child with a lot of anxiety which stems from present circumstances. I think Mark is working very extensively at an identification and ego development. By that I mean he is in the process of finding out who he is. . . ." "Mark has more anxiety than usual, in an abnormal amount. He had had, I think, much concern about the uncertainty of his own future. . . ." "I think his ego development, his personality development is much more likely to be secure and strong if Mark is in an arrangement which has a strong degree of permanency. I think the unsettled conditions throughout Mark's life up to this point will cumulatively become more and more detrimental if they are allowed to persist." "I think if Mark were four years younger, five years younger, I think this might be relatively unimportant, or less important, because there would be time to make up for whatever deficiencies might occur because of moving from one place to another." "When I use the phrase, 'If Mark is disrupted at this point' I meant that if Mark's environment is grossly changed at this point, if he is withdrawn from the parental

figure as established in his own mind, if he is withdrawn from a stable environment, if he must be moved to another environment."

"I have seen children who have been about the same age as Mark who have shown much more instability than he has. I do not mean to imply that I would call him exceptionally unstable, I think he falls within the normal range. I think he is making considerable progress and would become a valuable member of society. I think he is a very bright youngster. I think he has a lot of things going for him. He has a very good imagination, he approaches problems rather constructively, he knows how to learn which is important."

3. "In this case, I would not feel that the Bannister's age was in any way disqualifying. It would seem to me the experience they have had as parents, their own stability, their own status, removes several elements that often get in the way of parent-child relations. I would think the age would possibly be an asset, and certainly not a liability."

4. "If one or both of the Bannisters should die, couldn't take care of him, you ask if the transition at ten or twelve or fourteen would be much greater than at seven. The only way I can answer it again is to say it would be dependent upon the number of years Mark had to spend with the Bannisters. If he were to make the internalizing, you say ten or twelve, the transition took him three to five years to develop his strength, his ego strength, to develop his personality, I would think it would be less detrimental at that point because he would be in much better control of his environment than he is now."

5. "I would agree with your statement that continual contacts with the natural father, even though they are not in the same location, has an important element to play in that he still knows Hal Painter as his father, but let me add this: from long-time separation where fathers were separated because of war circumstances, we have many studies of this, we know that where contact was made with/by fathers to their children, that these ultimately had to be reinforced by the mother in order for those to be meaningful contacts, whether these were letter or telephone."

6. "I asked Mark on many occasions about his father. He was confused about his father and didn't know what to call him. He spoke of him as Hal. He didn't think it was quite right to speak of him as Hal, or father didn't seem quite right.... He remembers his father's visits here as being very short. This is his term not mine. He said he could not depend on his father. I am not sure he said it in that way, but essentially he said, 'He tells me he is coming, then he doesn't come when he says he is coming.' I think that is his major criticism of his father."

Mark, I Love You

In 1967 Hal Painter published a memoir entitled *Mark, I Love You* (Simon & Schuster). The following facts are taken from it.

Hal Painter first met his in-laws at his wedding in Alaska. He describes them as "civil and polite," but "glum, distant and uneasy." After the wedding, Jeanne wanted to buy a house; Hal wanted to move to Eskimo country "to live for a time with the last American nomads ... and to write a book about them." They bought a house, and soon Mark was born. However, Jeanne found the house, which was in the country outside Anchorage, lonely. She hated the outhouse. This, and financial problems, caused them to leave the house and helped account for their decision to move to Bremerton, a small town in Washington. There Hal took a job as a copy editor, a job he hoped would leave him time to write short stories. Hal, however, found Bremerton petty, provincial, and repressive; his job was "hell," albeit a "tepid hell." Jeanne disliked the house Hal had rented. Hal was soon fired because he didn't fit in and was indifferent to his work.

In Moses Lake, a town sixty miles away, Hal found a job covering local news. He hated the town and the work, and his "depressions and rages" upset Jeanne, who was lonely in the town and who worked, apparently part-time, for a newspaper eighty miles away. At Jeanne's suggestion, he applied for and received a job writing for Washington State University, in Pullman. Jeanne worked part-time for a paper in Spokane. Hal and Jeanne liked Pullman. However, Hal was soon fired, perhaps because of his incorrect punctuation, perhaps for the political opinions he advanced in editorials in the university news bulletin. Hal decided to try to work as a freelance writer and photographer, while Jeanne worked as a reporter in Moscow, Idaho, which is eight miles from Pullman. While in Pullman, Jeanne and Hal made wills naming the Bannisters guardians of the children (Mark's sister was by then about three years old) in the event that both Jeanne and Hal died. They would have preferred to name one of Jeanne's cousins, since the cousin and her husband were more of an age to be parents than the Bannisters and since they shared the Painters' views. However, their lawyer told them that doing so would be difficult. Shortly thereafter Jeanne and her daughter were killed in an automobile accident. After the funeral, Mr. Bannister seemed concerned about Mark's future and asked to take Mark to Iowa until Hal could make new arrangements. He invited Hal to come to Iowa as well. Hal declined. He did, however, feel closer to the Bannisters than ever before.

After struggling to get his financial situation straightened out, Hal took Mark to California for a "vacation in the sun." For a few weeks they stayed at Hal's foster parents' house near Santa Rosa. Then Hal rented a cabin in Sonoma County. Next he bought a sailboat on which he and Mark seem to have lived. Hal found his photo-journalism unsuccessful and came to dislike the pictures he had taken. He then moved into an apartment (retaining the boat) and took a job on a Contra Costa newspaper whose staff he liked. However, suburbia was intolerable. Apparently Mark was looked after at least part of the time by Hal's foster parents. They offered to care for Mark permanently, but Hal disagreed with his foster parents about how Mark should be raised. Hal "wanted desperately for Mark to have at least the trappings of security, a home with a man and a woman...." To the dismay of his foster parents, he chose the Bannisters to provide it, partly because he was anxious "to preserve in Mark all that was left of my wife." He called them and asked them to come to California to pick up Mark.

For the next year Hal lived on his boat. He did not write Mark regularly but called him occasionally. The Bannisters paid for Mark's support. Near the end of the year Hal met Marylyn, the woman who was to become his second wife. Hal was anxious for Mark to have a mother, and soon they were married.

Sometime before the marriage, Hal talked by phone with Mr. Bannister. Mr. Bannister seemed to express doubts about returning Mark to Hal's custody. Hal immediately consulted a lawyer, who told him to simply take Mark back. That September, Hal went to Ames. The Bannisters told him they wanted to adopt Mark. Hal refused to agree, and he returned to California, leaving Mark in Iowa, with Mark's future a subject of disagreement between Painter and the Bannisters.

Hal married Marylyn in November. In May they drove to Ames. The Bannisters refused to give up Mark, and Hal went to see a local attorney, who advised him just to take Mark. Hal and Marylyn tried to take Mark from Mark's school but were prevented from doing so since only the person who had registered a child at the school could remove him. Hal's attorney then sought writ of habeas corpus.

Hal reports that litigation eventually cost more than $3,500 at a time when he was making about $8,500 a year. (His attorney worked at reduced rates.) He says he could not afford to hire a psychologist to counter Dr. Hawks' testimony. The trial lasted five days and apparently involved testimony not just from Hawks but evidence gathered by the Bannisters about Hal's life up to that point and depositions Hal had gathered on the same subject. Hal testified; Mr. and Mrs. Bannister testified, as did their housekeeper, their neighbor, and the school bus driver (who was also the minister of the Congregational church at which Mr. Bannister taught Sunday school).

About two weeks after the trial, the trial judge awarded Hal custody. The Bannisters appealed and won. The Iowa Supreme Court heard the case in October 1965; its decision issued in February 1966. The decision received national attention. This reaction is summarized in a case comment in 79 Harv L Rev 1710, 1711 n3 (1966):

> The popular press ... has allowed its alarm at the tone which underlies the opinion to obscure ... possible justifications for the decision. See, *e.g.*, The New Yorker, April 2, 1966, p. 36:
>
>> I have a small daughter, you know, as well as a foreign car, and I tell you I dare not put the one inside the other and drive to Iowa for very fear that some party of milk-fed vigilantes will stop the car, wrest the child from me, and install her in some Iowagonconian institution where they will initiate her into the twin mysteries of raising corn and fattening hogs. I have, in fact, told my little girl

that she will never see Iowa. Naturally, it came as a frightful blow, but you will be happy to hear that she is able to sit up now and take a little clear broth.

McCall's magazine apparently paid Hal to agree to an interview with Jessica Mitford, a defense fund was formed, and a lawyer from the Washington firm of Covington & Burling offered to handle a petition to the United States Supreme Court. In November 1966, the Court denied the petition.

SECTION 2. THE BEST–INTEREST STANDARD AND THE PROBLEM OF DISCRETION

The good lady, for a moment, made no reply: her silence was a grim judgement of the whole point of view. "Poor little monkey!" she at last exclaimed; and the words were an epitaph for the tomb of Maisie's childhood. She was abandoned to her fate. What was clear to any spectator was that the only link binding her to either parent was this lamentable fact of her being a ready vessel for bitterness, a deep little porcelain cup in which biting acids could be mixed. They had wanted her not for any good they could do her, but for the harm they could, with her unconscious aid, do each other. She should serve their anger and seal their revenge, for husband and wife had been alike crippled by the heavy hand of justice, which in the last resort met on neither side their indignant claim to get, as they called it, everything.

Henry James
What Maisie Knew

A. STATING THE PROBLEM

The judge and the widow went to law to get the court to take me away from him and let one of them be my guardian; but it was a new judge that had just come, and he didn't know the old man; so he said courts mustn't interfere and separate families if they can help it; said he'd druther not take a child away from its father. So Judge Thatcher and the widow had to quit on the business.

That pleased the old man till he couldn't rest. He said he'd cowhide me till I was black and blue if I didn't raise some money for him. I borrowed three dollars from Judge Thatcher, and pap took it and got drunk and went a-blowing around and cussing and whooping and carrying on; and he kept it up all over town, with a tin pan, till most midnight; then they jailed him, and next day they had him before court, and jailed him again for a week. But he said he was satisfied; said he was boss of his son, and he'd make it warm for him.

Mark Twain
Huckleberry Finn

As you learned in *Painter*, the standard rule of American law is that disputes over the custody of a child should be resolved according to the best interests of the child. However, this broadly phrased standard lacks the specific content which might accurately guide courts. In this Section, we will do two things. First, we will survey the law of child custody. Second, we will examine a central criticism of that law's best-interest standard—namely, that it is indeterminate and therefore unsatisfactory. We will thus try to understand how the standard is applied, how well it works, and whether it can be given more precise content. In particular, we will ask whether the best-interest standard can be given greater specificity by being put in terms of rules or in terms of rights. We will review some of the most influential attempts to amplify or replace the best-interest standard and cases in which those attempts have been applied. In reading them, you should remember you have two goals. The first is to learn the doctrines for which the cases stand. The other is to get a sense of the kind of problems courts confront in applying the best-interest standard so that you may think fruitfully about the indeterminacy problem.

B. THE PROBLEM OF DISCRETION: THE SOLUTION OF RULES AND RIGHTS

[T]hanks to the limited desire for its company expressed by the step-parent, the law of its little life, its being entertained in rotation by its father and its mother, wouldn't easily prevail. Whereas each of these persons had at first vindictively desired to keep it from the other, so at present the re-married relative sought now rather to be rid of it—that is to leave it as much as possible, and beyond the appointed times and seasons, on the hands of the adversary; which malpractice, resented by the latter as bad faith, would of course be repaid and avanged by an equal treachery. The wretched infant was thus to find itself practically disowned, rebounding from racquet to racquet like a tennis-ball or a shuttlecock.

Henry James
What Maisie Knew

Insofar as the best-interest standard is indeterminate, child-custody cases are likely to be decided according to the discretion of the trial judge. This is not necessarily bad. However, even the judge will need some criteria to use in deciding what the child's best interest is. And perhaps those criteria should be legislatively or judicially imposed on trial judges. How then, might we govern judicial discretion? Two methods are generally available. The first is to write rules that constrain discretion. These rules might either amplify the meaning of the best-interest standard or set up a different standard. The second method is to acknowledge the claims of some contenders for custody that they have rights either to custody or to some special consideration in custody disputes. (Of course, these two methods may be combined in a variety of ways. For example, the presumption that a mother ought to be accorded custody of her young children has often been justified both on the grounds that doing so will serve the best interests of the children and that the mother has a special entitlement to custody the father does not.)

(1) An Opening Statement

We begin considering the tension between discretion, rules, and rights with a lucid statement of the indeterminacy of the best-interest standard and of the advantages and disadvantages of reducing that indeterminacy through rules.

ROBERT H. MNOOKIN
CHILD CUSTODY ADJUDICATION: JUDICIAL FUNCTIONS IN THE FACE OF INDETERMINACY

39 Law and Contemporary Problems 227 (1975)

II. An Analysis of Present-day Custody Standards

A. How Custody Disputes Contrast With Traditional Adjudication

At the core of adjudication is the notion that government exercises authority through a process in which the persons affected can participate. Each party has an "institutionally guaranteed ... opportunity to present proofs and arguments for a decision in his favor." A neutral judge resolves the dispute by ascertaining past events and evaluating those past events against articulated and described legal standards that are generally applicable. As part of this process, the judge is obliged to reconcile the rules used to evaluate these past events with those announced and applied in earlier disputes of the same sort. The parties then usually may ask some higher court to review the decision to determine whether the appropriate rules were applied and, to a limited extent, whether the past events were accurately ascertained. Child-custody disputes resolved under the broad best-interests-of-the-child principle differ from this model of adjudication in several closely interrelated ways.

1. *"Person–Oriented" Not "Act–Oriented" Determinations*

The first and most striking difference relates to a distinction suggested by Lon Fuller: custody disputes under the best-interests principle require "person-oriented," not "act-oriented," determinations. Most legal rules require determination of some event and are thus "act-oriented." A "person-oriented" rule, on the other hand, requires an evaluation of the "whole person viewed as a social being." Several of the other important ways in which child-custody disputes differ from the paradigm of adjudication follow from this feature of person-rather than act-orientation.

Normally, adjudication involves application of act-oriented rules and thus avoids broad evaluation of a litigant as a social being. For example, in a dispute in which Adams sues Brown alleging that Brown trespassed on land that Adams owns, Brown may defend on the ground that Adams six years earlier had given him permission to cross over the land and that Brown had done so daily ever since. To decide this case, a judge will seek to determine what actually happened between Adams and Brown. If the evidence indicates that in some way Adams may have assented to Brown's entering the property, the judge will consider what act or acts are sufficient to make entry lawful. Is acquiescence enough? For how long must it take place? Does the law require some formal means of granting permission in order to grant a permanent right to cross the Adams property? In deciding this kind of litigation, it will not be remotely relevant which disputant has more money, is more humane, works harder, gives more to charity, follows better religious practices, or takes better care of his house. The resolution will only be person-oriented to the extent that the judge must evaluate each as a social being in order to determine whether one should be considered more credible than the other.

Resolution of a custody dispute by the best-interests-of-the-child principle stands in sharp contrast to the foregoing. In a divorce custody, fight, a court *must* evaluate the attitudes, dispositions, capacities, and shortcomings of each parent to apply the best-interest standard. Indeed, the inquiry centers on what kind of person each parent is, and what the child is like. That there is, however, nothing inherent in custody disputes requiring resolution by a person-oriented rule is shown by the nineteenth-century examples of act-oriented rules for custody disputes between a child's parents.

2. *Predictions Not Determinations of Past Acts*

Adjudication usually requires the determination of past acts and facts, not a prediction of *future* events. Applying the best-interests standard requires an individualized prediction: with whom will this child be better off in the years to come? Proof of what happened in the past is relevant only insofar as it enables the court to decide what is likely to happen in the future. While most disputes resolved by adjudication do not require predictions, there are other areas of the law that involve legal standards that do. The standards governing preventive detention, pretrial detention, and sentencing are conspicuous examples. The Clayton Act by its terms condemns practices where "the effect ... may be substantially to lessen competition, or to tend to create a monopoly." Where courts are required to make predictions, however, they often attempt to formulate rules of thumb or presumptions that make the outcome turn in a systematic way on the showing of certain ascertainable facts about the past. Under the Clayton Act, for example, rules for horizontal mergers, in effect, presume adverse competitive effects from a demonstration that the merging companies presently have a particular share of existing markets. More generally, when courts are required to make predictions, they often attempt to develop subsidiary rules that relate certain ascertainable facts about the present or past in a systematic way to the future. They thus do not purport to make individualized predictions, but rather apply rules.

3. *Interdependence of Outcome—Affecting Factors*

Because custody disputes involve *relationships* between people, a decision affecting any one of the parties will often necessarily have an effect on the others. The resolution of a custody dispute may permanently affect—or even end—the parties' legal relationship; but the social and psychological relationships will usually continue. The best-interests principle requires a prediction of what will happen in the future, which, of course, depends in part on the future behavior of the parties. Because these parties will often interact in the future, this probable interaction must be taken into account in deciding what the outcome is to be. For example, awarding custody to the mother may affect the father's behavior, which, in turn, can affect the mother's behavior and the child. The possibility of such feedback must be considered in applying the best-interests standard. Most disputes resolved by adjudication do not require predictions involving appraisals of future relationships where the "loser's" future behavior can be an important ingredient.

4. *Findings, Precedent, and Appellate Review*

A determination that is person-oriented and requires predictions necessarily involves an evaluation of the parties who have appeared in court. This has important consequences for the roles of both precedent and appellate review in custody cases. The result of an earlier case involving different people has limited relevance to a subsequent case requiring individualized evaluations of a particular child and the litigants. Prior reported cases now provide little basis for controlling or predicting the outcome of a particular case. Moreover, the trial court in custody disputes is often not required to make specific findings of fact, much less write an opinion about the case or reconcile what has been done in this case with what has happened before.

All of this makes the scope of appellate review extremely limited. Because the trial court's decision involves an assessment of the personality, character, and relationship of people the judge has seen in court, appellate courts are extremely loath to upset the trial court's determination on the basis of a transcript. In the words of an English judge, "So much may turn, consciously or unconsciously, on estimates of character which cannot be made by those who have not seen or heard the parties." As Professor Fuller has written, "It would be hard [for an appellate court to pass an intelligent judgment on the trial court's decision] unless it were prepared to summon the husband, wife and child before it and try the case over again." For this reason, the often-stated rule is that an appellate court cannot interfere with the determination of a trial judge in a custody dispute unless the lower court has exercised its discretion on some wrong general principle or taken an inappropriate factor into account. But since only the broadest principle is typically announced in these decisions, it is difficult to know when a trial judge has acted upon some inappropriate principle or factor. Constrained little by precedent or appellate review, the trial court's discretion is very wide indeed.

5. *Participation by All Affected Parties*

Normally, parties most obviously affected by a dispute have a right to participate in the adjudicatory process. The issue in a child-custody dispute is what will become of the child, but ordinarily the child is not a true participant in the process. While the best-interests principle requires that the primary focus be on the interests of the child, the child ordinarily does not define those interests himself, nor does he have representation in the ordinary sense. Even in states that allow for independent representation for the child in the dispute, the role of the child's advocate is different from that in normal adjudication. A lawyer usually looks to his client for instructions about the goals to be pursued. Except in the case of older children, a child's representative in a custody dispute must himself normally define the child's interests.

B. The Indeterminacy of Present-day Standards

Lon Fuller has suggested that when a judge decides about custody under the best-interests principle, he is:

> [N]ot applying law or legal rules at all, but is exercising administrative discretion which by its nature cannot be rule-bound. The statutory admonitions to decide the question of custody so as to advance the welfare of the child is as remote from being a rule of law as an instruction to the manager of a state-owned factory that he should follow the principle of maximizing output at the least cost to the state.

Insofar as a court assumes responsibility for seeing how a child is to be raised, it is assuming a managerial role.

When a judge must resolve a custody dispute, he is committed to making a choice among alternatives. The very words of the best-interests-of-the-child principle suggest that the judge should decide by choosing the alternative that "maximizes" what is best for a particular child. Conceived this way, the judge's decision can be framed in a manner consistent with an intellectual tradition that views the decision process as a problem of rational choice. In analyzing the custody decision from this perspective, my purpose is not to describe how judges in fact decide custody disputes nor to propose a method of how they should. Instead, it is to expose the inherent indeterminacy of the best-interests standard.

1. *Rational Choice*

Decision theorists have laid out the logic of rational choice with clarity and mathematical rigor for prototype decision problems. The decision-maker specifies alternative outcomes associated with different courses of action and then chooses that alternative that "maximizes" his values, subject to whatever constraints the decision-maker faces. This involves two critical assumptions: first, that the decision-maker can specify alternative outcomes for each course of action; the second, that the decision-maker can assign to each outcome a "utility" measure that integrates his values and allows comparisons among alternative outcomes. Choice does not require certainty about the single outcome that will in fact flow from a particular action. Treating uncertainty as a statistical problem, models have been developed that allow decisions to be made on the basis of "expected" utility. This requires that the decision-maker be able to specify the probability of each possible outcome for a particular course of action. The utility of each possible outcome is then discounted by its probability.

Decision-making under this model also implies certain things about the process. The decision-maker will be receptive and sensitive to informational requirements and will modify his outcome calculations as new information becomes available:

> The quintessential analytic decision-maker is one who strains towards as complete an understanding as possible of the causal forces which determine outcomes. He seeks to predict the flow of events and, where he has leverage, to manipulate them to his advantage. The processing of information on making decisions is all done for the purposes of constructing and improving the blueprint from which the optimal choice emerges.

Unlike adjudication, rational choice does *not* require participation of the affected parties, the use of precedents or rules, or review; today's decision need not be reconciled with similar decisions made earlier.

2. *A Custody Determination Under the Best–Interests-of-the-Child Principle*

Assume that a judge must decide whether a child should live with his mother or his father when the parents are in the process of obtaining a divorce. From the perspective of rational choice, the judge would wish to compare the expected utility for the child of living with his mother with that of living with his father. The judge would need considerable information and predictive ability to do this. The judge would also need some source for the values to measure utility for the child. All three are problematic.

a. The Need for Information: Specifying Possible Outcomes

In the example chosen, the judge would require information about how each parent had behaved in the past, how this behavior had affected the child, and the child's present condition. Then the judge would need to predict the future behavior and circumstances of each parent if the child were to remain with that parent and to gauge the effects of this behavior and these circumstances on the child. He would also have to consider the behavior of each parent if the child were to live with the other parent and how this might affect the child. If a custody award to one parent would require removing the child from his present circumstances, school, friends, and familiar surrounding, the judge would necessarily wish to predict the effects these changes would have on the child. These predictions would necessarily involve estimates of not only the child's mutual relationships with the custodial parent, but also his future contacts with the other parent and siblings, the probable number of visits by the noncustodial spouse, the probable financial circumstances of each of the spouses, and a myriad of other factors.

One can question how often, if ever, any judge will have the necessary information. In many instances, a judge lacks adequate information about even the most rudimentary aspects of a child's life with his parents and has still less information available about what either parent plans in the future. This is particularly true in many juvenile court proceedings where, at the time of the dispositional hearing, the judge typically has no information about where the child will be placed if removal is ordered. The judge usually knows nothing about either the characteristics of the foster family or how long that family will want or be able to keep the child. Indeed, in these custody cases, the court is normally comparing an existing family with an unknown alternative.

b. Predictions Assessing the Probability of Alternative Outcomes

Obviously, more than one outcome is possible for each course of judicial action, so the judge must assess the probability of various outcomes and evaluate the seriousness of possible benefits and harms associated with each. But even where a judge has substantial information about the child's past home life and the present alternatives, present-day knowledge about human behavior provides no basis for the kind of individualized predictions required by the best-interests standard. There are numerous competing theories of human behavior, based on radically different conceptions of the nature of man, and no consensus exists that any one is correct. No theory at all is considered widely capable of generating reliable predictions about the psychological and behavioral consequences of alternative dispositions for a particular child.

While psychiatrists and psychoanalysts have at times been enthusiastic in claiming for themselves the largest possible role in custody proceedings, many have conceded that their theories provide no reliable guide for predictions about what is likely to happen to a particular child. Anna Freud, who has devoted her life to the study of the child and who plainly believes that theory can be a useful guide to treatment, has warned: "In spite of ... advances there remain factors which make clinical foresight, *i.e.*, prediction, difficult and hazardous," not the least of which is that "environmental happenings in a child's life will always remain unpredictable since they are not governed by any known laws. . . ."

The difficulty of making accurate predictions is shown clearly by a study undertaken by Joan Macfarlane and her associates in Berkeley, California. Using various tests and interviews, the Berkeley group, during a thirty-year period, studied a group of 166 infants born in 1929. Their objective was to observe the growth—emotional, mental, and physical—of normal people. As Arlene Skolnick observed, "Over the years this study has generated several significant research findings, but the most surprising of all was the difficulty of predicting what thirty-year-old adults would be like even after the most sophisticated data had been gathered on them as children."

Various studies have attempted to trace personality development to specific antecedent variables to show that these variables have the same effects on different children. This connection is now widely questioned by experimental psychologists such as H. R. Schaffer, who thinks that infants experience external events in individual ways. The implication of this for prediction is described very well by Skolnick: "[I]f the child selectively interprets situations and events, we cannot confidently predict behavior from knowledge of the situation alone."

c. Values to Inform Choice: Assigning Utilities to Various Outcomes

Even if the various outcomes could be specified and their probability estimated, a fundamental problem would remain unsolved. What set of values should a judge use to determine what is in a child's best interests? If a decision-maker must assign some measure of utility to each possible outcome, how is utility to be determined?

For many decisions in an individualistic society, one asks the person affected what he wants. Applying this notion to custody cases, the child could be asked to specify those values or even to choose. In some cases, especially those involving divorce, the child's preference is sought and given weight. But to make the child responsible for the choice may jeopardize his future relationship with the other parent. And we often lack confidence that the child has the capacity and the maturity appropriately to determine his own utility.

Moreover, whether or not the judge looks to the child for some guidance, there remains the question whether best interests should be viewed from a long-term or a short-term perspective. The conditions that make a person happy at age seven to ten may have adverse consequences at age thirty. Should the judge ask himself what decision will make the child happiest in the next year? Or at thirty? Or at seventy? Should the judge decide by thinking about what decision the child as an adult looking back would have wanted made? In this case, the preference problem is formidable, for how is the judge to compare "happiness" at one age with "happiness" at another age?

Deciding what is best for a child poses a question no less ultimate than the purposes and values of life itself. Should the judge be primarily concerned with the child's happiness? Or with the child's spiritual and religious training? Should the judge be concerned with the economic "productivity" of the child when he grows up? Are the primary values of life in warm, interpersonal relationships, or in discipline and self-sacrifice? Is stability and security for a child more desirable than intellectual stimulation? These questions could be elaborated endlessly. And yet, where is the judge to look for the set of values that should inform the choice of what is best for the child? Normally, the custody statutes do not themselves give content or relative weights to the pertinent values. And if the judge looks to society at large, he finds neither a clear consensus as to the best child rearing strategies nor an appropriate hierarchy of ultimate values.

It thus seems clear that a judge in a child-custody case is in a more difficult position than Professor Fuller's factory manager told to maximize his output or profits. While the factory manager's problems of prediction are formidable, he at least has a measure to compare the relative value of possible outcomes. Physical output or money profits, given existing resources, can be maximized. But in a child-custody dispute, what comparable measure does a judge have in a society that lacks a clearly defined and integrated set of values about what is good for particular individuals?

3. *Why Some Custody Cases Are Easy to Decide*

An inquiry about what is best for a child often yields indeterminate results because of the problems of having adequate information, making the necessary predictions, and finding an integrated set of values by which to choose. But some custody cases may still be comparatively easy to decide. While there is no consensus about what is best for a child, there is much consensus about what is very bad (*e.g.*, physical abuse); some short-term predictions about human behavior can be reliably made (*e.g.*, chronic alcoholism or psychosis is difficult quickly to modify). Asking which alternative is in the best interests of a child may have a rather clear-cut answer in situations where one claimant exposes the child to substantial risks of immediate harm and the other claimant already has a substantial personal relationship with the child and poses no such risk. In a private dispute between two parents, for example, if a judge could predict that one parent's conduct would seriously endanger the child's health, it would not be difficult to conclude that the child's expected utility would be higher if he went with the other parent, whose conduct did not, even without the necessity of defining utility carefully. More generally, where one alternative plainly risks irreversible effects on the child that are bad and the other does not, there is no need to make longer-term predictions or more complicated psychological evaluations of what is likely to happen to the child's personality.

But to be easy, a case must involve only one claimant who is well known to the child and whose conduct does not endanger the child. If there are two such claimants or none, difficult choices remain. Most custody disputes pose difficult choices. In child-neglect cases, for example, the existing home may clearly be far from "optimal," but placing the child with a foster family unknown to the child poses serious risks as well. Without knowing the long-term effects of foster care on children, for example, how is the judge to decide in all but the most obvious cases whether a four-year-old child is better off removed from the parental custody of neglectful parents whose conduct does not endanger the child's physical health? And in many private disputes, the court must often choose between parties who each offer advantages and disadvantages, knowing that to deprive the child completely of either relationship will be disruptive. In a divorce custody fight, for example, where the mother is overprotective, possessive, and insecure and the father is demanding, aggressive, and hard-driving, how is the judge to decide where to place a seven-year-old child?

III. Implications of Indeterminacy

A. Would Rules Be Better?

Custody disputes are now decided on the basis of broad, person-oriented principles that ask for highly individualized determinations. The trial judge has broad discretion, but the question asked often has no meaningful answer. What are some of the implications of the use of indeterminate standards in custody disputes? Would more precise standards that ask an answerable question be better? As Professors Hart and Sacks have noted, even where a general standard is "avowedly indeterminate," a legislature or court may develop "subsidiary guides" that "take the form both of more nearly precise principles and policies ... and of specific rules and standards." Indeed, a normal element of the adjudicatory process is the formulation of intermediate premises or rules that are then tested and elaborated by application in individual cases.

More rule-like standards would avoid or mitigate some obvious disadvantages of adjudication by an indeterminate principle. For one thing, the use of an indeterminate standard makes the outcome of litigation difficult to predict. This may encourage more litigation than would a standard that made the outcome of more cases predictable. Because each divorcing parent can often make plausible arguments why a child would be better off with him or her, a best-interests standard probably creates a greater incentive to litigate than would a rule that children should go to the parent of the same sex. Similarly, a broad, individualized child-neglect standard that gives very great discretion to a juvenile court to remove a child from parental custody, may encourage social workers, probation officers, and other state officials to seek intervention in a broader range of cases than might a narrow standard.

An indeterminate standard raises a number of questions related to fairness that better defined and less discretionary standards could minimize. Inherent in the application of a broad, person-oriented principle is the risk of retroactive application of a norm of which the parties affected will have had no advance notice. This may be unfair because (1) the private parties may have no opportunity to conform their private conduct to the norm subsequently applied by a particular judge; and (2) during the litigation itself, a party may not have an opportunity to address or question the aspect of the case that the court uses as a basis for decision.

Indeterminate standards also pose an obviously greater risk of violating the fundamental precept that like cases should be decided alike. Because people differ and no two custody cases are exactly alike, the claim can be made that no process is more fair than one requiring resolution by a highly individualized, person-oriented standard. But with an indeterminate standard, the same case presented to different judges may easily result in different decisions. The use of an indeterminate standard means that state officials may decide on the basis of unarticulated (perhaps even unconscious) predictions and preferences that could be questioned if expressed. Because of the scope of discretion under such a standard, there is a substantial risk that decisions will be made on the basis of values not widely shared in our society, even among judges.

A simulation study that analyzed the factors influencing the decision whether to provide a child with certain services within the child's own home or instead remove the child to foster care demonstrates the risks of a broadly discretionary standard. In this study, three child welfare professionals, each with at least five years' experience, were independently given the actual files for ninety-four children from fifty families. Each was asked to decide whether the child should be removed from parental custody and put into foster care or whether, instead, services should be provided within the home. The three agreed in less than one-half of the cases (forty-five out of ninety-four). Even more significantly, when each was asked to indicate the factors influencing the decision, the study concluded, "even in cases in which they agreed on the decision, [they] did not identify the same factors as determinate."

This analysis shows the importance of who has the authority to decide what is best for a particular child, and under what circumstances. Today, custody disputes are ultimately assigned to courts for resolution, suggesting that a trial judge has the primary authority to decide, although it is not clear how decision-making responsibility is in fact shared by the trial judge with various other professionals (social workers, psychologists, psychiatrists) who also participate in the process. Implicit in some suggested reforms is the notion that the power to decide should be shifted from the judge to some other state official with different professional training. While judges may be ill-equipped to develop and evaluate information about the child, having some other state official decide or making various procedural adjustments (such as giving counsel to the child, providing better staff to courts, or making the proceedings more or less formal) will not cure the root problem. The indeterminacy flows from our inability to predict accurately human behavior and from a lack of social consensus about the values that should inform the decision. Procedural adjustments may make the system fairer and more efficient and may avoid some conspicuously erroneous determinations—goals worth pursuing. But neither greater use of existing expertise nor better procedures will make an indeterminate question answerable for an individual case.

Unlike procedural changes, adjudication by a more determinate rule would confront the fundamental problems posed by an indeterminate principle. But the choice between indeterminate standards and more precise rules poses a profound dilemma. The absence of rules removes the special burdens of justification and formulation of standards characteristic of adjudication. Unfairness and adverse consequences can result. And yet, rules that relate past events or conduct to legal consequences may themselves create substantial difficulties in the custody area. Our inadequate knowledge about human behavior and our inability to generalize confidently about the relationship between past events or conduct and future behavior make the formulation of rules especially problematic. Moreover, the very lack of consensus about values that makes the best-interests standard indeterminate may also make the formulation of rules inappropriate: a legal rule must, after all, reflect some social value or values. An overly ambitious and indeterminate principle may result in fewer decisions that reflect what is known to be desirable. But rules may result in some conspicuously bad decisions that could be avoided by a more discretionary standard. What balance should be struck?

Notes and Questions on the Best–Interest Standard

Many criticisms of the best-interest standard and of child-custody decision-making can be understood in terms of the rationales for the principle of family autonomy with which you are by now familiar. Consider, for example, the following:

The Privacy Problem. Child-custody decisions are likely to intrude on a family's privacy in many ways. Like any investigation by a public agency into a family, the child-custody decisions expose family members to public (or at least semi-public) scrutiny of their lives. But attempts to discover where the child's best interests lie often demand a deeper scrutiny of people's lives and feelings in the form of investigations by psychologists or psychiatrists. Decision-makers commonly want to inquire into feelings which family members may prefer to keep from each other and even from themselves. A hint of these problems may be sensed from a story of one former family-court judge:

> The last case I decided as a family court judge involved a schizophrenic mother, diagnosed by some expert witnesses as being in remission but by others as having residual symptoms. She was intelligent and lucid.... This mother had what most parents in her situation lack: an assertive attorney who would neither concede the case on the basis of the diagnosis nor take the mother through the motions of a *pro forma* defense. She was therefore required to sit through four days of testimony designed to prove her worst fear: that she was hopelessly insane.

Peggy C. Davis, *Use and Abuse of the Power to Sever Family Bonds*, 12 Rev L & Soc Change 557, 557–58 (1983–84). This example suggests how the criticisms of the best-interest standard we have been reviewing might be understood in terms of the privacy problem. How can they also be understood in terms of the information, expertise, standards, and exacerbation problems and the autonomy and pluralism principles?

(2) A Statutory Solution

We have seen two academics trying to cope with the problem of discretion and the best-interest standard; let us now see how our two exemplars of modern trends in the law—the UMDA and the ALI Principles—try to cope with it.

UNIFORM MARRIAGE AND DIVORCE ACT

Section 401. [*Jurisdiction; Commencement of Proceeding.*]

(d) A child custody proceeding is commenced in the [________] court:

(1) by a parent, by filing a petition

(i) for dissolution or legal separation; or

(ii) for custody of the child in the [county, judicial district] in which he is permanently resident or found; or

(2) by a person other than a parent, by filing a petition for custody of the child in the [county, judicial district] in which he is permanently resident or found, but only if he is not in the physical custody of one of his parents.

Section 402. [*Best Interest of Child.*]

The court shall determine custody in accordance with the best interest of the child. The court shall consider all relevant factors including:

(1) the wishes of the child's parent or parents as to his custody;

(2) the wishes of the child as to his custodian;

(3) the interaction and interrelationship of the child with his parent or parents, his siblings, and any other person who may significantly affect the child's best interest;

(4) the child's adjustment to his home, school, and community; and

(5) the mental and physical health of all individuals involved.

The court shall not consider conduct of a proposed custodian that does not affect this relationship to the child.

Section 404. [*Interviews.*]

(a) The court may interview the child in chambers to ascertain the child's wishes as to his custodian and as to visitation. The court may permit counsel to be present at the interview. The court shall cause a record of the interview to be made and to be part of the record in the case.

(b) The court may seek the advice of professional personnel, whether or not employed by the court on a regular basis. The advice given shall be in writing and made available by the court to counsel upon request. Counsel may examine as a witness any professional personnel consulted by the court.

Section 405. [*Investigations and Reports.*]

(a) In contested custody proceedings, and in other custody proceedings if a parent or the child's custodian so requests, the court may order an investigation and report concerning custodial arrangements for the child. The investigation and report may be made by [the court social service agency, the staff of the juvenile court, the local probation or welfare department, or a private agency employed by the court for the purpose].

(b) In preparing his report concerning a child, the investigator may consult any person who may have information about the child and his potential custodial arrangements. Upon order of the court, the investigator may refer the child to professional personnel for diagnosis. The investigator may consult with and obtain information from medical, psychiatric, or other expert persons who have served the child in the past without obtaining the consent of the parent or the child's custodian;

but the child's consent must be obtained if he has reached the age of 16, unless the court finds that he lacks mental capacity to consent. If the requirements of subsection (c) are fulfilled, the investigator's report may be received in evidence at the hearing.

Section 407. [*Visitation.*]

(a) A parent not granted custody of the child is entitled to reasonable visitation rights unless the court finds, after a hearing, that visitation would endanger seriously the child's physical, mental, moral, or emotional health.

(b) The court may modify an order granting or denying visitation rights whenever modification would serve the best interest of the child; but the court shall not restrict a parent's visitation rights unless it finds that the visitation would endanger seriously the child's physical, mental, moral, or emotional health.

Section 408. [*Judicial Supervision.*]

(a) Except as otherwise agreed by the parties in writing at the time of the custody decree, the custodian may determine the child's upbringing, including his education, health care, and religious training, unless the court after hearing, finds, upon motion by the noncustodial parent, that in the absence of a specific limitation of the custodian's authority, the child's physical health would be endangered or his emotional development significantly impaired.

(b) If both parents or all contestants agree to the order, or if the court finds that in the absence of the order the child's physical health would be endangered or his emotional development significantly impaired, the court may order the [local probation or welfare department, court social service agency] to exercise continuing supervision over the case to assure that the custodial or visitation terms of the decree are carried out.

Section 409. [*Modification.*]

(a) No motion to modify a custody decree may be made earlier than 2 years after its date, unless the court permits it to be made on the basis of affidavits that there is reason to believe the child's present environment may endanger seriously his physical, mental, moral, or emotional health.

(b) If a court of this State has jurisdiction pursuant to the Uniform Child Custody Jurisdiction Act, the court shall not modify a prior custody decree unless it finds, upon the basis of facts that have risen since the prior decree or that were unknown to the court at the time of entry of the prior decree, that a change has occurred in the circumstances of the child or his custodian, and that the modification is necessary to serve the best interest of the child. In applying these standards the court shall retain the custodian appointed pursuant to the prior decree unless:

(1) The custodian agrees to the modification;

(2) the child has been integrated into the family of the petitioner with consent of the custodian; or

(3) the child's present environment endangers seriously his physical, mental, moral, or emotional health, and the harm likely to be caused by a change of environment is outweighed by its advantages to him.

(c) Attorney fees and costs shall be assessed against a party seeking modification if the court finds that the modification action is vexatious and constitutes harassment.

AMERICAN LAW INSTITUTE PRINCIPLES OF MARITAL DISSOLUTION

2002

§ 2.02 Objectives

(1) The primary objective of this Chapter is to serve the child's best interests.

(2) A secondary objective of this Chapter is to achieve fairness between the parents.

§ 2.03 Definitions

For purposes of this Chapter, the following definitions apply.

(1) Unless otherwise specified, a *parent* is either a legal parent, a parent by estoppel, or a de facto parent.

(a) A *legal parent* is an individual who is defined as a parent under other state law.

(b) A *parent by estoppel* is an individual who, though not a legal parent, is

(i) liable for child support under Chapter 3; or

(ii) lived with the child for at least two years and

(a) over that period had a reasonable good-faith belief that he was the child's biological father, based on marriage to the mother or on the actions or representations of the mother, and fully accepted parental responsibilities consistent with that belief, and

(b) thereafter continued to make reasonable, good faith efforts to accept responsibilities as the child's father, even if that belief no longer existed; or

(iii) lived with the child since the child's birth, holding out and accepting full and permanent responsibilities as a parent, as part of a prior co-parenting agreement with the child's legal parent (or, if there are two legal parents, both parents) to raise a child together each with full parental rights and responsibilities, when the court finds that recognition as a parent is in the child's best interests; or

(iv) lived with the child for at least two years, holding out and accepting full and permanent responsibilities as a parent, pursuant to an agreement with the child's parent (or, if there are two legal parents, both parents), when the court finds that recognition as a parent is in the child's best interests.

(c) A de facto parent is an individual other than a legal parent or a parent by estoppel who, for a significant period of time not less than two years,

(i) lived with the child and,

(ii) for reasons primarily other than financial compensation, and with the agreement of a legal parent to form a parent-child relationship, or as a result of a complete failure or inability of any legal parent to perform caretaking functions,

(a) regularly performed a majority of the caretaking functions for the child, or

(b) regularly performed a share of caretaking functions at least as great as that of the parent with whom the child primarily lived.

[There is no 2.]

(3) A parenting plan is a set of provisions for allocation of residential responsibility and decision-making authority on behalf of a child and for resolution of subsequent disputes between the parents.

(4) Residential responsibility refers to physical custodianship and supervision of a child. It usually includes, but does not necessarily require, overnight responsibility.

(5) Decision-making authority refers to authority for making significant life decisions on behalf of the child, including the child's education and health care.

(6) Caretaking functions are tasks that contribute to the care of the child and involve interaction with the child or decisionmaking on the child's behalf, such as

(a) meal preparation and feeding, bedtime and wake-up routines, care of child when sick or hurt, bathing, grooming, personal hygiene, dressing, recreation and play, physical safety, transportation, and other functions that meet the daily physical needs of the child;

(b) direction of the child's various developmental needs, including the acquisition of motor and language skills, toilet training, self-confidence and maturation;

(c) discipline, instruction in manners, assignment and supervision of chores, and other tasks that attend to the child's needs for behavioral control and self-restraint;

(d) arrangement of the child's education, including remedial or special services appropriate to the child's needs and interests and supervision of homework;

(e) the development and maintenance of appropriate interpersonal relationships with peers, siblings, and adults;

(f) arrangement of health care;

(g) moral guidance; and

(h) arrangement and supervision of alternative care by a family member, baby-sitter, or other child care provider or facility.

(7) Parenting functions are tasks that serve the needs of the child or the child's residential family, including

(a) caretaking functions, as defined in paragraph (6);

(b) provision of economic support;

(c) participation in decision-making regarding the child's welfare;

(d) maintenance or improvement of the family residence, home or furniture repair, home improvement projects, car repair and maintenance, yard work, and house cleaning;

(e) financial planning and organization, food and clothing purchasing, cleaning and maintenance of clothing, and other tasks supporting the consumption and savings needs of the family; and

(f) other functions usually performed by a parent or guardian that are important to the child's welfare and development.

(8) Domestic Abuse is the infliction of physical injury, or of reasonable fear of physical injury, by a present or former member of a child's household against a child or another member of the household. The requirement that physical injury, or reasonable fear thereof, has been inflicted is satisfied by proof of conviction for crimes that the state shall designate for this purpose, including but not limited to the crimes of assault, battery, kidnapping, malicious mischief, reckless endangerment, sexual assault, rape, and stalking. Action taken by a person for reasonable self-protection, or the protection of another person, is not domestic abuse.

Topic 2 Parenting Plan

From Preliminary Draft No. 7, 1998

§ 2.06 Parenting Plan

(1) A parent seeking a judicial allocation of residential responsibility or decisionmaking authority under this Chapter should file with the court a proposed parenting plan. Two or more parents may file a joint plan. A plan not joined in by all parents should be supported by an affidavit containing, to the extent known or reasonably discoverable by the filing parent,

(a) the name, address, and length of residence of the person or persons with whom the child has lived for the 24 months preceding the filing of the action under this Chapter;

(b) the name and address of each of the child's parents and any other individuals with standing to participate in the action;

(c) a description of the allocation of caretaking and other parenting responsibilities performed by each person named in paragraphs (a) and (b) during the 24 months preceding the filing on an action under this Chapter;

(d) a description of the work and child-care schedules of any person seeking an allocation of residential responsibility, and any expected changes to these schedules in the near future;

(e) a description of the child's school and extra-curricular activities;

(f) a description of any of the circumstances set forth in § 2.13 which are present; and

(g) a description of the areas of agreement and disagreement with any other parenting plan submitted in the case.

(2) Upon motion of a parent and after consideration of the evidence, the court should order a parenting plan consistent with the provisions of §§ 2.09–2.14, containing

(a) a provision for the child's living arrangements and each parent's residential responsibility, which shall include either

(i) a residential schedule that designates in which parent's home each minor child will reside on given days of the year; or

(ii) a formula or method for determining such a schedule in sufficient detail that, if necessary, the schedule can be enforced in subsequent proceedings by the court.

(b) an allocation of decision-making authority as to significant matters reasonably likely to arise with respect to the child; and

(c) a provision consistent with § 2.08 for resolution of disputes that arise under the plan and for violations of the plan.

(3) A parenting plan may, at the court's discretion, contain provisions that address matters that are expected to arise in the event of a parent's relocation, or to provide for future modifications in the parenting plan if specified contingencies occur.

(4) Upon motion of a parent at any time prior to the order of a parenting plan, the court may order a temporary allocation of residential responsibility or decision-making authority as the court determines is in the child's best interests, considering the factors in §§ 2.09 and 2.10. Such an order ordinarily should not preclude access by a parent who has been exercising a reasonable share of parenting functions. Upon credible evidence of one or more of the circumstances set forth in § 2.13, the court shall issue a temporary order limiting or denying access by one

parent to the child, in order to protect the child or the other party, pending adjudication of the underlying facts.

§ 2.08 Court-ordered Services

(1) The court may inform the parents, or require them to be informed, about mediation or other non judicial procedures designed to help them achieve an agreement. The court may not require a parent to participate in mediation or in another non judicial procedure involving face-to-face negotiations.

(2) A mediator may not conduct a mediation, even by parental agreement, without first screening for domestic abuse. If credible evidence thereof exists, the mediator should take steps

(a) to ensure the voluntary consent of the victim of the abuse to participate in the mediation, and to any agreement reached as a result of the mediation; and

(b) to protect the safety of the victim.

(3) A mediator may not make a recommendation to the court and may not reveal information that either parent has disclosed during mediation under a reasonable expectation of confidentiality except, upon questioning by the court, if relevant to a finding under § 2.07 (1)(a) or (b).

(4) The court may require the parents to attend parenting education classes for instruction about the impact of family dissolution on children and on how to meet the needs of children facing family dissolution.

(5) The services or classes described under paragraphs (1) and (4) may be ordered only if available at no cost or at a cost that is reasonable in light of the financial circumstances of each parent. Where one parent's ability to pay for such services is significantly greater than the other, the court may order that parent to pay some or all of the expenses of the other.

§ 2.09 Criteria for Parenting Plan—Residential Provisions

(1) To the extent not resolved by an agreement by the parents under § 2.07, the court shall make residential provisions in the parenting plan that it determines are in the child's best interests, subject to § 2.13 and § 2.14, and in light of

(a) the caretaking functions each parent performed for the child before their separation or, if the child never lived with both parents, before the filing of the action;

(b) the amount of residential time that will allow the child to maintain a meaningful relationship with each parent;

(c) the quality of the emotional attachments of each parent to the child;

(d) each parent's attitudes and abilities with respect to the child, including the ability to provide for the child's special needs;

(e) the child's preference, taking into account the child's age and level of maturity and the reasonableness of the preference;

(f) significant relationships of the child, including those with siblings and other relatives;

(g) the proximity of the parents' residences, their schedules, and other factors relating to the child's need for stability at home, school, and in the community; and

(h) the conflict level between the parents and their willingness to cooperate with one another.

(2) In considering the factors set forth in paragraph (1), the court shall give greatest weight to factor (a), except that it shall allocate to a legal parent who has exercised a reasonable share of parenting functions for the child, sufficient residential responsibility to satisfy factor (b). Except as provided in this paragraph, other factors in paragraph (1) may not substantially override factors (a) and (b) unless shown to be necessary to the child's welfare. Unless the parents have agreed to it, the court shall not order provisions involving substantially equal amounts of residential responsibility if, upon consideration of factors (g) and (h) and the parents' economic circumstances, it determines that the provisions are not in the child's best interests or are impractical.

(3) If a parent relocates or proposes to relocate to a residence at a distance that will impair the ability of the other parent to exercise the amount of residential responsibility that would otherwise be ordered pursuant to paragraphs (1) and (2), the court shall consider the additional factors set forth in § 2.20(4).

(4) The provisions of paragraph (2), requiring the court to give greatest weight to the factor set forth in paragraph (1)(a), shall not take account of residential arrangement arising from temporary arrangements after separation, made either with or without a court order. The court may take account of the child's adjustment to the temporary arrangements and of deficiencies in the compliance of any parent with any temporary order or with the parents' consensual arrangements.

§ 2.13 Parenting Plan—Limiting Factors

(1) The court shall limit or deny access and responsibility of a parent who would otherwise be allocated responsibility under a parenting plan, to the extent required, to secure the safety and welfare of the child or of a child's parent, where it finds that interests of the child would be served by such limit or denial, in light of credible evidence that the parent to be limited

(a) has abused, neglected, or abandoned a child, as defined by state law;

(b) has inflicted domestic abuse, or allowed another to inflict domestic abuse, as defined in § 2.03(8);

(c) has an impairment resulting from drug, alcohol, or other substance abuse that interferes with the parent's ability to perform caretaking functions; or

(d) has interfered persistently with the other parent's access to the child, except in the case of actions taken in the good faith belief that they are necessary to protect the safety of child or the interfering parent or another family member, pending adjudication of the facts underlying that belief.

(2) Limitations imposed by the court under this section shall be reasonably calculated to protect the child or a child's parent from physical, sexual, or emotional abuse or harm. Among the limitations that the court shall consider are

(a) an adjustment of the residential responsibility of the parents, including the allocation of exclusive residential responsibility to one of them;

(b) supervision of contacts between the parent and the child;

(c) exchange of the child between parents through an intermediary, or in a protected setting;

(d) restraints on the parent from contacting or visiting the other parent or the child, including a denial of all contact between the parent and the child;

(e) a requirement that the parent complete a program of intervention for perpetrators of domestic violence, for drug or alcohol abuse, or program designed to correct another factor;

(f) a requirement that the parent abstain from possession or consumption of or non-prescribed drugs during the period of parent-child contact and in the24–hour period immediately preceding such contact;

(g) denial of overnight residential responsibility;

(h) restrictions on the presence of specific persons while the parent is with the child

(i) a requirement that the parent post a bond to secure return of the child following a period of parent-child contact or to secure other performance required by the court; or

(j) any other constraints or conditions that the court deems necessary to provide for the safety of the child, a child's parent, or any person whose safety immediately affects the child's welfare.

§ 2.14 Criteria for Parenting Plan—Prohibited Factors

In issuing orders under this Chapter, the court shall disregard

(1) the race or ethnicity of a parent or of the child, except as necessary to meet the child's special needs relating to the child's race or ethnicity;

(2) the sex of a parent or of the child, except as necessary to meet special developmental needs relating to the child's gender identity;

(3) the religion of a parent or of the child, except to the minimum degree necessary to protect a child from manifest harm or to protect the child's ability to practice a religion to which the child has made a substantial and meaningful commitment;

(4) the sexual conduct or sexual orientation of a parent, except as necessary to protect a child from demonstrated harm; and

(5) the parents' relative earning capacities or financial circumstances, except insofar as the combined financial resources of the parents set practical limits on the feasible residential arrangements.

§ 2.18 Modification Upon Showing of Changed Circumstances

(1) A court may modify a parenting plan order if it finds, on the basis of facts that were not known or have arisen since the entry of the order and were not anticipated in the parenting plan, that a substantial change has occurred in the circumstances of the child of one or both parents and that a modification is necessary to the child's welfare.

(2) A court may modify a parenting plan, even if it does not make the findings required in paragraph (1), if it finds that the plan is manifestly harmful to the child's best interests.

(3) Unless the parents have agreed otherwise, the following circumstances ordinarily do not justify a significant modification of a parenting plan:

(a) loss of a job by a parent or other circumstance resulting in an involuntary loss of income, by loss of employment or otherwise, affecting the parent's economic status;

(b) a parent's remarriage or cohabitation; or

(c) choice of reasonable caretaking arrangements for the child by a legal parent, including the child's placement in day care.

(4) The existence of a limiting factor, as defined in § 2.13(1), after a parenting plan has been ordered constitutes a substantial change of circumstances under paragraph (1) of this section.

§ 2.20 Relocation of a Parent

(1) The relocation of a parent constitutes substantially changed circumstances under this section only when it significantly impairs another parent's ability to exercise responsibilities that parent has been exercising under a parenting plan.

(2) Unless otherwise ordered by the court, a parent who has responsibility under a parenting plan who changes, or intends to change, residences for more than ninety days must give sixty days advance notice, or the most notice possible under the circumstances, to any other parent with responsibility under the same parenting plan. Notice shall include the relocation date and, unless excused by the court pursuant to

limitations that have been ordered by the court or that would be justified under § 2.13, the address of the new residence. A parent who fails to comply with the notice requirements of this section without good cause may be required to pay reasonable expenses and attorney's fees of the other parent attributable to such failure, and may be subject to other sanctions, including contempt of court, as appropriate under this Chapter.

(3) When changed circumstances are shown under paragraph (1), the court should, if practical, revise the parenting plan so as to both accommodate the relocation and maintain the same proportion of residential responsibility being exercised by each of the parents.

(4) When the relocation constituting changed circumstances under Paragraph (1) renders it impractical to maintain the same proportion of residential responsibility being exercised by each of the parent, the court shall modify the parenting plan in accordance with the child's best interests, as defined in § 2.09 and § 2.10, and in accordance with the following principles:

(a) A parent who has been exercising primary residential responsibility for the child should be allowed to relocate with the child so long as it is for a legitimate purpose and shall be able to relocate to a location that is reasonable in light of the purpose. A relocation is for a legitimate purpose if it is to be close to family or other support networks, for significant health reasons, to protect the safety of the child or another member of the child's household, to pursue an employment or educational opportunity, or to be with one's spouse [or spouse equivalent, if such is defined in Chapter 6] who is established, or who is pursuing an employment or educational opportunity, in another location. The relocating parent has the burden of proving the legitimacy of any other purpose. A move with a legitimate purpose is reasonable unless its purpose is shown to be substantially achievable without moving, or by moving to a location that is substantially less disruptive of the other parent's relationship to the child.

(b) If a relocation of a parent is for a legitimate purpose and to a location that is reasonable in light of the purpose, and if the parent have been exercising equal or nearly equal residential responsibility and the relocation requires the allocation of primary residential responsibility to one parent, the court shall select that parent based on the criteria set forth in § 2.09 and taking into account the effects of the relocation on the child.

(c) If a parent establishes that the purpose for the relocation of another parent is pretextual or not legitimate, or not to a relocation that is reasonable in light of the purpose, the court may consider modifications to the parenting plan in accordance with the child's best interests, based on the factors set forth in § 2.09(1) and the effects of the relocation on the child. Among the modifications the court may consider is a reallocation of primary residential responsibility, effective if and when the relocation occurs, but such a reallocation should not be ordered if the relocating parent demonstrates that the child's best interests would be served by the relocation.

(d) The court shall attempt to minimize the impairment to a parent-child relationship caused by a parent's relocation through alternative arrangements for the exercise of custodial responsibility appropriate to the parents' resources and circumstances and the developmental level of the child.

§ 2.21 Allocations of Responsibility to Individuals Other Than Legal Parents

Tentative Draft No. 4, 2000

(1) The court should allocate responsibility to a legal parent, a parent by estoppel, or a de facto parent as defined in § 2.03, in accordance with the same standards set forth in §§ 2.09 through 2.14, except that

(a) it should not allocate the majority of custodial responsibility to a de facto parent over the objection of a legal parent or a parent by estoppel who is fit and willing to assume the majority of custodial responsibility unless

(i) the legal parent or parent by estoppel has not been performing a reasonable share of parenting functions, as defined in § 2.03(6), or

(ii) the available alternatives would cause harm to the child; and

(b) it should limit or deny an allocation otherwise to be made if, in light of the number of other individuals to be allocated responsibility, the allocation would be impractical in light of the objectives of this Chapter.

(2) A court should not allocate responsibility to an individual who is not a legal parent, a parent by estoppel, or a de facto parent, over a parent's objection, if that parent is fit and willing to care for the child, unless

(a) the individual is a grandparent or other relative who has developed a significant relationship with the child and

(i) a legal parent or parent by estoppel consents to the allocation, and

(ii) the parent objecting to the allocation has not been performing a reasonable share of parenting functions for the child; or

(b) the individual is a biological parent of the child who is not the child's legal parent but who has an agreement with a legal parent under which the individual retained some parental rights or responsibilities; or

(c) the available alternatives would cause harm to the child.

Notes and Questions About Section 401

In these questions and those to follow we explore the rules of child custody (and the problem of indeterminacy) by examining the UMDA's provisions.

(1) What limits does Section 401(d) place on standing to begin a child-custody action? Are those limits drawn wisely?

(2) Should third parties ever be able to overcome the presumption in favor of natural parents? Consider several third-party custody and visitation issues.

An unusual standing case is *Hardy v. Arcemont*, 444 SE2d 327 (Ga App 1994). Arcemont's child was conceived by Mrs. Hardy during her marriage to Dr. Hardy. When Dr. Hardy discovered his wife's infidelity, he filed for and was granted a divorce. At his request, the couple's separation agreement and final decree both recited that there were no children born of the marriage. Nonetheless, both Hardy and Arcemont paid child support, visited the child, and were regarded by the boy as his father. Mrs. Hardy died of cancer and on her deathbed executed a statement saying (inaccurately) that Hardy was the child's father and that she wanted Hardy to take custody. The court found Hardy did not have standing to intervene, since he was estopped from claiming parenthood by the separation agreement.

In *Grissom v. Grissom*, 886 SW2d 47 (Mo App 1994) the trial court refused to let a divorced couple's teenaged children participate in custody proceedings. A psychologist who had counseled the three oldest testified that the visitation the court had ordered would be counter-productive because of the children's antagonistic feelings. After years of disputes involving allegations of sexual abuse and motions to hold the custodial mother in contempt, the parents settled their dispute.

Matter of J.C., 417 S2d 529 (Miss 1982), asked whether foster parents could adopt an infant, one of eight children of its natural parents, even though the foster parents had signed a contract agreeing not to seek to adopt their foster child. The foster parents had had custody of the child for all but first seven weeks of her first 15 months. The court allowed the adoption. The dissent wrote that the decision would disrupt the foster care system, since it would allow these people to "jump ahead" of other prospective adoptive parents. See also *In re Haun*, 286 NE2d 478 (Ohio App 1972).

In re Francisco A., 866 P2d 1175 (NM App 1993), involved children in state custody who were placed in foster care with Mr. and Mrs. Vest. The Vests petitioned to adopt in 1986, but the mother's parental rights were not terminated until 1988. By that time Mr. Vest had died, so the children were removed from Mrs. Vest's home despite her continued petition to adopt and placed with the Runyons, who later were granted adoption. The court held a hearing in October of 1990 at which the children, questioned *in camera*, said they would like to remain with Runyons but wished to continue visits with Ms. Vest. The court held that visitation was appropriate.

As you know from *Troxel* (which you read in Chapter 8), standing issues arise not just when people seek custody of children but also when they seek a right to visit them. *Troxel* gives you a good sense of how states have dealt with grandparents' standing to petition for visitation rights. Standing to seek visitation was an issue in a more unusual situation in *L. v. G.*, 497 A2d 215 (NJ Super 1985). The father of six girls remarried after his first wife's death. The oldest girls did not get along with their stepmother and moved out of the house as soon as they reached their majority, so that ultimately four of them lived together. These older children were allowed to visit their younger sisters at their father's home with his or their stepmother's supervision. They were granted standing to sue for outside-the-home visitation rights even though no divorce or adoption proceeding was pending.

JURISDICTION: A BRIEF GUIDE TO A COMPLICATED QUESTION

When the authors were in law school in the 1970s, one of the major topics of family law courses was jurisdiction. Today, because states' divorce laws and property regimes are quite similar, there is much less wielding of jurisdictional tools in the typical divorce. Nevertheless, because family law is written by state legislatures and courts, our federalism creates interstate differences in legal rules. For example, an examination of divorce rates and the success of child support enforcement reveals dramatic differences among states. Margaret F. Brinig and F. H. Buckley, *No-Fault Laws and At–Fault People*, 18 Intl Rev L & Econ 325 (1998). We will therefore sketch some of the major jurisdictional issues a modern family practitioner may encounter. To do this, we proffer a series of questions that can help unravel a complex case, and citations for major cases references to discussions of these questions elsewhere in this casebook.

(1) Is there jurisdiction to grant a divorce or an annulment? *Williams v. North Carolina*, 325 US 226 (1945), held that domicile of one of the parties in a jurisdiction was sufficient for divorce as long as actual or constructive notice was given the defendant. By statute, annulment of voidable marriages usually works the same way. There may be exceptions for persons serving in the Armed Forces, who may be (a) domiciled in a state but stationed elsewhere or (b) residing in a state pursuant to military orders. See, e.g., Va Code Ann § 20–97 (2005).

If the plaintiff seeks to annul a void marriage, personal jurisdiction may suffice. *Whealton v. Whealton*, 432 P2d 979 (Cal 1967); *Sacks v. Sacks*, 263 NYS2d 891 (NY App 1965)(personal jurisdiction necessary); *Flaxman v. Flaxman*, 273 A2d 567 (NJ 1971)(requires personal jurisdiction). This is on the theory that if the marriage is void, there is no status within the state that will give the court jurisdiction over the marital res.

(2) May alimony be awarded at some time following a valid divorce? Yes, (a) if the statute does not require that it be granted simultaneously with the divorce or (b) if the divorce was ex parte, *Estin v. Estin*, 334 US 541 (1948)(divisible divorce), and (1) if doing so is allowed by the law of the recipient spouse's domicile, *Vanderbilt v. Vanderbilt*, 354 US 416 (1957); see also *Newport v. Newport*, 245 SE2d 134 (Va 1978), and (2) the recipient spouse has personal jurisdiction over the obligor, either through personal service or service under the long-arm statute. No, if there was personal jurisdiction over the recipient in the divorce proceedings and the right to alimony was not granted or reserved in the decree. See, e.g., *Osborne v. Osborne*, 207 SE2d 875 (Va 1974).

(3) Must a valid alimony degree be given full faith and credit by another state? Yes, if payments are past due and the amount due is not modifiable. *Sistare v. Sistare*, 218 US 1 (1910). No, if the amounts past due are modifiable (i.e., if the defendant may assert defenses to avoid payment of these past due amounts) or if the recipient seeks amounts due in the future. However, the obligor's home state may give the decree comity. See, e.g., *Scott v. Sylvester*, 257 SE2d 774 (Va 1979).

(4) What jurisdiction is necessary for enforcement of a foreign alimony obligation? (a) Enforcement actions require personal jurisdiction, *Griffin v. Griffin*, 327 US 220 (1946), and notice, for example, by personal service as required by the long-arm statute, (b) the method must be within the enforcing state's statutory scheme, *Picker v. Vollenhover*, 290 P2d 789 (Or 1955), and (c) the modification procedure is not against the enforcing state's public policy, *id.*

(5) How does a party get child-support jurisdiction? (a) Child support requires in personam jurisdiction, so that incidental contacts with the state are not sufficient. *Kulko v. Superior Court*, 436 US 84 (1978). That jurisdiction may be obtained under the long-arm statute if the statute meets due process requirements. For example, see Va Code Ann § 8.01–328.1 (2005). (b) There may also be jurisdiction under the Reciprocal Uniform Enforcement of Support Act or Uniform Interstate Family Support Act. See the discussion in Chapter 11. (c) If enforcing a property settlement or separation agreement, the party may proceed as with any other contract.

(6) How does a party enforce an interstate child support order? (a) If the order is final once it is due and payable (i.e., if the obligor can assert no defenses), it is enforceable through the usual remedies available for judgments plus special ones such as garnishment and tax intercepts required by the Social Security Act, as well as through the contempt power. (b) The order for child support is always modifiable, so if seeking prospective relief, the foreign state need only grant it comity. Frequently states will give such an order comity. See *Scott v. Sylvester, supra*. (c) Contempt requires personal service unless one of the reciprocal acts is being used. (d) The uniform acts are not supposed to be used to modify out of state orders.

(7) Where does jurisdiction lie for child-custody determinations? The older rule is that they require in personam jurisdiction, *May v. Anderson*, 345 US 528 (1953). More recently, some states have allowed a "status adjudication" when one parent and the child were domiciled in the state. *Perry v. Ponder*, 604 SW2d 306 (Tex Civ App 1980). Even where there is personal jurisdiction, the appropriate forum will be the child's home state, usually the place where the child has lawfully resided for the last six months. Uniform Child Custody Jurisdiction Act (see, e.g., Va Code §§ 20–146.1 et seq. (2005)) Full faith and credit must be given to a valid foreign decree under the Parental Kidnapping Prevention Act, 28 USC § 1738A (2006).

The celebrated case of *In re Baby Girl Clausen (DeBoer v. Schmidt)*, 501 NW2d 193 (Mich App 1993), affd in part, vac in part, and remanded, 502 NW2d 649 (Mich 1993), is an example of jurisdictional problems in the adoption context. The child ("Baby Jessica") was born in February 1989, in Iowa. Her biological mother (Cara) immediately placed the child for adoption. When asked to name the father, Cara gave a name. After she and the named "father" executed consents for adoption, the DeBoers were granted custody of the child and returned to their home in Michigan. In February 1991, the DeBoers filed for adoption in Iowa. Shortly thereafter, Cara sought to revoke her consent. She then revealed she had lied about the identity of the child's father, who was Daniel Schmidt. Daniel worked at the same place as Cara and knew she was pregnant but believed that he was not the father. He filed in Iowa seeking to intervene in the DeBoer's adoption proceeding. In January 1992, the Iowa trial court voided the adoption because Daniel's parental rights had never been terminated and because Cara had signed her consent to adoption before the statutory post-birth waiting period had expired. The DeBoers appealed to the Iowa Supreme Court, which rejected their argument that a "best interests of the child" analysis governed the issue of termination.

On the same day their rights were terminated in Iowa, the DeBoers filed a petition in Michigan under the Uniform Child Custody Jurisdiction Act (UCCJA). They argued that Michigan had jurisdiction since the child had resided there for all but three weeks of her life. The Michigan court entered an ex parte order that Daniel not remove the child from the county. He filed an action to dissolve the preliminary injunction and to recognize and enforce the Iowa order granting him custody. Daniel argued that his parental rights to develop a relationship with the child had been denied and that the DeBoers lacked standing to initiate a custody dispute. Daniel ultimately prevailed in the Michigan Supreme Court because under the UCCJA and the Parental Kidnapping Prevention Act Michigan was precluded from exercising jurisdiction if there was a pending proceeding in another state. Further, the court reasoned that the DeBoers lacked standing to bring their Michigan action because the Iowa decision had stripped them of any claim to custody.

The court concluded "it is now time for the adults to move beyond saying that their only concern is the welfare of the child" and to assure that the transfer of custody caused minimal disruption of the child's life. The practical effect, the press reported, was to forcibly remove a terrified two-year-old child from the home into which she had been placed by her biological mother, just days after birth, and in which she had lived happily all of her life. Fortunately, the dire predictions of media and legal scholars seem to have proved erroneous. By the end of 1994, the child, now known as Anna Schmidt, had adjusted well to her new home. Greg Smith, *Baby Jessica Takes to a New Life, New Name*, Los Angeles *Times*, August 7, 1994, A10, col 1.

Notes and Questions About Section 402

(1) Does a trial court have to make a specific finding as to each factor?

(2) The UMDA provides that the wishes of the parents should be taken into account. One way parents may effectuate their wishes (when they can agree) is to enter into an agreement allocating the custody of their children. Courts may refuse to enforce these agreements, but as a practical matter they are usually well pleased to enforce them, partly on the theory that the parents will make a better decision than a court and partly because it relieves the court of a burdensome problem.

(3) The UMDA provides that the wishes of the child are to be taken into account. Such a requirement is embodied in the statutes, judicial opinions, or judicial practice of perhaps every jurisdiction. The older the child, the more effective the child's preference is likely to be.

One study suggests that "the movement toward allowing the child to have a role in the custody decision" has two bases. "In part, it reflects a growing skepticism about the paternalism of traditional legal policy toward children." Second,

> [t]he history of custody law is one of optimism followed by disappointment as the law has searched for an optimal means of resolving custody disputes. The tender years presumption, the best interest of the child standard, and a presumption favoring joint custody have each in turn been embraced with enthusiasm; however, each has proved unsatisfactory, either intrinsically or in application. The search continues for a custody rule that will result in the "right" decision without increasing the already considerable destructive impact of divorce on children. Some observers argue that a rule recognizing the child's preference as a primary factor in the custody decision will achieve this elusive goal.

Elizabeth S. Scott, N. Dickon Repucci, and Mark Aber, *Children's Preference in Adjudicated Custody Decisions*, 22 Ga L Rev 1035, 1039–40 (1988).

Nevertheless, the practice has its complexities and even its critics. One concern is that children's decisions will be affected by trivial, short-term, or undesirable factors:

> Decision theory would suggest that children at the time of divorce may be influenced by short-term cognitive and emotional biases that poten-

> tially distort the decision making process. Decision makers tend to weigh heavily data that is vivid or directly related to immediate experience and to undervalue abstract or remote information. The context of divorce may lead younger children particularly to weigh heavily the loss of the absent parent or to be heavily influenced by transitory anger at the "guilty" parent. Moreover, the "week-end" parent who entertains the child and imposes few rules may seem more attractive than the parent associated with the school week routine. Choices may be affected by sympathy for the parent who has been left by the other or for the parent who has not been chosen by the other children.

Id. at 1055. Thus one court rejected a child's preference where the girl "was ten years old at the time of the hearing and easily influenced. For example, one of her reasons for preferring her mother's home was the accessibility of boating, fishing and swimming facilities on the lake near which the mother's trailer home is located." *Metz v. Morley*, 289 NYS2d 364 (NY App Div 1968).

Another common concern is presented by *Jordana v. Corley*, 220 NW2d 515 (ND 1974). In that case, their mother told a five-year-old and an eight-year-old she would commit suicide if she were not given custody. "Although the boys expressed a preference to remain with their mother, the trial judge gave little weight to such preference because he believed it was due to the fear that their mother would carry out her threat of suicide." The appellate court found the trial court had been correct, since, given the mother's threat, the children's preference was not "freely given." A dissenting justice would have gone farther:

> I do not believe it is beneficial for courts to ask children what their preferences are as to custody.... In the first place, it must create a feeling of guilt in any child to have to disappoint one of two parents he loves by expressing a preference for the other. Psychological problems can be expected whether the child makes the choice or refuses to do so. In the second place, if the child knows (and he usually does) that placements are not final and that he may be asked in the future to express a preference, he may consciously or unconsciously use that knowledge to extort favors from one or both parents—not a cheerful harbinger of a normal relationship with either parent.

How strictly ought the child's preferences heeded? In *In re Marriage of Ellerbroek*, 377 NW2d 257 (Iowa App 1985), James, "an extremely intelligent, articulate, and well-behaved sixteen-year-old," was "positive and firm in his position that he wants to live with his father." He threatened to run away if made to live with his mother. He had an "excellent relationship" with his father. The trial court awarded custody to his mother, and the appellate court affirmed, saying that it looked at several factors. These included the fact that awarding James to his father would separate him from his sister, that his father had "exhibited violent behavior toward his wife and children," that his father was living with a woman "whose abilities as a step-mother are not shown," that his father had "exhibited irresponsible and immature behavior since the parties' separation (although there was 'no evidence of immature actions following [the father's] treatment' " at the Menninger Clinic), that James "is a child who feels concern for others and is anxious to please them," and the a psychologist recommended that the mother have custody. Was the case correctly decided?

(4) Are the UMDA factors each accorded their correct weight? Are they accorded any weight at all? How should a court decide how much weight each factor should be given?

(5) Does the UMDA's list take all the relevant factors into account? Consider the following factors which the UMDA does not specifically mention. Do they fit within the factors the UMDA does mention? Should they have been mentioned specifically? Are they factors which can and should legitimately be taken into account?

(a) If we are to consult the child's best interests, shouldn't the relative wealth of the parties be relevant? There is a good deal of legal authority to the contrary. For instance, the New York Court of Appeals wrote, "[P]etitioner's poverty ... must not be held against her. Such socioeconomic factors, unless sufficient to establish neglect or unfitness of the parent under the specific circumstances of a particular case, are irrelevant and impermissible considerations." *Matter of Adoption of L.*, 462 NE2d 1165, 1170 (NY 1984). Other courts have a somewhat less strict standard: "In a custody proceeding, the sole permissible inquiry into the relative wealth of the parties is whether either parent is unable to provide adequately for the child; unless the income of one party is so inadequate as to preclude raising the children in a decent manner, the matter of relative income is irrelevant." *Brooks v. Brooks*, 466 A2d 152, 156 (Super Ct Pa 1983). And the Michigan Child Custody Act of 1970 requires courts to take into account the "capacity and disposition of competing parties to provide the child with food, clothing, medical care ... , and other material needs."

Other things being equal (and probably even if some things aren't equal), wouldn't most children prefer to live in a well-to-do household than a poor one? In "In 1993, 75% of America's entering collegians declared that an 'essential' or 'very important' life goal was 'being very well off financially' This goal topped a list of 19 possible life objectives, exceeding the rated importance even of 'raising a family' and 'helping others in difficulty.' Most adults share this materialism, believing that increased income would make them happier. Few agree that money can buy happiness, but many agree that a little more money would make them a little happier." David G. Myers and Ed Diener, *Who Is Happy?*, 6 Psychological Science 10, 12–13 (1995). (It should, however, be said that the same source reports that although "the correlation between income and happiness is not negative, it is modest.")

In a capitalist society is this sentiment irrational? Consider the following passage from the philosopher John Rawls:

> [P]rimary goods ... are things which it is supposed a rational man wants whatever else he wants. Regardless of what an individual's rational plans are in detail, it is assumed that there are various things which he would prefer more of rather than less. With more of these goods men can generally be assured of greater success in carrying out their intentions and in advancing their ends, whatever these ends may be. The primary social goods, to give them in broad categories, are rights and liberties, opportunities and powers, income and wealth.

A Theory of Justice 92 (Harv U Press, 1971). Or, more succinctly, "Wine maketh merry: but money answereth all things." Ecclesiastes X:19. As we said in the questions that followed *Painter*, money may not buy happiness, but it does improve access to health care, education, and so on. Thus, whether one uses a best-interest standard or a child's-experience standard, won't it be appropriate sometimes to take wealth into account in making child-custody decisions? Do you see any problems with making the wealth of the claimants a legitimate criterion in custody decisions? One court has written,

> Economic matters are of considerable consequence in child-rearing, but not preponderantly more important than other factors. Indeed, it can be argued that economic circumstances never should be conclusively determinative. The reason is plain. In most cases the mother will be disadvantaged.... [T]he danger in placing undue reliance on economic circumstances is its potential prejudicial effect upon the child's best interests. The party with the more modest economic resources should not be excluded from equal consideration as the custodial parent.

Dempsey v. Dempsey, 292 NW2d 549, 554 (Mich App 1980).

Where the custody dispute is between natural parents, the relative wealth of the parties can, to some extent, be dealt with through the court's power to order one party to pay the other child support. But this solution is not always available or effective. For instance, the wealth of one of the parent's households may come from income of a second spouse. Or the poverty of one of the parent's households might come from that parent's improvidence in handling money, including income from child-support payments. Where the contest is not between natural parents, courts usually lacks the authority to order child support at all.

(b) Should the kind of physical environment each contender can offer the child be taken into account?

(c) Should the ability of each parent to spend time with the child when he or she becomes the child's custodian matter? Should the ability of each parent to provide a home in which a parent or a step-parent can provide full-time care for a child count? In *Bonjour v. Bonjour*, 592 P2d 1233 (Alaska 1979), the trial court awarded custody to the father in part because he could "provide in his family unit a surrogate mother in Susan who is a full-time homemaker...."

In the custody of Lindsey, Joseph is placed in a day care center for a good portion of a day while Lindsey is working." 592 P2d at 1237. There are journalistic reports of cases in which working mothers have lost custody of their children because judges found they worked too many hours. Barbara Vobejda and D'Vera Cohn, *As Custody Laws Level the Field, Father Often Does Better*, Washington Post, at A1 col 1 (November 15, 1994).

(d) Should the ability of each parent to provide care from both a man and a woman be taken into account?

(e) Should the willingness of each parent to allow the other parent to visit the child matter? Alaska, for example, requires a trial court to consider "The willingness and ability of each parent to facilitate and encourage a close and continuing relationship between the other parent and the child." Alaska Stat § 25.24.150 (2005). A Missouri court, to take another example, modified an order granting custody to the mother and instead awarded custody to the father because the mother had impeded the father's visitation privileges. *Garrett v. Garrett*, 464 SW2d 740 (Mo App 1971).

(f) Should one's skill as a parent be taken into account? How should that skill be judged?

(g) Should siblings be kept together? In *In re M.*, 416 NE2d 669, 673 (Ohio Com Pl 1979), the court said siblings "have a right to the companionship of each other. A child should grow up as a part of its natural family and the role of the state should be to do everything that can be done to support the family and hold it together."

(h) The Michigan Child Custody Act of 1970 requires courts to consider the "length of time the child has lived in a stable satisfactory environment and the desirability of maintaining continuity." Why did the UMDA omit this factor?

(i) The Comment to section 402 says, "Although none of the familiar presumptions developed by the case law are mentioned here, the language of the section is consistent with preserving such rules of thumb. The preference for the mother as custodian of young children when all things are equal, for example, is simply a shorthand method of expressing the best interest of children...." What good is a rule of thumb if it is not stated? Why did the drafters of the UMDA omit it?

(j) The Michigan Child Custody Act of 1970 requires courts to consider the "moral fitness of the parties involved." What does this mean? How is a court to determine moral fitness? Is it appropriate for the court to do so? In one well-known case, *Bottoms v. Bottoms*, 457 SE2d 102 (Va 1995), the Supreme Court of Virginia reaffirmed the principle that "among the factors to be weighed in determining unfitness are the parent's misconduct that affects the child, neglect of the child, and a demonstrated unwillingness and inability to promote the emotional and physical well-being of the child. Other important considerations include the nature of the home environment and moral climate in which the child is to be raised." In *Bottoms*, the court was concerned (among other things) with the mother's living arrangements. The court noted that it had previously said that living daily in a lesbian household might impose a burden upon a child because of the "social condemnation" attached to such an arrangement, "which will inevitably afflict the child's relationships with its 'peers and with the community at large.' " The court did not retreat from that statement and found that such a result was likely under the facts.

(k) The UMDA instructs courts not to "consider conduct of a proposed custodian that does not affect his relationship to the child." The Comment to section 402 explained that the "last sentence of the section changes the law in those states which continue to use fault notions in custody adjudication. There is no reason to encourage parties to spy on each other in order to discover marital (most commonly, sexual) misconduct for use in a custody contest." Section 402 is in force in Illinois and was interpreted by the Illinois Supreme Court in *Jarrett v. Jarrett*, 400 NE2d 421 (Ill 1979). When Jacqueline and Walter Jarrett were divorced, Jacqueline received custody of their three daughters, who were then seven, ten, and twelve years old. Five months after the divorce, Jacqueline told Walter that her boyfriend, Wayne Hammon, was moving in. Walter then asked the court for custody of his daughters. The trial court agreed, the intermediate appellate court reversed, and the Illinois Supreme Court upheld the trial court. As you read the opinion, you should ask: Is the behavior at issue in *Jarrett* relevant to custody decisions? Does it directly affect the children? Indirectly?

JARRETT v. JARRETT

Illinois Supreme Court, 1979
400 NE2d 421

UNDERWOOD, JUSTICE:

The chief issue in this case is whether a change of custody predicated upon the open and continuing cohabitation of the custodial parent with a member of the opposite sex is contrary to the manifest weight of the evidence in the absence of any tangible evidence of contemporaneous adverse effect upon the minor children. Considering the principles previously enunciated, and the statutory provisions, and prior decisions of the courts of this State, we conclude that under the facts in this case the trial court properly transferred custody of the Jarrett children from Jacqueline to Walter Jarrett.

The relevant standards of conduct are expressed in the statutes of this State: Section 11:8 of the Criminal Code of 1961 (Ill. Rev. Stat. 1977, ch. 38, par. 11:8) provides that "[a]ny person who cohabits or has sexual intercourse with another not his spouse commits fornication if the behavior is open and notorious." In *Hewitt v. Hewitt* (1979), 394 N.E.2d 1204, we emphasized the refusal of the General Assembly in enacting the new Illinois Marriage and Dissolution of Marriage Act (Ill. Rev. Stat. 1977, ch. 40, par. 101 *et seq.*) to sanction any nonmarital relationships and its declaration of the purpose to "strengthen and preserve the integrity of marriage and safeguard family relationships" (Ill. Rev. Stat. 1977, ch. 40, par. 102(2)).

Jacqueline argues, however, that her conduct does not affront public morality because such conduct is now widely accepted, and cites 1978 Census Bureau statistics that show 1.1 million households composed of an unmarried man and woman, close to a quarter of which also include at least one child. This is essentially the same argument we rejected last term in *Hewitt v. Hewitt* (1979), and it is equally unpersuasive here. The number of people living in such households forms only a small percentage of the adult population, but more to the point, the statutory interpretation urged upon us by Jacqueline simply nullifies the fornication statute. The logical conclusion of her argument is that the statutory prohibitions are void as to those who believe the proscribed acts are not immoral, or, for one reason or another, need not be heeded. So stated, of course, the argument defeats itself. The rules which our society enacts for the governance of its members are not limited to those who agree with those rules—they are equally binding on the dissenters. The fornication statute and the Illinois Marriage and Dissolution of Marriage Act evidence the relevant moral standards of this State, as declared by our legislature. The open and notorious limitation on the former's prohibitions reflects both a disinclination to criminalize purely private relationships and a recognition that open fornication represents a graver threat to public morality than private violations. Conduct of that nature, when it is open, not only violates the statutorily expressed moral standards of the State, but also encourages others to violate those standards, and debases public morality. While we agree that the statute does not penalize conduct which is essentially private and discreet, Jacqueline's conduct has been neither, for she has discussed this relationship and her rationalization of it with at least her children, her former husband and her neighbors. It is, in our judgment, clear that her conduct offends prevailing public policy.

Jacqueline's disregard for existing standards of conduct instructs her children, by example, that they, too, may ignore them, and could well encourage the children to engage in similar activity in the future. That factor, of course, supports the trial court's conclusion that their daily presence in that environment was injurious to the moral well-being and development of the children.

It is true that, as Jacqueline argues, the courts have not denied custody to every parent who has violated the community's moral standards, nor do we now intimate a different rule. Rather than mechanically denying custody in every such instance, the courts of this State appraise the moral example currently provided and the example which may be expected by the parent in the future. We held in *Nye v. Nye* (1952), 105

N.E.2d 300, that past moral indiscretions of a parent are not sufficient grounds for denying custody if the parent's present conduct establishes the improbability of such lapses in the future. This rule focuses the trial court's attention on the moral values which the parent is actually demonstrating to the children.

At the time of this hearing, however, and even when this case was argued orally to this court, Jacqueline continued to cohabit with Wayne Hammon and had done nothing to indicate that this relationship would not continue in the future. Thus the moral values which Jacqueline currently represents to her children, and those which she may be expected to portray to them in the future, contravene statutorily declared standards of conduct and endanger the children's moral development.

Questions About Section 404

(1) In *Rose v. Rose*, 340 SE2d 176 (W Va 1985), Mrs. Rose had left Mr. Rose because of her relationship with another man. Their ten-year-old son, Brian, first chose to live with his mother. "However, after a talk between Brian and Mr. Rose, in which Mr. Rose explained to Brian that Brian's mother had left Mr. Rose for another man, Brian changed his mind and decided to stay with his father." The judge interviewed Brian in chambers, excluded counsel, but made a verbatim record of the interview. The judge awarded physical custody to Mr. Rose, holding that Brian's preference overcame the primary-caretaker presumption that benefitted Mrs. Rose. The West Virginia Supreme Court upheld this procedure and result.

The dissent, however, criticized both. The dissent reproduced the complete transcript of the judge's interview with Brian:

THE COURT: Now, have you thought about with which parent you would like to live?

ANSWER: Yes.

THE COURT: Have you made a decision with regard to which parent you would like to live with?

ANSWER: Yes.

THE COURT: Without telling me why, which parent would you rather live with?

ANSWER: With my dad.

THE COURT: Now tell me why?

ANSWER: I don't like Denver [the new social companion] and I don't like what went on.

THE COURT: Have you spent any time with Denver?

ANSWER: No, but I have been with him at fireworks and I didn't like him. I stayed away from him.

THE COURT: Is there anything else you'd like to tell me?

ANSWER: No.

THE COURT: That is all the questions I want to ask you, Brian.

The dissent argued that the judge's failure to probe further left the court with "no indication in the record of the basis for the child's animosity toward the new boyfriend.... It is unimaginable that a child's dislike of his or her primary caretaker's casual acquaintances could alone form a rational basis for rebuttal of the primary caretaker presumption."

Brian was apparently a more-than-usually-bright ten-year-old. Why should he not have been examined in the usual way—in open court, in the presence of the parties and their counsel, and subject to cross-examination? Or, failing that, in chambers but examined and cross-examined by both counsel? Couldn't the judge protect the child from over-zealous interrogation?

On the other hand, aren't there reasons Brian's testimony should have been more completely protected? Wouldn't he be able to testify more freely and openly if he did not have to worry about displeasing one of his parents? Should Brian's testimony therefore be kept from everyone except the judge? Should it be kept from the litigants but not their counsel? Should the parents be judicially ordered not to ask Brian what he said?

As Mrs. Rose's lawyer, how would you deal with this very harmful testimony? How would you deal with it under any of the alternative rules we have explored?

Are you satisfied by the inquiry the judge conducted? Are you persuaded Brian genuinely wanted to live with his father? That this preference was deep and lasting? That Brian's reasons are good ones? That Brian has not been improperly influenced to testify for his father? If you are not satisfied by the judge's interview of Brian, how would you have done better?

Questions About Section 405

(1) Section 405 represents one solution to the information and expertise problems. The reasoning behind it is that, if courts lack the information and expertise they need to decide custody cases, why not assign experts to collect information and make recommendations to courts? How well does the solution work? Robert J. Levy, *Custody Investigations in Divorce Cases*, 1985 ABF Res J 713, reports on an important attempt to answer that question through an empirical study of 629 divorce cases in Hennepin County, Minnesota, where investigations are conducted by the Hennepin County Department of Court Services. Professor Levy points out that investigators face the same indeterminacy problems judges do but that judges "have been given authority, in democratic fashion, to decide custody cases" and that "judges usually make these choices only after a trial at which the contesting parties have had an opportunity to test the witnesses ... and

to establish value priorities for the case that are different from those the judge might establish without a trial." He notes that in the overwhelming majority of cases there is no trial and that the report of the investigator can be greatly influential in these cases because the parties realize that, should they go to trial, the judge is likely to give the investigator's report considerable weight.

Professor Levy finds the power this gives the investigator disturbing because he sees many dangers in "the caseworker's informal decision-making role." Among them:

> [T]he investigation and reporting that influence the negotiation and decision can be selective and distorting; the evaluations and the recommendations can be biased by the investigator's personal values ... ; families can be subjected to authoritarian child-saving supervision, while the divorce is pending as well as postdecretally, without substantive or procedural safeguards.

Investigations might help solve the information problem, but Professor Levy concludes, "Too few of the cases are finally contested to compensate fully for the expense of a substantial bureaucracy." Investigations might also help solve the expertise problem, but Professor Levy believes that "the caseworkers' psychological interpretations ... were so unreliable that it is fair at least to wonder whether judges should be encouraged to derive assurance from such sources."

Professor Levy doubts that the situation

> can be improved by better education of professional staff, lower staff-client ratios, or more in-service training. For too many years, in too many contexts—juvenile courts, mental institutions, prisons—such hopes (and sometimes seductive promises) have delayed or obstructed essential reform. Moreover, the lower status professionals accord to public agency employment (impeding employment of highly qualified professionals) and the civil service protection afforded public agency employees (impeding elimination of professionals who perform poorly) make any promise of in-service improvement suspect.... [T]he manipulative and coercive child protection practices in which the Hennepin County caseworkers indulged during 1970 are likely to occur regularly no matter how much improvement there may be in hiring, in-service training, or supervision.

Professor Levy does, however, find

> good reason to believe that custody investigators can "mediate" (e.g., arrange the settlement of) some custody disputes which even a pair of extremely "nonadversarial" lawyers cannot or have not been able to settle—because an investigator can "reassure" a parent whose concern is only the care the children are likely to receive after the divorce and because the investigator can subtly coerce a settlement.... Unfortunately, the mediative endeavor was accompanied, in some cases, by unpleasant coercive and punitive behavior.

How does the UMDA address the kinds of problems Professor Levy describes? Is it successful? What further safeguards would you propose? Is section 405 necessary in light of section 404(b)?

Questions About Section 407

(1) As section 407 suggests, American courts generally award visitation rights to the non-custodial parent. *Frail v. Frail*, 370 NE2d 303 (Ill App 1977), illustrates that preference at work. After the Frails' divorce, Mrs. Frail received custody of her two children. Two years later, Mrs. Frail was charged with murdering her second husband, and Mr. Frail was accorded custody. Mrs. Frail was sentenced to prison for fourteen to twenty years. Mr. Frail "reported that the children (then nine and eleven) became upset when they visited their mother at the county jail and that they did not wish to visit her again while she was so confined." (The court treated this testimony "with some suspicion," for reasons that it did not explain.) The court ordered visitation twice a month, since it believed that "the visitation can be a rewarding experience for both parent and child in the present case.... To deny visitation, as the [father] urges, might well in effect be a permanent denial to [Mrs. Frail] of all rights to her children during the remainder of their minority, because they would reach majority long before she served her minimum term of 14 years." Was the court correct?

(2) Here, again, the enforcement problem may be severe. The custodial parent can easily interfere with the non-custodial parent's visit. How may and should a court enforce its order?

(a) A visitation order is a judicial order like any other, and courts may enforce it through the contempt power. What difficulties might this pose?

(b) Should visitation be linked to child support? Litigants in child support cases sometimes claim that if the noncustodial parent violates a child support order, the custodial parent should not have to permit visitation. Professor Czapanskiy argues that this reasoning violates the principle of doing what is best for the child, since linking payment of child support and visitation could result in the child losing two advantages: the support and contact with the noncustodial parent. Karen Czapanskiy, *Child Support and Visitation: Rethinking the Connections*, 20 Rutgers L J 619 (1989).

(c) Should custodial parents who interfere with the other parent's ability to visit their children lose custody where the non-custodial parent would be a fit parent? A court which reversed a custody decision partly on such grounds wrote, "If a court entrusts one parent with major custody of minor children and that parent's conduct with respect thereto deprives or materially abrogates the other parent's custodial and visitation rights granted by the decree, the court is not limited to mere punitive measures but may modify the decree to assure performance of those portions of its judgment designed to promote the welfare of the children." *Garrett v. Garrett*, 464 SW2d 740 (Mo App 1971).

(d) Parents have a remedy in tort against anyone who abducts or entices their child away from them and thereby interferes with the relationship between parent and child. This tort remedy extends to non-custodial parents who abduct or entice their own children away from the custodial parent. Applying the cause of action against custodial parents who interfere with visitation rights has not found judicial favor. Should it? In *Sheltra v. Smith*, 392 A2d 431 (Vt 1978), the Vermont Supreme Court found that a mother who alleged that the father prevented her from seeing or communicating with her daughter had stated a cause of action for intentional infliction of emotional distress. To what extent should this precedent be applied and extended? See also *Kajtazi v. Kajtazi*, 488 F Supp 15 (EDNY 1978); *Lloyd v. Loeffler*, 694 F2d 489 (7th Cir 1982); *Raftery v. Scott*, 756 F2d 335 (4th Cir 1985). This series of federal cases has allowed noncustodial parents to sue for damages when they have been denied visitation rights, usually when the other parent has hidden the children or taken them out of the country. The intentional torts used for the actions have included alienation of affections, interference with family relationships, and intentional infliction of emotional distress.

(e) California's Family Code permits courts to order compensation for denial of visitation rights, although this is limited to out-of-pocket costs. Cal Fam Code § 3028 (2006). Is this provision practical?

(3) What if a custodial parent defeats the non-custodial parent's visitation rights by moving away from the area where the non-custodial parent lives? One solution to that problem is embodied in statutes like New Jersey's law prohibiting the custodial parent from removing a minor child from the jurisdiction "without the consent of both parents, unless the court, upon cause shown shall otherwise order." NJ Stat Ann § 9:2–2 (2006). In enforcing that statute in *Cooper v. Cooper*, 491 A2d 606, 610–11 (NJ 1984), the New Jersey Supreme Court noted that courts "differed on what constitutes sufficient cause for removal." It observed that Minnesota requires that a "custodial parent's motion to remove a child from the jurisdiction should be granted unless the noncustodial parent established, by a preponderance of the evidence, that the move would not be in the best interests of the child." However, "[o]ther states allow the child to accompany the custodial parent whenever the custodian has a legitimate reason and the move is consistent with the best interests of the child."

Another solution is found in *Courten v. Courten*, 459 NYS2d 464 (App Div 2d Dept 1983). There, the custodial mother moved from New York to California. According to the appellate court, the family court had seen

> no compelling reason to justify the mother's move. In support of its decision, it cited the mother's unimpressive efforts to obtain employment in a location which would not unduly interfere with the father's visitation, the likelihood that the mother's move was motivated by the presence in California of her fiancé whom she had met while still living in New York and the fact that the mother seemed intent upon depriving the father of access to the child as evidenced by her failure to bring the child to New York to visit with the father during the trial.

The appellate court sustained the family court's order shifting custody from the mother to the father:

> Disruption of the relationship between the noncustodial parent and the marital issue by relocation of the custodial parent in a distant jurisdiction will not be permitted unless a compelling showing of "exceptional circumstances" or a "pressing concern" for the welfare of the custodial parent and child is made warranting removal of the child to a distant locale.

Questions About the UMDA's Approach to Child Custody

(1) How would *Painter* have been decided under the UMDA?

(2) Does the UMDA satisfactorily balance the need for discretion on one hand and the need to give judges clear guidance and keep them from abusing their discretion on the other?

(3) A Psychological Standard

We have now completed our examination of the UMDA's solution to the problems of setting substantive standards for child-custody disputes and of solving the indeterminacy problem. We now turn to other solutions of those problems. We begin with an influential book—Joseph Goldstein, Anna Freud, and Albert J. Solnit, *Beyond the Best Interests of the Child* (Free Press, 1973). Nadine Taub wrote more than a decade after the book had appeared that "the authors have had an impact on the law governing child welfare decisions that would exceed any academician's wildest expectations. As one commentator observed, every subsequent proposal for reform of the child welfare system has drawn its vocabulary and central ideas from Goldstein, Freud, and Solnit's conceptual framework." *Assessing the Impact of Goldstein, Freud, and Solnit's Proposals: An Introductory Overview*, 12 Rev of L & Social Change 485, 485 (1983–84). Professor Taub added, "The transformation of child welfare decision-making into a single-minded search for the psychological parent(s) is apparent in decisions applying psychological parenting theory in custody disputes arising out of divorce proceedings. It is also found increasingly in decisions resolving custody disputes between parents and third parties." In short, the book is influential enough to assign in its entirety and short enough to make such an assignment practical. Here, however, we only have space to summarize its arguments.

When the book was published, Joseph Goldstein was a professor of law, science, and social policy at Yale; Anna Freud (the daughter of

Sigmund Freud) was a leading figure in child psychoanalysis; and Albert Solnit was director of the Yale University Child Study Center. The book was written to remedy what its authors saw as the law's failure to heed children's psychological welfare when making decisions about children.

The authors begin by stating two beliefs. The first is that child-custody decisions should be made in the service of children and not adults, in important part because well-raised children make good parents, thus benefitting society. (Later, the authors say that another reason is that "[a]dults have deeply ingrained irrational reservations about the primacy of children's needs. These reservations—ambivalent feelings—cannot be guarded against except by clear and compelling priorities once there is a conflict about the child's placement.") The author's second belief is that parents have a "right to raise their children as they see fit, free of government intrusion" and that government is ill-suited to regulate the relationship between parents and children.

The authors then draw some conclusions about children from psychoanalytic theory, theory they think "provides a valuable body of generally applicable knowledge about a child's needs." Children, the authors say, have a different sense of time from adults: they are less able than adults to postpone gratification and less tolerant of lengthy separations. Children are less able than adults to understand rationally the events in their lives, are likelier to interpret those events egocentrically, and are more susceptible to emotional anxieties. Children "will freely love more than one adult only if the individuals in question feel positively to one another." Young children do not recognize blood ties: "What registers in their minds are the day-to-day interchanges with the adults who take care of them and who, on the strength of these become the parent figures to whom they are attached." When a child regularly receives affection and other emotional needs from the day-to-day caretaker, that caretaker (whether biological parent or not) becomes the child's "psychological parent." Children develop normally only if their relationships (particularly with the psychological parent) and surroundings remain stable. Children's development also depends on being wanted. A "wanted child" develops the self-esteem necessary for happiness in later life; an unwanted child does not. The authors invent the term "common-law adoptive parent" to "designate those psychological parent-child relationships which develop outside of either placement by formal adoption or by the initial assignment of a child to his biological parents." Citing *Painter v. Bannister*, the authors say such relationships can arise where a parent confides a child to a friend or relative for "an extended period."

The authors propose guidelines for custody decisions. The guidelines "rest on the belief that children whose placement becomes the subject of controversy should be provided with an opportunity to be placed with adults who are or are likely to become their psychological parents." Because stable relationships are necessary for normal child development, custody decisions should promote "continuity of relationships." That principle has several implications.

First, custody should be awarded to the psychological parent, whether that person is a biological parent, an adoptive parent, a foster parent, a "common-law" parent, or anyone else.

Second, a decision about custody should be "final and unconditional." Courts should not reconsider custody awards, even when the circumstances of the would-be custodians change. Adoptions should become final when the child is placed with the adoptive parents. There can be temporary placements. Foster care (both formal less formal) would be permissible. But preserving the tie between the child and the child's psychological parent is crucial. Should that tie break, the goal should be to make permanent whatever new tie has replaced the old one.

The principle of continuity has, for the authors, a third implication: Courts should not award non-custodial parents visitation rights; the decision to allow such visits should be left entirely to the custodial parent. This is because "[c]hildren have difficulty in relating positively to, profiting from, and maintaining the contact with two psychological parents who are not in positive contact with each other." Giving the custodial parent authority to decide whether the non-custodial parent may visit the child will help prevent destructive conflicts of loyalties. In any event, a "visiting" parent is ill-situated to be an effective psychological parent.

Because children have a quickened perception of time and need stability and continuity, custody decisions should be made with "all deliberate speed." Custody in divorce cases should thus be decided on an emergency basis in a separate proceeding held before the actual divorce proceeding. Adoptions could ideally be arranged even before the child is born as expeditiously as possible. Standards for deciding whether a parent has abandoned a child should be shifted toward "the individual child's tolerance of absence and sense of abandonment and away from the adult's intent to abandon or an agency's failure to encourage a relationship."

Because of the expertise and information problems, the state is ill-equipped to make wise decisions for the child. Thus, courts should abandon the best-interest standard, for the more modest but more realistic standard of the "least detrimental alternative." This standard is preferable because it reminds the court of the risks to the child in custody conflicts and because the latter best-interest standard has been used in ways disserve children and allow the interests of the contending adults to be taken into account. The "least detrimental alternative" is "that specific placement and procedure for placement which maximizes, in accord with the child's sense of time and on the basis of short-term predictions given the limitations of knowledge, his or her opportunity for being wanted and for maintaining on a continuous basis a relationship with at least one adult who is or will become his psychological parent."

When there is a legal dispute over custody, the child should be a party to the proceedings and be represented before the court by someone expert in child development. This is necessary because once parents come into conflict over their child, they can no longer be relied on to represent the child's interests in a conflict-free way.

Notes and Questions on Goldstein, Freud, and Solnit

(1) It is standard law that in a custody dispute between natural parents and "strangers," the natural parents have special status. That special status varies from state to state. The parental preference is stated in its strongest form by the Nebraska Supreme Court, which held in *Nielsen v. Nielsen*, 296 NW2d 483, 488 (Neb 1980), that "courts may not properly deprive a parent of the custody of a minor child unless it is affirmatively shown that such parent is unfit to perform the duties imposed by the relationship, or has forfeited that right." This holding attracted a dissent from a justice who argued that "we do a grave injustice to a parent when we require a court to make an affirmative finding of 'unfitness' before custody may be changed.... [T]he overwhelming impression left by the cases is that a finding of 'unfitness' implies that the parent is morally corrupt or emotionally unstable." That justice added that "there may be instances where permitting a child to remain with a fit, proper, and suitable parent may not be in the child's best interests and we should not so tie the hands of the courts who must hear the evidence and decide each individual case, one by one."

The New York Court of Appeals has a less stringent standard. It writes, "It has long been the law in this State that a parent has 'a right to the care and custody of a child, superior to that of all others, unless he or she has abandoned that right or is proved unfit to assume the duties and privileges of parenthood.' In the absence of 'surrender, abandonment, persisting neglect, unfitness or other like extraordinary circumstances,' a parent may not be denied custody." *Matter of Adoption of L.*, 462 NE2d 1165, 1169 (NY 1984). That court adds, "In *Matter of Bennett v. Jeffreys*, 356 NE2d 277, this court held that a 'disruption of custody over an extended period of time' could amount to an extraordinary circumstance sufficient to justify inquiry into whether custody with a nonparent would best serve the child's interests." But the same court also says, "While 'the child may be so long in the custody of the nonparent' that separation from the natural parent amounts to an extraordinary circumstance, especially when 'the psychological trauma of removal is grave enough to threaten destruction of the child,' nevertheless ... this court has always adhered to the view that natural parents are generally best qualified to care for their own children unless disqualified by 'gross misconduct'...."

Other jurisdictions articulate the parental preference more weakly. As you recall, the Iowa Supreme Court in *Painter* spoke of "the presumption of parental preference." The Connecticut Supreme Court states, "In any controversy between a parent and a stranger, the parent 'should have a strong initial advantage, to be lost only where it is shown that the child's welfare plainly requires custody to be placed in the stranger.'" *Hao Thi Popp v. Lucas*, 438 A2d 755, 758 (Conn 1980). Maryland law establishes a presumption in favor of the natural parent. One Maryland intermediate appellate court commented: "Too often those skilled at law treat all presumptions as decisive irrespective of the evidence, and fail to recognize that for the most part they are merely guidelines by which to reason, conclusive only in the absence of evidence to the contrary and are aught but one more auncel weight in the judicial balance. In the natural parent context it is nothing more than a burden-placing device." *Ross v. Hoffman*, 364 A2d 596, 600 (Ct Spec App Md 1976).

California Fam Code § 3040 (West 2006) provides an order of preference for awarding custody: "(1) to both parents jointly, or to either of them; (2) to the person or persons in whose home the child has been living in a stable and wholesome environment; (3) to any other person or persons deemed by the court to provide adequate and proper care and guidance." Where on the continuum does this standard fall?

The parental preference can also be promoted by procedural devices. Thus some statutes limit standing to bring an action for custody of a child. As you know, the UMDA permits anyone other than a parent to bring such an action "only if [the child] is not in the physical custody of one of his parents." UMDA § 401(d).

How do these principles work out in practice? You've already read of several cases which partially answer that question, and we will now look at two cases presenting conflicts between a natural parent and someone who is not a natural parent. In *In re Marriage of Allen*, 626 P2d 16 (1981), the Washington Court of Appeals stated its standard of review for such cases: "Great deference is accorded to parental rights, based upon constitutionally protected rights to privacy and the goal of protecting the family entity." The court said that "two factors would outweigh the deference normally given parents' rights." The first is parental unfitness. The second is circumstances in which "the child's growth and development would be detrimentally affected by placement with an otherwise fit parent." The court thus awarded custody to a step-parent where the trial court had found that the child's "future development would be detrimentally affected by placement with his father" and where the child "had become integrated into the family unit." Commenting on the latter factor, the court said,

> Where the reason for deferring to parental rights—the goal of preserving families—would be ill-served by maintaining parental custody, as where a child is integrated into the nonparent's family, the de facto family relationship does not exist as to the natural parent and need not be supported.... As noted in *In re Aschauer*, 611 P2d 1245, 1250 n. 5 (Wash 1980):

> [I]t was formerly thought that blood ties between parent and child were extremely important. Now it is learned that kinship is not as important as stability of environment and care and attention to the child's needs. *See* J. Goldstein, A. Freud, A. Solnit, *Beyond the Best Interests of the Child* (1973).

Is the Washington court's standard reasonable? Does its second factor for denying a natural parent custody, when coupled with its rationale, dilute the natural parent's claims too greatly? Consider the facts of the case.

Joe and Dana Allen's child Joshua was born September 11, 1971. He was profoundly deaf. When Joe and Dana were divorced, Dana received custody of Joshua. However, she found coping with her deaf child difficult. She first placed Joshua with her mother, then she transferred custody of him to Joe, who left him with Dana's mother. On August 26, 1974, Joe married Jeannie. Joe brought Joshua to live with him and adopted Jeannie's three children. In 1978, Jeannie petitioned for divorce and for custody of all four children. A court-ordered evaluation found both Joe and Jeannie "suitable parents." The trial court granted Jeannie custody of her three children and of Joshua. The appellate court reviewed some of the facts of the case:

> Shortly after Joshua joined the home of Joe and Jeannie, she began to help him learn sign language. Joshua was only 3 years old at the time and his intellectual development was behind that of normal hearing children of a similar age. Jeannie worked hard to find special training for Joshua. Due to her efforts, special training was provided in the public school for Joshua, involving one-on-one tutoring.... Jeannie had taken special classes and had provided additional training and tutoring on her own. She had gone substantially in debt in order to pay for the special tools and training necessary to help Joshua learn. Her efforts have attracted the state-wide attention of those interested in programs for deaf children....
>
> At the time of trial, Joshua ... was at a level of intellectual development equivalent to that of hearing children his age.... Jeannie and her three children use sign language as fluently as ordinary speech. All have the habit of "signing" everything they say in Joshua's presence, so that he participates in the conversations. Joe, too, has some sign language capability, but it is described as minimal....
>
> Joe's attitude toward Joshua's future development is described as apathetic and fatalistic.

Let us now look at the preference for the natural parent from a different angle by reading *Dyer v. Howell*, 184 SE2d 789 (Va 1971). Charles G. Dyer, Jr., and Emma Lane were married when he was sixteen and she was fifteen. On November 11, 1964, their daughter Kathryn was born. On November 30, 1965, Charles killed Emma. Kathryn was placed with a couple named Howell. On January 11, 1967, Charles was found not guilty by reason of insanity of Emma's murder. On August 3, 1967, he was released from the state hospital on the grounds that he was not mentally ill and was "mentally competent." (He remained under a psychiatrist's care until September 1969.) On November 10, 1967, the juvenile court awarded the Howells custody of Kathy.

On June 28, 1968, Charles married Carole Williams. In April 1969 they had a son. In December 1969, Charles petitioned for custody of Kathryn, Carole petitioned to adopt her, and the Howells also petitioned to adopt her. The court denied the first two of these petitions and granted the third.

DYER v. HOWELL

Virginia Supreme Court, 1971
184 SE2d 789

CARRICO, JUSTICE.

This controversy involves questions of the custody and adoption of Kathryn Lynn Dyer (Kathy), now seven years old. The three appeals before us bring up for review (1) the trial court's denial of a petition filed by Charles G. Dyer, Jr., natural father of Kathy, praying that her custody be changed from Thomas C. and Rebecca Lane Howell, the child's maternal aunt and uncle, to himself, (2) its denial of the petition of Carole Williams Dyer, present wife of the natural father, for adoption of Kathy, and (3) its granting of the petition of the Howells for the adoption of Kathy.

The evidence shows that Charles G. Dyer, Jr., married his first wife, Emma Lane Dyer, in March, 1964, when he was sixteen and she was fifteen years of age. On November 11, 1964, Kathryn Lynn Dyer, the infant around whom this controversy revolves, was born to this couple.

On November 30, 1965, Dyer killed his wife. On that day, upon a petition filed by a police officer alleging that Kathy was "without proper parental care and supervision," the Juvenile and Domestic Relations Court of Henrico County assumed Kathy's custody. She was placed in "the temporary custody of the Henrico County Probation Department," which in turn placed her with the Howells, where she has resided ever since.

Pursuant to an agreement with the Howells, Dyer was permitted the privilege of having Kathy visit with him. However, this privilege was later terminated on the advice of a child psychiatrist because the visits with the father were upsetting Kathy.

On January 21, 1966, the Howells petitioned the trial court for the adoption of Kathy. This proceeding was delayed in order to obtain Dyer's consent to and ascertain his feelings about such adoption. When a welfare report disclosed his opposition to the adoption, the case was continued generally.

On January 11, 1967, Dyer was tried in the Circuit Court of Henrico County for the murder of his wife and was found not guilty by reason of insanity. He was committed to a state hospital where he remained until

August, 1967. On August 3, 1967, the court entered an order reciting that Dyer was not "mentally ill" but was "mentally competent" and providing that he be "forthwith discharged and released." The order further provided that Dyer report to Dr. James Asa Shield, a psychiatrist, for such examination and treatment as the doctor deemed necessary. Dyer remained under Dr. Shield's care until September, 1969.

Following his discharge and release by the Circuit Court, Dyer was summoned to Juvenile Court for a hearing concerning Kathy's custody. On November 10, 1967, that court formally awarded Kathy's custody to the Howells. An appeal was taken from this award but the appeal was later withdrawn.

On June 28, 1968, Dyer married Carole Williams, and in April, 1969, a son was born to them. In December, 1969, Dyer filed his present petition for change of Kathy's custody. He also filed an answer to the Howell petition for adoption, stating his opposition thereto. Then Carole Williams Dyer filed her petition for adoption of Kathy, attaching Dyer's consent.

In March, 1970, the three cases, *i.e.*, the Howell petition for adoption, Dyer's petition for change of custody, and Mrs. Dyer's petition for adoption, came on to be heard together. In August, 1970, the trial court announced its decision in a written opinion.

The court found that it would not be in the best interests of Kathy to alter her custody. It therefore denied Dyer's petition for a change of custody and Mrs. Dyer's petition for adoption. The court further found that "the future welfare of the infant in question will be best promoted" by granting the Howell adoption petition and that the natural father's consent thereto was being withheld contrary to the child's best interests. The court accordingly granted the Howell petition for adoption of Kathy. The rulings were incorporated in orders entered November 2, 1970.

It is from these rulings that the Dyers appeal. Their assignments of error present two questions: (1) Did the trial court err in refusing Dyer's petition for a change of Kathy's custody and in consequently refusing Mrs. Dyer's petition for adoption? (2) Did the trial court err in then granting the Howell petition for adoption?

We first decide the propriety of the refusal to change custody from the Howells to Dyer.

The parties are in disagreement over what rule of law is applicable to disposition of the custody question. Dyer contends that the usual rule applicable in custody disputes between parents, *i.e.*, that the welfare of the child is of paramount concern, is inapplicable here where he, as the surviving natural parent, is seeking a change of custody from those not occupying parental status. The rule here, Dyer says, citing *Judd v. Van Horn*, 195 Va. 988, 81 S.E.2d 432 (1954), is that he, as the natural parent, is entitled to custody unless it is proved that he is unfit, the law presuming that the best interests of the child will be served by placing her in his custody. The burden was upon the Howells, Dyer argues, to prove his unfitness; they failed to carry that burden and he should have been awarded immediate custody of Kathy.

The Howells, on the other hand, contend, citing *Forbes v. Haney*, 204 Va. 712, 133 S.E.2d 533 (1963), that the proper rule is that the welfare of the child is the paramount consideration and that where such welfare would best be served by denying custody to the parent, the technical rights of the latter may be disregarded. The Howells argue that it was shown, and the trial court found, that Kathy's best interests would be served by permitting her to remain in their custody. This being so, the Howells say, it was proper to deny Dyer's petition for change of custody.

We need not stop to resolve what appears to be a conflict between the rule set forth in *Judd v. Van Horn*, and that set forth in *Forbes v. Haney*. There is a legal factor in this case which makes the *Judd* rule inapplicable in any event and requires that our decision be controlled by the *Forbes* rule. That factor is that the order of the Juvenile Court of November 10, 1967, formally divested Dyer of custody of Kathy and awarded her custody to the Howells. For Dyer to be entitled to a later change of custody, the burden was upon him to show that circumstances had so changed that it would be in Kathy's best interests to transfer her custody to him. Thus, the rule of decision in this case is that the welfare of the child is the paramount consideration.

At trial, Dyer did show that his circumstances had changed from the time the Juvenile Court divested him of Kathy's custody. He had attended college for one year and had secured gainful employment. He had remarried and become the father of a second child. His wife was also gainfully employed. He had purchased an old home in New Kent County, was restoring it, and was planning to move his family there. He had been discharged by his psychiatrist, who considered him "competent to be a father." And during the time his privilege of visiting with Kathy was in effect, a strong bond of affection had developed between them.

That was the bright side of Dyer's picture, as shown by the evidence. On the other side, it was shown that Kathy's visits with Dyer produced "a great deal of anxiety and tension" in the child, a condition which improved after the visits were terminated. It was also shown that Dyer had contributed nothing to the support of Kathy after he had become gainfully employed. And although Mr. and Mrs. Dyer were described as "a charming couple," it was stated that their marriage had "not been tested."

It was Dyer's plan, if awarded the custody of Kathy, to enroll her in private school in New Kent County. However, he had made no provision for the $500 annual tuition required for that purpose. In fact, in the contemplated move to New Kent, Mrs. Dyer planned to quit work, thus reducing the family's income to a level insufficient to meet living expenses, even without Kathy's presence in the household.

Further, there was testimony from a psychiatric expert called as a witness by Dyer that the latter was involved in "an undifferentiated family ego mass'' with his parents. This was described as a situation ''where there is a kind of sticky emotional thing working within a family where'' the members ''are so tied in with each other emotionally that no one can operate individually without having some fear or trepidation about getting the rest of the system upset.'' Although the witness stated that Dyer was ''attempting to make a greater differentiation of self,'' he also said that Dyer's emotional involvement with his family was ''basically the type of circumstance that . . . occurred in the Dyer home at the time that Mr. Dyer killed his first wife.''

In contrast, Kathy's situation in the Howell home presented quite a different picture. Kathy went to live with the Howells when she was one year old. At time of trial, she had been in their home almost 4 1/2 years. It was described as ''the only home she has ever known.'' She looked upon Mr. and Mrs. Howell as her father and mother and upon their daughter, Rachel, two years old, as her sister. In turn, Mr. and Mrs. Howell regarded Kathy as their own daughter.

The Howells had been married approximately 6 years at time of trial, and their marriage was described as ''settled.'' They were depicted as ''a very stable and ambitious young couple'' with income sufficient to provide for support of their family, including Kathy, and a comfortable home adequate for their needs.

A child psychiatrist called as a witness by the Howells testified that Kathy was ''emotionally the child of'' the Howells ''to whom she has deep and important and the essential mother-father ties.'' The witness stated that Kathy had become ''quite stable'' under the care of the Howells. When asked what would be the effect upon Kathy of removing her from the Howell home, the witness replied, ''It would be catastrophic.''

In settling this custody dispute, the trial court was vested with wide discretion. This was necessarily so because the determination of what was in Kathy's best interests was basically a factual matter, in the resolution of which the opportunity of the trial judge to see the witnesses and hear them testify was, as shown by his written opinion, of crucial importance.

The judgment of the trial court denying Dyer's petition for a change of custody is presumed to be correct, and we cannot disturb it unless plainly wrong or without evidence to support it. And the burden is upon Dyer to show that it is wrong.

With these principles in mind, we hold that the trial court did not err in ruling that the best interests of Kathy would not be served by transferring her custody to Dyer. In so holding, we have not overlooked the expressed and obviously sincere desire of the father to have the child with him or his claimed right as the natural parent, which in different circumstances we would respect, to be awarded her custody. But we cannot regard the proposed transfer of custody to him as other than a problematical experiment, in the failure of which the welfare of the child might well be seriously jeopardized.

We conclude, therefore, that the trial court properly denied Dyer's petition for change of custody. It follows that the consequent denial of Mrs. Dyer's petition for adoption was also proper.

This brings us to the question whether the trial court erred in allowing the adoption of Kathy by the Howells.

The record shows that the Howells had met all the technical requirements of Code § 63.1–220 *et seq.*, relating to adoption, except the requirement of Code § 63.1–225 that parental consent be obtained. Dyer contends that the adoption by the Howells should not have been granted without his consent.

Code § 63.1–225 further provides, however, that if the court finds that the consent of the parent "is withheld contrary to the best interests of the child ... the court may grant the petition without such consent." Thus the question becomes whether the trial court properly ruled that Dyer's consent to the adoption of Kathy by the Howells was withheld contrary to her best interests.

In addition to the evidence previously outlined on the custody question, the trial court had before it two reports of welfare authorities recommending the adoption of Kathy by the Howells. From these reports and the other evidence before the court, it is clear that the one thing for which the welfare of Kathy cries out is permanent stability in proper surroundings. It is problematical that she could get that stability in Dyer's home. She can get it in the Howell home.

To deny the adoption by the Howells now, against the possibility that Dyer might at some unknown time in the future be able to prove himself entitled to a change of custody, would be to deny Kathy, contrary to her best interests, the security and stability she so desperately needs. So the trial court was warranted in holding that Dyer's consent to the Howell's adoption of Kathy was being withheld contrary to her best interests and in granting the adoption without such consent.

The judgment in each of the three cases will be affirmed.

Questions on Goldstein, Freud, and Solnit

(1) What principles undergird this "standard law" giving natural parents a presumptive claim to custody? Is it a rule of judicial efficiency? A rule based on a generalization about what is most commonly in children's best interests? On some view of a special moral interest parents have in maintaining their relationship with their children? Does it have a constitutional basis? (Recall *Prince v. Massachusetts*, 321 US 158, 166 (1944): "It is cardinal with us that the custody, care and nurture of the child reside first in the parents....") Assume *arguendo* that Goldstein, Freud, and Solnit are right about the centrality of the psychological parent and the child's need for stability. Is their model statute preferable to the "standard law" we cited above?

(2) Goldstein, Freud, and Solnit argue for requiring custody trials and appeals to be "conducted as rapidly as is consistent with responsible

decisionmaking." What should this mean? Consider the following problem. In 1963 and 1964 children were born in Czechoslovakia to Bedrich and Vlasta G. In 1968, Bedrich emigrated to California while Vlasta stayed in Czechoslovakia. On July 8, 1969, Bedrich died. The children were to some extent looked after by their paternal grandparents, who had preceded their son to the United States, but the children lived with foster parents. For some time, Vlasta did not know the location of her children, although she continued to search for them. The California authorities knew of Vlasta's existence but did little to notify her of the whereabouts of her children. When Vlasta located her children, she brought an action to recover them. She first appeared (by counsel) before a court on November 4, 1971. Eventually Vlasta appealed a decision against her to the California Supreme Court. That court handed down its opinion on June 20, 1974. It held that the superior court had, in its order of March 15, 1972, failed to make a statutorily required finding that awarding custody to Vlasta would be "detrimental to the child" and had instead simply used the best-interest standard. The court also said,

> Both the mother and the foster parents have urged us not to remand this case to the superior court but to render a final custody decision ourselves. Unfortunately, we cannot do so. This issue of custody is one committed to the discretion of the trial court. Only in an exceptional case, in which the record so strongly supported a denial of that claim by the trial court that it would constitute an abuse of discretion may an appellate court itself decide who should be granted custody; plainly the present case does not fall under that exception.

In re B.G., 523 P2d 244, 258 (1974).

The dissent agreed with the majority's description of the superior court's statutory obligations, but the dissent argued,

> Instead of reversing, we should affirm the trial court's order by entering a formal finding of detriment, as permitted by Code of Civil Procedure section 909. That section provides: " ... [t]he reviewing court may make findings of fact contrary to or in addition to those made by the trial court.... This section shall be liberally construed to the end among others that, where feasible, causes may be finally disposed of by a single appeal and without further proceedings in the trial court except where in the interests of justice a new trial is required on some or all of the issues."
>
> This case is particularly appropriate for utilizing the procedure set forth in section 909. First, both sides join in the unusual request that this court dispose of the matter without remand, suggesting they are satisfied the record is complete following their 11–day trial.
>
> More importantly, the trial judge, though he did not use the magic word *detrimental*, did expressly find an award to nonparents was required for the best interests of the children and in effect clearly determined detriment would result should the children be returned to the natural mother.... He outlined the facts bearing on fitness and further explained his decision by referring to the psychiatrist's testimo-

ny concluding it would be "definitely harmful to the children to return them to Czechoslovakia with their mother."

Should the supreme court have decided the case itself? Would it be fair to decide the case using a standard the parties might not have had a chance to consult before deciding what arguments to make? Or, given the breadth of the best-interest standard, is it likely the parties had already presented all the arguments and evidence they could? Should the fact that both the mother and the foster parents asked the supreme court to decide the case be dispositive? Was there a judicial interest in remanding the case for "further proceedings consistent with this opinion?" Did the children have an interest here?

(3) The problem of litigation delay has another aspect. While a child-custody case is being decided, the children have to live somewhere. If the courts want to preserve the bonds that commonly form between custodian and child, the person who has custody of the children during the litigation will be advantaged. When the litigation lasts for years, that advantage can be critical. Should the court allow the custodian during litigation the benefit of that advantage? Goldstein, Freud, and Solnit would presumably say yes, since for them what matters is the psychological bonds that have formed between custodian and child. The New York Court of Appeals disagreed:

> While it is true in the instant case that the child has not been in his mother's custody since birth almost four years ago, and has remained with the respondents [would-be adoptive parents] for that entire period, it is nonetheless also true that petitioner requested her infant's return within three weeks of his birth and has persisted since that time in seeking to regain custody, as well as visiting the child regularly since she arrived in New York City.

Matter of Adoption of L., 462 NE2d 1165, 1169 (NY 1984). The court acknowledged that a child could be in a non-parent's care long enough to create "extraordinary circumstances" that would justify denying a natural parent custody. But the court said, "When in a case such as this, the separation between the natural parent and child is not in any way attributable to a lack of interest or concern for the parental role, that separation does not amount to an extraordinary circumstance and, indeed, deserves little significance." The court concluded:

> [T]he resolution of custody disputes such as this one ought not to provide an incentive for those who have attempted to take the law into their own hands. Here, the respondents disregarded the natural mother's entreaties for her child's return and assiduously avoided contact with her, her attorney and the jurisdiction of the California courts.... The mere passage of time cannot undo the wrong thus visited upon the natural mother and ultimately upon the child as well, and ought not now to redound to the respondents' benefit.

Is a custody dispute an adversary proceeding like any other, in which fairness to both contestants is essential and in which unfair behavior by one party may properly be punished by denying that party some or all of what he or she is seeking? Or is the only proper consideration the best interest of the child, so that fairness to the contestants becomes irrelevant and so that a misbehaving litigant may only be punished insofar as punishment is consistent with the best result for the child? The New York court seems to hint that its result is in the child's best interest. In what sense?

Should it matter whether the party adverse to the natural parent is a state agency which has, deliberately or not, delayed the decision of a case? See *In re Juvenile Appeal*, 420 A2d 875 (Conn 1979). Should the court rule that "temporary arrangements under circumstances of extraordinary need should not put parents in the position of risking permanent loss of their children due to the intervention of the state"?

(4) What unanticipated consequences might the Goldstein, Freud, and Solnit statute have?

(a) Might it make parents less willing to compromise in divorce disputes, since the losing parent would give up all rights in the child?

(b) Might it make it harder for parents in times of hardship to confide their children temporarily to the care of others, since the temporary caretakers might become the psychological parents and thus the legal custodians?

(c) Would it make child-support duties harder to enforce and less just, since the non-custodial parent would have no right to see his or her children?

(5) Goldstein, Freud, and Solnit's statute would deprive courts of much of the discretion that they have traditionally had in resolving child-custody disputes. Is this desirable?

(6) Because they would require courts to decide who a child's psychological parent is, Goldstein, Freud, and Solnit's proposals might transfer a significant part of a court's power to decide custody cases to psychologists and psychiatrists. Is this desirable?

(a) How easy is it to decide who the "psychological parent" is? What should a court do if the child has two "psychological parents"? If the child has no "psychological parents"?

(b) Is there really a difference between the "least detrimental alternative" and the best-interest standard?

(c) At this point, recall the question about the Jewish children of Dutch foster parents after World War II we asked after *Painter v. Bannister*. The Dutch government ruled that these children should be returned to their parents or placed with relatives. On Goldstein, Freud, and Solnit principles, was the Dutch government correct?

(d) If a non-custodial parent has no legally enforceable visitation rights, should he or she have legally enforceable support duties?

(7) How would *Painter v. Bannister* have been decided under Goldstein, Freud, and Solnit's approach? Was *Painter* decided under it?

The Psychological Evidence About Child Custody

Although there is now abundant literature on the children of divorced parents, it does not answer the hard questions of child-custody law. Ideally, such studies should involve large groups of children randomly selected, studied over long periods, and compared with control groups. Few studies meet these criteria. Even when the people undertaking a study are able, many things impede success. Projects that meet the criteria we described require, for instance, huge amounts of time and money. Because these studies are not laboratory experiments but rather studies of people actually living their lives, it can be hard to keep track of subjects and confine people to the categories of the study. For example, an inquiry into the child-rearing success of single mothers must cope with the fact that many single mothers may remarry during the study. In addition, some subjects have not been investigated. There is, to take one instance, little evidence about the success of single fathers of infants. In addition, there are normative questions about how to measure success. Professor Chambers thus concludes that "the recent research provides little more basis for rules than did the research available [twenty years ago]. There is even a danger that the recent research could deceive us into inappropriate conclusions." David L. Chambers, *Rethinking the Substantive Rules for Custody Disputes in Divorce*, 83 Mich L Rev 477, 514 (1984).

(4) The Tender–Years Presumption

One of the oldest rules that has been used to reduce the indeterminacy of the best-interest standard is the tender-years doctrine. That doctrine expresses a preference that mothers receive custody of young children. The doctrine has been attacked in recent years, in significant part because it is thought to offend principles of gender equality and to be an inadequate surrogate for the best-interests principle. The doctrine has in some jurisdictions been abolished legislatively. In other jurisdictions, it has been abolished by judicial decisions that find the presumption unsatisfactory on policy grounds. In yet other jurisdictions, the presumption has been found to conflict with the fourteenth amendment's equal protection clause as it has been interpreted in cases like *Orr v. Orr*, 440 US 268 (1979). Finally, in some jurisdictions the presumption has fallen before state equal-rights amendments.

Despite the waning doctrinal strength of the tender-years presumption, women are far likelier than men to become custodians of their children. There are many reasons. One is probably a persisting sense that obtaining custody is generally more important for women than for men. The economist Victor Fuchs, for instance, argues that women have a higher preference for custody than men. *Women's Quest for Economic Equality* (Harv U Press, 1988). Another reason lies in a widespread, continuing perception that it is generally better for children (especially young children) to be cared for by their mothers than their fathers. To help us assess these ideas, we will read a judicial defense of the tender-years presumption, albeit one that was legislatively invalidated shortly after it was written. W Va Code § 48–2–15 (1980).

J.B. v. A.B.

West Virginia Supreme Court of Appeals, 1978
242 SE2d 248

NEELY, JUSTICE:

The record shows that the parties were married in 1968 and that they had one child, a girl born in 1970. In September 1975 the parties separated and their child remained with the appellant wife.... The circuit court granted a divorce to the appellee husband and awarded him custody of the child, subject to the appellant's reasonable visitation rights. It was a specific finding of the circuit court that the appellant was not a fit person to have permanent custody of the child.

The trial court relied upon one incident of sexual misconduct on the part of the wife as grounds for awarding custody to the husband....

There was voluminous evidence in this case regarding the conduct of the parties which, except for this one incident of sexual misconduct, demonstrates nothing more than aggravated strife between two adults who quarreled, fought, and even on occasion physically abused one another. The evidence shows that the child received from both parents the type of affection and care which this society expects of competent parents. In fact both parties conceded that the other party was a perfectly fit "baby sitter" for the child, and the trial judge noted in his memorandum of opinion that both parties "took good care of the child when they had the child with them" and "both parties loved the child." The evidence covering the aggravated strife between the adults was offered to establish relative degrees of parental competence; however, it was essentially stipulated that the mother was fit, so the evidence of the parties' treatment of one another was introduced primarily to establish fault on the part of each party to the marriage in the hope that the child would be awarded to the less blameworthy party....

I

The appellee's primary argument in support of the ruling of the trial court is that our presumption of law that a mother is the natural custodian of children of tender years is unconstitutional, *State ex rel. Watts v. Watts*, 77 Misc.2d 178, 350 N.Y.S.2d 285 (N.Y.C.Fam.Ct.1973) or that if the presumption is constitutional, it is certainly unwise. As the proper standard for determining constitutionality is whether the presumption furthers, in a rational way, a legitimate public purpose, we can say that the question of constitutionality and the question of wisdom are inextricably intertwined.

In the first instance, it is incorrect to characterize the presumption as denying the equality of competing parents' rights to have custody of their children, since all parental rights in this respect are subordinate to the interests of the innocent children....

Even if we were to concede, however, that the parents' rights to custody of their children should be subjected to an equal protection analysis, there is no doubt that the presumption would withstand judicial scrutiny. So far, the United States Supreme Court has not decided that gender is a suspect category for equal protection purposes or that classifications based on sex must be subjected to strict scrutiny. It does appear, however, that the United States Supreme Court is examining gender-based distinctions under more stringent standards than the "rational basis" standard of review ordinarily applied to non-suspect categories. The emerging middle level standard is that " ... classifications by gender must serve important governmental objectives and must be substantially related to the achievement of those objectives." ...

The sociological, biological and evidentiary reasons which are discussed in the following sections provide sufficient grounds for sustaining the presumption, in the absence of compelling and preponderant evidence of a superior alternative.

II

... Even though lifestyles are rapidly changing, and men are now performing tasks which, as recently as ten years ago, were almost exclusively performed by women, we nonetheless are persuaded that the primary responsibility for the maintenance of the house and the care and upbringing of minor children in this society still rests with the woman, even though simultaneously, as in this case, the woman may be earning an outside income. The socialization patterns which prevailed during the formative years of the current generation of parents with young children encouraged women to develop certain attitudes such as surpassing patience and a high tolerance for a close, grating, aesthetically unpleasant, and frequently oppressive, yet nonetheless absolutely indispensable physical relationship with children. We are not being normative in our reliance upon the socialization process; we merely avail ourselves of it for the benefit of young children in the same way that a physicist relies upon the law of gravity or a doctor relies upon osmosis. When the socialization pattern changes to the extent that the traditional roles of mother and father are reversed with such frequency that the presumption no longer bears any relation to reality, then the law, perforce of changed circumstances will inevitably change.

Certainly the generalities which we infer from the socialization pattern alone, absent other considerations, would be slender reeds upon which to base our rule. However, there are other factors which militate in favor of the presumption and against the available alternatives. From a strictly biological perspective, children of the suckling age are necessarily accustomed to close, physical ties with their mothers, and young children, technically weaned, are accustomed to the warmth, softness, and physical affection of the female parent. The welfare of the child seems to require that if at all possible we avoid subjecting children to the trauma of being wrenched away from their mothers, upon whom they have naturally both an emotional and physical dependency. While a child is usually emotionally dependent upon his father, he seldom has the same physical dependency which he has upon his mother.

We have unsuccessfully been called upon to reconcile the welfare of children with the vindication of an ideal of non-gender-based societal roles. However, society is sharply divided about the desirability of such an ideal, and its implementation even among those strongly committed to the ideal is yet highly experimental. In order to reinforce the non-discriminatory nature of our presumption, it is important to remember that we are talking about a rule which operates in a situation where both parents are fit. In order to be fit, it is obvious that a mother must be willing to offer the type of closeness and physical contact which we assume on the part of mothers. Where a mother is emotionally unsupportive, fails to provide routine cleanliness, fails to prepare nourishing food, or otherwise demonstrates her unfitness, the presumption, by its own terms, will not apply.

All exceptions to the contrary notwithstanding, families in which the traditional roles of mother and father are reversed are extraordinary, at least in West Virginia. In the case before us we are not asked to inaugurate a new rule of law based upon preponderant, reliable social and biological evidence proving that our prior rule is unserviceable; rather, we are asked to inaugurate a new rule, the rationale for which is unsupported by preponderant creditable evidence. In this type of situation tradition and precedent, representing the collective wisdom of this society, provide an appropriate guide for our decision.

III

. . . The concept of "tender years" is somewhat elastic; obviously an infant in the suckling stage is of tender years, while an adolescent fourteen years of age or older is not, as he has an absolute right under *W.Va.Code*, 44§ 10–4 (1923) to nominate his own guardian. Between the two extremes are children who are more or less capable of expressing a preference concerning their custody. Where a child is under the age which entitles him to nominate his own guardian, but is, nonetheless, sufficiently mature that he can intelligently express a voluntary preference for one parent, then the trial judge is entitled to give that preference such weight as circumstances warrant, and where such child demonstrates a preference for the father, the trial judge is entitled to conclude that the presumption in favor of the mother is rebutted.

IV

. . . Recognizing the imperfections of our own materials we can justify our presumption only on the grounds that the presumption will achieve greater justice over a wider spectrum of cases than the alternative of endless hearings about issues which cannot, in any meaningful sense, be satisfactorily resolved in the adversary system. The presumption in favor of the mother, while obviously subject to challenge, is no more subject to challenge than expert testimony, the demeanor of the parties, or the competence of counsel.

... The fact finding process of courts is imperfect at best; it is unacceptable when the decision to be rendered has both subjective and objective elements, the mix of which is almost impossible to preordain by general rules, and the outcome almost uncontrollable by appellate review. If nothing else, the presumption provides a definite standard and a predictable result which is not conceivably related to the trial court's knowledge of the families involved, a serious problem whenever we are dealing with men, no matter how honest, in a rural setting where courts and litigants are frequently well known to one another.

If this Court felt that rational child custody decisions could be made in close cases by having each spouse attempt to prove himself or herself a relatively more competent custodian than the other, we might be inclined to question more critically our reliance on the presumption of maternal preference. As matters stand now, however, there is no reliable way to determine a custodian's degree of relative competence with respect to individual children except, possibly, by the use of behavioral science methods. Unfortunately, behavioral science has not advanced to the point where it can really help courts confronted by difficult child custody decisions. In fact, behavioral science is yet so inexact that we are clearly justified in resolving certain custody questions on the basis of prevailing cultural attitudes which give preference to the mother as custodian of young children.

The basic problem with behavioral science assessment of parental fitness and predictions of custody arrangements best suited to promote children's welfare is the "empirical findings directly or indirectly relevant to questions for which judges deciding difficult [custody] cases need answers are virtually nonexistent." Okpaku, *Psychology: Impediment or Aid in Child Custody Cases?*, 29 Rutgers L.J. 1117 at 1140 (1976). Existing theoretical research in this area is seriously deficient, and research opportunities for those hoping to improve on past efforts are inherently limited by the confidentiality of custody proceedings.

Because of the lack of relevant empirical data, expert witnesses in the behavioral sciences can contribute very little to the resolution of difficult custody problems, despite the inclination of some courts to rely on expert testimony in this area. For an expert to form an opinion concerning the most desirable custody alternative, he must first assess the personalities of the adults involved and the emotional adjustment of the children. Normally the assessment is done by the use of in-depth interviewing or psychological testing. The expert must then integrate his assessments of the individuals with general personality theory as a basis for predicting future behavior patterns and the consequences those behavior patterns have upon the children's emotional well-being. At this point, however, the trial court confronts the insurmountable obstacle that there are no reliable, empirical studies that can be used to predict the consequences of an adult's assumed future behavior upon a child. The end result is that " ... without empirical data specifying how adult behavior affects children, the behavioral science expert is without a scientific basis for an opinion on any issue in a difficult case." *Id.* at 1143.

V

In the case before us we have one isolated instance of sexual misconduct which in the context of this case is a wrong against the husband, but totally unrelated to the mother's relationship with her child....

While the appellant's conduct in this case might be outrageous to some, reasonable men would differ about whether it were sufficiently outrageous, *per se*, to lead us to conclude she is an unfit custodian, given the lack of consensus about these matters in contemporary society. In this type of situation, where we are drawing the inference that immoral behavior, *per se*, makes a person unfit as a guardian of a child of tender years, the only workable standard for the rebutting of the presumption is that the conduct must be so outrageous that reasonable men cannot differ about its deleterious affect upon the child.

Questions on the Tender Years Presumption

(1) Suppose the tender-years presumption is truly best for young children. Does the fact the presumption conflicts with the constitutional requirement of gender neutrality and with the social goal of gender equality mean the tender-years presumption should be abolished? In *Palmore v. Sidoti*, 466 US 429 (1984), the Court seemed to hold that even though it might be in a white child's best interest to be placed in the custody of her white father instead of the custody of her white mother who was living with (and later married) a black man, the Constitution prohibited a court from considering race in making custody decisions. Ought race and gender be treated similarly for these constitutional purposes?

(2) Professor Chambers reports that one study "found that, in general, the children within their sample who lived with parents of the same sex were less anxious, less demanding, and less angry; were warmer and more honest; and displayed higher levels of maturity, self-esteem, and social conformity than the children living with parents of the opposite sex." David L. Chambers, *Rethinking the Substantive Rules for Custody Disputes in Divorce*, 83 Mich L Rev 477, 512 (1984). If this study is correct, what role should gender play in custody decisions?

(5) The Replication Strategy

As the tender-years presumption has been weakened by constitutional attacks and changing social attitudes, courts have intensified their search for an alternative to it. One strategy is to try to replicate after divorce the custodial arrangements that prevailed while the parents were married. This strategy has four primary attractions. First, it seems to relieve courts of perplexing and onerous questions about what is best for children. Second, today's conventional wisdom holds that disruptions in children's lives should be minimized, and retaining the primary caretaker as primary custodian seems to minimize disruptions. Third, the replication strategy can be justified as doing a kind of justice between the parents. Fourth, the strategy seems to solve the discretion problem by providing an objective standard. We will consider two versions of this strategy. The first is the primary-caretaker principle.

(a) The Primary–Caretaker Standard

The first of our "replication" standards is the principle that the primary caretaker should receive custody. That principle has never triumphed legislatively, but it has appealed to and continues to influence courts. The principle has received its fullest exposition in West Virginia—which, ironically, has now statutorily dropped the principle in favor of the second replication standard, the ALI's. Minnesota experimented with the presumption for four years in the late 1980s and now retains a passing reference to it as the third of thirteen factors in Minn Stat Ann § 518.17 (2006). A Washington statute requires courts to give preeminent weight to the prevailing parent-child relationship, including the responsibility each parent assumed for caring for the child. Wash Rev Code Ann § 26.09.187(3) (West 2006). However, the Washington Supreme Court held in *In re Marriage of Kovacs*, 854 P2d 629, 632 (Wash 1993), that the statute does not enact a presumption in favor of the primary caretaker. Other courts, including those in North Dakota, Indiana, Utah, Vermont, Ohio, and Pennsylvania, have given priority to primary caretaking even without an explicit statutory command to do so.

We begin our investigation of the primary-caretaker standard with *Garska v. McCoy*. It is a West Virginia case that is no longer good law in West Virginia, but it remains the leading case on the subject.

GARSKA v. McCOY

West Virginia Supreme Court of Appeals, 1981
278 SE2d 357

NEELY, JUSTICE:

The appellant, Gwendolyn McCoy, appeals from an order of the Circuit Court of Logan County which gave the custody of her son, Jonathan Conway McCoy, to the appellee, Michael Garska, the natural father. While in many regards this is a confusing case procedurally, since the mother and father were never married, nonetheless it squarely presents the issue of the proper interaction between the 1980 legislative amendment to *W.Va.Code*, § 48–2–15 (1980) which eliminates any gender based presumption in awarding custody and our case of *J. B. v. A. B.*, 242 S.E.2d 248 (1978) which established a strong maternal presumption with regard to children of tender years.

In February, 1978 the appellant moved from her grandparents' house in Logan County, where she had been raised, to Charlotte, North Carolina to live with her mother. At that time appellant was 15 years old and her mother shared a trailer with appellee, Michael Garska. In March, Gwendolyn McCoy became pregnant by Michael Garska and in June, she returned to her grandparents' home in West Virginia.

The appellant received no support from the appellee during her pregnancy, but after she gave birth to baby Jonathan the appellee sent a package of baby food and diapers. In subsequent months the baby developed a chronic respiratory infection which required hospitalization and considerable medical attention. Gwendolyn's grandfather, Stergil Altizer, a retired coal miner, attempted to have his great-grandson's hospitalization and medical care paid by the United Mine Workers' medical insurance but he was informed that the baby was ineligible unless legally adopted by the Altizers.

In October, 1979 Gwendolyn McCoy signed a consent in which she agreed to the adoption of Jonathan by her grandparents, the Altizers. Upon learning of the adoption plan, the appellee visited the baby for the first time and began sending weekly money orders for $15. The Altizers filed a petition for adoption in the Logan County Circuit Court on 9 November 1979 and on 7 January 1980 the appellee filed a petition for a writ of habeas corpus to secure custody of his son.

Both the adoption and the habeas corpus proceedings were consolidated for hearing and the circuit court dismissed the adoption petition upon finding that the baby had not resided with the Altizers for the requisite six months before the filing of the petition, under *W.Va.Code*, 48–4–1(c) (1976), since Gwendolyn McCoy had moved away from their home for a short period. The circuit court heard testimony from three witnesses on the father's petition to be awarded custody of the child and then adjourned the hearing without a decision. The hearing on the habeas corpus petition resumed on 27 May 1980 and the circuit court awarded custody of Jonathan McCoy to the appellee based upon the following findings of fact:

(a) The petitioner, Michael Garska, is the natural father of the infant child, Jonathan Conway McCoy;

(b) The petitioner, Michael Garska, is better educated than the natural mother and her alleged fiancé;

(c) The petitioner, Michael Garska, is more intelligent than the natural mother;

(d) The petitioner, Michael Garska, is better able to provide financial support and maintenance than the natural mother;

(e) The petitioner, Michael Garska, can provide a better social and economic environment than the natural mother;

(f) The petitioner, Michael Garska, has a somewhat better command of the English language than the natural mother;

(g) The petitioner, Michael Garska, has a better appearance and demeanor than the natural mother;

(h) The petitioner, Michael Garska, is very highly motivated in his desire to have custody of the infant child, and the natural mother had previously executed an adoption consent, for said child

I

It is now time to address explicitly the effect which the strong presumption in favor of the primary caretaker parent articulated in *J. B. v. A. B., supra* has upon the equity of divorce and child custody dispositions. In this regard we must be concerned not only with those disputes which are decided by trial judges in court but also with all those cases which are settled outside of court in reliance on the rules we generate.

The loss of children is a terrifying specter to concerned and loving parents; however, it is particularly terrifying to the primary caretaker parent who, by virtue of the caretaking function, was closest to the child before the divorce or other proceedings were initiated. While the primary caretaker parent in most cases in West Virginia is still the mother, nonetheless, now that sex roles are becoming more flexible and high-income jobs are opening to women, it is conceivable that the primary caretaker parent may also be the father. If the primary caretaker parent is, indeed, the father, then under *W.Va.Code*, 48–2–15 (1980) he will be entitled to the alimony and support payments exactly as a woman would be in similar circumstances.

Since the parent who is not the primary caretaker is usually in the superior financial position, the subsequent welfare of the child depends to a substantial degree upon the level of support payments which are awarded in the course of a divorce. Our experience instructs us that uncertainty about the outcome of custody disputes leads to the irresistible temptation to trade the custody of the child in return for lower alimony and child support payments. Since trial court judges generally approve consensual agreements on child support, underlying economic data which bear upon the equity of settlements are seldom investigated at the time an order is entered. While *Code*, 48–2–15 (1980) speaks in terms of "the best interest of the children" in every case, the one enormously important function of legal rules is to inspire rational and equitable settlements in cases which never reach adversary status in court.

If every controversy which arose in this society required court resolution, the understaffed judiciary would topple like a house of cards. It is only voluntary compliance with the criminal law and the orderly settlement of private affairs in the civil law which permits the system to function at all. Consequently, anytime a new statute is passed or a new rule of common law developed, both legislators and judges must pay careful attention to interpreting it in a way which is consonant with equity in the area of private settlements.

Syl. pt. 2 of *J. B. v. A. B., supra,* attempted to remove from most run-of-the-mine divorce cases the entire issue of child custody. Certainly if we believed from our experience that full-blown hearings on child custody between two fit parents would afford more intelligent child placement than an arbitrary rule, we would not have adopted an arbitrary rule. However, it is emphatically the case that hearings do not enhance justice, particularly since custody fights are highly destructive to the emotional health of children. Furthermore, our mechanical rule was really quite narrowly drawn to apply only to those cases where voluminous evidence would inevitably be unenlightening. We limited the mechanical rule to the custody of children who are too young to formulate an opinion concerning their own custody and, further, we limited it to cases where an initial determination had been made that the mother was, indeed, a fit parent. While in *J. B. v. A. B., supra,* we expressed ourselves in terms of the traditional maternal preference, the Legislature has instructed us that such a gender based standard is unacceptable. However, we are convinced that the best interests of the children are best served in awarding them to the primary caretaker parent, regardless of sex.

Since trial courts almost always award custody to the primary caretaker parent anyway, establishment of certainty in this regard permits the issues of alimony and support to stand upon their own legs and to be litigated or settled upon the merits of relevant financial criteria, without introducing into the equation the terrifying prospect of loss to the primary caretaker of the children. As we noted in *J. B. v. A. B., supra* at 242 S.E.2d 255, "empirical findings directly or indirectly relevant to questions for which judges deciding difficult (custody) cases need answers are virtually nonexistent." The 1980 Amendment to *Code,* 48–2–15 was not intended to disturb our determination that in most instances the issue of child custody between two competent parents cannot be litigated effectively. Its intent was merely to correct the inherent unfairness of establishing a gender-based, maternal presumption which would defeat the just claims of a father if he had, in fact, been the primary caretaker parent.

II

In setting the child custody law in domestic relations cases we are concerned with three practical considerations. First, we are concerned to prevent the issue of custody from being used in an abusive way as a coercive weapon to affect the level of support payments and the outcome of other issues in the underlying divorce proceeding. Where a custody fight emanates from this reprehensible motive the children inevitably become pawns to be sacrificed in what ultimately becomes a very cynical game. Second, in the average divorce proceeding intelligent determination of relative degrees of fitness requires a precision of measurement which is not possible given the tools available to judges. Certainly it is no more reprehensible for judges to admit that they cannot measure minute gradations of psychological capacity between two fit parents than it is for a physicist to concede that it is impossible for him to measure the speed of an electron. Third, there is an urgent need in contemporary divorce law for a legal structure upon which a divorcing couple may rely in reaching a settlement.

While recent statutory changes encourage private ordering of divorce upon the "no-fault" ground of "irreconcilable differences," *W.Va. Code*, 48–2–4(a)(10) [1977], our legal structure has not simultaneously been tightened to provide a reliable framework within which the divorcing couple can bargain intelligently. Nowhere is the lack of certainty greater than in child custody. Not very long ago, the courts were often intimately involved with all aspects of a divorce. Even an estranged couple who had reached an amicable settlement had to undergo "play-acting" before the court in order to obtain a divorce. Now, however, when divorces are numerous, easy, and routinely concluded out of court intelligible, reliable rules upon which out-of-court bargaining can be based must be an important consideration in the formulation of our rules.

Since the Legislature has concluded that private ordering by divorcing couples is preferable to judicial ordering, we must insure that each spouse is adequately protected during the out-of-court bargaining. Uncertainty of outcome is very destructive of the position of the primary caretaker parent because he or she will be willing to sacrifice everything else in order to avoid the terrible prospect of losing the child in the unpredictable process of litigation.

This phenomenon may be denominated the "Solomon syndrome," that is that the parent who is most attached to the child will be most willing to accept an inferior bargain. In the court of Solomon, the "harlot" who was willing to give up her child in order to save him from being cleaved in half so that he could be equally divided, was rewarded for her sacrifice, but in the big world out there the sacrificing parent generally loses necessary support or alimony payments. This then must also be compensated for "in the best interests of the children." Moreover, it is likely that the primary caretaker will have less financial security than the nonprimary caretaker and, consequently, will be unable to sustain the expense of custody litigation, requiring as is so often the case these days, the payments for expert psychological witnesses.

Therefore, in the interest of removing the issue of child custody from the type of acrimonious and counter-productive litigation which a procedure inviting exhaustive evidence will inevitably create, we hold today that there is a presumption in favor of the primary caretaker parent, if he or she meets the minimum, objective standard for being a fit parent as articulated in *J. B. v. A. B., supra,* regardless of sex. Therefore, in any custody dispute involving children of tender years it is incumbent upon the circuit court to determine as a threshold question which parent was the primary caretaker parent before the domestic strife giving rise to the proceeding began.

While it is difficult to enumerate all of the factors which will contribute to a conclusion that one or the other parent was the primary caretaker parent, nonetheless, there are certain obvious criteria to which a court must initially look. In establishing which natural or adoptive parent is the primary caretaker, the trial court shall determine which parent has taken primary responsibility for, *inter alia*, the performance of the following caring and nurturing duties of a parent: (1) preparing and planning of meals; (2) bathing, grooming and dressing; (3) purchasing, cleaning, and care of clothes; (4) medical care, including nursing and trips to physicians; (5) arranging for social interaction among peers after school, i.e. transporting to friends' houses or, for example, to girl or boy scout meetings; (6) arranging alternative care, i.e. babysitting, day-care, etc.; (7) putting child to bed at night, attending to child in the middle of the night, waking child in the morning; (8) disciplining, i.e. teaching general manners and toilet training; (9) educating, i.e. religious, cultural, social, etc.; and, (10) teaching elementary skills, i.e., reading, writing and arithmetic.

In those custody disputes where the facts demonstrate that child care and custody were shared in an entirely equal way, then indeed no presumption arises and the court must proceed to inquire further into relative degrees of parental competence. However, where one parent can demonstrate with regard to a child of tender years that he or she is clearly the primary caretaker parent, then the court must further determine only whether the primary caretaker parent is a fit parent. Where the primary caretaker parent achieves the minimum, objective standard of behavior which qualifies him or her as a fit parent, the trial court must award the child to the primary caretaker parent.

Consequently, all of the principles enunciated in *J. B. v. A. B., supra*, are reaffirmed today except that wherever the words "mother," "maternal," or "maternal preference" are used in that case, some variation of the term "primary caretaker parent," as defined by this case should be substituted. In this regard we should point out that the absolute presumption in favor of a fit primary caretaker parent applies only to children of tender years. Where a child is old enough to formulate an opinion about his or her own custody the trial court is entitled to receive such opinion and accord it such weight as he feels appropriate. When, in the opinion of the trial court, a child old enough to formulate an opinion but under the age of 14 has indicated a justified desire to live with the parent who is not the primary caretaker, the court may award the child to such parent.

III

In the case before us it is obvious that the petitioner was the primary caretaker parent before the proceedings under consideration in this case arose, and there is no finding on the part of the trial court judge that she is an unfit parent. In fact, all of the evidence indicates that she mobilized all of the resources at her command, namely the solicitous regard of her grandparents, in the interest of this child and that she went to extraordinary lengths to provide for him adequate medical attention and financial support. While, as the trial court found, the educational and economic position of the father is superior to that of the mother, nonetheless, those factors alone pale in comparison to love, affection, concern, tolerance, and the willingness to sacrifice—factors about which conclusions can be made for the future most intelligently upon a course of conduct in the past. At least with regard to the primary caretaker parent there is a track record to which a court can look and where that parent is fit he or she should be awarded continued custody.

Certainly the record in the case before us does not demonstrate any intent by the mother to abandon the child through permitting him to be adopted by the grandparents; it is well recognized that mothers in penurious circumstances often resort to adoption in order to make the child eligible for social security or union welfare benefits, all of which significantly enhance the child's opportunities in life. Absent an explicit finding of intent to abandon we cannot construe manipulation of the welfare system to direct maximum benefits towards this child as anything other than a solicitous concern for his welfare.

Questions on the Primary–Caretaker Standard

(1) How strong is the primary-caretaker standard? Could it be used by a non-parent to defeat a claim of a parent? To defeat the (separate) claims of both parents? Would *any* primary caretaker have standing to participate in a child-custody suit? To initiate one?

(2) What is the relationship of the primary-caretaker standard to the other principles that may give meaning to the best-interest principle?

(a) Some jurisdictions have sought to channel parents into joint custody. Could such efforts co-exist with a flat rule in favor of the primary caretaker?

(b) What should the relation be between the primary-caretaker standard and the well-established principle that siblings should usually have the same custodian? Suppose two siblings came to have different primary caretakers but wished to live together?

(c) What status should children's preferences have in a jurisdiction that uses the primary-caretaker standard? The universal American understanding is that those preferences are to be heeded in some way. Yet children do not universally prefer their custodial parent.

(d) What should a court do when the primary caretaker is unwilling to allow visitation but the secondary caretaker is willing? Visitation is ordinarily considered desirable for the child and the non-custodial parent. There are even occasional intimations that non-custodial parents have some sort of constitutional right to visitation.

(e) Is the primary-caretaker standard anything more than the maternal preference in disguise? Is it enough that it phrases the preference in gender-neutral terms? Are the goals of the tender-years presumption satisfactorily served by a favoring the primary caretaker?

(3) What should happen to the standard where the primary caretaker seems likely to be a bad custodian? For example, the primary caretaker might have serious psychological problems. One response would be to make an exception to the primary-caretaker standard for unfitness. But unfitness is usually defined by abuse and neglect standards, which tend to be narrow. What would be done where the primary-caretaker mother has married a man who has been convicted of sexually molesting his own children and who is not "cured" and where the father has a good relationship with the children and can offer them an excellent home?

(4) What place would fairness to the litigants have in a jurisdiction using the primary-caretaker standard? The best-interest standard suggests that those issues are subordinate to the child's welfare. But a number of people have argued (with some force) that those interests should be relevant. Certainly some of the most wrenching custody cases arise where a parent has involuntarily lost contact with the child and then recovers it after someone else has become the child's primary caretaker. What would be the status of such parents under a primary-caretaker rule? How would the problem of litigation delay be handled? What if an initial judicial ruling places custody in the hands of one contender and that delays in litigation then allow that contender to become a primary caretaker.

(5) Would a well-enforced primary-caretaker rule encourage both parents to be devoted to their children? Or might the parent who was not the primary caretaker come to feel less responsibility for the child even during the marriage? Do custody rules have any effect at all on marital behavior?

(6) Is it fair to ignore, as the primary-caretaker rule seems to do, the ways parents who are not primary caretakers may contribute to the care of their children? Even if those contributions may generally be ignored, what ought a court do in a particularly compelling case? (It is often said that women who give up careers to be with their families should be compensated in dividing marital property. Should men who give up being with their families to have a career that will support that family be compensated in deciding child custody?)

(7) How easy will it be to tell the primary caretaker from the secondary caretaker? As Professor Clark observes, "Determination of which parent is the primary caretaker . . . is not easy for the increasingly common contemporary family in which both spouses work outside the home and share the care of the children." Homer H. Clark, 2 *The Law of Domestic Relations in the United States* 500 (West, 1987). In *Brooks v. Brooks*, 466 A2d 152 (Super Ct Pa 1983), for instance, the mother had

been the primary caretaker from the children's births in 1969 and 1972 until June 1980, when the father became the primary caretaker (with the help of a live-in babysitter). A hearing was held in July 1981. Who was the primary caretaker? (Does the reason for the change in custody matter?) Or consider the work of one court that has been enthusiastic about the primary-caretaker principle. It said that "it is incumbent upon the circuit court to determine as a threshold question which parent was the primary caretaker parent before the domestic strife giving rise to the proceeding began." *Graham v. Graham*, 326 SE2d 189 (W Va 1984), quoting *Garska v. McCoy*, 278 SE2d 357, 363 (W Va 1981). Why is this the rule? Does it make sense from the child's point of view? How long do you have to have been a primary caretaker to qualify?

(8) What if there is no primary caretaker? Sometimes the primary caretaker will have died. Sometimes the primary caretaker will not want or be able to have custody (because the caretaker is ill or jailed, for example). Sometimes the child simply will not have had any real caretaker. Sometimes the parents have contributed equally to raising the child.

(9) Is there adequate public support for the primary-caretaker standard not just as a factor to consider but as an exclusive or even a primary rule?

(10) Is the primary-caretaker standard supported by adequate evidence? After a careful survey, Professor Chambers concludes that "on the basis of the current empirical research alone, there is ... no solid foundation for concluding that children, even young children, will be typically better off if placed with their primary caretaker." David L. Chambers, *Rethinking the Substantive Rules for Custody Disputes in Divorce*, 83 Mich L Rev 477, 560 (1984). Should this matter?

(11) We said at the beginning of this section that one attraction of the primary-caretaker principle was that it seemed to cabin judicial discretion. As one judge writes,

> Minnesota's experience exemplifies the tension in child custody law between a need for predictable results and an equally compelling need to freely consider variations in each family situation. The supreme court intended for the primary caretaker preference to provide a "bright line" standard for child custody decisionmaking and to thereby reduce litigation and provide more predictable results. The court's intent, however, conflicted with desires for trial court discretion sufficient to serve the varied, best interests of children.

Cary Crippen, *Stumbling Beyond Best Interests of the Child: Reexamining Child–Custody Standard–Setting in the Wake of Minnesota's Four Year Experiment with the Primary Caretaker Preference*, 75 Minn L Rev 427, 429 (1990). The Minnesota Supreme Court's hopes were dashed, according to Judge Crippen, because of "the lack of a usable definition of primary caretaking, which is necessary to achieve any of the standard's asserted benefits." Judicial discretion survived, and litigation thus flourished. *Pikula v. Pikula*, 374 NW2d 705 (Minn 1985), which established the Minnesota presumption, is said to have inspired a river of contests about who changed the diapers more often, and so on.

(b) The ALI Standard

As the questions we have just asked suggest, the primary-caretaker standard presents a number of difficulties. One logical response to many of those difficulties runs like this: Many of the awkwardnesses of the primary-caretaker principal comes from its winner-take-all quality. We don't want one parent to win and one to lose. That is neither good for the children nor fair to the parents. As you will recall, § 2.09(1) of the ALI Principles (which we read earlier in this chapter at page 840) instructs courts to give preponderant weight to "the caretaking functions each parent performed for the child before their separation." The ALI custody standard has now been adopted by West Virginia. W Va Code 48–9–101 to 48–9–604 (2006).

Notes and Questions on the ALI Standard

(1) Does the ALI "proportional representation" approach solve the problems of the primary-caretaker principle?

(2) The ALI Principles distinguish between "caretaking functions" and "parenting functions." Custody is to be awarded primarily in terms of the former. The ALI Principles announce, "A secondary objective of this Chapter is to achieve fairness between the parents." Do the Principles achieve that objective? Recall Jerry (of the Linda and Jerry mediation). He worked long hours. He may well have thought he did so to support his family. He may not have wanted to work so hard and might rather have spent his time with his family. Is it fair to him to count this against him in allocating custody?

(3) Did Linda nevertheless "earn" custody of Kenny by being his primary caretaker? Women may feel particularly sensitive about this issue because, just as men historically obtain status from their jobs, women's status has historically been measured by their success as parents. Should this affect our understanding of "fairness between the parents"?

(4) Are these considerations of "fairness between parents" overcome by a belief that the child needs stability?

(5) How should *Garska* be decided under the ALI Principles?

(6) The Child's Preference

One solution to the problem of custody disputes is to take the choice out of the hands of both the litigants and the courts. One way to do this is to give the choice to the child. This device is used in some form throughout the United States. At this point, then, you should review what you learned about the child's preference. Question (3) of the "Notes and Questions About Section 402" of the UMDA considers the authority of that preference. "Questions About Section 404" of the UMDA investigates how the child's preference is to be discovered.

Many state statutes, like the UMDA, recognize that a child's choice of custodial parent ought to matter in custody decisions. Generally, the older the child, the more weight is given their views. Courts in the past have been cautious in allowing children's testimony for several reasons, including concerns that involving the children in litigation is itself detrimental that causing them to choose between their parents may harm them emotionally, and that allowing younger children to influence the court's decision may inspire contests of gift-giving between the parents. For an argument that older children are nevertheless able to determine their own interests see Wendy Anton Fitzgerald, *Maturity, Difference, and Mystery: Children's Perspectives and the Law*, 36 Ariz L Rev 11 (1994).

There is one device for taking the child's preference into account we have not discussed. That is having the child represented by an attorney during the proceedings. In a number of states, statutes confide the appointment of such an attorney, or "guardian ad litem," to the discretion of the trial court. Section 310 of the UMDA states, "The court may appoint an attorney to represent the interests of a minor or dependent child with respect to his support, custody, and visitation."

What are the duties of the guardian ad litem? One court concluded

> that a guardian ad litem . . . is in every sense the child's attorney, with not only the power but the responsibility to represent his client zealously and to the best of his ability. Like any other attorney he should, upon appointment, investigate the facts thoroughly, a responsibility which ordinarily should include home visits and a private interview with the child with no one else present. When he feels it necessary, he should consult with non-legal experts—psychologists, social workers, physicians, school officials, and others. He should exercise his best professional judgment on what disposition would further the best interests of the child, his client, and at the hearing vigorously advocate that position before the court. With this responsibility necessarily goes the power to conduct discovery, to subpoena witnesses and present their testimony, to cross-examine witnesses called by other parties, and to argue his position to the court.

Veazey v. Veazey, 560 P2d 382, 387 (Alaska 1977).

Since calls for them first started appearing in academic journals thirty years ago, guardians ad litem have proliferated in cases involving children. For example, the Iowa Code includes twelve separate occasions when GALs may be used, including minors' petitions to obtain abortions without parental consent, child-abuse assessments, juvenile-justice proceedings, parental-rights terminations, child-custody and visitation matters (including visitation by a parent who murdered the other parent), adoption, paternity determinations, cases involving the liability of parents for acts of children, and cases involving children who are victims of crime. The list in Virginia includes many of these categories and adds surrogacy proceedings and proceedings to collect child support. According to Linda D. Elrod and Robert G. Spector, *A Review of the Year in Family Law: Century Ends with Unresolved Issues*, 33 Fam LQ 865, 909 & Chart 2 (2000), attorneys for children or guardians ad litem are required in 39 states plus the District of Columbia.

Because restricting guardianship to attorneys would be expensive, many states allow non-lawyers to be appointed after special training. The use of non-lawyers does present unauthorized practice of law problems. However, volunteer programs like CASA (Court Appointed Special Advocates) have been well regarded in child abuse and neglect cases and are encouraged by the American Bar Association. As CASA's website reports:

> Concerned over making decisions about abused and neglected children's lives without sufficient information, a Seattle judge conceived the idea of using trained community volunteers to speak for the best interests of these children in court. So successful was this Seattle program that soon judges across the country began utilizing citizen advocates. In 1990, the U.S. Congress encouraged the expansion of CASA with passage of the Victims of Child Abuse Act. Today more than 900 CASA programs are in operation, with 42,400 women and men serving as CASA volunteers.

Veazey suggests the guardian ad litem's client is the child. Ordinarily an attorneys take instruction from their clients and pursues those goals the clients choose. But many children in custody actions are entirely unable to express an opinion, and many others may be too young to formulate a wise one. How, then, ought guardians ad litem decide how to represent their clients? *Veazey* says they "should exercise their "best professional judgment." But what in lawyers' professional training equips them to reach a judgment about child custody? We have been reading vigorous attacks on the ability of anyone—court, expert, or even parent—to decide what is best for a child. Why might we allow guardians ad litem to make such a decision? We have been much concerned with the scope of a judge's discretion in custody cases. Ought we be also concerned the guardian's discretion?

What should guardians do if they disagree with their client? The solution of the Virginia Supreme Court Rule 8.6 is that the guardian must "vigorously represent" the child, though the guardian must inform the court when the position conflicts with the guardian's assessment of the child's interests and welfare. In *In re Davis*, 465 A2d 614 (Pa 1983), the attorney appointed to represent the child objected to his testifying. The Pennsylvania Supreme Court wrote, "[C]ounsel does the child a disservice if he does not take care to submit the child's viewpoint/preference to the court, offer whatever reasonable support may exist for that viewpoint, and explain why counsel's opinion as to the 'best interests' differs from that of the child/client." But if the guardian may disregard the client's instructions to the extent of arguing against the client's position, why must he put the client on the stand when he thinks that injures the client's interests? For a description of how children actually work with their lawyers, see Emily Buss, *Confronting Developmental*

Barriers to the Empowerment of Child Clients, 84 Cornell L Rev 895 (1999).

Although children have an interest in their parents' divorce that may be recognized by the appointment of a guardian ad litem, children are not ordinarily thought of as litigants. For example, in *Grissom v. Grissom*, 886 SW2d 47 (Mo App 1994), the trial court refused to let a divorced couple's teenaged children participate in ongoing prolonged disputes (involving charges of sexual abuse) about visitation.

Are the guardian ad litem's responsibilities only to the client? One court suggests that "the guardian ad litem should also assist the court and the parties in reaching a prompt and fair determination, while minimizing the acrimony during this process." *Provencal v. Provencal*, 451 A2d 374, 377 (NH 1982). Does this duty conflict with the guardian's responsibilities to the client? Should the guardian's recommendation have special weight as coming from "a presumably disinterested, qualified person whose only concern was the welfare of the child"? *Metz v. Morley*, 289 NYS2d 364, 368 (Sup Ct App Div 1968).

How should a judge think about whether to appoint a guardian ad litem? Is a guardian likely to bring to the case enough useful information or ideas that would otherwise not surface to justify the cost in time, money, and resources? Proponents of GALs cite cases like *Marriage of Reinhart v. Reinhart*, 617 NW2d 907 (Wis App 2000). There, the mother left the marital home when her husband literally pointed a gun at her head. The children, at the father's request, stayed during the predivorce separation with his parents. Both the father and the grandparents did what they could to "improperly influence" the children and to "sabotage their relationship" with the mother. Without the guardian's support and investigation, the mother, who was faced with the husband's threats of violence and his family's hostility, would probably not have been able to make out a winning case. In *Serl v. Oles*, 2000 WL 973096 (Wash App), the mother had consistently attempted to restrict or eliminate the father's visitation. She once moved to a domestic violence shelter, home schooled the children, removed them from public places where he might be able to have contact with them, and finally moved from Utah to Washington. The guardian ad litem was able to ferret out her false allegation that the father had abused the children.

On the other hand, guardians for children in these hotly contested cases may be expensive, may not be not efficient, and sometimes may be counterproductive. One family-court judge writes, "There is little that counsel for the child can contribute to the fact finding unless by some mere fortuity he is better prepared on the case than the other attorneys or is a more competent interrogator. Thus he often sits mute at the counsel table during the fact finding." Nanette Dembitz, *Beyond Any Discipline's Competence*, 83 Yale L J 1304, 1312 (1974). In *Cyr v. Cyr*, 432 A2d 793, 798 (Me 1981), the court observed that the trial court

> was deluged with testimony from lay and expert witnesses concerning the relative capabilities of the Cyrs as parents. Neither party to this

bitterly contested custody proceeding had any incentive to minimize his own contributions to the children's welfare or to conceal any subversions of that welfare by the other spouse. An investigator from the Maine Department of Human services offered a neutral opinion of the children's best interest. The trial justice could reasonably have predicted that a guardian ad litem for the children would provide little additional information while substantially increasing the contentiousness of the hearing.

The most significant problem with GALs is that they may add cost without benefit. Occasionally, however, they may be actively troublesome. Consider *Perez v. Perez*, 769 S2d 389 (Fla App 1999), a case with good descriptions of the functions of both guardians and court-appointed attorneys for children. There, the guardian apparently sided with the father. This would hardly be remarkable except, among other things, that the guardian tried to evade the court's orders and advised the father not to return the children to the mother after a visitation period. In *Davis v. Davis*, 711 NYS2d 663 (App Div 2000), an attorney was appointed guardian ad litem in a contested custody case. Eventually the husband paid the GAL $1500 to write a report in the husband's favor. The husband did not disclose to the wife or the court that he had retained the attorney, who, in his words, was performing a useful function and not being compensated. The appellate court held that the trial court erred in not disqualifying the guardian because of the conflict of interest.

How does the appointment of a guardian fit with all the ideas we have discussed about parental rights and the superior judgment of parents about their children? Is there a kind of affront to parents in appointing someone to litigate on their child's behalf against them and then (as is customary) to charge them for that lawyer's services?

For more on representing children, see Chapter 10's discussion of the role of the guardian *ad litem* in child abuse and neglect cases.

(7) Joint Custody

As of 2000, every state allows some form of "joint custody," but most simply authorize it as a possible alternative rather than favor it. A number of states have some kind of presumption or preference in favor of joint physical custody. Five states, the largest of which is California, presume joint custody is in the child's best interests only when both parents favor it. Six others, including Iowa, New Mexico and the District of Columbia, allow the presumption to be overcome by a preponderance of the evidence.

A strong statutory preference for joint custody is:

> The court shall order that the parental responsibility for a minor child be shared by both parents unless the court finds that shared parental responsibility would be detrimental to the child. Evidence that a parent has been convicted of a felony of the third degree or higher involving domestic violence, as defined in s. 741.28 and chapter 775, or meets the

> criteria of s. 39.806(1)(d), creates a rebuttable presumption of detriment to the child. If the presumption is not rebutted, shared parental responsibility, including visitation, residence of the child, and decisions made regarding the child, may not be granted to the convicted parent.... If the court determines that shared parental responsibility would be detrimental to the child, it may order sole parental responsibility and make such arrangements for visitation as will best protect the child or abused spouse from further harm.

Fla Stat Ann § 61.13(2)(b)(2) (West 2005).

At the insistence of father's rights groups, significantly stronger presumptions of joint custody have been enacted in several states. See Iowa Code § 598.41 (2005); Me. Rev. Stat. Ann. Tit. 19–A § 1653 (2006). Further, litigation in nearly all jurisdictions challenges all but equal joint physical custody so long as both parents are fit, based on the parental autonomy doctrines discussed in connection with *Troxel* and *Elk Grove.* (For news on the class action suits, see http://www.indianacrc.org.) To date, the constitutional litigation has been unsuccessful. For some examples, see Urso v. Illinois, 2004 WL 2658395 (ND Ill, Kennelly, J.), (42 USC § 1331), dismissed for lack of subject matter jurisdiction (Oct. 7, 2004); Creed v. Wisconsin, 04–00917 (ED Wis Curran, J.), dismissed with prejudice Sept. 24, 2004 (same); Ward v. Louisiana, 04–CV–2697 (ED La)(Fulton, J.); Martin v. Florida, 04–CV–22385 (SD Fla Jordan, J.)(42 USC § 1985); and In re Marriage of Arnold, 679 NW2d 296 (Wis App), *review denied,* 679 NW2d 547, *cert. denied,* 543 U.S. 873 (2004) (denial of equal custody challenged under substantive due process). The *Arnold* court wrote:

> With our standard of review in place, we hold that David has not met his heavy burden. First, the facts of this case are distinguishable from those in *Troxel.* A dispute between a parent and grandparents represents a far different dynamic than the dispute between two natural parents with equal rights after a divorce. The grandparents in *Troxel* simply did not have a fundamental right to the care and custody of the children as do the parents here. So, when the *Troxel* court was speaking of fundamental rights in the raising of children, it was speaking to the existing disparity between natural parents and grandparents.
>
> Second, insofar as disputes between natural parents are concerned, while parents do have a natural right to care and custody of their children, this does not mean that parents have a "fundamental right" to "equal placement periods" after divorce. David has not demonstrated why, following a divorce between parents, the state does not have the right to arbitrate any dispute those parents may have over what happens to their children. *See LeClair v. LeClair,* 137 N.H. 213, 624 A.2d 1350, 1357 (N.H.1993) ("The legislature contemplated the need to have ... heightened judicial control over divorced families because of unique problems that exist in a home that is split by divorce."). We conclude that David has not met his heavy burden to show why the state should be foreclosed from allowing its courts to set placement schedules commensurate with the best interests of the children even if it means less than equal placement. His substantive due process argument fails.

The Iowa statute, Iowa Code § 598.41 (2006) signed by the governor in 2004, provides in relevant part, that absent a history of domestic abuse:

5. a. If joint legal custody is awarded to both parents, the court may award joint physical care to both joint custodial parents upon the request of either parent. Prior to ruling on the request for the award of joint physical care, the court may require the parents to submit, either individually or jointly, a proposed joint physical care parenting plan. A proposed joint physical care parenting plan shall address how the parents will make decisions affecting the child, how the parents will provide a home for the child, how the child's time will be divided between the parents and how each parent will facilitate the child's time with the other parent, arrangements in addition to court-ordered child support for the child's expenses, how the parents will resolve major changes or disagreements affecting the child including changes that arise due to the child's age and developmental needs, and any other issues the court may require. If the court denies the request for joint physical care, the determination shall be accompanied by specific findings of fact and conclusions of law that the awarding of joint physical care is not in the best interest of the child.

b. If joint physical care is not awarded under paragraph "a", and only one joint custodial parent is awarded physical care, the parent responsible for providing physical care shall support the other parent's relationship with the child. Physical care awarded to one parent does not affect the other parent's rights and responsibilities as a joint legal custodian of the child. Rights and responsibilities as joint legal custodian of the child include, but are not limited to, equal participation in decisions affecting the child's legal status, medical care, education, extracurricular activities, and religious instruction.

As you read the following case, consider whether a presumption of joint physical custody makes sense when the parties do not want it. For a discussion of the effects of Oregon's modification of its custody rules to encourage mediation, more sharing of time with children, and enforcement of visitation awards (called parenting time), see Margaret F. Brinig, *Does Parental Autonomy Require Equal Custody at Divorce*? 65 La L Rev 1345 (2005). The article concludes that children likely do not receive any real psychological benefit, that the costs of divorce (including legal fees) increase, and that both spouses have incentives to avoid mediation and the joint custody regime by claiming domestic violence.

Because of these statutes and because of the factors that motivated these statutes, there is an increasing tendency for couples to agree on and courts to order joint physical custody. In the 46,172 divorces recorded in 1995 in four states (Connecticut, Montana, Oregon and Virginia), 27% of the custody awards were joint. A study of 300 cases from Washington (which has a presumption of joint custody) revealed that 30% had awards of more than 20% of custodial time to each parent. Jane W. Ellis, *Plans, Protections and Professional Intervention: Innova-*

tions in Divorce Custody Reform and the Role of Legal Professionals, 24 U Mich JL Ref 65 (1990).

MURRAY v. MURRAY

Court of Appeals of Tennessee, 2000
2000 WL 827960

CANTRELL, J.

Following divorce, the court granted joint custody of the two children of the marriage to both parents, with the mother receiving primary physical custody. After problems arose with the joint custody arrangement, the parents both filed petitions to modify the divorce decree. The trial court responded by dividing custody equally between the parties. We reverse, and grant custody to the father, with reasonable visitation for the mother.

I.

Mark and Alma Murray married, divorced, and married again. Their son, Clint, was born in July of 1986. Their son, Mark Jr., was born in June of 1988. A final decree of divorce, filed on December 16, 1997, ended their second marriage. The court's order gave effect to the parties' marital dissolution agreement, which gave the parents joint custody of their two boys, with the mother to exercise primary physical custody. The father was ordered to pay child support.

Despite continuing tensions between the parties, they managed to cooperate reasonably well on matters of visitation and support. The parties had full-time jobs with different hours, and they had to alternate care of the children in a way that would not interfere with their job responsibilities. Mr. Murray always paid his child support on time, and he gave Ms. Murray additional financial help when she needed to move into a new apartment.

The situation changed in June of 1998 when Alma Murray began dating Patrick Neiswinter. Mr. Murray strongly objected to the fact that his former wife allowed Mr. Neiswinter to spend nights in her apartment when the children were present. For her part, Alma Murray no longer felt that she had to rely on Mark Murray for help with child care, and she stopped communicating with him about the children, and became less cooperative on matters of visitation. For example, she and Mr. Neiswinter took the boys on a camping trip in Virginia over the Labor Day weekend without telling Mr. Murray, and this apparently reduced his scheduled visitation.

On September 16, 1998, Mark Murray filed a Petition to Modify the final decree of divorce. He contended that it was not in the best interest of the children to be exposed to immoral behavior by the mother, and he asked the court to order her to "cease having men she is not married to spending the night at her home in the presence of the children or, in the alternative, that the children not be forced to spend the night in the home of their mother's boyfriend or any other man."

On December 18, Alma Murray filed an answer and counterclaim. The answer admitted that she "allowed one man, who she has a steady serious relationship with, sleep on the downstairs couch in her residence," but denied the allegations of immoral conduct. The counterclaim asked the court to award her 50% of the proceeds from the husband's sale of a piece of property in Georgia, where the parties had previously lived.

On February 18, 1999, Mark Murray filed an amended petition, in which he asked to be granted primary custody of the children. Mr. Murray alleged that he had asked both Ms. Murray and Mr. Neiswinter to discontinue the overnight visits while the children were in the house, and that they had agreed, but had not kept the agreement. Instead, they continued to live together on a nearly full-time basis in Ms. Murray's house. Mark Murray also claimed that Alma Murray had repeatedly interfered with his right to get information from the children's school, that she had allowed them to accumulate frequent and excessive absences from school, that she maintained a dirty or messy house that was not a suitable environment for the children, and that she was financially irresponsible.

The hearing of this case was conducted on May 12, 1999. During her testimony, Alma Murray admitted to her sexual relationship with Patrick Neiswinter, and referred to him as her fiancé. At the conclusion of testimony, the trial court took the case under advisement for 30 days, and implied that if Ms. Murray and Mr. Neiswinter married during those 30 days instead of waiting until a planned wedding date of October 2, he would be more sympathetic to her arguments.

Alma Murray married Patrick Neiswinter on May 28, 1999, and filed proof of the marriage with the court. On July 6, 1999, the trial court entered an order giving the parties what it termed "divided custody" of the children, but which appears to be just another form of joint custody. By the terms of the order, Mark Murray would have sole care and custody of the children during the fall school term, and Alma Murray Neiswinter would have the same custody during the spring term. The summer months would be equally divided between the parties. Each party would pay child support to the other during the other party's period of custody, and would be entitled to specified visitation during that period. An amended order, filed July 28, 1999, included more specific detail regarding schooling and visitation. Both parties appealed.

II.

The parties are equally unhappy with the decision of the trial court, and both agree that joint custody is not in the best interest of the children. Interestingly, the trial judge himself stated at the conclusion of the May 12 hearing that "there is no way that joint custody is going to continue to work in this case. I don't think it ever really operated or worked," and "joint custody is an onerous burdensome method of raising children between divorced people. It rarely really works."

It is unclear why the trial judge chose, despite his own grave reservations, to order a joint custody arrangement in this case. Perhaps he ruled as he did because of the difficulty of choosing one parent over another, when both parties appear from the record to be loving, concerned parents, who are obviously eager to do their best for the children.

In any case, the parties appear to be in agreement that it would be in the best interest of the children for the court to grant custody to only one parent. Of course they disagree as to which of them is the more suitable parent to exercise that custody.

Before dealing with that difficult question, however, we must first dispose of a threshold matter raised by Ms. Murray. She argues that it was error as a matter of law for the court to remove the children from her primary custody, in the absence of proof that her behavior poses a risk of danger to their mental or emotional well-being. She relies for this argument upon the case of *Musselman v. Acuff*, 826 S.W.2d 920 (Tenn. Ct.App.1991), in which this court used just such language in reversing a trial court's change of custody. We also held that the cohabitation of a parent with a person of the opposite sex does not, in and of itself, constitute a change of circumstances that would justify a change of custody.

We note that the custody statute, Tenn.Code. Ann. § 36–6–101, merely states in reference to modification of an order of custody and child support that "[s]uch decree shall remain within the control of the court and be subject to such changes or modifications as the exigencies of the case may require."

Our courts have interpreted the term "exigencies" in that section to refer to new facts or changed conditions which emerged after the initial custody order, and which could not have been anticipated by it. Such changes in circumstances may include "the unworkability of joint custody because of the recalcitrance of one or both parents."

The *Musselman* case can easily be distinguished from the present one by its unusual facts. In that case, the trial court terminated the sole custody that a mother had exercised over her son since he was an infant, and placed it in a father who had a history of untreated alcohol and drug abuse. The mother had remarried, and lived in New Mexico. The father, likewise remarried, apparently lived in Tennessee. The trial court's decision was based primarily upon the fact that the mother had become involved in sexual relationships with several men before getting married. This court appropriately reversed the trial court, finding nothing in the mother's conduct to justify the drastic remedy ordered by the trial court.

In the present case, both parents participated in bringing up their children both before and after the divorce. The father lives in Franklin, and the mother in Brentwood, so even with custody granted to one or the other, reasonable visitation will ensure that both will have a continuing role to play in their children's lives. It is apparent that a change of custody in this case need not have the drastic effect on the children that could have resulted from the trial court's order in the *Musselman* case.

It should be self-evident that it would be unwise for the courts to alter child custody orders because of minor changes in the lives of the custodians or children, even if those changes were unanticipated by the decree, or else every new circumstance would be an occasion for renewal of the struggle over custody. But we believe that the failure of joint custody in this case is not a small matter, and that it provides ample reason for crafting a different arrangement.

III.

The paramount consideration in child custody cases is always the best interest of the child or children. In cases in which the children are fortunate enough to have two capable and fit parents ready to assume custody, the job of the court is to weigh the comparative fitness of the parents, and choose the one best able to meet the children's needs.

The legislature has set out a list of factors for the courts to consider in determining the best interest of the child. Tenn.Code. Ann. § 36–6–106. [We omit the court's list of the now-standard statutory factors.]

The proof shows that both parties are able to offer their children a generous amount of love and affection, and that both are equally disposed to furnish their children with food, clothing, medical care, education and other necessities of life. We believe, however, that course of events following the divorce demonstrates that the father is in a better position to offer them the continuity and consistency that they require.

After the parties separated, the children continued to live with their mother in the Franklin apartment the parents had shared as a couple. Mr. Murray moved temporarily into a Brentwood apartment with a man who belonged to his church. Later, the mother fell behind in her rent. She moved out of her apartment without paying the rent, and after a move to Robertson County did not work out, she called upon Mr. Murray to help her move back to Williamson County. They found a duplex, and Mr. Murray paid the first month's rent in addition to his regular monthly child support payment.

Meanwhile, Mr. Murray's father moved to Tennessee, and he and Mr. Murray bought a new home in a Franklin subdivision, in close proximity to a neighborhood school. Larry Murray is retired, and while he did not testify at trial, it was clear from the mother's testimony that she regards him as a reasonable man who loves his grandchildren, and who can be trusted to take care of them when Mark Murray is unavailable.

The mother obviously has a problem handling money and meeting all the commitments involved in running a household. The apartment complex in which she had lived sued her for failure to pay the rent, and obtained a $2,000 judgment. Williamson County Medical Center also obtained a judgment against her. Her drivers license was suspended because of unpaid traffic citations, and for failure to pay damages from a 1997 accident. Since then, she had been driving around with a suspended license. On one occasion, the electricity in her apartment was turned off for non-payment of the bill. Interestingly, Patrick Neiswinter admitted that he has also had financial problems for several years, and that his car was recently repossessed.

Both parties hold down full-time jobs. Mark Murray works for Saturn. His job often requires that he work overtime. Alma Murray's job with Astra Pharmaceuticals involves frequent travel. After separation and divorce, the parties had to adjust their visitation schedule to ensure that one would be on the scene to take care of the children when the other was unavailable. As a result, Mr. Murray exercised more visitation than was contemplated by the court's order, and Alma Murray did not object.

After Mr. Neiswinter arrived on the scene, Alma Murray would leave the children in his care when she had to go on business trips, sometimes without even telling Mr. Murray that she would be gone. Mr. Neiswinter also works for Astra Pharmaceuticals, so this has sometimes meant his leaving the children unattended while he was at the office, even though Mr. Murray or his father might have been able to look after them if they had been contacted. Alma Murray often had trouble getting the children to school on time, and they accumulated a large number of absences and tardies during the school year. Patrick Neiswinter apparently did no better.

It appears that after establishing a relationship with Patrick Neiswinter, Alma Murray attempted to exclude Mark Murray from her life and that of her children as much as possible. Such an attempt is in direct contradiction to a very important factor in determining child custody, "the willingness and ability of each of the parents to facilitate and encourage a close and continuing parent-child relationship between the child and the other parent, consistent with the best interest of the child." Tenn.Code. Ann. § 36–6–106(10).

We note that Alma Murray testified that Patrick Neiswinter has established a strong and loving bond with her children, and his testimony confirmed that. Such a bond with a stepfather can be very helpful to children, but not at the cost of erasing the bond with a loving natural father.

We believe that the trial court erred in ordering joint custody in this case. We also believe that Mark Murray is the most suitable person to exercise custody of the two children. We are mindful of the importance of the relationship between the children and their mother, but we believe that Mr. Murray will be able to (and must) foster that relationship while exercising custody. We, therefore, reverse the trial court's order of custody and award primary custody of the children to Mark Murray. The cause will be remanded for the trial court to determine the child support to be paid by Ms. Murray and an appropriate visitation schedule.

Notes and Questions on **Murray**

(1) One thing we know about divorcing couples is that they have decided that they cannot continue to live together. Little that happens to them between that decision and the time their divorce becomes final will make it easier for them to cooperate. Joint custody, as *Murray* suggests, puts a premium on such cooperation. What implications does this have for joint custody?

(a) Does this mean courts should be reluctant to order joint custody unless they have some evidence that the parents are essentially well disposed to each other and will be able to cooperate?

(b) Should courts order joint custody in spite of these problems in the hopes that parents' animosities will cool over time?

(c) Should courts order joint custody in spite of these problems because it is important to children to maintain contact with both parents?

(d) Should courts order joint custody in spite of these problems because it is important to each parent to maintain contact with his or her children?

(2) Most parents want the best for their children, and it is becoming part of the conventional wisdom that continued ties with both parents are part of that best. And not all spouses leave their marriages in a rage at each other. But even with good intentions, cooperation between divorced parents depends on trust. Recall the excerpt from the mediation between Jerry and Linda we reprinted in Chapter 1. Did Linda mistrust Jerry so much that joint custody of their child was doomed? Recall, for example, that Linda was upset by Jerry's choice of day care for their child, by his unreliability, by what she believed was his untruthfulness, and by much else.

(3) Even when joint custodians do not actively distrust each other, they may find much to trouble them in each other's behavior. As Ann Estin reports from her own divorce practice,

> Mothers often experienced enormous difficulty in accepting the unorthodox parenting methods of their ex-spouses. For any practicing attorney, these complaints are familiar: "All they had for dinner was Coke and potato chips!," "They never go to bed on time at his house, and they're always exhausted when they come back to me on Sunday night," "Can you believe it? He *took a five-year-old* to see *Robocop*! Can't I do anything about it?"

Bonding After Divorce: Comments on Joint Custody: Bonding and Monitoring Theories, 73 Ind L J 441, 450 (1998). Problems of this kind plague primary custodians and "visitors." How much more severe are they likely to be if parents really share custody?

(4) Is joint custody a snare for trial (and even appellate) judges because it offers too easy a way out of hard choices? Is that what happened in *Murray?*

(5) Should a court order joint custody where the parents want it but the children do not, assuming the children are old enough to form opinions that would ordinarily be regarded as worth listening to?

(6) What incentive structure does a presumption in favor of joint custody create? For an article exploring how joint custody might change men's incentives to invest in their families during marriage and after divorce (thus lowering the divorce rate and raising the incidence of child support compliance), see Margaret F. Brinig and F.H. Buckley, *Joint Custody: Bonding and Monitoring Theories*, 73 Ind L J 393 (1998). The authors present some empirical evidence (state cross-sectional rate data) that in states where joint custody is awarded more often (or which have laws specifically mentioning joint physical custody as an option), two things are likely to happen. One is that the divorce rate is significantly lower, holding usual causes for divorce constant and using a number of different statistical techniques. The other is that the child support enforcement data show a higher percentage of paid non-AFDC child-support awards, again holding a number of other variables constant. The authors explain the child support results using the Weiss and Willis/Seltzer arguments that appear at the beginning of Chapter 11. These are that parents will be more apt to comply with court orders for support if they have closer relationships with their children and if they can see how their child-support money is spent. The divorce-rate theory involves a bonding hypothesis modeled after the hands-tying of Jon Elster and Anthony Kronman. As applied here, this theory predicts that parents who expect to maintain a close relationship with their children even if they divorce are apt to invest more heavily in their relationships (with both the children and the other parent) and to feel guiltier about how divorce would adversely affect the children. For an argument that continued contact and the status associated with joint decision making are important for fathers and should enhance their payment of child support, see Solangel Maldonado, *Beyond Economic Fatherhood: Encouraging Divorced Fathers to Parent,* 152 U Pa L Rev 921 (2005).

(7) It is often easy to change the law; it is even more often hard to change human behavior. Does joint custody in fact have the effects posited for it, or for that matter, any effects at all? Eleanor E. Maccoby and Robert H. Mnookin, *Dividing the Child: Social and Legal Dilemmas of Custody* (Harv U Press, 1992), reports that although California couples frequently agree to joint custody, and courts order it in divorce decrees, the couples settle into patterns following divorce that are remarkably like the sole custody awards of prior years. Their findings are similar to those of Judith Seltzer, *Legal Custody Arrangements and Children's Economic Welfare*, 96 Am J Sociology 895 (1991), which discovered very few differences in physical custody arrangements but some difference in payments by noncustodial fathers, and Margaret F. Brinig and Michael V. Alexeev, *Trading at Divorce: Preferences, Legal*

Rules and Transaction Costs, 8 Ohio St J on Disp Res 279 (1993), which found that custody agreements in Virginia (which had no statutory presumption in favor of joint custody) were nearly identical to those in Wisconsin (which did have such a statutory presumption). It seems likely that this apparent failure of legal reform to change legal practice tells us something about joint custody. What?

(8) When joint custody was first proposed, its advocates had high hopes that it would do wonderful things for both parents and children. The ALI Principles' § 2.06 Reporter's Notes, Comment a, at 74–75 (Tent Draft No 3, Part I, 1998), reports on a study of joint custody in Washington which found that joint custody did not seem to improve children's and parent's adjustment to divorce or the quality of the relationship between divorced parents and their children. (The study is Anna L. Davis et al., *Mitigating the Effects of Divorce on Children Through Family-Focused Court Reform* 229–30 (1997).) A meta-analysis by Paul R. Amato and Joan G. Gilbreth, *Nonresident Fathers and Children's Well-Being: A Meta-Analysis*, 61 J Marriage & Family 557, 569 (1999), found that "[h]ow often fathers see their children is less important than what fathers do when they are with their children." These findings are confirmed by Margaret F. Brinig, *Does Parental Autonomy Require Equal Custody at Divorce?* 65 La L Rev 1345, 1362–69 (2005). Using a large, nationally representative data set involving young people in grades 7–12, Brinig found that the number of nights (over several times a year) spent with noncustodial fathers had no significant effects on the children's depression, alcohol, tobacco and marijuana use, tendency towards juvenile delinquency, or morbidity (the fear of dying or being killed young). What did matter significantly for depression, juvenile delinquency and morbidity was how close the child felt to the biological father.

(9) What should parents who have joint custody but disagree about a problem do? Consider the attempt in *Griffin v. Griffin*, 699 P2d 407 (Colo 1985), to solve the problem by entering into a separation agreement. The agreement provided that the local court should have "continuing jurisdiction ... to enforce the rights of either party to joint decision making, visitation and custody...." Then it provided that "[b]oth parents shall fully and equally participate in the education of their child. Schools shall be selected jointly." When the mother selected the Vidya School (which was sponsored by the Boulder Tibetan Buddhist Community), the father objected and went to court to enforce the agreement. The Colorado Supreme Court refused to do so: "[S]uch agreements are unenforceable because the court has no power to force the parties to reach agreement and cannot grant a remedy." The court added, "Enforcing an agreement, such as this one, that requires the parents to meet and agree after they already have demonstrated their inability to agree exposes the child to further discord and surrounds the child with an atmosphere of hostility and insecurity." Do you agree? We have said that one of family law's central functions is the arbitral function. What other techniques might be open to couples with joint

custody for resolving their disputes? Can these problems be avoided by carefully selecting only those couples especially well suited for joint custody? To answer some of these questions consider Robert E. Emery et al, *Child Custody Mediation and Litigation: Custody, Contact and Coparenting 12 Years After Initial Dispute Resolution*, 69 J Consulting & Clinical Psych 323 (1991). Robert Emery and his colleagues from the University of Virginia report on a small study comparing the adjustment of children and parents who were randomly assigned to mediate or litigate their contested child custody cases, with the effects measured both close to the time of divorce and twelve years later. The children whose parents had been assigned to mediation (with highly motivated mediators) were far more likely to see their fathers once a week or more than either the litigation group or a national sample, to celebrate holidays and significant events with them, to discuss important questions with them and have the fathers involved in all aspects of their education.

(10) One of the most frequently litigated issues surrounding joint custody (and custody generally) involves relocation. The frequency of these disputes is hardly surprising. Comment (a) to ALI Principles § 2.20, page 359, notes that between 1985 and 1990 almost half the country changed living quarters, and 20 percent of them (10% of the whole country) moved across state lines. Figures for families who have experienced divorce are higher. It appears that 75% of custodial mothers move at least once within four years of separation or divorce, and over half of them move again. Anne L. Spitzer, *Moving and Storage of Postdivorce Children: Relocation, The Constitution and The Courts*, 1985 Ariz St L J 1, 3.

The New York Court of Appeals exclaimed in *Tropea v. Tropea*, 665 NE2d 145 (NY 1996), that these cases "present some of the knottiest and most disturbing problems that our courts are called upon to resolve." To be sure, courts are always bemoaning the burden of their decisions. But these cases do present conflicts in which everyone has a legitimate and conflicting interest. The custodial parents commonly have legitimate personal and professional reasons for wanting to move. The non-custodial parents commonly loath the idea of losing touch with their children. And because the stakes are so high for both sides, these disputes wind up in court with sad frequency.

If the children have reached the wanting stage, they commonly want both parents to be happy. The children may themselves be happier if their custodial parent is happier. On the other hand, they may also suffer from another disruption after the disruption of divorce. In a leading case, *In re Marriage of Burgess*, 913 P2d 473 (Cal 1996), California adopted a rule presuming that relocation was in the child's best interests. This rule has been promptly criticized. For example, Richard A. Warshak, *Social Science and Children's Best Interests in Relocation Cases:* Burgess *Revisited*, 34 Family LQ 83 (2000), criticizes the studies by Judith Wallerstein that bolstered the California rule and contends for a case-by-case examination of relocation decisions.

(11) We have already encountered the relocation problem in Jerry and Linda's mediation, which we described in Chapter 1. Jerry moved 1,000 miles away from the marital home. Should he be able to do that and remain a joint custodian?

Relocation has increasingly become a "hot" issue as more and more parents struggle with custody orders of various kinds. The California courts have both led and reflected the trends for treatment of relocation issues. Here is one well-known pronouncement on the topic:

IN RE MARRIAGE OF LaMUSGA

Supreme Court of California, 2004

32 Cal 4th 1072, 88 P3d 81, 12 Cal Rptr 3d 356

MORENO, J.

In the present case, the superior court ordered that primary physical custody of two minor children would be transferred from their mother to their father if their mother moved to Ohio. The Court of Appeal reversed, holding that if the custodial parent "has a good faith reason to move . . . the custodial parent cannot be prevented, directly or indirectly, from exercising his or her right to change the child's residence" unless the noncustodial parent makes a "substantial showing" that a change of custody is "essential" to prevent detriment to the children. We granted review to determine whether the Court of Appeal in the present case misapplied our holding in *Burgess*. We conclude that it did and reverse its judgment.

I. Facts

Susan and Gary LaMusga married on October 22, 1988, and had two children: Garrett, who was born on May 5, 1992, and Devlen, who was born two years later to the day on May 5, 1994. The mother filed an amended petition for dissolution of marriage on May 10, 1996, and requested sole physical custody of the children, who were living with her in the family residence. The father objected and requested joint legal and physical custody.

The parties were unable to agree on a visitation schedule and, pursuant to a court order, stipulated to the appointment of Philip Stahl, Ph.D, a licensed psychologist, to conduct a child custody evaluation. Pending this evaluation, the parties agreed to a visitation schedule under which the children would be with their father every Wednesday from 3:30 p.m. to 7:30 p.m. and Sunday from 10 a.m. to 5 p.m. The mother asserted that even this limited visitation with the father was detrimental to the children, causing Garrett to become overly aggressive, disorganized, unfocused, and to regress in toilet training, and causing Devlen to develop a facial tick, a stutter, and a squint.

In a report dated October 10, 1996, Dr. Stahl observed that "there has been a great deal of verbal hostility between Mr. and Mrs. LaMusga for years, at times escalating to some pushing and shoving between them.... Both acknowledge that communication has deteriorated completely and that there is no trust between them. Mrs. LaMusga is concerned that Mr. LaMusga lives in an unsafe environment, doesn't take adequate care of the boys and is not responsive to their needs. She would prefer that his time be even more limited."

"Additionally, Ms. LaMusga has expressed a desire to move with the boys to the Cleveland, Ohio, area.... [P] In contrast, Mr. LaMusga is quite upset that she wants to take the boys to Cleveland, and describes the environment there as hostile to him. He believes that Ms. LaMusga has attempted to alienate him from both the boys and ... is quite concerned that, if she does get to move, he'll end up having no relationship with his boys whatsoever."

Dr. Stahl opined that, in general, both the mother and the father were "good enough parents," but noted that the mother was "struggling with supporting and encouraging frequent and continuing contact between" the children and their father. Dr. Stahl believed that "each parent has different positive qualities to give to the children and that it is in the children's best interest to maintain a relationship with each of them as they continue to grow." But he noted his concern "about the dynamic of conflict between Mr. and Ms. LaMusga and its impact on the children. They don't speak to one another, their conflict does filter down to the children, and the children do show some evidence of anxiety related to this. Additionally, their charges and counter-charges reflect the extent to which both parents are willing to go to make the other look bad, something that is clearly detrimental to Garrett and Devlen.... [T]he conflict level between the parents is the single-most significant problem, and it has been going on for years."

Following a hearing on November 14, 1996, the superior court awarded the parties joint legal custody of the children, with the mother having "primary physical custody."[1] With the mother's agreement, the father's visitation was increased over a period of months to a final schedule of every Tuesday and Wednesday from 4 p.m. to 7:30 p.m. and every other weekend from Friday at 5 p.m. to Sunday at 6 p.m.

1. The provisions in the Family Code governing custody of children do not use the term "primary physical custody." (*In re Marriage of Richardson (2002) 102 Cal. App.4th 941, 945, fn. 2.)* Rather, the code uses the terms "joint physical custody," which "means that each of the parents shall have significant periods of physical custody" (*Fam. Code, § 3004*), and "sole physical custody," which "means that a child shall reside with and be under the supervision of one parent, subject to the power of the court to order visitation" (*Fam. Code, § 3007*). The term "primary physical custody" does appear in *Family Code section 4045*, subdivision (d)(3), which grants the Judicial Council the authority to review the statewide uniform child support guidelines.

Judgment subsequently was entered dissolving the marriage as of December 31, 1997.

On July 6, 1998, the parties stipulated that during the summer, the father would have custody of the children from July 9–15 and August 21–27, 1998, and the mother would have custody of the children from July 17–23 and August 13–19, 1998. The preexisting custody and visitation schedule would apply at all other times. On November 15, 1998, the father filed an order to show cause to have the court establish a holiday visitation schedule, which it did by an order issued on December 8, 1998.

The mother subsequently married Todd Navarro and, on September 16, 1999, gave birth to a daughter. The father also remarried. His wife, Karin, has a daughter from her prior marriage.

On February 13, 2001, the mother filed an order to show cause to modify the visitation order to permit her to relocate with the children to Cleveland, Ohio. She alleged that she had family in the Cleveland area and her husband had received an offer for a more lucrative job there. She noted in her supporting declaration that Dr. Stahl had been reappointed and was conducting an evaluation to determine whether the father's visitation should be increased.

The father objected to the mother's plan to move the children to Ohio and asked that primary custody of the children be transferred to him if the mother moved to Ohio. The father declared that the mother had attempted to alienate him from their sons since their separation and feared that moving the boys to Ohio would result in his "being lost as their father."

On February 26, 2001, Dr. Stahl submitted a supplemental report that did not address the mother's proposal to move to Ohio, which she had made less than two weeks earlier. Dr. Stahl stated that the parents were "at a continued impasse"; the father wanted "equal joint custody of the boys" while the mother wanted to discontinue the boys' midweek visits with their father. He reported some disturbing aspects of the boys' relationship with their father, noting that the boys were very critical of their father, but almost always in rather vague terms. Dr. Stahl observed, however, that the children "seemingly had a good time at their father's home." Once, Dr. Stahl "observed Devlen being affectionate with his dad, but he later denied it." . . .

Dr. Stahl recommended that the father be awarded longer periods of visitation and raised the possibility of transferring primary physical custody of the children to their father if the situation did not improve, stating: "Research suggests that alienated children do better with longer rather than shorter blocks of time with each parent, and also that it's helpful if fathers participate with children in the schooling.... I would recommend a schedule in which they are with their father every other week from Thursday after school until return to school on Monday morning and every other week from Thursday after school until Friday morning. Not only does this reduce the number of transitions that need to take place with the parents together, but it also broadens the blocks of time that they are with their dad. It also keeps mother as the primary parent, which is consistent for them." Dr. Stahl noted that if the situation did not improve, he might recommend either "a truly joint custody arrangement" or giving "primary custody" to the father.

Following a hearing on March 19, 2001, the father's visitation was increased as recommended by Dr. Stahl. The court again reappointed Dr. Stahl "to provide a focused evaluation on the issue whether the relocation of the parties' two minor children is in the best interest of said children."

Dr. Stahl's June 29, 2001, supplemental report notes that the mother has wanted to move ever since the divorce but waited, at Dr. Stahl's urging, until the children were older. The move would improve her family's "economic standard of living, and ... inherent quality of life...." The mother "believes that she will have no difficulty supporting the boys in their relationship with their dad," asserting "that she has always supported the boys in their relationship with their dad, and that she is not a contributor to any alienation that the boys might feel. [P] Not surprisingly, Mr. LaMusga doesn't see things the same way.... He is opposing the move, especially at this time, because he worries that the boys will regress in their relationship with him, especially after making tremendous progress in their work with Dr. Tuggle [the boys' therapist].... He feels strongly that a disruption now will break the bond that is developing." ...

Dr. Stahl opined that if the boys were permitted to move to Ohio: "The primary loss for the boys will be related to the growing and improving relationship with their dad. I suspect that they'll have few problems adjusting to a new school, friends, or activities, but it may be hard for them to deal with the emerging change in their relationship with their dad. The relationship currently is tenuous at best, for all of the reasons I outlined in the original update, and it is unlikely that there will be no impact to their relationship.... [P] The underlying risk, however, is that, with absence, they will regress to a more detached and disconnected state with their father. With regular and somewhat increased contact, there is improvement in the relationships. However, this improvement is tenuous, and I am concerned that the move will interrupt any progress that might be occurring at the present time."

Although the mother stated that she wanted to move to Ohio because that "is where she is originally from and where she has family support," Dr. Stahl suggested an additional motive: "Underneath, however, it has always appeared that [the mother] has wanted to move so that she can remove herself and the boys from the day-to-day interactions with [the father]. She has difficulty dealing with him and prefers to have as little communication with him as possible." ...

Acknowledging that there was "no good solution in this matter," Dr. Stahl observed that "there is a risk that both moving or not moving may create a significant change" in the children's relationship with their father, stating, "It's difficult to predict which way this will go. Mother believes that the boys will be less rejecting of their dad if they move and father believes that a move will put the nail in the coffin of their relationship. I suspect that neither of them is accurate and the actual reaction of the boys will be based on how the parents handle their issues over time....

On August 23, 2001, a hearing was held in the superior court on the mother's request to move the children's residence to Ohio. The mother declared that her husband had accepted a position as sales manager at a Toyota dealership in Cleveland, Ohio in March 2001 and had been living in Cleveland with her family since then....

The superior court ruled as follows: "The issue is not whether either of these parents are competent and qualified to be custodial parents, I think the evidence indicates that they are. That is not the question. [P] The question is whether there is sufficient evidence at this point to determine, one, that the best interests of the children is served by relocating with Mother to Ohio, or whether the best interests are served by the—a change of physical custody if [the mother] is to relocate."

The court acknowledged that the mother is not purposely trying to alienate the children from their father, but noted that the mother's inability to "let go" of her anger toward the father caused her to project those feelings onto their children and to reinforce the children when they expressed negative feelings toward their father. "That aligns the children with one parent and results in a strained or hostile relationship with the other parent." The court also acknowledged that this was not "a bad faith move away. I don't think this is an instance where [the mother is] attempting to relocate with the children for the specific purpose of limiting their contact or relationship with their father. I think it's far more subtle than that.... "

"The primary importance, it seems to me at this point, is to be able to reinforce what is now a tenuous and somewhat detached relationship with the boys and their father.... [P] I think the concerns about the relationship being lost if the children are relocated at this time are realistic.... [P] Therefore, I think that a relocation of the children out of the State of California, the distance of 2000 miles is—would inevitably under these circumstances be detrimental to their welfare. It would not promote frequent and continuing contact with the father, and I would deny the request to relocate the children. [P] If [the mother] wishes to relocate to the state of Ohio, certainly she is entitled to do that. Should she choose to do so, then I would implement the recommendations contained in Dr. Stahl's supplemental report of June 29th of 2001 which would provide for the primary physical custody of the children, at least during the school year, to Mr. Lamusga.... [P] [I]f [the mother] decides not to relocate, then the existing custodial arrangement will remain."

The mother appealed and the Court of Appeal reversed the judgment. The Court of Appeal applied the deferential abuse of discretion standard of review we recognized in *In re Marriage of Burgess*, *supra*, 13 Cal.4th 25, 32: "The precise measure is whether the trial court could have reasonably concluded that the order in question advanced the 'best interest' of the child." But the appellate court concluded that "although the [superior] court referred several times during the hearing to 'best interest' as the applicable standard, its order was not truly based on that criterion as it applies in the context of this custodial parent's relocation." The Court of Appeal concluded that the superior court "neither proceeded from the presumption that Mother had a right to change the residence of the children, nor took into account this paramount need for stability and continuity in the existing custodial arrangement. Instead, it placed undue emphasis on the detriment that would be caused to the children's relationship with Father if they moved." We granted review.

Shortly after we granted review, the mother filed a notice of abandonment of her appeal, supported by a declaration stating that she no longer intended to move to Ohio, but intended to move to Arizona instead. She asked this court to dismiss the appeal. The father objected. We denied the mother's motion to dismiss the appeal. The mother's counsel later sent to this court a copy of a letter dated July 8, 2003, informing the father that the mother and their children had moved to Arizona. Upon the request of the mother, and without objection by the father, we have taken judicial notice of an order of the superior court filed on August 29, 2003, permitting the children to live with the mother in Arizona "temporarily" pending our ruling in the present proceedings.

Despite the fact that it appears that the mother no longer intends to move to Ohio, the matter under review is not moot. It remains possible that the mother could chose to move to Ohio, and she has changed the residence of the children to Arizona. Accordingly, the issue of whether it is in the children's best interests to modify the custody order if the mother changes the residence of the children is not moot. In any event, we may decline to dismiss a case that has become moot "where the appeal raises issues of continuing public importance." This appeal certainly does.

II. Discussion

In *In re Marriage of Burgess, supra, 13 Cal.4th 25* (*Burgess*), the mother was awarded temporary sole physical custody of the couple's two children upon the dissolution of their marriage. Seven months later, the mother informed the court that she had accepted a job transfer and planned to move with the children to Lancaster, California, which was about a 40–minute drive from the couple's former home in Tehachapi. She explained that her new job would be "career advancing" and that moving to Lancaster would afford the children greater access to medical care, extracurricular activities, private schools, and day care facilities. The father objected and asked that sole physical custody of the children be transferred to him, contending that he could not maintain his current visitation schedule if the children moved to Lancaster.

The superior court awarded the mother sole physical custody of the children and modified the father's visitation schedule. The court found

" 'that it is in the best interest of the minor children that the minors be permitted to move to Lancaster with the [mother] and that the [father] be afforded liberal visitation.' " The father appealed and the Court of Appeal reversed, holding that the mother had failed to sustain her burden of showing that moving the children to Lancaster was " 'reasonably necessary.' " We granted review and reversed the judgment of the Court of Appeal.

We observed that "[i]n an initial custody determination, the trial court has 'the widest discretion to choose a parenting plan that is in the best interest of the child.' (*Fam. Code, § 3040*, subd. (b).) It must look to *all the circumstances* bearing on the best interest of the minor child." Citing *Family Code section 7501*, which states that "[a] parent entitled to custody of a child has a right to change the residence of the child, subject to the power of the court to restrain a removal that would prejudice the rights or welfare of the child," we noted that the court must also consider "the presumptive right of a custodial parent to change the residence of the minor children, so long as the removal would not be prejudicial to their rights or welfare. Accordingly, in considering all the circumstances affecting the 'best interest' of minor children, it may consider any effects of such relocation on their rights or welfare."

In reviewing the superior court's ruling, we applied "the deferential abuse of discretion test." "The precise measure is whether the trial court could have reasonably concluded that the order in question advanced the 'best interest' of the child.".) We concluded that the superior court had not abused its discretion. "After extensive testimony from both parents, the trial court not unreasonably concluded that it was in the 'best interest' of the minor children that the father and the mother retain joint legal custody and that the mother retain sole physical custody, even if she moved to Lancaster."

We rejected the Court of Appeal's holding that the mother was required to show that it was "necessary" for her to move to Lancaster: "The trial court must—and here it did—consider, among other factors, the effects of relocation on the 'best interest' of the minor children, including the health, safety, and welfare of the children and the nature and amount of contact with both parents. We discern no statutory basis, however, for imposing a specific additional burden of persuasion on *either* parent to justify a choice of residence as a condition of custody." We observed that the statutory policy promoting "frequent and continuing contact with both parents" (*Fam. Code, § 3020*) does not limit "the trial court's broad discretion to determine, in light of *all* the circumstances, what custody arrangement serves the 'best interest' of minor children." Rather, we noted, *Family Code section 3040*, subdivision (b), expressly provides the court with " 'the widest discretion to choose a parenting plan that is in the best interest of the child.' " Although *Burgess* involved an initial determination of custody, we held that "the same conclusion applies when a parent who has sole physical custody under an *existing* judicial custody order seeks to relocate: the custodial parent ... bears no burden of demonstrating that the move is 'necessary.' " But we recognized that, as with any allegation that "changed circumstances" warrant a modification of an existing custody order, the noncustodial parent has a substantial burden to show that " 'some significant change in circumstances indicates that a different arrangement would be in the child's best interest.' " The changed circumstance rule provides "that once it has been established that a particular custodial arrangement is in the best interests of the child, the court need not reexamine that question. Instead, it should preserve the established mode of custody unless some significant change in circumstances indicates that a different arrangement would be in the child's best interest. The rule thus fosters the dual goals of judicial economy and protecting stable custody arrangements." "In a 'move-away' case, a change of custody is not justified simply because the custodial parent has chosen, for any sound good faith reason, to reside in a different location, but only if, as a result of relocation with that parent, the child will suffer detriment rendering it ' "essential or expedient for the welfare of the child that there be a change." ' "

We were quick to emphasize, however, that "bright line rules in this area are inappropriate: each case must be evaluated on its own unique facts. Although the interests of a minor child in the continuity and permanency of custodial placement with the primary caretaker will most often prevail, the trial court, in assessing 'prejudice' to the child's welfare as a result of relocating even a distance of 40 or 50 miles, may take into consideration the nature of the child's existing contact with both parents ... and the child's age, community ties, and health and educational needs. Where appropriate, it must also take into account the preferences of the child."[3]

Recently, the Legislature codified our decision in *Burgess* by amending *Family Code section 7501* to add subdivision (b), which reads: "It is the intent of the Legislature to affirm the decision in *In re Marriage of Burgess (1996) 13 Cal.4th 25,* and to declare that ruling to be the public policy and law of this state." (*Fam. Code, § 7501,* as amended by Stats. 2003, ch. 674, § 1.)

The Courts of Appeal have applied the rules we stated in *Burgess* on numerous occasions. In all but two cases (*In re Marriage of Williams (2001) 88 Cal.App.4th 808* and *In re Marriage of Campos (2003) 108 Cal.App.4th 839,* which are discussed below), the Courts of Appeal have affirmed the superior court's exercise of discretion....

The difficulty of the task facing the courts in these matters is exemplified by the quandary posed in *In re Marriage of Abargil (2003) 106 Cal.App.4th 1294,* which the Court of Appeal correctly observed would challenge the wisdom of King Solomon. The parents were both

3. We noted that "[a] different analysis may be required when parents *share* joint physical custody of the minor children under an existing order and in fact, and one parent seeks to relocate with the minor children." In such cases, if it is shown that the best interests of the children require modification or termination of the order, the court "must determine de novo what arrangement for primary custody is in the best interest of the minor children."

Israeli citizens who came to the United States on tourist visas and overstayed. They married and had a son. When they separated, the child lived primarily with the mother and visited the father. The mother returned to Israel to nurse her dying mother, taking the boy with her. While she was in Israel, the father filed for divorce. When the mother attempted to return to California, she was barred from entering the United States for 10 years as a sanction for having overstayed her visa. This sanction was stayed, however, to permit her to return to California to litigate the custody of the child. The father asserted that he would be unable to visit his son if he moved to Israel, because the father was applying for permanent residency in the United States and could not leave the country for an extended time.

Following a five-day trial, the court permitted the child to move to Israel with the mother, noting that she had been the child's primary caregiver and finding that she was more likely to facilitate visitation with the father than if the parental roles were reversed. The Court of Appeal affirmed, holding that the superior court's finding that moving to Israel with the mother was in the child's best interests was supported by substantial evidence.

In only two cases have the Courts of Appeal reversed the superior court's exercise of discretion, and both cases involved unusual circumstances.

In *In re Marriage of Williams, supra,* 88 Cal.App.4th 808, the superior court permitted two of the couple's four children to move to Utah with their mother, but ordered the other two children to remain in Santa Barbara with their father. This apparent attempt at compromise pleased no one. On appeal by the father, both parents asserted that the superior court abused its discretion. The Court of Appeal agreed, holding that the superior court's order was not supported by "compelling circumstances warranting the separation of the siblings." The Court of Appeal noted, however: "Had the family law court allowed all of the children to either reside in Santa Barbara or move to Utah, we could easily affirm on the deferential standard of appellate review."

The other case in which the Court of Appeal reversed the superior court was *In re Marriage of Campos*, *supra*, 108 Cal.App.4th 839. The father in that case sought modification of a child custody and visitation order relating to his sons, aged 15 and 12, after their mother announced she would move with the children from Santa Barbara to Moorpark, about two hours away by car. The superior court summarily denied the request, finding that the mother did not have a bad faith reason for the move. The Court of Appeal reversed and remanded the matter for an evidentiary hearing to determine whether the proposed move would be detrimental to the welfare of the children. The Court of Appeal recognized that even when the custodial parent has a good faith reason for the proposed move, "a change of custody may be ordered in a 'move away' case where, as a result of the move, the children will suffer detriment rendering a change of custody essential or expedient for their welfare."

"In a move away case, the trial court must always consider whether a custodial parent is acting in bad faith. It must also always consider whether 'as a result of relocation with [the custodial] parent, the child will suffer detriment rendering it" 'essential or expedient for the welfare of the child that there be a change.' " ' "

The Court of Appeal in the present case held that the superior court abused its discretion in ordering that primary physical custody of the children would be transferred to the father if the mother moved to Ohio. The Court of Appeal concluded that the superior court "neither proceeded from the presumption that Mother had a right to change the residence of the children, nor took into account this paramount need for stability and continuity in the existing custodial arrangement. Instead, it placed undue emphasis on the detriment that would be caused to the children's relationship with Father if they moved." We disagree.

We reaffirm our statement in *Burgess* that "the paramount need for continuity and stability in custody arrangements]—and the harm that may result from disruption of established patterns of care and emotional bonds with the primary caretaker—weigh heavily in favor of maintaining ongoing custody arrangements." But there is nothing in the record before us that indicates that the superior court failed to consider the children's "interest in stable custodial and emotional ties" with their mother. The court carefully considered the comprehensive reports prepared by Dr. Stahl and the evidence submitted by both parties. The court placed "primary importance" on the effect the proposed move would have on "what is now a tenuous and somewhat detached relationship with the boys and their father," concluding that the proposed move would be "extremely detrimental" to the children's welfare because it would disrupt the progress being made by the children's therapist in promoting this relationship. The superior court found that it was "realistic" to be concerned that the proposed move could result in the relationship between the father and the children "being lost." In future cases, courts would do well to state on the record that they have considered this interest in stability, but the lack of such a statement does not constitute error and does not indicate that the court failed to properly discharge its duties.

Contrary to the conclusion of the Court of Appeal, the superior court did not place "undue emphasis" on the detriment to the children's relationship with their father that would be caused by the proposed move. The weight to be accorded to such factors must be left to the court's sound discretion. The Court of Appeal erred in substituting its judgment for that of the superior court.

Noting that the superior court relied on the history of animosity between the parents, and the mother's failure to foster and encourage a healthy relationship between the children and their father, the Court of Appeal quoted the superior court's comment: " 'Clearly if the parties had been co-parenting with the children and cooperative in this matter, under those circumstances there might well be a presumptive right' for

Mother to relocate with the children." The Court of Appeal concluded that the superior court improperly punished the mother for her past conduct by transferring primary physical custody of the children to their father. We disagree.

The Court of Appeal correctly noted that the superior court's function in determining custody is not to reward or punish the parents for their past conduct, but to determine what is in the best interests of the children. (*In re Marriage of Condon*, *supra*, 62 Cal.App.4th 533, 553.) But this does not mean that the court may not consider the past conduct of the parents in determining what future arrangement will be best for the children. (See *In re Marriage of Abargil, supra, 106 Cal.App.4th 1294, 1299* [finding that the mother respected the father's relationship with his son and was likely to foster continuing contact between them, noting her past efforts to nurture that relationship, and contrasting the father's disparagement of the mother's parenting skills]; *In re Marriage of Lasich*, *supra*, 99 Cal.App.4th 702, 719 [noting that the mother had never tried to block the father from exercising his visitation rights]; *In re Marriage of Bryant*, *supra*, 91 Cal.App.4th 789, 792 [noting in permitting a change of the child's residence that the mother had not "unreasonably interfered with [the father's] visitation with the children].) Clearly, the court must consider the past conduct of the parents in fashioning a custody order that serves the best interests of the children.

In the present case, the superior court recognized that "[t]he issue is not whether either of these parents are competent and qualified to be custodial parents.... [P] The question is whether ... the best interests of the children is served by relocating with Mother to Ohio, or whether the best interests are served by ... a change of physical custody if [the mother] is to relocate." There is nothing in the record before us that indicates the superior court acted out of a desire to punish or reward either parent. But the mother's past conduct indicated that it was unlikely that she would follow through on her promises to encourage the children's relationship with their father if they moved to Ohio. Dr. Stahl testified that "there is no evidence that I've seen in the five years that I've known this family that [the mother] will really do what she said she will do. In terms of being supportive of the boys' relationship with their father in a way that truly will reduce the loyalty conflicts and truly will help them ... feel better about things with him."

The superior court did misspeak, however, in stating that the mother might have had a presumptive right to relocate with the children if the parents had co-parented cooperatively. The mother—as the parent with primary physical custody of the children—had a presumptive right to change the children's residence unless the proposed move "would result in 'prejudice' to [the children's] 'rights or welfare.' " (*Burgess*, *supra*, 13 Cal.4th at p. 38.) But we are convinced, after examining the entire record, that the court's imperfect choice of words in this single regard does not indicate that the court misperceived the standard for determining the question before it. The court was correct that the situation might have been far different had the parents shown a history of cooperative parenting. If that had been the case, it might have appeared more likely that the detrimental effects of the proposed move on the children's relationship with their father could have been ameliorated by the mother's efforts to foster and encourage frequent, positive contact between the children and their father. But the court reasonably concluded that the present case presented the opposite situation. The parents' history of animosity and the mother's consistent attempts to limit contact between the children and their father indicated that the proposed move would be detrimental to the children. Essentially, the court concluded that the mother's past conduct made it unlikely that she would facilitate the difficult task of maintaining the father's long-distance relationship with the boys.

The Court of Appeal was concerned about the superior court's reliance upon the detriment to the children's relationship with their father that would be caused by the proposed move, because "[t]here is inevitably a significant detriment to the relationship between the child and the noncustodial parent" whenever the custodial parent relocates with the children. The Court of Appeal observed that "if evidence of some detriment due to geographical separation were to mandate a change of custody, the primary custodial parent would never be able to relocate." We agree. We do not suggest that a showing that a proposed move will cause detriment to the relationship between the children and the noncustodial parent *mandates* a change in custody. But it is within the wide discretion of the superior court to order a change of custody based upon such detriment, if such a change is in the best interests of the children in light of all the relevant factors.

It is instructive to compare the present case to *In re Marriage of Edlund & Hales*, *supra*, which involved similar circumstances. The mother in *Edlund* wished to move with her child to another state where her fiance had accepted a job and was already living and where they would have a lower cost of living, allowing her to stay at home with her children rather than working full time outside the home. A mediator found that " 'the mother does not appear to have negative motives for the move, i.e., [to] frustrate contact between the father and the child' " and an evaluator opined that the mother "was sincere about her reasons for moving." Significantly, the court relied upon the evaluator's opinion that the mother had not attempted to limit the father's visitation in the past, noting that the mother " 'did not express any anger or upset' " with the father and " 'acknowledged the importance of his role as Natalie's father. She endorsed their relationship and believes it is paramount for them to continue to have a strong bond. There is no evidence that [the mother] has frustrated or endeavored to limit or prohibit [the father's] custodial time with Natalie in the past.' " Finally, the evaluator noted that the father " 'would experience great difficulty' " if he were given primary physical custody of the child. Although the superior court questioned the mother's judgment, it permitted the mother to change the residence of the child.

The Court of Appeal in *Edlund* affirmed, concluding that the superior court had not abused its discretion: "After a thorough review of the record, we are satisfied that the trial court carefully considered all the factors bearing on Natalie's best interest, and that its decision was supported by substantial evidence of the strength and primacy of the bond between Natalie and her mother, [the mother's] proven ability to provide and care for Natalie on a full-time basis, and the overwhelming, undisputed proof that [the father] was not adequately prepared to assume primary physical custody of his daughter. Thus, we conclude the trial court did not abuse its discretion by issuing a move-away order in the circumstances of this case."

The *Edlund* court considered the detriment to the child's relationship with her father that was likely to result from the move, but correctly concluded that, under the circumstances of that case, this was insufficient to alter its holding: "we cannot imagine a case in which a child with any meaningful relationship with the noncustodial parent would not be 'significantly negatively impacted' by a good faith decision by a custodial parent to move, over the noncustodial parent's objection, to a distant location. But if the evidence of 'detriment' contained in [the evaluator's] report were sufficient to support denial of a move-away order in this case, no primary custodial parent would *ever* be able to secure such an order."

We agree that, considering all of the circumstances in *Edlund*, the superior court in that case did not abuse its discretion in permitting the change in the child's residence, but the Court of Appeal in *Edlund* may have inadvertently generated some confusion when it stated as a general conclusion: "The showing of 'changed circumstances' required of the noncustodial parent must consist of more than the fact of the proposed move." If we interpret this statement narrowly, it certainly is true. The mere fact that the custodial parent proposes to change the residence of the child does not automatically constitute "changed circumstances" that require a reevaluation of an existing custody order. A proposed change in the residence of a child can run the gamut from a move across the street to a relocation to another continent. As we have noted, the noncustodial parent has the burden of showing that the planned move will cause detriment to the child in order for the court to reevaluate an existing custody order.

But some courts have mistakenly interpreted the above quoted statement in *Edlund* more broadly to mean that the likely consequences of a proposed move can never constitute changed circumstances that justify a reevaluation of an existing custody order. (*In re Marriage of Abrams, supra*, 105 Cal.App.4th 979, 988 ["it is not enough to show the child has a meaningful relationship with the noncustodial parent and will be 'negatively impacted' by the custodial parent's good faith decision to move. If this were sufficient to support denial of a move-away order, no primary custodial parent would ever be able to secure such an order"]; *In re Marriage of Lasich, supra*, 99 Cal.App.4th 702, 711 ["Relocation alone cannot prove detriment because no move-away request could succeed under that standard," citing *In re Marriage of Edlund & Hales, supra,* 66 Cal.App.4th 1454].) This is incorrect. The likely consequences of a proposed change in the residence of a child, when considered in the light of all the relevant factors, may constitute a change of circumstances that warrants a change in custody, and the detriment to the child's relationship with the noncustodial parent that will be caused by the proposed move, when considered in light of all the relevant factors, may warrant denying a request to change the child's residence or changing custody. The extent to which a proposed move will detrimentally impact a child varies greatly depending upon the circumstances. We will generally leave it to the superior court to assess that impact in light of the other relevant factors in determining what is in the best interests of the child.

The Court of Appeal in the present case held that the father bore the burden of showing "that modification of custody is essential for the child's welfare," citing our statement in *Burgess* that a change of custody in a move-away case is justified "only if, as a result of relocation with that parent, the child will suffer detriment rendering it ' "essential or expedient for the welfare of the child that there be a change.' " " It is significant that the Court of Appeal reduced the phrase "essential or expedient" that we used in *Burgess* to simply "essential." In doing so, the Court of Appeal placed too great a burden on the noncustodial parent in a move-away case. . . .

The Court of Appeal in the present case further concluded that the superior court improperly used its conditional order transferring primary physical custody to the father as a device to restrain the mother from relocating. We agree that a court must not issue such a conditional order for the purpose of coercing the custodial parent into abandoning plans to relocate. Nor should a court issue such an order expecting that the order will not take effect because the custodial parent will choose not to relocate rather than lose primary physical custody of the children. But there is nothing in the record before us that indicates the superior court did so in the present case. The father had long sought joint physical custody or, barring that, increased visitation, and the superior court had slowly but consistently increased the time the children spent at their father's residence. The court found that both parties were "good enough" parents to their children. There is nothing to indicate that the order transferring primary physical custody of the children to the father if the mother relocated was issued to coerce the mother into abandoning her plans to move.

The mother places great emphasis on the superior court's finding that she was not acting in "bad faith." The father contends that the "bad faith test" announced in *Burgess* "is generally unworkable." We discussed good faith and bad faith in two footnotes in our opinion in *Burgess*.

In rejecting the argument that a parent who wishes to change the residence of a child bears the burden of proving the move is "necessary," we noted that such a rule would encourage costly litigation and would "require the trial courts to 'micromanage' family decisionmaking by second-guessing reasons for everyday decisions about career and family." (*Burgess*, *supra*, 13 Cal.4th at p. 36.) In a footnote, we observed that "the parties continue to dispute whether the mother's change of employment was merely a 'lateral' move or was 'career enhancing.' The point is immaterial. Once the trial court determined that the mother did not relocate in order to frustrate the father's contact with the minor children, but did so for sound 'good faith' reasons, it was not required to inquire further into the wisdom of her inherently subjective decision-making."

We then stated that a decision to change a child's residence ordinarily does not reflect upon the parent's suitability to retain primary physical custody. We pointed out in another footnote, however: "An obvious exception is a custodial parent's decision to relocate simply to frustrate the noncustodial parent's contact with the minor children.... Even if the custodial parent is otherwise 'fit,' such bad faith conduct may be relevant to a determination of what permanent custody arrangement is in the minor children's best interest."

We referenced these discussions of good faith and bad faith in our formulation of the rule: "In a 'move-away' case, a change of custody is not justified simply because the custodial parent has chosen, for any sound good faith reason, to reside in a different location, but only if, as a result of relocation with that parent, the child will suffer detriment rendering it ' "essential or expedient for the welfare of the child that there be a change." '

The Courts of Appeal have correctly applied these rules, but in one published decision the Court of Appeal overstated the importance of an absence of bad faith.

In *In re Marriage of Bryant, supra, 91 Cal.App.4th 789,* the superior court awarded primary physical custody to the mother who intended to move with the children to New Mexico to be with her family. A custody evaluation revealed that the mother had been the "primary parent," having had "a greater level of involvement in the children's lives" than the father and that it would be "detrimental to the children to make a 'radical shift' to [the father] as the primary parent." The evaluator saw no reason to believe that the move would end the children's relationship with their father. The superior court found that the mother "was not motivated to move by bad faith" and had not "unreasonably interfered with [the father's] visitation with the children."

The Court of Appeal affirmed, correctly noting that "the trial court has ' "the widest discretion to choose a parenting plan that is in the best interest of the child." ' This requires the court to consider all the circumstances." But the Court of Appeal went on to overstate the importance of the superior court's finding that the mother was not acting in bad faith, holding that that once the superior court found that the mother was not acting in bad faith," [n]o further inquiry [into the reasons for the proposed move] was necessary or appropriate. Rejecting the father's contention that the court should "consider the reason for the move in light of the circumstances of the case," the Court of Appeal stated: "except to show that the move is not in bad faith, the reason is irrelevant."[4]

This is not what we said in *Burgess*; we said simply that a finding that a reason for the proposed move constitutes bad faith "may be relevant" in determining custody arrangements. While we noted that the court need not evaluate the wisdom of the custodial parent's decision-making, we did not say that the reasons for a proposed move are irrelevant if the custodial parent is acting in good faith.

Absolute concepts of good faith versus bad faith often are difficult to apply because human beings may act for a complex variety of sometimes conflicting motives. As the superior court in the present case observed after finding that the mother was not acting in bad faith because she had legitimate reasons for the move and was not acting for the specific purpose of limiting the father's contact with his children: "I think it's far more subtle than that...." As Dr. Stahl stated in his evaluation: "On the surface, the reasons for the move are clear. [The mother] has always wanted to move to Ohio to be closer to her sister and family.... [Her husband] has received a good job opportunity in Cleveland, which he has taken. Their economic standard of living, and the inherent quality of life, will improve under such circumstances. All of these are reasonable reasons to make the move. [P] Underneath, however, it has always appeared that [the mother] has wanted to move so that she can remove herself and take the boys from the day-to-day interactions with [the father]. She has difficulty dealing with him and prefers to have as little communication with him as possible."

Even if the custodial parent has legitimate reasons for the proposed change in the child's residence and is not acting simply to frustrate the noncustodial parent's contact with the child, the court still may consider whether one reason for the move is to lessen the child's contact with the noncustodial parent and whether that indicates, when considered in light of all the relevant factors, that a change in custody would be in the child's best interests.[5]

The foregoing cases, many of which involve heart-wrenching circumstances, remind us that this area of law is not amenable to inflexible

4. In *Cassady v. Signorelli, supra, 49 Cal.App.4th 55,* the Court of Appeal commented on the wisdom of the mother's proposal to move with her child to Florida to pursue a career as a parapsychologist, referring to the "mother's somewhat whimsical plans," but it is clear from a full reading of the opinion that the appellate court affirmed the superior court's denial of the mother's request to move the child's residence because it agreed that the mother was not seriously seeking employment as a parapsychologist and "simply wishe[d] to get away from father by moving elsewhere." Although the Court of Appeal did not use the term "bad faith," it concluded that the mother's proposed move was "an apparent pretext to defeat visitation."

5. We have no occasion in this case to consider circumstances in which a reason for a proposed move is to minimize contact with a noncustodial parent who has engaged in a pattern of abuse of the custodial parent or the children or who has a substance abuse problem.

rules. Rather, we must permit our superior court judges—guided by statute and the principles we announced in *Burgess* and affirm in the present case—to exercise their discretion to fashion orders that best serve the interests of the children in the cases before them. Among the factors that the court ordinarily should consider when deciding whether to modify a custody order in light of the custodial parent's proposal to change the residence of the child are the following: the children's interest in stability and continuity in the custodial arrangement; the distance of the move; the age of the children; the children's relationship with both parents; the relationship between the parents including, but not limited to, their ability to communicate and cooperate effectively and their willingness to put the interests of the children above their individual interests; the wishes of the children if they are mature enough for such an inquiry to be appropriate; the reasons for the proposed move; and the extent to which the parents currently are sharing custody.

III. Disposition

The judgment of the Court of Appeal is reversed and the matter is remanded to that court with directions to affirm the superior court's postjudgment order transferring custody of the children to the father if the mother moves to Ohio. On remand, the superior court should consider the views expressed in this opinion and may consider the parties' present circumstances in issuing any further custody and visitation order.

Kennard, J., dissenting:

A mother who had been the primary caretaker of her two children since their birth, and who had never violated the trial court's visitation orders, wanted to provide a better life for her children by moving with them to another state where she had relatives and where her new husband had accepted a better paying job. Concerned that his tenuous relationship with the children would be weakened, the children's father objected. After a hearing, the trial court ordered that custody of the children be transferred to the father in the event the mother moved. The majority holds the trial court did not abuse its discretion in so ruling. I disagree.

When it explained its ruling, the trial court said that moving the children to another state could damage the children's relationship with their father, but the court never mentioned the potential harm to the children from losing their mother as their primary caretaker, despite undisputed evidence that this harm would be significant. The majority acknowledges that the trial court was required to consider this detriment—indeed it acknowledges " 'the *paramount* need for continuity and stability in custody arrangements' "—but it *assumes* the trial court adequately considered this point.

In a matter of this importance, involving the custody and welfare of minor children, a reviewing court should not make such a speculative assumption. When a trial court's explanation for exercising its discretion in a particular way does not mention a critical matter that the court was bound to consider, and does not accurately state the controlling legal standard, a reviewing court cannot simply ignore these omissions. When, as here, the appellate record raises substantial doubts that the trial court applied the proper legal principles and policies that should have guided its decision, reversal is required....

II

A parent with custody of minor children has a "presumptive right" to change the children's residence. (*In re Marriage of Burgess (1996) 13 Cal.4th 25, 32, 38;* see also *Fam. Code, § 7501.*) A noncustodial parent opposing such a change of residence bears the initial burden of showing that the move will cause some detriment to the children. Once this showing of detriment has been made, the trial court must then weigh the likely effects on the child's welfare from moving with the custodial parent, against the likely effects from a change in custody. Only if the child's interests are better served by changing custody than by relocating with the custodial parent may a court order custody transferred to the other parent.

Here, the trial court's explanation for its ruling shows that it properly considered how relocation to Ohio might detrimentally affect the children—including the impact on their tenuous relationship with their father. But the trial court was also required to weigh this detriment against the detriment that would result from removing the boys from the mother's custody. This the court did not do. In its statement of reasons, the court said: "So I don't think that I have any real question as to the qualifications or competence of either parent, that is not the issue before me. *The issue is the effect on these children of relocating, and the effect of the relationship with their father if they are permitted to relocate.*" (Italics added.) But the effect of the relocation on the children's relationship with the father was not *the* issue before the court. Rather, it was just one of the potential detriments shown by the evidence that the trial court was required to consider. Equally important was the potential detriment from disrupting the existing custodial arrangement by transferring custody from the mother to the father.

This court has stressed that the "the paramount need for continuity and stability in custody arrangements—and the harm that may result from disruption of established patterns of care and emotional bonds with the primary caretaker—weigh heavily in favor of maintaining ongoing custody arrangements." Here, the trial court's explanation for its ruling provides no assurance that the trial court gave any weight to the importance of continuity and stability in custody arrangements....

Questions on LaMusga

(1) Is the litigation surrounding relocation inevitable? Is it a manifestation of continued struggles between unhappy former spouses, i.e., a desire for control? Is it a manifestation of the increased sharing of parenting that spouses (and former spouses) do?

(2) Does the *LaMusga* court correctly set the presumption here?

(3) *Burgess* suggests that so long as not motivated by malice, custodial parental decisions about relocation should be honored. Does this disadvantage men? Children?

A somewhat controversial study (why?) of college students whose parents divorced reports that those whose parents have not relocated do better. See Sanford L. Braver, Ira Mark Ellman and William V. Fabricius, *Relocation of Children after Divorce and Children's Best Interests: New Evidence and Legal Considerations*, 17 J Fam Psych 206 (2003).

(4) The ALI Principles § 2.20 permits relocation when it does not significantly impair either parent's ability to exercise responsibilities as before. If, as in Jerry's case, the move will make frequent exchanges of custody onerous, should it be prohibited?

(5) In § 2.20(4), the ALI Principles allow relocation of the parent "exercising a significant majority" of custodial responsibility even where the proportions of custodial responsibilities will change "so long as that parent shows that the relocation is in good faith for a legitimate purpose and to a location that is reasonable in light of the purpose." What happened to the *summum bonum* of custody law—the child's best interest? Is this an area where we are willing to subordinate the child's interests to the parent's? Is that wrong?

(6) Some relocating parents have argued, and some courts have agreed, that restrictions upon their travel are unconstitutional. See, e.g., *Jaramillo v. Jaramillo*, 823 P2d 299, 305 (NM 1991); *Holder v. Polanski*, 544 A2d 852, 856 (NJ 1988).

(8) The Parental Interest

We have been examining rules designed to make the best-interest standard more determinate. We will now examine rights which could have the same effect. We will begin with an argument which draws on familiar rights ideas—ideas about parental rights. Some of the rationales we developed for parental rights rested on the belief that parents have special interests in their children. What should happen to those interests in custody decisions? The best-interest standard implies they should be ignored. Is that consonant with the family law you are learning? Is it good social policy?

The following case rests on ideas about the child's best interest. But there are also elements of concern about the parents' interests.

IN RE MARRIAGE OF LEVIN

California Court of Appeals, 1980
162 Cal Rptr 757

COBEY, ACTING PRESIDING JUSTICE.

FACTS

Mona Beth Levin, the subject of this appeal, was born to Paula and Barry Levin on May 12, 1975. Paula, the previous December when 4 1/2 months pregnant, had suffered an intracerebral hemorrhage (stroke) and as a result thereof was hospitalized in three different hospitals and one convalescent home in New York City and Los Angeles from December 1974 to June 1976.

Barry took care of Mona during the approximately 13 months of Paula's hospitalization that followed Mona's birth. In New York City he was assisted by a homemaker who was with Mona five days a week, Monday through Friday, 9 am to 5 pm and in Los Angeles, a month after their arrival in January 1976, he had similar assistance for six days a week from a trained professional attendant who was there, however, primarily to assist Paula. He also used in Los Angeles a professional baby-sitter two or three afternoons a week and occasionally on weekends. After Paula joined the household of Barry and Mona in June 1976, Barry had the help of the attendant but Paula insisted that Barry generally take care of her personal needs.

On or about March 8, 1977, Barry, with Mona, moved to another apartment and Paula then moved in with her aforementioned mother, Mrs. Singer. Shortly thereafter Barry's parents moved in with him and Mona. Mona has her own separate bedroom in this apartment which has two bathrooms. As already mentioned Barry also uses a professional baby-sitter in order to have some uninterrupted working time. Also, as we have already noted, as soon as Mona reached the age of two years in May 1977, Barry enrolled her in a nursery school which she attends 6 to 7 hours a day, 4 1/2 days a week. Apparently Barry has had a very warm and loving relationship with Mona. During the extensive period when he has been the only parent in the household, he has been an excellent mother as well as a father to her. He has been teaching her to play the piano and they often listen at home together to classical music. He also paints with her. Mona appears to be a very happy child with a strong attachment to her father. Barry makes a comparatively modest living at home as a free lance manuscript editor and promotional writer. He earned about three years of college credits.

Paula, a very bright young woman, and a former preschool and elementary school teacher in Spain and Chicago, has a B.A. in education and a graduate language and cultural certificate from the University of Madrid. She speaks four to five languages. At the time of the custody hearing under review, namely February 1978, she was generally confined to a wheelchair but she could walk a few hundred feet by herself. She needs assistance, however, in turning and in getting up from her wheelchair. She has permanently lost much of her vision in her right eye and is unable to see things to her left without turning her head. The prognosis though then was that she would eventually be able to walk with a cane. These physical limitations mean that she will need assistance for some time both for herself and in caring for Mona. She can prepare Mona's meals, however, and feed her. She can also dress Mona with some difficulty. She does need assistance in bathing Mona but she can and does play with her in a great variety of ways and makes a point of teaching her in the course of this play. She also paints with Mona.

Their relationship is a very warm and loving one. Mona has no aversion to her mother's wheelchair. Mona also has a close and loving relationship with her Grandmother Singer and with her mother's home attendant as well. Mona enjoys the well equipped play area and pool next to the apartment building where her mother lives and she plays there in safety with her peers. Mona is already bi-lingual. She converses with her mother in English and with her mother's attendant in Spanish.

The expert opinion in this case was numerically heavily in favor of Paula. The physician in charge of Paula's rehabilitation told the court's child custody investigator that Mona would be better off with her mother. A husband and wife team of psychologists reported observing a very warm and natural relationship between Paula and Mona and both opined that a child of Mona's age should generally be with her parents rather than in a nursery school and that Mona's hours in attendance there were too long in any event. The psychiatrist on Paula's rehabilitation team was of the view that generally the mother-child relationship was crucial for a child during its first three and perhaps four years of life and that taking Mona from Paula would deprive Paula of "the only meaning to her suffering." The court's child custody investigator likewise recommended that Mona be given to Paula, but her only criticism of Barry as a parent was his aforementioned sending Mona to nursery school as he did. On the other hand, a psychiatrist who had interviewed Barry at length and observed him with Mona thought that Barry was the primary psychological parent of Mona and that he possessed a greater capacity for tending to Mona's needs and could provide her with more normal physical togetherness.

On March 31, 1977, some three weeks after the Levins separated, Barry was awarded pendente lite custody of Mona, but she was to spend alternate weekends with Paula. Four months later Paula's visitation rights were substantially increased. After the four-day custody hearing two years ago, the trial court awarded permanent custody of Mona to Barry on the ground that Mona's best interests so dictated (see Civ.Code, § 4600, subd. (b)) but Paula's substantial visitation rights on alternate weekends, vacations and holidays were expressly continued....

B. The Trial Court's Error

At the conclusion of the child custody hearing before it, the trial court tried at some length to explain to the Levins the award it was about to make. It stated that its decision in this respect was based "100 percent on the welfare of the child" (see Civ.Code, § 4600, subd. (b)) and it remarked that both parents were good parents. It thereafter referred to the conclusions of Barry's expert witness that Mona knew Barry better than Paula because she had spent more time with him. It subsequently, however, concluded its remarks by saying:

"I don't know whether I, as the judge, would have the right to say to this child, 'I am going to give you the opportunity during much of your week, during a substantial majority of your time of learning to deal with difficulties and adversities.' Even though we know that children of the poor do as well as children of the rich, maybe better, still a judge can't say to a child, 'You be poor.' I can't do that.

"Where I have nothing else to choose between the two, and let's assume that is what I had, how can I say to the child, 'I am going to put you with a parent where you are going to have more responsibilities. I am not going to let you be with a parent that has more freedom of movement. Why? For your own good.' . . .

"But as a judge faced with the responsibility of deciding what to do with a child of two years and nine months, why should I say to that child, 'I am not going to give you the same kind of freedom. I am going to give you to a parent that does not have as much freedom.' I can't do that. My conscience wouldn't let me do that.

"I find that kind of freedom must be what the court should take into consideration. It's not just the fact of tying shoes. Nobody knows better than Mrs. Levin how many difficulties are involved in any handicap more than the average, and I don't have any real doubt.

"I was anxious to learn as much as I could about these people. I have learned as much as I can. I feel that in the best interest of this child she should be with the father. And I do that not because of the handicap but because of the limitations that the handicap imposes upon what I conceive to be the most normal, possible life for a child."

From these concluding remarks of the trial court which we have just quoted, it is quite apparent that it based its permanent custody award of Mona to Barry on "the limitations that the handicap imposes upon what I conceive to be the most normal, possible life for a child." As we read *Carney* this is an impermissible basis for a child custody award where one parent is physically handicapped. It does not represent an accommodation of the apparently conflicting public policies of the best interests of the child and the handicapped parent's right not to be deprived of her child because of that handicap. Under *Carney*, as we have already indicated, a trial court must determine whether the handicapped parent's condition will in fact have "a substantial and lasting adverse effect on the best interests of the child." In making this determination the court must consider the fact that the essence of parenting is ethical, emotional, and intellectual guidance of the child something which, by and large, is generally unrelated to the physical handicap of a parent.

The trial court, though, in this case, unlike *Carney*, did have a sound basis upon which it might have properly awarded permanent custody of Mona to Barry. This was that except for approximately nine months of Mona's life, she had largely been solely in Barry's custody and he had apparently done an excellent job of parenting during those years. A child's custody, especially that of a comparatively young child, should not be changed except for very compelling reasons. Stability and security in a child's environment are essential for both a child's happiness and its proper development.

But Paula is entitled to a new custody hearing in view of the improper basis that the trial court chose in this case. Custody of Mona should remain with Barry, however, pending a hearing for the reasons just stated.

The new permanent custody award will be entirely up to the trial court which will have two more years of Mona's childhood to weigh. We recommend strongly to both Barry and Paula that one or both apply at such hearing for joint custody of Mona since joint custody has so very recently become the preferred type of custody in California and could possess obvious advantages in this case.

(9) The Parental Right

As you now know, the child's best interest is the predominant—and sometimes sole—criterion in child custody cases. Yet—as you also know from reading Part II—there is in the American constitutional and moral tradition material that suggests that parents have—at least in some circumstances—a special claim to the companionship and custody of their offspring. In this section, we will explore some of the times and ways the law might recognize that tradition. We begin with one of the Supreme Court's principal pronouncements on the subject.

(a) The Unmarried Father

LEHR v. ROBERTSON

Supreme Court of the United States, 1983
463 US 248

STEVENS, JUSTICE. . . .

Jessica M. was born out of wedlock on November 9, 1976. Her mother, Lorraine Robertson, married Richard Robertson eight months after Jessica's birth. On December 21, 1978, when Jessica was over two years old, the Robertsons filed an adoption petition in the Family Court of Ulster County, New York. The court heard their testimony and received a favorable report from the Ulster County Department of Social Services. On March 7, 1979, the court entered an order of adoption. In this proceeding, appellant contends that the adoption order is invalid because he, Jessica's putative father, was not given advance notice of the adoption proceeding.

The State of New York maintains a "putative father registry." A man who files with that registry demonstrates his intent to claim paternity of a child born out of wedlock and is therefore entitled to receive notice of any proceeding to adopt that child. Before entering Jessica's adoption order, the Ulster County Family Court had the putative father registry examined. Although appellant claims to be Jessica's natural father, he had not entered his name in the registry.

In addition to the persons whose names are listed on the putative father registry, New York law requires that notice of an adoption proceeding be given to several other classes of possible fathers of children born out of wedlock—those who have been adjudicated to be the father, those who have been identified as the father on the child's birth certificate, those who live openly with the child and the child's mother and who hold themselves out to be the father, those who have been identified as the father by the mother in a sworn written statement, and those who were married to the child's mother before the child was six months old. Appellant admittedly was not a member of any of those classes. He had lived with appellee prior to Jessica's birth and visited her in the hospital when Jessica was born, but his name does not appear on Jessica's birth certificate. He did not live with appellee or Jessica after Jessica's birth, he has never provided them with any financial support, and he has never offered to marry appellee. Nevertheless, he contends that the following special circumstances gave him a constitutional right to notice and a hearing before Jessica was adopted.

On January 30, 1979, one month after the adoption proceeding was commenced in Ulster County, appellant filed a "visitation and paternity petition" in the Westchester County Family Court. In that petition, he asked for a determination of paternity, an order of support, and reasonable visitation privileges with Jessica. Notice of that proceeding was served on appellee on February 22, 1979. Four days later appellee's attorney informed the Ulster County Court that appellant had commenced a paternity proceeding in Westchester County; the Ulster County judge then entered an order staying appellant's paternity proceeding until he could rule on a motion to change the venue of that proceeding to Ulster County. On March 3, 1979, appellant received notice of the change of venue motion and, for the first time, learned that an adoption proceeding was pending in Ulster County.

On March 7, 1979, appellant's attorney telephoned the Ulster County judge to inform him that he planned to seek a stay of the adoption proceeding pending the determination of the paternity petition. In that telephone conversation, the judge advised the lawyer that he had already signed the adoption order earlier that day. According to appellant's attorney, the judge stated that he was aware of the pending paternity petition but did not believe he was required to give notice to appellant prior to the entry of the order of adoption.

Thereafter, the Family Court in Westchester County granted appellee's motion to dismiss the paternity petition, holding that the putative father's right to seek paternity " ... must be deemed severed so long as an order of adoption exists." Appellant did not appeal from that dismissal. On June 22, 1979, appellant filed a petition to vacate the order of adoption on the ground that it was obtained by fraud and in violation of his constitutional rights. The Ulster County Family Court received written and oral argument on the question whether it had "dropped the ball" by approving the adoption without giving appellant advance notice. After deliberating for several months, it denied the petition, explaining its decision in a thorough written opinion.

The Appellate Division of the Supreme Court affirmed.

The New York Court of Appeals also affirmed by a divided vote....

I

The intangible fibers that connect parent and child have infinite variety. They are woven throughout the fabric of our society, providing it with strength, beauty, and flexibility. It is self-evident that they are sufficiently vital to merit constitutional protection in appropriate cases. In deciding whether this is such a case, however, we must consider the broad framework that has traditionally been used to resolve the legal problems arising from the parent-child relationship.

In the vast majority of cases, state law determines the final outcome. Rules governing the inheritance of property, adoption, and child custody are generally specified in statutory enactments that vary from State to State. Moreover, equally varied state laws governing marriage and divorce affect a multitude of parent-child relationships. The institution of marriage has played a critical role both in defining the legal entitlements of family members and in developing the decentralized structure of our democratic society. In recognition of that role, and as part of their general overarching concern for serving the best interests of children, state laws almost universally express an appropriate preference for the formal family.

In some cases, however, this Court has held that the Federal Constitution supersedes state law and provides even greater protection for certain formal family relationships. In those cases, as in the state cases, the Court has emphasized the paramount interest in the welfare of children and has noted that the rights of the parents are a counterpart of the responsibilities they have assumed. Thus, the "liberty" of parents to control the education of their children that was vindicated in *Meyer v. Nebraska* and *Pierce v. Society of Sisters* was described as a "right, coupled with the high duty, to recognize and prepare [the child] for additional obligations." The linkage between parental duty and parental right was stressed again in *Prince v. Massachusetts*, 321 U.S. 158, 166 (1944), when the Court declared it a cardinal principal "that the custody, care and nurture of the child reside first in the parents, whose primary function and freedom include preparation for obligations the state can neither supply nor hinder." In these cases the Court has found that the relationship of love and duty in a recognized family unit is an interest in liberty entitled to constitutional protection. See also *Moore v. City of East Cleveland*, 431 U.S. 494 (1977)(plurality opinion). "[S]tate intervention to terminate [such a] relationship ... must be accomplished by procedures meeting the requisites of the Due Process Clause." *Santosky v. Kramer*, 455 U.S. 745, 752 (1982).

There are also a few cases in which this Court has considered the extent to which the Constitution affords protection to the relationship between natural parents and children born out of wedlock. In some we have been concerned with the rights of the children. In this case, however, it is a parent who claims that the state has improperly deprived him of a protected interest in liberty. This Court has examined the extent to which a natural father's biological relationship with his illegitimate child receives protection under the Due Process Clause in precisely three cases: *Stanley v. Illinois*, 405 U.S. 645 (1972), *Quilloin v. Walcott*, 434 U.S. 246 (1978), and *Caban v. Mohammed*, 441 U.S. 380 (1979).

Stanley involved the constitutionality of an Illinois statute that conclusively presumed every father of a child born out of wedlock to be an unfit person to have custody of his children. The father in that case had lived with his children all their lives and had lived with their mother for eighteen years. There was nothing in the record to indicate that Stanley had been a neglectful father who had not cared for his children. Under the statute, however, the nature of the actual relationship between parent and child was completely irrelevant. Once the mother died, the children were automatically made wards of the state. Relying in part on a Michigan case recognizing that the preservation of "a subsisting relationship with the child's father" may better serve the child's best interest than "uprooting him from the family which he knew from birth," the Court held that the Due Process Clause was violated by the automatic destruction of the custodial relationship without giving the father any opportunity to present evidence regarding his fitness as a parent.

Quilloin involved the constitutionality of a Georgia statute that authorized the adoption of a child born out of wedlock over the objection of the natural father. The father in that case had never legitimated the child. It was only after the mother had remarried and her new husband had filed an adoption petition that the natural father sought visitation rights and filed a petition for legitimation. The trial court found adoption by the new husband to be in the child's best interests, and we unanimously held that action to be consistent with the Due Process Clause.

Caban involved the conflicting claims of two natural parents who had maintained joint custody of their children from the time of their birth until they were respectively two and four years old. The father challenged the validity of an order authorizing the mother's new husband to adopt the children; he relied on both the Equal Protection Clause and the Due Process Clause. Because this Court upheld his equal protection claim, the majority did not address his due process challenge. The comments on the latter claim by the four dissenting Justices are nevertheless instructive, because they identify the clear distinction between a mere biological relationship and an actual relationship of parental responsibility.

Justice Stewart correctly observed:

"Even if it be assumed that each married parent after divorce has some substantive due process right to maintain his or her parental relationship, cf. *Smith v. Organization of Foster Families*, 431 U.S. 816 (opinion concurring in judgment), it by no means follows that each unwed parent has any such right. *Parental rights do not spring full-blown from the biological connection between parent and child. They require relationships more enduring.*"

In a similar vein, the other three dissenters in *Caban* were prepared to "assume that, *if and when one develops*, the relationship between a father and his natural child is entitled to protection against arbitrary state action as a matter of due process."

The difference between the developed parent-child relationship that was implicated in *Stanley* and *Caban*, and the potential relationship involved in *Quilloin* and this case, is both clear and significant. When an unwed father demonstrates a full commitment to the responsibilities of parenthood by "com[ing] forward to participate in the rearing of his child," *Caban*, his interest in personal contact with his child acquires substantial protection under the due process clause. At that point it may be said that he "act[s] as a father toward his children." *Id.* But the mere existence of a biological link does not merit equivalent constitutional protection. The actions of judges neither create nor sever genetic bonds. "[T]he importance of the familial relationship, to the individuals involved and to the society, stems from the emotional attachments that derive from the intimacy of daily association, and from the role it plays in 'promot[ing] a way of life' through the instruction of children as well as from the fact of blood relationship." *Smith v. Organization of Foster Families for Equality and Reform*, 431 U.S. 816 (1977)(quoting *Wisconsin v. Yoder*, 406 U.S. 205 (1972)).

The significance of the biological connection is that it offers the natural father an opportunity that no other male possesses to develop a relationship with his offspring. If he grasps that opportunity and accepts some measure of responsibility for the child's future, he may enjoy the blessings of the parent-child relationship and make uniquely valuable contributions to the child's development. If he fails to do so, the Federal Constitution will not automatically compel a state to listen to his opinion of where the child's best interests lie.

In this case, we are not assessing the constitutional adequacy of New York's procedures for terminating a developed relationship. Appellant has never had any significant custodial, personal, or financial relationship with Jessica, and he did not seek to establish a legal tie until after she was two years old. We are concerned only with whether New York has adequately protected his opportunity to form such a relationship.

II

The most effective protection of the putative father's opportunity to develop a relationship with his child is provided by the laws that authorize formal marriage and govern its consequences. But the availability of that protection is, of course, dependent on the will of both parents of the child. Thus, New York has adopted a special statutory scheme to protect the unmarried father's interest in assuming a responsible role in the future of his child.

After this Court's decision in *Stanley*, the New York Legislature appointed a special commission to recommend legislation that would accommodate both the interests of biological fathers in their children and the children's interest in prompt and certain adoption procedures. The commission recommended, and the legislature enacted, a statutory adoption scheme that automatically provides notice to seven categories of putative fathers who are likely to have assumed some responsibility for the care of their natural children. If this scheme were likely to omit many responsible fathers, and if qualification for notice were beyond the control of an interested putative father, it might be thought procedurally inadequate. Yet, as all of the New York courts that reviewed this matter observed, the right to receive notice was completely within appellant's control. By mailing a postcard to the putative father registry, he could have guaranteed that he would receive notice of any proceedings to adopt Jessica. The possibility that he may have failed to do so because of his ignorance of the law cannot be a sufficient reason for criticizing the law itself. The New York legislature concluded that a more open-ended notice requirement would merely complicate the adoption process, threaten the privacy interests of unwed mothers, create the risk of unnecessary controversy, and impair the desired finality of adoption decrees. Regardless of whether we would have done likewise if we were legislators instead of judges, we surely cannot characterize the state's conclusion as arbitrary.

Appellant argues, however, that even if the putative father's opportunity to establish a relationship with an illegitimate child is adequately protected by the New York statutory scheme in the normal case, he was nevertheless entitled to special notice because the court and the mother knew that he had filed an affiliation proceeding in another court. This argument amounts to nothing more than an indirect attack on the notice provisions of the New York statute. The legitimate state interests in facilitating the adoption of young children and having the adoption proceeding completed expeditiously that underlie the entire statutory scheme also justify a trial judge's determination to require all interested parties to adhere precisely to the procedural requirements of the statute. The Constitution does not require either a trial judge or a litigant to give special notice to nonparties who are presumptively capable of asserting and protecting their own rights. Since the New York statutes adequately protected appellant's inchoate interest in establishing a relationship with Jessica, we find no merit in the claim that his constitutional rights were offended because the family court strictly complied with the notice provisions of the statute.

The Equal Protection Claim

The concept of equal justice under law requires the State to govern impartially.... The sovereign may not draw distinctions between individuals based solely on differences that are irrelevant to a legitimate governmental objective. Specifically, it may not subject men and women to disparate treatment when there is no substantial relation between the disparity and an important state purpose.

The legislation at issue in this case, sections 111 and 111a of the New York Domestic Relations Law, is intended to establish procedures for adoptions. Those procedures are designed to promote the best interests of the child, protect the rights of interested third parties, and ensure promptness and finality. To serve those ends, the legislation guarantees to certain people the right to veto an adoption and the right to prior notice of any adoption proceeding. The mother of an illegitimate child is always within that favored class, but only certain putative fathers are included. Appellant contends that the gender-based distinction is invidious.

As we noted above, the existence or nonexistence of a substantial relationship between parent and child is a relevant criterion in evaluating both the rights of the parent and the best interests of the child. In *Quilloin v. Walcott*, we noted that the putative father, like appellant, "ha[d] never shouldered any significant responsibility with respect to the daily supervision, education, protection, or care of the child. Appellant does not complain of his exemption from these responsibilities...." We therefore found that a Georgia statute that always required a mother's consent to the adoption of a child born out of wedlock, but required the father's consent only if he had legitimated the child, did not violate the Equal Protection Clause. Because, like the father in *Quilloin*, appellant has never established a substantial relationship with his daughter, the New York statutes at issue in this case did not operate to deny appellant equal protection.

We have held that these statutes may not constitutionally be applied in that class of cases where the mother and father are in fact similarly situated with regard to their relationship with the child. In *Caban v. Mohammed*, the Court held that it violated the Equal Protection Clause to grant the mother a veto over the adoption of a four-year-old girl and a six-year-old boy, but not to grant a veto to their father, who had admitted paternity and had participated in the rearing of the children. The Court made it clear, however, that if the father had not "come forward to participate in the rearing of his child, nothing in the Equal Protection Clause [would] preclude[ ]the State from withholding from him the privilege of vetoing the adoption of that child."

Jessica's parents are not like the parents involved in *Caban*. Whereas appellee had a continuous custodial responsibility for Jessica, appellant never established any custodial, personal, or financial relationship with her. If one parent has an established custodial relationship with the child and the other parent has either abandoned or never established a relationship, the Equal Protection Clause does not prevent a state from according the two parents different legal rights.

WHITE, MARSHALL AND BLACKMUN, JUSTICES, dissenting.

I

It is axiomatic that "[t]he fundamental requirement of due process is the opportunity to be heard 'at a meaningful time and in a meaningful manner.' "As Jessica's biological father, Lehr either had an interest protected by the Constitution or he did not. If the entry of the adoption order in this case deprived Lehr of a constitutionally protected interest, he is entitled to notice and an opportunity to be heard before the order can be accorded finality.

According to Lehr, he and Jessica's mother met in 1971 and began living together in 1974. The couple cohabited for approximately 2 years, until Jessica's birth in 1976. Throughout the pregnancy and after the birth, Lorraine acknowledged to friends and relatives that Lehr was Jessica's father; Lorraine told Lehr that she had reported to the New York State Department of Social Services that he was the father. Lehr visited Lorraine and Jessica in the hospital every day during Lorraine's confinement. According to Lehr, from the time Lorraine was discharged from the hospital until August, 1978, she concealed her whereabouts from him. During this time Lehr never ceased his efforts to locate Lorraine and Jessica and achieved sporadic success until August, 1977, after which time he was unable to locate them at all. On those occasions when he did determine Lorraine's location, he visited with her and her children to the extent she was willing to permit it. When Lehr, with the aid of a detective agency, located Lorraine and Jessica in August, 1978, Lorraine was already married to Mr. Robertson. Lehr asserts that at this time he offered to provide financial assistance and to set up a trust fund for Jessica, but that Lorraine refused. Lorraine threatened Lehr with arrest unless he stayed away and refused to permit him to see Jessica. Thereafter Lehr retained counsel who wrote to Lorraine in early December, 1978, requesting that she permit Lehr to visit Jessica and threatening legal action on Lehr's behalf. On December 21, 1978, perhaps as a response to Lehr's threatened legal action, appellees commenced the adoption action at issue here.

The majority posits that "[t]he intangible fibers that connect parent and child . . . are sufficiently vital to merit constitutional protection *in appropriate cases*." It then purports to analyze the particular facts of this case to determine whether appellant has a constitutionally protected liberty interest. We have expressly rejected that approach. In *Board of Regents v. Roth*, 408 U.S. 564, 570–571 (1972), we stated that although "a weighing process has long been a part of any determination of the form of hearing required in particular situations, . . . to determine whether due process requirements apply in the first place, we must look not to the 'weight' but to the nature of the interest at stake . . . to see if the interest is within the Fourteenth Amendment's protection. . . ."

The "nature of the interest" at stake here is the interest that a natural parent has in his or her child, one that has long been recognized and accorded constitutional protection. We have frequently "stressed the importance of familial bonds, whether or not legitimized by marriage, and accorded them constitutional protection." If "both the child and the [putative father] in a paternity action have a compelling interest" in the accurate outcome of such a case, *ibid*, it cannot be disputed that both the child and the putative father have a compelling interest in the outcome of a proceeding that may result in the termination of the father-child relationship. "A parent's interest in the accuracy and justice of the decision to terminate his or her parental status is ... a commanding one." *Lassiter v. Department of Social Services*, 452 U.S. 18, 27 (1981). It is beyond dispute that a formal order of adoption, no less than a formal termination proceeding, operates to permanently terminate parental rights.

Lehr's version of the "facts" paints a far different picture than that portrayed by the majority. The majority's recitation, that "[a]ppellant has never had any significant custodial, personal, or financial relationship with Jessica, and he did not seek to establish a legal tie until after she was two years old," *ante*, at 2994, obviously does not tell the whole story. Appellant has never been afforded an opportunity to present his case. The legitimation proceeding he instituted was first stayed, and then dismissed, on appellees' motions. Nor could appellant establish his interest during the adoption proceedings, for it is the failure to provide Lehr notice and an opportunity to be heard there that is at issue here. We cannot fairly make a judgment based on the quality or substance of a relationship without a complete and developed factual record. This case requires us to assume that Lehr's allegations are true—that but for the actions of the child's mother there would have been the kind of significant relationship that the majority concedes is entitled to the full panoply of procedural due process protections.

I reject the peculiar notion that the only significance of the biological connection between father and child is that "it offers the natural father an opportunity that no other male possesses to develop a relationship with his offspring." *Ante*, at 2993. A "mere biological relationship" is not as unimportant in determining the nature of liberty interests as the majority suggests.

"[T]he usual understanding of 'family' implies biological relationships, and most decisions treating the relation between parent and child have stressed this element." *Smith v. Organization of Foster Families.* The "biological connection" is itself a relationship that creates a protected interest. Thus the "nature" of the interest is the parent-child relationship; how well-developed that relationship has become goes to its "weight," not its "nature." Whether Lehr's interest is entitled to constitutional protection does not entail a searching inquiry into the quality of the relationship but a simple determination of the fact that the relationship exists—a fact that even the majority agrees must be assumed to be established.

Beyond that, however, because there is no established factual basis on which to proceed, it is quite untenable to conclude that a putative father's interest in his child is lacking in substance, that the father in effect has abandoned the child, or ultimately that the father's interest is not entitled to the same minimum procedural protections as the interests of other putative fathers. Any analysis of the adequacy of the notice in this case must be conducted on the assumption that the interest involved here is as strong as that of any putative father. That is not to say that due process requires actual notice to every putative father or that adoptive parents or the State must conduct an exhaustive search of records or an intensive investigation before a final adoption order may be entered. The procedures adopted by the State, however, must at least represent a reasonable effort to determine the identity of the putative father and to give him adequate notice.

II

In this case, of course, there was no question about either the identity or the location of the putative father. The mother knew exactly who he was and both she and the court entering the order of adoption knew precisely where he was and how to give him actual notice that his parental rights were about to be terminated by an adoption order. Lehr was entitled to due process, and the right to be heard is one of the fundamentals of that right, which "has little reality or worth unless one is informed that the matter is pending and can choose for himself whether to appear or default, acquiesce or contest."

The State concedes this much but insists that Lehr has had all the process that is due to him. It relies on § 111–a, which designates seven categories of unwed fathers to whom notice of adoption proceedings must be given, including any unwed father who has filed with the State a notice of his intent to claim paternity. The State submits that it need not give notice to anyone who has not filed his name, as he is permitted to do, and who is not otherwise within the designated categories, even if his identity and interest are known or are reasonably ascertainable by the State.

I am unpersuaded by the State's position. In the first place, § 111–a defines six categories of unwed fathers to whom notice must be given even though they have not placed their names on file pursuant to the section. Those six categories, however, do not include fathers such as Lehr who have initiated filiation proceedings, even though their identity and interest are as clearly and easily ascertainable as those fathers in the six categories. Initiating such proceedings necessarily involves a formal acknowledgment of paternity, and requiring the State to take note of such a case in connection with pending adoption proceedings would be a trifling burden, no more than the State undertakes when there is a final adjudication in a paternity action. Indeed, there would appear to be more reason to give notice to those such as Lehr who acknowledge paternity than to those who have been adjudged to be a father in a contested paternity action.

The State asserts that any problem in this respect is overcome by the seventh category of putative fathers to whom notice must be given, namely those fathers who have identified themselves in the putative father register maintained by the State. Since Lehr did not take advantage of this device to make his interest known, the State contends, he was not entitled to notice and a hearing even though his identity, location and interest were known to the adoption court prior to entry of the adoption order. I have difficulty with this position. First, it represents a grudging and crabbed approach to due process. The State is quite willing to give notice and a hearing to putative fathers who have made themselves known by resorting to the putative fathers' register. It makes little sense to me to deny notice and hearing to a father who has not placed his name in the register but who has unmistakably identified himself by filing suit to establish his paternity and has notified the adoption court of his action and his interest. I thus need not question the statutory scheme on its face. Even assuming that Lehr would have been foreclosed if his failure to utilize the register had somehow disadvantaged the State, he effectively made himself known by other means, and it is the sheerest formalism to deny him a hearing because he informed the State in the wrong manner.

No state interest is substantially served by denying Lehr adequate notice and a hearing. The State no doubt has an interest in expediting adoption proceedings to prevent a child from remaining unduly long in the custody of the State or foster parents. But this is not an adoption involving a child in the custody of an authorized state agency. Here the child is in the custody of the mother and will remain in her custody. Moreover, had Lehr utilized the putative father register, he would have been granted a prompt hearing, and there was no justifiable reason, in terms of delay, to refuse him a hearing in the circumstances of this case.

The State's undoubted interest in the finality of adoption orders likewise is not well served by a procedure that will deny notice and a hearing to a father whose identity and location are known. As this case well illustrates, denying notice and a hearing to such a father may result in years of additional litigation and threaten the reopening of adoption proceedings and the vacation of the adoption. Here, the Family Court's unseemly rush to enter an adoption order after ordering that cause be shown why the filiation proceeding should not be transferred and consolidated with the adoption proceeding can hardly be justified by the interest in finality. To the contrary, the adoption order entered in March, 1979, has remained open to question until this very day.

Questions on Lehr

(1) *Lehr* leaves many questions unanswered. For example, the Court's treatment of its precedent is controversial. The Court's opinion tries to distinguish *Stanley*, *Quilloin*, and *Caban*. But is its distinction persuasive?

(2) *Lehr* does not clearly state the origin of the parental right it recognizes. Nor does the Court fully explicate the nature of the parent's

right. Is it the right to the companionship of one's child? To make decisions about one's child? Suppose, as the dissent argued, that the mother deliberately prevented the unmarried father from seeing his child. Would the case be the same? In other words, does the unmarried father's right arise only out of the developed relationship between father and child, or does it also arise out of the good-faith efforts of the father to create such a relationship? What if the mother puts the child up for adoption at birth? What if she refuses to reveal the father's identity? Consider the following case:

IN RE PETITION OF DOE (BABY RICHARD CASE)

Supreme Court of Illinois, 1994
638 NE2d 181

HEIPLE, J.

Otakar [Kirchner] and Daniella [Janikova] began living together in the fall of 1989, and Daniella became pregnant in June of 1990. For the first eight months of her pregnancy, Otakar provided for all of her expenses.

In late January 1991, Otakar went to his native Czechoslovakia to attend to his gravely ill grandmother for two weeks. During this time, Daniella received a phone call from Otakar's aunt saying that Otakar had resumed a former romantic relationship with another woman.

Because of this unsettling news, Daniella left their shared apartment, refused to talk with Otakar on his return, and gave birth to the child at a different hospital than where they had originally planned. She gave her consent to the adoption of the child by the Does, telling them and their attorney that she knew who the father was but would not furnish his name. Daniella and her uncle warded off Otakar's persistent inquiries about the child by telling him that the child had died shortly after birth.

Otakar found out that the child was alive and had been placed for adoption 57 days after the child was born. He then began the instant proceedings by filing an appearance contesting the Does' adoption of his son. As already noted, the trial court ruled that Otakar was an unfit parent under section 1 of the Adoption Act (the Act) (750 ILCS 50/1 (West 1992)) because he had not shown a reasonable degree of interest in the child within the first 30 days of his life. Therefore, the father's consent was unnecessary under section 8 of the Act (750 ILCS 50/8 (West 1992)).

The finding that the father had not shown a reasonable degree of interest in the child is not supported by the evidence. In fact, he made various attempts to locate the child, all of which were either frustrated or blocked by the actions of the mother. Further, the mother was aided by the attorney for the adoptive parents, who failed to make any effort to ascertain the name or address of the father despite the fact that the mother indicated she knew who he was. Under the circumstances, the father had no opportunity to discharge any familial duty.

In the opinion below, the appellate court, wholly missing the threshold issue in this case, dwelt on the best interests of the child. Since, however, the father's parental interest was improperly terminated, there was no occasion to reach the factor of the child's best interests. That point should never have been reached and need never have been discussed.

Unfortunately, over three years have elapsed since the birth of the baby who is the subject of these proceedings. To the extent that it is relevant to assign fault in this case, the fault here lies initially with the mother, who fraudulently tried to deprive the father of his rights, and secondly, with the adoptive parents and their attorney, who proceeded with the adoption when they knew that a real father was out there who had been denied knowledge of his baby's existence. When the father entered his appearance in the adoption proceedings 57 days after the baby's birth and demanded his rights as a father, the petitioners should have relinquished the baby at that time. It was their decision to prolong this litigation through a lengthy, and ultimately fruitless, appeal.

The adoption laws of Illinois are neither complex nor difficult of application. Those laws intentionally place the burden of proof on the adoptive parents in establishing both the relinquishment and/or unfitness of the natural parents and, coincidentally, the fitness and the right to adopt of the adoptive parents. In addition, Illinois law requires a good-faith effort to notify the natural parents of the adoption proceedings. These laws are designed to protect natural parents in their preemptive rights to their own children wholly apart from any consideration of the so-called best interests of the child. If it were otherwise, few parents would be secure in the custody of their own children. If best interests of the child were a sufficient qualification to determine child custody, anyone with superior income, intelligence, education, etc., might challenge and deprive the parents of their right to their own children. The law is otherwise and was not complied with in this case.

Notes and Questions on the **Baby Richard Case**

(1) The Baby Richard case had been preceded by a similar case, the Baby Jessica case. *In re Clausen*, 502 NW2d 649 (Mich 1993). In both cases, the eventual result was that a child was taken from the only home it had ever known and placed with parents it had never known. Both cases provoked considerable public attention and distress. They also provoked legislative responses intended to make such cases less likely. Professor Meyer reports:

> Most states followed one or both of two basic strategies. The first strategy was to reduce the ability of unwed fathers to block adoptions by expanding the statutory grounds for excluding them from the adoption process. Along these lines, some states broadened the statutory grounds

for terminating the legal rights of biological parents, such as child "abandonment" or parental "unfitness." Many states also rushed to enact measures specifically aimed at unwed fathers, providing for a waiver of legal rights in the adoption process of any putative father who failed to take prescribed steps to assert his interest in custody. The second basic legislative strategy was to mitigate the harm in those cases where adoptions could not go forward, typically by providing for the possibility of long-term custody with the caregivers who had sought to adopt.

David D. Meyer, *Family Ties: Solving the Constitutional Dilemma of the Faultless Father*, 41 Ariz L Rev 753, 770 (1999).

(2) How does the result in the Baby Richard case fit with the principle that the child's best interest is the touchstone in custody cases?

(a) Is the result ultimately consistent with that touchstone? For example, is the court assuming that it is in the child's best interest to be brought up by the child's natural parents?

(b) Is the result ultimately inconsistent with that touchstone? Consider again the material you have read about "psychological parents." Can it be in a child's best interests to take it away from the only parents it has ever known, particularly after years have passed? If *Doe is* inconsistent with the child's best interest, is it rightly decided? Why should the child's interest always trump everyone else's?

(3) In the Baby Jessica case (which we mentioned in Question (1)), the mother, Cara Clausen, gave up the baby for adoption without telling the father, Dan Schmidt (the father). However, they eventually married and together sought custody of Jessica. They won and renamed the child Anna. A news story reported that Anna had not since seen the would-be adoptive parents and that the Schmidts were divorcing. Rick Smith, *Parents of 9–Year–Old Once Known as Baby Jessica Are Granted a Divorce*, The Des Moines Register, Saturday, March 11, 2000.

(b) The Unmarried Father and the Married Mother

We have been reading cases in which an unmarried mother gave her child up for adoption and before the unmarried father was given a chance to assert a claim to custody. But such situations are not the only ones in which the unmarried father might find his claim barred. Consider the following case. The first opinion you will read is by Justice Scalia, who wrote an opinion which the Chief Justice joined in its entirety and in which Justices O'Connor and Kennedy joined except for a footnote in which Justice Scalia discussed the role historical analysis should play in identifying fundamental rights in substantive due process cases.

MICHAEL H. v. GERALD D.

Supreme Court of the United States, 1989
491 US 110

SCALIA, J.

[In 1976, Gerald D. ("a top executive in a French oil company") married Carole D. ("an international model"). In 1978, "Carole became involved in an adulterous affair with a neighbor, Michael H." In 1981, she had a child, Victoria D. "Gerald was listed as father on the birth certificate and has always held Victoria out to the world as his daughter." However, a blood test soon revealed "a 98.07% probability that Michael was Victoria's father."

During the next three years, Victoria stayed with Carole, but Carole moved among the households of Gerald, Michael, and "yet another man, Scott K." We cannot tell just how much contact Michael had with Victoria during this period. Justice Scalia's plurality opinion speaks of "the relationship established between a married woman, her lover and their child, during a three-month sojourn in St. Thomas, ... [and] during a subsequent 8–month period when, if he happened to be in Los Angeles, he stayed with her and the child." Justice Brennan's dissent said, "the evidence is undisputed that Michael, Victoria, and Carole did live together as a family; that is, they shared the same household, Victoria called Michael 'Daddy,' Michael contributed to Victoria's support, and he is eager to continue his relationship with her."

So eager was Michael that he "filed a filiation action ... to establish his paternity and right to visitation." To cut a long and tumultuous story short, "[i]n June 1984, Carole reconciled with Gerald and joined him in New York, where they now live with Victoria and two other children since born into the marriage." Michael's filiation action encountered a California statute providing "that 'the issue of a wife cohabiting with her husband, who is not impotent or sterile, is conclusively presumed to be a child of the marriage'.... The presumption may be rebutted by blood tests, but only if a motion for such tests is made, within two years from the date of the child's birth, either by the husband or, if the natural father has filed an affidavit acknowledging paternity, by the wife." In 1985 the trial court rejected Michael's claim; in 1987 an appellate court affirmed and the California Supreme Court denied certiorari.]

We address first the claims of Michael. At the outset, it is necessary to clarify what he sought and what he was denied. California law, like nature itself, makes no provision for dual fatherhood. Michael was seeking to be declared the father of Victoria. The immediate benefit he evidently sought to obtain from that status was visitation rights. But if Michael were successful in being declared the father, other rights would follow—most importantly, the right to be considered as the parent who should have custody.

Michael contends as a matter of substantive due process that, because he has established a parental relationship with Victoria, protection of Gerald's and Carole's marital union is an insufficient state interest to support termination of that relationship. This argument is, of course, predicated on the assertion that Michael has a constitutionally protected liberty interest in his relationship with Victoria.

Thus, the legal issue in the present case reduces to whether the relationship between persons in the situation of Michael and Victoria has been treated as a protected family unit under the historic practices of our society, or whether on any other basis it has been accorded special protection. We think it impossible to find that it has.

We have found nothing in the older sources, nor in the older cases, addressing specifically the power of the natural father to assert parental rights over a child born into a woman's existing marriage with another man. [E]ven in modern times—when, as we have noted, the rigid protection of the marital family has in other respects been relaxed—the ability of a person in Michael's position to claim paternity has not been generally acknowledged.

[Moreover, what Michael must establish] is not that our society has traditionally allowed a natural father in his circumstances to establish paternity, but that it has traditionally accorded such a father parental rights, or at least has not traditionally denied them. Even if the law in all States had always been that the entire world could challenge the marital presumption and obtain a declaration as to who was the natural father, that would not advance Michael's claim. Thus, it is ultimately irrelevant, even for purposes of determining current social attitudes towards the alleged substantive right Michael asserts, that the present law in a number of States appears to allow the natural father—including the natural father who has not established a relationship with the child—the theoretical power to rebut the marital presumption. What counts is whether the States in fact award substantive parental rights to the natural father of a child conceived within, and born into, an extant marital union that wishes to embrace the child. We are not aware of a single case, old or new, that has done so. This is not the stuff of which fundamental rights qualifying as liberty interests are made.

In *Lehr v. Robertson*, we observed that "[t]he significance of the biological connection is that it offers the natural father an opportunity that no other male possesses to develop a relationship with his offspring," and we assumed that the Constitution might require some protection of that opportunity. Where, however, the child is born into an extant marital family, the natural father's unique opportunity conflicts with the similarly unique opportunity of the husband of the marriage; and it is not unconstitutional for the State to give categorical preference to the latter. In *Lehr* we quoted approvingly from Justice Stewart's dissent in *Caban v. Mohammed*, to the effect that although " '[i]n some circumstances the actual relationship between father and child may suffice to create in the unwed father parental interests comparable to those of the married father,' " " 'the absence of a legal tie with the mother may in such circumstances appropriately place a limit on whatever substantive constitutional claims might otherwise exist.' " In accord with our traditions, a limit is also imposed by the circumstance that the mother is, at the time of the child's conception and birth, married to, and cohabitating with, another man, both of whom wish to raise the child as the offspring of their union. It is a question of legislative policy and not constitutional law whether California will allow the presumed parenthood of a couple desiring to retain a child conceived within and born into their marriage to be rebutted.

We do not accept Justice BRENNAN's criticism that this result "squashes" the liberty that consists of "the freedom not to conform." It seems to us that reflects the erroneous view that there is only one side to this controversy—that one disposition can expand a "liberty" of sorts without contracting an equivalent "liberty" on the other side. Such a happy choice is rarely available. Here, to provide protection to an adulterous natural father is to deny protection to a marital father, and vice versa. If Michael has a "freedom not to conform" (whatever that means), Gerald must equivalently have a "freedom to conform." One of them will pay a price for asserting that "freedom"—Michael by being unable to act as father of the child he has adulterously begotten, or Gerald by being unable to preserve the integrity of the traditional family unit he and Victoria have established. Our disposition does not choose between these two "freedoms," but leaves that to the people of California. Justice BRENNAN's approach chooses one of them as the constitutional imperative, on no apparent basis except that the unconventional is to be preferred.

JUSTICE STEVENS, concurring in the judgment.

I think cases like *Stanley v. Illinois*, and *Caban v. Mohammed* demonstrate that enduring "family" relationships may develop in unconventional settings. I therefore would not foreclose the possibility that a constitutionally protected relationship between a natural father and his child might exist in a case like this. Indeed, I am willing to assume for the purpose of deciding this case that Michael's relationship with Victoria is strong enough to give him a constitutional right to try to convince a trial judge that Victoria's best interest would be served by granting him visitation rights. I am satisfied, however, that the California statute, as applied in this case, gave him that opportunity.

JUSTICE BRENNAN, with whom JUSTICE MARSHALL and JUSTICE BLACKMUN join, dissenting.

[T]o describe the issue in this case as whether the relationship existing between Michael and Victoria "has been treated as a protected family unit under the historic practices of our society, or whether on any other basis it has been accorded special protection" is to reinvent the wheel. The better approach—indeed, the one commanded by our prior cases and by common sense—is to ask whether the specific parent-child relationship under consideration is close enough to the interests that we already have protected to be deemed an aspect of "liberty" as well. On the facts before us, therefore, the question is not what "level of generality" should be used to describe the relationship between Michael and Victoria, but whether the relationship under consideration is sufficiently substantial to qualify as a liberty interest under our prior cases.

On four prior occasions, we have considered whether unwed fathers have a constitutionally protected interest in their relationships with their children. See *Stanley v. Illinois, Quilloin v. Walcott, Caban v. Mohammed*, and *Lehr v. Robertson*. Though different in factual and legal circumstances, these cases have produced a unifying theme: although an unwed father's biological link to his child does not, in and of itself, guarantee him a constitutional stake in his relationship with that child, such a link combined with a substantial parent-child relationship will do so. "When an unwed father demonstrates a full commitment to the responsibilities of parenthood by 'com[ing] forward to participate in the rearing of his child,' ... his interest in personal contact with his child acquires substantial protection under the Due Process Clause. At that point it may be said that he 'act[s] as a father toward his children.' "*Lehr v. Robertson*, quoting *Caban v. Mohammed*. This commitment is why Mr. Stanley and Mr. Caban won; why Mr. Quilloin and Mr. Lehr lost; and why Michael H. should prevail today. Michael H. is almost certainly Victoria D.'s natural father, has lived with her as her father, has contributed to her support, and has from the beginning sought to strengthen and maintain his relationship with her.

Claiming that the intent of these cases was to protect the "unitary family," the plurality waves *Stanley, Quilloin, Caban*, and *Lehr* aside. In evaluating the plurality's dismissal of these precedents, it is essential to identify its conception of the "unitary family." If, by acknowledging that *Stanley* et al. sought to protect "the relationships that develop within the unitary family," ibid., the plurality meant only to describe the kinds of relationships that develop when parents and children live together (formally or informally) as a family, then the plurality's vision of these cases would be correct. But that is not the plurality's message. Though it pays lip service to the idea that marriage is not the crucial fact in denying constitutional protection to the relationship between Michael and Victoria, the plurality cannot mean what it says.

The evidence is undisputed that Michael, Victoria, and Carole did live together as a family; that is, they shared the same household, Victoria called Michael "Daddy," Michael contributed to Victoria's support, and he is eager to continue his relationship with her. Yet they are not, in the plurality's view, a "unitary family," whereas Gerald, Carole, and Victoria do compose such a family. The only difference between these two sets of relationships, however, is the fact of marriage. The plurality, indeed, expressly recognizes that marriage is the critical fact in denying Michael a constitutionally protected stake in his relationship with Victoria: no fewer than six times, the plurality refers to Michael as the "adulterous natural father" (emphasis added) or the like. However, the very premise of *Stanley* and the cases following it is that marriage is not decisive in answering the question whether the Constitution protects the parental relationship under consideration. These cases are, after all, important precisely because they involve the rights of unwed fathers. It is important to remember, moreover, that in *Quilloin, Caban,* and *Lehr,* the putative father's demands would have disrupted a "unitary family" as the plurality defines it; in each case, the husband of the child's mother sought to adopt the child over the objections of the natural father. Significantly, our decisions in those cases in no way relied on the need to protect the marital family. Hence the plurality's claim that *Stanley, Quilloin, Caban,* and *Lehr* were about the "unitary family," as that family is defined by today's plurality, is surprising indeed.

The plurality's exclusive rather than inclusive definition of the "unitary family" is out of step with other decisions as well. This pinched conception of "the family," crucial as it is in rejecting Michael's and Victoria's claims of a liberty interest, is jarring in light of our many cases preventing the States from denying important interests or statuses to those whose situations do not fit the government's narrow view of the family. From *Loving v. Virginia,* 388 U.S. 1 (1967), to *Levy v. Louisiana,* 391 U.S. 68, (1968), and *Glona v. American Guarantee & Liability Ins. Co.,* 391 U.S. 73, (1968), and from *Gomez v. Perez,* 409 U.S. 535 (1973), to *Moore v. East Cleveland,* 431 U.S. 494, (1977), we have declined to respect a State's notion, as manifested in its allocation of privileges and burdens, of what the family should be. Today's rhapsody on the "unitary family" is out of tune with such decisions .

JUSTICE WHITE, with whom Justice Brennan joins, dissenting.

Like Justices BRENNAN, MARSHALL, BLACKMUN, and STEVENS, I do not agree with the plurality opinion's conclusion that a natural father can never "have a constitutionally protected interest in his relationship with a child whose mother was married to, and cohabiting with, another man at the time of the child's conception and birth." Prior cases here have recognized the liberty interest of a father in his relationship with his child. In none of these cases did we indicate that the father's rights were dependent on the marital status of the mother or biological father. The basic principle enunciated in the Court's unwed father cases is that an unwed father who has demonstrated a sufficient commitment to his paternity by way of personal, financial, or custodial responsibilities has a protected liberty interest in a relationship with his child.

We have not before faced the question of a biological father's relationship with his child when the child was born while the mother was married to another man. On several occasions however, we have considered whether a biological father has a constitutionally cognizable interest in an opportunity to establish paternity. *Stanley v. Illinois* recognized the biological father's right to a legal relationship with his illegitimate child, holding that the Due Process Clause of the Fourteenth Amendment entitled the biological father to a hearing on his fitness before his illegitimate children could be removed from his custody. We rejected the State's treatment of Stanley "not as a parent but as a stranger to his children."

Quilloin v. Walcott also expressly recognized due process rights in the biological father, even while holding that those rights were not impermissibly burdened by the State's application of a "best interests of the child" standard. *Caban v. Mohammed* invalidated on equal protection grounds a statute under which a man's children could be adopted by their natural mother and her husband without the natural father's consent.

In *Lehr v. Robertson*, though holding against the father in that case, the Court said clearly that fathers who have participated in raising their illegitimate children and have developed a relationship with them have constitutionally protected parental rights. Indeed, the Court in *Lehr* suggested that States must provide a biological father of an illegitimate child the means by which he may establish his paternity so that he may have the opportunity to develop a relationship with his child. The Court upheld a stepparent adoption over the natural father's objections, but acknowledged that "the existence or nonexistence of a substantial relationship between parent and child is a relevant criterion in evaluating both the rights of the parent and the best interests of the child." There, however, the father had never established a custodial, personal, or financial relationship with his child. Lehr had never lived with the child or the child's mother after the birth of the child and had never provided any financial support.

In the case now before us, Michael H. is not a father unwilling to assume his responsibilities as a parent. To the contrary, he is a father who has asserted his interests in raising and providing for his child since the very time of the child's birth. In contrast to the father in Lehr, Michael had begun to develop a relationship with his daughter. There is no dispute on this point. Michael contributed to the child's support. Michael and Victoria lived together (albeit intermittently, given Carole's itinerant lifestyle). There is a personal and emotional relationship between Michael and Victoria, who grew up calling him "Daddy." Michael held Victoria out as his daughter and contributed to the child's financial support. The mother has never denied, and indeed has admitted, that Michael is Victoria's father. *Lehr* was predicated on the absence of a substantial relationship between the man and the child and emphasized the "difference between the developed parent-child relationship that was implicated in *Stanley* and *Caban*, and the potential relationship involved in *Quilloin* and [*Lehr*]." "When an unwed father demonstrates a full commitment to the responsibilities of parenthood by 'com[ing] forward to participate in the rearing of his child,' his interest in personal contact with his child acquires substantial protection under the Due Process Clause." The facts in this case satisfy the *Lehr* criteria, which focused on the relationship between father and child, not on the relationship between father and mother. Under *Lehr* a "mere biological relationship" is not enough, but in light of Carole's vicissitudes, what more could Michael have done? It is clear enough that Michael more than meets the mark in establishing the constitutionally protected liberty interest discussed in *Lehr* and recognized in *Stanley v. Illinois* and Caban v. Mohammed. He therefore has a liberty interest entitled to protection under the Due Process Clause of the Fourteenth Amendment.

Notes and Questions on Michael H.

(1) Was it *morally* correct for Michael H. to seek to maintain ties with his daughter after her mother reunited with her husband? Was it *morally* correct for him to bring the legal action he brought? What relationship with his daughter and her mother and the mother's husband did he expect to have if he won the suit?

(2) What were Victoria's best interests? What were her legal rights? Did she have any kind of constitutional claim? To continued contact with her biological father? To an undisturbed relationship with her biological mother and *de facto* father?

(3) The dissent in *Michael H.* criticizes the majority for its "myopic" view of families. Is the state constitutionally inhibited from preferring some kinds of families to others? For an extended discussion of the state's interest in *Michael H.*, see Chapter 13.2.D.

(5) What effect, if any, does *Troxel v. Granville* (which we read in Chapter 7), have on *Michael H.*?

(6) *Michael H.* is the United States Supreme Court's latest word on the unmarried father and the married mother. However, a number of state supreme courts have also dealt with the issue. In *Callender v. Skiles*, 591 NW2d 182, 188 (Iowa 1999), for example, the unmarried father persuaded a court to order a blood test which established that he was the father of the child. He sought not only custody, visitation, and child support, but also an order terminating the parental rights of the mother's husband. The court observed, "Some jurisdictions follow the line of reasoning established in *Michael H.* and hold statutes which deny a putative father standing constitutional under the state or federal constitutions." And it noted, "On the other hand, it has been recognized that a statutory scheme depriving a putative father of standing to rebut the marital presumption or establish paternity violates portions of the state constitution." (The Iowa Supreme Court held that the father had a right under the state constitution to a hearing in which to argue for the claims he had made.)

(7) Who is a natural parent? Consider *C.M. v. C.C.*, 377 A2d 821 (Juvenile & Dom Rel Ct, Cumberland Cty, NJ 1977). In that case, C.C. and C.M. had been seeing each other for approximately two years. She (C.C.) "wanted a child and wanted him [C.M.] to be the father, but did not want to have intercourse with him before their marriage." The couple went to a sperm bank, which refused them the use of their facilities. "Over a period of several months, C.C. went to C.M.'s apartment where they attempted the artificial insemination. C.M. would stay in one room while C.C. went to another room to attempt to inseminate

herself with semen provided by C.M." These attempts were eventually successful. C.M. claimed that he had always assumed that he would act as the child's father; C.C. claimed "that C.M. was to be only a visitor in her home—much as any of her other friends." The relationship between the two ended, and C.M. went to court to seek visitation rights. The court held in favor of C.M., reasoning that "a man is [not] any less a father because he provides the semen by a method different from that normally used." Is this right? Should C.M. be liable for child support?

(8) To what extent should our understanding of child-custody law be altered in light of the constitutional protection of parental rights?

(a) The UMDA inferentially recognizes the importance of parental custody agreements, and the ALI (along with a number of states) does so expressly. Can these agreements be thought of as analogous to a joint decision made by still-married parents about any important aspect of their child's welfare? The latter decision would (unless it amounted to abuse and neglect) be constitutionally insulated from governmental review. Is there any reason a parental custody agreement should not be similarly insulated?

(b) Goldstein, Freud, and Solnit's proposals in some cases result in the denial of custody to parents who are not "unfit." Is this constitutionally permissible?

(c) Joint-custody rules, in at least some of their forms, attempt to ensure that *both* parents will continue to be parents in the fullest sense possible to the fullest extent possible. Is this constitutionally required?

(d) Do parents have a constitutional right to visitation? This question was addressed in an unusual form in *Franz v. United States*, 707 F2d 582 (DC Cir 1983). When William and Catherine Franz were divorced, Catherine apparently received custody of their three children and William apparently was awarded visitation privileges, privileges he proceeded to use for four or five years. Catherine apparently married one Charles Allen, "a contract killer in the employ of leaders of organized crime." In 1978, Allen agreed "to testify in a federal criminal trial in return for the relocation and protection of himself, Catherine, and Catherine's three children." The family was relocated, leaving William unable to exercise his visitation privileges. The U.S. Marshal's Service, which was responsible for the relocation, refused to arrange for William to visit the children without Catherine's consent, which she withheld. William brought suit against the United States seeking damages and declaratory and injunctive relief. The court wrote a lengthy opinion which included the following:

> The first of the three factors [which account for the court's skepticism of governmental interference with parent-child relations]—the existence of a tradition of respect for the institution in question—provides us little guidance. It seems undeniable that recognition of the sanctity of the bond between a child and his non-

custodial parent is far less firmly embedded in our cultural heritage than respect for the autonomy of the relations between a child and parent in a nuclear family. But that discrepancy is readily explainable on the basis of the relative rarity, in United States society in the past, of regularly exercised "visitation rights." Recognition of the need to adjust the meaning of the Constitution to conform to changes in social life requires, in this in stance, that we eschew reliance on history.

Reference to the second of the three factors is more productive of insight. Neither of the two complementary social functions fulfilled by traditional parent-child relations [socialization and preserving cultural heterogeneity] would appear to be specially dependent upon non-interference with the bond between a child and his non-custodial parent.

The force of the third consideration [the importance to both parent and child of the emotional bond between them] is somewhat harder to assess.... [I]n short, it appears impossible to say with any confidence that the concerns that underlie our willingness to accord "fundamental" status to parent-child bonds are any less telling when the relationship in question consists of mere "visitation." ...

[W]e conclude that the constitutional interests asserted by the plaintiffs are, in critical respects, roughly comparable to the interests of a parent and child in a viable nuclear family. We stress, however, that our analysis extends only to the question of the constitutional status of the right of a non-custodial parent and his or her children not to be totally and permanently prevented from ever seeing one another.... [W]e do not mean to suggest that a parent (or child) has a "fundamental right" to maintain visitation privileges in any particular way.

The court concluded that the federal government is constitutionally required to provide a hearing and that it must show that the governmental interest in the Witness Protection Program would in each specific case "be promoted in ways sufficiently substantial to warrant overriding basic human liberties."

In a "separate statement" which expressed a variety of doubts about the majority's opinion, Judge Bork wrote,

The Court has never enunciated a substantive right to so tenuous a relationship as visitation by a non-custodial parent. The reason for protecting the family and the institution of marriage is not merely that they are fundamental to our society but that our entire tradition is to encourage, support, and respect them. That cannot be said of broken homes and dissolved marriages.

Indeed, the majority takes the usual argument for creating fundamental rights and runs it backwards. Fundamental rights are usually grounded in the existence of a tradition of respect for the cultural institution in question. The majority notes that there is no comparable tradition of respect for the bond between a child and his non-custodial parent.... But the majority turns the difficulty to advantage by prophesying a continuing trend toward divorce and hence the increased social importance of the "broken" family. This, the majority declares, is sufficient to permit ignoring the absence of a strong tradition with respect to non-custodial parents....

The argument of the majority opinion also rests heavily upon the importance of the emotional bond between the non-custodial parent and the child.... It would be well, however, if there were some additional analysis indicating how this form of emotional distress differs from others that the majority does not, I assume, wish to make the foundation for additional fundamental rights. Suppose, for example, that a mother brought suit protesting her son's induction into a dangerous branch of the armed services.... Though the majority emphasizes the narrowness of its reasoning, it does so merely by assertion; it does not identify any limiting principles that would prevent its reasoning from being applied to situations like the one just described....

The decisive argument against judicial creation of a substantive constitutional right of a non-custodial parent to visit his or her children is that it is likely to make many state law denials of a right of visitation, or of custody, subject to federal constitutional challenge—a challenge based not upon the need for adequate procedures but upon some federal substantive standard. The majority states that its principle is limited to cases of *permanent* severance of the relation between parent and child, but it is doubtful that the underlying rationale permits the principle so to be confined.... Once this substantive right is in place, a state will have to muster a "compelling need" whenever it wishes significantly to deny visitation rights or custody to one parent.

(10) Racial and Religious Matching

A number of jurisdictions have adopted rules that require courts to take race and religion into account when making decisions about child custody and adoption. These rules are analyzed at length in Chapter 12.

SECTION 3. ALTERNATIVE REPRODUCTIVE TECHNIQUES: REVIEWING OLD ISSUES THROUGH NEW PROBLEMS

And Laban had two daughters: the name of the elder was Leah, and the name of the younger was Rachel. Leah was tender eyed; but Rachel was beautiful and well favoured. And Jacob loved Rachel; and said, I will serve thee seven years for Rachel thy younger daughter. And Laban said, It is better that I give her to thee; than that I should give her to another man; abide with me. And Jacob served seven years for Rachel; and they seemed unto him but a few days, for the love he had to her.

And Jacob said unto Laban, Give me my wife, for my days are fulfilled, that I may go in unto her. And Laban gathered together all the men of the place, and made a feast. And it came to pass in the evening, that he took Leah his daughter, and brought her to him; and he went in unto her. And Laban gave unto his daughter Leah Zilpah his maid for an handmaid. And it came to pass, that in the morning, behold, it was Leah: and he said to Laban, What is this thou has done unto me? Did not I serve with thee for Rachel? Wherefore then has thou beguiled me? And Laban said, It must not be so done in our country, to give the younger before the firstborn. Fulfil her week, and we will give thee this also for the service which thou shalt serve with me yet seven other years. And Jacob did so, and fulfilled her week; and he gave him Rachel his daughter to wife also. And Laban gave to Rachel his daughter Bilhah his handmaid to be her maid. And he went in also unto Rachel, and he loved also Rachel more than Leah, and served with him yet seven other years.

And when the Lord saw that Leah was hated, he opened her womb: but Rachel was barren. And Leah conceived, and bare a son, and she called his name Reuben: for she said, Surely the Lord hath looked upon my affliction; now therefore my husband will love me. And she conceived again, and bare a son; and said, Because the Lord hath heard that I was hated, he hath therefore given me this son also: and she called his name Simeon. And she conceived again, and bare a son; and said, Now this time will my husband be jointed unto me, because I have born him three sons: therefore was his name called Levi. And she conceived again, and bare a son: and she said, Now I will praise the Lord: therefore she called his name Judah; and left bearing.

And when Rachel saw that she bare Jacob no children, Rachel envied her sister; and said unto Jacob, Give me children, or else I die. And Jacob's anger was kindled against Rachel: and he said, Am I in God's stead, who hath withheld from thee the fruit of the womb? And she said, Behold my maid Bilhah, go in unto her; and she shall bear upon my knees, that I may also have children by her. And she gave him Bilhah her handmaid to wife: and Jacob went in unto her. And Bilhah conceived, and bare Jacob a son. And Rachel said, God hath judged me, and hath also heard my voice, and hath given me a son: therefore called she his name Dan. And Bilhah Rachel's maid conceived again, and bare Jacob a second son. And Rachel said, With great wrestlings have I wrestled with my sister, and I have prevailed: and she called his name Naphtali. When Leah saw that she had left bearing, she took Zilpah her maid, and gave her Jacob to wife. And Leah said, A troop cometh: and she called his name Gad. And Zilpah Leah's maid bare Jacob a son. And Leah said, Happy am I, for the daughters will call me blessed. . . .

Genesis 29:16–35; 30:1–13

When law confronts new problems, its assumptions often emerge with fresh clarity. When law confronts new problems, it is often forced to make new calculations about what it should value. The emergence of newly practical alternatives to coital reproduction exemplifies that process. For that reason, we will close our examination of the law of child custody by looking at what the law's response to those alternatives reveals about its assumptions and its goals.

A. SURVEYING THE FIELD

O brave new world,

That has such people in it.

William Shakespeare
The Tempest

This chapter may have convinced you that custody disputes between ordinary parents of ordinarily reproduced children can be complex and troubled enough. But, of course, disputes over responsibility for children have become yet more complex and troubled as less orthodox means of reproduction have become increasingly available. Three of these means are worth some attention. Consider, then, the following introduction to these issues:

MARSHA GARRISON LAW MAKING FOR BABY MAKING: AN INTERPRETIVE APPROACH TO THE DETERMINATION OF LEGAL PARENTAGE

113 Harvard Law Review 835 (2000)

I. The Revolution in Reproduction

A. *Artificial Insemination*

Artificial insemination (AI) is the oldest and most popular means of technological conception. An estimated 20,000 to 30,000 children are born in the United States each year following AI with sperm provided by donors (AID), and tens of thousands more following AI with sperm donated by husbands (AIH).

Although AIH and AID both offer an infertile couple increased odds of conceiving a child, they produce different results and different legal issues. The husband and wife who conceive using AIH are both genetic parents of the child, and thus, under traditional family law principles, they are also his legal parents. With AID, however, only the wife is genetically related to the child. Thus, under prevailing law at the time AID came into widespread use, her husband's parental status was unclear.

During the 1970s, the states began to enact legislation that clarified the AID child's legal parentage. The 1973 Uniform Parentage Act (UPA), for example, provided that "[i]f, under the supervision of a licensed physician and with the consent of her husband, a wife is inseminated artificially with semen donated by a man not her husband, the husband is treated in law as if he were the natural father of a child thereby conceived." As of 1998, fifteen states had adopted the UPA or a virtually identical standard, and fifteen others had enacted similar statutes that varied by eliminating the licensed physician requirement.

Although the AID statutes resolved the status issue that courts initially confronted, they failed to resolve a host of other legal questions that might arise from the use of AID—and which increasingly do. The status issues posed by AID today reflect a shift in its usage. Advances in the treatment of male infertility have markedly reduced the number of married couples who seek AID, while a remarkable change in parenting norms has greatly expanded the number of would-be parents who seek AID for reasons unrelated to infertility: many of these new AID applicants are single women who wish to achieve pregnancy but have no male partner; others are parties to a surrogate parenting agreement; and an occasional applicant wishes to become pregnant using sperm from a deceased partner. Many of these new users continue to employ sperm banks and physician assistance in order to ensure donor screening and anonymity, but others rely on known donors and perform AID at home without physician involvement.

The larger legal context has also shifted. As AID developed during the 1950s and 60s, its practitioners followed the model pioneered by adoption agencies. In both contexts, the goal was to provide would-be parents with the closest possible substitute for their own biological child; secrecy, participant anonymity, and physical-trait "matching" were employed to achieve these ends. But while AID practitioners still follow the old model, adoption practice has turned away from it. The federal government has severely restricted racial matching in adoption, and disclosure increasingly replaces secrecy; agencies and experts now counsel openness about the adopted child's origins, and adoption statutes have accordingly moved toward open records and even "open adoption," in which the biological parent retains some form of contact with the child after her adoptive placement.

The legal status of unmarried biological fathers has shifted even more dramatically. Although both AID users and adoptive parents could afford to ignore biological fathers during the 1950s and 60s—in most states unmarried fathers had no legal rights whatsoever, the Supreme Court has since held that an unmarried father who has "grasp[ed] th[e] opportunity [to develop a relationship with his child] and accept[ed] some measure of responsibility for the child's future" is entitled to constitutional protection. A number of state courts have accordingly voided adoptions when the unmarried father had no notice of the proceeding and promptly came forward to obtain custody. Courts have also permitted challenges to the marital presumption of legitimacy, and even sperm donors who have asserted claims to visitation or custody have sometimes been recognized as legal parents.

Current AID statutes were not drafted with an eye to either the new users or the new legal context in which AID occurs. Most do not address the paternity of an AID child born to an unmarried woman. Nor do current statutes typically provide guidance either on the AI donor's rights to a relationship with his biological child or the child's rights to information about her origins. In sum, current law on artificial insemination provides an extremely limited response to an isolated legal issue; it fails to assimilate AID into the broader set of legal principles governing parental rights and relationships.

B. *In Vitro Fertilization*

While AI avoids sex, in vitro fertilization (IVF) moves the entire process of conception outside the body. In IVF, ovarian stimulation is followed by the collection of eggs ready for fertilization. The process of fertilization takes place in vitro in a laboratory; some or all of the resulting preembryos are then implanted into the uterus or fallopian tubes. The first IVF birth occurred in 1978 in Great Britain. Since then, tens of thousands of children conceived through IVF have been born in the United States alone.

Like AI, IVF was originally employed by married couples with fertility problems; thus the first IVF baby, Louise Brown, was conceived using Mrs. Brown's ova in combination with her husband's sperm. But as with AI, the uses of IVF have expanded. Because IVF takes the process of conception outside the body, it permits the use of donated eggs (the analog to AID); this practice has expanded dramatically because IVF success rates for older women substantially increase when the eggs of younger women are employed. IVF also permits the use of another woman to gestate the fetus; although less common than IVF with donated ova, this practice, too, has increased. The net result is a confusing array of "parents"; for example, would-be parents A and B might obtain sperm from Man C and eggs from Woman D, then have a doctor implant the resulting preembryos in Woman E to be carried to term. And, as with AI, today's IVF users are not necessarily married couples with fertility problems. A and B might be a gay couple, or A and B might be simply A, a single man or woman.

The parenting possibilities created by IVF present a host of legal issues. One set of questions relates to the legal parentage of children born through IVF. While arguably more complex, these questions are similar to those raised by AID. But IVF also poses altogether new legal problems relating to the status of preembryos created in vitro. Were these preembryos within her body, the pregnant woman could choose to abort them or carry them to term. When they are outside the womb, the woman's rights are less clear.

Courts have begun to address the legal issues raised by IVF, but legislatures have thus far been almost entirely inactive. The Tennessee Supreme Court has ruled that preembryos created through IVF and frozen for future use are neither persons nor property; when a married couple that had donated genetic material for the creation of such preembryos later divorced, the court held that, based on the facts and lack of an agreement regarding disposition of the preembryos, the spouse who wished to destroy the preembryos was entitled to do so over the objection of the other spouse. The California Supreme Court has held that a baby born using IVF and a gestational surrogate was the legal child of the genetic parents, and a lower court in New York has ruled that a woman who bore a child through IVF using donated ova was the child's legal mother. A case involving the parentage and custody of twins born to a woman who underwent IVF with "donated" preembryos that had allegedly been cryopreserved only for the future use of the genetic parents is currently before the California courts, but has not yet been resolved.

C. *Pregnancy for Another: The Various Forms of Surrogacy*

Surrogacy—bearing a child for someone else—stands in contrast to AI and IVF in that it requires no technology at all. The Biblical Sarah, Rachel, and Leah all made use of surrogates—their handmaids—in order to produce children for their husbands; conception was achieved sexually rather than technologically. Modern surrogacy, however, invariably involves conception through AI. In the case of gestational surrogacy, in which the woman who gives birth is not genetically related to the child she bears, IVF is employed as well.

Modern surrogacy also differs from that of Biblical times in its reliance on contract. Biblical surrogacy involved an informal understanding between the infertile woman, her husband, and her handmaid, but surrogacy today is almost invariably conducted on the basis of a formal, written document specifying rights and obligations. Surrogacy today is also commercial: contracts almost always require payments both to the woman who will bear the child and to a service that has brokered the arrangement.

Commercial, contract surrogacy emerged in the United States in the late 1970s. Although its use has spread, the number of surrogate births remains small in comparison to those obtained through AI and IVF alone; in 1993 the Center for Surrogate Parenting estimated that 4000 surrogate births had occurred in the United States.

Public attention became focused on surrogacy as a result of the widely-publicized case of *In re Baby M*, [537 A2d 1227 (NJ 1988)] involving the legality of an agreement by a "surrogate" mother to relinquish the child she had conceived through AI to the sperm donor and his wife in return for $10,000. Perhaps because of the media attention, state legislatures reacted to surrogacy with greater speed than they have reacted to AI and IVF. By 1987, at least seventy-two bills pertaining to surrogacy had been introduced in Congress, state legislatures and the District of Columbia; today, nearly half of the states have statutes regulating surrogacy. Almost all of these statutes declare commercial surrogacy contracts void and unenforceable. Some additionally criminalize participation in and/or brokering of a surrogacy agreement. A few explicitly permit noncommercial surrogacy. And three states (New Hampshire, Nevada, and Virginia) permit some forms of commercial surrogacy, although all allow the birth mother to rescind the surrogacy contract within a specified time period.

Most surrogacy laws assume that the "surrogate" birth mother is genetically related to the child; they thus fail to address the increasingly common phenomenon of gestational surrogacy. With gestational surrogacy, it is possible for a child to have three "mothers"—one who is genetically related to the child, one who gave birth to the child, and one who planned the pregnancy and intended the child to be hers. It is also possible for a child to have three "fathers"—one related to the child genetically, one married to the woman who gave birth to it, and one who planned the pregnancy and intended it to be his. Current law, even in states with statutes governing surrogacy, typically fails to offer clear (or even murky) answers as to the rights and obligations of these various parties.

Notes and Questions on Alternative Reproductive Technology

(1) As Professor Garrison reports, state legislatures have responded to the challenges of surrogacy in various ways. Some states have banned surrogacy entirely. For instance, NY Dom Rel Law §§ 122 et seq (McKinney 2006), provides, "Surrogate parenting contracts are hereby declared contrary to the public policy of this state, and are void and unenforceable." Some states authorize enforcement of surrogacy contracts that meet prescribed standards. For example, Va Code Ann § 20–160.B.4 (2005) allows enforcement where the arrangement is not for financial gain, and NH Rev Stat Ann § 168–B:25V (2005) recognizes reimbursement for actual lost wages, attorneys' fees, and counseling or home studies. The Uniform Parentage Act provision appears in Utah Code §§ 78–45g–801 et seq. (2005). It provides for court validation and payment of related healthcare expenses until the birth of the child.

(2) In *Davis v. Davis*, 842 SW2d 588 (Tenn 1992), the attempts of a married couple, Mary Sue and Junior Davis, to have a child through IVF had yielded a number of frozen embryos (zygotes). The parties then decided to divorce. Mrs. Davis wanted to donate the zygotes to another woman, but Mr. Davis did not want to become a father. The Tennessee Supreme Court held for Mr. Davis. It said that a woman's right to privacy does not encompass a general right to procreate and that Junior's right not to become an unwilling parent outweighed Mrs. Davis's right to donate the zygotes.

Kass v. Kass, 696 NE2d 174 (1998), involved a couple who, before beginning IVF, had signed forms that required the consent of both parties before the clinic could release the zygotes to either party and that gave the clinic permission to donate the zygotes for research if the parties did not reach an agreement. After divorce, Maureen Kass, who was forty years old and regarded the frozen zygotes as her best hope of having children, sought the zygotes without her former husband's permission. A New York trial court awarded them to her over her ex-husband's objection, holding that the consent forms were so badly drafted that they were unenforceable and noting that the constitutional right of privacy, which includes both a right to procreate and a right not to become a parent against one's will, supported her claim. The court said a husband has no right to procreate or avoid procreation because he has no role in the decision to have an abortion. On appeal, however, the judgment was reversed. The New York Court of Appeals unanimously held that the parties' clearly expressed intent that the IVF clinic be able to donate the zygotes for research controlled, that the woman's constitutional right to procreative privacy and bodily integrity was not implicated, and that the zygotes were not "persons" in the constitutional sense.

(3) The legal problems presented by the new reproductive technology are about to become yet more complex, for it has become possible to take sperm from a dead man. The first fetus known to be produced by the posthumous removal of gametes was due in March, 1999. The sperm donor, the woman's husband, died in 1994. However, within 30 hours of his death his wife asked that his sperm be removed in order to permit her to undergo IVF at some later date. Four years later she conceived using his sperm. Post-mortem removal of gametes has recently become prominent enough that the American Society of Reproductive Medicine has developed a protocol—"Posthumous Reproduction"—to govern it. Although reliable estimates of the number of postmortem removals are difficult to come by, a 1997 study conducted by the University of Pennsylvania's Center for Bioethics found that at least fourteen clinics in eleven states had performed the procedure.

(4) Although posthumous sperm donation is too novel to have produced case law, much less legislation, posthumous reproduction has reached the courts in a different guise. Consider the facts of *Hecht v. Superior Court*, 16 Cal App 4th 836, 20 Cal Rptr 2d 275 (1993):

> At the age of 48, William E. Kane took his own life on October 30, 1991, in a Las Vegas hotel. For about five years prior to his death, he had been living with petitioner, 38-year-old Deborah Hecht. Kane was survived by two college-aged children of his former wife whom he had divorced in 1976.
>
> In October 1991, decedent deposited 15 vials of his sperm in an account at California Cryobank, Inc., a Los Angeles sperm bank (hereinafter sperm bank). On September 24, 1991, he signed a "Specimen Storage Agreement" with sperm bank which provided in pertinent part that "In the event of the death of the client [William E. Kane], the client instructs the Cryobank to: ... [¶] Continue to store [the specimens] upon request of the executor of the estate [or] [r]elease the specimens to the executor of the estate." A provision captioned "Authorization to Release Specimens" states, "I, William Everett Kane, ... authorize the [sperm bank] to release my semen specimens (vials) to Deborah Ellen Hecht. I am also authorizing specimens to be released to recipient's physician Dr. Kathryn Moyer."
>
> On September 27, 1991, decedent executed a will which was filed with the Los Angeles County Superior Court and admitted to probate. The will named Hecht as executor of the estate, and provides, "I bequeath all right, title, and interest that I may have in any specimens of my sperm stored with any sperm bank or similar facility for storage to Deborah Ellen Hecht."
>
> An October 21, 1991 letter signed by Kane and addressed to his children stated: "I address this to my children, because, although I have only two, Everett and Katy, it may be that Deborah will decide—as I hope she will—to have a child by me after my death. I've been assidu-

ously generating frozen sperm samples for that eventuality. If she does, then this letter is for my posthumous offspring, as well, with the thought that I have loved you in my dreams, even though I never got to see you born."

After several pages of childhood memories and family history, the letter stated: "So why am I checking out now? Basically, betrayal, over and over again, has made me tired. I've picked up some heavyweight enemies along the way—ranging from the Kellys of the world, to crazies with guns, to insurance companies, to the lawyers that have sucked me dry.... I don't want to die as a tired, perhaps defeated and bitter old man. I'd rather end it like I have lived it—on my time, when and where I will, and while my life is still an object of self-sculpture—a personal creation with which I am still proud. In truth, death for me is not the opposite of life; it is a form of life's punctuation."

Kane committed suicide on October 30, 1991, in Las Vegas, Nevada. On November 18, 1991, Robert L. Greene was appointed special administrator of the estate of William Everett Kane. On December 3, 1991, William Kane, Jr., and Katharine Kane each filed separate will contests.

Katharine Kane and William Kane, Jr., filed a statement of interested parties in which they argued that ordering destruction of decedent's sperm would "help guard the family unit in two different ways": First, such an order would prevent the birth of children who will never know their father and "never even have the slightest hope of being raised in a traditional family." Second, such an order would "prevent the disruption of existing families by after-born children," and would "prevent additional emotional, psychological and financial stress on those family members already in existence." They characterized the desire to father children after one's death as "egotistic and irresponsible," and stated that they "have lost their father to a tragic death which Hecht could easily have prevented; they do not wish to suffer any more at her hands. Further, they do not wish to be troubled for the rest of their lives with worries about the fate of their half-sibling(s)."

What should the court have done? (What it did was award ownership of the frozen sperm to the girlfriend on the grounds that the sperm were property subject to the probate court's jurisdiction and that public policy did not forbid Hecht to be artificially inseminated with it.) Does reproductive material—and particularly do fertilized eggs—have any of the quality of "human life"? The *Davis* court, for instance, said that "preembryos are not, strictly speaking, either 'persons' or 'property,' but occupy an interim category that entitles them to special respect because of their potential for human interest." Can genetic material be owned? Can it be the subject of binding contracts? Should its control be determined according to the usual rules of child custody?

Recent articles on artificial reproductive technology include Susan B. Apel, *Cryopreserved Embryos: A Response to "Forced Parenthood" and the Role of Intent*, 39 Fam. LQ 663 (2005)(arguing that the intended parent doctrine should not be used to deny children born of ART a legal father); Susan L. Crocklin, The *"Embryo" Wars: At the Epicenter of*

Science, Law, Religion, and Politics, 39 Fam LQ 599 (2005); and Ellen Waldman, *The Parent Trap: Uncovering the Myth of "Coerced Parenthood" in Frozen Embryo Disputes*, 53 Am L Rev 1021 (2004).

B. DILEMMAS OF SURROGACY

It is a wise father that knows his own child.

William Shakespeare
The Merchant of Venice

At base, surrogacy presents two categories of legal problems. The first is the question whether surrogate contracts ought to be legally enforceable. The second is how custody should be allocated in the event of a surrogate pregnancy where a contract does not determine the result. As you know from reading Professor Garrison's article, the first of these questions is settled by statute in many jurisdictions. Typically, however, surrogacy first achieved prominence as a legal issue in a case—*Matter of Baby M.*, 537 A2d 1227 (NJ 1988). There a married woman (Mary Beth Whitehead) entered into a contract in which she agreed to be impregnated by artificial insemination with sperm coming from the husband of another married couple (the Sterns). When the child was born, the woman refused to give the child to the couple. The New Jersey Supreme Court held that the contract was unenforceable because it conflicted with New Jersey statutes concerning adoption and the termination of parental rights and with public policy concerning families and the formation of contracts. For example, the court said, "This is the sale of a child, or, at the very least, the sale of a mother's right to her child," which New Jersey law prohibited. The court then treated the case as a child-custody dispute and awarded custody to the biological father. More recently, two cases from the California courts have addressed these issues:

JOHNSON v. CALVERT

Supreme Court of California, 1993
851 P2d 776

PANELLI, JUSTICE.

FACTS

Mark and Crispina Calvert are a married couple who desired to have a child. Crispina was forced to undergo a hysterectomy in 1984. Her ovaries remained capable of producing eggs, however, and the couple eventually considered surrogacy. In 1989 Anna Johnson heard about Crispina's plight from a coworker and offered to serve as a surrogate for the Calverts.

On January 15, 1990, Mark, Crispina, and Anna signed a contract providing that an embryo created by the sperm of Mark and the egg of Crispina would be implanted in Anna and the child born would be taken into Mark and Crispina's home "as their child." Anna agreed she would relinquish "all parental rights" to the child in favor of Mark and Crispina. In return, Mark and Crispina would pay Anna $10,000 in a series of installments, the last to be paid six weeks after the child's birth. Mark and Crispina were also to pay for a $200,000 life insurance policy on Anna's life.

The zygote was implanted on January 19, 1990. Less than a month later, an ultrasound test confirmed Anna was pregnant.

Unfortunately, relations deteriorated between the two sides. Mark learned that Anna had not disclosed she had suffered several stillbirths and miscarriages. Anna felt Mark and Crispina did not do enough to obtain the required insurance policy. She also felt abandoned during an onset of premature labor in June.

In July 1990, Anna sent Mark and Crispina a letter demanding the balance of the payments due her or else she would refuse to give up the child. The following month, Mark and Crispina responded with a lawsuit, seeking a declaration they were the legal parents of the unborn child. Anna filed her own action to be declared the mother of the child, and the two cases were eventually consolidated. The parties agreed to an independent guardian ad litem for the purposes of the suit.

The child was born on September 19, 1990, and blood samples were obtained from both Anna and the child for analysis. The blood test results excluded Anna as the genetic mother. The parties agreed to a court order providing that the child would remain with Mark and Crispina on a temporary basis with visits by Anna.

At trial in October 1990, the parties stipulated that Mark and Crispina were the child's genetic parents. After hearing evidence and arguments, the trial court ruled that Mark and Crispina were the child's "genetic, biological and natural" father and mother, that Anna had no "parental" rights to the child, and that the surrogacy contract was legal and enforceable against Anna's claims. The court also terminated the order allowing visitation. Anna appealed from the trial court's judgment. The Court of Appeal for the Fourth District, Division Three, affirmed. We granted review.

Discussion: Determining Maternity Under the Uniform Parentage Act

The Uniform Parentage Act (the Act) was part of a package of legislation introduced in 1975 as Senate Bill No. 347. The legislation's purpose was to eliminate the legal distinction between legitimate and illegitimate children.

Civil Code sections 7001 and 7002 replace the distinction between legitimate and illegitimate children with the concept of the "parent and child relationship." The "parent and child relationship" means "the legal relationship existing between a child and his natural or adoptive parents incident to which the law confers or imposes rights, privileges, duties, and obligations. It includes the mother and child relationship and the father and child relationship." "The parent and child relationship extends equally to every child and to every parent, regardless of the marital status of the parents." The "parent and child relationship" is thus a legal relationship encompassing two kinds of parents, "natural" and "adoptive."

Passage of the Act clearly was not motivated by the need to resolve surrogacy disputes, which were virtually unknown in 1975. Yet it facially applies to any parentage determination, including the rare case in which a child's maternity is in issue.

Anna, of course, predicates her claim of maternity on the fact that she gave birth to the child. The Calverts contend that Crispina's genetic relationship to the child establishes that she is his mother. Counsel for the minor joins in that contention and argues, in addition, that several of the presumptions created by the Act dictate the same result. As will appear, we conclude that presentation of blood test evidence is one means of establishing maternity, as is proof of having given birth, but that the presumptions cited by minor's counsel do not apply to this case.

We turn to those few provisions of the Act directly addressing the determination of maternity. "Any interested party," presumably including a genetic mother, "may bring an action to determine the existence ... of a mother and child relationship." Civil Code section 7003 provides, in relevant part, that between a child and the natural mother a parent and child relationship "may be established by proof of her having given birth to the child, or under [the Act]." Apart from Civil Code section 7003, the Act sets forth no specific means by which a natural mother can establish a parent and child relationship. However, it declares that, insofar as practicable, provisions applicable to the father and child relationship apply in an action to determine the existence or nonexistence of a mother and child relationship. Thus, it is appropriate to examine those provisions as well.

A man can establish a father and child relationship by the means set forth in Civil Code section 7004. Paternity is presumed under that section if the man meets the conditions set forth in section 621 of the Evidence Code. The latter statute applies, by its terms, when determining the questioned paternity of a child born to a married woman, and contemplates reliance on evidence derived from blood testing. Alternatively, Civil Code section 7004 creates a presumption of paternity based on the man's conduct toward the child (e.g., receiving the child into his home and openly holding the child out as his natural child) or his marriage or attempted marriage to the child's natural mother under specified conditions.

In our view, the presumptions contained in Civil Code section 7004 do not apply here. They describe situations in which substantial evidence points to a particular man as the natural father of the child. In this case, there is no question as to who is claiming the mother and child relationship, and the factual basis of each woman's claim is obvious. Thus, there is no need to resort to an evidentiary presumption to ascertain the identity of the natural mother. Instead, we must make the purely legal determination as between the two claimants.

Significantly for this case, Evidence Code section 892 provides that blood testing may be ordered in an action when paternity is a relevant fact. When maternity is disputed, genetic evidence derived from blood testing is likewise admissible. The Evidence Code further provides that if the court finds the conclusions of all the experts, as disclosed by the evidence based on the blood tests, are that the alleged father is not the father of the child, the question of paternity is resolved accordingly. By parity of reasoning, blood testing may also be dispositive of the question of maternity. Further, there is a rebuttable presumption of paternity (hence, maternity as well) on the finding of a certain number of genetic markers.

[W]e are left with the undisputed evidence that Anna, not Crispina, gave birth to the child and that Crispina, not Anna, is genetically related to him. Both women thus have adduced evidence of a mother and child relationship as contemplated by the Act. Yet for any child California law recognizes only one natural mother, despite advances in reproductive technology rendering a different outcome biologically possible.

We see no clear legislative preference in Civil Code section 7003 as between blood testing evidence and proof of having given birth. "May" indicates that proof of having given birth is a permitted method of establishing a mother and child relationship, although perhaps not the exclusive one. The disjunctive "or" indicates that blood test evidence, as prescribed in the Act, constitutes an alternative to proof of having given birth.

Because two women each have presented acceptable proof of maternity, we do not believe this case can be decided without enquiring into the parties' intentions as manifested in the surrogacy agreement. Mark and Crispina are a couple who desired to have a child of their own genes but are physically unable to do so without the help of reproductive technology. They affirmatively intended the birth of the child, and took the steps necessary to effect in vitro fertilization. But for their acted-on intention, the child would not exist. Anna agreed to facilitate the procreation of Mark's and Crispina's child. The parties' aim was to bring Mark's and Crispina's child into the world, not for Mark and Crispina to donate a zygote to Anna. Crispina from the outset intended to be the child's mother. Although the gestative function Anna performed was necessary to bring about the child's birth, it is safe to say that Anna would not have been given the opportunity to gestate or deliver the child had she, prior to implantation of the zygote, manifested her own intent to be the child's mother. No reason appears why Anna's later change of heart should vitiate the determination that Crispina is the child's natural mother.

We conclude that although the Act recognizes both genetic consanguinity and giving birth as means of establishing a mother and child relationship, when the two means do not coincide in one woman, she who intended to procreate the child—that is, she who intended to bring about the birth of a child that she intended to raise as her own—is the natural mother under California law.

[A]s Professor Shultz recognizes, the interests of children, particularly at the outset of their lives, are "[un]likely to run contrary to those of adults who choose to bring them into being." Thus, "[h]onoring the plans and expectations of adults who will be responsible for a child's welfare is likely to correlate significantly with positive outcomes for parents and children alike." [*Reproductive Technology and Intent–Based Parenthood: An Opportunity for Gender Neutrality*, 1990 Wisconsin L Rev 297.] Under Anna's interpretation of the Act, by contrast, a woman who agreed to gestate a fetus genetically related to the intending parents would, contrary to her expectations, be held to be the child's natural mother, with all the responsibilities that ruling would entail, if the intending mother declined to accept the child after its birth. In what we must hope will be the extremely rare situation in which neither the gestator nor the woman who provided the ovum for fertilization is willing to assume custody of the child after birth, a rule recognizing the intending parents as the child's legal, natural parents should best promote certainty and stability for the child.

In deciding the issue of maternity under the Act we have felt free to take into account the parties' intentions, as expressed in the surrogacy contract, because in our view the agreement is not, on its face, inconsistent with public policy.

Preliminarily, Mark and Crispina urge us to interpret the Legislature's 1992 passage of a bill that would have regulated surrogacy as an expression of this state's public policy despite the fact that Governor Wilson's veto prevented the bill from becoming law. Senate Bill No. 937 contained a finding that surrogate contracts are not against sound public and social policy .

In the Governor's veto message we find, not unequivocal agreement with the Legislature's public policy assessment, but rather reservations about the practice of surrogate parenting. "Comprehensive regulation of this difficult moral issue is premature." ... Given this less than ringing endorsement of surrogate parenting, we conclude that the passage of Senate Bill No. 937, in and of itself, does not establish that surrogacy contracts are consistent with public policy.

Anna urges that surrogacy contracts violate several social policies. Relying on her contention that she is the child's legal, natural mother, she cites the public policy embodied in Penal Code section 273, prohibiting the payment for consent to adoption of a child. She argues further that the policies underlying the adoption laws of this state are violated by the surrogacy contract because it in effect constitutes a prebirth waiver of her parental rights.

We disagree. Gestational surrogacy differs in crucial respects from adoption and so is not subject to the adoption statutes. The parties voluntarily agreed to participate in vitro fertilization and related medical procedures before the child was conceived; at the time when Anna entered into the contract, therefore, she was not vulnerable to financial inducements to part with her own expected offspring. As discussed above, Anna was not the genetic mother of the child. The payments to Anna under the contract were meant to compensate her for her services in gestating the fetus and undergoing labor, rather than for giving up "parental" rights to the child. Payments were due both during the pregnancy and after the child's birth. We are, accordingly, unpersuaded that the contract used in this case violates the public policies embodied in Penal Code section 273 and the adoption statutes. For the same reasons, we conclude these contracts do not implicate the policies underlying the statutes governing termination of parental rights.

It has been suggested that gestational surrogacy may run afoul of prohibitions on involuntary servitude. Involuntary servitude has been recognized in cases of criminal punishment for refusal to work. We see no potential for that evil in the contract at issue here, and extrinsic evidence of coercion or duress is utterly lacking. We note that although at one point the contract purports to give Mark and Crispina the sole right to determine whether to abort the pregnancy, at another point it acknowledges: "All parties understand that a pregnant woman has the absolute right to abort or not abort any fetus she is carrying. Any promise to the contrary is unenforceable." We therefore need not determine the validity of a surrogacy contract purporting to deprive the gestator of her freedom to terminate the pregnancy.

Finally, Anna and some commentators have expressed concern that surrogacy contracts tend to exploit or dehumanize women, especially women of lower economic status. Anna's objections center around the psychological harm she asserts may result from the gestator's relinquishing the child to whom she has given birth. Some have also cautioned that the practice of surrogacy may encourage society to view children as commodities, subject to trade at their parents' will.

We are all too aware that the proper forum for resolution of this issue is the Legislature, where empirical data, largely lacking from this record, can be studied and rules of general applicability developed. However, in light of our responsibility to decide this case, we have considered as best we can its possible consequences.

We are unpersuaded that gestational surrogacy arrangements are so likely to cause the untoward results Anna cites as to demand their invalidation on public policy grounds. Although common sense suggests that women of lesser means serve as surrogate mothers more often than do wealthy women, there has been no proof that surrogacy contracts exploit poor women to any greater degree than economic necessity in general exploits them by inducing them to accept lower-paid or otherwise undesirable employment. We are likewise unpersuaded by the claim that surrogacy will foster the attitude that children are mere commodities; no evidence is offered to support it. The limited data available seem to reflect an absence of significant adverse effects of surrogacy on all participants.

The argument that a woman cannot knowingly and intelligently agree to gestate and deliver a baby for intending parents carries overtones of the reasoning that for centuries prevented women from attaining equal economic rights and professional status under the law. To resurrect this view is both to foreclose a personal and economic choice on the part of the surrogate mother, and to deny intending parents what may be their only means of procreating a child of their own genes. Certainly in the present case it cannot seriously be argued that Anna, a licensed vocational nurse who had done well in school and who had previously borne a child, lacked the intellectual wherewithal or life experience necessary to make an informed decision to enter into the surrogacy contract.

Constitutionality of the Determination That Anna Johnson Is Not the Natural Mother

Anna argues at length that her right to the continued companionship of the child is protected under the federal Constitution.

Anna relies mainly on theories of substantive due process, privacy, and procreative freedom, citing a number of decisions recognizing the fundamental liberty interest of natural parents in the custody and care of their children. (See, e.g., *Santosky v. Kramer; Lassiter v. Department of Social Services; Smith v. Organization of Foster Families; Stanley v. Illinois.)* Most of the cases Anna cites deal with the rights of unwed fathers in the face of attempts to terminate their parental relationship to their children. (See, e.g., *Stanley v. Illinois; Quilloin v. Wallcott; Caban v. Mohammed; Lehr v. Robertson.)* These cases do not support recognition of parental rights for a gestational surrogate. Although Anna quotes language stressing the primacy of a developed parent-child relationship in assessing unwed fathers' rights, certain language in the cases reinforces the importance of genetic parents' rights. "The significance of the biological connection is that it offers the natural father an opportunity that no other male possesses to develop a relationship with his offspring. If he grasps that opportunity and accepts some measure of responsibility for the child's future, he may enjoy the blessings of the parent-child relationship and make uniquely valuable contributions to the child's development."

Anna's argument depends on a prior determination that she is indeed the child's mother. Since Crispina is the child's mother under California law because she, not Anna, provided the ovum for the in vitro fertilization procedure, intending to raise the child as her own, it follows that any constitutional interests Anna possesses in this situation are something less than those of a mother. As counsel for the minor points out, the issue in this case is not whether Anna's asserted rights as a natural mother were unconstitutionally violated, but rather whether the determination that she is not the legal natural mother at all is constitutional.

Anna relies principally on the decision of the United States Supreme Court in *Michael H. v. Gerald D.,* 491 U.S. 110 (1989), to support her claim to a constitutionally protected liberty interest in the companionship of the child, based on her status as "birth mother." In that case, a plurality of the court held that a state may constitutionally deny a man parental rights with respect to a child he fathered during a liaison with the wife of another man, since it is the marital family that traditionally has been accorded a protected liberty interest, as reflected in the historic presumption of legitimacy of a child born into such a family. The reasoning of the plurality in *Michael H.* does not assist Anna. Society has not traditionally protected the right of a woman who gestates and delivers a baby pursuant to an agreement with a couple who supply the zygote from which the baby develops and who intend to raise the child as their own; such arrangements are of too recent an origin to claim the protection of tradition. To the extent that tradition has a bearing on the present case, we believe it supports the claim of the couple who exercise their right to procreate in order to form a family of their own, albeit through novel medical procedures.

Moreover, if we were to conclude that Anna enjoys some sort of liberty interest in the companionship of the child, then the liberty interests of Mark and Crispina, the child's natural parents, in their procreative choices and their relationship with the child would perforce be infringed. Any parental rights Anna might successfully assert could come only at Crispina's expense. As we have seen, Anna has no parental rights to the child under California law, and she fails to persuade us that sufficiently strong policy reasons exist to accord her a protected liberty interest in the companionship of the child when such an interest would necessarily detract from or impair the parental bond enjoyed by Mark and Crispina.

Amicus curiae ACLU urges that Anna's right of privacy, embodied in the California Constitution (Cal. Const., art. I, § 1), requires recognition and protection of her status as "birth mother." . . . Amicus curiae appears to assume that the choice to gestate and deliver a baby for its genetic parents pursuant to a surrogacy agreement is the equivalent, in constitutional weight, of the decision whether to bear a child of one's own. We disagree. A woman who enters into a gestational surrogacy arrangement is not exercising her own right to make procreative choices; she is agreeing to provide a necessary and profoundly important service without (by definition) any expectation that she will raise the resulting child as her own.

Drawing an analogy to artificial insemination, Anna argues that Mark and Crispina were mere genetic donors who are entitled to no constitutional protection. That characterization of the facts is, however, inaccurate. Mark and Crispina never intended to "donate" genetic material to anyone. Rather, they intended to procreate a child genetically related to them by the only available means. Civil Code section 7005, governing artificial insemination, has no application here.

Finally, Anna argues that the Act's failure to address novel reproductive techniques such as in vitro fertilization indicates legislative disapproval of such practices. Given that the Act was drafted long before such techniques were developed, we cannot agree. Moreover, we may not arrogate to ourselves the power to disapprove them. It is not the role of the judiciary to inhibit the use of reproductive technology when the Legislature has not seen fit to do so; any such effort would raise serious questions in light of the fundamental nature of the rights of procreation and privacy. Rather, our task has been to resolve the dispute before us, interpreting the Act's use of the term "natural mother" when the biological functions essential to bringing a child into the world have been allocated between two women. . . .

DISPOSITION

The judgment of the Court of Appeal is affirmed.

[The concurring opinion of Justice Arabian is omitted.]

KENNARD, J, dissenting. . . .

II. THIS OPINION'S APPROACH

The determination of a question of parental rights to a child born of a surrogacy arrangement was before the New Jersey Supreme Court in *Matter of Baby M.* (1988) 109 N.J. 396 [537 A.2d 1227], a case that received worldwide attention. But in the surrogacy arrangement at issue there the woman who gave birth to the child, Marybeth Whitehead, had been impregnated by artificial insemination with the sperm of the intending father, William Stern. Whitehead thus provided the genetic material and carried the fetus to term. This case is different, because here those two aspects of the female role in reproduction were divided between two women. This process is known as "gestational" surrogacy, to distinguish it from the surrogacy arrangement involved in *Baby M*. . . .

IV. POLICY CONSIDERATIONS. . . .

Surrogacy proponents generally contend that gestational surrogacy, like the other reproductive technologies that extend the ability to procreate to persons who might not otherwise be able to have children, enhances "individual freedom, fulfillment and responsibility." Under this view, women capable of bearing children should be allowed to freely agree to be paid to do so by infertile couples desiring to form a family; see also Posner, Economic Analysis of Law (3d ed. 1986) p. 139; Landes & Posner, The Economics of the Baby Shortage (1978) 7 J. Legal Stud. 323. The "surrogate mother" is expected "to weigh the prospective investment in her birthing labor" before entering into the arrangement, and, if her "autonomous reproductive decision" is "voluntary," she should be held responsible for it so as "to fulfill the expectations of the other parties...." (Shalev, Birth Power: The Case for Surrogacy.).

One constitutional law scholar argues that the use of techniques such as gestational surrogacy is constitutionally protected and should be restricted only on a showing of a compelling state interest. (Robertson, Procreative Liberty and the Control of Conception, Pregnancy, and Childbirth (1983) 69 Va.L.Rev. 405.) Professor Robertson reasons that procreation is itself protected under decisions of the United States Supreme Court that affirm the basic civil right to marry and raise children. (Robertson, citing *Meyer v. Nebraska; Skinner v. Oklahoma; Stanley v. Illinois.*) From this premise, he argues that the right to procreate should extend to persons who cannot conceive or bear children.

Professor Robertson's thesis of broad application of the right of privacy for all procreational techniques has been questioned, however, in light of recent United States Supreme Court jurisprudence. (See *Medical Technology*, supra, 103 Harv.L.Rev. 1525, 1530, citing *Michael H. v. Gerald D.* (1989) 491 U.S. 110, as evidence of the high court's reluctance "to extend the right of privacy to new relationships and activities" that the court has not perceived to merit "traditional protection.")

Surrogacy critics, however, maintain that the payment of money for the gestation and relinquishment of a child threatens the economic exploitation of poor women who may be induced to engage in commercial surrogacy arrangements out of financial need. Some fear the development of a "breeder" class of poor women who will be regularly employed to bear children for the economically advantaged. Others suggest that women who enter into surrogacy arrangements may underestimate the psychological impact of relinquishing a child they have nurtured in their bodies for nine months.

Gestational surrogacy is also said to be "dehumanizing" and to "commodify" women and children by treating the female reproductive capacity and the children born of gestational surrogacy arrangements as products that can be bought and sold. The commodification of women and children, it is feared, will reinforce oppressive gender stereotypes and threaten the well-being of all children. Some critics foresee promotion of an ever-expanding "business of surrogacy brokerage."

Whether surrogacy contracts are viewed as personal service agreements or agreements for the sale of the child born as the result of the agreement, commentators critical of contractual surrogacy view these contracts as contrary to public policy and thus not enforceable.

Organizations representing diverse viewpoints share many of the concerns highlighted by the legal commentators. For example, the American Medical Association considers the conception of a child for relinquishment after birth to pose grave ethical problems. Likewise, the official position of the Catholic Church is that surrogacy arrangements are " 'contrary to the unity of marriage and to the dignity of the procreation of the human person.' " (Magisterium of the Catholic Church, Instruction on Respect for Human Life in Its Origin and on the

Dignity of Procreation: Replies to Certain Questions of the Day 25 (Feb. 22, 1987).)

The policy statement of the New York State Task Force on Life and the Law sums up the broad range of ethical problems that commercial surrogacy arrangements are viewed to present: "The gestation of children as a service for others in exchange for a fee is a radical departure from the way in which society understands and values pregnancy. It substitutes commercial values for the web of social, affective and moral meanings associated with human reproduction.... This transformation has profound implications for child-bearing, for women, and for the relationship between parents and the children they bring into the world. Surrogate parenting allows the genetic, gestational and social components of parenthood to be fragmented, creating unprecedented relationships among people bound together by contractual obligation rather than by the bonds of kinship and caring.... Surrogate parenting alters deep-rooted social and moral assumptions about the relationship between parents and children.... [It] is premised on the ability and willingness of women to abdicate [their parental] responsibility without moral compunction or regret [and] makes the obligations that accompany parenthood alienable and negotiable." (New York State Task Force on Life and the Law, Surrogate Parenting: Analysis and Recommendations for Public Policy (May 1988).

Proponents and critics of gestational surrogacy propose widely differing approaches for deciding who should be the legal mother of a child born of a gestational surrogacy arrangement. Surrogacy advocates propose to enforce pre-conception contracts in which gestational mothers have agreed to relinquish parental rights, and, thus, would make "bargained-for intentions determinative of legal parenthood." Professor Robertson, for instance, contends that "The right to noncoital, collaborative reproduction also includes the right of the parties to agree how they should allocate their obligations and entitlements with respect to the child. Legal presumptions of paternity and maternity would be overridden by this agreement of the parties."

Surrogacy critics, on the other hand, consider the unique female role in human reproduction as the determinative factor in questions of legal parentage. They reason that although males and females both contribute genetic material for the child, the act of gestating the fetus falls only on the female. Accordingly, in their view, a woman who, as the result of gestational surrogacy, is not genetically related to the child she bears is like any other woman who gives birth to a child. In either situation the woman giving birth is the child's mother. Under this approach, the laws governing adoption should govern the parental rights to a child born of gestational surrogacy. Upon the birth of the child, the gestational mother can decide whether or not to relinquish her parental rights in favor of the genetic mother.

V. Model Legislation

The debate over whom the law should recognize as the legal mother of a child born of a gestational surrogacy arrangement prompted the

National Conference of Commissioners on Uniform State Laws to propose the Uniform Status of Children of Assisted Conception Act. (9B West's U. Laws Ann. (1992 Supp.) Uniform Status of Children of Assisted Conception Act (1988 Act) pp. 122–137 [hereafter also USCACA].) This model legislation addresses many of the concerns discussed above.

The commissioners gave careful consideration to the competing interests of the various participants in assisted conception arrangements, and sought to accommodate those interests in the model legislation. Their overriding concern, however, was the well-being of children born of gestational surrogacy and other types of assisted conception. As the foreword to the model legislation notes, the extraordinary circumstances of these children's births deprive them of parentage in the traditional sense. Thus, the intent of the proposed legislation was to define with precision the legal status of these children as well as to codify the rights of the other participants in a surrogacy arrangement. The commissioners proposed alternative versions of the USCACA: one that would disallow gestational surrogacy and another that would permit it only under court supervision.

In its key components, the proposed legislation provides that "a woman who gives birth to a child is the child's mother" unless a court has approved a surrogacy agreement before conception. In the absence of such court approval, any surrogacy agreement would be void. If, however, the arrangement for gestational surrogacy has court approval, "the intended parents are the parents of the child."

To obtain court approval, the parties to the surrogacy arrangement must file a petition. The model legislation provides for the court to appoint a guardian ad litem for the intended child and legal counsel for the surrogate mother. Before approving a surrogacy arrangement, the trial court must conduct a hearing and enter detailed findings, including the following: medical evidence shows the intended mother's inability to bear a child or that for her to do so poses an unreasonable risk to the unborn child or to the physical or mental health of the intended mother; all parties to the surrogacy agreement (including the surrogate's husband if she has one) meet the standards of fitness of adoptive parents; the agreement was voluntary and all parties understand its terms; the surrogate mother has undergone at least one successful pregnancy and medical evidence shows that another pregnancy will not endanger her physical or mental health or pose an unreasonable risk to the unborn child; and all parties have received professional mental health counseling pertaining to the effect of the surrogacy arrangement. These provisions serve to minimize the potential for overreaching and to ensure that all parties to a surrogacy arrangement understand their respective roles and obligations.

The USCACA offers predictability in delineating the parentage of children born of gestational surrogacy arrangements. Under the model legislation, if enacted, there would never be a question as to who has the legal responsibility for a child born of a gestational surrogacy arrangement: If the couple who initiated the surrogacy had complied with the provisions of the legislation, they would be the child's legal parents. If they had not, the rights and responsibilities of parenthood would go to the woman who gave birth to the child and her spouse.

Because the California Legislature has not enacted the Uniform Status of Children of Assisted Conception Act, its provisions were not followed in this case.

VI. The Uniform Parentage Act

The only California statute defining parental rights is the Uniform Parentage Act (hereafter also UPA). The Legislature enacted the UPA to abolish the concept of illegitimacy and to replace it with the concept of parentage. The UPA was never intended by the Legislature to govern the issues arising from new reproductive technologies such as gestational surrogacy. Nevertheless, the UPA is on its face broadly applicable, and it is in any event the only statutory guidance this court has in resolving this case.

The provisions of the UPA "extend equally to every child and to every parent, regardless of the marital status of the parents." The parent-child relationship defined by the UPA accords a child's parents both rights and obligations. A primary focus of the UPA is the determination of paternity and enforcement of financial responsibility.

When a child is born by gestational surrogacy, as happened here, the two women who played biological roles in creating the child will both have statutory claims under the UPA to being the child's natural mother. The UPA permits a woman to establish that she is "the natural mother" of a child by "proof of ... having given birth to the child...." Thus, a gestational mother qualifies as a "natural mother" under the statute. (Ibid.) Alternatively, the UPA allows a woman to prove she is a mother in the same manner as a man may prove he is a father. A man may demonstrate he is a child's natural father through genetic marker evidence derived from blood testing. Accordingly, a genetic mother may also demonstrate she is a child's natural mother through such genetic evidence. Here, both Anna, the gestational mother, and Crispina, the genetic mother, have offered proof acceptable under the UPA to qualify as the child's natural mother.

By its use of the phrase "the natural mother," however, the UPA contemplates that a child will have only one natural mother. But the UPA provides no standards for determining who that natural mother should be when, as here, two different women can offer biological proof of being the natural mother of the same child under its provisions. Thus, the UPA by its terms cannot resolve the conflict in this case.

VII. Analysis of the Majority's "Intent" Test

Faced with the failure of current statutory law to adequately address the issue of who is a child's natural mother when two women qualify under the UPA, the majority breaks the "tie" by resort to a criterion not found in the UPA—the "intent" of the genetic mother to be the child's mother.

This case presents a difficult issue. The majority's resolution of that issue deserves serious consideration. Ultimately, however, I cannot agree that "intent" is the appropriate test for resolving this case.

The majority offers four arguments in support of its conclusion to rely on the intent of the genetic mother as the exclusive determinant for deciding who is the natural mother of a child born of gestational surrogacy. Careful examination, however, demonstrates that none of the arguments mandates the majority's conclusion.

The first argument that the majority uses in support of its conclusion that the intent of the genetic mother to bear a child should be dispositive of the question of motherhood is "but-for" causation. Specifically, the majority relies on a commentator who writes that in a gestational surrogacy arrangement, "the child would not have been born but for the efforts of the intended parents."

The majority's resort to "but-for" causation is curious. The concept of "but-for" causation is a "test used in determining tort liability...." In California, the test for causation is whether the conduct was a "substantial factor" in bringing about the event. Neither test for causation assists the majority, as I shall discuss.

The proposition that a woman who gives birth to a child after carrying it for nine months is a "substantial factor" in the child's birth cannot reasonably be debated. Nor can it reasonably be questioned that "but for" the gestational mother, there would not be a child. Thus, the majority's reliance on principles of causation is misplaced. Neither the "but for" nor the "substantial factor" test of causation provides any basis for preferring the genetic mother's intent as the determinative factor in gestational surrogacy cases: Both the genetic and the gestational mothers are indispensable to the birth of a child in a gestational surrogacy arrangement.

Behind the majority's reliance on "but-for" causation as justification for its intent test is a second, closely related argument. The majority draws its second rationale from a student note: " 'The mental concept of the child is a controlling factor of its creation, and the originators of that concept merit full credit as conceivers.' "

The "originators of the concept" rationale seems comfortingly familiar. The reason it seems familiar, however, is that it is a rationale that is frequently advanced as justifying the law's protection of intellectual property. As stated by one author, "an idea belongs to its creator because the idea is a manifestation of the creator's personality or self." Thus, it may be argued, just as a song or invention is protected as the property of the "originator of the concept," so too a child should be regarded as belonging to the originator of the concept of the child, the genetic mother.

The problem with this argument, of course, is that children are not property. Unlike songs or inventions, rights in children cannot be sold for consideration, or made freely available to the general public. Our most fundamental notions of personhood tell us it is inappropriate to treat children as property. Although the law may justly recognize that the originator of a concept has certain property rights in that concept, the originator of the concept of a child can have no such rights, because children cannot be owned as property. Accordingly, I cannot endorse the majority's "originators of the concept" or intellectual property rationale for employing intent to break the "tie" between the genetic mother and the gestational mother of the child.

Next, the majority offers as its third rationale the notion that bargained-for expectations support its conclusion regarding the dispositive significance of the genetic mother's intent. Specifically, the majority states that " 'intentions that are voluntarily chosen, deliberate, express and bargained-for ought presumptively to determine legal parenthood.' "

It is commonplace that, in real or personal property transactions governed by contracts, "intentions that are voluntarily chosen, deliberate, express and bargained-for" ought presumptively to be enforced and, when one party seeks to escape performance, the court may order specific performance. But the courts will not compel performance of all contract obligations. For instance, even when a party to a contract for personal services (such as employment) has wilfully breached the contract, the courts will not order specific enforcement of an obligation to perform that personal service. The unsuitability of applying the notion that, because contract intentions are "voluntarily chosen, deliberate, express and bargained-for," their performance ought to be compelled by the courts is even more clear when the concept of specific performance is used to determine the course of the life of a child. Just as children are not the intellectual property of their parents, neither are they the personal property of anyone, and their delivery cannot be ordered as a contract remedy on the same terms that a court would, for example, order a breaching party to deliver a truckload of nuts and bolts.

Thus, three of the majority's four arguments in support of its exclusive reliance on the intent of the genetic mother as determinative in gestational surrogacy cases cannot withstand analysis. And, as I shall discuss shortly, the majority's fourth rationale has merit, but does not support the majority's conclusion. But before turning to the majority's fourth rationale, I shall discuss two additional considerations, not noted by the majority, that in my view also weigh against utilizing the intent of the genetic mother as the sole determinant of the result in this case and others like it.

First, in making the intent of the genetic mother who wants to have a child the dispositive factor, the majority renders a certain result preordained and inflexible in every such case: as between an intending genetic mother and a gestational mother, the genetic mother will, under the majority's analysis, always prevail. The majority recognizes no meaningful contribution by a woman who agrees to carry a fetus to term for the genetic mother beyond that of mere employment to perform a specified biological function.

The majority's approach entirely devalues the substantial claims of motherhood by a gestational mother such as Anna. True, a woman who enters into a surrogacy arrangement intending to raise the child has by her intent manifested an assumption of parental responsibility in addition to her biological contribution of providing the genetic material. But the gestational mother's biological contribution of carrying a child for nine months and giving birth is likewise an assumption of parental responsibility. A pregnant woman's commitment to the unborn child she carries is not just physical; it is psychological and emotional as well. The United States Supreme Court made a closely related point in *Lehr v Robertson,* explaining that a father's assertion of parental rights depended on his having assumed responsibility for the child after its birth, whereas a mother's "parental relationship is clear" because she "carries and bears the child." This court too has acknowledged that a pregnant woman and her unborn child comprise a "unique physical unit" and that the welfare of each is "intertwined and inseparable." Indeed, a fetus would never develop into a living child absent its nurturing by the pregnant woman. A pregnant woman intending to bring a child into the world is more than a mere container or breeding animal; she is a conscious agent of creation no less than the genetic mother, and her humanity is implicated on a deep level. Her role should not be devalued.

To summarize, the woman who carried the fetus to term and brought a child into the world has, like the genetic mother, a substantial claim to be the natural mother of the child. The gestational mother has made an indispensable and unique biological contribution, and has also gone beyond biology in an intangible respect that, though difficult to label, cannot be denied. Accordingly, I cannot agree with the majority's devaluation of the role of the gestational mother.

I find the majority's reliance on "intent" unsatisfactory for yet another reason. By making intent determinative of parental rights to a child born of a gestational surrogacy arrangement, the majority would permit enforcement of a gestational surrogacy agreement without requiring any of the protections that would be afforded by the Uniform Status of Children of Assisted Conception Act. Under that act, the granting of parental rights to a couple that initiates a gestational surrogacy arrangement would be conditioned upon compliance with the legislation's other provisions. They include court oversight of the gestational surrogacy arrangement before conception, legal counsel for the woman who agrees to gestate the child, a showing of need for the surrogacy, medical and mental health evaluations, and a requirement that all parties meet the standards of fitness of adoptive parents.

In my view, protective requirements such as those set forth in the USCACA are necessary to minimize any possibility in gestational surrogacy arrangements for overreaching or abuse by a party with economic advantage. As the New Jersey Supreme Court recognized, it will be a rare instance when a low income infertile couple can employ an upper income surrogate. (*Matter of Baby M.*, supra, 537 A.2d 1227, 1249.) The model act's carefully drafted provisions would assure that the surrogacy arrangement is a matter of medical necessity on the part of the intending parents, and not merely the product of a desire to avoid the inconveniences of pregnancy, together with the financial ability to do so. Also, by requiring both pre-conception psychological counseling for all parties and judicial approval, the model act would assure that parties enter into a surrogacy arrangement only if they are legally and psychologically capable of doing so and fully understand all the risks involved, and that the surrogacy arrangement would not be substantially detrimental to the interests of any individual. Moreover, by requiring judicial approval, the model act would significantly discourage the rapid expansion of commercial surrogacy brokerage and the resulting commodification of the products of pregnancy. In contrast, here the majority's grant of parental rights to the intending mother contains no provisions for the procedural protections suggested by the commissioners who drafted the model act. The majority opinion is a sweeping endorsement of unregulated gestational surrogacy.

The majority's final argument in support of using the intent of the genetic mother as the exclusive determinant of the outcome in gestational surrogacy cases is that preferring the intending mother serves the child's interests, which are " '[u]nlikely to run contrary to those of adults who choose to bring [the child] into being.' " I agree with the majority that the best interests of the child is an important goal; indeed, as I shall explain, the best interests of the child, rather than the intent of the genetic mother, is the proper standard to apply in the absence of legislation. The problem with the majority's rule of intent is that application of this inflexible rule will not serve the child's best interests in every case.

I express no view on whether the best interests of the child in this case will be served by determining that the genetic mother is or is not the natural mother under California's Uniform Parentage Act. It may be that in this case the child's interests will be best served by recognizing Crispina as the natural mother. But this court is not just making a rule to resolve this case. Because the UPA does not adequately address the situation of gestational surrogacy, this court is of necessity making a rule that, unless new legislation is enacted, will govern all future cases of gestational surrogacy in California. And all future cases will not be alike. The genetic mother and her spouse may be, in most cases, considerably more affluent than the gestational mother. But "[t]he mere fact that a couple is willing to pay a good deal of money to obtain a child does not vouchsafe that they will be suitable parents...." It requires little imagination to foresee cases in which the genetic mothers are, for example, unstable or substance abusers, or in which the genetic mothers' life circumstances change dramatically during the gestational mothers' pregnancies, while the gestational mothers, though of a less advantaged socioeconomic class, are stable, mature, capable and willing to provide a loving family environment in which the child will flourish. Under those circumstances, the majority's rigid reliance on the intent of the genetic mother will not serve the best interests of the child.

VIII. The Best Interests of the Child

As I have discussed, in California the existing statutory law applicable to this case is the Uniform Parentage Act which was never designed to govern the new reproductive technology of gestational surrogacy. Under the UPA, both the genetic mother and the gestational mother have an equal right to be the child's natural mother. But the UPA allows one natural mother for each child, and thus this court is required to make a choice. To break this "tie" between the genetic mother and the gestational mother, the majority uses the legal concept of intent. In so doing, the majority has articulated a rationale for using the concept of intent that is grounded in principles of tort, intellectual property and commercial contract law.

But, as I have pointed out, we are not deciding a case involving the commission of a tort, the ownership of intellectual property, or the delivery of goods under a commercial contract; we are deciding the fate of a child. In the absence of legislation that is designed to address the unique problems of gestational surrogacy, this court should look not to tort, property or contract law, but to family law, as the governing paradigm and source of a rule of decision.

The allocation of parental rights and responsibilities necessarily impacts the welfare of a minor child. And in issues of child welfare, the standard that courts frequently apply is the best interests of the child. Indeed, it is highly significant that the UPA itself looks to a child's best interests in deciding another question of parental rights. This "best interests" standard serves to assure that in the judicial resolution of disputes affecting a child's well-being, protection of the minor child is the foremost consideration. Consequently, I would apply "the best interests of the child" standard to determine who can best assume the social and legal responsibilities of motherhood for a child born of a gestational surrogacy arrangement.

The determination of a child's best interests does not depend on the parties' relative economic circumstances, which in a gestational surrogacy situation will usually favor the genetic mother and her spouse. (See *Matter of Baby M.*, supra, 537 A.2d at p. 1249.) As this court has recognized, however, superior wealth does not necessarily equate with good parenting.

Factors that are pertinent to good parenting, and thus that are in a child's best interests, include the ability to nurture the child physically and psychologically, and to provide ethical and intellectual guidance. Also crucial to a child's best interests is the "well recognized right" of every child "to stability and continuity." The intent of the genetic mother to procreate a child is certainly relevant to the question of the child's best interests; alone, however, it should not be dispositive.

Here, the child born of the gestational surrogacy arrangement between Anna Johnson and Mark and Crispina Calvert has lived continuously with Mark and Crispina since his birth in September 1990. The trial court awarded parental rights to Mark and Crispina, concluding that as a matter of law they were the child's "genetic, biological and natural" parents. In reaching that conclusion, the trial court did not treat Anna's statutory claim to be the child's legal mother as equal to Crispina's, nor did the trial court consider the child's best interests in deciding between those two equal statutory claims. Accordingly, I would remand the matter to the trial court to undertake that evaluation....

I would reverse the judgment of the Court of Appeal, and remand the case to the trial court for a determination of disputed parentage on the basis of the best interests of the child.

Notes and Questions on Johnson v. Calvert

(1) The court is faced with a conflict between two women who have a legitimate claim to be considered the mother of the child under California statutes. Does there have to be only one mother? Does it really matter which of them is "the mother" in this case? Isn't the issue not who is the mother, but who should have custody? We face custody cases between two parents all the time without feeling obliged to say one is the parent and the other is not. How would the case look if Crispina and Mark had decided to divorce and no longer wanted custody of the child. Would we still say that Anna was not the "mother"?

(2) Why does intent seem to be the test for parenthood in *Johnson*? Don't people become parents entirely without intending to all the time?

IN RE MARRIAGE OF BUZZANCA

California Court of Appeal, 1998
72 Cal Rptr 2d 280

SILLS, PRESIDING JUSTICE.

INTRODUCTION

Jaycee was born because Luanne and John Buzzanca agreed to have an embryo genetically unrelated to either of them implanted in a woman—a surrogate—who would carry and give birth to the child for them. After the fertilization, implantation and pregnancy, Luanne and John split up, and the question of who are Jaycee's lawful parents came before the trial court.

Luanne claimed that she and her erstwhile husband were the lawful parents, but John disclaimed any responsibility, financial or otherwise. The woman who gave birth also appeared in the case to make it clear that she made no claim to the child.

The trial court then reached an extraordinary conclusion: Jaycee had no lawful parents. First, the woman who gave birth to Jaycee was not the mother; the court had—astonishingly—already accepted a stipulation that neither she nor her husband were the "biological" parents. Second, Luanne was not the mother. According to the trial court, she could not be the mother because she had neither contributed the egg nor given birth. And John could not be the father, because, not having contributed the sperm, he had no biological relationship with the child. . . .

Case History

John filed his petition for dissolution of marriage on March 30, 1995, alleging there were no children of the marriage. Luanne filed her response on April 20, alleging that the parties were expecting a child by way of surrogate contract. Jaycee was born six days later. In September 1996 Luanne filed a separate petition to establish herself as Jaycee's mother. Her action was consolidated into the dissolution case. In February 1997, the court accepted a stipulation that the woman who agreed to carry the child, and her husband, were not the "biological parents" of the child. At a hearing held in March, based entirely on oral argument and offers of proof, the trial court determined that Luanne was not the lawful mother of the child and therefore John could not be the lawful father or owe any support. . . .

Discussion

The Statute Governing Artificial Insemination Which Makes a Husband the Lawful Father of a Child Unrelated to Him Applies to Both Intended Parents In This Case

Perhaps recognizing the inherent lack of appeal for any result which makes Jaycee a legal orphan, John now contends that the surrogate is Jaycee's legal mother; and further, by virtue of that fact, the surrogate's husband is the legal father. His reasoning goes like this: Under the Uniform Parentage Act (the Act), and particularly as set forth in section 7610 of California's Family Code, there are only two ways by which a woman can establish legal motherhood, i.e., giving birth or contributing genetically. Because the genetic contributors are not known to the court, the only candidate left is the surrogate who must therefore be deemed the lawful mother. And, as John's counsel commented at oral argument, if the surrogate and her husband cannot support Jaycee, the burden should fall on the taxpayers.

The law doesn't say what John says it says. It doesn't say: "The legal relationship between mother and child shall be established only by either proof of her giving birth or by genetics." The statute says "may," not "shall," and "under this part," not "by genetics." Here is the complete text of section 7610: "The parent and child relationship may be established as follows: [¶] (a) Between a child and the natural mother, it may be established by proof of her having given birth to the child, or under this part. [¶] (b) Between a child and the natural father, it may be established under this part. [¶] (c) Between a child and an adoptive parent, it may be established by proof of adoption."

The statute thus contains no direct reference to genetics (i.e., blood tests) at all. The *Johnson* decision teaches us that genetics is simply subsumed in the words "under this part." In that case, the court held that genetic consanguinity was equally "acceptable" as "proof of maternity" as evidence of giving birth.

It is important to realize, however, that in construing the words "under this part" to include genetic testing, the high court in Johnson relied on several statutes in the Evidence Code (former Evid.Code, §§ 892, 895, and 895.5) all of which, by their terms, only applied to paternity. It was only by a "parity of reasoning" that our high court concluded those statutes which, on their face applied only to men, were also "dispositive of the question of maternity." . . .

In addition to blood tests there are several other ways the Act allows paternity to be established. Those ways are not necessarily related at all to any biological tie. Thus, under the Act, paternity may be established by:

—marrying, remaining married to, or attempting to marry the child's mother when she gives birth (see § 7611, subds. (a) & (b));

—marrying the child's mother after the child's birth and either consenting to being named as the father on the birth certificate (§ 7611, subd. (c)(1)) or making a written promise to support the child (see § 7611, subd. (c)(2)).

A man may also be deemed a father under the Act in the case of artificial insemination of his wife, as provided by section 7613 of the Family Code. To track the words of the statute: "If, under the supervision of a licensed physician and surgeon and with the consent of her husband, a wife is inseminated artificially with semen donated by a man not her husband, the husband is treated in law as if he were the natural father of a child thereby conceived." . . .

[I]it is, of course, true that application of the artificial insemination statute to a gestational surrogacy case where the genetic donors are unknown to the court may not have been contemplated by the legislature. Even so, the two kinds of artificial reproduction are *exactly* analogous in this crucial respect: Both contemplate the procreation of a child by the consent to a medical procedure of someone who intends to raise the child but who otherwise does not have any biological tie.

If a husband who consents to artificial insemination under section 7613 is "treated in law" as the father of the child by virtue of his consent, there is no reason the result should be any different in the case of a married couple who consent to in vitro fertilization by unknown donors and subsequent implantation into a woman who is, as a surrogate, willing to carry the embryo to term for them. The statute is, after all, the clearest expression of past legislative intent when the legislature did contemplate a situation where a person who caused a child to come into being had no biological relationship to the child.

Indeed, the establishment of fatherhood and the consequent duty to support when a husband consents to the artificial insemination of his wife is one of the well-established rules in family law. The leading case in the country . . . is *People v. Sorensen*, 68 Cal.2d 280, 66 Cal.Rptr. 7, 437 P.2d 495, in which our Supreme Court held that a man could even be criminally liable for failing to pay for the support of a child born to his wife during the marriage as a result of artificial insemination using sperm from an anonymous donor.

In *Sorensen*, the high court emphasized the role of the husband in *causing* the birth, even though he had no biological connection to the child: "[A] reasonable man who . . . actively participates and consents to his wife's artificial insemination in the hope that a child will be produced whom they will treat as their own, *knows that such behavior carries with it the legal responsibilities of fatherhood and criminal responsibility for nonsupport.*" (emphasis added.) The court went on to say that the husband was "directly responsible" for the "existence" of the child and repeated the point that "without defendant's active participation and consent the child would not have been procreated."

Sorensen expresses a rule universally in tune with other jurisdictions. . . .

It must also be noted that in applying the artificial insemination statute to a case where a party has caused a child to be brought into the world, the statutory policy is really echoing a more fundamental idea—a sort of *grundnorm* to borrow Hans Kelsen's famous jurisprudential word—already established in the case law. That idea is often summed up in the legal term "estoppel." . . .

There is no need in the present case to predicate our decision on common law estoppel alone, though the doctrine certainly applies. The estoppel concept, after all, is already inherent in the artificial insemination statute. In essence, Family Code section 7613 is nothing more than the codification of the common law rule articulated in *Sorensen*: By consenting to a medical procedure which results in the birth of a child—which the *Sorensen* court has held establishes parenthood by common law estoppel—a husband incurs the legal status and responsibility of fatherhood.

John argues that the artificial insemination statute should not be applied because, after all, his wife did not give birth. But for purposes of the statute with its core idea of estoppel, the fact that Luanne did not give birth is irrelevant. The statute contemplates the establishment of lawful fatherhood in a situation where an intended father has no biological relationship to a child who is procreated as a result of the father's (as well as the mother's) *consent* to a medical procedure.

Luanne is the Lawful Mother of Jaycee, Not the Surrogate, and Not the Unknown Donor of the Egg

In the present case Luanne is situated like a husband in an artificial insemination case whose consent triggers a medical procedure which results in a pregnancy and eventual birth of a child. Her motherhood may therefore be established "under this part," by virtue of that consent. In light of our conclusion, John's argument that the surrogate should be declared the lawful mother disintegrates. The case is now postured like the *Johnson v. Calvert* case, where motherhood could have been "established" in either of two women under the Act, and the tie broken by noting the intent to parent as expressed in the surrogacy contract. The only difference is that this case is not even close as between Luanne and the surrogate. Not only was Luanne the clearly intended mother, no bona fide attempt has been made to establish the surrogate as the lawful mother.

We should also add that neither could the woman whose egg was used in the fertilization or implantation make any claim to motherhood, even if she were to come forward at this late date. Again, as between two women who would both be able to establish motherhood under the Act, the Johnson decision would mandate that the tie be broken in favor of the intended parent, in this case, Luanne.

Our decision in In re *Marriage of Moschetta*, 25 Cal.App.4th 1218, 30 Cal.Rptr.2d 893, relied on by John, is inapposite and distinguishable. In *Moschetta*, this court held that a contract giving rise to a "traditional" surrogacy arrangement where a surrogate was simply inseminated with the husband's sperm could not be *enforced* against the surrogate by the intended father. In order for the surrogate not to be the lawful mother she would have to give the child up for adoption. In *Moschetta*, the surrogate was the mother both by birth and genes; the woman contemplated as the intended mother in the surrogacy contract gave up any claim to the child. In fact, at the appellate level, she went so far as to file a brief in favor of the birth mother's claim.

Moschetta is inapposite because this court never had occasion to consider or discuss whether the original intended mother's participation in the surrogacy arrangement, which brought about the child's birth, might have formed the basis for holding her responsible as a parent. She had given up her claim; the issue was not before the court. Unlike the *Johnson* case there was no tie to break between two women both of whom could be held to be mothers under the Act. . . .

Moschetta is distinguishable because it involved the claim of a woman who both gave birth to the child, "contributed" the egg, and who wanted the child enough to go to court to seek custody. The only alternative was a woman who did not give birth, did not contribute genes, and who gave up her claim. Only if the surrogacy contract were *specifically enforced* in *Moschetta* could this court have ruled in favor of the father's claim to *exclusive* parenthood.

There is a difference between a court's *enforcing* a surrogacy agreement and making a legal determination based on the intent *expressed in* a surrogacy agreement. By the same token, there is also an important distinction between enforcing a surrogacy contract and making a legal determination based on the fact that the contract itself *sets in motion* a medical procedure which results in the birth of a child.

In the case before us, we are not concerned, as John would have us believe, with a question of the enforceability of the oral and written surrogacy contracts into which he entered with Luanne. This case is not about "transferring" parenthood pursuant to those agreements. We are, rather, concerned with the consequences of those agreements as *acts* which *caused the birth* of a child....

Notes and Questions on Surrogacy and the Functions of Family Law

The cases you have read provide a good introduction to the standard arguments about surrogacy. Here we want to offer another view of the subject by asking how surrogacy looks from the perspective of the functions of family law.

(1) *The Facilitative Function.* Isn't surrogacy a classic example of the facilitative function at work? Someone, usually an infertile couple, wants children, a desire the Supreme Court repeatedly speaks respectfully of. Someone else can help the couple have children. The law can offer them its services in writing and enforcing a contract that will allow the couple to get what they want in exchange for giving the surrogate something she wants. Isn't this just one more development in the contractualization of family law, a development so central to that field that it is one of our recurring themes?

In the article we excerpted earlier, Professor Garrison helpfully reviews and criticizes this argument:

> A number of commentators have proposed that the parental rights of those who conceive technologically should be governed by contract principles.... Relying on the claim that technological conception "dramatically extend[s] affirmative intentionality" by "eliminat[ing] uncertainty regarding procreative intention," Schultz urges that "[w]ithin the context of artificial reproductive techniques, intentions that are voluntarily chosen, deliberate, express and bargained-for ought presumptively to determine legal parenthood." [Marjorie Maguire Schultz, *Reproductive Technology and Intent–Based Parenthood: An Opportunity for Gender Neutrality*, 1990 Wis L Rev 297.] ...
>
> Schultz is undeniably right that parentage law has traditionally relied on presumed, rather than actual, intent. Procreation has been thought part of the state-imposed marriage contract, and even unmarried persons who engage in sexual intercourse have been presumed to consent to the risk of procreation. Indeed, courts have uniformly imposed parental responsibilities on men who were legally incapable of consenting to sexual intercourse and those who had been tricked into fathering a child; they have refused to honor nonpaternity agreements whether made before or after the child's conception. Even in cases of adoption, in which legislatures have required actual consent both to

> relinquish and accept parental rights, the parties' intentions are insufficient to effect a rights transfer; a showing of compliance with other state requirements designed to protect the child's and parties' interests must also be made.
>
> Schultz's claim that technological conception presents "differences in moral and factual legitimacy" that require a more important—indeed, determinative—role for contract rests on much weaker ground, however. Undeniably, it is easier to assess intention when conception occurs technologically than when it occurs sexually. But it is not easier to assess intention in a case of technological conception than it is in a case of adoption. Nor does the pool of would-be parents who adopt differ markedly from those who conceive technologically: both groups include single individuals who want to parent without a partner and couples who already have genetically related children, but both are also dominated by couples who have tried and failed to conceive sexually.
>
> Schultz's claim for contract thus comes down to the argument that reliance on intention is desirable. But she does not explain why reliance on intention is uniquely desirable for determining the parentage of technologically conceived children; although some areas of family law do increasingly rely on private ordering, parentage and parental obligation are not among them. Here, family law simply has not "favor[ed] the fulfillment of individual purposes and the amplification of individual choice." Indeed, under current law, no contract regarding a child's custody, support, or legal status is per se enforceable; unenforceability applies whether the contract was negotiated prenatally or postnatally, and whether or not there is clear evidence of pre-contract parental intentions. Nor does Schultz address children's rights and interests, the basis for restrictions on parental contract rights. . . .

The argument that surrogacy contracts are desirable may be enhanced with arguments that people have a constitutional right to enter into them. You have already read statements of this position. Again, Professor Garrison comments on it:

> Robertson [the principal proponent of the rights-position] fails to note that the Supreme Court has never employed his proposed test either when reviewing state laws limiting access to abortion and contraception, the context in which the procreative liberties doctrine developed, or when addressing parental rights more generally. Although the Court has held that state abortion and contraception regulations implicate a "zone of privacy created by several fundamental constitutional guarantees" and thus must be "narrowly drawn" to express only "compelling state interests," it has never mandated Robertson's "substantial harm to tangible interests" test as a basis for state regulation in this area. Indeed, in recent years, the Court has retreated from the position that "compelling" interests are required to justify government restrictions on procreational choice, holding that state abortion limitations are valid unless they impose an "undue burden" on a woman's right to terminate an unwanted pregnancy. The Court has also consistently held that government may prefer one form of procreational choice over another in funding medical services.

Although the evidence is sparse, it seems probable that the procreative liberties doctrine would preclude explicit state restrictions on family size. The Court has already noted that a birth control requirement and a birth control ban are logically equivalent; a complete state ban on access to reproductive technology thus would also be constitutionally suspect, as it would deprive the infertile of their only chance at genetic parenthood. Gender-based access restrictions, such as rules denying access to reproductive technology if a wife is post-menopausal but granting it if a husband is of post-menopausal age, might also constitute impermissible gender discrimination.

Nonetheless, given that traditional restrictions on choice of a sexual partner—prohibitions on prostitution, incest, fornication, statutory rape, adultery—all appear to be valid, there is no obvious reason why restrictions on choice of a technological "partner" would not also be valid, including restrictions disallowing the sale of genetic material and imposing "time and manner" requirements. Nor does the Court's procreative liberties doctrine pose any apparent bar to state rules defining parental status. While Robertson and other advocates of a rights-based approach to technological conception have sometimes assumed that freedom to engage in a particular reproductive practice automatically implies recognition of parental status, the procreational liberties doctrine in fact mandates no such thing. The Supreme Court has simply never held that the right to bear a child ensures the right to have one's parental status recognized. Instead, in another line of cases involving claims by unmarried fathers, the Court has made it clear that "the mere existence of a biological link" is inadequate to ensure parental rights. . . .

Our tradition of deference to individual decisions about coital procreation and parenting undeniably supports equivalent deference to individual choice in the use of technological conception. But deference does not imply abdication of any regulatory role. Indeed, parents who want to adopt, the "traditional" method of achieving parenthood noncoitally, face a maze of state regulations, including rules imposing waiting periods before an adoption is finalized, voiding parental consents obtained prenatally, permitting rescission of parental consent within stated time limits, and requiring adoption through an intermediary agency. Under Robertson's view of the procreative liberties doctrine, all of these rules should fail. Baby selling prohibitions would also be unconstitutional under Robertson's proposed standard, as children whose parents want to sell them are not likely to be better off remaining in parental custody. . . .

(2) *The Protective Function*. Ultimately, the arguments for letting the facilitative-function work depend not on the merits of doing so (which are numerous), but on the costs (which look daunting). In other words, many lawmakers have been reluctant to recognize surrogacy contracts because of the demands of family law's protective function. Two groups may need protection—the children who may be born of surrogacy contracts and the surrogates who may give birth to them. Professor Garrison is again our guide. She observes that only

a few contract advocates, notably Professors Epstein and Posner, have gone so far as to argue that all current restraints on parental contract rights, including babyselling prohibitions, should be abolished. Professor Epstein, for example, urges that:

> [t]he most that can be said is that money may create some kind of conflict of interest between parent and child, so that the sale will be made to a higher bidder when the child would be better off in the care of a lower bidder. Yet ... the decisions made in the gray [adoption] market suggest that this concern is overblown.... One can find cases in which ostensible sales seem abusive per se.... But the use of these extreme examples should not discredit the general practice in its far more benign form. [Richard Epstein, *Surrogacy: The Case for Full Contractual Enforcement*, 81 Va L Rev 2305 (1995).]

Epstein ignores the historical evidence, which shows that adoption regulation arose precisely because market transactions did not adequately protect children's interests. The fact that today's highly regulated adoptions generally produce good results, even if some money surreptitiously changes hands, hardly provides a testimonial to the merits of an unregulated contract regime. There is no reason to suppose that would-be parents utilizing technological conception to obtain a child more frequently possess inadequate parenting skills than would-be adoptive parents. But neither is there reason to suppose the reverse; in each context, the vast majority of intended parents are able and well-motivated, but a few are not.

Nor is it obvious how contract advocates could demonstrate that their proposed approach adequately addresses the interests of children who will be the subject of parental agreements. Our legal system rarely tolerates a contract that binds a nonsignatory; only when a guardian or conservator is appointed for an incompetent may an unconsenting adult be contractually bound by someone else. In such a case, the guardian or conservator is bound to act as a fiduciary, not a self-interested actor.

Another set of risks to children can be identified by asking how surrogacy contracts fare when considered in terms of the enforcement problem. What if, for example, the father breaches and refuses to accept the child on the grounds, for example, that the child was born with a birth defect? Would specific performance make any sense? Would money damages compensate the mother adequately? Would the child have any remedies for the damage done to him or her by his or her father's rejection? What if the father defends on the grounds that the child isn't his? Consider the case of Alexander Malahoff, who wanted to strengthen his marriage by acquiring a child. (His marriage in fact ended during the pregnancy of the surrogate mother.) The baby was born with microcephaly (an unusually small head and possible mental retardation), and Malahoff refused to accept the child and ordered the hospital not to treat the baby for a life-threatening infection. (The surrogate mother agreed to permit the infection to be treated, and the hospital obtained court permission for treatment.) Malahoff, the surrogate mother, and the surrogate mother's husband went on the Phil Donahue show, where they received the results of tests that indicated that the surrogate mother's husband was the baby's father. (A similar problem was presented by the birth of a baby who had antibodies that made it more than likely that the baby would develop AIDS. Both the father and the mother rejected the child.)

A similar approach can help us see why the protective function might be invoked in the interests of surrogates. For example, what if the mother breaches and refuses to transfer the child, as Mary Beth Whitehead did in the *Baby M* case and Anna Johnson did in *Johnson v. Calvert*? Given the strength of attachment which such a mother may have developed, is specific performance not a cruel remedy? And if the mother had the kind of money needed to pay damages, is it likely she would have entered into the contract in the first place?

This leads us to the question whether surrogates can, as we might say, give informed consent to the contract. Can they, that is, fully realize what they are agreeing to do? In Mary Beth Whitehead, *A Mother's Story: The Truth About the Baby M Case* (St. Martin's Press, 1989), the surrogate mother in the Baby M. case said that it "wasn't until the day I delivered my daughter that I fully comprehended the fact that it wasn't Betsy Stern's baby. It was the joy, and the pain, of giving birth that finally made me realize I wasn't giving Betsy Stern *her* baby, I was giving her *my* baby." Ms. Whitehead came to feel that all through her pregnancy "I had suppressed the reality; I had denied my feelings." One night soon after Baby M. was born Ms. Whitehead woke from her sleep and found herself

> lying in a pool of milk.... I knew it was time to feed my baby. I knew she was hungry, but I could not hear her crying. The room was quiet as I sat up in the bed, alone in the darkness, with the milk running down my chest and soaking my nightgown. I held out my empty arms and screamed at the top of my lungs, "Oh God, what have I done—I want my baby."

(3) *The Arbitral Function.* It should now be clear how severely surrogacy contracts may tax the arbitral function of family law. When these contracts work, they may well leave everybody better off. The surrogate has money and the satisfaction of bringing a much wanted child into the world. The couple have what they probably wanted intensely—a child. The child has adoring and gratified parents who have tried uncommonly hard to become parents. When these contracts do not work, however, the consequences for all concerned may be savage, and some systematic way of resolving their intense disagreements will become essential. The questions this raises, of course, are whether the contracts that go wrong are so costly the state might try to prevent them altogether and whether satisfactory standards can be devised for resolving such disputes.

(4) *The Expressive Function.* Many of the expressive-function objections to surrogacy derive from an "anticommodification" argument, an argument you have already encountered in the opinions in *Johnson v.*

Calvert. Professor Garrison writes, "A number of commentators on technological conception have relied, either wholly or partially, on the claim that reproductive capacity constitutes an attribute, like sexuality or a body part, that is so bound up with an individual's personhood that it should not be the subject of market transactions." The leading work on commodification is Margaret Jane Radin, *Market-Inalienability*, 100 Harv L Rev 1849 (1987). She suggests "the possibility that paid surrogacy should be completely prohibited because it expresses an inferior conception of human flourishing" and that surrogacy may create "a domino effect of commodification in rhetoric that leaves us all inferior human beings." She explains, "The most credible fear of a domino effect—one that paid surrogacy does share with commissioned adoption—is that all women's personal attributes will be commodified." She concedes that putting a price on "surrogates' services will not immediately transform the rhetoric in which women conceive of themselves and in which they are conceived, but that is its tendency." She believes that "[t]his fear, even though remote, seems grave enough to take steps to ensure that paid surrogacy does not become the kind of institution that could permeate our discourse." She is particularly concerned that while surrogates "may feel they are fulfilling their womanhood by producing a baby for someone else, ... they may actually be reinforcing oppressive gender roles," partly because "paid surrogacy within the current gender structure may symbolize that women are fungible baby-makers for men whose seed must be carried on."

Professor Garrison has some doubts about the anticommodification approach:

> As critics of the anticommodification claim have noted, however, it is not so easy to articulate a clear definition of what is fundamental to personhood and what is not. "[H]eight, eye color, race, intelligence, and athletic ability"—which Radin fears might be monetized through commercial surrogacy—are already monetized in the employment market on a daily basis. Nor can we point to historical continuity in those aspects of personhood that are legally unmarketable. Blood was marketable (although with price controls) until health concerns led to bans on payment.

Professor Radin's criticisms of commodification also raise questions about why people seek the services of a surrogate and why they agree to become surrogates. We have only anecdotal information about this, but here are two brief reports:

> William and Elizabeth Stern [the contracting couple in *Baby M.*] were married in July 1974, having met at the University of Michigan, where both were Ph.D. candidates. Due to financial considerations and Mrs. Stern's pursuit of a medical degree and residency, they decided to defer starting a family until 1981. Before then, however, Mrs. Stern learned that she might have multiple sclerosis and that the disease in some cases renders pregnancy a serious health risk. Her anxiety appears to have exceeded the actual risk, which current medical authorities assess as minimal. Nonetheless that anxiety was evidently quite real, Mrs.

> Stern fearing that pregnancy might precipitate blindness, paraplegia, or other forms of debilitation. Based on the perceived risk, the Sterns decided to forego having their own children. The decision had special significance for Mr. Stern. Most of his family had been destroyed in the Holocaust. As the family's only survivor, he very much wanted to continue his bloodline.

And the surrogate in that case explained her motives this way: "I thought that this was something I could do to improve the lives of an infertile couple and at the same time help my own family economically. It seemed like a good way to provide extra opportunities to my children.... But most important was the fact that, at that time, I genuinely believed that this was a way for me to help to better the world." She reported, "By the time the clinic completed its screening, I was so anxious to help and so convinced that the child wasn't mine that I didn't even think about the terms of the contract. I even told the Sterns I didn't want the money."

(5) *The Channelling Function*. Professor Radin suggests ways in which permitting or even encouraging surrogacy might affect our views about the kinds of social institutions (particularly parenthood) the law may wish to channel people into:

> Perhaps a more visionary reason to consider prohibiting all surrogacy is that the demand for it expresses a limited view of parent-child bonding; in a better view of personal contextuality, bonding should be reconceived. Although allowing surrogacy might be thought to foster ideals of interrelationships between men and their children, it is unclear why we should assume that the ideal of bonding depends especially on genetic connection. Many people who adopt children feel no less bonded to their children than responsible genetic parents; they understand that relational bonds are created in shared life more than in genetic codes. We might make better progress toward ideals of interpersonal sharing—toward a better view of contextual personhood—by breaking down the notion that children are fathers'—or parents'—genetic property.

A Note on Adoption

Although relationships come in many varieties, only two flavors are legally families: connections of consanguinity (blood) and affinity (ties created by law as the result of emotional relationships, i.e., marriage and adoption). Most children are children by blood and are reared by their birth parents. Adoption, on the other hand, creates a bond between parent and child by operation of law. Though adoption of adult heirs was relatively common in ancient Rome, adoption of children has come relatively recently to both England and the United States. Because the legal practice dates only from the mid-nineteenth century, it is not part of the common law heritage. Consequently, courts granting adoptions must have special jurisdiction and must follow statutory formulations. As the cases put it, "adoption is a creature of statute."

Because all of us are born into families and legally can only possess one set of parents at a time, adoption involves two steps. The first is the breaking of the ties with birth parents, the second the legal forging of bonds to the new, or adoptive, parents. There are interesting questions involving both steps scattered throughout this casebook. Surrogacy contracts, discussed above, affect this "supply side" of the market. Voluntary termination of parental rights, or consent to adoption, suggests questions about transactions costs as well as price mechanisms that would encourage adoptive placement as opposed to abortion or single parenting. The involuntary termination of parental rights, which leads to adoption or foster care, is discussed in Chapter 10. Transracial adoption questions, discussed in Chapter 12, affect the "demand side," since they speak to the ability of interested couples to adopt particular children. Visitation and standing questions appear earlier in this chapter.

Most second-step discussions focus on the problems generated by the prohibition of explicit pricing mechanisms like the black market in babies. In the adoption market, children cannot be individually priced, even though fees are often charged to the adoptive parents that can cover birth expenses and the agencies' costs. This second adoption step has always been heavily regulated. Not only must the court granting adoption create the legal relationship, but statutes require that adoptions be "in the best interests of the child." This gives the state, or its agency delegates, power to investigate adoptive parents for fitness and to ration children on the basis of characteristics like stability, race, and religion.

The following discussion presents some of the recurrent questions in the law of adoption. Although there is a shortage of adoptable children, many children are not adopted even after their birth parents' rights end. These "special needs" children may be nonwhite, older, or in large sibling groups that need placement together. Most often, though, they are handicapped in some way. In a market for babies these children would fetch a negative price—adoptive parents would be paid to take them. In the adoption market, where explicit pricing is prohibited, agencies may attempt to portray these children in a more desirable light than the adoptive parents find justifiable. Hence the problem of "wrongful adoption." Once the child "wrongfully" is placed with the adoptive parents and a major problem is discovered, the question becomes one of remedy. In some cases, adoptions are annulled because of agency misrepresentation or nondisclosure. In a growing number of "wrongful adoption" cases, although the adoption remains intact, distressed adoptive parents have sued the placing agencies.

Courts have allowed recovery in five of the ten cases reported before mid–1994. *Burr v. Board of Co. Comm'rs*, 491 NE2d 1101 (Ohio 1986); *Meracle v. Children's Service* Soc, 437 NW2d 532 (Wis 1989); *Michael J. v. County of Los Angeles Dep't of Adoptions*, 247 Cal Rptr 504 (Cal App 1988)(no summary judgment against parents); *MH v. Caritas Family Services*, 488 NW2d 282 (Minn 1992)(no summary judgment against parents); *Gibbs v. Ernst*, 615 A2d 851 (Pa Cmwlth 1992)(summary judgment against parents improper). In three of these successful suits, the child involved had life-threatening diseases. *Burr v. Board of Co. Comm'rs, supra* (Huntington's Disease); *Meracle v. Children's Service Soc, supra* (Huntington's Disease); *Michael J. v. County of Los Angeles Dep't of Adoptions, supra* (Sturge–Weber syndrome). In all these cases, the agencies deliberately misinformed the parents that the child was healthy. The parents were able to recover for past or future medical expenses although the agencies were not "guarantors of the child's health." Although the agencies knew of the genetic or other problems, the parents could not have discovered them through their own diligence.

In the other half of the reported cases, the parents' suit was barred. *Engstrom v. Iowa*, 461 NW2d 309 (Iowa 1990); *Allen v. Children's Services*, 567 NE2d 1346 (Ohio App 1990); *Adoption of Baby Boy C.*, 596 NYS2d 56 (App Div 1993); *April v. Associated Catholic Charities*, 629 So2d 1295 (La App 1993); *Foster v. Bass*, 575 So2d 967 (Miss 1990). In some of these cases, the defects were not substantial, although the parents would not have wished them. For example, one child was deaf, *Allen v. Children's Services, supra,* while another turned out to be unavailable for adoption because his father had never given consent. *Foster v. Bass*, supra. In others, although the agencies might have negligently failed to discover the problem, plaintiffs could not show fraud. Perhaps the agency was not the "least cost avoider," given the difficulty of placing these children. The *Bass* court wrote:

> In short, to impose liability in a case such as this would in effect make the adoption agency a guarantor of the infant's future good health ... To do so would put adoption agencies in a quagmire because they want to continue to perform this service. Yet, they could not afford an unreasonable responsibility of guaranteeing the health of a child. Even natural parents are without this guarantee.

Fraud in adoption resembles fraud in marriage in many respects, but the fact that children are involved, who have their own interests if not their own rights changes the set of possible remedies. In most cases, returning the children to their birth parents or the agencies placing them presents an unacceptable alternative, because, as we have seen, children need stability, particularly early in their lives. Disabled children, the subject of these cases, may need a stable loving home even more than most. Rescission of the adoption contract therefore loses power as a device because of the "externalities" involved.

The special needs of these hard-to-place infants creates another barrier to recovery: a heightened burden of proof of fraud. Particularly if the adoptive parents were willing to accept a special needs child, courts will be reluctant to penalize the agency by a finding of fraud with its concomitant damages, even if the agency withheld critical information. If these "wrongful adoption" cases became too routine, the government would have fewer incentives to attempt adoptive placement of disabled children, thus forcing more of them to remain in permanent foster care.

Finally, as in the "wrongful life" cases brought a generation ago, the courts in the adoption-fraud cases confront situations where the damages are hard to measure. Even if the child possesses some trait the adoptive parent wished to avoid, he or she is nonetheless a human being capable of giving and receiving love. As they do in the case of "wrongful life" children, courts typically find that the positive aspects of having a child outweigh the negative. On the whole, the child is a net benefit to the adoptive parents despite the agency's misinformation.

In addition to race and religion, which we discuss at length in Chapter 12, contemporary courts face other pluralism questions in deciding which of several people should adopt. One of the most frequent questions involves adoption by gay or lesbian partners of a natural parent. The court finalized the adoption in *Adoption of Tammy*, 619 NE2d 315 (Mass 1993), where the two women in question were both biologically related to the five-year-old child. The court further held that "when a natural parent is a party to a joint adoption petition, that parent's legal relationship to the child does not terminate on entry of the adoption decree." In *Adoptions of BLVB*, 628 A2d 1271 (Vt 1993), the court held that "when the family unit is comprised of the natural mother and her [lesbian] partner, and the adoption [by the partner] is in the best interests of the children, terminating the natural mother's right is unreasonable and unnecessary." A psychologist who had evaluated the family unit testified that "it was essential for the children to be assured of a continuing relationship" and recommended that the "adoptions be allowed for the psychological and emotional protection of the children."

Even when adoptions are finalized, all contacts with the birth family do not necessarily end. For example, more and more states are allowing contact with natural grandparents under statutes permitting the grandparents to get court-ordered visitation following divorce or death of a natural parent. See, e.g., *In re Nearhoof*, 359 SE2d 587 (W Va 1987). One court permitted visitation of her former foster children by a foster parent who was unable to adopt the children because her husband died during the period in which the social services department attempted to terminate the natural mother's rights. *In re Francisco A.*, 866 P2d 1175 (NM App 1993).

Many state statutes permit children to inherit from their birth parents under intestate succession, particularly when the adoption is by a blood relative or stepparent. This may present the problem of what is called dual inheritance, since the child might receive two shares of the deceased's estate. For a good description of the problem (under a now defunct statute), see *In re Estate of Cregar*, 333 NE2d 540 (Ill App 1975), which allowed recovery through both natural and adoptive parents. Contrast this view with *Hall v. Vallandingham*, 540 A2d 1162 (Md App 1988), which barred the adopted child's inheritance from the natural parent.

In order to facilitate inheritance from adoptive parents, as well as to make useful information available and to satisfy the natural parents' and children's curiosity, more and more states are permitting parents to leave identifying information with adoption agencies. See, e.g., Va Code

Ann § 63.2–1247 (2005). The Second Circuit has held, however, that there is no constitutional right to receive such identifying information. *Alma Society v. Mellon*, 601 F2d 1225 (2 Cir 1979); see also *In re Roger B.*, 418 NE2d 751 (Ill 1981), *appeal dism'd*, 454 US 806 (1981).

A last problem involves the remedy called "equitable adoption," which permits children whose parents placed them for adoption to claim the benefits the children would have received if the legal adoption had taken place. Usually such children seek recovery from their would-be parents at the time the parents die. However, in *Estate of McConnell*, 268 F Supp 346 (DDC 1967), the "sisters" of the child who thought he had been adopted sued the estate. These women were the natural children of a couple who did not fulfill their promise to adopt and were the only living "relatives" of Edward McConnell, who died wealthy and intestate. The "sisters" were not permitted to inherit the estate. The right to claim equitable adoption belongs only to the wronged person, not those claiming through the parents who did not fulfill their obligations.

Adoption and Consent

We have now encountered a number of circumstances in which parents give up their children to other people. Surrogacy contracts are one vivid example. The adoption cases like the Baby Richard and Baby Jessica cases are another. And we will see in the next chapter that parents accused of abusing or neglecting their children often give up temporary custody of them and even cede their parental rights. It is self-evidently desirable that when parents do these things, they do so after at least considering their options carefully. On the other hand, once the children have been placed with new custodians, it is also desirable that that placement not be disturbed. Every state requires that parents relinquishing a child for adoption voluntarily consent. For example, Colo Rev Stat 19–1–103 (2006) provides in § 28: " 'Consent' means voluntary, informed, written consent." What that means generally is not well defined in the statutes and consequently has been defined through case law. To give you a sense of the problems that arise in these cases, we present two illuminating fact patterns:

HUEBERT v. MARSHALL

Illinois Court of Appeals, 1971
270 NE2d 464

... Sara Elizabeth Marshall was born on April 17, 1969. The natural parents, Paula and Tim Marshall, were very happy about the birth. Tim is 26 and has a high school education, and Paula is 24 and has had one year of college. They have one other child, Erica, who is five years old.

After leaving the hospital, Paula stayed with Tim's parents for four days. She appeared to be disorganized but happy. About a week after giving birth she called her doctor about her weight. On his advice she began taking Eskatrol (diet pills) and Diuril (a diuretic). She continued the medication about ten to fourteen days and lost about fifteen pounds.

On Friday, April 25, Tim told Paula he had lost his job and that he was going to leave her. He said he "didn't feel capable of handling the job or the situation of being married, and wanted to get out of Chicago and get out of the situation I was in." Paula was disbelieving and became hysterical.

On Monday, April 28, Julie Brown went to see Paula and found she was still in the same condition. Julie tried to calm her down and told her she should never have had the baby. She said she knew of a couple who had wanted to adopt a baby but were unable to because it was stillborn. Julie told Paula the Hueberts were good people, that they would provide a good home for the baby and would be good parents.

Julie had been a good friend for about three years and saw Paula about two or three times a week. Tim and Paula and Julie and her husband had gone out together from time to time, but Julie had been divorced from her husband on January 30, 1969, after being separated about a year. However, Paula did not know that Julie and her own husband, Tim, had become emotionally involved and had discussed the possibility of meeting in California.

On Monday, April 28, Paula talked with Judy Ripp and said she was worried that she would not be able to support herself and two children. She was very distraught during this period, and Judy was unable to reason with her.

On April 29, Paula called Julie and asked if the people still wanted a baby. Julie said she thought so but did not want to call unless Paula was really sure. Later that morning Paula called Julie and said she would like her to call the Hueberts. At this time Julie cautioned Paula not to talk to anyone because "they'll just talk you out of it." Mrs. Huebert did not at any time ask Julie Brown what her interest was in arranging the adoption, nor did she try to ascertain what it might have been.

Mr. James R. Donnelly, the Hueberts' attorney, called Paula at about 1:30 that same day and told her he was representing some people who wanted to adopt a baby and that he had made an appointment for her to go downtown to the Cook County Department of Public Aid. Paula said she could not make any decisions and would have to talk to her husband. Mr. Donnelly did not ask whether she was represented by counsel or whether she had had any independent advice.

When Tim Marshall came home, Paula told him what had happened, and he called Mr. Donnelly. Tim told him he could not make a decision at that time and would call him back. Paula then told Tim she could not "take it with the baby. I'm too upset. You have lost your job and you are leaving me. I don't know what to do. It's the best thing for the baby. These people want a baby and they are able to take care of the baby and I'm not." Tim called Mr. Donnelly back and was told they had to be "interviewed" at the Department of Public Aid. When questioned about whether there was a waiting period in this situation, Mr. Donnelly said it would be six months before it would be final. Mr. Donnelly and Julie Brown were the only ones Tim and Paula talked to about the possible adoption.

On April 30, Tim and Paula went to the Department of Public Aid. They were interviewed separately by Helene Schimmeyer. Each interview took about fifteen or twenty minutes. Paula testified she was not alert during the session: "I was strange. I wasn't me." She also said she cried about 50% of the time. Paula and Tim then went in together, and Mrs. Schimmeyer said, "You have lost your job and you are thinking of leaving." Tim said, "Yes, I think so." She said, "All right," and led them down the hall to see Mrs. Wideikis who handled the signing of the consent papers. Mrs. Wideikis explained the finality of their actions, but Tim did the talking for both, since Paula seemed distant and was not reacting. This interview lasted five to ten minutes. Each signed two "copies" of the consents. Two of the forms were complete except for the names of the adopting parents, which were inserted by Mrs. Schimmeyer after the forms were signed. Two of the forms lacked the names of the adopting parents and information as to the sex and place of birth of the child. No alternative suggestions for dealing with the situation were offered at any of the interviews.

Afterwards Tim called Mr. Donnelly to tell him they had signed the papers. Tim said, "Does the other couple get the baby now?" Donnelly said, "Well, now there is a trial period before it's theirs."

Paula called her mother when they got home to tell her what they had done. After the conversation, Paula told Tim she would not let the baby out of the door, and that her mother would take care of the baby.

Julie Brown came to the apartment at 8:00 or 9:00 P.M. to pick up the baby. Tim handed it over while Paula just sat there with a blank stare. Julie again repeated not to talk to anybody.

On May 1, Paula went to Judy Ripp's apartment and told her about the interview. Judy asked, "Didn't these people offer you a foster home or a marriage counselor or something," and Paula said, "No." Judy asked, "If they had offered it to you would you have done it?" Paula said, "In a minute."

MEYERS v. GEORGIA

Georgia Court of Appeals, 1971
183 SE2d 42

The mother in this case was unmarried, 23 years of age, and suffered an estranged relationship with her parents who lived in her home state of Iowa. She received a master's degree in teaching exceptional children from a university in Colorado, where conception took place. She had lived in Atlanta on a prior occasion and came here after graduation, holding a "T–5" teaching certificate in this state. Although she suspected she was pregnant, she was not able to admit it positively to herself until the eighth month; and, trapped in a sort of emotional isolation booth, unable to confide in her parents or anyone else except a friend in Colorado with whom she corresponded, she somehow concealed her pregnancy from co-workers and casual friends.

On December 18, 1970, she worked until 5 p.m., went to her apartment and waited alone. The child was born normally at 11:40 that night, after which she was exhausted and in a daze. She tried to get cleaned up and held the child in her arms until sometime after 6 a.m. It appeared to be perfectly healthy, but she felt it should go to the hospital. It was her thought that the Suicide Prevention Bureau would be the only agency that would listen to her, secure medical facilities quickly, and give her advice. Accordingly, she telephoned them from a telephone booth, explaining the situation and notifying them that the child would be left in the booth. She then left it in a basket, wrapped in a blanket, with a note and $25 in cash. Approximately ten minutes later the child was picked up by the police, whom the Suicide Prevention Bureau had notified, and taken to the hospital, where it was examined and found to be in good health.

After leaving the child, the mother cleaned her apartment and went to work. Several days later she heard on the radio that the policeman on duty at the hospital when the child was brought in was interested in adopting it. Apparently at this point she began to think more clearly about her life and the possibilities of keeping the child, and started an investigation of the home of the policeman. She conversed over the phone with the policeman's wife, and at this point she determined that she could offer the child a better home and a better life than these people. The policeman's wife displayed a hostile attitude toward the mother's actions in coming forward, and threatened criminal action; so the mother telephoned her parents in Iowa, told them she had a problem that she could not handle alone or explain over the telephone and requested that her mother come to Atlanta. The mother's father chartered a plane, and her mother came to Atlanta, where, after the situation was explained to her, she began calling various city and county officials in behalf of her daughter, who was working. By December 28, 1970, some nine days after the call to the Suicide Prevention Bureau, appellant's mother succeeded in locating the probation officer of Fulton Juvenile Court who was assigned to this case and had a conference with her, and the child's mother followed up with another conference the next day.

At a hearing on January 13, the mother appeared, represented by counsel, but the policeman seeking custody was not present nor were other necessary witnesses. The hearing was continued until February 4, by which time the policeman had lost interest in the matter. Also by this time, the mother had moved from her old apartment, which excluded children, to a larger apartment where children were welcome. In addition, the mother had accomplished the following: made arrangements with a day-care center for child care during her working hours; consulted a professional counselor, whom she felt could be depended upon in the future to help her with problems that might arise; consulted a physician for a physical examination and was pronounced in good health; made arrangements with her friend in Colorado to act as the guardian of the child in the event of the mother's death; and placed funds in escrow to begin a trust fund for the child's education. . . .

Questions on Consent to Adoption

(1) If you were the judge in these two cases, would you decide either of these surrenders was voluntary?

(2) In what sense did the mother in these cases relinquish her child voluntarily? In what sense did she do so voluntarily? Will there ever be cases in which she did so *entirely* voluntarily? If not, just how voluntary does the surrender have to be? Can you find help in the standards of voluntariness used in other areas of the law? The test used in deciding whether contracts were voluntarily entered into? In deciding whether constitutional rights were voluntarily waived? In deciding, for example, whether a confession has been voluntarily made?

(3) In thinking about what standard you want to use, how should you factor in the interests of the child? What are the interests of the child?

(4) Suppose you are the attorney for a couple who want to adopt a child. You want to be sure the biological mother will not be able to contest the adoption. What procedures would you advise the county social services authorities to follow to secure a truly voluntary consent?

(5) The courts in *Huebert* and *Meyers* returned the children to their birth mothers. Were the courts unduly influenced by sympathy for the two young mothers? Would they have decided the cases the same way if the fathers were the ones who wished to revoke consent? Should they have?

(6) In the summer of 1999 a series of dead and abandoned babies was found in Houston. Barbara Whitaker, *Death of Unwanted Babies Brings Plea to Help Parents*, . . . NY Times, March 6, 2000. Texas Penal Code § 22.041(h) now makes it "an affirmative defense to prosecution under Subsection (b) [for abandonment of a child] that the actor voluntarily delivered the child to an emergency medical services provider." If the "actor" was the mother, should she be taken to have ceded any claim she had to the child?

SECTION 4. DISCRETION, RULES, AND LAW: CHILD–CUSTODY DECISIONS AND THE BEST–INTEREST STANDARD

Arbitrary decision, wilful and lawless, is the enemy of liberty; but discretionary judgement is its essential servant.

William Letwin
Policy-Making, Discretionary Judgement and Liberty

A. INTRODUCTION

Many of the foremost students of family law—including Robert H. Mnookin, *Child-Custody Adjudication: Judicial Functions in the Face of Indeterminacy,* 39 L & Contemp Probs 226 (1975); Robert A. Burt, *Experts, Custody Disputes, & Legal Fantasies*, 14 The Psychiatric Hospital 140 (1983); David L. Chambers, *Rethinking the Substantive Rules for Custody Disputes in Divorce*, 83 Mich L Rev 477, 481 (1984); and Mary Ann Glendon, *Fixed Rules and Discretion in Contemporary Family Law and Succession Law*, 60 Tulane L Rev 1165, 1181 (1986)—have criticized the best-interest standard on the grounds that its indeterminacy allows judges too much discretion in deciding custody cases. The materials that follow have two purposes. The first is to help you evaluate this criticism. The second is to provide a broader understanding of the tension between discretion and rules so that you can analyze it as it appears elsewhere in family law and in law generally.

These materials have a theme, albeit a simple one. It is that the relationship between discretion and rules in American law is complex. We will suggest that the critics of the best-interest standard fail to appreciate this complexity. Nevertheless, the critics may ultimately be correct in thinking judges today have too much leeway in making custody decisions.

B. THE SOURCES OF DISCRETION

In this section, we take a preliminary look at the problem of discretion in custody litigation. First, we provide working definitions of discretion and some related ideas. Second, we explore the sources of discretion. Why is discretion created? How is it created? These inquiries reveal both that discretion has many prolific sources and that child-custody decisions are particularly discretionary.

(1) Some Working Definitions

We first need working definitions of our terms. These definitions must be very rough ideal types because there is rarely a pure rule or pure discretion, and most cases are decided according to a complex mix of rules and discretion. Then, the ideal type of a "rule" is an authoritative, mandatory, binding, specific, and precise direction which tells a judge how to decide a case or resolve a legal issue. See Frederick Schauer, *Playing by the Rules: A Philosophical Examination of Rule-Based Decisionmaking in Law and in Life* (Oxford U Press 1991). Discretion describes those "cases as to which a judge, who has consulted all relevant legal materials, is left free by the law to decide one way or another." Kent Greenawalt, *Discretion and Judicial Decision: The Elusive Quest for the Fetters That Bind Judges*, 75 Colum L Rev 359, 365 (1975).

On the continuum between rules and discretion are a number of intermediate categories. Some of these can be derived from the work of Professor Dworkin. For instance, he calls "a 'policy' that kind of standard that sets out a goal to be reached, generally an improvement in some economic, political, or social feature of the community...." Ronald Dworkin, *Taking Rights Seriously* 22 (Harv U Press 1977). He calls "a 'principle' a standard that is to be observed, not because it will advance or secure an economic, political, or social situation deemed desirable, but because it is a requirement of justice or fairness or some other dimension of morality." He distinguishes policies and principles from rules: "Rules are applicable in an all-or-nothing fashion. If the facts a rule stipulates are given, then either the rule is valid, in which case the answer it supplies must be accepted, or it is not, in which case it contributes nothing to the decision." Policies and principles, on the other hand, "do not set out legal consequences that follow automatically when the conditions provided are met."

For our purposes, policies and principles are less directive rules. There are also more directive versions of discretion. Professor Dworkin calls our working definition the "strong" form of discretion. But he also remarks two "weak" forms of discretion: "Sometimes we use 'discretion' in a weak sense, simply to say that for some reason the standards an official must apply cannot be applied mechanically but demand the use of judgment." The other weak sense refers to occasions when "some official has final authority to make a decision and cannot be reviewed and reversed by any other official."

(2) The Sources of Discretion

We will now glance at the sources of discretion. Often there is a direct and deliberate grant of discretionary authority to a decision-maker. We will identify four ideal types of directly and deliberately created discretionary authority. The first is distinguishable from the others by its distance from the ordinary principles of "law" in Western industrialized countries. The rest are distinguishable from the others by the reason for the grant of discretionary authority.

The first kind of directly and deliberately created discretionary authority is the most complete and the most foreign to our legal system: It may be believed that decision-makers can be found who are wise, who understand the principles of justice, and already know or are well-placed to discover the relevant facts, sometimes through some personal connection with the parties or through personal inquiry of people who know them. When discretion to decide cases is accorded to such people, what Max Weber called khadi-justice has been created. As Professor Kronman describes Weber's understanding of it, khadi-justice is

> adjudication of a purely *ad hoc* sort in which cases are decided on an individual basis and in accordance with an indiscriminate mixture of legal, ethical, emotional and political considerations.... Khadi-justice is irrational in the sense that it is peculiarly ruleless; it makes no effort to base decisions on general principles, but seeks, instead, to decide each

> case on its own merits and in light of the unique considerations that distinguish it from every other case. The characterization of khadi-justice as a substantive form of law-making highlights another of its qualities, namely, its failure to distinguish in a principled fashion between legal and extra-legal (ethical or political) grounds for decision. It is the expansiveness of this form of adjudication—its willingness to take into account all sorts of considerations, non-legal as well as legal—which gives it its substantive character; the idea of a limited and self-contained "legal" point of view is foreign to all true khadi-justice.

Anthony T. Kronman, *Max Weber* 76–77 (Stan U Press 1983). King Solomon's custody decision exemplifies khadi justice. Even his technique was a classic khadi technique: "when stories are told of really clever *qadis* they often involve the *qadi* trapping one of the parties in a display of his true character." Lawrence Rosen, *Equity and Discretion in a Modern Islamic Legal System*, 15 L & Society Rev 217, 231 (1980–81).

The second kind of direct and deliberate grant of discretionary authority is more characteristic of Western legal systems. It is "rule-failure" discretion. It is created where cases arise in circumstances so varied, so complex, and so hard to anticipate that satisfactory rules that would accurately guide decision-makers to correct results and only to correct results in a sufficiently large number of cases cannot be written. This second kind of grant differs from khadi-justice in several ways. The first is in the motive for its creation. Discretionary authority is accorded the khadi partly because of his special personal qualities and status. While American judges are expected to have a "judicial temperament," discretionary authority is accorded them more because of the difficulty of writing rules than because of those qualities. A judicial temperament is thought necessary because discretion must be exercised; the judicial temperament does not justify the exercise of discretion. A second difference between the two kinds of justice is that, unlike the khadi, the American judge is not expected to bring personal knowledge of the parties and their situation to bear. A third difference is that while khadi-justice is "peculiarly ruleless," American justice is as little ruleless as possible. A final difference is that, unlike the khadi, the American judge ought not consult "non-legal" considerations.

The best-interest principle in its pure form may be based on such reasoning. The UMDA's custody guidelines (which confide decisions to the court's discretion and provide a list of factors to consider in exercising it) can also be rationalized on these grounds. That is, those guidelines seem to acknowledge the desirability of cabining discretion but to concede the impossibility of doing so very effectively.

A direct and deliberate grant of discretionary authority may also be made where the decision-maker will develop out of its experience with individual cases over long periods of time a better understanding than anyone else could acquire of the recurring problems and where the decision-maker should develop rules for itself as it goes along. This may be called "rule-building" discretion. It is the theory of common-law adjudication. Proponents of statutes like the UMDA may hope that courts will develop custody rules as they accumulate experience.

Finally, a direct and deliberate grant of discretionary authority may be made where the members of the governmental body responsible for instructing the decision-maker cannot agree on rules or even guidelines and therefore deliberately pass responsibility to the decision-maker. We may call this "rule-compromise" discretion. The longevity of the best-interest standard in the face of so much criticism may be partly explained by the inability of legislators to agree on a replacement.

Discretionary authority may also be created in less direct and deliberate ways. It often grows out of the institutional structure of decision. For example, where a decision-maker is not subject to review, the decision-maker has discretion in one of Professor Dworkin's "weak senses." As Justice Jackson put it, "We are not final because we are infallible, but we are infallible only because we are final." *Brown v. Allen*, 344 US 443, 450 (1953) (Jackson, J, concurring). In any kind of litigation, this form of discretion will eventually be exercised. It may be exercised sooner than usual in custody litigation because the parties often cannot afford litigation and because the greater-than-usual deference to trial-court decisions probably deters appeals. Also, there is a greater need for an immediate decision in child-custody cases than in many other kinds of litigation: the child needs stability, and the parents to need repose.

In addition, any decision-maker, not just the last, will derive discretion from other "structural" sources. Indeed, in some ways the first decision-maker has the greatest discretion. First, someone must find facts, and fact-finding is quite a discretionary process, since it requires making complicated judgments: Deciding what actually happened involves judgments about what evidence to hear, what evidence to regard as relevant, what evidence to regard as reliable, to say nothing about drawing final conclusions about what actually happened. In most hierarchical situations, it will be impractical to keep re-gathering evidence, so many of these discretionary decisions will be effectively unreviewable. In custody litigation, this fact-finding authority is enhanced by the usual understanding that the trial court's opportunity to see and hear witnesses gives its conclusions special reliability.

The second reason the first decision-maker has great discretion is that someone must select the relevant rules, and this must initially be the fact-finder, since one cannot know what facts are relevant until the rules to which the facts are relevant have been identified. Where, as in custody law, rules are formulated in broad terms, this power to identify the rules to be applied can be significant.

Third, someone must decide *how* to apply the rule to the facts. As Professor Cooper writes, "It is now common to recognize that there is a third category, law application, that has the characteristics of both law-making and fact-finding." Edward H. Cooper, *Civil Rule 52(a): Rationing and Rationalizing the Resources of Appellate Review*, 63 Notre Dame

L Rev 645, 658 (1988). This requires complicated decisions which demand judgment and which hence create discretion. And where, as in custody law, multiplicitous and uncertain facts must be applied to broad rules, the scope for discretion swells.

The argument that discretion is an inherent part of deciding cases may be stated in still a stronger way. The power to identify the relevant rules and then to apply them to the facts is the power to *interpret* law. It is sometimes said language is so imprecise and interpretation potentially so free that even rules cannot cabin discretion. This is not the place to enter the jurisprudential debate that assertion raises. However, our investigation of discretionary decisions in custody cases should suggest something about the forces that limit as well as the forces that produce discretion.

In this section, then, we have seen that discretionary authority may be directly and deliberately created and that it also arises inevitably out of the very process of deciding cases. Both sources have helped make child-custody decisions, particularly those under the best-interest standard, discretionary. In other words, the critics of the best-interest standard are clearly right when they say that decisions under it are crucially discretionary.

C. DISCRETION IN CONTEXT

Most lawyers have pledged their faith to the concept of rules and the doctrine of due process; correspondingly, they are dubious about discretion. The critics of the best-interest test draw on that faith and those doubts. The critics seek to show that custody litigation is unduly discretionary by suggesting that the best-interest principle grants more discretion to judges than American law generally countenances. We will now propose that discretion plays a larger, richer part in American law than critics of the best-interest principle may credit.

(1) The Ubiquity of Discretion

The most imposing allocation of discretion in our system is to the government from "the people." The allocation is phrased in the broadest and haziest terms, if it is phrased at all. It is, within constitutional bounds, an allocation of plenary authority.

A principal part of that discretion is accorded to the legislature. It principally exercises its discretion in making laws. But it also commonly delegates vast swaths of discretion to administrative agencies. Sometimes this is discretion to make rules, as testified by acres of trees that died so that the C.F.R. might live. Sometimes it is discretion to adjudicate, as the Social Security Administration, the Veterans Administration, the NLRB, and many more, show.

In addition, the executive branch exercises discretion quite apart from legislative grants of authority. Part of it discretion is spent participating in legislating. But discretion is also assumed in the ordinary process of enforcing legislation. In the sociological literature, the police exemplify this kind of discretion. Police discretion begins at the administrative level. Police agencies have, for example, discretion to be proactive or reactive. Individual officers have substantial discretion in their work. As Professor Reiss indicates,

> Although police departments are organised around a centralised command and control where subordinates must follow orders, the bulk of police officers are dispersed in field assignments.... Most police officers work most of the time without direct supervision. Their discretionary decisions, thus, are not generally open to review by superiors.... Even when evidence of activity is submitted, such as in an arrest report, the capacity to review discretion is limited. There is no simple way to determine the facts in police encounters with citizens, the alternatives available to make choices, and their behaviour.

Albert J. Reiss, Jr., *Discretionary Justice in the United States*, 2 Intl J Criminology & Penology 181, 190–91 (1974).

Individual officers enjoy discretion even in the parts of their work that seem most strictly constrained by procedural regulations: "[I]n practice, when enforcing the law, the police exercise enormous discretion to arrest. Field observation studies of police decisions to arrest demonstrate this point: in one such study, the police released roughly one-half of the persons they suspected of committing crimes...." Nor is police authority limited to enforcing the law:

> [I]n times of crisis or emergency in non-criminal matters, local police in the United States are called upon to exercise discretion in performing a variety of services. These include intervention in conflicts between members of families, landlords and tenants, and employers and employees, as well as assistance in sickness, in tracing missing persons, and in dealing with the plight of animals or hazardous situations.

It is judicial discretion with which lawyers are peculiarly familiar. As we have seen, great discretion is confided to judges. For instance, many common-law areas are presumptively confided to the courts, sometimes so much so that it is the legislature, not the judiciary, which acts interstitially. Courts often acquire discretion even where the legislature is the prime mover, as Professor Chayes observes: "In enacting fundamental social and economic legislation, Congress is often unwilling or unable to do more than express a kind of general policy objective or orientation.... [T]he result is to leave a wide measure of discretion to the judicial delegate. The corrective power of Congress is also stringently limited in practice." Abram Chayes, *The Role of the Judge in Public Law Litigation*, 89 Harv L Rev 1281, 1314 (1976).

Judges also have discretion in fact-finding, especially, but not exclusively, when there is no jury. Further, judges exercise (sometimes along with juries) a generous discretion in "law application"—that vast borderland between "fact" and "law" that is created by standards like the "reasonable" in torts or the "rule of reason" in anti-trust law. Finally, considerable discretion is confided to judges in some kinds of remedy-giving. For example, both the decision to grant injunctive relief and shape are richly discretionary. Since an injunction can be an attempt to regulate the parties well into the future in considerable complexity, and since the role of injunctive relief has swollen recent years, this discretionary power can be impressive.

But judicial discretion is exercised outside of trials. For instance, judges exercise wide discretion in semi-administrative matters. In the criminal justice system, Reiss remarks, "main forms of discretion that they exercise are by decisions to: (1) detain defendants, grant bail or release them on their own recognisance; (2) dismiss matters or bind over at preliminary hearing; (3) accept pleas of guilty or to find guilty or not guilty in bench trials; (4) rule on matters of substance and procedure during trial proceedings; (5) decide the fate of defendants found guilty...."

Nor are judges the only actors in the judicial branch to make discretionary decisions. Juries not only make some of the same discretionary decisions judges do, but they are less subject to review when they make them. Lawyers too are endowed with significant kinds of discretion. Most prominently, prosecutors exercise discretion in such matters as deciding whether to file or drop charges and in plea bargaining. But defense counsel also commonly have discretion in preparing the defense and in plea bargaining and giving advice.

Finally, actors outside the legal system wield discretion in ways that affect it. For instance, the law has cooperated in making social and semilegal institutions of such radically discretionary enterprises as arbitration, mediation, and conciliation. Ordinary citizens retain a good deal of discretion about the work of the criminal and civil justice systems, since these systems primarily depend for their workload on the initiative of citizens. And insofar as citizens enter contracts, they exercise discretion in creating publicly enforced private government.

The significance of discretion in the American legal system can be illuminated by comparing it to civil-law systems. Particularly as opposed to such systems, our common-law system seems designed to promote the exercise of discretion. For one thing, the common law seems particularly suited to preserve doctrinal flexibility. Dean Levi expressed a standard common-law outlook when he wrote,

> The categories used in the legal process must be left ambiguous in order to permit the infusion of new ideas. And this is true even where legislation or a constitution is involved. The words used by the legislature or the constitutional convention must come to have new meanings.... In this manner the laws come to express the ideas of the community and even when written in general terms, in statute or constitution, are molded for the specific case.

Edward H. Levi, *An Introduction to Legal Reasoning* 4 (U Chi Press 1949).

Common-law decision-making also seems well adapted to allowing judges to respond to the claims of justice in a particular case where a rule fails to do so. The discretion of the common-law decision-maker is preserved out of an almost deliberate preference for subtly distinguishing cases so that justice can be individualized.

Discretion is at the heart of the common-law system for still more reasons: Much fact-finding is done by the jury, a lay group which cannot be effectively reviewed and which allows in a highly discretionary way for the injection of "community values." As Mirjan R. Damaska writes, "It is this openness to ordinary community judgments that may well be more deeply engrained or more canonical in Anglo–American legal culture than the more visible arabesques of pleading, or the exquisite refinements of evidentiary rules." *The Faces of Justice and State Authority* 42 (Yale U Press, 1986).

Furthermore, unlike civil-law judges, common-law judges are not supervised in a systematic, hierarchical way. In civil-law countries, the judge is a bureaucrat who hopes to make a career by moving up the hierarchy of judicial jobs. In common-law countries, the judge is brought in after achieving stature in another branch of the legal profession. The judge may not much expect a promotion, any chances for it may depend on the vagaries of politics. The common-law system in fact, if not in logical necessity, also preserves judicial discretion by limiting the scope of review of trial-court findings of fact. In civil-law systems, in contrast, the trial court assembles a factual record which is passed on to the appellate court, which may review that record *de novo*.

The common law accords judges more discretionary authority than civil law in part because common-law courts have subsumed the courts of chancery. The law of equity was designed from the beginning to respond to instances in which common-law rules prove too rigid. It expands judicial discretion to ensure flexibility in the decision of individual cases and in remedial relief.

One scholar argues that the discretionary powers of Anglo–American judges is expanding:

> It is my thesis that the balance between principle and pragmatism in the judicial process has shifted markedly since the beginning of the last century. In the first half of the nineteenth century, I suggest the courts were inclined to resolve the conflict by adhering to principle. They were less concerned with doing justice in the particular case and more concerned with the impact of their decision in the future. In modern times, by contrast, I suggest that the courts have become highly pragmatic and a great deal less principled. Nor has the change been carried through by the courts alone. At virtually every point it has been assisted by legislation.

P.S. Atiyah, *From Principles to Pragmatism: Changes in the Function of the Judicial Process and the Law*, 65 Iowa L Rev 1249, 1251 (1980). As Professor Atiyah explains, "Rules of procedure and evidence tend increasingly to be subject to discretion rather than fixed rule; and even where there are rules they tend increasingly to be of a prima facie nature, rules liable to be displaced where the court feels they may work injustice." Professor Atiyah associates this with a change in the prominence of two of the law's functions. Law "provides a means of settling disputes by fair and peaceful procedures...." But "the judicial process is part of a complex set of arrangements designed to provide incentives and disincentives for various types of behavior." Professor Atiyah suggests that the former function has acquired a much more prominent position relative to the latter function than it used to have. And since the latter works through rules and the former through "pragmatism," the scope of discretion has ballooned.

Perhaps inevitably, the burgeoning of discretion is associated with a new attitude toward the authority of rules. Professor Atiyah quotes Keynes, who, speaking of the friends of his youth, said:

> "We claimed ... the right to judge every individual case on its merits, and the wisdom, experience and self-control to do so successfully. This was a very important part of our faith, violently and aggressively held, and for the outer world it was our most dangerous characteristic. We repudiated entirely customary morals, conventions and traditional wisdom.... [W]e recognized no moral obligation on us, no inner sanction, to conform or to obey. Before heaven we claimed to be our own judge in our own case."

As Professor Atiyah concludes, "Modern man is unwilling to accept the authority of a principle whose application seems unjust in a particular case, merely because there might be some beneficial long-term consequence which he is unable to identify or even perceive."

Professor Schauer places the growing power of discretion in the context of the history of American legal thought. He detects

> a tradition in American law and legal theory that not only connects [Ronald] Dworkin in interesting ways with the work of theorists as diverse as Lon Fuller and Duncan Kennedy, but also has important points of contact with American Legal Realism and the Aristotelian conception of equity. The tradition starts with an intuitively appealing goal—getting *this case* just right. But that goal and the tradition embracing it are in tension with the very idea of a rule, for implicit in rule-based adjudication is a tolerance for some proportion of wrong results, results other than the results that would be reached, all things other than the rule considered, for the case at hand. In many of the most important areas of American adjudication, the tolerance for the wrong answer has evaporated, often for good reason, and the current paradigm for adjudication in the American legal culture may already have departed from rule-bound decisionmaking. This new paradigm instead stresses the importance not of deciding the case according to the rule, but of tailoring the rule to fit the case. Instead of bowing to the inevitable resistance of rules, the new paradigm exalts reasons without the mediating rigidity of rules, thus avoiding the occasional embarrassment generated by rules. And because this new jurisprudence treats what looks like rules as continuously subject to molding in order best to maintain the purposes behind those rules in the face of a changing world, we can say that what emerges is a jurisprudence not of rules but of reasons.

Frederick Schauer, *The Jurisprudence of Reasons*, 85 Mich L Rev 847, 847 (1987)(review of Ronald Dworkin, *Law's Empire*).

(2) Discretion and the Forms of Adjudication

We have been testing the claim that the discretionary best-interest principle falls outside the mainstream of American law by describing the context of discretion in that law. We will now examine that claim in a more concrete forms. Professor Mnookin seeks to show custody litigation is unduly discretionary by contrasting it to "traditional adjudication." First, "[m]ost legal rules require determination of some event and are thus 'act-oriented.' " But custody adjudication "centers on what kind of person each parent is, and what the child is like," and is thus "person-oriented." Second, traditional "adjudication usually requires the determination of *past* acts and facts," but custody adjudication requires "a prediction of *future* events." Third, custody adjudication involves "appraisals of future relationships where the 'loser's' future behavior can be an important ingredient," but most traditional adjudication does not. Fourth, in traditional adjudication precedents matter, but in custody litigation "[t]he result of an earlier case involving different people has limited relevance to a subsequent case requiring individualized evaluations of a particular child and the litigants." Fifth, "[n]ormally, parties most obviously affected by a dispute have a right to participate in the adjudicatory process," but children do not truly participate in custody adjudications.

There are two difficulties with the contrast Professor Mnookin draws between "traditional" and custody adjudication. The first concerns his description of traditional litigation. First what does mean by "traditional" litigation? Is that litigation as uniform and narrowly focused as he suggests? Does his description surely fit some kinds of litigation, particularly criminal prosecutions and some tort actions. But much of what he probably means by traditional adjudication lacks the qualities he thinks define it, and there are many kinds of traditional litigation in which elements of traditional adjudication seem missing. As he acknowledges, courts consider " 'the whole person viewed as a social being' "on a number of important occasions in traditional adjudication: "The standards governing preventive detention, pretrial detention, and sentencing are conspicuous examples."

Consider how the law of nuisance fits Professor Mnookin's description of traditional adjudication. Nuisance law may not be "person-oriented," but to call it "act-oriented" seems inadequate, since nuisance suits inquire into a continuing relationship between landowners. Nuisance law does require a determination of past acts, but it also frequently requires a determination of the future effects of remedies. In such determinations, "the 'loser's future behavior can be an important ingredient." Precedents are surely relevant in nuisance cases, but nuisance law is so reliant on ideas about reasonableness and balancing social goods and costs that "[t]he result of an earlier case involving different people [often] has limited relevance." And parties vitally affected by a nuisance action (like the employees of a cement factory that might be bankrupted by the suit) cannot participate in the litigation. In short, there are many areas—prominently including the law of contract, bankruptcy, partnership, corporations, important parts of property, and family law in general—that regulate the continuing relations of people and which thus poorly fit Professor Mnookin's paradigm of traditional adjudication.

The second difficulty with the contrast between traditional and custody litigation is that so much modern litigation isn't traditional. Professor Chayes has pointed to the growing predominance of "public law" litigation. Abram Chayes, *The Role of the Judge in Public Law Litigation*, 89 Harv L Rev 1281 (1976). This litigation includes "[s]chool desegregation, employment discrimination, and prisoners' or inmates' rights cases" as well as "[a]ntitrust, securities fraud and other aspects of the conduct of corporate business, bankruptcy and reorganizations, union governance, consumer fraud, housing discrimination, electoral reapportionment, [and] environmental management" cases. Public-law litigation significantly resembles Professor Mnookin's paradigm of custody litigation, for it is not "act-oriented"; it looks crucially to future, not past, events; it features interdependent, outcome-affecting factors, it often finds precedent a poor guide to decision, and it excludes affected parties.

Let us fill out these points slightly. Public-law litigation may not always be "person-oriented," but it is not "act-oriented," and it is often complex-entity oriented. In public-law adjudication, "[t]he fact inquiry is not historical and adjudicative but predictive and legislative," and the decree that concludes litigation often "seeks to adjust future behavior, not to compensate for past wrong." The public-law decree "provides for a complex, on-going regime of performance rather than a simple, one-shot, one-way transfer," and that regime regulates "an elaborate and organic network of interparty relationships." In public law, "the judge will not, as in the traditional model, be able to derive his responses directly from the liability determination, since ... the substantive law will point out only the general direction to be pursued and a few salient landmarks to be sought out or avoided." Finally, public law remedies "often hav[e] important consequences for many persons including absentees." (Indeed, much of the conventional objection to public-law litigation is exactly that many parties, including the public at large, that have an interest in litigation are unrepresented in it.)

D. THE LIMITATIONS ON DISCRETION

We have been suggesting that discretion is more deeply and widely embedded in American law than critics of the best-interest principle say. But our argument so far only raises questions about why discretion is so pervasive, whether it can be avoided, and why it seems to be tolerable even in large doses. In this section, we will say that part of the answer is that limitations on discretion are as inevitable and abundant as its sources of, and that discretionary decisions are rarely as unfettered as they look.

Discretion is regularly cabined, cribbed, and confined in multitudinous ways. "Complete freedom—unfettered and undirected—there never is. A thousand limitations—the product some of statute, some of precedent, some of vague tradition or of an immemorial technique—encompass and hedge us even when we think of ourselves as ranging freely and at large.... Narrow at best is any freedom that is allotted to us." Benjamin N. Cardozo, *The Growth of the Law* 61 (Yale U Press, 1924). What are some of those thousand limitations on discretion?

The first limitation on discretion lies in the power to select the people who exercise discretion. We know this limitation best in the Presidential appointment of Supreme Court Justices. Though Presidents have sometimes been unpleasantly surprised, they have gotten what they wanted more than is conventionally supposed. Life tenure dampens the power of selection in reducing discretion, but most state-court judges do not have life tenure. On the contrary, many of them must regularly be re-selected. The effectiveness of the appointment power is enhanced where the decision-maker will face only one kind of decision. Where the decision-maker makes many kinds of decisions, it is hard to learn all the decider's views in advance and to find someone who has *all* the right views. Specialized family courts make it easier to choose judges whose views on family law issues are predictable.

The second limitation on discretion lies in socializing and training of decision-makers. Decision-makers do not operate in a vacuum; they are products of their environment, and their environment has many shared social norms. Some of these speak directly to the substantive issues to be decided. Others speak to the way *any* issue may be decided: "Almost any situation in which a person acts ... makes relevant certain standards of rationality, fairness, and effectiveness." Ronald Dworkin, *Taking Rights Seriously* 33 (Harv U Press, 1977). Most decision-makers in an industrialized western democracy, and certainly governmental decision-makers, are thought obliged to make decisions that are rational by the standards of the society and that accord with its basic institutions.

Judges are affected not only by their socialization as twentieth-century Americans, but also by their legal training and the norms that training inculcates. These include "procedural" norms that tell the decision-maker what kinds of evidence and reasoning are permissible. Thus one commentator notes that

> Parliament can entrust some discretionary latitude where the repository of the discretion by reason of his antecedents and training, is a part and product of the system itself which we call the common law. The fact that under that system appointees to the bench must first have been in actual practice in the very courts of which they are to become members can only confirm the likelihood that they will continue to speak with much the same voice as their predecessors.

H.A. Finlay, *Judicial Discretion in Family and Other Litigation*, 2 Monash L Rev 221, 222 (1976). In the United States, a system of national law schools offering intensive training (particularly in the first year) contributes to the universality and stability of these norms. And while they generally lack comparable specialized training beyond law-school, judges learn on the job a further set of professional norms, some formally articulated, some simply internalized.

A third limitation on discretion lies in the judicial decisions are subject to. Some of this criticism is scholarly. But judges hear from the local bar and their colleagues on the bench. "The inscrutable force of professional opinion," Justice Cardozo wrote, "presses upon us like the atmosphere, though we are heedless of its weight." Benjamin N. Cardozo, *The Growth of the Law* 61 (Yale U Press, 1924). Nor is criticism of judges confined to the legal profession: Prominent and consequential decisions can provoke politicians, journalists, and other interested publics, including the public at large. Judges may even hear from friends and family.

A fourth limitation on discretion grows out of the decision-maker's internal dynamics. Decision-makers are often constrained by the structure and imperatives of the institutions they are part of and of their own psychology. Efficiency concerns, boredom, laziness, a wish to avoid responsibility, and more can drive decision-makers toward relying on their own earlier decisions in factually similar cases. In other words, decision-makers usually have strong incentives to develop their own rules, their own common-law, even if constraints on discretion are not forced on them from the outside. The more work a court must do, the less time it will have for the work of exercising unfettered discretion. A court may exercise discretion in deciding how to decide cases, but it will have an incentive to construct principles of decision that are easily applicable and to defer to other decision-makers. Thus courts deciding custody cases massively approve custody agreements worked out by divorcing parents.

Another institutional factor that constrains discretion is the institution's need to coordinate several decision-makers or to coordinate the same decision-maker's decisions over time. Because of the strength in American law of the principle that like cases should be treated alike, this pressure to coordinate decisions is widely and intensely felt.

Furthermore, all people try to make sense of the world by categorizing the events and problems they encounter. Judges are no different. Their categories can become rules of decision which govern, or at least influence, how issues are resolved. Such categories arise out of a judge's general experience with the world. They also arise directly out of a judge's experience of deciding custody cases. For example, a judge who regularly awarded custody to alcoholic contenders and then regularly found the parties returning to court with more problems might become discouraged from awarding custody to alcoholics.

A fifth constraint on discretion is that no governmental decision-maker acts entirely alone and that, shared power constrains each decision-maker's scope of discretion. The most obvious consequential example of this constraint is the authority of the legislature to write rules which a court must follow. But this fifth constraint appears in other forms.

Sometimes this fifth constraint works "jurisdictionally." Courts lack authority to decide many kinds of family disputes, even if they nominally involve enforcing a contract, e.g., *Kilgrow*. These cases are implicitly, and sometimes explicitly, rationalized on the theory that "family government is recognized by law as being as complete in itself as the State government is in itself." *North Carolina v. Rhodes*. Thus the discretion even of a court deciding a custody question is limited by this "jurisdictional" principle.

This fifth restraint on discretion also operates where a decision-maker has "jurisdiction" but shares it with another governmental decision-maker. For instance, a department of social services can alter a custody battle by initiating proceedings to terminate one parent's parental rights, and its failure to do so will limit (although not eliminate) a court's authority to deny a non-custodial parent visiting rights. That department of social services can also limit judicial discretion by issuing a report on a potential custodian.

Sometimes this fifth constraint works by giving other branches power to retaliate against the judiciary. At its most extreme, this can involve impeaching judges or depriving courts of jurisdiction. But it can also operate less dramatically. For instance, even county commissioners can in some jurisdictions deprive a family court of the funds court would like to allocate.

Courts share authority not just with other governmental agencies, but even with the litigants. Litigants' decisions determine what disputes will be brought to a court. This sounds obvious and trivial, but only about ten percent of divorces are actually litigated. Where cases are litigated, the parties crucially affect the evidence the court hears and the legal arguments it is asked to resolve. Both the introduction and the omission of important facts cabin a court's decisions. In custody disputes expert testimony may be particularly limiting. When Mr. Painter failed to provide a psychologist to contradict the confident Dr. Hawks, Mr. Painter made it harder for the trial judge to find for him and, in the mind of the Iowa Supreme Court, impossible for it to sustain the trial court. (In custody cases, the frequent presence of a guardian *ad litem* further expands this kind of constraint on judicial discretion. The guardian speaks with the moral force accorded to those who are supposed to be disinterested and can take positions and make arguments that the decision-maker must at least explain away.)

Litigants set other limits on judicial discretion. Sometimes they have things the court wants, like the ability to settle a case. Sometimes they can resist judicial orders. This problem is particularly acute in family law, where the court often depends on cooperation from the litigants. The unfortunate Morgan–Foretich case is only a lurid example of a larger problem. *Morgan v. Foretich*, 546 A2d 407 (DC App 1988).

The sixth limitation on discretion is created by the hierarchical organization of the judiciary. Because it is widely acknowledged, we need say little about it. Intermediate appellate courts review trial-court procedures, opinions, and holdings, and supreme courts review appellate courts. In extreme cases of judicial misbehavior, disciplinary proceedings may be brought or judges may be impeached.

The seventh limitation on discretion arises where a court must follow a set of procedures. These procedures may be self-imposed or externally imposed. Some procedures limit discretion by telling the court how to conduct its inquiry. These procedures may limit the evidence that may be received, specify who may make arguments, state who must receive notice of the proceedings, identify the litigant who speaks first, and so on. The underlying idea is that if a decision-maker follows the right procedure, the right decision is likelier to be made. In other words, procedural rules limit substantive discretion.

Other procedures constrain discretion by telling the decision-maker what procedures to follow in deciding a case. One such requirement is the obligation to justify decisions, particularly to in writing. The process of explaining affects the decision-maker, if only because writing clarifies thought. It also subjects the decision-maker to criticism from the parties and the public and to review from a hierarchical superior.

The eighth limitation on discretion is to provide guidelines for decisions. Decision-makers are commonly furnished at least with a statement of the purposes and goals the decision is intended to serve. The best-interest principle exemplifies such a statement. And also commonly, decision-makers will be provided with (or will construct) a statement of second-level considerations thought generally to promote those purposes and goals. The UMDA's factors to consider in custody decisions are an example.

The ninth limitation on discretion is to state rules written at some level of detail that instruct the decision-maker what to do when faced with particular facts. This limitation is in some senses the polar opposite of discretion.

The tenth limitation on discretion is to accord rights to a disputant. Rights transfer partial and sometimes complete responsibility for a decision from government to an individual. If there is a constitutional right to enter into binding surrogate-mother contracts, for example, judicial limited.

In this discussion, we saw that discretion has prolific sources and pervades American law. We asked how such broad discretion is tolerable. In this section, we have seen part of the answer—that discretion is almost always limited by a multiplicity of factors.

E. THE ADVANTAGES OF DISCRETION

Discretionary authority pervades American law and multitudinous limitations on discretion make it less alarming than it sometimes seems. But to evaluate the critics' charges, we need a more accurate understanding of how to choose the mix of discretion and rules to prefer in an area of law. We will start by sketching the general attractions and the drawbacks of discretion.

The attractions of discretion are well known. The first is negative—rules have disadvantages and can malfunction. Sometimes rule-makers fail to anticipate the problems a rule is written to solve. Discretion can fill gaps in rules. Sometimes two or more rules simultaneously apply but dictate conflicting results. Discretion can permit the decision-maker to resolve the conflict. Sometimes the way a rule is written will, applied to a particular case, produce a result that conflicts with the rule's purpose. Discretion can allow the decision-maker to promote the purpose of the rule. Sometimes the way a rule is written will, applied to a particular case, produce a result that conflicts with our understanding of what justice is. Discretion can allow the decision-maker to do justice. And sometimes the circumstances in which a rule must be applied will be so complex that a rule cannot be written that works effectively. Discretion frees the decision-maker to deal with that complexity.

The advantages of discretion can be put more positively. Discretion can lead to better decisions because they can be tailored to the circumstances of the case. Discretion gives the decision-maker flexibility to do justice. It does so not just by allowing a decision-maker to consider all the individual circumstances that ought to affect a decision but that could not be listed by rules. It also does so by allowing a decision-maker repeatedly to see how well a decision worked and to adjust future decisions to respond to the new information. Discretion may also conduce to better decisions by discouraging bureaucratic ways of thinking and by making the decision-maker's job attractive to able people.

One study of the criminal-justice system has summarized the advantages of discretion with special passion:

> The solace of standardized rules and procedures is largely illusory. Rigid rules tend to ossify individual responsibility and discourage individualistic thinking. Those who would shrink discretion obey the precept: 'Treat likes alike.' However, the overriding lesson of experience in our criminal justice operation is that every case is different. The major worry is that the people out there dealing with the problems will lose their appreciation of the differences between the cases and will begin reacting to them as repetitive. There is nothing quite like a good set of rules *cum* guidelines to bring common elements to the fore and obscure differences. If nothing else, our experience with mandatory minimums in drug sentencing should have taught the sterility of the reduced factor method of response. The learned fact should be that crimes and criminals emerge from a rich variety of circumstances. Separately and in combination, the variants can never be fully anticipated or assessed; yet they are often critical to forming the just response.

H. Richard Uviller, *The Unworthy Victim: Police Discretion in the Credibility Call,* 47 L & Contemp Probs 15, 32 (1984).

F. THE DRAWBACKS OF DISCRETION

What then are the drawbacks of discretion? The most prominent drawback hardly needs elaboration: It makes it easier than rules usually do for a decision-maker to employ illegitimate considerations. Less prominently, discretion may have bad psychological effects on the decision-maker. Discretion is power, and power corrupts.

But the drawbacks of discretion can also be phrased in terms of the advantages rules offer. We will consider six. First, rules can contribute to the legitimacy of a decision. In a democracy, power flows from the people. The closer a decision is to the people, the more secure its legitimacy. Legislative rules are likely to be "closer" than administrative or judicial decisions.

The second advantage of rules is that rule-makers may be better situated than decision-makers to decide what justice is both in an individual case and in general. Rule-makers typically have more time than decision-makers to evaluate a problem, which can allow them to survey more elements of the problem and think about them more reflectively. Rule-makers may have more resources for gathering information. They may be better able to bring together the whole range of social groups interested in the a problem.

Nor does one always get the best view of a problem by looking at a particular instance. This is the point of many criticisms of the common-law method of developing rules. For instance, a decision-maker in a particular case may be distracted from a just decision by the special but irrelevant circumstances of the particular litigants. Sometimes these can be plainly irrelevant factors. But many chance characteristics of the litigants or their circumstances may influence a decision in a way that, on a longer view, we would think wrong. For example, many people argue that the marital misbehavior of a spouse which does not directly and evidently affect a child has too often diverted courts from consulting only the child's best interest.

The third advantage of rules relates to our basic assumption that like cases should be treated alike. One way to try to ensure that they are is writing rules instead of allowing decision-makers decide case by case what principles to apply to what fact situations and how. Rules suppress differences of opinion about what works to serve what purpose, about how to balance factors, and what justice requires; these differences could otherwise lead to different results in similar cases. Rules also serve as record-keeping devices, devices that are more efficient and therefore more likely to be used effectively than an elaborate system of precedent. Rules coordinate the decisions of multiple decision-makers and one decision-maker over time.

The fourth advantage of rules is that they serve the planning function better than discretionary decisions. The people and institutions affected by a need to know in advance how a case will be decided so that they may plan their lives and work in accordance with the rules. On the whole, rules give better warning than discretionary decisions because they are likelier to provide clear and complete information about what a court will do. (One important reason common-law adjudication works is that rules are eventually adduced.)

The fifth attraction of rules is that they are, on average, more efficient than discretion, for rules institutionalize experience. A rule can distill a long process of decisions. Decision-makers exercising discretion, unless they consult some rules, have to go through the entire process for each decision, even though it means duplicating that process each time. Further, rules help the decision-maker (and the litigants) select only those arguments and facts that will be relevant. In short, as Whitehead wonderfully said,

> It is a profoundly erroneous truism, repeated by copy-books and by eminent people when they are making speeches, that we should cultivate the habit of thinking about what we are doing. The precise opposite is the case. Civilization advances by extending the number of important operations which we can perform without thinking about them. Operations of thought are like cavalry charges in a battle—they are strictly limited in number, they require fresh horses, and must only be made at decisive moments.

Alfred North Whitehead, *An Introduction to Mathematics* 61 (Oxford U Press, 1958).

Sixth and finally, rules serve social purposes discretionary decisions generally serve less well. Rules are often an announcement about how people should behave, an announcement that attempts to affect behavior. Rules communicate this information more clearly and emphatically and are more easily recognized as commands than a series of individual decisions from which general principles must be drawn.

G. CHOOSING BETWEEN DISCRETION AND RULES IN CUSTODY LAW

You have now learned a great deal about the place of discretion in American law and about the merits of rules and discretion. You should now be using what you have learned choose between discretion and rules in custody law. The following questions should help you do so.

(1) The Advantages of Discretion

The core advantage of discretion is its flexibility, its ability to allow the decision-maker to do justice in the individual case. Here, the great drawback of the best-interest standard—its "indeterminacy"—becomes its great advantage. Professor Cooper's praise of Rule 52(a) of the Federal Rules of Civil Procedure[1] offers a nice analogy. He attributes the

1. "Findings of fact ... shall not be set aside unless clearly erroneous, and due regard shall be given to the opportunity of the trial court to judge of the credibility of the witnesses."

enormous success of that rule to "the fact that the 'clearly erroneous' phrase has no intrinsic meaning. It is elastic, capacious, malleable, and above all variable. Because it means nothing, it can mean anything and everything that it ought to mean. It cannot be defined, unless the definition might enumerate a nearly infinite number of shadings along the spectrum of working review standards." Edward H. Cooper, *Civil Rule 52(a): Rationing and Rationalizing the Resources of Appellate Review*, 63 Notre Dame L Rev 645, 645 (1988).

But do custody decisions require flexibility? *Are* custody decisions so multifarious that no rules can be written for them? Don't custody cases, like most cases, form patterns that can be the bases for rules? Even if judges need flexibility in assessing all the errant but relevant facts that present themselves, do they also need the flexibility in developing second-level that the best-interest principle seems to give them? Should courts have this latter kind of discretion because of their considerable experience with custody problems? Should they have both kinds of discretion to allow them to respond to the particular values of the community in which they work? To respond to the particular values of the family whose dispute they are helping to settle? On this last point, consider the argument that

> the litigants ... are bound by something they helped to make. Moreover, the examples or analogies urged by the parties bring into the law the common ideas of the society. The ideas have their day in court, and they will have their day again. This is what makes the hearing fair, rather than any idea that the judge is completely impartial, for of course he cannot be completely so.

Edward H. Levi, *An Introduction to Legal Reasoning* 5 (U Chi Press, 1949).

(2) The Advantages of Rules

The first advantage of rules which we discussed is that they can contribute to the legitimacy of a decision by bringing the standard closer to the source of legitimacy. Would rules lend greater legitimacy to custody decisions than discretionary decisions made under the best interest standard? Isn't it a classic problem with discretion that it permits the substitution of private for public rules? On the other hand, how often does this substitution actually occur? In writing generally about legal decisions, Professors Lempert and Sanders conclude that

> rules of decision as well as methods of presentation apparently make a difference in the way evidence is used.... At times such ideas are debunked by lawyers and nonlawyers alike on the theory that lay people will decide cases as they see fit and that nothing will alter this. This 'perfidy' theory of human behavior finds little support in the previous data. Decision rules structure the problem the fact finder must resolve, and so alter the ways in which cases are decided.

Richard Lempert and Joseph Sanders, *An Invitation to Law and Social Science* 75 (Longman, 1986).

Is this enough? How many "wrong" decisions ought it take to make us want to reduce judicial discretion? Even if we decide to reduce judicial discretion, should we do so rules judges must follow in all cases or by writing rules which prohibit judges from relying on specifically enumerated factors that we want to exclude from custody decisions?

The second advantage of rules is that rule-makers may be better situated than decision-makers to decide what justice is. Is this true in the instance of child custody? Are legislators better situated to write general policy on custody than judges? Are appellate court judges better situated to write that policy than trial court judges? Doesn't the answer depend on the qualities and abilities of the people who occupy those posts? Doesn't it also depend on how possible it is to write good rules? Consider again the alternatives to the best-interest principle. Does any of them strike you as an adequate substitute? Some combination? Would the substitutes you considered really reduce discretion?

The third advantage of rules is that they promote treating like cases alike. How well does this advantage of rules apply? What does "alike" mean in custody cases? Should urban and rural cases be treated similarly? May the value preferences of local communities or the litigants themselves be taken into account even if this produces different results around a state? How strong is a litigant's interest in being treated like other litigants in custody cases?

How strong is the child's interest in being treated like other children? It will often be difficult to say about custody disputes that one child is getting a better deal than another. It will probably be more accurate to say that one child's case was decided in one plausible way and that another child's in another plausible way. How is either child injured? Have the children have been treated alike in that each court has tried in reasonable ways to do its best for each child?

The fourth advantage of rules is that they make it easier for people to anticipate how their case will be decided and thus plan their lives and to avoid the unfairness of retroactivity. How important is this in custody disputes? Do people really plan their lives in a marriage with an eye to the rules governing divorce? Are there cases in which a parent might need to know in advance how a court would decide a custody dispute? Was *Painter* such a case?

Even if couples do not rely on custody rules in planning their behavior during marriage, won't they rely on them once they have decided to divorce? Won't they negotiate with an eye to what they think a court will do? And wouldn't predictable rules reduce bargaining costs and the ability of one of the parties to abuse the bargaining process? Won't uncertainty benefit the stronger party? Won't it benefit the party who cares least about the children? But how unpredictable are discretionary decisions? And doesn't predictability have an important drawback—that it reduces the parties' freedom to bargain toward the ends that they prefer?

The fifth advantage of rules is that they can be more efficient than discretion. In custody cases need quick and inexpensive resolutions. But would cumbersome rules and elaborate procedures be more efficient than judicial discretion? Are rules more efficient than discretion only where the rule is fairly simple? In the custody context, does such a rule give up too much in precision? What number of suboptimal results is outweighed by what number of cases in which delay is avoided?

Part of the answer to that question depends on how costly suboptimal results are. What, then, is the state trying to achieve through custody law? Each function of family law is implicated: (1) The protective function is represented by the state's interest in protecting children from living in harmful circumstances and in ensuring that responsibility for every child is clearly assigned to a specific person. (2) The arbitral function is represented by the state's interest in giving would-be custodians a means of resolving their dispute. (3) The facilitative function is represented by the state's interest in allowing parents to arrange in legally binding form the terms under which care for and access to their child is to be assured. (4) The channelling function is represented by the state's interest in directing people toward the "best" forms of child custody. (5) The expressive function is represented by the state's interest in stating the importance of children's interests in divorce disputes and in emphasizing the responsibility both parents have for their children. How severe might be failures to serve those functions effectively?

Finally, rules serve social purposes discretionary decisions can serve less well. Principally, rules guide social conduct better than discretionary decisions. But don't the rules governing child-custody disputes have to do primarily with settling a dispute, not guiding social conduct? Could the indeterminate best-interest standard itself serve important social functions by standing for the proposition that children's needs may be unclear and may conflict with their parent's needs, but nevertheless should predominate?

H. CONCLUSION

Where should all this leave us? It may be unreasonable to expect to find happiness at either end of the continuum between discretion and rules. It may not even be possible to find either end in actual operation. As we saw, discretion has many sources and limitations. These sources and limitations are so numerous, so embedded in the American system of law-making, that they are essentially inevitable.

Suppose judges had no rule of decision at all. They would nevertheless bring with them some fairly systematic ideas about what made for fair decisions. And they would feel under several kinds of internal and external pressure to make decisions in ways that fit some fairly systematic ideas about children and parents. Judges under these circumstances might borrow and develop rules of their own. Thus it may be a false opposition to say we have a choice between rules and discretion. Rather, we may have a choice between rules formally and systematically applied and rules adopted informally and perhaps unsystematically.

In fact, we have already rejected the most discretionary kind of plausible decision, one we live with in many kinds of cases—a jury decision. The jury decision is made by people who have not been selected to make any particular kind of decision, who have not been socialized in making decisions according to law, who have not been trained in making legal decisions, who are not readily or systematically subject to criticism, who need not have explain their decision, who are not subject to many kinds of hierarchical authority, who never have to make a decision of this sort again and who thus are not under institutional pressures toward consistency, and so on. Juries are checked only in that they are supposed to represent community sentiment, they are instructed on the law by a judge, they explain their decisions to each other, and they are subject to reversal by the trial judge or an appellate court if they pass the outer bounds of rationality.

On the other hand, as the complexities of Section 2 of this Chapter may suggest, it is also unlikely that any rule could ever be so simple and so mechanically enforced as to deprive judges of the discretion to make or apply law. Even the tender-years presumption was only a presumption, and parental unfitness and even marital fault were grounds for rebutting it. Similarly, even the preference for the natural parent over another contender is sometimes overcome

Nor would we have trouble rejecting the least discretionary system—the coin toss. As Professor Mnookin suggests, the coin toss is unsatisfactory because, even if we don't know what is best for children, we have a pretty clear idea what is worst. We also have some reasonably good ideas about some things that are good—affection, stability, and so on—and want to see them provided when we can.

In fact, the present custody regime is much more a mix of discretion and rules than one might gather from the critics of the best-interest standard. The critics assume the principle is applied as if it meant what it says and as if it were all that is said. But the discretionary aspects of the principle are frequently tempered. For instance, jurisdictions institute rules or presumptions. Sometimes these are positive instructions, like the preference for joint custody, the primary-caretaker rule, the tender-years presumption, and so on. Sometimes these are negative instructions, like the UMDA's prohibition on taking marital fault into account. Other jurisdictions adopt guidelines listing factors. But even though guidelines may do little solve the indeterminacy problem, and even though the best-interest standard is indeterminate, these indeterminate standards gain meaning through judicial interpretation which evolves into rules.

In the end, the Court's statement in *Commissioner v. Duberstein*, 363 US 278 (1960), may be worth remembering. There, the Court was asked by the government to accept a new test which, "while apparently simple and precise in its formulation, depends frankly on a set of 'principles' or 'presumptions' derived from the decided cases, and concededly subject to various exceptions; and it involves various corollaries, which add to its detail." The Court responded,

> Decision of the issue presented in these cases must be based ultimately on the application of the fact-finding tribunal's experience with the mainsprings of human conduct to the totality of the facts of each case. The nontechnical nature of the statutory standard, the close relationship of it to the data of practical human experience, and the multiplicity of relevant factual elements, with their various combinations, creating the necessity of ascribing the proper force to each, confirm us in our conclusion that primary weight in this area must be given to the conclusions of the trier of fact.

BIBLIOGRAPHY

Adoption. For a fascinating and controversial insight into the adoption market, see Elisabeth Landes and Richard Posner, *The Economics of the Baby Shortage*, 7 J Legal Stud 323 (1978). This is the original "baby selling" article. It contends that many problems of the current adoption system (and even the frequency of abortion) could be diminished by an explicit price system. In *Unwed Fathers and Adoption: A Theoretical Analysis in Context*, 72 Tex L Rev 967 (1994), Deborah L. Forman argues that "substantial commitment" is the standard that should be applied before unwed fathers are given a major decisionmaking role in their children's lives. Richard J. Delaney and Frank R. Kunstal, *Troubled Transplants: Unconventional Strategies for Helping Disturbed Foster and Adopted Children* (U Southern Maine, 1993), argues for shortening the time children spend in foster care before permanent placement. For a wide-ranging account of adoption, including an influential section on transracial adoption, see Elizabeth Bartholet, *Family Bonds: Adoption and the Politics of Parenting* (Houghton Mifflin, 1993). For a response to problems like the Baby Jessica case, see David D. Meyer, *Family Ties: Solving the constitutional Dilemma of the Faultless Father*, 41 Ariz L Rev 753 (1999).

Surrogate Motherhood. A relatively early but quite useful perspective on the issue is in Martha A. Field, *Surrogate Motherhood: The Legal and Human Issues* (Harv U Press, 1988). For a contrary view, see Carmel Shalev, *Birth Power: The Case for Surrogacy* (Yale U Press, 1989). The natural mother in the *Baby M.* case proffers her memoirs in Mary Beth Whitehead, *A Mother's Story: The Truth About the Baby M Case* (St. Martin's Press, 1989). For a feminist view of surrogacy, consider Joan Mahoney, *An Essay on Surrogacy and Feminist Thought*, 16 Law, Med & Health Care 81 (1988). Professor Mahoney explores the problems of exploitation, control over one's own body, and perpetuation of traditional gender roles that are problematic for feminists in the surrogacy context. Martha Garrison, *Surrogate Parenting: What Should Legislatures Do?* 22 Family LQ 149 (1988), argues that state legislatures should take a moderate approach and should use existing adoption, parental fitness, and "best interests" standards in resolving surrogacy issues. Margaret F. Brinig, *A Maternalistic Approach to Surrogacy*, 81 Va L Rev 2377 (1995), evaluates surrogacy from a law-and-economics perspective and concludes surrogacy is a "demerit good" that should not be forbidden but should be discouraged.

Custody. For thoughtful reflections on a difficult subject, see Elizabeth S. Scott, *Pluralism, Parental Preference, and Child Custody*, 80 Calif L Rev 615 (1992). Katharine T. Bartlett, *Re-Expressing Parenthood*, 98 Yale L J 293 (1988), argues that custody rules should not encourage parental possessiveness and self-centeredness. For a related view, see *John Elster, Solomonic Judgments: Against the Best Interests of the Child*, 54 U Chi L Rev 1 (1987). Catherine R. Albiston and Eleanor E. Maccoby, *Does Joint Legal Custody Matter*, 2 Stanford L & Policy Rev 167 (1990), found that changing custody standards did not make an appreciable difference in divorce settlements or actual, as opposed to court-ordered, custody and visitation patterns. Margaret F. Brinig and F.H. Buckley, *Joint Custody: Bonding and Monitoring Theories*, 73 Ind L J 393 (1998), argues that parents who expect to receive at least partial custody of their children are apt to bond more strongly with them during marriage (and thus be less likely to divorce). June Carbone, *From Parents to Partners* (Columbia U Press, 2000), shows how welfare policies, custody laws, and women's roles in the household and labor force interact to influence both marriage and childrearing. Scott Altman, *Should Child Custody Rules be Fair?* 35 J Family L 325 (1997), suggests that if the child's best interest is truly the main concern, outcomes (and therefore rules) should not necessarily reward the parent who has invested the most. For a more complete examination of discretion and child custody, see Carl E. Schneider, *Discretion, Rules, and Law: Child Custody and the UMDA's Best–Interest Standard*, 89 Mich L Rev 2215 (1991). Margaret F. Brinig, Carl E. Schneider and Lee E. Teitelbaum, *Family Law in Action: A Reader* 341 (Anderson, 1999) reviews several theoretical and empirical discussions of child custody law.

Empirical Research on Custody. For one of many studies on the effect of divorce on children, see Mavis Hetherington, Martha Cox, and Roger Cox, *Long-Term Effects of Divorce and Remarriage on the Adjustment of Children*, 24 J Amer Academy of Child Psychiatry 518 (1985). It concludes that divorce is almost always more harmful to children over the long run than remaining in an intact relationship, unless the dissolved marriage was characterized by violence and hostility. Judith Wallerstein, *The Long–Term Effects of Divorce on Children: A Review*, 30 J Amer Academy of Child & Adolescent Psychiatry 349 (1991), finds that children of divorce frequently reflect their parents' problems in their own adult relationships.

Gender and Custody. For an early view of how gender differences might affect custody rules, see John S. Murray, *Improving Parent and Child Relationships Within the Divorced Family: A Call for Legal Reform*, 19 U Mich JL Ref 563 (1986). Professor Murray advocates custodial arrangements after divorce that mimic as closely as possible those enjoyed while the family was intact. Jerry McCant, *The Cultural Contradiction of Fathers as Non–Parents*, 21 Family LQ 127 (1987), argues that society criticizes fathers for taking only financial roles in their children's lives but does not support them when they attempt to nurture their children. For three perspectives on the special role of motherhood in contemporary American law, see Mary Becker, *Maternal Feelings: Myth, Taboo, and Child Custody*, 1 Rev L & Women's Stud 133 (1992); Karen Czapanskiy, *Volunteers and Draftees: The Struggle for Parental Equality*, 38 UCLA L Rev 1415 (1991); and Carol Sanger, *M is for the Many Things*, 1 Rev L & Women's Stud 15 (1992).

Visitation by Third Parties. John DeWitt Gregory, *Blood Ties: A Rationale for Child Visitation by Legal Strangers*, 55 Wash & Lee L Rev 351 (1998), discusses the importance of relationships outside the nuclear family.

General. Margaret F. Brinig, Carl E. Schneider and Lee E. Teitelbaum, *Family Law in Action: A Reader* Chapter 97–134 (Anderson, 1999), includes excerpts discussing unwed parents, adoption, and step-parenting.

Chapter X

CHILD ABUSE AND NEGLECT: PROTECTING CHILDREN AND THE DILEMMA OF DUE PROCESS

One morning when I went into the parlour with my books, I found my mother looking anxious, Miss Murdstone looking firm, and Mr. Murdstone binding something round the bottom of a cane—a lithe and limber cane, which he left off binding when I came in, and poised and switched in the air....

'Now, David,' he said—and I saw that cast again as he said it—'you must be far more careful to-day than usual.' He gave the cane another poise, and another switch; and having finished his preparation of it, laid it down beside him, with an impressive look, and took up his book.

This was a good freshener to my presence of mind, as a beginning. I felt the words of my lessons slipping off, not one by one, or line by line, but by the entire page; I tried to lay hold of them; but they seemed, if I may so express it, to have put skates on, and to skim away from me with a smoothness there was no checking....

He walked me up to my room slowly and gravely—I am certain he had a delight in that formal parade of executing justice—and when we got there, suddenly twisted my head under his arm.

'Mr. Murdstone! Sir!' I cried to him. 'Don't! Pray don't beat me! I have tried to learn, sir, but I can't learn while you and Miss Murdstone are by. I can't indeed!'

'Can't you, indeed, David?' he said. 'We'll try that.'

He had my head as in a vice, but I twined round him somehow, and stopped him for a moment, entreating him not to beat me. It was only for a moment that I stopped him, for he cut me heavily an instant afterwards, and in the same instant I caught the hand with which he held me in my mouth, between my teeth, and bit it through. It sets my teeth on edge to think of it.

He beat me then as if he would have beaten me to death. Above all the noise we made, I heard them running up the stairs, and crying out—I heard my mother crying out—and Peggotty. Then he was gone;

and the door was locked outside; and I was lying, fevered and hot, and torn, and sore, and raging in my puny way, upon the floor.

Charles Dickens
David Copperfield

We move now to child abuse and neglect, a topic that could in some ways be thought of as an extension of the topic of child custody. The law of abuse and neglect, to be sure, governs the state's response when parents fail to care for or even injure their children. But in practice this turns into a question about custody. At the extremes of abuse and neglect, the question becomes who should have custody instead of the parents. Even where the punishment has been less severe, the question will be what limits should be placed on the parents' custodial authority.

Thus a primary theme of the law of abuse and neglect is the tension between discretion and rules. We will again ask how much discretion judges and other officials need to do good and how rules might be written to keep them from doing harm. But abuse and neglect law brings two new elements to rules and discretion. The first arises because child abuse is in some respects a criminal offense, and even where the offense isn't criminal, it can have consequences that resemble those of criminal offenses. (Most significantly, the state can deprive parents of their children.) Thus this chapter returns us to the theme we discussed in connection with spousal abuse—how far family problems should be handled through the criminal law or even through civil proceedings. In addition, we will encounter a new theme—What does due process require of a legal system responding to abuse and neglect through criminal or quasi-criminal means?

The second new element occurs because the law of abuse and neglect involves more than a simple suit between two litigants before a judge. Rather, it governs several bureaucracies and numerous individuals. One way to limit bureaucratic power is due process. This gives us another reason to take up the theme of due process.

Abuse and neglect law is a fertile and complex source for investigating due process. This is for a reason we are already know from our discussion of rights and neonatal euthanasia. Ordinarily, we think of due process (outside civil litigation) as protecting a single individual against a governmental bureaucracy. But here we have three actors. One is the state. The other two are individuals—the parent and the child—whose interests may be in conflict with each other. Here, then, it can no longer be assumed that increasing due process rights will improve the welfare, autonomy, and power of individuals against the state. Indeed, the state's very purpose in acting is supposed to be to increase the welfare of one individual (the child) against another (the abusive parent).

We begin our investigation with a story that sketches the social problem of child abuse and neglect the system which attempts to respond to parental failures and cruelties. As you read, keep in mind several questions. Are the parents in the story treating their children improperly? Is their behavior so improper that the state ought to abandon its presumption that the family should be autonomous and that parental action is in the child's best interest and intervene to protect the children? Should the state take the children away from their parents? Permanently? Is the state's process a good one? Does it fully protect all the rights and interests of all the private parties and of society at large? Does it operate efficiently? How could it be improved? What role do lawyers play? Do they help the system perform fairly, effectively, and efficiently?

SECTION 1. INTRODUCTION: THE ABUSE AND NEGLECT CASE OF JESSIE BOND

I condemn all violence in the education of a tender soul which is being trained for honor and liberty. There is a sort of servility about rigor and constraint; and I hold that what cannot be done by reason, and by wisdom and tact, is never done by force.

Michel de Montaigne
Of the Affection of Fathers for their Children

This opening section is intended to introduce you—briefly—to the social dimensions of child abuse and neglect, to the structure of abuse and neglect law, and to the child-protection system. Our vehicle for doing so will be the hypothetical case of Jessie Bond. This case cannot be said to be "typical," because abuse and neglect cases vary greatly. However, the case exemplifies some of the salient kinds of abuse and neglect and the stages through which abuse and neglect cases pass.

On June 5, 2006, Jessie Bond's daughter Dorothy Rose was born in the Magdala City Hospital. When Dorothy was born, the obstetrician, Evan Luke, noticed she had symptoms of having been prenatally exposed to drugs. She was lethargic and had a low birth weight, a skull defect, a congenital heart lesion, an abnormal cardiorespiratory pattern, and withdrawal symptoms. Blood and urine tests showed Dorothy had significant traces of cocaine. These tests were first seen by Camilla Lellis, the head nurse in the hospital's maternity ward, and on June 6 she showed the tests to Dr. Luke. Dr. Luke remarked that, like the other 11 percent of the babies born in the state in 2006 exposed to cocaine as fetuses, Dorothy would have an increased chance of retarded growth, feeding problems, behavioral problems, learning disabilities, congenital malformations (particularly of the gastrointestinal and genitourinary tracts), and of dying from sudden-infant-death syndrome.

The Federal Child Abuse Prevention and Treatment Act, 42 USCA § 5101 et seq, conditions federal funds for child-protection projects on state adoption of reporting statutes. Section 11166 of the Hutchins Penal

Code (which follows the California Child Abuse & Neglect Reporting Act, Cal Penal Code §§ 11166 et seq (West 2006)) states:

> (a) Except as provided in subdivision (d), a mandated reporter shall make a report to an agency specified in Section 11165.9 whenever the mandated reporter, in his or her professional capacity or within the scope of his or her employment, has knowledge of or observes a child whom the mandated reporter knows or reasonably suspects has been the victim of child abuse or neglect. The mandated reporter shall make an initial report to the agency immediately or as soon as is practicably possible by telephone and the mandated reporter shall prepare and send, fax, or electronically transmit a written followup report thereof within 36 hours of receiving the information concerning the incident ..... For the purposes of this article, "reasonable suspicion" means that it is objectively reasonable for a person to entertain such a suspicion, based upon facts that could cause a reasonable person in a like position, drawing, when appropriate, on his or her training and experience, to suspect child abuse. For the purpose of this article, the pregnancy of a minor does not, in and of itself, constitute the basis of reasonable suspicion of sexual abuse.
>
> (b) Any child care custodian, health practitioner, or employee of a child protective agency ... who has knowledge of or who reasonably suspects that mental suffering has been inflicted on a child or his or her emotional well-being is endangered in any other way, may report such known or suspected instance of child abuse to a child protective agency....
>
> (e) Any commercial film and photographic print processor who has knowledge of or observes, within the scope of his or her professional capacity or employment, any film, photograph, video tape, negative or slide depicting a child under the age of 16 years engaged in an act of sexual conduct shall report such instance of suspected child abuse....
>
> (g) Any other person who has knowledge of or observes a child whom he or she knows or reasonably suspects has been a victim of child abuse may report the known or suspected instance of child abuse to a child protective agency.

Section 11172 of the Hutchins Penal Code (2006) provides:

> (a) No mandated reporter shall be civilly or criminally liable for any report required or authorized by this article, and this immunity shall apply even if the mandated reporter acquired the knowledge or reasonable suspicion of child abuse or neglect outside of his or her professional capacity or outside the scope of his or her employment. Any other person reporting a known or suspected instance of child abuse or neglect shall not incur civil or criminal liability as a result of any report authorized by this article unless it can be proven that a false report was made and the person knew that the report was false or was made with reckless disregard of the truth or falsity of the report, and any person who makes a report of child abuse or neglect known to be false or with reckless disregard of the truth or falsity of the report is liable for any damages caused .....

Section 11171.2(b) provides:

> Neither the physician-patient privilege nor the psychotherapist-patient privilege applies to information reported pursuant to this article in any court proceeding or administrative hearing.

Section 11165 of the Code defines child care custodian broadly to include, for example, teachers, teacher's aides, a variety of school employees, and people providing day care for children. Section 11165(21) defines health practitioner broadly to include, for example, doctors, dentists, psychiatrists, psychologists, optometrists, nurses, dental hygienists, marriage, family and child counselors, paramedics and religious practitioners who diagnose, examine or treat children.

Ms. Lellis and Dr. Luke were not sure whether using cocaine while pregnant constituted child abuse in Hutchins. Ms. Lellis was uncertain whether to report a conversation she had with Jessie. Shortly after Jessie had arrived in the hospital, Ms. Lellis had stopped by to chat. Jessie had asked whether she could speak confidentially to Ms. Lellis, since some things were worrying her. Ms. Lellis said of course. Jessie said that, in the last few years, she had been living with Alan Kane and that he was a drug dealer. She denied she herself was a drug addict, but she said she had been convicted of possession of crack cocaine and given a suspended sentence. She said one reason she was worried about Alan was that she thought he was sexually abusing her daughter Catherine. She said she wanted help, and asked Ms. Lellis for it. Ms. Lellis believed she could get her into a special hospital program she helped administer that provided psychological counselling and social services to addicted mothers. However, Ms. Lellis was afraid Jessie would be alienated from the program if she found out Ms. Lellis had reported the conversation to the authorities.

Because Ms. Lellis and Dr. Luke were uncertain of their responsibilities under the reporting statute, they went to the hospital administrator's office, which in turn consulted the hospital's lawyer, Tom More. More advised Lellis, Luke, and the hospital that, although the statute did not in specific terms require that evidence of prenatal drug use be reported, the local juvenile courts were treating such behavior as child abuse and that it was becoming local practice to report it. And More advised Lellis that in light of section 11171(b) she should report the conversation she had had with Jessie. More added that, not only did the statute carry criminal penalties for failures to report, but that *Landeros v. Flood*, 551 P2d 389 (Cal 1976), was widely cited for the proposition that someone's failure to report child abuse as required raises a presumption in a tort action by the child that that person has not exercised due care.

Despite More's advice, Lellis told the Department of Social Services (on June 7 by phone and later in writing, as the statute required) only that blood tests indicated Dorothy had been exposed to cocaine. In addition, the hospital concluded Dorothy's condition required that she be kept in the hospital, especially since they doubted Jessie's ability to care for any child, much less one with Dorothy's problems. A Hutchins statute permits a hospital to detain a child when it "believes the facts so warrant." The hospital thus placed a "twenty-four hour hold" on Dorothy.

After Lellis's report about Dorothy, the Department began an investigation. Responsibility for the investigation was assigned to Louise Marillac, a social worker, on June 9. However, Marillac had several other cases to investigate that seemed more pressing, since Marillac assumed Dorothy would be safe in the hospital. On June 14, Marillac opened her investigation: This is her report:

> I first visited the Magdala City Hospital and called on Ms. Camilla Lellis, the head nurse in the maternity ward. She showed Dorothy to me. Dorothy is still suffering from the effects of her mother's cocaine use, and her prognosis remains uncertain.
>
> I then went to see Jessie. She lives in a two-bedroom apartment which is an incredible mess. The beds are unmade, the dishes are unwashed, the floors are unswept, garbage litters the floor, bugs crawl everywhere, glass from a broken window lies on the floor of the living room, and drug paraphernalia sits on the bathroom washstand. I looked into the backyard and saw a decomposing cat. Jessie was not home. Ethel Bond, Jessie's mother, was. She is an angry woman. She told me in voluble terms that Jessie had come home from the hospital a few days earlier but had left right away and not returned. Ethel said Jessie had left her three children—Andrew, Bartholomew, and Catherine—in the care of Jessie's boyfriend, Alan Kane. But, Ethel said, Alan is a drug dealer who often stays away from home for hours at a time. When he is at home, he sometimes gets drunk and beats Jessie. Ethel said Jessie is a drug addict who had been in several detoxification programs but had always gone back to drugs. Ethel had been obliged to take care of the children, as has often happened in the past. She said her daughter had always been irresponsible and hard to live with, and if it weren't for her grandchildren, she would be done with Jessie.
>
> At this point, Jessie walked in. When she discovered who I was, she was belligerent and said furiously that she was a good mother who loved her children and took good care of them. When I told her we had proof Dorothy tested positive for cocaine, she explained that the night before Dorothy's birth, she felt extremely uncomfortable and wanted to "get my pregnancy over with." Following advice she had heard on the street, she smoked some crack to bring on labor and anesthetize herself to the pain of childbirth.
>
> When I told Jessie her mother had said she had left the children uncared for, she told me that Alan was perfectly capable of taking care of the children, whom he loved as though they were his own. When I told Jessie her mother said she was a drug addict, Jessie denied it and said Ethel was always trying to alienate the children from her and Alan. She loudly denied Alan was a drug dealer. Then Ethel said Jessie knew perfectly well Alan had been sexually molesting Catherine for the last two years. Jessie hotly denied this.

> While Jessie and Ethel were fighting, I got Catherine off into a corner to ask her a few questions. I asked her whether everything was O.K. at home. She said it was. I asked her whether she liked Alan. She said she did, but she didn't seem to mean it. I asked her whether Alan sometimes touched her in ways she didn't like. She said he didn't. I told her it was important to tell me the truth, whatever she had promised anybody else about keeping secrets. Catherine then started to cry.
>
> At that moment, Alan walked in. Jessie told him that I was a social worker and that Ethel had accused him of sexually abusing Catherine. Alan became dangerously angry and told me I'd better clear out if I didn't want big trouble. The situation had clearly become impossible, so I left. I reported everything to my supervisor, Paula Vincent. She and I agreed the children needed to be gotten out of the household quickly. We thought about exercising our power to remove children from their home without a judicial order, but we weren't sure we met the two requirements that Hutchins imposes on such removals: the child must be in imminent danger and there can be no time to get a court order.
>
> Happily, we got a court order quickly from Judge John Capistran. Taking the court order, I went with two police officers to Jessie's house and removed all three children. I told her the children were being taken into protective custody on an emergency basis until there could be a hearing. The next day Catherine was examined by a doctor, who found no evidence of sexual abuse.

A few days later, Catherine was examined by Al Liguori, a child psychologist. This is his report:

> I began with a free play period in which I observed Catherine playing with toys and dolls. This was to allow Catherine time to relax. Next, I gave her anatomically correct dolls and asked her to undress them and name their body parts. This allowed me to learn her terminology in order to facilitate clear communication. I then asked her to describe different types of touching—nice, not nice, or confusing—using the dolls as models. Next, I asked her to name the dolls and to name one of the dolls Alan. I then tried to get Catherine to re-enact the instances of abuse with the dolls, but she was not yet able to do this. I also used hypothetical and multiple-choice questions to assist her in her disclosures. I assured her that, whatever Alan may have told her, she would be doing the right thing by telling me about what he had done to her.
>
> Having set the stage, I asked Catherine whether Alan had ever touched her in a way she didn't like. She said no. I asked her if she knew what it meant to tell the truth. When she said she did, I reminded her I wanted her to tell the truth to me and that nothing bad would happen to her if she did. She still said Alan hadn't molested her. I then reminded her that, when she played with the dolls, the Alan doll had touched the Catherine doll in several ways. I said, "Alan kissed you, didn't he?" She said yes. I said, "He took your clothes off, didn't he?" She said yes. Further questions and answers along this line, and Catherine's play with dolls, show that Alan has for several years been molesting Catherine and that the molestation included fondling, kissing,

and oral sex. In particular, Catherine could describe each kind of abuse with some particularity.

Questions of this kind may seem overly directive to lawyers. But they may be necessary to detect sexual abuse:

> Since children are often very reluctant to talk about the matters in issue, the interviewer applies a degree of coaxing and pressure on the child to overcome this reticence. This encouragement to answer may involve leading or hypothetical questions or questions designed to elicit a different answer to one already given. It is felt by the clinic that such pressure is necessary to enable the child finally to make statements against another family member; as one of the clinic staff has put it, it is necessary to match the trauma which the child has suffered through the abuse by placing equal pressure on the child to talk about what occurred.

Douglas and Willmore, *Diagnostic Interviews as Evidence in Cases of Child Sexual Abuse*, 17 Fam L 151 (1987), quoted in Robert J. Levy, *Using "Scientific" Testimony to Prove Child Sexual Abuse*, 23 Fam L Q 383, 399 (1989).

My diagnosis is confirmed by the fact Catherine seems to be describing a series of incidents. "Since so much intrafamilial and sexual abuse involves a progression of acts over time, from fondling to oral contact, to penetration, a young child's description of such a sequence would raise the index of suspicion that the incidents really did occur." Mary de Young, *A Conceptual Model for Judging the Truthfulness of a Young Child's Allegations of Sexual Abuse*, 56 Am J Orthopsychiatry 553, 553 (1983). In addition, Catherine is the kind of child who is especially likely to have been sexually abused. Such children "would include a young child who has little accurate sexual knowledge, has few self-protective coping skills, has been sexually abused before, has a step-father living in the home, or has a weak or conflictual bond with the mother." Id at 557.

It is true Catherine has often denied she has been abused. But this is in fact one of the characteristics of the "sexual abuse accommodation syndrome," several of whose characteristics Catherine also displays. This syndrome is explained in layman's terms in *People v. Bowker*, 249 Cal Rptr 886, 888 (Cal App 4 Dist 1988):

> Stage one is secrecy, an element inherent in the adult-child relationship, where a child understands certain things should not be disclosed. Stage two is helplessness, the absence of power a child has in a relationship with a parental figure or trusted adult. The first two stages are present in every child and establish a child's potential to become a victim of sexual abuse. Stages three through five occur as the result of abuse. Entrapment and accommodation, the third stage, occurs after the child fails to seek protection. Stage four, delayed disclosure, occurs when the child tells someone about the abuse. In retraction, the final stage, the child denies abuse has occurred.

> Not only is delayed disclosure an aspect of the syndrome, so also is conflict and unconvincing exposure. Catherine presents the classic elements of this syndrome. And it is not surprising that Catherine won't tell people what Alan did to her. Alan may well have threatened her if she did tell anyone, or she may have felt ashamed of what had happened, or she may have believed it was her fault. Nor would it be surprising if she recanted. Fear of Alan, negative reactions from her family, and the unpleasantness of legal proceedings all might encourage her to do so.

After talking with the psychologist, Catherine was interviewed by a medical social worker and a juvenile division police officer. Catherine repeatedly denied that she had been sexually abused.

The Department of Social Services and the local prosecutor now had to decide which category of abuse and neglect law to use. First, the department had to decide whether to use the criminal law. First, child abuse might violate generally applicable provisions of the criminal law, particularly statutes criminalizing assault, homicide, and sexual molestation. The tendency, however, is not to use such provisions unless the assault is serious. Second, child abuse might violate criminal provisions written expressly to prohibit cruelty to children. Third, child abuse might violate statutes intended to protect children from sexual abuse, including statutory rape laws and statutes prohibiting incest.

Less drastically, the department could proceed civilly. It could petition a court to find that Catherine had been abused or neglected and that the court therefore had jurisdiction to issue orders to protect her. These could range from orders removing Catherine from Jessie's home to orders requiring that Jessie have various social services.

The department's least drastic alternative was to ask Jessie to ask for help. Where the department's services are voluntarily requested, no court order is necessary. One scholar estimates that

> [p]robably more parents seek help from the child welfare system than are coerced into accepting it.... Sometimes the parent cannot obtain the help—housing, daycare, a homemaker—necessary to continue caring for the child at home. Sometimes the parent cannot cope with the child's disability or behavior problem. Sometimes the parent decides, for reasons good or bad, that he is unwilling or unable to care for the child at present. And sometimes the request for placement represents a plea bargain of sorts, in which the parent agrees to placement rather than contest an imminent abuse or neglect action.

Marsha Garrison, *Child Welfare Decisionmaking: In Search of the Least Drastic Alternative*, 75 Geo L J 1745, 1807 (1987).

Another category of statutes, while not strictly part of abuse-and-neglect law, shares some of its characteristics. One example is explained by the court in *In the Interest of Polovchak*, 432 NE2d 873, 877 (Ill App 1981):

> Section 2–3(a) of the Juvenile Court Act (the Act) defines a minor otherwise in need of supervision as, *inter alia*, "any minor under 18

> years of age who is beyond the control of his parents, guardian or other custodian." Allegations that a minor is otherwise in need of supervision must be proven at an adjudicatory hearing by a preponderance of the evidence. If the court finds that the minor is a person in need of supervision and that it is in the best interest of the minor and the public that he be made a ward of the court, the court shall adjudge the minor a ward and proceed to a dispositional hearing.
>
> At proceedings under the Act, the minor and his parents have the right to be present, to be heard, to present evidence material to the proceedings, to cross-examine witnesses, to examine pertinent court files and records, and to be represented by counsel.

As Professor Clark cogently explains, these statutes have been widely criticized:

> A fair sample of the criticism would include assertions that the statutes are so general that they permit all sorts of harmless conduct to be prosecuted; that the courts process as CHINS [children in need of supervision] or PINS [persons in need of supervision] children who should be handled as either neglected or delinquent; conversely that these children are treated like delinquents with respect to disposition; that the courts permit the proceedings to be used as a threat or as punishment for the child without making an investigation of the causes and circumstances of the child's conduct, the implication being that the fault often lies with the parents rather than the child; that the remedies available to and applied by the courts are not effective, or harm rather than help the child; and that the ungovernable child should be a responsibility of other community organizations or of the schools rather than the courts.

1 Homer H. Clark, Jr., *The Law of Domestic Relations in the United States* 617 (West, 1987). Professor Clark nevertheless finds "logic to providing state support for parental authority. In other contexts the law places heavy responsibility upon parents.... It is hardly unreasonable for the state to provide such remedies as it can to help parents meet these responsibilities."

To help it decide which choice to select, the Department of Social Services prepared a case assessment which included a family history, a statement of the different versions of the family's situation, and an evaluation of Jessie Bond's ability to care for her children. The family history said Jessie was born April 13, 1980, in Magdala, in the state of Hutchins. On November 30, 1996, when she was sixteen, she had her first child, whom she called Andrew X. Bond. Despite his birth, Jessie eventually finished high school. Shortly after she did, on August 24, 1998, her second child, Bartholomew Nathanael, was born. On November 25, 2000, a third child, Catherine Alexandra, was born. Jessie did not know where any of the fathers of her children were except Alan (who was Dorothy's father). After Jessie graduated from high school, she occasionally held part-time jobs, but her income came primarily from AFDC. She and her children had moved repeatedly from apartment to apartment. The three children did not seem to be in particularly bad health, but Andrew had missed a good deal of school. All the children said they loved their mother and Alan and did not want to be separated from them.

The department concluded it was more important to help Jessie and her family than prosecute them. Jessie clearly was not going to ask for help. It seemed even the threat of prosecution would not drive her to doing so. Since this was not a case in which PINS jurisdiction was appropriate, the department was left with the alternative of a civil proceeding against the parents. The department then had to decide what approach that proceeding should take. Essentially, there were three choices: to try to provide the family with services that would help them solve their problems, to remove the children from their home but provide services that would help the parents solve their problems so the children could return, and to remove the children with the expectation of terminating parental rights.

Although the department doubted that the many problems of Jessie's family could be solved, it believed families should be preserved whenever possible. The department thus chose the second alternative. It forwarded its recommendation to the district attorney's office, since that office would be responsible for litigating the case. That office had also learned of the case from the police investigation. The district attorney reviewed the record and considered whether to bring criminal prosecutions. Two memoranda were written on that subject.

MEMORANDUM

TO: The District Attorney

FROM: Laetitia Minton, Assistant District Attorney

DATE: July 27, 1990

RE: Prosecutions of Jessie Bond & Alan Kane

I favor prosecutions in these two cases. These parents have both abused and neglected their children. Jessie abused Dorothy by taking drugs before Dorothy was born; Alan abused Catherine by sexually molesting her. Both neglected all the children by failing to provide proper care. However, I am arguing here only for criminal prosecution on the abuse charges.

At heart, my reasons for favoring prosecution are those I surveyed in my memorandum to you on prosecuting A.B. Shrode for spouse abuse [see Chapter 3]. I incorporate that memo by reference.

I favor prosecutions because they are demanded under each of the rationales for criminal punishment. The first of these rationales is retribution. "The retributive view rests on the idea that it is right for the wicked to be punished: because man is responsible for his actions, he ought to receive his just deserts." Herbert L. Packer, *The Limits of the Criminal Sanction* 37 (Stan U Press, 1968). Child abuse is particularly wicked, for child abusers are the very people responsible for the children who are abused, and they are exploiting the weakness of children and the strength of their position. These factors combine to justify retribution or even command it.

The second and third rationales for criminal punishment are general and specific deterrence. The tendency has been not to prosecute child-abuse cases. This has sent just the wrong message. Child abusers may not be altogether rationally calculating people, but they must still be affected by knowing that abusers risk jail and disgrace. Even if child abusers are impervious to such disincentives, prosecutions could help deter people by operating at a deeper, earlier level. As Professor Packer wrote,

> The existence of a "threat" helps to create patterns of conforming behavior and thereby to reduce the number of occasions on which the choice of a criminal act presents itself.... [F]requently ... we automatically and without conscious cognition follow a pattern of learned behavior that excludes the criminal alternative without our even thinking about it. Indeed, the arguments for the efficacy of deterrence may become stronger the more one departs from a rational free-will model and the more one accepts an unconsciously impelled, psychological determinism as an accurate description of human conduct.... Guilt and punishment are, after all, what the superego is all about.

The fourth rationale for criminal punishment is incapacitation. If a parent is in jail, he cannot abuse his children. If the "risks of reabuse ... are high," incapacitation seems desirable. The practice has often been to remove children from their homes to protect them from their abusers. It will often be preferable to remove the abuser from the home while leaving the children, at least where another parent can care for them. This promotes the children's crucial interest in stability.

The fifth rationale for criminal punishment is rehabilitation. I would not argue that prosecution or even jail by itself will rehabilitate abusers. But criminal prosecutions can help start people down the road to rehabilitation by forcing them to realize that they have done something wrong. Further, many abusers will not undertake serious therapy until compelled to do so by a criminal prosecution.

In any event, the tendency of the law is and should be toward intervention to protect children from prenatal drug abuse and sexual abuse. It has been estimated that the former problem affects 375,000 babies a year, and jurisdictions have responded in several ways. *In re Smith*, 492 NYS2d 331, 335 (Fam Ct 1985), for example, "holds that an unborn child is a 'person,' and, thereby, entitled to the protection" of the abuse and neglect laws such that the mother's prenatal alcohol use constituted neglect. *In re Baby X*, 293 NW2d 736, 739 (Mich App 1980), reasoned, "Since prior treatment of one child can support neglect allegations regarding another child, ... prenatal treatment can be considered probative of a child's neglect as well." The court thus held "that a newborn suffering narcotics withdrawal symptoms as a consequence of prenatal maternal drug addiction may properly be considered a neglected child. . . ." Illinois defines as a neglected or abused minor "any newborn infant whose blood or urine contains any amount of a controlled substance. . . ." 705 Ill Comp Stat 405/2–3(c) (2005). At least one mother has been convicted of two felony counts of delivering a controlled substance to her child through the umbilical cord. (The theory of the prosecution apparently was that that delivery was made in the time between the child's birth and the cutting of the umbilical cord. The conviction was reversed on appeal. *Johnson v. State*, 602 S2d 1288 (Fla 1992).)

If this precedent is unpersuasive, hear the mother of a child born with Fetal Alcohol Syndrome:

> Knowing what I know now, I am sure that even when I drank hard, I would rather have been incarcerated for nine months and produce a normal child than bear a human being who would, for the rest of his or her life, be imprisoned by what I had done. I would certainly go to jail for nine months now if it would make Adam whole. For those still outraged at this position, those so sure, so secure in opposition, I say the same thing I say to those who would not allow a poor woman a safe abortion and yet have not themselves gone to adoption agencies and taken in the unplaceable children, the troubled, the unwanted:
>
> If you don't agree with me, then please, go and sit beside the alcohol-affected while they try to learn how to add.

Louise Erdrich, *Foreword*, Michael Dorris, *The Broken Cord* xviii (Harper Perennial, 1989).

As to prosecuting Alan Kane for sexually abusing Catherine, I think little need be said. This is outrageous criminal behavior. The arguments I made above about the purposes of criminal punishment apply with special force to sexual abuse of children under the abuser's care.

True, there are evidentiary difficulties. Catherine has been and presumably will be an equivocal and ambivalent witness. But this can be explained in terms of the abuse-accommodation syndrome. We will need to rely heavily on the psychologist's testimony. The standard test for the admissibility of scientific principles is the *Frye* test, which requires any such principle to be "sufficiently established to have gained general acceptance in the particular field in which it belongs." *Frye v. United States*, 293 F 1013, 1014 (DC Cir 1923). There is precedent holding that evidence about the accommodation syndrome is admissible. *People v. Luna*, 250 Cal Rptr 878 (Cal App 5 Dist 1988); *Keri v. Georgia*, 347 SE2d 236 (Ga App 1986).

In the end, I acknowledge that people abuse children for reasons we do not well understand and that go deep into their social situation and psychological make-up. But I believe that, short of insanity, people are responsible for their acts and that you cannot organize a society on the principle that they aren't. I concede that we do not have irrefutable evidence that criminal punishment deters, but I think we are entitled, in the absence of clear evidence, to act on our best reasoning. And even though I cannot prove criminal prosecution "works," neither can its proponents prove therapy "cures."

In addition, our response to child abuse must emphasize that it is *wrong*. Some of my feelings are captured in this passage:

> If society feels strongly enough about the impropriety of certain conduct, it may choose to express this norm through the criminal law even though the behavior is largely invisible and will be reduced only through effective operation of other institutions of control. Laws against incest and child beating are good examples.... The benefits consist of the value of society in reaffirming certain norms, together with a reinforcement of self-restraint by those who accept society's judgment.

National Commission on Marihuana and Drug Abuse, *Drug Use in America: Problem in Perspective* 255 (1973), quoted in Michael P. Rosenthal, *Physical Abuse of Children by Parents: The Criminalization Decision*, 7 Am J Crim L 141, 146 (1979).

MEMORANDUM

TO: The District Attorney
FROM: Felicity Bold, Assistant District Attorney
DATE: July 31, 1999
RE: Prosecutions of Jessie Bond & Alan Kane

Once again, I'm afraid I have to disagree with Laetitia. I oppose prosecution in these two cases. I too have said what I have to say about prosecutions in family cases in my earlier memo. But, like Laetitia, I have a few further points.

To begin, I will respond to Laetitia's arguments from the rationales for criminal punishment. First, quite apart from my doubts about whether retribution justifies punishment, I doubt it justifies punishing child abusers. Laetitia's quote says that "because man is responsible for his actions, he ought to receive his just deserts." But, while child abuse is horrible, I doubt that most child abusers are fully responsible for what they do. Many child abusers were themselves abused as children. This is part of the larger argument that most child abuse is motivated by psychological forces beyond the control of the abusers. That is vividly illustrated by this case. Jessie passed cocaine on to Dorothy not because she wanted to hurt Dorothy, but because she could not control her own addiction to cocaine. Alan sexually abused Catherine not because he wanted to hurt her, but because he was psychologically disturbed and sexually dysfunctional.

My response to Laetitia's general-deterrence argument builds on what I have just said. As Professor Packer noted, "[W]here the prohibited conduct is the expression of sufficiently compulsive drives, deterrence is made possible, if at all, only by cruelly rigorous enforcement, widespread repression, and a considerable drain on human and economic resources...." Herbert L. Packer, *The Limits of the Criminal Sanction* 45 (Stan U Press, 1968). Child abuse is probably just such a case, for, as Professor Rosenthal writes, "[M]uch child abuse appears to be impulsive rather than planned behavior. Certainly, extreme stress contributes to a good deal of abuse...." Michael P. Rosenthal, *Physical Abuse of Children by Parents: The Criminalization Decision*, 7 Am J Crim L 141, 150 (1979). And about specific deterrence, Professor Rosenthal observes, "Commentators on child abuse usually take the view that imprisonment is not likely to deter the convicted abuser from committing further acts of abuse," although he warns that "these views often seem to be impressionistic." He also notes that "it is sometimes said that the risks of reabuse in abusing families are high."

I respect Laetitia's point about incapacitation. And I agree that sometimes the best solution is to remove the abuser from the home. But this can often be done without criminal prosecution. And even where removing the abuser isn't possible, it may still be better for children to remove the children from their home rather than use so draconian an approach as jail. Jail injures children by cruelly separating them from their parent (a separation for which children will often feel responsible).

Finally, like Professor Packer, I see it as a primary objection to "making rehabilitation the primary justification for punishment ... that we do not know how to rehabilitate offenders.... The more we learn about the roots of crime, the clearer it is that they are non-specific, that the social and psychic springs lie deep within the human condition." We know particularly little about rehabilitating child abusers. Professor Rosenthal cites a study which "takes the position that '[W]e know little about the causes and dynamics of child abuse and even less about effective social intervention and treatment.' " While I favor doing everything we can to treat abusers, I doubt we can feel confident enough about our rehabilitative powers to rely on them to justify criminal prosecutions.

More specifically, Laetitia argues that the trend is toward bringing governmental power to bear against women who use drugs and alcohol while pregnant. That may be the trend, but I doubt it is desirable. First, such prosecutions seem incompatible with *Roe v. Wade*. Second, it's wrong to punish people criminally or quasi-criminally for things they can't help, a pregnant addict cannot help taking drugs, especially since treatment for drug addiction can be hard to come by. Third, I am concerned with the precedent such prosecutions and abuse-and-neglect actions set. If we prosecute pregnant women for using drugs, should we also prosecute them for drinking alcohol? For smoking cigarettes? Drinking coffee? Eating a poor diet? Parachute or bungee-jumping? Failing to get prenatal care? Failing to agree to have a Caesarean section where that seemed medically indicated? Failing to agree to *in utero* surgery where that seemed medically necessary? Using prescription drugs that help the mother but damage the fetus? (See *Grodin v. Grodin*, 301 NW2d 869 (Mich App 1980)). Fourth, fear prosecutions and abuse-and-neglect actions will deter pregnant addicts from seeking help. Fifth, even if pregnant women should be subject to criminal or civil sanctions for using drugs, our statute does not proscribe that conduct with enough clarity to give defendants fair notice.

A number of cases support my position. *Reyes v. Superior Court*, 141 Cal Rptr 912, 913 (Cal App 1977), held "that the word 'child' as used in Penal Code section 273a(1) was not intended to refer to an unborn child and that petitioner's prenatal conduct does not constitute felonious child endangering within contemplation of the statute." *Cox v. Court of Common Pleas*, 537 NE2d 721, 725 (Ohio App 1988), held that a juvenile court lacked jurisdiction to "compel a pregnant woman to take action for the alleged benefit of her unborn child."

As to the prosecution for sexual abuse, I have two problems. The first has to do with the quality of the evidence. A review of that evidence suggests Catherine will not make a good witness or even that she will say she was abused. And I distrust the main evidence, the psychologist's report. I am persuaded by Professor Levy's case against such reports. For example, he argues that the "sexual abuse accommodation syndrome" was never intended by its originator, Roland Summit, to be used to diagnose sexual abuse and that "Summit did not compare the proven cases of child sexual abuse in which the syndrome was observed with proven cases in which the syndrome was not observed. Nor did he provide any information about unproven allegation cases or cases involving false allegations in which the child nonetheless exhibited some or all symptoms of the syndrome." Robert J. Levy, *Using "Scientific" Testimony to Prove Child Sexual Abuse*, 23 Fam L Q 383, 393 (1989). Thus a number of courts have refused to allow the syndrome to be used to establish that a child had been sexually abused. Thus the court in *People v. Bowker*, 249 Cal Rptr 886, 891 (Cal App 4 Dist 1988) said, "It is one thing to say that child abuse victims often exhibit a certain characteristic or that a particular behavior is not inconsistent with a child having been molested. It is quite another to conclude that where a child meets certain criteria, we can predict with a reasonable degree of certainty that he or she has been abused." That court spoke of the danger of presenting such evidence to the jury, saying that "the jurors' education and training may not have sensitized them to the dangers of drawing predictive conclusions" and that the jury might not know that "although victims of child abuse generally exhibit a particular type of behavior, that behavior is also found in significant numbers of children who have not been molested."

Professor Levy also argues that the literature "inspires little confidence regarding the validity of *any* proposition concerning the meaning of children's play with anatomically correct dolls," although he acknowledges that the trend seems to be toward admitting testimony about such play. Finally, Professor Levy fears experts on child sexual abuse are over-committed for professional and even economic reasons to discovering instances of sexual abuse. He tells the story of a

> child sexual abuse expert, the supervisor of a medical school evaluation and treatment facility, [who] came to see me.... She was scheduled, she told me, to give a deposition the following week in a classic case: the child had made accusations of sexual abuse as well as accusations of a host of other abnormal behaviors—devil worship, fetishistic and occult

rituals, activities with human excrement. She indicated that she planned to testify only to the child's complaints of sexual abuse and not to the child's other disclosures. When I asked why, she answered that describing all the facts would only undermine the child's credibility. The problem here is not that some professionals may be dishonest; the problem, rather, is that many of these experts are so committed to child protection that neither their judgment nor their statements can be trusted.

My second problem with prosecuting Alan Kane for sexually abusing Catherine echoes the reasons Professor Wald gives for de-criminalizing sexual abuse. He observes that "any intervention, insofar as it requires the child to tell his or her story to the police, welfare workers, and court, may cause more trauma than parental behavior." Michael Wald, *State Intervention on Behalf of "Neglected" Children: A Search for Realistic Standards*, 27 Stan L Rev 985, 1025 (1975). He adds that "criminal prosecution will often result in the father's imprisonment. Several recent reports contend that splitting up the family and imprisoning the father may add to the child's problems. Meaningful treatment has to involve the entire family. In addition, the child may suffer guilt feelings over the parent's imprisonment." He concludes, as I do, that the "availability of neglect proceedings through which the child can be protected negates, from the child's perspective, the need for criminal proceedings."

In the end, I agree with Professor Myers:

> The belief that the legal system can cope with child abuse is unfounded because reliance on the law ignores the deep social and psychological roots of abuse. The legal system has an important role to play, but the ultimate solution lies in a greater understanding of human behavior, a genuine societal commitment to programs aimed at prevention, education and economic equality, and a humane and therapeutically oriented approach to deviant behavior. The law is a blunt and punitive instrument, ill-suited to the achievement of such far-reaching social reorganization.

John E.B. Myers, *The Legal Response to Child Abuse: In the Best Interest of Children?*, 24 J Fam L 149, 179 (1985–86). Thus, like Professor Myers, I would reject

> the punitive, accusatory, stigmatizing atmosphere of the criminal justice system in favor of the positive approach of therapeutic intervention. The result of adopting such an approach should be a substantial reduction in the trauma experienced by children. Rather than spending time and resources preparing children for the rigors of the legal process, energy would be directed toward therapy for the child, the family and the abuser.... [M]ost children would be spared involvement in the criminal system. The need to repeat the story to police officers, social workers, attorneys, judges, grand juries and rooms full of strangers would be eliminated. Gone also would be the ordeal of cross-examination and face-to-face confrontation with the defendant. The healing process would begin immediately, and would not be interrupted by adversary proceed-

ings in which the child becomes the enemy of the defendant, an especially sad result when the defendant is a relative or parent.

On reading these two memos, the district attorney decided not to prosecute Jessie or Alan criminally. Meanwhile, Ms. Marillac (the social worker responsible for the Bond case) had prepared a petition detailing the bases on which the department wanted the court to take jurisdiction over the Bond children. The petition stated numerous grounds: (1) that Jessie had exposed Dorothy to cocaine, (2) that Alan had sexually abused Catherine, (3) that Jessie had failed to prevent Alan from doing so, (4) that the four children were neglected because they were not provided with attentive care and healthy surroundings, and (5) that Jessie was unable, because of her addiction to drugs, to care for her children. The petition alleged that because of these factors there would be a risk of serious harm to the children were they returned home immediately. This petition was written in layman's terms so that Jessie and Alan would understand its meaning. It was served on both of them, and an unsuccessful attempt was made to discover the names of the fathers of the first three children so they could also be notified.

The petition was first considered at a preliminary hearing that Hutchins statutes required whenever a child was removed from home. The state was represented by Laetitia Minton, the assistant district attorney whose memo you just read. She argued that there was probable cause to believe that the petition's allegations were true and that they constituted abuse and neglect. Jessie, who was not represented by counsel, denied all the allegations. Alan was not present. Judge Capistran held that Ms. Minton's showings were successful and that the petition should be filed.

Judge Capistran issued a number of orders. He ordered that custody of the children should temporarily remain with the department (which had placed the children with interim foster parents). He ordered that all the family members be psychologically evaluated and that Jessie and Alan participate cooperatively in the services and programs the department provided. He ordered Jessie to obtain an apartment in which the children might suitably live, to refrain from using any controlled substance, and to submit to regular drug tests. He ordered Alan to refrain from attempting to see Catherine. He ordered the department to provide all services necessary to assist in reunifying the family and to provide for Jessie and Alan to visit the children (excepting Alan's visits to Catherine). As Hutchins statutes provided, he ordered that Jessie be provided with counsel at county expense since she could not afford a lawyer, and he appointed a guardian ad litem to represent the children. Finally, he set trial for September 25.

In mid-September, a pretrial conference was held in which the lawyers agreed on the issues to be addressed at trial but did not agree on any settlement. Jessie's lawyer reported that he had talked to Alan and that Alan had no intention of appearing and did not wish to be represented or to make any claim to custody.

At the trial Ms. Minton sought to prove the factual allegations made in the petition and to show that returning the children to their home would create a reasonably likely risk of harm. She called as witnesses Dr. Luke, Ms. Lellis (the nurse), Ms. Marillac (the social worker), Ethel Bond (Jessie's mother), and Mr. Liguori (the psychologist). She also introduced evidence that Jessie had failed to find a new place to live and had failed some, but not all, of her drug tests.

Jessie's lawyer vigorously cross-examined Ms. Minton's witnesses and called two of Jessie's neighbors and Jessie herself. The neighbors testified that Jessie was a loving mother who cared faithfully for her children. Jessie made a sympathetic impression. She denied that Alan had sexually abused Catherine, much less that she had known about any abuse. She denied she was a drug addict and repeated her explanation of how Dorothy had tested positive for cocaine. She said that she tried to keep the apartment in good shape, but that it was difficult to bring up four children on so little money. Jessie's lawyer introduced evidence that Jessie had kept all her appointments to visit her children and that she was embarked on a drug-treatment program. He also reported that he had attempted to subpoena Alan but he could not locate him. The children's guardian ad litem cross-examined all the witnesses briefly but introduced none of her own.

Judge Capistran held that the state had carried its burden of proof and that the children were abused and neglected. He thus concluded that the court had jurisdiction in the case.

The trial lasted two days. On the third day, a hearing was held to decide what the disposition of the children should be. At this hearing the rules of evidence were relaxed so that, for example, hearsay evidence might be admitted. The state urged that the children be kept in foster care. Jessie's lawyer argued that the children should be returned to Jessie under supervision by the department and with the provision of services to the family, including the services of a visiting nurse and a part-time housekeeper. The guardian ad litem argued that the children should be kept in foster care but that Jessie should be allowed increasingly long visits so that her ties with her children could be maintained (and, in Dorothy's case, created).

Judge Capistran found that the department had made reasonable efforts to return the children to Jessie but that conditions had not changed enough to justify returning the children. He reaffirmed the orders he had made at the preliminary hearing and stipulated that the department should continue to provide Jessie with a drug-treatment program. He also ordered the department to have Catherine participate in group counselling for sexually abused girls and to have Dorothy provided treatment for her prenatal ingestion of drugs.

As you will recall, Jessie's children were placed in the custody of the Department of Social Services. Children can come into the care of the state when they are orphaned, when they are abandoned by their parents, when the state removes them from their parents' home to prevent parental abuse or neglect, and when the state terminates their parents' rights. It is now often thought that institutionalization harms children, and thus the state generally attempts to place children in foster homes if adoptive parents cannot readily be found or if the children might eventually be returned to their parents.

After the court proceeding about which you have just read, there were periodic review hearings according to a schedule set in Hutchins statutes. Those statutes (which responded to requirements in the federal Adoption Assistance and Child Welfare Act of 1980, 42 USC § 675 (1997)) provide that the hearings should inquire into whether the case plan established at the disposition phase of the trial is being complied with and whether it should be amended. At the first of these hearings, Ms. Marillac testified that the children had been transferred from their interim foster homes into long-term foster homes. The two boys were kept together, Catherine was in another home, and Dorothy had been released from the hospital into a third home.

Eventually, the department concluded that the children would never be able to return to Jessie's care. The department therefore decided to propose that Jessie's and Alan's parental rights be terminated. The Hutchins Juvenile Code permitted termination of the rights of parents in the following circumstances, among others:

> § 712A.19b(3)(b)(ii). A parent who had the opportunity to prevent the physical injury or physical or sexual abuse failed to do so and the court finds that there is a reasonable likelihood that the child will suffer injury or abuse in the foreseeable future if placed in the parent's home.
>
> § 712A.19b(3)(c). The parent was a respondent in a proceeding brought under this chapter, 182 or more days have elapsed since the issuance of an initial dispositional order, and the court, by clear and convincing evidence, finds ... [that]
>
> > (1) The conditions that led to the adjudication continue to exist and there is no reasonable likelihood that the conditions will be rectified within a reasonable time considering the age of the child.
>
> § 712A.19b(3)(d). The parent, without regard to intent, fails to provide proper care or custody for the child and there is no reasonable expectation that the parent will be able to provide proper care and custody within a reasonable time considering the age of the child.

The department sent its recommendation to the district attorney's office, which concurred. Ms. Minton met with Ms. Marillac and reviewed the case record. To help her decide which grounds to emphasize, what her strategy ought to be, which witnesses to call, and what evidence to introduce, she prepared the following notes:

Code §	Supporting Facts	Evidence	Witnesses
(b)(ii)	Jessie knew Alan was sexually molesting Catherine	Marillac report	Ms. Lellis

Code §	Supporting Facts	Evidence	Witnesses
	Catherine sexually molested	Psych report	Mr. Liguori Ethel Bond Catherine?
(c)(I)	In-patient drug treatment failed. Positive drug screens. Has not yet found suitable housing. Neither Jessie nor Alan has participated in psych. evaluation as court ordered.	Marillac report	Ms. Marillac
(3)(d)	Jessie exposed Dorothy to cocaine.	Medical reports	Nurse/Doctor
	Jessie living with known drug dealer.	Police reports	Jessie Ms. Lellis Ethel Bond
	Jessie convicted for possession of crack.	Police report	Find out!
	Filthy house. Drug paraphernalia scattered around house. Children left alone. Jessie a coke addict.	Marillac report	Ms. Marillac /Ethel Bond

Ms. Minton decided to emphasize the third statutory ground: that Jessie Bond had failed to provide proper care and custody. Jessie's problems with drug addiction, her frequent unexplained absences from her house and children, and the unhealthy conditions in the house seemed to Ms. Minton an adequate basis for termination on proper-care-and-custody grounds. She was reluctant to rest too much on the argument that Jessie had failed to protect Catherine from sexual abuse since it might be hard to prove that Catherine was sexually abused and that Jessie had known about it. And Ms. Minton was reluctant to rest too much on the argument that Jessie had failed to rectify the conditions that led to the original petition, since, although Jessie had not complied with all the court's orders, she had taken the required drug tests and kept pretty much to the visitation schedule.

Ms. Minton then talked with the witnesses she planned to call in the trial, and she put together the evidence of Jessie's addiction to drugs and her failings as a parent. Ms. Minton asked Ms. Marillac to let her know about any changes in the case. Ms. Minton then prepared for her cross-examination of the expert witnesses at the trial and for anything Jessie's attorney might argue by doing research on the sexual abuse of children and on prenatal exposure to drugs.

One problem confronting Ms. Minton was whether to call Catherine. She felt she should have at least one child testify to the conditions in which the children were being raised, Alan's violent nature, and the frequency with which Jessie absented herself. And Catherine was the most logical witness to testify that Alan had sexually abused her. Ms. Minton talked to the children's attorney and Catherine's therapist. Their advice was equivocal, but it persuaded Ms. Minton that Catherine should be able to testify effectively. Ms. Minton also concluded that Catherine could testify on the stand, and not on videotape or closed-circuit television, especially since the courtroom was small and few people would be present. Ms. Minton arranged for Catherine to wait in a small office near the courtroom so she could be separated from the other witnesses, for Catherine to testify first in the morning, so she wouldn't have to endure a long wait, for Catherine to be allowed to take frequent breaks, and for Catherine's attorney to bring her to the courtroom the day before the trial to familiarize her with the room.

Ms. Minton then drafted opening and closing statements and prepared notes for her direct and cross examinations. Particularly since this was a jury case, she tried to put the opening statement in simple, clear language. She also tried to adhere to the requirement that it not be argumentative. This was her first draft.

> Good morning members of the jury, your honor, counsel. I am Laetitia Minton. I am from the District Attorney's office, and I am representing the people and the Department of Social Services.
>
> Today you will be hearing testimony about four children: Andrew, Bartholomew, Catherine, and Dorothy Bond. Your decision will be crucial to the lives of these children. I ask that you listen attentively, that you consider all the evidence you hear, and that you refrain from reaching a decision until the end of the trial.
>
> Andrew, Bartholomew, Catherine, and Dorothy are the children of Jessie Bond. Until recently, they lived with Jessie and her boyfriend, Alan Kane. He is Dorothy's father, but the fathers of the other three children are unknown.
>
> You will hear testimony that when Dorothy was born a few months ago, tests showed she had been exposed to cocaine. This was because her mother used crack during her pregnancy. This prenatal exposure to cocaine, you will learn, can cause horrible birth and learning defects. It may affect Dorothy every day of her life.
>
> You will also learn that the children lived with their mother and Mr. Kane in a filthy apartment scattered with broken glass, drug paraphernalia, and trash. You will learn that Ms. Bond often left her children to go out in search of drugs. Sometimes Mr. Kane would care for the four. But sometimes he would fail to do so, and they would be left alone until their grandmother, Ethel Bond, would discover them without food, without diapers, without clean clothes.
>
> And you will hear that Catherine, who is only seven years old, was repeatedly molested sexually by Mr. Kane. Although Ms. Bond was aware of this abuse, she failed to do anything to prevent it. She never called the police, she never called a rape hot line, she never told her doctor, she never left Mr. Kane.
>
> You will make a most important decision about these children. We ask you to serve their best interests by deciding that Jessie Bond's

parental rights to her four children and Alan Kane's rights to Dorothy should be terminated.

The children's attorney, Nicholas Myra, faced several perplexing questions. He was notified by certified mail that a termination petition had been filed. He found himself with many unanswered questions. What harm had the children actually suffered in the past? What harm would they actually suffer if returned home? What were the chances that at least Jessie might escape her drug addiction and become a satisfactory parent? Had the Department of Social Services done all it could to help Jessie and Alan comply with Judge Capistran's orders? What would happen to the children if Jessie's parental rights were terminated? Could the costs to the children of litigation somehow be reduced? What, in sum, were the children's interests?

To help with these questions, Mr. Myra interviewed the children. He called the foster parents and arranged to see the children in their foster homes so that that neutral and unthreatening venue might promote open and frank interviews. He asked the foster parents to prepare the children for his visit so they would not be anxious.

His visit with Catherine began with a conversation about her new kitten and how she liked school. He told her that he understood that she was probably confused and worried about all the things that had already happened to her but that his job was to try to make things less confusing and distressing. He explained he wanted her to understand the purpose of the hearing and to tell him what messages to relay to the judge. He explained that, since being in court can be frightening, he would talk to the judge so she wouldn't have to. He added that there were no right or wrong answers, but that he needed to understand her opinions so that he could best represent her in court.

Catherine was happy in her placement and wanted to stay there "forever." She said she missed her mother "a little bit," but didn't miss Alan, since "he made me feel bad." She did miss her grandmother, however, wanted to see her a lot, and wanted to live with her.

Andrew and Bartholomew told Mr. Myra that they missed their mother very much and wanted to go home. They said they liked their foster mother but loved Jessie much more. At the end of the interview, Mr. Myra asked them if they had any questions. They asked why they couldn't go home. He explained that although their mother loved them very much, she couldn't take care of them right now because she was having a lot of problems.

Mr. Myra's conversations with the foster parents revealed that Catherine's foster parents found her difficult. They expected to care for her for the foreseeable future but not to adopt her. The boys' foster parents were fond of them and hoped to adopt them if everything worked out. Dorothy's foster parents felt they could not say what their relations with her would be. Mr. Myra also talked with Jessie's mother, who said she could not care for of any of the children full-time.

Mr. Myra then reflected that a lawyer's obligation is ordinarily to represent the client's wishes. But these clients were all young enough that their ability to make wise decisions might be doubted. He eventually came down in favor of parental termination, but he decided to recommend that an attempt be made to find an adoptive home where at least the three older children could remain together.

Because the lawyer who had earlier represented Jessie and Alan was no longer available, a new lawyer, Breton Ives, had been appointed. He asked the couple for a copy of the termination petition. He then asked for a general description of what had happened. They told him about Dorothy's birth, about her exposure to cocaine because of Jessie's use of crack, about the allegations of sexual abuse, and about the social worker's visit to their home. He let them answer in a free-flowing, if disjointed and prolonged, narrative, asking only a few open-ended questions to help them relate the full story.

Mr. Ives then led the two through a detailed chronological overview of their family history. He asked them about the fathers of Andrew, Bartholomew, and Catherine, about Alan's relationship with the children, and about Jessie's and Alan's use of drugs. He asked specific questions designed to clarify obscure points.

He then asked them how they wanted things to come out. They told him they wanted all the children returned, although they said that if that were impossible, they would like their children to be able to visit them at home with increasing frequency.

This interview convinced Mr. Ives that a lawyer representing both Jessie and Alan would have a conflict of interest. He thought that Jessie's best defense would be that she was relatively innocent, that Alan was to blame for Catherine's sexual abuse and Jessie's drug problems, and that without Alan, Jessie might be a satisfactory mother. He told them he would represent Jessie and request another attorney for Alan.

At a subsequent meeting, Jessie told Mr. Ives that Alan probably had abused Catherine but that she had not known for sure and that she was frightened into silence because of Alan's quick temper and violent ways. Mr. Ives concluded that the best defense on this score was that Jessie was simply seeking to protect herself and her children from violence and that a modestly educated, unemployed woman with three children and few resources cannot easily leave the man she is living with. Mr. Ives asked Jessie for the names of family or friends who could testify to Alan's dangerous character.

As to her failure to change, Jessie said she had taken the drug tests the court had ordered, although she had failed some of them. She repeated several times that she really wanted to get free of drugs but that the treatment programs just hadn't been successful. She said she had been unable to follow up on one program with the required outpatient counselling because of a lack of transportation. She said she had not undergone the psychological evaluation that was a prerequisite to another program because Ms. Marillac had failed to set up the necessary appointment. She said she had stayed with Alan because she couldn't find suitable housing away from him. She said, however, that Alan had now left her. She explained that Ms. Marillac was supposed to have helped her find new housing but hadn't and that, having lost her AFDC when she lost her children, she couldn't afford better housing.

Mr. Ives decided to make two arguments: First, that Catherine had not actually been sexually abused, that even if she had been, Jessie had not known about it, and that even if she had known she could not have been expected to prevent it. Second, that Jessie had tried to comply with all the court's orders and to make herself a suitable parent, that whatever failures she had suffered were due to her poverty and the inattentiveness of the Department of Social Services, that with help she could overcome her problems, and that with Alan's departure the conditions in her home would not harm the children.

Mr. Ives sought to strengthen his case by putting Jessie directly in contact with a private agency that he thought could help her find housing. He also made an appointment for her to have a psychological evaluation that might provide evidence of her parental capacities. And he encouraged her to enroll in another drug-treatment program.

When Jessie left his office, Mr. Ives made a list of things to do. The list included talking to a child psychologist about interviewing victims of sexual abuse, doing research on the reliability of children as witnesses in sexual abuse cases, trying to locate the fathers of the children, hiring an expert witness who might testify that Catherine had not been sexually assaulted, assembling evidence that Jessie had tried to comply with the court's orders, talking to people Jessie had said could testify to Alan's violent temper, and preparing a witness list.

Mr. Ives then decided to develop his arguments by drafting a closing argument. This was his first draft:

> Today we are here to decide whether Jessie Bond's parental rights should be terminated. Today you will decide whether Jessie will lose Andrew, Bartholomew, Catherine, and Dorothy. Your decision will affect Jessie and her children for the rest of their lives.
>
> The burden is on the prosecution to prove by clear and convincing evidence that there are legal grounds for terminating Jessie's parental rights. But the evidence you have heard does not reach that standard.
>
> The testimony showed that Dorothy Rose, Jessie's newborn daughter, was unfortunately exposed to cocaine before she was born. Everyone agrees this was a terrible thing. But remember Jessie testified that she smoked crack only at the very end of her pregnancy, when it would least affect the growth and development of her child. And remember she used cocaine only because she had wrongly been told it would speed up labor and anesthetize her to the pain of delivery. Remember too that, since her pregnancy, Jessie has worked hard to free herself of drugs. She has entered drug-treatment programs and successfully completed them. But Jessie has not received the help she needs from the Department of Social Services, so she has not always been able to stay free of drugs.

Some of the most disturbing testimony you heard was that Alan was sexually molesting Catherine, that Jessie knew about it, and that she did nothing to stop him. But I ask you to look carefully at that testimony. You will find no convincing evidence that Catherine was actually molested or that Jessie knew about it.

The main testimony that Catherine was molested came from the psychologist, Mr. Liguori. But he didn't ask Catherine what had happened. He told her what had happened and bullied and cajoled her into agreeing. He relies on what he calls the "sexual abuse accommodation syndrome." But we all know that the fact that Catherine may have some characteristics in common with sexually abused children does not prove she was sexually abused, any more than the fact that Catherine has a cough means she has tuberculosis. In fact, Mr. Liguori seems to be a psychologist who finds sexual abuse wherever he looks. Each of the fourteen times he has testified in court, he has testified for the prosecution that a child was sexually abused. He does this even though he has no special training in the sexual abuse of children.

Even if Alan did abuse Catherine (and remember no one has proved that he did), what evidence is there that Jessie knew about it? The only testimony seems to be from Jessie's mother. And Jessie and her mother have been on bad terms for a long time.

Even if Jessie knew something was wrong with the way Alan was treating Catherine (and remember no one has shown this), what should Jessie have done? She was afraid of Alan and of what he might do to her and her children. She relied on Alan's financial support. Maybe this frightened woman who had so few choices in life made the wrong decision, but her attempt to do what she thought was best should not be turned into grounds for taking away her children forever.

Today, it is not our job to punish, but to cure. How can we best help these four children pursue a happy, healthy life? What are their best interests? In the end, what is best for children is to be with their mother, to maintain their ties to the person who is most important in their lives. Jessie has problems and will need help solving them. She has already begun to solve them on her own. And—what is most important—she is a loving parent. She deserves a chance to be one, and her children deserve the chance to have her. Let Jessie, Andrew, Bartholomew, Catherine, and Dorothy be a family again.

Having this closing argument to guide him, Mr. Ives prepared notes for his cross-examination of Mr. Liguori. Mr. Ives sought to ask only questions to which he knew the answer and which did not invite the witness to expound broadly, for he remembered the famous story of the cross-examiner who had violated those rules:

Cross-examiner: You say my client bit off the plaintiff's ear?

Witness: Yes.

Cross-examiner: Did you actually see him do it?

Witness: No.

Cross-examiner: Then how can you possibly say he bit it off?

Witness: I saw him spit it out.

Among the questions Mr. Ives prepared were these: Mr. Ives, isn't it true that you have testified in fourteen sexual abuse cases? And that all fourteen times were for the prosecution?

Mr. Ives, are you a child psychologist? Isn't it also correct that you have had no special training in child sexual abuse? That you have never written an article on child sexual abuse? That you've never taught a course on child sexual abuse? You don't even specialize in child sexual abuse, do you? Isn't it true that most of your cases concern mental illness in children, not sexual abuse?

Isn't it correct that you base your opinion that Catherine was sexually abused on the fact she displayed some characteristics of the so-called "sexual abuse accommodation syndrome"? Isn't it true that child psychologists disagree about how to identify a child who has been sexually abused? And isn't it true that many psychologists discourage using the accommodation syndrome to diagnose sexual abuse?

Isn't it true that children commonly associate dolls with playing? And that they associate dolls with fantasy? But isn't it true that you used dolls in your interview with Catherine? And isn't it right that you told Catherine to call one of the dolls Alan? That you didn't give her a chance to name them? That she didn't come up with the idea of naming one of them Alan? That you tried to get Catherine to reenact any abuse that had occurred? Didn't she refuse to do so at first? And isn't it true that when you asked her if Alan had ever touched her in a way she didn't like, she said no? And that even after you discussed telling the truth with her, she still said Alan hadn't hurt her? That Catherine only admitted to any abuse when you asked the leading question, "Alan kissed you, didn't he?" And isn't it true that you failed to videotape this interview with Catherine?

At the termination hearing, Ms. Minton called Ms. Marillac as her leading witness. Ms. Marillac said Jessie had entered an in-patient drug-treatment facility but had tested positive for drugs two weeks after her discharge. By the time of the hearing, eight of her drug screens were negative, four were positive for cocaine, and two were positive for barbiturates. Ms. Marillac testified that Jessie, who had apparently left Alan, had moved into an apartment that was smaller than her previous one and in no better shape. She further testified that the children were doing reasonably well in foster care (although Catherine's foster parents had become unable to care for her and she had been transferred to a new set) and that the boys' foster parents wished to adopt them.

On cross-examination by Jessie's lawyer, Ms. Marillac acknowledged that Jessie had kept most of her appointments to visit her children. Jessie testified that she had entered another drug-rehabilitation program. The director of a job-training program testified that Jessie had been doing well in it. Jessie's lawyer argued that these facts and the fact she had left Alan would let her care for her children within six to twelve months. Mr. Myra, the guardian ad litem, argued Jessie's and Alan's parental rights should be terminated. Alan could not be located.

Judge Capistran found that there was clear and convincing evidence the children would not be able to return safely to their mother in the foreseeable future, that Jessie's drug addiction made her an unsuitable parent unable to protect her children from harm, and that there was no prospect she would be able to provide her children a suitable place to live. The judge found that Alan had abandoned the children. He therefore terminated Jessie's and Alan's parental rights. Finally, at a dispositional hearing, Judge Capistran ordered that custody of the children be continued in the department. The department told him that it was working toward the adoption of the two boys and that the two girls would remain with foster parents who intended to keep them permanently but not adopt them.

SECTION 2. DEFINING CHILD ABUSE AND NEGLECT

It is curious, the degree—I will not say of actual hardship, but of squalor and neglect—that was taken for granted in upper-class schools of that period. Almost as in the days of Thackeray, it seemed natural that a little boy of eight or ten should be a miserable, snotty-nosed creature, his face almost permanently dirty, his hands chapped, his nails bitten, his handkerchief a sodden horror, his bottom frequently blue with bruises.

George Orwell
Such, Such Were the Joys

A. DRAFTING STATUTORY STANDARDS

"And what does the boy say?" said my aunt. "Are you ready to go, David?"

I answered no, and entreated her not to let me go. I said that neither Mr. nor Miss Murdstone had ever liked me, or had ever been kind to me.... I said that I had been more miserable than I thought anybody could believe who only knew how young I was. And I begged and prayed my aunt ... to befriend and protect me, for my father's sake.

"Mr. Dick," said my aunt; "what shall I do with this child?"

Mr. Dick considered, hesitated, brightened, and rejoined, "Have him measured for a suit of clothes directly."

"Mr. Dick," said my aunt; triumphantly, "give me your hand, for your common sense is invaluable."

Charles Dickens
David Copperfield

Although the case of Jessie Bond and her children was not unusual, it came to the attention of an organization of parents who had had dealings with the Hutchins Department of Social Services, an organization of foster parents, an organization of social workers, and an organization of lawyers who regularly served as guardians *ad litem* in abuse and neglect cases. All these groups felt the process by which the Bond case was handled was less than perfect. All were interested in what kind of due process protection should be provided in abuse and neglect cases. Because of the publicity surrounding several nationally publicized abuse or neglect cases, the discontent with the Bond case eventually came to the attention of the Social Welfare Committee of the Hutchins Senate. That committee has undertaken to review the Hutchins abuse and neglect statute. You have been appointed counsel to that committee and been asked to draft an ideal statute as a starting point for discussion.

(1) The Scope of the Social Problem

To get some idea of the extent of the social problem of abuse and neglect, you first consult National Center on Child Abuse and Neglect, *Study Findings: Study of National Incidence and Prevalence of Child Abuse and Neglect: 1988*. This study attempted to measure the number of abused or neglected children known over the course of a year to child-protective-service agencies, to other investigatory agencies, and to professionals in schools, hospitals, and other "major agencies." The study found that, of all the children in the population,

.25% had been sexually abused.

.35% had been emotionally abused. Specifically, .018% were tied up or confined to an enclosed area, .23% were verbally or emotionally assaulted, and .1% were emotionally abused in other ways.

.91% had been physically neglected. Specifically, .11% were refused health care, .06% received delayed health care, .03% were abandoned, .07% were ejected from their homes, .05% were subjected to some other kind of denial or failure of parental custody, .3% were inadequately supervised, and .35% were physically neglected in other ways.

.46% had been educationally neglected. Specifically, .35% were permitted chronic truancy, .11% were not properly enrolled in school, and .01% were not accorded proper attention to their special educational needs.

.35% had been emotionally neglected. Specifically, .08% were given inadequate nurturance or affection, .04% lived in the presence of chronic or extreme spouse abuse, .07% were encouraged or permitted to use drugs or alcohol, .04% were permitted other maladaptive behavior, .04% were refused psychological care, .04% were given only delayed psychological care, and .09% were subject to some other form of emotional neglect.

.06% had been subject to general or unspecified neglect. This category was "[u]sed for neglect allegations not classifiable elsewhere, for lack of preventive health care, and for unspecified forms of neglect. . . ."

.07% had been subject to other or unspecified maltreatment.

In sum, 1.07% had been abused and 1.59% had been neglected. However, a child who was both abused and neglected was counted in both categories, and a given child could be placed in more than one sub-category. The study concluded that 2.52% of the children in the population had been abused or neglected that year.

The study also provided figures on the seriousness of the abuse or neglect. Of all the children in the population, .002% died of maltreatment. "Injury/impairment was defined as serious when it involved a life-threatening condition, represented a long-term impairment of physical, mental, or emotional capacities, or required professional treatment aimed at preventing such long-term impairment." Serious injury was suffered by .25%. "Moderate injuries/impairments were those which persisted in observable form (including pain or impairment) for at least 48 hours. For example, bruises, depression or emotional distress (not serious enough to require professional treatment), and the like." Moderate injury was suffered by 1.51%. "The nature of the maltreatment itself gave reasonable cause to assume that injury/impairment probably occurred" to .28%. The study estimated that .47% were "endangered but not yet injured/impaired. . . ."

The study found that the child's race or ethnicity had no effect on maltreatment, nor did it matter whether the child lived in an urban or rural county. Girls were likelier to be abused than boys, primarily because girls were likelier to be sexually abused than boys. Older children were likelier to be abused than very young children, but very young children were likelier to die from maltreatment. Children from large families were more likely than children from small families to suffer maltreatment. Family income was the family characteristic most strikingly associated with maltreatment. The study reported that 5.4% of the children from lower-income families (i.e., families with incomes under $15,000) experienced maltreatment, compared with .79% of the children from higher-income families (i.e., families with incomes over $15,000.) Children from lower-income families were 4.5 times as likely to be abused as children from higher-income families. Lower-income children were more than four times as likely as higher-income children to be physically abused or sexually abused and more than five times as likely to be emotionally abused. Lower-income children were about nine times as likely to be neglected, almost twelve times as likely to be physically neglected, almost eight times as likely to be educationally neglected, and more than four times as likely to be emotionally neglected. Children from lower-income families were three times as likely to die from maltreatment, more than six times as likely to be seriously injured, and more than five and a half times as likely to be moderately injured. Finally, there is evidence that children are considerably more likely to be abused by parents' cohabitants than by their own parents. See Margaret F. Brinig and F.H. Buckley, *Parental Rights and The Ugly Duckling*, 1 J L & Fam Stud 41 (1999).

(2) Three Statutes

To get some sense of the problems other people have encountered drafting abuse and neglect statutes and some idea of how they have attempted to solve them, you will study two statutory approaches which represent strongly different attitudes. The first is embodied in two state statutes, the second in a model code, the third in a federal statute.

(a) The Broad Grant of Authority

MICHIGAN CODE, SECTION 712A.2 (2006)

Sec. 2. The [Family division of the Circuit Court] has the following authority and jurisdiction:

(b) Jurisdiction in proceedings concerning a juvenile under 17 years of age found within the county:

(1) Whose parent or other person legally responsible for the care and maintenance of the juvenile, when able to do so, neglects or refuses to provide proper or necessary support, education, medical, surgical, or other care necessary for his or her health or morals, who is subject to a substantial risk of harm to his or her mental well-being, who is abandoned by his or her parents, guardian, or other custodian, or who is without proper custody or guardianship. As used in this sub-subdivision:

(A) "Education" means learning based on an organized educational program that is appropriate, given the age, intelligence, ability, and psychological limitations of a juvenile, in the subject areas of reading, spelling, mathematics, science, history, civics, writing, and English grammar.

(B) "Without proper custody or guardianship" does not mean a parent has placed the juvenile with another person who is legally responsible for the care and maintenance of the juvenile and who is able to and does provide the juvenile with proper care and maintenance.

(2) Whose home or environment, by reason of neglect, cruelty, drunkenness, criminality, or depravity on the part of a parent, guardian, nonparent adult, or other custodian, is an unfit place for the juvenile to live in.

(3) Whose parent has substantially failed, without good cause, to comply with a limited guardianship placement plan described in section 5205 of the estates and protected individuals code . . . regarding the juvenile.

UTAH CODE ANN § 62A–4a–203.5 (2006)

(2) [T]the division shall file a petition for termination of parental rights with regard to:

(a) an abandoned infant; or

(b) a parent, whenever a court has determined that the parent has:

(i) committed murder or child abuse homicide of another child of that parent;

(ii) committed manslaughter of another child of that parent;

(iii) aided, abetted, attempted, conspired, or solicited to commit murder, child abuse homicide, or manslaughter against another child of that parent; or

(iv) committed a felony assault or abuse that has resulted in serious physical injury to another child of that parent, or to the other parent of that child.

(b) The Narrow Grant of Authority

INSTITUTE OF JUDICIAL ADMINISTRATION AND THE AMERICAN BAR ASSOCIATION JUVENILE JUSTICE STANDARDS PROJECT, STANDARDS RELATING TO ABUSE AND NEGLECT

Part I: General Principles

1.1 Family autonomy.

Laws structuring a system of coercive intervention on behalf of endangered children should be based on a strong presumption for parental autonomy in child rearing. Coercive state intervention should occur only when a child is suffering specific harms as defined in Standard 2.1. Active state involvement in child care or extensive monitoring of each child's development should be available only on a truly voluntary basis, except in the situations described by these standards.

1.2 Purpose of intervention.

Coercive state intervention should be premised upon specific harms that a child has suffered or is likely to suffer.

1.3 Statutory guidelines.

The statutory grounds of coercive intervention on behalf of endangered children:

A. should be defined as specifically as possible;

B. should authorize intervention only where the child is suffering, or there is a substantial likelihood that the child will imminently suffer, serious harm;

C. should permit coercive intervention only for categories of harm where intervention will, in most cases, do more good than harm.

1.4 Protecting cultural differences.

Standards for coercive intervention should take into account cultural differences in childrearing. All decisionmakers should examine the child's needs in light of the child's cultural background and values.

1.5 Child's interests paramount.

State intervention should promote family autonomy and strengthen family life whenever possible. However, in cases where a child's needs as defined in these standards conflict with his/her parents' interests, the child's needs should have priority.

1.6 Continuity and stability.

When state intervention is necessary, the entire system of intervention should be designed to promote a child's need for a continuous, stable living environment....

1.8 Accountability.

The system of coercive state intervention should be designed to insure that all agencies, including courts, participating in the intervention process are held accountable for all of their actions.

Part II: Statutory Grounds for Intervention

2.1 Statutory grounds for intervention.

Courts should be authorized to assume jurisdiction in order to condition continued parental custody upon the parents' accepting supervision or to remove a child from his/her home only when a child is endangered in a manner specified in subsections A.-F.:

A. a child has suffered, or there is a substantial risk that a child will imminently suffer, a physical harm, inflicted nonaccidentally upon him/her by his/her parents, which causes, or creates a substantial risk of causing disfigurement, impairment of bodily functioning, or other serious physical injury;

B. a child has suffered, or there is a substantial risk that the child will imminently suffer, physical harm causing disfigurement, impairment of bodily functioning, or other serious physical injury as a result of conditions created by his/her parents or by the failure of the parents to adequately supervise or protect him/her;

C. a child is suffering serious emotional damage, evidenced by severe anxiety, depression, or withdrawal, or untoward aggressive behavior toward self or others, and the child's parents are not willing to provide treatment for him/her;

D. a child has been sexually abused by his/her parent, or a member of his/her household, or by another person where the parent knew or should have known and failed to take appropriate action (alternative: a child had been sexually abused by his/her parent or a member of his/her household, and is seriously harmed physically or emotionally thereby);

E. a child is in need of medical treatment to cure, alleviate, or prevent him/her from suffering serious physical harm which may result in death, disfigurement, or substantial impairment of bodily functions, and his/her parents are unwilling to provide or consent to the medical treatment;

F. a child is committing delinquent acts as a result of parental encouragement, guidance, or approval.

2.2 Need for intervention in specific case.

The fact that a child is endangered in a manner specified in Standard 2.1 A.-F. should be a necessary but not sufficient condition for a court to intervene. To justify intervention, a court should also have to find that intervention is necessary to protect the child from being endangered in the future. This decision should be made in accordance with the standards proposed in Part VI.

Part VI: Dispositions

6.1 Predisposition investigation and reports.

A. Predisposition investigation.

After the court has entered a finding pursuant to Standard 5.4 F. that a child is endangered, it should authorize an investigation to be conducted by the probation department to supply the necessary information for an order of disposition.

B. Predisposition report.

The predisposition report should include the following information:

1. a description of the specific programs and/or placements, for both the parents and the child, which will be needed in order to prevent further harm to the child, the reasons why such programs and/or placements are likely to be useful, the availability of any proposed services, and the agency's plans for ensuring that the services will be delivered;

2. a statement of the indications (e.g., specific changes in parental behavior) that will be used to determine that the family no longer needs supervision or that placement is no longer necessary;

3. an estimate of the time in which the goals of intervention should be achieved or in which it will be known they cannot be achieved.

4. In any case where removal from parental custody is recommended, the report should contain:

a. a full description of the reasons why the child cannot be adequately protected in the home, including a description of any previous efforts to work with the parents with the child in the home, the "in-home treatment programs," e.g., homemakers, which have been considered and rejected, and the parents' attitude toward placement of the child;

b. a statement of the likely harms the child will suffer as a result of removal (this section should include an exploration of the nature of the parent-child attachment and the anticipated effect of separation and loss to both the parents and the child);

c. a description of the steps that will be taken to minimize harm to the child that may result if separation occurs.

5. If no removal from parental custody is recommended, the report should indicate what services or custodial arrangements, if any, have been offered to and/or accepted by the parents of the child.

C. The investigating agency should be required to provide its report to the court and the court should provide copies of such report to all parties to the proceedings.

6.2 Proceeding to determine disposition.

Following a finding pursuant to Standard 5.4 that a child is endangered, the court should, as soon as practicable, but no later than [forty-five] days thereafter, convene a hearing to determine the disposition of the petition. If the child is in emergency temporary custody, the court should be required to convene the hearing no later than [twenty] working days following the finding that the child is endangered....

6.3 Available dispositions.

A. A court should have at least the following dispositional alternatives and resources:

1. dismissal of the case;

2. wardship with informal supervision;

3. ordering the parents to accept social work supervision;

4. ordering the parents and/or the child to accept individual or family therapy or medical treatment;

5. ordering the state or parents to employ a homemaker in the home;

6. placement of the child in a day care program;

7. placement of the child with a relative, in a foster family or group home, or in a residential treatment center.

B. A court should have authority to order that the parent accept, and that the state provide, any of the above services.

C. It should be the state's responsibility to provide an adequate level of services.

6.4 Standards for choosing a disposition.

A. General goal.

The goal of all dispositions should be to protect the child from the harm justifying intervention in the least restrictive manner available to the court.

B. Dispositions other than removal of the child.

In ordering a disposition other than removal of the child from his/her home, the court should choose a program designed to alleviate the immediate danger to the child, to mitigate or cure any damage the child has already suffered, and to aid the parents so that the child will not be endangered in the future. In selecting a program, the court should choose those services which least interfere with family autonomy, provided that the services are adequate to protect the child.

C. Removal.

1. A child should not be removed from his/her home unless the court finds that:

a. the child has been physically abused as defined in Standard 2.1 A., and there is a preponderance of evidence that the child cannot be protected from further physical abuse without being removed from his/her home; or

b. the child has been endangered in one of the other ways specified by statute and there is clear and convincing evidence that the child cannot be protected from further harm of the type justifying intervention unless removed from his/her home.

2. Even if a court finds subsections 1.a. or b. applicable, before any child is removed from his/her home, the court must find that there is a placement in fact available in which the child will not be endangered.

3. The court should not be authorized to remove a child when the child is endangered solely due to environmental conditions beyond the control of the parents, which the parents would be willing to remedy if they were able to do so.

4. Those advocating removal should bear the burden of proof on all these issues.

6.5 Initial plans.

A. Children left in their own home.

Whenever a child is left in his/her own home, the agency should develop with the parent a specific plan detailing any changes in parental behavior or home conditions that must be made in order for the child not to be endangered. The plan should also specify the services that will be provided to the parent and/or the child to insure that the child will not be endangered....

B. Children removed from their homes.

Before a child is ordered removed from his/her home, the agency charged with his/her care should provide the court with a specific plan as to where the child will be placed, what steps will be taken to return the child home, and what actions the agency will take to maintain parent-child ties. Whenever possible, this plan should be developed in consultation with the parent, who should be encouraged to help in the placement....

1. The plan should specify what services the parents will receive in order to enable them to resume custody and what actions the parents must take in order to resume custody.

2. The plan should provide for the maximum parent-child contact possible, unless the court finds that visitation should be limited because it will be seriously detrimental to the child.

3. A child generally should be placed as close to home as possible, preferably in his/her own neighborhood, unless the court finds that placement at a greater distance is necessary to promote the child's well-being. In the absence of good cause to the contrary, preference should be given to a placement with the child's relatives.

6.6 Rights of parents, custodians, and children following removal.

A. All placements are for a temporary period. Every effort should be made to facilitate the return of the child as quickly as possible....

D. Unless a child is being returned to his/her parents, the child should not be removed from a foster home in which he/she has resided for at least one year without providing the foster parents with notice and an opportunity to be heard before a court. If the foster parents object to the removal and wish to continue to care for the child, the child should not be removed when the removal would be detrimental to the child's emotional well-being.

Part VII: Terminations of Parental Rights....

8.2 Voluntary termination (relinquishment).

A. The court may terminate parental rights based on the consent of the parents....

B. The court should accept a relinquishment or voluntary consent to termination of parental rights only if:

1. The parents appear personally before the court in a hearing that should be recorded pursuant to Standard 5.3 C. The court should address the parents and determine that the parents' consent to the termination of parental rights is the product of a voluntary decision. The court should address the parents in language calculated to communicate effectively with the parents and determine:

a. that the parents understand that they have the right to the custody of the child;

b. that the parents may lose the right to the custody of the child only in accordance with procedures set forth in Standard 8.3;

c. that relinquishment will result in the permanent termination of all legal relationship and control over the child....

C. If the court is satisfied that the parents voluntarily wish to terminate parental rights, the court should enter an interlocutory order of termination. Such order should not become final for at least thirty days, during which time the parents may, for any reason, revoke the consent....

E. Regardless of the provisions of Standard 8.2 B. 1.–2., a court should not be authorized to order termination if any of the exceptions in Standard 8.4 are applicable.

8.3 Involuntary termination. . . .

B. Procedure. . . .

2. Petitioner. The following persons are eligible to file a petition under this Part:

a. an agency that has custody of a child;

b. either parent seeking termination with respect to the other parent;

c. a foster parent or guardian who has had continuous custody for at least eighteen months who alleges abandonment pursuant to Standard 8.3 C. 1. c. or a foster parent or guardian who has had continuous custody for at least three years who alleges any other basis for termination;

d. a guardian of the child's person, legal custodian, or the child's guardian ad litem appointed in a prior proceeding.

3. Prosecutor. . . . The prosecutor may refuse to file a petition only on the rounds of legal insufficiency.

4. Parties. The following should be parties to all proceedings to terminate parental rights:

a. the child;

b. the child's parents, guardians, custodian, and, if relevant, any other adults having substantial ties to the child who have been assuming the duties of the caretaking role;

c. the petitioner.

5. Service of summons and petition. . . . The summons should advise the parents of the purpose of the proceedings and of their right to counsel. . . .

7. Appointment of counsel for child. Counsel should also be appointed at public expense to represent the child identified in the petition, as a party to the proceedings. No reimbursement should be sought from the parents or the child for the cost of such counsel, regardless of their financial resources. . . .

11. Appointment of independent experts. Any party to the proceeding may petition the court for appointment of experts, at public expense, for independent evaluation of the matter before the court. . . .

14. Burden of proof. The burden should rest on the petitioner to prove by clear and convincing evidence allegations sufficient to support the petition.

15. Evidence. Only legally relevant material and competent evidence, subject to cross-examination by all parties, may be admissible to the hearing. . . .

16. Findings. If the trier of fact, after a hearing, determines that facts exist sufficient to terminate parental rights pursuant to the standards set out in Standard 8.3C., the court should convene a dispositional hearing in accordance with Standard 8.5.

If the finder of fact determines that facts sufficient to terminate parental rights have not been established, the court should dismiss the petition.

C. Basis for involuntary termination.

Before entering an interlocutory order of termination of parental rights, a court, after a hearing, must find one or more of the following facts:

1. The child has been abandoned. For the purposes of this Part, a child has been abandoned when:

a. his/her parents have not cared for or contacted him/her, although the parents are physically able to do so, for a period of [sixty] days, and the parents have failed to secure a living arrangement for the child that assures the child protection from harm that would authorize a judicial declaration of endangerment pursuant to Standard 2.1;

b. he/she has been found to be endangered pursuant to Part V and has been in placement, and the parents for a period of more than one year have failed to maintain contact with the child although physically able to do so, notwithstanding the diligent efforts of the agency to encourage and strengthen the parental relationship; or

c. he/she has been in the custody of a third party without court order, or by court order pursuant to Standard 10.7, for a period of eighteen months, and the parents for a period of more than eighteen months have failed to maintain contact with the child although physically able and not prevented from doing so by the custodian.

2. The child has been removed from the parents previously under the test established in Standard 6.4 C., has been returned to his/her parents, has been found to be endangered a second time, requiring removal, has been out of the home for at least six months, and there is a substantial likelihood that sufficient legal justification to keep the child from being returned home, as specified in Standard 6.4 C., will continue to exist in the foreseeable future.

3. The child has been found to be endangered in the manner specified in Standard 2.1 A., more than six months earlier another child in the family had been found endangered under 2.1 A., the child has been out of the home for at least six months, and there is a

substantial likelihood that sufficient legal justification to keep the child from being returned home, as specified in Standard 6.4 C., will continue to exist in the foreseeable future.

4. The child was found to be endangered pursuant to Standard 5.4, the child has been in placement for two or more years if under the age of three, or three or more years if over the age of three, the agency has fulfilled its obligations undertaken pursuant to Standard 6.5 b., and there is a substantial likelihood that sufficient legal justification to keep the child from being returned home, as specified in Standard 6.4 c., will continue to exist in the foreseeable future.

5. The child has been in the custody of a third party without court order, or by court order pursuant to Standard 10.7, for a period of three years, the third party wishes to adopt the child, and

a. the parents do not want or are unable to accept custody at the present time;

b. return of the child to the parents will cause the child to suffer serious and sustained emotional harm; or

c. the child is twelve years or older and wants to be adopted.

6. The child has been in voluntary placement by court order pursuant to Standard 10.7 for a period of three years and

a. the parents do not want or are unable to accept custody at the present time;

b. return of the child to the parents will cause the child to suffer serious and sustained emotional harm; or

c. the child is twelve years or older and wants to be adopted.

8.4 Situations in which termination should not be ordered.

Even if a child comes within the provisions of Standard 8.2 or 8.3, a court should not order termination if it finds by clear and convincing evidence that any of the following are applicable:

A. because of the closeness of the parent-child relationship, it would be detrimental to the child to terminate parental rights;

B. the child is placed with a relative who does not wish to adopt the child;

C. because of the nature of the child's problems, the child is placed in a residential treatment facility, and continuation of parental rights will not prevent finding the child a permanent family placement if the parents cannot resume custody when residential care is no longer needed;

D. the child cannot be placed permanently in a family environment and failure to terminate will not impair the child's opportunity for a permanent placement in a family setting;

E. a child over age ten objects to termination.

8.5 Dispositional proceedings.

A. Predisposition report

Upon a finding that facts exist sufficient to terminate parental rights, the court should order a complete predisposition report prepared by the probation department for the dispositional hearing. . . .

B. Dispositional hearing.

A dispositional hearing should be held within [forty-five] days of the finding pursuant to Standard 8.3 B. 16. . . .

8.6 Interlocutory order for termination of parental rights; appeals.

A. If the court after a hearing finds that one or more of the bases exist pursuant to Standard 8.3 C. and that none of the bases in Standard 8.4 C. is applicable, it should enter an interlocutory order terminating parental rights. . . .

B. Appeals. An appeal may be taken as of right from a court order entered pursuant to Standard 8.3 B. 16., 8.6, or 8.7. . . .

8.7 Actions following termination.

A. When parental rights are terminated, a court should order the child placed for adoption, placed with legal guardians, or left in long-term foster care. Where possible, adoption is preferable. However, a child should not be removed from a foster home if the foster parents are unwilling or unable to adopt the child, but are willing to provide, and are capable of providing, the child with a permanent home, and the removal of the child from the physical custody of the foster parents would be detrimental to his/her emotional well-being because the child has substantial psychological ties to the foster parents.

B. When an adoption or guardianship has been perfected, the court should make its interlocutory order final and terminate its jurisdiction over the child. If some other long-term placement for the child has been made, the court should continue the hearing to a specific future date not more than one year after the date of the order of continued jurisdiction. After the hearing, the court should extend the interlocutory order to a specified date to permit further efforts to provide a permanent placement, or vacate the interlocutory order and restore parental rights to the child's parents.

Part IX: Criminal Liability for Parental Conduct

9.1 Limiting criminal prosecutions.

Criminal prosecution for conduct that is the subject of a petition for court jurisdiction filed pursuant to these standards should be authorized only if the court in which such petition has been filed certifies that such prosecution will not unduly harm the interests of the child named in the petition.

Part X: Voluntary Placement

10.1 Definition

For purposes of this Part, "voluntary placement" is any placement of a child under twelve years of age into foster care when the placement is made at the request of the child's parents and is made through a public or state supported private agency without any court involvement....

10.3 Preplacement inquiries.

Prior to accepting a child for voluntary placement, the agency worker should:

A. Explore fully with the parents the need for placement and the alternatives to placement of the child.

B. Prepare a social study on the need for placement; the study would explore alternatives to placement and elaborate the reasons why placement is necessary. However, a child may be placed prior to completion of the social study if the child would be endangered if left at home or the parents cannot care for the child at home even if provided with services.

C. Review with an agency supervisor the decision to place the child.

D. Determine that an adequate placement is in fact available for the child.

10.4 Placement agreements.

When a child is accepted for placement, the agency should enter into a formal agreement with the parents specifying the rights and obligations of each party. The agreement should contain at least the following provisions:

A. a statement by the parents that the placement is completely voluntary on their part and not made under any threats or pressure from an agency;

B. a statement by the parents that they have discussed the need for placement, and alternatives to placement, with the agency worker and have concluded that they cannot care for their child at home;

C. notice that the parents may resume custody of their child within forty-eight hours of notifying the agency of their desire to do so;

D. a statement by the parents that they will maintain contact with the child while he/she is in placement;

E. a statement by the agency that it will provide the parents with services to enable them to resume custody of their child;

F. notification to the parents of the specific worker in charge of helping them resume custody and an agreement that the agency will inform the parents immediately if there is a change in workers assigned to them;

G. a statement that if the child remains in placement longer than six months, the case will automatically be reviewed by the juvenile court, and that termination of parental rights might occur if the child remains in placement for eighteen months if the parents have failed to maintain contact or after three years even if the parents have maintained contact.

10.5 Parental involvement in placement.

The agency should involve the parents and the child in the placement process to the maximum extent possible, including consulting with the parents and the child, if he/she is of sufficient maturity, in the choice of an appropriate placements, and should request the parents to participate in bringing the child to the new home or facility. Preference should be given to the placement of choice of the parents and the child, in the absence of good cause to the contrary.

10.6 Written plans.

Within two weeks of accepting a child for placement, the agency and parents should develop a written plan describing the steps that will be taken by each to facilitate the quickest possible return of the child and to maximize parent-child contact during placement....

10.7 Juvenile court supervision.

No child should remain in placement longer than six months unless the child is made a ward of the juvenile court, and the court, at a hearing in which both the parents and child are represented by counsel, finds that continued placement is necessary....

(c) Broadening Authority Again

The Adoption and Safe Families Act is one of those statutes which amends many other statutes in ways too gruesomely complex to summarize intelligibly. Nevertheless, it is an important statute at least because it represents a sea change in attitudes about the legal response to child abuse. More precisely, it represents a sense that the spirit of the IJA/ABA Standards had gone too far, that solicitude for parents' prerogatives had too often deterred government from intervening to protect children from their parents. For example, in introducing AFSA, its cosponsor, Rep. Dave Kemp, said,

> In 1980, the pendulum moved toward "family reunification." While this is a goal we should strive to achieve, it should not come at the cost of our children. Since 1980 news stories in each of our states have highlighted the problems associated with reasonable efforts. According to the National Committee to Prevent Child Abuse, in 1995, 1,248 children died as a result of abuse or neglect.

THE ADOPTION AND SAFE FAMILIES ACT OF 1997

US Public Laws, 105th Congress—First Session, 1997

SEC. 101. CLARIFICATION OF THE REASONABLE EFFORTS REQUIREMENT.

(a) IN GENERAL.—Section 471(a)(15) of the Social Security Act (42 U.S.C. 671(a)(15)) is amended to read as follows:

"(15) provides that—

"(A) in determining reasonable efforts to be made with respect to a child, as described in this paragraph, and in making such reasonable efforts, the child's health and safety shall be the paramount concern;

"(B) except as provided in subparagraph (D), reasonable efforts shall be made to preserve and reunify families. . . .

"(D) reasonable efforts of the type described in subparagraph (B) shall not be required to be made with respect to a parent of a child if a court of competent jurisdiction has determined that—

"(i) the parent has subjected the child to aggravated circumstances (as defined in State law, which definition may include but need not be limited to abandonment, torture, chronic abuse, and sexual abuse);

"(ii) [the parent has committed murder of another child of the parent, committed voluntary manslaughter of another child of the parent, aided or abetted, attempted, conspired, or solicited to commit such a murder or such a voluntary manslaughter, or committed a felony assault that has resulted in serious bodily injury to the child or to another child of the parent, or has had parental rights terminated with respect to another child of the parent] . . . ."

SEC. 103. STATES REQUIRED TO INITIATE OR JOIN PROCEEDINGS TO TERMINATE PARENTAL RIGHTS FOR CERTAIN CHILDREN IN FOSTER CARE.

(a) REQUIREMENT FOR PROCEEDINGS.—Section 475(5) of the Social Security Act (42 U.S.C. 675(5)) is amended— . . .

"(E) in the case of a child who has been in foster care under the responsibility of the State for 15 of the most recent 22 months, or, if a court of competent jurisdiction has determined a child to be an abandoned infant (as defined under State law) or has made a determination that the parent has committed murder of another child of the parent, committed voluntary manslaughter of another child of the parent, aided or abetted, attempted, conspired, or solicited to commit such a murder or such a voluntary manslaughter, or committed a felony assault that has resulted in serious bodily injury to the child or to another child of the parent, the State shall file a petition to terminate the parental rights of the child's parents (or, if such a petition has been filed by another party, seek to be joined as a party to the petition), and, concurrently, to identify, recruit, process, and approve a qualified family for an adoption, unless—

"(i) at the option of the State, the child is being cared for by a relative;

"(ii) a State agency has documented in the case plan (which shall be available for court review) a compelling reason for determining that filing such a petition would not be in the best interests of the child; or

"(iii) the State has not provided to the family of the child, consistent with the time period in the State case plan, such services as the State deems necessary for the safe return of the child to the child's home, if reasonable efforts of the type described in section 471(a)(15)(B)(ii) are required to be made with respect to the child." . . .

TITLE II—INCENTIVES FOR PROVIDING PERMANENT FAMILIES FOR CHILDREN

SEC. 201. ADOPTION INCENTIVE PAYMENTS. [42 U.S.C. (the Social Security Act) was amended by adding a new section 473A providing for state grants to any state that meets incentive eligibility requirements. A state becomes incentive-eligible for a fiscal year if: it has an approved plan for moving children out of foster care and into permanent homes, the number of foster-child adoptions during the fiscal year exceeds the "base number" set for the state by the Secretary of Health and Human Services, and the state provides health coverage for special needs children.]

(a) IN GENERAL.—Section 1130(a) of the Social Security Act (42 U.S.C. 1320a–9) [was amended to give States the authority to conduct demonstration projects, including kinship care projects under 42 USCA § 5113].

Reports on kinship care projects shall contain each State's policy regarding kinship care, the characteristics of the kinship care providers . . . ; the characteristics of the household of such . . . ; how much access to the child is afforded to the parent from whom the child has been removed; the cost of, and source of funds for, kinship care (including any subsidies such as medicaid and cash assistance); the permanency plan for the child and the actions being taken by the State to achieve the plan; the services being provided to the parent from whom the child has been removed; and the services being provided to the kinship care provider; and are to specifically note the circumstances or conditions under which children enter kinship care.

[Family reunification services were authorized under 42 USCA § 629a only for the 15–month period that begins on the date that the child enters foster care. These services are to include individual, group, and family counseling; inpatient, residential, or outpatient substance abuse treatment services; mental health services; assistance to address domestic violence; services designed to provide temporary child care and therapeutic services for families.

The Social Security Act, 42 USCA § 671, was amended as follows:]

SEC. 401. PRESERVATION OF REASONABLE PARENTING.

Nothing in this Act is intended to disrupt the family unnecessarily or to intrude inappropriately into family life, to prohibit the use of reasonable methods of parental discipline, or to prescribe a particular method of parenting.

The heart of the AFSA, then, is section 101 (encoded as 42 USC. § 671(a)(15) (a)), which provides that "in determining reasonable efforts to be made with respect to a child, as described in this paragraph, and in making such reasonable efforts, the child's health and safety shall be the paramount concern." The significance of subsection (a) becomes clearer when one reads that subsection (b) provides that "reasonable efforts shall be made to preserve and reunify families." To put the point crudely, the statute's supporters regarded it as calling for protecting children first, then protecting parents' interest in being reunited with their children. (How do you think the drafters of the IJA/ABA Standards would respond?) The statute goes on to spell out when "reasonable efforts" aren't necessary. This includes cases in which a parent has been convicted of a variety of assaults on or homicides of another sibling or a custodial parent, in which a parent has been convicted of a serious assault on the child, or has had lost parental rights to another child. The second part of the act provides substantial financial incentives for states to move children expeditiously out of foster care and into adoption. Here again the statute is intended to reduce what has been thought to be an undue reluctance to separate abusive and neglectful parents from their children and to free children for adoption.

Notes and Questions on the Adoption and Safe Families Act

(1) In *United States v. Morrison*, 529 US 598 (2000), a former university student brought an action under the Violence Against Women Act against students who allegedly raped her. In a 5–4 opinion by Chief Justice Rehnquist, the Court held that the Commerce Clause did not grant Congress authority to enact the Act's civil remedies, since the Act did not regulate activity that substantially affected interstate commerce, nor did the enforcement clause of the Fourteenth Amendment provide Congress with authority to enact the provision. Is the ASFA constitutional, since adoptions and parental-rights terminations are primarily confided to the states? The statute in Morrison was enacted on the authority of the Commerce Clause and the Fourteenth Amendment,

while the ASFA conditioned grants of federal funds on states' compliance with its provisions. Does this distinguish the two statutes? Should Congress nevertheless refrain from acting out of federalism concerns?

(2) Is AFSA likely to be effective? Jess McDonald, Director of the Illinois Department of Children, and Family Services, testified on behalf of the American Public Welfare Association (APWA), where he served as Chair of the Children and Family Services Committee of APWA's National Council of State Human Service Administrators (upper level state administrators of welfare and child protective programs. He noted:

> Between June of 1986 and June of 1995, the size of the substitute care population [i.e., children in the custody of the state human services department] in Illinois expanded at an average annual rate of 15 percent—from 13,734 children to 47,862 children. Since July of 1995, through a variety of legislative and administrative changes, we have been able to hold annual caseload growth to below 5 percent.

Is this a relevant statistic? Further, Mr. McDonald testified that:

> We fully support changing the federal law to require a permanency hearing at 12 months rather than at 18 months. This requirement places a reasonable, albeit challenging, expectation on the system and charges us to be more expeditious in moving children to permanency. The Subcommittee should be aware that this requirement is going to be especially difficult for many urban systems where the courts are backlogged and reportedly are unable to devote no more than five minutes to each case.

How can courts do an adequate job if they can devote no more than five minutes to each case? Note that the Senate compromised here by using a 15–month time period.

(3) Mr. McDonald testified strongly and at some length about kinship care:

> Illinois has been approved for a child welfare demonstration waiver and is seeking to address the issues of kinship care through a program of subsidized guardianship. Illinois has identified over 16,000 children who have been in state custody for longer than two years and living in the home of a relative for more than one year. In a survey of this population that we conducted in 1994, fully 85 percent of relatives said that the best plan for these children was to remain with them until they were fully grown. The problem is that the special character and dynamics of kinship foster care make it difficult to move large numbers of children into permanent homes through the established channel of adoption. While our research shows that many more relatives are willing to consider adoption than previously supposed, significant proportions still are uncomfortable with this approach. Families fear becoming embroiled in an adversarial process that pits parents against sons and daughters, siblings against sisters and brothers. Many relatives,especially grandparents, find formal adoption to be an unnecessary bureaucratic imposition. They feel that their relationship to the children is already permanently sealed by virtue of their blood ties. Many relatives find subsidized guardianship an attractive permanency option that would add legal

permanence to existing family relationships which is less disruptive of customary kinship norms than adoption. We expect that as many as 4,000 families will avail themselves of this option under our waiver demonstration over the next five years. Together with improved adoption rates, subsidized guardianship will help bring permanence to the lives of more than 8,000 children who otherwise would have spent their childhood in long-term foster care.

Notes and Questions on Three Statutory Approaches to Child Abuse

(1) When a jurisdiction substitutes one statute for another, lawyers must analyze the changes the new statute works. As counsel to the committee, you need to bring to bear on the statutes the skills that analysis calls for. What are the differences between the statutes? (For convenience we will treat the Michigan and Utah statutes as a single statute.) The Michigan/Utah and IJA/ABA approaches are obviously radically different in virtually every respect. The former is, of course, the traditional approach. The latter was born out of unhappiness with that approach. Now, a reaction has set in to the IJA/ABA approach.

(2) What differences do you see in the attitudes of the statutes toward parents' and children's interests and rights? Which statute protects which of those interests and rights better?

(3) What differences do you see in how the statutes choose between discretion and rules? Which of the statutes is preferable?

(4) What differences do you see in the statutes' attitudes toward due process? Which of the statutes is preferable?

(3) Testing the Statutory Approaches: The Case of Cornilous

The following case became something of a *cause célèbre*, at least in the Washington, D.C., area. It is a case from which observers have drawn radically different conclusions. It is a case that has influenced state and federal legislation. What does it tell us about the three statutes we have just studied and the attitudes that underlie them?

IN RE: ADOPTION NO. 12612

Court of Appeals of Maryland, 1999
725 A2d 1037

WILNER, J.

This contested custody dispute, between the birth mother of a young child and the woman who has been the child's principal care giver for most of his life, involves the construction of Maryland Code, § 9–101 of the Family Law Article. Ultimately at issue is whether the Circuit Court for Montgomery County erred in awarding custody of the child to his birth mother, notwithstanding (1) that she had murdered another of her children six years earlier, (2) while on probation for that crime, she engaged in a scheme of credit card fraud, leading to her conviction of mail fraud, and (3) other circumstances relating to her conspicuous lack of success in raising children. In an unreported opinion, the Court of Special Appeals, stressing the deference to be accorded to a trial judge's conclusion, affirmed that judgment. Because we conclude that the circuit court erred in failing to comply with § 9–101, as we construe it, we shall direct that the judgment of that court be vacated and the case remanded for further proceedings.

BACKGROUND

The child whose custody is at issue is Cornilous Pixley, who is now three years old. The contestants here are Latrena Pixley, his birth mother, and Laura Blankman, his principal caregiver since Cornilous was three-and-a-half months old.

Ms. Pixley was born in June, 1973. Her upbringing was neither stable nor happy. She informed the court's adoption investigator in this case that her mother is an active alcoholic and drug abuser and has been incarcerated at least four times. Her father, also a drug abuser who apparently has never been gainfully employed, has been incarcerated on a number of occasions, and her brother, who had previous incarcerations for drug distribution, was serving time for assault and violation of probation. Her father left when Ms. Pixley was but three or four years old. The family moved often, and Ms. Pixley went to at least six schools before dropping out at the end of the eleventh grade. At 14, she attempted to commit suicide by swallowing Tylenol pills. At 15, she was pregnant. By the time she was 23, she had four children by four different men, none of whom she either married or lived with for very long.

Ms. Pixley's first child, Carlos, was born in June, 1989, when Ms. Pixley was 16. Carlos remained with her for about a year, until she relinquished physical custody of the child to his paternal grandparents. She did that, she said, because she was pregnant with her second child and her mother, who had applied for social service benefits for Carlos, was using all of the money to buy drugs. The second child, Edward, was born in July, 1990; Ms. Pixley had just turned 17. In May, 1992, Ms. Pixley was living in the District of Columbia with a drug user named Terrell Cooper, although she was carrying the child of one Keith Scott. She had terminated her relationship with Mr. Scott because Scott did not want Edward in his apartment. On May 6, 1992, her daughter, Nakya, was born. Ms. Pixley did not want the child and allowed Mr. Scott to take her from the hospital.

When Nakya was five weeks old, Ms. Pixley agreed to watch her for a few days, while Mr. Scott was in New York. Along with the child, Scott brought a few cans of milk and some diapers. When he did not return in a week, Ms. Pixley called, and Scott said that he would come for the child, but he never did. Ms. Pixley ran out of formula and diapers, although she had other food in the apartment. On June 19, 1992—the day after Ms. Pixley called Scott—Nakya woke up crying. Ms. Pixley tried giving the child some water, to no avail. Her telephone had been disconnected. She went to a neighbor's apartment to use the telephone, but the neighbor was not then at home. Although Ms. Pixley had previously received assistance from Maryland social service agencies with respect to Carlos and Edward, she made no attempt to contact any District of Columbia social service agency or to seek assistance from any other neighbor, and she had said nothing to her boyfriend before he left for work earlier that morning.

In short, other than seeking out one neighbor, she did nothing to obtain assistance for Nakya. Instead, she placed the child in her crib and smothered her with a blanket, keeping the blanket over Nakya's head for about a half hour. Edward was in the apartment at the time; there is some dispute whether he witnessed the murder of his infant sister.

Eventually, Ms. Pixley stuffed the dead child in a trash bag, put her into a dumpster, and returned to the apartment to await the arrival of her boyfriend. When her boyfriend returned, she made dinner for him, for Edward, and for herself, and then the three of them visited the boyfriend's sister until two o'clock in the morning. Not until the next day did she inform her boyfriend of what she had done. After discovering the body in the dumpster, the boyfriend called his uncle, who called the police. Ms. Pixley was arrested. When asked by the police why she had killed Nakya, she said "I don't know."

It is at this point that the lives of Ms. Pixley and Ms. Blankman first converge. Ms. Blankman, at the time, was a 22–year-old college student who, while on a summer break, was doing an internship at the Washington, D.C. public defender's office. She worked with Lisa Greenman, Ms. Pixley's attorney in the murder case. In the course of assisting Ms. Greenman, Ms. Blankman got to know Ms. Pixley, and a friendship developed between them. Ms. Blankman completed her internship in July or August and returned to school, but she and Ms. Pixley continued to correspond by mail.

Although she may have attended a hearing of some kind involving Ms. Pixley during another break, her next recollection of meeting Ms. Pixley was in the fall of 1995, when, by happenstance, she encountered her in Washington while crossing the street.

Ms. Pixley was on the street due to the outcome of the criminal case. In June, 1993—a year after the murder—Ms. Pixley pled guilty to second degree murder. The full record of that proceeding in the Superior Court of the District of Columbia is not in the record before us, but it appears that, at sentencing, Judge Mitchell was persuaded by a psychiatric assessment that Ms. Pixley was suffering from postpartum depression when she murdered Nakya. That assessment was accepted by the circuit court in this case. Judge Mitchell sentenced Ms. Pixley to prison for a period of from five to fifteen years but then suspended execution of that sentence in favor of her serving weekends at a halfway house for three years and five years of probation. Because of her obligation to spend weekends at the halfway house, Ms. Pixley signed a stipulation that she was unable to care for Edward, who was placed in foster care. Ms. Pixley visited with Edward frequently in the beginning. The visits were suspended for a time due to Edward having nightmares, but were reinstated until eventually terminated by the District of Columbia court. Ms. Pixley had not seen Edward since June, 1996. At some point, the social service plan was changed from reunification to termination of her parental rights.

In October, 1993, Ms. Pixley started a job training program at Arch Training Center. When the training program ended in the summer of 1994, she was offered a position at Arch and began employment there. At some point in late February, 1995, while still on probation from the murder conviction, she commenced a scheme of credit card fraud. She obtained the names, addresses, birth dates, and social security numbers of four or five other Arch employees from the company's computer files, prepared and mailed credit card applications in their names, received credit cards, and charged merchandise on those cards, directing that some of the merchandise be sent to her grandmother's home. Through such a scheme, she obtained a VCR and various other household appliances. Ms. Pixley admitted that she did not purchase anything that was necessary for her children, that she already had credit on her own and did not need additional credit cards, and that she simply did not expect to get caught.

In April, 1995, Arch discovered what she had done and accepted her resignation in lieu of discharge. She lied to her probation officer about the reason for her termination, informing him that she left in order to return to school full time and thereby concealing her criminal behavior. She was then pregnant with her fourth child, Cornilous, fathered by a man she had known for only a short period. Although she informed one of her expert witnesses, Dr. Feister, that this pregnancy also was unintentional—"that she did not want to be pregnant [because] she felt she couldn't care for Edward and another baby too"—she testified, and informed other people, that the pregnancy was planned, although she gave different reasons at different times for why she wanted to get pregnant. At one point, she said that it was because she was lonely and wanted company. At another time, she said that life was good and, after having the child, she wanted to marry the father. The father denied that the pregnancy was planned and that he and Ms. Pixley were ever engaged. Whatever were her intentions when she became pregnant, she terminated the relationship with the father prior to Cornilous's birth, and, indeed, there is some discrepancy in her story as to how and when that occurred. In August, 1995, she decided, unilaterally, to resume custody of Carlos, without informing his grandparents; while exercising visitation, she refused to return him to the grandparents' home. That triggered the involvement of a social service agency, the opening of a neglect case in the District of Columbia, and the return of Carlos to the custody of his grandparents, following which the neglect case was terminated.

The women's paths crossed again in the fall of 1995. Ms. Pixley was then pregnant with Cornilous. Ms. Blankman said that she received an unexpected invitation to a baby shower for Ms. Pixley, which she attended. Ms. Pixley invited Ms. Blankman to attend her in the delivery room, and Ms. Blankman made an effort to be present but arrived about a half hour after the baby was born. Cornilous was born in January, 1996. Judge Mitchell allowed Ms. Pixley to remain at home only for the first two weekends and then insisted that she resume her weekends at the halfway house. At Ms. Pixley's request, Ms. Blankman began caring for Cornilous on most of the weekends, picking him up from Ms. Pixley on Friday afternoon and returning him on Monday morning. When, on two occasions, Ms. Blankman was unavailable, the child was placed in an institution for the weekend. No family member came forth to care for the child. In light of what had happened to Nakya and in order to assist Ms. Pixley with Cornilous during the week, the District of Columbia Department of Health and Human Resources arranged for social workers from the Department's Families Together program to have almost daily contact with Ms. Pixley and with Cornilous—to visit her home and to transport her to therapy sessions and other places.

In March, 1996, Ms. Pixley's credit card fraud came to the attention of Federal agents, on the complaint of one of the persons defrauded, and, on March 12, Ms. Pixley was arrested and charged with mail fraud. As a result, in May, Judge Mitchell revoked her probation and directed execution of the five-to-fifteen year prison sentence. When other persons desired by Ms. Pixley proved unwilling to care for Cornilous and no family member volunteered to assist, Ms. Pixley, through a friend, asked Ms. Blankman to care for him on a full-time basis, which she agreed to do. That arrangement was to last only while Ms. Pixley was in jail. In July, 1996, she was sentenced on the mail fraud charge to two months incarceration—one month in jail and one month in a halfway house, consecutive to the sentence being served for the murder—and ordered to pay a total of $1,139 in restitution. In January, 1997, however, Judge Mitchell reduced the murder sentence to two years, to be served at a halfway house. In March, after Ms. Pixley served the two months on the mail fraud conviction, she reported to the halfway house prescribed by Judge Mitchell but was not accepted because the facility could not accommodate Judge Mitchell's requirement that she remain there for two years. She was then re-incarcerated, in default of an acceptable halfway house arrangement, until November, 1997, when she was released to Milestone Place.

Ms. Blankman continued to care for Cornilous during this period. Initially, despite considerable inconvenience, she brought the child to visit Ms. Pixley at the District of Columbia jail on a regular basis, twice a week. In October, 1996, however, she decided to keep Cornilous, and the visits became less frequent, finally ending in December. Ms. Blankman concealed her intent from Ms. Pixley, fearing that, if she disclosed her intent, Ms. Pixley would revoke her consent to Cornilous remaining in her custody.

In October, she told Judge Mitchell that she was caring for the child only while Ms. Pixley was in jail and that Ms. Pixley and Cornilous should be reunited. By December, Ms. Blankman had effectively cut off all contact with Ms. Pixley; she changed her telephone number from one unlisted number to another and declined to respond to a letter from Ms. Pixley. In February, 1997, when it appeared that Ms. Pixley might be on the verge of being released into a halfway house, Ms. Blankman filed a petition for the adoption and, in the alternative, for custody of Cornilous. She was permitted to retain custody of Cornilous pending the litigation, subject to weekly supervised visitation with Ms. Pixley.

Although permanent custody was an alternative request, the case was tried principally as a contested adoption case. Ms. Blankman was seeking to terminate Ms. Pixley's parental rights and adopt Cornilous. The child's father consented to and recommended the adoption, but Ms. Pixley vigorously contested it. In addition to reports and recommendations from the guardian ad litem appointed for Cornilous and the court's adoption investigator, who reached opposite conclusions, a great deal of evidence was presented by psychologists, a psychiatrist, and social service workers regarding the parties, Cornilous, and what was in Cornilous's best interest. Apart from the facts recited above, it was essentially conceded that Carlos, Edward, and Cornilous had never been physically abused or neglected by Ms. Pixley, except to the extent that her absence due to incarceration rendered her unable to care for Edward or Cornilous. It was also conceded that the visits Ms. Pixley had with Cornilous while he was in Ms. Blankman's care were positive ones. Ms. Blankman stated that Ms. Pixley appeared to be a good, loving, and nurturing mother to him during those visits, that she was always happy to see him, that she held him appropriately, and that she never abused him. Ms. Blankman said that she knew from the beginning that she would have to return the child and that she had been warned by friends about the danger of becoming too involved with him.

By the time of trial, Ms. Blankman, then 27, had accepted employment as a police officer candidate for Montgomery County and was in training at the police academy; she expected to graduate in March, 1998. She remained unmarried and lived in a three-bedroom house with her mother. She was a college graduate with a good job and an unblemished background. Ms. Pixley was living at Milestone Place, which permits children to visit but not to reside there. If she were to receive custody of Cornilous, another facility, acceptable to Judge Mitchell, would have to be found. She had obtained her GED, was taking courses at the University of the District of Columbia, and was working part-time at a retail store for $6.15 an hour.

Cornilous's guardian ad litem recommended that the adoption petition be granted. In a written report summarizing the historical facts and her conversations with various witnesses and therapists, the guardian concluded, among other things, that Ms. Pixley had not been cooperative in releasing information, that she "is more concerned about her liberty than she is about reunification with Cornilous," that "Cornilous has been used by her as a legal tool to help her be released from prison for almost two years," that she had not remained involved with the child to the extent possible, and that, in general, Ms. Pixley "is not looking out for Cornilous' best interests, rather she is looking out for herself." She stated that, if the court were to deny the petition for adoption, it should find that Ms. Pixley was "fit and capable of being Cornilous' primary caretaker," but concluded, overall, that the facts "support a finding by the Court of exceptional circumstances warranting the termination of parental rights." In that regard, she observed:

"The minor child has been away from Respondent for approximately nineteen months due to her own criminal conduct, resulting in incarceration. The minor child was less than four-months old when Petitioner assumed his care, thus, Petitioner is the only mother he has known. Although Respondent has been attempting to reclaim the minor child, she has not been in a position to reclaim the child until her recent release from incarceration. A change of custody would be detrimental to Cornilous because of both the strong emotional ties he has developed toward Petitioner and because of the unstable situation he would be placed in if placed in the custody of Respondent. Finally, the genuineness of Respondent's desire to have the minor child is lacking."

As noted, the court's adoption investigator reached a very different conclusion. She expressed "grave concerns in regard to [Ms. Blankman's] insensitivity to adoption issues and her inability to stay within normal societal boundaries." She was concerned that Ms. Blankman "would befriend a murderer via her place of work/education" and then betray that friendship. She felt that Ms. Blankman had betrayed a trust by presenting herself as a friend to Ms. Pixley, someone she could turn to for help, "and now is trying to take her child from her." The investigator regarded Ms. Blankman as deceitful and as "basically an informal foster parent who became too attached and is not willing to let go" and admonished that "this should not be allowed." She noted that Ms. Blankman "believes that Cornilous is her son," that "she gets very upset when the term foster mother or foster care is used in describing the placement situation," and that "Ms. Blankman does not appear open to compromising in any way with Ms. Pixley." As to Ms. Pixley, the investigator determined that she had done "all that the court, DHS, her therapist, and society had asked of her," yet it appeared that "a vast number of people, including [Ms. Blankman], feel that she has not been punished enough." The investigator noted that Ms. Pixley had never abused or neglected Cornilous, that she had excellent reports from her case manager at Milestone Place, and, what can only be regarded as an understatement of classic proportions, that "this would be a non-case if the murder had not occurred."

In her testimony, the investigator expressed the belief that a child should not be adopted if there is a family member available to raise the child, and she viewed Ms. Pixley's aunt as an available resource. She believed that the wealth of services that Ms. Pixley would need in order to raise Cornilous would somehow be available in the District of Columbia, and, if they were not, perhaps Ms. Pixley could move to Maryland and stay with her aunt (whose telephone was "blocked" to preclude her adolescent son from receiving collect calls from prisoners). When questioned about her assumption that Ms. Pixley could move from Milestone Place to another facility that provided adequate services and allowed children in residence, she stated that she was unaware that the facility then under consideration did not have staff on duty full time, but only from ten to six o'clock, or that ex-offenders and recovering addicts also would be living there. She said that made no difference to her. The investigator made clear that any transfer of custody to Ms. Pixley would have to be gradual.

A great deal of evidence was taken with respect to all of the parties. Dr. Ronald Wynne, a clinical psychologist who, in 1995, had evaluated Ms. Pixley's parenting competence for the D.C. Superior Court in connection with what should be done with Edward, concluded that she was angry, mistrustful, and hyper-vigilant, and that she found it hard to establish intimacy with other people. Although he concluded that she did not have an elevated potential to be physically abusive, he opined that she was not realistic about what to expect from a child and he was not very hopeful that reunification with Edward would be successful. He concluded that she needed a lot of "bolstering" but did not believe that the District of Columbia social service agencies would be able to provide the needed support.

A similar assessment came from Dr. Richard Gelles, a sociologist and teaching (but not clinical) psychologist. At the request of the D.C. authorities, Dr. Gelles had investigated and made recommendations with respect to Edward. In his May, 1996 report, he concluded that Ms. Pixley was unable to maintain adequate care for either Carlos or Edward, and he expressed "deep concerns" about the safety of Cornilous as well. Testifying in this case, he said that his particular area of expertise was family violence, and, from the research he conducted, he had developed certain risk factors for predicting the recurrence of child abuse and neglect. The best predictor, he said, was past behavior, but he identified a number of other factors as well, including age, education, income below the poverty level, number of children in the family, early onset of child-bearing, unwanted children, social isolation and lack of social support, various personality characteristics, unrealistic expectations with respect to child development, having been a victim of domestic violence, and stressful circumstances.

Upon his review of the various reports, Dr. Gelles concluded that Ms. Pixley was not a consistent, caring, concerned caretaker with acceptable parenting skills, that she could not meet Cornilous's best interest in the context of a halfway house setting, and that, although it was unlikely that she would fatally attack Cornilous, he would be in danger of maltreatment in other ways. Dr. Gelles's principal concern was that Cornilous would be neglected. In particular, he opined that the probability of neglect by Ms. Pixley was "quite a bit above 51%," that the probability of fatal attack was "quite a bit below 50%," but the probability of other physical abuse was "above 51%." In large measure, this view was prompted by his conclusion that, if severe maltreatment has already occurred, the likelihood of recurring maltreatment begins at 50%. Dr. Gelles expressed the belief that depression, which was offered as the explanation for the murder of Nakya, explains only about 10% of child abuse, implying that successful treatment of that problem would not substantially reduce the risk of further maltreatment....

Ms. Pixley's case was supported principally by Dr. Susan Feister, a psychiatrist who had evaluated Ms. Pixley in the fall of 1996 and had done an update evaluation in December, 1997, and by Joanne Bragg, a counselor who provided ongoing therapy to Ms. Pixley since 1994. Dr. Feister had testified for Ms. Pixley in January, 1997, before Judge Mitchell, and concluded then that she would not be a danger to herself or anyone else, including her children. She opined in this case that Ms. Pixley had no personality disorders and that, "with appropriate therapeutic intervention," Ms. Pixley "would be able to appropriately parent her child." Dr. Feister expressed the belief that Cornilous began bonding with Ms. Pixley while still in utero, that that bonding continued in the first months of his life, and that it remained strong. On cross-examination, she disputed that Ms. Pixley had "murdered" Nakya, insisting that she had only "killed" her. Dr. Feister acknowledged that Cornilous's growing up with the woman who had killed his sister, gave away his brother, Carlos, lost custody of his brother, Edward, and had engaged in credit card fraud could have "a profound effect" on the child, and that those "complicated issues" would need to be dealt with by Ms. Pixley. She also acknowledged that bonding and attachment issues represented a small part of her clinical practice and that she was not a person having "a tremendous amount of expertise in such issues...."

Ms. Bragg, a licensed professional counselor with a degree in agency counseling who referred to herself as a "psychotherapist," stated that she had provided individual psychotherapy to Ms. Pixley since 1994. She believed that Ms. Pixley could live in the community with Cornilous, basing that opinion on the fact that she had lived with the child in the community prior to her incarceration. Ms. Bragg described Ms. Pixley, as of 1994, as young, immature, impulsive, exercising poor judgment, and in need of both psychotherapy and pervasive socialization, but said that she had matured "to become a very responsible young woman." Although she expressed the belief that Ms. Pixley had "been as honest with me as she possibly could," she acknowledged that Ms. Pixley had not told her about the credit card fraud until after she lost her job, that she had not discussed her plan to become pregnant with Cornilous or her relationship with Cornilous's father, and that Ms. Pixley had not been entirely truthful with respect to her attempt to regain custody of Carlos.

Principally upon this evidence, the court rendered its decision on December 22, 1998. In conformance with how the case had been tried, the court's focus was on the petition for adoption, and its analysis was keyed to the factors set forth in § 5–312 of the Family Law Article with respect to unconsented independent adoptions. In summary, that section permitted such an adoption by a person who had exercised physical care and custody of the child for at least six months if the court found, by clear and convincing evidence, that (1) it was in the child's best interest to terminate the natural parent's rights; (2) the child had been out of the parent's custody for at least one year; (3) the child had developed significant feelings toward and emotional ties with the adopting parent; and (4) the natural parent had failed to maintain meaningful contact with the child despite an opportunity to do so, had repeatedly failed to contribute to the physical care and support of the child although financially able to do so, or had been convicted of child abuse of "the child."

The court began by announcing its general finding that Ms. Blankman had failed to meet her burden of proof. It noted the presumption that it is in the best interest of a child to be raised by the natural parent—a presumption "rooted in a belief that there is a greater desire on the part of the natural parent to properly care for the child"—and acknowledged that the presumption may be overcome by evidence that the natural parent is unfit or of exceptional circumstances. It identified ten factors to consider in determining whether exceptional circumstances exist and made findings with respect to them, as follows:

(1) Length of time the child has been away from the natural parent: The court found that Cornilous had been away from Ms. Pixley for 20 months, but concluded that, given his young age, that factor did not weigh in favor of severing the parental ties.

(2) Age of child when care assumed by third party: Cornilous was between three and four months old when placed in Ms. Blankman's care and thus, according to the court, had no concept of time or abandonment.

(3) Emotional effect on child of change of custody: The court found that Cornilous had established a strong bond with Ms. Blankman and would suffer a negative emotional effect from a change. The court noted that the experts disagreed on the magnitude of that effect, but accepted Dr. Feister's view that the effect would be short-lived.

(4) Delay in natural parent's attempt to regain custody: Ms. Pixley acted promptly when informed of Ms. Blankman's attempt to adopt Cornilous.

(5) Nature and strength of ties between child and third party: The court found that the ties with Ms. Blankman were strong but were never exclusive; i.e., Ms. Pixley had always remained involved in Cornilous's life.

(6) Intensity and genuineness of parent's desire to have the child: Based on its assessment of Ms. Pixley's conduct and demeanor, the court rejected the guardian ad litem's view and found Ms. Pixley's desire genuine and not just for purposes of escaping incarceration.

(7) Stability and certainty as to child's future: That factor, the court held, weighed in Ms. Blankman's favor. Ms. Blankman had a good home and stable employment, whereas Ms. Pixley's arrangements had "an element of uncertainty." Ms. Blankman had been law-

abiding and Ms. Pixley clearly had not. Nonetheless, the court did not give singular significance to that factor. It seemed to assume that the wealth of therapy and other services that Ms. Pixley would need would, in fact, be provided. It declared that her living environment was "very much a factor of socioeconomic factors" beyond her control and therefore deserving of little weight; that the murder of Nakya was the product of postpartum depression and did not "pose a threat of death or fatal abuse" to Cornilous; that it was not likely, in light of her progress in therapy, that Ms. Pixley would neglect Cornilous; and that the credit card offense showed poor judgment but did not suffice to forfeit her rights to the child. Although noting that Ms. Pixley's current job was temporary, the court observed that she had "taken advantage of opportunities presented to her to make herself more employable, having obtained her GED since she came under the court's jurisdiction and having enrolled in college classes in computer at [University of District of Columbia]." Finally, as to this factor, the court found no history of drug or alcohol abuse by Ms. Pixley.

(8) Effect of having one or both relationships continue: The court found that the long-term benefit of Cornilous being raised by Ms. Pixley outweighed the short-term detriment that would be caused by severing his ties with Ms. Blankman.

(9) Abandonment: The court found no abandonment by Ms. Pixley.

(10) Failure to support or visit the child: The court found that Ms. Pixley supported and visited the child as best she could. It attributed the 11 times she was late for visitation to factors beyond her control.

Upon this analysis, and returning to the statutory factors, the court declared that Ms. Blankman had failed to show, by clear and convincing evidence, that it was in Cornilous's best interest to terminate Ms. Pixley's parental rights, that Ms. Pixley failed to maintain meaningful contacts with the child, or that she failed to contribute to his physical care and support, though financially able to do so. Acknowledging Ms. Blankman's subjective belief that she had been acting in Cornilous's best interest, the court found that her assessment was "colored by her emotional attachment to Cornilous and, therefore, in that sense, her self-interest." It retained Ms. Blankman as a temporary guardian and directed counsel, with the assistance of Dr. Jacobs, to formulate a transition plan for returning custody of Cornilous to Ms. Pixley within 60 days. The court did not mention in its remarks § 9–101 or § 9–101.1 of the Family Law Article and made no specific findings with respect to those statutes.

In response to a motion to stay, the court addressed a number of issues raised by Ms. Blankman, among them being that the court had applied a clear and convincing evidence standard, which was appropriate with respect to the adoption petition but not with respect to custody. The court denied that it had applied that standard with respect to the issue of custody and stated in a supplemental opinion and order its finding that Ms. Blankman "failed to establish by a preponderance of the evidence that [Ms. Pixley] was unfit or that exceptional circumstances existed as of December 22, 1997." It repeated its conclusion that it was in Cornilous's best interest that he be returned to Ms. Pixley. The court denied the motion for stay and directed a transitional arrangement looking toward a complete transfer of custody by April, 1998. Ms. Blankman did not raise the application of §§ 9–101 or 9–101.1 in her motion to stay, and the court made no comment with respect to them.

As we observed, the Court of Special Appeals affirmed the circuit court judgment, concluding that, to the extent § 9–101 was applicable, the court complied with the statutory requirements, the court was not clearly erroneous in its fact-finding, and the court gave appropriate consideration to Nakya's murder and to Ms. Pixley's handling of Carlos and Edward. We granted certiorari to consider three issues: (1) is § 9–101 applicable; (2) if applicable, did the court comply with its mandate; and (3) did the court err in applying the common law presumption favoring custody with Ms. Pixley in light of the fact that she murdered one of her other children? Because of our conclusions with respect to § 9–101, we need not address the third question.

DISCUSSION

As the Court of Special Appeals noted, § 9–101 of the Family Law Article needs to be considered together with § 9–101.1.

Section 9–101 provides:

> (a) In any custody or visitation proceeding, if the court has reasonable grounds to believe that a child has been abused or neglected by a party to the proceeding, the court shall determine whether abuse or neglect is likely to occur if custody or visitation rights are granted to the party.
>
> (b) Unless the court specifically finds that there is no likelihood of further child abuse or neglect by the party, the court shall deny custody or visitation rights to that party, except that the court may approve a supervised visitation arrangement that assures the safety and the physiological, psychological, and emotional well-being of the child.

Section 9–101.1, after defining the term "abuse," provides, in subsections (b) and (c):

> (b) In a custody or visitation proceeding, the court shall consider, when deciding custody or visitation issues, evidence of abuse by a party against:
>
> (1) the other parent of the party's child;
>
> (2) the party's spouse; or
>
> (3) any child residing within the party's household, including a child other than the child who is the subject of the custody or visitation proceeding.

(c) If the court finds that a party has committed abuse against the other parent of the party's child, the party's spouse, or any child residing within the party's household, the court shall make arrangements for custody or visitation that best protect:

(1) the child who is the subject of the proceeding; and

(2) the victim of the abuse.

Ms. Blankman looks to the requirement of § 9–101(b) that, when the court has reasonable grounds to believe that a child has been abused or neglected by a party, it "shall" deny custody to that party unless it specifically finds that there is "no likelihood" of further child abuse or neglect by that party. Nakya, she contends, was a child of Ms. Pixley who, by virtue of her murder, was certainly abused by Ms. Pixley. It was therefore incumbent on the court to deny Ms. Pixley custody of Cornilous unless it made the requisite finding that there was no likelihood of further abuse or neglect on the part of Ms. Pixley. The court never made such a finding, she avers, and its judgment was therefore infected with legal error. The court's finding that there was no threat of "death or fatal abuse," she argues, does not suffice.

Ms. Pixley responds that (1) Ms. Blankman did not properly raise this issue in the circuit court and has therefore waived her right to raise it on appeal; (2) even if preserved, § 9–101(b) applies only when the child previously abused is the same child whose custody is currently under consideration, which is not the case here; and (3) the court essentially made the requisite finding and, if it did not, the error was harmless.

Preservation

When, in February, 1997, Ms. Blankman filed her petition for adoption, she was concerned that Ms. Pixley would immediately reassert her parental right to custody of Cornilous, so she filed with that petition, prior to its service on Ms. Pixley, an ex parte petition for temporary custody pending the litigation. In that ex parte petition, she urged that it was in Cornilous's best interest to remain in her temporary custody and, in support of that averment, she cited §§ 9–101 and 9–101.1, together, for the proposition that the court must consider previous acts of abuse and neglect of "other children" when ruling on custody and visitation and must deny custody to the abusive party unless it finds no likelihood of further abuse or neglect. The court awarded Ms. Blankman temporary custody but provided for supervised visitation by Ms. Pixley. In September, 1997, Ms. Pixley requested that she be given extended, unsupervised visitation, and, in response to that motion, Ms. Blankman again cited both § 9–101 and § 9–101.1, averring that, in light of Ms. Pixley having murdered another child, the court must make a specific finding that there was no likelihood of further abuse. The point was argued by her at the hearing on the motion.

That was the last time she mentioned § 9–101, however. It was not argued at trial, and, as noted, it was not argued in Ms. Blankman's motion to stay the court's order. The guardian ad litem never mentioned it in her report to the court, or in her testimony. Nonetheless, it had been brought to the judge's attention in the context of both custody and visitation, albeit in pendente lite proceedings. Also significant is the fact that Ms. Pixley never raised the preservation issue in the Court of Special Appeals, and that court ruled on the applicability and satisfaction of § 9–101. Indeed, the first question raised in Ms. Blankman's petition for certiorari was whether the Court of Special Appeals erred in its ruling. Ms. Pixley did not raise the preservation question in her answer to the petition for certiorari or in a cross-petition. The issue was mentioned by her for the first time in her brief in this Court. Even assuming that the statutory direction is a matter that could be waived, these circumstances militate against our declining to address the substantive issue on the ground of waiver or non-preservation.

Applicability of § 9–101

On the merits of the issue, Ms. Blankman points out that § 9–101(a) requires that if the court has reasonable grounds to believe that "a" child has been abused or neglected, it must, under subsection (b), deny custody to the party responsible for that abuse or neglect unless it finds no likelihood of further abuse or neglect by that party. Use of the indefinite article "a" in subsection (a), she urges, evidences a legislative intent that the abuse of any child by the party suffices to invoke the requirement of subsection (b). She cites Wright v. State, 349 Md. 334, 355, 708 A.2d 316, 326 (1998) and Webster's dictionary for the proposition that the indefinite article "a" connotes a broader universe than the definite article "the." She notes, as well, the anomaly that would accrue from a contrary interpretation, of a custody case involving two or more children, only one of whom had previously been abused or neglected by a party. Only that child, and not his or her siblings, would have the benefit of the statute, which could lead to the children being split and the non-abused or non-neglected children being placed in danger.

Ms. Pixley offers a triple response. First, relying to some extent on the legislative history of § 9–101, she avers that the Legislature's concern behind that statute was over the child who previously had been abused, and she therefore construes the article "a" in subsection (a) as meaning the child whose custody or visitation is at issue. She observes that to require a specific finding that there is no likelihood of further abuse or neglect to a child who has not previously been abused or neglected stretches the statute beyond its plain meaning. Second, she urges that §§ 9–101 and 9–101.1 must be read together, that § 9–101.1 clearly and unmistakably covers the situation of another child of the party having been abused and yet does not require the specific finding stated in § 9–101. Ms. Blankman's reading of § 9–101, she posits, would render § 9–101.1 surplusage. Those responses focus on statutory construction. Ms. Pixley also contends that, to read § 9–101 as applying to what she regards as "3rd party cases" would render the statute unconstitutional, as it would overcome the presumption favoring a natural parent on the basis of just one factor, rather than on the basis of the overall best interest of the child....

We find no patent ambiguity in the wording of § 9–101. Ordinarily, as Ms. Blankman points out, use of the indefinite article "a" indicates an intent that the noun following not be individualized or restricted; the word "a," when so used, is often the equivalent of "any." That reading is not called into question or made ambiguous, as Ms. Pixley suggests, by the reference in § 9–101(b) to "further" abuse. The statute dictates that, if the court, in a custody or visitation proceeding, has reasonable grounds to believe that a child—any child—has been abused or neglected by a party to the proceeding, the court must determine whether abuse or neglect is likely to occur if custody or visitation rights are granted to that party—the party responsible for the abuse or neglect. Unless the court specifically finds that there is no likelihood of further abuse or neglect by that party, it must deny custody or visitation rights to that party except for a supervised visitation arrangement that assures the safety and the physiological, psychological, and emotional well-being of the child. It is not, as Ms. Pixley suggests, a matter of looking at the prospect of further abuse of a child who has never been abused; rather, it is a matter of assuring that the party responsible for abusing or neglecting a child in the past will not abuse or neglect the child or children whose custody or visitation is within the court's control, whether or not they were the ones subjected to the previous abuse or neglect. The focus is not on a particular child but on the party guilty of the previous abuse or neglect.

The legislative history of § 9–101 supports that plain reading of the statute. Senate Bill 320 (1984), which was enacted as § 9–101, was one of several bills recommended to the General Assembly in the Preliminary Report of the Governor's Task Force on Child Abuse and Neglect. The bill was enacted precisely in the form recommended by the Task Force. It is clear from the Preliminary Report that the Task Force's concern was not just the particular child who may have been abused or neglected but all minor children in the household of the abuser....

This construction of § 9–101 does not, as Ms. Pixley suggests, make § 9–101.1 superfluous. Although that section certainly does address the kind of situation at issue here—abuse directed against a child other than the one whose custody or visitation is at issue—it has a much broader focus. Section 9–101.1, first enacted in 1991 and strengthened in 1995, deals not just with abuse by a party that has been directed against a child but also with abuse by that party directed against the other parent of the child or the party's current spouse. The legislative history of § 9–101.1 indicates recognition by the Legislature of a deep concern over the effect on a child of being in the maelstrom of any domestic violence within the home, including the abuse of adults and other children, whether or not those victims are related to the child whose custody or visitation is at issue. Testimony and letters presented to the legislative committees both in 1991 and in 1995 stressed the adverse effects on children from abusive households generally, not only the psychological harm derived from witnessing violence directed against other household members, but also the greater likelihood, statistically demonstrated, that violence directed against others, including adults in the home, will eventually be directed against them as well, and the need for courts to give due consideration to such violence in determining what is in a child's best interest. The legislative decision to include abuse directed against siblings within the ambit of § 9–101.1, as part of the more comprehensive reach of that section, in no way suggests that such abuse is not also within the ambit of § 9–101. Construing § 9–101 in the manner urged by Ms. Blankman does not make either statute superfluous or inconsistent with the other.

We find no greater merit in Ms. Pixley's constitutional argument. She seems to acknowledge that, if restricted to the situation where the child whose custody or visitation is at issue was abused, the statute would pass constitutional muster and finds a problem only when custody is denied because the parent has abused another child. We fail to see the distinction. As a preface, it is important to note that § 9–101 does not provide a basis for terminating parental "rights," does not capriciously interfere with a parent's fundamental liberty interest in raising his or her child, and does not set an impossible burden for a parent. A parent, after all, has no right, fundamental or otherwise, to abuse or neglect his or her children.

Significant abuse or neglect of a child may lead to the termination of parental rights and it may lead to the loss of custody upon a finding by a Juvenile Court that the child is in need of assistance. In a contested custody action between private individuals, evidence of abuse or neglect has always been relevant under general equitable principles with respect both to the fitness of a parent to have or retain custody and to the general consideration of the child's best interest. Even without regard to § 9–101, if the court concludes that there is a likelihood of a party subjecting a child to abuse or neglect, whether that conclusion is drawn from evidence of past abuse directed against the child whose custody or visitation is at issue or against another child, it has been authorized to deny custody to and limit visitation with that party.

Section 9–101 focuses the court's attention and gives clear direction in the exercise of its discretion. It does not set an insurmountable burden; even upon substantial evidence of past abuse or neglect, it does not require a finding that further abuse or neglect is impossible or will, in fact, never occur, but only that there is no likelihood—no probability—of its recurrence. Webster defines likelihood as probability, something that is likely to happen. Nor would § 9–101, under our construction, tie the court's hands or substitute a single, arbitrary factor for the governing best interest analysis, as Ms. Pixley contends. If the law may properly presume that, in the absence of clear and convincing evidence to the contrary, a child's best interest is served by being in the custody of a birth parent rather than someone else, it may, in light of the evidence presented to the Legislature, also presume that a child's best interest is not served by placing the child in the custody of someone with a history of abusing children, absent a finding that further abuse by that party is not likely. Section 9–101 does not scrap the overall best interest of the child standard in favor of another single, alternative standard, as suggested by Ms. Pixley, and it does not absolutely preclude a parent who has previously abused or neglected his or her child from ever having custody or visitation. It merely requires the court, when faced with a history of child abuse or neglect by a party seeking custody or visitation, to give specific attention to the safety and well-being of the child in determining where the child's best interest lies and not place the child in harm's way. There is nothing unconstitutional about that requirement.

We conclude, therefore, that § 9–101 applies when the abuse was directed against a sibling of the child, in this instance, Nakya. The court was therefore obliged to determine "whether abuse or neglect is likely to occur if custody or visitation rights" were granted to Ms. Pixley, and, unless it specifically found that "there is no likelihood of further child abuse or neglect" by her, to deny custody and unsupervised visitation.

Compliance With § 9–101

Ms. Pixley urges that, even if § 9–101 is applicable, it was satisfied. The court's finding that she did not pose "a threat of death or fatal abuse to Cornilous" coupled with its finding that the concerns expressed by Ms. Blankman's witnesses were unconvincing and the absence of any evidence that Cornilous, Carlos, or Edward were ever abused, was the equivalent, she says, of a finding that there was "no likelihood of further abuse or neglect." We do not agree. The statute requires, when there are reasonable grounds to believe that a child has been abused or neglected, that the court make a specific finding of "no likelihood of further child abuse or neglect by the party." The statute requires more than a finding that Ms. Pixley posed no threat of death or fatal abuse, and it does not envision an appellate court assuming the required finding from other disparate statements by the trial judge.

The fact is that no witness, even those testifying for Ms. Pixley, opined that there was no likelihood of further abuse or neglect by Ms. Pixley. At best, they concluded that Ms. Pixley had made significant progress in socialization and parenting skills and believed that, if she continued in therapy and received the other extensive services she required, she would be able to raise Cornilous appropriately. Significantly, although the court found the views of Ms. Pixley's witnesses to be more accurate than those of Ms. Blankman's witnesses, it made clear that it was "not persuaded to accept either set of experts in toto." We do not find in this record anything approaching an acceptable equivalent to the required statutory finding, and, for that reason, must direct that the judgment be vacated and the case remanded for further proceedings.

On remand, the court may take evidence with respect to the current situation. It will have to determine from all of the evidence whether, in light of Ms. Pixley's murder—not killing, but murder—of Nakya, there is any likelihood of her abusing or neglecting Cornilous. Obviously, in light of the findings it makes and articulates, the court will have to take account of the requirements of §§ 9–101 and 9–101.1....

Continuing Proceedings in the Cornilous Case

Since the decision you have just read, Cornilous has been in Ms. Blankman's custody. Ms. Pixley has been forbidden to have contact with a 9–year-old son in foster care, and she has had no contact with another child who lives with his father's family.

On January 12, 2000, Montgomery County Circuit Court Judge Louise G. Scrivener granted "sole legal custody" to Ms. Blankman. Manuel Perez–Rivas, *Pixley Denied Custody of Son*, The Washington Post, January 12, 2000 (2000 WL 2279444). (The original judge in the case had by this point recused himself.)

> Scrivener ruled that Pixley, 26, has not established enough of a track record to be a full-time parent to Cornilous, who will turn 4 this month, despite indications that she has begun to turn her life around. The judge's order maintains the child's current living arrangements, in which he spends six days a week with Blankman, 29 ... and one day a week with his biological mother. [Ms. Pixley was required to show she had food, electricity, a phone, and $50 in cash before each visit.]
>
> "Ms. Pixley impressed the Court as someone who is sincerely motivated to learn how to care for herself and her son," Scrivener wrote in a 10–page ruling. But she added later, "This Court cannot find that there is no likelihood of neglect of Cornilous where the track record of any type of stability and responsibility is barely begun."

The ruling was apparently crucially influenced by the testimony of a court-appointed psychologist who said he did not think Ms. Pixley would abuse her child but that she was likely to neglect him if allowed custody for extended periods. The judge "said ... the boy appears 'stable, loved and loving,' which she credited to" Ms. Blankman. Jennifer Andes, *Mom Who Killed Daughter Loses Son*, AP Online, January 12, 2000 (2000 WL 3305616).

The decision found that it was in Cornilous's best interests to maintain a relationship with Ms. Pixley. The judge "urged both Ms. Pixley and Ms. Blankman to end their conflict and ordered both to attend at least five sessions of family therapy." According to another article, Manuel Perez–Rivas, *Pixley Could Win Son, Experts Say*, Washington Post, January 13, 2000, Ms. Pixley's attorney "was skeptical about the two women's ability to cooperate ... 'We think this competition is going to be ongoing,' he said."

The "opinion laid out the progress Pixley has made in her efforts at rehabilitation. It also emphasized that Blankman is not the boy's mother and outlined some of the criticism leveled by Pixley's attorneys against her, all of which are factors that could be crucial if there is a future review." Such a review is possible at any time. "Under Maryland law, to regain custody, Pixley would have to prove that there has been a material change in circumstances. Lawyers disagreed, however, on whether it would be enough for Pixley to continue to show improvement in her condition...."

The "criticism leveled by Ms. Blankman's attorneys" is described in Arlo Wagner, *Pixley Loses Custody*, The Washington Times, Wednesday, January 12, 2000 (2000 WL 4145889): "Officer Blankman has been attempting to 'drive a wedge between mother and son since 1996, Mr. Hall [Ms. Pixley's attorney] said, adding that she changed his name to Joshua, dedicated him in her church and enrolled him in preschool without Pixley's consent." We are specifically told: "Judge Scrivener criticized Officer Blankman for trying to change Cornilous' name and withholding visitation with Pixley. However, the judge pointed out that 'none of Cornilous' extended family offered to take care of him when his mother went to jail." In addition, the judge thought Ms. Pixley "does not have a sufficient understanding" "about Cornilous' black race." The judge explained, "Simply being 'colorblind' or feeling that you are a person who is not conscious of the racial differences is not enough," Judge Scrivener said, adding that "Cornilous needs to understand the significance and learn the 'pride in his race' as he grows older."

Finally, Manuel Perez–Rivas, *Mother Who Killed Daughter Dealt Loss in Custody Case*, The Washington Post, Wednesday, July 12, 2000, reports that Judge Scrivener found Ms. Pixley in contempt of court for failing to attend the therapy sessions the judge had ordered. Ms. Pixley's attorney said, "The reason she didn't do it was that I advised her to not go because the [January] order's on appeal." Oral arguments in the appeal are scheduled for October 2000.

Some Responses to the Cornilous Case

The Maryland legislature, in 1998 Md. Laws 629, amended Md Fam Code 5–312 to provide that in determining whether to grant adoptions courts must make a "specific finding as to whether or not the return of a child to the custody of the natural parent poses an unacceptable risk to the future safety of the child." The court must give primary consideration to the safety and health of the child. Section 5–312 "applies only to independent adoptions in which a natural parent affirmatively withholds consent by filing a notice of objection." In such cases (and in other cases if the agency having jurisdiction consents), the court may grant an adoption over the natural parent's objection if the child has been out of his or her custody for at least a year, it is in the best interests of the child to do so, the child has developed significant feelings toward and emotional ties with the petitioner, and the natural parent has not maintained meaningful contact despite the opportunity to do so, has repeatedly and volitionally failed to contribute to the child's physical care and support, has been convicted of child abuse of the child or another child of the natural parent, has subjected the child to torture, chronic abuse, sexual abuse, or chronic neglect, or has been convicted of family violence against the other natural parent (or anyone who resides in the household of the other natural parent), or who has involuntarily lost parental rights to another sibling.

According to Daniel LeDuc, *New Child Custody Standard Sought*, The Washington Post, Thursday, January 29, 1998, at D05, "Supporters said the proposals [since enacted] are a response to two highly publicized child abuse cases in Montgomery County and another in Baltimore County last year in which a child died." The report noted that "the plan would also bring Maryland into compliance with new federal legislation that requires states to give priority to children's safety over parents' rights in order to receive federal money for foster care and adoption services."

The Cornilous case has also been mentioned in testimony during Congress's consideration of legislation to reform the District of Columbia foster care system.

Notes and Questions on the Cornilous *Case*

(1) We said this case had become a *cause célèbre* in Washington. It is one partly because both sides have their supporters. The National Center for Adoption was at least at one point raising funds for Cornilous Pixley's legal defense fund (presumably to support Ms. Blankman's position). Ms. Pixley seems to have been represented by lawyers acting *pro bono*. What are the arguments on both sides?

(2) How does this case affect your thinking about the statute you are responsible for drafting? How would the case be decided under each of the statutory schemes you have studied?

(a) Would the state have had any difficulty under the Michigan/Utah statute in obtaining authority to intervene in the case? In terminating Ms. Pixley's parental rights? What would the state have had to prove at each stage? Does the statute adequately balance the interests of both parents and children? Does the statute infringe parents' constitutional rights? Does the statute wisely resolve the tension between discretion and rules we discussed in Chapter 9?

(b) Would the state have had any difficulty under the IJA/ABA statute in obtaining authority to intervene in the case? In terminating Ms. Pixley's parental rights? What would the state have had to prove at each stage? Does the statute adequately balance the interests of both parents and children?

(i) The IJA/ABA standards make it much harder than the Michigan/Utah statute for the government to separate parents and children. Does this mean the statute sacrifices children to the interests of parents? Or does the statute crucially assume that it is generally in the children's interests to be with their parents, not easily to be separated from their parents, and to be returned to their parents as quickly as possible? Recall the rationales for parents' rights we developed in Chapter 8.

(ii) Is the IJA/ABA necessary to protect parents' constitutional rights?

(iii) The IJA/ABA standards try to make it hard for the government to separate parents and children partly out of the fear that the government will use its power against poor and minority parents. Is that what is happening here? Ms. Pixley's lawyers claimed Ms. Blankman was not a fit mother partly on the grounds that, because she was white, she could not adequately raise a black child. In addition, Manuel Perez–Rivas, *Mother Testifies in Montgomery Custody Case*, The Washington Post, Friday, December 17, 1999 (1999 WL 30308990), reports that

> issues such as income and race have surfaced occasionally in this custody case pitting a white woman from a middle-class Montgomery County neighborhood against a black woman living in one of the District's most disadvantaged communities. Both those issues surfaced in yesterday's arguments.
>
> Before Pixley took the stand, her attorneys called her aunt, Linda Lateef, to the stand.
>
> Lateef broke down in tears as she told the court that African Americans have suffered through years of forced separations, evoking the era of slavery.
>
> "What scares me is that he is going to be ripped away from my family, and we are never going to see him again," Lateef said.

(We will take up this problem in detail in Chapter 12.)

(iv) It seems apparent that the drafters of the IJA/ABA standard thought carefully about the tension between discretion and rules. Were their conclusions wise?

(c) How would the Adoption and Safe Families Act affect the decision in the Cornilous case? How would the Maryland statute enacted in response to the ASFA and the Cornilous case? Those statutes are particularly intended to give the state authority to act to protect the siblings of a child who has been abused or murdered. Is it wise as a matter of policy and permissible as a matter of constitutional law for the state to limit or terminate parents' rights when the parents have not specifically injured the child the state seeks to protect? Suppose there is unrebutted expert testimony that the parent is unlikely to injure that child. May the state nevertheless argue that the parent is a *morally* unfit guardian?

(d) The factors listed in the various sections of Maryland Code 9–101 are typical of modern state statutes involving involuntary termination. Do they help the court reach a coherent decision in this case? Do they satisfactorily resolve the tension between rules and discussion? The tension between the parents' interests and the children's interests?

(e) Texas Hum Resources Code § 40.001(5) before its revision in 2005, stated that the goal of " '[f]amily preservation' includes the protection of parents and their children from needless family disruption because of unfounded accusations of child abuse or neglect. It does not include the provision of state social services for the rehabilitation of parents convicted of abusing or neglecting their children." After its revision, the provision states:

> (5) "Family preservation" includes the provision of services designed to assist families, including adoptive and extended families, who are at risk or in crisis, including:
>
> > (A) preventive services designed to help a child at risk of foster care placement remain safely with the child's family; and
> >
> > (B) services designed to help a child return, when the return is safe and appropriate, to the family from which the child was removed.

What does the change in language signify? Would either version change the [the continue with existing text of (e)?

Does this change the way that the Cornilous case would have been resolved? How does it compare with the Adoption and Safe Families Act, § 401: "Nothing in this Act is intended to disrupt the family unnecessarily or to intrude inappropriately into family life, to prohibit the use of reasonable methods of parental discipline, or to prescribe a particular method of parenting?"

(3) Would the pilot program for kinship care set by the Adoption and Safe Families Act adequately respond to the concerns of Ms. Pixley's supporters? Kinship care is loosely defined as long-term (or "permanent") foster-care placement with relatives. The idea is that kinship care will substitute for adoption by third parties and that it will give children the advantages of continuity with their families and connection with their ethnic community, both of which are absent in the usual agency adoption. (The relatives may be financially unable or unwilling to adopt the child because they would then lose a foster-care subsidy.) Critics of the practice fear that kinship care may make it difficult to keep the child safe from an abusive birth parent, that it may deprive the child of the sense of finality and permanence that may come with being adopted as a child rather than cared for as a relative, and that the child may suffer if the relative has biological children with whom the child must compete for resources and attention. Is ASFA's kinship-care program likely to undermine the other sections of the statute that promote adoption, or does it represent a reasonable compromise?

(a) Did kinship care work for the Pixley children? How? Was it available for Cornilous?

(b) Would it have worked in the case of the Bond children? Specifically, could Jessie's mother have acted as a caretaker for them? What assistance would have been needed to make this possible?

(4) Has Judge Scrivener handled the case properly? Should Ms. Pixley be encouraged to think she may be able to regain custody of her son? Should the boy be visiting with Ms. Pixley? The boy's court-appointed lawyer was reported to have said that Judge Scrivener's plan was the "best arrangement" and that it would preserve his "Mommy" relationships with both women. She is also quoted as saying, "Both women need to facilitate an environment where Cornilous does not feel guilty about loving either one.... I think there needs to be a resolution. He's been in litigation for three of the four years of his life." Is preserving the boy's ties with both women likely to promote "a resolution"?

B. SOME REPRESENTATIVE ABUSE AND NEGLECT SITUATIONS

He must have known me had he seen me as he was wont to see me, for he was in the habit of flogging me constantly. Perhaps he did not recognize me by my face.

Anthony Trollope
Autobiography

You have been asked to begin drafting your statute by defining abuse and neglect. One of the primary components of due process is the notice clearly written standards supply. However, defining child abuse and devising a legal response that deals effectively with it but that does not interfere with parental prerogatives are woefully problematic enterprises.

You have read several statutory approaches to these problems. To help you further analyze them and to help you think about the definition of abuse and neglect, you need some idea of what kinds of situations those statutes affect. You have therefore assembled the following examples of behavior that might constitute abuse and neglect. How would each of these cases be resolved under each of the statutes? (1) Would there have been intervention in the family in the first place? Under what specific statutory authority? Ought intervention be possible? (2) Would the child have been removed from the parental home? (3) Would parental rights have been terminated?

(1) *Suttles v. Suttles*, 748 SW2d 427 (Tenn 1988), was a divorce action. Dennis Suttles got into an argument with his wife. Her father intervened. Suttles (whom the court refers to as "Defendant")

> drew a pistol and shot her father in the chest. He then abducted Plaintiff [his wife] and their son in his car and led the police on a high speed chase. During the course of the chase, Defendant threatened his [three-year-old] son with the pistol and shot at Plaintiff when she tried to protect the child. As a result of the chase, the Defendant wrecked his car, injuring both Plaintiff and their son. At some point during this

incident, Defendant choked his son but was restrained by Plaintiff and the police before the child was seriously injured.

(Suttles was convicted on four counts of assault with intent to commit murder in the first degree with a firearm on his wife and child. The trial court ordered that the child be made available for "reasonable visitation" with the father, who had been imprisoned. The appellate court ordered "at least monthly" visitation. The Tennessee Supreme Court ordered that visitation be "suspended until a change of circumstances can be shown" but said that "to prevent the bonds between Defendant and child from being severed completely, he is free to communicate with his child by telephone or mail or other means approved by the trial court.")

(2) Suppose a father and mother become involved in an altercation while the mother is holding their child. With no desire to hurt the child, the father strikes at the mother with his fist. Again with no desire to harm the child, the mother moves in such a way that the blow falls on the child. The child is seriously injured.

(3) Suppose a father has been kept up all night caring for a colicky child. The child is sitting in a high chair. The father hurriedly, carelessly, and roughly lifts the child out of the chair, not noticing that the child's leg is caught in it. The child's leg is broken.

(4) Suppose a mother becomes angry at her young, deaf child while doing the ironing. She throws the hot iron at the child as hard as she can, but she misses. The child's back is turned at the time, and thus the child never knows the iron has been thrown.

(5) William Lewis, once an appliance repairman and a barber, established a twenty-two acre religious commune. The commune had roughly one hundred members, called Black Hebrew Israelite Jews. Lewis called himself "prophet" and apparently exercised great influence over the members of the commune. *People v. Yarbough*, 384 NW2d 107 (Mich App 1986), reports that, on June 29, 1983, John Yarbough, the son of Ethel Mae Yarbough, was beaten "with a tree limb approximately four feet long and an inch to an inch and a half in diameter" by three male members of the camp because he refused to work. "In the days following the beating, John refused to eat and suffered episodes of vomiting, involuntary bowel movements and stumbling and falling down." Over those days, John was beaten again by men in the commune, including Lewis. On July 3, when John failed to go for the walk his mother had ordered, she "hit him with a stick approximately 18 inches long and an inch to 2 inches in diameter." By the afternoon of July 4, John was dead. The injuries he suffered at his mother's hands "resulted in brain edema, kidney, heart and pulmonary failure, which, in conjunction with internal hemorrhage, were apparently the cause of death." The mother was convicted of manslaughter, and two of the three men who had beaten John on June 29 were convicted of child cruelty (the third apparently turned state's evidence).

Lewis and the community believed in strict physical discipline (of adults as well as children) as a religious matter. Lewis cited *Deuteronomy* 21:18–21:

> If a man have a stubborn and rebellious son, which will not obey the voice of his father, or the voice of his mother, and that, when they have chastened him, will not hearken unto them: Then shall his father and his mother lay hold on him, and bring him out unto the elders of his city, and unto the gate of his place; And they shall say unto the elders of his city, This our son is stubborn and rebellious, he will not obey our voice; he is a glutton, and a drunkard. And all the men of his city shall stone him with stones, that he die: so shalt thou put evil away from among you; and all Israel shall hear, and fear.

Lewis stated "that God killed him [John]. So if God tells us to put the rod on him then the rod doesn't—the rod don't—kill him." Eleven of the sixty-six children in the commune showed signs of physical abuse. What should be done with Yarbough's other children? With the abused children? With the children who showed no signs of abuse?

(6) D.M.C. is a nine-year-old boy. *In Interest of D.M.C.*, 438 NE2d 254 (Ill App 1982), reports that

> D.M.C.'s parents had disciplined him by means of a leather belt, at least fifty strokes each and perhaps as many as one hundred strokes each, administered to the boy's unclothed buttocks and rear and side thighs. Photographs introduced in evidence showed the entire area to be solidly bruised....
>
> Testimony was introduced which indicated the child was hyperactive and perhaps had a learning disability "in the social behavior realm." The parents are both professional psychologists and have educational training and professional experience in dealing with hyperactive and learning-disabled children. Testimony indicated that they believed he had a high threshold of pain. The mother testified that she, the father, and the child all bruise easily and that she used the belt instead of her hand because she had bruised her hand spanking the child in the past.
>
> The incident that triggered the punishment involved the boy's having taken his father's cowboy hat to school for "Show and Tell" without permission and then having lied to cover up....
>
> [T]he father testified that ten or twelve strokes were not enough because "I wasn't getting any reaction. I wasn't getting any tears; I wasn't getting any yelling...."
>
> The boy testified that on the day of the "spanking" he told his parents it was hurting but they didn't stop. He said he cried afterwards but not while they were hitting him with the belt. He said he really didn't know why, "it's just that it wouldn't come out."

(The trial court held this "excessive corporal punishment" amounting to physical abuse. It placed the child in the custody of the department of child and family services, ordered family counselling, and intended to review the case in five months to see if the child could be returned to the family. The appellate court affirmed. It also noted testimony "about the child's guilt feelings over the cost of foster care to his parents and his feeling that ... the ... proceedings killed his grandfather who was very ill at the time. The child testified that he would not report it even if he were spanked many times again.")

(7) In *In Interest of Aaronson*, 382 NE2d 853 (Ill App 1978), "The State alleged appellant beat his children [ages 10, 9, and 7] by striking them on the buttocks with a belt and board." There was apparently no evidence of scars or bruising.

(The appellate court noted the Supreme Court "recently affirmed a decision holding the paddling of students in public schools ... did not constitute cruel and unusual punishment in violation of the Eighth Amendment. *Ingraham v. Wright*, 430 US 651 [1977]." The court concluded, "Certainly, paddling one's own children cannot be the basis of a charge of child abuse and neglect in the absence of clear evidence the paddling was vicious or for other than disciplinary reasons.")

(8) Suppose the parent occasionally spanks the child but uses no implements and leaves no marks.

(9) A mother discovered her seven-year-old son had committed various petty thefts and had lied about them. She dressed him to look like a pig, tied his hands behind him, placed him on a bench in front of their apartment, and hung a sign on him which read: "I'm a dumb pig. Ugly is what you will become every time you lie and steal. Look at me squeal. My hands are tied because I cannot be trusted. This is a lesson to be learned. Look. Laugh. Thief. Stealing. Bad boy." The mother explained that her own parents had punished her in this way and that she wanted the boy to learn "that lying and stealing make you ugly like Pinocchio."

While the press reports are not entirely clear, it appears that the mother was arrested, that her children were taken from her and put in foster homes, and that a charge of child endangerment was dismissed in exchange for a plea of guilty to lying to a police officer during a traffic stop (for which the mother was fined $500 and placed on three years probation). Cf. *In re Shane T.*, 453 NYS2d 590 (Brooklyn Co 1982), which involved a father who continually taunted his fourteen-year-old son, even in public, calling him "queer," a "fag," and a "faggot." The boy ended up in therapy and the mother was unable or unwilling to stop the taunting. The child was declared dependent as to both parents, the mother because she had not protected her child.

(10) The following are the facts of *Wisconsin v. Kruzicki*, 561 NW2d 729 (Wis 1997):

> The petitioner was an adult carrying a viable fetus with a projected delivery date of October 4, 1995. Based upon observations made while providing the petitioner with prenatal care, her obstetrician suspected that she was using cocaine or other drugs. Blood tests performed on May 31, June 26, and July 21, 1995, confirmed the obstetrician's suspicion that the petitioner was using cocaine or other drugs.

On July 21, 1995, the obstetrician confronted the petitioner about her drug use and its effect on her viable fetus. The petitioner expressed remorse, but declined the obstetrician's advice to seek treatment. On August 15, 1995, a blood test again confirmed that the petitioner was ingesting cocaine or other drugs. Afterward, the petitioner canceled a scheduled August 28, 1995, appointment, and rescheduled the appointment for September 1, 1995. When she failed to keep the September 1 appointment, her obstetrician reported his concerns to Waukesha County authorities.

On September 5, 1995, the Waukesha County Department of Health and Human Services (the County) filed a "MOTION TO TAKE AN UNBORN CHILD INTO CUSTODY," pursuant to Wis. Stat. § 48.19(1)(c) (2005). In its motion, the County requested an order "removing the above-named unborn child from his or her present custody, and placing the unborn child" in protective custody. The motion was supported by the affidavit of the petitioner's obstetrician, which set out the obstetrician's observations and medical opinion that "without intervention forcing [the petitioner] to cease her drug use," her fetus would suffer serious physical harm.

In an order filed on September 6, 1995, the juvenile court directed that:

> the [petitioner's] unborn child ... be detained under Section 48.207(1)(g), Wis. Stats., by the Waukesha County Sheriff's Department and transported to Waukesha Memorial Hospital for inpatient treatment and protection. Such detention will by necessity result in the detention of the unborn child's mother.

Later that same day, before the protective custody order was executed, the petitioner presented herself voluntarily at an inpatient drug treatment facility. As a result, the juvenile court amended its order to provide that detention would be at the inpatient facility. The court further ordered that if the petitioner attempted to leave the inpatient facility or did not participate in the facility's drug treatment program, then both she and the fetus were to be detained and transported to Waukesha Memorial Hospital....

After several appeals, the case reached the Wisconsin Supreme Court, which declined to read the local abuse statute (Wis Stat § 48.02(2)) to apply to a fetus. Subsequently, we learn from Lisa Sink, *Mom Misses Court Date, Loses Parental Rights to Son*, Milwaukee Journal–Sentinel, June 24, 1997, at pg 1, that "[T]he notorious Waukesha 'cocaine mom' Monday lost her rights to the custody of her son as she missed the final court hearing on the matter, saying she overslept." This was the final termination hearing in the case. Lisa Sink reported in the same paper on September 26, 1997, that the child's father, who had signed away his parental rights to the child, had been arrested and charged with possession of cocaine. And on December 16, 1997, the same reporter noted that the woman was again pregnant and had been charged with possession of drug paraphernalia. Released on bail, she tested positive for drugs in February 1998, when she also lost an appeal from the termination decision. Lisa Sink, *'Cocaine Mom' Loses Custody Plea*, Milwaukee Journal–Sentinel, March 14, 1998. Pursuant to a court order, she entered a drug treatment facility in April, gave birth to her second son, and remained at the facility until her case on the drug charges came to trial in June. We also know that another of her children won a countywide contest for the best poster against drug abuse. Lisa Spice, *Son of 'Cocaine Mom' Wins Anti–Drug Contest; DARE Judges Pick Boy's Artwork out of More than 900 Anonymous Entries*, Milwaukee Journal–Sentinel, October 27, 1998, at 1. Finally, the Wisconsin legislature passed a bill allowing detention of pregnant women in 1998, 1997 Act 292, §§ 18 to 20, eff. July 1, 1998; see Wis Stat Ann § 48.02 (1996 Supp).

(11) The following are the facts of *Smith v. Indiana*, 408 NE2d 614 (Ind App 1980):

> On February 19, 1978, Defendant [Lawanna Smith] resided in an apartment in Indianapolis with her son, Eric, and her boyfriend, Lawrence Burkhalter. Eric was four years old; Burkhalter was 29 years old and unemployed.... Defendant was showing Eric a book and attempting to have Eric spell the word "butterfly".... When Eric could not spell it correctly, Burkhalter took the child into the bathroom, filled the tub with water, and ordered Eric to undress and get in the tub. Burkhalter repeatedly dunked Eric's head under the water while urging him to correctly spell the word.... Burkhalter took off his pants and entered the tub, placing his knee upon Eric's stomach.... At one point Eric slipped and bumped his head on the tub. Defendant witnessed this entire episode, but did nothing to protect Eric or restrain Burkhalter, except to ask Burkhalter on several occasions to stop. Finally, Eric spelled the word correctly, and Defendant removed him from the tub....
>
> Burkhalter then kicked Eric, knocking him to the floor, and repeatedly kicked and struck him all over his body. Eric would stand up and Burkhalter would strike him down again. This happened repeatedly. Burkhalter also struck Eric on the face. Defendant also witnessed this abuse, protesting verbally several times but failing to intercede in any other manner....
>
> The day after the beating, doctors performed abdominal surgery, a tracheotomy, and brain surgery.... Eric underwent additional surgery on March 17 and May 2 to relieve complications resulting from the collection of fluids on his brain....
>
> Eric was found dead in his hospital bed on May 26.

Smith was convicted of the felonies of neglect of a dependent and involuntary manslaughter, despite, *inter alia*, an argument that "her personality was meek, timid, and dependent."

(12) Review now problems (6)-(10). Suppose that in each of those cases the injuries to the child had not been caused by the parent, but rather that, as in *Smith*, the parent had failed to prevent the injuries.

(13) In *In the Matter of the Welfare of S.G. and K.G.*, 390 NW2d 336 (Minn App 1986), we read:

> Mr. G. and Mrs. G. have three children. In January 1985, when the neglect petition was filed in this case, S.G. was fifteen and K.G. was eleven. The youngest child, D.G., a son, was two....
>
> On January 2, 1985, Mr. G. informed his daughters that household discipline was going to be enforced more strictly in the future. He and his wife then left to go shopping. After they left, S.G. packed up some of her things and went to the home of an adult friend a few miles away. S.G. told her friend, who had previously suspected sexual abuse in S.G.'s household, that her father had been sexually abusing her. The friend called Beltrami County Social Services, who in turn called the sheriff's department.
>
> The sheriff's department investigator spoke with S.G. that day. She told him that her father had been sexually abusing her since she was in the fourth or sixth grade. According to S.G., the abuse started when her father sought to explain the facts of life to her. As he did so, he began giving her an "example" of what he was talking about, and touched her on her breasts and in her genital area. The activity continued from that point and progressed to the stage where he had intercourse with her when she was ten or twelve. After that, he had intercourse with her about once a week....
>
> By this time, S.G.'s parents had returned home and were looking for her. The sheriff's department called them at home and asked them to come to the Beltrami County Law Enforcement Center, where they both gave voluntary statements denying the abuse occurred. Mr. G. was taken into custody and placed in the Beltrami County jail.
>
> The investigators went to the family's home that evening, executed a search warrant, and interviewed S.G.'s twelve-year-old sister, K.G. K.G. stated that she had shared a bed with her sister until about two years ago. She said that her father would climb into the bed at night and kiss S.G. and get on top of her. She said that her father would have no clothes on and that her sister had her nightgown pulled up.
>
> About two years before the petition was filed, in March of 1983, K.G. was interviewed in the principal's office at her school by Gail Hendershot, a county social services worker. K.G. told Ms. Hendershot that her father had been having sex with S.G. since S.G. was in about the third grade; that her father would climb into bed and climb over her to get to S.G.; that S.G. cried or had a stomachache or headache after intercourse; that her mother sent K.G. out of the house on one occasion so that the father could abuse S.G.; that once, on a trip, the father and S.G. had gone into the woods and had come out carrying a blanket....

(The appellate court upheld an order finding that S.G. and K.G. were neglected children and placing legal custody of the two girls in the county for placement in foster homes. The trial court also ordered that the girls begin psychological treatment, that the girls not return home "until treatment for the family has progressed to the point that replacement in the home is appropriate," and that the parents not have contact with the children until the court permitted it. The appellate court cited testimony that K.G. "exhibited many of the characteristics of a secondary victim of sexual abuse, i.e., a sibling in a family where sexual abuse has occurred, but who has not been directly approached sexually." The court said those characteristics "include family isolation; lack of a desire to grow up; feelings of guilt and shame; increased household activities; anger; pseudo-Maturity [sic]; poor self and body image; dependence; unmet emotional needs; and extremism regarding sexual activities." The court found it "totally inconceivable that it would be in the best interests of S.G. and K.G. to be returned to the custody of their natural parents in light of the court's finding of sexual abuse.")

What if parents respond to their young son's questions about how babies are made by taking him into the bedroom and demonstrating? *Chesebrough v. State*, 255 S2d 675 (Fla 1971), involved the parents' prosecution for committing a "lewd and lascivious act" in the presence of a minor. The parents were convicted despite claims of a right to educate their children about human sexuality.

(14) Consider again the case of Jessie and Catherine Bond. Suppose Jessie certainly knew Alan was sexually abusing Catherine.

(In a case with such facts, *In Interest of Cook*, 304 NW2d 390 (Neb 1981), the Nebraska Supreme Court sustained the termination of the mother's parental rights:

> The record shows that Yvonne [the mother] was more interested in preserving her relationship with Joseph [the father] than in protecting the child. The fact that Yvonne claimed ignorance of but a few of the incidents that had occurred demonstrated her inability to deal with the realities of the situation. She was unwilling to do anything to remedy the situation other than urge Joseph to seek counseling and attempt to be more "watchful" of the child.

The dissent, however, argued, "A moderately educated woman with small children, no means of support, and no place to go does not quickly remove herself from the family home for whatever reason." The dissent would have "delayed terminating the parental rights of the mother in this case for at least an additional 6 months to see whether the mother and her child could not have been successfully reunited.")

(15) Consider again the case of Alan Kane and Catherine Bond. As you will recall, Catherine was not Kane's own child, but Dorothy was. Should Kane's abuse of Catherine (assuming that he did abuse her) be grounds for proceedings directed toward his relationship with Dorothy?

(16) The opinion in *Fabritz v. Traurig*, 583 F2d 697 (4th Cir 1978), reports that Virginia Fabritz lived with her three-year-old daughter Windy with Thomas Crockett and his wife, Ann. She left Windy with the Crocketts to go to a funeral, and when she returned Windy "looked unwell." At 2:30 that afternoon,

> Windy began to suffer with cramps and to her mother seemed feverish with the flu. At this time she noted the bruises on her body. After

> bathing her, Fabritz put her to bed or on a couch. Soon afterwards, Windy was seen to have gotten up and curled herself in a blanket on the floor. At 5:00 the child was semi-conscious and improved, sitting up for a brief interval after receiving some liquid nourishment. Near 6:00 that afternoon, Windy vomited and showed she was not feeling well. At 7:00 she was put back to bed. . . .
>
> Fabritz twice telephoned Connie Schaeffer, a neighbor, for assistance, telling her of the child's flu and of her worsening condition. On arrival Schaeffer, too, saw that Windy had a fever. Asked about the bruises on Windy, the mother replied, "Tommy hits hard." They bathed her in alcohol and put her to bed. . . .
>
> Schaeffer testified at trial that she did not know what was the matter with Windy, and had left the Crockett house without suggesting medical assistance. . . . Ann Crockett arrived home and discussed with Fabritz the procurement of medical attention. . . . The two concluded it was necessary to seek help. Ann called the County Hospital. . . .

Windy was declared dead on arrival at the hospital. She died from a blow to the abdomen with a blunt instrument, "possibly a fist, rupturing the duodenum and leading to death from peritonitis." Crockett was charged but acquitted. "At one juncture Fabritz remarked that she had not taken Windy to the hospital because Fabritz 'was too ashamed of the bruises' on her body."

(Fabritz was convicted of child abuse for failing to get medical help. In a habeas action, the Fourth Circuit found the evidence "utterly bare of proof of a consciousness of criminality during her bedside vigil." Chief Judge Haynsworth dissented. His opinion relies on the facts above and adds, "Tommy Crockett was the lover of both of the women who shared the house with him. Thus, she explained to the neighbor that she had not sought a physician's help because she was ashamed of the bruised condition of the child's body and that if the child were seen by a physician she would have to explain the origin of the bruises.")

(17) How would you answer the questions we posed above in the context of Phillip B.'s parent's decision not to allow him to have an operation to treat his heart condition? (See Ch. 8.)

(18) In *In re Hudson*, 126 P2d 765 (Wash 1942), we read:

> Patricia Hudson was born August 8, 1930, with a congenital deformity consisting of an abnormal growth of her entire left arm which made that arm much longer and larger than the right arm and rendered it absolutely useless. . . .
>
> . . . [Physicians testified] that the child appears to be frail and is suffering from the effects of "this enormously heavy, useless extremity," which, for the sake of her general health should be removed. The two physicians were of the opinion that the child will remain in a rather weakened condition and that she will be an easy prey for infection by reason of her affliction; that her heart is burdened by reason of having to pump blood through the large left arm; that her chest and spine are becoming deformed from carrying the enormous weight; that there is no

method, other than amputation of the left arm, of treating the condition; and that under present circumstances it will be impossible for the child to take her place in society and live a normal life. While they testified that there is a fair degree of risk of life involved in the operation, both physicians recommended removal of the arm, having in mind the child's welfare.

> Summarized, the testimony of Patricia's seven brothers and sisters ... is that the deformity was a handicap to their sister in her association with other people; that Patricia had many times expressed the wish for removal of the left arm and frequently wept because of her affliction.

Patricia's father wanted to "leave the entire matter to the judgment of the court." Her mother "opposed the operation because she thought there was 'too much of a chance on her life,' " although " 'if as the child grows older, and if she is not happy about it, and if it is her own wish to do it, I would then consent to it, because then I would feel that she had done it herself, and not me.' "

The dissent in *Hudson* added a number of facts. Patricia's left arm was ten times the size of the right and was nearly as large as her body. One doctor testified that "the prognosis for life is not nearly as good as it would be if she did not have to nourish this enormous thing with her own little body." Patricia had a home teacher " 'because she was jeered at by the other children in the school, and she could not stay there. . . .' " One of Patricia's sisters said that

> once in a while she is allowed the freedom of going without her wrap, and if there is a knock on the door she runs like an animal to get in her smock before anyone can see her, because she is so horrified about it. . . . And it keeps her out of life, and it will keep her out of everything eventually, because she cannot help taking that with her in life.

(The Washington Supreme Court reversed the trial court's finding that Patricia was a "dependent child," saying that parents have a "paramount right ... to decide questions affecting the welfare of their children. . . ." The dissent said that Patricia

> is entitled to be put in a condition where she can run and play, attend public school, and take part in school activities. She is entitled to a healthy body, to secure a good education, to take her place in American society, to grow up as a normal American girl, to get married, and to have a home and children. Without an operation all these are denied to her and she is condemned to travel along life's pathway a hopeless cripple, an object of pity dependent upon either private or public charity.)

(19) The opinion in *In re Rotkowitz*, 25 NYS2d 624 (Dom Rel Ct 1941), reports the case of a child who had a "deformity of the right lower extremity" which had been caused by polio. Medical evidence stated that an operation "is absolutely necessary to stabilize the foot and prevent aggravation and extension of the deformity." That evidence further stated that the operation "is not a serious one" and that "the condition will become worse as time goes by unless operative correction is had

now.'' The father opposed to the operation but did not give a reason. The mother favored the operation.

(The trial court found the operation in the child's best interests and ordered it.)

(20) In *In re D.L.E.*, 645 P2d 271 (Colo 1982), twelve-year-old D.L.E. had epilepsy. His

> adoptive mother, J.E., has refused to comply with a program of medical treatment for D.L.E. Various religious tenets of the sect [to which she belongs] eschew medical care or treatment and provide for faith healing. Neither D.L.E. nor his mother believes that medical treatment is warranted for his condition. They both believe that prayer and assistance by church elders will improve his condition.

Under a court order which was later reversed, D.L.E. took Dilantin, an anti-convulsant. When he stopped taking it,

> he went into a state of status epilepticus with resulting dysfunction, including a stroke which caused permanent flaccid paralysis of his left arm and leg, a nerve injury which restricted movement in his right arm, a dislocated jaw, and continued seizure activity.... Because of frequent focal seizures, the right side of D.L.E.'s brain was not functioning at least forty percent of the time.... [A] physician testified that if D.L.E. suffered a focal seizure while eating, there was a reasonable medical probability that he would choke.

Colorado child-protection law provided:

> Notwithstanding any other provision of this title, no child who in good faith is under treatment solely by spiritual means through prayer in accordance with the tenets and practices of a recognized church or religious denomination by a duly accredited practitioner thereof shall, for that reason alone, be considered to have been neglected within the purview of this title.

How would you answer our standard questions? How would you answer them in the absence of the statutory provision? Suppose D.L.E. had died in the way the physician warned of. Is his mother guilty of either manslaughter or homicide?

(The Colorado Supreme Court held D.L.E. should have been adjudicated a dependent and neglected child: ''[T]he meaning of the statutory language, 'for that reason alone,' is quite clear. It allows a finding of dependency and neglect for other 'reasons,' such as where the child's life is in imminent danger, despite any treatment by spiritual means.'')

(21) *In re S.L.*, 419 NW2d 689 (SD 1988), presented the case of a boy, S.L., who by the time of the appellate opinion was seven years old. His mother (whom the court refers to as ''Mother'')

> was locking S.L. in his upstairs bedroom each night from about 9 p.m., apparently out of a concern that S.L. might fall down the stairway in the home because the stairs did not have a hand rail. S.L. was therefore restrained from using the bathroom, sometimes on into the night. With

> some frequency, Mother was also shutting S.L. in his closet and calling him dirty names through the door.

In addition, "Mother was inflicting physical harm on herself by burning herself with cigarettes and cutting herself with knives or razor blades, often in front of the children." On one occasion, S.L.'s mother "mutilated some of S.L.'s personal possessions in his presence, including his teddy bear and some art work he had brought home."

(On this and other evidence, the South Dakota Supreme Court upheld the termination of the mother's parental rights.)

(22) In *People v. Warner*, 424 NE2d 747 (Ill App 1981), the defendant, Larry Warner was accused of unlawful restraint. He lived with his two children and a woman and her four children. In June and July, Jesse, one of the woman's sons

> was confined to his bedroom for approximately 30 days, and Sarah [one of the woman's daughters] was confined to her bedroom for one week, as punishment for "stealing food from the family kitchen...."
>
> [D]uring the time Jesse was confined to his room, he was allowed to leave the room once a day to use the bathroom, food was brought to him, and he was not allowed to see or talk to anyone other than the defendant.... [T]he windows and door in Jesse's room were closed, and the windows were covered with plastic until the last week of his confinement when a fan was placed in the room. Throughout the 30-day period, Jesse was permitted to leave his bedroom for one visit to defendant's mother's grave and "some trips to the park or to shop...."
>
> [The woman] testified that during the restriction period, Jesse appeared "peaked, white and almost comatose," and Sarah broke out in a heat rash.
>
> Defendant cites Dr. Benjamin Spock, *Baby and Child Care* (2d ed. 1968), as authority for his first argument that he did not commit the offense of unlawful restraint by confining Jesse and Sarah to their bedrooms as a means of discipline. Dr. Spock recognized some form of confinement as an appropriate form of punishment although he neither encouraged nor condemned it.

(The appellate court upheld defendant's conviction, since the "jury could have concluded that it was not reasonable to confine a child to an unventilated bedroom during the summer for the greater part of one month, or even for the one week that Sarah was confined.")

(23) Professor Wald posits the case of "two preteen children [who] are afraid to live at home because their mother believes that they are about to be kidnapped and, in order to prevent the kidnapping, she never allows them to leave the house." Michael S. Wald, *Thinking About Public Policy Toward Abuse and Neglect of Children: A Review of* Before the Best Interests of the Child, 78 Mich L Rev 645, 666 (1980).

(24) Professor Wald also puts the case of "a young boy [who] is frequently absent from school, and when he attends school he sits alone in the corner because the parent makes him wear dresses."

(25) *Leone v. Dilullo*, 365 SE2d 39 (SC App 1988), reports the case of Marie Dilullo, who was robbed of her rent money, was evicted, lost her job, went on welfare, and asked her brother and sister-in-law to care for her four-and three-year-old children until she could do so herself. In May 1980, the children moved from Dilullo's home in Connecticut to the Leone's home in South Carolina. Over the next five years, Dilullo provided no support for the children, sent the girl a dress in December 1984 but never sent the boy anything, never visited the children, never sent them a letter, made only "a few intermittent telephone calls over the years," and never sought custody.

(The appellate court upheld an order terminating Dilullo's parental rights and allowing the Leones to adopt the children. It found Dilullo's argument that she had couldn't afford to keep in touch with her children unconvincing. "For example, she admitted the Leones had not discouraged her from calling the children, claiming she failed to call only because she had no money to pay for it and she did not have a telephone. Yet she also admitted that during the two years she was married to Mr. Dilullo . . . she had financial support and a telephone.")

(26) Consider again the case of Phillip B., but ignore the issue whether the parents should have consented to Phillip's heart treatment.

(27) In *Matter of A.M.K.*, 312 NW2d 840 (Wis App 1981), "Mr. K. was convicted of the second-degree murder of his wife, K.A.K. [the mother of Mr. K's six-year-old son], and was sentenced to eighteen years in prison." Mr. K. had "spent many years in both juvenile and criminal institutions for crimes ranging from grand theft to sexual intercourse with a minor, battery to his wife, and second degree murder." Should it matter whether Mr. K. has some plan for caring for his child? Whether Mr. K. had had no criminal record except the murder of his wife? Whether Mr. K. had been sentenced to eighteen years in prison only for the murder of someone he did not know?

(The appellate court sustained the trial court's termination of parental rights. It cited approvingly the trial court's finding of unfitness grounded on "Mr. K's 'potentially long prison sentence,' his history of violence, his inability to care for his son in the foreseeable future and the psychological trauma he has caused his son.")

(28) *In re Jason B.*, 458 NYS2d 180 (Fam Ct 1983), reports that while nine-month-old Jason's mother was receiving treatment at the North Richmond Community Mental Health Center, she said,

> "What do I have to do to get help, something stupid like dangling one of my kids over the ferry?" Noting that the respondent [mother] was "in crisis" and capable of hurting the children, a social worker from North Richmond filed a report of suspected child abuse or mistreatment.
>
> Responding to this report, Ronald Haucke, a caseworker . . ., visited the respondent at her home. She stated to him that she was "very depressed," "wanted to end it all," and would "take the children with her." Respondent now maintains that she never intended to hurt her

children and points to the fact that there is no evidence of any past or present injury to them.

In 1976, Jason's mother had been hospitalized for seventeen days for schizophrenia. A few months after the incident described above, she was again admitted to St. Vincent's with complaints of "feeling depressed, insomnia, and unable to function or care for her children." The observation was further made that she was "vaguely suicidal." A final diagnosis of "Major Depression, Recurrent with Psychotic Features" was reached.

(The family court held that Jason and his siblings were neglected, saying, "Since the parent made the threat, it is only reasonable that she be required to come forward to satisfy the Court that the children are, and will be, safe," and adding that it was "her special ongoing vulnerability to depression that leads the Court to conclude that these children of tender age, are in danger.")

(29) In *Oregon v. Goff*, 686 P2d 1023 (Ore 1984), Tina Marie Goff left her eight-year-old and twenty-two-month-old children alone at 9:30 Halloween night to go to a nearby tavern. She left the number of the tavern and a neighbor for the eight-year-old to call in case there was any problem. Between 10:45 and 11:00 two of Goff's friends stopped by the house to pick up a camera. Everything seemed fine. Goff had eight or nine beers and returned home at 2:00 A.M. She found the house on fire. Both children died. The fire was caused by matches which were used by the three adult smokers who lived in the house.

(The Oregon Supreme Court sustained Goff's conviction of criminal child neglect: "Every responsible adult should know that fire is a likely danger when children are left alone with access to matches." The court added, "The fact that the defendant went to a party at a tavern is directly relevant to the justifiability of the risk." Compare *New Jersey Division of Youth & Family Services v. B.W.*, 384 A2d 923 (NJ Juv & Dom Rel 1977). Although two of her children had died in a fire while she went to the movies with her boyfriend and B.W. was found guilty of involuntary manslaughter, her parental rights to her remaining children were left intact. B.W. maintained an unbroken record of visitation with her children. The children were increasingly difficult to return to foster care and jumped up and down and raced around when they were to see their mother. When the children returned to B.W.'s care, substantial homemaker services had to be provided by social services.)

(30) *Harper v. Department of Human Resources*, 285 SE2d 220 (Ga App 1981) is worth reading virtually in its entirety:

> This is an appeal from a judgment of the Juvenile Court of Fulton County severing parental rights under Code § 24A–3201 (a)(2) which sanctions the procedure where the child is a deprived child "and the court finds that the conditions and causes of the deprivation are likely to continue or will not be remedied and that by reason thereof the child is suffering or will probably suffer serious physical, mental, moral or emotional harm." A deprived child may mean one who "is without

proper parental care or control, subsistence, education as required by law, or other care or control necessary for his physical, mental or emotional health or morals."

In brief summary, the appellant mother completed nine years of public school. Her first husband abandoned her and her second was in prison at the time of this hearing. She lives in a trailer without water or toilet facilities in the rear of her mother's yard. She has three children by her first husband. The little girl is with her. One boy is in a home for mental retardates. The child involved here, referred to as M.S.S., was five years old at the time he was removed from appellant's custody. In the past five years since that time appellant has visited him between four and six times. The child looked forward to her visits with dread, nightmares, and fantasies of violence. The family has been the subject of long term cooperation between the Protective Services' Branch of the Department of Family & Children Services of Fulton County, the Georgia Mental Health Institute, a specially selected team of foster parents chosen to work closely with the mental health branches in the interests of M.S.S., and at least two therapists at all times, one assigned to the appellant and another to the child and foster parents. During this time definite improvement was shown. The child was able to attend a public school rather than a special school; his behavior and attention span increased and hyperactivity decreased due to medication and training, and he gained a belated control over most bodily functions. Opinion evidence and other circumstances support the conclusion that the child dreads return to the mother, regresses when forced into her company, and that the appellant, who was offered therapy sessions, soon drops out, and also fails to stay gainfully employed although she is able to work, and when she works earns in the neighborhood of $400 per month. On the other hand, the record reflects that medication and drugs were given to the child by the state agencies, at different times, to control hyperactivity in amounts of ½ of a 5 milligram tablet of dexedrine in the morning before breakfast and two 37.5 milligrams of cylert before breakfast, and as needed, one at 7:00 p.m. in the evening with foster parents medicating him on weekends. In lengthy testimony the mother stated that she had only been permitted to see Shane six times since April of 1976, although many requests have been made. The mother contended that Shane had been coached on what to say and not to speak to his mother; that the mother generally indicated the endless and useless counseling and therapy as a condition precedent to see the child was part of the problem, not a solution, and it was so time consuming that she had lost several jobs because of it; that agencies and psychologists had done "me dirty as all get out about my child" and that she had to put a stop to agency involvement with her other child, Tammy, who is at home with her, and that the state had turned her child against her.

The child's therapist testified at length concerning fantasies and nightmares of the child involving the fear that his mother would kidnap him, and fear that she would kill him and his brother. The appellant herself testified that she did at one time take a knife in the presence of the children with the intention of taking her own life but did not threaten them with it. The objection to the testimony of the expert witness on the ground of hearsay was properly denied, as it tended to reflect the medical history reasonably pertinent to the diagnosis and treatment of the child (Code § 38–315). The testimony of the child might be the best testimony as to the mother-child relationship.

We are alert to the danger of severing parental ties without necessity, and to the ruling in *Ray v. Department of Human Resources*, that there is "some required showing of parental unfitness caused either by intentional or unintentional misconduct . . . or by what is tantamount to physical or mental incapacity to care for the child." This child has been in the foster home and/or under the control of the state for over four years and he has made satisfactory improvement. There is no evidence to reflect that this would not have been the case if custody and care had remained in the mother for motivation and self-determination involving the family, both mother and child. The case of *Collins v. Martin*, 267 S.E.2d 858 (Ga App 1980), appears to be applicable in this case: "The appellant's conduct, while not exemplary, cannot be said to be so profoundly detrimental or egregious as to permanently terminate her rights to her child."

Having only a ninth-grade education, living in a trailer without water or toilet facilities in the rear of her mother's yard, not holding a steady job, and with a husband in prison are the only reasons shown to sever parental rights as required under *Ray* and *Chancey, supra*. In our opinion, these reasons are totally insufficient to trigger the drastic action of severing parental rights. No other misconduct or physical or mental disability of the mother is shown. Factually, the child seems to have emotional difficulties, fantasies, and nightmares; but these are problems of the child, not the mother.

(31) Consider again the case of Jessie Bond. Eliminate from that case the sexual abuse and prenatal drug abuse charges and assume Jessie's parental problems are attributable to her drug addiction.

(32) In *State ex rel. Paul v. Department of Public Welfare*, 170 S2d 549 (La App 1965), the plaintiff was a thirty-five-year-old unmarried woman whose baby was taken from her a few days after he was born. The evidence was

> that plaintiff is in good physical health. She has a congenital motor speech defect, however, which is of such a nature that it is impossible for her to speak words or to communicate orally with anyone other than her mother, who has learned to understand what plaintiff is trying to say. Plaintiff has . . . an I.Q. of about 45 and a mental age of about 7.3 years. . . .
>
> Plaintiff lives in a small house with her 72–year-old mother and with two of her sisters, and both of these sisters have a lower level of intelligence than does plaintiff. . . . The mother is classified as mentally dull, but she has a higher intelligence quotient than any of the daughters. . . .

Psychologists and lay witnesses indicate that she [plaintiff] is able to perform work in a field ... without supervision. She also is able to cook and to can or preserve fruits and vegetables. She unquestionably loves the child and wants to obtain custody of it....

Dr. Ralph Ware, a psychiatrist ... testified that she walks well, handles her hands well, knows the time of day, knows the difference between hot and cold, knows the day of the week, and she can perform common ordinary tasks at home well, such as cleaning, cooking, canning, bathing and dressing. In his opinion, plaintiff could handle the bringing up of this child.... He concedes that plaintiff could not teach the child to speak, that she could not help him with his school lessons, and that the environment is not good, but he feels that plaintiff can take care of the physical needs of the child, and that she can provide a mother's love.

Dr. Robert H. Cassell [a psychologist] ... feels that ... plaintiff would not be able to function if something of a non-routine nature occurred. She, for instance, could not determine when the child was sick, what is dangerous and what is not dangerous, or when the child should be taken to a doctor....

Mr. Bernard Phelps, a psychologist ... testified that awarding custody of the child to plaintiff would result in "utter havoc for the child's concern, for the parent's concern, and some question as to the survival of the infant."

(The appellate court upheld the trial court's denial of a writ of habeas corpus because of evidence the plaintiff "would not be able to provide some of the training which the child must have, such as the ability to speak or to properly care for him in case of sickness or emergencies." There was a concurrence which reads more like a dissent.)

(33) *Matter of R.W.*, 772 P2d 366 (NM App 1989), reports that

R.W. is the second of three children born to mother and her husband. When he was 27 days old, mother noticed R.W. would not eat, was always sleeping, and generally appeared to her to be very ill. She took him to the hospital, and the doctors decided to keep him there. R.W. was diagnosed at that time as having nonorganic failure to thrive. While he was still in the hospital, mother was served with a summons in a neglect action. Ultimately, mother entered into a stipulated judgment, under which R.W. was adjudicated neglected....

[At a subsequent termination hearing], Mary Steir, Ph.D., a psychologist and professor at the University of New Mexico, ... explained that children are diagnosed with this condition when they have failed to gain weight as expected and there is no organic cause for the failure to gain weight. In these circumstances, it is believed that the failure to gain weight results from some sort of parental interactional patterns, not the failure to provide enough nourishment or food....

The department's other witnesses in this case included Debbie Sanchez, a teacher from the Peanut Butter and Jelly Preschool, an organization that provides parent skills training, and Wilma McBride, the family life coordinator from the Young Children's Health Center, Department of Pediatrics at the University of New Mexico Medical School, who facilitated visitation between mother and R.W. while he was in the custody of the department and placed in a foster home. Both witnesses expressed the opinion that mother's inability to understand and provide for R.W.'s needs had not improved, despite psychological counseling and classes in parenting skills.

(The appellate court upheld the trial court's termination of the mother's parental rights. It cited the evidence of "Ms. McBride, who had worked with mother and R.W. intensively during the period of time from October 1986 through March 1987, . . . that such a return [of R.W. to the mother] would have a negative impact on R.W. and that he would have a difficult time developing the skills he would need to survive in the family." The court noted "that R.W.'s older and younger siblings are still living with mother and are acknowledged to be physically healthy." But it said that,

> while the department has not moved to take either of the other children into custody, mother's relationship with both has been the subject of intervention by teachers at the Peanut Butter and Jelly Preschool and the Young Children's Health Center. Further, there was testimony that R.W.'s siblings have been able to adapt to the family's lifestyle because they have more assertive personalities than R.W. and because they have remained part of the family unit since birth.)

Compare *New Jersey Div. Youth and Fam Serv. v. A.W. and R.W.*, 512 A2d 438 (NJ 1986), where the mother was so limited that the children did not know that an object dropped under a table remained in existence, were not toilet trained, and could not even speak at the ages of three and four. The mother's rights were severed although the court pointed out that mere poverty would not justify removal of a child, much less termination of parental rights.

(34) *In re Barbara M*, 494 NYS2d 968 (Fam Ct 1985), relates the story of fourteen-year-old Barbara M., who one year was absent from school 74 full days and 26 half days. There was evidence that she

> suffered from various ailments, including: upper respiratory infection, viral pneumonia, repeated ear and throat infections, strep throat, and allergies, as well as a staph infection in her nose and a swollen face, causing her left eye to be swollen shut for almost a month. She had her tonsils and adenoids surgically removed. Barbara was treated by Dr. Nagy eleven times during the year and, upon referral for possible rheumatoid arthritis, was treated approximately once a month by a Dr. Cohen.... She has also shown symptoms of a persistent low grade fever.

(The family court found that Barbara was not a person in need of supervision, since she "suffered extraordinary, numerous ailments during the 1983–1984 school term . . . [,] remained away from school with the consent of her parent.... [and since the school district's] rules provide that illness is a permissible excuse from attendance...." However, the court required the department of social services "to conduct a child protective investigation to determine whether Barbara M is a neglected child, in that her parent failed to obtain home tutoring.")

(35) *In re Yardley*, 149 NW2d 162 (Iowa 1967), reports that Wanda Yardley divorced her husband in 1963 because he was living with another woman and received custody of their six children. Subsequently, she had another child out of wedlock. "The house was found to be cluttered and untidy, the kitchen had unwashed dishes piled up, the beds were unmade and without sheets or proper bedding. In 18 to 25 visits to the home ... petitioner [the Department of Social Welfare] found it in much the same condition as at first." Wanda had the help of eighteen-year-old Helen Guard in caring for the children. "Helen admitted as a witness [that] a divorced man named Buck stayed with her in the back bedroom all of about three or four nights. The children who usually slept in that bed were required to give it up on these occasions." Wanda went to bars two or three nights a week, leaving around 8:30 or 9:00 and returning around 11:30 to 1:00. On other occasions she would stay away from home all night.

(The Iowa Supreme Court approved intervention, the children lacked "parental direction, moral guidance and good example." However, the court remanded "for the taking of additional evidence ... as to whether conditions in the home and Wanda's conduct ... are such that custody of the children should be returned to her....")

(36) *In Interest of Polovchak*, 432 NE2d 873 (Ill App 1981) reports that Michael and Anna Polovchak came to the United States from the Ukraine with their three children in January 1980. At some point, the parents apparently told the children the family was going to return to the Ukraine. Anna Polovchak testified that, on July 14, 1980, she had come home to find Natalie (then seventeen) and Walter (twelve) removing their things from the family apartment with the help of the children's cousin (who until two days earlier had been living with the Polovchaks). The cousin told Mrs. Polovchak that Walter was not being forced to do anything. The cousin and the two children then went to the cousin's apartment. There they stayed until July 18, when, at Michael's request, the police came to the apartment and took Walter to the police station. "Walter said he had run away because he did not want to return to the Ukraine with his family." Walter later testified that he "did not like the Ukraine because 'there aren't many things to be bought there.' "

(This is not a true abuse and neglect case. The issue was whether Walter was a "minor in need of supervision." Apparently her parents did not insist that Natalie accompany them back to Russia, and in any event, she reached the age of majority by the time the case was litigated.)

The appellate court reversed the lower court's finding that Walter was a minor in need of supervision and rejected the state's argument "that Walter was a runaway and needed to be protected by the State from the considerable dangers existent to all runaways." The court said Walter's "single act of leaving the family residence ... was an exaggerated manifestation of parent-child conflict and was not sufficient to bring him within the jurisdiction of the court." It added that the expert witnesses agreed "Walter was not beyond his parents' control."

> We have serious doubt as to whether the State would have intervened in this realm of family life and privacy had the parents' decision to relocate involved a move to another city or state. The fact that the parents had decided to move to a country which is ruled under principles of government which are alien to those of the United States of America should not compel a different result.

The dissent put the facts in a different light:

> While his mother stood by, apparently unable to control the situation, Walter packed and left home. Several days later, still unable to control the situation, the parents were compelled to seek out the authorities in order to locate the boy. When the police found Walter, he still refused to return home. And in court, Walter stated that he would leave again if forced to return home.

And the dissent was convinced that "where a boy fled home under circumstances such as these but because his family was moving to another state, a juvenile court's decision that supervision over the child was required never would be disturbed by a reviewing court."

Walter remained in the United States until he reached his majority. He recounts his experiences in *Freedom's Child: A Courageous Teenager's Story of Fleeing His Parents—and the Soviet Union—to Live in America* (Random House, 1988).

(37) Now review the questions we have just studied. Suppose in each of those cases where it is plausible to do so that the state is moving to protect not the child who was injured, but rather that child's sibling. Would and should the same result be reached in each case?

C. EVALUATING THE APPROACHES TO ABUSE AND NEGLECT

Having tested each statutory approach in a range of cases, you should reach conclusions about each approach and to formulate your own. What are the assumptions of each approach? What strengths and weaknesses do you see in each? How could each be improved? The following questions should help you answer these queries.

Questions on Abuse and Neglect

(1) Do all the statutes restrict the state's power to protect children too greatly? David Gil, an expert on child abuse, suggests that it be defined as "any act of commission or omission . . . which deprives children of equal rights and liberties and/or interferes with their optimal development." In social terms, is this a good definition? In legal terms?

(2) The *Standards* postpone intervention as long as possible. Is that a good idea? The commentary to section 1.3 explains that "because our limited knowledge of child rearing practices and child development

renders predictions of future harm a very difficult endeavor, coercive intervention should be restricted to situations where harm has occurred or is imminent." Further, "[b]y limiting intervention to situations where the harm is serious, we can assume that intervention will generally do more good than harm." On the other hand, it is said that a "typical pattern of abuse involves a continuing series of assaults, escalating in severity. Neglect is an even more obvious case of a chronic condition." Richard Bourne and Eli H. Newberger, *"Family Autonomy" or "Coercive Intervention"? Ambiguity and Conflict in the Proposed Standards for Child Abuse and Neglect*, 57 BU L Rev 670, 685 (1977). If this is true, should we intervene before the child's distress and even danger become acute?

(3) The commentary to *Standards* section 1.2 says "most state statutes define the grounds for intervention in terms of parental behavior or home conditions without requiring a showing that the child is being harmed by the behavior of the parent or conditions in the home." In contrast, section 1.2 of the *Standards* expressly states that "[c]oercive intervention should be premised upon specific harms that a child has suffered or is likely to suffer." Is the *Standards* approach always preferable?

There is one circumstance when the *Standards* do not require serious demonstrable harm before intervention. Section 2.1.D authorizes intervention merely on a showing of sexual abuse, although an alternative would require showing serious emotional or physical harm. The commentary explains why the alternative might be adopted:

> [T]he available studies come to diverse findings regarding the negative impact of sexual "abuse." While some studies find significant harm, other commentators concluded that the children studied suffered no significant short or long-term negative effects. Moreover, the process of intervention may be more disturbing to the child than the sexual activity.... Finally, there is little evidence of the efficacy of treatment programs following intervention which might justify the added trauma. Neither is there evidence that the activity, once discovered, will be continued.

The commentary then defends its "broader basis for intervention." First, sexual abuse "is usually only one of several negative factors operative in families where this conduct occurs," thus justifying "singling out these families for special attention." Second, once the sexual abuse is discovered, "it may be essential to intervene in order to assess the impact of the discovery on the child and to insure that the conduct is discontinued." Third, juvenile court proceedings are generally preferable to criminal proceedings against the abusing parent.

Could the *Standards* reasoning about sexual abuse be applied to the other situations? Consider the following criticism:

> [E]xclusive reliance on the short number of symptoms listed would preclude intervention in many cases in which the evidence suggests that it is appropriate. In infants these particular symptoms may be impossi-

ble to detect, while other symptoms, such as feeding and sleep disturbances or developmental delay will be more appropriate and more easily measurable indicators of harm. Even for older children, other symptoms—serious school problems, major problems in cognitive development, poor results on psychological tests, for example—may be more reliable indicators of harm than vaguely defined states such as depression or withdrawal.

Requiring symptomological evidence in every case also prevents intervention before serious damage has been done, even in instances where eventual harm is virtually guaranteed. An infant living alone with an acutely psychotic parent, for example, is in danger of serious harm.

Marsha Garrison, *Child Welfare Decisionmaking: In Search of the Least Drastic Alternative*, 75 Geo L J 1745, 1798–99 (1987).

(4) What standards of clarity does the Constitution impose on the statutes we are considering? Professor Clark reports that "the cases have nearly always held that the statutes are sufficiently definite to give persons of ordinary intelligence fair notice of what the legislature is forbidding." Homer H. Clark, Jr., 1 *The Law of Domestic Relations in the United States* 606 (West, 1987). A different answer is given in *Alsager v. District Court of Polk County, Iowa*, 406 F Supp 10 (SD Iowa, 1975). The Iowa statute provided for termination of parental rights where "the parents have substantially and continuously refused to give the child necessary parental care and protection" and where "the parents are unfit by reason of debauchery, intoxication, habitual use of narcotic drugs, repeated lewd and lascivious behavior, or other conduct found by the court likely to be detrimental to the physical or mental health or morals of the child." The court found that those standards "are susceptible to multifarious interpretations which prevent the ordinary person from knowing what is and is not prohibited," that they "afford state officials with so much discretion in their interpretation and application that arbitrary and discriminatory parental terminations are inevitable," and that they "serve to inhibit parents in the exercise of their fundamental right to family integrity." The court further found that there had been no "state court construction [of the statute] restricting the vague standards to constitutionally permissible bounds." The court thus concluded the statute was void for vagueness.

(5) The *Standards* appear to be animated by a deep skepticism of state intervention and by a feeling that even abused or neglected children are likely to be best served by being left with their parents. Professor Michael Wald, a co-reporter for the *Standards*, defended both views in two influential articles. *State Intervention on Behalf of "Neglected" Children: A Search for Realistic Standards*, 27 Stan L Rev 985 (1975); *State Intervention on Behalf of "Neglected" Children: Standards for Removal of Children from Their Homes, Monitoring the Status of Children in Foster Care, and Termination of Parental Rights*, 28 Stan L Rev 623 (1976).

Professor Wald begins with a familiar theme—that we know little about how children develop or how to influence that development. He reasons that, if we don't know how to help children, we should be reluctant to try. He argues that attempts to do so have meant that "coercive intervention frequently results in placing a child in a more detrimental situation than he would be in without intervention." One important reason is that separating children from their parents is "per se damaging." Another reason is that the primary state alternative to the child's own home—foster homes—"are subject to a number of defects." These include the difficulty of finding good foster parents, the risk of multiple placements, and the conflict children may feel in having two sets of parents. Further, the "success of several experimental programs in treating parents while safely keeping the child in the home holds out the promise that the trauma of removal can be avoided."

Even where children are not removed from their homes, intervention is problematic: "Despite approximately 70 years of experience, there is remarkably little evidence demonstrating the usefulness of social work intervention, particularly with regard to 'soft' services [like counselling and education, as opposed to things like money and medical care]." And there is "substantial evidence ... that many public social work agencies have untrained or poorly trained staff." In addition, "[w]hile there is no empirical evidence demonstrating that social workers act in a discriminatory manner, many commentators believe that social work agencies apply middle-class standards to poor and minority parents and attempt to change their lifestyles to meet middle-class norms."

Insofar as the *Standards* intend that the government not intervene in families more than it must to accomplish legitimate purposes, they are hardly controversial. There is substantial agreement that being separated from parents can hurt children and that the foster system can work badly. But do the *Standards* nevertheless set too high a barrier to intervention? Professor Marsha Garrison has argued that they do. *Child Welfare Decisionmaking: In Search of the Least Drastic Alternative*, 75 Geo L J 1745 (1987).

Professor Garrison's starting point resembles Professor Wald's: "The experts do not agree on the long-term effects of many child rearing practices, or on the efficacy of various treatment strategies. One of the few points on which they do generally agree is the present difficulty of predicting adult personality on the basis of childhood experiences." She adds that "most of the research is simply not very good: control groups are frequently lacking, follow-up is often inadequate, and variable methods of measuring outcomes make comparisons extremely difficult." And like Professor Wald, Professor Garrison points to the "high caseloads, rapid staff turnover, and inadequate training among workers." In fact, "child welfare administration has been consistently characterized by its noncompliance with legal standards."

However, Professor Garrison believes Professor Wald overstates the risks of intervention. She believes continuity benefits children but is not the only, or even the most important, thing that is good for them. She recites evidence "that inadequate care poses greater risks than discontinuity." Nor have "researchers generally ... found that children suffer status anxiety based simply on the conditional and impermanent nature of foster care placement." She finds the evidence on foster care at worst equivocal, with the best studies reporting foster care doesn't hurt children and may help them. Nor can she find much evidence that interventions that do not remove children from their homes generally harm children.

Professor Garrison emphasizes the risks of non-intervention. She cites evidence "that researchers have failed to find large numbers of children receiving child welfare services on frivolous grounds." She notes that those children typically live in circumstances neither they nor their parents can cope with well, circumstances that have been linked with developmental deficiencies in children. Professor Garrison is skeptical of providing services to parents as a substitute for removing children from the home, since "the evidence suggests that only a minority of parents show significant improvement as a result of intervention programs."

Professor Wald himself recently participated in a study comparing children in foster care with abused or neglected children who were not removed from their homes and whose parents received services in their homes. This study concluded,

> Looking only at what happened to the children from the time we first saw them until the end of the study, two years later, there was not a great deal of difference between home and foster care. On *average*, there was little change in the relative well-being of each group of children. However, those changes that did occur favored foster care....
>
> The outcomes for those children who remained at home throughout the two years were mixed, at best. Nearly half the children were subjected to some degree of abuse or continued neglect, though none of the children suffered serious harm. Yet despite the fact that many of the home environments remained only marginally adequate, there was, on average, no deterioration in the well-being of the home children in most areas of development. The only clear area of decline was in social behavior at school....
>
> ... [H]ome placement, even with services to the family, did not help the children overcome their academic, emotional, and social problems....
>
> In most aspects of development, the white foster children were better off at the end than at the beginning.... There was some improvement in both the physical health and the academic performance of the white foster children, though few children either at home or in foster care had health problems, and most children in both settings continued to experience academic difficulties. Perhaps more significant, the foster children reported increased personal satisfaction during the two years.... [T]hey consistently seemed somewhat more satisfied than

the home children. There also seemed to be much less adult-child conflict in the foster setting.

Michael S. Wald, J.M. Carlsmith, and P.H. Leiderman, *Protecting Abused and Neglected Children* 183–84 (Stan U Press, 1988). How ought these findings and Professor Garrison's criticisms affect your thinking about the ABA *Standards*?

(6) Consider again the *Harper* case from Question 30, above.

(a) Is *Harper* rightly decided? On what theory is it decided?

(i) Is this simply a question of burden of proof? Is the problem simply that the Department of Human Services failed to show that the child would not have improved "if custody and care had remained in the mother for motivation and self-determination involving the family, both mother and child"?

(ii) Is the court concerned because the parent is not "at fault"? Is that what "misconduct" means under the statute?

(iii) Is the court concerned because there is not "physical or mental disability"? Mrs. Harper is in fact raising one child, which seems to suggest that she is not unable to raise a child.

(iv) Is the court swayed by the presumption of parental fitness?

(b) What does the court anticipate will happen next in *Harper*?

(c) What, do your answers to these questions suggest about the Michigan statute and the Standards?

(7) Professor Wald writes that

the great majority of neglect cases involve very poor families who are usually receiving welfare.... In addition to the problems directly caused by poverty—poor housing, inadequate medical care, poor nutritional practices—many of these parents can best be described as extremely 'marginal' people, that is, they are continually at the borderline of being able to sustain themselves—economically, emotionally, and mentally.

Their plight is reflected in their home situations. Their homes are often dirty and run-down. Feeding arrangements are haphazard. One or both parents may have a drinking or drug problem, suffer from mental illness, or be retarded, which may affect the quality of their child care. If there are two parents, constant bickering and fighting may occur, or the husband may periodically disappear. Often the children's lives are marked by uncertainty and chaos.

Such parents may provide little emotional support for their children. While the children may not be physically abused, left unattended, dangerously malnourished, or overtly rejected, they may receive little love, attention, stimulation, or emotional involvement. The children do not usually evidence emotional damage as serious as that previously discussed. However, they may be relatively listless and may perform poorly in school and in social relations.

State Intervention on Behalf of "Neglected" Children: A Search for Realistic Standards, 27 Stan L Rev 985, 1021 (1975). Is it realistic and desirable for the state to exert intensive and prolonged efforts to keep children in their families when their families face the problems Professor Wald describes? Would it be wrong for the state not to make such efforts?

Drafting a Definition of Abuse and Neglect

You are now ready to draft the section of your statute that defines abuse and neglect. What does your statute say? Do your definitions define abuse and neglect with enough specificity to give parents adequate notice and judges adequate guidance? Do your definitions encompass all the situations in which the state ought to intervene but exclude all the situations in which it ought not intervene? Do your definitions give officials and judges enough discretion to intervene in situations you have not anticipated but not so much discretion as to encourage improper intervention? Are your definitions worded clearly enough to prevent problems in interpreting them? Will your definitions be workable in the context of reporting statutes as well as abuse and neglect statutes?

How do your definitions differ from those you have already read? In what ways are your definitions superior? What are the assumptions on which your definitions are based? Will your statute be able to win enough support to be adopted? What resistance might there be to your statute once it is enacted?

SECTION 3. PROCEDURAL STANDARDS FOR INTERVENTION

Well, pretty soon the old man was up and around again, and then he went for Judge Thatcher to make him give up that money, and he went for me, too, for not stopping school. He catched me a couple of times and thrashed me, but I went to school just the same, and dodged him or out-run him most of the time. I didn't want to go to school much, before, but I reckoned I'd go now to spite pap. That law trial was a slow business; appeared like they warn't ever going to get started on it; so every now and then I'd borrow two or three dollars off of the judge for him, to keep from getting a cowhiding. Every time he got money he got drunk; and every time he got drunk he raised Cain around town; and every time he raised Cain he got jailed. He was just suited—this kind of thing was right in his line.

Mark Twain
Adventures of Huckleberry Finn

You should now establish procedural standards for intervention in abuse and neglect cases for your model statute. As we learned in examining discretion and rules in the context of child custody, one way to limit discretion is to establish procedures officials must follow. And it is the essence of due process to provide subjects of government action with procedural protections. In addition, good procedures should lead to good decisions.

Many of these procedures limit the state's power to intervene in the family. They protect parents in the exercise of their parental rights. They benefit children by discouraging the state from intervening where intervention would do no good or do harm. Yet these same procedures can inhibit the state when its intervention would protect children from serious harm. The following materials should help you explore these tensions so you can decide how your statute should resolve them.

A. PROCEDURES BEFORE JUDICIAL PROCEDURES BEGIN

I have taught them the duties of the family, of parent and child, and husband and wife; and how can I bear to have this open acknowledgment that we care for no tie, no duty, no relation, however sacred, compared with money? I have talked with Eliza about her boy—her duty to him as a Christian mother, to watch over him, pray for him, and bring him up in a Christian way; and now what can I say, if you tear him away, and sell him, soul and body, to a profane, unprincipled man, just to save a little money?

Harriet Beecher Stowe
Uncle Tom's Cabin

(1) The Reporting Acts

As public concern about child abuse has grown, so has the scope of abuse and neglect reporting acts which we discussed in Section 1 of this Chapter. What kinds of abuse or neglect ought your statute require people to report? Who ought to be obliged to report abuse or neglect? What penalties ought there be for failures to report? What costs do such statutes impose? The following questions are designed to raise some of these issues in a useful form.

Questions on Reporting

(1) Suppose you are the lawyer for Dr. P and Ms. L in the following case (taken from Anonymous, *Should Child Abuse Always Be Reported?*, 13 Hastings Center Rep 19 (1983)). What would you advise?

> Kim S, age fifteen, was brought by her mother to the OB–GYN clinic at a state university medical center, located about twenty miles from the family's small rural town. Kim told Dr. P that she was pregnant, and that her eighteen-year-old brother was the father. She claimed that her brother forced her to have sexual relations with him, though without violence. Kim also claimed that she had resisted his advances, but finally submitted when her brother threatened to reveal an important secret Kim had shared with him earlier.
>
> Both embarrassed and afraid of reprisals, Kim had initially decided to tell no one about the incident. Slightly more than two months later, when she realized that she might be pregnant, Kim told her mother about the assault. Mrs. S confronted her son, who admitted that the

incest had taken place. He claimed, however, that his sister was a willing partner. Mrs. S then contacted the medical center.

After hearing the details of the incident, Dr. P spoke about the possibility of an abortion and offered to help make the arrangements. Both Kim and her mother agreed to an abortion. Dr. P then invited a hospital social worker, Ms. L, to join the conversation. Dr. P stated that Kim had apparently been abused; the hospital staff was therefore obligated by state law to report the incident to the state Department of Family and Children's Services (DFCS).

Mrs. S immediately became visibly upset and told Dr. P and Ms. L that if the case were reported to DFCS "our lives will be ruined. We know people who work in that office of our county, and the news will spread like wildfire." Mrs. S then went on to explain that the family was well known and respected in their small town, and that any publicity about the incident would place an unbearable burden upon the family members. She argued that the family was capable of handling its own problems without interference from a state agency, and that she had already made an appointment for the family to meet with a counselor. Mrs. S also questioned whether her son's actions technically constituted abuse. She pointed out that this sort of incident is not uncommon between siblings and that her son had not intended to harm his sister.

Should Dr. P and Ms. L report what they have learned to the DFCS? What other routes might they, ought they, be able to pursue?

(2) Do the reporting acts go far enough? Professor Wald reports that

several nationally respected scholars have recently suggested the establishment of monitoring systems to screen all children for developmental progress at regular intervals starting at birth. For example, one prominent physician advocates having health visitors regularly visit every home to check on the well-being of children. The Joint Commission on Mental Health of Children has recommended the establishment of neighborhood children's councils to check on the development of all children in their respective service areas and to "take full responsibility for seeing that each child gets all appropriate helping services."

State Intervention on Behalf of "Neglected" Children: A Search for Realistic Standards, 27 Stan L Rev 985, 990–91 (1975).

B. PROCEDURES AFTER JUDICIAL PROCEEDINGS BEGIN

Your first duty is to be humane. Love childhood. Look with friendly eyes on its games, its pleasures, its amiable dispositions....

This is the time to correct the evil inclinations of mankind, you reply. Suffering should be increased in childhood when it is least felt, to reduce it at the age of reason. But how do you know that all the fine lessons with which you oppress the feeble mind of the child will not do more harm than good?

Jean Jacques Rousseau
Emile

(1) The Role of Counsel

Another question to consider in drafting your model statute is what role to allot to lawyers. This question is more complex than it might first appear. Abuse and neglect and termination proceedings are judicial processes in which parents' legal rights are at stake and which raise issues lawyers are specially trained to deal with. Further, it is a standard part of due-process thinking that people who have been haled into court by the government have a right to counsel. But the ultimate purpose of abuse and neglect law is presumably to protect children from their parents where that is necessary and to help parents deal better with their children where that is possible. These are not goals lawyers are generally trained to promote. To put the conflict differently, the government's response to the abuse and neglect of children might be seen as primarily therapeutic, while the orientation of lawyers is generally not therapeutic. One might even say the adversarial orientation of lawyers regularly bring them into conflict with therapeutic attitudes and goals.

(a) The Constitutional Framework

In thinking about the role lawyers will play under your model statute, remember the question has a constitutional dimension. The following case discusses that dimension in the context of the question whether a parent subject to termination proceedings who cannot afford a lawyer is constitutionally entitled to have one paid for by the state.

LASSITER v. DEPARTMENT OF SOCIAL SERVICES

Supreme Court of the United States, 1981
452 US 18

STEWART, JUSTICE. . . .

II

For all its consequence, "due process" has never been, and perhaps can never be, precisely defined. "[U]nlike some legal rules," this Court has said, due process "is not a technical conception with a fixed content unrelated to time, place and circumstances." *Cafeteria Workers v. McElroy*, 367 US 886, 895. Rather, the phrase expresses the requirement of "fundamental fairness," a requirement whose meaning can be as opaque as its importance is lofty. Applying the Due Process Clause is therefore an uncertain enterprise which must discover what "fundamental fairness" consists of in a particular situation by first considering any relevant precedents and then by assessing the several interests that are at stake.

A

The pre-eminent generalization that emerges from this Court's precedents on an indigent's right to appointed counsel is that such a right has been recognized to exist only where the litigant may lose his physical liberty if he loses the litigation. Thus, when the Court overruled the principle of *Betts v. Brady*, 316 US 455, that counsel in criminal trials need be appointed only where the circumstances in a given case demand it, the Court did so in the case of a man sentenced to prison for five years. *Gideon v. Wainwright*, 372 US 335. And thus *Argersinger v. Hamlin*, 407 US 25, established that counsel must be provided before any indigent may be sentenced to prison, even where the crime is petty and the prison term brief.

That it is the defendant's interest in personal freedom, and not simply the special Sixth and Fourteenth Amendments right to counsel in criminal cases, which triggers the right to appointed counsel is demonstrated by the Court's announcement in *In re Gault*, 387 US 1, that "the Due Process Clause of the Fourteenth Amendment requires that in respect of proceedings to determine delinquency *which may result in commitment to an institution in which the juvenile's freedom is curtailed*," the juvenile has a right to appointed counsel even though proceedings may be styled "civil" and not "criminal." *Id.*, at 41 (emphasis added). Similarly, four of the five Justices who reached the merits in *Vitek v. Jones*, 445 US 480, concluded that an indigent prisoner is entitled to appointed counsel before being involuntarily transferred for treatment to a state mental hospital. The fifth Justice differed from the other four only in declining to exclude the "possibility that the required assistance may be rendered by competent laymen in some cases." *Id.*, at 500 (separate opinion of Powell, J.).

Significantly, as a litigant's interest in personal liberty diminishes, so does his right to appointed counsel. In *Gagnon v. Scarpelli*, 411 US 778, the Court gauged the due process rights of a previously sentenced probationer at a probation-revocation hearing. In *Morrissey v. Brewer*, 408 US 471, 480, which involved an analogous hearing to revoke parole, the Court had said: "Revocation deprives an individual, not of the absolute liberty to which every citizen is entitled, but only of the conditional liberty properly dependent on observance of special parole restrictions." Relying on that discussion, the Court in *Scarpelli* declined to hold that indigent probationers have, *per se*, a right to counsel at revocation hearings, and instead left the decision whether counsel should be appointed to be made on a case-by-case basis.

Finally, the Court has refused to extend the right to appointed counsel to include prosecutions which, though criminal, do not result in the defendant's loss of personal liberty. The Court in *Scott v. Illinois*, 440 US 367, for instance, interpreted the "central premise of *Argersinger*" to be "that actual imprisonment is a penalty different in kind from fines or the mere threat of imprisonment," and the Court endorsed that premise as "eminently sound and warrant[ing] adoption of actual imprisonment as the line defining the constitutional right to appointment of counsel." *Id.*, at 373. The Court thus held "that the Sixth and Fourteenth Amendments to the United States Constitution require only that no indigent criminal defendant be sentenced to a term of imprisonment unless the State has afforded him the right to assistance of appointed counsel in his defense." *Id.*, at 373–374.

In sum, the Court's precedents speak with one voice about what "fundamental fairness" has meant when the Court has considered the right to appointed counsel, and we thus draw from them the presumption that an indigent litigant has a right to appointed counsel only when, if he loses, he may be deprived of his physical liberty. It is against this presumption that all the other elements in the due process decision must be measured.

B

The case of *Mathews v. Eldridge*, 424 US 319, 335, propounds three elements to be evaluated in deciding what due process requires, viz., the private interests at stake, the government's interest, and the risk that the procedures used will lead to erroneous decisions. We must balance these elements against each other, and then set their net weight in the scales against the presumption that there is a right to appointed counsel only where the indigent, if he is unsuccessful, may lose his personal freedom.

This Court's decisions have by now made plain beyond the need for multiple citation that a parent's desire for and right to "the companionship, care, custody and management of his or her children" is an important interest that "undeniably warrants deference and, absent a powerful countervailing interest, protection." *Stanley v. Illinois*, 405 US 645, 651. Here the State has sought not simply to infringe upon that interest but to end it. If the State prevails, it will have worked a unique kind of deprivation. A parent's interest in the accuracy and injustice of the decision to terminate his or her parental status is, therefore a commanding one.

Since the State has an urgent interest in the welfare of the child, it shares the parent's interest in an accurate and just decision. For this reason, the State may share the indigent parent's interest in the availability of appointed counsel. If, as our adversary system presupposes, accurate and just results are most likely to be obtained through the equal contest of opposed interests, the State's interest in the child's welfare may perhaps best be served by a hearing in which both the parent and the State acting for the child are represented by counsel, without whom the contest of interests may become unwholesomely unequal. North Carolina itself acknowledges as much by providing that where a parent files a written answer to a termination petition, the State must supply a lawyer to represent the child.

The State's interests, however, clearly diverge from the parent's insofar as the State wishes the termination decision to be made as economically as possible and thus wants to avoid both the expense of appointed counsel and the cost of the lengthened proceedings his presence may cause. But though the State's pecuniary interest is legitimate, it is hardly significant enough to overcome private interests as important as those here, particularly in light of the concession in the respondent's brief that the "potential costs of appointed counsel in termination proceedings . . . is [*sic*] admittedly *de minimis* compared to the costs in all criminal actions."

Finally, consideration must be given to the risk that a parent will be erroneously deprived of his or her child because the parent is not represented by counsel. North Carolina law now seeks to assure accurate decisions by establishing the following procedures: A petition to terminate parental rights may be filed only by a parent seeking the termination of the other parent's rights, by a county department of social services or licensed child-placing agency with custody of the child, or by a person with whom the child has lived continuously for the two years preceding the petition. A petition must describe facts sufficient to warrant a finding that one of the grounds for termination exists, and the parent must be notified of the petition and given 30 days in which to file a written answer to it. If that answer denies a material allegation, the court must, as has been noted, appoint a lawyer as the child's guardian *ad litem* and must conduct a special hearing to resolve the issues raised by the petition and the answer. If the parent files no answer, "the court shall issue an order terminating all parental and custodial rights . . . ; provided the court shall order a hearing on the petition and may examine the petitioner or others on the facts alleged in the petition." Findings of fact are made by a court sitting without a jury and must "be based on clear, cogent, and convincing evidence." Any party may appeal who gives notice of appeal within 10 days after the hearing.

The respondent argues that the subject of a termination hearing—the parent's relationship with her child—far from being abstruse, technical, or unfamiliar, is one as to which the parent must be uniquely well informed and to which the parent must have given prolonged thought. The respondent also contends that a termination hearing is not likely to produce difficult points of evidentiary law, or even of substantive law, since the evidentiary problems peculiar to criminal trials are not present and since the standards for termination are not complicated. In fact, the respondent reports, the North Carolina Departments of Social Services are themselves sometimes represented at termination hearings by social workers instead of by lawyers.

Yet the ultimate issues with which a termination hearing deals are not always simple, however commonplace they may be. Expert medical and psychiatric testimony, which few parents are equipped to understand and fewer still to confute, is sometimes presented. The parents are likely to be people with little education, who have had uncommon difficulty in dealing with life, and who are, at the hearing, thrust into a distressing and disorienting situation. That these factors may combine to overwhelm an uncounseled parent is evident from the findings some courts have made. Thus, courts have generally held that the State must appoint counsel for indigent parents at termination proceedings. The respondent is able to point to no presently authoritative case, except for the North Carolina judgment now before us, holding that an indigent parent has no due process right to appointed counsel in termination proceedings.

C

The dispositive question, which must now be addressed, is whether the three *Eldridge* factors, when weighed against the presumption that there is no right to appointed counsel in the absence of at least a potential deprivation of physical liberty, suffice to rebut that presumption and thus to lead to the conclusion that the Due Process Clause requires the appointment of counsel when a State seeks to terminate an indigent's parental status. To summarize the above discussion of the *Eldridge* factors: the parent's interest is an extremely important one (and may be supplemented by the dangers of criminal liability inherent in some termination proceedings); the State shares with the parent an interest in a correct decision, has a relatively weak pecuniary interest, and, in some but not all cases, has a possibly stronger interest in informal procedures; and the complexity of the proceeding and the incapacity of the uncounseled parent could be, but would not always be, great enough to make the risk of an erroneous deprivation of the parent's rights insupportably high.

If, in a given case, the parent's interests were at their strongest, the State's interests were at their weakest, and the risks of error were at their peak, it could not be said that the *Eldridge* factors did not overcome the presumption against the right to appointed counsel, and that due process did not therefore require the appointment of counsel. But since the *Eldridge* factors will not always be so distributed, and since "due process is not so rigid as to require that the significant interests in informality, flexibility and economy must always be sacrificed," *Gagnon v. Scarpelli*, 411 US at 788, neither can we say that the Constitution requires the appointment of counsel in every parental termination proceeding. We therefore adopt the standard found appropriate in *Gagnon v. Scarpelli*, and leave the decision whether due process calls for the appointment of counsel for indigent parents in termination proceedings to be answered in the first instance by the trial court, subject, of course, to appellate review.

[A long and agitated dissent by Justice Blackmun is omitted.]

Questions on Lassiter

(1) What the court has essentially done in *Lassiter* is to adopt the old *Betts v. Brady*, 316 US 455 (1942), standard that was rejected for criminal cases in *Gideon v. Wainwright*, 372 US 335 (1963). Given the eventual fate of *Betts*, why do you think the court decided *Lassiter* as it did?

(2) Would this case have been decided differently had the plaintiff been more sympathetic? Should her unsympathetic qualities have deterred public interest lawyers from taking her case to the Supreme Court?

(3) Should William Lassiter have been represented by counsel? Was he constitutionally entitled to be? Ought he have been statutorily entitled?

(4) Does the Court apply the *Eldridge* standard correctly?

(5) Would providing defendants with counsel improve the quality of the decision whether to terminate parental rights? If so, how? If not, why not?

(6) In *M. L. B. v. S. L. J.*, 519 US 102 (1996), the Supreme Court decided that an indigent appealing from a decision terminating her parental rights so that the children's father's second wife could adopt them must be provided a transcript. The grounds for termination were a "substantial erosion of the relationship between the parent and child" caused at least in part by the parent's abuse, neglect, or abandonment of the child. Mississippi, where the case was originally heard, allowed defendants in trial courts to proceed *in forma pauperis* but would not prepay the more than $2500 in fees for the record preparation required for an appeal. The Court reasoned that (1) terminating a parent's rights was irremediably destructive of the most fundamental family relationship, (2) the risk of error in such cases was considerable, (3) only a transcript could reveal the sufficiency of the evidence, (4) there were few appeals in such cases, and (5) in light of prior Supreme Court decisions, it would be anomalous to hold that a transcript need not be prepared for the mother.

(b) The Role of Lawyers: The Example of the Jessie Bond Case

To think more concretely about the lawyer's role in abuse and neglect cases, we return to the case of Jessie Bond. We will examine problems each of the lawyers in that case encountered. We will emphasize one kind of problem—how should lawyers decide what position to take and what to do if the client prefers another position? We generally expect lawyers to take whatever position their clients want. But, the problem is not always so easily resolved in abuse and neglect cases.

Laetitia Minton: Assistant District Attorney

Laetitia Minton represented the state. Who is "the state"? Who decides what the state wants? One candidate is the Department of Social Services. The department is the agency primarily responsible for helping parents cope with raising children and for protecting children from their parents. The department's employees are presumably trained in the sociological and psychological bases for child abuse and neglect, and therefore they are presumably better equipped than lawyers to decide what will best serve parents and children. In addition, the department may have dealt with the parent for some time and have accumulated much information about the parent and the parent's situation. So should Ms. Minton's client be the department and should she take her instructions from it?

The contrary argument might note that the department's social workers are government employees who enjoy a good deal of discretion and wield a good deal of power over the lives of parents and children. Their discretion and power are not easily constrained, since many of those parents are poorly situated to resist. The parents are often unrepresented, and judges often do not review what has happened until fairly late and even then may not make a thorough review. Thus, the argument would go, the department should not have the power to instruct the district attorney, but rather the district attorney should have independent power to decide when and how to bring proceedings against parents. The district attorney's office would thus check the department.

Compare the relationship between the police and the district attorney in bringing criminal prosecutions. Like the department, the police exercise considerable power which can be hard to constrain. District attorneys are supposed to make independent decisions to prosecute to protect citizens from over-zealous police.

Another reason not to make the department the district attorney's client is that the question whether and how to bring an abuse and neglect action is not purely a therapeutic one; it is also a legal one. The district attorney, unlike the department's employees, is trained to decide whether there are legal grounds for a proceeding. But how is the district attorney supposed to resolve questions about what will be best for the parents and children involved? Should the district attorney simply accept whatever representations the department's social workers make?

How will your statute resolve these questions? Will you make the department the client, with a client's ordinary power to instruct the client's attorney? Will you give the client's power to the district attorney? Can you find some third way?

Nicholas Myra: Lawyer to the Children

Like Laetitia Minton, Nicholas Myra needed to decide who his clients were and how he should respond to their instructions. Nominally, his clients were Andrew (who was eleven), Bartholomew, (eight), Catherine (seven), and Dorothy (a few months). Could he represent all four children simultaneously? The children said they wanted different things. The two boys wanted to live with their mother, while Catherine seemed not to. Could Myra effectively argue for termination of Jessie's parental rights as to Catherine but not to the boys? Should he ask the court to appoint another lawyer to represent some of the children?

We have been implicitly assuming Mr. Myra should accept his clients' instructions. These clients, however, are all children who might not be capable, intellectually or emotionally, of understanding their own situation or interests. Rule 1.14(a) of the Model Rules of Professional Conduct states: "When a client's ability to make adequately considered decisions in connection with the representation is impaired, whether because of minority, mental disability or for some other reason, the lawyer shall, as far as reasonably possible, maintain a normal client-lawyer relationship with the client." The comment to the rule says, "If the person has no guardian or legal representative, the lawyer often must act as de facto guardian. Even if the person does have a legal representative, the lawyer should as far as possible accord the represented person the status of client, particularly in maintaining communication."

How ought this rule be applied to Mr. Myra's problem? Dorothy clearly cannot make decisions. But can Andrew, who is eleven? How should Mr. Myra decide whether Andrew has that capacity? Should he ask what weight the law gives to decisions of children of that age in similar circumstances? Should he evaluate Andrew's general intelligence and maturity? Should he evaluate how wise a decision Andrew is making in this particular circumstance?

Insofar as Mr. Myra must decide what would be best for these four children, how should he do so? Does anything equip Mr. Myra to decide what will be in the children's interests? Does the law provide him with substantive standards that will help? Should he presume, subject to rebuttal by conflicting evidence, that it will be in the best interest of his clients to stay with their natural parents? Should he accept the law's usual assumption that parents know their children better than anyone else and thus know better what their children need? Should he assume the children would want him to give some deference to their parents?

Should Mr. Myra be able to hire a psychologist to evaluate the children? Is a psychologist better equipped than a lawyer to gauge the children's interests? What if Mr. Myra's psychologist disagrees with all the other psychologists who have evaluated the children? Should Mr. Myra make his own investigation? Besides talking to his clients, should he talk to Jessie, Alan, Jessie's mother, the neighbors, Dr. Luke, the foster parents, any children of the foster parents, or the relevant social workers?

Would Mr. Myra be doing his job adequately if he did not take a position on behalf of his clients, but rather tried to place as much information as possible in front of the court? Each of the other lawyers would presumably be arguing for a position and thus might be unwilling to introduce some facts and to ask some questions. Would Mr. Myra's freedom from having to argue a position eventually benefit the children by furnishing the ultimate decision-maker the best possible evidence?

Ultimately, Mr. Myra argued that Jessie's parental rights should be terminated as to all the children. He thus ignored the wishes of the two boys. Was Mr. Myra's decision in accord with Model Rule 1.14? Were his decisions correct?

Breton Ives: Lawyer to Jessie Bond

Mr. Ives, as you may remember, originally represented both Jessie and Alan. He decided that he could not represent both. Was this decision correct under Model Rule 1.7? If the state, Jessie, Alan, and each of the four children is represented by a lawyer, will the court have more and better information? Will a better decision thus be reached? Enough better to justify the cost?

Jessie told Mr. Ives she wanted to keep custody of her children. Suppose he believed this would not be in her children's interests or that it would not be in her own interests. Rule 2.1 of the Model Rules of Professional Conduct states, "In representing a client, a lawyer shall exercise independent professional judgment and render candid advice. In rendering advice, a lawyer may refer not only to law but to other considerations such as moral, economic, social and political factors, that may be relevant to the client's situation." The comment explains that, "[a]lthough a lawyer is not a moral advisor as such, moral and ethical considerations impinge upon most legal questions and may decisively influence how the law will be applied." Under Model Rule 2.1, is Mr. Ives obliged to tell Jessie what he thinks? Is he entitled to tell her what he thinks where the basis of his opinion lies in his personal beliefs rather than in the law? Is he entitled to refuse to represent her unless she accepts his views of what she should ask for? How would you answer these questions if Mr. Ives' client were Alan?

Suppose next no lawyer had been appointed to represent the children. Should Mr. Ives recommend to the court that such counsel be appointed? Would such a recommendation be contrary to Jessie's expressed interests and therefore barred? Would such a recommendation be based on information Mr. Ives obtained from Jessie and thus breach his duty of confidentiality?

Suppose that Mr. Ives were representing Jessie and Alan but that the state had no evidence Alan was molesting Catherine. Suppose Alan told you he had been molesting Catherine and Jessie said she knew he had been molesting Catherine but was afraid to do anything about it. Rule 1.6 of the Model Rules of Professional Conduct states:

> (a) A lawyer shall not reveal information relating to representation of a client unless the client consents after consultation, except for disclosure that are impliedly authorized in order to carry out the representation, and except as stated in paragraph (b).
>
> (b) A lawyer may reveal such information to the extent the lawyer reasonably believes necessary:
>
>> (1) to prevent the client from committing a criminal act that the lawyer believes is likely to result in imminent death or substantial bodily harm....

What should Mr. Ives do, under Rule 1.6? Does the Rule lead to a good result? These questions are discussed in Ruth Fleet Thurman, *Incest and Ethics: Confidentiality's Severest Test*, 61 Denver L J 619 (1984). See also *Committee on Professional Ethics v. Hurd*, 375 NW2d 239 (Iowa 1985), where a lawyer was disbarred, *inter alia*, for telling the judge and opposing counsel in a contested custody case that it was untrue that his client was being investigated for sexual abuse. In fact, he was defending the client, who had been indicted a few days earlier.

(2) Child Witnesses and the Confrontation Clause

One of the central causes of the enforcement problem is that information about what goes on in the family is likely to be limited to family members. They may have abundant reasons for not wishing to tell what they know. In child-abuse cases, and particularly in sexual-abuse cases, the enforcement problem can be exacerbated by the special drawbacks of children as witnesses: Even adults have surprising difficulties in reporting accurately events they have witnessed. There is even more doubt about the reliability of children. In addition, children are particularly vulnerable witnesses who may need special protections against the pains of the judicial process. To these dangers are added our concerns—traditionally embodied in the various constitutional protections given defendants in criminal cases—that innocent people not be convicted of crimes or otherwise made to suffer at the hands of the law.

The dilemma can be put somewhat differently. Accuracy in determining whether a parent has abused his child sexually is necessary. First, it is in the parent's interest for all the reasons parents may want the companionship and care of their children, reasons we recognize by according parents rights. Further, to be falsely accused of abusing one's own child, and particularly sexually abusing one's own child, is to be wrongly accused of something especially dreadful. Second, accurate determinations of abuse are in the child's interest. This is true not only where the parent has actually abused the child and where the parent must be separated from the child, but also where the parent has not abused the child and where it is thus presumptively in the child's interest to have the parent's companionship and care.

All these problems present themselves when a parent is criminally charged with child abuse, particularly sexual abuse. The sixth amendment to the Constitution provides: "In all criminal prosecutions, the accused shall enjoy the right ... to be confronted with the witnesses against him." In *Coy v. Iowa*, 487 US 1012 (1988), the Court reviewed the conviction of a man charged with sexually assaulting two thirteen-year-old girls. When they testified, a large screen was placed between them and the defendant. The Court said this violated the Confrontation Clause.

The Court said that a face-to-face encounter was at the core of the Confrontation Clause: "Shakespeare was ... describing the root meaning of confrontation when he had Richard the Second say: 'Then call them to our presence—face to face, and frowning brow to brow, ourselves will hear the accuser and the accused freely speak....' "The Court reasoned that a witness "may feel quite differently when he has to repeat his story looking at the man whom he will harm greatly by distorting or mistaking the facts...." The Court concluded, "That face-to-face presence may, unfortunately, upset the truthful rape victim or abused child; but by the same token it may confound and undo the false accuser, or reveal the child coached by a malevolent adult." The Court acknowledged "that rights conferred by the Confrontation Clause are not absolute, and may give way to other important interests," but the Court implied this was not true of the core right of face-to-face confrontation.

In *Maryland v. Craig*, 497 US 836 (1990), a woman was charged with sexually abusing a six-year-old child who attended her child-care center. A Maryland statute allowed child witnesses to testify on one-way closed circuit television where "testimony by the child victim in the courtroom will result in the child suffering serious emotional distress such that the child cannot reasonably communicate." The Court said that the "central concern of the Confrontation Clause is to ensure the reliability of the evidence...." It found that "Maryland's procedure preserves all of the other elements of the confrontation right: the child witness must be competent to testify and must testify under oath; the defendant retains full opportunity for contemporaneous cross-examination; and the judge, jury, and defendant are able to view (albeit by video monitor) the demeanor (and body) of the witness as he or she testifies." Further, the Maryland procedure furthered the compelling state interest of protecting children from the trauma of testifying. The Court noted that

> [t]hirty-seven States ... permit the use of videotaped testimony of sexually abused children; 24 States have authorized the use of one-way closed circuit television testimony in child abuse cases; and 8 States authorize the use of a two-way system in which the child-witness is permitted to see the courtroom and the defendant on a video monitor and in which the jury and judge is permitted to view the child during the testimony.

Justice Scalia's dissent (which was joined by Justices Brennan, Marshall, and Stevens) argued that the question wasn't what the purpose of the Confrontation Clause is, but rather what the clause says, and that what it says is that defendants will have a right to confront their accusers. And to "say that a defendant loses his right to confront a witness when that would cause the witness not to testify is rather like saying that the defendant loses his ... right not to give testimony against himself when that would prove him guilty."

Justice Scalia believed the state's interest was not protecting children from the trauma of testifying, but rather convicting more defendants. The

> interest on the other side is also what it usually is when the State seeks to get a new class of evidence admitted: fewer convictions of innocent defendants.... Some studies show that children are substantially more vulnerable to suggestion than adults, and often unable to separate recollected fantasy (or suggestion) from reality. The injustice their erroneous testimony can produce is evidenced by the tragic Scott County investigations of 1983–84, which disrupted the lives of many (as far as we know) innocent people in the small town of Jordan, Minnesota.... Specifically, 24 adults were charged with molesting 37 children. In the course of the investigations, 25 children were placed in foster homes. Of the 24 indicted defendants, one pleaded guilty, two were acquitted at trial, and the charges against the remaining 21 were voluntarily dismissed.... A report by the Minnesota Attorney General's office ... describes an investigation full of well-intentioned techniques employed

> by the prosecution team, police, child protection workers, and foster parents, that distorted and in some cases even coerced the children's recollection. Children were interrogated repeatedly, in some cases as many as 50 times; answers were suggested by telling the children what other witnesses had said; and children (even some who did not at first complain of abuse) were separated from their parents for months....
>
> As children continued to be interviewed the list of accused citizens grew. In a number of cases, it was only after weeks or months of questioning that children would 'admit' their parents abused them....
>
> [S]ome children were told by their foster parents that reunion with their real parents would be hastened by "admission" of their parents' abuse.

The Court again encountered the Confrontation Clause in *Idaho v. Wright*, 497 US 805 (1990). Wright had been convicted of helping her co-conspirator rape her 5 1/2 and 3 1/2–year-old daughters. The trial court decided the younger daughter was "not capable of communicating to the jury." However, it allowed a doctor who had examined her to testify to how she had responded to a series of questions he had asked her. Justice O'Connor's opinion for the Court stated that "[t]o be admissible under the Confrontation Clause, hearsay evidence used to convict a defendant must possess indicia of reliability by virtue of its inherent trustworthiness...." The Court held there were inadequate "particularized guarantees of trustworthiness" to make this hearsay admissible under that standard. The Court mentioned "the presumptive unreliability of the out-of-court statements and ... the suggestive manner in which Dr. Jambura conducted the interview." He described his conversation:

> She started to carry on a very relaxed animated conversation. I then proceeded to just gently start asking questions about, "Well, how are things at home," you know, those sorts. Gently moving into the domestic situation and then moved into four questions in particular, as I reflected in my records, "Do you play with daddy? Does daddy play with you? Does daddy touch you with his pee-pee? Do you touch his pee-pee?"

The dissent argued that the Court erred in looking solely to the "inherent trustworthiness" of the hearsay and in refusing to consider corroborating evidence in assessing trustworthiness.

(3) The Burden of Proof

SANTOSKY v. KRAMER

Supreme Court of the United States, 1982
455 US 745

JUSTICE BLACKMUN delivered the opinion of the Court.

Under New York law, the State may terminate, over parental objection, the rights of parents in their natural child upon a finding that the child is "permanently neglected." N.Y. Soc. Serv. Law §§ 384–b.4.(d), 384–b.7.(a) (McKinney Supp.1981–1982)(Soc. Serv. Law). The

New York Family Court Act § 622 (McKinney 1975 and Supp. 1981–1982)(Fam. Ct. Act) requires that only a "fair preponderance of the evidence" support that finding. Thus, in New York, the factual certainty required to extinguish the parent-child relationship is no greater than that necessary to award money damages in an ordinary civil action.

Today we hold that the Due Process Clause of the Fourteenth Amendment demands more than this. Before a State may sever completely and irrevocably the rights of parents in their natural child, due process requires that the State support its allegations by at least clear and convincing evidence.

I

A

New York authorizes its officials to remove a child temporarily from his or her home if the child appears "neglected," within the meaning of Art. 10 of the Family Court Act. Once removed, a child under the age of 18 customarily is placed "in the care of an authorized agency," usually a state institution or a foster home. At that point, "the state's first obligation is to help the family with services to ... reunite it...." But if convinced that "positive, nurturing parent-child relationships no longer exist," the State may initiate "permanent neglect" proceedings to free the child for adoption.

The State bifurcates its permanent neglect proceeding into "factfinding" and "dispositional" hearings. At the factfinding stage, the State must prove that the child has been "permanently neglected," as defined by Fam. Ct. Act §§ 614.1.(a)-(d) and Soc. Serv. Law § 384–b.7.(a). See Fam. Ct. Act § 622. The Family Court judge then determines at a subsequent dispositional hearing what placement would serve the child's best interests.

At the factfinding hearing, the State must establish, among other things, that for more than a year after the child entered state custody, the agency "made diligent efforts to encourage and strengthen the parental relationship." The State must further prove that during that same period, the child's natural parents failed "substantially and continuously or repeatedly to maintain contact with or plan for the future of the child although physically and financially able to do so." Should the State support its allegations by "a fair preponderance of the evidence," the child may be declared permanently neglected. That declaration empowers the Family Court judge to terminate permanently the natural parents' rights in the child. Termination denies the natural parents physical custody, as well as the rights ever to visit, communicate with, or regain custody of the child.

New York's permanent neglect statute provides natural parents with certain procedural protections. But New York permits its officials to establish "permanent neglect" with less proof than most States require. Thirty-five States, the District of Columbia, and the Virgin Islands currently specify a higher standard of proof, in parental rights termination proceedings, than a "fair preponderance of the evidence." The only analogous federal statute of which we are aware permits termination of parental rights solely upon "evidence beyond a reasonable doubt." Indian Child Welfare Act of 1978, Pub.L. 95–608, § 102(f), 92 Stat. 3072, 25 U.S.C. § 1912(f)(1976 ed., Supp.IV). The question here is whether New York's "fair preponderance of the evidence" standard is constitutionally sufficient.

B

Petitioners John Santosky II and Annie Santosky are the natural parents of Tina and John III. In November 1973, after incidents reflecting parental neglect, respondent Kramer, Commissioner of the Ulster County Department of Social Services, initiated a neglect proceeding under Fam. Ct. Act § 1022 and removed Tina from her natural home. About 10 months later, he removed John III and placed him with foster parents. On the day John was taken, Annie Santosky gave birth to a third child, Jed. When Jed was only three days old, respondent transferred him to a foster home on the ground that immediate removal was necessary to avoid imminent danger to his life or health.

In October 1978, respondent petitioned the Ulster County Family Court to terminate petitioners' parental rights in the three children. Petitioners challenged the constitutionality of the "fair preponderance of the evidence" standard specified in Fam. Ct. Act § 622. The Family Court Judge rejected this constitutional challenge, and weighed the evidence under the statutory standard. While acknowledging that the Santoskys had maintained contact with their children, the judge found those visits "at best superficial and devoid of any real emotional content." After deciding that the agency had made " 'diligent efforts' to encourage and strengthen the parental relationship," he concluded that the Santoskys were incapable, even with public assistance, of planning for the future of their children. The judge later held a dispositional hearing and ruled that the best interests of the three children required permanent termination of the Santoskys' custody.

Petitioners appealed, again contesting the constitutionality of § 622's standard of proof. The New York Supreme Court, Appellate Division, affirmed, holding application of the preponderance-of-the-evidence standard "proper and constitutional." *In re John A.A.*, 75 App. Div.2d 910, 427 N.Y.S.2d 319, 320 (1980). That standard, the court reasoned, "recognizes and seeks to balance rights possessed by the child . . . with those of the natural parents. . . ."

The New York Court of Appeals then dismissed petitioners' appeal to that court "upon the ground that no substantial constitutional question is directly involved." We granted certiorari to consider petitioners' constitutional claim.

II

Last Term in *Lassiter v. Department of Social Services*, 452 U.S. 18 (1981), this Court, by a 5–4 vote, held that the Fourteenth Amendment's

Due Process Clause does not require the appointment of counsel for indigent parents in every parental status termination proceeding. The case casts light, however, on the two central questions here—whether process is constitutionally due a natural parent at a State's parental rights termination proceeding, and, if so, what process is due.

In *Lassiter*, it was "not disputed that state intervention to terminate the relationship between [a parent] and [the] child must be accomplished by procedures meeting the requisites of the Due Process Clause." The absence of dispute reflected this Court's historical recognition that freedom of personal choice in matters of family life is a fundamental liberty interest protected by the Fourteenth Amendment.

The fundamental liberty interest of natural parents in the care, custody, and management of their child does not evaporate simply because they have not been model parents or have lost temporary custody of their child to the State. Even when blood relationships are strained, parents retain a vital interest in preventing the irretrievable destruction of their family life. If anything, persons faced with forced dissolution of their parental rights have a more critical need for procedural protections than do those resisting state intervention into ongoing family affairs. When the State moves to destroy weakened familial bonds, it must provide the parents with fundamentally fair procedures.

In *Lassiter*, the Court and three dissenters agreed that the nature of the process due in parental rights termination proceedings turns on a balancing of the "three distinct factors" specified in *Mathews v. Eldridge*, 424 U.S. 319, 335 (1976): the private interests affected by the proceeding; the risk of error created by the State's chosen procedure; and the countervailing governmental interest supporting use of the challenged procedure. While the respective *Lassiter* opinions disputed whether those factors should be weighed against a presumption disfavoring appointed counsel for one not threatened with loss of physical liberty, that concern is irrelevant here. Unlike the Court's right-to-counsel rulings, its decisions concerning constitutional burdens of proof have not turned on any presumption favoring any particular standard. To the contrary, the Court has engaged in a straight-forward consideration of the factors identified in *Eldridge* to determine whether a particular standard of proof in a particular proceeding satisfies due process.

In *Addington v. Texas*, 441 U.S. 418 (1979), the Court, by a unanimous vote of the participating Justices, declared: "The function of a standard of proof, as that concept is embodied in the Due Process Clause and in the realm of factfinding, is to 'instruct the factfinder concerning the degree of confidence our society thinks he should have in the correctness of factual conclusions for a particular type of adjudication.'" *Addington* teaches that, in any given proceeding, the minimum standard of proof tolerated by the due process requirement reflects not only the weight of the private and public interests affected, but also a societal judgment about how the risk of error should be distributed between the litigants.

Thus, while private parties may be interested intensely in a civil dispute over money damages, application of a "fair preponderance of the evidence" standard indicates both society's "minimal concern with the outcome," and a conclusion that the litigants should "share the risk of error in roughly equal fashion." When the State brings a criminal action to deny a defendant liberty or life, however, "the interests of the defendant are of such magnitude that historically and without any explicit constitutional requirement they have been protected by standards of proof designed to exclude as nearly as possible the likelihood of an erroneous judgment." The stringency of the "beyond a reasonable doubt" standard bespeaks the "weight and gravity" of the private interest affected, society's interest in avoiding erroneous convictions, and a judgment that those interests together require that "society impos[e] almost the entire risk of error upon itself."

The "minimum requirements [of procedural due process] being a matter of federal law, they are not diminished by the fact that the State may have specified its own procedures that it may deem adequate for determining the preconditions to adverse official action." *Vitek v. Jones*, 445 U.S. 480, 491 (1980). Moreover, the degree of proof required in a particular type of proceeding "is the kind of question which has traditionally been left to the judiciary to resolve." *Woodby v. INS*, 385 U.S. 276 (1966). "In cases involving individual rights, whether criminal or civil, '[t]he standard of proof [at a minimum] reflects the value society places on individual liberty.'" *Addington v. Texas*, 441 U.S., at 425.

This Court has mandated an intermediate standard of proof—"clear and convincing evidence"—when the individual interests at stake in a state proceeding are both "particularly important" and "more substantial than mere loss of money." *Addington v. Texas*, 441 U.S., at 424. Notwithstanding "the state's 'civil labels and good intentions,'" the Court has deemed this level of certainty necessary to preserve fundamental fairness in a variety of government-initiated proceedings that threaten the individual involved with "a significant deprivation of liberty" or "stigma."

In *Lassiter*, to be sure, the Court held that fundamental fairness may be maintained in parental rights termination proceedings even when some procedures are mandated only on a case-by-case basis, rather than through rules of general application. But this Court never has approved case-by-case determination of the proper standard of proof for a given proceeding. Standards of proof, like other "procedural due process rules[,] are shaped by the risk of error inherent in the truth-finding process as applied to the generality of cases, not the rare exceptions." *Mathews v. Eldridge*, 424 U.S., at 344 (emphasis added). Since the litigants and the factfinder must know at the outset of a given proceeding how the risk of error will be allocated, the standard of proof necessarily must be calibrated in advance. Retrospective case-by-case review cannot preserve fundamental fairness when a class of proceedings is governed by a constitutionally defective evidentiary standard.

III

In parental rights termination proceedings, the private interest affected is commanding; the risk of error from using a preponderance standard is substantial; and the countervailing governmental interest favoring that standard is comparatively slight. Evaluation of the three *Eldridge* factors compels the conclusion that use of a "fair preponderance of the evidence" standard in such proceedings is inconsistent with due process.

A

"The extent to which procedural due process must be afforded the recipient is influenced by the extent to which he may be 'condemned to suffer grievous loss.' "Whether the loss threatened by a particular type of proceeding is sufficiently grave to warrant more than average certainty on the part of the factfinder turns on both the nature of the private interest threatened and the permanency of the threatened loss.

Lassiter declared it "plain beyond the need for multiple citation" that a natural parent's "desire for and right to 'the companionship, care, custody, and management of his or her children' "is an interest far more precious than any property right. When the State initiates a parental rights termination proceeding, it seeks not merely to infringe that fundamental liberty interest, but to end it. "If the State prevails, it will have worked a unique kind of deprivation.... A parent's interest in the accuracy and justice of the decision to terminate his or her parental status is, therefore, a commanding one."

In government-initiated proceedings to determine juvenile delinquency, civil commitment, deportation, and denaturalization, this Court has identified losses of individual liberty sufficiently serious to warrant imposition of an elevated burden of proof. Yet juvenile delinquency adjudications, civil commitment, deportation, and denaturalization, at least to a degree, are all *reversible* official actions. Once affirmed on appeal, a New York decision terminating parental rights is *final* and irrevocable. Few forms of state action are both so severe and so irreversible.

Thus, the first *Eldridge* factor—the private interest affected—weighs heavily against use of the preponderance standard at a state-initiated permanent neglect proceeding. We do not deny that the child and his foster parents are also deeply interested in the outcome of that contest. But at the factfinding stage of the New York proceeding, the focus emphatically is not on them.

The factfinding does not purport—and is not intended—to balance the child's interest in a normal family home against the parents' interest in raising the child. Nor does it purport to determine whether the natural parents or the foster parents would provide the better home.

Rather, the factfinding hearing pits the State directly against the parents. The State alleges that the natural parents are at fault. Fam. Ct. Act § 614.1.(d). The questions disputed and decided are what the State did—"made diligent efforts," § 614.1.(c)—and what the natural parents did not do—"maintain contact with or plan for the future of the child." § 614.1.(d). The State marshals an array of public resources to prove its case and disprove the parents' case. Victory by the State not only makes termination of parental rights possible; it entails a judicial determination that the parents are unfit to raise their own children.

At the factfinding, the State cannot presume that a child and his parents are adversaries. After the State has established parental unfitness at that initial proceeding, the court may assume at the *dispositional* stage that the interests of the child and the natural parents do diverge. See Fam. Ct. Act § 631 (judge shall make his order "solely on the basis of the best interests of the child," and thus has no obligation to consider the natural parents' rights in selecting dispositional alternatives). But until the State proves parental unfitness, the child and his parents share a vital interest in preventing erroneous termination of their natural relationship. Thus, at the factfinding, the interests of the child and his natural parents coincide to favor use of error-reducing procedures.

However substantial the foster parents' interests may be, cf. *Smith v. Organization of Foster Families*, 431 U.S., at 845–847, they are not implicated directly in the factfinding stage of a state-initiated permanent neglect proceeding against the natural parents. If authorized, the foster parents may pit their interests directly against those of the natural parents by initiating their own permanent neglect proceeding. Fam. Ct. Act § 1055(d); Soc. Serv. Law §§ 384–6.3(b), 392.7.(c). Alternatively, the foster parents can make their case for custody at the dispositional stage of a state-initiated proceeding, where the judge already has decided the issue of permanent neglect and is focusing on the placement that would serve the child's best interests. Fam. Ct. Act §§ 623, 631. For the foster parents, the State's failure to prove permanent neglect may prolong the delay and uncertainty until their foster child is freed for adoption. But for the natural parents, a finding of permanent neglect can cut off forever their rights in their child. Given this disparity of consequence, we have no difficulty finding that the balance of private interests strongly favors heightened procedural protections.

B

Under *Mathews v. Eldridge*, we next must consider both the risk of erroneous deprivation of private interests resulting from use of a "fair preponderance" standard and the likelihood that a higher evidentiary standard would reduce that risk. See 424 U.S., at 335. Since the factfinding phase of a permanent neglect proceeding is an adversary contest between the State and the natural parents, the relevant question is whether a preponderance standard fairly allocates the risk of an erroneous factfinding between these two parties.

In New York, the factfinding stage of a state-initiated permanent neglect proceeding bears many of the indicia of a criminal trial. The Commissioner of Social Services charges the parents with permanent neglect. They are served by summons. The factfinding hearing is conducted pursuant to formal rules of evidence. The State, the parents, and the child are all represented by counsel. The State seeks to establish a series of historical facts about the intensity of its agency's efforts to reunite the family, the infrequency and insubstantiality of the parents' contacts with their child, and the parents' inability or unwillingness to formulate a plan for the child's future. The attorneys submit documentary evidence, and call witnesses who are subject to cross-examination. Based on all the evidence, the judge then determines whether the State has proved the statutory elements of permanent neglect by a fair preponderance of the evidence.

At such a proceeding, numerous factors combine to magnify the risk of erroneous factfinding. Permanent neglect proceedings employ imprecise substantive standards that leave determinations unusually open to the subjective values of the judge. In appraising the nature and quality of a complex series of encounters among the agency, the parents, and the child, the court possesses unusual discretion to underweigh probative facts that might favor the parent. Because parents subject to termination proceedings are often poor, uneducated, or members of minority groups, such proceedings are often vulnerable to judgments based on cultural or class bias.

The State's ability to assemble its case almost inevitably dwarfs the parents' ability to mount a defense. No predetermined limits restrict the sums an agency may spend in prosecuting a given termination proceeding. The State's attorney usually will be expert on the issues contested and the procedures employed at the factfinding hearing, and enjoys full access to all public records concerning the family. The State may call on experts in family relations, psychology, and medicine to bolster its case. Furthermore, the primary witnesses at the hearing will be the agency's own professional caseworkers whom the State has empowered both to investigate the family situation and to testify against the parents. Indeed, because the child is already in agency custody, the State even has the power to shape the historical events that form the basis for termination.

The disparity between the adversaries' litigation resources is matched by a striking asymmetry in their litigation options. Unlike criminal defendants, natural parents have no "double jeopardy" defense against repeated state termination efforts. If the State initially fails to win termination, as New York did here, it always can try once again to cut off the parents' rights after gathering more or better evidence. Yet even when the parents have attained the level of fitness required by the State, they have no similar means by which they can forestall future termination efforts.

Coupled with a "fair preponderance of the evidence" standard, these factors create a significant prospect of erroneous termination. A standard of proof that by its very terms demands consideration of the quantity, rather than the quality, of the evidence may misdirect the factfinder in the marginal case. Given the weight of the private interests at stake, the social cost of even occasional error is sizable.

Raising the standard of proof would have both practical and symbolic consequences. The Court has long considered the heightened standard of proof used in criminal prosecutions to be "a prime instrument for reducing the risk of convictions resting on factual error." An elevated standard of proof in a parental rights termination proceeding would alleviate "the possible risk that a factfinder might decide to [deprive] an individual based solely on a few isolated instances of unusual conduct [or] ... idiosyncratic behavior." "Increasing the burden of proof is one way to impress the factfinder with the importance of the decision and thereby perhaps to reduce the chances that inappropriate" terminations will be ordered.

The Appellate Division approved New York's preponderance standard on the ground that it properly "balanced rights possessed by the child ... with those of the natural parents...." By so saying, the court suggested that a preponderance standard properly allocates the risk of error between the parents and the child. That view is fundamentally mistaken.

The court's theory assumes that termination of the natural parents' rights invariably will benefit the child. Yet we have noted above that the parents and the child share an interest in avoiding erroneous termination. Even accepting the court's assumption, we cannot agree with its conclusion that a preponderance standard fairly distributes the risk of error between parent and child. Use of that standard reflects the judgment that society is nearly neutral between erroneous termination of parental rights and erroneous failure to terminate those rights. For the child, the likely consequence of an erroneous failure to terminate is preservation of an uneasy status quo. For the natural parents, however, the consequence of an erroneous termination is the unnecessary destruction of their natural family. A standard that allocates the risk of error nearly equally between those two outcomes does not reflect properly their relative severity.

C

Two state interests are at stake in parental rights termination proceedings—a *parens patriae* interest in preserving and promoting the welfare of the child and a fiscal and administrative interest in reducing the cost and burden of such proceedings. A standard of proof more strict than preponderance of the evidence is consistent with both interests.

"Since the State has an urgent interest in the welfare of the child, it shares the parent's interest in an accurate and just decision" at the *factfinding* proceeding. *Lassiter v. Department of Social Services*, 452

U.S., at 27. As *parens patriae*, the State's goal is to provide the child with a permanent home. Yet while there is still reason to believe that positive, nurturing parent-child relationships exist, the *parens patriae* interest favors preservation, not severance, of natural familial bonds. "[T]he State registers no gain towards its declared goals when it separates children from the custody of fit parents." *Stanley v. Illinois*, 405 U.S., at 652.

The State's interest in finding the child an alternative permanent home arises only "when it is clear that the natural parent cannot or will not provide a normal family home for the child." Soc. Serv. Law § 384–b.1.(a)(iv)(emphasis added). At the factfinding, that goal is served by procedures that promote an accurate determination of whether the natural parents can and will provide a normal home.

Unlike a constitutional requirement of hearings or court-appointed counsel, a stricter standard of proof would reduce factual error without imposing substantial fiscal burdens upon the State. As we have observed, 35 States already have adopted a higher standard by statute or court decision without apparent effect on the speed, form, or cost of their factfinding proceedings.

Nor would an elevated standard of proof create any real administrative burdens for the State's factfinders. New York Family Court judges already are familiar with a higher evidentiary standard in other parental rights termination proceedings not involving permanent neglect. See Soc. Serv. Law §§ 384–b.3.(g), 384–b.4.(c), and 384–b.4.(e)(requiring "clear and convincing proof" before parental rights may be terminated for reasons of mental illness and mental retardation or severe and repeated child abuse). New York also demands at least clear and convincing evidence in proceedings of far less moment than parental rights termination proceedings. See, *e.g.*, N.Y. Veh. & Traf. Law § 227.1 (McKinney Supp. 1981)(requiring the State to prove traffic infractions by "clear and convincing evidence"); see also *Ross v. Food Specialties, Inc.*, 6 N.Y.2d 336, 341, 160 N.E.2d 618, 620 (1959)(requiring "clear, positive and convincing evidence" for contract reformation). We cannot believe that it would burden the State unduly to require that its factfinders have the same factual certainty when terminating the parent-child relationship as they must have to suspend a driver's license.

IV

The logical conclusion of this balancing process is that the "fair preponderance of the evidence" standard prescribed by Fam. Ct. Act § 622 violates the Due Process Clause of the Fourteenth Amendment. The Court noted in *Addington*: "The individual should not be asked to share equally with society the risk of error when the possible injury to the individual is significantly greater than any possible harm to the state." Thus, at a parental rights termination proceeding, a near-equal allocation of risk between the parents and the State is constitutionally intolerable. The next question, then, is whether a "beyond a reasonable doubt" or a "clear and convincing" standard is constitutionally mandated.

In *Addington*, the Court concluded that application of a reasonable-doubt standard is inappropriate in civil commitment proceedings for two reasons—because of our hesitation to apply that unique standard "too broadly or casually in noncriminal cases," and because the psychiatric evidence ordinarily adduced at commitment proceedings is rarely susceptible to proof beyond a reasonable doubt. To be sure, as has been noted above, in the Indian Child Welfare Act of 1978, Pub.L. 95–608, § 102(f), 92 Stat. 3072, 25 U.S.C. § 1912(f)(1976 ed., Supp.IV), Congress requires "evidence beyond a reasonable doubt" for termination of Indian parental rights, reasoning that "the removal of a child from the parents is a penalty as great [as], if not greater, than a criminal penalty...." H. R. Rep. No. 95–1386, p. 22 (1978). Congress did not consider, however, the evidentiary problems that would arise if proof beyond a reasonable doubt were required in all state-initiated parental rights termination hearings.

Like civil commitment hearings, termination proceedings often require the factfinder to evaluate medical and psychiatric testimony, and to decide issues difficult to prove to a level of absolute certainty, such as lack of parental motive, absence of affection between parent and child, and failure of parental foresight and progress. The substantive standards applied vary from State to State. Although Congress found a "beyond a reasonable doubt" standard proper in one type of parental rights termination case, another legislative body might well conclude that a reasonable-doubt standard would erect an unreasonable barrier to state efforts to free permanently neglected children for adoption.

A majority of the States have concluded that a "clear and convincing evidence" standard of proof strikes a fair balance between the rights of the natural parents and the State's legitimate concerns. We hold that such a standard adequately conveys to the factfinder the level of subjective certainty about his factual conclusions necessary to satisfy due process. We further hold that determination of the precise burden equal to or greater than that standard is a matter of state law properly left to state legislatures and state courts.

We, of course, express no view on the merits of petitioners' claims. At a hearing conducted under a constitutionally proper standard, they may or may not prevail. Without deciding the outcome under any of the standards we have approved, we vacate the judgment of the Appellate Division and remand the case for further proceedings not inconsistent with this opinion.

Questions on Santosky

(1) Before parents' rights can be terminated under the scheme reviewed in *Santosky*, four hearings are necessary—two fact-finding proceedings and two disposition proceedings, one of each for the decision to remove the child from the parents' home and one of each for the

decision to terminate parental rights. At each stage the parents have a right to a lawyer, paid for by the state if necessary. At each stage, many of the same issues will presumably be discussed. The state has the burden of helping re-unite the parents with the children after they have been removed from the home, and the state has the burden of proof as to every issue. Given all this, is a high standard of proof necessary to do justice to the parents?

(2) Consider again the facts recited in Question 1. Is the state constitutionally entitled to terminate parental rights using less elaborate procedures? Is the state constitutionally entitled to terminate parental rights using less demanding substantive standards? If so, why must the state by clear and convincing evidence prove allegations it is not constitutionally required to prove at all? Or does *Santosky* indicate that New York's procedures and substantive standards are the constitutional minimum? If so, is *Santosky* correctly decided?

(3) The point of establishing a burden and standard of proof is generally to allocate the risk of error. In the cases to which Justice Blackmun analogizes—civil commitment, deportation, denaturalization, juvenile delinquency—there is a conflict between society and an individual. The question is whether an individual will suffer a loss of freedom or whether society will suffer the disadvantages of an unrestrained instance of deviance. In those cases, the high standard of proof is a way for society to take the risk of error upon itself. In *Santosky*, however, the real question is whether the child will be better off with his parents or whether the child will risk injury if he is with his parents. The risk of error is with the child, not primarily with the state. If this analysis is correct, Justice Blackmun's reasoning and analogies seem inappropriate. Is this analysis correct? If so, what ought the standard of proof be constitutionally? Prudentially?

(4) Much of the implicit rationale for *Santosky* is that the higher standard of proof on which the Court insists will produce more accurate decisions. How? Does a higher standard of proof provide either more and better information or a wiser weighing of information?

(5) Why is "clear and convincing" the correct standard? Given the Court's statements about the importance of the parental right, why doesn't it insist on "beyond a reasonable doubt"?

(6) As a practical matter, does the standard of proof matter?

(7) After *Santosky*, what standard of proof must be used when a court decides whether to take jurisdiction of a child on abuse and neglect grounds? When a court decides to remove a child from the parent's home?

(8) What procedural devices do the ABA *Standards* use?

SECTION 4. THE PRIVATE–LAW REMEDY

Children begin by loving their parents; after a time they judge them; rarely, if ever, do they forgive them.

Oscar Wilde
A Woman of No Importance

So far, you have been reading about administrative action to prevent and correct child abuse. Another perspective on the problem may be had by examining the possibility of giving children a tort remedy either directly against abusive parents or indirectly by bringing an action against the state for failing to protect the child against the parents. At common law, children could sue their parents in tort, but in the United States the rule has for some time been that children may not do so. The modern trend, however, has been toward allowing such suits. Some jurisdictions have abolished parental immunity to a considerable extent, others have made exceptions to it, as by permitting children to sue dead or divorced and non-custodial parents or to sue for injuries caused in automobile accidents. Some courts distinguished between torts committed in the exercise of parental authority and discretion (when suit is not permitted) and those not (when suit is permitted). Others have permitted suits only where the parental relationship has already been disrupted. The following case wrestles with these problems.

BURNETTE v. WAHL

Supreme Court of Oregon, 1978
588 P2d 1105

HOLMAN, JUSTICE.

Three identical cases have been consolidated for appeal. Plaintiffs are five minor children aged two to eight who, through their guardian, are bringing actions against their mothers for emotional and psychological injury caused by failure of defendant-mothers to perform their parental duties to plaintiffs. Plaintiffs appeal from orders of dismissal entered after demurrers were sustained to the complaints and plaintiffs refused to plead further.

The complaints allege that plaintiffs are in the custody of the Children's Services Division of the Department of Human Resources of the State of Oregon and are wards of Klamath County Juvenile Court....

It is significant that plaintiffs' complaints do not allege that proceedings for the termination of the defendants' parental rights have taken place. In such circumstances, it would be exceedingly unwise for this court to step in and to initiate a new and heretofore unrecognized cause of action in a field of social planning to which the legislature has devoted a great deal of time and effort in evolving what appears to be an all-encompassing plan. Those persons designated by statute for aiding the plaintiffs in these cases have not yet taken the step for which the plan provides when there is no longer any hope of reestablishing these children in a family unit with their mothers. Tort actions such as the present ones might well be destructive of any plans the social agencies and the juvenile court might have for these children. It is inappropriate for this court to insert a new cause of action into the picture....

In addition, there is a limitation to the extent to which use may be made of tort actions for the purpose of accomplishing social aims. If there is ever a field in which juries and general trial courts are ill equipped to do social engineering, it is in the realm of the emotional relationship between mother and child. It is best we leave such matters to other fields of endeavor. There are certain kinds of relationships which are not proper fodder for tort litigation, and we believe this to be one of them. There are probably as many children who have been damaged in some manner by their parents' failure to meet completely their physical, emotional and psychological needs as there are people. A tort action for damages by emotionally deprived persons against their parents is, in our opinion, not going to solve the social problem in the same manner in which the legislature is attempting to solve it....

LINDE, J., dissenting.

With due respect, I cannot subscribe to the court's opinion.

The simple issue before us is whether a young child who allegedly has suffered severe mental and emotional injuries as a result of being deserted and abandoned by a parent acting "maliciously, intentionally, and with cruel disregard of the consequences"—conduct which the legislature has declared to be a crime—may upon proper proof hold the parent responsible in damages for these severe mental and emotional injuries. Contrary to the majority opinion, I believe that these allegations, which plead a violation of ORS 163.535, state a claim on which a child so injured may go to trial.

In reaching this conclusion, I differ with the majority's treatment of its two crucial premises: (1) the source of civil liability for violation of criminal laws, and (2) the significance to be accorded to Oregon's child protection laws....

It should be noted at the outset that awarding civil damages for violations of prohibitory laws is not an uncommon or radical theory of recovery. The question when the victim of criminal or otherwise prohibited conduct may recover damages from the wrongdoer is increasingly important in many areas of law. In a number of recent cases the issue has occupied the United States Supreme Court and the federal courts, whose greater attention to statutory premises of liability probably reflects the fact that these courts are not empowered to formulate common law torts unrelated to the Constitution or laws of the United States. Thus the Supreme Court has also referred to potential civil liability under state law as one factor in determining whether such liability arises implicitly from an act of Congress. Apart from these differences, however, federal and state courts face the same question when prohibitory legislation implies a civil liability toward those for whose protection the legislation is enacted and when it does not. The answer depends first on whether a legislative policy to allow or to deny a civil remedy can be discerned in the text or the legislative history of the statute. If neither can be discerned, then it depends on whether the plaintiff belongs to the class for whose special protection the statute was enacted and whether the civil remedy would contribute to or perhaps detract from achieving the object of the legislation....

Of course, the question of civil recovery for breach of a statutory duty can be an issue only when the legislation itself is silent on the point. If the legislature either provides for a civil remedy or clearly indicates that it means other provisions for enforcement to be complete and exclusive, there is nothing for a court to decide. It would help to clarify not only private rights but also the particular public policy if the legislative assembly as a routine step in the drafting of penal legislation faced the question of its civil consequences, or alternatively, if it were to enact a general formula for determining these consequences when a statute is otherwise silent.

Unfortunately legislatures do neither, but nothing can be inferred from that fact, given the existing practice of recognizing such consequences when the nature of the protective statute appears to imply them. The majority overstates the case when it equates legislative silence with an "underlying assumption ... that it was not intended that the statute create any civil obligation or afford civil protection against the injuries which it was designed to prevent." Nor does it follow, when a court finds that the duty created or defined by the statute does imply a civil cause of action, that the court is engaged in pronouncing common law. The difference between a new common law theory of recovery in tort or otherwise and a civil claim based on a statute is obvious: The latter claim stands and falls with the statute from which it is implied, and it will disappear as soon as the amendment or repeal of the statute indicates a reconsideration of the previous public policy. Thus, while a court is often left at large to divine the implications of a statutory policy, it is equally an overstatement to say that the court simply makes its own judgment whether to "create a cause of action" deriving "solely" from the court's own appraisal whether additional protection for the claimed interest is "necessary and desirable."

The relevance of criminal or regulatory laws to civil liability is more complex than merely being an element "taken into consideration by the court in deciding whether a common law action should be established," as the majority puts it. Such laws express distinct kinds of policies. First, the most familiar criminal laws are redefinitions of common-law crimes against private persons or property. They have equally familiar civil analogues in common-law torts. Only "victimless crimes" and crimes deemed to endanger the public as a collectivity, such as bribery, counterfeiting, or tax evasion, are likely to lack a corresponding civil liability. Violations of game laws or environmental protection laws may be other examples. Second, regulatory laws specify standards of socially responsible conduct for the protection of persons endangered by the conduct. While the tort standard may go further, we have recognized the force of the criminal or regulatory standard in negligence cases even when it was set by agencies or local governments that presumably could not themselves create civil liability whether or not they had such an intent. Third, governmental sanctions, penal or otherwise, may be enacted to add governmental enforcement to the recognized obligations of a relationship existing apart from the legislation. In such a situation the "underlying assumption," to use the majority's phrase, is hardly that the penal sanction makes the civil obligation unnecessary. Rather, the statute shows that the obligation is considered of such importance that it deserves enforcement by public prosecution.

The child protection laws. It can hardly be questioned that a statute like 163.535, which makes it a crime intentionally to desert and abandon a child, is of the third kind. It and the related sections did not enact a novel prohibition against parental neglect for the convenience of the general public or the protection of taxpayers. They enacted a legislative definition and public enforcement of certain minimal obligations of an existing relationship. Jurisprudentially it might be said that parents have a duty not to abandon and desert their young children because ORS 163.535 makes it a crime to do so, but a legislator would surely think ORS 163.535 should make it a crime to abandon and desert a child because the parent's existing duty—the duty to the child, not to the state—deserved governmental reenforcement. It is the parent's duty thus recognized under Oregon law that plaintiffs invoke in these cases.

The majority does not really deny that ORS 163.535 constitutes such a legislative recognition and reenforcement of the parent's private obligation to the child, not of some socially convenient behavior. Rather, the majority would deny a remedy for the intentional breach of this obligation on the ground that other public policies militate against such a remedy. Upon examination, the majority's statutory citations refer to the single policy of maintaining and preserving the position of the child within a functioning family as long as this is possible. Without in any way questioning that this is indeed the state's public policy, I do not agree that it supports the conclusion that the legislature meant to deny the child a remedy for injuries from a parent's unlawful acts.

First, it must be kept in mind what conduct violates ORS 163.535. The statute makes it a felony to desert one's child with intent to abandon it. Of course, we have no evidence of the actual facts in these cases, but the allegations are that defendants did desert and abandon their children "maliciously, intentionally, and with cruel disregard of the consequences." If that is true, the parents have in fact ended the family unit, so that solicitude about not impairing it by litigation may sacrifice the children's legal rights to a pious hope. Contrary to the majority, I do not believe it is this court's own judgment of the possible effects of litigation on family relations that matters (a question on which counsel was unable to enlighten us and that, if taken seriously, is hardly within judicial notice) but rather what view of these effects may be attributed to the legislature. More important for interpreting the legislative policy, however, the statute means that a district attorney or grand jury on the alleged facts could prosecute the parents for a felony. It is incongruous to hold that the legislature provided for a felony prosecution of parents who egregiously violate a duty toward their children, but that it meant to exclude civil actions on behalf of the maliciously abandoned children for fear of impairing the family unit. To hold that the plaintiffs cannot invoke this duty, one must assume a legislative policy that a deserted and abandoned child (or a guardian on its behalf) should ask a district attorney to seek the criminal punishment of the parent for this desertion, but that the child should have no claim that would be of any benefit to itself. That seems too unlikely a policy to attribute to the legislature without some showing that it was intended.

Moreover, the majority's premise proves too much. For purposes of the issue of law before us on these demurrers, it can be assumed that the plaintiffs have suffered actual, demonstrable injuries of a kind for which the law provides money damages against defendants other than parents, that defendants have assets from which these real injuries of the plaintiffs could be compensated, and that defendants caused these injuries by intentionally breaching a specific duty toward plaintiffs that is recognized in Oregon law. Perhaps the explanation for the majority's unwillingness to follow these assumptions to their conclusion is that the injuries alleged are psychological and emotional rather than physical. But if a civil remedy is denied on the majority's premise that it is precluded by a state policy of preserving family unity, that premise would apply equally to bar recovery of damages by a child crippled by physical abuse. And despite the majority's reference to statutory proceedings for the termination of parental rights, it is at least questionable that a termination proceeding would create rights to a financial recovery to compensate for such very real and costly harm caused before the termination proceeding.

Although the majority does not say so, its premise is the equivalent of the doctrine of intrafamily tort immunity which Oregon has abandoned at least with respect to intentional torts, though attributed here to a supposed legislative policy subordinating legal claims of children against their parents to reliance on "protective social services." I perceive no such prescribed reliance on social services when parents who have deliberately mistreated their children in a manner made criminal by statute have the assets to be responsible for the harm caused thereby. In my view, plaintiffs have alleged at least one triable cause of action arising from an alleged intentional violation of duties recognized in ORS 163.535. Therefore, the demurrers should have been overruled.

Questions on **Burnette v. Wahl**

(1) What difficulties do you see with a precedent which allows children to sue their parents? How far might and should such a precedent be extended? On what principles might that extension be limited?

(2) What advantages do you see in a precedent which allows children to sue their parents? Might such a precedent help deter parents from abusing their children? Might it provide some relief for abused children?

(3) Does it matter if the abuse is physical, as opposed to psychological? See *Ankenbrandt v. Richards*, 504 US 689 (1992), which holds that a federal court could entertain a tort suit against a father and stepmother of two girls who had allegedly been physically and sexually abused. What if the parents are deceased, so that only the abuser's estate is being sued? *Mahnke v. Moore*, 77 A2d 923 (Md 1951), concerned a father who brutally murdered a child's mother in the child's presence. The child was kept with the body for several days, after which the father drove both child and the body to New Jersey, where he committed suicide in the child's presence. The child, through her next friend, was permitted to sue the father's estate in tort. See also *Doe v. Holt*, 418 SE2d 511 (NC 1992)(claim for damages arising from the father's rape and sexual molestation was not barred by parental immunity).

(4) What should the statute of limitations be in cases like *Burnette*? Some feel that children who discover through psychiatric treatment or hypnotism that their parents have sexually abused them many years before should be able to sue them and testify against them about their possibly reawakened memories, which may have been suppressed because of Post–Traumatic Stress Disorder. Cases involving the statute of limitations include *Johnson v. Johnson*, 701 F Supp 1363 (ND Ill 1988)(applying Illinois law and finding that Illinois courts would toll limitations where the plaintiff suppressed memories of abuse); *Meiers-Post v. Schafer*, 427 NW2d 606 (Mich App 1988)(discovery rule applies where plaintiff repressed the memory of the abuse and the allegations were corroborated by other evidence); *Ault v. Jasko*, 637 NE2d 870 (Ohio 1994)(daughter permitted to sue father for sexual abuse beginning when she was age 12; the cause of action did not accrue until she reached age 29, when she was first able to verify sexual abuse after psychotherapy). Some state statutes specifically relax the limitations period in such cases. Cal Civ Proc Code § 340.1 (2006); 720 Ill Comp Stat § 513–6 (2005); Utah Code Ann § 76.1–303.5 (2006); Va Code Ann § 8.01–249(6) (2006). See generally Jacqueline Kanovitz, *Hypnotic Memories and Civil Sexual Abuse Trials*, 45 Vand L Rev 1185 (1992), which advocates admitting such testimony when safety devices are used to filter out false claims. A more critical discussion is found in Tracey Thompson, *Delayed Lawsuits of Sexual Abuse on the Rise*, Washington Post, August 14, 1991 at B1. For a detailed examination of several cases involving claims of "recovered memory" and a highly skeptical analysis of the reliability of such claims, see Frederick Crews, *The Revenge of the Repressed*, New York Review of Books at 54 (Nov. 17, 1994); and Frederick Crews, *The Revenge of the Repressed: Part II*, New York Review of Books at 49 (December 1, 1994).

(5) What are the particular evidentiary problems posed in cases involving torts between family members? Should there be a ban against

testimony in the civil context? The criminal case? Should the standard be any different if we are considering the testimony of one spouse that may adversely affect the other? For a comprehensive study of these and other problems in the context of spousal privilege, see Milton C. Regan, Jr., *Alone Together: Law and the Meanings of Marriage*, (Oxford U Press, 1999). Professor Regan discusses the communications and adverse testimony privileges in terms of what he calls the internal stance ("the perception of empathetic identification and unselfish concern by one's partner") and the external stance ("a standpoint from which a person can independently evaluate the moral demands made by the relationships in which she is involved"). The communications privilege bars either spouse from divulging the contents of privately made communications. The adverse testimony privilege, where available, allows a defendant spouse (or, more often, only the witness spouse) to refuse to testify against the other.

(6) Parents who abuse may well be unable to pay even for the out-of-pocket costs of physical or psychiatric treatment for the victims of their abuse. For example, household insurance typically excludes injuries relating from intentional wrongdoing. Many of the worst abusers may be incarcerated and therefore unable to pay for the damage they inflicted.

The material you have been reading deals with remedies an abused child might (eventually, at least) have against the abusive parent. The material you are about to read asks what remedies such a child might have against a state agency which failed to protect the child against such a parent.

DeSHANEY v. WINNEBAGO CO DEPT OF SOC SERVS

Supreme Court of the United States, 1989
489 US 189

REHNQUIST, J.:

Petitioner is a boy who was beaten and permanently injured by his father, with whom he lived. Respondents are social workers and other local officials who received complaints that petitioner was being abused by his father and had reason to believe that this was the case, but nonetheless did not act to remove petitioner from his father's custody. Petitioner sued respondents claiming that their failure to act deprived him of his liberty in violation of the Due Process Clause of the Fourteenth Amendment to the United States Constitution. We hold that it did not.

I

The facts of this case are undeniably tragic. Petitioner Joshua DeShaney was born in 1979. In 1980, a Wyoming court granted his parents a divorce and awarded custody of Joshua to his father, Randy DeShaney. The father shortly thereafter moved to Neenah, a city located in Winnebago County, Wisconsin, taking the infant Joshua with him. There he entered into a second marriage, which also ended in divorce.

The Winnebago County authorities first learned that Joshua DeShaney might be a victim of child abuse in January 1982, when his father's second wife complained to the police, at the time of their divorce, that he had previously "hit the boy causing marks and [was] a prime case for child abuse." The Winnebago County Department of Social Services (DSS) interviewed the father, but he denied the accusations, and DSS did not pursue them further. In January 1983, Joshua was admitted to a local hospital with multiple bruises and abrasions. The examining physician suspected child abuse and notified DSS, which immediately obtained an order from a Wisconsin juvenile court placing Joshua in the temporary custody of the hospital. Three days later, the county convened an ad hoc "Child Protection Team"—consisting of a pediatrician, a psychologist, a police detective, the county's lawyer, several DSS caseworkers, and various hospital personnel—to consider Joshua's situation. At this meeting, the Team decided that there was insufficient evidence of child abuse to retain Joshua in the custody of the court. The Team did, however, decide to recommend several measures to protect Joshua, including enrolling him in a preschool program, providing his father with certain counselling services, and encouraging his father's girlfriend to move out of the home. Randy DeShaney entered into a voluntary agreement with DSS in which he promised to cooperate with them in accomplishing these goals.

Based on the recommendation of the Child Protection Team, the juvenile court dismissed the child protection case and returned Joshua to the custody of his father. A month later, emergency room personnel called the DSS caseworker handling Joshua's case to report that he had once again been treated for suspicious injuries. The caseworker concluded that there was no basis for action. For the next six months, the caseworker made monthly visits to the DeShaney home, during which she observed a number of suspicious injuries on Joshua's head; she also noticed that he had not been enrolled in school, and that the girlfriend had not moved out. The caseworker dutifully recorded these incidents in her files, along with her continuing suspicions that someone in the DeShaney household was physically abusing Joshua, but she did nothing more. In November 1983, the emergency room notified DSS that Joshua had been treated once again for injuries that they believed to be caused by child abuse. On the caseworker's next two visits to the DeShaney home, she was told that Joshua was too ill to see her. Still DSS took no action.

In March 1984, Randy DeShaney beat 4-year-old Joshua so severely that he fell into a life-threatening coma. Emergency brain surgery revealed a series of hemorrhages caused by traumatic injuries to the head inflicted over a long period of time. Joshua did not die, but he suffered brain damage so severe that he is expected to spend the rest of his life confined to an institution for the profoundly retarded. Randy DeShaney was subsequently tried and convicted of child abuse.

Joshua and his mother brought this action under 42 U.S.C. § 1983 in the United States District Court for the Eastern District of Wisconsin against respondents Winnebago County, DSS, and various individual employees of DSS. The complaint alleged that respondents had deprived Joshua of his liberty without due process of law, in violation of his rights under the Fourteenth Amendment, by failing to intervene to protect him against a risk of violence at his father's hands of which they knew or should have known. The District Court granted summary judgment for respondents.

The Court of Appeals for the Seventh Circuit affirmed, holding that petitioners had not made out an actionable § 1983 claim for two alternative reasons. First, the court held that the Due Process Clause of the Fourteenth Amendment does not require a state or local governmental entity to protect its citizens from "private violence, or other mishaps not attributable to the conduct of its employees." In so holding, the court specifically rejected the position endorsed by a divided panel of the Third Circuit ... that once the State learns that a particular child is in danger of abuse from third parties and actually undertakes to protect him from that danger, a "special relationship" arises between it and the child which imposes an affirmative constitutional duty to provide adequate protection. Second, the court held, in reliance on our decision in *Martinez v. California*, 444 U.S. 277 (1980), that the causal connection between respondents' conduct and Joshua's injuries was too attenuated to establish a deprivation of constitutional rights actionable under § 1983. The court therefore found it unnecessary to reach the question whether respondents' conduct evinced the "state of mind" necessary to make out a due process claim.

Because of the inconsistent approaches taken by the lower courts in determining when, if ever, the failure of a state or local governmental entity or its agents to provide an individual with adequate protective services constitutes a violation of the individual's due process rights, and the importance of the issue to the administration of state and local governments, we granted certiorari. We now affirm.

II

The Due Process Clause of the Fourteenth Amendment provides that "[n]o State shall ... deprive any person of life, liberty, or property, without due process of law." Petitioners contend that the State deprived Joshua of his liberty interest in "free[dom] from ... unjustified intrusions on personal security," by failing to provide him with adequate protection against his father's violence. The claim is one invoking the substantive rather than the procedural component of the Due Process Clause; petitioners do not claim that the State denied Joshua protection without according him appropriate procedural safeguards, but that it was categorically obligated to protect him in these circumstances.

But nothing in the language of the Due Process Clause itself requires the State to protect the life, liberty, and property of its citizens against invasion by private actors. The Clause is phrased as a limitation on the State's power to act, not as a guarantee of certain minimal levels of safety and security. It forbids the State itself to deprive individuals of life, liberty, or property without "due process of law," but its language cannot fairly be extended to impose an affirmative obligation on the State to ensure that those interests do not come to harm through other means. Nor does history support such an expansive reading of the constitutional text. Like its counterpart in the Fifth Amendment, the Due Process Clause of the Fourteenth Amendment was intended to prevent government "from abusing [its] power, or employing it as an instrument of oppression." Its purpose was to protect the people from the State, not to ensure that the State protected them from each other. The Framers were content to leave the extent of governmental obligation in the latter area to the democratic political processes.

Consistent with these principles, our cases have recognized that the Due Process Clauses generally confer no affirmative right to governmental aid, even where such aid may be necessary to secure life, liberty, or property interests of which the government itself may not deprive the individual. As we said in *Harris v. McRae*: "Although the liberty protected by the Due Process Clause affords protection against unwarranted government interference ..., it does not confer an entitlement to such [governmental aid] as may be necessary to realize all the advantages of that freedom." 448 U.S. at 317–318. If the Due Process Clause does not require the State to provide its citizens with particular protective services, it follows that the State cannot be held liable under the Clause for injuries that could have been averted had it chosen to provide them. As a general matter, then, we conclude that a State's failure to protect an individual against private violence simply does not constitute a violation of the Due Process Clause.

Petitioners contend, however, that even if the Due Process Clause imposes no affirmative obligation on the State to provide the general public with adequate protective services, such a duty may arise out of certain "special relationships" created or assumed by the State with respect to particular individuals. Petitioners argue that such a "special relationship" existed here because the State knew that Joshua faced a special danger of abuse at his father's hands, and specifically proclaimed, by word and by deed, its intention to protect him against that danger. Having actually undertaken to protect Joshua from this danger—which petitioners concede the State played no part in creating—the State acquired an affirmative "duty," enforceable through the Due Process Clause, to do so in a reasonably competent fashion. Its failure to discharge that duty, so the argument goes, was an abuse of governmental power that so "shocks the conscience," as to constitute a substantive due process violation.

We reject this argument. It is true that in certain limited circumstances the Constitution imposes upon the State affirmative duties of care and protection with respect to particular individuals....

But these cases afford petitioners no help. Taken together, they stand only for the proposition that when the State takes a person into its custody and holds him there against his will, the Constitution imposes upon it a corresponding duty to assume some responsibility for his safety and general well-being. The rationale for this principle is simple enough: when the State by the affirmative exercise of its power so restrains an individual's liberty that it renders him unable to care for himself, and at the same time fails to provide for his basic human needs—e.g., food, clothing, shelter, medical care, and reasonable safety—it transgresses the substantive limits on state action set by the Eighth Amendment and the Due Process Clause. The affirmative duty to protect arises not from the State's knowledge of the individual's predicament or from its expressions of intent to help him, but from the limitation which it has imposed on his freedom to act on his own behalf. In the substantive due process analysis, it is the State's affirmative act of restraining the individual's freedom to act on his own behalf—through incarceration, institutionalization, or other similar restraint of personal liberty—which is the "deprivation of liberty" triggering the protections of the Due Process Clause, not its failure to act to protect his liberty interests against harms inflicted by other means.

The *Estelle-Youngberg* analysis simply has no applicability in the present case. Petitioners concede that the harms Joshua suffered occurred not while he was in the State's custody, but while he was in the custody of his natural father, who was in no sense a state actor. While the State may have been aware of the dangers that Joshua faced in the free world, it played no part in their creation, nor did it do anything to render him any more vulnerable to them. That the State once took temporary custody of Joshua does not alter the analysis, for when it returned him to his father's custody, it placed him in no worse position than that in which he would have been had it not acted at all; the State does not become the permanent guarantor of an individual's safety by having once offered him shelter. Under these circumstances, the State had no constitutional duty to protect Joshua.

It may well be that, by voluntarily undertaking to protect Joshua against a danger it concededly played no part in creating, the State acquired a duty under state tort law to provide him with adequate protection against that danger.... But the claim here is based on the Due Process Clause of the Fourteenth Amendment, which, as we have said many times, does not transform every tort committed by a state actor into a constitutional violation. A State may, through its courts and legislatures, impose such affirmative duties of care and protection upon its agents as it wishes. But not "all common-law duties owed by government actors were ... constitutionalized by the Fourteenth Amendment." Because, as explained above, the State had no constitutional duty to protect Joshua against his father's violence, its failure to do so—though calamitous in hindsight—simply does not constitute a violation of the Due Process Clause.

Judges and lawyers, like other humans, are moved by natural sympathy in a case like this to find a way for Joshua and his mother to receive adequate compensation for the grievous harm inflicted upon them. But before yielding to that impulse, it is well to remember once again that the harm was inflicted not by the State of Wisconsin, but by Joshua's father. The most that can be said of the state functionaries in this case is that they stood by and did nothing when suspicious circumstances dictated a more active role for them. In defense of them it must also be said that had they moved too soon to take custody of the son away from the father, they would likely have been met with charges of improperly intruding into the parent-child relationship, charges based on the same Due Process Clause that forms the basis for the present charge of failure to provide adequate protection.

The people of Wisconsin may well prefer a system of liability which would place upon the State and its officials the responsibility for failure to act in situations such as the present one. They may create such a system, if they do not have it already, by changing the tort law of the State in accordance with the regular lawmaking process. But they should not have it thrust upon them by this Court's expansion of the Due Process Clause of the Fourteenth Amendment.

Affirmed.

JUSTICE BRENNAN, with whom JUSTICE MARSHALL and JUSTICE BLACKMUN join, dissenting.

"The most that can be said of the state functionaries in this case," the Court today concludes, "is that they stood by and did nothing when suspicious circumstances dictated a more active role for them." Because I believe that this description of respondents' conduct tells only part of the story and that, accordingly, the Constitution itself "dictated a more active role" for respondents in the circumstances presented here, I cannot agree that respondents had no constitutional duty to help Joshua DeShaney.

It may well be, as the Court decides, that the Due Process Clause as construed by our prior cases creates no general right to basic governmental services. That, however, is not the question presented here; indeed, that question was not raised in the complaint, urged on appeal, presented in the petition for certiorari, or addressed in the briefs on the merits. No one, in short, has asked the Court to proclaim that, as a general matter, the Constitution safeguards positive as well as negative liberties....

The Court's baseline is the absence of positive rights in the Constitution and a concomitant suspicion of any claim that seems to depend on such rights. From this perspective, the DeShaneys' claim is first and foremost about inaction (the failure, here, of respondents to take steps to protect Joshua), and only tangentially about action (the establishment of a state program specifically designed to help children like Joshua). And from this perspective, holding these Wisconsin officials liable—where the only difference between this case and one involving a general claim to protective services is Wisconsin's establishment and operation of a program to protect children—would seem to punish an effort that we should seek to promote.

I would begin from the opposite direction. I would focus first on the action that Wisconsin has taken with respect to Joshua and children like him, rather than on the actions that the State failed to take. Such a method is not new to this Court. Both *Estelle v. Gamble* and *Youngberg v. Romeo* began by emphasizing that the States had confined J. W. Gamble to prison and Nicholas Romeo to a psychiatric hospital. This initial action rendered these people helpless to help themselves or to seek help from persons unconnected to the government. Cases from the lower courts also recognize that a State's actions can be decisive in assessing the constitutional significance of subsequent inaction. For these purposes, moreover, actual physical restraint is not the only state action that has been considered relevant. . . .

Wisconsin has established a child-welfare system specifically designed to help children like Joshua. Wisconsin law places upon the local departments of social services such as respondent (DSS or Department) a duty to investigate reported instances of child abuse. While other governmental bodies and private persons are largely responsible for the reporting of possible cases of child abuse, Wisconsin law channels all such reports to the local departments of social services for evaluation and, if necessary, further action. Even when it is the sheriff's office or police department that receives a report of suspected child abuse, that report is referred to local social services departments for action, the only exception to this occurs when the reporter fears for the child's immediate safety. In this way, Wisconsin law invites—indeed, directs—citizens and other governmental entities to depend on local departments of social services such as respondent to protect children from abuse.

The specific facts before us bear out this view of Wisconsin's system of protecting children. Each time someone voiced a suspicion that Joshua was being abused, that information was relayed to the Department for investigation and possible action. When Randy DeShaney's second wife told the police that he had "hit the boy causing marks and [was] a prime case for child abuse," the police referred her complaint to DSS. When, on three separate occasions, emergency room personnel noticed suspicious injuries on Joshua's body, they went to DSS with this information. When neighbors informed the police that they had seen or heard Joshua's father or his father's lover beating or otherwise abusing Joshua, the police brought these reports to the attention of DSS. And when respondent Kemmeter, through these reports and through her own observations in the course of nearly 20 visits to the DeShaney home, id., at 104, compiled growing evidence that Joshua was being abused, that information stayed within the Department—chronicled by the social worker in detail that seems almost eerie in light of her failure to act upon it. (As to the extent of the social worker's involvement in, and knowledge of, Joshua's predicament, her reaction to the news of Joshua's last and most devastating injuries is illuminating: "I just knew the phone would ring some day and Joshua would be dead.")

Even more telling than these examples is the Department's control over the decision whether to take steps to protect a particular child from suspected abuse. While many different people contributed information and advice to this decision, it was up to the people at DSS to make the ultimate decision (subject to the approval of the local government's corporation counsel) whether to disturb the family's current arrangements. When Joshua first appeared at a local hospital with injuries signaling physical abuse, for example, it was DSS that made the decision to take him into temporary custody for the purpose of studying his situation—and it was DSS, acting in conjunction with the corporation counsel, that returned him to his father. Unfortunately for Joshua DeShaney, the buck effectively stopped with the Department.

In these circumstances, a private citizen, or even a person working in a government agency other than DSS, would doubtless feel that her job was done as soon as she had reported her suspicions of child abuse to DSS. Through its child-welfare program, in other words, the State of Wisconsin has relieved ordinary citizens and governmental bodies other than the Department of any sense of obligation to do anything more than report their suspicions of child abuse to DSS. If DSS ignores or dismisses these suspicions, no one will step in to fill the gap. Wisconsin's child-protection program thus effectively confined Joshua DeShaney within the walls of Randy DeShaney's violent home until such time as DSS took action to remove him. Conceivably, then, children like Joshua are made worse off by the existence of this program when the persons and entities charged with carrying it out fail to do their jobs.

It simply belies reality, therefore, to contend that the State "stood by and did nothing" with respect to Joshua. Through its child-protection program, the State actively intervened in Joshua's life and, by virtue of this intervention, acquired ever more certain knowledge that Joshua was in grave danger. These circumstances, in my view, plant this case solidly within the tradition of cases like *Youngberg* and *Estelle*.

It will be meager comfort to Joshua and his mother to know that, if the State had "selectively den[ied] its protective services" to them because they were "disfavored minorities," their § 1983 suit might have stood on sturdier ground. Because of the posture of this case, we do not know why respondents did not take steps to protect Joshua; the Court, however, tells us that their reason is irrelevant so long as their inaction was not the product of invidious discrimination. Presumably, then, if respondents decided not to help Joshua because his name began with a "J," or because he was born in the spring, or because they did not care enough about him even to formulate an intent to discriminate against him based on an arbitrary reason, respondents would not be liable to the

DeShaneys because they were not the ones who dealt the blows that destroyed Joshua's life.

I do not suggest that such irrationality was at work in this case; I emphasize only that we do not know whether or not it was. I would allow Joshua and his mother the opportunity to show that respondents' failure to help him arose, not out of the sound exercise of professional judgment that we recognized in *Youngberg* as sufficient to preclude liability, but from the kind of arbitrariness that we have in the past condemned....

As the Court today reminds us, "the Due Process Clause of the Fourteenth Amendment was intended to prevent government 'from abusing [its] power, or employing it as an instrument of oppression.' "My disagreement with the Court arises from its failure to see that inaction can be every bit as abusive of power as action, that oppression can result when a State undertakes a vital duty and then ignores it. Today's opinion construes the Due Process Clause to permit a State to displace private sources of protection and then, at the critical moment, to shrug its shoulders and turn away from the harm that it has promised to try to prevent. Because I cannot agree that our Constitution is indifferent to such indifference, I respectfully dissent.

JUSTICE BLACKMUN, dissenting.

Today, the Court purports to be the dispassionate oracle of the law, unmoved by "natural sympathy." But, in this pretense, the Court itself retreats into a sterile formalism which prevents it from recognizing either the facts of the case before it or the legal norms that should apply to those facts. As Justice Brennan demonstrates, the facts here involve not mere passivity, but active state intervention in the life of Joshua DeShaney—intervention that triggered a fundamental duty to aid the boy once the State learned of the severe danger to which he was exposed.

The Court fails to recognize this duty because it attempts to draw a sharp and rigid line between action and inaction....

Like the antebellum judges who denied relief to fugitive slaves, the Court today claims that its decision, however harsh, is compelled by existing legal doctrine. On the contrary, the question presented by this case is an open one, and our Fourteenth Amendment precedents may be read more broadly or narrowly depending upon how one chooses to read them. Faced with the choice, I would adopt a "sympathetic" reading, one which comports with dictates of fundamental justice and recognizes that compassion need not be exiled from the province of judging....

Poor Joshua! Victim of repeated attacks by an irresponsible, bullying, cowardly, and intemperate father, and abandoned by respondents who placed him in a dangerous predicament and who knew or learned what was going on, and yet did essentially nothing except, as the Court revealingly observes, "dutifully recorded these incidents in [their] files." It is a sad commentary upon American life, and constitutional principles—so full of late of patriotic fervor and proud proclamations about "liberty and justice for all"—that this child, Joshua DeShaney, now is assigned to live out the remainder of his life profoundly retarded. Joshua and his mother, as petitioners here, deserve—but now are denied by this Court—the opportunity to have the facts of their case considered in the light of the constitutional protection that 42 U.S.C. § 1983 is meant to provide.

Questions on DeShaney

(1) The Supreme Court opinion concentrates on problems, practical as well as legal, that would surface if government agencies were responsible for non-action, as well as misfeasance. If social workers could be sued for being too intrusive (by the parents) or not intrusive enough (by the children), would people be deterred from entering the profession?

(2) In some ways *DeShaney* is reminiscent of a series of cases (most involving state law questions) dealing with third party beneficiary actions. In *H.R. Moch Co. v. Rensselaer Water Co*, 159 NE 896 (NY 1928), the New York Court of Appeals refused to allow a private citizen to enforce the contract made between the utility and the city after his building burned down because of a lack of water pressure. Although the contract had been for individual citizens' benefit, they were not "intended beneficiaries." The price citizens paid for water, like the taxes we pay for social services, did not include the premium needed to cover suits like those.

(3) Is the Court correct in assuming the other remedies available to children like Joshua, including removal and termination of parental rights, will usually be optimal? Or, as Justice Blackmun suggests, does the holding mean that help for Joshua, and children like him, will remain illusory?

(4) *DeShaney*, of course, does not prevent states from waiving sovereign immunity in suits against welfare officials who did not take action when they might have. It merely held that the failure of the Wisconsin officials to act did not deprive him of his liberty in violation of the due process clause and thus did not give rise to § 1983 damages. The following materials, again from Wisconsin, explore the relief available under state law.

KARA B. v. DANE COUNTY

Supreme Court of Wisconsin, 1996
555 NW2d 630

JON P. WILCOX, J. . . .

The relevant facts are not in dispute. In 1989 and 1990, Kara B. and Mikaela R. were adjudged to be children in need of protection or services in separate juvenile court proceedings, and were placed in the temporary custody of the Dane County Department of Social Services for foster home placement. Kara B., a seven year old girl, was placed in a licensed foster home operated by Roxanne Smit on March 28, 1989, and remained there until July 14, 1990. Mikaela R., an eleven year old girl, was placed in the Smit home on June 11, 1990. She remained there until December 18, 1990, when she fled after being sexually assaulted at knifepoint by two men in the basement of the home. The men were known to have a history of physically and sexually abusing children. In the course of investigating the assault, police contacted Kara B., who told them that she too had been sexually abused by Smit and by a man who had lived in the foster home during the course of her stay there.

In separate actions brought under 42 U.S.C. § 1983 and state-law negligence and professional malpractice claims, Kara B. and Mikaela R. sued Dane County for damages resulting from physical and sexual abuse that occurred during their separate stays in the Smit foster home. In the case brought by Kara B., the circuit court, Judge Mark A. Frankel, granted Dane County's motion for summary judgment dismissing the § 1983 claims. The court concluded that the Dane County public officials were entitled to qualified immunity because Kara B. had not shown that the public officials had violated a clearly established constitutional right. In Mikaela R.'s case, a second circuit court, Judge Gerald C. Nichol, denied Dane County's motion for summary judgment. This decision was based on the circuit court's determination that the Dane County public officials were not entitled to qualified immunity because they had a clearly established constitutional duty to protect Mikaela R. while she was in the Smit home, and that a reasonable jury could have found that the Dane County public officials had violated that duty.

The court of appeals held that: (1) the Dane County public officials were not entitled to qualified immunity from the 42 U.S.C. § 1983 claims brought by Kara B. and Mikaela R. because the public officials were accused of violating a clearly established right, (2) the public officials' conduct should be assessed based on a professional judgment standard, and (3) Dane County was not entitled to qualified immunity. Dane County petitioned for review and we granted the petition on January 16, 1996.

I.

The first issue that we address is whether the Dane County public officials are entitled to qualified immunity. The issue of qualified immunity is a question of law to be decided by the court. This court decides questions of law independently and without deference to the lower courts.

The doctrine of qualified immunity protects public officials from civil liability if their conduct does not violate a person's clearly established constitutional or statutory right. Qualified immunity is designed to allow public officials to perform their duties without being hampered by the expense or threat of litigation. In *Harlow*, the Supreme Court explained the importance of qualified immunity:

> It cannot be disputed seriously that claims frequently run against the innocent as well as the guilty—at a cost not only to the defendant officials, but to society as a whole. These social costs include the expenses of litigation, the diversion of official energy from pressing public issues, and the deterrence of able citizens from acceptance of public office. Finally, there is the danger that fear of being sued will "dampen the ardor of all but the most resolute, or the most irresponsible [public officials], in the unflinching discharge of their duties."

Harlow v. Fitzgerald, 457 U.S. 800, 807, 814, 73 L. Ed. 2d 396, 102 S. Ct. 2727 (1982).

In *Davis v. Scherer,* 468 U.S. 183, 82 L. Ed. 2d 139, 104 S. Ct. 3012 (1984), the Supreme Court further elaborated on the goal of qualified immunity: "the qualified immunity doctrine recognizes that officials can act without fear of harassing litigation only if they reasonably can anticipate when their conduct may give rise to liability for damages and only if unjustified lawsuits are quickly terminated." *Id. at 195.* Although qualified immunity plays a crucial role in allowing our government and its public officials to function effectively and efficiently, it is not absolute.

Qualified immunity does not protect public officials who have allegedly violated someone's clearly established constitutional right. *Anderson v. Creighton,* 483 U.S. 635, 639 (1987). This, in part, stems from the fact that officials may reasonably anticipate that violation of a clearly established constitutional right will give rise to liability. As the Supreme Court stated in *Harlow*, "if the law was clearly established, the immunity defense ordinarily should fail, since a reasonably competent public official should know the law governing his conduct." *Harlow*, 457 U.S. at 818–19. The parties dispute whether the constitutional right of foster children to safe and secure placement in a foster home was clearly established in 1989. Thus, we must determine whether the constitutional right in question was clearly established to decide whether the Dane County public officials are entitled to qualified immunity....

In *Burkes*, this court considered what constitutes a clearly established constitutional right for purposes of qualified immunity. This court stated:

> "Government officials are not protected from suit for civil damages (that is, they do not have the defense of qualified immunity) when at the time they acted they knew or should have known that the action would deprive the employee of a constitutional right. The relevant inquiry, then, is whether a reasonable state official could have believed his or her act was constitutional "in light of clearly established law and the information [he or she] possessed" at the time of the official's action."

185 Wis.2d at 326, quoting *Anderson,* 483 U.S. at 641. This court also specified what case law is relevant in making such a determination:

> "In determining whether it was objectively legally reasonable for public officials to conclude that a particular decision was lawful, we must

examine the information they possessed in light of the established case law at the time. In this case, the question is whether, in June 1989, the defendants knew or should have known that a decision to discharge the plaintiff ... would be unlawful." 185 Wis.2d at 326–27.

Consequently, we must determine whether, in March 1989, existing case law had clearly established a constitutional right for a foster child to be placed in a safe and secure foster home to such an extent that a reasonable public official would have been put on notice that violation of such a right could lead to liability....

Although we do not believe it impossible, or even improbable, that a reasonable social worker would have been aware of the natural application of *Youngberg* to foster children, we do not believe that prior to *DeShaney v. Winnebago County Dep't of Social Services,* 489 U.S. 189 (1989), the constitutional right to reasonably safe and secure placement in a foster home had reached the level of clearly established. We also do not believe that *DeShaney*, if viewed in isolation from the cases that preceded it, is sufficient to clearly establish such a constitutional right. However, when *Estelle*, *Youngberg*, *Taylor*, *Doe*, and *DeShaney* are read together a constitutional right is clearly established....

When this reasoning is examined in the context of *Estelle*, *Youngberg*, *Taylor*, and *Doe*, it is apparent that the *DeShaney* decision completed the clear establishment of a constitutional right to safe and secure placement in a foster home. There can be no doubt that the explicit holding of *DeShaney*—that the state assumes responsibility for an individual's safety when that individual is taken into custody by the state—provided public officials with adequate notice....

If the Dane County public officials had considered the holding of *DeShaney* and the trend established by *Estelle*, *Youngberg*, *Taylor*, and *Doe* when they took Kara B. and Mikaela R. into custody, they would have certainly expected to assume some responsibility for their safety.

Dane County points out that the *DeShaney* Court did not directly confront the application of the state's duty to those in its custody to the foster home setting. We do not discount this fact; however, it was not necessary for the circuit court to directly consider the issue to clearly establish a constitutional right. See *Anderson, 483 U.S. at 640* ("This is not to say that an official action is protected by qualified immunity unless the very action in question has previously been held unlawful....")

In sum, we believe that the trend beginning with *Estelle* and ending with *DeShaney* created a clearly established right. The first significant steps toward establishing this right were taken by the Supreme Court in *Estelle* and *Youngberg*. The *Doe* court then recognized a constitutional right of foster children. The *Taylor* court moved the right closer to being clearly established by the explicit extension of the *Youngberg* reasoning to foster children. The Supreme Court provided the final link in *DeShaney*. Accordingly, we conclude that Kara B. and Mikaela R. had a clearly established constitutional right under the Due Process Clause to safe and secure placement in a foster home.

II.

The next issue that we address is the appropriate scope of the public officials' constitutionally imposed duty to place foster children in a safe and secure environment. Constitutional issues are questions of law that this court reviews without deference to the holdings of the lower courts.

Dane County argues that a deliberate indifference standard should be used to evaluate whether the foster children's rights were violated. The plaintiffs assert that a professional judgment standard is appropriate. We hold that those entrusted with the task of ensuring that children are placed in a safe and secure foster home owe a constitutional duty that is determined by a professional judgment standard....

These are young children, taken by the state from their parents for reasons that generally are not the fault of the children themselves. The officials who place the children are acting in the place of the parents.

We agree that *Youngberg* is more closely analogous to claims involving foster children than *Estelle.* We also find compelling the argument that foster children should be entitled to greater rights than prisoners. Accordingly, we conclude that the duty of public officials to provide foster children with a safe and secure placement is based on a professional judgment standard.

As we conclude that the professional judgment standard should be applied, we need not address whether Dane County did not act with deliberate indifference as a matter of law.

Questions on Private Remedies

(1) Would this case help Joshua, or someone in his position? Joshua had once been removed from his father. Is return of the child to a parent the same as placement in a foster home as far as government tort liability is concerned?

(2) In *Barillari* v. *City of Milwaukee*, 533 NW2d 759 (Wis 1995), the same court found the city immune in a case where a young woman was murdered by her abusive boyfriend. The police had promised to apprehend and arrest the boyfriend for sexual assault and failed to do so or to notify the woman or her mother that he had not been arrested. Wis Stat § 893.80 (2006) limits liability to $50,000 for actions against municipalities or other government agencies. Does this limitation preclude any meaningful remedy in egregious cases like Joshua's?

(3) Section 4 prohibits actions "for the intentional torts of [the state's] officers, officials, agents or employees" or "for acts done in the exercise of legislative, quasi-legislative, judicial or quasi-judicial functions." Would Winnebago County be immune under this section, as the City of Milwaukee was in *Barillari*, because the (non)actions involving Joshua were within the agency's discretion?

(4) The statute's counterpart in Maryland, Md Cts and Judicial Proceedings Code Ann § 5–303 (2006), disallows claims for punitive damages and limits liability of a local government to $200,000 for each individual claim and $500,000 for all the claims that arise from the same occurrence. The statute also relaxes the intent standard, for under it there can be no claims under the statute for official actions done with actual malice.

(5) The Iowa sovereign immunity statute, Iowa Code Ann 669.14 (2005), disallows actions against the state for "negligent supervision" or for behavior involving official discretion. For example, setting the terms and conditions of parole for a prisoner was a discretionary function for which State was immune from liability. For example, in *Sheerin v. State*, 434 NW2d 633 (Iowa 1989), the suit's theory was that the state had negligently failed to supervise the parolee adequately or to provide adequate treatment and that the state was therefore liable for the death of a co-worker the parolee stabbed. The court held that the state was immune from this cause of action. Would such a theory exempt Winnebago County for liability for Joshua's injuries?

SECTION 5. DILEMMAS OF DUE PROCESS

The worse the society, the more law there will be. In Hell there will be nothing but law, and due process will be meticulously observed.

Grant Gilmore
The Ages of American Law

STUDIES IN LEGAL CHANGE: THE COURTS AND PUBLIC INTEREST LITIGATION

Like any legal institution, courts can be an instrument of legal change. Courts have increasingly become such an instrument, in part because lawyers have sought to make them so. We will now read a fascinating case involving public-interest lawyers who sought to change the New York foster-care system through judicial reform. This reading will provide further insights into the foster-care system and into the doctrine of due process.

SMITH v. ORGANIZATION OF FOSTER FAMILIES FOR EQUALITY AND REFORM

Supreme Court of the United States, 1977
431 US 816

BRENNAN, J.:

Appellees, individual foster parents[1] and an organization of foster parents, brought this civil rights class action pursuant to 42 U.S.C. s

1. Appellee Madeleine Smith is the foster parent with whom Eric and Danielle Gandy have been placed since 1970. The Gandy children, who are now 12 and 9

1983 in the United States District Court for the Southern District of New York, on their own behalf and on behalf of children for whom they have provided homes for a year or more. They sought declaratory and injunctive relief against New York State and New York City officials, alleging that the procedures governing the removal of foster children from foster homes provided in N.Y.Soc.Serv. Law §§ 383(2) and 400 (McKinney 1976), and in 18 N.Y.C.R.R. § 450.14 (1974) violated the Due Process and Equal Protection Clauses of the Fourteenth Amendment. The District Court appointed independent counsel for the foster children to forestall any possibility of conflict between their interests and the interests asserted by the foster parents. A group of natural mothers of children in foster care were granted leave to intervene on behalf of themselves and others similarly situated.

A divided three-judge District Court concluded that "the pre-removal procedures presently employed by the State are constitutionally defective," holding that "before a foster child can be peremptorily transferred from the foster home in which he has been living, be it to another foster home or to the natural parents who initially placed him in foster care, he is entitled to a hearing at which all concerned parties may present any relevant information to the administrative decisionmaker charged with determining the future placement of the child," *Organization of Foster Families v. Dumpson*, 418 F.Supp. 277, 282 (1976). Four appeals to this Court were taken from the ensuing judgment declaring the challenged

years old respectively, were voluntarily placed in foster care by their natural mother in 1968, and have had no contact with her at least since being placed with Mrs. Smith. The foster-care agency has sought to remove the children from Mrs. Smith's care because her arthritis, in the agency's judgment makes it difficult for her to continue to provide adequate care. A foster-care review proceeding under N.Y.Soc.Serv. Law § 392 (McKinney 1976), see infra, at 2103–2104, resulted in an order, subsequent to the decision of the District Court, directing that foster care be continued and apparently contemplating, though not specifically ordering, that the children will remain in Mrs. Smith's care. *In re Gandy*, Nos. K–26 63/74 S, K–26 64/74 S (Fam.Ct.N.Y.Cty., Nov. 22, 1976).

Appellees Ralph and Christiane Goldberg were the foster parents of Rafael Serrano, now 14. His parents placed him in foster care voluntarily in 1969 after an abuse complaint was filed against them. It is alleged that the agency supervising the placement had informally indicated to Mr. and Mrs. Goldberg that it intended to transfer Rafael to the home of his aunt in contemplation of permanent placement. This effort has apparently failed. A petition for foster-care review under Soc.Serv. Law § 392 filed by the agency alleges that the Goldbergs are now separated, Mrs. Goldberg having moved out of the house, taking her own child but leaving Rafael. The child is now in a residential treatment center, where Mr. Goldberg continues to visit him. App. to Reply Brief for Appellants in No. 76–180.

Appellees Walter and Dorothy Lhotan were foster parents of the four Wallace sisters, who were voluntarily placed in foster care by their mother in 1970. The two older girls were placed with the Lhotans in that year, their two younger sisters in 1972. In June 1974, the Lhotans were informed that the agency had decided to return the two younger girls to their mother and transfer the two older girls to another foster home. The agency apparently felt that the Lhotans were too emotionally involved with the girls and were damaging the agency's efforts to prepare them to return to their mother. The state courts have ordered that all the Wallace children be returned to their mother, *State ex rel. Wallace v. Lhotan*, 51 A.D.2d 252, 380 N.Y.S.2d 250, appeal dismissed and leave to appeal denied, 39 N.Y.2d 705, 384 N.Y.S.2d 1027, 349 N.E.2d 882 (1976). We are told that the children have been returned and are adjusting successfully.

statutes unconstitutional and permanently enjoining their enforcement. The New York City officials are appellants in No. 76–180. The New York State officials are appellants in No. 76–183. Independent counsel appointed for the foster children appeals on their behalf in No. 76–5200. The intervening natural mothers are appellants in No. 76–5193. We noted probable jurisdiction of the four appeals. We reverse.

I

A detailed outline of the New York statutory system regulating foster care is a necessary preface to a discussion of the constitutional questions presented.

A

The expressed central policy of the New York system is that "it is generally desirable for the child to remain with or be returned to the natural parent because the child's need for a normal family life will usually best be met in the natural home, and . . . parents are entitled to bring up their own children unless the best interests of the child would be thereby endangered," Soc.Serv. Law § 384–b(1)(a)(ii) (McKinney Supp. 1976–1977). But the State has opted for foster care as one response to those situations where the natural parents are unable to provide the "positive, nurturing family relationships" and "normal family life in a permanent home" that offer "the best opportunity for children to develop and thrive."

Foster care has been defined as "(a) child welfare service which provides substitute family care for a planned period for a child when his own family cannot care for him for a temporary or extended period, and when adoption is neither desirable nor possible." Child Welfare League of America, *Standards for Foster Family Care Service*, 5 (1959). Thus, the distinctive features of foster care are, first, "that it is care in a family, it is noninstitutional substitute care," and, second, "that it is for a planned period either temporary or extended. This is unlike adoptive placement, which implies a permanent substitution of one home for another."

Under the New York scheme children may be placed in foster care either by voluntary placement or by court order. Most foster care placements are voluntary. They occur when physical or mental illness, economic problems, or other family crises make it impossible for natural parents, particularly single parents, to provide a stable home life for their children for some limited period. Resort to such placements is almost compelled when it is not possible in such circumstance to place the child with a relative or friend, or to pay for the services of a homemaker or boarding school.

Voluntary placement requires the signing of a written agreement by the natural parent or guardian, transferring the care and custody of the child to an authorized child welfare agency. Although by statute the terms of such agreements are open to negotiation, it is contended that agencies require execution of standardized forms. The agreement may provide for return of the child to the natural parent at a specified date or upon occurrence of a particular event, and if it does not, the child must be returned by the agency, in the absence of a court order, within 20 days of notice from the parent.

The agency may maintain the child in an institutional setting, but more commonly acts under its authority to "place out and board out" children in foster homes. Foster parents, who are licensed by the State or an authorized foster-care agency, provide care under a contractual arrangement with the agency, and are compensated for their services. The typical contract expressly reserves the right of the agency to remove the child on request. Conversely, the foster parent may cancel the agreement at will.

The New York system divides parental functions among agency, foster parents, and natural parents, and the definitions of the respective roles are often complex and often unclear. The law transfers "care and custody" to the agency, but day-to-day supervision of the child and his activities, and most of the functions ordinarily associated with legal custody, are the responsibility of the foster parent. Nevertheless, agency supervision of the performance of the foster parents takes forms indicating that the foster parent does not have the full authority of a legal custodian. Moreover, the natural parent's placement of the child with the agency does not surrender legal guardianship; the parent retains authority to act with respect to the child in certain circumstances. The natural parent has not only the right but the obligation to visit the foster child and plan for his future; failure of a parent with capacity to fulfill the obligation for more than a year can result in a court order terminating the parent's rights on the ground of neglect.

Children may also enter foster care by court order. The Family Court may order that a child be placed in the custody of an authorized child-care agency after a full adversary judicial hearing under Art. 10 of the New York Family Court Act, if it is found that the child has been abused or neglected by his natural parents. §§ 1052, 1055. In addition, a minor adjudicated a juvenile delinquent, or "person in need of supervision" may be placed by the court with an agency. §§ 753, 754, 756. The consequences of foster-care placement by court order do not differ substantially from those for children voluntarily placed, except that the parent is not entitled to return of the child on demand pursuant to Soc.Serv.Law § 384–a(2)(a); termination of foster care must then be consented to by the court.

B

The provisions of the scheme specifically at issue in this litigation come into play when the agency having legal custody determines to remove the foster child from the foster home, either because it has determined that it would be in the child's best interests to transfer him to some other foster home, or to return the child to his natural parents in accordance with the statute or placement agreement. Most children are removed in order to be transferred to another foster home. The procedures by which foster parents may challenge a removal made for that purpose differ somewhat from those where the removal is made to return the child to his natural parent.

Section 383(2) provides that the "authorized agency placing out or boarding (a foster) child . . . may in its discretion remove such child from the home where placed or boarded." Administrative regulations implement this provision. The agency is required, except in emergencies, to notify the foster parents in writing 10 days in advance of any removal. The notice advises the foster parents that if they object to the child's removal they may request a "conference" with the Social Services Department. The department schedules requested conferences within 10 days of the receipt of the request. The foster parent may appear with counsel at the conference, where he will "be advised of the reasons (for the removal of the child), and be afforded an opportunity to submit reasons why the child should not be removed." The official must render a decision in writing within five days after the close of the conference, and send notice of his decision to the foster parents and the agency. The proposed removal is stayed pending the outcome of the conference.

If the child is removed after the conference, the foster parent may appeal to the Department of Social Services for a "fair hearing," that is, a full adversary administrative hearing, under Soc.Serv.Law § 400, the determination of which is subject to judicial review under N.Y.Civ.Prac. Law §§ 7801 et seq. (McKinney 1963); Art. 78; however, the removal is not automatically stayed pending the hearing and judicial review. This statutory and regulatory scheme applies statewide. In addition, regulations promulgated by the New York City Human Resources Administration, Department of Social Services Special Services for Children (SSC) provide even greater procedural safeguards there. Under SSC Procedure No. 5 (Aug. 5, 1974), in place of or in addition to the conference provided by the state regulations, the foster parents may request a full trial-type hearing before the child is removed from their home. This procedure applies, however, only if the child is being transferred to another foster home, and not if the child is being returned to his natural parents.

Nevertheless, nothing in either the statute or the regulations limits the availability of these procedures to transfers within the foster-care system. Each refers to the decision to remove a child from the foster family home, and thus on its face each would seem to cover removal for the purpose of returning the child to its parents. Furthermore, it is undisputed on this record that the actual administrative practice in New York is to provide the conference and hearing in all cases where they are requested, regardless of the destination of the child. In the absence of authoritative state-court interpretation to the contrary, we therefore assume that these procedures are available whenever a child is removed from a foster family home.

One further preremoval procedural safeguard is available. Under Soc.Serv.Law § 392, the Family Court has jurisdiction to review, on petition of the foster parent or the agency, the status of any child who has been in foster care for 18 months or longer. The foster parents, the natural parents, and all interested agencies are made parties to the proceeding. After hearing, the court may order that foster care be continued, or that the child be returned to his natural parents, or that the agency take steps to free the child for adoption. Moreover, § 392(8) authorizes the court to issue an "order of protection" which "may set forth reasonable conditions of behavior to be observed for a specified time by a person or agency who is before the court." Thus, the court may order not only that foster care be continued, but additionally, "in assistance or as a condition of" that order that the agency leave the child with the present foster parent. In other words, § 392 provides a mechanism whereby a foster parent may obtain preremoval judicial review of an agency's decision to remove a child who has been in foster care for 18 months or more.

C

Foster care of children is a sensitive and emotion-laden subject, and foster-care programs consequently stir strong controversy. The New York regulatory scheme is no exception. New York would have us view the scheme as described in its brief:

> "Today New York premises its foster care system on the accepted principle that the placement of a child into foster care is solely a temporary, transitional action intended to lead to the future reunion of the child with his natural parent or parents, or if such a reunion is not possible, to legal adoption and the establishment of a new permanent home for the child."

Some of the parties and amici argue that this is a misleadingly idealized picture. They contend that a very different perspective is revealed by the empirical criticism of the system presented in the record of this case and confirmed by published studies of foster care.

From the standpoint of natural parents, such as the appellant intervenors here, foster care has been condemned as a class-based intrusion into the family life of the poor. See, e.g., Jenkins, *Child Welfare as a Class System, in Children and Decent People* 3 (A. Schorr ed. 1974). And see generally ten Broek, *California's Dual System of Family Law: Its Origins, Development and Present Status* (pt. I), 16 Stan.L.Rev. 257 (1964); (pt. II), 16 Stan.L.Rev. 900 (1964); (pt. III), 17 Stan.L.Rev. 614 (1965). It is certainly true that the poor resort to foster care more often than other citizens. For example, over 50% of all children in foster care in New York City are from female-headed families receiving Aid to Families with Dependent Children. Foundation for Child Development, *State of the Child: New York City* 61 (1976). Minority families are also more likely to turn to foster care; 52.3% of the children in foster care in New York City are black and 25.5% are Puerto Rican. Child Welfare

Information Services, *Characteristics of Children in Foster Care*, New York City Reports, Table No. 2 (Dec. 31, 1976). This disproportionate resort to foster care by the poor and victims of discrimination doubtless reflects in part the greater likelihood of disruption of poverty-stricken families. Commentators have also noted, however, that middle-and upper-income families who need temporary care services for their children have the resources to purchase private care. The poor have little choice but to submit to state-supervised child care when family crises strike.

The extent to which supposedly "voluntary" placements are in fact voluntary has been questioned on other grounds as well. For example, it has been said that many "voluntary" placements are in fact coerced by threat of neglect proceedings[34] and are not in fact voluntary in the sense of the product of an informed consent. Studies also suggest that social workers of middle-class backgrounds, perhaps unconsciously, incline to favor continued placement in foster care with a generally higher-status family rather than return the child to his natural family, thus reflecting a bias that treats the natural parents' poverty and lifestyle as prejudicial to the best interests of the child. Levine, *Caveat Parents: A Demystification of the Child Protection System,* 35 U.Pitt.L.Rev. 1, 29 (1973). This accounts,[35] it has been said, for the hostility of agencies to the efforts of natural parents to obtain the return of their children.

Recent legislative reforms in New York that decrease agencies' discretion to retain a child in foster care are apparently designed to meet these objections. For example, Soc.Serv.Law § 384–a(2)(a) gives parents of children in voluntary foster placement greater rights to the return of their children. Since the statute permits placement agreements of varied terms, however, and since many children in foster care are not voluntarily placed, there may still be situations in which the agency has considerable discretion in deciding whether or not to return the child to the natural parent. The periodic court review provided by s 392 is also intended in part to meet these objections, but critics of foster care have argued that given the heavy caseloads, such review may often be perfunctory. Mnookin, *Child-Custody Adjudication: Judicial Functions in the Face of Indeterminacy*, 39(3) Law & Contemp. Probs. 226, 274–275 (1975) (hereafter *Mnookin II*). Moreover, judges too may find it difficult, in utilizing vague standards like "the best interests of the child," to avoid decisions resting on subjective values.

Appellee foster parents as well as natural parents question the accuracy of the idealized picture portrayed by New York. They note that children often stay in "temporary" foster care for much longer than

34. See, e.g., the case of Rafael Serrano, the foster child of appellees Ralph and Christiane Goldberg, n. 1, supra.

35. Other factors alleged to bias agencies in favor of retention in foster care are the lack of sufficient staff to provide social work services needed by the natural parent to resolve their problems and prepare for return of the child; policies of many agencies to discourage involvement of the natural parent in the care of the child while in foster care; and systems of foster-care funding that encourage agencies to keep the child in foster care. Wald 677–679. See also E. Sherman, R. Neuman, & A. Shyne, *Children Adrift in Foster Care: A study of Alternative Approaches* 4–5 (1973).

contemplated by the theory of the system. See, e.g., Kadushin 411–412; *Mnookin I* [Mnookin, Foster Care In Whose Best Interests?, 43 Harv. Educ.Rev. 599, 600 (1973)] 610–613. The District Court found as a fact that the median time spent in foster care in New York was over four years. Indeed, many children apparently remain in this "limbo" indefinitely. *Mnookin II* 226, 273. The District Court also found that the longer a child remains in foster care, the more likely it is that he will never leave: "(T)he probability of a foster child being returned to his biological parents declined markedly after the first year in foster care." See also E. Sherman, R. Neuman, & A. Shyne, *Children Adrift in Foster Care: A Study of Alternative Approaches* 3 (1973); Fanshel, T*he Exit of Children from Foster Care: An Interim Research Report*, 50 Child Welfare 65, 67 (1971). It is not surprising then that many children, particularly those that enter foster care at a very early age and have little or no contact with their natural parents during extended stays in foster care, often develop deep emotional ties with their foster parents.[40]

On the other hand, too warm a relation between foster parent and foster child is not the only possible problem in foster care. Qualified foster parents are hard to find, and very little training is provided to equip them to handle the often complicated demands of their role; it is thus sometimes possible that foster homes may provide inadequate care. Indeed, situations in which foster children were mistreated or abused have been reported. And the social work services that are supposed to be delivered to both the natural and foster families are often limited, due to the heavy caseloads of the agencies. Given these problems, and given that the very fact of removal from even an inadequate natural family is often traumatic for the child, it is not surprising that one commentator has found "rather persuasive, if still incomplete, evidence that throughout the United States, children in foster care are experiencing high rates of psychiatric disturbance." Eisenberg, *The Sins of the Fathers: Urban Decay and Social Pathology*, 32 Am.J. of Orthopsychiatry 5, 14 (1962).

Yet such ties do not seem to be regarded as obstacles to transfer of the child from one foster placement to another. The record in this case indicates that nearly 60% of the children in foster care in New York City have experienced more than one placement, and about 28% have experienced three or more. The intended stability of the foster-home management is further damaged by the rapid turnover among social work professionals who supervise the foster-care arrangements on behalf of the State. Moreover, even when it is clear that a foster child will not be returned to his natural parents, it is rare that he achieves a stable home

40. The development of such ties points up an intrinsic ambiguity of foster care that is central to this case. The warmer and more homelike environment of foster care is intended to be its main advantage over institutional child care, yet because in theory foster care is intended to be only temporary, foster parents are urged not be become too attached to the children in their care. *Mnookin I* 613. Indeed, the New York courts have upheld removal from a foster home for the very reason that the foster parents had become too emotionally involved with the child. *In re Jewish Child Care Assn. (Sanders)*, 5 N.Y.2d 222, 183 N.Y.S.2d 65, 156 N.E.2d 700 (1959). See also the case of the Lhotans, named appellees in this case, n. 1, supra.

life through final termination of parental ties and adoption into a new permanent family.

The parties and amici devote much of their discussion to these criticisms of foster care, and we present this summary in the view that some understanding of those criticisms is necessary for a full appreciation of the complex and controversial system with which this lawsuit is concerned. But the issue presented by the case is a narrow one. Arguments asserting the need for reform of New York's statutory scheme are properly addressed to the New York Legislature. The relief sought in this case is entirely procedural. Our task is only to determine whether the District Court correctly held that the present procedures preceding the removal from a foster home of children resident there a year or more are constitutionally inadequate. To that task we now turn.

II

A

Our first inquiry is whether appellees have asserted interests within the Fourteenth Amendment's protection of "liberty" and "property."

The appellees have not renewed in this Court their contention, rejected by the District Court, that the realities of the foster-care system in New York gave them a justified expectation amounting to a "property" interest that their status as foster parents would be continued. Our inquiry is therefore narrowed to the question whether their asserted interests are within the "liberty" protected by the Fourteenth Amendment.

The appellees' basic contention is that when a child has lived in a foster home for a year or more, a psychological tie is created between the child and the foster parents which constitutes the foster family the true "psychological family" of the child. See J. Goldstein, A. Freud, & A. Solnit, *Beyond the Best Interests of the Child* (1973). That family, they argue, has a "liberty interest" in its survival as a family protected by the Fourteenth Amendment. Cf. *Moore v. City of East Cleveland,* 431 U.S. 494. Upon this premise they conclude that the foster child cannot be removed without a prior hearing satisfying due process. Appointed counsel for the children, however, disagrees, and has consistently argued that the foster parents have no such liberty interest independent of the interests of the foster children, and that the best interests of the children would not be served by procedural protections beyond those already provided by New York law. The intervening natural parents of children in foster care also oppose the foster parents, arguing that recognition of the procedural right claimed would undercut both the substantive family law of New York, which favors the return of children to their natural parents as expeditiously as possible, and their constitutionally protected right of family privacy, by forcing them to submit to a hearing and defend their rights to their children before the children could be returned to them....

We therefore turn to appellees' assertion that they have a constitutionally protected liberty interest in the words of the District Court, a "right to familial privacy," in the integrity of their family unit. This assertion clearly presents difficulties.

B

It is, of course, true that "freedom of personal choice in matters of . . . family life is one of the liberties protected by the Due Process Clause of the Fourteenth Amendment." There does exist a "private realm of family life which the state cannot enter," *Prince v. Massachusetts*, 321 U.S. 158, 166 (1944), that has been afforded both substantive and procedural protection. But is the relation of foster parent to foster child sufficiently akin to the concept of "family" recognized in our precedents to merit similar protection? Although considerable difficulty has attended the task of defining "family" for purposes of the Due Process Clause, see *Moore v. City of East Cleveland*, supra, 431 U.S., pp. 495 (plurality opinion of Powell, J.); 531 (Stewart, J., dissenting); 541 (White, J., dissenting), we are not without guides to some of the elements that define the concept of "family" and contribute to its place in our society.

First, the usual understanding of "family" implies biological relationships, and most decisions treating the relation between parent and child have stressed this element. *Stanley v. Illinois*, 405 U.S. 645, 651 (1972), for example, spoke of "(t)he rights to conceive and to raise one's children" as essential rights, citing *Meyer v. Nebraska*, 262 U.S. 390 (1923), and *Skinner v. Oklahoma, ex rel. Williamson*, 316 U.S. 535 (1942). And *Prince v. Massachusetts,* 321 U.S., at 166, stated:

> "It is cardinal with us that the custody, care and nurture of the child reside first in the parents, whose primary function and freedom include preparation for obligations the state can neither supply nor hinder."

A biological relationship is not present in the case of the usual foster family. But biological relationships are not exclusive determination of the existence of a family. The basic foundation of the family in our society, the marriage relationship, is of course not a matter of blood relation. Yet its importance has been strongly emphasized in our cases:

> "We deal with a right of privacy older than the Bill of Rights older than our political parties, older than our school system. Marriage is a coming together for better or for worse, hopefully enduring, and intimate to the degree of being sacred. It is an association that promotes a way of life, not causes; a harmony in living, not political faiths; a bilateral loyalty, not commercial or social projects. Yet it is an association for as noble a purpose as any involved in our prior decisions." *Griswold v. Connecticut,* 381 U.S. 479 (1965).

See also *Loving v. Virginia*, 388 U.S. 1 (1967).

Thus the importance of the familial relationship, to the individuals involved and to the society, stems from the emotional attachments that derive from the intimacy of daily association, and from the role it plays in "promot(ing) a way of life" through the instruction of children, *Wisconsin v. Yoder*, 406 U.S. 205 (1972), as well as from the fact of blood relationship. No one would seriously dispute that a deeply loving and interdependent relationship between an adult and a child in his or her care may exist even in the absence of blood relationship. At least where a child has been placed in foster care as an infant, has never known his natural parents, and has remained continuously for several years in the care of the same foster parents, it is natural that the foster family should hold the same place in the emotional life of the foster child, and fulfill the same socializing functions, as a natural family. For this reason, we cannot dismiss the foster family as a mere collection of unrelated individuals.

But there are also important distinctions between the foster family and the natural family. First, unlike the earlier cases recognizing a right to family privacy, the State here seeks to interfere, not with a relationship having its origins entirely apart from the power of the State, but rather with a foster family which has its source in state law and contractual arrangements. The individual's freedom to marry and reproduce is "older than the Bill of Rights," *Griswold v. Connecticut, supra*, 381 U.S., at 486. Accordingly, unlike the property interests that are also protected by the Fourteenth Amendment *cf. Board of Regents v. Roth*, 408 U.S., at 577, the liberty interest in family privacy has its source, and its contours are ordinarily to be sought, not in state law, but in intrinsic human rights, as they have been understood in "this Nation's history and tradition." *Moore v. City of East Cleveland*, 431 U.S., at 503. Here, however, whatever emotional ties may develop between foster parent and foster child have their origins in an arrangement in which the State has been a partner from the outset. While the Court has recognized that liberty interests may in some cases arise from positive-law sources, *see, e.g., Wolff v. McDonnell*, 418 U.S. 539, 557 (1974), in such a case, and particularly where, as here, the claimed interest derives from a knowingly assumed contractual relation with the State, it is appropriate to ascertain from state law the expectations and entitlements of the parties. In this case, the limited recognition accorded to the foster family by the New York statutes and the contracts executed by the foster parents argue against any but the most limited constitutional "liberty" in the foster family.

A second consideration related to this is that ordinarily procedural protection may be afforded to a liberty interest of one person without derogating from the substantive liberty of another. Here, however, such a tension is virtually unavoidable. Under New York law, the natural parent of a foster child in voluntary placement has an absolute right to the return of his child in the absence of a court order obtainable only upon compliance with rigorous substantive and procedural standards, which reflect the constitutional protection accorded the natural family. Moreover, the natural parent initially gave up his child to the State only on the express understanding that the child would be returned in those circumstances. These rights are difficult to reconcile with the liberty interest in the foster family relationship claimed by appellees. It is one thing to say that individuals may acquire a liberty interest against arbitrary governmental interference in the family-like associations into which they have freely entered, even in the absence of biological connection or state-law recognition of the relationship. It is quite another to say that one may acquire such an interest in the face of another's constitutionally recognized liberty interest that derives from blood relationship, state-law sanction, and basic human right an interest the foster parent has recognized by contract from the outset. Whatever liberty interest might otherwise exist in the foster family as an institution, that interest must be substantially attenuated where the proposed removal from the foster family is to return the child to his natural parents.

As this discussion suggests, appellees' claim to a constitutionally protected liberty interest raises complex and novel questions. It is unnecessary for us to resolve those questions definitively in this case, however, for like the District Court, we conclude that "narrower grounds exist to support" our reversal. We are persuaded that, even on the assumption that appellees have a protected "liberty interest," the District Court erred in holding that the preremoval procedures presently employed by the State are constitutionally defective.

III

Where procedural due process must be afforded because a "liberty" or "property" interest is within the Fourteenth Amendment's protection, there must be determined "what process is due" in the particular context. The District Court did not spell out precisely what sort of preremoval hearing would be necessary to meet the constitutional standard, leaving to "the various defendants state and local officials the first opportunity to formulate procedures suitable to their own professional needs and compatible with the principles set forth in this opinion." The court's opinion, however, would seem to require at a minimum that in all cases in which removal of a child within the certified class is contemplated, including the situation where the removal is for the purpose of returning the child to his natural parents, a hearing be held automatically, regardless of whether or not the foster parents request a hearing; that the hearing be before an officer who has had no previous contact with the decision to remove the child, and who has authority to order that the child remain with the foster parents; and that the agency, the foster parents, and the natural parents, as well as the child, if he is able intelligently to express his true feelings, and an independent representative of the child's interests, if he is not, be represented and permitted to introduce relevant evidence.

It is true that "(b)efore a person is deprived of a protected interest, he must be afforded opportunity for some kind of a hearing, 'except for extraordinary situations where some valid governmental interest is at stake that justifies postponing the hearing until after the event.' "*Board of Regents v. Roth*, 408 U.S., at 570 n.7; quoting *Boddie v. Connecticut*,

401 U.S. 371, 379 (1971). But the hearing required is only one "appropriate to the nature of the case." "(D)ue process is flexible and calls for such procedural protections as the particular situation demands." Only last Term, the Court held that "identification of the specific dictates of due process generally requires consideration of three distinct factors: First, the private interest that will be affected by the official action; second, the risk of an erroneous deprivation of such interest through the procedures used, and the probable value, if any, of additional or substitute procedural safeguards; and finally, the Government's interest, including the function involved and the fiscal and administrative burdens that the additional or substitute procedural requirement would entail." *Mathews v. Eldridge*, 424 U.S. 319, 335, 96 S.Ct. 893, 903, 47 L.Ed.2d 18 (1976). Consideration of the procedures employed by the State and New York City in light of these three factors requires the conclusion that those procedures satisfy constitutional standards.

Turning first to the procedure applicable in New York City, [it] provides that before a child is removed from a foster home for transfer to another foster home, the foster parents may request an "independent review." Such a procedure would appear to give a more elaborate trial-type hearing to foster families than this Court has found required in other contexts of administrative determinations. The District Court found the procedure inadequate on four grounds, none of which we find sufficient to justify the holding that the procedure violates due process....

Outside New York City, where only the statewide procedures apply, foster parents are provided not only with the procedures of a preremoval conference and postremoval hearing provided by 18 N.Y.C.R.R. § 450.10 (1976) and Soc.Serv.Law § 400 (McKinney 1976), but also with the preremoval judicial hearing available on request to foster parents who have in their care children who have been in foster care for 18 months or more, Soc.Serv.Law § 392. As observed supra, a foster parent in such case may obtain an order that the child remain in his care.

The District Court found three defects in this full judicial process. First, a § 392 proceeding is available only to those foster children who have been in foster care for 18 months or more. The class certified by the court was broader, including children who had been in the care of the same foster parents for more than one year. Thus, not all class members had access to the § 392 remedy. We do not think that the 18–month limitation on § 392 actions renders the New York scheme constitutionally inadequate. The assumed liberty interest to be protected in this case is one rooted in the emotional attachments that develop over time between a child and the adults who care for him. But there is no reason to assume that those attachments ripen at less than 18 months or indeed at any precise point. Indeed, testimony in the record as well as material in published psychological tests, see, e. g., J. Goldstein, A. Freud, & A. Solnit, *Beyond the Best Interests of the Child* 40–42, 49 (1973), suggests that the amount of time necessary for the development of the sort of tie appellees seek to protect varies considerably depending on the age and previous attachments of the child. In a matter of such imprecision and delicacy, we see no justification for the District Court's substitution of its view of the appropriate cutoff date for that chosen by the New York Legislature, given that any line is likely to be somewhat arbitrary and fail to protect some families where relationships have developed quickly while protecting others where no such bonds have formed. If New York sees 18 months rather than 12 as the time at which temporary foster care begins to turn into a more permanent and family-like setting requiring procedural protection and/or judicial inquiry into the propriety of continuing foster care, it would take far more than this record provides to justify a finding of constitutional infirmity in New York's choice.

The District Court's other two findings of infirmity in the § 392 procedure have already been considered and held to be without merit. The District Court disputed defendants' reading of s 392 as permitting an order requiring the leaving of the foster child in the same foster home. The plain words of the statute and the weight of New York judicial interpretation do not support the court. The District Court also faulted § 392, as it did the New York City procedure, in not providing an automatic hearing in every case even in cases where foster parents chose not to seek one. Our holding sustaining the adequacy of the city procedure applies in this context as well.

Finally, the § 392 hearing is available to foster parents, both in and outside New York City, even where the removal sought is for the purpose of returning the child to his natural parents. Since this remedy provides a sufficient constitutional preremoval hearing to protect whatever liberty interest might exist in the continued existence of the foster family when the State seeks to transfer the child to another foster home, a fortiori the procedure is adequate to protect the lesser interest of the foster family in remaining together at the expense of the disruption of the natural family.

We deal here with issues of unusual delicacy, in an area where professional judgments regarding desirable procedures are constantly and rapidly changing. In such a context, restraint is appropriate on the part of courts called upon to adjudicate whether a particular procedural scheme is adequate under the Constitution. Since we hold that the procedures provided by New York State in § 392 and by New York City's SSC Procedure No. 5 are adequate to protect whatever liberty interest appellees may have, the judgment of the District Court is

Reversed.

Questions on Smith v. Offer

1. Why might we say that this case is a study in social welfare law? Is it because the proceedings involved poor children? Because the children were in foster care? Or is the real problem here that there were many constitutional interests in play, some of which conflicted?

2. An important book chapter by David Chambers and Michael Wald, "*Smith v. Offer:* A Case Study of Children in Foster Care," from *In the Interests of Children* (Freeman, 1981), discusses the conflicting roles that lawyers who were usually on the same (public interest) side were at odds in this litigation. The agency head from New York City noted "Everyone, including myself, was in the wrong role—they really were. I felt I was always a defender of due-process and here I was, you know, stone-walling. By the end I was saying, "I don't care what it takes, we're going to beat this one." Does this conflict—or reversal—of roles characterize social welfare cases?

3. Did the Supreme Court get the balance right in *Smith v. OFFER*? Whose rights are foremost, those of the child or those of the parent? Which set of parents? After this case, do you suppose that foster parents have any liberty rights?

4. Studies indicate that children in foster care do not fare as well as children in birth families (though some of this difference is undoubtedly due to "selection effects"—the children in foster care have already been through a lot or they would still be living with their parents) or in families created by adoption. How would you explain this difference? Does the moving between foster homes characterized in *Smith v. OFFER* (a lack of stability criticized by Goldstein, Freud and Solnit in *Beyond the Best Interests of the Child*) make the difference? Could it be the lack of a sense of really belonging? For a review of the literature and an attempt to answer some of these questions empirically, see Margaret F. Brinig and Steven L. Nock, *How Much Does Legal Status Matter? Adoptions by Kin Caregivers*, 36 Family L Q 449 (2002).

Due Process and Family Law

You have now read a good deal about the tension between our concern that parents be accorded adequate due-process protections and our concern that children should be protected, about due-process devices as a way of improving the state's child-protection efforts, and about courts as agents of legal change. What follows is a portion of Professor Schneider's review of a book by Professor Robert Mnookin and others called *In the Interest of Children.* The book is a fascinating collection of studies of public-interest litigation over children's issues. Professor Schneider's review considers what the book suggests about due-process constraints on child-protection programs.

CARL E. SCHNEIDER
LAWYERS AND CHILDREN: WISDOM AND LEGITIMACY IN FAMILY POLICY

84 Michigan Law Review 919 (1986)

However troubling it is that lawyers who are freed to formulate positions on public policy seem ill-suited to do so, the adversary process and judicial insight might nevertheless flush out all that judges need to know to make wise policy. *In the Interest of Children*, however, suggests reasons to doubt that this happens. We begin with the set of reasons that has to do with a court's ability to collect and interpret information in test-case litigation.

The first kind of problem in this respect was that these proceedings too often lacked the virtues and yet had the faults of an adversary system of justice. For example, an adversary system depends on a rough equality between the lawyers for each side. But in each of these cases, the government's lawyers seem to have been badly outmatched: The public interest lawyers tended to come from better law schools and to have greater resources—money, time, research services, and the like—than their opponents. Thus, the state's position often seems to have been, relatively, weakly presented. An adversary system, particularly one relied on to formulate social policy in a large and baffling area, also depends on some genuine adverseness between the parties to generate evidence and sharpen argument. In these cases, however, the evidence presented to the courts was limited by the fact that, at some point in each of the cases, the parties had only slight differences. In *Goss*, for instance, the school committee early in the litigation adopted disciplinary procedures somewhat more favorable than those the Supreme Court eventually ordered, and throughout the litigation the defendants "perceived the case as having only one issue: did Ohio law grant them autonomy in maintaining discipline in the schools?" The defendants (and concomitantly the plaintiffs) therefore introduced virtually no evidence to the court. Even in *Pennhurst*, the defendants said they wanted and intended to do what the plaintiffs asked—close the institution. Consequently, "there was virtually no controversy about institutional closure until some considerable time after the trial had ended."

Not only were some of the adversary system's advantages for collecting information absent in these cases, but some of its impediments were present. In each case, for example, the lawyers seem not to have believed that representing the public interest obliged them to depart from the usual practice of exploiting every ethical litigational advantage. Thus lawyers for children opposed the appointment of additional lawyers who might have represented more fully the interests of all the children in the class, attempted to limit the witnesses and issues presented to courts, and used technicalities to prevent a case from being heard on appeal.

This brings us to the second kind of limit on the court's ability to collect information in test-case litigation involving children: The hearing in each of the cases was stunningly inadequate. In none of the cases was there a genuine trial of the major issues at stake; except for *Pennhurst*, hearings lasted from only one to three days. This brevity was sometimes commanded by the court and sometimes caused by the parties. In either event, the court learned little about the named parties, the class, the immediate problem, or the larger social issues. Much of the evidence presented related to the named plaintiffs, partly for tactical reasons and partly, one suspects, because that is what lawyers customarily do. Yet in test-case litigation, anecdotes about a few individuals can rarely be enlightening and are often misleading. And little though the trial judges could have learned from these hearings, the appellate judges who finally decided those cases surely learned even less, since it is unlikely that they read the full trial record.

The third limit on the judicial capacity to collect information is that to ask lawyers in "social policy" cases to be genuinely and thoroughly illuminating is to ask a great deal. Each author of *In the Interest of Children* devastatingly shows the inadequacy of the social information presented in these cases. To some extent, systematic evidence was simply unavailable. To a considerable extent, the lawyers failed to grasp the relevance of what was available or to use experts to inform themselves and the court. Where systematic evidence was available and where lawyers tried to use it, its complexity and ambiguity prevented lawyers from effectively gathering, analyzing, and presenting it, and courts from assimilating it.

Judicial understanding of the social problems presented by test-case litigation for children seems, then, to be hampered by severe problems in acquiring information and ideas. These problems are simultaneously exacerbated and eased (or evaded) by a set of judicial (and lawyer's) attitudes that might be called hyper-rationalism.

Hyper-rationalism is essentially the substitution of reason for information and analysis. It has two components: first, the belief that reason can reliably be used to infer facts where evidence is unavailable or incomplete, and second, the practice of interpreting facts through a set of artificial analytic categories. The first component of hyper-rationalism has three related aspects. In its first aspect, it is the assumption that systematic evidence is generally superfluous to understanding social problems, since the behavior of people and institutions can be logically inferred from a general understanding of how people and institutions work. In its second aspect, it is the assumption that, in the absence of a general understanding of how people and institutions work, anecdotal evidence is generally sufficient, since the behavior of people and institutions can be logically inferred from a few examples of their actual behavior under the relevant circumstances. In its third aspect, it is the assumption that a description of social reality articulated in one case may be taken as demonstrated fact in subsequent cases; it is, in other words, the application of *stare decisis* to evidence about social behavior.

All three attitudes recurred in the cases described in *In the Interest of Children* and are manifest in the evidence presented to and recited by the judges. These attitudes are not, of course, uniquely judicial; they are probably common among public officials, who must formulate policy quickly and who are often temperamentally disinclined to learn about an issue through systematic reading. However, these attitudes are more problematic when held by judges, who lack the general administrative experience and the particular subject-matter expertise that officials can use in interpreting sketchy information and who are ill-situated to revise a policy as experience with it teaches new lessons.

The second component of hyper-rationalism is the practice of analyzing social problems in terms of a small set of legal categories. Legal categories are troublesome and necessary for the same reason—they are a limited set of abstractions from social reality. Legal categories may be specially awkward when the law makes policy for families, since many of the values of family life are notoriously nonlegal and extra-rational. But even aside from this difficulty, drawbacks of analyzing a social problem in terms of the legal categories available sound in *In the Interest of Children*. For instance, judicial policymaking was repeatedly impaired by the fact that each of the five cases concerned (and the plaintiffs' lawyers and many of the judges were primarily interested in) a perplexing social problem, but the legal issue the cases presented was rarely an apt means of addressing that problem: The legal issue often spoke only indirectly to the social problem; to resolve the legal issue in a way that contributed to resolving the social problem often would have required a remedy far beyond judicial authority; and to define the legal issue so as to give a court scope in solving the social problem often risked creating legal doctrines with unanticipated and unwanted consequences. This point is made with particular clarity by Professors Wald and Chambers in their discussion of *OFFER*, but it was or could have been made by each of the authors. *Bellotti* is centrally about the dilemmas of adolescent pregnancy; *Pennhurst* about the best ways of treating the extraordinarily various handicaps of the retarded; *Norton* about how the interests of mothers and children receiving welfare can be reconciled and served; *Goss* about how schools should handle the difficulties caused by integration and by changes in social attitudes towards discipline and education. Yet the legal issue in each case was defined in terms of (usually procedural, sometimes substantive) due process, and each case was in part resolved by a provision for some kind of hearing.

Due process devices were prominent in these cases not only because due process is the most convenient and plausible category for judicially addressing problems of family policy; due process also allows judges to hope that the social complexity which escapes their immediate understanding and reach will be taken into account in the newly revised process of decision. Yet, on the evidence of these cases, that hope seems unfounded. Few foster parents have used the hearing assured by *OFFER*; virtually every girl who sought judicial authorization for an abortion after *Bellotti* received it; hardly any mothers have fully pursued the procedural rights they secured in the process of which *Norton* was a part, and Professor Sugarman questions whether the fight over the *Norton* regulations "has made any important difference"; and Professor Zimring and Mr. Solomon conclude that "what many commentators have called 'proceduralism' did students very little good but even less palpable harm." These results accord with Dean Yudof's conclusion that "[e]xperience with recent federal acts creating procedural rights for parents suggests that few take advantage of these statutory rights" and with Professor Mashaw's observation that "[t]he *Goldberg* requirement of extensive pretermination hearings has not produced a huge, or even very substantial, increase in the number of hearings held."

The difficulties presented by both components of judicial hyper-rationalism can be seen by examining another common feature of these cases. Each case, with the possible exception of *Bellotti*, has centrally to do with a bureaucracy. In each case, a court was asked to make a bureaucracy work "better." Few judges are equipped by training, experience, or temperament to understand bureaucracies. Nevertheless, their hyper-rationalism allows them to believe that their experience with conducting or evaluating trials makes them expert in governmental procedure of all kinds.

The quality of bureaucratic work depends on the characteristics of the particular bureaucracy, of its staff, and of its leaders. But because judges believe they can understand how all bureaucracies work through *a priori* reasoning, they resist inquiring into the individual character of a bureaucracy. Further, because judges are bound to use a limited number of legal categories in dealing with bureaucracies, it is hard for judges to interpret the law in a way that allows for variations between bureaucracies and within a single bureaucracy over time. The upshot of this, as we have just seen, is that judges try to improve bureaucracies by imposing on them procedures that are, at best, *pro forma* or unused. The judicial cure for the ills of bureaucracy is more bureaucracy.

Not only does hyper-rationalism lead courts to impose on bureaucracies and their clients procedures which are, like the hearings described above, unused or meaningless. It also allows courts to underestimate greatly both the difficulties of persuading a bureaucracy to act in the way a court wishes and the resourcefulness of recusant bureaucrats. In other words, because courts substitute anecdote for evidence and legal categories for social analysis, they do not ask why bureaucrats think and act as they do. And because courts do not understand the assumptions of and pressures on bureaucrats, courts are ill-fitted to win their cooperation (and, because of the paucity of judicial remedies and the scarcity of judicial time, ill-equipped to coerce it).

OFFER exemplifies many of these features of the hyper-rational approach to bureaucracies. In that case, the social problem was to ensure that foster children are wisely treated, and thus a central question was whether hearings would improve the bureaucracy's decisions. That question was to be answered for the whole country on the basis of evidence about only two bureaucracies and of a small set of legal assumptions about how hearings generally affect bureaucratic decisions. But it depends on an almost endless number of considerations, many of which will vary from one bureaucracy to another and within a single bureaucracy over time. Will a hearing officer make a better decision than a case worker? Can anything systematic be learned about the comparative sensitivity, training, experience, energy, or judgment of those two bureaucrats? Is the hearing officer a worn-out caseworker or a caseworker whose ability has been rewarded by promotion? Is a caseworker's personal acquaintance with the people involved a help or a hindrance? How important is speed in making a decision? How will hearings affect the morale of caseworkers? Their attitudes toward their clients? Their willingness to take necessary risks? Will the prospect of hearings encourage the caseworker to think more carefully, or merely to avoid making reviewable decisions? To follow rules more faithfully, or to doctor the paper record? Will hearings lead to the formulation of clearer standards for the removal of children? Are clearer standards better standards, or is it preferable to use vaguer standards that preserve a measure of discretion? Is the cost of hearings worth the price? Would the money have been better spent hiring another caseworker? Hiring another supervisor? Improving training programs? Improving record-keeping? Raising salaries to attract abler caseworkers? Does the usefulness of hearings vary with the size of the bureaucracy? Will hearings affect a bureaucracy's ability to recruit and retain foster parents? Its ability to persuade natural parents to put children in foster care? And so on and on.

In these two sections, we have been examining how judicial understanding of public policy affecting children may be limited by judicial problems in acquiring and analyzing evidence. We have seen that for structural and attitudinal reasons, judges are exposed to only a fraction of the information that they need and that they rely on an analytic framework which is often incomplete and ill-fitting. An obvious source of both information and analysis is the social sciences, and these cases often do indicate that the social sciences need to be better used. But I am not arguing that courts should simply shift the burden of decision onto the social sciences. For familiar and understandable reasons, social science evidence is too incomplete, social science theory is too fragile, and social science value choices are too problematic to justify such a tactic.

Nor does my criticism of the incompleteness of the information, analysis, and remedies in these cases imply that the only good policy is a global one, one that tries conclusively to understand and finally to solve the whole problem all at once. On the contrary, there is much to be said for incrementalism, for what Professor Lindblom, in a famous article, called "the science of muddling through." Because incrementalism is a relatively cautious and modest approach to social policy, it seems plausible that courts might be able to make workable contributions to child welfare through incremental changes in policy. But even an incrementalist approach ought to be informed by the best available evidence and the most appropriate analytic framework. It is the apparent failure to achieve that level of understanding that raised questions about whether, even used incrementally, "test-case litigation [is] a sensible way to promote the welfare of children."

Incrementalism is less promising a method of judicial child welfare reform than it might first seem for another reason. Incrementalism requires flexibility and a close and constant attention to the problem being addressed, so that changes can be made as successes and failures emerge. In some ways, courts seem well suited to those requirements. Indeed, the traditional explanation of common law development neatly fits the incrementalist model. That explanation sees courts as deciding a long series of cases each dealing with a small part of a social problem.

From the series of holdings courts gradually induce a principle which is itself susceptible to gradual change as further holdings are assimilated.

As a description of how courts actually decide cases, this theory obviously has many deficiencies, but it may help direct us toward two impediments to successful incrementalism in test-case litigation over children's policy. First, such litigation is constitutional, not common law, litigation, and as such it tends to be deductive, not inductive. The Constitution provides not only a text to apply, but embodies principles of importance. This makes it easier for courts to feel they are equipped to deal with whole problems and not just increments of problems (since the text and principles presumably preempt many of the aspects of a problem that might otherwise be addressed incrementally) and it makes it harder for courts to respond flexibly (because it is harder to back down over an issue of principle and because of the need to maintain consistent application of a principle over the entire range of assimilable problems). Second, there may simply be too few cases to generate real familiarity with many of the problems children's policy raises and to allow for frequent small adjustments of policy. From this point of view, test-case litigation involving numerous enforcement cases (like *Brown*) ought, *ceteris paribus*, to produce better judicial policy than litigation (like *OFFER, Bellotti, Norton*, and *Goss*) resolved in relatively few cases. Similarly, test-case litigation involving institutions (like *Pennhurst*) ought to produce better judicial policy than other such reform efforts (again, like *OFFER, Bellotti, Norton*, and *Goss*), at least to the extent that the intensive interaction between court and institution which is thought to typify institutional litigation forces the court to learn in detail about the particular entity it seeks to change. Yet even these instances of better judicial policy (if such they be) import their own limits: only a greatly expanded judiciary could afford such attention to more than a very few areas of litigation, and it is exactly the intensity of judicial involvement that has provoked criticism of the school desegregation and institutional cases.

Questions On Due Process

(1) One limitation of judicial reform is that its remedies are limited. Where due process is at stake, a hearing is the likeliest remedy. Would more and fuller hearings help improve the quality of child-custody decisions in the foster-care system?

(a) Will hearings improve decisions because any transfer is likely to be bad, and hearings make transfers less likely?

(b) Will hearings impair decisions because transfers are likely to increase the natural parents' chances of retrieving their children, and hearings make transfers less likely?

(c) Will hearings make social workers more careful to make considered decisions and to document them thoroughly and thus to make wiser decisions? Will hearings simply make social workers more careful to make a good paper record without improving the quality (although increasing the cost) the decisions? Will hearings be too infrequent to affect social workers at all?

(d) Will hearings tax limited agency resources and thus lead to less satisfactory decisions?

(e) Will hearings make it harder for social workers to remove children from unsatisfactory foster homes and thus lead to less satisfactory decisions?

(f) Will hearings make it harder for social workers to act when they perceive that a child is in danger but cannot fully document that perception, and will hearings thus lead to less satisfactory decisions?

(g) Will hearings make it harder for social workers to act on their class biases and thus lead to more satisfactory decisions?

(h) Will hearings produce different, but not necessarily better, decisions than those already made by social workers, given the indeterminacy in child-custody decisions and the advantages of the social worker who is on the spot and has dealt with the parties for some time?

(i) Will hearings discourage social workers from going to the trouble to seek transfers, even where the transfer may be desirable, and will hearings thus lead to less satisfactory decisions?

(j) Will hearings be conducted by former social workers whose preconceptions will be so similar to those of present social workers that hearings will make little difference? Will hearings be conducted by social workers who were kicked upstairs because they weren't doing well in the field, and will hearings thus lead to less satisfactory decisions? Will hearings be conducted by social workers who were promoted from the field because of the excellence of their judgment, and will hearings thus lead to better decisions?

(k) Will hearings make it harder for parents to retrieve their children from the foster-care system and thus deter them from confiding their children to foster care?

(l) Will hearings be so rarely demanded that their increased availability will make no difference? Recall that in New York informal hearings were already available at the time of *Smith v. OFFER* and that they were used in less than one percent of the transfers. And that when New York City adopted more formal pre-termination hearings, only two to three percent of terminations were preceded by hearings, while another two to three percent were settled before hearings.

(2) Can we answer the questions in Question 1, since the circumstances of agencies vary from place to place and from time to time?

(3) What costs do due-process remedies impose? Consider the following criticism of the ABA *Standards*:

> [A] single agency could be called upon to perform an initial investigation of a report of abuse and, if court action ensues, the agency must submit an investigative plan, conduct a detailed investigation, analyze the services available and their possible impact, and submit specific treatment of placement plans and periodic post-disposition reports. Moreover, agency personnel may be required to attend hearings at as many as four stages of the initial proceedings, as well as at periodic reviews of agency provision of services or placement. These procedures are designed to make the agency more accountable to courts. The net result, however, is so to burden the agency that it will be less capable of offering quality services to needy families than it is at present.

Richard Bourne and Eli H. Newberger, *"Family Autonomy" or "Coercive Intervention"? Ambiguity and Conflict in the Proposed Standards for Child Abuse and Neglect*, 57 BU L Rev 670, 677–78 (1977).

(4) *DeShaney* illustrates the trade-offs that must be made when constitutional rights conflict: there, the right of parents to raise their children without untoward governmental intrusion and the right of children like Joshua to live free of parental abuse. In refusing to allow Joshua's § 1983 action, the Court seems to be choosing the presumption in favor of parental privacy. One criticism of *DeShaney* might be that the Court has chosen the wrong set of rights, or overprotected the parents'. Does either harm that might result seem serious? Least remediable?

(5) Another way of considering this problem is through the mathematical foundations underlying the burden of proof. The most famous modern example of such analysis is *In re Winship*, 397 US 358 (1970), where the Court states that the risk that one innocent juvenile might be convicted outweighs the harm caused by freeing ten guilty youths using a burden of proof less than "beyond a reasonable doubt." As the Court said, quoting from *Speiser v. Randall*, 357 US 513, 525–526 (1958):

> There is always in litigation a margin of error, representing error in factfinding, which both parties must take into account. Where one party has at stake an interest of transcending value—as a criminal defendant his liberty—this margin of error is reduced as to him by the process of placing on the other party the burden of . . . persuading the factfinder at the conclusion of the trial of his guilt beyond a reasonable doubt. Due process commands that no man shall lose his liberty unless the Government has borne the burden of . . . convincing the factfinder of his guilt.

In mathematical or statistical terms, this convention is called setting the null hypothesis. The null hypothesis is chosen by imagining which of two errors would be more serious. In *Winship*, for example, the more serious error is declaring the innocent youth a juvenile delinquent. By the choice of the null hypothesis this type of error is designated Type I error, with the result that protecting against this type of error receives significant due process protection (the most substantial burden of proof). In the *DeShaney* set of facts, the Court seems to be choosing Mr. DeShaney's chance of wrongfully being deprived of custody of Joshua (since a criminal conviction for abuse is not the focus of the case) as more significant than the possible harm to Joshua from nonaction. In other words, the preference is in favor of a not-intrusive-enough government over one that is overly intrusive. Is this preference correct? The one most helpful for families generally? Is the *DeShaney* situation so unusual that it is not worth upsetting the rules that might be appropriate in the vast majority of cases?

SECTION 6. CONCLUSION

Because his mother drank, Adam is one of the earth's damaged. Did his mother have the right to take away Adam's curiosity, the right to take away the joy he could have felt at receiving a high math score, in reading a book, in wondering at the complexity and quirks of nature? Did she and his absent father have the right to make him an outcast among children, to make him friendless, to make of his sexuality a problem more than a pleasure, to slit his brain, to give him violent seizures?

Louise Erdrich
Foreword to *The Broken Cord*, by
Michael Dorris

Parental rights face their harshest test when parents have abused or neglected their children. The following questions are designed to help you think about how strong parental rights are under those circumstances and about the law's response to abused and neglected children.

(1) Our first justification for parental rights is that parents know their child and their child's situation better than anyone else can, since they have cared for and lived with their child from his birth. How convincing is this justification in the context of child abuse and neglect?

(a) What difference does it make if the knowledge is not being put to good use or is even being put to bad use? Is it even clear that parents who neglect their children really know the important things about them? Are parents who are disturbed enough to abuse or neglect their children capable of seeing their children clearly?

(b) Even if parents don't know their child well, will they still know the child better than "the state" can? How satisfactory are the state's means of finding out about the child?

(2) Our second justification for parental rights is that decisions about children implicate questions about child development and family interactions about which judges and bureaucrats are not expert. How convincing is this in abuse and neglect cases?

(a) Abuse and neglect cases are generally handled by specialized courts whose judges have an incentive and opportunity to become experienced in the problems of abused children and learned in the psychological literature about them. And abused children are generally brought within the responsibility of a department of social services which is equipped with social workers and a variety of at least nominal experts.

(b) It is possible to doubt the expertise of the people the state employs to deal with child abuse. But is there any reason to think parents understand child development and family interactions better than state's judges, social workers, psychiatrists, and the like, particularly where the parents at issue have abused their child?

(c) Even if the state's employees are not expert in child development and family interactions, should the state be inhibited from dealing with child abuse and neglect? Aren't there many kinds of harms to children which don't take an expert to identify? Or is the problem that it takes an expert to know how to deal with children who have been harmed?

(3) The third justification for parental rights lies in the difficulty of devising standards to govern judicial or administrative decisions.

(a) The first version of this justification is that the situations in which children live are so various, complex, and unpredictable that no adequately comprehensive, detailed, and principled standards could be drawn up to guide courts or agencies in making decisions about children.

(i) One response to this version is, so what? Why should the fact that children can be harmed in many ways prevent us from protecting children from all kinds of harms? One answer to this question that, in the absence of standards, judges and other officials have too much discretion. This answer takes us back to the problems we discussed in considering the tension between rules and discretion. How does that discussion apply to abuse and neglect cases?

(ii) A second response to this version is again to ask, so what? Perhaps we cannot write a standard that will foresee all the kinds of abuse and deal with them. But can we draw up a standard that will deal with the major kinds? The IJA/ABA Standards attempt to do this in a rigorous way. Are they successful? If not, what does their failure tell us?

(b) A second version of this justification is that in a large pluralistic society no satisfactory social agreement can be reached about what kind of adult we want children to become, about what child-rearing techniques will rear what kind of adults, or about what child-rearing techniques are appropriate. But even if we cannot reach a "satisfactory" social agreement on these questions, we may still be able to deal with the abuse and neglect of children. Can't we reach agreement about many things that are bad for children, even if we don't fully agree about what's good for them?

(4) The third justification for parental rights is the enforcement problem.

(a) One version of this justification is that much of the interaction between parents and children takes place in private and that government therefore cannot easily find out and affect what is going on. Child abuse and neglect exemplifies this problem. But what follows? Should the government not attempt to prevent harm to children because the task is difficult?

(b) A second version of this justification is that much of what influences parental behavior concerns psychological motives which are both strong and unrecognized and which thus are so difficult for people to control that even governmental sanctions may be bootless. Again, this may be true, but what flows from it? Should government intervene less, or more? If parents cannot control what they do to children, should the state be more willing to remove children from their homes?

(c) A third version of this justification is that parents often feel their upbringing of their children is not the concern of outsiders (and particularly not government's business), so that parents resist attempts to enforce government rules and decisions. This can mean that evidence to use in prosecutions will be elusive. Are there ways to reduce parental resistance?

(d) A fourth version of this justification is that governmental attempts to enforce rules against parents may provoke parents to retaliate (consciously or unconsciously) against the very people the government is trying to protect—the children. Alternatively, a punished parent (particularly a jailed parent) may be unable to care for the child at all. But how should these possibilities affect the authority of parents and the intervention of the state?

(5) The fifth justification for parental rights is that governmental intervention might exacerbate family conflict. Will intervention, by bringing into the family outsiders from social workers to prosecutors, disrupt the crucial stability of the relationship between parent and child? Does intervention injure parents' position as stable authority figures? How important is stability (compared to abuse or neglect)? How important is the child's continuing contact with and regard for the parent?

(6) The sixth justification for parental rights is that government intervention injures the family by diminishing its privacy. Douglas Besharov argues:

> To determine whether a particular child is in danger, caseworkers must inquire into the most intimate personal and family matters. Often, it is necessary to question friends, relatives, and neighbors, as well as school teachers, daycare personnel, doctors, clergymen, and others who know the family.

Richard Wexler, a reporter in Rochester, New York, tells what happened to Kathy and Alan Heath (not their real names): "Three times in as many years, someone—they suspect an 'unstable' neighbor—has called in anonymous accusations of child abuse against them. All three times, those reports were determined to be 'unfounded,' but only after painful investigations by workers.... The first time the family was accused, Mrs. Heath says, the worker spent almost two hours in my

> house going over the allegations over and over again.... 'She went through everything from a strap to an iron, to everything that could cause bruises, asking me if I did those things. [After she left] I sat on the floor and cried my eyes out. I couldn't believe that anybody could do that to me.' "Two more such investigations followed.
>
> The Heaths say that even after they were "proven innocent" three times, the county did nothing to help them restore their reputation among friends and neighbors who had been told, as potential "witnesses," that the Heaths were suspected of child abuse.

Douglas J. Besharov, *Unfounded Allegations—A New Child Abuse Problem*, The Public Interest 18, 23 (Spring, 1986). How important is privacy compared to the harms suffered by an abused or neglected child?

(7) The seventh justification for parental rights is that it is normatively preferable for people to organize their own intimate lives. Can this justification survive abuses of parental authority?

(8) The eighth justification for parental rights is that allowing families freedom promotes pluralism. Part of the impetus for proposals like the ABA *Standards* comes from the fear that broadly written standards will lead to interventions on purely "cultural" grounds. But how far should pluralist values prevent us from dealing with child abuse and neglect? Some of what we call abuse and neglect may be acceptable in some American subcultures. Can pluralism justify allowing one child to suffer harms other children would be protected from?

BIBLIOGRAPHY

Foster Care. Richard J. Delaney and Frank R. Kunstal, *Troubled Transplants: Unconventional Strategies for Helping Disturbed Foster and Adopted Children* (U Southern Maine, 1993), argues for shortening the time children spend in foster care before permanent placement. For another view of foster and extended family care, see Katharine T. Bartlett, *Rethinking Parenthood as an Exclusive Status: The Need for Legal Alternatives when the Premise of the Nuclear Family has Failed*, 70 Va L Rev 879 (1984). Professor Bartlett suggests giving greater legal recognition to adults other than parents who may have been important in children's lives.

Child Abuse. Child abuse is studied in a series of (sometimes rather technical) essays in Dante Cicchetti and Vicki Carlson, eds, *Child Maltreatment: Theory and Research on the Causes and Consequences of Child Abuse and Neglect* (Cambridge U Press, 1989). Barbara J. Nelson, *Making an Issue of Child Abuse: Political Agenda Setting for Social Problems* (U Chi Press, 1984), studies the way child abuse becomes a political issue. A needed check on our insular view of our child-abuse problem may be found in the essays in Jill E. Korbin, *Child Abuse and Neglect: Cross Cultural Perspectives* (U Cal Press, 1981). Richard Rhodes, a noted journalist, has written a remarkable memoir of his troubled childhood in *A Hole in the World: An American Boyhood*

(Touchstone, 1990). For an economic perspective on children at risk, see Victor Fuchs and Diane M. Reklis, *America's Children: Economic Perspectives and Policy Options*, 255 Science 41 (1992), surveys the grim statistics of children living in poverty, particularly those living with single parents. Jane Hamilton, *A Map of the World* (Anchor 1994), presents a fictional account of a family whose security is destroyed by an accusation of child abuse.

Termination of Parental Rights. For provocative answers to a rhetorical question, see Marsha Garrison, *Why Terminate Parental Rights?*, 35 Stan L Rev 423 (1983).

Discretion. A modern judge's perspective on the subject is Aharon Barak, *Judicial Discretion* (Yale U Press, 1989). A broader legal perspective is D.J. Galligan, *Discretionary Powers: A Legal Study of Official Discretion* (Oxford U Press, 1990).

Chapter XI

CHILD SUPPORT AND THE ENFORCEMENT PROBLEM

The gruel disappeared; the boys whispered to each other, and winked at Oliver; while his next neighbours nudged him. Child as he was, he was desperate with hunger, and reckless with misery. He rose from the table; and advancing to the master, basin and spoon in hand, said: somewhat alarmed at his own temerity:

"Please, sir, I want some more."

Charles Dickens
Oliver Twist

SECTION 1. THE DIMENSIONS OF THE RESPONSIBILITY

As for me, I think it is cruelty and injustice not to receive them [children] into a share and association in our goods, and as companions in the understanding of our domestic affairs, when they are capable of it, and not to cut down and restrict our own comforts in order to provide for theirs, since we have begotten them to that end.

Michel de Montaigne
Of the Affection of Fathers for Their Children

A. WHAT OUGHT THE BASIC SUPPORT STANDARD BE?

Partly for the reasons adduced by the court in *McGuire* (in Chapter 4) and partly for the reasons we considered in discussing the law of parents and children, American family law has been reluctant to impose particular child-support obligations on parents of an intact family. Such parents must supply the child's necessaries and must meet whatever minimum standards abuse-and-neglect statutes set. More is not legally required. The law has, however, long placed child-support obligations on the non-custodial parent—generally the father—following divorce.

(1) The Rise of Child–Support Guidelines

How much do noncustodial parents owe their children? Traditionally, that question has been decided case by case. The UMDA exemplifies that approach:

UNIFORM MARRIAGE AND DIVORCE ACT

Section 309. [*Child Support.*] In a proceeding for dissolution of marriage, legal separation, maintenance, or child support, the court may order either or both parents owing a duty of support to a child to pay an amount reasonable or necessary for his support, without regard to marital misconduct, after considering all relevant factors including:

(1) the financial resources of the child;

(2) the financial resources of the custodial parent;

(3) the standard of living the child would have enjoyed had the marriage not been dissolved;

(4) the physical and emotional condition of the child and his educational needs; and

(5) the financial resources and needs of the noncustodial parent.

As the UMDA suggests, the traditional standard for setting child support rested on the child's needs (evaluated in terms of the child's standard of living during the marriage) and the parents' ability to pay. (Since both parents are obligated to support their children, the ability of both the non-custodial and the custodial parent to pay is relevant. Any income of the child's may be taken into account if the parents cannot provide for him out of their own resources.) This loose standard leaves much—everything?—to the court's discretion. The court may be guided, but is not bound, by whatever agreement the parents have worked out. Courts have not, until recently, generally been provided with guidelines, beyond the limited kind of considerations listed in statutes like the UMDA. However, title IV–D of the Social Security Act now requires states to develop such guidelines, and these guidelines are sometimes to be treated as rebuttable presumptions. Finally, the court may modify support orders when the parent's ability or the child's need changes.

As guidelines for child-support decisions have proliferated, they have assumed a good deal of importance. However, there are many ways of writing such guidelines. In the article that follows, Marsha Garrison, one of the consultants to the ALI Principles project, provides several valuable kinds of information. First, she describes the several kinds of child-support guidelines. Second, she criticizes both the theory behind the "first generation" child support formulas and the impact of the federally mandated guidelines. Third, she argues that the law of child support should reflect the same principles that animate modern marriage and divorce legislation.

MARSHA GARRISON
AN EVALUATION OF TWO MODELS OF PARENTAL OBLIGATION

86 California Law Review 41 (1998)

The article examines this question: How much do parents owe their children? It describes the historical development of the child support obligation and current support "guidelines," mandated by Congress with the hope of raising support levels. It utilizes several distributive justice theories to evaluate the guidelines, concluding that they fail under any approach. The article explains that all of the surveyed distributive justice theories lead to one of two support models. The "Community Model" bases the support obligation on family membership and mandates income sharing as a basic approach. The "Autonomy Model" bases the support obligation on both the societal burden produced by nonsupport and the nonsupporting parent's contractual obligations to the custodial parent; it mandates public assistance (or poverty) prevention and contract enforcement as basic goals....

How much do parents owe their children? Does parental obligation derive primarily from the burdens that a child may impose on society and on the other parent, or from parent's and child's joint membership in a sharing community? ...

Over the past twenty years, both the federal and state governments have enacted laws designed to improve [the] dismal record [of collecting child-support payments]. While the reform effort has altered many aspects of child support practice, the most sweeping shift has been in the determination of support award values. Traditional support laws urged consideration of the child's needs, prior standard of living, and parental resources, but left to judicial discretion the task of translating these factors into a dollars and cents payment schedule. Today, based on directives from Congress, each state has adopted numerical guidelines governing the value of child support. While these guidelines need only establish a rebuttable presumption as to the child support amount, deviation must be justified in a written decision.

While Congress adopted the numerical guidelines requirement with the aim of significantly increasing award levels and decreasing award variability, available evidence suggests that these goals have not been met. Awards calculated under existing guidelines do not appear to differ dramatically from those produced under earlier discretionary standards. Many guidelines fail to ensure that children are protected from poverty, even when parental income is adequate to meet that goal. Moreover, they often improve the living standard of the child support obligor, while causing that of his child to plummet. Today's child support laws thus prefer the interests of the nonresident parent to those of the child, the custodial parent, and the public.

Are these results fair? ... Current guidelines ... lack an articulated theory of the support obligation to ground their design and justify their results. Most were derived from economic models of household expenditure in intact families, not from a decision about what income allocation would be fair in a divided family. The literature on child support today thus focuses almost exclusively on details—child care costs, extraordinary medical expenses, joint custody, extended visitation—without regard to basic goals or principles....

I. Child Support in Retrospect: The Development of the Child Support Obligation

A legal child support obligation might be derived from any of three parental duties—to the child, to the other parent, or to the community. The first child support laws relied exclusively on the parent's community obligations. But, from time to time, support laws have relied on each form of parental obligation .....

C. The Modern Era: The Guidelines Movement and Growing Disparity in the Status of Spouses and Children

In the late 1970s, the federal government began, for the first time, to collect national data on child support awards and payments. The impetus for both this data collection effort and the new wave of child support laws that accompanied it was concern over rising rates of single parenting and welfare dependence—the same concern that motivated earlier support laws. It is thus unsurprising that reforms were initiated by the federal government, which today foots most of the bill for welfare payments to children, instead of the states, which traditionally have made child support law.

While sixteenth-century lawmakers focused on public support institutions and their nineteenth century counterparts on private support obligations, contemporary policymakers have taken a hybrid approach.... [J]ust as contemporary welfare law has abandoned individualized assessment of need in favor of standardized eligibility criteria and grants, Congress required numerical guidelines to replace discretionary decisionmaking....

[T]he new federal requirements applied exclusively to child support, eroding the prior consistency between child and spousal support principles. Although contemporary alimony law has moved toward standards based on need instead of fault, it is still highly discretionary. In contrast to the Congressional emphasis on increasing child support levels, the major alimony innovation during this period was the durational award, designed to limit alimony payments to a fixed period of economic "rehabilitation."

The joint economic interests of children and their mothers have not substantially abated, however. Although the percentage of fathers awarded custody has increased substantially, the number of children who live in a father-only household is still small. As a result of these conflicting trends, the tension between alimony and child support principles has intensified....

As a result of these various trends, laws governing economic relations within the family no longer evidence common assumptions and consistent goals. Child support is subject to increasing state regulation aimed at raising support levels, while spousal support is increasingly viewed as a limited, need-based remedy. Spouses are now seen as members of a sharing community who should divide the fruits of their relationship equally, while parents are still treated as autonomous individuals with far more limited obligations....

II. The New Child Support Guidelines: Their Development and Effects

A. Current Child Support Guidelines: The Basic Model

When Congress mandated the development of numerical support guidelines in the mid 1980s, it did not specify a particular formula or model. As a result, each state ... had to resolve—explicitly or implicitly—these questions: To whom does the income of individual family members belong? Exactly what do parents owe their children and each other? What do they owe the public, that may be forced to pick up the tab for children's needs that parents have failed to meet? ...

In the early days of the guidelines movement, scholars ... offered legislators a variety of policy options. Some advocated an "equal outcomes" model aimed at achieving equal living standards for the child and noncustodial parent. Others advocated a "continuity-of-expenditure" approach, which based the support obligation on typical child-related expenditure within intact, two-parent families. And others urged that the new guidelines seek, above all else, to ensure that the supported child did not become impoverished as a result of parental separation. While these approaches garnered the most attention, legislators could also have opted for a utilitarian model or one that aimed at ensuring the child a minimally adequate income.

But while the range of policy options was extensive, policy debate was muted and rarely focused either on the underlying choice between individualist and sharing norms within the family or on the ordering of community and familial obligation....

One reason for the constricted debate was the speed with which the guidelines movement came to fruition. Prior to 1984, when Congress first required states to adopt advisory support guidelines, only a handful of states and localities utilized guidelines of any description; within a few months of the October 1989 deadline imposed by Congress, all states had adopted guidelines meeting the federal requirement....

The continuity-of-expenditure model was expressed in two different guideline formulae. Under the "percentage-of-obligor-income" formula, the child support obligation is stated as a percentage that varies with the number of children to be supported. The percentages are based on a variety of consumer surveys and purport to represent typical expenditure patterns in intact families....

The "income-shares" formula similarly utilizes standard percentages that are applied to parental income and vary depending on the number of children. But an income shares formula typically requires more information and arithmetic. The percentages are calculated to exclude child-care costs and any costs associated with extraordinary medical care on the theory that these, potentially very large, expenses are too variable to permit standardization. The percentages are also variable and, in most versions, regressive, with lower percentages applicable to higher incomes. The support calculation takes into account the incomes of both parents, with the final award obtained by prorating the percentage-based support obligation plus child-care costs according to the percentage of family income contributed by each. Awards calculated under income shares guidelines thus represent a compromise between standardization and individualized case processing.

In sum, continuity-of-expenditure guidelines, although motivated by a common aim, vary substantially in their methodology, complexity, and results. The same facts, about the same family, may yield an altogether different child support award.

In contrast to the diversity of continuity-of-expenditure formulae, the poverty prevention approach is reflected in only one guideline formula, the so-called "Melson" model. This formula, pioneered in Delaware by Judge Elwood F. Melson, Jr. for use in his own courtroom, was the first guideline to be adopted statewide. In revised form, it is still in effect in Delaware and has been adopted in three other states. The formula establishes "primary support" values designed to meet the minimum needs of one adult and one or more children. The adult primary support value is first subtracted from each parent's income; the remainder is then applied, in proportion to the parents' relative incomes, to the basic child support obligation. The Melson formula does not take poverty prevention as its only goal, however. If the child support obligor still has available income, a fixed percentage of that income, based on those utilized by the percentage-of-obligor-income model, is then added to the basic support obligation. The Melson formula thus seeks to avert impoverishment of the noncustodial parent and the child, in that order. A secondary goal is income sharing in relation to expenditure patterns within the intact family....

All of the states have thus far adopted either the Melson formula or a variant of the continuity-of-expenditure model. Thus despite the fact that the guidelines legislation evidenced no central philosophy and required no particular approach, all state guidelines today aim, to some extent, at maintaining continuity of child-related expenditure; in a handful, poverty-prevention is also an articulated goal.

B. What the Guidelines Have Accomplished

Although research reports analyzing the impact of the new guidelines are still few in number, available reports suggest that child support awards remain highly variable and that the average value of awards has increased modestly but not dramatically. Despite predictions by some experts that guidelines would triple child support values, increases to date have fallen far short of that level. In some states, average award levels apparently did not increase at all after guidelines were introduced. In others, increases were registered by some income groups but not others. Moreover, a significant proportion of the increase in average child support values that researchers have noted may simply be due to the imposition of token, rather than zero-dollar, awards in cases of unemployed or female noncustodial parents. . . .

To be sure, some of the reasons for these results lie outside the reach of any law governing child support values. Variation in award levels, for example, results in large part from the process of individual negotiation that determines the vast majority of child support awards. Many parents who negotiate support awards are poorly informed about the relevant legal standards. In a large, and apparently growing, proportion of the cases, lawyer representation is available to only one—or neither—parent. Under these circumstances, the resources and attitudes of each parent may play important roles in determining child support outcomes and produce results that bear little relationship to the outcomes that lawmakers intended to achieve. Aggregate outcomes are also affected by the failure of many support-eligible parents to seek awards. More than four out of ten mothers—and more than three-quarters of those never-married—have not obtained a child support award. Some of these mothers could not find the father or believed that he was unable to pay; others report that they simply did not want to pursue an award. Thus, even with an excellent rule, the attitudes and behavior of custodial parents may preclude excellent results.

Moreover, even the best possible child support rule is powerless to ensure that children are adequately supported when family income is inadequate. Children who were poor before family dissolution (or nonformation) will remain poor. Because both divorce and nonmarital childbearing are more common among low-income families, the extent of unpreventable poverty in the support-eligible population is substantial. The problem of preexisting poverty is also exacerbated by the loss of economies of scale that accompanies family break-up. Two households cannot live as cheaply as one; thus the federal poverty level for a family of three is approximately 50% less than that of a family of one and a family of two. For the family that had barely averted poverty when together, dissolution ensures that some, if not all, family members will thereafter be poor.

Because of these factors limiting the extent to which a child support rule can achieve its intended results, the new support guidelines must be judged primarily on the basis of the results sought rather than those achieved. But today's guidelines appear to be lacking even by this measure. First, the level of support mandated frequently does not protect children from poverty. One recent review, which evaluated all state guidelines in effect in 1989–90, concludes that none required lower-income noncustodial parents to provide enough child support to ensure either a poverty-level or a "minimum decent living" standard for two children. While this goal might have been unobtainable in some of the cases to which the guidelines were applied, in others it was not. A significant number of states also failed to ensure that children in middle-income families enjoyed a minimum decent living standard. Moreover, awards calculated under the guidelines produced a dramatic decline in children's living standard as compared to that of the noncustodial parent. On average, awards under the guidelines reviewed caused children's living standards to decline by 26% while noncustodial parents' improved by 34%. . . .

C. The Reasons for the Results

The failure of current guidelines to ensure that children do not bear the brunt of family dissolution is sobering but not surprising: current guidelines were not designed either to achieve a minimum decent living standard for children or to ensure that the economic burden of family dissolution is equitably distributed; the methodology that they employ is inherently ill-adapted to accomplishing either of these other goals.

The estimates of child-related expenditure on which current guidelines rely are based on predictions of how much more income a two-parent household, with a given level of expenditure, would need in order to add a new family member and maintain its standard of living. But single parents appear to spend a considerably larger fraction of their incomes on children than do two-parent households. Moreover, more than 90% of typical family expenditure represents goods such as housing, transportation, and utility payments that cannot easily be allocated to specific family members. The estimates thus describe only the marginal, or extra, costs associated with a new family member, not the per person allocation of family resources.

These marginal cost estimates all derive from one or another "household equivalence scale," devised by economists to permit living standard comparisons when households are not the same size. These scales were not intended as a basis for assessing child support, and have major limitations when used for that purpose. Although their assumptions and results vary substantially, such scales do offer a basis for predicting how much more income a family (say, John and Mary) will need in order to add a new member (Baby, for example) and maintain its current living standard. They also enable us to predict Baby's standard of living when she joins the family. But they tell us nothing about Baby's living standard if her parents separate, dividing the family and its income. Unless the same income base is available in Baby's new household—an unlikely result given prevailing custody patterns and gender-based wage differentials—her living standard must, of necessity, change.

Current child support guidelines thus "severely penalize children for being in the custody of a parent who has less income, and reward them for living with the parent who has more."

D. Why the Success of the Continuity-of-Expenditure Model? . . .

There are two different approaches one might employ in resolving these underlying issues of justice. One method treats child support policy as a question of distributive justice, focusing on the determination of which child support principles are most fair to the parties involved. Another is the familiar approach of policy science and political debate, that proceeds by articulating and critiquing goals, assumptions, expected outcomes, and implementational problems. . . . On many issues of public concern—taxation, affirmative action, welfare policy—we routinely employ both types of analysis. This dual approach is the one I will utilize here. . . .

III. Child Support as Distributive Justice: Issues and Theories

A. The Family and Justice. . . .

Because of its primacy, political philosophers have written extensively about the parent-child relationship. At least since the Enlightenment, they have tended to assume that parents owe to their children an obligation of care, protection, and education. But agreement on the existence of parental obligation has not produced a uniform theory (or even an array of competing accounts) of either the extent of parental obligation or its relationship to marital and community obligations.

One explanation for this theoretical gap can be found in the tendency to assume that family relationships are governed by altruism rather than by the constraints of formal justice. Although this tendency has abated in contemporary discussions of marriage, it is still dominant in discussions of the parent-child tie. . . .

D. Child Support Past and Present: The Legacy of Locke and its Transformation

[T]he perspective [on distributive justice that is] most compatible with the law on the books is undeniably the libertarian. This is the only perspective that assumes, as does past and current support law, that parents are individually entitled to their income; it is the only perspective that views child support as a taking which demands a justification; it is the only perspective that measures the child support obligation based on public expense and private contractual obligation. . . .

In order to fully justify traditional support law within a libertarian framework, one must ... assume a duty owed by the parent directly to the child. While modern libertarians have seldom addressed this issue, their Enlightenment forebears were firmly committed to an ethic of parental obligation. John Locke, the most important source of libertarian property concepts, rejected absolute parental authority just as he rejected monarchical authority: though a parent "may dispose of his own

Possessions as he pleases, when his Children are out of danger of perishing for want," Locke held, "[t]he Nourishment and Education of their Children, is a Charge so incumbent on Parents for their Childrens [sic] good, that nothing can absolve them from taking care of it." Nor did Locke view the child's claim as extending "only to a bare Subsistence but [instead] to the conveniences and comforts of Life, as far as the conditions of their Parents can afford it." Traditional support law is thus most easily characterized as a Lockean construct: while it is firmly committed to an individual entitlement approach to parental income, it is also firmly committed to the view that parental duty is an inviolable obligation owed directly to the child and measured by parental ability to pay.

Current guidelines retain much of the Lockean perspective. They presuppose a parental obligation running directly to the child, assume a parent's entitlement to his income, and base the support obligation on parental spending patterns. They depart from Locke, however, by favoring the parent's needs over those of the child.... Under these formulae, even the parent whose children burden the community through receipt of public assistance may owe no, or token, child support if his own income falls below the statutory personal support allowance. Perhaps more importantly, Locke measured the support obligation by what the parent could afford, a child-centered metric that hints at an underlying sharing norm. Continuity-of-expenditure guidelines, by contrast, measure support by the extra expenses induced by the birth of a child in an intact....

E. Current Guidelines: A Failure by Any Measure

In evaluating current guidelines, it is important to keep in mind that they are grounded in a philosophical tradition that emphasizes property rights and individual autonomy. These aspects of the Lockean tradition clearly retain a powerful grip on the American imagination, fueling distrust of "big government" and a tendency to look to individual behavior as a reason for and solution to social problems. Indeed, one way to understand the federal child support initiatives is as an attempt to explain and reverse a rising tide of children's poverty through the behavior of individual "deadbeat dads." ...

Even within a libertarian framework, however, current guidelines fall short. Libertarian child support would be set at a level that prevents welfare dependence and/or poverty; support awards—like the results of traditional child support laws—would be regressive, to the point at which work and payment disincentives dictate otherwise. Even the Melson formula, the only current guideline that takes poverty prevention as its primary goal, does not meet these requirements....

Within any other distributive justice framework—utilitarian, egalitarian, contractarian—current guidelines would have to be scrapped. All of these nonlibertarian approaches require a sharing norm and yield some version of the equal outcomes model. The individual entitlements assumption of current guidelines is so inconsistent with this approach that revision would not be possible....

IV. Autonomy or Community: What Child Support Model Do We Want?

...

B. Contemporary Attitudes Toward Child Support

Information on public attitudes toward child support determinations is available from only two public opinion polls, neither of which focused on attitudes toward child support policy goals. The more detailed ... is the 1985 Wisconsin Survey of Children, Incomes, and Program Participation (CHIPPS).... Approximately three-quarters of the respondents indicated that the value of the support obligation should vary with a shift in either the cost-of-living or the noncustodial parent's income. About the same percentage indicated that the support obligation should also vary based on the value of the custodial parent's income. By contrast, only 36.5% reported that a noncustodial father's remarriage should affect the support award....

Respondents appeared to believe that the value of support should not be restricted to a minimum basic needs package; that the support obligation should be based on, and updated to take account of, the current incomes and circumstances of family members; that the support calculation should include a comparative element that takes into account the circumstances of both segments of the divided family; and, finally, that a parent should contribute something to his child's support, even if he is worse-off than the child. Except for the respondents' insistence on support payment by a worse-off parent, these trends are all more consistent with a community than an autonomy model. While they do not clearly support an equal outcomes support formula, they do strongly support an approach that treats the divided family as one family, and which adjusts the support payment to equitably balance the claims of all family members.

To supplement the published survey data on child support, I conducted a survey on attitudes toward child support in my Fall 1997 Family Law class.... In response to the question, "[p]lease choose the goal you believe most important in formulating a child support rule," 42% of the respondents indicated that the child support amount should be set at a level that will "maintain the standard of living the child enjoyed prior to parental separation;" 58% indicated that the support amount should "equalize the living standard of the child and his or her noncustodial parent." None of the respondents indicated that child support should be set at an amount that would "ensure that the child's basic needs are met," "maintain the non-custodial parent's child-related expenditure at what it would be in an intact family," or "ensure that the child does not burden the community by becoming a recipient of public assistance." ...

C. Evidence from Related Areas of Law

Another way of evaluating the choice between community and autonomy is by analogy: Which approach is more consistent with other laws governing the parent-child relationship? Which is more consistent with the assumptions upon which family law generally relies?

1. Parental Rights and Obligations: Tradition and Trends

American law has generally followed a tradition of deference to parental decision-making.... This tradition of deference to parental decision making is, of course, highly compatible with the minimalist, parent-centered approach that underlies traditional support law and the autonomy-focused support models ...

While the tradition of deference to parents is still strong, for at least the past two centuries it has been on the decline.... By the late nineteenth century, parental authority had been circumscribed by laws dealing with child labor, education, and neglect, and the last three decades have witnessed a wave of new limitations on parental prerogatives.... Within the past two decades, the Supreme Court has also ruled that parents may not veto a mature minor's reproductive decisions, and that a parent's entitlement to commit his child to a mental institution is not absolute. In sum, deference to parental authority has reached an historic low.

The decline in parental authority has been accompanied by a shift in rhetoric. Recent commentators on parental rights may disagree about the scope and content of parental authority, but they are virtually unanimous in the view that parental rights derive from, and are limited by, the child's needs. This child-centered perspective on parents' rights has produced an altered account of parenthood as a functional status, rather than one derived from biology or legal entitlement. The new perspective has increasingly led courts to limit the rights of parents who have failed to accept parental responsibilities and to grant "parental" rights to nonparents....

These various manifestations of a child-centered approach to parental rights support a community-based support model more than an autonomy-based one. But the child-centered perspective also represents only a trend, not a consistent, established tradition.

2. Economic Entitlements Based on Family Membership: Can Inconsistent Rules Be Justified?

Community is clearly the emerging norm in rules governing marriage. Does logic mandate a similar approach to the parent-child relationship or can an inconsistent approach be justified?

At first glance, the differences between marriage and parenting stand out more than the similarities. The oft-cited basis for a community model of marriage is the evolution of marriage toward a "partnership of equals" norm. But parents and children are neither relational equals nor partners who have chosen each other in an arms-length transaction....

While inequality and lack of choice factually distinguish the parent-child relationship from that of a married couple, these differences do not necessarily justify departure from the community ideal now applicable to marriage. The roots of parent-child inequality lie in the child's dependence, which is itself the source of both the parental support obligation and the parental altruism norm. Parent-child inequality could thus justify a legal regime requiring more sharing behavior toward a child than toward a marital partner, but not one that requires less. Moreover, ... [t]he community conception of marriage ... ultimately derives from social values, not from spousal equality or choice....

Perhaps the best evidence on sharing expectations comes from research on beliefs about distributive justice. Jennifer Hochschild, who studied American attitudes toward distributive justice in a wide range of institutions, has reported that within the nuclear family "strict equality and need predominate" as norms to which individuals profess allegiance. While parents often "leaven [their] focus on equality with discipline," they also believe that "[all family] members deserve equal amounts of the good being divided" and should "sacrifice equal amounts of satisfaction when necessary." ...

Like the trend toward a child-centered approach to parents' rights, ... various manifestations of less hierarchical relationships between parents and children support a community support model more than they do an autonomy-based approach. The autonomy model relies on a "Father Knows Best" conception of the family in which parental rights go hand-in-hand with the assumption that parents will know, and act on, their children's best interests. By contrast, the community model—like the egalitarian family—assumes neither parental wisdom nor altruism; parents are expected to share, no more and no less.

D. Applying the Community Principle to Child Support: Problems and Prospects

So far, we have seen that the community support models meet public policy goals better than does the autonomy approach. The community models satisfy the poverty prevention aims of the autonomy approach as well as the autonomy approach itself. They do a much better job of increasing support awards, the policy goal that motivated the guidelines movement in the first place. Based on the sparse evidence available, the community models more closely match public opinion trends. Finally, they appear to comport with evolving family law and cultural norms better than does the autonomy approach. These various advantages all argue strongly in favor of a community-based support policy.

1. Community vs. Clean Break

A community approach would apply to the parent-child relationship differently than it does to the husband-wife relationship, a difference that may negatively affect its political acceptability. With marriage partners, the community approach demands equal sharing only at the time the relationship terminates; although an aggrieved spouse may seek the imposition of a constructive trust to prevent the dissipation of marital assets, division takes place at divorce or death. While case law is sparse, courts have been extremely loathe to interfere with actual spending patterns in an intact marriage. The rhetoric of community emphasizes the commitments made during marriage, but the application of a community approach focuses on the severance of those commitments. The result is that the community approach, applied to marriage, is entirely consistent with the current view of divorce as a "clean" relational break.

By contrast, the child support obligation arises when parent and child live physically apart in an intact legal relationship; a "winding-up," like that which occurs at divorce or spousal death, is inappropriate. In this context, the community principle would apply to income, not property; sharing would take place over time, not all at once; the emphasis would be on relational continuity, not severance. The result is conflict with the current ideal of divorce as a clean relational break; the community models of child support assume that both parents will remain part of one family.

This aspect of the community models, which runs counter to a deep current in contemporary culture, will almost certainly ensure opposition to its adoption. Couples who divorce typically want a clean break and, for the growing population of never-married parents, there will seldom be an ongoing familial relationship to continue. Indeed, legislative rejection of the equal outcomes approach during the period when guidelines were first adopted may have stemmed more from opposition to this emphasis on relational continuity than the "hidden alimony" issue identified by commentators; all child support models benefit the custodial parent, but not all treat that parent as an ongoing member of the support obligor's family.

While the tension between the community principle and clean break philosophy is an undeniable political disadvantage, it is not, in my view, a disadvantage on the merits. Although the desire for a clean break from a former spouse is understandable, the attainment of that aim requires abandonment of parental commitments. The parent who maintains a relationship with his child must maintain a relationship with the child's other parent. Visits and vacations must be planned; decisions about the child's education and medical care must be made. Nor can one parent always avoid the other at the school play, the Little League game, or the hospital bedside. Even when support obligations have terminated as a result of the child's maturity, parents will—or should—share graduation ceremonies, weddings, and grandchildren....

2. Community vs. the Reality of Separation

The fact that the child support obligation arises in the context of a disrupted relationship offering neither parent nor child the opportunities for noneconomic sharing available in an intact family raises a more fundamental issue: Is it fair to treat parent and child as an ongoing familial community when they lack the opportunities for day-to-day intimacy and sharing offered by a residential relationship, and may never have had such opportunities? The issue is presented most starkly in the case of nonmarital childbearing, where the noncustodial parent may never have had a residential relationship with the child or even the other parent.

In looking at this question, it is important to keep in mind that a community child support model does not uniformly disadvantage noncustodial parents as compared to an autonomy-based approach. Noncustodial parents who earn a relatively high percentage of family income will initially pay more support under a community approach, but the noncustodial parent whose former spouse remarries, whose own income declines, or who has additional children—situational shifts to which the autonomy-focused models are insensitive and that today produce cries of unfairness from noncustodial parents—will over time fare better under a community model than under an autonomy-focused approach. The community model also places the noncustodial parent on a footing equal to that of his child and former spouse; he is not expected to shoulder a significant child support burden when they are better off than he is.

Nor is the community model, when applied to marriage, restricted to those relationships that have in fact provided intimacy and sharing. The couple whose marriage is marked by distrust, withholding, violence, or even prolonged separation is treated as a community just as is the couple whose relationship involves genuine mutuality. It is the fact of marriage, not its quality, that has triggered the community standard.

The law has looked to the existence of, rather than the circumstances surrounding, the marriage both to avoid difficult fault judgments and to emphasize the centrality of marital status as the basis for application of the community principle. There are strong reasons for applying this status-oriented approach to the parent-child relationship as well. First, the parent-child relationship may well be, in our mobile and divorce-prone society, the most permanent of ties. For both parent and child, the relationship is unique and, in many cases, irreplaceable. Parent and child will have only one opportunity to experience this relationship; for the child, there may be no other opportunity to relate to a parent-figure of this gender. The quality of the relationship and the range of parental substitutes also lie entirely outside the child's control.

While the child's options for replacing a parent are fewer than those of a spouse who is dissatisfied with a marriage partner, the relationship is of even greater importance. A wealth of data, from diverse sources and theoretical schools, uniformly demonstrates the centrality of the parent-child relationship as a determinant of the child's personality, resilience, and relationships with others....

Finally, to restrict application of the community principle to cases in which the parent-child relationship closely approximates that of a harmonious intact family—one with a successful joint custody arrangement, for example—would reward the wrong kind of parental behavior. Although some commentators have speculated that the increased incidence of "casual" parenting may produce a more limited child support obligation, it is no accident that it has instead spurred a new wave of interest in child support....

[T]o the extent that concerns relating to one or another difference between parenting and marriage leave the rule-making authority unprepared to adopt a community support model mandating full equality, the limited equality model, reliant on a community norm but offering greater deference to the noncustodial parent, is available. This approach, which might be justified based on the continuity of the parent-child relationship, still offers substantial improvements over both current guidelines and the autonomy approach in terms of child support outcomes....

Questions on Models of Parental Obligation

(1) Can the duty to pay child support square with the principle of family autonomy? The idea of community that Professor Garrison suggests ought to dominate parent-and-child as well as marriage law has always conflicted with the principle that the family is "a little Commonwealth" into which outsiders—the state—ought intervene only rarely. Does her discussion of Locke, whose thoughts on families we encountered at the beginning of Chapter 8, help resolve this tension?

(2) We encounter once again our old friend, the tension between discretion and rules. The traditional method of setting child support was, as UMDA section 309 suggests, magnificently discretionary: "reasonable or necessary." You don't get much more discretionary than that. And no one supposed that the little list of factors the court was supposed to consult would much discipline its decisions. Some time ago, it became clear that judicial decisions were producing troublesome results. First, awards were inconsistent. Second, they were insufficient. A central solution to these problems has been to swing from one end of the discretion-rules continuum to the other. We now have guidelines laid out neatly in charts. And the ALI piles yet a further complexity on rules on top of the charts. Yet Professor Garrison tells us, "Awards calculated under existing guidelines do not appear to differ dramatically from those produced under earlier discretionary standards." How can this be? Recall that Professor Garrison also delivered the bad news that equitable-distribution principles altered property distribution in New York very little. Do her reasons for that failure of legal rules to work in expected ways help us understand this one?

(a) Is the problem that these cases are too complex to settle in advance with binding rules, however elaborate?

(b) Is the problem that judges do what they like whatever the rules instruct them to do?

(c) Is the problem not with using rules instead of discretion, but with the particular rules that have been chosen?

(d) Does the problem lie in some features of the economic and social situation of divorcing parents which judicial discretion and binding rules are alike unable to alter?

(3) The federal statutes that mandate guidelines, and, as we shall see presently, specify enforcement mechanisms, conflict with another principle we've encountered before—the idea that family law ought to primarily be state law and that each state should be able to experiment and to put into law the preferences of its own citizens. Should we care?

(4) Professor Garrison suggests that child support, in its current incarnation, conflicts with one of the newer rationales for alimony, the rehabilitation standard. Is this observation accurate? Are the two distinguishable because the husband-wife relationship ends at divorce while the parent-child one changes but continues? Or does Professor Garrison convince you that both policies should be reformulated to reflect ideas of community?

(5) Does it make any sense to talk about rationales for child support without even considering which policies might better promote payment (or collection) of the amount ordered?

BALL v. MINNICK

Supreme Court of Pennsylvania, 1994
648 A2d 1192

MR. JUSTICE CAPPY.

This case presents us with the opportunity to elucidate the scope of our current support guidelines contained in Rule 1910.16–1 et seq. of the Pennsylvania Rules of Civil Procedure.[1] More specifically, we must determine whether the trial court correctly ordered child support in an amount lower than the guideline figure suggests. For reasons other than those relied upon by the learned Superior Court, we agree that the order of the trial court must be reversed. Accordingly, we affirm, in part, the Order of the Superior Court.

In October, 1989, appellant, Teresa Ball, filed a petition for modification of child support with respect to her and appellee's two children, both of whom were, at that time, living with appellant. An Order

1. [Ed.] Pa.R.C.P. § 1910.16–4 provides:

(a) If the amount of support deviates from the amount of support determined by the guidelines, the trier of fact shall specify, in writing, the guideline amount of support, and the reasons for, and findings of fact justifying, the amount of the deviation.

(b) In deciding whether to deviate from the amount of support determined by the guidelines, the trier of fact shall consider

(1) unusual needs and unusual fixed obligations;

(2) other support obligations of the parties;

(3) other income in the household;

(4) ages of the children;

(5) assets of the parties;

(6) medical expenses not covered by insurance;

(7) standard of living of the parties and their children; and

(8) other relevant and appropriate factors, including the best interests of the child or children.

requiring appellee to pay $500.00 per month was entered upon recommendation of a Domestic Relations Hearing Officer. Believing that the award was too high, appellee sought a de novo hearing in the Court of Common Pleas of Westmoreland County. Following the hearing, the trial court ordered appellee to pay $400.00 per month, while the guidelines suggested the amount of $513.00 per month. In its opinion in support of its order, the trial court found the following:

> Plaintiff resides with her husband, their child and the two children of the parties who are the subject of the current support order. Plaintiff has been employed as a waitress, and has a minimum wage earning capacity. She is currently off work after having surgery, but plans to return to work in the near future. Her present husband is not employed and no explanation of his status was presented at trial. It is axiomatic that he has a duty to contribute to the support of his wife and child. The total monthly budget of Plaintiff's household is $850.00 per month. The parties' children constitute forty per cent of that household, and the sum of $340.00 per month reflects their reasonable needs. The Court has concluded that the reasonable needs of the children are about $400.00 per month.
>
> Defendant earns $1,705.00 per month. He resides with his wife and her two children from a prior union. Application of the support guidelines at $1,705.00 per month for defendant and $400.00 per month earning capacity for plaintiff suggests an Order of $513.00 per month.

This Court is aware that the guidelines are a starting point only. The Court has considered the expenses of both parties and their standard of living. It is clear that an Order of $400.00 per month meets all the basic needs of the children, so that any contribution made by plaintiff will serve to enhance the standard of living of the children. The Court believes that an award in the guideline amount would require this defendant to pay 60% of the expenses of Plaintiff's household, and thus subsidize plaintiff's current husband and their child. Considering all factors, this Court concluded that an Order of $400.00 per month for two children is fair and reasonable.

Appellant appealed that decision to the Superior Court arguing that the trial court erred in awarding only $400.00 per month. A majority of the Superior Court, which heard the case en banc, reversed and remanded the matter for further proceedings. In doing so, it found that while child support could be determined in numerous ways including, inter alia, the implementation of the support guidelines, Pa.R.C.P. 1910.16–1 et seq., or the formula set forth in *Melzer v. Witsberger*, 480 A.2d 991 (1984), the trial court here erred by not considering all the relevant factors. Specifically, the Superior Court found that the trial court failed to consider the income of each parent's respective spouses and also failed to support its award by not setting forth sufficient detail regarding the reasonable needs of these two children. With respect to the applicability of the guidelines, the Superior Court held as follows:

> Thus we conclude the guidelines are not mandatory, but a starting point and by implication they cannot and do not supersede *Melzer* or deny the trial judge or hearing officer of the discretion to mold support orders to meet the specific conditions of the parties.

The Superior Court went on to state that "the traditional broad discretion in the trial court to determine these matters remains unrestricted."

In so holding, the Superior Court misperceives the effect of the adoption of the guidelines and sets forth an incorrect statement of the law. First, with respect to the viability of the *Melzer* formula, the Superior Court ignores the clear and unambiguous language of the guidelines and corresponding rules. In *Melzer v. Witsberger*, this Court set forth a formula for determining child support obligations based upon the reasonable needs of the particular child or children involved together with the respective abilities of each parent to support their children. In 1989, however, this Court adopted the support guidelines found at Pa.R.C.P. 1910.16–1 et seq. Rule 1910.16–5 specifies in detail the applicability of the guidelines. Initially, the rule makes clear that the *Melzer* formula applies only where the parties' combined income exceeds the amount of the guideline income figures. Thus, the Superior Court erred in holding that the guidelines do not supersede the *Melzer* formula. The clear and unambiguous wording of Rule 1910.16–5 provides that the *Melzer* formula is no longer viable where the parties' incomes fall within the guideline figures. This is true even where the finder of fact, upon application of the guideline rules, determines that a deviation from the recommended guideline figure is warranted.

The Superior Court also erred with respect to its conclusion that the trial judge or hearing officer's discretion remains inviolate irrespective of the adoption of the guidelines and accompanying rules. Rule 1910.16–1 explicitly states that the amount of support, whether it be child support, spousal support or alimony pendente lite, shall be determined in accordance with the support guidelines which consist of not only the grids set forth in Rule 1910.16–2 and the formula set forth in Rule 1910.16–3, but also Rule 1910.16–5 which discusses in detail the operation of the guidelines. The rules make clear that the amount of support as determined from the support guidelines is presumed to be the appropriate amount of support and that any deviation must be based on Rule 1910.16–4.

In the instant case, the trial court deviated from the support guidelines by awarding monthly support of $400 rather than the guideline amount of $513. The sole issue before this Court is thus whether this case presents any basis for deviation.

The standard of appellate review of child support matters has not changed; a reviewing court must continue to apply an abuse of discretion standard. A support order will not be disturbed on appeal unless the trial court failed to consider properly the requirements of the Rules of Civil Procedure Governing Actions for Support, Pa.R.C.P. 1910.1 et seq., or abused its discretion in applying these Rules.

As we said previously, deviations are governed by Rule 1910.16–4 in support proceedings involving parties whose incomes fall within the guideline figures. Subsection (b) of this Rule sets forth the only factors that a trier of fact may consider in determining whether to deviate. The trier of fact is required to consider all relevant factors and any one factor alone will not necessarily dictate that the amount of support should be other than the guideline figure. Rather, the trier of fact must carefully consider all the relevant factors and make a reasoned decision as to whether the consideration thereof suggests that there are special needs and/or circumstances which render deviation necessary. Furthermore, where the trier of fact does determine that the circumstances warrant a departure from the guideline amount, the justification for any such deviation must be explicitly set forth in writing, giving particular attention to those factors which this Court, in adopting the guidelines, has specifically deemed relevant. See Pa.R.C.P. 1910.164(a). General references to the effect that "all relevant factors have been considered" is wholly insufficient.

The presumption is strong that the appropriate amount of support in each case is the amount as determined from the support guidelines. However, where the facts demonstrate the inappropriateness of such an award, the trier of fact may deviate therefrom. This flexibility is not, however, intended to provide the trier of fact with unfettered discretion to, in each case, deviate from the recommended amount of support. Deviation will be permitted only where special needs and/or circumstances are present such as to render an award in the amount of the guideline figure unjust or inappropriate.

In the instant matter, there was no evidence presented which established any special obligations or special circumstances justifying an award lower than the recommended guideline figure. The trial court's primary reason for deviating from the support guidelines was that the basic needs of the children could be met by a payment of less than the guideline amount. This is an impermissible basis for deviating from the guidelines.

Under established Pennsylvania case law, a parent has a duty to provide for the reasonable needs of his or her children to the best of his or her ability. This support obligation is not limited to the basic necessities of life. The children's reasonable needs include any expenditure that will reasonably further the child's welfare. Thus, unless a child enjoys an unusually high standard of living, the amount of the support obligation is based on a parent's ability to pay child support rather than the amount of money required to pay for those essential and nonessential items that would reasonably further the child's welfare.

The support guidelines were promulgated pursuant to the Act of October 30, 1985, as amended, 23 Pa.C.S. § 4322, which provides that child and spousal support shall be awarded pursuant to statewide guidelines as established by general rule by the Supreme Court of Pennsylvania. This legislation provides that:

> [t]he guideline[s] shall be based upon the reasonable needs of the child or spouse seeking support and the ability of the obligor to provide support. In determining the reasonable needs of the child or spouse seeking support and the ability of the obligor to provide support, the guideline[s] shall place primary emphasis on the net incomes and earning capacities of the parties, with allowable deviations for unusual needs, extraordinary expenses and other factors, such as the parties' assets, as warrant special attention.

The support guidelines are based on the principle embodied in the case law that the financial support of a child is a primary obligation of each parent. Since the child's needs receive priority, the support obligation consists of that portion of the parents' incomes that is reasonably available for child support. This approach is also mandated by 23 Pa.C.S. § 4322, which provides for the reasonable needs of a child to be determined through the use of the guidelines that place primary emphasis on the net incomes and earning capacities of the parents.

As the Explanatory Comment to Rule 1910.16–1 notes, the child support guidelines are based on the Income Shares Model developed by the Child Support Guidelines Project of the National Center for State Courts, the premise of which is that there should be available for the needs of a child of separated parents the same proportion of parental income that would have been available for the needs of that child if the parents lived together. The guidelines assume that similarly situated parties, at least with respect to income levels, will have similar reasonable needs and expenses. The reasonable needs of the child as well as the reasonable expenses of the obligor are factored into the support guidelines. The support guideline amount is presumed to be (1) a payment which the obligor can reasonably afford and (2) a payment that is reasonably necessary to further the child's welfare. The clear intent of the guidelines, therefore, was to do away with individual, case-by-case determinations of just what constitutes the reasonable needs and expenses of the particular parties involved and thus to limit the trial court's discretion. In other words, the trier of fact need not, nor should he or she, consider in the first instance, the actual expenses of the parties in an effort to establish the reasonable needs of a particular child. Instead, the trier of fact must assume initially that the guideline amount constitutes the amount necessary to meet the reasonable needs of the child.

Under Rule 1910.16–4, a court may not deviate from the guidelines on the ground that the child does not need this amount of money. This is not a factor that is set forth in Rule 1910.16–4 (b). While subsection (7) of that Rule which references the standard of living of the parties might seem at first blush to support the trial court's reasoning, we find that given the premises on which the guidelines are based, subsection (7) was not intended to justify the downward modification of the guideline figures absent a showing of special needs and/or circumstances. Again, the purpose of the support guidelines is to make available for the children's reasonable needs the full amount of the guideline figure unless unusual obligations of the obligor limit his or her ability to pay the guideline amount.

Since the trial court considered a factor that should not have been considered in entering the support award here, an abuse of discretion is readily apparent. Moreover, as there were no additional relevant factors which would support the trial court's award, application of the above principles dictates that an award in the amount of the appropriate guideline figure should have been awarded. Accordingly, for reasons other than those articulated by the learned Superior Court, the decision of the Superior Court reversing the trial court's award is affirmed. The case is remanded for the imposition of an award in the amount of the appropriate guideline figure.

JUSTICE FLAHERTY, dissenting.

I emphatically dissent. The support guidelines provide a starting point to calculate what child support should be paid in a given case. There is, as the majority states, a presumption that the guidelines are correct, but this presumption can always be rebutted by a presentation of facts in the case which suggest that the amount paid should be more or less than the guideline.

The guiding principle is that the absent parent should pay his or her fair share of what is required to support the children.

In many cases, that need is uncertain and so the guidelines are relied upon. In this case, the need is defined. The custodial parent, the mother, tells us, through submission of her monthly budget, that she requires $850 per month to support her family of five. Because only two of these five people are the non-custodial father's responsibility to support, the trial court properly multiplied the required $850 by 40%, the percentage of the mother's new family represented by the non-custodial father's children. This calculation yields the amount of $340. Out of an abundance of caution, the court then increased that amount to $400 per month.

This calculation and reasoning process were entirely proper. The whole purpose of the guidelines and of support hearings generally is to determine what amount of money is needed to support the children and to require both parents to pay their fair share of that need. This is exactly what the trial court did.

Furthermore, the trial court properly explained its deviation from the guideline. As Rule 1910.16–4 (7) requires, the court must consider, inter alia, "standard of living of the parties and their children." In basing its order on the monthly budget for the family as presented by the mother, the court appropriately considered the standard of living of the parties and their children.

The majority "finds" that subsection (7) of Rule 1910.16–4 cannot be used to justify a downward modification of the guideline. The justification for this remarkable determination is "the premises on which the guidelines are based." Needless to say, this justification justifies nothing. By definition, a guideline must be able to be modified upwards or downwards, depending on the facts of the case.

Generally, I agree with the majority's conclusion that "the purpose of the support guidelines is to make available for the children's reasonable needs the full amount of the guideline figures unless unusual obligations of the obligor limit his or her ability to pay the guideline amount," but this has no application where the parties tell us what amount is needed to support the children and that amount is different from the guideline.

The trial court is correct in reasoning that on the facts of this case, if the father were required to pay the guideline amount, he would, in effect, be subsidizing the mother's new husband and child in addition to supporting his own children. Such a result defies rationality.

Questions on Ball *and Support Guidelines*

(1) Among other things, *Ball* involves the question whether the remarriage of the custodial parent should affect the noncustodial parent's support obligation. As the court below noted, "the trial court failed to consider the income of each parent's respective spouses." Should the remarriage of either parent (or a parents' assumption of responsibility for additional children) affect the amount of child support owed? *Ball's* answer, and that of most state courts, is that the guidelines are presumptive only. In individual cases, where the needs of the children or justice warrant, guideline amounts can be adjusted.

(2) Should stepparents be responsible, in any way, for contributing to the income that is available for guideline purposes? We have already seen that the ALI Principles § 302A, Comment b, notes that generally stepparents are not responsible for contributing (though some states do mandate contribution when the child would otherwise be on public assistance).

(3) Another question that may not be answered by the Guidelines is what to do if the parents' combined incomes exceed what is strictly necessary to provide for the child's well-being or to maintain the child's previous standard of living. States have dealt with this question in various ways. One is to provide for a sliding percentage scale (rather like a regressive income tax amount). Thus, Va Code § 20–108.2 (B) (2006), provides that for a family of four whose gross income is $75,000 monthly, child support will be $2,222 for the first $10,000 (or 22%), plus $780 for the second $10,000 (or 7.8%), plus $600 for the third $10,000 (or 6 %), plus $1800 for the last $45,000 (or 4%). Thus the total amount awarded would be $5400.

(4) What if the parties' income changes so that the amount awarded is no longer within the statutory guidelines? Should this be enough of a change of circumstances to warrant a modification? For a case that says that it is, see, e.g., *Milligan v. Milligan*, 407 SE2d 702 (Va App 1991).

(5) Do the guidelines affect an agreement between the parties for, say, a lower amount? *Watson v. Watson*, 436 SE2d 193 (Va App 1993), held that the guideline amount must first be calculated so the court can determine whether the amount set is in the children's best interests. See also *Slonka v. Pennline*, 440 SE2d 423 (Va App 1994), which holds that even in a shared custody case, the guideline amounts should be considered first.

(2) The ALI and Child Support

We turn now to the ALI's attempt to improve the way the amount of child support is set.

AMERICAN LAW INSTITUTE PRINCIPLES OF THE LAW OF FAMILY DISSOLUTION § 3.05

(2002)

§ 3.05 The Child Support Formula

(1) The basic child support obligation should be determined by a rule of statewide application, expressed as a formula.

(2) The formula should include two parts: a *preliminary assessment* and a *reduction mechanism*.

(3) The *preliminary assessment*, expressed as a percentage of obligor income, combines two elements: a *base* and a *supplement*.

(a) The *base* is the percentage of obligor income that, if paid as child support, would ensure all parties the same standard of living if before payment of child support, the parents had equal incomes.

(b) The *supplement* is an additional percentage of obligor income that, when added to the base percentage, tends to ensure that the child enjoys: (i) a minimum decent standard of living when the combined income of both parents is sufficient to achieve such result without impoverishing either parent; and (ii) a standard of living not grossly inferior to that of the other income parent.

(4) The *reduction mechanism* contains two elements: a *reduction fraction* and a *harmonizing factor*.

(a) The numerator of the *reduction fraction* is the amount by which the residential parent's income exceeds that parent's *income exemption*. The denominator is the sum of the numerator and the support obligor's income. The *income exemption* is the amount necessary to provide the residential parent with a minimum decent standard of living.

(b) The *harmonizing factor*, which is expressed as a decimal greater or smaller than 1, is a technical adjustment necessary to ensure that the formula would reduce the supplement to zero if the incomes of the parents were equal before the payment of child support.

(5) To establish the basic child-support obligation, the child-support formula should determine the dollar amount of the obligor's preliminary assessment; multiply it by the reduction fraction to establish a preliminary reduction; multiply the preliminary reduction by the harmonizing factor to establish a final reduction; and then subtract the final reduction from the preliminary assessment.

(6) When the residential parent has income in excess of the income exemption, the amount of child support required by the formula should be adjusted to apportion between the parents, according to their relative incomes, expenditure for child care required by the residential parent's employment or vocational education. Adjustment for the nonresidential parent's proportional share of child-care expenditure should operate only to offset any reduction of the preliminary assessment under Paragraph (5). It should not create a support obligation greater than the amount of the unreduced preliminary assessment.

(7) Expenditure for medical and dental care should not be included within the formula. The child-support rules should require that such expenditure be treated as additional child support. When a child is covered by a parent's health insurance, or when health insurance for a child is available at reasonable cost to a parent through employment or otherwise, that parent should be required to maintain or to acquire such insurance. The cost of the child's portion of a premium for medical or dental insurance, if paid directly by a parent, and expenditure for uninsured medical and dental care for the child should be shared by the parents according to their relative incomes.

(8) The following types of expenditure are not included within the formula and the child support rules should provide that they may be treated as additional child support and apportioned to the parents according to their relative incomes and the other equities of the case:

(a) expenditure that is appropriate in light of the special needs or gifts of the child, and

(b) expenditure for long-distance travel required to exercise custodial responsibility.

(9) In allocating responsibility for additional expenditure under Paragraphs (6) and (8) of this section, the child support required by the formula should be treated neither as income to the payee parent nor as a deduction from the income of the payor parent, and the residential parent's entire income, including the income exemption, should be counted.

§ 3.07 Presumptive Effect of Child–Support Formula

(1) The child-support rules should provide that the obligation established by the child support formula is presumptively just and appropriate. Unless the presumption is rebutted as provided in this section, the

amount determined by the formula should be incorporated in the child-support award.

(2) The presumption established by Paragraph (1) is a presumption affecting the burden of proof. It is rebuttable only by proof that, taking into account the interests of the child, the amount determined by the formula would be unjust or inappropriate, under the particular circumstances of the case, for one or more of the following reasons:

(a) the support obligor has extraordinarily high income and the amount determined under the formula exceeds an amount necessary to insure that (i) the child enjoys a standard of living that is both adequate and not grossly inferior to that of the support obligor and (ii) the child's § 3.12 life opportunities are adequately secured;

(b) the child has independent income and not taking that income into account would work a hardship on the support obligor;

(c) the support obligor's income is insufficient to maintain the obligor at federal poverty level and, in lieu of applying the formula, a small fixed amount is established as a nominal support obligation; or

(d) the parents have agreed to a greater amount, or the parents have agreed to a lesser amount and their agreement has been reviewed and approved by the trier of fact pursuant to § 3.13

(e) by court order under § 3.11, or by agreement of the parties, sale of the family residence is deferred for the benefit of a child, and deferred sale results in housing savings or additional housing costs under § 3.11(7), which are allocated to the parents under § 3.11(8);

(3) The child-support rules should require that, when departing from the formula as permitted by Paragraph (2) of this section, the court state in writing all of the following:

(a) the amount of support that would have been ordered under the formula, and the amounts of income, as defined by §§ 3.14–3.16, that are used in determining the amount due under the formula;

(b) the amount of support actually ordered; and

(c) the reasons for the difference.

Notes and Questions on ALI § 3.05

(1) As you can see, calculations of child support are to be based upon guidelines set by each state. Current state guidelines typically begin by trying to establish the amount the parents together earn each month. Then, typically, a chart is consulted. The row headings in the chart are income categories; the column headings are numbers of children. The boxes represent the amount that would be spent on each child in the family *if the parents lived together.* To find the amount the noncustodial parent presumptively owes one multiplies the amount in the chart by his percentage of the couple's gross income. For an example of this kind of guideline, see Va Code Ann § 20–108.2 (2006). For a

slightly more complicated version (which features a separate chart for each number of children in which rows represent the custodial parent's net monthly income and columns represent the noncustodial parent's net monthly income), see Iowa Rule 9.2 (2006). The Iowa Code follows the guidelines with a worksheet. Since these are presumptive amounts, they may be adjusted to take into account expenses like extraordinary medical and dental expenditures, child care costs, and health care costs.

Contemporary guidelines, we said, commonly use as their baseline the amount that would be spent on the child in an intact household. ALI § 3.05, on the other hand, seeks to equalize standards of living between the two households. This requires knowing the difference between the obligor's and the obligee's income, the standards of living that could be expected given the two incomes, and the basic percentage of income that would be spent on the child *to equalize these two standards of living*. In addition, where possible, the ALI assesses a supplemental amount to insure the child a "minimum decent standard of living." And, following current practice, presumptive guideline amounts are to be adjusted to accommodate the child's special expenses or assets.

(2) Illustration 5 to § 3.05, Tent Draft No 3, Pt. II, 1998, at 37, shows how the calculation works and how much the amount will differ from traditional child support awards:

> 5. James, the nonresidential parent, has monthly net income of $1,600 and Martha, the residential parent, who is employed full-time at low wages, has net income of $800. They have one child. Because Martha's income is below the $1,000 income exemption, the nonresident parent pays the full preliminary assessment, $544 (34% of obligor income). After payment of child support, the residential household has income of $1,344 and the nonresidential parent has income of $1,056. Applying the Bureau of Labor Standards household-equivalence table, the residential household will experience a 20 percent decline in standard of living, and the nonresidential parent will experience a six percent decline. Because both households have relatively low incomes, it is also appropriate to evaluate the outcome in terms of basic adequacy, defined as income of at least 150 percent of poverty threshold. Applying the poverty threshold equivalence table, the total income of the residential household after payment of child support is 149 percent of poverty threshold, while the remaining income of the nonresidential parent is 150 percent of poverty threshold.
>
> A first generation Marginal Expenditure [or current Guidelines] formula, in contrast, would require the nonresidential parent to pay $320 (20% of net obligor income). After payment of child support, the residential household would have income of $1,120 and the nonresidential parent would have income of $1,280. Applying the Bureau of Labor Standards household-equivalence table, the residential household would experience a 33 percent decline in standard of living and the nonresidential parent would experience a 13 percent increase. The income of the residential household would be 124 percent of poverty threshold, and

the income of the nonresidential parent would be 182 percent of poverty threshold.

Questions on Deviations from Presumptive Amounts under Section 3.10

(1) If you represented a parent, would you be able to calculate the guideline amount owed under this section and § 3.05 easily? Reliably? To put the question differently, does this calculation strike you as a tiny bit complicated? This tendency toward elaborately complicated rules is quite characteristics of the ALI Principles. Does their complication add to or detract from their usefulness?

(2) Should the child support obligation ever be below some token amount? In 2000, the Virginia legislature amended its child support guidelines to set awards at zero for truly impecunious fathers who are incarcerated, institutionalized in a mental health facility, or permanently and totally disabled. Va Code Ann § 20–108.2B (2006). This means their parental rights are less likely to be terminated for nonsupport.

(3) Should a generous grandparent's gift (particularly the gift of a custodial parent's parent) reduce the obligation of a noncustodial parent, since the child will then have his or her own resources? Is it good for parents to feel they must make some sacrifices for the children, quite apart from the children's economic need?

B. WHAT OUGHT THE LIMITS OF THE STANDARD BE?

We have now examined the basic rules for setting child support. We will now consider some important questions about the limits of the support the law should require.

(1) A Duty to Earn?

Some noncustodial parents attempt to reduce their child-support obligations by reducing their income. Here is one particularly ingenious attempt.

PENCOVIC v. PENCOVIC

Supreme Court of California, 1955
287 P2d 501

TRAYNOR, JUSTICE.

Plaintiff and defendant were married in 1937 and had two children, a son and a daughter. In 1944 plaintiff obtained a divorce and was given custody of the children, who were then six and four years of age respectively. Defendant was ordered to pay $20 per month for the support of each child. He made one payment, entered the army, and authorized an allotment for his children. From the time of his discharge late in 1945 until 1951 he made no payments for the support of his children, who depended in part on assistance from Alameda County. In

1951 the county instituted criminal proceedings against him. He was found guilty of nonsupport and ordered to pay $20 per month for each child in accordance with the divorce decree and $10 per month for each child for unpaid arrearages. Since then plaintiff has received $30 per month for each child from defendant through the probation officer of Alameda County.

In November 1953 plaintiff filed an affidavit alleging that her earning capacity had been impaired in an automobile accident, that the children required more money for their support, and that she believed that defendant's income was $1,000 per month. She requested the court to increase the support for the children to $100 per month for each child. The court ordered defendant to show cause why he should not be punished for contempt for disobedience of the original support order and why that order should not be modified as requested by plaintiff. After a hearing on the orders to show cause, the court discharged the contempt citation and ordered defendant to pay $50 per month for the support of each child and plaintiff's costs and fees for her attorney. Defendant appeals.

Section 139 of the Civil Code provides: "That portion of the decree of judgment making any such (support) allowance or allowance ... may be modified or revoked at any time at the discretion of the court. ..." In the exercise of its discretion, the trial court must consider the needs of the dependents and the ability of the husband to meet those needs. Its orders, however, need not be based upon the actual income or property of the husband, but may be based solely upon his ability to earn money. No abuse of discretion is disclosed by the record in this case. There is ample evidence of changed circumstances and of defendant's financial ability to meet his children's needs and of his ability to earn money in the future.

The two children, now teenagers attending high school, have greater needs for food, clothing, and medical services than at the date of the original order. Living expenses are greater, but their mother, who has been their chief source of support, was permanently disabled in an automobile accident, spent a year and one half in a hospital, and is $1,000 in debt for the care of the children and the payment of hospital bills. She is employed as a Blue Cross Hospital clerk at $200 a month, but because of her injury cannot work steadily. For two and one half years she was completely unemployed and her earnings for the past year have been less than $150 a month. Since it now costs $127 a month for the care of the son and $118 a month for the care of the daughter, she has been unable to feed and clothe herself and the children on her earnings.

When plaintiff obtained the interlocutory decree, defendant told her that he would "plan his life accordingly so he would be protected." He said that he would "form this organization where people would give all their possessions into the organization and he would be the head of the organization, nothing would be in his name, everything would be in the name of the organization, yet he would have them arrange for all the money he wanted to use any time he wanted it."

Defendant's principal contention is that he has neither money nor property nor earnings and that he is therefore without ability to pay the increased amounts. At no time has he contended that he is unable to earn sufficient money to support the children. In 1941 and 1942 he was employed at the shipyards in Oakland as a timekeeper, and at the time of the divorce he was working as a machinist's helper for about $75 a week. Shortly after the divorce he changed his name to Krishna Venta and founded a religious society, the "W.K.F.L. Fountain." (The letters stand for wisdom, knowledge, faith, and love.) The society was incorporated in 1951 and is governed by a board of directors and officers. Defendant is the treasurer of the society and its spiritual leader or "Master." Neither he nor any one connected with the society receives a salary as such. About 100 members reside at a home maintained by the society at Canoga Park in Ventura County. They have a communal system of living and none of them works on the outside. All food, clothing, and medical care are provided by the society. Funds are obtained from new members, who transfer all their property to the society on being admitted to membership, and from gifts, plays presented by the members, and donations received for fighting fires. Defendant and his present wife and their young daughter occupy a small room and five other children of defendant's sleep in a garage made into a bedroom with three other children living at the society's home. Defendant makes periodic automobile trips to Denver to carry on the work of the society. Occasionally he stops at Las Vegas and Reno to gamble, and on some occasions the society and various persons have advanced him money for that purpose, but he has never won. In Las Vegas he once lost $2,900 and in payment drew checks on a bank in which he had no funds. The society paid part of the amount due on the checks and no civil action or criminal charges were brought against defendant for issuing them. The society paid the cost of a trip by defendant to Europe in 1949, a trip to South America in 1951, and trips in 1952 to 54 cities in the United States to study fire equipment and fire departments and to advance the cause of the society. A member of the board of directors usually accompanies him on trips and handles temporal matters. For all contributions that he receives and for all his expenditures defendant accounts to the board of directors, and there is no evidence of unauthorized use of society funds. The society pays all of defendant's expenses, including the $60 per month for the support of his children ordered at the criminal proceeding, and at the time of that proceeding it also supplied him with funds with which to buy gifts for his children, ice skates costing $65 for his daughter and a wrist watch, tennis shoes, and other gifts for his son. It also paid the fees for his attorney in both the 1951 and present proceedings.

Although defendant contends that the support he receives from the society constitutes only a gift to him and that his services are in turn rendered gratuitously, the trial court could reasonably infer from the foregoing evidence that he is in fact receiving compensation from the society for the services he renders as its spiritual leader or 'Master.' Moreover, in the past this compensation has been measured by defendant's needs, including his obligation to support his children. Accordingly, the trial court could reasonably conclude that the amount of his compensation would be increased to meet any additional obligation imposed upon him, and his reasonable expectation of securing such additional compensation could properly be considered in determining his ability to pay. Under these circumstances the fact that the society is not obligated to support defendant's children is immaterial, for in fact it has adopted as the measure of his compensation his needs, including his obligation to support his children. The society and defendant, by determining the compensation by reference to defendant's needs instead of by adopting a fixed rate, cannot compel the court to ignore the fact that under their existing arrangement defendant's compensation as measured by his needs includes his obligation to support his children.

Even if the trial court concluded, however, that defendant was not receiving compensation, but only gifts, and that the society would not provide him with additional funds to discharge the increased support award, its order would not constitute an abuse of discretion. Defendant is an able-bodied man, and the trial court could reasonably conclude that he had the earning capacity to discharge the obligation of the support award. By refusing for religious reasons to seek or accept gainful employment defendant may not evade that obligation. Although the guarantee of religious freedom of the First Amendment of the Constitution of the United States is binding on the states under the due process clause of the Fourteenth, the states may nevertheless regulate conduct for the protection of society, and insofar as such regulations are directed towards a proper end and are not discriminatory, they may indirectly affect religious activities without infringing the constitutional guarantee. Although freedom of conscience and the freedom to believe are absolute, the freedom to act is not. Certainly there are few interests of greater importance to the state than the proper discharge by parents of their duties to their children, and the Constitution does not compel the subordination of the statutory duty of a parent to support his child to a rule of religious conduct prohibiting gainful employment.

Defendant contends finally that the order increasing the amount of the support award is inconsistent with the order discharging the contempt citation, on the ground that the court stated with respect to the alleged contempt that he did not "think there has been any showing ... of ability to pay." Since defendant was paying $20 per month on the accrued arrearages in addition to the $40 per month currently due under the original order, the contempt citation was presumably based on his failure to pay all of the balance of the accrued arrearages. There is no direct evidence of the amount of such arrearages but it may be inferred that it is in excess of $2,000. Accordingly, it cannot be said that the trial court's conclusion that defendant was unable to pay all of the accrued arrearages was inconsistent with its implied finding that he was currently able to pay the increased monthly award.

The orders are affirmed.

Notes and Questions on Pencovic

(1) What happens under conventional child-support guidelines if the noncustodial parent has an income of zero at the time of trial and under the guidelines would owe nothing? A number of cases hold that a presumptive income will be calculated if income is "voluntarily" lowered for college attendance, see *Hur v. Virginia Dept. of Social Servs*, 409 SE2d 454 (Va 1991); the noncustodial parent leaves a high paying job to stay home with a child of a second marriage, *Brody v. Brody*, 432 SE2d 20 (Va App 1993); or the unemployment is due to the noncustodial parent's imprisonment, *L.C.S. v. S.A.S.*, 453 SE2d 580 (Va App 1995)(attorney father convicted of sexually abusing of one of the couple's children and third parties).

(2) Would the result in *Pencovic* be the same if the religion were a more traditional one? What if Pencovic had been an Orthodox Jewish rabbinical scholar rather than "Krishna Ventna"? What if his post-divorce occupation and life were consistent with those he followed before the parties separated? For a case with similar facts to these hypothetical ones, see *Goldberger v. Goldberger*, 624 A2d 1328 (Ct App Md 1993):

> A parent who chooses a life of poverty before having children and makes a deliberate choice not to alter that status after having children is also "voluntarily impoverished." Whether the voluntary impoverishment is for the purpose of avoiding child support or because the parent simply has chosen a frugal lifestyle for another reason, doesn't affect that parent's obligation to the child. Although the parent can choose to live in poverty, that parent cannot obligate the child to go without the necessities of life.

(3) Compare the Court's remark in *Prince v. Massachusetts*, which we read in Chapter VII: "Parents may be free to become martyrs themselves. But it does not follow they are free, in identical circumstances, to make martyrs of their children before they have reached the age of full and legal discretion when they can make that choice for themselves."

(4) How far should one follow the principle that parents who voluntarily impoverish themselves must still pay child support? Should a parent be told to work longer hours? To work at a better paying job?

(2) What Duty to Educate?

One of the substantive child support questions that has produced much litigation and significant legislative attention involves the duty of divorced parents to provide for their children's college education. For most people even fifty years ago, post-secondary education would have seemed a luxury no parent should be required to supply. Today, when far more Americans attend college, tuition costs have swollen, and the divorce rate has soared, the issue has become more complicated. Children are already the "victims" of their parents' decision to divorce. Should they be further disadvantaged by being denied the higher education necessary to achieve most American dreams (and attract a swankier mate)? On the other hand, once a household breaks in two at divorce, many parents who might have afforded college before they separated now must make even greater sacrifices to do so. We examine three states' attempts to grapple with this problem.

IOWA CODE ANN § 598.21F (2005)

1. The court may order a postsecondary education subsidy if good cause is shown.

2. In determining whether good cause exists for ordering a postsecondary education subsidy, the court shall consider the age of the child, the ability of the child relative to postsecondary education, the child's financial resources, whether the child is self-sustaining, and the financial condition of each parent. If the court determines that good cause is shown for ordering a postsecondary education subsidy, the court shall determine the amount of subsidy as follows:

(a) The court shall determine the cost of postsecondary education based upon the cost of attending an in-state public institution for a course of instruction leading to an undergraduate degree and shall include the reasonable costs for only necessary postsecondary education expenses.

(b) The court shall then determine the amount, if any, which the child may reasonably be expected to contribute, considering the child's financial resources, including but not limited to the availability of financial aid whether in the form of scholarships, grants, or student loans, and the ability of the child to earn income while attending school.

(c) The child's expected contribution shall be deducted from the cost of postsecondary education and the court shall apportion responsibility for the remaining cost of postsecondary education to each parent. The amount paid by each parent shall not exceed thirty-three and one-third percent of the total cost of postsecondary education.

3. Subsidy payable. A postsecondary education subsidy shall be payable to the child, to the educational institution, or to both, but shall not be payable to the custodial parent.

4. Repudiation by child. A postsecondary education subsidy shall not be awarded if the child has repudiated the parent by publicly disowning the parent, refusing to acknowledge the parent, or by acting in a similar manner.

5. Obligations of child. The child shall forward, to each parent, reports of grades awarded at the completion of each academic session, within ten days of receipt of the reports. Unless otherwise specified by the parties, a postsecondary education subsidy awarded by the court shall be terminated upon the child's completion of the first calendar year of course instruction if the child fails to maintain a cumulative grade point average in the median range or above during that first calendar year.

Questions about Iowa's Solution for College Education for Children of Divorce

(1) What does "acting in a similar manner" mean in subsection (4)? In *Milne v. Milne*, 556 A2d 854, 859 (Pa Super 1989), the trial court reported:

> Karen Milne separated from her husband, appellee David Milne, IV, in December, 1984 after a twenty-two year marriage. During their marriage, the couple had two children. At the time of the separation, the younger child, Caleb Milne, was a senior in high school. At first, Caleb continued to reside in the marital home with his mother. However, Caleb became estranged from his mother and, in March of 1985, he voluntarily moved in with his father. Karen Milne testified that prior to Caleb's departure, he engaged in several arguments with her which erupted into physical attacks on her. On one occasion, Caleb spit in his mother's face. More than once, he pushed her so that she fell down and at least twice, he struck her.
>
> After Caleb left his mother's house, he ceased all communication with her. In the fall of 1985, he entered the University of Richmond in Virginia. He completed his freshmen year there, attaining a 3.0 grade point average. All of Caleb's expenses during his freshmen year were paid for by his father, whom Caleb lived with during the time he was not in residence at the university.
>
> In February of his freshmen year, David Milne, IV, filed a petition for special relief on behalf of his son. This petition requested the court to issue an order permitting Caleb access to his mother's house to obtain his personal belongings. In support of the petition, Caleb appeared in court to testify against his mother.
>
> During the summer following Caleb's freshmen year in college, Caleb was admitted to Occidental College in California for the completion of his undergraduate studies. When this college admitted him, he filed a complaint in child support against his mother and father to secure financial assistance in meeting his anticipated college expenses at Occidental College. He specifically alleged that his mother had neglected her duty to sufficiently support him.

The court was not charmed by the father's plea to have the mother pay a portion of the college expenses:

> That any father would condone, let alone encourage, a son who has so abused his mother in taking legal action against her shocks the sensibilities of this writer. [The father had encouraged the son to sue the mother to get his belongings from her home.] The dissent would add insult to injury by finding that Caleb is entitled to exact funds for college from his mother's already strained resources. Such compounding of the tragedy of this family cannot be countenanced. To do so would be to relieve Caleb of any responsibility for his actions, which were taken as an adult, however embittered. Neither the passage of time, so favored as a panacea by the dissent, nor Caleb himself have done anything to mitigate the harm of his actions.

Should the parent be able to refuse to send to college a child who, for example, refuses to discuss college activities?

(2) Can a child sue as a beneficiary of his parent's separation agreement? *Drake v. Drake*, 455 NYS 2d 420 (App Div 1982), said no where the contract provided for support until the child reached 21 so long as he was a full-time college student. *Drake* did cite a number of cases in which children were permitted to recover if the payments were specifically for college tuition and also noted that the principle extended to other "direct benefit" cases (like providing for the child in a will or making the child the beneficiary of a life insurance policy). A more recent but similar case is *Chen v. Chen*, 893 A2d 87 (Pa 2006).

In each of the following cases, the noncustodial parent challenges on constitutional grounds his obligation to provide college educational support.

CURTIS v. KLINE

Supreme Court of Pennsylvania, 1995
666 A2d 265

ZAPPALA, JUSTICE. In *Blue v. Blue*, 532 Pa. 521, 616 A.2d 628 (1992), we declined to recognize a duty requiring a parent to provide college educational support because no such legal duty had been imposed by the General Assembly or developed by our case law. As a result of our Blue decision, the legislature promulgated Act 62 of 1993. Section 3 of the Act states:

> (a) General rule—a court may order either or both parents who are separated, divorced, unmarried or otherwise subject to an existing support obligation to provide equitably for educational costs of their child whether an application for this support is made before or after the child has reached 18 years of age.

The issue now before us is whether the Act violates the equal protection clause of the Fourteenth Amendment of the United States Constitution. The Court of Common Pleas of Chester County held that it did, resulting in this direct appeal....

The essence of the constitutional principle of equal protection under the law is that like persons in like circumstances will be treated similarly. However, it does not require that all persons under all circumstances enjoy identical protection under the law. The right to equal protection under the law does not absolutely prohibit the Commonwealth from classifying individuals for the purpose of receiving different treatment and does not require equal treatment of people having different needs. The prohibition against treating people differently under the law does not preclude the Commonwealth from resorting to legislative classifications, provided that those classifications are reasonable rather than arbitrary and bear a reasonable relationship to the object of the legislation. In other words, a classification must rest upon some ground of difference which justifies the classification and have a fair and substantial relationship to the object of the legislation.

Judicial review must determine whether any classification is founded on a real and genuine distinction rather than an artificial one. A classification, though discriminatory, is not arbitrary or in violation of the equal protection clause if any state of facts reasonably can be conceived to sustain that classification. In undertaking its analysis, the reviewing court is free to hypothesize reasons the legislature might have had for the classification. If the court determines that the classifications are genuine, it cannot declare the classification void even if it might question the soundness or wisdom of the distinction.

We are also mindful of the different types of classifications and the standards according to which they are weighed:

The types of classifications are: (1) classifications which implicate a "suspect" class or a fundamental right; (2) classifications implicating an "important" though not fundamental right or a "sensitive" classification; and (3) classifications which involve none of these. *Id.* Should the statutory classification in question fall into the first category, the statute is strictly construed in light of a "compelling" governmental purpose; if the classification falls into the second category, a heightened standard of scrutiny is applied to an "important" governmental purpose; and if the statutory scheme falls into the third category, the statute is upheld if there is any rational basis for the classification. In this instance, we are satisfied that Act 62 neither implicates a suspect class nor infringes upon a fundamental right. Neither the United States Constitution nor the Pennsylvania Constitution provides an individual right to post-secondary education.

Likewise, the classification does not implicate an important though not fundamental right. Consequently, Act 62 must be upheld if there exists any rational basis for the prescribed classification. It is in this context that we review the Act's creation of a duty, and more significantly a legal mechanism for enforcement of that duty, limited to situations of separated, divorced, or unmarried parents and their children.

In applying the rational basis test, we have adopted a two-step analysis. First, we must determine whether the challenged statute seeks to promote any legitimate state interest or public value. If so, we must next determine whether the classification adopted in the legislation is reasonably related to accomplishing that articulated state interest or interests.

The preamble to Act 62 sets forth the legislature's intention "to codify the decision of the Superior Court in the case of *Ulmer v. Sommerville*, ... and the subsequent line of cases interpreting *Ulmer* prior to the decision of the Pennsylvania Supreme Court in *Blue v. Blue* ..." It also states:

> Further, the General Assembly finds that it has a rational and legitimate governmental interest in requiring some parental financial assistance for a higher education for children of parents who are separated, divorced, unmarried or otherwise subject to an existing support obligation.

This latter statement begs the question of whether the legislature actually has a legitimate interest in treating children of separated, divorced, or unmarried parents differently than children of married parents with respect to the costs of post-secondary education.

Appellant argues that with the passage of Act 62 the legislature may have chosen to treat the children of married families and divorced/unmarried families differently, not as a preference towards the latter, but out of deference to the Commonwealth's strong interest in protecting the intact marital family unit from governmental interference. Alternatively, Appellant argues that the legislature may have determined that children in non-intact or non-marital families require educational advantages to overcome disadvantages attendant to the lack of an intact marital family. The critical consideration is whether either of these bases or any other conceivable basis for distinction in treatment is reasonable.

Act 62 classifies young adults according to the marital status of their parents, establishing for one group an action to obtain a benefit enforceable by court order that is not available to the other group. The relevant category under consideration is children in need of funds for a post-secondary education. The Act divides these persons, similarly situated with respect to their need for assistance, into groups according to the marital status of their parents, i.e., children of divorced/separated/never-married parents and children of intact families.

It will not do to argue that this classification is rationally related to the legitimate governmental purpose of obviating difficulties encountered by those in non-intact families who want parental financial assistance for post-secondary education, because such a statement of the governmental purpose assumes the validity of the classification. Recognizing that within the category of young adults in need of financial help to attend college there are some having a parent or parents unwilling to provide such help, the question remains whether the authority of the state may be selectively applied to empower only those from non-intact families to compel such help. We hold that it may not. In the absence of an entitlement on the part of any individual to post-secondary education, or a generally applicable requirement that parents assist their adult children in obtaining such an education, we perceive no rational basis for the state government to provide only certain adult citizens with legal means to overcome the difficulties they encounter in pursuing that end.

It is not inconceivable that in today's society a divorced parent, e.g., a father, could have two children, one born of a first marriage and not residing with him and the other born of a second marriage and still residing with him. Under Act 62, such a father could be required to provide post-secondary educational support for the first child but not the second, even to the extent that the second child would be required to forego a college education. Further, a child over the age of 18, of a woman whose husband had died would have no action against the mother to recover costs of a post-secondary education, but a child over the age of 18, of a woman who never married, who married and divorced, or even who was only separated from her husband when he died would be able to maintain such an action. These are but two examples demonstrating the arbitrariness of the classification adopted in Act 62.

In *LeClair v. LeClair,* 137 N.H. 213, 624 A.2d 1350 (1993), the New Hampshire Supreme Court was faced with the issue of the constitutionality of a state statute regarding post-secondary educational support. Initially, it must be noted that the Court decided this appeal based upon the New Hampshire constitution even though the appellant contended that the statute denied him equal protection under both the federal and state constitution.

The underlying premise upon which the New Hampshire Supreme Court undertook its constitutional analysis of the post-secondary educational support scheme was that the legislation created two classifications: married parents and divorced parents. The object of the legislation was to protect children of divorced parents from being unjustly deprived of opportunities they would otherwise have had if their parents had not divorced. The statute was promulgated to ensure that children of divorced families are not deprived of educational opportunities solely because their families are no longer intact. The result is a heightened judicial involvement in the financial and personal lives of divorced families with children that is not necessary with intact families with children. The New Hampshire Supreme Court concluded that because of the unique problems of divorced families, the legislature could rationally conclude that absent judicial involvement, children of divorced families may be less likely than children of intact families to receive post-secondary educational support from both parents.

With all due respect to our sister state, we must reject the New Hampshire Supreme Court's analysis in *LeClair*. The discriminatory classification adopted by our legislature is not focused on the parents but rather the children. The question is whether similarly situated young adults, i.e. those in need of financial assistance, may be treated differently.

Ultimately, we can conceive of no rational reason why those similarly situated with respect to needing funds for college education, should be treated unequally. Accordingly, we agree with the common pleas court and conclude that Act 62 is unconstitutional.

IN RE MARRIAGE OF CROCKER

Court of Appeals of Oregon, 1998
971 P2d 469

ARMSTRONG, J. Mother appeals from a judgment dismissing her motion to modify child support. The trial court concluded that the statute authorizing the modification, ORS 107.108,[2] was unconstitutional. We reverse. . . .

Article I, section 20, provides that "[n]o law shall be passed granting to any citizen or class of citizens privileges, or immunities, which, upon the same terms, shall not equally belong to all citizens."

Father's challenge to ORS 107.108 is based on a contention that the statute grants an immunity to a class of people rather than to specific people, and that there is no rational basis for the distinction that the statute makes among classes of people. Given that focus, father must establish the following in order to prevail on his claim that ORS 107.108 violates Article I, section 20: (1) that ORS 107.108 grants to a class of people an immunity that is not granted to the class to which father belongs; (2) that the class to which father belongs is a "true class," i.e., one that is based on personal or social characteristics that exist independently of the distinctions created by the statute; and (3) that " 'the distinction between classes . . . has no rational foundation in light of the [statute's] purposes.' " . . .

Considering the statute in context, however, suggests that that may not be the case. ORS 109.155 gives courts authority to order support for children attending school by parents who never married, so that class of parents is in the same position as are the parents in father's class. Moreover, the state suggests that ORS 108.110 could be construed to authorize courts to require married parents of children attending school to support their children. If that were the case, there would be no difference in treatment among the relevant classes of people, because all parents of children attending school would be in the same position as are the parents in father's class. . . .

Although the statute appears to apply to all married people, an examination of its history leads us to conclude that it applies only to married people who are living apart.

In sum, under the statutory scheme, families comprised of married people who live together and who have at least one child attending school are treated differently from those comprised of at least one such child whose parents are married but do not live together, are divorced or separated, or have never married. Relevant to this case, married parents

2. Section 1 provides that "[i]n addition to any other authority of the court, the court may enter an order against either parent, or both of them, to provide for the support or maintenance of a child attending school."

who are living together are given an immunity from an obligation to support their children attending school that is not given to divorced or separated parents.

We conclude that father is a member of a "true class." The class is comprised of people who, like father, are divorced parents of children attending school. They can be identified by their status as divorced parents of such children and not by the challenged law. Because father and the other members of his class could still be identified by their shared personal characteristics if the legislature repealed ORS 107.108, they comprise a "true class."

Because ORS 107.108 can be understood to give an immunity to married, cohabiting parents of children attending school that it does not give to father's "true class," we must determine whether the difference in treatment between the two classes of parents violates Article I, section 20. Father does not contend, and the trial court did not conclude, that the classifications in this case are based on characteristics that require anything other than an evaluation for whether there is a rational basis for the distinction that the legislature has made among classes of people. Consequently, we consider only whether ORS 107.108 violates Article I, section 20, on the ground that there is no rational basis for the distinction that it draws.

Father does not dispute that the state has an interest in having a well-educated populace. Although children aged 18 to 21 have no general right to have their parents pay for them to attend school, it cannot reasonably be disputed that the state has an interest in having parents support their children in that endeavor. ORS 107.108 advances that interest by providing the means for some children to attend school. The issue, then, is whether the statutory scheme by which the state has chosen to advance that interest—a scheme that distinguishes among true classes—is rational. Father argues that it is not. He notes that many children attending school are in need of financial support and argues that there is no rational reason to target for assistance only those children whose parents are divorced, separated, or unmarried or are married but living apart. The trial court agreed. We do not.

We conclude that the statutory distinction is rational. Even if most divorced or separated parents could cooperate sufficiently to decide whether to support their children attending school, legislators could rationally believe that, because of the nature of divorce and separation, there will be instances in which children will not receive support from their parents to attend school precisely because the parents are divorced or separated, despite the fact that the parents have the resources to provide the support and it is in the children's best interest for them to do so. It might be that, although both parents agree that they should support their child attending school, they disagree on how much each of them should contribute, so that one or both of them contribute nothing. It might be that the nature of the relationship between the parents is so acrimonious that they refuse to agree on anything. It might be that the parent who did not have custody when the child was a minor is unwilling to provide support precisely because he or she did not have custody. It might be that one of the parents who, when married, considered support for his or her child attending school to be a moral obligation, now considers it to be only a legal obligation and, hence, that the parent will provide support only if ordered to do so by a court. In short, legislators could rationally envision situations in which, but for the fact that a child's parents are divorced or separated, the parents would support the child while the child attends school. In that situation, the parents' marital status operates to thwart the state's interest in having parents support their children while the children are attending school. Providing courts with the authority to require those parents to support their children attending school is a rational response to that problem.

Deciding not to give courts authority to require parents from intact families to provide the same support is rational as well. Legislators could rationally assume that, in most instances, parents in intact families will be able to make reasonable decisions about whether to support their children attending school.

Moreover, whatever the reasons those parents might decide not to provide that support, legislators could rationally believe that there will seldom be a situation in which, but for the fact that a child's parents are married and living together, the parents would have provided financial support to their child while the child attends school. In other words, the marital status of parents who are living together would not be expected to make them less willing to support their children attending school, but the marital status of divorced or separated parents could have that effect.

In sum, legislators could rationally believe that the most efficient way to advance the state's interest in having parents support their children attending school is to rely on parents to make those decisions in intact families and on courts to make those decision for families that are not intact. That policy decision does not become irrational simply because, on occasion, some married parents who have the resources to support their children attending school will refuse to do so. Nor does it become irrational simply because, under ORS 107.108, on occasion, a court may require separated or divorced parents to support their children attending school even when the parents' refusal to provide that support is for reasons completely unrelated to the separation or divorce. A statute does not have to be perfect in order for it to be rational. In other words, there does not have to be a perfect correlation between the state's interest and the means it uses to advance that interest. To a certain extent, the statute can be underinclusive or overinclusive, as long as the distinction that it makes among classes is reasonably related to a legitimate state interest. As we have already explained, ORS 107.108 is reasonably related to such an interest.

The distinction embodied in the statutes governing support for children attending school is analogous to the distinction that the legislature has made between married and divorced parents with respect to support for their minor children.

Every parent has an obligation to care for his or her minor child. The state has a legitimate interest in ensuring that parents fulfill that obligation. Nonetheless, when a child's parents are married, the state generally does not interfere with the parents' decisions on how best to meet their financial obligations to their children. However, when parents divorce or separate, the state assumes that, as a result of the divorce or separation, many of them will no longer be able to work together to make responsible decisions about how to support their children. Accordingly, the state does not wait to see whether, despite the divorce or separation, the parents can decide how to meet their financial obligations to their children. Instead, it steps in to dictate how they will do that by authorizing courts to enter support orders that establish how much money each parent must contribute each month toward the care of the parent's children. Even though some married parents do not make appropriate decisions about how to care for their children and many divorced parents unquestionably do make appropriate decisions, the state has distinguished between parents with respect to their child-support obligations based on their marital status. Although not perfect, the distinction is rationally related to a legitimate state interest. So is the one in this case....

Questions on Crocker *and* Kline

(1) Does the requirement of the Iowa statute that each parent and the child pay one-third of the expenses of a college education strike you as an equitable solution to the problems posed by these cases?

(2) Which of the two opinions frames the issue most persuasively? Why does only one court find that the statute meets the rational basis test?

(a) *Crocker* says that "legislators could rationally believe that the most efficient way to advance the state's interest in having parents support their children attending school is to rely on parents to make those decisions in intact families and on courts to make those decision for families that are not intact. *Kline*, however, criticizes "[t]he result [of] a heightened judicial involvement in the financial and personal lives of divorced families with children that is not necessary with intact families with children." Do the reasons courts do not generally attempt to regulate the financial decisions made in intact families (see, e.g., *Kilgrow* and *McGuire*) apply to families where the parents have divorced?

(b) What happened to the principle that adults are responsible for themselves and thus for supporting themselves? If the parents no longer have any legal authority over their children, should they have financial responsibility for them? Some states require parents to support adult children who cannot support themselves because, for example, they are disabled. (Other states are silent on the issue.) Is the duty to pay for a college education at all analogous?

(3) Should a parent ordered by a court to pay for a child's college education be able to choose what kind of college the child will attend? Should, for example, the parent be able to veto the child's choice of a college the parent finds offensive on religious grounds?

(4) What if the child elects very expensive private schools rather than those bargains in higher education, state universities? In the frequently cited case of *Rohn v. Thuma*, 408 NE2d 578 (Ind App 1980), the father proffered tuition for his sons' education at Indiana University. They had been accepted to and were attending the University of Chicago and Vassar College. The court did not find the father in contempt since the parties' separation agreement was ambiguous about the kind of education for which the father was responsible, but the court did suggest that the mother might be able to obtain more money from the father to pay for the private schools since he clearly had the ability to do so.

SOLOMOND v. BALL

Court of Appeals of Virginia, 1996
470 SE2d 157

SAM W. COLEMAN, III, J.

This domestic relations appeal involves the obligation of a noncustodial parent to pay an amount of child support in excess of the amount provided by the presumptive guidelines under Code § 20–108.2. The trial court ordered the increase in the noncustodial parent's child support, which deviated from the guidelines, to enable the parents' two children to transfer from one private school to a more expensive private school of the custodial parent's choice. We hold that the trial court erred by increasing the noncustodial parent's monthly support obligation because no showing was made on the record of an adequate reason to further deviate from the presumptive amount of support.

In addition, the father appeals the trial court's holding that he was $100 in arrears for his January 1995 support payment. We affirm that holding.

FACTS AND PROCEEDINGS

John Paul Solomond and C. Louise Ball were divorced in 1988. The divorce decree granted Ball custody of their two sons, Phillip McCown Solomond and Matthew Brady Solomond. In 1994, Ball filed a motion to increase child support because Phillip and Matthew had been accepted at Corpus Christi School, a private Catholic school. Prior to the fall of 1994, both children had attended public school, where they had performed well academically.

As a result of the 1994 modification hearing, the trial court held that Phillip's and Matthew's acceptances to attend Corpus Christi were material changes in circumstances that justified modifying the existing child support order. The court determined that the presumptive amount of child support that Solomond was expected to pay according to the guidelines was $1,171 per month, based upon Solomond's actual monthly income and Ball's actual and imputed income of $1,952 per month. However, because the children incurred substantial additional educational expenses by attending Corpus Christi, and because Ball's actual annual income was only $18,000, the trial court held that the presumptive guideline amount would be "unjust and inappropriate." Specifically, the court stated that it was deviating from the guidelines because it would be in the children's "best interests to take advantage of the educational opportunity" offered by attending Corpus Christi. Consequently, the court ordered that Solomond "should pay 70% of all school-related costs, including but not limited to expenses of tuition, uniforms, books, transportation, supplies, registration and testing fees, and field trips as such expenses and costs are due." In addition, the court held that "if the children succeed in gaining entrance to another school whose tuition is higher, this would constitute a sufficient change in circumstances to re-evaluate the percentage each parent would be required to contribute." Solomond objected to the court's 1994 modification order, but he did not appeal from it.

In March 1995, Ball filed a motion to increase child support by adjusting the percentage of tuition that Solomond would be required to pay because Phillip had been accepted to St. Stephen's, another private school, for the 1995–96 school year and Matthew had been placed on the school's waiting list. Because the tuition at St. Stephen's is "considerably higher" than the tuition at Corpus Christi, Ball petitioned the court to increase the percentage of the children's educational expenses to be paid by Solomond.

Solomond responded by requesting that the trial court vacate the August 1994 modified child support order that required him to pay seventy percent of the children's educational expenses, and he also requested that the court enter an order limiting his child support obligation to the presumptive amount under the guidelines. Solomond argued that the evidence did not show that it was necessary or justified for the children to attend private school, much less to transfer from Corpus Christi to St. Stephen's. Furthermore, he asserted that his income and financial resources were inadequate to send the children to private school, particularly to pay the increased expenses to attend St. Stephen's.

The trial court held that Phillip's admission to St. Stephen's and Matthew's placement on the waiting list constituted a material change in circumstances, and that it would be in the "best interests" of the children "to take advantage of this educational opportunity." Accordingly, the court modified the child support order to require Solomond to pay, in addition to the presumptive amount provided by the guidelines, the children's yearly educational expenses in the amount of seventy percent of the first $8,000 in expenses and fifty percent of expenses exceeding $8,000.

PRIVATE SCHOOL EXPENSES . . .

In *Smith v. Smith,* 18 Va. App. 427, 444 S.E.2d 269 (1994), we held that "implicit in the [child support] statutory scheme is that educational expenses are included in the presumptive amount of child support as calculated under the Code." Code § 20–108.1(B) expressly provides that when a trial court deviates from the presumptive amount recommended by the guidelines, it must provide written findings of fact that "shall give a justification of why the order varies from the guidelines." Furthermore, "a conclusory written statement of [the trial court's] findings" is not sufficient to justify deviating from the presumptive guideline amount.

In determining whether a noncustodial parent should be required to pay support to provide for a child's private educational expenses, other jurisdictions have held that two conditions must exist: "demonstrated need of the child, and the parent's ability to pay." These courts have considered factors such as the availability of satisfactory public schools, the child's attendance at private school prior to the separation and divorce, the child's special emotional or physical needs, religious training, and family tradition. We find these factors relevant not only for determining whether a demonstrated need has been shown for the child to attend private rather than public school, but also for determining whether there is justification for requiring a parent to pay for a child to transfer to a more expensive private school. When a parent proposes to have a child transfer to another private school and that change will have a significant effect on the parents' support obligations, the trial court must consider, together with each parent's ability to pay, whether a reason or need is shown to justify a change of schools before increasing a noncustodial parent's support obligation.

Here, the trial court's only stated reason for increasing the amount of the father's child support obligation was the conclusion "that it would be in [Phillip's and Matthew's] best interest to be able to take advantage of this opportunity." The court made no written findings of fact, as required by Code § 20–108.1, that justified further deviation from the guidelines to require Solomond to pay an additional amount of child support. Although Ball attended St. Stephen's and testified that it is "the preferred institution," the record does not demonstrate a need of either child that was not being adequately met at Corpus Christi, and that would be served by transferring to St. Stephen's. The only fact the record establishes is that the tuition at St. Stephen's is "considerably higher" than that at Corpus Christi. Accordingly, the record does not support the trial court's finding and provides no "justification" for the holding that it would be in the best interests of Phillip or Matthew to transfer from Corpus Christi to St. Stephen's. Thus, we reverse the modification order and remand the support issue for the court to reinstate a support order at the amount previously established by the August 1994 order. . . .

Questions on Solomond v. Ball

(1) What does the opinion mean when it says the trial court imputed income to the custodial wife? Why would it have done so? According to Va Code Ann § 20–108.1(B)(3) (2006), income is imputed "to a party who is voluntarily unemployed or voluntarily under employed; provided that income may not be imputed to the custodial parent when the child is not in school, child care services are not available and the cost of such child care services are not included in the computation." Ms. Ball is an attorney in practice with her father and brother.

(2) The Virginia guidelines considered in *Solomond* excepted custodial parents who stayed home with pre-school aged children from the imputed-income regime. What if the *noncustodial* parent married a woman with an income higher than his and then decided to stay home to care for the children of his second marriage? A New York case, *Felisa L.D. v. Allen M.*, 433 NYS2d 715 (NY Fam Ct 1980), decided that while it was fine for the former husband to choose to become a child-care provider for his second family, his second spouse's income could be reached for child support.

(3) Although the parties did not pay much out-of-pocket to litigate this case, because both appeared *pro se*, with a little imagination you could approximate its cost in terms of lost work time, judicial time (in a jurisdiction with a crowded docket), and court fees and costs for both the original hearing and the appeal. Would this sum be larger than the amount the custodial wife sought? Must the children necessarily have been aware of their parents' litigation? Was there a cost to them?

(4) A public education is free (if we leave taxes to the side). For the school year 1999–2000, tuition at Corpus Christi School was $3,036 per child per year. For the same time period, tuition for a junior high school student at St. Stephen's was $14,190 per student per year. The noncustodial father was being asked to pay 70% of each of these fees. (The calculation was presumably derived as the percentage of their combined income earned by him.) We know Ms. Ball's actual and imputed income was just under $24,000, so his must have been about $78,000. Would an intact family earning $102,000 per year be likely to spend $28,000 on their children's junior high school tuition?

(5) Could the parents have had any motive for this litigation other than a disagreement about their children's junior high school education?

(3) Who Is a Parent?

A different kind of problem in the limits of child-support is presented by the following cases:

IN THE MATTER OF PAMELA P. v. FRANK S.

Family Court, New York County, 1981
443 NYS 2d 343

NANETTE DEMBITZ, JUDGE:

The question in the instant paternity suit is whether a father should be liable for the support of his out-of-wedlock child, even though the mother accomplished her plan to have a baby by deliberately and falsely representing to him that she was using contraception.

Petitioner mother contends that the evidence as to her purposeful deceit, even if credited, is irrelevant to a father's statutory duty to support his progeny. Respondent father, on the other hand, emphasizes that the Constitution as interpreted by the United States Supreme Court guarantees to men as well as to women the freedom to choose whether or not to beget a child. He therefore argues that a support order burdening him with an attribute of parenthood despite petitioner's interference with his right to avoid procreation, would violate the Constitution.

Research has disclosed no New York case involving the question at bar, and no out-of-state decision except one by an intermediate California court. While that court upheld a mother's contention that her alleged deception of the father was irrelevant, the decision ignored both the law of fraud and deceit and the Constitutional issue. Both common law and constitutional principle must in this court's opinion influence the construction of the paternity statute, and they require curtailment of respondent's support obligation because of petitioner's purposeful misrepresentation. However, the court must, for reasons concerning the welfare of the child, reject respondent's argument that his duty of support can be entirely eliminated.

Before discussing the legal issues the findings as to respondent's paternity and petitioner's intentional deceit will be summarized.

Findings as to Respondent's Paternity and Petitioner's Deceit

Respondent's paternity was clearly and convincingly established by credible and uncontroverted evidence. Petitioner, who is an unmarried airline flight attendant based in New York City, lived with respondent in 1973–74 in Switzerland and thereafter saw him approximately once a year when he came from Europe to New York. Besides her testimony that she had sexual intercourse only with respondent during the period for conception of the child born on March 15, 1980, the Human Leukocyte Antigen bloodmatching test showed the high probability of respondent's paternity.

As to petitioner's deception, respondent testified that on the crucial night, which followed a long separation, he asked petitioner before they had sexual intercourse what she was doing in regard to contraception, and she replied that she was "on the pill." Petitioner conceded in her testimony that she was not using birth control pills or any other contraception, and that her sexual intercourse with respondent occurred during the most fertile phase of her monthly reproductive cycle. However, she denied recollection of any question by respondent about contraception.

A witness who under the circumstances of his appearance seemed completely credible, testified that he had broken off a sexual relationship with petitioner approximately two months before the date of the child's conception, because she told him she was no longer taking birth control pills and wanted to have a baby. When he said he was unwilling to father her child, she replied, according to his testimony, that she would have a child with S, the respondent, whether he wanted her to or not, and that she would refrain from telling him she was off of birth control pills. In the context of this testimony as well as the total testimony as to petitioner and respondent's relationship and conversations, the evidence is entirely clear and convincing that petitioner falsely told respondent she was "on the pill" and thereby purposely deceived him with regard to contraception; the court so finds.

Legal Consequences of Petitioner's Deceit

A. Exceptions to Absolute Rule of Parental Responsibility

As petitioner argues, the paternity statute, like provisions for support of legitimate children, states a father's duty of support in terms of an unequivocal obligation (Fam. Ct. Act, sec. 545). Nevertheless, respondent is correct in his contention that the courts have grafted some exceptions onto the statutes; and the question at bar is whether a deception such as petitioner's should, like a few other circumstances unmentioned by the legislative draftsmen, ground an exception. The statutory silence on this point is unpersuasive either way. At the time the paternity statute was written, "modern methods of contraception" were unknown; their free discussion was far in the future; conduct like petitioner's could hardly have been visualized. And the law of support has accommodated itself to achieve equitable results in the light of scientific progress.

Pertinent to respondent's claim to exemption from the support obligation, are the rulings suspending a father's duty of payment when the custodial mother wrongfully deprives him of visitation with the child. There the courts, recognizing the practical benefit to the custodial mother of a child support order against the father, apply common law precepts as to reciprocal rights and duties between the parties. Those precepts and the underlying principle that the father's statutory support obligation can be drastically affected by the custodial mother, are also reflected in the landmark decision in *Boden v. Boden* (42 N.Y.2d 210, 213) emphasizing the effect of a separation agreement on the father's basic duty to the child.

Common-law concepts as to fraud and deceit likewise warrant weight, in this court's opinion, in determining support obligations. These standards, embodying enduring ethical values, apply throughout the domestic relations law. Thus, despite the sanctity of an adoption in establishing a parental relationship and obligation, an adoption has always been voidable for fraud.

The chief ingredient of fraud and deceit was here clearly and convincingly established by petitioner's premeditated, deliberate and intentional misrepresentation for the purpose of influencing respondent to act for her benefit. It is true that one factor in a suit for fraud—action in reliance on the misrepresentation—has not been convincingly proved. Though petitioner probably estimated respondent correctly when she decided to deceive him to gain her goal, he apparently realized the possible ineffectiveness of birth control pills; and it cannot be concluded with certainty that her misrepresentation was the "but-for" cause of respondent's risking sexual intercourse with her without himself using contraception. However, the requirement of proximate causation seems pertinent only to the justification for damages for a deception; it is inapposite in considering the relevant question here: the law's accepted standards for right conduct between individuals.

Petitioner's planned and intentional deceit bars her, in this court's opinion, from financial benefit at respondent's expense. The usual rule in apportioning support, that parents must make equivalent financial sacrifices to support their child, is therefore held inapplicable in the instant case (see Point C below as to appropriate standard for support order). Petitioner's wrong towards respondent precludes her transfer to him of her financial burden for the child she alone chose to have. Consistent with the judicial function of following an equitable approach in support cases, this court must consider "the inequitable conduct of one who invokes its relief ..." The question suggested by the attorneys as to whether this ruling would apply to a married couple need not be answered here; but it may be noted that marriage is ordinarily deemed to represent a willingness to procreate.

B. Constitutional Impact of Petitioner's Deceit

In construing support statutes, the courts must be alert not only to common law but to Constitutional principles.

Constitutional doctrine as to procreative freedom has developed mainly in the context of women's rights. There can be no question, however, that the Fourteenth Amendment to the Constitution guarantees to a man equally with a woman freedom of choice to use contraception and avoid procreation. (See *Eisenstadt v. Baird*, 405 U.S. 438, 448–49, 453; *Carey v. Population Services*, 431 U.S. 678, 684–91). It is likewise established constitutional doctrine that "The prohibitions of the Fourteenth Amendment ... includes action of state courts ...", and that a court order sanctioning a private individual's act violates the Constitution whenever official action having by itself a similar impact would be unconstitutional (see *Shelley v. Kraemer*, 334 U.S. 1, 18). And (see *Bowman v. Davis*, 48 Ohio St.2d 41, 46), holding that the court would impermissibly infringe on a Constitutional right if it denied liability for medical malpractice regarding a patient's "choice not to procreate."

Under the *Shelley* principle the question is whether petitioner's deception interfered with respondent's right of free choice regarding procreation to such an extent that an order in petitioner's favor would be unconstitutional. Here there was no outright barrier to respondent's resort to contraception or to abstinence. Nor would a court order in petitioner's favor impinge as crucially on constitutional rights as the order sought in *Shelley*; there denial of relief deprived the private act—a restrictive covenant—of retrospective as well as prospective effect. Nevertheless, petitioner did bar respondent from full and true freedom of choice by deceiving him as to the procreative facts, and her intention undoubtedly was to deprive him of a free choice. "[R]estrictions ... (that) could not be squared with the requirements of the Fourteenth Amendment if imposed by state statute" cannot be implemented by court order (*Shelley*, 334 U.S. at p. 11); and a law with the purpose and the likely effect of curtailing free choice as to procreation, would assuredly be unconstitutional. Thus, *Shelley* is pertinent, for an order in petitioner's favor, enforceable by the Court's contempt power would condone, encourage, and put the "imprimatur of the State" upon interference with reproductive choice (see *Shelley*, 334 U.S. at p. 20). Since a support order benefitting petitioner would raise Constitutional doubt under the Fourteenth Amendment, it should be denied.

C. Separate Interests of Petitioner and Child

Unquestionably, as petitioner argues, a paternity case is chiefly concerned with the welfare of the child; and denial of financial benefit to petitioner mother in accordance with the above conclusion, must be accomplished without detriment to the child.

Respondent argues that his complete exemption from financial responsibility would not harm the child because petitioner's income would, if necessary, be supplemented by public assistance. It is true, as respondent contends, that an infringement of constitutional rights cannot be justified merely by the State's interest in saving money (see *Goldberg v. Kelly*, 397 U.S. 254, 265–66). That principle however is inapposite here because relegation of the child to public assistance would affect a more fundamental State interest than the fiscal.

The ancient and enduring interest here at stake is parental support for helpless children—the sharing of parental means with an infant—with State care only as a last resort. Research reveals no prior consideration of parental obligation from a constitutional standpoint; but clearly, the duty of support fits into the legal framework as a reciprocal of the fundamental constitutional right to beget and raise children. Public concern with the child support obligation thus corresponds in intensity with the major significance of that constitutional right in a democratic, non-statist society. Accordingly, this court views enforcement of the parental support duty as a compelling State interest that justifies diminution of the right to free procreative choice.

In defining that duty the legislature and the courts have established the standard of fair and reasonable parental support in accordance with the parent's means, and this criterion must under the constitution apply to an illegitimate child equally with the legitimate. Thus the child herein cannot be relegated to a public assistance standard. However, since it is consistent with the support rulings in this state to give weight to petitioner's deceit (Point A above), it is in this court's opinion constitutional to deny her application for child support provided that the basic objective of satisfying the child's fair and reasonable needs can nevertheless be met. Accordingly, under a reasonable and valid accommodation of principles, a support order will be entered against respondent only if petitioner's means are insufficient to answer such needs.

Because need above a subsistence level is a flexible concept, standards of living must be considered. The child is entitled in this court's opinion to no less a standard of living than his father's, because it indicates the likely level that the child would enjoy if he had been born into the still-prevalent circumstance of an intact family or a father willingly sharing his custody and care. However, the father's standard would under this reasoning set a maximum as well as a minimum limit on his duty of child support, even if his standard is more modest, as in this case it may be, than his means require. A hearing is scheduled to determine whether the financial facts justify entry of a support order in accordance with this opinion.

IN THE MATTER OF L. PAMELA P. v. FRANK S.

State of New York Court of Appeals, 1983
449 NE2d 713

WACHTLER, JUDGE.

The issue on this appeal is whether a father, whose paternity of a child has been established, may assert, as a defense to his support obligation the deliberate misrepresentation of the mother concerning her use of contraception. We agree with the Appellate Division that the mother's alleged deceit has no bearing upon a father's obligation to support his child or upon the manner in which the parents' respective support obligations are determined. The order of the Appellate Division should therefore be affirmed.

Following a hearing on the paternity petition, Family Court made an order of filiation, having found by clear and convincing evidence that respondent is the father of petitioner's child. Thereafter respondent endeavored to establish that petitioner, intending to have respondent's child regardless of his wishes, misrepresented to him that she was using contraception. Although petitioner conceded that she was not, at the time of conception, using any form of birth control, she denied that any conversation concerning contraception took place.

Family Court found that petitioner had purposely deceived respondent with regard to her use of contraception and that this wrongful conduct should weigh in respondent's favor in determining the parents' respective support obligations. Thus, the Family Court held that the general rule that the apportionment of child support obligations between parents is to be based upon the parents' means would not be applicable to the present case; rather, it held that an order of support would be entered against the father only in the amount by which the mother's means were insufficient to meet the child's needs.

The Appellate Division modified Family Court's order, striking the defense of fraud and deceit and increasing the child support award accordingly. Noting that the only factors to be considered by Family Court in fixing an award of child support are the needs of the child and the means of the parents, the Appellate Division held that the father's allegations concerning the mother's fraud and deceit had no relevance to the determination of his obligation to support the child.

Although at one time the objective of paternity proceedings was merely to prevent a child born out of wedlock from becoming a public charge, it is now well established that the appropriate emphasis must be upon the welfare of the child. The primary purpose of establishing paternity is to ensure that adequate provision will be made for the child's needs, in accordance with the means of the parents.

This overriding concern for the child's welfare is reflected in the provisions of article 5 of the Family Court Act. Once paternity is established, section 545 requires the court to "direct the parent or parents possessed of sufficient means or able to earn such means to pay . . . a fair and reasonable sum according to their respective means as the court may determine and apportion for such child's support and education, until the child is twenty-one." Thus, in determining the parents' obligations to support their child, the statute mandates consideration of two factors—the needs of the child for support and education and the financial ability of the parents to contribute to that support. The statute does not require, nor, we believe, does it permit, consideration of the "fault" or wrongful conduct of one of the parents in causing the child's conception. The purpose of the paternity proceeding and the imposition of support obligations being the protection of the child, the Family Court, as a court of limited jurisdiction, is simply not the proper forum for adjudicating disputes existing solely between the parents.

Respondent argues, however, that petitioner's intentional misrepresentation that she was practicing birth control deprived him of his constitutional right to decide whether to father a child. Recognizing that petitioner herself engaged in no State action by her conduct, respondent urges that imposition of a support obligation upon him under these circumstances constitutes State involvement sufficient to give vitality to his constitutional claim.

Assuming, without deciding, that sufficient State action is present in this case we conclude that respondent's contentions fall short of stating any recognized aspect of the constitutional right of privacy.

Clearly, respondent has a constitutionally protected right to decide for himself whether to father a child (*Carey v. Population Servs. Int.*, 431 U.S. 678; *Eisenstadt v. Baird*, 405 U.S. 438, 453). This right is deemed so fundamental that governmental interference in this area of decision-making may be justified only by compelling State interests (*Carey v. Population Servs. Int., supra*, at p. 686). Yet, the interest protected has always been stated in terms of governmental restrictions on the individual's access to contraceptive devices (*Griswold v. Connecticut*, 381 U.S. 479; *Eisenstadt v. Baird, supra*; *Carey v. Population Servs. Int., supra*). It involves the freedom to decide for oneself, without unreasonable governmental interference, whether to avoid procreation through the use of contraception. This aspect of the right of privacy has never been extended so far as to regulate the conduct of private actors as between themselves. Indeed, as the Appellate Division recognized, judicial inquiry into so fundamentally private and intimate conduct as is required to determine the validity of respondent's assertions may itself involve impermissible State interference with the privacy of these individuals (see, also, *Stephen K. v. Roni L.*, 105 Cal.App.3d 640).

The interest asserted by the father on this appeal is not, strictly speaking, his freedom to choose to avoid procreation, because the mother's conduct in no way limited his right to use contraception. Rather, he seeks to have his choice regarding procreation fully respected by other individuals and effectuated to the extent that he should be relieved of his obligation to support a child that he did not voluntarily choose to have. But respondent's constitutional entitlement to avoid procreation does not encompass a right to avoid a child support obligation simply because another private person has not fully respected his desires in this regard. However unfairly respondent may have been treated by petitioner's failure to allow him an equal voice in the decision to conceive a child, such a wrong does not rise to the level of a constitutional violation.

Accordingly, the order of the Appellate Division should be affirmed, with costs.

Notes and Questions on Pamela P.

(1) Does the trial court's decision convince you in its non-constitutional aspects?

(a) Is the exception to section 545 for situations in which custodial parents refuse visitation rights apposite to the situation in this case? Is the exception even desirable?

(b) Is the exception to section 545 for situations in which the parties work out support arrangements between themselves relevant to the situation in this case?

(c) Is the court's fraud argument sound if reliance, a substantive part of an action for fraud, has not, according to the court itself, been proved?

(d) Is the trial court's solution likely to make sense? What award ought to issue, according to the court's theory?

(2) Does the trial court's decision convince you in its constitutional aspects?

(a) Is the state action argument persuasive here? Isn't this an example of the over-extension of state action whose possibility was a central criticism of *Shelley v. Kraemer*?

(b) What is the constitutional right at issue here? Does the Constitution guarantee a full and informed choice as to every decision about reproduction, or does it only guarantee some freedom of government interference in choices about reproduction?

(c) Even if there is a constitutional right of the kind the trial court seems to identify, does a compelling state interest override the right? An interest in ensuring that children are well-supported? In encouraging in parents a strong sense of responsibility for their children?

(3) The "Frank S." about whom you have been reading is the New York City police whistle-blower Frank Serpico. J. Thomas Oldham and Davis S. Caudill, *Reconnaissance of Public Policy Restrictions Upon Enforcement of Contracts Between Cohabitants*, 18 Family L Q 93, 140 n152 (1984).

(4) Is a father constitutionally entitled to be relieved of support obligations if the mother refused the father's request that she obtain an abortion during her first trimester? See, for a negative answer, *In the Interest of S.P.B.*, 651 P2d 1213 (Colo 1982); or *In the Matter of Godwin*, 567 P2d 144 (Or App 1977). When the couple divorced, the wife was pregnant with the couple's child. Although willing to pay for his toddler's support, Mr. Godwin sought an order relieving him of his duty to pay for the support of the unborn child. His theory, rejected by the court of appeals, was that his wife alone could determine whether to carry the baby to term. Although he was willing to pay for an abortion, the father did not see why he should have to support the additional child he would have elected to abort.

AMERICAN LAW INSTITUTE
PRINCIPLES OF FAMILY DISSOLUTION

(2002)

§ 3.03 Estoppel to Deny Parental Support Obligation

(1) The court may in exceptional cases impose a parental support obligation upon a person who may not be the child's parent under state law, but whose prior course of affirmative conduct equitably estops that person from denying a parental support obligation to the child. Such estoppel may arise when:

(a) there was an explicit or implicit agreement or undertaking by the person to assume a parental support obligation to the child;

(b) the child was born during the marriage or cohabitation of the person and the child's parent; or

(c) the child was conceived pursuant to an agreement between the person and the child's parent that they would share responsibility for raising the child and each would be a parent to the child.

Only the child and the child's parents have standing to assert an estoppel under this section.

(2) In deciding whether to impose a support obligation under this section, the court should consider

(a) whether the person and the child act toward each other as parent and child and, if so, the duration and strength of that behavior,

(b) whether the parental undertaking of the person supplanted the child's opportunity to develop a relationship with an absent parent and to look to that parent for support;

(c) whether the child otherwise has two parents who owe the child a duty of support and are able and available to provide support; and

(d) any other facts that may relate to the equity of imposing a parental-support duty on the person.

(3) No continuing obligation to support a child arises merely from a person's former cohabitation with or marriage to the child's parent.

Comment . . .

b. Stepparents. This section is not intended to create a general stepparent duty of support that survives the domestic relationship of the child's legal parent and the stepparent. In most such cases, state law and the Principles impose no continuing duty of child support on the stepparent. The stepparent who marries a legal parent who already has a child from a prior relationship necessarily shares resources with the child's household, and hence the child, during the continuance of the marriage. This sharing alone is an insufficient basis for imposing a support obligation that survives the termination of the relationship of the adult parties. However, in rare cases a stepparent may behave in a manner that should equitably estop the stepparent from disclaiming a support obligation to a stepchild after the termination of the stepparent's marriage to the legal parent. . . .

d. *Husbands whose wives bear extramarital children during marriage*. Historically the law conclusively presumed that the husband was the father of a child born to his wife so long as the husband and wife were living together at the time of conception or birth. Effectively, this was a substantive rule of law: The husband cohabiting with a wife was designated the legal father of child born to his wife. This rule survives in only a minority of states. In many states, a divorcing husband may avoid his support obligation to "a marital child". This practice may disrupt a long-established relationship between a child and a man who has occupied the social role of father.

This section should discourage belated inquiries into the biological paternity of marital children, undertaken long after the family relationship has been well established as a social reality. It discourages such inquiries because they do not defeat a claim against a husband for child support. This section would be invoked by a wife or marital child only when, at divorce, a husband seeks to prove that he is not the biological father of a marital child. Procedurally, once a responsive motion is made under this section, a jurisdiction may appropriately require that genetic testing, or the admission of genetic evidence, be postponed until a motion under this section has been decided. This section does not determine "legal paternity," which is a matter outside the scope of these Principles. It merely imposes a parental support obligation upon persons who should be equitably estopped to deny the obligation. Nevertheless, much of the motive for paternity determination disappears once a motion is granted under this section. A husband estopped to deny a support obligation under this section may reasonably choose to relinquish his inquiry into biological paternity in order to enjoy a parental relationship with the child he is required to support.

Notes and Questions on ALI § 3.02A

(1) Comment (d) to § 3.02A proposes exceptions to the rule that in many states allows a divorcing husband who is not the biological father of a child born during the marriage to disclaim any obligation to support the child. In some states there is a conclusive (or very strong) presumption that a child born into a marriage is the legitimate child of the husband.

(2) Does the imposition of a child support duty upon a third party disrupt the ability of the parent to direct and control the upbringing of the child? Should the duty of support bring with it a right to visitation?

(3) If grandparents and other third parties win the right to visit a child should they also be required to help support the child?

SECTION 2. SOME APPROACHES TO ENFORCEMENT

A father has only done a third of his duty when he begets children and makes provision for them. To his species he owes men; to society he owes social beings; to the state he owes citizens. Every person who fails to pay this triple debt is blameworthy, even more so if he only pays it in part.

Jean Jacques Rousseau
Emile

We have now completed our inquiry into how much child support noncustodial parents owe their children. That inquiry revealed that it is widely believed that child-support orders usually are set quite low. Nevertheless, many divorced parents fail to make significant proportions of their child-support payments. This failure has two proximate causes. First, most parents work hard to support one household and are hard pressed to support two households.

Second, some non-custodial parents will not pay even what they can afford to pay. How can this be, given the law's assumption that parents' natural affection for their children leads them to treat their children lovingly and solicitously? People who adopt the more pessimistic view of human nature we described in Chapter 2 may attribute parental failures to support children to frailties of human character. In addition, that failure is presumably exacerbated by the animosity many parents feel toward each other, compounded by their knowledge that part of what they pay supports the former spouse as well as the children. To some extent, it is presumably because non-custodial parents tend to become distanced from their children physically, socially, and emotionally, so that their sense of obligation is diminished by their diminished sense of attachment. They may further reason, in the language of the economist, that custodial parents get the consumption benefit (that non-custodial parents accordingly lose) of being with the children most of the time. In addition, obligors may be discouraged by their inability to monitor whether the money is being spent "in the best interests" of the child.

In any event, there is today surprising agreement across the political spectrum that parents ought at least to pay what they owe and there has been considerable indignation that they do not do so. This has led to a variety of measures to enforce child-support orders. They reflect an intriguing range of responses to the enforcement problem that dogs family law, and we will therefore consider several of them with some care.

A. THE MICHIGAN APPROACH

Traditionally, child-support orders have been enforced primarily at the behest of the custodial parent, who may seek a civil contempt order to coerce payment and a criminal contempt order to punish nonpayment. The contempt remedy has traditionally been supplemented by devices like writs of execution, attachment, and bonds for security. However, custodial parents generally lack the resources to pursue these remedies successfully. Michigan has attacked the problem by establishing an office called the Friend of the Court, which initiates actions to collect child-support payments, and by jailing non-payers. Professor Chambers evaluates the Michigan experiment in his book *Making Fathers Pay*:

DAVID L. CHAMBERS
WHAT MAKES FATHERS PAY?

(University of Chicago Press, 1979)

What all the Michigan counties have in common is the agency known as the Friend of the Court, which is charged with disbursing child support payments that do come in and pursuing payments that don't.

Barry County, with thirty-eight thousand residents in 1970, had the smallest population of any of our twenty-eight counties. Rural, but without particularly fertile soil, it has recently suffered Michigan's common problem of high levels of unemployment. At the time we coded the county's payment records in 1974, Barry's Friend of the Court had six full-time employees: Gerald Mahler, the head of the agency; two full-time bookkeepers; two persons with training as social workers who performed home visits; and a deputized enforcement officer, Mr. Sunior, who previously had been in police work. Mr. Mahler know personally most of the families who had been in his caseload for several years. Younger staff members knew the remaining families Mr. Mahler did not. When he and I crossed the courthouse square into a coffee shop, he exchanged "good morning" with other customers and then leaned over and said, "I won't tell you who, but there are three people in my caseload in here now." Later, when he and I reviewed some payment records I had found somewhat confusing, he remembered most of the specific events in men's lives that had produced the puzzling entries.

Barry's system of contacts with divorced families was thoroughgoing. The staff conducted two home visits with the custodial parent before divorce and annual visits thereafter, taking a particularly disdainful view of custodial mothers who lived with men to whom they were not married. They monitored the father's payments even more closely than the mother's sex life. The man who missed more than a couple of payments was sent a warning, whether the mother had complained or not. If he failed to respond to the warning, he received an order to show cause, directing him to appear at a hearing. If he again failed to respond, a warrant was issued for his arrest. (In many counties the Friends of the Court use the civil equivalent of a warrant known as a writ of attachment. Mahler used warrants because "most people think an attachment is some sort of order to pick up a chair or a car.")

Those brought to court when significantly in arrears stood a high probability of being sentenced to jail for contempt. During 1974, twenty-five men, or one in eight of those who ended the year paying less than 80 percent of everything due, were sentenced to jail. The two judges in Barry typically imposed sentences of thirty days on those they held in contempt, and most men purchased their early release by making a substantial lump-sum payment. Barry also extradited men who fled to other states, an expensive proposition, since two officers had to travel to the other state. Barry nonetheless brought back nine men during 1975 at an average cost of about seven hundred dollars. With a smile, Mahler explained that, during the winter, he rarely has difficulty finding officers willing to travel to somewhat warmer places to pick up miscreants.

Wayne County is seventy times as populous as Barry and, though the two counties are similar in the seriousness with which they take the enforcement of support orders, there are many differences in their approaches. In 1974, Wayne's Friend of the Court had three hundred employees spread across several floors of two downtown buildings in Detroit. If paternity cases are included, the agency had a caseload of well over 120,000, by far the largest in the state. Unlike Barry, Wayne kept all payment records on computer. Also unlike Barry, but like nearly half the counties in our sample, Wayne removed from its active files cases that hadn't been paying for some substantial period, and stored them in a separate location. (We went to those separate locations—in Wayne, to tier after tier in the dusty basement of the old county courthouse—to include such cases proportionately in our sample.) Wayne had its own staff of arresting officers and mailed nearly twenty-five thousand orders to show cause during 1974. Its twenty-eight judges sentenced around nine hundred men to jail for contempt. Nine hundred is a large number, but if the Wayne judges had followed Barry's pattern in sentencing to jail one of every eight men who had paid less than 80 percent of everything owed during the year, they would have sentenced over eight thousand men, not nine hundred, during the year. Wayne's scale is too vast for intimacy. The head of the agency, a lawyer earning over forty thousand dollars a year, not only did not know very many of the divorced persons in his caseload, he barely knew, and could hardly have been expected to have known, all his employees.

The other twenty-six counties also exhibited diverse approaches to collection and enforcement. As of 1974, several large counties did not have computerized records, but several much smaller counties did. Half the counties sent warnings to nonpaying fathers whose former wives were not on welfare only on the request of the mother. The other half, which we called "self-starting," had a system similar to Barry's in which they acted to warn nonpaying fathers after a fixed number of weeks of nonpayment had gone by. Many counties had no arresting officers of their own and relied solely on the local sheriff; and so forth. One need not be a sophisticated social theorist to hypothesize that these differences of approach might well produce differences in rates of collection.

The counties also differed greatly among themselves in the extent of their reliance on court hearings and jail for persons who failed to respond to warning letters. The tool that agencies use to force men to come to a hearing is an "order to show cause," an order directing the man to "show cause" to the judge why he should not be held in contempt. In each county, we counted these orders or obtained a count from the agency. Some agencies, we found, sent few orders, but their counties' judges jailed a large portion of the persons brought for hearings. Other agencies mailed large numbers of orders, up to eight times as many in relation to the size of their caseload, but their judges sent few men to jail. Still others did little of either or a great deal of both. When they did sentence men to jail, judges in almost all counties fixed a dollar figure short of the full arrearage that they would accept for early release, but the dollar amounts they demanded varied greatly, as did the jail terms they imposed as the alternative to the payment on the arrearage. In many counties, judges almost never imposed sentences of six months or more. In a few, however, judges routinely imposed sentences of a year, the maximum permitted by law.

There was one further aspect of the child support system that varied across counties and, though on the face of it this aspect had nothing directly to do with enforcement, it might well have exerted an effect on collections. As we mentioned earlier, men paying child support on behalf of children receiving welfare benefits have a disincentive to pay not shared by other men. The disincentive flows from the fact that the payments are never received by the child but are forwarded by the Friend of the Court directly to the welfare department. The father's payments make no difference in the standard of living of his child. While this policy exists in all Michigan counties—indeed, in every county in every state—there was great variation among the counties in the portion of the caseload that involved welfare cases. The one piece of information in addition to payments that we coded for every case in our own samples was whether the children in the case were currently receiving welfare benefits. In several counties we found that fewer than 20 percent of mothers were receiving assistance; in several others, more than 40 percent received assistance. The rate of welfare receipt was high not only in Wayne County but also in several rural counties where unemployment was high and earnings comparatively low....

Why Rates Of Collection Differ....

When we completed a long series of regression analyses of our own data, three factors stood out as powerfully related to the levels of collections of support....

The first of the three was an aspect of the enforcement process: counties that initiated enforcement efforts in nonwelfare cases without waiting for complaints from the mothers collected more than those that relied on complaints. These fourteen aggressive Friends of the Court, with what we have called "self-starting" systems, monitored men's payments and, after a few weeks of missed payments or the accumulation of an arrearage of a certain amount (say a hundred dollars), sent a warning notice to the nonpaying parent.

The second significant factor was linked to the first. It was the county's rate of jailing (in relation to its population). We reported above a strong positive correlation between collections and the rate of jailing. After controlling for other factors, we found that counties that jailed more men collected at higher rates—if, but only if, they also had self-starting enforcement systems. A county had to have both a self-starting enforcement system and a substantial rate of jailing in order to add appreciably to collections. Counties with a high jail rate but no self-starting system of warnings collected little, if any, more than counties that jailed almost no one.

The third factor was population—the larger the county, the lower the collections. For example, none of the seven highest collecting counties had populations larger than 70,000. Conversely, nine of the ten lowest collecting counties had populations greater than 100,000.

These three factors account for over 60 percent of the variation in payment rates among the counties. Put another way, within our sample, if one knew a county's population, whether its Friend of the Court was "self-starting," and the frequency of jailing, one could typically predict within a few percentage points the average proportion of the amounts men owed that the county actually collected.

One other factor aids slightly in explaining differences in collections. When unemployment rates are higher, collections are lower. It is not, of course, surprising that payments should be lower in places where unemployment is high. What was surprising to us was that unemployment rates did not account for more of the differences among the counties. When we included unemployment rates with our other factors, we could account for differences among the counties only to a slightly greater degree than we could using the three dominant factors alone. What was also surprising to us was that among several unemployment figures we had for each county the figure that served to account for some differences was the 1970 unemployment rate rather than the rate for the exact months in 1974 or 1975 for which we had coded payments. The figures for 1974–75 were not merely contemporaneous with our payment data but were also much more varied than the rates for 1970.

The rate of jailing makes a difference in collections, but how much of a difference? As we have said, our analysis indicates that, for purposes of measuring differences, the jail rate and the factor of a self-enforcement process cannot be separated. When taken jointly, and when population and unemployment are also taken into account, counties with both a high jailing rate and a self-starting policy collected an average of 25 percent more per case than was collected by the counties that did not have both. For a county such as Genesee that collected $17.3 million in 1974 from all fathers, this finding suggests that had Genesee not been a high-jailing, self-starting county it would probably have collected about $3.5 million less than it did. That is a lot of money.

A Self–Starting Enforcement Process, the Rate of Jailing, and Population

We have dismembered a complex process—the payments across counties of divorced parents toward the support of their children. Payments go down with higher population, up with a self-triggering warning system, down with more unemployment, and up with more jailing. Though our findings have surface plausibility, those who cherish the complexity of humanity will be pleased that when we peered more deeply into our pool of data we found the waters muddier than they initially appeared.

In the first place, it is important to remember that while these variables explain much about the differences in the rates of collections, they do not explain everything. Consider just a couple of comparisons among our counties. One non-self-starting county collected more than 20 percent more than another non-self-starting county, despite the fact that the higher-collecting county was considerably larger and jailed far fewer men. Similarly, as between two other counties of closely similar population, both with high rates of jailing, the non-self-starting county collected more, not less, than the self-starting county. Clearly, other factors are also at work that we cannot fully identify. Had we information about the portion of fathers in our counties' caseloads who had moved out of the county or about actual rates of unemployment for the men in our samples, we might have been able to account for more of the differences.

Moreover, with each of our three most important factors relating to collections, there are problems in interpreting the factor's significance.

Our finding that counties whose Friends of the Court initiated enforcement without awaiting complaints collected more money than other counties is, at first glance, hardly surprising. One anomaly nonetheless persists about this self-starting factor. We defined a "self-starting" county as one in which the Friend of the Court initiated enforcement efforts in nonwelfare cases without awaiting complaint from the custodial parent. We excluded welfare cases from the definition of a self-starting county because all Friends of the Court had self-triggering systems for initiating enforcement in welfare cases. Given our definition, one would have expected that when we analyzed the welfare cases from our samples in the twenty-eight counties, the self-starting factor would not have helped sort the high-and low-collecting counties. In fact, however, the self-starting factor is nearly as significant an explainer of the variations among counties in their collections in the welfare cases as it is for the caseload as a whole. This finding suggests that the counties that are self-starting simply collect support in both welfare and nonwelfare cases more effectively for reasons related to, but distinct from, the self-starting attribute alone. Several other aspects of the enforcement process—thoroughness of bookkeeping, size of the enforcement staff and dollar expenditures in relation to caseload, and so forth—correlate mildly with performance and with the self-starting factor. It appears that "self-starting" may simply capture best the sum of the attributes of an efficient and persistent organization.

That the presence of an effective collection organization and the rate of jailing work hand in hand is also not surprising. Under a self-starting enforcement system, a larger portion of men who falter are told to "pay up." The high rate of jailing seems to add, "and we really mean it." Neither message has potency without the other. We had expected, however, that the rate of jailing would not have been the only way to convey "we really mean it," but at least within our study no other aggressive aspect of the enforcement system served anywhere nearly as well to explain the differences in overall collections.

We looked, for example, at the use of orders to show cause—the orders to appear at hearings issued when men fail to respond to warning letters. As noted above, we had a reasonably accurate count of such orders during the same period for which we counted jailings and found that counties varied widely in their rate of use of such orders and in the ratio of orders to subsequent sentences to jail. We had hypothesized that, because they were sent to many more people than were actually jailed, the orders themselves, with their stern and official directive to appear in court, might well have served to communicate more effectively than the sentencing rate itself the seriousness of the enforcement agency. We found, however, that neither the rate of orders to show cause nor any combination of the show-cause rate and jail rate (to measure the conviction rate among those ordered to appear at hearings) helped sort the higher—from the lower—collecting counties nearly as well as the jail rate.

On the other hand, we found that long sentences to jail also appear to make no difference. An index that weighted the rate of jailing in each county by the average length of sentences imposed was far less valuable in explaining variations in county collections than the jailing rate alone and added nothing to the explained variation in the collection rate when used with the rate of jailing controlled. We will have more to say in Chapter 9 about sentence length when we look to see whether it has an effect on the men actually jailed. For now, we can state that, within the range of measures available to us, it is the sentence to jail rather than the length of the sentence that appears to communicate the necessity of paying.

It remains possible, nonetheless, that some unmeasured aspect of the enforcement process less stringent than jailing explains what the jailing rate appears to explain. We were, for example, unable to count the number of warning letters mailed in the twenty-eight counties during either a year we studied or any other year. We thus could not calculate the rate at which the agency sent warnings in relation to the number of cases in the caseload or in relation to the number of cases with arrears at some point during the year. Nor were we able to determine for each county the average time between the development of an arrearage and the mailing of a warning. While we believe it probable that our self-starting factor would correlate strongly and positively with each of these desirable measures, had we been able to develop them, the self-starting factor is unsubtle in its form—every county either was or was not self-starting in our definition. There were no gradations. It is thus possible that one or more of these other dimensions of the enforcement process would account for all or some part of the differences in collections that we have attributed to the rate of jailing.

A problem for analysis would persist even if we had found that the rate of jailing in our twenty-eight counties failed to explain variations in collections but that measures of milder enforcement efforts were powerful explainers of variation. Since the form warning-letters in nearly all counties carried threats of judicial action that many recipients probably read as a threat of jail, a finding that the heavy use of nonpenal enforcement efforts, but not the jail rate, helped sort the higher—from the lower—collecting counties could have either of two very different meanings. It could mean that the threat of jail was truly irrelevant and that men can be propelled toward payment by reminders alone, or it could mean that letters threatening judicial action are sufficient in themselves to create the fear of jail, regardless of the actual rate of jailing. If the latter were the case, then, even though the actual jail rate would not have affected collections, collections would still decline if jail were removed as a legally permissible sanction and men under orders learned of the change in the law.

The final significant factor apparently affecting collection was the county's population. Our findings suggest that even if two counties have a self-starting system of enforcement, jail at the same rate, and have the same rate of unemployment, the less populous county will still collect more money. Why should this be so? The lower collections in populous counties is unlikely to be attributable to lower incomes among the persons in our large-county samples. Among our counties, the portions of the population living in poverty were larger and median incomes were appreciably lower in the smaller counties than in the large ones. It is, of course, possible that our samples mirror unevenly the income levels and unemployment rates of their counties as a whole and that a disproportionate number of poor people are among the divorcing population in the large but not the small counties. Although that interpretation is possible, it receives no support from other data within our own samples.

Another possible explanation for lower payments in more populous counties was also untestable. Within Genesee County, we found that men who left the county after divorce paid dramatically less well than men who stayed.

It is possible that the portion of parents under orders who left town after divorce was much greater in the more populous counties than in the less populous ones. Unfortunately we have no reliable figures on out-migration either for the fathers in *our* samples or for the counties generally. The only migration figures available from census data are those for net migrations projection of the probable net number of people moving into and people moving out of a county between decennial censuses. For what it is worth, we found that only a small portion of the divorced men in Genesee moved away after divorce. For only about one-sixth of the men do we have any indication that they established residence outside Genesee County at any point during the life of their order, and some of these returned while the order was still in force....

Among all the explanations for the relevance of population, it is our best guess that the correct explanation lies in a greater insulation of city dwellers from the enforcement process. In several of the small counties such as Barry, but in none of the large, the director of the Friend of the Court knew personally a significant portion of the men in his county's caseload, a fact that probably affected some of the men under orders.

The difference for the parent in the smaller county is probably not merely that someone whose esteem he values knows whether he is paying. It is also likely that he believes—correctly—that he is easily located. Staffs of the Friend of the Court in populous counties often reported grave difficulties in finding nonpayers, even when they had remained within the county.

Remember Barry County, our least populous county, where the Friend of the Court nodded to his clients in the coffee shop. Barry was our highest-collecting county—87 percent was collected of everything owed, almost eighteen dollars of every twenty dollars ordered was actually paid. Someone on the staff of the agency knew where almost every father lived, worked, or drank. And then recall Wayne County, seventy times more residents, over one hundred thousand cases, three hundred employees. Wayne was our lowest-collecting county—45 percent was collected, only nine dollars of every twenty dollars ordered was actually paid. And yet both counties took enforcement seriously. Barry did jail more persons in relation to its population and did have a self-starting enforcement system of much longer-standing, but the massive differences in collections between them is almost certainly attributable in large part to Barry's cozy manageability and Wayne's impersonal vastness.

Lessons from the Twenty–Eight County Study

In Chapter 5, we offered a startling comparison of payments in Genesee County, Michigan, and Dane County, Wisconsin. Genesee's payments started fairly high—in the first year fathers paid on the average about two-thirds of all they owed—and then, wonder of wonders, improved slightly over time. Payments in Dane started somewhat less well—in the first year fathers paid about half of all that was due—and then got steadily worse. The differences now seem more comprehensible. Since Dane's population was half that of Genesee, with unemployment no higher, the results of our study of twenty-eight Michigan counties support our original hypothesis that the collection system is critical.

In Dane County there was an agency, an office of the court that received payments from fathers, but it had no enforcement duties. Dane mothers not receiving welfare benefits, like mothers in most of the country today, had to turn to private enforcement mechanisms—typically a lawyer—that were no more satisfactory in Wisconsin in 1965 than they had been in Michigan fifty years before. The only vestige of an enforcement system was the prosecutor's office. Focusing on the small portion of fathers whose families received welfare and on fathers charged with other criminal offenses more difficult to prove, the prosecutor secured the jailing of as many men in Dane in relation to the caseload as had the Friend of the Court in Genesee. The remaining fathers—those without other pending criminal charges and whose wives did not receive welfare—were essentially immune from serious enforcement.

The contrast between Dane and Michigan thus suggests two significant conclusions that complement and clarify our findings. The first is that simply having a full-time enforcement agency available, at least at the mother's request, will exert an immense effect on payments. Dade County collected far less per case that Wayne County, ten times its size. Had Dane been a Michigan county with a Friend of the Court and with the same population and the same rate of unemployment it had in 1970, our study suggests that, even if it had been a low-jailing, non-self-starting county, it would probably have collected over 60 percent of all that was ordered (not the 30 percent it in fact received in an average year). Within Michigan, we found that the degree of the agency's organization and tenacity makes a difference. The comparison suggest that just having some sort of integrated collection and enforcement system charged with enforcement is itself critical. It suggests, in short, that places that collect little today might collect a great deal more simply by creating such a full-time agency with responsibilities for all areas of enforcement.

The second message from Dane concerns the effects of jail as an instrument of enforcement. We found within Michigan that in the absence of a self-starting enforcement system, a heavy jailing rate makes little difference in collections. The Wisconsin county, collecting so little but jailing as many men as Genesee, corroborates our own tentative conclusion about the utility of jail as an instrument of collection except when potential offenders come to believe that they are likely to end up there. That belief apparently does not arise for most men from the mere fact that many other men are jailed but rather from the coupling of jailing with an effective warning system pointing toward one's own confinement.

Washtenaw County, Michigan, also offers us some further, more subtle lessons. Washtenaw, in which we drew, as in Genesee, a detailed random sample, was also one of the counties in our twenty eight-county sample. The enforcement systems in Genesee and Washtenaw differed greatly. Two differences are familiar to the reader. For several years up to and including the years we studied, Washtenaw had not been a "self-starting" county: a woman not receiving public assistance had to make a complaint by letter or telephone before a form notice of arrearage was sent to the father, and she had to complain again, this time in writing, before a nonresponding father was sent an order to show cause. Moreover, although many Washtenaw men in the caseload had been arrested for nonsupport—often through the serving of a warrant when arrested for an altogether different offense like a traffic violation—Washtenaw's judges jailed far fewer persons for nonsupport. In the year that Genesee's judges sentenced 224 men, Washtenaw's sentenced no more than five.

In Washtenaw, as in Genesee and Dane, as time passed after the entry of a support order, some men ceased to pay, some began to pay, and some kept paying at the same rate. A comparison of overall patterns of payment performance of parents in Genesee and Washtenaw over the lives of their decrees sheds more light about the effects of a zealous enforcement process, for Washtenaw comes much closer to Genesee but still exhibits important differences.

In the first year in each county most men are paying either nearly everything or nearly nothing, and over the years more and more men end at the extremes, drawn into or falling out of the payment system. The difference between the two counties, subtle but distinct, lies in the changing proportion of fathers paying at high and low rates. In Genesee in the first year, as viewed earlier in figure 5.1, half the men are high payers and 16 percent are low payers. By the sixth year, even more men—close to 60 percent—are high payers and 24 percent are low. The mean level of payments rises slightly over the years, from .67 up to .72. In Washtenaw, the pattern is better than Genesee's in the beginning but worse in the end. In the first year, 56 percent are high payers and only 12 percent are low payers. By the sixth year, however, the portion of high payers has slipped to 46 percent and the portion of low payers has risen dramatically to 36 percent. The mean level of payments falls somewhat every year, beginning at .70 but ending at .53. Were we able to control for population and unemployment, the earlier results suggest that Washtenaw, both smaller and with less unemployment, would appear even worse.

The patterns of payments in the two counties over time suggest that, in each county, a substantial number of men consciously or unconsciously tested the enforcement system in the early years. In Genesee, many were burned and moved toward full payments. In Washtenaw, many who paid erratically apparently found that their haphazard payments were ignored or followed by hollow threats or that, even if they were arrested, they were released and then forgotten.

Table 6.2 illustrates the same point in somewhat different form. It reveals the pattern of payments in individual cases in the same two counties, showing the number of men in each county who started in the first years of the order paying at either high or low rates and whether they were still paying at high or low rates by the sixth and seventh years. The difference between the two counties does not lie in the men who started at high rates. In each county, 49 percent of the men started in the first year paying 80 percent or more of the amount due. Of these men who started at high rates, only slightly more of Washtenaw's than Genesee's slid into lower payments. The noteworthy difference lies rather in the men who started at a low rate of payment. In each county 51 percent of the men start low, but in Genesee County more than half of this low-starting group ends up as high payers whereas in Washtenaw only about one-fourth of the low payers move up.

Table 6.2 Payment Trends. Genesee and Washtenaw Random Samples

Percent of Men in Caseload Whose Payment Rate:	**Genesee County**	**Washtenaw County**
Starts high, ends high	39%	35%
Starts high, ends low	10	14
Starts low, ends high	28	13
Starts low, ends low	23	38
Totals	100%	100%
	N=229	N=167

High = Payment rate was 80% or more of amount due.

Low = Payment rate was less than 80% of the amount due.

Start = Average for each person of payment rate in year of final order and first year thereafter. In cases with missing data for either year, the payment rate of the other year was used.

End = Average for each person of the payment rate in sixth and seventh year after the year of the final order. In cases with missing data for either year, the payment rate of the other year was used.

What this pattern suggests, when taken together with Eckhardt's findings in Dane County, Wisconsin, is that when there is no enforcement system at all (Dane) most men who pay well at the outset will fall by the wayside. On the other hand, if there is some enforcement system, even of the passive sort found in Washtenaw County, most high payers will stay high payers. The presence of an especially rigorous system, such as that in Genesee, makes little difference to those who start at a high level so long as there is at least some system. For those men who start badly, however, only an ardent enforcement system serves to bring many up to high payment levels. These findings are consistent with a hypothesis that, while it takes some effort to maintain payers in a pattern of steady payment behavior voluntarily begun, it takes far more effort to undo an established pattern of poor payment. Washtenaw's system is sufficiently effective to sustain the high starters but insufficient to turn around many of the low.

Dollar Costs and Returns of Jailings

Within Michigan, counties that jail large numbers of men collect more than those that do not. It remains possible that the counties that use jail will show a net loss for their policy because the dollar costs of jailing exceed the returns. In fact, the gains in dollars are almost certainly far greater than the dollar costs....

Questions on Jailing and Compliance

(1) How persuasive is the evidence Professor Chambers uses to bolster his argument? Is it bothersome that it is from two similar, Midwestern states? That some is statistical, some very anecdotal?

(2) Are you surprised by Chambers' finding that jailing itself matters, but not the time actually spent in jail? This agrees with the law and

economics approach to sentencing found, for example, in Gary Becker, *Crime and Punishment: An Economic Approach*, 76 J Pol Econ 169 (1968).

(3) Would you expect Chambers' findings to be replicated fifteen or twenty years later? In other words, are they still valid now that national attitudes about "deadbeat dads" have changed, at least in the eyes of the popular press? In *The Market for Deadbeats*, 25 J Legal Stud 201 (1996), Margaret F. Brinig and F.H. Buckley re-explore some of the problems Chambers found. Looking at national data for a twelve year period, they found results much like Chambers' for unemployment and rural populations. They also found that there were lower rates of collection in Western states, in those where there was no-fault divorce, and in those without statutes allowing joint custody.

B. THE WISCONSIN APPROACH

Another state's experiment is described and condemned in this case:

ZABLOCKI v. REDHAIL

Supreme Court of the United States, 1978
434 US 374

MARSHALL, JUSTICE:

At issue in this case is the constitutionality of a Wisconsin statute, Wis.Stat. §§ 245.10(1), (4), (5)(1973), which provides that members of a certain class of Wisconsin residents may not marry, within the State or elsewhere, without first obtaining a court order granting permission to marry. The class is defined by the statute to include any "Wisconsin resident having minor issue not in his custody and which he is under obligation to support by any court order or judgment." The statute specifies that court permission cannot be granted unless the marriage applicant submits proof of compliance with the support obligation and, in addition, demonstrates that the children covered by the support order "are not then and are not likely thereafter to become public charges." No marriage license may lawfully be issued in Wisconsin to a person covered by the statute, except upon court order; any marriage entered into without compliance with § 245.10 is declared void; and persons acquiring marriage licenses in violation of the section are subject to criminal penalties.

After being denied a marriage license because of his failure to comply with § 245.10, appellee brought this class action under 42 U.S.C. § 1983, challenging the statute as violative of the Equal Protection and Due Process Clauses of the Fourteenth Amendment and seeking declaratory and injunctive relief. The United States District Court for the Eastern District of Wisconsin held the statute unconstitutional under the Equal Protection Clause and enjoined its enforcement. 418 F.Supp. 1061 (1976). We noted probable jurisdiction, and we now affirm.

I

Appellee Redhail is a Wisconsin resident who, under the terms of § 245.10, is unable to enter into a lawful marriage in Wisconsin or elsewhere so long as he maintains his Wisconsin residency. The facts, according to the stipulation filed by the parties in the District Court, are as follows. In January 1972, when appellee was a minor and a high school student, a paternity action was instituted against him in Milwaukee County Court, alleging that he was the father of a baby girl born out of wedlock on July 5, 1971. After he appeared and admitted that he was the child's father, the court entered an order on May 12, 1972, adjudging appellee the father and ordering him to pay $109 per month as support for the child until she reached 18 years of age. From May 1972 until August 1974, appellee was unemployed and indigent, and consequently was unable to make any support payments.

On September 27, 1974, appellee filed an application for a marriage license with appellant Zablocki, the County Clerk of Milwaukee County, and a few days later the application was denied on the sole ground that appellee had not obtained a court order granting him permission to marry, as required by § 245.10. Although appellee did not petition a state court thereafter, it is stipulated that he would not have been able to satisfy either of the statutory prerequisites for an order granting permission to marry. First, he had not satisfied his support obligations to his illegitimate child, and as of December 1974 there was an arrearage in excess of $3,700. Second, the child had been a public charge since her birth, receiving benefits under the Aid to Families with Dependent Children program. It is stipulated that the child's benefit payments were such that she would have been a public charge even if appellee had been current in his support payments.

On December 24, 1974, appellee filed his complaint in the District Court, on behalf of himself and the class of all Wisconsin residents who had been refused a marriage license pursuant to § 245.10(1) by one of the county clerks in Wisconsin. Zablocki was named as the defendant, individually and as representative of a class consisting of all county clerks in the State. The complaint alleged, among other things, that appellee and the woman he desired to marry were expecting a child in March 1975 and wished to be lawfully married before that time. The statute was attacked on the grounds that it deprived appellee, and the class he sought to represent, of equal protection and due process rights secured by the First, Fifth, Ninth, and Fourteenth Amendments to the United States Constitution....

II

In evaluating §§ 245.10(1), (4), (5) under the Equal Protection Clause, "we must first determine what burden of justification the classification created thereby must meet, by looking to the nature of the classification and the individual interests affected." Since our past decisions make clear that the right to marry is of fundamental importance, and since the classification at issue here significantly interferes with the exercise of that right, we believe that "critical examination" of the state interests advanced in support of the classification is required.

The leading decision of this Court on the right to marry is *Loving v. Virginia*, 388 U.S. 1 (1967). In that case, an interracial couple who had been convicted of violating Virginia's miscegenation laws challenged the statutory scheme on both equal protection and due process grounds. The Court's opinion could have rested solely on the ground that the statutes discriminated on the basis of race in violation of the Equal Protection Clause. But the Court went on to hold that the laws arbitrarily deprived the couple of a fundamental liberty protected by the Due Process Clause, the freedom to marry. The Court's language on the latter point bears repeating:

> "The freedom to marry has long been recognized as one of the vital personal rights essential to the orderly pursuit of happiness by free men.
>
> "Marriage is one of the 'basic civil rights of man,' fundamental to our very existence and survival." *Id.*, at 12, quoting *Skinner v. Oklahoma ex rel. Williamson*, 316 U.S. 535, 541 (1942).

Although *Loving* arose in the context of racial discrimination, prior and subsequent decisions of this Court confirm that the right to marry is of fundamental importance for all individuals. Long ago, in *Maynard v. Hill*, 125 U.S. 190 (1888), the Court characterized marriage as "the most important relation in life," and as "the foundation of the family and of society, without which there would be neither civilization nor progress." In *Meyer v. Nebraska*, 262 U.S. 390 (1923), the Court recognized that the right "to marry, establish a home and bring up children" is a central part of the liberty protected by the Due Process Clause, and in *Skinner v. Oklahoma ex rel. Williamson, supra*, marriage was described as "fundamental to the very existence and survival of the race."

More recent decisions have established that the right to marry is part of the fundamental "right of privacy" implicit in the Fourteenth Amendment's Due Process Clause. In *Griswold v. Connecticut*, 381 U.S. 479 (1965), the Court observed:

> "We deal with a right of privacy older than the Bill of Rights—older than our political parties, older than our school system. Marriage is a coming together for better or for worse, hopefully enduring, and intimate to the degree of being sacred. It is an association that promotes a way of life, not causes; a harmony in living, not political faiths; a bilateral loyalty, not commercial or social projects. Yet it is an association for as noble a purpose as any involved in our prior decisions."

Cases subsequent to *Griswold* and *Loving* have routinely categorized the decision to marry as among the personal decisions protected by the right of privacy. For example, last Term in *Carey v. Population Services International*, 431 U.S. 678 (1977), we declared:

> "While the outer limits of [the right of personal privacy] have not been marked by the Court, it is clear that among the decisions that an individual may make without unjustified government interference are personal decisions 'relating to marriage', *Loving v. Virginia*, procreation, *Skinner v. Oklahoma ex rel. Williamson*, contraception, *Eisenstadt v. Baird*, family relationships, *Prince v. Massachusetts*, and child rearing and education, *Pierce v. Society of Sisters*; *Meyer v. Nebraska.*"

It is not surprising that the decision to marry has been placed on the same level of importance as decisions relating to procreation, childbirth, child rearing, and family relationships. As the facts of this case illustrate, it would make little sense to recognize a right of privacy with respect to other matters of family life and not with respect to the decision to enter the relationship that is the foundation of the family in our society. The woman whom appellee desired to marry had a fundamental right to seek an abortion of their expected child, see *Roe v. Wade, supra*, or to bring the child into life to suffer the myriad social, if not economic, disabilities that the status of illegitimacy brings, see *Trimble v. Gordon*, 430 U.S. 762, 768–770, and n. 13 (1977); *Weber v. Aetna Casualty & Surety Co.*, 406 U.S. 164, 175–76 (1972). Surely, a decision to marry and raise the child in a traditional family setting must receive equivalent protection. And, if appellee's right to procreate means anything at all, it must imply some right to enter the only relationship in which the State of Wisconsin allows sexual relations legally to take place.

By reaffirming the fundamental character of the right to marry, we do not mean to suggest that every state regulation which relates in any way to the incidents of or prerequisites for marriage must be subjected to rigorous scrutiny. To the contrary, reasonable regulations that do not significantly interfere with decisions to enter into the marital relationship may legitimately be imposed. The statutory classification at issue here, however, clearly does interfere directly and substantially with the right to marry.

Under the challenged statute, no Wisconsin resident in the affected class may marry in Wisconsin or elsewhere without a court order, and marriages contracted in violation of the statute are both void and punishable as criminal offenses. Some of those in the affected class, like appellee, will never be able to obtain the necessary court order, because they either lack the financial means to meet their support obligations or cannot prove that their children will not become public charges. These persons are absolutely prevented from getting married. Many others, able in theory to satisfy the statute's requirements, will be sufficiently burdened by having to do so that they will in effect be coerced into forgoing their right to marry. And even those who can be persuaded to meet the statute's requirements suffer a serious intrusion into their freedom of choice in an area in which we have held such freedom to be fundamental.

III

When a statutory classification significantly interferes with the exercise of a fundamental right, it cannot be upheld unless it is supported by sufficiently important state interests and is closely tailored to effectuate only those interests. Appellant asserts that two interests are served by the challenged statute: the permission-to-marry proceeding furnishes an opportunity to counsel the applicant as to the necessity of fulfilling his prior support obligations; and the welfare of the out-of-custody children is protected. We may accept for present purposes that these are legitimate and substantial interests, but, since the means selected by the State for achieving these interests unnecessarily impinge on the right to marry, the statute cannot be sustained.

There is evidence that the challenged statute, as originally introduced in the Wisconsin legislature, was intended merely to establish a mechanism whereby persons with support obligations to children from prior marriages could be counseled before they entered into new marital relationships and incurred further support obligations. Court permission to marry was to be required, but apparently permission was automatically to be granted after counseling was completed. The statute actually enacted, however, does not expressly require or provide for any counseling whatsoever, nor for any automatic granting of permission to marry by the court, and thus it can hardly be justified as a means for ensuring counseling of the persons within its coverage. Even assuming that counseling does take place—a fact as to which there is no evidence in the record—this interest obviously cannot support the withholding of court permission to marry once counseling is completed.

With regard to safeguarding the welfare of the out-of-custody children, appellant's brief does not make clear the connection between the State's interest and the statute's requirements. At argument, appellant's counsel suggested that, since permission to marry cannot be granted unless the applicant shows that he has satisfied his court-determined support obligations to the prior children and that those children will not become public charges, the statute provides incentive for the applicant to make support payments to his children. This "collection device" rationale cannot justify the statute's broad infringement on the right to marry.

First, with respect to individuals who are unable to meet the statutory requirements, the statute merely prevents the applicant from getting married, without delivering any money at all into the hands of the applicant's prior children. More importantly, regardless of the applicant's ability or willingness to meet the statutory requirements, the State already has numerous other means for exacting compliance with support obligations, means that are at least as effective as the instant statute's and yet do not impinge upon the right to marry. Under Wisconsin law, whether the children are from a prior marriage or were born out of wedlock, court-determined support obligations may be enforced directly via wage assignments, civil contempt proceedings, and criminal penalties. And, if the State believes that parents of children out of their custody should be responsible for ensuring that those children do not become public charges, this interest can be achieved by adjusting the criteria used for determining the amounts to be paid under their support orders.

There is also some suggestion that § 245.10 protects the ability of marriage applicants to meet support obligations to prior children by preventing the applicants from incurring new support obligations. But the challenged provisions of § 245.10 are grossly underinclusive with respect to this purpose, since they do not limit in any way new financial commitments by the applicant other than those arising out of the contemplated marriage. The statutory classification is substantially over-inclusive as well: Given the possibility that the new spouse will actually better the applicant's financial situation, by contributing income from a job or otherwise, the statute in many cases may prevent affected individuals from improving their ability to satisfy their prior support obligations. And, although it is true that the applicant will incur support obligations to any children born during the contemplated marriage, preventing the marriage may only result in the children being born out of wedlock, as in fact occurred in appellee's case. Since the support obligation is the same whether the child is born in or out of wedlock, the net result of preventing the marriage is simply more illegitimate children.

Questions on **Zablocki**

(1) Instead of employing the usual "necessary to serve a compelling state interest" standard of review, the Court in *Zablocki* uses a "closely tailored to support a sufficiently important state interest" standard. Why?

(2) What state interests does the state assert the statute serves? What other interests might it serve? Are these "sufficiently important"?

(3) The Court says the state has alternative enforcement mechanisms that make the statute unnecessary. What does the Court have in mind? Are the alternatives effective enough to make the statute unnecessary?

(4) Consider the Court's argument that the statute is underinclusive.

(a) In what way is the statute underinclusive? Why is it relevant that it is? What would a statute that was not underinclusive look like? Why would such a statute be preferable to the actual statute?

(b) Is there a plausible reason for singling out child-support payments for special treatment?

(5) Assume that the Wisconsin statute had an exemption for those who did not meet the statutory criteria but who were truly unable to

make their child-support payments. Would the statute still be unconstitutional?

(6) Since *Zablocki*, Wisconsin has sought other ways to encourage parents to support their children (and protect its fisc). Wis Stat § 49.90(2)(1987) requires a parent of a dependent person under 18 to maintain the dependent's child to the extent the dependent cannot do so. Further, in its controversial "bridefare" legislation, the state has removed welfare disincentives that discourage young couples from marrying, Wis Stat §§ 49.19 et seq. (2006). See generally Rogers Worthington, *Wisconsin's Big Cheese: Can Wisconsin Gov. Tommy Thompson Ride Welfare Reform into the White House?*, Chicago Tribune, April 10, 1994, at E8.

(7) In *State v. Oakley*, 629 N.W.2d 200 (Wis. 2001), *cert. denied, Oakley v. Wisconsin*, 537 U.S. 813 (2002), the Wisconsin Supreme Court divided along gender lines when it considered whether as a condition of probation, a father of nine children who had intentionally failed to pay child support could be required to avoid having other children unless he showed he could support that child and his other children. The Wisconsin Court, in light of the unique circumstances and "extraordinarily troubling record manifesting his disregard for the law" found that the condition was not overly broad and was reasonably related to Oakley's rehabilitation. Oakley, whose conviction was for intentionally refusing to pay child support, could have been imprisoned for six years (eliminating his right to procreate altogether). The majority found this condition was not invalid under the given facts. Dissenting, Justice Bradley emphasized the fundamental right at issue: the right to have children. Citing *Skinner v. Oklahoma*, 316 U.S. 535 (1942), the court found that the means of effecting the governmental interest in requiring parents to support their children was not drawn narrowly enough to meet heightened scrutiny. Justice Sykes, also dissenting, could not distinguish these conditions from those found unconstitutional in *Zablocki*. As in *Zablocki*, less restrictive means were available such as executing a wage assignment, intercepting tax refunds, placing liens on personal property and finding him in civil contempt. If he did not maintain employment and make payments, his probation could be revoked. Is the difference between *Oakley* and *Zablocki* what the court suggests, that Oakley would otherwise have been in prison where he could have been unable to procreate, while Zablocki was absolutely prohibited from marrying? That Oakley was a "convicted individual," with a lesser liberty interest, while Zablocki was not? That Zablocki did not have a realistic way to fulfill the conditions for marrying, while Oakley could have at least made an attempt to pay back the support? That the children of Zablocki's current relationship would be worse off without the marriage, while Oakley's children would not be better off if he had additional children?

C. THE INTERSTATE APPROACH

One problem with enforcing a child support order in our large and federal country is that a parent who owes support can often escape the jurisdiction of the court that issued the order and can elude the custodial parent. Many custodial parents lack the resources to track down an absent spouse or to pay for bringing suit against him in a distant state. And while the full faith and credit clause of Article IV of the Constitution requires each state to accord final judgments of courts from foreign states the same authority as judgments from their own courts, child support orders, which generally are modifiable, have not always been regarded as final judgments. The argument is that, since the order is subject to change in the original court, the second court cannot know how to interpret or enforce it. Child support orders were made subject to the full faith and credit clause by the 1984 Child Support Enforcement Amendments, 42 USCA § 666 (a)(9). But even where the clause makes an order enforceable, there remain the problems of locating the absent parent and suing him in a distant place.

One of the oldest and most successful attempts to ameliorate these difficulties was the Uniform Reciprocal Enforcement of Support Act (URESA). This legislation, along with its successor, the Revised Uniform Reciprocal Enforcement of Support Act (RURESA), sought to promote interstate cooperation in establishing and enforcing child support orders through uniform laws. To meet the same goal more effectively, the Uniform Interstate Family Support Act (UIFSA) was formulated in 1992 and revised in 1996. The states universally adopted UIFSA, if only because Congress required them to enact UIFSA to remain eligible for federal funding for child-support enforcement. UIFSA incorporates the basic programs of its predecessor acts and introduces new concepts to improve the enforcement capabilities of individuals seeking court-ordered child (or spousal) support.

UIFSA's basic programs include: (1) a procedure for registering an existing support order in a foreign state so that it may be enforced by a tribunal in that state and an informal procedure through which an obligee may enforce an existing order through direct filing either with the obligor's employer in the foreign state or with an enforcement agency of the foreign state; (2) a civil enforcement procedure for modifying orders (in very limited circumstances) when the non-registered party is in a different state; and (3) a procedure ("rendition") to extradite obligors charged with criminal non-support.

Long Arm Jurisdiction

One important addition to the scheme originally provided for by URESA is the establishment of long-arm jurisdiction over an absent nonresident for support-order or parentage proceedings. Section 201. One of the deficiencies of the previous system was that establishing jurisdiction over obligors who moved from state to state was quite difficult and depended on each state's personal jurisdiction statute. Not only was this provision added to assist those seeking enforcement of support orders over (often absent) non-residents, it was also added to promote UIFSA's aim of eliminating multiple orders (that might have been issued from different state courts after a *de novo* review under

URESA). Also, a long-arm statute helps to convert what would be a two-state lawsuit into a single-state proceeding. Under this new regime, once jurisdiction over a respondent is established (an easy hurdle to clear, given the statute's broad language), the court may seek out evidence, order discovery, and receive testimony with the statutorily mandated assistance and cooperation of other state courts. Section 202, 316, 318.

Continuing Exclusive Jurisdiction and the Establishment of a Controlling Order

As we said, UIFSA aims to eliminate the possibility of multiple orders governing the same parent and same child. In addition to providing a basis for asserting personal jurisdiction over non-resident respondents, UIFSA introduced the concept of "continuing, exclusive, jurisdiction." Section 205. This provision is arguably the most crucial aspect of UIFSA because the tribunal that issued an order will now retain the ability to modify it no matter where the respondent resides. Section 206(b). The order may not be modified by any other state's tribunal except in very limited circumstances. Sections 205 and 609–614. The role of the foreign state (where the obligor lives) thus becomes one of enforcement only. The forum state applies its law regarding enforcement, but the law of the state that issued the order continues to control the order's substance. Section 603. Moreover, courts are required to cooperate with or defer to other courts that may be hearing the same matter in order to avoid competing support orders. Priority is given to the court in the child's current home state. Section 204.

Continuing exclusive jurisdiction over child-support orders may be lost in certain circumstances. The parties may file with the issuing state's tribunal their written consent to waive the order. Section 205(b). If the order is thus lawfully amended, the original court may only enforce payment of money owed before the order's modification, enforce nonmodifiable aspects of the order, or provide appropriate relief for violations occurring before the modification. Section 205(c). Spousal-support orders are treated differently under UIFSA, since the parties may not waive jurisdiction by mutual agreement. Section 205(f). Moreover, tribunals in states that did not issue the spousal-support order may not modify it. Section 206(c).

A Question on the UIFSA Modification Provisions

(1) Why are spousal support (alimony) orders treated differently under UIFSA in regard to continuing exclusive jurisdiction and the ability of a non-issuing state to modify the order?

(a) The Commentary to the statute says that spousal-support laws vary much more from state to state than child-support schemes. Further, a change in the obligor's income, the most common reason for modifying child support, usually will not affect spousal support. Modification is therefore more common in child-support cases. Does that answer the question?

(b) Or is there something intrinsically different about child and spousal support? The answer cases sometimes give is that the relationship between parent and child does not terminate at divorce, while that between the two spouses ends. *Cole v. Cole*, 409 A2d 734 (Md Ct Spec App 1979); *Conway v. Conway*, 395 SE2d 464 (Va Ct App 1990).

Recognition of a Single Order

Because URESA could give rise to multiple orders for the same set of parents and children, UIFSA includes a provision that lets multiple orders be merged into a single order. Section 207. This device (which is intended to ease the transition from URESA to UIFSA) is known as recognition of the "controlling" child-support order, identifies the single order that will be suitable for enforcement under the UIFSA system. When more than one order exists for the same parent and the same child, UIFSA sets up a priority system designed to identify the controlling order. Section 207(b). The statute gives primacy to the state entitled to continuing exclusive jurisdiction under UIFSA. If more than one tribunal would meet the definition, the statute provides that if the child's current home state has issued an order, that order controls. Otherwise, the most recently issued order controls. Section 207(b)(1), (2).

Direct Enforcement of Support Orders

Under URESA, an order could only be enforced if it was registered by the obligee in the foreign state. UIFSA only requires registration if the individual seeks to enforce an order judicially (as opposed to directly). Section 601–604. One of the central of goals of UIFSA is to allow individuals to initiate enforcement actions without involving the judicial process. Therefore, UIFSA prescribes two procedures for pursuing enforcement of an order in a foreign state. In the first, the order may be sent directly to the obligor's employer for immediate withholding of earnings without a hearing unless the employee objects. Sections 501–506. The second procedure allows an individual or a support-enforcement agency (which the Social Security Act requires each state to create) to seek direct administrative enforcement of the order. Section 507. In either of these procedures, the individual owed support is not the only one entitled to seek enforcement. Enforcement may also be sought by an attorney (suing for attorney's fees) or an interested agency, including the state if the obligee receives public assistance. Section 101(12)(ii).

Registration of Support Orders and Civil Enforcement

To utilize the judicial system to enforce an order, one must first register the order in the foreign state. This process is substantially the same as it was under URESA and requires filing (1) a letter requesting that the order be registered and enforced, (2) two copies (one certified) of the order(s) to be registered, together with any modifications of the order, (3) an affidavit by the party seeking registration or a certified statement by the custodian of records stating the amount owed, the name of and other identifying information about the obligor and obligee, and information regarding where payments should be sent. Section 602. The non-registering party is given 20 days to assert any defenses, after which a hearing will be held. Section 605(b)(2). The non-registering party may only raise defenses relating to the validity of enforcement of the original order. If the non-registering party does not respond, or if the defenses are rejected, the order is enforced as if it were an order issued by that state. Section 603. The receiving state court only applies the law of the forum in procedural matters such as evidence rules and other procedures required for enforcement hearings. The substance of the order remains intact and subject to the law of the issuing tribunal. Section 604. Again, the foreign state's tribunal may not modify the order according to the forum's local law unless the issuing state has lost continuing exclusive jurisdiction. Section 205(b).

Notes and Questions on Enforcement of Support Under UIFSA

(1) Imagine you are a father on the move. Does the knowledge that the child support order can follow you affect your attitude about your duty of support? Does the ability of your spouse or other interested party (including the state if the spouse receives public assistance) to file the order directly with your employer for immediate garnishment of your wages? Will these make you more likely to pay or merely less likely to let your former spouse discover your whereabouts?

(2) One of the obligee's problems under RURESA was that if the obligor moved to a state that was sympathetic to wandering fathers or had a lower standard of living, the original order could be frustrated by the local court's battery of defenses, by cavalier attitudes about the needs of the child, or by the cost of living in the obligee's state. For a discussion of these matters, a theory about why some states may actually try to attract "deadbeats," and some empirical findings suggesting differences in political goals and social norms among states, see Margaret F. Brinig and F.H. Buckley, *The Market for Deadbeats*, 25 J Legal Stud 201 (1996).

(3) One reason for UIFSA procedures like interstate registration is that they save the obligee money, time, and effort compared to a traditional lawsuit brought against the obligor in his home state. What other benefits can you see? Are there situations where interstate registration and enforcement would be unwise? (The next section may help you see some of these.)

(4) Does the mechanical routine of the procedure help or hurt the obligee? The obligor? How? What does the possibility for direct enforcement add to the analysis? (Remember Professor Chambers' study of enforcement in Michigan and the importance of a non-bureaucratic approach.)

Civil Enforcement

In order to initiate a civil enforcement proceeding under UIFSA, the individual seeking enforcement (usually the obligee) begins by filing a petition in his or her home state. The pleadings and other documents must contain identifying information regarding the obligor, the obligee, and affected children including their names, addresses and social security numbers. Section 311. If this information is not known, the state information agency may be consulted. Section 310. This agency, commonly the attorney general's office of the state's social services agency, must help locate the obligor and forward the papers to the proper tribunal. Section 310. To address the increasing awareness of domestic violence and other related fears, UIFSA added a provision that the identifying information will not be disclosed when the health, safety, or liberty of a party is in danger. Section 312. The tribunal receiving the petition in the individual's home state is the "initiating tribunal" and must forward three copies of the petition and accompanying documents to the responding tribunal or the appropriate support-enforcement agency in the responding state. Section 304. Under URESA, the initiating tribunal had to make a preliminary finding on the merits of the petition. This procedure was seen as mechanical at best and served little good, so the drafters of UIFSA reduced the initiating tribunal to a purely ministerial body.

The court or agency in the foreign state receiving the petition and the accompanying documentation is the "responding tribunal." The responding tribunal causes the petition or pleading to be filed and notifies the petitioner where and when it was filed. Section 305(a). As we said a moment ago, the responding tribunal follows the procedural law of its state, unless a provision of UIFSA addresses a question (like the prohibition of conditioning visitation on payment of support). Section 305(d).

The order is substantively interpreted under the law of the issuing state. The exception to this choice of law rule involves the statute of limitations to apply in cases involving arrearage—the statute which provides for the longer time period for filing controls. Section 604. If it is likely that the non-registering party (often the obligor) might flee the jurisdiction, his physical seizure is left up to the civil laws of the forum state. Section 305(b)(9).

Because the responding state may not modify the order unless the issuing state has lost continuing exclusive jurisdiction (through either the filed written consent of the parties or because neither party still resides in the issuing state and the responding tribunal has personal jurisdiction over both parties), the hearing is limited to enforcement of the support order. Sections 605–608. Also, the hearing itself is limited solely to the enforcement of support orders. Thus, no collateral actions like visitation matters may be addressed by the court. Section 305(d). (However, the UIFSA does authorize tribunals to establish parentage in interstate proceedings even when there is no pending support proceeding. Section 701.)

The actual hearing resembles an ordinary support hearing, except that the petitioner (obligee) is absent. The obligee is entitled to be represented by the enforcement agency of the state. Obligee's counsel must present credible, admissible evidence to prove the petition's allegations. This is usually accomplished primarily through depositions and interrogatories. Similarly, the obligor may cross-examine the obligee through interrogatories and depositions. The witness may also testify by telephone or other electronic means. Section 316. Again, the tribunals must cooperate and assist with discovery requested by a sister tribunal under UIFSA. Sections 317–318.

The obligor usually does not appear or appears and admits owing a duty of support. The court then issues a judgment and provides a remedy. In the less usual case, the respondent enters a denial or defense or files responsive pleadings. The primary defenses commonly used relate to the existence of a duty of support. UIFSA specifically prohibits the respondent from disputing parentage if it has been previously determined pursuant to the law. Section 315. However, the respondent can assert compliance with an existing support order or that the child has reached the age of majority (defined by the issuing state). The respondent may also attempt to introduce evidence that shows substantial compliance with the support order if he has provided benefits in kind, established a trust, or made payment to the child or to the child's creditors on the child's behalf.

If the respondent seeks to modify the order due to a change in circumstances such as loss of a job, or birth of more children, the respondent may initiate proceedings in the issuing state, or the state with continuing exclusive jurisdiction, to modify the order. The responding tribunal will defer to the tribunal having the authority to modify the order. Section 204, 609–614. Most often the obligor will allege he is unable to pay. If newly acquired obligations (e.g., more children) are the source of this inability, the court is likely to reject this defense on the grounds that the obligor was aware of his support duty when he undertook the new responsibilities. If, on the other hand, the obligor has lost his job or become disabled, the court is more likely to be receptive. Inability to pay usually does not relieve the obligor of his duty to pay, but it can often forestall contempt charges and may help show that an existing support order should be modified. However, even where the support order is modified, the obligor may remain responsible for the arrearage accumulated under the old order, particularly if the inability to pay is temporary. In addition, child-support debts cannot be discharged in bankruptcy. 42 USC § 656. Again, modification may only be considered by the tribunal having continuing exclusive jurisdiction under the limited circumstances provided for by UIFSA. Sections 605–614.

Where there is no move to modify the order, the tribunal may at the close of the (enforcement) hearing grant any remedy allowed by its state law or any of the eleven specifically mentioned remedies in UIFSA, including the withholding of income and civil or criminal contempt orders. It may require the obligor to seek appropriate employment by specified methods or award attorney's fees and other costs. Section 305(b). The specifically listed remedies are designed to supplement state laws which do not provide for such a remedy. A catch-all phrase allowing "any other available remedy" permits the enforcing tribunal to use any remedy allowed under their state law.

Questions on the Methods of Enforcement Under UIFSA

(1) What problems can you see with a hearing at which only one party appears? With an advocate who has never met his or her client? What does UIFSA's summary procedure do to the adversarial process? How could these objections be overcome? How would overcoming them affect the procedure as it is now?

(2) Imagine you are an attorney in a responding jurisdiction assigned to represent an obligee from another state in a UIFSA proceeding. What will your attitude be toward her case? How hard will you try to locate the obligor? Will the fact that you have never met her affect the zeal with which you pursue her case?

(3) Is it just to require the obligor to support children whose address he is not even told? In other words, should child support be awarded even when visitation is not? Under what circumstances?

(4) Should an obligor be able to relocate to a state having a lower age of majority, say, 18, and avoid payment of a child-support obligation that goes until 21? What if the state in which the obligor lives does not require payment of college expenses, but the "initiating" state does? What if the child and custodial parent (the obligee) have moved to the state with the higher age of majority? What happens under UIFSA in such cases?

(5) Now suppose you are a judge in a UIFSA hearing. How will the obligee's absence affect your decision? With whom will your sympathies most likely lie? How can you overcome this tendency and remain objective?

(6) Now take the position of an obligor who is an absent divorced parent. Does this process treats you fairly? Do the limitations on the defenses available to you leave you adequate opportunity to present your case? Is it fair that this issue must be decided separately from issues of custody, visitation, divorce, and property settlement? How does your inability to confront your former spouse directly affect your attitude towards these proceedings?

Criminal Procedures Under UIFSA

UIFSA makes no substantive changes in URESA's "rendition" procedures. This remains a little-used device that provides for the extradition of parents charged with criminal nonsupport. As is usual in extraditions, the governor of the responding state surrenders the accused to the governor of the initiating or "demanding" state. However, as is not usual in extraditions, the extraditing state need not show that the parent has fled from justice or that the parent was present in the extraditing state when the offense occurred. Section 801. The governor of the responding state need not extradite the obligor if the obligor can show that he has prevailed in a previous support action or that he is currently complying with an existing support order. The governor may also inquire into the effectiveness of utilizing a civil-support action before surrendering the parent, since the criminal rendition provision was designed to impose criminal liability only where existing civil measures were unsuccessful. Section 802.

Questions on Criminal Proceedings Under UIFSA

(1) What social or legal advantage is there in extraditing the parent who owes support? See Professor Chambers' article, above, for a discussion of the relationship between support collection and the jailing of delinquent fathers. Does an extradition provision enhance or detract from Professor Chambers' position in the excerpt?

(2) Under what circumstances would a civil remedy be more effective than extradition or other criminal measures? What factors should a governor consider in making the extradition decision?

A Problem

David and Denise were married for 18 years before their divorce, which was granted by State A, their state of residence. Their sons, John and Jeff, were then 16 and 8. Denise retained custody of both children. The divorce was reasonably amicable, and David and Denise reached an informal agreement about child support and visitation. Three years later, David discovered that Denise had been having an extramarital affair during most of their marriage and is under psychiatric care for alcoholism. Infuriated, he has refused to continue to pay support. Denise fears he will bring a lawsuit for custody of the children. Consequently, she has moved to State B without telling David her new address. This has effectively prevented him from visiting the boys. However, because she has left her job in State A, she is forced to apply for welfare benefits in State B. The welfare office in State B has initiated a UIFSA action on behalf of Denise and the children.

Contemplate the effect of UIFSA on this fact situation by considering the following questions:

(1) Should David be able to raise a defense based upon Denise's obstruction of the relationship between David and his sons? Upon her marital misconduct? Should the fact that misconduct might be admissible if she had initiated the action in State A make a difference?

(2) If the age of majority in State B is 21 and in State A is 18, should David be required to pay child support for John, who is now 19, because of Denise's choice of homes? (UIFSA would not permit this). Suppose the age of majority in State A is 21 and in State B is

18? Should David be relieved of three years of supporting John because of Denise's move? (UIFSA would not permit this either).

(3) Should David be able to assert as a defense that he has been paying John's college tuition and putting money in a bank account for Jeff's education? If the children have an absolute right to support from their father, do they have a right to a specific type of support (money rather than education or insurance or vice versa)? Should the fact that they are receiving public assistance affect this decision?

A Concluding Note

There are two ways of enforcing interstate support obligations. The first method is through the interstate statutory system that you have been reading about—UIFSA. However, even where this system operates relatively inexpensively, the payee spouse may be unable to collect the full amount authorized by the initiating state. Further, the payee must rely on the collection mechanism of the payor state. Some states are far more efficient in collection than others. The 1998 Report of the Office of Child Support Enforcement shows a variance in collections ranging from less than 12% of total non-TANF court orders to 84%.

The second method of enforcing interstate support obligations relies on the full faith and credit clause of the Constitution (Art IV, § 6) for enforcing final judgments made with personal jurisdiction over the obligor. *Kulko v. Superior Court*, 436 US 84 (1978). The entire amount of arrearages may be collected after being reduced to a final judgment. Some states, however, permit the payor to raise defenses even after payment is due, so that the judgement is not necessarily final without a further hearing, which also requires personal jurisdiction or at least notice. *Griffin v. Griffin*, 327 US 220 (1946).

Some states go beyond UIFSA requirements and grant comity even for prospective orders for child support. See, e.g., *Scott v. Sylvester*, 257 SE2d 774 (Va 1979). Such accommodations, which treat another state's order like a domestic one, are usually found between neighboring states or those having frequent contact, at least in the child-support context.

D. THE FEDERAL APPROACH

(1) Introduction

The enormous and increasing number of children not receiving parental support came to the attention of Congress primarily in the form of a fiscal fact—the crescendoing cost of Aid to Families with Dependent Children (AFDC). AFDC was devised during the Depression to support orphans and was never expected to be a major social welfare program. However, the number of children receiving AFDC who were left with only one parent because of divorce, separation, or abandonment as well as those born out of wedlock increased dramatically, from 818,000 in 1950 to 6,062,000 in 1974. In 1974, only 26.4% were the beneficiaries of child support orders, and few of those orders were enforced. In 1981, one child in five was living with only one parent, and it was estimated in 1983 that half of all children born would sometime live in a single parent family headed by a female.

Providing assistance to these children burdened federal and state budgets. In 1981, 7.7 million children were receiving AFDC, and between 1960 and 1983, the cost of AFDC payments increased from $1.0 billion to $13.8 billion. Lawmakers agreed that absent parents not only owed it to their children to support them, but also owed it to the American taxpayers. Out of this agreement came the federal child-support enforcement program, Title IV–D of the Social Security Act, which was signed into law in early 1975 and amended significantly in 1981 (Omnibus Budget Reconciliation Act), 1984 (Child Support Enforcement Amendments), and 1988 (Family Support Act). 42 USCA §§ 651–669. Using this program, states may and in many respects must collect child or spousal support payments owed families on whose behalf AFDC, Medicaid, or foster care payments have been made. A November 1975 Senate Finance Committee staff report summarized Congress's intentions:

> The committee believed that all children have the right to receive support from their fathers. The committee bill is designed to help children attain this right, including the right to have their fathers identified so that support can be obtained. The immediate result will be a lower welfare cost to the taxpayer but, more importantly, as an effective support collection system is established fathers will be deterred from deserting their families to welfare and the children will be spared the effects of family breakup.

The federal program primarily gives states the means to enforce child support obligations more efficiently. Relatively effective enforcement measures are mandated, and states must comply or risk losing funding for their AFDC programs. 42 USCA § 666. Recognizing the difficulties with the RURESA program and other attempts at interstate enforcement—cumbersome procedures, the difficulties encountered locating the absent parent, and the risk of apathy towards these cases in overworked prosecutors' offices—the program commands states to utilize enforcement programs such as tax-refund interception and income-withholding for interstate cases as well as single state cases. 42 USCA § 654 (8)(C). In addition, a parent-locator service was established to assist state agencies and other obligees find the obligor, his social security number, and his employer. 42 USCA § 653. The federal program also provides states with funding and incentive payments, technical assistance for upgrading data management capabilities, and information gathered by the Office of Child Support Enforcement. 42 USCA § 652.

The federal government has continued to tinker with these enforcement remedies. In addition to the remedies described above and those traditionally available for enforcing contractual obligations, the child support enforcement arsenal includes deductions from federal civil service retirement pay, 5 USCA § 8346 (1994); from income from United

States or District of Columbia employment, 42 USCA § 659 (since 1975); and from tax refunds which are subject to qualified domestic relations orders, 26 USCA § 414. Under 42 USCA § 666 (7), which prescribes procedures for wage withholding, child-support garnishment is to be given priority over any other kind of garnishment.

The federal program establishes guidelines and minimum standards for state programs and requires them to establish a child-support enforcement office, commonly called the IV–D agency, to administer the state program. 42 USCA § 654. AFDC recipients must assign both child and spousal support entitlements to this agency for collection. The state agency collects the support from the obligor to reimburse the state for public assistance paid to the obligee, although the state can collect spousal support only if the recipient is a custodial parent. Non–AFDC recipients can register with the agency for child-support enforcement assistance, usually upon the payment of a fee. 42 USCA § 654 (6). AFDC recipients and other obligees registered with the IV–D agency for child support enforcement services are called IV–D agency clients. Some enforcement programs are available to non-clients. Families that do not receive public assistance are granted access to these enforcement measures in hopes that some families which would otherwise be forced onto the welfare rolls will remain self-supporting.

The federal program also recognizes that one of the biggest problems facing obligees wishing to enforce support orders is delay, particularly delay caused by crowded dockets. The program calls for expedited procedures for establishing and enforcing child support orders. § 666 (a)(2). These usually involve quasi-judicial procedures and personnel, the nature and precise responsibilities of which vary from state to state. Orders entered in an abbreviated quasi-judicial procedure must be given the same force and effect as other court orders. However, procedural safeguards must be observed. States must resolve 90% of all cases within three months and 100% of all cases within one year or lose funding for AFDC, unless an exception is granted by the Department of Health and Human Services.

States are encouraged to set up child-support clearinghouses—agencies through which child support payments can be made so that a clear record of payments is available. § 666 (c). This service is to be available to all parents, regardless of IV–D client status or of whether arrearages have accumulated. Such a system can be helpful to both obligors and obligees, particularly when questions of delinquency arise.

Congress has strengthened the national commitment to child-support enforcement by providing for withholding or garnishment where child support is owed by employees of the federal government and the District of Columbia and by members of the military. 42 USCA §§ 659, 661, 665. Congress has also granted federal courts jurisdiction over child-support enforcement cases certified by the Secretary of Health and Human Services, whatever the amount in controversy. 42 USCA § 660. Finally, Congress put national resources at the disposal of the states, including the newly formed parent-locator service, the power to intercept federal income tax refunds of delinquent obligors, statistics available to the federal government, and money. These resources are available because of the political support for this program, support due partly to the fact that collecting child support both benefits the fisc and enforces a widely approved obligation.

The federal legislation also recognizes that a major problem with child support had been the disparity of amounts awarded. The Act thus requires states to adopt guidelines for child-support awards. § 667. These guidelines cannot simply list factors to consider when making awards, but must be actual formulas for calculating amounts. They must serve as rebuttable presumptions in setting support awards.

Another facet of the Child Support Enforcement Program deals with establishing paternity to help the growing number of children born out of wedlock, particularly those who end up on the welfare rolls, by establishing the child's paternity so a child support order can be entered. The mother of a child born out of wedlock must disclose the putative father's name to receive AFDC benefits unless good cause (e.g., rape, incest) can be shown. The state then brings a paternity suit to establish the identity of the child's legal father and his obligation to pay child support. The program encourages states to devise a simple process whereby fathers can voluntarily acknowledge paternity and a simple procedure for establishing paternity in contested cases. § 668. With current technology, paternity can be established quite accurately with blood-group or genetic tests. The state pays for such tests where the mother receives AFDC but may charge a fee to cover the cost of genetic paternity tests for other cases. The federal government provides subsidies ranging to 90% of the cost of tests. The federal program also requires states to permit paternity suits at least until the child's eighteenth birthday. § 666 (a)(5). This followed the striking down by the Supreme Court of one, two, and six year statutes of limitations for paternity suits on equal protection grounds. *Mills v. Habluetzel*, 456 US 91 (1982); *Pickett v. Brown*, 462 US 1 (1983); and *Clark v. Jeter*, 486 US 456 (1988). In some limited circumstances, a finding of paternity can lead to a retroactive child-support award.

These enforcement measures are the cornerstone of the federal child-support enforcement program. Read the following discussions carefully, and consider the implications for each of the parties involved—the obligor, the obligee, the children, and the various governments. Also pay close attention to the changes in relations between state and federal governments caused by these programs.

(2) Wage or Income Withholding

One of the major enforcement measures mandated by the 1984 Child Support Amendments and the Family Support Act of 1988 is wage or income withholding. Withholding of various kinds had for some time been used in many states, among them New York and California. In New

York City, collection rates were 80% for support orders with an automatic wage withholding provision, but only 40% for those without. However, there were problems with employer cooperation and the voluntary nature of most of those programs. In addition, judges often feared employers would fire or refuse to hire parents subject to wage withholding. The federal legislation attempts to solve those problems and to make wage or income withholding the enforcement measure of choice.

Title 42 USCA, Chapter 7, Title IV–D, § 666 (a)(1), requires each state to phase in the use, among other enforcement measures, of income withholding (and, under (b)(8), withholding from other forms of income, like commissions). Subparagraph (8) provides that child support orders enforced by the IV–D agency generally must "include provision for withholding from wages, in order to assure that withholding as a means of collecting child support is available if arrearages occur without the necessity of filing application for services under this part." Orders must include withholding provisions even if the obligee is not receiving enforcement assistance from the IV–D agency.

Under the program, an amount equal to the sum of the support obligation and any fee payable to the employer is withheld from wages due the obligor. § 666 (b). If there are arrearages, an additional amount may be withheld as well. However, the total amount withheld is ordinarily limited to the maximum garnishable amount permitted by the Consumer Credit Protection Act, i.e. 60% of disposable income or 50% of disposable income if the obligor has a second family.

Wage withholding must be automatically available to all IV–D clients. It must also be available to non-clients (the general public) upon filing with the IV–D agency. In neither case may a state require an applicant for a withholding order to obtain an amendment of the original support order or seek any other court or administrative action by the entity which issued the order. § 666 (b)(2).

The 1988 Family Support Act added a provision that eased wage withholding. The wages of any parent under any support order that is issued or modified after that date and which is being enforced by the IV–D agency is subject to withholding whether or not the parent is in arrears, except where (1) one party shows and the court finds that there is good cause not to require income withholding or (2) both parties agree in writing on alternative arrangements. § 666 (b)(3)(A). In cases not covered by this provision, states must make wages subject to withholding the moment arrearages equal the amount of support due for one month, although states may, if they wish, select an even earlier point to begin withholding. In effect, the federal government is permitting the states to have mandatory immediate wage withholding in all cases. Withholding can also be commenced without regard to whether arrearages have accumulated at the request of the absent, obligated parent or, if the state approves, at the request of the custodial parent. § 666 (b)(3)(B).

Withholding measures must comply with state procedural-due-process requirements, and the state must notify obligees that they are subject to wage withholding and that they may challenge withholding "on the grounds that withholding (including the amount to be withheld) is not proper in the case involved because of mistakes of fact." § 666 (b)(4)(A). The state must review any such contention within forty-five days, must tell the parent of its decision and the date withholding will begin, and must provide the parent any information provided to the parent's employer. § 666 (b)(4)(A).

The withholding program must be administered by a state agency or by a private agency operating under state supervision (e.g., a bank or financial institution). Amounts withheld must be expeditiously disbursed, and the agency collecting and distributing such funds must be publicly accountable and capable of recording and monitoring support payments. § 666 (b)(5).

Since employer cooperation was a major problem encountered by states attempting to initiate wage withholding mechanisms, the Act insists that the state provide sanctions should an employer fail to cooperate. "The employer must be held liable to the State for any amount which such employer fails to withhold from wages due an employee following receipt by such employer of proper notice...." § 666 (b)(6)(C). In addition, "[p]rovision must be made for the imposition of a fine against any employer who discharges from employment, refuses to employ, or takes disciplinary action against any absent parent subject to wage withholding required by this subsection because of the existence of such withholding and the obligations or additional obligations which it imposes upon the employer." § 666 (b)(6)(D).

The Act also provides that child-support payments collected this way take priority over any other legal claim under state law against the same wages. § 666 (b)(7). This is consistent with other provisions, such as § 656, which provides that child-support debts are not dischargeable in bankruptcy.

This enforcement mechanism also works in interstate cases. § 666 (b)(9) provides that "such system will include withholding from income derived within such State in cases where the applicable support orders were issued in other States, in order to assure that child support owed by absent parents in such State or any State will be collected without regard to the residence of the child for whom the support is payable or such child's custodial parent."

Questions on Wage Withholding

(1) You are the attorney for a father during a divorce proceeding. The mother will retain custody of the couple's two minor children. How will you advise your client in light of these provisions? Which of the income-withholding provisions most affects your client's interests?

(2) You represent the mother. How does automatic income withholding affect your client's interests? How will you advise her?

(3) Taking the position of the father, think about your reaction to these provisions. How does this program affect your attitudes toward child support, your children, your former spouse, and the law?

(4) Now assume the role of a delinquent absent parent whose wages are subject to withholding. What is your reaction to the program? Does it depend on the reason you have fallen behind? Is your reaction different if you have a second family? Does withholding make it easier or harder to pay child support if you have a second family? Consider *Felisa L.D. v. Allen M.*, 433 NYS2d 715 (NY Fam Ct 1980). When the parties divorced, the mother received custody, and the father was ordered to pay child support. He remarried and remained at home to care for the young children of the second marriage. His new wife was employed. The court noted that the theory behind New York's equitable distribution law is that marriage is an economic partnership, so that all property and money accumulated during the marriage belong to both spouses jointly. Therefore, the court reasoned that the $10,300 annual earnings of the second wife could be used by the husband to meet his support obligations.

(5) You are an attorney for the local IV–D agency who is responsible for collecting child support on behalf of welfare recipients. Does this program make your job easier? In what cases do you foresee difficulties?

(3) Tax Refund Offset

42 USCA § 664 was introduced as part of the Omnibus Budget Reconciliation Act of 1981 and has been revised several times. It enacts a program designed to intercept federal (and state—see § 666 (a)(3)(A)) tax refunds due to delinquent obligors and to apply the proceeds to child support (and occasionally spousal support) obligations due to obligees or to state agencies providing public assistance to obligees. Tax refund interception offers advantages: it is an administrative, rather than a judicial, remedy which requires little effort or information on the part of the obligee and which can be carried out with comparatively little additional effort by the bureaucracy. However, it cannot be used to collect ongoing child-support obligations, and it can be used only when arrearages of $500 or more have accumulated.

State IV–D agencies are designated to identify cases in which federal income tax refund offsets may be used. Before referring a case to the Secretary of Treasury, the state must notify the obligor that support delinquencies will be recovered from any refund owed him. The notice must also tell him how he can contest the state's determination of how much he owes and how he can protect the portion of the refund owed another person if a joint return was filed. § 664 (a)(1) authorizes the Secretary of Treasury, upon notice from a state IV–D agency that sufficient arrearages have accrued under a child or spousal support obligation which has been assigned to the state, to withhold that amount from a federal income tax refund due the obligor. § 664 (a)(2) authorizes such action for non-agency clients wishing to collect child (but not spousal) support due. The Secretary of Treasury must notify the obligor whose refund has been intercepted and anyone with whom that obligor may have filed a joint return. The money collected is then paid to the state agency for distribution. Where support payments have not been assigned to the state for collection, the Secretary of the Treasury may charge the obligee a fee of $25. 42 USCA § 666 (a)(3) requires states to implement a similar program for refunds of state income tax. This program must be available to all obligees, including those not IV–D clients, although a fee may be charged non-clients.

The tax refund offset program has occasioned much litigation. There has been debate about what steps, beyond prior notice of the interception, are necessary to satisfy due process requirements. Because the obligor had due process protection when the original child support obligation was imposed, some courts set relatively low standards for due process in intercept cases. However, this is not the case when the offset involves a joint return and the property rights of a non-obligated taxpayer are involved. Cases such as *Coughlin v. Regan*, 584 F Supp 697 (D Me 1984), *aff'd*, 768 F2d 468 (1st Cir 1985); and *Jahn v. Regan*, 584 F Supp 399 (ED Mich 1984), led to amendments of the law to provide explicit safeguards for the portions of refunds due non-obligated taxpayers in the case of joint returns.

(4) Parent Locator Service

One frustration encountered by parents or state agencies trying to enforce support orders is locating the absent parent. Many custodial parents find themselves financially strapped, particularly when support payments are delinquent, and cannot afford to track down the obligor. The Parent Locator Service, created within the Department of Health and Human Services as part of the federal Child Support Enforcement program, lessens that burden by putting the data resources of the federal government at the disposal of local child-support enforcement agencies. In addition, all states must provide parent locator services which can draw information from state records as well as from the federal parent locator. 42 USCA § 654 (8). These services are available to all parents seeking to enforce support orders, not just those receiving AFDC benefits.

Section 653 (a) establishes HHS's parent locator service, "which shall be used to obtain and transmit to any authorized person ... information as to the whereabouts of an absent parent for the purpose of enforcing support obligations against such parent." Subsection (d) allows the Secretary to decide how applications must be made and what information or documentation the applicant must provide. A search may be initiated by the parent, guardian, attorney, or agent of the child to whom support is owed, even if a court order for support has not been issued. States seeking to recover amounts due in child and spousal support assigned to them and courts having authority to enter a support order against an absent parent may also use the service. § 653 (c).

Once the request is filed, the Secretary of HHS may release the social security number and address and employer of any absent parent if that information is available from the files of HHS or the files of "any of the departments, agencies, or instrumentalities of the United States or any State." § 653 (e)(1). The only exception is when the release of information would "contravene national policy or security interests of the United States or the confidentiality of census data." § 653 (b)(2). Special provisions are made for "prompt access for the Secretary ... to the wage and unemployment compensation claims information and data maintained by or for the Department of Labor or State employment security agencies." § 653 (e)(3). A fee may be charged to parents but not to states or courts.

The Department must arrange with state child-support enforcement agencies for those agencies to accept requests for information about absent parents and to transmit those requests to HHS.

Other amendments to the Social Security Act provide that states must cooperate in providing wage and unemployment compensation information to the parent locator service or risk losing funding for unemployment compensation. 42 USCA § 503 (h). Since November 1990 all state laws regulating birth certificates have required the disclosure of the parents' social security numbers or a showing of why they should not be disclosed. The numbers are to be released or used only in enforcing a child support order. 42 USC § 405 (2000).

Questions on the Parent Locator Service

(1) What objections might be raised against this program? What about privacy rights? Interaction among agencies of the federal government? Federalism? What considerations balance these objections?

(2) Even an "omniscient" program needs a starting point. As a IV–D attorney, what information would you seek from an obligee in order to utilize the parent locator service? When would the program be most helpful?

(3) Recall that birth certificates of children born after November 1990 will include the social security numbers of both parents, which are to be used only in the event of a child support order. What does this say about our attitudes towards parents and parenting? The rights of children? Does this indicate a loss of faith in the traditional family or an affirmation of it?

A Problem

Melissa and Chris married in 1988. Chris is a petty officer in the Navy, and Melissa is a bank teller. They have three children, Katie (1990), Patrick (1992), and Megan (1994). After seven years of marital strife primarily about Chris's frequent absences from home, they got divorced in 1995. Melissa retains custody of the children. Chris was ordered to pay child support and granted reasonable visitation rights.

In 1996, Chris remarried; his wife Alyce has a daughter, Amanda (1993), from her first marriage. While Alyce had worked as a waitress, after the birth of a son, Eddie (1997), they have decided she should stay home with the children, and the family is supported solely by Chris's pay and sporadic child-support payments from Amanda's father. The budget is tight, and Alyce resents the monthly payments made to Melissa and her children, particularly when she and her children must economize. Chris resents having to send money to Melissa and the children. Alyce's former husband does little to support Amanda. In addition, he thinks about Melissa and the children less and less, as his time when he is not at sea is consumed with his new family and responsibilities. He found himself "forgetting" to send support checks, first occasionally, when his new family faced some big expense, then regularly.

Meanwhile, Melissa is having difficulty raising the children on her own. She continues to work at the bank, but child care expenses are large. She has had to sell their townhouse and move with the children to a cramped apartment in a less desirable location. She depends on the child-support payments for basic living expenses, and when the checks do not arrive, she is frantic and must do without or ask her relatives for loans and other assistance. When Chris begins to miss payments regularly, she turns to the local IV–D agency for enforcement assistance.

Questions on the Problem

(1) You are the IV–D attorney to whom Melissa turns. What advice will you give to her? What sorts of enforcement measures do you think will be most effective in this case?

(2) Suppose that Chris's child support payments are 30% of his income (not unlikely with 3 children) and that their payment means severe hardship for his new family. Is he justified in denying support to his "old" family in order to support his "new" family? Should Alyce be forced to go to work so that Chris can pay his child support? How many people can have legitimate claims upon Chris's income for support? Whose claims should take precedence?

The Problem Continued

In 1998 Melissa marries Michael, a wealthy officer at the bank where she works. They think it would be inappropriate for her to work there, and she is content to stay home with the children. In 1999 Melissa and Michael have a son, Andrew. Even without Melissa's salary, Michael is well able to support her and all four children at a level higher than Chris could. Chris's child support payments, now regularly made through income withholding by the Navy, are put in a special account which Michael and Melissa intend to give to Katie, Patrick and Megan when they are of age. The children rarely see Chris and begin to look to Michael for emotional as well as financial support.

At the same time, Chris's family is under further economic strain from the birth of Amy in 1999. Alyce is still not working. Attempts to collect child support from Amanda's father have been fruitless, as he has fled the state and efforts to trace him have come to naught. Chris does not resent Melissa's remarriage, but he feels it isn't fair that he must pay child support when the children have another source of support. While income withholding makes paying the child support easier, he finds it difficult to deny his new family money they truly need to make payments to other children whom he rarely sees and who apparently have no current "need" for the money.

Questions on the Problem Continued

(1) How does Melissa's second family affect your perception of Chris's child support obligation? Does Michael's relative affluence affect Chris's duty to support the children? Does the fact Chris's payments are saved rather than spent mean the children have no needs?

(2) What does the federal legislation reveal about the legal perceptions of child support? In that view, is a father ever relieved of the duty to support his children? Should he be?

(3) Suppose Melissa and Michael got divorced. Who would be responsible for supporting Katie, Patrick and Megan? If you say Michael, on what do you base his duty to support those children?

A Second Problem

Nicole was 16, unmarried, and a high school student when her baby, Sam, was born. She assumed the father was her former boyfriend, Tim, now in the Army and stationed in another state. She had broken up with him shortly before she discovered she was pregnant, and because he was far away physically and emotionally she never told him about the child. While she named Tim as the father for the birth certificate, she thought her pregnancy might have resulted from a short fling with Joe, a college student she met at a cousin's wedding in another city.

After the baby was born, Nicole continued living with her parents. Her mother agreed to help with Sam if Nicole continued to go to school. However, Nicole found the arrangement difficult. She and her parents argued about the baby, and she resented the interference Sam represented in her life. Her parents finally told her to find a job or leave their house. Her skills were marginal, but she found a part-time job as a telemarketer. This worked as long as her mother cared for Sam while she was at work. However, when Nicole was 20 and Sam was 4, Nicole's grandmother became ill and came to live with Nicole's parents. Nicole was told she was no longer welcome at home.

Mother and child moved in with a friend, but she could not afford rent, food, and child care on her income. She applied for AFDC benefits. She was eligible but was required to provide information for a paternity suit so a child-support order could be established. She named Tim as the father. The IV–D agency initiated a paternity suit.

Questions on the Second Problem

(1) As the IV–D attorney, what will your primary concerns be when attempting to establish a child support order in this case? What enforcement tools will you need to use? How will you advise Nicole?

(2) From Tim's perspective, what will your primary concerns be?

(3) As Tim's attorney, how will you advise him?

The Second Problem Continued

The blood tests performed to establish paternity prove Tim could not be Sam's father. The IV–D agency presses Nicole to name the real father. Nicole admits that Joe might be the father, but she knows only his name and the city where she met him. The IV–D agency uses the parent locator service and learns Joe is still living there. He is a promising young stock broker, newly married. The state institutes a paternity suit to establish a child support order, and a blood test confirms Joe is Sam's father.

Questions on the Second Problem Continued

(1) What are the short-and long-term ramifications of this paternity suit?

(2) How will establishing of a support order affect Nicole's life? Joe's life? Sam's life?

(3) What is the state's interest in this paternity suit? Are there times the state should not pursue such suits? Is this one?

(4) What does the state's willingness (indeed eagerness) to pursue such suits say about the rights of children? About state power? About privacy?

And a Third Problem

Steve and Anne Lewis married in 1975. They had three children before they divorced in 1984. Anne was awarded custody, and Steve was ordered to pay child support and granted reasonable visitation rights. In 1989, Steve's child support payments stopped.

Questions on the Third Problem

As Anne's attorney, how will you help her enforce her child support order in the following situations?

(1) Anne knows Steve is a car salesman in Hutchins, which is not her home state. His income is derived solely from commissions. In Hutchins, income-withholding can be instituted against commissions. Now suppose that in Hutchins income withholding is applicable to wage income only.

(2) Steve is an auto worker. When Anne last heard from him, he was working for Ford in Detroit, but her contacts there tell her he has moved and left no forwarding address. Anne knows that he has received unemployment compensation in the past. She also knows his union affiliation. Now suppose Anne knows he now works for Nissan in Tennessee.

(3) Steve is a major league baseball player. Anne knows where he is from watching the nightly news. His contract negotiations are publicized and she knows how much income he receives.

(4) Steve is a policy analyst in the diplomatic corps. When he last contacted her, he was assigned to the mission in Liberia. Anne has no idea where he is. Now suppose she knows he is in Washington. Suppose she knows he is in Indonesia. Suppose she knows he has left government service. Suppose she suspects he really works for the CIA.

(5) Steve's last job was as a waiter. He has always been a drifter and has always preferred to be paid in cash, which he doesn't report to the government. Anne has no idea where he is. Suppose Anne knows the last city in which he worked.

(6) Steve is a salaried computer programmer who lives in the same city as Anne and works for the same company. Suppose he has moved. Suppose Anne knows he is in the Army Reserves.

(7) Steve is a dentist with his own practice.

BIBLIOGRAPHY

Payment of Child Support. Judith A. Seltzer et al., *Family Ties after Divorce: The Relationship between Visiting and Paying Child Support*, 51 J Marriage & Family 1013 (1989), argues that the more frequent and lengthy the visitation, the more will be paid in support. Margaret F. Brinig, Carl E. Schneider and Lee E. Teitelbaum, *Family Law in Action: A Reader* 301–40 (Anderson, 1999), includes articles that show how the way we invest in children has changed and how child support might better be enforced. For two economists' views of why noncustodial parents don't pay child support, see Yoram Weiss and Robert Willis, *Children as Collective Goods in Divorce Settlements*, 3 J Lab Econ 268 (1985). The article suggests that noncustodial parents fail to pay child support because they cannot monitor how these payments are being spent and because they know that part of every dollar sent for child support will go for goods enjoyed by the custodial parent. Milton C. Regan, *The Boundaries of Care: Constructing Community After Divorce*, 31 Houston L Rev 425 (1994), suggests that while divorce severs some aspects of a couple's relationship, other parts continue so that the parent-child community is not the only one to survive divorce.

Collection of Child Support. An extensive study of the success of recent efforts to improve the system for the support of children is Andrea H. Beller and John W. Graham, *Small Change: The Economics of Child Support* (Yale U Press, 1993). Professor Chambers' book, of which you read an excerpt, is reviewed by Professor Mnookin in 48 U Chi L Rev 338 (1981). For a look at the problems procedural associated with child-support enforcement, see Gary B. Melton, *Children, Families and the Courts in the Twenty-First Century*, 66 S Cal L Rev 1993 (1993), which advocates rules to cope with today's complex and stress-filled families.

Chapter XII

PARENT, CHILD, COMMUNITY, STATE: DILEMMAS OF PLURALISM

There she lies, the great Melting–Pot—listen! . . . There gapes her mouth . . . the harbor where a thousand mammoth feeders come from the ends of the world to pour in their human freight. Ah, what a stirring and a seething! Celt and Latin, Slav and Teuton, Greek and Syrian, black and yellow. . . . Yes, East and West, and North and South, the palm and the pine, the pole and the equator, the crescent and the cross—how the great Alchemist melts and fuses them with his purging flame! Here shall they all unite to build the Republic of Man and the Kingdom of God. Ah, Vera, what is the glory of Rome and Jerusalem where all nations and races come to worship and look back, compared with the glory of America, where all races and nations come to labour and look forward!

Israel Zangwill
The Melting–Pot

Throughout this casebook, the issue of pluralism has lain in the background and has often been propelled into the foreground. In this chapter, we will examine the intersection of pluralism and family law in a concentrated way. We will do so by considering two contexts: first, where parental authority to control children's education meets the state's authority to ensure that children achieve some minimal education; second, where religion, race, and ethnicity become issues in disputes over the custody or adoption of a child.

SECTION 1. EDUCATION AND CULTURAL CONFLICT

It is so generally taken for granted that a life strictly dedicated to religion is stiff and dreary, that I may have some difficulty in persuading my readers that . . . we were always cheerful and often gay. . . . My Father and Mother lived so completely in the atmosphere of faith, and were so utterly convinced of their intercourse with God, that, so long as that intercourse was not clouded by sin, to which they were delicately

> *sensitive, they could afford to take the passing hour very lightly. They would even, to a certain extent, treat the surroundings of their religion as a subject of jest, joking very mildly and gently about such things as an attitude at prayer or the nature of a supplication. . . .*
>
> *The mere fact that I had no young companions, no story books, no outdoor amusements, none of the thousand and one employments provided for other children in more conventional surroundings, did not make me discontented or fretful, because I did not know of the existence of such entertainments. In exchange, I became keenly attentive to the limited circle of interests open to me.*
>
> **Edmund Gosse**
> *Father and Son*

In all states parents are obliged by law to send their children to school, usually until the children are sixteen. As you remember from *Pierce v. Society of Sisters*, parents are constitutionally entitled to send their children to private schools, but the state may set minimum standards for them. What if, however, the parents refuse to send their children to school altogether, and claim a religious basis for doing so? A classic case—*Wisconsin v. Yoder*—examines that question, which we further explore with a decision—*Mozert v. Hawkins County Board of Education*—that raises similar issues in what may be an even more challenging context.

WISCONSIN v. YODER

Supreme Court of the United States, 1972
406 US 205

BURGER, C.J. . . .

Respondents Jonas Yoder and Wallace Miller are members of the Old Order Amish religion, and respondent Adin Yutzy is a member of the Conservative Amish Mennonite Church. They and their families are residents of Green County, Wisconsin. Wisconsin's compulsory school-attendance law required them to cause their children to attend public or private school until reaching age 16 but the respondents declined to send their children, ages 14 and 15, to public school after they completed the eighth grade. The children were not enrolled in any private school, or within any recognized exception to the compulsory-attendance law, and they are conceded to be subject to the Wisconsin statute.

On complaint of the school district administrator for the public schools, respondents were charged, tried, and convicted of violating the compulsory-attendance law in Green County Court and were fined the sum of $5 each. Respondents defended on the ground that the application of the compulsory-attendance law violated their rights under the First and Fourteenth Amendments. The trial testimony showed that respondents believed, in accordance with the tenets of Old Order Amish communities generally, that their children's attendance at high school, public or private, was contrary to the Amish religion and way of life.

They believed that by sending their children to high school, they would not only expose themselves to the danger of the censure of the church community, but, as found by the county court, also endanger their own salvation and that of their children. The State stipulated that respondents' religious beliefs were sincere.

In support of their position, respondents presented as expert witnesses scholars on religion and education whose testimony is uncontradicted. They expressed their opinions on the relationship of the Amish belief concerning school attendance to the more general tenets of their religion, and described the impact that compulsory high school attendance could have on the continued survival of Amish communities as they exist in the United States today. The history of the Amish sect was given in some detail, beginning with the Swiss Anabaptists of the 16th century who rejected institutionalized churches and sought to return to the early, simple, Christian life de-emphasizing material success, rejecting the competitive spirit, and seeking to insulate themselves from the modern world. As a result of their common heritage, Old Order Amish communities today are characterized by a fundamental belief that salvation requires life in a church community separate and apart from the world and worldly influence. This concept of life aloof from the world and its values is central to their faith.

A related feature of Old Order Amish communities is their devotion to a life in harmony with nature and the soil, as exemplified by the simple life of the early Christian era that continued in America during much of our early national life. Amish beliefs require members of the community to make their living by farming or closely related activities. Broadly speaking, the Old Order Amish religion pervades and determines the entire mode of life of its adherents. Their conduct is regulated in great detail by the *Ordnung*, or rules, of the church community. Adult baptism, which occurs in late adolescence, is the time at which Amish young people voluntarily undertake heavy obligations, not unlike the Bar Mitzvah of the Jews, to abide by the rules of the church community.

Amish objection to formal education beyond the eighth grade is firmly grounded in these central religious concepts. They object to the high school, and higher education generally, because the values they teach are in marked variance with Amish values and the Amish way of life; they view secondary school education as an impermissible exposure of their children to a "worldly" influence in conflict with their beliefs. The high school tends to emphasize intellectual and scientific accomplishments, self-distinction, competitiveness, worldly success, and social life with other students. Amish society emphasizes informal learning-through-doing; a life of "goodness," rather than a life of intellect; wisdom, rather than technical knowledge; community welfare, rather than competition; and separation from, rather than integration with, contemporary worldly society.

Formal high school education beyond the eighth grade is contrary to Amish beliefs, not only because it places Amish children in an environment hostile to Amish beliefs with increasing emphasis on competition in class work and sports and with pressure to conform to the styles, manners, and ways of the peer group, but also because it takes them away from their community, physically and emotionally, during the crucial and formative adolescent period of life. During this period, the children must acquire Amish attitudes favoring manual work and self-reliance and the specific skills needed to perform the adult role of an Amish farmer or housewife. They must learn to enjoy physical labor. Once a child has learned basic reading, writing, and elementary mathematics, these traits, skills, and attitudes admittedly fall within the category of those best learned through example and "doing" rather than in a classroom. And, at this time in life, the Amish child must also grow in his faith and his relationship to the Amish community if he is to be prepared to accept the heavy obligations imposed by adult baptism. In short, high school attendance with teachers who are not of the Amish faith—and may even be hostile to it—interposes a serious barrier to the integration of the Amish child into the Amish religious community. Dr. John Hostetler, one of the experts on Amish society, testified that the modern high school is not equipped, in curriculum or social environment, to impart the values promoted by Amish society.

The Amish do not object to elementary education through the first eight grades as a general proposition because they agree that their children must have basic skills in the "three R's" in order to read the Bible, to be good farmers and citizens, and to be able to deal with non-Amish people when necessary in the course of daily affairs. They view such a basic education as acceptable because it does not significantly expose their children to worldly values or interfere with their development in the Amish community during the crucial adolescent period. While Amish accept compulsory elementary education generally, wherever possible they have established their own elementary schools in many respects like the small local schools of the past. In the Amish belief higher learning tends to develop values they reject as influences that alienate man from God.

On the basis of such considerations, Dr. Hostetler testified that compulsory high school attendance could not only result in great psychological harm to Amish children, because of the conflicts it would produce, but would also, in his opinion, ultimately result in the destruction of the Old Order Amish church community as it exists in the United States today. The testimony of Dr. Donald A. Erickson, an expert witness on education, also showed that the Amish succeed in preparing their high school age children to be productive members of the Amish community. He described their system of learning through doing the skills directly relevant to their adult roles in the Amish community as "ideal" and perhaps superior to ordinary high school education. The evidence also showed that the Amish have an excellent record as law-abiding and generally self-sufficient members of society.

Although the trial court in its careful findings determined that the Wisconsin compulsory school-attendance law "does interfere with the freedom of the Defendants to act in accordance with their sincere religious belief" it also concluded that the requirement of high school attendance until age 16 was a "reasonable and constitutional" exercise of governmental power, and therefore denied the motion to dismiss the charges. The Wisconsin Circuit Court affirmed the convictions. The Wisconsin Supreme Court, however, sustained respondents' claim under the Free Exercise Clause of the First Amendment and reversed the convictions. A majority of the court was of the opinion that the State had failed to make an adequate showing that its interest in "establishing and maintaining an educational system overrides the defendants' right to the free exercise of their religion."

I

There is no doubt as to the power of a State, having a high responsibility for education of its citizens, to impose reasonable regulations for the control and duration of basic education. See, *e.g., Pierce v. Society of Sisters*, 268 U.S. 510, 534 (1925). Providing public schools ranks at the very apex of the function of a State. Yet even this paramount responsibility was, in *Pierce*, made to yield to the right of parents to provide an equivalent education in a privately operated system. There the Court held that Oregon's statute compelling attendance in a public school from age eight to age 16 unreasonably interfered with the interest of parents in directing the rearing of their offspring, including their education in church-operated schools. As that case suggests, the values of parental direction of the religious upbringing and education of their children in their early and formative years have a high place in our society. See also *Ginsberg v. New York*, 390 U.S. 629 (1968); *Meyer v. Nebraska*, 262 U.S. 390 (1923). Thus, a State's interest in universal education, however highly we rank it, is not totally free from a balancing process when it impinges on fundamental rights and interests, such as those specifically protected by the Free Exercise Clause of the First Amendment, and the traditional interest of parents with respect to the religious upbringing of their children so long as they, in the words of *Pierce*, "prepare (them) for additional obligations."

It follows that in order for Wisconsin to compel school attendance beyond the eighth grade against a claim that such attendance interferes with the practice of a legitimate religious belief, it must appear either that the State does not deny the free exercise of religious belief by its requirement, or that there is a state interest of sufficient magnitude to override the interest claiming protection under the Free Exercise Clause. Long before there was general acknowledgment of the need for universal formal education, the Religion Clauses had specifically and firmly fixed the right to free exercise of religious beliefs, and buttressing this fundamental right was an equally firm, even if less explicit, prohibition against the establishment of any religion by government. The values underlying these two provisions relating to religion have been zealously protected, sometimes even at the expense of other interests of admittedly high social importance. The invalidation of financial aid to parochial schools by government grants for a salary subsidy for teachers is but one example of the extent to which courts have gone in this regard, notwithstanding that such aid programs were legislatively determined to be in the public interest and the service of sound educational policy by States and by Congress. *Lemon v. Kurtzman*, 403 U.S. 602 (1971); *Tilton v. Richardson*, 403 U.S. 672 (1971). See also *Everson v. Board of Education*, 330 U.S. 1, 18 (1947).

The essence of all that has been said and written on the subject is that only those interests of the highest order and those not otherwise served can overbalance legitimate claims to the free exercise of religion. We can accept it as settled, therefore, that, however strong the State's interest in universal compulsory education, it is by no means absolute to the exclusion or subordination of all other interests. *E.g., Sherbert v. Verner*, 374 U.S. 398 (1963); *McGowan v. Maryland*, 366 U.S. 420, 459 (1961)(separate opinion of Frankfurter, J.); *Prince v. Massachusetts*, 321 U.S. 158, 165 (1944).

II

We come then to the quality of the claims of the respondents concerning the alleged encroachment of Wisconsin's compulsory school-attendance statute on their rights and the rights of their children to the free exercise of the religious beliefs they and their forbears have adhered to for almost three centuries. In evaluating those claims we must be careful to determine whether the Amish religious faith and their mode of life are, as they claim, inseparable and interdependent. A way of life, however virtuous and admirable, may not be interposed as a barrier to reasonable state regulation of education if it is based on purely secular considerations; to have the protection of the Religion Clauses, the claims must be rooted in religious belief. Although a determination of what is a "religious" belief or practice entitled to constitutional protection may present a most delicate question, the very concept of ordered liberty precludes allowing every person to make his own standards on matters of conduct in which society as a whole has important interests. Thus, if the Amish asserted their claims because of their subjective evaluation and rejection of the contemporary secular values accepted by the majority, much as Thoreau rejected the social values of his time and isolated himself at Walden Pond, their claims would not rest on a religious basis. Thoreau's choice was philosophical and personal rather than religious, and such belief does not rise to the demands of the Religion Clauses.

Giving no weight to such secular considerations, however, we see that the record in this case abundantly supports the claim that the traditional way of life of the Amish is not merely a matter of personal preference, but one of deep religious conviction, shared by an organized group, and intimately related to daily living. That the Old Order Amish daily life and religious practice stem from their faith is shown by the fact that it is in response to their literal interpretation of the Biblical injunction from the Epistle of Paul to the Romans, "be not conformed to this world.... " This command is fundamental to the Amish faith.

Moreover, for the Old Order Amish, religion is not simply a matter of theocratic belief. As the expert witnesses explained, the Old Order Amish religion pervades and determines virtually their entire way of life, regulating it with the detail of the Talmudic diet through the strictly enforced rules of the church community.

The record shows that the respondents' religious beliefs and attitude toward life, family, and home have remained constant—perhaps some would say static—in a period of unparalleled progress in human knowledge generally and great changes in education. The respondents freely concede, and indeed assert as an article of faith, that their religious beliefs and what we would today call "lifestyle" have not altered in fundamentals for centuries. Their way of life in a church-oriented community, separated from the outside world and "worldly" influences, their attachment to nature and the soil, is a way inherently simple and uncomplicated, albeit difficult to preserve against the pressure to conform. Their rejection of telephones, automobiles, radios, and television, their mode of dress, of speech, their habits of manual work do indeed set them apart from much of contemporary society; these customs are both symbolic and practical.

As the society around the Amish has become more populous, urban, industrialized, and complex, particularly in this century, government regulation of human affairs has correspondingly become more detailed and pervasive. The Amish mode of life has thus come into conflict increasingly with requirements of contemporary society exerting a hydraulic insistence on conformity to majoritarian standards. So long as compulsory education laws were confined to eight grades of elementary basic education imparted in a nearby rural schoolhouse, with a large proportion of students of the Amish faith, the Old Order Amish had little basis to fear that school attendance would expose their children to the worldly influence they reject. But modern compulsory secondary education in rural areas is now largely carried on in a consolidated school, often remote from the student's home and alien to his daily home life. As the record so strongly shows, the values and programs of the modern secondary school are in sharp conflict with the fundamental mode of life mandated by the Amish religion; modern laws requiring compulsory secondary education have accordingly engendered great concern and conflict. The conclusion is inescapable that secondary schooling, by exposing Amish children to worldly influences in terms of attitudes, goals, and values contrary to beliefs, and by substantially interfering with the religious development of the Amish child and his integration into the way of life of the Amish faith community at the crucial adolescent stage of development, contravenes the basic religious tenets and practice of the Amish faith, both as to the parent and the child.

The impact of the compulsory-attendance law on respondents' practice of the Amish religion is not only severe, but inescapable, for the Wisconsin law affirmatively compels them, under threat of criminal sanction, to perform acts undeniably at odds with fundamental tenets of their religious beliefs. Nor is the impact of the compulsory-attendance law confined to grave interference with important Amish religious tenets from a subjective point of view. It carries with it precisely the kind of objective danger to the free exercise of religion that the First Amendment was designed to prevent. As the record shows, compulsory school attendance to age 16 for Amish children carries with it a very real threat of undermining the Amish community and religious practice as they exist today; they must either abandon belief and be assimilated into society at large, or be forced to migrate to some other and more tolerant region.

In sum, the unchallenged testimony of acknowledged experts in education and religious history, almost 300 years of consistent practice, and strong evidence of a sustained faith pervading and regulating respondents' entire mode of life support the claim that enforcement of the State's requirement of compulsory formal education after the eighth grade would gravely endanger if not destroy the free exercise of respondents' religious beliefs.

III

Neither the findings of the trial court nor the Amish claims as to the nature of their faith are challenged in this Court by the State of Wisconsin. Its position is that the State's interest in universal compulsory formal secondary education to age 16 is so great that it is paramount to the undisputed claims of respondents that their mode of preparing their youth for Amish life, after the traditional elementary education, is an essential part of their religious belief and practice. Nor does the State undertake to meet the claim that the Amish mode of life and education is inseparable from and a part of the basic tenets of their religion—indeed, as much a part of their religious belief and practices as baptism, the confessional, or a sabbath may be for others.

Wisconsin concedes that under the Religion Clauses religious beliefs are absolutely free from the State's control, but it argues that "actions," even though religiously grounded, are outside the protection of the First Amendment. But our decisions have rejected the idea that religiously grounded conduct is always outside the protection of the Free Exercise Clause. It is true that activities of individuals, even when religiously based, are often subject to regulation by the States in the exercise of their undoubted power to promote the health, safety, and general welfare, or the Federal Government in the exercise of its delegated powers. See, *e.g.*, *Gillette v. United States*, 401 U.S. 437 (1971); *Braunfeld v. Brown*, 366 U.S. 599 (1961); *Prince v. Massachusetts*, 321 U.S. 158 (1944); *Reynolds v. United States*, 98 U.S. 145 (1879). But to agree that religiously grounded conduct must often be subject to the broad police power of the State is not to deny that there are areas of conduct protected by the Free Exercise Clause of the First Amendment and thus beyond the power of the State to control, even under regulations of general applicability. This case, therefore, does not become easier because respondents were convicted for their "actions" in refusing to send their children to the public high school; in this context belief and action cannot be neatly confined in logic-tight compartments.

Nor can this case be disposed of on the grounds that Wisconsin's requirement for school attendance to age 16 applies uniformly to all citizens of the State and does not, on its face, discriminate against religions or a particular religion, or that it is motivated by legitimate secular concerns. A regulation neutral on its face may, in its application, nonetheless offend the constitutional requirement for governmental neutrality if it unduly burdens the free exercise of religion. *Sherbert v. Verner, supra*; cf. *Walz v. Tax Commission*, 397 U.S. 664 (1970). The Court must not ignore the danger that an exception from a general obligation of citizenship on religious grounds may run afoul of the Establishment Clause, but that danger cannot be allowed to prevent any exception no matter how vital it may be to the protection of values promoted by the right of free exercise. By preserving doctrinal flexibility and recognizing the need for a sensible and realistic application of the Religion Clauses

> "we have been able to chart a course that preserved the autonomy and freedom of religious bodies while avoiding any semblance of established religion. This is a 'tight rope' and one we have successfully traversed." *Walz v. Tax Commission, supra*, at 672.

We turn, then, to the State's broader contention that its interest in its system of compulsory education is so compelling that even the established religious practices of the Amish must give way. Where fundamental claims of religious freedom are at stake, however, we cannot accept such a sweeping claim; despite its admitted validity in the generality of cases, we must searchingly examine the interests that the State seeks to promote by its requirement for compulsory education to age 16, and the impediment to those objectives that would flow from recognizing the claimed Amish exemption.

The State advances two primary arguments in support of its system of compulsory education. It notes, as Thomas Jefferson pointed out early in our history, that some degree of education is necessary to prepare citizens to participate effectively and intelligently in our open political system if we are to preserve freedom and independence. Further, education prepares individuals to be self-reliant and self-sufficient participants in society. We accept these propositions.

However, the evidence adduced by the Amish in this case is persuasively to the effect that an additional one or two years of formal high school for Amish children in place of their long-established program of informal vocational education would do little to serve those interests. Respondents' experts testified at trial, without challenge, that the value of all education must be assessed in terms of its capacity to prepare the child for life. It is one thing to say that compulsory education for a year or two beyond the eighth grade may be necessary when its goal is the preparation of the child for life in modern society as the majority live, but it is quite another if the goal of education be viewed as the preparation of the child for life in the separated agrarian community that is the keystone of the Amish faith. See *Meyer v. Nebraska.*

The State attacks respondents' position as one fostering "ignorance" from which the child must be protected by the State. No one can question the State's duty to protect children from ignorance but this argument does not square with the facts disclosed in the record. Whatever their idiosyncrasies as seen by the majority, this record strongly shows that the Amish community has been a highly successful social unit within our society, even if apart from the conventional "mainstream." Its members are productive and very law-abiding members of society; they reject public welfare in any of its usual modern forms. The Congress itself recognized their self-sufficiency by authorizing exemption of such groups as the Amish from the obligation to pay social security taxes.

It is neither fair nor correct to suggest that the Amish are opposed to education beyond the eighth grade level. What this record shows is that they are opposed to conventional formal education of the type provided by a certified high school because it comes at the child's crucial adolescent period of religious development. Dr. Donald Erickson, for example, testified that their system of learning-by-doing was an "ideal system" of education in terms of preparing Amish children for life as adults in the Amish community, and that "I would be inclined to say they do a better job in this than most of the rest of us do." As he put it, "These people aren't purporting to be learned people, and it seems to me the self-sufficiency of the community is the best evidence I can point to—whatever is being done seems to function well."

We must not forget that in the Middle Ages important values of the civilization of the Western World were preserved by members of religious orders who isolated themselves from all worldly influences against great obstacles. There can be no assumption that today's majority is "right" and the Amish and others like them are "wrong." A way of life that is odd or even erratic but interferes with no rights or interests of others is not to be condemned because it is different.

The State, however, supports its interest in providing an additional one or two years of compulsory high school education to Amish children because of the possibility that some such children will choose to leave the Amish community, and that if this occurs they will be ill-equipped for life. The State argues that if Amish children leave their church they should not be in the position of making their way in the world without the education available in the one or two additional years the State requires. However, on this record, that argument is highly speculative. There is no specific evidence of the loss of Amish adherents by attrition, nor is there any showing that upon leaving the Amish community Amish children, with their practical agricultural training and habits of industry and self-reliance, would become burdens on society because of educational shortcomings. Indeed, this argument of the State appears to rest primarily on the State's mistaken assumption, already noted, that the

Amish do not provide any education for their children beyond the eighth grade, but allow them to grow in "ignorance." To the contrary, not only do the Amish accept the necessity for formal schooling through the eighth grade level, but continue to provide what has been characterized by the undisputed testimony of expert educators as an "ideal" vocational education for their children in the adolescent years.

There is nothing in this record to suggest that the Amish qualities of reliability, self-reliance, and dedication to work would fail to find ready markets in today's society. Absent some contrary evidence supporting the State's position, we are unwilling to assume that persons possessing such valuable vocational skills and habits are doomed to become burdens on society should they determine to leave the Amish faith, nor is there any basis in the record to warrant a finding that an additional one or two years of formal school education beyond the eighth grade would serve to eliminate any such problem that might exist.

Insofar as the State's claim rests on the view that a brief additional period of formal education is imperative to enable the Amish to participate effectively and intelligently in our democratic process, it must fall. The Amish alternative to formal secondary school education has enabled them to function effectively in their day-to-day life under self-imposed limitations on relations with the world, and to survive and prosper in contemporary society as a separate, sharply identifiable and highly self-sufficient community for more than 200 years in this country. In itself this is strong evidence that they are capable of fulfilling the social and political responsibilities of citizenship without compelled attendance beyond the eighth grade at the price of jeopardizing their free exercise of religious belief. When Thomas Jefferson emphasized the need for education as a bulwark of a free people against tyranny, there is nothing to indicate he had in mind compulsory education through any fixed age beyond a basic education. Indeed, the Amish communities singularly parallel and reflect many of the virtues of Jefferson's ideal of the "sturdy yeoman" who would form the basis of what he considered as the ideal of a democratic society. Even their idiosyncratic separateness exemplifies the diversity we profess to admire and encourage.

The requirement for compulsory education beyond the eighth grade is a relatively recent development in our history. Less than 60 years ago, the educational requirements of almost all of the States were satisfied by completion of the elementary grades, at least where the child was regularly and lawfully employed. The independence and successful social functioning of the Amish community for a period approaching almost three centuries and more than 200 years in this country are strong evidence that there is at best a speculative gain, in terms of meeting the duties of citizenship, from an additional one or two years of compulsory formal education. Against this background it would require a more particularized showing from the State on this point to justify the severe interference with religious freedom such additional compulsory attendance would entail.

We should also note that compulsory education and child labor laws find their historical origin in common humanitarian instincts, and that the age limits of both laws have been coordinated to achieve their related objectives. In the context of this case, such considerations, if anything, support rather than detract from respondents' position. The origins of the requirement for school attendance to age 16, an age falling after the completion of elementary school but before completion of high school, are not entirely clear. But to some extent such laws reflected the movement to prohibit most child labor under age 16 that culminated in the provisions of the Federal Fair Labor Standards Act of 1938. It is true, then, that the 16-year child labor age limit may to some degree derive from a contemporary impression that children should be in school until that age. But at the same time, it cannot be denied that, conversely, the 16-year education limit reflects, in substantial measure, the concern that children under that age not be employed under conditions hazardous to their health, or in work that should be performed by adults.

The requirement of compulsory schooling to age 16 must therefore be viewed as aimed not merely at providing educational opportunities for children, but as an alternative to the equally undesirable consequence of unhealthful child labor displacing adult workers, or, on the other hand, forced idleness. The two kinds of statutes—compulsory school attendance and child labor laws—tend to keep children of certain ages off the labor market and in school; this regimen in turn provides opportunity to prepare for a livelihood of a higher order than that which children could pursue without education and protects their health in adolescence.

In these terms, Wisconsin's interest in compelling the school attendance of Amish children to age 16 emerges as somewhat less substantial than requiring such attendance for children generally. For, while agricultural employment is not totally outside the legitimate concerns of the child labor laws, employment of children under parental guidance and on the family farm from age 14 to age 16 is an ancient tradition that lies at the periphery of the objectives of such laws. There is no intimation that the Amish employment of their children on family farms is in any way deleterious to their health or that Amish parents exploit children at tender years. Any such inference would be contrary to the record before us. Moreover, employment of Amish children on the family farm does not present the undesirable economic aspects of eliminating jobs that might otherwise be held by adults.

IV

Finally, the State, on authority of *Prince v. Massachusetts*, argues that a decision exempting Amish children from the State's requirement fails to recognize the substantive right of the Amish child to a secondary education, and fails to give due regard to the power of the State as *parens patriae* to extend the benefit of secondary education to children regardless of the wishes of their parents. Taken at its broadest sweep, the Court's language in *Prince*, might be read to give support to the

State's position. However, the Court was not confronted in *Prince* with a situation comparable to that of the Amish as revealed in this record; this is shown by the Court's severe characterization of the evils that it thought the legislature could legitimately associate with child labor, even when performed in the company of an adult. The Court later took great care to confine *Prince* to a narrow scope in *Sherbert v. Verner*, when it stated:

> "On the other hand, the Court has rejected challenges under the Free Exercise Clause to governmental regulation of certain overt acts prompted by religious beliefs or principles, for 'even when the action is in accord with one's religious convictions, (it) is not totally free from legislative restrictions.' *Braunfeld v. Brown*, 366 U.S. 599, 603. The conduct or actions so regulated have invariably posed some substantial threat to public safety, peace or order. See, *e.g., Reynolds v. United States*, 98 U.S. 145; *Jacobson v. Massachusetts*, 197 U.S. 11; *Prince v. Massachusetts*, 321 U.S. 158. . . . "

This case, of course, is not one in which any harm to the physical or mental health of the child or to the public safety, peace, order, or welfare has been demonstrated or may be properly inferred. The record is to the contrary, and any reliance on that theory would find no support in the evidence.

Contrary to the suggestion of the dissenting opinion of Mr. Justice Douglas, our holding today in no degree depends on the assertion of the religious interest of the child as contrasted with that of the parents. It is the parents who are subject to prosecution here for failing to cause their children to attend school, and it is their right of free exercise, not that of their children, that must determine Wisconsin's power to impose criminal penalties on the parent. The dissent argues that a child who expresses a desire to attend public high school in conflict with the wishes of his parents should not be prevented from doing so. There is no reason for the Court to consider that point since it is not an issue in the case. The children are not parties to this litigation. The State has at no point tried this case on the theory that respondents were preventing their children from attending school against their expressed desires, and indeed the record is to the contrary. The State's position from the outset has been that it is empowered to apply its compulsory-attendance law to Amish parents in the same manner as to other parents—that is, without regard to the wishes of the child. That is the claim we reject today.

Our holding in no way determines the proper resolution of possible competing interests of parents, children, and the State in an appropriate state court proceeding in which the power of the State is asserted on the theory that Amish parents are preventing their minor children from attending high school despite their expressed desires to the contrary. Recognition of the claim of the State in such a proceeding would, of course, call into question traditional concepts of parental control over the religious upbringing and education of their minor children recognized in this Court's past decisions. It is clear that such an intrusion by a State into family decisions in the area of religious training would give rise to grave questions of religious freedom comparable to those raised here and those presented in *Pierce v. Society of Sisters*, 268 U.S. 510 (1925). On this record we neither reach nor decide those issues.

The State's argument proceeds without reliance on any actual conflict between the wishes of parents and children. It appears to rest on the potential that exemption of Amish parents from the requirements of the compulsory-education law might allow some parents to act contrary to the best interests of their children by foreclosing their opportunity to make an intelligent choice between the Amish way of life and that of the outside world. The same argument could, of course, be made with respect to all church schools short of college. There is nothing in the record or in the ordinary course of human experience to suggest that non-Amish parents generally consult with children of ages 14–16 if they are placed in a church school of the parents' faith.

Indeed it seems clear that if the State is empowered, as *parens patriae*, to "save" a child from himself or his Amish parents by requiring an additional two years of compulsory formal high school education, the State will in large measure influence, if not determine, the religious future of the child. Even more markedly than in *Prince*, therefore, this case involves the fundamental interest of parents, as contrasted with that of the State, to guide the religious future and education of their children. The history and culture of Western civilization reflect a strong tradition of parental concern for the nurture and upbringing of their children. This primary role of the parents in the upbringing of their children is now established beyond debate as an enduring American tradition. If not the first, perhaps the most significant statements of the Court in this area are found in *Pierce v. Society of Sisters*, in which the Court observed:

> "Under the doctrine of *Meyer v. Nebraska*, 262 U.S. 390, we think it entirely plain that the Act of 1922 unreasonably interferes with the liberty of parents and guardians to direct the upbringing and education of children under their control. As often heretofore pointed out, rights guaranteed by the Constitution may not be abridged by legislation which has no reasonable relation to some purpose within the competency of the State. The fundamental theory of liberty upon which all governments in this Union repose excludes any general power of the State to standardize its children by forcing them to accept instruction from public teachers only. The child is not the mere creature of the State; those who nurture him and direct his destiny have the right, coupled with the high duty, to recognize and prepare him for additional obligations."

The duty to prepare the child for "additional obligations," referred to by the Court, must be read to include the inculcation of moral standards, religious beliefs, and elements of good citizenship. *Pierce*, of course, recognized that where nothing more than the general interest of the parent in the nurture and education of his children is involved, it is beyond dispute that the State acts "reasonably" and constitutionally in requiring education to age 16 in some public or private school meeting the standards prescribed by the State.

However read, the Court's holding in *Pierce* stands as a charter of the rights of parents to direct the religious upbringing of their children. And, when the interests of parenthood are combined with a free exercise claim of the nature revealed by this record, more than merely a "reasonable relation to some purpose within the competency of the State" is required to sustain the validity of the State's requirement under the First Amendment. To be sure, the power of the parent, even when linked to a free exercise claim, may be subject to limitation under *Prince* if it appears that parental decisions will jeopardize the health or safety of the child, or have a potential for significant social burdens. But in this case, the Amish have introduced persuasive evidence undermining the arguments the State has advanced to support its claims in terms of the welfare of the child and society as a whole. The record strongly indicates that accommodating the religious objections of the Amish by forgoing one, or at most two, additional years of compulsory education will not impair the physical or mental health of the child, or result in an inability to be self-supporting or to discharge the duties and responsibilities of citizenship, or in any other way materially detract from the welfare of society.

In the face of our consistent emphasis on the central values underlying the Religion Clauses in our constitutional scheme of government, we cannot accept a *parens patriae* claim of such all-encompassing scope and with such sweeping potential for broad and unforeseeable application as that urged by the State.

V

For the reasons stated we hold, with the Supreme Court of Wisconsin, that the First and Fourteenth Amendments prevent the State from compelling respondents to cause their children to attend formal high school to age 16. Our disposition of this case, however, in no way alters our recognition of the obvious fact that courts are not school boards or legislatures, and are ill-equipped to determine the "necessity" of discrete aspects of a State's program of compulsory education. This should suggest that courts must move with great circumspection in performing the sensitive and delicate task of weighing a State's legitimate social concern when faced with religious claims for exemption from generally applicable education requirements. It cannot be overemphasized that we are not dealing with a way of life and mode of education by a group claiming to have recently discovered some "progressive" or more enlightened process for rearing children for modern life.

Aided by a history of three centuries as an identifiable religious sect and a long history as a successful and self-sufficient segment of American society, the Amish in this case have convincingly demonstrated the sincerity of their religious beliefs, the interrelationship of belief with their mode of life, the vital role that belief and daily conduct play in the continued survival of Old Order Amish communities and their religious organization, and the hazards presented by the State's enforcement of a statute generally valid as to others. Beyond this, they have carried the even more difficult burden of demonstrating the adequacy of their alternative mode of continuing informal vocational education in terms of precisely those overall interests that the State advances in support of its program of compulsory high school education. In light of this convincing showing, one that probably few other religious groups or sects could make, and weighing the minimal difference between what the State would require and what the Amish already accept, it was incumbent on the State to show with more particularity how its admittedly strong interest in compulsory education would be adversely affected by granting an exemption to the Amish. *Sherbert v. Verner, supra.*

Nothing we hold is intended to undermine the general applicability of the State's compulsory school-attendance statutes or to limit the power of the State to promulgate reasonable standards that, while not impairing the free exercise of religion, provide for continuing agricultural vocational education under parental and church guidance by the Old Order Amish or others similarly situated. The States have had a long history of amicable and effective relationships with church-sponsored schools, and there is no basis for assuming that, in this related context, reasonable standards cannot be established concerning the content of the continuing vocational education of Amish children under parental guidance, provided always that state regulations are not inconsistent with what we have said in this opinion.

[The concurring opinions of Justice Stewart and Justice White are omitted.]

DOUGLAS, J., dissenting in part.

I

I agree with the Court that the religious scruples of the Amish are opposed to the education of their children beyond the grade schools, yet I disagree with the Court's conclusion that the matter is within the dispensation of parents alone. The Court's analysis assumes that the only interests at stake in the case are those of the Amish parents on the one hand, and those of the State on the other. The difficulty with this approach is that, despite the Court's claim, the parents are seeking to vindicate not only their own free exercise claims, but also those of their high-school-age children.

It is argued that the right of the Amish children to religious freedom is not presented by the facts of the case, as the issue before the Court involves only the Amish parents' religious freedom to defy a state criminal statute imposing upon them an affirmative duty to cause their children to attend high school.

First, respondents' motion to dismiss in the trial court expressly asserts, not only the religious liberty of the adults, but also that of the children, as a defense to the prosecutions. It is, of course, beyond question that the parents have standing as defendants in a criminal prosecution to assert the religious interests of their children as a defense. Although the lower courts and a majority of this Court assume an identity of interest between parent and child, it is clear that they have treated the religious interest of the child as a factor in the analysis.

Second, it is essential to reach the question to decide the case, not only because the question was squarely raised in the motion to dismiss, but also because no analysis of religious-liberty claims can take place in a vacuum. If the parents in this case are allowed a religious exemption, the inevitable effect is to impose the parents' notions of religious duty upon their children. Where the child is mature enough to express potentially conflicting desires, it would be an invasion of the child's rights to permit such an imposition without canvassing his views. As in *Prince v. Massachusetts*, 321 U.S. 158, it is an imposition resulting from this very litigation. As the child has no other effective forum, it is in this litigation that his rights should be considered. And, if an Amish child desires to attend high school, and is mature enough to have that desire respected, the State may well be able to override the parents' religiously motivated objections.

Religion is an individual experience. It is not necessary, nor even appropriate, for every Amish child to express his views on the subject in a prosecution of a single adult. Crucial, however, are the views of the child whose parent is the subject of the suit. Frieda Yoder has in fact testified that her own religious views are opposed to high-school education. I therefore join the judgment of the Court as to respondent Jonas Yoder. But Frieda Yoder's views may not be those of Vernon Yutzy or Barbara Miller. I must dissent, therefore, as to respondents Adin Yutzy and Wallace Miller as their motion to dismiss also raised the question of their children's religious liberty.

II

This issue has never been squarely presented before today. Our opinions are full of talk about the power of the parents over the child's education. See *Pierce v. Society of Sisters*, 268 U.S. 510; *Meyer v. Nebraska*, 262 U.S. 390. And we have in the past analyzed similar conflicts between parent and State with little regard for the views of the child. See *Prince v. Massachusetts, supra*. Recent cases, however, have clearly held that the children themselves have constitutionally protectable interests.

These children are "persons" within the meaning of the Bill of Rights. We have so held over and over again. In *Haley v. Ohio*, 332 U.S. 596, we extended the protection of the Fourteenth Amendment in a state trial of a 15-year-old boy. *In re Gault*, 387 U.S. 1, 13, we held that "neither the Fourteenth Amendment nor the Bill of Rights is for adults alone." In *In re Winship*, 397 U.S. 358, we held that a 12-year-old boy, when charged with an act which would be a crime if committed by an adult, was entitled to procedural safeguards contained in the Sixth Amendment.

In *Tinker v. Des Moines Independent Community School District*, 393 U.S. 503, we dealt with 13-year-old, 15-year-old, and 16-year-old students who wore armbands to public schools and were disciplined for doing so. We gave them relief, saying that their First Amendment rights had been abridged.

> "Students in school as well as out of school are 'persons' under our Constitution. They are possessed of fundamental rights which the State must respect, just as they themselves must respect their obligations to the State."

In *Board of Education v. Barnette*, 319 U.S. 624, we held that school-children, whose religious beliefs collided with a school rule requiring them to salute the flag, could not be required to do so. While the sanction included expulsion of the students and prosecution of the parents, *id.*, at 630, the vice of the regime was its interference with the child's free exercise of religion. We said: "Here . . . we are dealing with a compulsion of students to declare a belief." In emphasizing the important and delicate task of boards of education we said:

> "That they are educating the young for citizenship is reason for scrupulous protection of Constitutional freedoms of the individual, if we are not to strangle the free mind at its source and teach youth to discount important principles of our government as mere platitudes."

On this important and vital matter of education, I think the children should be entitled to be heard. While the parents, absent dissent, normally speak for the entire family, the education of the child is a matter on which the child will often have decided views. He may want to be a pianist or an astronaut or an oceanographer. To do so he will have to break from the Amish tradition.

It is the future of the student, not the future of the parents, that is imperiled by today's decision. If a parent keeps his child out of school beyond the grade school, then the child will be forever barred from entry into the new and amazing world of diversity that we have today. The child may decide that that is the preferred course, or he may rebel. It is the student's judgment, not his parents', that is essential if we are to give full meaning to what we have said about the Bill of Rights and of the right of students to be masters of their own destiny. If he is harnessed to the Amish way of life by those in authority over him and if his education is truncated, his entire life may be stunted and deformed. The child, therefore, should be given an opportunity to be heard before the State gives the exemption which we honor today.

The views of the two children in question were not canvassed by the Wisconsin courts. The matter should be explicitly reserved so that new hearings can be held on remand of the case.

III

I think the emphasis of the Court on the "law and order" record of this Amish group of people is quite irrelevant. A religion is a religion irrespective of what the misdemeanor or felony records of its members might be. I am not at all sure how the Catholics, Episcopalians, the Baptists, Jehovah's Witnesses, the Unitarians, and my own Presbyterians would make out if subjected to such a test. It is, of course, true that if a group or society was organized to perpetuate crime and if that is its motive, we would have rather startling problems akin to those that were raised when some years back a particular sect was challenged here as operating on a fraudulent basis. *United States v. Ballard*, 322 U.S. 78. But no such factors are present here, and the Amish, whether with a high or low criminal record, certainly qualify by all historic standards as a religion within the meaning of the First Amendment.

The Court rightly rejects the notion that actions, even though religiously grounded, are always outside the protection of the Free Exercise Clause of the First Amendment. In so ruling, the Court departs from the teaching of *Reynolds v. United States*, 98 U.S. 145, 164, where it was said concerning the reach of the Free Exercise Clause of the First Amendment, "Congress was deprived of all legislative power over mere opinion, but was left free to reach actions which were in violation of social duties or subversive of good order." In that case it was conceded that polygamy was a part of the religion of the Mormons. Yet the Court said, "It matters not that his belief [in polygamy] was a part of his professed religion: it was still belief and belief only."

Action, which the Court deemed to be antisocial, could be punished even though it was grounded on deeply held and sincere religious convictions. What we do today, at least in this respect, opens the way to give organized religion a broader base than it has ever enjoyed; and it even promises that in time *Reynolds* will be overruled.

In another way, however, the Court retreats when in reference to Henry Thoreau it says his "choice was philosophical and personal rather than religious, and such belief does not rise to the demands of the Religion Clauses." That is contrary to what we held in *United States v. Seeger*, 380 U.S. 163, where we were concerned with the meaning of the words "religious training and belief" in the Selective Service Act, which were the basis of many conscientious objector claims. We said:

> "Within that phrase would come all sincere religious beliefs which are based upon a power or being, or upon a faith, to which all else is subordinate or upon which all else is ultimately dependent. The test might be stated in these words: A sincere and meaningful belief which occupies in the life of its possessor a place parallel to that filled by the God of those admittedly qualifying for the exemption comes within the statutory definition. This construction avoids imputing to Congress an intent to classify different religious beliefs, exempting some and excluding others, and is in accord with the well-

established congressional policy of equal treatment for those whose opposition to service is grounded in their religious tenets."

Welsh v. United States, 398 U.S. 333, was in the same vein, the Court saying:

> "In this case, Welsh's conscientious objection to war was undeniably based in part on his perception of world politics. In a letter to his local board, he wrote: 'I can only act according to what I am and what I see. And I see that the military complex wastes both human and material resources, that it fosters disregard for (what I consider a paramount concern) human needs and ends; I see that the means we employ to "defend" our "way of life" profoundly change that way of life. I see that in our failure to recognize the political, social, and economic realities of the world, we, as a nation, fail our responsibility as a nation.' "

The essence of Welsh's philosophy, on the basis of which we held he was entitled to an exemption, was in these words:

"I believe that human life is valuable in and of itself; in its living; therefore I will not injure or kill another human being. This belief (and the corresponding 'duty' to abstain from violence toward another person) is not 'superior to those arising from any human relation.' On the contrary: *it is essential to every human relation.* I cannot, therefore, conscientiously comply with the Government's insistence that I assume duties which I feel are immoral and totally repugnant."

I adhere to these exalted views of "religion" and see no acceptable alternative to them now that we have become a Nation of many religions and sects, representing all of the diversities of the human race. *United States v. Seeger*, 380 U.S., at 192–93 (concurring opinion).

Notes and Questions on Yoder

(1) Why did the Court decide *Yoder* as it did? Is its opinion so elaborately circumscribed that the case has little significance beyond its facts?

(a) Was the Court simply impressed by the weakness of the state's interests? For most children, the difference between what the parents wanted and the state required was only one or two years of school.

(i) What if the parents had wished to educate their children only enough to enable them to work on a farm run on pre-modern principles—only enough, perhaps, to be able to read and write?

(ii) How well did the Court distinguish *Prince v. Massachusetts,* the major precedent against its holding in *Yoder*?

(iii) The Court does not distinguish *Reynolds*, another contrary precedent. Can it be distinguished?

(b) Was the Court in *Yoder* simply impressed by the piety, industriousness, and law-abidingness of the Amish?

(i) The Court says, "A way of life, however virtuous and admirable, may not be interposed as a barrier to reasonable state regulation of education if it is based on purely secular considerations. . . ." Why is a group whose objections to compulsory education are religious exempted from that requirement while a group whose objections are equally serious and sincere but secular not exempted? Is the difference the First Amendment's Free Exercise Clause? What about the parents' Fourteenth Amendment rights? Their freedom-of-association rights?

(ii) The Court says, "It cannot be overemphasized that we are not dealing with a way of life and mode of education by a group claiming to have recently discovered some 'progressive' or more enlightened process for rearing children for modern life." Why is the length of time the Amish have lived as they do relevant? Because it demonstrates the sincerity of Amish beliefs? Because it gives the Court ample basis for evaluating the effectiveness of Amish education? Because the Court feared extensions of the *Yoder* principle to cases it did not foresee?

(c) Was the Court in *Yoder* impressed by the parents' rights? If so, what does the Court believe those rights are?

(2) Courts have sometimes held that parents may be required to send their children to school even where parents have argued that they would prefer to educate their children at home and that they will give their children a better education than the public schools would. Can these holdings be reconciled with *Yoder?*

Home schooling is an increasingly popular method of educating children whose parents are dissatisfied with public schools for religious or educational reasons. Relying on *Pierce*, *Meyer*, and *Yoder*, a number of cases have challenged statutes requiring certification or other regulation of teachers and curriculum. For example, *People v. DeJonge*, 501 NW2d 127 (Mich 1993) ruled Michigan's teacher-certification requirement unconstitutional under the First Amendment when applied to families who wished to educate their children at home but whose religious convictions prohibited the use of certified instructors. The DeJonges began home teaching in 1984 to give their children a Christ-centered education. They used materials from an Illinois organization, and proposed monitoring by individualized standardized achievement testing.

However, the same court found that the certification requirement did not unconstitutionally interfere with parents' Fourteenth Amendment right to direct their children's education when home schooling was not done for religious reasons. The court reasoned that the Fourteenth Amendment does not provide parents a fundamental right to direct their children's secular education, so the state regulation needed only to pass a rational-relationship test. *People v. Bennett*, 501 NW2d 106 (Mich 1993).

In any event, the trend has been toward statutory accommodation of home schooling, not least because home schoolers are effective lobbyists in federal and state legislatures. Daniel Golden, *Social Studies: Home Schoolers Learn How to Gain Clout Inside the Beltway*, Wall Street Journal, April 24, 2000, at A1: "Pennsylvania Congressman Bill Goodling, chairman of the House Committee on Education and the Workforce, calls home schoolers the most effective educational lobby on Capitol Hill." Va Code Ann § 22.1–254.1 (2006) provides:

> A. Any parent of any child ... may elect to provide home instruction in lieu of school attendance if he (i) holds a baccalaureate degree in any subject from an accredited institution of higher education; or ... (iv) provides a program of study or curriculum which, in the judgment of the division superintendent, includes the standards of learning objectives adopted by the Board of Education for language arts and mathematics and provides evidence that the parent is able to provide an adequate education for the child....
>
> C. The parent who elects to provide home instruction shall provide the division superintendent by August 1 following the school year in which the child has received home instruction with either (i) evidence that the child has attained a composite score in or above the fourth stanine on a battery of achievement tests which have been approved by the Board of Education for use in the public schools; or (ii) an evaluation or assessment which, in the judgment of the division superintendent, indicates that the child is achieving an adequate level of educational growth and progress....

Va Code Ann § 22.1–254 (2006) provides in relevant part:

> B. A school board shall excuse from attendance at school:
>
> 1. Any pupil who, together with his parents, by reason of bona fide religious training or belief is conscientiously opposed to attendance at school. For purposes of this subdivision, "bona fide religious training or belief" does not include essentially political, sociological or philosophical views or a merely personal moral code....

The Home School Legal Defense Association estimates that 1.5 million of the 53 million schoolchildren in the country are taught at home; the Department of Education estimated 750,000 in 1996. Home schoolers generally do well on standardized tests. Daniel Golden, *Class of Their Own: Home–Schooled Pupils Are Making Colleges Sit Up and Take Notice,* Wall Street Journal, February 11, 2000, at A1. On the SAT, they scored an average 1,083 (verbal 548, math 535), 67 points above the national average of 1,016. On the ACT, home schoolers scored 23.4 in English, well above the 20.5 national average; and 24.4 in reading, compared with a national mean of 21.4. The gap was closer in science (21.9 vs. 21.0), and home schoolers scored below the national average in math, 20.4 to 20.7. Home schoolers also get into college. Golden's article cites a recent survey by the National Center for Home Education, a Virginia-based advocacy group, which found that 68% of colleges accept parent-prepared transcripts or portfolios in place of an accredited diploma. That includes Stanford University, which in 1999 accepted 27% of the home-schooled applicants who sought admission—nearly double its normal acceptance rate.

(3) *Yoder* can be read as based not so much on parents' rights, but on the rights of the Amish as a group. Seen in this light, *Yoder* serves a constitutional interest in pluralism.

(a) What is the textual basis for a constitutional interest in pluralism? Is it exclusively to be found in the religion clauses of the First Amendment? If so, is the constitutional interest in pluralism exclusively religious? Is the textual basis also to be found in the Fourteenth Amendment? If so, how is it derived from the Amendment and what is its nature?

(b) What is "pluralism"? Is it an interest in protecting social differences of all kinds? Is it only an interest in protecting diverse groups? Particular kinds of diverse groups?

(c) Why might we want to protect pluralism? What limits ought there be to pluralism?

(d) Does *Yoder* actually promote pluralism? *Yoder* may increase the range of choices for adults who are or may wish to become Amish, but it may diminish the range of choices for the children of the Amish. *Pierce* said the Constitution "precludes any general power of the State to standardize its children." Is standardization less troublesome when the standardizer is a church instead of the state? (The problem of standardization here is further complicated by the point emphasized in the opinion, that the Amish bring up their children almost hyper-conventionally.)

(4) *Yoder* is in part about the role of communities in socializing children and in providing meaning in the lives of adults. But which is the relevant community in *Yoder*? Is it the Amish community, whose long struggle for stability and autonomy the Court describes? Is it the local school district and the state of Wisconsin, which wish to incorporate the children of the Amish into their common life? Is it the national community, whose opportunities may be partially closed to the children of the Amish by the practices of the Amish community?

(a) The ideal and tendency of American constitutional law and national politics in the twentieth century has been to make available to all American citizens the social, economic, and intellectual benefits of a modern, industrialized society. A crucial means of accomplishing this goal has been to try to assure that all children receive the kind of education that will give them access to those benefits. The Court wrote in *Brown v. Board of Education*, 347 US 483, 493 (1954): "In these days it is doubtful that any child may reasonably be expected to succeed in life if he is denied the opportunity of an education. Such an opportunity, where the state has undertaken to provide it, is a right which must be made available to all children." Is the Court's opinion in *Yoder* inconsistent with this vision of American life and with its opinion in *Brown*?

(b) Philip B. Kurland, *The Supreme Court, Compulsory Education, and the First Amendment's Religion Clauses*, W Va L Rev 213, 234 (1973), argues:

> The Court [in *Yoder*] made no mention of the public school systems as a means of integrating a larger community. It disregarded *Brown v. Board of Education*, just as it rejected the arguments in the released-time cases that suggest that religion is a divisive force that can and frequently does fragment the larger community. The distinction between religious separation and racial separation was never clearly delineated.... Is there the possibility that the Court will allow blacks and Chinese to opt out of the public school systems in order to maintain their communities?

(5) *Yoder* could also be understood as a children's rights case. How convincing would such an understanding be?

(a) Can a fourteen-year-old form the understanding of religious ideas necessary to evaluate the religious component of the decision to leave school early? Is it a relevant question that many religions make fourteen the age of entry into adult participation in the religion? Do adolescents have the independence from parental and community pressure necessary for a genuinely personal decision?

(b) Can a fourteen-year-old adequately understand the non-religious consequences of leaving school early? Justice Douglas suggests there is some evidence that "the moral and intellectual maturity of the 14-year-old approaches that of the adult." But what does that mean?

(i) Does the maturity of the fourteen-year-old go further than providing an abstract understanding of moral and intellectual problems? Is such an understanding enough? Even if the adolescent can reason like an adult, does the adolescent have the experience with the world to make a wise decision? Does an adolescent brought up in the restricted world of an Amish family have that experience?

(ii) Are adolescents under emotional and social pressures—to assert independence, to benefit from dependence—that affect their decisions and that adults commonly feel less severely? Do adolescents benefit from being able to assert themselves while knowing that adults will help protect them from unwise decisions?

(c) As a practical matter, to what extent can the state remove the decision whether a child is to attend school from the parents? If the parent and the child agree and are adamant, the state's enforcement power will be severely tested, as the experience with the Amish suggests. The state is soon left with the alternative of jailing parents or acceding to them. If the parents and the child disagree, the enforcement problem is still severe, since the parent is well situated to pressure the child, and the state is ill-situated to find out about the pressure and to prevent it. Is it the better part of valor for the state to concede the issue to the parents?

(d) What effect would according children a right to decide against their parents' wishes to attend school have?

(i) Would according children such a right damage family autonomy and family privacy? Would such an effect be undesirable?

(ii) Would according children such a right change the balance of power within families? Undesirably?

(e) Would denying children the right to decide against their parents' wishes harm children?

(i) If it would harm children not to attend school until the age of sixteen, is the solution to give children a right to decide or for the state to enforce compulsory-education laws?

(ii) Would denying children the right to decide deprive them of a necessary attribute of human dignity?

(6) How far may *Yoder* be extended beyond the Amish context? What if a fully trained but uncertified teacher wants to educate her children at home because she is a Calvinist? What if the children perform above grade level?

(7) Wisconsin's compulsory education statute now permits home schooling without certification or testing where the primary purpose is to provide private or religious-based education and the program provides at least 875 hours of instruction each school year organized in a sequentially progressive curriculum that includes instruction in reading, language arts, mathematics, social studies, science, and health. No instruction is required in "any concept, topic or practice in conflict with the program's religious doctrines." Wis Stat § 118.165 (2006). Should a divorcing parent be able to seek spousal support in order to remain home to educate the children under this statute? Under what circumstances?

MOZERT v. HAWKINS COUNTY BOARD OF EDUCATION

United States Court of Appeals, Sixth Circuit, 1987
827 F2d 1058

[A group of parents and students brought a § 1983 action against a school system which required students to read the Holt, Rinehart and Winston series of readers in the first through eighth grades. The plaintiffs did not "belong to a single church or denomination, but all consider themselves born-again Christians." One plaintiff, Mrs. Frost, "stated that the offending materials fell into seventeen categories which she listed. These ranged from such familiar concerns of fundamentalist Christians as evolution and 'secular humanism' to less familiar themes such as 'futuristic supernaturalism,' pacifism, magic and false views of death." Mrs. Frost and another witness, Mr. Mozert, "testified under cross-examination that the plaintiff parents objected to passages that expose their children to other forms of religion and to the feelings, attitudes and values of other students that contradict the plaintiffs' religious views without a statement that the other views are incorrect and that the plaintiffs' views are the correct ones."]

Lively, C.J. . . .

The district court held that the plaintiffs' free exercise rights have been burdened because their "religious beliefs compel them to refrain from exposure to the Holt series," and the defendant school board "has effectively required that the student plaintiffs either read the offensive texts or give up their free public education." *Mozert v. Hawkins County Public Schools*, 647 F.Supp. 1194, 1200 (E.D.Tenn.1986). In reaching this conclusion the district court analogized the plaintiffs' position to that of a sabbatarian who was denied unemployment compensation benefits for refusing to work on Saturdays, *Sherbert v. Verner*, 374 U.S. 398 (1963), a Jehovah's Witness who was denied unemployment compensation benefits after quitting a job that required him to work on military tanks, *Thomas v. Review Board*, 450 U.S. 707 (1981), and a conscientious objector who refused to participate in ROTC training, *Spence v. Bailey*, 465 F.2d 797 (6th Cir.1972).

The district court went on to find that the state had a compelling interest "in the education of its young," but that it had erred in choosing "to further its legitimate and overriding interest in public education by mandating the use of a single basic reading series" in the face of the plaintiffs' religious objections. The court concluded that the proof at trial demonstrated that the defendants could accommodate the plaintiffs without material and substantial disruption to the educational process by permitting the objecting students to "opt out of the school district's reading program," and meet the reading requirements by home schooling. . . .

III.

A.

The first question to be decided is whether a governmental requirement that a person be exposed to ideas he or she finds objectionable on religious grounds constitutes a burden on the free exercise of that person's religion as forbidden by the First Amendment. . . .

The plaintiffs did not produce a single student or teacher to testify that any student was ever required to affirm his or her belief or disbelief in any idea or practice mentioned in the various stories and passages contained in the Holt series. . . .

[T]he plaintiffs' own testimony casts serious doubt on their claim that a more balanced presentation would satisfy their religious views. . . . It is clear that to the plaintiffs there is but one acceptable view—the Biblical view, as they interpret the Bible. Furthermore, the plaintiffs view every human situation and decision, whether related to personal belief and conduct or to public policy and programs, from a theological or religious perspective. Mrs. Frost testified that many political issues have theological roots and that there would be "no way" certain themes could be presented without violating her religious beliefs. She identified such themes as evolution, false supernaturalism, feminism, telepathy and magic as matters that could not be presented in any way without offending her beliefs. . . .

B.

In this case the district court erroneously applied decisions based on governmental requirements that objecting parties make some affirmation or take some action that offends their religious beliefs. In *Sherbert* the burden on the plaintiff's right of free exercise consisted of a governmental requirement that she either work on her Sabbath Day or forfeit her right to benefits. Similarly, in *Thomas* the plaintiff was denied a benefit for refusing to engage in the production of armaments. In each case the burden on the plaintiff's free exercise of religion consisted of being required to perform an act which violated the plaintiff's religious convictions or forego benefits. Ms. Sherbert was not merely exposed to the view that others in the work force had no religious scruples against working on Saturdays and Mr. Thomas was not merely exposed to government publications designed to encourage employees to produce armaments. In each case there was compulsion to do an act that violated the plaintiff's religious convictions. In *Hobbie v. Unemployment Appeals Commission of Florida*, 107 S.Ct. 1046 (1987), the Supreme Court reaffirmed its holdings in *Sherbert* and *Thomas*, emphasizing that in both cases there was compulsion either to do an act that was prohibited by the plaintiff's religion or to modify his or her behavior and violate religious beliefs. In *Spence* this court upheld a conscientious objector's right not to be required to participate in his high school's ROTC program. The court found that Spence's claim resembled Sherbert's "since it compels the conscientious objector either to engage in military training contrary to his religious beliefs, or to give up his public education." It is clear that it was being compelled *to engage* in military training, not being exposed to the fact that others do so, that was found to be an unconstitutional burden.

In *Sherbert*, *Thomas* and *Hobbie* there was governmental compulsion to engage in conduct that violated the plaintiffs' religious convictions. That element is missing in the present case. . . .

D.

The third Supreme Court decision relied upon by the plaintiffs is the only one that might be read to support the proposition that requiring mere exposure to materials that offend one's religious beliefs creates an unconstitutional burden on the free exercise of religion. *Wisconsin v. Yoder*, 406 U.S. 205 (1972). However, *Yoder* rested on such a singular set of facts that we do not believe it can be held to announce a general rule that exposure without compulsion to act, believe, affirm or deny creates an unconstitutional burden. The plaintiff parents in *Yoder* were Old

Order Amish and members of the Conservative Amish Mennonite Church, who objected to their children being required to attend either public or private schools beyond the eighth grade. Wisconsin school attendance law required them to cause their children to attend school until they reached the age of 16. Unlike the plaintiffs in the present case, the parents in *Yoder* did not want their children to attend any high school or be exposed to any part of a high school curriculum. The Old Order Amish and the Conservative Amish Mennonites separate themselves from the world and avoid assimilation into society, and attempt to shield their children from all worldly influences. The Supreme Court found from the record that—

> [C]ompulsory school attendance to age 16 for Amish children carries with it a very real threat to undermining the Amish community and religious practice as they exist today; they must either abandon belief and be assimilated into society at large, or be forced to migrate to some other and more tolerant region.

As if to emphasize the narrowness of its holding because of the unique 300 year history of the Old Amish Order, the Court wrote:

> It is one thing to say that compulsory education for a year or two beyond the eighth grade may be necessary when its goal is the preparation of the child for life in modern society as the majority live, but it is quite another if the goal of education be viewed as the preparation of the child for life in the separated agrarian community that is the keystone of the Amish faith.

This statement points up dramatically the difference between *Yoder* and the present case. The parents in *Yoder* were required to send their children to some school that prepared them for life in the outside world, or face official sanctions. The parents in the present case want their children to acquire all the skills required to live in modern society. They also want to have them excused from exposure to some ideas they find offensive. Tennessee offers two options to accommodate this latter desire. The plaintiff parents can either send their children to church schools or private schools, as many of them have done, or teach them at home. Tennessee law prohibits any state interference in the education process of church schools:

> The state board of education and local boards of education are prohibited from regulating the selection of faculty or textbooks or the establishment of a curriculum in church-related schools.

TCA 49–50–801(b). Similarly the statute permitting home schooling by parents or other teachers prescribes nothing with respect to curriculum or the content of class work.

Yoder was decided in large part on the impossibility of reconciling the goals of public education with the religious requirement of the Amish that their children be prepared for life in a separated community. As the Court noted, the requirement of school attendance to age 16 posed a "very real threat of undermining the Amish community and religious practice as they exist today...." No such threat exists in the present case, and Tennessee's school attendance laws offer several options to those parents who want their children to have the benefit of an education which prepares for life in the modern world without being exposed to ideas which offend their religious beliefs....

KENNEDY, J., concurring.

I agree with Chief Judge Lively's analysis and concur in his opinion. However, even if I were to conclude that requiring the use of the Holt series or another similar series constituted a burden on appellees' free exercise rights, I would find the burden justified by a compelling state interest....

BOGGS, J., concurring.

I concur with my colleagues that Hawkins County is not required by the Constitution to allow plaintiffs the latitude they seek in the educational program of these children. However, I reach that result on a somewhat different view of the facts and governing principles here....

If the situation of these children is not a burden on their religious exercise, it must be because of a principle applicable to all religious objectors to public school curricula. Thus, I believe a deeper issue is present here, is implicitly decided in the court's opinion, and should be addressed openly. The school board recognizes no limitation on its power to require any curriculum, no matter how offensive or one-sided, and to expel those who will not study it, so long as it does not violate the Establishment Clause. Our opinion today confirms that right, and I would like to make plain my reasons for taking that position....

Questions on Mozert

(1) The Supreme Court said in *Thomas v. Review Board*, 450 US 707 (1981), "When deciding a free exercise claim ... it must be determined whether the government action does, in fact, create a burden on the litigant's exercise of his religion." And it said, "Where the state conditions receipt of an important benefit upon conduct proscribed by a religious faith, or where it denies such a benefit because of conduct mandated by religious belief, ... such a burden upon religion exists." If parents can show that their public school curriculum systematically affronts the religious beliefs in which they are raising their children, have the parents shown an infringement of their free exercise rights, an infringement that under *Yoder* must be accommodated?

(2) What is the state interest here? Is it more than the expense of alternative reading programs? Isn't this the kind of "mere administrative cost" that regularly fails to meet the standard of a state interest significant enough to override a right?

(3) Suppose the administrative cost of alternatives is significant, but that the parents who object to the public school's reading curriculum will educate their children at home. Should they have a constitutional

right to do so, if they can show that their children read as well as children in public schools?

(4) Suppose parents want their children educated in a church school, but the church school refuses to hire certified teachers because the training conflicts with the denomination's religious principles. Do the parents have a constitutional right to send their children to such a school? What if the school's students do as well on standardized tests as students in public schools?

(5) What is the relevant community in *Mozert*? Are the plaintiffs asserting any community interest? If so, how does that interest differ from the community interest asserted in *Yoder*?

(6) Former Mich Stat Ann § 15.2782 allowed local school districts to teach sex hygiene as part of their physical education program but provided that "it is hereby expressly prohibited to any person to offer or give any instruction in . . . birth control or offer or deliver any advice or information with respect to said subject." Was the statute constitutional? See *Mercer v. Michigan State Board of Educ.*, 379 F Supp 580 (ED Mich 1974), aff'd mem, 419 US 1081 (1974). Michigan's current statute, Mich Comp Laws § 380.1507 (1993), allows instruction in sex education including "family planning," but provides in (8) that "clinical abortion shall not be considered a method of family planning, nor shall such abortion be taught as a method of reproductive health." Is this statute constitutional?

SECTION 2. RACIAL AND RELIGIOUS MATCHING IN CHILD CUSTODY AND ADOPTION

There is no such thing as an American nation. Poles form a nation, but the United States is a country, under one government, inhabited by representatives of different nations.... I do not think that there will be amalgamation, one race composed of many. The Poles, Bohemians, and so forth, remain such, generation after generation.

Howard Kallen

Some states have statutes that contemplate that race will be a factor in adoption placements, and the practice of many agencies is to match children of one race with adoptive parents of the same race. In addition, there is case law suggesting that racial matching should be a factor in child-custody decisions. Racial matching is favored by groups such as the National Association of Black Social Workers, which fears that minority children may lose their identities in white households. There are, however, a disproportionate number of minority children available for adoption, and there are constitutional questions about the practice of matching.

A special case for racial matching is presented by cases involving Indians. That special case has been addressed by a federal statute, the Indian Child Welfare Act. It seeks to assure that Indian children will be cared for by Indian custodians.

Finally, some state statutes not only contemplate religious matching, but affirmatively favor it. Delaware requires that children be placed with parents who share the children's religion unless the natural parents do not care, and other states require that religious matching be done "when practicable." And, since many adoption agencies are affiliated with religious groups, religious matching is a common practice.

Each of these practices raises questions about the intersection of pluralism and family law. As you read the materials that follow, you should ask yourself what principles of pluralism should organize your analysis.

(a) Racial Matching

Before we look at race as a factor in child-custody law (including the law of adoption), we need a brief background. According to Professor Margaret Howard, "most adoption statutes make no mention of race." *Transracial Adoption: Analysis of the Best Interests Standard*, 59 Notre Dame L Rev 503, 516 (1984). However, for many years, the usual practice of adoption agencies was not to permit transracial adoptions. In part, this was because of their adherence to the doctrine of matching, which held that adopted children should be as much like their adoptive parents as possible. "The idea was that parents and child could establish a better relationship if differences were minimized. The idea was plausible since there is evidence that similarity is important in selecting friends and spouses." Jacqueline Macaulay and Stewart Macaulay, *Adoption for Black Children: A Case Study of Expert Discretion*, 1 Research in Law & Sociology 265, 280 (1978).

In the late 1950s and early 1960s, it began to be argued that many children of minority races needed adoptive homes, and transracial adoptions began to be essayed. By the middle to late 1960s, "transracial adoption seemed to be the 'in' thing for progressive agencies." Id at 283. At this point, however, there was a "counterrevolution ... sparked by the National Association of Black Social Workers (NABSW)." Id at 287. The NABSW vowed to "work to end this particular form of genocide." Howard, 59 Notre Dame L Rev at 518.

"This counterrevolution cut transracial adoption by 39% in a single year, just when the movement seemed to be growing rapidly." Macaulay and Macaulay, *Adoption for Black Children* at 287–88. In response to the suggestion that there were many black children who would be better off with even white adoptive parents than living in institutions or in perpetual foster care, critics of transracial adoption argued for increasing the number of black adoptive parents through such reforms as having adoptions of black children handled only by black social workers and subsidizing adoptions of black children by black parents.

Professor Howard concludes that "[c]urrent figures are hard to locate, but only a small number of transracial placements are still being made. Since no data suggest that more black homes have become available, the inevitable conclusion is that adoptable black children remain in foster homes and institutions." The Macaulays report that "[m]ost estimates find that from one-third to one-half of the adoptable children in foster care are black."

What, then, is the law governing racial matching? The Supreme Court has not considered the constitutionality of racial (or religious) matching. It has, however, decided the following case.

PALMORE v. SIDOTI

Supreme Court of the United States, 1984
466 US 429

BURGER, C.J.

We granted certiorari to review a judgment of a state court divesting a natural mother of the custody of her infant child because of her remarriage to a person of a different race.

I

When petitioner Linda Sidoti Palmore and respondent Anthony J. Sidoti, both Caucasians, were divorced in May 1980 in Florida, the mother was awarded custody of their three-year-old daughter.

In September 1981 the father sought custody of the child by filing a petition to modify the prior judgment because of changed conditions. The change was that the child's mother was then cohabiting with a Negro, Clarence Palmore, Jr., whom she married two months later. Additionally, the father made several allegations of instances in which the mother had not properly cared for the child.

After hearing testimony from both parties and considering a court counselor's investigative report, the court noted that the father had made allegations about the child's care, but the court made no findings with respect to these allegations. On the contrary, the court made a finding that "there is no issue as to either party's devotion to the child, adequacy of housing facilities, or respect[a]bility of the new spouse of either parent."

The court then addressed the recommendations of the court counselor, who had made an earlier report "in [another] case coming out of this circuit also involving the social consequences of an interracial marriage. *Niles v. Niles*, 299 So.2d 162." From this vague reference to that earlier case, the court turned to the present case and noted the counselor's recommendation for a change in custody because "[t]he wife [petitioner] has chosen for herself and for her child, a life-style unacceptable to her father *and to society*.... The child ... is, or at school age will be, subject to environmental pressures not of choice."

The court then concluded that the best interests of the child would be served by awarding custody to the father. The court's rationale is contained in the following:

> "The father's evident resentment of the mother's choice of a black partner is not sufficient to wrest custody from the mother. It is of some significance, however, that the mother did see fit to bring a man into her home and carry on a sexual relationship with him without being married to him. Such action tended to place gratification of her own desires ahead of her concern for the child's future welfare. *This Court feels that despite the strides that have been made in bettering relations between the races in this country, it is inevitable that Melanie will, if allowed to remain in her present situation and attains school age and thus more vulnerable to peer pressures, suffer from the social stigmatization that is sure to come.*"

The Second District Court of Appeal affirmed without opinion, thus denying the Florida Supreme Court jurisdiction to review the case. We granted certiorari, and we reverse.

II

The judgment of a state court determining or reviewing a child custody decision is not ordinarily a likely candidate for review by this Court. However, the court's opinion, after stating that the "father's evident resentment of the mother's choice of a black partner is not sufficient" to deprive her of custody, then turns to what it regarded as the damaging impact on the child from remaining in a racially-mixed household. This raises important federal concerns arising from the Constitution's commitment to eradicating discrimination based on race.

The Florida court did not focus directly on the parental qualifications of the natural mother or her present husband, or indeed on the father's qualifications to have custody of the child. The court found that "there is no issue as to either party's devotion to the child, adequacy of housing facilities, or respect[a]bility of the new spouse of either parent." This, taken with the absence of any negative finding as to the quality of the care provided by the mother, constitutes a rejection of any claim of petitioner's unfitness to continue the custody of her child.

The court correctly stated that the child's welfare was the controlling factor. But that court was entirely candid and made no effort to place its holding on any ground other than race. Taking the court's findings and rationale at face value, it is clear that the outcome would have been different had petitioner married a Caucasian male of similar respectability.

A core purpose of the Fourteenth Amendment was to do away with all governmentally imposed discrimination based on race. Classifying persons according to their race is more likely to reflect racial prejudice than legitimate public concerns; the race, not the person, dictates the category. Such classifications are subject to the most exacting scrutiny; to pass constitutional muster, they must be justified by a compelling governmental interest and must be "necessary ... to the accomplishment" of its legitimate purpose.

The State, of course, has a duty of the highest order to protect the interests of minor children, particularly those of tender years. In common with most states, Florida law mandates that custody determinations be made in the best interests of the children involved. The goal of granting custody based on the best interests of the child is indisputably a substantial governmental interest for purposes of the Equal Protection Clause.

It would ignore reality to suggest that racial and ethnic prejudices do not exist or that all manifestations of those prejudices have been eliminated. There is a risk that a child living with a step-parent of a different race may be subject to a variety of pressures and stresses not present if the child were living with parents of the same racial or ethnic origin.

The question, however, is whether the reality of private biases and the possible injury they might inflict are permissible considerations for removal of an infant child from the custody of its natural mother. We have little difficulty concluding that they are not. The Constitution cannot control such prejudices but neither can it tolerate them. Private biases may be outside the reach of the law, but the law cannot, directly or indirectly, give them effect. "Public officials sworn to uphold the Constitution may not avoid a constitutional duty by bowing to the hypothetical effects of private racial prejudice that they assume to be both widely and deeply held." *Palmer v. Thompson*, 403 U.S. 217, 260–61 (1971)(White, J., dissenting).

This is by no means the first time that acknowledged racial prejudice has been invoked to justify racial classifications. In *Buchanan v. Warley*, 245 U.S. 60 (1917), for example, this Court invalidated a Kentucky law forbidding Negroes from buying homes in white neighborhoods.

> "It is urged that this proposed segregation will promote the public peace by preventing race conflicts. Desirable as this is, and important as is the preservation of the public peace, this aim cannot be accomplished by laws or ordinances which deny rights created or protected by the Federal Constitution." *Id.*, at 81.

Whatever problems racially-mixed households may pose for children in 1984 can no more support a denial of constitutional rights than could the stresses that residential integration was thought to entail in 1917. The effects of racial prejudice, however real, cannot justify a racial classification removing an infant child from the custody of its natural mother found to be an appropriate person to have such custody.

A Note on Palmore *on Remand*

During the litigation of *Palmore*, Mr. Sidoti received custody of his daughter Melanie. By the time the case returned to the trial court, Mr. Sidoti, his new wife, and Melanie had moved to Texas. Eventually, the Florida trial court declined jurisdiction in favor of the relevant Texas trial court, saying, "Regardless of whether Texas or Florida is found to be Melanie's 'home state', she has in fact resided in Texas with Mr. Sidoti for some 20 months. Accordingly substantial evidence concerning her *present* care, protection, training and personal relationship would be more readily available in Texas than in Florida." *Palmore v. Sidoti*, 472 So2d 843, 845 (Fla App Dist Ct 1985).

Questions on Palmore

(1) What is the Court's reasoning in *Palmore*? The Court begins by stating that racial classifications "must be justified by a compelling governmental interest and must be 'necessary ... to the accomplishment' of their legitimate purpose." The Court then evidently proceeds to apply that test. The Court first concludes that "[t]he goal of granting custody based on the best interests of the child is indisputably a substantial governmental interest for purposes of the Equal Protection Clause." Is the use of "substantial" instead of "compelling" a hint that the governmental interest is not strong enough? Or does the Court intend to say that there is a compelling governmental interest and that the only question is whether the "necessary" part of the test is met? The Court then immediately says that the injuries to the child that result from racial biases are not "permissible considerations." How does this fit into the strict-scrutiny test the Court says it is applying? Does it speak to necessity? Or is it a statement that the test is being abandoned? Why is the test abandoned here when it presumably works elsewhere? What is being substituted for the test?

(2) Assume that the lower courts were correct in believing that living in a racially mixed household would create difficulties for the child. Assume further that all the other possible factors were so evenly balanced that those assumed difficulties would be dispositive. Would the holding in *Palmore* still be justified? If so, why ought we in this case abandon the presumption that is so central to child-custody law—that the child's best interest should be the pre-eminent consideration in child-custody disputes?

The Statutory Law of Racial Matching

In 1996, racial matching policies encountered an unexpected setback from a surprising person and a surprising part of government. The surprising person was Senator Howard Metzenbaum, whose solidly leftist voting record might seem to have placed him with the generally leftist forces that supported racial matching. The surprising part of government was the federal government, whose entry into an area historically confided to the states was hardly unprecedented but was hardly inevitable. The following statute was the result of legislation Senator Metzenbaum introduced:

MULTIETHNIC PLACEMENT ACT OF 1996

Public Law 104–188, Small Business Job Protection Act of 1996

Sec. 1808. REMOVAL OF BARRIERS TO INTERETHNIC ADOPTION.

(a) State Plan Requirements. Section 471(a) of the Social Security Act (42 U.S.C 671(a)) is amended—

(3) by adding at the end the following:

(18) ... neither the State nor any other entity in the State that receives funds from the Federal Government and is involved in adoption or foster care placements may—

(A) deny to any person the opportunity to become an adoptive or a foster parent, on the basis of the race, color, or national origin of the person, or of the child, involved; or

(B) delay or deny the placement of a child for adoption or into foster care, on the basis of the race, color, or national origin of the adoptive or foster parent, or the child, involved....

(c) 42 USC 1996b Civil Rights.

(1) Prohibited conduct.—A person or government that is involved in adoption or foster care placements may not—

(A) deny to any individual the opportunity to become an adoptive or a foster parent, on the basis of the race, color, or national origin of the individual, or of the child, involved; or

(B) delay or deny the placement of a child for adoption or into foster care, on the basis of the race, color, or national origin of the adoptive or foster parent, or the child, involved.

(2) Enforcement.—Noncompliance with paragraph (1) is deemed a violation of title VI of the Civil Rights Act of 1964.

(3) No effect on the Indian Child Welfare Act of 1978.—This subsection shall not be construed to affect the application of the Indian Child Welfare Act of 1978.

This statute might seem to moot out any discussion of transracial adoption. It has not done so. First, cases of many sorts remain which the statute does not control but in which racial-matching ideas may be influential. Consider, for instance, the Cornilous case we discussed in Chapter 10. Consider also a custody dispute between a white mother and a black father over their children.

Second, the statute seems to have encountered resistance. David Crary, *Interracial Adoption Debate Plagues Family*, Harrisburg Patriot, July 3, 2000, at B20 (2000 WL 9351525), reports that

> four years later, the congressional initiative remains divisive. The National Association of Black Social Workers [NABSW], backed by many white colleagues, opposes interracial adoption except as a last resort. Some prominent advocates of interracial adoption are upset, contending that the Health and Human Services Department has undermined congressional intent with halfhearted enforcement of the new rules.
>
> "Nothing has frustrated me more in the entire time I've been in Washington than the unwillingness of those at the policy-making level and out in the field to enforce the law," said former Sen. Howard Metzenbaum, the Ohio Democrat who initiated the legislation in 1994.
>
> He asserts that the black social workers' position is shared by many black civil servants serving under Health and Human Services Secretary Donna Shalala.

This article reports that 51% of the 117,000 children in foster care waiting for adoption in 1995 were black and that "[b]lack children wait longer than whites; relatively few are the infants and toddlers so prized by many adoptive parents; and most have medical or developmental problems." It said that the NABSW "shares a yearning to get black children out of foster care. But it says the priority should be to place them with black families who have a better understanding of racism and black culture."

Nor is it evident that all the states have embraced the spirit of the Multiethnic Placement Act. After that statute was passed, for example, Minnesota rewrote its statute governing racial matching, Minn Stat § 259.29 subd 2 (2005), to require that the "child-placing agency shall consider placement, consistent with the child's best interests and in the following order, with (1) a relative or relatives of the child, or (2) an important friend with whom the child has resided or had significant contact." Is this just common sense? Is it an attempt to make transracial adoption less likely without expressly mentioning it?

The continuing, often bitter, controversy over transracial adoption suggests the third reason it remains worth our attention—few issues raise questions at the intersection of family law and pluralist principle more forcefully. The topic raises challenging questions about who should be considered a member of an ethnic community, about the claims ethnic communities may make on the larger society and on its members, and about how to understand the interests of children of those communities.

The Case Law of Racial Matching

Before *Palmore* was decided, a number of cases held that race could be consulted in decisions about child custody and adoption. These cases typically fall into three categories. First are those cases like *Palmore* in which one white parent is having an affair with or has married someone of a different race, and the other white parent argues that the child will suffer from the social strains arising out of the situation. Second are cases in which parents who are of different races contend for custody of their child, with the minority parent contending that the child is also of the minority race and therefore will be better off with the minority parent. As to these cases, one court wrote that "the general rule appears to be that race is simply one factor among many others which should be considered in determining what is in the child's best interest." *Farmer v. Farmer*, 439 NYS2d 584, 588 (Sup Ct, Trial Term 1981). Third are adoption cases in which a white couple seek to adopt a child of a minority race and are resisted either on the theory that someone of the minority race is available to adopt the child or that white couples ought not be allowed to adopt children of minority races whatever the availability of minority adoptive parents.

A leading example of the third pattern is *Petition of R.M.G.*, 454 A2d 776 (DC App 1982). "D," the child, was "born on September 22, 1977, to unwed, teenage, black parents." D's mother gave her up for adoption without notifying D's father, who had moved to Cleveland. On January 6, 1978, the District of Columbia Department of Human Services placed D with white foster parents. When they received D, she was suffering from nausea and diarrhea and was lethargic, underweight, and showing signs of mental retardation. On April 26, 1978, the foster parents petitioned to adopt D. The Department recommended that the petition be approved. At the foster mother's insistence, however, the Department notified the child's natural father of the adoption. The father objected, and D's paternal grandmother and her husband sought, with the father's support, to adopt D. The Department recommended that their petition be approved instead of the foster parents'.

The foster parents were a colonel and his wife who had three children of their own and who had already adopted another black child. By the time of the adoption hearing in April 1979, D's health was good, she had "bloomed enormously," and her intelligence had turned out to be "high average to above average." The trial court found that, "[a]s a direct result of [the foster parents'] love, affection and special efforts, the child prospered to her present state of good health." The foster parents "had begun 'an affirmative program' with their adopted male child. For example, [the foster mother] had obtained pre-school black history and coloring books for their son. She testified, 'I make sure he knows that he's not white. I don't care how long he lives with us, he's black, and he's beautiful, and he's ours.' "

The paternal grandmother had eight children and was living with two of her nine grandchildren. She said she could take a leave of absence from her job to be with D. Both the grandmother and her husband said they wanted to and could raise D.

The trial court said both families had "shown love and concern for the child" and were "reasonably stable." It wrote,

> The question of race is important.... [T]here are not conclusive absolutes to be drawn on the basis of race. It would seem, however, entirely reasonable that as a child grows older the ramifications of this problem would increase. At a later stage, notwithstanding love and affection, severe questions of identity arising from the adoption and race most

> probably would evolve. In the world at large, as the circle of contacts and routines widens, there are countless adjustments which must be made. Given the circumstances in this case, the child's present status is relatively secure and carefree. The future, in each of its stages—childhood, adolescence, young adulthood, etc.—would likely accentuate these vulnerable points.

On June 1, 1979, the trial court held in favor of adoption by the grandmother and her husband.

D was still with her foster parents by the time of the oral argument in the District of Columbia Court of Appeals on January 29, 1981. That court did not hand down an opinion until December 29, 1982. Each of the three members of the panel wrote a separate opinion; however, they agreed that race was a factor that could be taken into account.

Judge Ferren's opinion found that racial classifications are presumptively invalid and must be necessary to serve a compelling state interest. The opinion concluded that "advancement of a child's best interest is a 'compelling' governmental interest." In asking whether taking race into account was necessary, Judge Ferren wrote,

> [A]doptees often find it difficult to establish a sense of identity. "Identity," in this context, has at least three components: (1) a sense of "belonging" in a stable family and community; (2) a feeling of self-esteem and confidence; and (3) "survival skills" that enable the child to cope with the world outside the family.... [A]doptive parents' attitudes ... affect, to a significant extent, whether the child will feel secure and confident in the family and community. Because race may be highly relevant to these parental attitudes ... it is relevant to the larger issue of the child's best interest....
>
> When considered among a number of factors, on the basis of evidence, without automatic or presumptive preference for an adoptive parent of a particular race, that criterion [race] does not reflect a "racial slur or stigma" against any group. It is a criterion that markedly contrasts with the impermissible use of race both in facially discriminatory statutes and in facially neutral statutes—some referring to race, others not—masking invidious racial discrimination in the law either as enacted or as administered.

However, because of the "very real risk of misuse—of discriminatory application—of a racial classification," Judge Ferren wished to require the appellate court to "be sure that the trial court has exercised its discretion within the range of permissible alternatives, based on all relevant factors and no improper factor." He concluded that "only through detailed written findings and conclusions will the trial court be able to explain its thinking process with sufficient clarity to assure the data needed for effective review."

Judge Ferren's opinion went on to require courts to

> make a three-step evaluation: (1) how each family's race is likely to affect the child's development of a sense of identity, including racial identity; (2) how the families compare in this regard; and (3) how

> significant the racial differences between the families are when all the factors relevant to adoption are considered together.

Judge Ferren concluded that the trial court "did not articulate the comparative analysis required by steps two and three" and thus that the case should be remanded.

Judge Mack concurred in Judge Ferren's conclusion that the case should be remanded, but Judge Mack saw "no need to reach the constitutional issue of equal protection." Judge Mack reasoned that since the adoption statute "*does not require* that the court give these [racial and religious] factors any consideration," the court was "not faced with a statutory scheme separating persons solely on the basis of racial classifications or an affirmative action program allegedly giving preference on the basis of racial classifications." Judge Mack instead reasoned that the trial court "employed the factor of race as an impermissible *presumption*." Judge Mack wished to "remand for a particularized determination, taking into consideration factors bearing uniquely upon this child's adjustment and development including the significance of giving 'full recognition to a family unit already in existence.'"

Judge Newman's opinion argued that "the Constitution does *not* require a court to ignore racial differences between prospective parent and child, to the extent that such differences must be observed in order to judge" the child's best interest. Judge Newman believed that a remand "will probably do no harm" but found it "unlikely that a wordier opinion will make it easier to detect and overturn abuses if and when they occur in the future."

Judge Newman would have affirmed the trial court's result. Judge Newman reasoned that strict scrutiny of the racial classification used in this case was not necessary because "the use of the racial factor does not stigmatize a particular racial group" and because, "though the consideration of race was not purposefully remedial, neither were its purpose and effect pernicious with respect to the distribution of burdens and benefits among racial groups." In these situations, "the consideration of race seeks not to improve the position of any particular racial group, but simply to protect the best interests of the child, of whatever race." But Judge Newman reasoned that, even if strict scrutiny were applied, protecting the child's best interests is a compelling state interest. That compelling interest, Judge Newman concluded, is served by considering race:

> Some of the risks of interracial adoption involve the child's development of identity (including racial and cultural identity), self-esteem, and a sense of belonging in the family.... One problem is the possibility that the child may not perceive herself as black or develop an identity as a black person. There was evidence at trial that the foster parents would make efforts to alleviate this possibility. Even if the child is made aware of her black identity, however, other problems might develop. The child would then have to cope with the fact that she is different from her parents. As one of the expert witnesses in this case testified:

> If a child has to start out, "I'm different. I'm special," that child is being deprived of a strong and healthy concept of self that they could have in an environment where they do not have to deal with that kind of division twenty-four hours a day.

Another aspect of the identity problem is the possibility that the child may experience a "conflict of loyalties" as she grows older.... [T]he child may be caught between two cultures and accepted by neither. Even if the white foster parents were able to nurture the child's ability to perceive herself as black, there is little they could do to prevent the ambivalent feelings and rejection she may experience later in life.

In addition to a strong sense of identity, the black child must learn to develop certain survival skills.... Blacks and other minorities develop survival skills for coping with ... racism, which they can pass to their children expressly, or more importantly, by unconscious example. Parents of interracial families may attempt to learn these lessons and then teach them, but most authorities recognize that this is an inferior substitute for learning directly from minority role models....

... When some people see a child whose race is different from that of his parents, they assume he is an illegitimate child or the product of a multi-racial marriage—circumstances they may disapprove of. Other people overreact in a well-meaning way, commenting on how wonderful it is to adopt a minority child. But however well-intentioned, such reactions have the effect of emphasizing to the child that he is "different," and can lead to a sense of isolation.

R.M.G. preceded *Palmore*. Would *Palmore* require a different result in *R.M.G.*? Another panel of the District of Columbia Court of Appeals appeared to think not, for in *Petition of D.I.S.*, 494 A2d 1316 (DC App 1985), it upheld an award of custody to a grandmother rather than to the child's white foster mother in part because of "the trauma [the child] would face in adolescence in searching for her roots if placed with [the foster mother], and [the grandmother's] greater ability to foster the child's sense of her Guyanese/Latino heritage." Neither the majority opinion nor Judge Ferren's concurrence mentioned *Palmore*.

Questions on Racial Matching

What all these cases—*Palmore, Farmer, R.M.G.*, and the rest—have in common is the argument that cultural ideas about race may make it in the child's best interests to be placed with members of the child's race. Is this principle correct?

(1) For lawyers, the legitimacy of *R.M.G.*'s principle must be measured against *Palmore*. Can *Palmore* be distinguished?

(a) Is *Palmore* indistinguishable because it states that racial classifications may not be used in making child-custody decisions? By its terms, the reasoning would go, *Palmore* speaks of doing away with "all governmentally imposed discrimination based on race." It also seems to condemn "racial classifications" and situations where "the race, not the person, dictates the category." Are *Palmore* and *R.M.G.* indistinguishable because in both cases the lower court argument is that children are better off when brought up by parents of their own race and when they are protected from social hostility to the racial composition of their household?

Marriage of Brown, 480 NE2d 246 (Ind App 1985), involved children of an interracial marriage. The black grandmother argued that "the best interests of the children would be served by rearing them in a black home in an integrated community." The court, however, declared itself "precluded from considering the merit or lack of merit in this contention," since *Palmore* "held that the reality of private biases based on race and the possible injury they might inflict were *not* permissible considerations for removing an infant child from the custody of its natural mother." The court rejected attempts to read *Palmore* narrowly, since "[i]t holds on equal protection grounds that race is not a permissible consideration to be employed by the courts in this context in determining custody."

Some confirmation of such a broad reading of *Palmore* may perhaps be inferred from the use of that case in two later cases. In the course of finding an affirmative-action plan unconstitutional, the four-Justice plurality in *Wygant v. Jackson Board of Education*, 476 US 267 (1986), cited *Palmore* for the proposition that "a 'core purpose of the Fourteenth Amendment' ... is to 'do away with all governmentally imposed discriminations based on race' " and for the proposition that the Court has subjected to strict scrutiny "the means chosen by a State to accomplish its race-conscious purposes." In a dissent in *Wygant*, Justice Stevens wrote that the equal protection clause "absolutely prohibits the use of race in many governmental contexts," including to decide "who may be fit parents." He also wrote that "consideration of whether the consciousness of race is exclusionary or inclusionary plainly distinguishes the Board's valid purpose in this case from a race-conscious decision that would reinforce assumptions of inequality." To this sentence he appended a footnote which began, "Cf. *Palmore*.... " Finally, in *Richmond v. J.A. Croson*, 488 US 469, 520 (1989), Justice Scalia's concurrence said: "The benign purpose of compensating for social disadvantages ... can no more be pursued by the illegitimate means of racial discrimination than can other assertedly benign purposes we have repeatedly rejected. See, *e.g.*, ... *Palmore v. Sidoti*...."

(b) Is *Palmore* distinguishable because it is about a child's interest in being brought up by her natural mother? The opinion's penultimate paragraph says that the effects of racial prejudice "cannot justify a racial classification removing an infant child from the custody of its natural mother found to be an appropriate person to have such custody." In other words, is *Palmore* distinguishable from those cases where a natural mother (or at least a natural parent) is not the losing contender? Many courts say that "the respective races of the participants is a *factor* to be considered in a child's placement determination but, *as with all factors, can be no more than that—a factor.*" *In re Davis*, 465 A2d 614, 622 (Pa 1983). Is *Palmore* simply saying that, by treating race as a factor that overrode the (powerful?) claim a natural mother would ordinarily have, the trial court was treating race as something more than "a factor"?

Does this distinction between *R.M.G.* and *Palmore* justify deciding *R.M.G.* in favor of the child's black grandmother? Or is the position of the white foster parents (who had had custody of the five-year-old child virtually all her life by the time of the appellate court's remand) close enough to the position of a natural mother to warrant a decision in their favor?

(c) Is *Palmore* distinguishable because the problem in that case was that the reality of the racial prejudice against the Palmores' marriage and its effects on the child are merely assumed, not proved? The opinion quotes Justice White speaking of " 'the hypothetical effects of private racial prejudice that [officials] assume to be both widely and deeply held.' "In *Palmore*, the objection may have been that "[c]lassifying persons according to their race is more likely to reflect racial prejudice than legitimate public concerns. . . ." Is this what the court means when it refers to racial classifications? In other words, is a classification saved from being a "racial classification" if specific, concrete harm can be shown in the particular case? Would *Palmore* have been decided differently if such harm could have been shown? If this was the basis for *Palmore*, why didn't the Court remand to give Mr. Sidoti a chance to show that such harm would result if his wife kept custody of their daughter?

Is *R.M.G.* distinguishable from *Palmore* because the expert testimony in it took the court beyond "risks" and "hypothetical effects" to specific, concrete harm? Since the experts were testifying to harms that were years in the future, should their testimony have that kind of effect?

(d) Is *Palmore* distinguishable because what was really at stake was the mother's constitutional right to associate with and marry anyone she chose? The mother's right to marry a black man and his right to marry her under *Loving v. Virginia*, 388 US 1 (1967)?

(e) Is *Palmore* distinguishable because its gravamen was that courts may not ratify private discrimination, whereas *R.M.G.* does not involve courts ratifying private discrimination? Was the trial court in *Palmore* "ratifying" the private discrimination? Could it be said that the court in *R.M.G.* also ratifying discrimination, since in it, as in *Palmore*, the court was accommodating a social situation that was the result of racial discrimination? Could both courts simply be taking into account the effects of discriminatory behavior in making custody decisions without expressing any approval of it?

The leading case in which the Court considered judicial "enforcement" of private discrimination is *Shelley v. Kraemer*, 334 US 1 (1948). There the court refused to enforce a racially restrictive covenant when the promisees sought to prevent a promisor from selling restricted land to a black purchaser. Is there the same kind and degree of "ratification" of private discrimination in *Shelley* and *Palmore*? In *Shelley*, for example, the covenant was racially discriminatory on its face and had as its direct purpose racial discrimination. In *Palmore*, was racial discrimination even the indirect purpose of the decision?

(2) How persuasive is the argument we summarized in describing *R.M.G.* that if racial matching is not practiced, children will suffer problems of social obloquy, identity, self-esteem, and adjustment? To refresh your memory, here is another formulation of the argument, this time by the National Association of Black Social Workers:

> Black children belong, physically, psychologically and culturally in Black families in order that they receive the total sense of themselves and develop a sound projection of their future. Human beings are products of their environment and develop their sense of values, attitudes and self concept within their family structures. Black children in white homes are cut off from the healthy development of themselves as Black people.

Reprinted in Margaret Howard, *Transracial Adoption: Analysis of the Best Interests Standard,* 59 Notre Dame L Rev 503, 517 (1984). Similarly, see Twila L. Perry, *The Transracial Adoption Controversy: An Analysis of Discourse and Subordination*, 21 NYU Rev of L & Soc Change 33 (1993–94).

(a) Professor Howard, in a summary of the literature, proffers a happier picture of transracial adoption than the opinions in *R.M.G.* (She relies most prominently on: L. Grow and D. Shapiro, *Black Children—White Parents: A Study of Transracial Adoption* (Child Welfare League of America, 1974); L. Grow and D. Shapiro, *Transracial Adoption Today: Views of Adoptive Parents and Social Workers* (Child Welfare League of America, 1975); R. Simon and H. Altstein, *Transracial Adoption* (Wiley, 1977); R. Simon and H. Altstein, *Transracial Adoption: A Follow–Up* (Lexington Books, 1981); D. Fanshel, *Far From the Reservation: The Transracial Adoption of American Indian Children* (Scarecrow Press, 1972).) She notes that "the commentators appear to agree that in-race placement is better for children, despite data suggesting that transracially adopted children adjust just as well as in-racially adopted children." She finds that "transracially adopted children, generally speaking, experience good emotional development." She reports one study which found 23% of its families "in trouble," but observes that race was a factor in only half of these situations and that there was no way of knowing how many of those problems arose out of the child's (often prolonged) experience in foster care. She also warns that "there is some evidence that minority children in general experience problems with self-esteem and emotional adjustment due to the effects of prejudice and racism," and thus "we cannot know whether these problems were caused by the transracial placement or whether the child would experience them anyway."

More specifically, Howard says that one study "found no correlation between racial composition of the neighborhood and any of their measures of the child's adjustment" and that another study "found that parents who adopted transracially perceived their friends and neighbors 'as having little interest in or reaction to their adopted child,' and only 10% reported negative feedback...." She quotes the Macaulays as stating that " 'two of the most common problems transracial parents reported were the discomfort of facing attributions of sainthood and moral superiority and the child-raising problem of gushing relatives and neighbors.' " Finally, she responds to the suggestion that "white adoptive parents are unable to transmit to the black adoptive child the tendency toward doubt and the temporary suspension of trust [and are thereby] failing to satisfy the 'psychosurvival' need of the black child" by describing a study which

> found that both white and non-white children raised in mixed-race families were less likely to have pro-white attitudes or to associate "white" with positive and desirable characteristics than were both white and non-white children generally. Thus the practice of transracial adoption attacked as destroying "psychosurvival skills" of black children may in itself contribute to such a change in attitudes that those skills become superfluous. Indeed, those skills might actually handicap the child's ability to learn "the role of the equal citizen."

(b) In evaluating the apparent conflict between Professor Howard's view of transracial adoptions and *R.M.G.*'s, we confront questions we have encountered before about how social science evidence should be used. As you might expect, the evidence about black children growing up in white homes is hard to evaluate. First, it is "impossible to define 'success' or to measure whether it is accomplished, or to define 'cultural identity' or to determine whether it is lost." Howard, 59 Notre Dame L Rev at 534 n.155. Second, it is hard to construct an adequate study design, one that would, for instance, factor out all the possible influences on a child's well-being except race. Third, too little research has actually been conducted.

The problem lies not just in the quality of the evidence, but in its assimilation by courts, as Professor Howard suggests:

> In *In re R.M.G.*, the trial court found it "interesting that all the experts who appeared in this matter agreed that not enough work has been done on the subject [of race] as it pertains to adoption" and expressed concern that "little medical or scientific attention has been devoted to this problem." Yet the trial court noted that "*[i]t would seem, however, entirely reasonable* that as a child grows older the ramifications of this problem would increase." The dissent was even more straightforward, acknowledging that "lack of empirical data is especially acute as regards the crucial adolescent years." Yet the dissent repeated the trial court's finding of *fact* that " 'severe

> questions of identity arising from the adoption and race most probably would evolve' "later and stated that "[t]he trial court's finding that such risks exist is more than amply supported by trial testimony." Thus, social science speculation is elevated to social science fact.

(All italics and brackets are Professor Howard's.) As to the theory that the problems of transracial adoptions become most acute when the child reaches adolescence, Professor Howard cites findings that "the longer children were in placement [and hence the older they were], the more likely they were to have higher scores on the researchers' measure for personal adjustment."

Serious as problems with the research are, what alternatives are available to a court? If a court ignores the social science evidence as unreliable, what evidence should it use instead? Is the lesson to be drawn from Professor Howard's story the modest one that social science evidence should be treated skeptically and that courts should remember the limits of what they (and we) know?

(3) How persuasive are the arguments in *R.M.G.* that living in a white home will cause serious identity problems for black children?

(a) Presumably all children who are separated from both natural parents, and possibly all children who are separated from one natural parent, face some "identity" questions. How much more is added to those questions by the racial factor in transracial adoptions?

(b) To most people, identity is a complex thing, compounded of all a person's experiences. How central is the racial component of identity? If we consider what Goldstein, Freud, and Solnit seemed to be saying about psychological parenthood, might we suppose that race will be a relatively minor part of a child's identity? Is the argument that people will inevitably build their identities on their understanding of their biological, their genetic, their racial origins? Or is the argument that black children will, as they grow up, build their identities on society's understanding that they are black? How will they perceive this understanding? How powerful an effect will it have?

(c) If race is destiny, how should we think about the identities of children of interracial marriages? Will they feel that they have a white identity as well as a black one? Would their search for that identity be impeded by life in a black household?

(d) How does the issue look if we reverse the races? That is, can it be argued that white children brought up in a black household will face social disapproval and identity problems? Ought black couples be allowed to adopt or win custody of white children?

(e) To what extent is it socially desirable to encourage people to think of themselves in racial terms?

(4) The question in thinking about *Palmore* and *R.M.G.* is not simply whether racial matching is good or bad, but also whether racial matching is better than the alternatives. A strict racial matching policy could mean that black children were kept in institutions or prolonged foster care instead of being adopted by white parents. What would Goldstein, Freud, and Solnit say about such a result? Would they be right?

As we wrote earlier, courts often say that "the respective races of the participants is a *factor* to be considered in a child's placement determination but, *as with all factors, can be no more than that—a factor.*" *In re Davis*, 465 A2d 614, 622 (Pa 1983). But how powerful a factor may and should race be? How should it be weighed against other factors? In *R.M.G.*, the child had been living for five years with the only parents she had ever known when the appellate court remanded the case. When, if at all, should the child's ties to her foster parents and her interest in stability outweigh her interest in being raised by people of her race?

Since *R.M.G.*, *Palmore*, and Professor Howard's writing, there have been developments on the issue of transracial placement on legal, practical, and academic fronts. Congress has taken action in the Howard M. Metzenbaum Multiethnic Placement Act of 1994, Pub L No 103–382, § 553(a)(1), 108 Stat. 3518, 4056 (repealed 1996) (providing that an agency that receives federal assistance may not "[c]ategorically deny to any person the opportunity to become an adoptive or a foster parent, solely on the basis of the race, color, or national origin of the adoptive or foster parent, or the child, involved." More recently, federal law has prevented states from prohibiting transracial adoption. See 42 USC § 671(a)(18)(A)-(B) (2005)). Some states, attempting to continue race preferences, give preference to adoptive parents who are kin or close friends, always in the goal of furthering the child's best interests. See Minn Stat § 259.29 (2005); Cal Fam Code § 7950 (West 2006). Meanwhile, the practice of kinship care, or fostering with relatives, has become the norm in some places when children can no longer reside with their birth families, particularly in the black community. Kinship care is an exception to the policies against any race matching, and is recognized by 42 USC § 675(1)(E). Ernestine F. Jones et al., Casey Family Programs, *The Kinship Report: Assessing the Needs of Relative Caregivers and the Children in their Care* 8–9 (2003) ("[Kinship care] appears to be growing at a remarkable rate. In 1998, an estimated 2.1 million children were living with relatives. By the year 2000, this figure had almost doubled: according to the U.S. Census Bureau, almost 4 million children were living with relatives other than birth parents."), available at http://www. casey.org/ Resources/Archive/ Publications/ KinshipReport. htmhttp://www.casey.org/ Resources/ Archive/ Publications/Kinship Report.htm. Important discussions of transracial adoption include: Elizabeth Bartholet, *Nobody's Children: Abuse and Neglect, Foster Drift, and the Adoption Alternative* (Beacon Books, 1999); Randall Kennedy, Interracial Intimacies: Sex, Marriage, Identity, and Adoption (Pantheon

Books, 2003) (reviewed by Margaret F. Brinig in The Child's Best Interests: A Neglected Perspective on Interracial Intimacies, 117 Harv L Rev 2129 (2004)); Rachel Moran, Interracial Intimacy: The Regulation of Race and Romance (U of Chicago Press 2001); and Rita J. Simon and Rhonda M. Roorda, *In Their Own Voices: Transracial Adoptees Tell Their Stories* (Columbia U Press, 2000). For a smattering of the law review literature, see Margaret F. Brinig and Steven L. Nock, *How Much Does Legal Status Matter? Adoptions by Kin Caregivers*, 36 Fam L Q 449 (2002) (including an empirical study on the relative strengths of adoption, kinship care and foster care for children of various ethnicities) and Dorothy Roberts, *The Genetic Tie*, 62 U Chi L Rev 209, 266–67 (1995)(maintaining that the interest in adopting children of color may stem from a desire to add excitement to white lives, while transracial "adoptions permit white families to embrace Black children without eliminating the structures that preserve white supremacy."). For a look at how poverty might be used to involve the state in families through subsidies in a kinship care program, see Dorothy E. Roberts, *Kinship Care and the Price of State Support for Children*, 76 Chi–Kent L Rev 1619 (2001).

(5) Does the reasoning of *R.M.G.* apply to children of other races? For example, does it apply to Indians? Asians? Ethnic groups that are not racially distinct? To Hispanics? Poles? Italians? Germans?

(6) May race—ought race—be relevant on the theory that that promotes the interests of the minority race? The NABSW statement we quoted above suggests it may and must be. That statement was based on

> 1. the necessity of self-determination from birth to death, of all Black people.
>
> 2. the need of our young ones to begin at birth to identify with all Black people in a Black community.
>
> 3. the philosophy that we need our own to build a strong nation.

Howard, 59 Notre Dame L Rev at 517. What legal precedent is there for such a position?

(a) Perhaps the best precedent for according special authority to a cultural group to socialize its members in order to preserve the group is *Wisconsin v. Yoder*. The Amish argued that if their children were required to stay in school after completing the eighth grade their children would be distanced from their religious community. And the Court found the Wisconsin statute posed "a very real threat of undermining the Amish community and religious practice." Is *Yoder* distinguishable from the racial matching cases?

(i) *Yoder* might be a parents-rights case rather than a group-rights case. The parents were prosecuted in their role as parents. Could *Yoder* be justified purely in terms of parents rights to control their children's religious and educational lives?

(ii) One distinction between the racial matching cases and *Yoder* is that no one can speak for American blacks as a group in the same way members of local Amish communities—particularly clergymen—might speak for those communities. (Not only are local Amish communities structured, they maintain homogeneity through systematic resistance to pluralizing influences and through splitting into separate communities when divided by doctrinal disputes.) Ought this distinction matter? How do we know that racial matching is in a race's interest? Insofar as racial matching is "separationist," there may be a significant number of blacks who oppose it. A significant number of blacks may believe that racial matching principles, while desirable in theory, undesirably prevent black children from finding stable homes. If so, to whom should a court look to find the voice of the group? How is the court to decide who speaks for the group?

(iii) One distinction between the racial matching cases and *Yoder* is that the Amish were unequivocally a "group," while the same cannot as readily be said of blacks. Consider, however, the following argument:

> There are natural classes, or social groups, in American society and blacks are such a group. Blacks are viewed as a group; they view themselves as a group; their identity is in large part determined by membership in the group; their social status is linked to the status of the group; and much of our action, institutional and personal, is based on these perspectives.
>
> . . . A social group . . . has two other characteristics. (1) It is an *entity*. . . . This means that the group has a distinct existence apart from its members, and also that it has an identity. It makes sense to talk about the group (at various points of time) and know that you are talking about the same group. . . . (2) There is also a condition of *interdependence*. The identity and well-being of the members of the group and the identity and well-being of the group are linked. Members of the group identify themselves—explain who they are—by reference to their membership in the group; and their well-being or status is in part determined by the well-being or status of the group.

Owen M. Fiss, *Groups and the Equal Protection Clause*, 5 Phil & Pub Affairs 107, 147 (1976).

Is Professor Fiss's argument enough to convince you that blacks qualify for group treatment on the principle of *Yoder*? Consider the following argument:

> Despite increasing references to "the black experience" and exhortations to solidarity, even the most ardent supporters of black unity acknowledge that it is a goal, not an established institution. Among American blacks today, differ-

> ences in economic status, geographical origin and current location, outlook, organizational ties, and education background are powerful centrifugal forces that black nationalist groups have not succeeded in neutralizing.... [B]lacks who are skeptical or distrustful of institutionalized unity can assert that the sudden acceptance by the government of the concept of black unity would be a massive intrusion into the area of black organization—not a merely passive acceptance of the authentic wishes of American blacks.

Boris I. Bittker, *The Case for Black Reparations* 74–75 (Random House 1973).

Professor Bittker's argument may be amplified by comparing the groups involved in the racial matching cases and in *Yoder*. The Amish live in communities that are geographically localized. They tend to be homogeneous in class terms. They share a powerful unifying religion and culture; they even have a separate language (German). Their communities are organized by religious and social institutions and hierarchies. Blacks, on the other hand, are distributed (though not always proportionately) geographically and socially throughout American society. They do not share a single religion, and whether they share a culture depends on what you mean by culture. No single black institution has the strength among American blacks the church has in Amish communities. Is a collectivity relatively this diffuse a "group" for the purpose of asserting the legal interests we are discussing?

(iv) One distinction between the racial-matching cases and *Yoder* is that the latter involves religion while the former involve race. Is this a distinction that ought to matter? Religion may be chosen; race usually cannot be. Is it one thing to treat people as a group when they have chosen to be one and another thing to treat them as a group when they have not chosen to be one?

(v) One distinction between the racial matching cases and *Yoder* is that the Amish could argue that the Wisconsin statute, because it had potentially serious effects on *all* the group's children, could jeopardize the group's existence, while it may be harder to argue that the law's practice in the relatively few child custody cases involving race would jeopardize the group's existence. In addition, Amish children who leave their religion and community cease to be Amish in most people's eyes; black children brought up by white parents will still be black in most people's eyes. Being black is a well-established social category in a way that being Amish is not. Is this distinction convincing?

(b) Is *Yoder* apposite and is *Palmore* distinguishable because the racial classification in *Palmore* disadvantages of someone who was associating with a black and thus indirectly disadvantages blacks whereas in *R.M.G.* the discrimination is designed to benefit black children and possible custodians? In other words, is *R.M.G.*'s racial classification justifiable on "affirmative action" grounds? The Supreme Court has decided a number of affirmative action cases. While it has rarely been able to find a majority in favor of any single position, its results establish that governments may sometimes take race into account. Are the racial matching cases distinguishable from the affirmative action cases?

(i) Insofar as we are justifying cases like *R.M.G.* on a group rights theory, we need to cope with statements like that of the four Justice plurality in *Richmond v. J.A. Croson Co.*, 488 US 469 (1989), which, in the course of finding that even benign racial classifications need to be strictly scrutinized, wrote, "the 'rights created by the first section of the Fourteenth Amendment are, by its terms, guaranteed to the individual. The rights established are personal rights.' *Shelley v. Kraemer*." (Justice Scalia wrote a concurrence implicitly affirming the plurality's statement.)

(ii) One of the judges in *R.M.G.* believed racial matching cases should be subject to strict scrutiny, one believed they need not be, and the third declined to reach the issue. Does the *Croson* rule that even benign racial classifications should be strictly scrutinized require a holding that racial matching is unconstitutional? Judge Ferren's opinion in *R.M.G.* finds that racial matching survives strict scrutiny because serving the child's best interest is a compelling state interest. But is racial matching necessary to serve that interest?

(iii) The argument for a standard lower than strict scrutiny is that benign discrimination ought not have to meet so onerous a standard. The plurality in *Croson*, however, (with the probable assent of Justice Scalia, who wrote separately) wrote,

> Absent searching judicial inquiry into the justification for ... race-based measures, there is simply no way of determining what classifications are "benign" or "remedial" and what classifications are in fact motivated by illegitimate notions of racial inferiority or simple racial politics. Indeed, the purpose of strict scrutiny is to "smoke out" illegitimate uses of race.

How should a court decide whether considering race in custody decisions is benign or malign? Consider the court's explanation in *Ward v. Ward*, 216 P2d 755, 756 (Wash 1950), for its decision to award custody of children of an interracial couple to the black father: "These unfortunate girls, through no fault of their own, are the victims of a mixed marriage and a broken home. They will have a much better opportunity to take their rightful place in society if they are brought up among their own people." Does the legitimacy of the result in cases like *Ward* and

R.M.G. depend on what language a court uses in explaining itself?

Or consider the statute at issue in *Compos v. McKeithen*, 341 F Supp 264 (ED La 1972): "A single person over the age of twenty-one years, or a married couple jointly, may petition to adopt any child of his or their race." La Rev Stat Ann § 9:422. Should we look to the legislative motive in deciding whether the statute is constitutional? Should we look to the Jim Crow past of Louisiana? Would a statute which was unconstitutional in Louisiana be constitutional in, say, Massachusetts?

(iv) Part of the argument for a weak standard of review for affirmative action programs is that when the majority legislates against its own interest a racial classification is less likely to be problematic. But, as the plurality in *Croson* noted, that argument seems greatly weakened when the governmental entity that adopted the program is controlled by members of a minority. Does that mean the level of scrutiny applied in *R.M.G.* should turn on the race of the judges making the decision?

(v) Another lesson of *Croson* seems to be, as the plurality in *Wygant v. Jackson Board of Education*, 476 US 267, 274 (1986), wrote, that there must be "some showing of prior discrimination by the governmental unit involved before allowing a limited use of racial classifications in order to remedy such discrimination." The evidence about past practice in the racial matching context is hardly clear cut, but a notable part of it suggests that past practice was to try to match children with parents of their own race, on the theory that that was in the child's interest. Does the fact that the grounds for this policy may have been partly racist show that the present racial matching policy is remedial?

(vi) An affirmative action case whose fact situation may be relevant to the racial matching cases is *Wygant v. Jackson Board of Education*, 476 US 267 (1986). There, the Court considered a lay-off provision in the Jackson teachers' collective bargaining agreement that called for "the layoff of tenured non-minority teachers while retaining minority teachers on probationary status." The court of appeals had "held that the Board's interest in providing minority role models for its minority students ... was sufficiently important to justify the racial classification...." Justice Stevens' dissent argued that "a school board may reasonably conclude that an integrated faculty will be able to provide benefits to the student body that could not be provided by an all-white, or nearly all-white faculty." There was no majority opinion, but the Court held that the lay-off provision was unconstitutional, five Justices were unpersuaded by the role model theory, and no one joined Justice

Stevens' opinion. May it be inferred from *Wygant* that racial-matching is also unconstitutional?

(vii) One factor that has surfaced repeatedly in the affirmative-action cases is a concern for the "legitimate firmly rooted expectation[s]" of the nonminorities who are disadvantaged by affirmative-action programs. Does *Smith v. OFFER* acknowledge such an expectation in people like the foster parents in *R.M.G.*?

(viii) May the affirmative-action cases be distinguished from the cases that endorse racial matching on the theory that the affirmative action cases can all be described as integrationist, while the racial matching cases can be described as separationist?

(ix) Concurring in *Croson*, Justice Scalia wrote, "The difficulty of overcoming the effects of past discrimination is nothing compared with the difficulty of eradicating from our society the source of those effects, which is the tendency—fatal to a nation such as ours—to classify and judge men and women on the basis of their country of origin or the color of their skin." Is the result in *R.M.G.* objectionable because it perpetuates that tendency? Or is Justice Scalia wrong?

(c) Assuming that blacks ought to be treated as a group for *Yoder* purposes, how ought courts decide who is a member?

(i) Is a child black if a child has preponderantly black ancestry? Some substantial black ancestry? Any black ancestry? Should the same test be used in deciding if a would-be custodian is black? For a detailed discussion, see F. James Davis, *Who Is Black? One Nation's Definition* (Pa St U Press, 1991).

(ii) What if a child belongs to more than one minority group? For example, what if the child's mother "is of Black, American Indian and Irish heritage" and the father is Jewish? *Tubwon v. Weisberg*, 394 NW2d 601, 604 (Minn App 1986).

(iii) If social definitions of and understandings about race are an important reason for taking race into account, should race be determined according to the social determinants of race? For example, should the child's physical appearance be dispositive? The physical appearance of a very young child does not always accurately foretell the adult's appearance. Should courts transfer custody where the court's prediction about the child's appearance changes?

If social definitions are relevant, the preponderance of children of interracial marriages will probably be regarded as black. Should the black parent have some presumption of custody?

(iv) May the parent or parents decide what the child's race is? Should a court ask what racial identity they attribute to the child? Should the court heed that attribution even when the parents are giving the child up for adoption? Should the court accept the parent's description of a child as white, or a parent's consent to a child's adoption by a white couple, even where the child would by all other standards be considered black?

(v) Can children choose their own racial identity?

(vi) How should the racial identity of the custodians be decided? Since the custodians will be adults, should we assume they are the final arbiters of their racial identity? Or, since much of the logic of racial matching is that society or racial antecedents impose a racial identity, should we look to social attitudes or racial antecedents? What should the rule of transracial adoption be where the would-be custodians are a couple of different races?

(vii) Does the awkwardness of this inquiry into racial identity suggest that the inquiry is not a proper one for a court to undertake? Professor Bittker argues that

> the adoption of a formal code of racial classification . . . would have calamitous consequences for the United States. It would ease the way to more and more private, public, and official distinctions between black and white. It would put pressure on millions of persons of mixed blood to make an official declaration of their racial origin, instead of allowing their allegiance to remain private, ambiguous, submerged, neglected, or changeable.

Bittker, *The Case for Black Reparations* at 97. Is this right?

(d) May the law and should the law attempt to protect members of a group from the effects of membership in the group?

(i) In discussing parental rights, we suggested that *Yoder* might disserve the interest in pluralism by allowing Amish parents to "standardize" their children by removing them from the larger community and the opportunities education through high school provides. If parents choose not to regard their children as members of a particular group, or if children choose not to regard themselves as members of a particular group, should that group be able to assert an interest in claiming them as members and in socializing them in membership? We sometimes think that what makes group membership important is that membership is voluntary. But in *Yoder* and the racial matching cases (at least as seen from the perspective we are examining), groups are arguing for the power to socialize children into membership.

(ii) There may be cases (*R.M.G.* may even be one) where, because of factors like the cost to the child of removing her from the people she has regarded as her parents all her life, it will not be in the child's interests but it will be in the group's interest for her to be placed black adoptive parents. How should a court respond? Should a court be willing to advance the interests of a group at the expense of an identifiable child?

(7) May race—ought race—be considered because doing so promotes the interests of the child's parents? Should the natural parents be able to specify the race of the adopting parents? Do parents give up all authority to make decisions for their children when they give up their children for adoption? Suppose the parents give up their children for adoption only on the condition that they be placed with parents of a particular race?

More specifically, consider again *R.M.G.* Suppose both natural parents had specified that they wished the foster parents to be able to adopt their daughter. Suppose that they said they did not care what the race of the adoptive parents was. What weight should be given to such a preference? In fact, the natural father supported his mother's petition. Suppose part of his reason was a preference that his daughter be brought up by a black family. What weight should be given such a preference?

(b) The Indian Child Welfare Act

We have been discussing racial matching in terms of black children. The issue also arises when the custody of Indian children is decided. Congress has sought to deal systematically with many problems we have discussed by passing the Indian Child Welfare Act of 1978, 25 U.S.C. §§ 1901–1963, portions of which are reproduced below:

INDIAN CHILD WELFARE ACT OF 1978

§ 1901. Congressional findings

Recognizing the special relationship between the United States and the Indian tribes and their members and the Federal responsibility to Indian people, the Congress finds— . . .

(2) that Congress, through statutes, treaties, and the general course of dealing with Indian tribes, has assumed the responsibility for the protection and preservation of Indian tribes and their resources; . . .

(4) that an alarmingly high percentage of Indian families are broken up by the removal, often unwarranted, of their children from them by nontribal public and private agencies and that an alarmingly high percentage of such children are placed in non-Indian foster and adoptive homes and institutions; and

(5) that the States, exercising their recognized jurisdiction over Indian child custody proceedings through administrative and judicial bodies, have often failed to recognize the essential tribal relations of Indian people and the cultural and social standards prevailing in Indian communities and families.

§ 1903. Definitions

For the purposes of this chapter, except as may be specifically provided otherwise, the term—

(1) "child custody proceeding" shall mean and include—

(i) "foster care placement" . . .

(ii) "termination of parental rights" . . .

(iii) "preadoptive placement" . . .

(iv) "adoptive placement" . . .

Such term or terms shall not include a placement based upon an act which, if committed by an adult, would be deemed a crime or upon an award, in a divorce proceeding, of custody to one of the parents. . . .

(3) "Indian" means any person who is a member of an Indian tribe, or who is an Alaska Native and a member of a Regional Corporation as defined in section 1606 of Title 43;

(4) "Indian child" means any unmarried person who is under age eighteen and is either (a) a member of an Indian tribe or (b) is eligible for membership in an Indian tribe and is the biological child of a member of an Indian tribe; . . .

§ 1911. Indian tribe jurisdiction over Indian child custody proceedings

(a) Exclusive jurisdiction

An Indian tribe shall have jurisdiction exclusive as to any State over any child custody proceeding involving an Indian child who resides or is domiciled within the reservation of such tribe, except where such jurisdiction is otherwise vested in the State by existing Federal law. Where an Indian child is a ward of a tribal court, the Indian tribe shall retain exclusive jurisdiction, notwithstanding the residence or domicile of the child.

(b) Transfer of proceedings; declination by tribal court

In any State court proceeding for the foster care placement of, or termination of parental rights to, an Indian child not domiciled or residing within the reservation of the Indian child's tribe, the court, in the absence of good cause to the contrary, shall transfer such proceeding to the jurisdiction of the tribe, absent objection by either parent, upon the petition of either parent or the Indian custodian or the Indian child's tribe: *Provided*, That such transfer shall be subject to declination by the tribal court of such tribe.

(c) State court proceedings; intervention

In any State court proceeding for the foster care placement of, or termination of parental rights to, an Indian child, the Indian custodian of the child and the Indian child's tribe shall have a right to intervene at any point in the proceeding. . . .

§ 1912. Pending court proceedings

(a) Notice; time for commencement of proceedings; additional time for preparation

In any involuntary proceeding in a State court, where the court knows or has reason to know that an Indian child is involved, the party seeking the foster care placement of, or termination of parental rights to, an Indian child shall notify the parent or Indian custodian and the Indian child's tribe,....

§ 1913. Parental rights; voluntary termination ...

(b) Foster care placement; withdrawal of consent

Any parent or Indian custodian may withdraw consent to a foster care placement under State law at any time and, upon such withdrawal, the child shall be returned to the parent or Indian custodian.

(c) Voluntary termination of parental rights or adoptive placement; withdrawal of consent; return of custody

In any voluntary proceeding for termination of parental rights to, or adoptive placement of, an Indian child, the consent of the parent may be withdrawn for any reason at any time prior to the entry of a final decree of termination or adoption, as the case may be, and the child shall be returned to the parent....

§ 1914. Petition to court of competent jurisdiction to invalidate action upon showing of certain violations

Any Indian child who is the subject of any action for foster care placement or termination of parental rights under State law, any parent or Indian custodian from whose custody such child was removed, and the Indian child's tribe may petition any court of competent jurisdiction to invalidate such action upon a showing that such action violated any provision of sections 1911, 1912, and 1913 of this title....

Notes and Questions on ICWA

(1) In thinking about racial matching in the context of black children, we considered questions designed to reveal the underlying problems racial matching involves. If we had more space, we would pose those questions again here, because ICWA implicitly provides one set of answers to them. You should at this point review those questions, asking yourself how ICWA would answer them and how those answers accord with the Constitution and with good social policy. How do ICWA's answers differ from the answers in the law of racial matching? What differences between the social, political, and legal situations of Indians and blacks might justify different approaches?

(2) In *Mississippi Band of Choctaw Indians v. Holyfield*, 490 US 30 (1989), the Supreme Court considered a problem which spoke to several tensions ICWA seeks to resolve. Twins were born out of wedlock to two members of the Mississippi Band of Choctaw Indians. Both parents were

residents and domiciles of the tribe's reservation. The mother went to a hospital two hundred miles from that reservation to give birth. Days after the twins were born, both parents consented to their adoption. The Holyfields petitioned to adopt the twins, and a Mississippi court granted the petition. Two months later, the tribe moved to vacate the decree, citing 25 USC § 1911(a). The Mississippi Supreme Court declined. It said the twins "were voluntarily surrendered and legally abandoned by the natural parents to the adoptive parents, and it is undisputed that the parents went to some efforts to prevent the children from being placed on the reservation as the mother arranged for their birth and adoption" off the reservation.

The United States Supreme Court reversed because the twins were domiciled on the reservation within the meaning of § 1911(a). Writing for a six-member majority, Justice Brennan said that "domicile is established by physical presence in a place in connection with a certain state of mind concerning one's intent to remain there," that the twins' parents were domiciled on the reservation, and that children take the domicile of their parents, that therefore the children were domiciled on the reservation even though they had never been there. The Court continued:

> Nor can the result be any different simply because the twins were "voluntarily surrendered" by their mother. Tribal jurisdiction under § 1911(a) was not meant to be defeated by the actions of individual members of the tribe, for Congress was concerned not solely about the interests of Indian children and families, but also about the impact on the tribes themselves of the large numbers of Indian children adopted by non-Indians.... The numerous prerogatives accorded the tribes through the ICWA's substantive provisions ... must, accordingly, be seen as a means of protecting not only the interests of individual Indian children and families, but also of the tribes themselves.
>
> In addition, it is clear that Congress' concern over the placement of Indian children in non-Indian homes was based in part on evidence of the detrimental impact on the children themselves of such placements outside their culture. Congress determined to subject such placements to the ICWA's jurisdictional and other provisions, even in cases where the parents consented to an adoption, because of concerns going beyond the wishes of individual parents....
>
> These congressional objectives make clear that a rule of domicile that would permit individual Indian parents to defeat the ICWA's jurisdictional scheme is inconsistent with what Congress intended.

Justice Brennan's opinion closed by acknowledging that it would "doubtless cause considerable pain" to separate the twins from the Holyfield's. His opinion pointed out, however, that the tribal court which was responsible for deciding the children's custody could take that fact into account.

Writing for the dissent, Justice Stevens began by describing the lengths to which the natural parents had gone to have the state court have jurisdiction. He said, "both parents appear before us today, urging that Vivian Holyfield be allowed to retain custody...." He urged that the Act not be construed to defeat the parents' wishes:

> The Act gives Indian tribes certain rights, not to restrict the rights of parents of Indian children, but to complement and help effect them. The Indian tribe may petition to transfer an action in state court to the tribal court, but the Indian parent may veto the transfer. § 1911(b). The Act provides for a tribal right of notice and intervention in involuntary proceedings but not in voluntary ones. §§ 1911(c), 1912(a). Finally, the tribe may petition the court to set aside a parental termination action upon a showing that the provisions of the ICWA that are designed to protect parents and Indian children have been violated. § 1914.
>
> While the Act's substantive and procedural provisions effect a major change in state child custody proceedings, its jurisdictional provision is designed primarily to preserve tribal sovereignty over the domestic relations of tribe members and to confirm a developing line of cases which held that the tribe's exclusive jurisdiction could not be defeated by the temporary presence of an Indian child off the reservation....
>
> If [the natural parents] had established a domicile off the Reservation, the state courts would have been required to give effect to their choice of jurisdiction; there should not be a different result when the parents have not changed their own domicile, but have expressed an unequivocal intent to establish a domicile for their children off the Reservation.

Justice Stevens concluded, "if both parents have intentionally invoked the jurisdiction of the state court in an action involving a non-Indian, no interest in tribal self-governance is implicated."

(3) The ICWA may be more easily understood with the following information from *Santa Clara Pueblo v. Martinez*, 436 US 49, 55–56 (1978):

> Indian tribes are "distinct, independent political communities, retaining their original natural rights" in matters of local self-government. Although no longer "possessed of the full attributes of sovereignty," they remain a "separate people, with the power of regulating their internal and social relations." They have power to make their own substantive law in internal matters and to enforce that law in their own forums.
>
> As separate sovereigns pre-existing the Constitution, tribes have historically been regarded as unconstrained by those constitutional provisions framed specifically as limitations on federal or state authority....
>
> [H]owever, Congress has plenary authority to limit, modify, or eliminate the powers of local self-government which the tribes otherwise possess.

In addition, as we saw in Chapter 3, these tribes are not only "distinct, independent political communities" with their own distinct cultural traditions; they also have distinct dispute-resolution principles and processes.

(4) The facts of *Martinez* raise another relevant issue. In that case, an Indian woman and her daughter had "brought suit in federal court against the tribe ... seeking declaratory and injunctive relief against enforcement of a tribal ordinance denying membership in the tribe to children of female members who marry outside the tribe, while extending membership to children of male members who marry outside the tribe." They claimed that the rule "discriminates on the basis of both sex and ancestry in violation of Title I of the Indian Civil Rights Act of 1968 (ICRA), 25 USC §§ 1301–1303 (1983), which provides in relevant part that '[n]o Indian tribe in exercising powers of self-government shall ... deny to any person within its jurisdiction the equal protection of its laws.' " The Court held that the ICRA does not "impliedly authorize such actions ... in federal courts." Ms. Martinez and her daughter were thus relegated to pursuing their claim in the tribal court. The Court's opinion noted that the ICRA does not incorporate the entire Bill of Rights; for instance, "the statute does not prohibit the establishment of religion.... "

In dissent, Justice White wrote, "Given Congress' concern about the deprivations of Indian rights by tribal authorities, I cannot believe, as does the majority, that it desired the enforcement of these rights to be left up to the very tribal authorities alleged to have violated them. In the case of the Santa Clara Pueblo, for example, both legislative and judicial powers are vested in the same body, the Pueblo Council."

(5) Jason Begay, *Foster Program Pairs American Indians*, Duluth News–Tribune, Monday, August 2, 1999, reports on the "Fond du Lac Foster Care Licensing and Placement Agency[, which] is the only agency in the nation that focuses on placing Indian children who live outside of their reservations with Indian foster homes." The agency reports that before it "was activated in 1991, nearly 70 percent of Indian children in out-of-home placement in St. Louis County were in non-Indian homes.... In 1996, 60 percent of those children were living in Indian homes." The agency's "homes are licensed based on standards set by the state of Minnesota but also must contain members of federally recognized tribes. That requirement complies with the Indian Child Welfare Act."

The article noted that

> [m]any tribes, including most Ojibwe bands in Wisconsin and Minnesota, have culturally based programs in their schools and community centers. There's a strong movement among the nation's 550 tribes to strengthen cultural ties as more tribal members move away from reservations. For example, 1,200—less than a third—of the Fond du Lac Band's 3,100 members live on the reservation. Growing up in a familiar culture is particularly important to American Indian children, said Robertson [the agency's "lead social worker"]. "How can you figure out

who you are when nobody looks like you? If you're surrounded by people who are totally unlike you?" she asked.

The article observed, "Despite the intent of the ICWA, the National Indian Child Welfare Association reported more than 50,000 Indian children lived away from their cultural roots as adoptees in non-Indian families in 1997." A county official was quoted as saying that any time the county social service authorities place an Indian child "we need concurrence with the tribe to make sure it's OK." He "said the county continues to seek an Indian home for a child even after he or she is placed in a non-Indian home."

As you may remember, the Multiethnic Placement Act's civil rights subsection "shall not be construed to affect the application of the Indian Child Welfare Act of 1978." Why? Do the arguments for the Fond du Lac program apply equally well to the placement of black children? Should we distinguish between programs that encourage placement within an ethnic community and rules that directly inhibit children from being placed or adopted outside such a community?

(c) Religion in Adoption and Child Custody Decisions

A number of states permit or encourage courts to take religion into account in making decisions about adoption and child custody. We will look at three areas in which questions about such policies arise.

The first area has to do with religious matching. Perhaps the most extensively litigated and discussed provision requiring that policy is Article VI, section 32 of the New York Constitution, which states that a child "shall be committed or remanded or placed, when practicable, in an institution or agency governed by persons, or in the custody of a person, of the same religious persuasion as the child." This provision and statutes implementing it were found constitutional in *Dickens v. Ernesto*, 281 NE2d 153 (NY 1972), and *Wilder v. Sugarman*, 385 F Supp 1013 (SDNY 1974). Statutes of this kind grow in part out of the fears, which in the nineteenth century could be quite strong, of the churches of immigrant groups that children of their members were being systematically placed for adoption in Protestant homes.

The second area in which religion has entered custody decisions involves cases in which the religious wants of the child have been heeded in choosing a custodian. There is overlap between this category and the preceding one, but the preceding category emphasizes simple matching, while this category emphasizes accommodating the child's developed religious beliefs.

The third area comprises situations in which the religiously motivated behavior of a would-be custodian is a basis for denying him or her custody. Typical cases in this category involve parents who are hostile on religious grounds to the other parent, custodians who limit the child's access to medical care in some way, and custodians who bring up the child in a markedly unusual way, often one that isolates or alienates the child from conventional society.

The questions that follow discuss the problems that arise in each kind of case. However, the questions are arranged to track the questions we asked about racial matching to make it easier for you to ask yourself whether racial and religious matching are similar.

Notes and Questions on Religion and Custody

(1) May religion be relevant to decisions about the custody of a child on grounds analogous to those in *R.M.G.*? Might a child brought up outside his or her own religion suffer problems of obloquy, identity, self-esteem, and adjustment? In *T. v. H.*, 245 A2d 221 (NJ Super Ch 1968), a Jewish father sought custody of his two children. Their Jewish mother had married a Gentile and moved to Kellogg, Idaho, where the children and their mother were the only Jews and had access only to two temples, each distant. In an elliptical opinion, the court held that "the religious education and religious environment of the children, eight and ten, [are] an important though not controlling factor" and awarded custody to the father.

On the other hand, in *In re Marriage of Gersovitz*, 779 P2d 883 (Mont 1989), the trial court had, when the child was three years old, devised a plan which placed the child in the Gentile mother's custody after he began school. The trial court had chosen the mother "because of her parenting abilities, her lack of animosity towards [the father] and her greater range of interests.... [The mother] appears to be more capable of allowing Alex to develop his own identity."

The Montana Supreme Court wrote,

> Jeremy [the Jewish father] argues that from the time of his birth, Alex [the child] has been raised Jewish, with the support and cooperation of both parents. He argues that being Jewish is not merely a religion, it is a way of life. Alex's full name, Alexander Samuel Gersovitz, is a Jewish name and he will be recognized by society as a Jew. Jeremy further states that Alex has been circumcised and has regularly and routinely been made a part of the Missoula Jewish community celebration of their faith.
>
> Jeremy argues that the District Court abused its discretion in concluding, for all practical purposes, that once Alex reaches school age, he should be raised in no religion, rather than the religion in which he has been raised since his birth. [The father] claims that because he has been separated from [the child], he will not be raised with sufficient knowledge of Judaism. This, he argues, will make it difficult, if not impossible, for Alex to live in the Jewish tradition, because a Jewish boy achieves religious responsibility at the age of thirteen when he celebrates his barmitzvah, becomes an adult and chooses his religion, Judaism.

The appellate court, however, held that the district court had not abused its discretion and that, "under the facts of this case, an award of custody for the purpose of religious education should not dominate other elements which comprise the best interests of this particular child."

The religion in both these two cases was Judaism. Does the *R.M.G.* rationale, if it applies at all to religions, apply only to religions like Judaism, which have a strong ethnic and cultural component? If Alex had not, as his father argued, been recognizable as a Jew, would the *R.M.G.* rationale apply? Or would Alex have known he was Jewish and thus suffered identity problems when not brought up as a Jew?

(2) May religion be taken into account to provide the child with a religious life when the child has arguably acquired his or her own religious faith? Alaska's child custody statute directs courts to consider "the ... religious ... needs of the child." The Alaska Supreme Court assessed that requirement in *Bonjour v. Bonjour*, 592 P2d 1233 (Alaska 1979). The trial court awarded custody of Michael Bonjour (five at the time of the trial, six and a half at the time of the appellate court opinion) to his father, Randall, a "devout Protestant" who was "involved in an organized religious community and has in the past been principally involved in Joseph's religious education." The appellate court found the statute facially constitutional:

> The tripartite test for judging governmental action allegedly violating the establishment clause was recently articulated in *Wolman v. Walter*, 433 U.S. 229, 236 (1977):
>
> > In order to pass muster, a statute [1] must have a secular legislative purpose, [2] must have a principal or primary effect that neither advances nor inhibits religion, and [3] must not foster an excessive government entanglement with religion.
>
> *Accord, Lemon v. Kurtzman*, 403 U.S. 602, 612–13 (1971)....
>
> Consideration of religion in child custody cases, properly limited to an examination of a child's actual religious needs, can further a secular purpose. The legislature's intent in passing AS 09.55.205 was to assure that the award of custody was in furtherance of the best interests of the child, a secular purpose.... To hold otherwise would be to sanction an unwarranted hostility toward religion and religious beliefs. *See Walz v. Tax Commission*, 397 U.S. 664, 672 (1970); *Zorach v. Clauson*, 343 U.S. 306, 313–14 (1952)....
>
> Here, however, the trial court made no finding that the child, Michael Bonjour, had any religious needs. In the absence of a finding of religious needs in fact, a presumption that a child "needs religion" converts the secular legislative purpose into a judicial preference for religion....
>
> Even if a secular purpose could be found in the trial court's action, its reliance upon the religious affiliations of the parties runs afoul of the second requirement, that the government action have a predominantly secular effect. Laws which incidentally coincide with some religious practices do not violate the establishment clause. *McGowan v. Mary-*

> *land*, 366 U.S. 420 (1961)(state statute providing for Sunday as common day of rest upheld). Similarly, programs which seek to accommodate the free exercise of religious beliefs and practices in general are not forbidden by the establishment clause. *Zorach v. Clauson*, 343 U.S. 306 (1952)(released time program which allowed children to leave public schools at designated times to receive religious instruction elsewhere upheld).... The principal or primary effect of giving preference to parents who are members of an "organized religious community" in child custody disputes ... goes beyond accommodation and benevolent neutrality towards religion, while not advancing any values protected by the free exercise clause.

The supreme court remanded, stressing "that the court must make a finding that the child has actual, not presumed, religious needs, and that one parent will be more able to satisfy those needs than the other parent. By actual religious needs, we refer to the expressed preference of a child mature enough to make a choice between a form of religion or the lack of it."

(a) How are a child's religious needs to be defined? In a footnote, the court in *Bonjour* said that, "given the age of the child, it seems highly improbable that the court could have found any religious needs on the part of [Michael]." *Was* Michael not "mature enough to make a choice"? Is the child's ability to make a choice the proper test? In *Gersovitz*, the father had argued that his at-least-equally-young son was Jewish because he had been raised Jewish, would be regarded as Jewish, and had been circumcised. Can a child's parent define the child's religious needs? Can the religion into which the child was born?

(b) The court in *Bonjour* says preference may not be given to parents simply because they are religious. Consider, however, *In re Adoption of "E,"* 279 A2d 785 (NJ 1971). There, the trial court "held that plaintiffs' lack of belief in a Supreme Being rendered them unfit to be adoptive parents." The New Jersey Supreme Court wrote,

> By basing his decision *solely* on the absence of the Burkes' belief in a Supreme Being and their lack of church affiliation, the trial court relied on a factor which cannot alone be determinative of the "best interests" of the child "E". We do not mean to suggest that a trial court may not probe into the religious background and convictions of prospective adopting parents.... Religion and morality are inextricably interwoven in the lives of most people in this country, and a high moral character of prospective adopting parents is an essential consideration in adoption proceedings....

... [Q]uestions concerning religion as it bears on ethics are not constitutionally forbidden because they serve a valid secular purpose.... [S]uch questions may be evidential of moral fitness to adopt in relation to how the applicants will conduct themselves as adopting parents.

(3) Can religion justify denying someone custody when that person's religion might have harmful secular effects on the child? In *Quiner v. Quiner*, 59 Cal Rptr 503 (Cal App 1967), both parents were members of a sect called the Plymouth Brethren. However, Mrs. Quiner belonged to a particularly strict subsect called the Exclusive Brethren. The Exclusive Brethren "dissociate" themselves from all who are not Exclusive Brethren. Mrs. Quiner said she "would teach [her son] to love his father as a son and as his father and to respect him in every way and to obey him. I would not teach him to hate his father at all." However, she "admitted she would keep him away from his father if she could," and she agreed that "children within the religious group [are] brought up to think that others outside the religious group [including Mr. Quiner] are unclean."

There was also evidence that Exclusive Brethren do "not affiliate with any outside organization" of any kind, vote or participate in "civic political or governmental activities," use any form "of public or private entertainment," have pets, or read anything except the Bible. Their children "are discouraged, if not forbidden as sinful, from participating in all forms of extracurricular activity." Their children "may not visit or play with other children in their homes, or in their own homes or elsewhere" except school.

The trial court held that the Quiners' child John Edward (who was around three years old at the time of the trial) should be placed in his father's custody. It observed that "mental welfare" was part of the child's best interests and that that term "includes the opportunities for intellectual, character and personality growth, and the development of those social graces and amenities without which one cannot live comfortably or successfully in a complex, integrated society." It concluded that

> the intellectually blighted social microcosm of the Exclusive Brethren in which John Edward would be forceably confined during his early years in [his mother's] custody is more than likely to retard his mental growth and personality development, would be inimical to his welfare, and would severely handicap him in later years in his struggle to achieve his goals of social and economic attainment.

The appellate court reversed:

> We are sensitive to the revelation ... that custody in the mother may breed in John Edward a lack of religious and filial rapport with his father and the father's parents, and may possibly breed definite antipathy to his father and his paternal grandparents.... We agree that this probability is not for the best interests of John Edward. We are aware, too, that it may be persuasively argued that custody in the father would have little or no effect on the child's affection for his mother....
>
> We assume that if the parties had remained married, and the father refused to observe the principle of separation, or if each had continued in the identical faith and accepted as part of that faith the principle of separation as zealously espoused by [the mother] alone, there could be no doubt that intervention by the state in John Edward's upbringing would not receive hospitable consideration in any court....

We have found no case, with [one] ... exception ... which even squints at holding that a court can take a child of tender years away from the mother because of a potential effect the religious views of the mother may have on the mental welfare of her child....

Precisely because a court cannot *know* one way or another, with any degree of certainty, the proper or sure road to personal security and happiness or to religious salvation, which latter to untold millions is their primary and ultimate best interest, evaluation of religious teaching and training and its projected as distinguished from immediate effect (psychologists and psychiatrists to the contrary notwithstanding) upon the physical, mental and emotional well-being of a child, must be forcibly kept from judicial determinations.... The record shows not even a remote suggestion of any lack of morality, character or competence on the part of either parent....

... Deprivation of the custody of a child is not a "slender" punishment: it is a heavy penalty to pay for the exercise of a religious belief, neither illegal nor immoral....

The fact that judged by the common norm, it may be logically concluded that custody in the father is for the child's best interests, does not warrant us in taking custody away from the mother when such an order must be bottomed on our opinion that the mother's religious beliefs and teachings, in their effect on the child, will continue to be contrary to the child's best interests.

(a) Was the appellate court correct in saying the trial court had "penalized" Mrs. Quiner? The dissent argued,

> The judgment of the trial court is neither designed, intended nor operative as a penalty upon appellant either for her religious beliefs or for her conduct.... Insofar as it may be said that the parent deprived of custody suffers a penalty, its infliction is simply an incidental and unavoidable consequence of the circumstances and the parental conduct which have imposed upon the trial court the painful necessity of awarding the custody to one and denying it to the other.

The dissent added that "if we are to speak in terms of penalties, what is there to say in justification of the penalty which the judgment of the majority would impose upon the father and the paternal grandparents because of *their* religious beliefs?" Is the dissent suggesting the majority's opinion, far from penalizing Mrs. Quiner, actively advantages her? That is, if Mrs. Quiner had had purely secular motives, she would probably have lost custody. Is the fact that she has religious motives insulating her from that result? Would there be any problem with a rule that said that conduct which would cause a court to decide against awarding custody where the conduct is motivated by secular factors should have the same consequence where the conduct is motivated by religious factors?

(b) One argument that was rejected in *Palmore* but that is made for racial matching is that without it the child may be stigmatized and distanced from the people with whom he or she has to deal. An important part of the trial court's reasoning in *Quiner* concerned such distancing. The trial court also said that "enforced public observance of religious taboos, seemingly irrational and deviating from the norm, by a bewildered young child while attending school, such as avoiding and refusing to eat with his classmates or taking part in extra scholastic and other youth activities, is likely to subject him to scorn and ridicule by thoughtlessly cruel classmates." Can *Palmore*, the racial-matching cases, and *Quiner* be distinguished? Is one distinction that children should be willing to bear stigma where it is ill-founded?

Ought the stigma and distancing arguments be ruled out altogether in these cases? Consider the court's comment in one Jehovah's Witnesses case: "We are not unaware that deviation from the normal often brings ridicule and criticism. We reject, however, the notion that it is necessarily the basis for implanting neuroses. Criticism is the crucible in which character is tested. Conformity stifles the intellect fathering decadency." *Smith v. Smith*, 367 P2d 230, 233 (Ariz 1961).

(c) In thinking about these problems, you may want a sense of some of the religious beliefs that arise in these cases. In *Burnham v. Burnham*, 304 NW2d 58 (Neb 1981), for instance, the wife was a member of "a sect calling itself the Tridentine Church, or the Fatima Crusaders." The Nebraska Supreme Court noted that the mother had concluded that her daughter was illegitimate because the mother and her husband had not been married in the Fatima Crusader Church, that the sect's views were anti-Semitic, that the mother was prepared to "cut [her daughter] out of her life if she disobeys the rules of the Tridentine Church," and that the mother's plan to send her daughter to "the Tridentine school in Coeur d'Alene, Idaho, would interfere with the father's rights of visitation." The court therefore awarded custody to the father.

There are also a number of cases in which spouses of Jehovah's Witnesses have argued that the unwillingness of that sect to allow blood transfusions endangered their children. One court sought to resolve the problem by ordering that the mother's consent to a transfusion would not be required, by "specifying conditions upon which any licensed physician ... may administer blood," and by requiring the wife to notify the husband when the children were ill or hospitalized. *Levitsky v. Levitsky*, 190 A2d 621, 627 (Md App 1963).

(d) Some courts have devised standards for cases where a custodian's religious beliefs seem injurious to the child. For example:

> [F]irst, ... the court must make a threshold factual determination that the child's temporal well-being is immediately and substantially endangered by the religious practice in question and, if that threshold determination is made, second, the court must engage in

> a deliberate and articulated balancing of the conflicting interests involved, to the end that its custody order makes the least possible infringement upon the parent's liberty interests consistent with the child's well-being. In carrying out that two-stage analysis, the trial court should make, on the basis of record evidence, specific findings of fact concerning its evaluation of all relevant considerations bearing upon its ultimate custody order.

Osier v. Osier, 410 A2d 1027, 1030 (Maine 1980).

(4) May religion be relevant if that conduces to the interests (or to serving the rights of) the parents? Standard constitutional law from *Meyer* and *Pierce* through *Yoder* suggests that parents have a right to determine the religious upbringing of their children. Where divorcing parents remain agreed on religious issues, religious issues are unlikely to arise in custody disputes. But how ought courts respond when parents disagree?

(a) The standard law is that the custodial parent determines the child's religious upbringing. Nevertheless, it is sometimes said, as in *Felton v. Felton*, 418 NE2d 606, 607–08 (Mass 1981), that the law

> tolerates and even encourages up to a point the child's exposure to the religious influences of both parents although they are divided in their faiths. This, we think, is because the law sees a value in "frequent and continuing contact" of the child with both its parents and thus contact with the parents' separate religious preferences. There may also be a value in letting the child see, even at an early age, the religious models between which it is likely to be led to choose in later life. And it is suggested, sometimes, that a diversity of religious experience is itself a sound stimulant for a child. In all events, the question that comes to the courts is whether, in particular circumstances, such exposures are disturbing a child to its substantial injury, physical or emotional, and will have a like harmful tendency for the future.

More concretely, in *Grayman v. Hession*, 446 NYS2d 505 (NY App Div 1982), a Jewish father had divorced a Gentile mother when their son was two years old. When the boy was seven, the father won a court order granting the father liberal visitation and requiring the mother to enroll the boy in an after-school Hebrew school. The appellate court found that the order was in the boy's best interest, since the mother had "either consented to or acquiesced in the religious training the child has undergone since birth," since the child would otherwise "receive no religious training," and since the mother's "recent move to Long Island seriously hinders [the father's] ability to continue his frequent visitations and religious training of his son. . . ."

In *Brown v. Szakal*, 514 A2d 81 (NJ Super Ch Div 1986), a court refused to order the non-Jewish father to observe the Sabbath and keep kosher when he visited his seven-and nine-year-old daughters. The court found that "absent a showing of emotional or physical harm to the children, courts in other jurisdictions will not impose upon the non-custodial parent the burden of policing the religious instructions of the custodial parent." The court said the children had not "reached an age, according to Jewish law, where they could be ecclesiastically culpable for non-observance." The court concluded, "In the absence of evidence that non-observance of Jewish law during visits with the father would endanger the children's physical, temporal or religious welfare, this court may not impose upon the father the affirmative obligation of observing the laws of his children's religion when he visits with the children."

(b) One way parents might exercise their right to direct their children's religious upbringing is through agreements. In *Spring v. Glawon*, 454 NYS2d 140, 142 (App Div 1982), the court said of a stipulation on divorce (stating that the child would have "no religious upbringing without the express written permission of the parties"), "While such agreements are not inviolate, before a court will substitute its judgment for that of the parents the burden is on the party seeking to modify or avoid the agreement to demonstrate that enforcement will not be in the best interest of the child."

However, in *Lynch v. Uhlenhopp*, 78 NW2d 491 (Iowa 1956), the court said that "the courts have generally refused to enforce agreements between the father and mother concerning the religious training of children." In *Lynch*, the husband and wife stipulated on divorce that "the care, custody and control of [the child] shall be awarded to the [mother, a Protestant,] and it is provided that the said child [who had been baptized a Catholic] shall be reared in the Roman Catholic Religion...." Some years later, the father brought a contempt action against the mother, claiming she had sent the boy to a Congregational Sunday school and summer Bible camp. The court found the agreement unenforceably vague. It asked a series of rhetorical questions: "How are we to determine what must be done to rear a child in any given religion? What constitutes 'rearing' a child in the religion or cultus of this church, or of any church? Must [the boy] be taken to church once a week, or once in two weeks, on Sunday?" "Is it required that he attend catechism class? Must he attend a parochial school ... ? What fast days must be observed, what Lenten observances followed?" The court thought that to answer these questions it would have to consult experts and that even experts might disagree.

In addition, the court reasoned that it was being asked to "actively enforc[e]" the agreement, but that the

> Supreme Court of the United States has said, in *Shelley v. Kraemer*, 334 U.S. 1, that this may not be done. In the words of ... *West Virginia State Board of Education v. Barnette*, 319 U.S. 624 [1943]: "If there is any fixed star in our constitutional

> constellation, it is that no official, high or petty, can prescribe what shall be orthodox in politics, nationalism, religion, or other matters of opinion or force citizens to confess by word or act their faith therein."

Was the agreement in *Lynch* constitutionally problematic in the way the covenant in *Shelley* was?

(5) In discussing racial matching, we asked whether race could be taken into account because doing so conduces to the minority race's interests. Do the problems with considering race to serve the interests of the relevant race apply to considering religion to serve the interests of the relevant religion? Does considering religion to serve the interests of the religion present other problems?

(a) Does it present Establishment Clause problems? What does *Yoder* say?

(b) How ought the religion's interests be determined? Should a representative of the religion participate in the case, much as Indian tribes participate in some custody cases?

(6) We have asked whether religion can be taken into account to serve the child's interests, to accommodate the parent's rights, and to promote the religion's interests. In each of these cases, and particularly in the last and first, it will be crucial to identify the child's religion. This is not always easy. Consider *In re Glavas*, 121 NYS2d 12 (Dom Rel Ct NYC 1953). Mr. Glavas was a member of the Greek Catholic Church who from time to time attended Roman Catholic churches. Mrs. Glavas was Jewish. Their son was "circumcised according to Jewish rites early in the year of 1948." Although the father had acquiesced in the ceremony, he was not present. In October 1952, the father, without the mother's consent, had the boy baptized by a Roman Catholic priest. Three months later, the father went to the Jewish Child Care Association to place the child with the Association for adoption. The father told the Association the boy was Jewish. At the trial, the father claimed the boy was Roman Catholic. The father "did not impress [the court] as being deeply concerned as to what denomination or religion his child should follow." The case came to the court on a neglect petition, and the court was required to place the child "in the custody of a person or persons of the same religious faith as that of the child." The court held the child was Jewish. Was he? Consider the various principles the court might consult.

(a) Is a child's religion the religion to which the child's parents belong when the child was born? What if the parents belong to different religions?

(b) Is a child's religion the religion in which the child is baptized?

(c) Is a child's religion the religion in which the child is raised?

(d) Is a child's religion the religion into which the child has been inducted according to the religion's own rules? In other words, is a child a Congregationalist if the child has been confirmed?

(e) Is a child's religion the religion which a religion says is the child's religion?

(f) Is a child's religion the religion the child's parents say is the child's religion?

(g) Is a child's religion the religion the child says is his or her religion?

(h) Ought a court (could a court) consult the child's best interests in answering these questions?

(i) Does the answer to these questions depend on the child's age?

(j) Does deciding what a child's religion is impermissibly or undesirably involve a court in questions of religious doctrine? Are these questions nevertheless questions a court must answer if a child's or parent's free-exercise rights are to be protected?

BIBLIOGRAPHY

Religious Pluralism. Professor Schneider examines many of the issues discussed in the religion part of these materials in *Religion and Child Custody*, 25 U Mich J L Ref 879 (1992).

Children's Rights. A recent collection of essays on children's rights, one which ranges into a variety of topics in the relation between children and the law, is Philip Alston, Stephen Parker, and John Seymour, *Children, Rights, and the Law* (Oxford U Press, 1992). Carol Sanger and Eleanor Willemsen, *Minor Changes: Emancipating Children in Modern Times,* 25 U Mich JL Ref 239 (1992), suggests that although much legal language is couched in terms of emancipating children, in fact many parents are simply abdicating their responsibility of caring for them. For a discussion of why children should be capable of bringing actions in their own right, see Wendy A. Fitzgerald, *Maturity, Difference, and Mystery: Children's Perspectives and the Law*, 36 Ariz L Rev 11 (1994). Professor Fitzgerald contends, among other things, that adolescent children ought to be able to determine the caretaker in their "best interests." Martha Minow, in *Rights of the Next Generation: A Feminist Approach to Children's Rights*, 9 Harv Women's L J 1 (1986), argues that children are legally disadvantaged much as women are and that mature minors should be given the freedom to make difficult choices. For a contrary view, see Barbara Bennett Woodhouse, *Children's Rights: The Destruction and Promise of Family*, 1993 BYU L Rev 497 (1993). As the title implies, Professor Woodhouse is skeptical that the current movement towards independence of children, will be helpful to the majority of children or to families in the long run.

Race and Adoption. For a wide-ranging account of adoption, including an influential section on transracial adoption, see Elizabeth Bartholet, *Family Bonds: Adoption and the Politics of Parenting* (Houghton Mifflin, 1993). For a contrasting perspective on adoption and race, see

Twila L. Perry, *The Transracial Adoption Controversy: An Analysis of Discourse and Subordination*, 21 NYU Rev L & Social Change 33 (1993–1994). An exceptionally interesting student note on transracial adoption is Kim Forde–Mazrui, Note, *Black Identity and Child Placement: The Best Interests of Black and Biracial Children*, 92 Mich L Rev 925 (1994). Nancy E. Dowd, *Family Bonds: Adoption and the Politics of Parenting* (Book Review), 107 Harv L Rev 913 (1994), provides a feminist approach to the problems of adoption, from both the birth mother and adoptive parent's perspectives.

Pluralism Generally. Margaret F. Brinig, Carl E. Schneider and Lee E. Teitelbaum, *Family Law in Action: A Reader* 79–116 (Anderson, 1999), presents discussions of various kinds of family forms. Many issues of pluralism are presented by Fannie Flagg's fictional account of a pre- and post-War Missouri community in *Welcome to the World, Baby Girl!* (Random House, 1998). Another well-told story, this time of how diverse members of a community treat a stranger literally dropped in their midst is Billie Letts, *Where the Heart Is* (Warner Books, 1995).

Part IV

CONCLUSION

And your business as thinkers is to make plainer the way from some thing to the whole of things; to show the rational connection between your fact and the frame of the universe. If your subject is law, the roads are plain to anthropology, the science of man, to political economy, the theory of legislation, ethics, and thus by several paths to your final view of life.

Oliver Wendell Holmes
The Profession of the Law

We have now completed our survey of family law, and you should now have a basic understanding of that subject. But these materials are designed to help you develop something more than a basic understanding of family law. They are also intended to help you think more fully about how the law conceives of the family, what social effects that conception has, how to generalize about the direction and working of family law, and how the family, the law, and society ought to interact in the last years of the twentieth century. This Conclusion, then, offers an opportunity to review what you have learned and to think systematically about those broader questions.

Chapter XIII

THE FAMILY, SOCIETY, AND THE LAW: IN CONCLUSION AND IN REVIEW

In order to know what [the law] is, we must know what it has been, and what it tends to become. We must alternately consult history and existing theories of legislation. But the most difficult labor will be to understand the combination of the two into new products at every stage.

Oliver Wendell Holmes
The Common Law

In this closing chapter you will have a chance to think about the family and society both descriptively and normatively. Descriptively, you should try to develop your own generalizations about what directions family law is taking, about what seems to motivate change in family law, and about how the law works when it tries to regulate families. Normatively, you should develop your own ideas about what direction family law should proceed in, about what purposes the law should serve in regulating the family, and about what limits there should be on the law's regulation of the family.

To help you with these problems, and to help you review what you have learned, this chapter contains two parts. In the first, you will use what you have read to review the themes and functions of family law and use the themes and functions of family law to review what you have read. In the second, you will read two attempts to generalize about family law.

SECTION 1. REVIEWING THE THEMES OF FAMILY LAW

The law is the witness and external deposit of our moral life.

Oliver Wendell Holmes
The Path of the Law

We said at the beginning of this book that there were several ideas or problems (which we have called themes) we would repeatedly encounter. We have given each of those themes special attention at an appropriate point. Now that you have studied all of family law you are ready to assess each of the themes as a whole, in relation to the other themes, and as a part of family law. In short summaries of each of these themes we will review briefly the forms in which we have encountered each theme.

A. FAMILY AUTONOMY: A PERVASIVE THEME

In introducing the theme of family autonomy, we said it pervaded family law. Has that turned out to be true? You should review each subject we have studied and ask whether the doctrine of family autonomy plays any important part in it.

To what degree is family autonomy possible? Dean Teitelbaum argued that the whole idea of "intervention" in the family was incoherent. His argument was that law is "constitutive" of the family, that both decisions to "intervene" in the family and decisions not to "intervene" in the family have significant consequences for families. How much truth is there in this argument? Assuming the assumptions of the argument are correct, does it follow that the doctrine of family autonomy is meaningless?

What limits does family law place on family autonomy? What interests does the state typically advance to justify infringements on it? The doctrine of family autonomy prevents the state from intervening in families on some occasions when intervention might have prevented some harm from occurring. When is this likely to happen? Is the doctrine worth its costs?

At this point you should review the eight rationales for the doctrine of family autonomy we have repeatedly used. What instances can you identify that show the strength of each rationales? That cast doubt on each of those rationales?

B. PRINCIPLE OF INDIVIDUAL AUTONOMY: A SECOND PERVASIVE THEME

The theme of individual autonomy pervades these materials. This is so true that any attempt at summary must fail. The theme does appear in some regular forms. For instance, we have repeatedly seen cases in which the problem has not been the relatively simple one presented in the "Mill paradigm," where a person confronts the state. Rather, the problem has been how to handle the conflicting but presumptively equal autonomy claims individuals might assert in families. Faced with these conflicts, the law has struggled to find a principle for resolving them. Sometimes the law attributes rights to one individual and not another. Sometimes the law conceives of one individual as in need of protection from the other. Often the law hopes the individuals can work out their claims on their own.

Is our social (and thus legal?) understanding of autonomy changing? Is autonomy increasingly viewed not just as something to which people are entitled, but as something they ought to want and even should be encouraged, taught, inveigled, or even compelled to exercise? This change might have many possible sources, but one of them is movement in social opinion toward the moral stance expressed by Isaiah Berlin, *Two Concepts of Liberty*, in *Four Essays on Liberty* 131 (Oxford U Press, 1969): "I wish my life and decision to depend on myself, not on external forces of whatever kind.... I wish, above all, to be conscious of myself as a thinking, willing, active being, bearing responsibility for his choices and able to explain them by reference to his own ideas and purposes."

Consider again the Appleby hypothetical from Chapter 1. One reason Mrs. Appleby might be thought wrong to oppose Mr. Appleby's request for a divorce is that she was herself responsible for the troubles she would face after a divorce. She would obviously suffer economically and socially were she to live alone. But she was vulnerable because of decisions she made during the marriage: She did not develop saleable skills; she did not make friends of her own; she did not develop a life of her own. People should maintain their independence, be their own person, and not rely for their happiness, worth, and identity on someone else. What provisions had Mrs. Appleby made for widowhood? Given today's divorce rate, should she think her marriage would last a lifetime?

Where else in the materials you have read do you see hints of such a development? Is it desirable? How might the law encourage or discourage it?

C. GENDER AND FAMILY LAW: A THIRD PERVASIVE THEME

We have been repeatedly concerned with what the role of women ought to be in the family and in society, and we have been centrally concerned with the law's attitude toward the role of women. Once again, you should review each of the subjects we have studied and ask whether and how it speaks to those questions. What patterns do you detect? What questions regularly present themselves? What answers?

For instance, consider this basic question: Should the law try to change the customary role of women in the family and society? Should the law decline to influence the role of women within families on the ground that how women and men live in families is not the government's business? Should the law seek to change the role of women in families and society by writing rules designed to protect women from some of the consequences of the social roles women have held in the past? Should the law seek to change the role of women in the family and society by treating women as though women's roles have already changed?

Or consider another basic question: To what extent *has* the law toward women changed? How can we generalize about the nature of that change?

Or consider yet another basic question: How might family law be organized to promote gender equality? Should family law be written in ways that are as gender neutral as possible? Or should family law be written in ways that systematically advantage women, on the grounds that women start off from a socially disadvantaged position and need the law's assistance to attain a position of equality with men? Is there some middle ground between these positions? For example, can family law allow for an individualized inquiry into whether particular women have been socially disadvantaged in some specific way that should be remedied by according those particular women some legal advantage? In what areas do these problems present themselves?

D. HUMAN NATURE AND FAMILY LAW: A FOURTH PERVASIVE THEME

All of family law might be interpreted in terms of the two views of human nature we have described, for those views speak crucially to basic attitudes toward governmental regulation. It is difficult to be definite on this subject, since most people would agree that human nature is no more purely vicious than purely virtuous. And it is rarely obvious what particular positions to infer from general principles, especially since so many factors influence one's conclusions about complicated subjects. Nevertheless, to put the point crudely, the more pessimistic your view of human nature, the more receptive you may be to placing constraints on human conduct. (Of course, life is complicated. That same view may also lead you—as it led the Framers—to fear placing power in the hands of government and may lead you—as it lead Mill—to fear social power as well.) Or, to put the point differently, the more pessimistic your view of human nature, the more receptive you may be to the protective and channeling functions of family law.

If you are such a pessimist, you may, in other words, look for ways of encouraging people to remain in marriages where divorce would injure children or spouses. You may believe that people can be deterred from abusing their spouses and children—if at all—only by considerable effort. You may believe that in "most marriages, even successful ones, one or both spouses will on occasion be tempted to engage in uncooperative behavior. The values of care, commitment, and responsibility translate into choices that may seem to offer remote rewards and high immediate costs." Elizabeth Scott, *Rehabilitating Liberalism in Modern Divorce Law*, 1994 Utah L Rev 687, 726. You may therefore hope to supervise the economic relations of spouses, at least on divorce, to minimize the damage they may do each other. And believing that the strong may too easily tyrannize the weak, you may be skeptical of expanding the scope of marital contracts. These concerns may be accentuated when you begin to think about parents and children, for you may doubt that the love most parents feel for most children most of the time will be constant or strong enough to assure that parents will put their children's interests before their own in custody disputes or that noncustodial parents will willingly help support children from whom they are separated.

The preceding paragraph briefly tours family law from the perspective of a true pessimist. How would such a tour look from the opposite perspective?

E. DEFINING THE FAMILY

We have implicitly asked how the law defines "family" throughout these materials, but we have not paused to ask that question explicitly. We will now do so. Therefore, our review of this theme will be more extended than our review of others.

Family law is often rebuked for defining family too narrowly. How narrow is the definition you discerned? How may the definition be changing? Why is the definition narrow (if it is)? How might it be broadened? Should it be? Why should it not be broadened? Does the law have "a" definition of the family? Does law have different definitions for different circumstances, so that (for example) someone who is a family member for purposes of a rent-control ordinance may not be a family member for purposes of inheritance? Does it help us to define family? What turns on the law's definition of family? How much difference does the law's definition make to the way people think about their family lives? How might changing that definition affect that thinking?

So far in talking about the definition of family, we have been asking who may be said to be a member of a family. But we must also ask another question—what makes family relationships different from other relationships? This leads us to ask what special obligations family members have toward each other. Much of the present doctrinal uncertainty and controversy in family law arises from changing ideas about what it means to be a member of a family.

To help you think about these issues, we propose two hypotheses for your evaluation: (1) the membership of the family is expanding; (2) the legal ties that bind family members to each other are diminishing. The following materials develop and debate these hypotheses. As you read the materials you should ask how far they support the hypotheses and whether what you have read in this casebook does so as well.

(1) The Expanding Definition of the Family

We have already learned a good deal about what it takes to make a marriage. We saw that every state establishes a legally defined relationship called marriage, that every state creates procedures for entering it, and that every state sets some prerequisites to it. Every state sets age limits, every state prohibits incestuous marriages (even though states may define "incestuous" somewhat differently), every state limits marriage to two partners, every state except Massachusetts requires that the partners be of opposite sexes. Further, every state establishes elaborate, judicially supervised procedures for ending marriages.

If these were the only regulations affecting the formation of marriage, it might be easy to say who was and was not a spouse. But these never were the only such rules. The law of putative marriage has long meant that some people whose entry into marriage was legally defective were nevertheless married. And the possibility of common-law marriage has long meant that some people who never tried to marry nevertheless could find themselves married. But today these two doctrines do not constitute a great exception to marriage as a clearly defined institution. For one thing, these doctrines do not affect many people. Very few people meet the requirements of putative marriage, relatively few people meet the requirements of common-law marriage, and many states have abolished common-law marriage. For another thing, those doctrines hardly change in the traditional understanding of marriage: Both putative and common-law marriage can be seen as efforts to *preserve* marriage as a clearly defined institution. The former attempted to assure the marital status of people who had made a reasonable, good-faith effort to marry; the latter to assure the marital status of people who over time actually treated themselves as married and were actually regarded as married by their community.

In the late twentieth century, however, a more serious challenge to marriage as a clearly defined institution has arisen. That challenge might be phrased this way: family law has traditionally treated a particular grouping of people as a "family." That grouping has been thought to serve particular functions. In fact, what is important about the grouping is its function, not its form. Thus a group of people which does not meet the standard definition of family but which serves the function families serve ought also to be treated as a "family." This is the "functional-equivalence" argument, which we encountered in Chapter 1, Section 2.C. One case in that section—*Braschi v. Stahl Associates*—dealt with ways the law might treat same-sex lovers as in some sense legally related.

The functional-equivalence argument's greatest expansion of the definition of family has been symbolized for us by *Marvin v. Marvin*. It seems to create an institution which has many (most? all?) of the substantive attributes of marriage but which can be entered without following any formal procedures and which can even be entered inadvertently. That principle has gained a great deal of currency, not just in judicial decisions, but also in municipal ordinances and administrative regulations. E.g., City of Ann Arbor, Michigan, Title IX, Ch. 110 (1991); City of Berkeley, California, Resolution No. 56,106; Memorandum of Understanding between the City of Los Angeles and the All City Employees Assoc., June 24, 1991. But how far does the *Marvin* principle extend? We have selected the following case to help you think about that question, since it may provide as ambitious an answer as any court has offered.

BUTCHER v. SUPERIOR COURT OF ORANGE COUNTY

California Court of Appeals, 1983
139 Cal App 3d 58

TROTTER, ASSOCIATE JUSTICE. . . .

Facts

Paul Forte was walking across the street when he was allegedly struck by Ralph Butcher's Volkswagen. Paul suffered a fractured neck, forearm and leg, and a severe cerebral contusion. Paul sued Butcher for personal injuries. Cindy Forte sued as Paul's wife for loss of consortium with Paul.

In pretrial discovery, Butcher learned that Cindy and Paul did not have a valid legal marriage, although Cindy testified at her deposition that she and Paul had a "common law" marriage.

Paul and Cindy began living together on September 11, 1969. Since that time, Cindy has used the name Forte. At the time of the accident, March 28, 1981, Paul and Cindy had been living together as husband and wife for 11 1/2 years. They had two children together, filed joint income tax returns, and maintained joint savings and checking accounts. Paul acknowledges and refers to Cindy as his wife. Cindy testified that she and Paul had a common law marriage, and she considered them to be married as of September 11, 1969.

Upon learning that there had been no valid legal marriage between Cindy and Paul, Butcher moved for summary judgment on Cindy's claim for loss of consortium. After argument, the trial court denied the motion for summary judgment. Defendant Butcher now petitions this court for a writ of mandate to compel the trial court to grant the motion for summary judgment.

Discussion

1. Theory of Consortium Cause of Action

Butcher argues that there can be no claim for loss of consortium without a valid legal marriage because the right to consortium grows out of the marriage.

The notion that a valid legal marriage is a prerequisite to the cause of action for loss of consortium has its origin in the common law view that the wife was more or less a servant or chattel of the husband, and that therefore he was entitled to an independent cause of action if the wife were injured, since the tortfeasor would have damaged the husband's property rights in the services and society of the wife.

The theory of the cause of action for loss of consortium has changed, however, since its early common law statement of proprietary entitlement. The wife is no longer a chattel or servant. The element of loss of services is no longer the essence of the cause of action. The real damage is to what may be called a relational interest. An interference with the continuance of the relation, unimpaired, may be redressed by a tort action.

There are many evidences of a shift from the proprietary entitlement theory of consortium to a relational interest theory. First were the cases which finally allowed the wife as well as the husband to state a claim for loss of consortium. The rule that the husband alone had such a cause of action has "no other justification than that of history.... The loss of 'services' is an outworn fiction, and the wife's interest in the undisturbed relation with her consort is no less worthy of protection than that of the husband."

The cases cited by Butcher for the proposition that a valid legal marriage is a prerequisite to a cause of action for loss of consortium involve injuries which occurred *before* the marriage.... For example, in *Donough v. Vile* (1948) 61 Pa.D. & C. 460, the wife had been injured before the marriage. The court held that the husband had no cause of action for loss of consortium. "Damages for the loss of consortium are intended to compensate for an injury done to the connubial relationship. It would therefore appear that where the marriage relationship does not exist at the time of the tort, a cause of action cannot be created by a marriage subsequent thereto."

This is no more than to state that the cause of action protects the parties' relational interest, and if the relationship did not exist at the time of the tort, a fortiori it could not be injured. In fact, application of this principle to all of the premarital injury cases would lead to the same result in each case. If the injury occurs before the relationship is established, when the parties are engaged, or acquainted, or perhaps total strangers to one another, then the interest in continuing the relationship undisturbed has not been injured....

Thus, while refusing to extend the doctrine beyond the bounds of legal marriage for policy reasons, courts have clearly recognized and redefined the theory of the tort to be an interference with the continuation of the relational interest.

2. *Policy Arguments*

We next address the argument that, even recognizing an unmarried person's interest in the continuation of the relationship with the nonmarital partner, policy reasons dictate limiting those interests to the legally married. Recent cases speak in terms of judicial line drawing; whether the line should be drawn to include or exclude the interest of a nonmarital cohabitant.

Some policy considerations which would arguably limit recognition of the relational interest to legally married couples are: (a) lack of precedent for extending the cause of action to unmarried couples, (b) the injury to the unmarried partner is too indirect, (c) the damages would be too speculative, (d) there is a danger of double recovery, (e) the cause of action would be extended to other classes of plaintiffs, and (f) public policy favors marriage.

The argument that recovery for loss of consortium in a nonmarital relationship breaks new ground and is without precedent, or that it should be left to legislative action "[i]n effect ... is a request that courts abdicate their responsibility for the upkeep of the common law. That upkeep it needs continuously, as this case demonstrates." (*People v. Pierce* (1964) 395 P.2d 893.) ...

[I]n terms of precedent, only one case has ever directly addressed the issue of loss of consortium with respect to unmarried cohabitants. That case is *Bulloch v. United States* (D.N.J.1980) 487 F.Supp. 1078, and there the court *allowed* the cohabitant wife's claim for loss of consortium.

In *Bulloch*, the cohabitants had been married for 20 years and were divorced. Shortly after the divorce was final, they agreed that they would reconcile and resume living together. Before they began living together again, the husband was injured. When he was discharged from the hospital, he moved back into the family home and the wife took care of him. From the time the husband moved back into the family home, the couple held themselves out as husband and wife. The federal court, purporting to apply New Jersey state law, held that the wife could maintain a cause of action for loss of consortium. The major factors weighing in the court's decision were: (1) that the policy of tort law is to compensate for injury, and that reward or punishment for a person's marital status is not relevant in assessing tortfeasor liability, (2) increasing court criticism of the traditional common law view of nonmarital relations, (3) public policy implications of two New Jersey cases that cohabitation should not be penalized, (4) similarities between the cohabitant's claim and the cases allowing the wife's right to sue for loss of consortium, (5) the similarities between cohabitation and marriage, and the dissimilarities of spousal-type relationships and other relationships like the parent-child relationship, and (6) the strong evidence of a nearly 30–year relationship upon which the court could evaluate the claim.

Although *Bulloch* is open to criticism for ignoring some prior New Jersey cases and as an inaccurate attempt to predict the direction state law would take, nevertheless, many of the reasons given by the *Bulloch* court are persuasive in finding that an unmarried cohabitant may state a cause of action for loss of consortium. The court accurately assessed the policy of tort law to compensate for injury and redress wrongs. Moreover, after cases like *Marvin v. Marvin* (1976) 557 P.2d 106, and *Ekalo v. Constructive Serv. Corp. of Am.* (1965) 215 A.2d 1, the general trend of the law has been to criticize and to change the traditional common law view of nonmarital relations. The court's reasoning that the nonmarital cohabitation relationship is similar to the spousal relationship, and is different from other relationships like the parent-child relationship, is both accurate and logical.

One who negligently causes a disabling injury to an adult may ... reasonably expect in our contemporary society that the injured person may be cohabiting with another without benefit of marriage. In *Drew v. Drake* (1980) 110 Cal.App.3d 555, the First District Court of Appeal denied recovery for an alleged negligent infliction of emotional distress by a de facto spouse who had witnessed the death of her housemate. Justice Poche dissented, stating: "Foreseeability of the risk is the issue. The formula for resolution given by the California Supreme Court in *Dillon v. Legg*" is controlling. The dissent further pointed out that the majority opinion in effect held "that unchurched male/female relationships cannot be close and that the tortfeasor could not foresee that his victim would have a close relationship with a person to whom she was not formally married. Giving full credit to the rarified air at the appellate level the conclusion reached here today is nevertheless astonishing: my majority colleagues have determined the incidence of cohabitation without benefit of clergy in contemporary California society to be so rare that it can be characterized as 'unexpected and remote.' I do not believe that this no marriage-no recovery rule is what the California Supreme Court meant when it ordered the courts of this state to carefully analyze on a case-by-case basis what the ordinary person should have foreseen. (*Dillon v. Legg, supra.*) This insistence on adherence to an older morality as the key to the courtroom was discarded shortly after the close of the Spanish Inquisition and is clearly not the law of this state." (*Drew v. Drake, supra*, 110 Cal.App. 3d 555, 558–559, dis. opin. of Poche, J.)

We adhere to the view that the courts must determine on a case-by-case basis what an ordinary person may reasonably foresee. The incidence of cohabitation without marriage in the United States increased by 800 percent between 1960 and 1970. The injury to the de facto spouse, like the injury to a legally married spouse, is real, direct, and foreseeable. We believe that, in the conditions of modern society, the possibility that an adult may be cohabiting with another is neither unexpected nor remote; in short, it is reasonably foreseeable....

It is further argued that if the cause of action is not restricted to legally married couples, there will be no limit to liability, and the cause of action would be unduly extended to brothers, sisters, aunts, cousins, coworkers, other friends and relatives. This "floodgates" argument was addressed specifically in *Borer v. American Airlines, Inc.*, 563 P.2d 858. There, the court held that, although the relationship to the injured person must be foreseeable in order to state a claim for loss of consortium, not every foreseeable relationship is covered. An injured person foreseeably has children, parents, brothers, sisters, aunts, uncles, cousins, in-laws, friends, colleagues, and other acquaintances who could foreseeably be affected by the injury. However, the spousal relationship is different in kind from any of these other relationships. If these other relationships were recognized, then the limit of tortfeasor liability would depend on such fortuitous circumstances as the number of children or siblings or other relatives an injured person may have, without regard to the level of culpability. (E.g., Patricia Borer had nine children. Other persons may have two, twelve, or none. This is not a proper basis upon which to determine the level of tortfeasor liability.) If the limits of liability were extended so far, the social costs would be dramatically increased in terms of higher insurance premiums, or in the form of more people running risks without insurance because of the higher premiums. For these reasons of social policy, the *Borer* court declined to extend the cause of action for loss of consortium to the parent-child relationship.

The crux of the *Borer* case is the distinction between a spousal relationship and the other relationships mentioned. However, as we noted earlier, the relationship of unmarried cohabitants possesses every characteristic of the spousal relationship except formalization. The sexual aspects of the relationship, which distinguish the spousal relationship from the parent-child or other relationships mentioned in *Borer*, are present in the relationship of unmarried cohabitants. Thus, if a proper test can be formulated for evaluating unmarried cohabitation relationships, there is no reason why a de facto spouse could not state a claim for loss of consortium without affecting the policy or the result in *Borer*.

The final argument is that public policy favors marriage over unmarried cohabitation relationships as shown by the workers' compensation death benefit statute and the wrongful death statutes. It is argued that those statutes which limit recovery to "heirs" as defined by the Probate Code, and cases applying them, evidence an intent or policy that the right to recover in consortium cases be limited to validly married spouses. However, the right to recover under the workers' compensation or wrongful death laws is wholly statutory, while the cause of action for loss of consortium is judge-made law. If defendant's argument is taken to its logical conclusion, the cause of action for loss of consortium would be defined by the legislative scheme under the workers' compensation and wrongful death statutes, and would include claims by children, parents, siblings, and others. These claims are plainly not allowed. Since the Legislature has not defined consortium rights by statute, the implication is rather that the statutory definitions employed in the workers' compensation and wrongful death statutes are not applicable to the cause of action for loss of consortium.

It is therefore left to us in common law tradition to construct a standard whereby such relationships may be evaluated so that a remedy be afforded for the redress of wrongs inflicted by tortious conduct.

3. *The Standard*

Obviously, cohabitation arrangements may be of many kinds, ranging from a "one-night stand" to and including relationships which have endured as long as or longer than most marriages. To allow all cohabitants to recover would pose severe practical problems in terms of limiting liability.

One standard which may be used to evaluate the cohabitation relationship is that the relationship must be both stable and significant.

If the plaintiff can show that the relationship meets both of these criteria, then he or she will have demonstrated the parallel to the marital relationship which will enable the court to find the elements of consortium and the damage to the relational interest.

Evidence of the stability and significance of the relationship could be demonstrated by the duration of the relationship; whether the parties have a mutual contract; the degree of economic cooperation and entanglement; exclusivity of sexual relations; whether there is a "family" relationship with children. While the particular items of evidence will vary from case to case, and some of these suggested criteria may be absent, and other different ones present, the plaintiff will bear the burden of demonstrating both that the relationship is stable and that it has those characteristics of significance which one may expect to find in what is essentially a de facto marriage.

In the case before us, however, we need not determine the effect of such evidence since we are concerned only with the denial of a summary judgment motion....

[W]e hold that an unmarried cohabitant may state a cause of action for loss of consortium by showing that the nonmarital relationship is both significant and stable.

Questions on Butcher

(1) *Butcher* purports to follow from *Marvin*. Does it?

(a) *Marvin* purports not to disturb California's abolition of common-law marriage. Does *Butcher*?

(b) *Marvin* purports to be consistent with the public policy in favor of marriage. Is *Butcher*?

(c) *Marvin* says that, had meretricious services been part of the consideration for the contract, that part of it would have been unenforceable. Is *Butcher* consistent with that?

(d) Does *Butcher* read *Marvin* as saying there is no great difference between marriage and long-term cohabitation? Would that be correct? Desirable? One that might distinguish marriage and long-term cohabitation is that marriage requires a public commitment to a life-long relationship which may be terminated only under the supervision of a court. Does that distinction bear any legal weight?

(2) Why are sexual relations controlling in *Butcher*? Can't friendships be as "stable and significant" as sexual relationships, and sometimes more so? Can't sexual relations be destabilizing?

(3) Does *Borough of Glassboro v. Vallorosi*, 568 A2d 888 (NJ 1990), reasonably extend the functional equivalence principle? Glassboro's zoning ordinance said only "families" could occupy homes in residential districts. The ordinance defined a family as "one or more persons occupying a dwelling unit as a single non-profit housekeeping unit, who are living together as a stable and permanent living unit, being a

traditional family unit or the function equivalency [sic] thereof." Each of ten college students signed a four-month lease on a house in a residential district. The New Jersey Supreme Court upheld the trial court's conclusion that the students were a family: "The students ate together, shared household chores, and paid expenses from a common fund." The court noted that two years after the lease was signed, the main renter withdrew from school and the students stopped using the house.

We have been discussing the expansion of family membership in terms of couples. But the adult-child dimension of the family has also been expanded. For example, judicial and legislative reforms have largely eliminated the legal differences between children born in and out of wedlock. The modern frequency of divorce has created situations in which the boundaries of "family" are blurred, as husbands and wives marry and remarry, bringing their children with them into new households. Some courts seem to be beginning to grant stepparents custody of their stepchildren. David L. Chambers, *Stepparents, Biologic Parents, and the Law's Perceptions of "Family" after Divorce*, in Stephen D. Sugarman, and Herma Hill Kay, *Divorce Reform at the Crossroads* 102 (Yale U Press, 1990). Professor Levy explores a number of other ways in which stepfamilies seem to be acquiring some of the legal characteristics of traditional families. Robert Levy, *Rights and Responsibilities for Extended Family Members*, 27 Family L Q 191 (1993). Perhaps yet more radically, *Smith v. OFFER* suggests that people who have been hired by the state to care for its wards—i.e., foster parents—might have some constitutional claim to maintain their relationship with the children they have been paid to care for.

Indeed, one might say there are ways in which the law has opened up the nuclear family to create a kind of legally recognized extended family. One classic constitutional statement of this development is *Moore v. City of East Cleveland*, 431 US 494 (1977), which we describe in our discussion of *Troxel* in Chapter 7. Similarly, courts have become much more willing to award visitation rights to people outside the traditional range of formerly-married natural parents, as in the *Baby M* case, where the court awarded custody of a child born out of a surrogate-mother contract to the contracting father (and, effectively, his wife) but ordered visitation for the surrogate mother (who had breached the contract by refusing to hand over the child). Even more spectacularly, it has also become commonplace for states to provide grandparents standing to seek visitation rights, as you will recall from reading *Troxel*. Open adoption similarly creates another novel kind of extended family.

(2) The Narrowing Obligations of the Family

We have been exploring the hypothesis that the law's definition of membership in the family has been expanding to include more people. We move now to investigate our second hypothesis—that the law imposes lighter duties and ties on family members. The most obvious example is no-fault divorce, which is intended to loosen the ties that bind husbands and wives and which, accompanied by changing social attitudes, has succeeded. Less intentionally—indeed, despite legal efforts to the contrary—the proliferation of divorce has separated parents from children. Although visitation rights are routinely awarded ordered after divorce, many non-custodial parents let them lapse.

The major exception to the movement we have been sketching lies in attitudes toward child support. As we have seen in Chapter 11, both state and federal governments have undertaken extensive efforts to compel divorced and unmarried fathers to help support their children. This development is hard to interpret, because it seems to conflict with several basic attitudes of modern family law. (For an elaboration of this point, see the discussion of support obligations in Carl E. Schneider, *Moral Discourse and the Transformation of American Family Law*, an article which is excerpted in Section 3 of this Chapter.)

The desire to give legal recognition to "functional families" contributes to the weakening bonds of family life at the same time it contributes to its weakening bounds. "Functional families" generally comprise people who have chosen *not* to subject themselves to all the obligations the law imposes on family members, and courts and legislatures have hesitated to insist on that rejected burden. Thus under *Marvin* cohabiting couples are subject only to duties they contractually assume or which a court decides are special equitable obligations. And couples like those in *Braschi* may have no duties at all.

Even within traditionally defined family, duties and ties may be diminishing, and not just in the important sense that the duty of permanence is now gone. For instance, the rationale for alimony has been thrown into doubt by the erosion of a common understanding about what obligations husbands and wives assume to each other and how long those obligations endure.

Is *Department of Human Resources v. Williams*, 202 SE2d 504 (Ga Ct App 1973), another example of this trend? The husband, who was receiving state money because he was "permanently and totally disabled," had "contracted with his wife for her domestic and personal care." The state contended state funds could not be used to pay for this contract, since "it was an unenforceable agreement to pay the wife for services she owed her husband irrespective of the contract." The court held that the wife's support duties did not encompass the care contracted for:

> No authorities cited by appellant hold that, under all circumstances, a husband's right to his wife's domestic services includes all services which she is capable of rendering that he may require.... It is law in Georgia that a husband is not entitled to the salary or wages of his wife, and shall not receive them without her consent.... Her surrendering of this legal right to become a personal attendant to her husband is sufficient consideration for the express contract of employment....

Consider yet a further example. A number of states used to have "family responsibility" statutes, many still do. They commonly required the adult children of indigents to help support their parents. However, as Professor Clark reports, criticism of these statutes "has had its effect upon courts and legislatures as shown by restrictive construction of the statutes, assertions of unconstitutionality, and total repeal of the statutes in some states...." Homer H. Clark, Jr., 1 *The Law of Domestic Relations in the United States* 489 (West, 1987).

Questions on the Narrowing Obligations of Family Members

(1) Is there a basis for imposing a legal duty to support indigent parents in the benefits parents furnished children while the children were growing up? Recall that in *Marvin* the California Supreme Court was willing to imply a contract in order to do fairness between the parties, even though the parties had not, even implicitly, contracted between themselves. Even if the relationship between parents and children do not give rise to a contract implied in law, is it enough to create a moral duty that can justify a statutorily imposed support obligation?

(a) Does it matter that parents commonly support their children voluntarily, out of love, and expecting no return? Do parents expect no return?

(b) Does it matter that parents commonly sacrifice their own interests to support their children?

(c) Does it matter that, whatever the parents' motives, they are legally obliged to support their children?

(d) Does it matter that whatever the parents gave the children received involuntarily, out of need and with no ability to refuse?

(2) That the fact that members of a family constitute an "economic unit" is sometimes a basis for imposing economic obligations on them. For example, that fact is used in divorces to oblige a spouse who has title to a piece of property to divide it with his or her spouse. To what extent does participation in an economic unit justify imposing support obligations?

(a) Are parents and children enough of an economic unit to justify requiring children support their indigent parents?

(b) Are step-parents and children enough of an economic unit to justify requiring step-parents to support their step-children?

(c) Are husbands and wives enough of an economic unit to justify imposing a support obligation in situations like those in *Williams*? Or was *Williams* driven by the court's desire to assist two needy people to get help from the state government?

(3) A statute imposing a support obligation on children of indigent parents might have relatively little effect, since such children might well do their best to support their parents even in the absence of a statute and might often be too poor to support their parents. Are statutes

imposing support obligations nevertheless justifiable because they affirm important principles and encourage people in meeting their support obligations?

One way of understanding this contraction of familial duties is by returning to a definitional difficulty we grappled with earlier: whether the family should be considered an "entity." Dean Teitelbaum's criticism of *McGuire v. McGuire* represents the increasingly favored view that the family is not an entity, but rather is a collection of individuals. This view is reflected in many of the areas we have studied. No-fault divorce represents a backing away from a conception of marriage as an indissoluble bond, as does the (partial) substitution of rehabilitative alimony for alimony as a wife's (forfeitable) entitlement. The contractualization of marriage may be seen as a recognition that marriage is not a status in which two people merge, but rather a negotiated arrangement between two people with distinct (even if mutually congruent) interests and with rights against each other. The conferral of constitutional rights to an abortion has, in *Danforth v. Planned Parenthood*, brought with it a legal statement that can be taken as recognizing the separateness of the interests of a husband and a wife in the fetus they have conceived. The increasing willingness to identify instances of child abuse may be regarded as a recognition that children can have separate interests from their parents' interests, a recognition that achieved particularly controversial statement in *Bellotti v. Baird*. In short, is not the law moving away from the entity view to the view Justice Brennan stated in *Eisenstadt v. Baird*: "[T]he marital couple is not an independent entity with a mind and a heart of its own, but an association of two individuals, each with a separate intellectual and emotional makeup"?

You should ask yourself two kinds of questions about the preceding paragraph. First, is it true? Does the paragraph accurately summarize the areas of law it says demonstrate a movement away from the entity view of the family? Can you find examples of movement *toward* the entity view? Second, is it good? Is it accurate to describe the family as simply a collection of individuals? Is it desirable—does it further important social goals—to describe the family as an entity? As a collection of individuals?

F. PRIVACY

In discussing privacy, we asked whether society actually values privacy. Does family law value it? In what areas of family law do privacy questions present themselves? How does the law handle them? In what ways does it protect privacy? Fail to protect it? Can you discern a trend? What costs does family law incur by attempting to protect privacy? What gains may come from those attempts?

Consider, for example, the following attempt to generalize about the theme of privacy: It is conventionally supposed the law values privacy more than it used to. The two main exhibits for this argument are the law of divorce (which by moving to no-fault divorce obviated the need for inquiries into some of the more intimate aspects of marriages) and the law of abortion (which by making abortion a right has eliminated a requirement imposed by some states that women seeking an abortion show they met one of the state's prerequisites to an abortion). But an argument can be constructed that the larger trend is actually toward a diminished place for privacy in family law.

Consider the law of divorce. No-fault *has* reduced the inquiry the state makes into the marriage to decide whether a divorce may be had. (That inquiry has not been eliminated, since many states retain fault-based divorce grounds.) However, the privacy-affecting inquiries needed to resolve the disputes that accompany divorce may have increased. In part this is because the inquiry needed to divide a divorcing couple's wealth under the traditional common-law and community-property systems was ordinarily limited to activities relating to property; the inquiry needed to divide marital property "equitably," on the other hand, seems to require a relatively broad inquiry into the couple's activities, even though marital fault may be excluded as a grounds for dividing property. Similarly, insofar as child-custody decisions are made in terms of the "best interests of the child" rather than a relatively automatic maternal preference, a broader inquiry into the life and character of the couple is possible. Child-support cases may also require courts to make decisions, such as those involving college educations, parents would ordinarily make on the basis of private considerations.

Another area in which privacy may have diminished is state regulation of spouse and child abuse. Both are prosecuted markedly more vigorously than before. All along the line—from initial contact with the police through sentencing—the criminal justice system's inquiries into abuse will be probing more deeply (even if desirably) than before into a family's privacy. Attempts to detect child abuse have extended the range of people obliged to be observant of families, since statutes require doctors, teachers, and others who regularly observe children to report suspected abuse.

Yet another development that may to have diminished family privacy is the contractualization of family law. Contracts may sometimes obviate the need for a judicial decision and may thus enhance a family's privacy. However, as the range of subjects amenable to contract increases, so does the range of subjects as to which judicial inquiry may be needed. A significant development is the *Marvin* doctrine. It not only brings a new group of people under judicial scrutiny, it also brings under that scrutiny kinds of contracts—oral and implied contracts—whose range had been limited in family law. As *Marvin II* suggests, this could explode the privacy of the cohabiting couple.

A miscellany of other reforms in family law may similarly affect privacy. For instance, the rise of open adoption seems likely to reduce the privacy of both the natural mother and the adopting parents. The increasing technical capacity to produce children in novel ways—through *in vitro* fertilization, for instance—brings into courts a whole category of new disputes—surrogate-mother contracts, for instance—many of which involve issues which can be resolved only with judicial inquiries into family life. More vigorous state and federal programs to collect child support involve record-keeping which reduces the privacy of the obligor and even the obligee. Even cases like *Bellotti v. Baird*, which increase the privacy of children who want abortions, involve judicial hearings which lessen the privacy of the children's parents.

G. CONTRACT AS AN ORDERING DEVICE

You know that contract potentially has a vast scope in family law. But just how vast? Which areas of family law have been contractualized? Which could be? Which areas ought not be? What distinguishes the areas that should be contractualized from those that should not be? What costs does contractualization impose? Can they be diminished? What advantages does contractualization bring? Are there less costly ways of achieving those advantages? To help you answer these questions, the following paragraph will remind you of some central features of contractualization.

Contract is ordinarily thought to have two normative advantages: it promotes freedom and the efficient organization of human affairs. It has practical advantages as well: it helps people communicate, it helps them plan, and it helps them resolve disputes. Contract has limits even in the commercial context: sometimes it is simply unnecessary; sometimes it is actively dysfunctional. Contract may not apply as well to family contexts as to commercial contexts: many family contracts are for longer terms than most business contracts; many family contracts will attempt to regulate relations that are more complex and unpredictable than most commercial relations; family contracts are infected by an altruism that inhibits the bargaining that makes business contracts work; family bargainers may be more vulnerable to each other than commercial contractors. There are also normative objections to applying commercial contract law to the family: in families, contracts may not promote freedom; business contracts may heighten attitudes toward people that ought to be inimical in family settings; contract can provide government with an opportunity for affecting the family through contract interpretation and enforcement. There are several standard arguments for limiting the range of family contracts: doing so may protect third parties, the parties themselves, and larger social interests. There are three standard mechanisms for limiting contracts: to decline to enforce contracts respecting certain subjects, to require contracts to meet procedural requirements, and to require contracts to meet standards of substantive fairness.

H. RIGHTS

We have seen that constitutional rights have assumed an eminent place in family law. In this review, our first inquiry about those rights should be a reassessment of their sources. The right that has most significantly affected family law is the right to privacy. What techniques of constitutional interpretation may be used to legitimate that right? The term "right of privacy" is of course not precise. How would you articulate the right to give it greater precision? What limits on the right does the Constitution establish?

Our second inquiry should be into the application of the right of privacy. Which family law issues have courts treated in constitutional terms? Which issues ought to be treated that way? For instance, what are the constitutional dimensions of the right to marry? Is there a constitutional right to polygamous marriage? To homosexual marriage? To incestuous marriage? A constitutional right to end a marriage? To no-fault divorce? To divorce counsel supplied by the state where a petitioner cannot afford one? Does the doctrine of family autonomy have a constitutional basis? If so, what consequences does that conclusion have? Is there a constitutional right to enter into enforceable contracts respecting one's marriage? To enter into enforceable contracts respecting *Marvin* relations? Do natural parents have a constitutional entitlement to the custody of their children such that they should win custody disputes with anyone who is not a natural parent unless the parent has acted in a way that justifies terminating the parent's rights? Do people who are the functional equivalent of natural parents have similar constitutional rights? Is there a constitutional right to enter into (and have enforced) surrogate-mother contracts? What constitutional rights do children have?

I. THE TENSION BETWEEN DISCRETION AND RULES

As we have repeatedly seen, family law exists in a tension between according judges discretion and limiting that discretion by requiring judges to follow rules. Consider how often that tension recurs.

The shift to no-fault divorce preferred a bright-line rule making divorce universally available to a rule that requires courts to decide case by case whether a divorce is proper. The family autonomy doctrine itself is a statement of the general desirability of depriving judges of discretion to make decisions for families. Similarly, *McGuire* is an even more explicit statement that it is better to have a bright-line rule excluding judges from reviewing the adequacy of spousal support except in the most egregious cases.

The tension between discretion and rules also appears in new approaches to spouse abuse. Thus policies that require the police to make arrests whenever they have a certain level of confidence that an assault has occurred and policies that require prosecutors to prosecute every time their evidence meets a certain standard deprive police and prosecutors of discretion to decide whether to arrest or prosecute.

The entire history of Anglo–American marital-property is a struggle between, on one hand, the desire to write simple, clear rules to guide litigants and courts and, on the other hand, the desire to handle the wide variety of circumstances in which marital-property cases arise and with the demands of justice in cases that do not fit anticipated patterns. For some time, both common-law and community property systems developed more and more elaborate rules to accommodate the latter interest while still primarily serving the former. With the popularity of equitable distribution systems, we seem to be in a period in which the latter interest has won pre-eminence.

Allowing couples to contract out of marital-property regimes relieves the law of resolving the tension between rules and discretion. However, as we saw, marital contracts do not wholly have that effect, since courts have felt obliged to look into both the substantive and procedural fairness of those contracts, an enterprise that has largely been left to judicial discretion. Interpreting *Marvin* contracts places an even greater burden on judicial discretion, since there will be generally be harder questions about whether a contract was intended in the first place, what the terms of the contract were, and whether the court should imply a contract in the absence of an express one.

As we saw in our study of child custody, that issue presents some of the most severe questions for the tension between discretion and rules. But similarly troubling questions are also presented in the law of child abuse and neglect. The core question is whether abuse and neglect should be narrowly defined to prevent intervention from occurring where it should not, or whether abuse and neglect should be broadly defined to prevent injury to children as completely as possible. Subsidiary questions involve such issues as how far discretion may be profitably limited by imposing procedural rather than substantive requirements.

Historically, setting child support has been left to judicial discretion, and the question of how to enforce those awards has been left to the discretion of the obligee and the court. Dissatisfaction with this allocation of tasks has led to guidelines that substitute rules for discretion in setting amounts and to practices that substitute automatic procedures for discretion in collecting support.

We may also be moving away from rules toward discretion in defining "family." Earlier law held that a family is a unit formed either by marriage or by (particularly close) blood relation. The tendency is to grant courts greater discretion in deciding what a family is, discretion courts have sometimes exercised by defining as a family functional equivalents of traditional families. The *Marvin* doctrine, for instance, can be understood in those terms, as can *Braschi v. Stahl Associates* and *Moore v. East Cleveland*.

What conclusions about discretion and rules can you draw from this survey? What advantages do rules have in family cases? What advantages does discretion have? Do you see a pattern that would explain the choices family law has made between rules and discretion? Do you see ways to accommodate the interest in rules and the interest in discretion?

J. DUE PROCESS

Due process has two aspects. In its first aspect, due process concerns the procedures the government must follow when it acts against a citizen. In its second aspect, due process concerns the procedures the government offers its citizens for resolving their legal disputes. Which of the areas we have studied present which kind of due-process problems? How were those problems resolved?

Both aspects of due process serve two functions. The first function is to set limits to the exercise of governmental power. This function is at the heart of the first aspect of due process, but it is also relevant to the second. This is because litigation between citizens in family law often turns on the substantive standards set by the government. For example, the government's power to effect an allocation of wealth between the parties to a divorce depends in part on the procedures available to the parties for asserting their interests. What other examples of this function as it is performed by both aspects of due process law have we encountered? How well has the function been performed?

Both aspects of due process serve a second function—improving judicial decisions. As you recall, the Court justified the due process requirements imposed on the government in *Santosky v. Kramer* in part on the theory that they would lead government to make a "better" decision. Similarly, it is often argued that providing children legal representation in a divorce promotes wiser child custody decisions. What other examples of this function as it is performed by both aspects of due process law have we encountered? How well has the function been performed?

Due process has its costs. In its less beneficial aspects, due process is called "bureaucracy" and "red tape." What are the costs of due process as we have encountered them? Are they worth paying?

K. THE ENFORCEMENT PROBLEM

At the beginning of this book, we said enforcement problems were as difficult and consequential in family law as in any other area of law. Consider the following examples.

Even in an area that seems as easy to control as entry into marriage, states have, for example, been reluctant actively to enforce restrictions against polygamous marriage. Widespread connivance by both bench and bar subverted restrictive divorce regimes so much and so long that that connivance became a central motive for no-fault divorce. The enforcement problem itself is important among the rationales for family autonomy, for reasons that *Kilgrow v. Kilgrow*, among other cases, illustrates. Controlling spouse abuse presents a long series of enforcement problems, many of which we investigated. Part of the reason for the court's decision in *McGuire v. McGuire* was probably the time and trouble the court might have incurred enforcing a support order. One attraction of resolving divorce disputes about wealth in terms of marital property distribution rather than alimony is that a lump-sum settlement relieves the court of the enforcement problems alimony orders can present. And one attraction of contract as a means of establishing rules for dividing marital property (or, as in *Marvin* cases, quasi-marital property) is that parties may be likelier to acquiesce to judicial orders where the parties have had a say in those orders.

The enforcement problem has also played a role in the constitutional law of the family. For instance, Justice Douglas used the unlikelihood of finding a legitimate enforcement mechanism as a reason for finding the statute in *Griswold v. Connecticut* unconstitutional. And part of the impetus for *Roe v. Wade* came from the Justices' knowledge that prohibitions of abortion failed to prevent a large number of abortions and that they posed risks to the women who obtained them.

Nor is the law of parent and child without its enforcement problems. For instance, the difficulties of detecting child abuse have led to reporting statutes. The difficulties of collecting child support have led to URESA, RURESA, UIFSA, and federal statutes and regulations. And the lack of a satisfactory remedy against custodial parents who refuse to abide by visitation orders has long baffled courts.

Even this long list of enforcement problems is hardly exhaustive. What other examples can you think of? Why does family law seem so prone to enforcement difficulties? What is the range of sanctions that are available to the state in family law situations? Are there approaches to securing its ends the state might find particularly effective in family settings? When should enforcement difficulties deter the state from trying to accomplish its ends?

L. PLURALISM

Pluralism refers to the value of preserving within a society some variety of culturally distinct groups. We have thought about the pluralism problem most directly in considering *Wisconsin v. Yoder*. There we had a culturally distinct group and a legal question that had to do with the ability of that group to survive. But we have also thought about the problem (directly or indirectly) in several other contexts. For instance, *Reynolds v. United States* presented in its time an arguably comparable pluralism problem. One argument for marital contracts could be that they allow members of cultural groups that favor traditional views about marriage to put their preferences into legally binding form. One justification for cases like *Meyer v. Nebraska* and *Pierce v. Society of Sisters* is that they make it easier for parents to pass on the cultural practices and beliefs of groups of which they are a part. The law of child medical care may also present pluralism questions. For example, ought parents who are Christian Scientists be relieved of the obligation to provide their children with medical care? Pluralism questions are even more directly raised by claims that racial and religious groups should be able to promote their perpetuation by ensuring that children who are members of their groups are adopted only by other members.

What issues does this catalog raise? If we are to treat pluralism as an important value, we will need to be able to define "culturally distinct group." What is a culture? (Recall that Chief Justice Burger's opinion in *Yoder* seemed to suggest that not just any group would be entitled to the protections *Yoder* assured the Amish.) How distinct must a culture be for its preservation to serve the goal of pluralism? Who speaks for a culture?

What ought the limits of pluralism be? How much power over its members (and over non-members) ought groups wield in the name of pluralism? Suppose the Amish wished to send their children to schools where only German was spoken? Suppose the Amish argued for the enforcement of antenuptial agreements whereby women ceded any claim to child custody because their religion confided responsibility for child-rearing to men?

How great are the advantages of pluralism? What are the benefits of preserving a diverse range of cultures? What are the costs of pluralism? Does the state have an interest in securing some elements of cultural commonality among its citizens?

M. A CONCLUDING NOTE: FAMILY LAW AND LEGAL CHANGE

Partly because family law has undergone (and may still be undergoing) a transformative change, we have emphasized to legal change. In part, we have been interested in the institutional aspects of legal change. We thus examined the adoption of no-fault divorce by state legislatures; the reform of abortion through judicial interpretation of the Constitution; and an attempt to reform the administration of foster-care programs by means of public-interest litigation. In looking at these examples of legal reform, we asked a number of questions you should reconsider now. For instance: Through what institutions can changes in family law be accomplished? How is responsibility for legal change allocated among those institutions? Are there some kinds of change which some institutions may legitimately undertake but other institutions may not? How well situated is each institution to accomplish such change? Are there some kinds of change some institutions have the practical capacity to undertake but other institutions lack? Are our legal institutions capable of working legal change quickly and efficiently?

We have also studied some of the doctrinal aspects of legal change. Thus we have tried to understand how fault-based divorce differs from no-fault divorce, how the law of alimony has evolved from (in principle) requiring alimony almost uniformly to (in principle) requiring alimony rarely, how equitable distribution differs from common law and community property systems and how equitable distribution came to its present prominence, how the role of contract within the family has expanded from its modest beginnings to its present rather promising vantage, how non-marital cohabitation has acquired legal status, how constitutional privacy emerged from the ashes of *Lochner*, how the tender years presumption has been (in principle) weakened by a search for other interpretations of and even alternatives to the best interest principle, how courts and legislatures have struggled to balance the interest in preventing child abuse with the interest in preventing parents from being wrongly deprived of their children, how we have moved from setting child support awards in a fairly ad hoc way toward setting them through guidelines, how we have experimented with different devices for enforcing child support duties, and how we increasingly hesitate to conceive of the family as an entity.

This is a large number of doctrinal changes. How do we make sense of them? Can you detect a pattern? Are we moving toward a coherent new general doctrine of family law? If so, what are its features? If not, what elements of incoherence, or inconsistency, and what lines of tension do you see?

These questions lead us to one more aspect of legal change we have considered: the relationship between social and legal change. We opened the material on the law of husband and wife by looking at the traditional social understanding (as embodied in the wedding service of the Book of Common Prayer) of what marriage means. We tried to identify those social views of human nature that undergirded traditional family law. We also asked you to describe changes in basic social views of human nature. Throughout the book we have tried to understand how those changing views help explain changes in the law.

The preceding paragraph describes broad social changes that may have affected the shape of family law in important but still indirect ways. We have also seen some reasonably direct examples of how specific changes in social behavior have been responsible for a change in family law. No-fault divorce, for instance, was in part a response to the *fait accompli* of a diminished social willingness to remain in marriages the parties wished to leave. In *Marvin v. Marvin*, the court expressly justified its change in the law in terms of changed rates of non-marital cohabitation. Changes in marital property law reflect the increased social power of the women's movement, as the UMDA's recognition of the economic significance of housework indicates. Child-abuse reporting statutes and other changes in child abuse law are partly responses to the development of groups of experts with a professional interest in the subject. Surrogate mother contracts are a response to technological change, e.g., the development of artificial insemination.

Sometimes, however, the social bases for changes in family law are obscure. Consider, for example, the contractualization of family law. What drives it? Are there shifts in basic social attitudes to which contractualization is a response? Are there specific social movements that seek contractualization? Are there legal developments outside family law that exert a gravitational pull toward contractualization? Is there some internal logic to family law that drive it toward contractualization?

The lists in the two preceding paragraphs are hardly more than illustrative. What other examples can you see in our materials of the interworking of social and legal change? What conclusions can you draw from them about the relationship of the two? How is social change reflected in the law? When is social change *not* reflected in the law? What are the mechanisms by which social change is translated into legal change? Does law operate on a logic (doctrinal or institutional) of its own, operate "independently" of social change? How does law affect social change? How much influence on social behavior does family law have?

SECTION 2. REVIEWING THE FUNCTIONS OF FAMILY LAW

The way to gain a liberal view of your subject is . . . to get to the bottom of the subject itself. The means of doing that are, in the first place, to follow the existing body of dogma into its highest generalizations by the help of jurisprudence; next, to discover from history how it has come to be what it is; and, finally, so far as you can, to consider the ends which the several rules seek to accomplish, the reasons why those ends are desired, what is given up to gain them, and whether they are worth the price.

Oliver Wendell Holmes
The Path of the Law

A. THE PROTECTIVE FUNCTION

The clearest examples of the protective function of family law are the law of spouse abuse and the law of child abuse. But family law deals with people in their most vulnerable moments, and the protective function appears in various guises throughout family law. One justification for the prohibition on polygamy which was reviewed in *Reynolds* was that the prohibition protected women from the risks of being plural wives. One function of the elaborate body of law that regulates alimony and the distribution of marital property is to protect the expectations and property of spouses who have relied on each other. And *Marvin* extends that protection to unmarried couples. Even when it is primarily the facilitative function that is being served—as in the law of marital contracts—the protective function is more prominent than it would be in analogous contexts outside family law. For instance, marital contracts must meet unusual procedural and substantive requirements designed to protect the weaker party. Virtually the whole law of parent and child can be seen as an exercise of the protective function. The law of child custody intends to prevent children from being placed with the less desirable of the two contenders. The law of child support intends to ensure that children are not immiserated.

Even where the state forebears to act, its forbearance is regularly justified in terms of the protective function. The doctrine of family autonomy assumes that the family can protect itself better than the state can, that it can make better decisions for itself than the state can. And insofar as the state's ability to protect children is limited, it is limited by the principle that children's parents protect them better than the state, that parents make better decisions for children than the state.

In introducing the five functions of law, we said the protective function of law may be the least controversial. But that function often seems problematic in family law. When family law seeks to protect adults, it opens itself to the charges of interfering with individual autonomy, to the charge of paternalism. Insofar as it seeks to protect children, it opens itself to charges of infringing with parental autonomy. Some of the reasons for these difficulties are familiar, for they are the arguments for family autonomy. In other words, the argument is that the state is ill-equipped to serve the protective function because it has difficulties collecting information, has difficulties interpreting information it does collect, lacks satisfactory standards for deciding what to protect a family member from, can't serve the protective function without damaging familial privacy, faces damaging enforcement problems, risks exacerbating the harm it wishes to prevent, and may erode individual autonomy during its protective efforts.

The ambiguities of the protective function are especially fierce in a number of issues involving the protection of women as a class. The opponents in these debates agree that women have historically been socially disadvantaged. But, as we have seen in our discussions of polygamy, alimony, contractualization, *Marvin*, child custody, and surrogate mother contracts, the opponents disagree about how the law should remove that disadvantage. One side argues that treating women equally in doctrine is to treat them differently in fact. This side contends that the law should recognize that women are often socially disadvantaged and that the law should compensate for this by according them legal advantages. Another side argues that treating women differently from men perpetuates the very attitudes that led to the social disadvantage in the first place. How would you resolve this dispute? Can you state a convincing principle to resolve it? More broadly, how would you resolve the tension between the protective function and the principle of family autonomy?

B. THE FACILITATIVE FUNCTION

In defining the facilitative function, we said its task is "not so much to regulate the behavior of citizens, as to create mechanisms that facilitate their organizing their lives and affairs in whatever ways they prefer." That function appears in various forms in family law. For instance, we have not discussed the critical body of laws which direct providing services to families, particularly to poor families. These services want to help recipients live their lives in the way they prefer despite their economic or social disadvantages. Child abuse laws that require the state to find ways of keeping abused or neglected children in their parents' home is one example of the facilitative function at work.

The centerpiece of the facilitative function is the law of contract. It confers on people the power of the state to assist them in maintaining a kind of private government. The law of contract has been altered to fit the family situation, but the alterations can serve the facilitative function. The procedural restrictions on marital contracts, for example, attempt to ensure that the parties have thought carefully and intelligently about their contract. The substantive restrictions on marital contracts attempt to do what the parties would have wanted had they anticipated an unexpected development. (Going a step further, substantive restrictions may promote the parties' intent to deal fairly with each other. This seems dangerously close to fiction, but it may work occasionally.) Finally, even refusals to make contract available are sometimes justified in facilitative terms. An implicit argument of *Kilgrow* (an argument made explicit in *Rhodes*) is that it can be better to refuse parties the services of the state in resolving their disputes because the parties achieve better solutions left to their own devices.

We earlier described a tension between the facilitative and the protective function. We traced some of that tension to the principle of family autonomy. But it may also be traced to problems in the law of contract. That is, contract may sometimes (often?) serve the facilitative function inadequately. Reviewing, how would you assess contract's success in serving the facilitative function? Do you see ways of adapting contract law so that it might serve it better? Or do the tensions between the protective function and the facilitative function suggest contract ought to have only a restricted scope?

C. THE ARBITRAL FUNCTION

When family law serves the arbitral function, it seeks to help family members resolve their disputes. The arbitral function is thus at the core of family law. Most of family law involves disputes over money and children between divorcing couples. Family law serves the arbitral function by providing a forum for those disputes and standards to be applied in adjudicating them. The arbitral function also works more obliquely—by providing couples standards to be used in organizing their affairs so disputes do not arise. In other words, if the law of marital property is clear enough and gives couples enough room to organize their affairs in a congenial way, they may not need the arbitral help of courts. As you see, this reasoning suggests how the facilitative function can serve the arbitral function.

Controversy over the arbitral function is concentrated in two areas. The first is over its scope. In other words, there is often disagreement over what disputes the government should help people resolve. We have encountered telling limits on the willingness to have government resolve family disputes. The principle of family autonomy and deference to parental rights combine to cause courts to decline to resolve disputes between husbands and wives over support, *McGuire*, between parents over their children's education, *Kilgrow*, and between parents and children, *Parham v. J.R.* And the arbitral function has been straightened by no-fault divorce, which limits judicial power to resolve disputes between husbands and wives about whether marriage should be dissolved.

We have, however, also seen expansions of the arbitral function. The more vigorous response to spouse abuse represents an unwillingness to leave some disputes to the disputants. The expansion of children's rights represents a greater willingness to provide a forum in which children can resolve conflicts with parents, see *Bellotti v. Baird*, as may the movement toward providing children with counsel in custody disputes. What other aspects of the dispute over the scope of the arbitral function have we encountered? Is there a principled way to talk about how to resolve them?

The second controversy over the arbitral function concerns how well government helps people resolve disputes. The major hope has been that some method of resolving disputes arising out of divorce might be found. There are numerous questions to consider here. How are divorce disputes settled in principle? In practice? What alternatives to the traditional judicial proceeding are there? What advantages do they offer? Spouses have elaborate rights. Can they be protected by non-judicial proceedings? The law of contract similarly creates rights, and it also creates opportunities for spouses to exploit each other. Can contractual rights be protected, can abuses of the power to contract be prevented, in non-judicial proceedings? Divorce disputes affect third parties, particularly children. Can their interests be assured in non-judicial proceedings?

D. THE CHANNELLING FUNCTION

When it serves the channeling function, family law creates social institutions designed to promote social goals and channels people into them. The channeling function flourished in traditional family law. The central social unit of traditional family law was life-long monogamous marriage. It was not created by law; it is an institution with roots deep in the social and religious history of the West. But family law promulgated rules designed to shape and sustain monogamous marriage: It established rules setting standards for entry into marriage. It created procedures to tell couples when they are married and to tell the world as well. It devised rules (particularly fault-based divorce law) to make marriage commitments permanent. It set up special categories of property to reflect the special relationship of marriage. It articulated prohibitions against non-marital sexual activity. It imposed (usually indirectly) rules for behavior within marriage—for example, rules obliging husbands and fathers to support their wives and children.

The channeling function does not principally work by direct governmental compulsion. People are not forced to marry. One can contract out (formally or informally) of a number of the rules designed to promote monogamous life-long marriage. Rather, the channeling function works by shaping an institution that has broad social support and that comes to seem so natural that people participate in it almost unreflectively. Imagine two nineteen-year-olds living in a state of nature who find themselves in love. They would have to work out for themselves how to express that love, how to structure their relationship, and how to decide what expectations they might reasonably have of each other for the future. The same couple in the United States in the second half of this century, however, would find a set of answers to all three questions presented by the institution of marriage. The institution would seem natural because most adults participated in it. The institution, in other words, would be part of a common social vocabulary.

The channeling function of traditional marriage also served social interests. That institution, for instance, established which people were specially responsible for which other people. In particular, it helped specify who was responsible for which children.

The channeling function also serves the facilitative function. The facilitative function offers people "mechanisms that facilitate their organizing their lives and affairs in whatever way they want." The social institutions sustained by family law give people models for organizing their lives. These models have been developed over time and have presumably worked tolerably well for many other people. They thus might well be superior to the models people invent for themselves.

These models have a second advantage:

> Without such institutions every individual would have to decide personally every detail about how to organize his life. "Today," Peter Berger writes, "it is not so much that individuals become convinced of their capacity and right to choose new ways of life, but rather that tradition is weakened to the point where they *must* choose between alternatives whether they wish it or not.... [O]ne of the most archaic functions of society is to take away from individuals the burden of choice." The point here is not that the burden of choice is in any particular instance intolerable; it is that at some point the combined burdens become intolerable, or at least become so numerous as to distract one from other significant choices and thus to detract from one's autonomy in other areas.

Carl E. Schneider, *State-Interest Analysis in Fourteenth Amendment "Privacy" Law: An Essay on the Constitutionalization of Social Issues*, 51 L & Contemp Probs 79, 121 (1988).

A third advantage of these models is that even if one invented satisfactory models for oneself, one could rarely live them alone:

> [A]s Martin Krygier writes, "There are many social situations where our decisions are strategically interdependent [with the decisions of other people].... [I]n such situations, *norms* will be generated which provide 'some *anchorage*; some preeminently conspicuous indication as to what action is likely to be taken by (most of) the others....' " The institutions created by such norms, then, enhance the level of available autonomy by improving the ability of people to predict and thus to rely on and cope with the behavior of other people.

Id. In other words, these models allow people to anticipate how other people will behave and to plan their lives accordingly.

One might compare the situation of the nineteen-year-old couple without channeling institutions to the situation of two people who are looking for recreation, who live in a society without tennis, and who are given three balls, two rackets, and one net. The two will no doubt be able to find some way of amusing themselves with these toys. But tennis is a good game partly because it has been developed over many years (in fact, centuries), and it is not likely that the two will invent on the instant as good a game. In addition, where tennis is a social institution, the two will have a much broader range of people with whom to enjoy their recreation. And part of the pleasure of tennis lies in knowing its history and in following its progress; it is a social pleasure.

In these ways, then, the channeling promotes the facilitative function. Channeling also serves the protective function. Law does not just help create a shell of an institution; it helps create institutions with rules. These rules can protect participants in the institution. Vigorous prosecution of spouse abusers shapes the channeling institution so that its participants understand its rules prohibit violence.

Channeling's worth crucially depends on the institutions it supports. Even if an institution serves the function's ends well, it must be evaluated in terms of *all* its social consequences. The law has supported institutions—pejoratively described as the bourgeois family—which have hardly been universally admired over the last two centuries. In the nineteenth century the family was assailed as a prison by the Romantics and as an instrument of oppression by the Marxists. Today, it is similarly assailed by the psychological left and feminists. If those charges are correct, the law's channeling power is, *pro tanto*, badly used.

The workings of the channeling function are complicated. Here are a few questions designed to help you think critically about it. First, we described how the channeling may have functioned in traditional family law. How is it functioning now? Second, we described ways the channeling function might serve the facilitative function. In what specific respects does it do so? How well does it do so? How might channeling disserve the facilitative function? Third, we described one way channeling might serve the protective function. In what other ways does it do so? How well does it do so? How else might it do so?

Finally, here is a brief case-study of channeling, one which uses a case many students believe is wrongly decided to test what may be channeling's outer limits. The case is *Michael H. v. Gerald D.*, 491 US 110 (1989), which we describe in Chapter 9.

In channeling terms, the state in *Michael H.* has two related "institutional" interests: first, an interest in preserving the stability of "marriage" in general and the marriage between Gerald and Carole in particular. Second, an interest in the security of "parenthood" in general and of the relationship between Victoria and her presumptive parents in particular. Both these interests might be reasonably adduced against allowing Michael either parental rights or a hearing.

A state exercising the channeling function may seek to nurture the bond between husbands and wives, to promote the strength and stability of marriages. The constitutional legitimacy of that aim seems confirmed by the many cases lauding a couple's constitutional interest in marriage. The state might conclude it would damage such relationships to require a couple to litigate with an outsider over the paternity of a child born to the wife during the marriage and to issue a governmental announcement that the child was the wife's but not the husband's. The damage might come from several sources. If the husband did not know of his wife's affair and that "his" child was not "his," he might feel acute pain. His reaction might be bitter and recriminating. The child might constantly remind him of his wife's infidelity. It would hardly be surprising for him to contemplate divorce.

Even if the husband already knew of his wife's affair, their marriage might still be harmed by the inquiry Michael sought. What couple would welcome such attention to their marriage and to the husband's cuckolded status? A core argument against fault-based divorce is that couples ought not have to make a public display of their private lives. Even if devices like concealing the parties' names were used, spouses would still reveal themselves to everyone in court. Further, litigation brings misery, and litigation over intimate subjects brings it abundantly. Misery cannot enhance the couple's marriage. Nor can compelling the wife to recount her betrayal of her marital loyalties. And a judicial inquiry would commonly come at the worst time—when the affair had recently ended, the wife had returned to her husband, and they were trying to reconstruct their marriage and their family life. And if the natural father won visitation rights, would the couple's marriage benefit from sharing child-rearing with the wife's former lover?

The California rule has other attractions. An abandoned lover might be bitter, and the rule protects the reunited couple against malicious (even if factually well-founded) suits by a vengeful lover. And the lover's allegation might be false. The rule protects couples from having to resist such accusations. Finally, there would always be a slim (roughly two percent) but relevant chance the blood test was wrong.

A state using the channeling function may also want a child in Victoria's situation to have two parents who are fully and reliably hers. She cannot live with both natural parents, but she has a natural mother who is married and that mother's husband has been caring for her. The state might conclude from the social experience with children of divorce that, while it can be hard to be raised by two people on difficult terms who live apart, it would be worse to be brought up by three people, two of whom (the two men) have reason to be on hostile terms, two of whom (the mother and the lover) have reason to be on tense terms, and two of whom (the mother and the husband) have reason to be on uneasy terms.

The dissent in *Michael H.* would presumably respond that the child's situation is secure because visitation would be ordered only if it were in the child's best interest. However, the state might reasonably conclude that the chances of visitation benefitting a child are small enough to justify a ban on an inquiry. The state might also believe that best interest decisions are uncertain enough to make it wise to avoid them in risky circumstances like these.

Further, Victoria's well-being and her relationship with Gerald and Carole, like their relationship with each other, might well be injured simply from having to endure a hearing. Like her parents, she has a privacy interest in avoiding the scrutiny hearings inflict and an interest in escaping litigation's horrors. Further, the ability of Victoria's caretakers to be good parents and to maintain an untroubled relationship with her is vulnerable to a hearing which so basically questions the relationships of everyone involved. Finally, until the hearing is concluded (and this litigation lasted something like seven years) the child would not know the status of her various parents. Such instability is now widely deplored.

In sum, California's rule buttresses two institutions: a version of marriage and a view of parenthood. It does so by refusing legal effect to some ways of entering parenthood. And it does so by restricting the forces that can impinge on participants in both institutions. Finally, the rule reaffirms in people's minds the social importance of marriage and its relationship with parenthood.

Not atypically, channeling operates here by disadvantaging the "alternative institution" Michael sought to create. It denied him the consolation of legally enforced contact with his child. This technique can be problematic. Is it here?

Michael knew when he had the affair with Carole that she was married, and, given the operation of the channeling function and the social assumptions on which it relied, he knew people commonly lack legal or even social rights in their married lovers' children. The California statute put him on constructive notice that any child he had with Carole would legally be considered a child of her marriage (unless one spouse repudiated the child). More, the child was conceived in an adulterous relationship, a relationship Justices have said in dictum the state may make criminal. Finally, Michael probably knew that asserting a claim to the child could harm the marriage he had already damaged. If expectation has anything to do with parental rights, as the Court sometimes seems to say, and if his moral situation is as we have suggested, his claim to parental status does not look so strong.

Is this explanation of *Michael H.* in channeling terms convincing? How might one criticize it?

E. THE EXPRESSIVE FUNCTION

The channeling function works by creating institutions that people are "channeled" into. The expressive function works by deploying the law's ability to impart ideas through words and symbols. The expressive function has two aspects: First, law's expressive abilities may be deployed because doing so gratifies those speaking through it. Second, law's expressive abilities may be sued to affect people's behavior.

Let us amplify this a bit. Expressive laws may be expressive in the narrowest sense: they may express the "personality" of citizens in the same way of art expresses the "personality" of the artist. But expressive laws may be also be much more instrumental. Then they influence behavior by encouraging people to think in a particular way. This can be done by passing laws that are in some way symbolic or that use a particular language or set of ideas (so that those ideas are brought more fully into public discourse). These laws often affirm or contradict an idea or way of acting. The Connecticut statute in *Griswold v. Connecticut* may well have been, at least in part, such a law, and the ERA surely carried considerable expressive freight as do laws criminalizing spouse abuse. Expressive laws may be used in a different way: law may be used symbolically or expressively by groups wishing to affirm their status as full-fledged or predominant members of the larger society. *Baker* and the statute enacted in response to it exemplify a struggle over this sort of expressive use of law.

Of course, many, probably most, laws perform multiple functions. Most laws intend to regulate behavior directly. But many laws also buttress direct regulation through an expressive element. And some of these laws may also allow their proponents to express ideas for the non-instrumental gratification that brings.

Partly because the instrumental and expressive motives are often mixed, a law's expressive and symbolic functions are often difficult to assess. Legislators rarely say they are passing a law for expressive or symbolic purposes, partly because such a motive may seem too trivial and partly because legislators may not fully realize they have such a motive. Sometimes laws are passed or retained *despite* their expressive or symbolic implications. No-fault divorce may have carried with it the expressive message that divorce ought to be relatively easy to obtain and that marriages break down for reasons generally unrelated to fault. However, a desire to communicate those ideas was not what most supporters of no-fault wished to convey.

An important part of the difficulty the supporters of no-fault faced was the inattentiveness of their audience—the public. Law is often not prominent enough in people's minds for its expressive and symbolic functions to matter. Sometimes a particular case is noticed by almost everyone. *Roe v. Wade* is probably an example. Sometimes a case will be important to a particular group and insignificant to the rest of the country. *Wisconsin v. Yoder* was presumably significant to the Amish and to some other sects, but probably didn't matter much to the rest of the country. Sometimes a series of cases begins to make an impression even though no particular case stands out. The school prayer cases may be an example. Nevertheless, law's output is vast, and most people know little about it. Even people who have an economic interest in knowing the law often do not. Robert Ellickson, for example, has conducted an extensive and fascinating study of ranchers and farmers in Shasta County, California. *Order Without Law: How Neighbors Settle Disputes* (Harv U Press, 1991). He concludes that virtually no one in Shasta County—ranchers, farmers, law enforcement officials, and lawyers—understands the rules governing liability for trespassing animals.

How well people grasp the expressive and symbolic elements of law depends on whether an idea can be communicated by a judicial holding or by a brief statement of a law, or whether the language or reasoning of the holding or law is what bears the expressive weight. The more precise the language and logic used in communicating the expressive idea, the less well it is likely to be understood, if only because most people don't read laws and cases. Many discussions of *Roe*, for instance, assume people pay attention to its language and reasoning. But how many non-lawyers have read the opinion? A similar problem is presented by *Marvin v. Marvin*. What most people probably took away from news accounts was the idea that "palimony" is available, that non-marital cohabitation is legally regarded as socially acceptable, and (probably, although less clearly) that formal marriage is less exalted in the law's eyes than before. The opinion's asseverations in favor of marriage will be entirely unknown.

On the other hand, the public's failure to read legal texts does not necessarily deprive those texts of their expressive importance. Interest groups may read those texts and communicate what they have learned to their followers. This has probably happened with *Roe v. Wade*. Furthermore, sometimes the law only wants to talk to particular groups. Most people probably do not know how child support obligations are enforced in their state. But divorced fathers are likely to hear about it from their wives, other divorced fathers, and their lawyers. And the expressive messages of opinions and laws are often aimed at the very people who do read cases and statutes. For example, judges write opinions to affect the way later judges interpret the law, and expressive and symbolic functions can influence law's later judges.

But the problem of the audience is hardly the only problem for anyone wishing to communicate an expressive message through law. For instance, it is often hard, given the limited expressive tools at hand, given the complexity of the message, and given the need to write rules of behavior at the same time you are writing expressive messages, to say all that you want to say and to say it cogently. For instance, a legislature writing a statute regulating surrogate mother contracts might want to say two things. First, to say to women that society does not approve of their being treated as mere means of production and that it wants women not to feel coerced by economic or social pressure into doing something they find degrading or immoral. Second, this legislature might want to say to women that society believes they are fully autonomous moral agents capable of deciding for themselves whether to enter into contracts. The former message might be expressively communicated by making surrogate-mother contracts unenforceable. The latter might be communicated by making them enforceable. It is not easy to see how you accomplish both purposes at once. On the other hand, every statute does not have to try to communicate every relevant message. The first of the two messages may seem particularly relevant to the surrogate-mother problem and may be susceptible of being delivered only in a few contexts. The second might be made in many other ways. Thus the first message may be the message that ought to be communicated in this particular context, without prejudice to the importance of the second.

Even apart from all these difficulties, it may be normatively inappropriate to use law in this expressive way. It may endow government with an ability to speak that ought to be reserved for private citizens. On the other hand: First, some governmental ends—preventing spouse abuse, for instance—seem so clearly and powerfully legitimate and may be pursued through so many other potent means that it seems anomalous to say government may not pursue them expressively. Second, can government prevent itself from acting expressively? Many legal acts carry a symbolic message whether that is intended or not.

This précis of the complexities of the expressive function leaves much unsaid. How has government spoken expressively through family law? What messages have been communicated? What normative problems do you see in using the law expressively? What practical problems?

SECTION 3. REVIEWING AMERICAN FAMILY LAW

The very name of moralist seems to have become a term of disparagement and to suggest a somewhat pretentious and a somewhat stupid, perhaps even a somewhat hypocritical, meddler in other men's lives. In the minds of very many in the modern generation moralists are set down as persons who, in the words of Dean Inge, fancy themselves attracted by God when they are really only repelled by man.

> **Walter Lippman**
> *A Preface to Morals*

To help you develop your own normative and descriptive generalizations about American family law, we will read three attempts to outline ways of viewing recent changes in that law. As you read them, you should ask yourself whether the changes Professors Schneider, Brinig and Bartlett identify are accurately described and whether they are normatively desirable. Even if what they say is correct, though, theirs are not the only ways of generalizing about family law. Thus as you read, you should formulate other generalizations about family law.

CARL E. SCHNEIDER MORAL DISCOURSE AND THE TRANSFORMATION OF AMERICAN FAMILY LAW

83 Michigan Law Review 1803 (1985)

A. INTROIT

To complain of the age we live in, to murmur at the present possessors of power, to lament the past, to conceive extravagant hopes of the future, are the common dispositions of the greatest part of mankind. . . .

> **Edmund Burke**
> *Thoughts on the Cause of the Present Discontents (1770)*

(1) The Hypothesis

We come now to the first formulation of my hypothesis. Four forces in American institutions and culture have shaped modern family law. They are the legal tradition of noninterference in family affairs, the ideology of liberal individualism, American society's changing moral beliefs, and the rise of "psychologic man." These forces have occasioned a crucial change: a diminution of the law's discourse in moral terms about the relations between family members, and the transfer of many moral decisions from the law to the people the law once regulated. I do not mean that this change is complete or will ever be completed. I do not suppose that it is occurring in every aspect of family law, or everywhere in the country with equal speed. I emphasize that there are other trends, and that there is a considered and considerable reaction to the trend impelled by a revived conservatism and a politicized fundamentalism. But I do suggest that the change is widespread jurisdictionally, institutionally, and doctrinally; that it is deep-seated; and that it is transforming family law.

In this paper, I will initially describe that change in order to demonstrate its strength and its scope. Then, since no area of law flows in a single uninterrupted stream, I will describe some of the eddies and cross-currents affecting moral discourse in family law. Next, I will explore some of the reasons for the present course of family law, hoping that that exploration will also yield a richer sense of the texture and complexity of the change. I will, however, postpone to a later paper the many troubling questions that family law must answer in assessing the wisdom of the change and in deliberating on responses to it.

Before we begin, let me warn against two possible (and related) misreadings of my hypothesis. The first stems from the fact that, as the word is used colloquially, "morality" is a good thing, and more morality is a better thing. Therefore, to say that the law is becoming quantitatively "less moral" seems to imply that the law is becoming qualitatively less good. In some ways this is perhaps true, but for reasons that are immediately obvious, or will shortly become so, it is in other ways surely false.

The second, closely related, misreading of my hypothesis is what might be called the *"O tempora, o mores"* problem. There is a tradition millennia old—and long honored in this country—of jeremiads against a failing moral order and exhortations to a return to the virtuous past. In light of that tradition, to describe a changing moral order risks implying a wish to restore the status quo ante. I do not wish to do so: I doubt that you can go home again, and even if you could, I doubt you would enjoy it.

B. THE STATEMENT OF THE THEME

(1) The Transformation of Family Law

Now and then it is possible to observe the moral life in process of revising itself, perhaps by reducing the emphasis it formerly placed upon one or another of its elements, perhaps by inventing and adding to itself a new element, some mode of conduct or of feeling which hitherto it had not regarded as essential to virtue.

Lionel Trilling
Sincerity and Authenticity (1972)

I have said that the tendency toward diminished moral discourse and transferred moral responsibility in family law is widespread, and I will now attempt to prove that proposition by briefly surveying family law. The survey will reveal that, in virtually every area of family law, this tendency has made itself felt; that in most areas, the tendency is a considerable one; and that in many areas, it is prepotent.

(a) The Law Surrounding Divorce

Divorce is among the clearest examples of the change I discern. For over a century, divorce law reflected and sought to enforce society's sense of the proper moral relations between husband and wife. Indeed, the law of divorce was virtually the only law that spoke directly or systematically to an ideal of marital relations. That ideal included duties of life-long mutual responsibility and fidelity from which a spouse could be relieved, roughly speaking, only upon the serious breach of a moral duty by the other spouse. In the last two decades, however, every state has statutorily permitted some kind of no-fault divorce. These reforms exemplify the trend I hypothesize because (1) they represent a deliberate decision that the morality of each divorce is too delicate and complex for public, impersonal, and adversarial discussion; (2) they represent a decision that the moral standard of life-long fidelity ought no longer be publicly enforced; and (3) they represent a decision to diminish the extent of mutual spousal responsibility that will be governmentally required.

It is, of course, true that no-fault divorce rests in part on a moral view about the relations of people to each other and about the proper scope of government influence over people's lives. Thus I am far from suggesting that the decision to adopt no-fault divorce was itself amoral or immoral. Rather, my point is that, before no-fault divorce, a court discussed a petition for divorce in moral terms; after no-fault divorce, such a petition did not have to be discussed in moral terms. Before no-fault divorce, the law stated a view of the moral prerequisites to divorce; after no-fault divorce, the law is best seen as stating no view on the subject. Before no-fault divorce, the law retained for itself much of the responsibility for the moral choice whether to divorce; after no-fault, most of that responsibility was transferred to the husband and wife.

The availability of no-fault divorce does not eliminate all the possible moral questions to be resolved when couples separate; judicial decisions concerning alimony or maintenance, marital-property division, and child custody and support all may raise such questions. The tendency in each of those areas is likewise toward diminished moral discourse. This trend in alimony law is in part caused by a significant change described in the preceding paragraph—namely, the decline in the belief that each spouse assumes lifelong responsibility for the other. This change has strengthened the disinclination of both courts and legislatures to award alimony for life (or until the remarriage of the recipient), may have led to an increased disinclination to award alimony at all, and has led to a preference for "rehabilitative" alimony (i.e., to awarding alimony only for "the time necessary to acquire sufficient education or training to enable the party seeking maintenance to find appropriate employment.") Further, just as legislatures relieved courts of the responsibility of evaluating the moral relationship of petitioners for divorce, so are they increasingly relieving courts of that responsibility for petitioners for alimony. Even when legislatures have not expressly done so, many courts have inferred from their state's no-fault divorce statute a legislative intent to eliminate considerations of marital fault in setting alimony. An analogous movement may be seen in the treatment of marital property upon divorce; both statute and case law increasingly require courts to ignore marital fault.

In child-custody law, moral discourse has been reduced by the legislative and judicial erosion as proper bases for decision of various issues of morality, particularly sexual morality, such as nonmarital cohabitation and homosexuality, which were once thought relevant. Thus the Uniform Marriage and Divorce Act (a "barometer of enlightened legal opinion") provides, "The court shall not consider conduct of a proposed custodian that does not affect his relationship to the child." As the Commissioner's Note explains, "This provision makes it clear that unless a contestant is able to prove that the parent's behavior in fact affects his relationship to the child (a standard which could seldom be met if the parent's behavior has been circumspect or unknown to the child), evidence of such behavior is irrelevant." Further, legislatures and courts have, by limiting discussion to the psychological well-being of the child, tried to close off the consideration of morals and values that the "best interests of the child" standard once seemed to invite. Thus the Uniform Marriage and Divorce Act, while requiring a court determining child custody to "consider all relevant factors," expressly mentions (besides the wishes of the child and his parents) the child's "interaction and interrelationship" with any relevant persons, the child's "adjustment to his home, school, and community," and the "mental and physical health" of all concerned.

(b) The Law Surrounding Support Obligations

Developments relevant to my thesis in the child-support area center on the survival of the belief in the parent's obligation to support the child during the child's minority. While my thesis would predict that that belief was waning, there is evidence to the contrary. For example, there has been much attention to and legislation for enforcing child support duties. Some legislatures and courts have expanded the legally imposed parental support duty to include the support of children through college and even law school. On the other hand, in this area the law's actual practice may be as telling as its enunciated principle, and even that principle is ambivalently regarded. As Professor Chambers reports, "In the United States in 1975, of five million mothers living with minor children and divorced, separated, remarried, or never married, only about one-fourth received child support payments of any kind during the year and, of those who received anything, fewer than half received thirty dollars or more a week." From this fact, from the low rate of visitation by noncustodial fathers, and from the increasing discontinuity of family arrangements, Professor Chambers predicts that legislatures might someday limit child-support obligations (and court-enforced visitation rights) to a short term, perhaps three or four years. He believes this change may be foreshadowed by the willingness of states "to recognize more explicitly the right of couples to agree by contract to vary otherwise applicable obligations of support," and he speculates that "[c]hild-support may come to be viewed in much the same way [as rehabilitative alimony]: aid during a period of transition until the custodial parent can achieve financial independence or enter a new relationship." He also observes that the increasing availability and acceptability of abortion and birth control may lead to a time when "a pregnant woman, not living with the father, who knows that the father has no desire to participate in the child's upbringing may be seen [in not aborting a child] as making a unilateral decision to bear a child and the responsibility for its birth and for raising it may be seen as hers alone." Two factors enhance this possibility: society's sense of a public responsibility to support children whose parents cannot support them, and the fact that the "[p]rivate law support obligations for spouses and children that remain rest less on ideas of moral and natural duty than they do on utilitarian notions."

The rise of public provision for the indigent, especially through Social Security, promoted a change in the law's moral impositions in another area related to support. Statutes were once common whose object was "to protect the public from loss occasioned by neglect of a moral or natural duty imposed on individuals," namely, the duty of adults to support parents or grandparents who cannot support themselves. Such statutes are now decreasingly common and are evidently rarely enforced.

Marital responsibilities may be said to have diminished in yet another respect. The law was once, and to a considerable extent still is, that a couple cannot contract to reduce the marital duties imposed by law. An exception to this rule has long been made for pre-and postnuptial contracts respecting property. Now, a second exception, fostered by both courts and legislatures, is developing that allows couples to agree to some nonproperty divorce terms. This modest increase in freedom to contract represents a slackening of legal attempts to regulate moral conduct, but, like most grants of freedom to contract, is not an unambiguous withdrawal from private affairs by the state: With the right to contract comes judicial supervision and interpretation of the contract, and that authority can provide judges with the opportunity to impose their own moral views. This judicial authority is exercised with special zeal in supervising contracts concerning obligations after divorce. Courts commonly require that the parties must either have made a fair agreement or must have understood both the economic circumstances of the other party and any rights waived in making the agreement.

(c) The Law Surrounding Nonmarital Relations

Changes in the law of nonmarital contracts likewise reveal a marked alteration in the law's moral viewpoint. It was once "well settled that neither a court of law nor a court of equity will lend its aid to either party to a contract founded upon an illegal or *immoral consideration*," and thus that "[a]n agreement in consideration of future illicit cohabitation between the plaintiffs is void." In the celebrated *Marvin* case, however, the California Supreme Court discovered that California had always used "a narrower and more precise standard: a contract between nonmarital partners is unenforceable only to the extent that it explicitly rests upon the immoral and illicit consideration of meretricious sexual services." The court offered to enforce oral contracts and contracts implied in fact, and it enticingly declined to "preclude the evolution of additional equitable remedies to protect the expectations of the parties to a nonmarital relationship in cases in which existing remedies may prove inadequate." Other states have widely, though not universally, followed suit. This approach, in effect if not precisely in terms, removes from judicial consideration a moral question ... whether a relationship is so offensive to morals that the state should decline to enforce contracts respecting it. However, here even more than in marital contracts, the elimination of one moral consideration could create more. This would be true even if judges needed do no more than supervise and interpret express written contracts; it would be truer if judges dealt only with implied contracts; it will be very true indeed if judges are actually to devise standards for "additional equitable remedies" even where no implied contract is found. This visitation of the law into the moral lives of the unmarried seems particularly piquant in view of the likelihood that they stay unmarried in part to avoid the legal consequences of marriage.

(d) The Law Surrounding Abuse of Children

The contraction of moral discourse in the law of child abuse and neglect may be illustrated by beginning with Joseph Story:

> [P]arents are intrusted with the custody of the persons, and the education, of their children; yet this is done upon the natural presumption, that the children will be properly taken care of, and will be brought up with a due education in literature, and morals, and religion; and that they will be treated with kindness and affection. But, whenever ... a father ... acts in a manner injurious to the morals or interests of his children; in every such case, the Court of Chancery will interfere....

Until recently, child abuse and neglect statutes used similarly broad criteria for legal intervention. Georgia's statute, for instance, still authorizes legal intervention on behalf of any child "without proper parental care or control, subsistence, education as required by law, or other care or control necessary for his physical, mental or emotional health or morals." And child-welfare officials and courts long intervened exactly in aid of a child's presumed moral welfare. The present trend of influential opinion is to define grounds for intervention specifically and narrowly so that the state may act only when the child suffers or risks severe physical or mental injury. Supporters of that approach urge it in part precisely because it lessens intervention on "moral" grounds:

> [A]ll intervention involves value judgments about appropriate childrearing practices and value choices about where and how a child should grow up. Considering the seriousness of the decision to intervene, intervention should be permissible only where there is a clear-cut decision, openly and deliberately made by responsible political bodies, that that type of harm involved justifies intervention. Such value judgments should not be left to the individual tastes of hundreds of nonaccountable decisionmakers.

Moral discourse about child abuse has diminished in another way. There has for some time been a tendency to discuss that issue not in moral, but in medical terms. In recent decades, many social issues have undergone such a shift. The shift in language about child abuse has been specially marked, however, because various kinds of experts—psychiatrists, psychologists, and social workers—have directly influenced the statutory, judicial, and administrative discourse about child abuse.

In the related area of child medical care, the direction of change is somewhat obscure, partly because there are few reported cases save those in which a parent has refused a child medical treatment for religious reasons. The paucity of cases may itself indicate the law's apprehension of the mine field of moral issues that questions of child medical care, and particularly questions of neonatal euthanasia, present. The dearth of cases seems especially significant since the incidence of legally consequential child medical care problems appears to have increased with recent advances in perinatal care and since public discussion about and awareness of those problems has certainly increased. . . .

(e) The Law Surrounding Sexual Relations and Reproduction

In a series of areas, the law's moral discourse has been restricted by narrower definitions of immorality. Perhaps the first change was in the law's treatment of contraception. In the late nineteenth century and into the twentieth century, dissemination of information about contraception was limited by both state and federal statute. In the 1920s and 1930s, an active and successful birth-control movement arose, and as contraception went "from private vice to public virtue," such statutes were repealed. The Supreme Court fired the coups de grace when, in *Griswold v.*

Connecticut and *Eisenstadt v. Baird*, it held that state regulations limiting access to contraception infringe the constitutional right to privacy.

A slower but still pronounced change has characterized laws prohibiting fornication, cohabitation, and adultery. While all states once had such statutes, fewer than a third have them now, and states that have not repealed them seem to enforce them rarely or sporadically. Although several Supreme Court Justices have said in dicta that such statutes are constitutional, the Court has never ruled on the question, and some commentators have argued and some courts have held to the contrary.

Laws against homosexuality may be in an earlier stage of a similar process. Although the Supreme Court summarily and delphically affirmed a lower-court ruling refusing to find Georgia's sodomy statute unconstitutional, a number of state courts have held that such statutes infringe the right of privacy, and a number of states and towns have written antidiscrimination statutes or ordinances protecting homosexuals.

The law's rescue from the moral difficulties of abortion was more abrupt. In the 1960s and early 1970s, a reform movement began to persuade state legislatures, most notably New York's, to liberalize abortion statutes. In 1973, however, the Supreme Court preempted that movement by holding in *Roe v. Wade* that women have a constitutional right to an abortion free from state regulation in the first trimester of pregnancy, and a right to an abortion under limited state regulation in the second trimester. *Roe* neatly exemplifies the diminution of moral discourse: it removed a major moral question from the law, and did so at a remarkable and revealing moment—exactly when debate about abortion in legislatures was developing vigorously and productively, and when judicial debate was too recent and unformed to give the Court the kind of guidance it ordinarily relies on. *Roe* exemplifies just as neatly the law's tendency to transfer moral decisions to the people the law once regulated, for *Roe* apparently rested partly on the belief that the pregnant woman could better make the moral decisions about abortion than the state, a belief the Court has carried to the point of protecting a "competent" minor's power to decide to have an abortion without parental guidance.

(f) Conclusion

This brief and allusive survey of family law illustrates how broad and deep the trend toward diminished moral discourse and transferred moral responsibility is. In the rest of this Part, I shall suggest two additional ways of analyzing the trend, shall deal with objections to my formulation of it, and shall attempt to articulate some of its complexities.

(2) Two Amplifications of the Hypothesis

All systems of ethics, no matter what their substantive content, can be divided into two main groups. There is the "heroic" ethic, which imposes on men demands of principle to which they are generally not able to do justice, except at the high points of their lives, but which serve as signposts pointing the way for man's endless striving. Or there is the "ethic of the mean," which is content to accept man's everyday "nature" as setting a maximum for the demands which can be made.

Max Weber
Letter to Edgar Jaffe (1907)

I have described a series of doctrinal developments that support the hypothesis that moral discourse in family law has diminished and that responsibility for moral decisions has been transferred from the law. This description not only supports that hypothesis; it also allows us to amplify it, for there has been an associated change in the nature of the moral discourse—namely, a change away from aspirational morality. The family law we inherited from the nineteenth century sought not just to regulate family life, but to set a standard of behavior not readily attainable. That law enunciated and sought to enforce an ideal of lifelong marital fidelity and responsibility. Attempts to diminish the responsibilities of one spouse to the other were denied legal force by prohibitions against altering the state-imposed terms of the marriage contract. Divorce was discouraged, was justified primarily by serious misconduct by a spouse, and was available only to the innocent. Marital responsibility in the form of alimony continued even where the marriage itself had ended. The old family law also enunciated what might be called an ascetic ideal. Sexual restraint in various forms was a prominent part of this ideal. Laws prohibiting fornication, cohabitation, and adultery confined sexual relations to marriage; laws declining to enforce contracts based on meretricious consideration and laws giving relief in tort for interference with the marital relationship sought to achieve the same effect indirectly. Sexual relations were confined to monogamous marriage by laws prohibiting polygamy and to exogamous marriage by laws prohibiting incest. Sexual relations were confined to conventional heterosexuality by sodomy laws. And laws regulating the sale of contraceptives and the use of abortions made the "risks" of normal sexual relations difficult to avoid. Sexual restraint, while central, was not the only feature of the law's ascetic ideal. That ideal also included, through child-custody law, a view of "good moral character" that valued the diligent, law-abiding, churchgoing citizen.

Modern family law, as this survey suggests, not only rejects some of the old standards as meaningless, undesirable, or wrong; it also hesitates to set standards that cannot readily be enforced or that go beyond the minimal responsibility expressed in the cant phrase, "Do your own thing, as long as you don't hurt anybody else." The standard embodied in that phrase, with its emphasis on its first clause, is emphatically not aspirational; that standard can instill neither the inspiration nor the empathy to encourage people to anticipate ways in which their conduct might be harmful, much less to shape their conduct so that it is actively helpful.

My survey of family law suggests a second amplification of my hypothesis. I have had to discuss the trend toward diminished moral discourse as though it were entirely disembodied, as though it had no social, economic, or political origins. Legal scholarship's unfortunate ignorance of the politics of family law, the numerous and complex origins of the posited trend, and the limited scope of this paper inhibit precision, and therefore I proffer only a limited working hypothesis. I hypothesize that the trend toward diminished moral discourse in family law is most actively promoted by lawyers, judges, and legal scholars who are, relative to the state legislators and judges who would otherwise, decide family law questions, affluent, educated, and elite. This group's views on family law questions are (relatively) liberal, secular, modern, and noninterventionist. Some confirmation of this hypothesis may be found in public opinion surveys that suggest that "community leaders" and members of the "legal elite" consistently have more liberal attitudes on family law questions than the "mass public." And it does seem likely, for instance, that judicial receptivity to unmarried cohabitation stems in part from the fact that judges' sons and daughters are members of one of the two groups in which nonmarital cohabitation is most common. Indeed, a good deal of change in family law may be attributable to the encounter of an upper-middle class whose mores are changing with traditional legal regulation of divorce, abortion, and contraception, and to the response of a more feminist upper-middle class to the law's failure to prevent spouse abuse, nonpayment of alimony, and inequitable allocation of marital property.

This hypothesis may help us glimpse some of the complexity of the trend toward diminished moral discourse. While a number of the developments I have described—the Supreme Court's privacy decisions, for example—clearly reduce moral discourse by eliminating or limiting important moral issues as bases for legal decision, legal (and political) discussion of some version of these issues has sometimes persisted. In general, however, such discussion has been relegated to those legal and political institutions that are relatively less "elite" (and that are relatively more accessible to their lower-middle-class constituents). And insofar as such discussion occurs in "elite" legal and political institutions—resistance to the Court's abortion decision is a prime example—we may expect those institutions to be divided along the class and cultural lines I have described....

C. THE THEME INVERTED: TWO COUNTER–TRENDS AND THEIR LIMITATIONS

I have suggested that family law has tended to diminish discourse about the moral relations of family members and to transfer moral decisions, and I have offered instances of that tendency. However, in Part II.C., I said that no area of law can be explained in terms of one trend and that no trend of importance lacks counter-trends of importance. To emphasize this point, and to place the tendency toward diminished moral discourse in context, I wish to explore two of its leading counter-trends.

(1) The Counter–Trends

In two areas of the law generally there has been especially active discourse about the moral relations between people. The first of these is contract law. That field has in recent decades seen, for example, a new eagerness to apply the doctrine of unconscionability, a keener hostility to contracts of adhesion, a readier eye for contractual liability on equitable grounds, and, as in landlord/tenant and labor law, a renewed willingness to use status-based ideas to help those the law takes to be helpless.

The second such field consists of the laws that grew out of the intense moralism of the civil rights movement. The purpose of a civil rights movement is by definition to alter the rights of citizens vis-a-vis their government. However, the larger purpose of our civil rights movement—and one of the means of accomplishing the governmental purpose—was to introduce a morality of equality into everyday life: into life at school; in neighborhoods; on buses, in department stores, and at lunch counters; in hotels and restaurants; at work, at play, and at home. Indeed, one tribute to the moral strength of that purpose has been the willingness of the law to serve it by expanding the state-action doctrine and the commerce clause. Courts making civil rights law have expressly sought to change popular attitudes by ending "the role-typing society has long imposed." Significantly, the movement and these legal reforms were resisted precisely on the grounds that "you can't legislate morality."

I suggest that these two areas of the law and the social ideas they symbolize have contributed elements of waxing enthusiasm for moral analysis in family law. It is in the areas of family law susceptible to contractual analysis that courts have been most inclined to examine the specifics of people's moral relations in search of a fair result. For example: courts have sought to reward the expectation interests of people who have supported their spouses through school, have countenanced contracts (have even been willing to imply contracts) between unmarried cohabitants have begun to allow parties to alter the contract of adhesion that is the marriage contract, and have closely supervised those alterations to prevent unconscionable contracts. The civil rights movement's egalitarian ethos has likewise vitalized moral discourse in some parts of family law. That ethos has hastened the reform of marital property law, alimony, child custody law, grandparents' visitation rights, the doctrine of necessaries, and various support requirements.

(2) Limits to the Counter–Trends

However appealing contractarian and egalitarian principles may be for family law, there are inherent limits on the capacity of each to reverse, or even greatly delay, the trend toward reduced moral discourse in family law. Many of these limits grow precisely out of the uneasy relationship between the egalitarian ethos and the contractarian ethos. Much of the moral strength and interest of the contractarian ethos is in fact drawn from the egalitarian ethos: Traditional contract law achieves its modern attraction by its distinction from status based means of social organization; "reformist" contract law achieves its attraction by more realistically assessing the original relative situations of the contracting parties. Significantly, however, reformist contract law's assessment of the contracting parties' situation results in differential treatment of the contracting parties based precisely on their status. Thus in landlord/tenant law, to take one example, both statute and case law have not only provided systematic protections for tenants qua tenants, but have made those protections unwaiveable.

Although reformist contract law is status based, it seems, because of its commercial nature, status based in a relatively inoffensive way. That law commonly deals with contracts between actors (usually an individual and a business) who are of disparate wealth, knowledge, and expertise and who have joined in only one kind of transaction (usually a rental or sale). Moreover, the fairness of the contract is commonly measurable straightforwardly, in economic terms.

In some ways, status based family law contracts share the attractions of their commercial counterparts. Those attractions arise particularly from the perception that, when the contracting parties are a man and a woman, the man is likely to have social and economic advantages that could affect the ultimate fairness of the contract. But there are dissimilarities between the family contract and the commercial contract that limit the former's attractiveness and its capacity to expand moral discourse in family law. First, given the large proportion of "relationships" that can usefully be called endogamous, and given the changing patterns of women's education and careers, the relative advantages of the parties to a family contract, especially at the time of the contract, are less palpably unequal than the relative advantages of the landlord and tenant or the customer and seller, and any inequalities that persist seem likely to diminish.

Second, and more important, even if we are convinced that the bargaining positions of the man and the woman are and will remain unequal, it is much harder in the family than the commercial situation to know what a fair contract would look like. This is because, unlike the commercial contract, the family contract is really about many kinds of transactions between the parties, the fairness of which can often not be measured in economic terms. Nor does the egalitarian ethos provide reliable standards for evaluating or reformulating family contracts: Egalitarianism can require the law to shape its doctrines so that they do not discriminate between similarly situated parties, but it cannot readily speak to the many ways in which members of a family may be differently situated, either by conduct (where, for instance, a spouse has wasted joint assets) or by status (where, for instance, one of the parties is incapable of contracting—an impediment that alone makes almost the whole of parent/child family law unsusceptible to contractual discourse), or, most important, by choice (where the parties have altered their positions by contract). In other words, egalitarianism provides only one, partial standard of decision.

This last factor reminds us that contract law itself sets limits on the moral inquiries the law should make, limits so significant that contractarianism is itself an important cause of the trend toward diminished moral discourse. Contract law embodies a moral preference for allowing the contracting parties to arrange their own affairs, a preference expressed, for instance, in the doctrines that a court will not investigate the adequacy of consideration and that a court will interpret a contract in light of the intent of the parties. Indeed, just that preference accounts for much of the eagerness to introduce contract principles into family law, and the preference seems specially apt in the family context, where people's reasons for choosing "unequal" contracts may be based on deep-seated and well-considered social and religious views. To the extent that an egalitarian ethos prevails over contract law's preference for effectuating the parties' intent, the problem of legally enforced paternalism will be raised. And that paternalism seems inconsistent with the egalitarian ethos itself.

A third relevant difference between commercial and family contracts is that, while we can plausibly encourage parties to a commercial contract to bargain at arm's length, to establish their rights against each other in writing in advance, and to enforce those rights in courts, the whole contractual approach will seem to many families (and possibly should seem to the law) inimical to good family relations. (Indeed, it may be inimical to good commercial relations.)

Thus, while family law is being transformed by the diminution of moral discourse in and the transfer of moral decision from many of its fields, there are at least two major sources of resistance to that trend. These two sources—contractarianism and egalitarianism—seem, however, to be subject to some inherent limitations. In any event, their continued influence on family law will depend on the unpredictable political future of this country, a subject mercifully outside the scope of this paper.

D. VARIATIONS ON THE THEME: SOME OBSERVATIONS ON THE CAUSES OF THE TREND

So far, I have attempted to show that family law is undergoing significant change—a trend toward diminished moral discourse and toward the transfer of moral decision. I have described that change, and I have placed it in the context of countervailing changes. I will next examine four features of American life that form yet a broader context of this change in family law—the legal tradition of noninterference in the family, the ideology of liberal individualism, society's changing moral views, and the rise of psychologic man....

(1) *The Rise of Psychologic Man*

(a) The Social Change

If man were independent, he could have no law but his own will, no end but himself. He would be a god to himself and the satisfaction of his own will the sole measure and end of all his actions.

John Locke
Ethica (1693)

When so little can be taken for granted, and when the meaningfulness of social existence no longer grants an inner life at peace with itself, every man must become something of a genius about himself. But the imagination boggles at a culture made up mainly of virtuosi of the self.

Philip Rieff
The Triumph of the Therapeutic (1966)

Sexual mores are not the only part of the old "family morality" to have lost their meaning; there has also been a larger shift from a "moral" to a "psychological" view of personal affairs. This shift is, of course, a cause (and probably also a consequence) of our changing view of sexual morals, it has sharpened our appreciation of the enforcement problem, and it shapes and is shaped by the tradition of liberal individualism. This shift may not be the most crucial cause of the trend away from moral discourse in family law; indeed, it is pointless to attempt such a distinction at this stage of our knowledge. However, the psychologic view merits particular attention here for several reasons. First, while psychology has, of all the social sciences, contributed most abundantly to family law scholarship, the consequences for family law of the psychologic view have not been sufficiently analyzed. Second, the rise of the psychologic view provokes specially intriguing questions about how ideas from "high" and "popular" culture enter legal thought and about the interplay between modes of popular and of legal thinking. Third, and perhaps most important, because the psychologic view interacts in important ways with each of the other origins of the trend, and because the psychologic view so directly affects the terms of modern discourse, a detailed study of its consequences for the law is an apt way to elaborate a description of the new discourse in family law. I shall therefore devote disproportionate space to it.

a. The complexities of the shift. The shift to psychologism has, of course, been described before, usually in apocalyptic woe or messianic joy. Nevertheless, the shift confounds description because it is intellectually fragmented and complex. Its patriarch and paradigm, surely, is Freud. But no important thought achieves social power undegraded, and Freud's thought has reached its present power in a gaudy array of vulgarizations which have, in the public mind, overwhelmed the sophisticated variants.

The shift further confounds description because it is also sociologically complex. Nevertheless, its scope and significance cannot be doubted. Thus three leading students of the shift announce "the introduction of the 'era of psychology.' "A 1957 study on which those scholars rely "spoke of a psychological orientation, as distinguished from material or moral orientations, and suggested that this way of looking at life experiences and life problems might increase significantly in the future." By 1976, they conclude, "this shift had indeed occurred."

b. From morals to medicine: the role of human happiness. For our purposes, a central feature of the psychologic view is that it replaces moral discourse with medical discourse and moral thought with therapeutic thought. That shift may usefully be understood in terms of the role attributed to human happiness in social life. The old view held that men and women were obligated to lead a good life as that was defined by religious or social convention. Happiness was not the purpose of these conventions, but was expected to be a by-product of performing one's duties. If it did not come, however, one would be consoled by knowing one had led the right kind of life. The psychologic view, at least in its ideal type, denies that there are religious or social conventions that are independently valid. It holds that life's goal is the search for personal well-being, adjustment, and contentment—in short, for "health." Adherence to a religious or social convention may serve that end, but if it does not, other paths to well-being should be tried and used. In short, says Rieff mordantly,

> [E]vil and immorality are disappearing, as Spencer assumed they would, mainly because our culture is changing its definition of human perfection. No longer the Saint, but the instinctual Everyman, twisting his neck uncomfortably inside the starched collar of culture, is the communal ideal, to whom men offer tacit prayers for deliverance from their inherited renunciations.

On the old view, the right life was difficult: one's duties were numerous and onerous (though not necessarily unpleasant); distractions from duty were numerous and dangerous. Thus codes of family morality were aspirational and ascetic. As Professor Rieff observes:

> Heretofore, the saving arrangements of Western culture have appeared as symbol systems communicating demands by stoning the sensual with deprivations, and were thus operated in a dynamically ambivalent mode. Our culture developed, as its general technique of salvation, assents to moral demands that treated the sensual part of the self as an enemy. From mastery over this enemy-self there developed some triumphant moral feeling; a character ideal was born.

The psychologic view concedes that "stoning the sensual with deprivations" can work, but doubts it will. That view sees the drive of the instincts as crucial to understanding human motivation, believes that confining the drive of the instincts tends to be unhealthy, and, more specifically, sees sexual expression as central to human happiness.

c. Antinomianism, pragmatism, and nonbinding commitments. In his search for health, psychologic man must be skeptical and analytic in method and pragmatic in evaluation. In particular, psychological man must learn not to judge himself, his relationships, or other people according to moral rules; to do so is dysfunctional, since it asks the wrong question ("Is it right?") and blinds him to the answers to the right question ("Does it work?"). In other words, psychological man cannot come to rest in any relationship, or any community, or any creed; he must keep asking whether they are working for him. This is the doctrine of "nonbinding commitments." Personal and familial relations, on this view, become "arrangement[s] of convenience designed to advance the personal satisfactions and self-fulfillment of [their] members."

d. The search for self and the psychologic view of human nature. In the psychologic view, happiness comes from discovering and expressing one's unique true self. That self is discovered by peeling off society's false impositions and is expressed by peeling off its false constraints. Among the false impositions and constraints to be peeled off in the search for the "more personalized self-consciousness" are the roles and statuses into which society places people. Thus Veroff, Douvan, and Kulka announce as one of their "central themes" that "[s]ocial organization, social norms, the adaptation to and successful performance of social roles all seem to have lost some of their power to provide people with meaning, identity elements, satisfaction. In fact, role and status designations have become objects of suspicion. . . ."

The psychologic attitude seems to imply an optimistic account of human nature; if its proponents thought people base and vile, they could hardly advocate a Hobbesian world without the Leviathan or be so cheery about man's quest to find and express himself. Much psychologic writing explicitly argues that human nature is benign enough that, freed of socially imposed constraints, men will behave better than they do now. This benignity is buoyed by faith in human malleability: If people behave badly, it is because of environmental factors, which can be manipulated, or because of patterns of thought and behavior, which can (on some therapeutic views) be changed even if they cannot be understood.

Yet psychologic man's view of human nature is profoundly ambivalent. Against the optimism described in the preceding paragraph are pitted a vivid sense of the power and ubiquity of the passions, a dark sense of their cruelty, and a resigned sense that character is irrevocably and inevitably formed by early and universal experiences. Psychologic man's strain of pessimism about individual human nature is matched by a strain of pessimism about the capacity of systematic social activity to enhance human happiness. Professor Allen, in explaining why psychologism has been inimical to penal rehabilitation, notes the movement's frequent anti-intellectualism, its absence of public purpose, and the perverse fact that it "has not generally nourished the autonomy of individuals but has expressed a weariness with self-hood." Even "contemporary expressions of confidence in human malleability are often accompanied by a pervasive pessimism about the effectiveness and integrity of social institutions."

e. The psychologic view of privacy. Psychologic man's ambivalence about human nature extends to his views about privacy. On one hand, searching for one's self and peeling off social constraints seem to require privacy, and "privacy" at least as a slogan has more social (and legal) cachet than it used to. But those most enthralled by the psychologic attitude seem the least interested in privacy, as we may infer from the phrase "let it all hang out," from the techniques of psychotherapy, from the proclivity to use those techniques in ordinary conversation, from the itch of celebrities to discuss the intimacies of their lives on television, from the eagerness of the rest of us to become celebrities by retailing and living the intimacies of our lives on television, from our willingness to tell survey researchers whatever they want to know, from the belief in first names at first sight, and from the compelled contemplation of intimate and ultimate questions imposed on us by the pictures of the dead, the dying, and the *deshabille* which accost us in the daily papers and the monthly magazines. And some sacrifice of privacy seems inherent in the free expression of one's true personality, in the desire to reduce the power of social roles, and in them instant intimacy with family, friends, and colleagues that is also part of the psychologic creed.

The apparent conflict in psychologic man's view of privacy may perhaps be resolved, however, if we recall that privacy has come to have two meanings. The first, conventional, meaning speaks to the secrecy in which one conducts one's affairs. The second, newer, meaning speaks directly to the ability to conduct one's affairs autonomously. It is privacy in the second meaning psychological man wants, for without autonomy his efforts to find and express himself may be thwarted. And it is privacy in the first meaning that psychological man does not need, for, to him, secrecy is desired by those who are ashamed of what they do, and psychologic man's moral relativism and his awareness that all men serve unconscious drives make shame shameful. *Honi soit qui mal y pense.*

f. A case study. Perhaps greater concreteness can be given to psychologic man by reporting one version of his rise. Professor Susman suggests that in the nineteenth century, "character" was the word most revelatory of the modal American type, but that in the twentieth century, that word was "personality." The nineteenth century held "that the highest development of self ended in a version of self-control or self-mastery, which often meant fulfilment through sacrifice in the name of a higher law, ideals of duty, honor, integrity. One came to selfhood through obedience to law and ideals." The words "most frequently related to the notion of character" were *"citizenship, duty, democracy, work, building, golden deeds, outdoor life, conquest, honor, reputation, morals, manners, integrity,* and above all, *manhood."* The twentieth century, on the other hand, "stressed self-fulfillment, self-expression, self-gratification. . . ." Its "essentially antinomian . . . vision . . . with its view not of a higher law but of a higher self, was tempered by the suggestion that the self ought to be presented to society in such a way as to make oneself 'well-liked.' "The adjectives most frequently associated with personality "suggest a very different concept from that of character: *fascinating, stunning, attractive, magnetic, glowing, masterful, creative, dominant, forceful*."

(b) The Legal Consequences of the Rise of Psychologic Man

> *The wisdom of the next social order, as I imagine it, would not reside in right doctrine, administered by the right men, who must be found, but rather in doctrines amounting to permission for each man to live an experimental life.... All governments will be just, so long as they secure that consoling plentitude of option in which modern satisfaction really consists. In this way the emergent culture could drive the value problem clean out of the social system and, limiting it to a form of philosophical entertainment in lieu of edifying preachment, could successfully conclude the exercise for which politics is the name.*
>
> **Philip Rieff**
> *The Triumph of the Therapeutic (1966)*

The legal consequences of a new character ideal are, inevitably, tangled and obscure, especially where that ideal is variously shaped and varyingly accepted. Nevertheless, the psychologic character ideal is now so well-established that its influence on the law is inescapable. That influence is exerted in two ways: first, lawmakers respond to changes in the behavior and beliefs of the people they seek to regulate. Second, the new ideal alters the language, assumptions, and acts of the lawmakers themselves. The legal effect of the psychologic view can thus be substantial. But my argument in this Part will be modest—not that the rise of psychologic man has, of its own force, created wholly new doctrine, but rather that it has, in concert with the other social forces I have described, shaped the ways we use doctrines and ideas already present in the law.

a. From morals to medicine. In the preceding section, I identified, to borrow Professor Boorse's words, "a strong tendency ... to debate social issues in psychiatric terms.... This growing preference for medicine over morals ... might be called the *psychiatric turn*." Of course, that "turn" itself constitutes a change in discourse, because it directly substitutes one kind of discourse for another. Consider, for instance, situations in which family law looks at the whole of someone's personality, as when it evaluates the suitability of a guardian or the best interests of a child. The psychologic approach looks to that person's "health," mental and physical, while the old view holds that the guardian's qualifications and the child's interests include (prominently) the state of his mind and his morals.

The medical view also discards the old view that there is such a thing as "moral character" and that it should be considered in, for instance, child-custody decisions. The idea of "moral character" assumes that moral qualities are relevant to every aspect of one's personality, and that one's moral nature is essentially unitary. The disuse of "moral character," then, marks a shift away from a broad, if not global, way of looking at personality. Thus the Michigan legislature once believed it had said enough when it authorized courts to commit neglected children to the care of "some reputable citizen of good moral character." And thus to be of bad moral character was, under the old view, almost to be barred from winning custody of a child. In the law's new view, however, moral character becomes, at best, one trait among many. At worst, the idea of moral character vanishes altogether, to be replaced by the view that a person's moral qualities are unrelated to each other. For instance, modern family law holds that even if you have erred morally the law cannot infer that you are likely to commit the same fault again, or that you are likely to commit other faults. The eclipse of "moral character" thus diminishes the quantum of moral discourse by depreciating the contribution of a person's moral nature to his entire personality and by removing from the law a useful (whether or not accurate) predictive theory.

Also implicit in the idea of "moral character" are the beliefs that one's moral nature is within one's own control, and that it is helpful to talk about one's conduct in moral terms. Psychologic man and, increasingly, the law doubt both of these beliefs. "No-fault" divorce, for instance, captures neatly the psychologic attitude toward the latter belief: There ought be no sense of guilt when a marriage doesn't work, because there was simply a technical dysfunction; there ought to be no sense of prolonged responsibility, because that would itself be dysfunctional; and there ought to be no regulation of those technical problems except, possibly, a technical one, i.e., counselling.

The law's turn from morals to medicine is further evidenced by the difficulty the law has with the view—implicit in the "moral character" idea—that moral conduct is within one's control. The medical viewpoint poses two (related) challenges to that belief: first, that some moral faults are illnesses, and therefore beyond one's responsibility; and second, that all behavior is determined by forces beyond one's control. The law, obviously, cannot fully accede to the second challenge, but family law, at least, has been influenced by both. This influence can be seen even in an area as instinct with moral problems and feeling as child abuse, where the law has "accepted in principle the therapeutic approach."

The "psychiatric turn" diminishes moral discourse in family law in yet another way. The tendency to see family law problems in medical terms readily leads law to rely on specialists from other disciplines—medicine, psychiatry, psychology, social work, and so on. As it relies on experts from these disciplines, the law adopts their language, thereby diminishing moral discourse. Further, the law to some extent confides direct power to such experts—to doctors admitting patients to state hospitals, to social workers, to probation officers—and to some extent relies on their recommendations. To the extent the law does so, it replaces legal discourse (with its traditionally substantial quantum of moral discourse) with the discourse of another discipline. That substitution is noticeable, for example, in child-custody law, where a psychiatric recommendation can seem so encompassing, so authoritative, and so portentous that it overwhelms all other considerations.

The celebrated case of *Painter v. Bannister*, for instance, is usually taken as an example of Iowa stubbornness and invincible provincialism. However, a careful reading reveals the central influence of the psychiatric testimony in the case. The court began by comparing the "philosophies" of Mark Painter's father and of his grandparents, conceded its preference for the "stable, dependable, conventional, middle-class, middle west" home of the grandparents, and said "security and stability in the home are more important than intellectual stimulation in the proper development of a child," but then stated that a father has a special claim to custody of his child. However, instead of resolving this moral and legal conflict, the court devoted the final two pages of the opinion to extensive quotations from the psychologist who had testified that the grandparents were the psychological parents and that "the chances are very high (Mark) will go wrong if he is returned to his father." With testimony of this astonishing scope and assurance, the court apparently felt itself relieved of further inquiry into the moral, social, and legal problems it faced.

b. Nonbinding commitments. A second consequence of the psychological view for my theory arises from the doctrine of "nonbinding commitments." That doctrine, fully accepted, could eliminate many of the moral problems over which family law has puzzled, since many of them have to do with how binding commitments should be, with whether, when, and how one spouse may leave another or a parent may leave child. The doctrine finds its legal analogues in the law's tendency to see families in terms of their individual members and not as units and in the legal tendency to make it easier to leave a family. Like the doctrine of nonbinding commitments, these legal tendencies are sustained by psychologic man's pragmatic view of personal relations—the view that a relationship should be maintained only if it "works," that "options" should be kept numerous and open to "facilitate personal growth," and that living in a family is a matter of psychological adjustment, a technical matter of finding happiness, not a matter of moral relations. This view prefers temporary marriages, temporary nonmarital arrangements, and temporary children, and the law is coming to accommodate it.

No-fault divorce exemplifies that accommodation, along with the various procedural reforms designed to make divorce speedy and simple. And coordinate with this view of no-fault divorce are its companions, the trend toward permitting couples to contract in anticipation of divorce, the trend toward short-term "rehabilitative" alimony, and whatever trend there may be toward diminished responsibility for child support after divorce. The law has also accommodated itself to the view of "marital" relations as temporary by creating—and, not inconsiderably, legitimizing—temporary alternatives to marriage. Finally, the dwindling of family-responsibility statutes reflects the temporary quality of family relations from a somewhat different angle.

The law's increasing propensity to see the family in terms of its component members rather than as an entity is specially visible in, and in part arises from, the law's increasing propensity to see issues in terms of individual rights. The Court's shift from *Griswold v. Connecticut* to *Eisenstadt v. Baird* (from its first modern "privacy" case to its second) catches those propensities near their origin. In *Griswold* (which held unconstitutional a statute criminalizing the use of contraceptives), the Court's discovery of a "right to privacy" was expressly the discovery of a special right, one "older than the Bill of Rights—older than our political parties, older than our school system," a right that grew out of the special relationship of marriage. The Court apostrophized marriage as "a coming together for better or for worse, hopefully enduring, and intimate to the degree of being sacred." Allowing police "to search the sacred precincts of marital bedrooms" would be "repulsive." But in *Eisenstadt*, where contraceptives were distributed to the unmarried, the Court held that the Equal Protection Clause requires that the right of access to contraceptives "must be the same for the unmarried and the married alike." The Court conceded that "in *Griswold* the right of privacy in question inhered in the marital relationship." However, the Court discarded Griswold's encomium to marriage for something akin to its opposite:

> [T]he marital couple is not an independent entity with a mind and heart of its own, but an association of two individuals each with a separate intellectual and emotional makeup. If the right of privacy means anything, it is the right of the individual, married or single, to be free from unwarranted governmental intrusion into matters so fundamentally affecting a person as the decision whether to bear or beget a child.

The law of abortion provides two further examples of situations in which the Supreme Court's "rights" perspective has encouraged it to regard the family as a collection of individuals. *In Planned Parenthood of Central Missouri v. Danforth*, the Court held unconstitutional a statute requiring a married woman seeking an abortion in the first twelve weeks of pregnancy to obtain her husband's consent, unless the abortion was necessary to preserve her life. The state had justified the statute on the grounds of its "perception of marriage as an institution" and its view that "any major change in family status is a decision to be made jointly by the marriage partners." The Court quoted the passage from *Eisenstadt* that I just quoted, and reasoned that "since the State cannot regulate or proscribe abortion during the first stage, when the physician and his patient make that decision, the State cannot delegate authority to any particular person, even the spouse, to prevent abortion during that same period." However desirable the Court's result may be, its reasoning is fragile. As Justice White noted in dissent, the state was not delegating a power, but rather "recognizing that the husband has an interest of his own in the life of the fetus...." But even Justice White seemed not to credit that the state might be trying to impose, however unwisely, the view that the husband and wife ought to make the decision together.

The second example from the abortion area is represented by *Bellotti v. Baird*. The Court's judgment in that case was that if a state "decides to require a pregnant minor to obtain one or both parents' consent to an abortion, it also must provide an alternative procedure whereby authorization for the abortion can be obtained."

These examples suggest that once a court sees a problem as a question of constitutional right, it is easily driven toward psychologic man's view of human relations—driven, that is, to treat the problem as one involving individuals, not families, to project an atomistic image of the family, and to regard family problems as matters to be settled between the law and a single member of the family. A constitutional right, after all, is a right an individual has against the government; that is the point of the state-action requirement. Where a right exists, we prima facie prefer the individual, as the law of substantive due process illustrates. But the rights schema is often inapposite in the family context, since there a right against the government is also a right against other family members. And because we dislike compromising a right against the government, we are inhibited from looking for ways to encourage compromises or even discussion within the family. Indeed, the very appeal to law—to an external set of standards enforced by might—is atomistic in that it circumvents the (no doubt idealized) standards of family decision: private persuasion and eventual accommodation based on solicitude for the person with whom one disagrees.

To put the point somewhat differently, our tendency to constitutionalize family law and thus to think of it in terms of rights means that, when the law transfers moral decisions, it transfers them to individuals rather than to families, thus sustaining the image of the family as a collection of discrete individuals. And the rights approach must be, in one sense, hostile to moral discourse, because the resolution of moral problems must commonly be particularistic and delicate, while the promulgation and enforcement of rights is often generalistic and insensitive to nuance.

Even where the "rights" approach is used to unite the components of the family in principle, it is likely to divide the members of the family in practice, because in such situations one member of the family is often using the law to force his way on others in the family. For example, those favoring visitation rights for grandparents justify them not only in terms of the interests of the child, but also in terms of the "rights" of the grandparents. Court-ordered visitation is presumably necessary only where the child's parent objects to such visitation, and we thus see the law compelling the parent to submit to the intrusion of that cliche and source of popular wit, the intermeddling in-law.

A final irony of the "rights approach" is that the situation in which it is used most often to unite the family—when parents' rights are invoked to limit the state's interference in the family—is also the situation in which it can be abused to mistreat or even eject a member of the family. This possibility is most grimly raised when parents refuse lifesaving medical aid for their children.

Family law's movement toward contract likewise comports with psychologic man's tendency to see the family as a collection of individuals united temporarily for their mutual convenience and armed with rights against each other. Contracts are, by definition, made between individuals competent to deal with each other at arm's length. Contracts by definition give each individual rights against the other. And contracts by doctrine may be renounced, as long as the breaching party gives the other the benefit of that part of the bargain that can be reduced to economic terms. Indeed, if the breaching party can compensate the other party and still come out ahead, it is thought economically efficient—that is, socially desirable—for him to do so.

Finally, psychologic man's view of families as made up of individuals is encouraged by and encourages egalitarianism. The practical problem with seeing the family as a unit is that units are often called upon to speak as units; and historically, when the family has spoken, the voice has been the husband's. Egalitarianism has had the greatest effect in financial matters, but it has also spurred the attack on spousal tort immunity, on the spousal testimonial privilege, and on the law's handling of spouse abuse. Egalitarianism may well be compatible with a view of the family as a unit; indeed, most modern views of the family as a unit are based on a view of husband and wife as equals. But family law's sense that the patriarchal concept of the family must be extirpated and compensated for has perhaps led to a form of egalitarianism whose effects can be atomistic.

c. The search for self. Psychologic man, as we have seen, constantly seeks to find his unique "true self," to escape society's imposed roles. Family law, increasingly, lets him do so. This helps explain some of the appeal of recent attempts to ensure accurate, individualized trials by expanding procedural rights, as the Court did in *Santosky v. Kramer*, *Lassiter v. North Carolina*, and *Stanley v. Illinois*. It also helps explain attempts to eliminate "stereotypes" as to child custody (by making inadmissible evidence about a parent's sexual habits where those habits do not demonstrably affect the parent's ability to raise children and by weakening the tender-years presumption), as to illegitimacy (by eliminating disabilities based on a characteristic outside the control of the person affected), as to alimony and spousal support (by eliminating the assumption that the man should support the woman), and as to age (by allowing children to have an abortion without telling their parents if they can convince a court they need one).

How these developments affect the quantum of moral discourse in the law is unclear. On one hand, treating people as they are individually rather than according to roles and generalizations could allow the law to make more complex moral judgments about them and their situations, and trials that produce more information about litigants might give courts more material with which to make fuller moral judgments.

On the other hand, the "stereotypes" being attacked could also be seen as generalized resolutions of particular moral questions, and the attacks on those stereotypes as attempts to eliminate those moral questions from the law's purview and to substitute an inquiry into the particular psychological characteristics of the litigants and a search for the psychologic solution that "works." Furthermore, the effect of individualizing decisions is clouded by our ignorance about how legal actors decide cases where no rules guide their discretion. While individualized decisions may permit more complex moral judgments, they may also make them less likely. Legal decisions are those made on the basis of rules, and legal decisionmakers thus tend to look for rules to guide them. Where a factor is not expressly embodied in a rule, it is perhaps likely to be excluded, at least from conscious decisionmaking. In other words, we simply do not know whether freeing the decisionmaker from generalizations and rules will liberate him to make richer moral judgments or simply restrict the set for moral standards he is willing the employ. Finally, while the law expends much effort elaborating and using procedures, it is not clear that the procedural reforms of family law actually alter the outcomes of cases. It is thus possible that family law's procedural reforms might, anticlimactically, have little effect of any kind of discourse.

d. Removing false constraints. A further consequence of the psychologic view is weightier than the preceding consequence, for insofar as the law responds to that view's command to peel off society's false constraints and to that view's preference for pragmatism and flexibility, the law will eliminate rules. Family law, as we have said, is gradually but widely doing just that. The most interesting evidence of the law's direction here is in the area of substantive due process, where the personal right to be free of a legal rule directly confronts the state's moral or social justification for the rule.

For present purposes, the significance of substantive due process is that the Court had used both sides of the substantive due process equation in ways that suggest a predisposition to peel off rules. The Court's treatment of the personal rights side of the equation has been expansive to an extent made remarkable by the obscure origins of the "right to privacy." Its handling of the state-interest side of the equation shares the imprecision of its handling of the rights side, but the former is as narrow as the latter is broad: The Court almost invariably finds that the state interests advanced in support of a statute that infringes on a "fundamental" constitutional right are insufficient to justify the statute. No doubt the Court sometimes peeks at the state's interests before it decides whether the right violated is fundamental. But as Professor Nagel showed in his celebrated Note, the Court's application of the state-interest test has been so mechanical, so clumsy, so literalistic, that one may infer that the Court is not sensitive to many of the moral purposes of states.

The removal of false constraints is, in part, a removal of the religious and social conventions that, we noted earlier, psychologic man need use only instrumentally and pragmatically. Psychologic man's antinomianism neatly complements the American commitment to pluralism. That antinomianism, in other words, like American pluralism, acknowledges the possible importance and usefulness of beliefs and conventions, but denies that any particular belief or convention has inherent or independent justification. Under both views, many beliefs and conventions should be available to be used in a society; none should be imposed by it.

e. The psychologic view of human nature. Another consequence of the psychologic view arises from psychological man's assessment of the goodness and perfectibility of human nature. Curiously, both sides of that ambivalence may diminish moral discourse in family law. First, insofar as the psychologic view is pessimistic about the malleability of man, and sees man as governed by passions he cannot understand and cannot resist, it calls for the law to make as few attempts to regulate him as possible. This is the attitude reflected in the aphorisms endemic in discussions of family law: "You can't change human nature." "You can't legislate morality." Psychologic man's particular pessimism about the capacity of social institutions is widely echoed in the increasingly expressed doubts about, for example, the state's ability to intervene satisfactorily in child custody disputes, to provide adequate foster care, or to furnish decently run, effective asylums for retarded or mentally ill children. This pessimism, in other words, increases sensitivity to the enforcement difficulties that, we have seen, recur in family law.

Second, insofar as the psychologic view is optimistic about man's nature, it would still require the law to make few attempts to guide or regulate him. Indeed, on this view it may be the constraints themselves that are the problem. Thus both consequences of the psychologic view diminish the desirability of regulation of families, and both therefore diminish the law's need to evaluate the moral problems of families.

f. The nature of privacy. The final consequence of the psychologic view concerns the fundamental rights side of the substantive due process test—specifically, the right to privacy. I said that the psychologic view's attitude toward privacy is paradoxical. That view seems at first to demand privacy, but its adherents seem not to seek it nor the doctrine, on reflection, to require it. For its part, the law has elevated "privacy" to a fundamental right. I suggest that the law's "privacy" is the kind of "privacy" the psychological view requires. That kind is not privacy in the sense of secrecy; secrecy psychologic man seems not to want, and the law abandoned it as a protected right when it moved from *Griswold* to *Eisenstadt*. The privacy psychologic man needs is the kind the law comes closer to granting—autonomy from state control. And this is the kind of privacy that, when elevated to a right, is peculiarly incompatible with the law's moral discourse, for once a right to autonomy from state control is found, the issue of state intervention on "moral" grounds vel non is largely resolved and the state's moral interest is virtually irrelevant.

g. A concluding comparison. I conclude our consideration of the legal reactions to the psychologic view of man by proposing a modest analogy between the rising view of family law and the rise of classical liberalism. Each has its prototypical man: psychologic man for one, economic man for the other. Those personality types are in Professor Rieff's view related: "We will recognize the case history of psychological man the nervous habits of his father, economic man: he is antiheroic, shrewd, carefully counting his satisfactions and dissatisfactions, studying unprofitable commitments as the sins most to be avoided." Each type believes the greatest good for the greatest number is to be had by allowing the market, in goods or in "interpersonal relations," to work as free of government regulation as possible. Each view is primarily associated with the bourgeoisie. Each favors the contract as the market's mechanism, and thus family law has seen the rise of the antenuptial contract, the postnuptial contract, contracts for surrogate motherhood, a contractual view of career choices made by husbands and wives, and hostility to contractors preferred by status. Both were born in attacks on an older system of law and mores; and both employ egalitarianism in making those attacks. Both raise the questions to which we will shortly turn.

(c) A Case Study: Roe v. Wade

Up to this point, I have described the trend toward diminished moral discourse in family law and the transfer of moral decision from family law in necessarily general terms. At this point, I will attempt to make the nature of the trend clearer through extended exegesis of a specific text. I have chosen *Roe v. Wade*, the Court's well-known abortion opinion, as that test. I have done so for several reasons. First, *Roe* is an important case, the opinion—whatever its quality—was carefully considered, and the opinion and the problems it raises will be familiar to many readers. Second, *Roe* exemplifies the trend toward diminished moral discourse well: it not only removes from the law's (if not politics') purview a major moral issue, it does so without addressing that moral issue. Third, *Roe* illustrates the fit between psychologic man and modern family law in general and between the psychologic view and substantive due process in particular.

I said earlier that an expansive treatment of the private-rights side of the substantive due process question typical of family law. Just how expansive that treatment is may be seen in *Roe*. The case turns on the constitutional "right to privacy," a right inferred from the fourteenth amendment's provision that no state may deprive a person of life, liberty, or property without due process of law. Since little in the language, structure, or intent of the clause establishes the nature or limits of that right, since the Court has never defined those limits, since the right has little to do with "privacy" in the colloquial sense, and since the right of privacy is a "greedy" one, the right has long seemed menacingly capacious. The Court in *Roe* opens its discussion of the right to privacy with a sentence that acknowledges that the Constitution mentions no such right. In its next two sentences, the Court attempts to identify the origin of the right:

> In a line of decisions ... going back *perhaps* as far as ... [1891], the Court has recognized that a right of personal privacy, *or* a guarantee of certain areas *or* zones of privacy, does exist under the Constitution. In varying contexts, the Court *or* individual Justices have, indeed, found *at least* the roots of that right in the First Amendment ... ; in the Fourth and Fifth Amendments ... ; in the penumbras of the Bill of Rights ... ; in the Ninth Amendment ... ; *or* in the concept of liberty guaranteed by the first section of the Fourteenth Amendment....

After this disjunctive jumble of precedent (which may establish no more than "the roots of that right"), and after adding that the right has "some extension to activities relating to" various family law issues, the Court closes its attempt to define and defend the right, having established neither the principle that limits it.

Nevertheless, the Court next says, "This right of privacy ... is broad enough to encompass a woman's decision whether or not to terminate her pregnancy." *Why* that right is "broad enough" the Court does not say. The Court does follow this sentence with a list of "detriments" a woman would suffer who could not have an abortion, and one may infer that it is the severity of the detriments that gives rise to the right. But while the Court cannot mean that "detriments" create rights—since all statutes impose "detriments," and since most "detriments" do not give rise to a legal right—the Court does not say why detriments create a right here, or why these particular detriments create this particular right.

One might suppose that *Roe* is an example of the trend toward transferring the moral decision whether a particular abortion is justifiable from the state to the citizen. That is, of course, its effect. But the Court seems uninterested in building any argument for the wisdom of such a transfer. Indeed, when the Court reflects on the nature of the decision whether to have an abortion, the "factors the woman and her responsible physician necessarily will consider in consultation" turn out to be those consonant with the psychologic viewpoint. That is, they are largely "therapeutic," having almost exclusively to do with the woman's medical and psychological health, although other factors presumably, if vaguely, enter in one sentence: "There is also the distress, for all concerned, associated with the unwanted child, and there is the problem of bringing a child into a family already unable, psychologically and otherwise, to care for it." But the central question of the morality of abortion itself, the subsidiary moral questions about the extent to which the woman's conduct and situation influence the morality of her particular abortion, and the moral questions about how the abortion affects the woman's relations with the father of the child are all conspicuously absent.

The Court's "therapeutic" viewpoint is similarly apparent in the centrality of the role it sees for the doctor. So powerful is that viewpoint that at one point the Court actually attributes primary responsibility for the decision to the doctor: "the attending physician, in consultation with his patient, is free to determine, without regulation by the State, that, in his medical judgment, the patient's pregnancy should be terminated." Significantly, the Court seems not to expect that the doctor will give the woman the empirical medical information as to the nature of fetal life about which he should be expert and which many people believe relevant to the moral propriety of abortion. Nor does the Court acknowledge that there is hardly any medical expertise, except where continued pregnancy will endanger the mother's health, relevant to the decision whether to have an abortion. Nevertheless, the Court stresses that the doctor will be consulted—will be worth consulting and available for consultation—on the psychological, social, and moral issues the Court believes are relevant to the decision.

When the Court in *Roe* turns to the state's interests, it feints toward dealing with the central moral question the case presents—whether abortions destroy something we value in the way we value human life. But the Court immediately veers off to ask whether the fetus is a "person" within the meaning of the fourteenth amendment, on the theory that, if it were, "of course . . . the fetus' right to life would . . . be guaranteed specifically by the Amendment." The Court then embarks on a macabre inquiry into whether the Constitution ever refers to a "person" when it also means a fetus. The Court canvasses, *inter alia*, the apportionment clause, the emolument clause, the electors provisions, the provision setting qualifications for the presidency, and the extradition provisions, and discovers that "in nearly all these instances, the use of the word is such that it has application only postnatally. None indicates, with any assurance, that it has any possible pre-natal application."

The Court then returns to its central moral problem, but declines to confront it:

> We need not resolve the difficult question of when life begins. When those trained in the respective disciplines of medicine, philosophy, and theology are unable to arrive at any consensus, the judiciary, at this point in the development of man's knowledge, is not in a position to speculate as to the answer.

Thus relying on its own incapacity to resolve the question of when life begins, and without explaining its reasoning, the Court says that "by adopting one theory of life, Texas may [not] override the rights of the pregnant woman that are at stake."

The Court's attitude in *Roe* fits well with the moral skepticism and relativism that are part of psychologic man's world view. Courts may reasonably respond to the increased respectability of those attitudes by looking skeptically at moral justifications for statutes. But they might just as reasonably respond by deferring to any plausible moral justification propounded by the branch of government whose function is to represent democratic opinion. This latter response seems particularly appropriate in *Roe*, for if "the respective disciplines of medicine, philosophy, and theology" can't agree, the legislature's choice must be backed by some substantial arguments from each discipline. Further, the legislature's choice can, in principle, be better informed than the Court's (because the legislature has, if it will use them, better facilities for gathering information), and it can, as it always has, represent public opinion as to how society should define and protect human life. In *Roe*, as in other substantive due process cases, the Court has avoided examining all the possible rationales for a statute, although conventional doctrine prescribes otherwise. And among the unexplored rationales is what is surely a common one—that the state is protecting the state's classic police power interest in morality. The Court has announced (in an obscenity case) that such a rationale is legitimate (although the Court did not decide whether it is also "compelling"). In sum, the Court uses the rhetorical device of implying that the legislature made an arbitrary choice between arbitrary definitions to avoid dealing directly either with the crucial moral issue presented by the case or with the justification for holding that the legislature could not legitimately consider and decide that moral issue.

The *Roe* Court's next steps further demonstrate the artificial, ad hoc nature of the Court's state-interest analysis and of the Court's refusal to explain its decision in moral (or even morally comprehensible) terms. Although the Court had denied that Texas could, by defining "life," deprive a woman of her right to decide whether to have an abortion, the Court next finds that Texas has an "important and legitimate interest in protecting the potentiality of human life," and that that interest "grows in substantiality as the woman approaches term, and at a point during pregnancy, . . . becomes 'compelling.' " The Court then holds that that point is reached at "viability," which the Court indicates is reached after twenty-four to twenty-eight weeks of pregnancy. "This is so because the fetus then presumably has the capability of meaningful life outside the mother's womb." The Court does not say why its definition of "meaningful life" (which deprives a woman of a constitutional right to an abortion in the last trimester) is reasonable when the legislature's is not. Nor does the Court say why the "potentiality of life" which the Court concedes exists through the second trimester is not something the state may protect.

One approach to these questions is suggested by the practice, in substantive due process cases, of striking the balance between the individual and the state "having regard to what history teaches are the traditions from which [the country] developed as well as the traditions from which it broker." On one view, then, courts might substitute an analysis of the law's historical treatment of a moral problem for a direct analysis of the moral problem itself. This might be the purpose of Justice Blackmun's curious historical excursion in *Roe*. However, the Court's use of history, for whatever purpose it is advanced, is disquieting. It begins by noting that, while the Persians severely punished abortion, the

Greeks and the Romans did not. Justice Blackmun agonizes for two pages over the awkwardness that the Hippocratic Oath flatly proscribes abortions. He concedes that with the rise of Christianity, "[t]he Oath 'became the nucleus of all medical ethics' and 'was applauded as the embodiment of truth,'" and he concedes that the oath is "a long-accepted and revered statement of medical ethics." Nevertheless, he discovers that "the late Dr. Edelstein" thought the oath "'a Pythagorean manifesto and not the expression of an absolute standard of medical conduct.'" He thinks this "a satisfactory and acceptable explanation of the Hippocratic Oath's apparent rigidity." It is revealingly indicative of the psychologic attitude of the opinion that that "apparent rigidity" is something that needs to be explained away instead of accepted as a statement of a considered moral judgment.

The Court then reports that the common law may have made abortion after quickening a crime; that in 1821 American states began to make such abortions criminal; and that, beginning in the middle of the nineteenth century, abortions before quickening were also made criminal. The Court concludes that "throughout the major portion of the 19th century, abortion was viewed with less disfavor than under most American statutes currently in effect." But the Court's own history demonstrates that abortion itself was condemned by the relevant ethical tradition for two thousand years, that never in the history of Anglo–American law was there any doubt about the state's power to prohibit abortion, that abortion before quickening was criminalized by statute in the early-middle nineteenth century, that abortion before quickening was criminalized as soon as anyone could diagnose pregnancy before quickening, and that abortion has been a felony in virtually every state for a century.

Finally, *Roe* is consonant with the psychologic viewpoint sociologically and tends to confirm the sociological amendment to the hypothesis propounded in Part II.B. Crudely put, the same groups that most partake of the psychologic outlook also have the most liberal views of abortion, while those groups that partake of it least have the most conservative views of abortion. Indeed, abortion is an issue that is being used in the political debate over the desirability of the psychologic world view, a debate in which positions are greatly influenced by social class.

My point is not to show yet again that the opinion in *Roe* is uncommonly unpersuasive. Rather it is to propose that the unpersuasiveness indicates that the explanation for the Court's result lies, more than usually, outside the realm of theories embedded in judicial decision. It is, further, to suggest that the result of *Roe* and the Court's attitude toward substantive due process doctrine are consonant with the viewpoint of psychologic man....

E. CODA

"And you, Mr. Arabin, what do you think?" said Eleanor....

"What do I think, Mrs. Bold?" and then he rumbled his money with his hands in his trowsers pockets, and looked and spoke very little like a thriving lover. "It is the bane of my life that on important subjects I acquire no fixed opinion. I think, and think, and go on thinking; and yet my thoughts are running ever in different directions. I hardly know whether or no we do lean more confidently than our fathers did on those high hopes to which we profess to aspire."

"I think the world grows more worldly every day," said Eleanor.

"That is because you see more of it than when you were younger. But we should hardly judge by what we see—we see so very very little." There was then a pause for a while, during which Mr. Arabin continued to turn over his shillings and half-crowns.

Anthony Trollope
Barchester Towers (1857)

In this paper, we have seen how family law has become ever more reluctant to discuss and resolve moral problems. We have seen that the trend has been impelled by legal, intellectual, and social attitudes of great strength and tenacity. We have noted forces that might reverse that trend, though we have discounted their strength. Finally, in the last section, we have glimpsed the troubling and intractable problems—legal, intellectual, and social—the trend ultimately raises.

"So [said the doctor]. Now vee may perhaps to begin. Yes?"

Perhaps few social forces have exerted as much influence on contemporary family law as the women's movement. The following article both details that influence and points to some of its complexity.

KATHARINE T. BARTLETT
FEMINISM AND FAMILY LAW

33 Family Law Quarterly 475 (1999)

I. Introduction

Feminism's principal contribution to the law of the family in the United States has been to open up that institution to critical scrutiny and question the justice of a legal regime that has permitted, even reinforced, the subordination of some family members to others. The family has long been idealized as a refuge—a "haven in a heartless world"—requiring privacy and freedom from public interference. It still is. Feminists have attempted to pierce this shield of privacy, to reach the injustice of family relationships and the law that permits them. They have questioned the premises of family privacy, insisting that just because relationships are private does not make them beyond public concern. They have challenged the inevitability or naturalness of family privacy, arguing that where the line is drawn between private and public is itself a highly discretionary, political act. And they have exposed the hypocrisy of a construct that purports to be neutral but that suppresses recognition of the kinds of harms from which women disproportionately suffer, while leaving room for prohibition of the kinds of harms men experience....

In the course of this analysis, I will stress not only common agendas and insights that feminism has brought to family law reform, but also tensions within feminist thought and practice. Feminists have disagreed, for example, over the extent to which sex differences exist, the origin of these differences, and the significance that should be given them. They have disputed the importance of sex neutrality in formulating solutions to women's subordination. They have debated the advantages and disadvantages of individual rights approaches to securing women's rights, and compared these to approaches that offer protection or benefits to women based on their characteristics as a group and to approaches based on relational or communitarian theories. They have argued about whether to promote woman's economic self-sufficiency and ability to compete in the workplace, or to affirm woman's maternal obligations and the public support necessary to help her meet them. They have questioned each other about who speaks for women, given their diversity and the conflicting nature of some of their interests. And they have disagreed about the extent to which traditional values, including marriage and the nuclear family, should be retained.

These tensions, many of them overlapping, reveal feminism not as a single set of commitments to a particular set of reforms, but as an open commitment to identifying the ways in which the law disadvantages women and to advocating changes to eliminate those disadvantages. Feminists work from a common hypothesis that "women have been, and still are, wrongly treated (or thought about, or regarded, or valued), and that this should be remedied," and they ask common questions to test this hypothesis. They do not necessarily reach the same answers, and the answers they reach may change over time, as circumstances change and experience teaches. But it is this common hypothesis and the set of questions asked to test it that bind feminists together in a more or less recognizable movement. This essay discusses some issues on which feminists have maintained a more or less common and consistent front, others as to which the common ground has shifted over time, and still others as to which the battles in which feminists have been engaged have been among themselves as well as between themselves and others. Understanding both the common ground and the points of dissension is important in comprehending both the past role of feminism in family law reform, and the role it is likely to take in the future.

II. Divorce....

Women's groups played a larger role in reforms associated with the consequences of divorce, including property distribution, alimony, child support, and custody. The objectives they sought with respect to these reforms were a mix of material and symbolic goals. In the case of property distribution, women's groups sought primarily to obtain a fairer (i.e., larger) share of assets for women at divorce.... Reform of the system for dividing property between divorcing spouses in the 1970s and 1980s was viewed both as a way to secure some source of support at divorce for women whose husbands failed to provide adequate alimony, and to correct the fundamental unfairness of a system that neither recognized the contributions of wives toward the accumulated property of their husbands nor gave wives any ownership interest in the assets acquired by their "partners" during the marriage. Most women's groups preferred a presumption in favor of equal division of the property acquired by either spouse during the marriage; some favored a more open-ended *equitable* division standard. All women's groups agreed, however, that radical change was required. By 1982, every state, by legislation or court decision, had adopted equitable distribution in one form or another.

Reform of the child support system was also viewed by feminist reformers as an issue of gender equity, to be addressed by improving the share of the economic pie for women and their custodial children. While the precise figures are disputed, scholars agree that the standard of living of women and their custodial children is likely to decline significantly at divorce, while the standard of living of custodial fathers either rises, or declines far less severely. Federal legislation was enacted in several different packages from 1975 through 1996 to attack the problem on several fronts, requiring states (1) to undertake more paternity actions and to obtain more child support orders, both against divorced fathers and never-married ones; (2) to establish mandatory, rebuttable guidelines in order to achieve more consistent and more adequate awards; and (3) to adopt stricter enforcement mechanisms, such as automatic income withholding. It is unclear how important the issue of gender equity was in the minds of legislators involved in passing this legislation; the politically conservative impulse to shift the burden of responsibility for poor children from the public to "deadbeat dads" surely provided the major impetus for child support reform. However, the ongoing (and somewhat disputed) public evaluation of the federal legislation has focused significantly on the impact of this legislation on the lives of single mothers and their children.

While women's groups used property distribution and child support reform to try to increase resources for women and children at divorce, feminist reform efforts in the areas of alimony and child custody in the 1970s and 1980s subordinated economic goals to ideological ones. Traditionally, the availability of alimony to an innocent, dependent wife represented part of the marital bargain whereby the wife gave up control of her property and wages permanently in exchange for lifelong support. Although this rationale was undermined once women could control their own property in marriage and once divorce was available to end marriage, it seemed clear that many divorced women would continue to need, and in some sense deserve, continuing support from their ex-husbands. Given that before no-fault divorce became available, alimony awards were rare, and low, and that, coincident with no-fault divorce, various factors combined to reduce still further the likelihood of obtaining a permanent and adequate alimony award, one might have expected feminists to exert pressure on the law to obtain higher and more adequate support amounts.

By and large, however, women's advocates did not seek to expand alimony but rather to contain it. The reasons were symbolic and strategic. One problem these advocates identified with alimony laws was that they promoted the damaging stereotype of the dependent wife. This was true especially in those states in which only men could be made to pay alimony, and only women could receive it. But even sex-neutral alimony statutes helped to legitimate the stereotype of women economically dependent upon their husbands, insofar as women were virtually the only beneficiaries. Thus, not only did feminists seek to eliminate sex bias in alimony statutes, but some supported restrictions on alimony, such as time limits and stricter eligibility requirements. This support was part of the strategy to increase women's share of the property divided at divorce. The premise of this strategy was that a one-time fair and equitable division of the property at divorce that recognized women's contribution to the couple's assets as a homemaker and parent would serve women's long-term economic interests better than having to rely for a monthly alimony check from a reluctant ex-husband. A fair property division also, it was hoped, would not stigmatize women as needy dependents. In short, even though dependence was an accurate reality for many women, feminists disfavored alimony both out of the fear that alimony only strengthened that reality, and out of the hope that property reform would be worth more to women than the monthly support checks they might give up.

The same (optimistic, some would say) impulse that led feminists to disfavor alimony as a solution to women's economic vulnerability at divorce also made them uncomfortable with custody presumptions that favored mothers over fathers at divorce. Children were viewed for some time as the natural property of their fathers, but between the mid-nineteenth century until the 1970s, mothers in virtually all jurisdictions were favored in custody cases, either through formal statutory presumptions or judicial convention. As other sex-based classifications fell to the equal rights campaign of the 1970s and 1980s, the explicit partiality of these presumptions and conventions came to seem untenable. A few feminist advocates briefly flirted with the possibility of joint custody as a gender-neutral solution that would encourage equal parenting roles, but most feminist advocates from the beginning of this period favored some version or another of the primary caretaker presumption. Neither type of presumption caught on, and most states continue to operate with the best-interests-of-the-child test in custody cases. The upshot is the almost complete elimination of statutory presumptions in favor of mothers, without a substitute standard to control bias against them.

B. Feminism and Reform....

The tension among feminists caused by multiple, sometimes conflicting goals has been apparent over the past decade especially in the criticisms that prominent feminists such as Martha Fineman and Mary Becker have made against women's advocates who fought for many of the reforms described in the prior section, for having been too concerned with sex neutrality and not concerned enough with women's material interests. It is not clear how fair this criticism is. As Joan Williams points out, feminists who have pursued sex-neutral solutions to women's unequal situations have always sought to advance women's material interests; they have just believed that the best way to do so is within a sex-neutral framework. In fact, those feminists who have been especially critical of the equality concept have urged solutions that are themselves consistent with formal equality. The wisdom of these measures, as with all other measures that feminists propose, turns not on whether or not men and women should be treated "equally," but on which equality solution is best. Of the positions feminists have taken on the legal issues raised by divorce, the revival of a maternal custody presumption would appear to be the only one that poses the stark choice between equal and special treatment.

Still, there are substantive differences between feminists that explain why one equality solution to a particular problem seems superior to another. Joan Williams puts her finger on one substantive difference when she distinguishes between *equal parenting* advocates and *maternalists*. Advocates of equal roles in the home and at work put a high priority on men sharing the burdens (and joys) of childrearing and family and women obtaining the opportunities of paid employment, viewing this shared role ideal as necessitating the elimination of not only barriers to women, but favored treatment as well. Maternalists believe the goal should not be to change women by directing them away from motherhood and women's work, but rather to support them when they take these traditional paths.

Another axis along which feminists differ substantively, and have long done so, concerns the appropriate role of the state. The tension has been especially apparent in the area of child support. Feminists have been supportive, in general, of efforts to obtain more adequate child support awards from fathers. Some feminists, however, have become increasingly critical of the emphasis placed on private resources as the way to address financial dependency by mothers and their children. They emphasize that a private system is inadequate in those many cases in which fathers are simply too poor to support their children. They argue also that dependency is an inevitable condition of children, the elderly, and the disabled and that women who meet the needs of dependents are satisfying a public function, deserving of public support. Martha Fineman couples this latter argument with the criticism that when mothers are forced to rely on *private* resources, they are inappropriately being forced to depend on a man and thus to conform to a nuclear family norm.

More generally, just how much support the law *should* give to the nuclear family has been a difficult issue for feminists. While most feminists generally support an expanded definition of family and the protection of voluntary relationships, whether or not they are centered on a married, heterosexual couple, feminists also believe that traditional nuclear families serve important societal goals. It has been said, however, that the "major theoretical contribution of contemporary feminism has been the identification of the family as a central institution of women's oppression." In keeping with this contribution, Martha Fineman has argued for the elimination of the nuclear family as the basic unit to which special property, tax, contract, and tort privileges and protections apply, in favor of the mother-child dyad as the privileged group.

It is perhaps surprising that Martha Fineman, who among influential, contemporary feminists has put the highest priority on protecting women in the exercise of their traditional maternal roles, seems the least supportive of traditional marriage. Conversely, the feminists who have been the most interested in eliminating traditional gender roles have tended to remain more loyal to the traditional, marriage-based family unit. It is also unexpected, in light of her strong maternalist identification, that Fineman has not been one of the feminists who supports a return to a maternal custody presumption. These incongruencies could be viewed as inconsistencies, but they are better understood as manifestations of the many traps feminists face in attempting to improve women's situation. The marriage reform trap presents one of the most difficult dilemmas: Is it better for women to save marriage without traditional gender roles, or to save traditional gender roles without marriage? One hundred and fifty years after Seneca Falls, these same questions continue to vex women's advocates.

III. Sex and Reproduction

A. *Reform and Reproductive Rights*

It has been one of feminism's greatest insights that society's norms with respect to sex and reproduction are central to women's oppression. Contemporary feminists describe a "sex/gender system," which rationalizes women's subordinate roles according to their biological functions, especially those related to sex and reproduction. In attempting to expose the sex/gender system, feminist scholars have emphasized how state policies with respect to contraception, abortion, and procreation have been political decisions, masked in medical or moral rhetoric. The link between restrictions on the medical practice of abortion that were in place in the nineteenth century and the desire to maintain women in their "place" are particularly well documented. More generally, women in the nineteenth century were portrayed by doctors as fragile and dominated by their reproductive process in order to justify restrictions on their reproductive choices. Women who did not conform to expected gender roles were deviants—promiscuous when their sexual activities exceeded the allowable boundaries, frigid or hysterical when they failed to fulfill their marital obligations. Restrictions on interracial marriage and on penalties against illegitimate children and their mothers also served, in their own ways, to channel permissible sexual and reproductive activity to uphold the sexual hierarchy....

A more radical, feminist pro-abortion movement beginning in the early 1970s ... [views abortion] as a matter of the right of determination of all women. This right, initially situated by the U.S. Supreme Court in the sanctity of the marriage bond between husband and wife, expanded into a freedom of intimate decision making centered in the individual woman, and later combined with the medicalized view of birth control and abortion to form the conceptual basis of the Supreme Court's decision in *Roe v. Wade*. The two frameworks have remained somewhat distinct orientations, however, with organizations such as the National Abortion Rights Advocacy League (NARAL) emphasizing the feminist commitment to the individual woman's autonomy and Planned Parenthood and other organizations favoring the medical model of reproductive rights.

B. Feminism and a New Generation of Reproductive Issues

Over the last two decades, feminist activity has been directed, for the most part, less at extending reproductive rights than at preserving them in the face of significant efforts at retrenchment. Soon after *Roe v. Wade*, it was established that, while the individual woman had a right to make the decision to have an abortion, the state could not be compelled to fund it. More recently, the U.S. Supreme Court in *Planned Parenthood of Southeastern Pennsylvania v. Casey* has altered the framework of *Roe v. Wade*, which had allowed women unlimited discretion to have an abortion at least in the first trimester of pregnancy, to permit state limits on abortion that do not constitute an "undue burden" on the women's autonomy rights. Under this evolving standard, courts have upheld, among other things, waiting period restrictions, rules requiring abortion providers to provide certain specified information to women seeking abortions, and prohibitions against the practice by traditional nonphysician abortion providers. In addition, prior U.S. Supreme Court decisions requiring a judicial bypass provision to parental consent restrictions have been altered to permit parental consent provisions with waiting periods even when these restrictions could cause substantial delays in obtaining an abortion. Efforts at enacting federal and state prohibitions directed against a particular method of late-term (or so-called "partial birth") abortions have been vigorously pursued, although to date, the constitutionality of this legislation is in doubt. Further, the exercise by many women of their reproductive rights has been frustrated by violence and threats of violence, and efforts to curb this violence have met with some resistance by courts.

As reproductive rights are being curtailed in many states, it is hard to imagine a future in which issues of reproductive control are evaluated absent their implications for women, and even harder to imagine a time in which there will not be overwhelming support among feminists for reproductive choice. The feminist responses to these efforts to curtail reproductive rights, however, have included serious review of the individual privacy and autonomy rationale of *Roe v. Wade*. This rationale has been blamed for the abortion-funding decisions and for the difficulty of developing a constitutional theory to compel the state to protect women who are physically threatened in their intimate relationships. With these failures in mind, some feminists have argued that equal protection is a better theory to support reproductive freedom than the right of privacy.

Other challenges to the privacy theory arose out of the branch of feminism associated with "different voice" theory or "relational feminism." Some feminists found in relational feminism an alternative justification for the woman's right to abortion; others worried that, by contrast to the appealing images of relational feminism, "choice" rhetoric feeds the unappealing image of mothers pursuing their own self-interest, which is being used to undercut many of women's hardwon rights. More recently, the reinvigoration of the view of an unwanted pregnancy as a bodily assault, from which a woman should be able to defend herself, has reinvigorated the autonomy perspective, within a framework in which the question of whether the fetus is a person is arguably avoided and the obligation of the state to support women seeking abortions more firmly secured.

A rethinking of the old frameworks has been forced not only by threats to women's abortion rights but by other factors, as well. One of these factors is the challenge to the established white, middle-class feminist community by nonwhite women and poor women; since this challenge, the question in evaluating the law relating to sex and reproduction is no longer simply how the law affects women in some general sense, but how it affects certain groups of women, such as those who cannot afford to exercise all of the "choices" the law makes available to them. A second factor has been the emergence of new reproductive technologies, technologies that do not require sex, or even a woman's body, and thus that change the relationship between reproduction and the oppression of women.

Both of these factors have sharpened the tension between autonomy and other potentially competing values and principles woman may care about. For example, new reproductive technologies raise issues about the possible exploitation of poor women, hired to bear children for couples who can afford to pay. An individual autonomy model emphasizes the value in affirming women's choices, including potentially unwise surrogacy arrangements, and the risk that protecting individual women from the choices they make demeans all women. Yet, such arrangements may enable some women to be exploited or to have to sacrifice their own reproductive freedom in order to facilitate the reproductive choices of other women. Debates over prostitution and the appropriate legal response to drug-abusing pregnant women have raised similar questions about the meaning of choice in sex and reproduction and how to protect women's interests when women live in very different economic circumstances....

IV. Domestic Violence

Feminists also have linked family violence with women's inequality and oppression. Traditionally, the law has viewed violence in the family as a private issue, into which the law should not intrude, for fear of exposing the family to "public curiosity and criticism" and thus undermining it. Feminists have shown that, to the extent family violence is beyond the reach of the law, men's abuse of and power over women is enabled and affirmed.

The ebbs and flows of legal responses to domestic violence have had more to do with shifts in political and social fashions in U.S. history than with the actual incidence of crime or knowledge about it. Thus, for example, late nineteenth-century campaigns against abuse of children and women were tied to the temperance movement, directed (with some condescension) against lower class families, and related more to the desire to domesticate the new, immigrant populations than with any more general concern about the problem of the subordination of women. By comparison, efforts to use the law to curb family violence in the last few decades of the twentieth century have been closely tied to feminist concerns about equality and individual autonomy for women. At the same time, part of the most recent case for regulating domestic violence has been the growing understanding that it is a more common, and more serious, problem than was previously assumed. Estimates of family assaults vary widely, but the Uniform Crime Reports indicate that, of all female murder victims in 1995, 26 percent were killed by husbands or boyfriends, and a report submitted to Congress in connection with the passage of the Violence Against Women Act of 1994 estimated that 3 to 4 million women are beaten by their husbands or boyfriends each year—an average of one every fifteen seconds.

Feminist successes in achieving reform in this area are quite impressive. The common law exemption for rape has been abrogated completely in at least twenty-four states and, in the remainder of the states, the exemption has been qualified by statute or judicial decision. All states now have procedures for obtaining civil protection orders that, under varying circumstances, can enjoin an abuser form harassing, threatening, or abusing a victim. The effectiveness of civil protection orders is limited, of course, by the willingness of the state to enforce them and the abuser to obey them, as well as by the resources and resilience of the victims and how well the victims stand up to the real or potential escalation of the violence. Still, police training, greater availability of shelters for battered women and their children, and public education efforts directed at both abusers and the abused have helped to improve attitudes and options in these regards.

By 1994 at least twenty-two states and the District of Columbia had statutes requiring mandatory, warrantless arrests in domestic violence situations. Depending on the statute, arrest may be mandated when the officer determines that a family violence crime has been committed, when there is probable cause that a protection order has been violated, where there is probable cause that an aggravated battery has occurred, or when the officer observes a recent physical injury. In addition, in a number of states, special domestic abuse statutes treat violence in the domestic context as a more serious offense that in other settings. Most states now have anti-stalking statutes.

The law has also become more responsive to the impact of domestic violence on the safety and welfare of children. At least two-thirds of the states require consideration of domestic violence in custody determinations. Many of these states impose a rebuttable presumption or an outright prohibition against an award of custody, or joint custody, to a perpetrator of domestic violence. A finding of domestic violence also increasingly affects the terms of visitation and whether or not a parent will be required to mediate a custody dispute.

These reforms have been viewed, uniformly, as matters of women's rights and have succeeded in large part because of lobbying by women's groups. The Violence Against Women Act of 1994 goes far in explicitly recognizing the link between violence against women and women's equality. Among its wide range of measures to address domestic violence, it creates a civil rights remedy for "crimes of violence motivated by gender." Under this provision, any person, including but not limited to a person who acts under color of state law, who commits a crime of violence "because of gender or on the basis of gender and due, at least in part, to an animus based on the victim's gender" is liable for "compensatory and punitive damages, injunctive and declaratory relief, and such other relief as a court may deem appropriate." ...

The most debated of [the "few substantive issues relating to domestic violence that have divided feminists"] ... is whether battered woman need their own law of self-defense or whether existing standards are adequate. Some advocates have urged a special "reasonable woman" or "reasonable battered woman" self-defense standard when the defendant woman has killed her abuser, on the grounds that the traditional doctrine of self-defense fails to account for gender differences, including women's lack of physical defense training, their weaker strength and battered women's particular perceptions of helplessness. A standard especially designed for women, however, concerns feminists committed to gender-neutral approaches, who fear that such rules emphasize women's passivity and thus reinforce the negative perceptions of women that encourage their unequal and abusive treatment....

Professor Brinig's book, *The Contract and the Covenant*, presents a view of families that in some ways is suggested by many of the questions in this casebook, particularly those in Chapters 1, 5 and 9. In her view, families are best understood in terms of covenant rather than contract. She argues that contractual analysis, particularly that designed for the commercial realm, does not suit families especially well. She makes three primary distinctions, which she illustrates throughout the book. First, families exist in and for the benefit of communities, while contracts need not. Second, family members, regardless of their legal status, remain permanently attached to each other emotionally and economically. Third, families that function well share unconditional love, rather than the exchange mentality typical even of long-term contracts. Here we present the conclusion of the book. References to Chapters are to chapters in her book.

MARGARET F. BRINIG
FROM CONTRACT TO COVENANT: BEYOND THE LAW AND ECONOMICS OF THE FAMILY

(Harvard University Press, 2000)

Predicting Family Law Reform

One of the more interesting observations about family law reform, modern or ancient, is that it always seems to benefit attorneys. In fact, to the extent that one can predict the future of family law, paying attention to what will cement family practices will prove most successful. Normal economic and even public predictors do not tend to fare as well, as I have observed in the past. For example, in my "Rings and Promises," I tried to predict which states abolished the breach of promise action that allowed women to sue if their fiancés were unwilling to go through with the planned marriage. About all I could tell was that these states had a much higher than average marriage rate (and some, for example, Nevada, actively encouraged marriages within its borders) and that some of them were centers for women's rights reform (as New York and California were; Illinois and Alabama were not). In "Marriage and Opportunism," Steven Crafton and I attempted to model states' enactment of no-fault legislation as a function of Catholicism, women in the labor force, the divorce-to-marriage ratio, and political liberalism. We could identify only the extremes of early enactment of no-fault legislation and the lack of no-fault. Allen Parkman speculated that divorce reform occurred in male-dominated legislatures, "in a process of benign neglect" reinforced by the lobbying efforts of male interest groups. (It is unclear why women could not also have organized. The fact that there were very few women on either the committee that recommended reform of California family law nor in the legislature may have been the difference.) Although I am not completely convinced by this analysis, I am more interested in his point that it was not merely the change in property and alimony laws that made the difference in people's attitudes about divorce, but also the push that the no-fault movement made toward negotiated settlements. Part of my paper on gender and divorce mediation involved identification of opponents to alternative dispute resolution of family law matters and proponents of the tax reform efforts in 1984 and 1986. Some of the results are outlined in the following paragraphs.

At first, the organized bar considered divorce mediation inconsistent with professional ethics on two grounds. First, non-attorney mediators would violate "unauthorized practice of law" rules. Second, attorneys would be unable to represent both (necessarily adversary) spouses, and would therefore be involved in conflicts of interest. Because of their extensive training in legal rules as opposed to counseling, lawyer-mediators would be unable to resist giving legal advice. Some non-lawyers, however, suspected that the protests of the organized bar were little more than a smoke screen to restrict entry into what had been lawyers' exclusive domain, since divorce in most cases does not raise difficult legal issues. Some lawyers were quite overt about their fears, calling mediation a "blot on the escutcheon."

In fact, lawyers ultimately capitulated to the inevitable, and most states now allow mediation by both attorney and non-lawyer mediators. But they have raised the stakes considerably for the non-lawyers. Since the advent of no-fault divorce, and contemporaneously with the rise of mediation, the practice of family law has shifted from being a rather disreputable one (only slightly above criminal defense work, and perhaps below "ambulance chasing" and loan collection in terms of public perception) to a practice that looks very much like a general business practice. The effective family law practitioner is not only counselor and strategist. He or she must also know a good deal about taxation, finance, and human capital theory, as we have seen in Chapter 6. In fact, the work in some states has spawned a valuation industry in which the experts also testify in business dissolutions.

And just when the complexities of property distribution began to be understood, Congress changed the tax laws relating to divorce. If we look carefully at this legislation, which disrupted the regime that had been in place since 1961, we see that there were no obvious gains by divorcing husbands or wives. A unitary payment of alimony and child support used to be taxable to the recipient and deductible by the payor under § 71. Now to be treated this way, payments need to be clearly related to the recipient, not the children. Further, property transferred from one spouse to the other incident to divorce used to be treated as a taxable event, with the capital gain payable by the original property holder. Now such a transfer is treated as a gift for income tax purposes: it is not taxable at the time of divorce, and the capital gain is realized when the property is sold to a third party. The first of these changes largely benefited wives, who pay less taxes on the amount received from former husbands. The second change largely benefited husbands, who used to have to both part with property held in their name and pay taxes on it. The legislation was promulgated by tax attorneys and the family law section of the American Bar Association, not by men's or women's groups. Attorneys were benefited by the reshuffled tax provisions because the changes were complex and probably beyond the competence of non-lawyer mediators, who previously had profited by the relative stability of divorce taxation.

Nor are my suspicions limited to the modern era. Eileen Spring, in her *Law, Land and Family*, has looked at a series of early laws ostensibly designed to benefit women. According to the legislative histories she discovered, the proponents were the solicitors, who eventually drew up the marriage settlements that guaranteed fixed sums for women marrying with estates. This practice, according to Spring, disadvantaged many if not most women since they were likely to have outlived their husbands and, absent the settlement, would have acquired the whole of the property rather than a certain small share in it.

Another instance of family law reform that apparently helped women was the institution of judicial divorce, beginning in the United States around 1830. Until then, aggrieved spouses who wished absolute divorces could only obtain these by legislative action after obtaining judicial decrees of separation. In every year since 1800, most divorce plaintiffs in this country have been wives. The legislative divorce practice was expensive, since the local legislator who would sponsor the bill of divorce would undoubtedly have to be paid. But unless she wished to remarry, the wife did not need an absolute divorce. Even earlier, if she could convince a judge that she had been deserted, abused, or that her husband was otherwise at fault, a wife could be awarded what today would be called a legal separation, which gave her an allowance out of the husband's estate. Because of the serious stigma associated with divorce (and remarriage), this was probably the most attractive alternative for all but the most desperate wives.

Why would lawyers, more than wives, prefer judicial divorces? First, there is a volume answer. Because the transactions costs for divorce were lowered substantially, there presumably would be more of them. In fact, Lawrence Friedman and Robert Percival show a gradually rising divorce rate during this period, which lasted from colonization until about 1880. The second pragmatic reason is that there was probably little an attorney could do for a wife beyond what was necessary for the legal separation when the task was to secure passage of a simple piece of legislation. (Sometimes the bills contained one sentence paragraphs allowing divorces for as many as ten couples, without even stating reasons for the divorce.) Once a suit was necessary, a new form of practice emerged, one that has been lucrative for attorneys for decades.

Some Candidates For Law Reform

We have already discussed the changes wrought by no-fault divorce, both in terms of their effects and the interest groups who lobbied for them. By now it should be obvious that I am concerned about the effects of no-fault divorce on marriages, as well as on divorced women and children. My partial solutions, discussed in Chapters 2 and 6, involve allowing couples to choose their divorce regime through a covenant marriage option, retaining or returning to fault in the granting of alimony or in the division of property, or explicitly recognizing investment in earning capacity.

There are other candidates for law reform that are worth mentioning. The first is the change in custody laws. One candidate for a substantive standard is joint custody. In empirical work discussed already in Chapters 6 and 7, I have found that joint custody laws discourage divorce and encourage payment of court-ordered child support. From the child's perspective, therefore, the data suggest that they are a desirable innovation, even without considering the obvious fact that children prosper most when they have contact with two parents. From the wife and mother's perspective, feminists criticize these laws because they apparently enhance the power of divorcing and divorced husbands. They argue that husbands may ask for joint custody they do not plan to exercise in order to extract favorable financial settlements. Further, they might use their increased power as decisionmakers to continue to control or harass their former wives. Empirical work is equivocal on the subject of the first concern. Maccoby and Mnookin found very little of the strategic bargaining through threats of seeking custody. However, in "Lurking in the Shadow," Scott Altman found that lawyers surveyed in California noted some such tactics (about twenty percent reported that they had seen this technique used against their clients). To date, no one has tested the second feminist contention: that joint legal custodians might use the opportunity to maintain power over their wives. Ira Lupu indicates a contrary benefit from the child's perspective: joint custody may act as a power balancer to assure that the child is given the best possible care. The alternative primary caretaker presumption has largely been untested except in terms of its allocational result: more mothers are awarded custody than under a best-interests or joint custody regime. Because the standard is indeterminate (it is difficult to know in all cases who the primary caretaker has been), there has been significantly more litigation in primary caretaker states.

Another possible reform is a statutory prohibition (or discouraging) of transracial adoption. This was briefly addressed in Chapter 3. While statutes like those in place in Minnesota would have the desired effect of keeping minority children in their communities, because there is a shortage of minority prospective adoptive parents and a queue of non-minority would-be parents, bans on transracial adoption also mean that some children who would otherwise be adopted must remain in foster care. If the problems of poverty leading to these children's placement with state agencies cannot be alleviated, adoption seems the second best choice from the individual child's perspective. Preference for same-race parents, like a religious preference, seems nonobjectionable, but if a same-race adoptive parent cannot be found in a short time, adoption by a different race parent should be allowed.

Welfare reform, as of the time of this writing, remains a volatile subject, with new federal legislation discussed in Chapter 3. My empirical work and reading suggests that the old system of AFDC deters men from being involved with their children either through paying court ordered child support (Chapter 5), through marrying the mothers (Chapter 6), or remaining married rather than divorcing (Chapter 6). These are clearly bad results worth remedying. However, the welfare caps that have been enacted in several states have not yet been shown to affect the unwed birth rate. (The "caps" put a ceiling on the amount that can be received, even if there are additional children). To the extent that women might go on having children even when on AFDC and even when there are caps in place, the people penalized are children. Reducing the AFDC subsidies (which would lower the amount available even for the first child and therefore reduce financial incentives for even the first pregnancy), or placing time limits on their receipt, as is required by the federal legislation, seem more humane ways of dealing with this important problem, and may in fact reduce unwed births.

My longtime state of Virginia is considering joining a number of other states in reforming alimony laws to make rehabilitative, as opposed to permanent, alimony the norm. The economic effects of alimony (even though at present only about a third of Virginia divorcing couples have alimony as part of their decrees) have been noted already, in Chapter 6. Alimony seems to be associated with more investment in marriage and in children, and with a lower incidence of spousal abuse. When children are involved, and a parent remains out of the job force or otherwise changes work to accommodate them, the loss is permanent. The custodial parent can never be "rehabilitated," for, as Victor Fuchs suggests, there is a lifetime loss of 1.5% for each year the parent remains out of the job market. Rehabilitative alimony also seems inappropriate for many older women who married and made investments in their marriage or their spouse based on the older system. While it might be perfectly appropriate for very short and childless marriages, the majority do not seem good candidates for rehabilitative alimony, as we discussed in Chapter 7.

A final possible set of law reforms involves transfer payments made to the elderly through Social Security and Medicare. Unquestionably both systems need reforming. There is tremendous waste in the provision of medical care for the elderly, and under-funding will bankrupt Social Security in another generation unless something is done. Were neither system in place, there would probably be private provision for old people—arguably, as we saw in Chapter 5, a good thing for both the elderly and minor children. However, as with welfare reform and alimony, one cannot change the rules midstream without tremendous hardship upon people who are already in the system. Other incentives for private care, like those discussed in Chapter 7, might work in a more just way than termination of the present system.

Conclusion

One of the rewards of a large project like this one is the learning that takes place as one writes. Although I had worked for several years on the application of contracts principles to family law, when I began this book in the spring of 1994, I had just completed my first work on the family covenant. At that point, I was still unsure how the permanence of covenant could be explained in an era of no-fault divorces and early emancipation of children. The metaphor of franchise came to me in the late spring of 1995. Now it is much easier to see how all these ideas fit together, how a change in one area of family law affects so many others, and even how economics can help predict the likely effects of proposed law reform efforts.

The more I teach and think about family law, the more I feel its interconnectedness. Just as I am not a rock or an island, no part of family law can ever be usefully "deconstructed" in isolation. For example, every time we change divorce law, there are obvious effects upon support and custody. Another ripple affects marriage—both when couples decide to marry and what they do once they are married. Further out lie the effects upon children born out-of-wedlock, juvenile delinquency, and, arguably, child and elder abuse.

How have we already made some choice as a nation? To the extent that the contract and the market-like sovereign nation model dominates today, it is the product of several forces, some directly and some only indirectly legal. The first is no-fault divorce. When it became easier for couples to separate and form new families, attachments to spouses and children became in many ways more contingent. Particularly for men, who seem to view attachment to children in terms of their current relationships, family life in many cases becomes discrete: rent-a-husband or rent-a-dad. The grand sweep of family life disappears. The next legal intervention is the whole set of laws that established Social Security and Medicare and made private pensions attractive for employers and workers. When we concentrate on saving for our own old age (voluntarily or through taxation), we both spend less on our children and trust less in our continued relationships with them. A third legal change has been the lowering of the age of emancipation to 18. What this does (besides the obvious political changes of increasing the number of young voters) is to make college more the child's responsibility than the parents' (except in cases of divorce), and remove any force from parental guidance about decisions like youthful marriage. We have a shorter time when our children are primarily our responsibility, and we have less time during which we can learn from each other and strengthen family bonds. Finally, and perhaps in response to the social changes I would argue were inevitably wrought by all these other legal choices, we have enacted a spate of child protective, parental responsibility and elder abuse prevention laws. These constrict the scope of family privacy and protect against what used to be unthinkable—the abandonment or mistreatment of our children or parents.

What, then, do we do? I read a story about a Scottish immigrant minister who built a house for his wife and children on an island in Lake Superior. Ninety years later, four generations of the family still come, each with fond memories of summer vacations spent there. Home places are like that—they bring us back from our Diaspora to a shared family experience. Even though most of us have lost the family farm, and certainly Lear's kingdom, we can still discover (or begin) family traditions, frequently centered around one place. Electronic mail can be a wonderful family unifier when physical closeness, though the best, is impossible.

Less concretely but more legally, we can encourage investment in our families, as I pointed out in the family law reform section of this chapter. Joint custody laws apparently motivate noncustodial parents (most of them fathers) to continue to support their children. A two-level divorce system, with divorce more difficult where there are children, or if a covenant marriage is selected at the beginning, also encourages healthier families. For example, the current Virginia and Tennessee statutes have a longer waiting period for divorces including minor children. The Louisiana and Arizona covenant marriage, discussed in Chapter 2, allows a no-fault divorce after a six-month separation only in standard marriages, while for covenant marriages the waiting period is two years. Another such family-reinforcing idea is the education deduction, particularly for college education. The federal government could authorize deductions for payments made to support elderly parents. The state might encourage low-interest loan programs for children who wish to build "in-law" additions to their homes? What about reducing inheritance taxes so that elderly people won't feel that they will lose a large part of what they have earned if they don't consume it during life?

As I pointed out in the last chapter, the system of family law I have proposed in this book in some ways reflects a "difference" feminist approach. It rejects bright line distinctions between married and unmarried, child and adult, parent and stranger. I maintain that family, and therefore family law, is continuous, not discrete. It is in fact a covenant that does not end, even if law says it does. Law has limits, and cannot always control the complex of human relationships we call families. In some senses, therefore, families are beyond law. To the extent that we must look elsewhere for satisfying explanations of love and the makeup of other utility functions, we have also ventured beyond economics.

Notes and Questions: Generalizing About Family Law

(1) Are the data assembled in these articles correct? Are they correctly analyzed? How might they alternatively be analyzed?

(a) Over fifteen years have passed since Professor Schneider wrote his article. Has moral discourse in family law continued to diminish?

(b) Professor Schneider emphatically does *not* argue that family law is necessarily without a moral basis. He only argues that family law speaks in moral language less frequently and that it has shifted some overtly moral decisions to the people the law once regulated. What moral justifications for the shape of contemporary family law can you imagine?

(c) Professor Bartlett argues that feminism has crucially shaped family law. What other forces might explain the developments she attributes to feminism? What other areas of law have been significantly affected by the rise of feminism in the late twentieth century?

(2) What differences do you see between the theses of Professors Schneider, Bartlett, and Brinig? Are they describing the same phenomena? What views of human nature do you suppose they hold?

(3) Are you convinced by Professor Brinig's rather cynical view about the origins of family law reform? She mentions no-fault divorce, some changes in the tax laws, and earlier legal developments in married woman's property and judicial divorces. Are there exceptions to the theory she posits? In particular, what do you suppose drove the current wave of ALI reform? If these changes become law, will lawyers benefit? Who will be the big winners and losers?

(4) Professor Brinig appears to take a child-centered rather than either a traditional or feminist view of custody law. Does this position (taken before the ALI custody project) conflict with Professor Bartlett's? (Note that Professor Bartlett was the Reporter for the custody chapter of the ALI Principles.) What about the "recognizing investment in earning capacity" point, which you may remember seeing argued in Chapter 4? Does it conflict with the "moral discourse" Professor Schneider writes about? Can you envision a family law scheme that will ensure gender justice and equality without undermining the vital role families play for children?

(5) Is Professor Brinig correct that families have lost many of the intergenerational benefits they produced until the twentieth century? If you believe she is correct, is this as important a loss as she suggests? Can you think of additional *legal* changes that would ameliorate the social situations she describes? Are these proposals politically realistic? Are they wise?

(6) Which of the changes described in these essays are normatively desirable? Undesirable?

(7) What other hypotheses about the present direction of family law might one advance?

(8) Many contemporary social critics seem convinced that the American family is collapsing. Many social critics past and present have argued that it should collapse. Is it collapsing?

(a) Is the current divorce rate persuasive evidence of the collapse of the American family?

(b) Is the modern family is collapsing because it has been deprived of most of the functions it used to serve? Is it true that the family has been deprived of a crucial number of its functions? How many functions need the family serve to flourish? Does the family now serve fewer functions, but serve them more intensively?

(c) Has affluence injured the family? Has it on the contrary made life in the modern family more rewarding?

(9) One concern about the American family concerns whether outside forces—governmental and social—"permeate" the family. In other words, social critics have wanted to discover and evaluate the extent to which governments and society participate—formally and informally—in the regulation of the family, the extent to which the family operates in privacy, and the extent of the family's autonomy. In what specific ways has government's permeation of the family increased?

(10) In what specific ways has government's permeation of the family decreased?

(11) In what specific ways has society's permeation of the family increased? Which of the following strike you as accurate generalizations and as evidence of that permeation? Can you identify others?

(a) Education, whether public or private, is not only conducted largely outside of the family, but it lasts much longer than it used to. Not only do many more people attend college and graduate school, but many more children attend pre-schools. In addition, schools now teach broader range of subjects than before; the call is for schools to educate "the whole child."

(b) Social critics like Christopher Lasch (in *Haven in a Heartless World* (Basic Books, 1977)) have argued that, as children spend proportionately more time outside of the home, peer groups gain greater influence not only on children, but on parents and on how parents raise children.

(c) As children and adults watch more television, the family becomes more susceptible to its influence on how its members behave and becomes more distracted from diversions in which family members deal more actively with each other.

(d) As it becomes increasingly common for both parents to work, as the family increasingly relies on the market rather than its own productive activities for all commodities, and as children have increasing market power, the market increasingly permeates the family.

(e) As the authority of experts waxes, as the number of aspects of life in which expert advice is thought necessary swells, professions increasingly permeate the family.

(f) As the desirability of privacy decreases, society increasingly permeates the family.

(12) How far—in what specific ways—has society's permeation of the family decreased? Is the fact that families are now generally more prosperous than before, with more job security, more retirement security, and more wealth, important in permitting families to resist the permeation of society?

(13) One view of the family is that it provides a haven from the world, particularly the world of commerce and employment. Is it realistic to expect the family to be such a haven? Desirable? What does it mean to

be a haven? Is the haven a haven for individualism? Can the family protect the individual, or does the family constrain the individual?

BIBLIOGRAPHY

There are not many attempts to look broadly at the whole range of family law. Two particularly worth reading are Mary Ann Glendon, *The Transformation of Family Law: State, Law, and Family in the United States and Europe* (U Chi Press, 1989), and Milton C. Regan, Jr., *Family Law and the Pursuit of Intimacy* (NYU Press, 1993).

For philosophical reflections on the family, see Jacob Joshua Ross, *The Virtues of the Family* (Free Press, 1994); Jean Bethke Elshtain, ed, *The Family in Political Thought* (U Mass Press, 1982); Philip Abbott, *The Family on Trial: Special Relationships in Modern Political Thought* (Pennsylvania State U Pa Press, 1981); Frederick Engels, *The Origins of the Family, Private Property, and the State* (Pathfinder Press, 1972). And for reflections on the literary view of the family, see Stephen Kern, *The Culture of Love: Victorians to the Moderns* (Harv U Press, 1992).

On changes in moral thinking in American society, see Gertrude Himmelfarb, *The De–Moralization of Society: From Victorian Virtues to Modern Values* (Knopf, 1995); James Q. Wilson, *The Moral Sense* (Free Press, 1993); Amitai Etzioni, *The Moral Dimension: Toward a New Economics* (Free Press, 1988).

For another view on what makes a family, see Margaret F. Brinig, *Status, Contract and Covenant (Book Review)*, 89 Cornell L Rev 601 (1994), suggesting that use of the concept of covenant may be a way to secure intimacy in relationships without reverting to concepts of patriarchy.

For a critique of law and economics approaches to the family, see Ann L. Estin, *Law and Obligation*, 43 Wm & Mary L Rev 989 (1995), who reviews the law and economics literature, and suggests which concepts are the most useful for family law.

For another look at children outside the traditional family setting, see James A. Rosenthal, Victor Groze and Gloria D. Aguilar, *Adoption Outcomes for Children with Handicaps*, 70 Child Welfare 623 (1991), which notes that children with handicaps frequently remain in foster care. Even when they are adopted, the adoptions fail more often than for healthy children.

*

Index

References are to Pages

References are to Pages

References are to Pages

References are to Pages

References are to Pages

†